THE COMPLETE BILL OF RIGHTS

THE DRAFTS, DEBATES, SOURCES, AND ORIGINS

THE
COMPLETE
BILL OF RIGHTS

THE DRAFTS, DEBATES, SOURCES, AND ORIGINS

Edited by

NEIL H. COGAN

David Lindsay Adams   Theresa Lynn Harvey
EDITORIAL ASSISTANTS

New York Oxford
OXFORD UNIVERSITY PRESS
1997

Oxford University Press

Oxford New York
Athens Auckland Bangkok Bogotá Bombay
Buenos Aires Calcutta Cape Town Dar es Salaam
Delhi Florence Hong Kong Istanbul Karachi
Kuala Lumpur Madras Madrid Melbourne
Mexico City Nairobi Paris Singapore
Taipei Tokyo Toronto Warsaw

and associated companies in
Berlin Ibadan

Copyright © 1997 by Oxford University Press, Inc.

Published by Oxford University Press, Inc.,
198 Madison Avenue, New York, New York 10016

Library of Congress Cataloging-in-Publication Data
The complete Bill of Rights : the drafts, debates,
sources, and origins / edited by Neil H. Cogan.
p. cm.
ISBN 0-19-510322-X
1. United States—Constitution—Amendments—1st–10th—Sources.
2. United States—Constitutional history—Sources.
3. Civil rights—United States—History—Sources.
I. Cogan, Neil H. (Neil Howard), 1944– .
KF4744 1997
342.73′085 [347.30285]—DC20 96-46588

11-26-97

Printing (last digit): 9 8 7 6 5 4 3 2 1

Printed in the United States of America
on acid free paper

*This book is dedicated to
my mother, Elizabeth,
and my late father, Jacob.*

"And you shall impress them upon your children."
—Deuteronomy 6:7

CONTENTS IN BRIEF

CONTENTS

CONTENTS

AMENDMENT I: Establishment and Free Exercise Clauses, *continued*

CONTENTS

Chapter 2

AMENDMENT I
FREE SPEECH AND FREE PRESS CLAUSES

AMENDMENT I: Free Speech and Free Press Clauses, *continued*

AMENDMENT I: Free Speech and Free Press Clauses, *continued*

Chapter 3

AMENDMENT I
ASSEMBLY AND PETITION CLAUSES

CONTENTS

Chapter 4
AMENDMENT II
KEEP AND BEAR ARMS CLAUSE

AMENDMENT II: Keep and Bear Arms Clause, *continued*

Chapter 5

AMENDMENT III
QUARTERING SOLDIERS CLAUSE

Chapter 6

AMENDMENT IV
SEARCH AND SEIZURE CLAUSE

CONTENTS

Chapter 7

AMENDMENT V
GRAND JURY CLAUSE

Chapter 8

AMENDMENT V
DOUBLE JEOPARDY CLAUSE

CONTENTS

Chapter 9

AMENDMENT V
SELF-INCRIMINATION CLAUSE

AMENDMENT V: Self-Incrimination Clause, *continued*

Chapter 10

AMENDMENT V
DUE PROCESS CLAUSE

AMENDMENT V: Due Process Clause, *continued*

Chapter 11

AMENDMENT V
TAKINGS CLAUSE

Chapter 12

AMENDMENT VI
CRIMINAL TRIAL CLAUSES

AMENDMENT VI: Criminal Trial Clauses, *continued*

AMENDMENT VI: Criminal Trial Clauses, *continued*

Chapter 13

AMENDMENT VII
CIVIL JURY TRIAL CLAUSES

CONTENTS

AMENDMENT VII: Civil Jury Trial Clauses, *continued*

CONTENTS

CONTENTS

AMENDMENT VII: Civil Jury Trial Clauses, *continued*

AMENDMENT VII: Civil Jury Trial Clauses, *continued*

Chapter 14

AMENDMENT VIII
BAIL/PUNISHMENT CLAUSES

CONTENTS

CONTENTS

CONTENTS

AMENDMENT IX
UNENUMERATED RIGHTS CLAUSE

AMENDMENT IX: Unenumerated Rights Clause, *continued*

Chapter 16

AMENDMENT X
RESERVATION OF POWERS CLAUSE

AMENDMENT X: Reservation of Powers Clause, *continued*

CONTENTS

AMENDMENT X: Reservation of Powers Clause, *continued*

ABBREVIATIONS OF SOURCES

Original Documents

Commentaries William Blackstone. *Commentaries on the Laws of England.* 4 vols. Oxford, 1765.

Congressional Register Thomas Lloyd, ed. *The Congressional Register.* 2 vols. New York, 1789.

Connecticut Acts *Acts and Laws of the State of Connecticut in America.* New London, 1784.

Connecticut Charter *The Charter Granted by His Majesty King Charles II to the Governour & Company of the English Colony of Connecticut in New-England in America.* New London, 1718.

Connecticut Code *Code of 1650 . . . Commonly Called Blue Laws.* Hartford, 1822.

Continental Congress Papers *Records of the Continental and Confederation Congresses and the Constitutional Convention, Miscellaneous Records of the Continental and Confederation Congresses.* Record Group 360, National Archives.

Daily Advertiser *Daily Advertiser.* New York, 1789.

Dall. A. J. Dallas, ed. *Reports of Cases Ruled and Adjudged in the Courts of Pennsylvania.* Vol. 1. Philadelphia, 1790.

Delaware Laws *Laws of the State of Delaware. . . .* New-Castle, 1797.

Ellsworth MS *Senator Oliver Ellsworth's Handwritten Notes of the Senate Amendments to the Proposed Bill of Rights.* Record Group 46, National Archives.

Eng. Rep. *The English Reports.* Vols 1–176. London, 1900–1930.

First Congress Journal *Journal of the First Congress of the American Colonies. . . .* New York, 1845.

Georgia Laws Robert Watkins and George Watkins, eds. *A Digest of the Laws of the State of Georgia. . . .* Philadelphia, 1800.

Gazette of the U.S. *Gazette of the United States.* Philadelphia, 1789.

HJ *Journal of the House of Representatives.* New York, 1789.

How. St. Tr. Thomas Bayly Howell, ed. *A Complete Collection of State Trials and Proceedings for High Treason and Other Crimes and Misdemeanors. . . .* London, 1814–1826.

Kirby (Conn.) Ephraim Kirby, ed. *Reports of Cases Adjudged in the Superior Court of the State of Connecticut from the Year 1785, to May, 1788.* Reprint. Harford, 1962.

Massachusetts Bay Charter *The Charter Granted by Their Majesties King William and Queen Mary to the Inhabitants of the Province of the Massachusetts-Bay in New England.* Boston, 1742.

Massachusetts Bay First Charter *The First Charter of the Province of Massachusetts Bay. . . .* London, 1774.

Massachusetts Colonial Laws William H. Whitmore, ed. *The Colonial Laws of Massachusetts* (1672). Reprint. Boston, 1890.

Massachusetts Convention *Debates and Proceedings in the Convention of the Commonwealth of Massachusetts Held in the Year 1788.* Boston, 1856.

Massachusetts Perpetual Laws *The Perpetual Laws of the Commonwealth of Massachusetts. . . .* Worcester, 1787.

N. C. (Mart.) *Cases Adjudged in the Superior Courts of Law and Equity and in the Court of Conference of North Carolina: From Nov. Term, 1788, to Dec. Term, 1894. . . .* Reprint. Raleigh, 1901.

New Hampshire Laws *The Laws of the State of New-Hamphire. . . .* Portsmouth, 1792.

New Haven's Lawes *New-Haven's Settling in New-England and Same Lawes for Government.* London, 1656.

New Jersey Acts Peter Wilson, ed. *Acts of the General Assembly of the State of New Jersey.* Trenton, 1784.

New Jersey Grants Aaron Leaming and Jacob Spicer, eds. *The Grants, Concessions, and Original Constitutions of the Province of New-Jersey. . . .* Philadelphia, 1758.

New-Plimouth Laws *The Book of the General Laws of . . . New-Plimouth. . . .* Cambridge, Mass., 1672.

New-Plymouth Declaration *A Declaration of the . . . Associates . . . of New-Plymouth . . . Together with the General Fundamentals of Their Laws.* Boston, 1773.

New Plymouth Laws William Brigham, ed. *The Compact with the Charter and Laws of the Colony of New Plymouth.* Boston, 1836.

New York Acts *The Laws and Acts of the General Assembly of the State of New York . . . 1691.* New York, 1694.

New York Daily Gazette *The New York Daily Gazette.* New York, 1789.

New York Laws *Laws of the State of New-York. . . .* 2 vols. New York, 1789.

North Carolina Acts Samuel Swann, ed. *A Collection of All the Public Acts of Assembly, of the Province of North Carolina: Now in Force and Use.* New Bern, N.C., 1751.

North Carolina Laws James Iredell, ed. *Laws of the State of North Carolina.* Edenton, N.C., 1791.

North Carolina State Records Walter Clark, ed. *The State Records of North Carolina.* 26 vols. Chapel Hill, 1886–1907. [Vol. 25, 1898, referenced.]

Penn Abstract *An Abstract or Abridgment of the Laws Made and Past by William Penn Absolute Proprietary . . . in the Year 1700.* Philadelphia, 1701.

Penn Charter *The Charter Privileges Granted by William Penn, Esq; to the Inhabitants of Pensilvania.* Philadelphia, 1741

Pennsylvania Acts, Dallas A. J. Dallas, ed. *The Acts of the General Assembly of the Commonwealth of Pennsylvania.* Philadelphia, 1791.

Pennsylvania Acts, McKean Thomas McKean, ed. *The Acts of the General Assembly of the Commonwealth of Pennsylvania.* Philadelphia, 1782.

Pennsylvania Charters   *The Charters of the Province of Pensilvania. . . .* Philadelphia, 1742.

Pennsylvania Frame   *The Frame of the Government of the Province of Pennsylvania.* N.p., 1682.

Printed SJ   *Journal of the First Session of the Senate of the United States of America. . . .* New York, 1789.

Quincy's Reports (Mass.)   Josiah Quincy, Jr., ed. *Reports of Cases Argued and Adjudged in the Superior Court of Judicature of the Province of Massachusetts Bay, Between 1761 and 1772.* Boston, 1865.

RG11   Certificates of Ratification of the Constitution and Bill of Rights and Related Correspondence and Rejections of Proposed Amendments. Record Group 11, General Records of the United States Government, National Archives.

RG46   Rough Copy of the Legislative Journal, Part of the First Session (March 4–September 10, 1789), and Transcribed and Corrected Copy of the Legislative Journal, First Session and Part of the Second Session (March 4, 1789–June 11, 1790). Record Group 46, General Records of the United States Government, National Archives.

Rhode Island Acts   *Acts and Laws, of His Majesties Colony of Rhode Island, and Providence-Plantations in America, Prefaced by the Charter Granted by His Majesty King Charles the Second, to the Colony of Rhode-Island and Providence-Plantations.* Boston, 1719.

Rhode Island Code   William R. Staples, ed. *Proceedings of the First General Assembly of "The Incorporation of Providence Plantations," and the Code of Laws Adopted by that Assembly in 1647.* Providence, 1847.

Rhode Island Records   *Records of the Colony of Rhode Island and Providence Plantation in New England.* Providence, 1856.

Rough SJ   *A Journal of the Senate Begun and Held at the City of New York, March 4th, 1789.* Record Group 46, National Archives [water damaged].

Smooth SJ   *A Journal of the Senate Begun and Held at the City of New York, March 4th, 1789.* Record Group 46, National Archives [corrected copy].

South Carolina Constitution   *An Act for Establishing the Constitution of the State of South-Carolina.* Charles-Town, 1778.

South Carolina Laws   John Grimké, ed. *The Public Laws of the State of South-Carolina.* Philadelphia, 1790.

South Carolina Provincial Laws   Nicholas Trott, ed. *The Laws of the Province of South-Carolina.* Charles-Town, 1736.

Tryals Per Pais   *Tryals Per Pais: Or, The Law of England Concerning Juries by Nisi Prius . . .* G.D. 3d ed. London, 1695.

Vermont Acts   *Acts and Laws of the State of Vermont in America.* [Dresden], 1779.

Virginia Acts   *A Collection of All Such Public Acts of the General Assembly, and Ordinances and Conventions of Virginia.* Richmond, 1785.

Virginia Laws   William Waller Hening, ed. *The Statutes at Large; Being a Collection of All the Laws of Virginia.* Vol. 1. Richmond, 1809.

Virginia Memorial and Remonstrance   *A Memorial and Remonstrance Presented to the General Assembly of the State of Virginia.* Worcester, Mass., 1786.

Virginia Religious Freedom Act *An Act for Establishing Religious Freedom, Passed . . . 1786.* Richmond, 1786.

Documentary Collections

Bowling & Veit Kenneth R. Bowling and Helen E. Veit, eds. *The Diary of William Maclay and Other Notes on Senate Debates.* Baltimore, 1988.

Boyd Julian P. Boyd, ed. *The Papers of Thomas Jefferson.* 26 vols. Princeton, 1950–1995.

Cooke James E. Cooke, ed. *The Federalist.* Cleveland, 1965.

Elliot Jonathan Elliot, ed. *The Debates in the Several State Conventions on the Adoption of the Federal Constitution. . . .* 5 vols, 2d ed. Reprint, New York, 1888.

Ford Paul Leicester Ford, ed. *Pamphlets on the Constitution of the United States, Published during Its Discussion by the People, 1787–88.* Reprint, Brooklyn, 1888.

Hobson & Rutland (or Rutland & Hobson) Charles F. Hobson and Robert A. Rutland, eds. *The Papers of James Madison.* Vols 11–12. Charlottesville, Va., 1977 and 1979.

Jensen Merrill Jensen, ed. *The Documentary History of the Ratification of the Constitution.* Vols. 1–3. Madison, Wis., 1976–1978.

Kaminski & Saladino John P. Kaminsky and Gaspare J. Saladino, eds. *The Documentary History of the Ratification of the Constitution.* Vols. 8–10 and 13–18. Madison, Wis., 1981–1995.

McMaster & Stone John Back McMaster and Frederick D. Stone, eds. *Pennsylvania and the Federal Constitution, 1787–88.* Lancaster, Penn., 1888.

Statutes at Large Richard Peters, ed. *The Public Statutes at Larg[e] of the United States of America. . . .* Vol 1. Boston, 1848.

Storing Herbert J. Storing, ed. *The Complete Anti-Federalist.* 7 vols. Chicago, 1981.

Tansill *Documents Illustrative of the Formation of the Union of the American States.* Washington, D.C., 1927.

Veit Helen E. Veit, Kenneth R. Bowling, and Charlene Bangs Bickford, eds. *Creating the Bill of Rights, The Documentary Record from the First Federal Congress.* Baltimore, 1991.

Documentary Locations

Ct Y Sterling Library, Yale University, New Haven, Connecticut.

DLC Library of Congress, Washington, D.C.

DNA National Archives, Washington, D.C.

DNDAR Daughter of the American Revolution, National Headquarters, Washington, D.C.

PHSP The Historical Society of Pennsylvania, Philadelphia, Pennsylvania.

PLC The Library Company of Philadelphia, Philadelphia, Pennsylvania.

PREFACE

THIS BOOK'S AIM IS TO PROVIDE THE MOST COMPLETE, ACCURATE, and accessible set of texts available for interpreting the Bill of Rights, the first ten amendments to the United States Constitution. Well into the third century since its ratification, the importance of and necessity for a collection such as this are as great as ever; indeed, because of the bill's continually increasing significance, perhaps the need for this book is greater than ever.

Significance of the Bill of Rights

Interpreting the Bill of Rights, which represented for Madison "the great rights of mankind," is of surpassing importance. Originally intended to limit the power of the federal government, most provisions of the bill now limit the power of *all* government within the United States—federal, state, and local. Put somewhat more didactically, the bill's limit upon power arises from the Constitution's principle of constitutional supremacy. By that principle, when a provision of federal, state, or local law—be it statute, rule, order, or other exercise of legal authority— conflicts with an applicable provision of the Bill of Rights, the latter deprives the former of some or all of its effect and thereby limits the power of government.

In the United States, at the turn of the twenty-first century, Americans file thousands of lawsuits each year in federal and state courts, asking judges to interpret the Bill of Rights in order to decide whether government has exceeded its power. In innumerable instances each day, Americans of all kinds—governors and legislators, school teachers and school children, police officers and motorists— ponder whether government, by the exercise of its authority, is violating the Bill of Rights and is, accordingly, acting beyond its constitutional powers. And they ponder how a judge, if presented with the question, would interpret the bill and decide the question.

The Inevitability of Interpretation and the Inevitability of Disagreement

Whether there is a conflict between a provision of federal, state, or local law and the Bill of Rights inevitably depends upon interpretation, including an interpretation of the applicable provision of the Bill of Rights. "'Tis funny about th' constitution," Finley Peter Dunne's Mr. Dooley said, "It reads plain, but no wan can undherstant it without an interpreter."

Not everyone agrees with Mr. Dooley. There are those who believe that judges do not interpret or, perhaps better, should not interpret. They should simply apply the applicable provision. But inevitably, even persons who agree that the task is simply to apply a provision engage in interpretation by their selection process, that is, by the dictionaries or treatises or cases they choose to read in order to learn the meaning of a provision, not to mention the personal experiences they bring to the reading process.

But even if we lay aside the controversy concerning the inevitability of interpretation, it is noteworthy and surprising that in the third century after the proposal and ratification of the Constitution and the Bill of Rights, significant controversy persists about such matters as whether there is an ultimate interpreter of the Constitution and Bill of Rights, and, if so, who that interpreter is. Related controversies concern the processes of constitutional interpretation and the proper texts to be used in constitutional interpretation.

The Importance of Originalism, More or Less

Regardless of whether the Supreme Court of the United States is the ultimate interpreter of the Constitution and Bill of Rights, as the Court itself has said, or whether each official sworn to uphold the Constitution is an interpreter of authority and competence equal to the Supreme Court, as several presidents and governors have said, most (but not all) interpreters agree that some form of originalism is the beginning, if not also the end, of interpretation. That is, most interpreters have said that one or more of the following conditions must be met in order to interpret a provision of the Constitution or Bill of Rights, with the important caveat that many would impose further conditions.

For some interpreters, originalism requires that one discern the original meaning of the applicable provision. This might require learning the meaning of words from contemporaneous dictionaries, examining the meaning of words in other constitutional and colonial provisions, provisions that were or might have been the source of the applicable provision or that simply show contemporaneous usage. And it might entail a study of words in caselaw and treatises, again in order to show contemporaneous usage.

For some interpreters, originalism requires that one seek the original intention of the drafters of the applicable provision, an intention that might differ from the meaning of the words. This inquiry might require, as above, reading the sources of the applicable provision. It might also involve reading the proposals for the provision and the provision's drafts as they made their way through the legislative process. And it might necessitate reading the discussion of the provision both by those engaged in the legislative process and by those outside the process who sought to influence the discussion or, at least, to comment on the discussion.

For some interpreters, originalism requires that one determine the original understanding of the ratifiers, an understanding that might differ from the original meaning of the words and the original intentions of the drafters of the provision. This might require reading many of the same materials described above. Unfortunately, in the case of the Bill of Rights, there is no record of the discussion by the ratifiers in the legislative chambers.

In addition, many interpreters, though holding to originalism in one or more of its senses, emphasize more strongly the principles of a particular provision and related provisions. Of course, to learn what those principles are one must read the materials described above. Some of these interpreters emphasize the meaning and understanding of the text and its principles over the centuries in the minds and lives of the people of the United States. Such a historical understanding can be gained through studying caselaw, legislation, and customs and their attendant applications, refinements, and discussions. And for some interpreters, the emphasis is some part or some variation of all of these.

The Need for a Set of Originalist Texts

However an interpreter approaches her or his task, whether as an originalist exclusively or partially, some set of complete, accurate, and accessible texts is necessary. But, once again, more than two hundred years after the proposal and ratification of the Bill of Rights, it is surprising—especially in light of the historic references to and reliance on originalism in some sense—that there is no satisfactory set of texts for these purposes.

While there have been authoritative sets of texts arranged in chronological order, the published materials do not provide all the texts that many interpreters would choose to read. For example, there is no place where one can read all the drafts of the provisions of the Bill of Rights. One must piece the drafts together from journals, newspaper reports, and manuscripts.

Moreover, even if one can gain access to a complete set of printed materials, they often do not provide accurate versions of what many interpreters would want. For example, there is no single source that provides all the pertinent constitutional and statutory sources for the Bill of Rights. One must seek out each state's legislative texts. And even if there are libraries where one can gather all the sources from each state's legislative texts, it is unlikely that, with the exception of a few libraries, one will find the sources in a form that would have been available to the framers of the Bill of Rights. Rather, the form of these texts that one finds reprinted in state legislative materials or in secondary sources often differs in grammar, wording, punctuation, and capitalization from pre-1791 versions.

Plainly, from what I have noted, there are significant problems of completeness, accuracy, and accessibility. When representing a client in my role as an advocate, both in district courts and courts of appeals, I have often wished that I could, within a reasonably brief period of time, have access to all the pertinent materials to assist me in illuminating for a court the bearing of a constitutional amendment upon the issue before the court. But that has not existed, leaving me dissatisfied that I had done all I could to represent my client well.

The Methodology of the Collection

To remedy these problems and to assist lawyers, judges, scholars, and lay persons, I have compiled and edited the materials in this book. While many interpreters—whether lawyers, judges, historians, political scientists, or scholars in other fields—use and value materials that appeared after the ratification of the Bill of Rights, I decided to limit these materials to those that are of significant use and value to originalists and the many non-originalists who include originalist texts in their interpretations and other work. Like any edition, there have been choices and difficulties.

To compile a reasonably complete set of relevant texts up to the point of ratification, I sought out those materials that were produced by members of the First Congress—the Congress that considered, passed, and sent to the state legislatures the proposed amendments to the Constitution. These materials consist of journals and manuscripts held by the National Archives in Washington, D.C., and pamphlets and manuscripts held by the Library of Congress. I also located the proposals for constitutional amendments submitted by the state conventions that considered ratification of the Constitution, also held by the National Archives.

Readers will note that I have included texts from three versions of the Senate Journals, which were written out by hand from notes and later printed. The first handwritten Senate Journal for the First Session of the First Congress, the session during which the amendments were considered, was damaged by water and was replaced by a second handwritten version. Because there are some differences between these handwritten versions, I have included both the first, designated the Rough Journal, and the second, designated the Smooth Journal, as well as the printed version.

For source texts, I sought out materials that would have been available to the members of the First Congress or with which they would have been familiar. With just a few exceptions, these consist of collections of constitutions, statutes, laws, and charters published before 1789 and available in libraries in New York and other important cities. In addition, these materials include such widely known and widely held texts as the basic English constitutional materials, Blackstone's *Commentaries on the Laws of England*, and American and English caselaw.

For the debate in the Congress, I sought out the four contemporaneous newspaper reports, not the report from the *Annals*, a frequent reference in interpretative decisions despite its later compilation. The newspaper reports are available on microfilm. For the debate in the ratifying conventions and in the press and pamphlets, I relied upon the excellent published collections now available. For letters and diaries, I did the same.

To compile an accurate set of texts, I examined the original documents myself, including the materials in the vaults of the National Archives and Library of Congress. Of course, the able staff of these institutions handled the documents with protective gear, but I was privileged to see the materials and compare them to my own texts. Despite these efforts, the reader should realize that seeing and comparing does not assure absolute accuracy or, better, agreed accuracy. Besides the errors to which we are all prone, differences of opinion inevitably arise regarding orthography. For example, it may sometimes be virtually impossible to distinguish whether a handwritten letter is capitalized or whether an aging mark is a semicolon, a comma, or a random mark or spot. I have used my best judgment. Others may disagree.

To limit this collection to a single volume, I have had to make some choices. While every draft, proposal, and congressional discussion is included, there may be some sources and some ratification and pamphlet debate that readers would have preferred that I include. Moreover, I have limited treatise discussion to

Blackstone's *Commentaries*, with an occasional additional reference, and I have limited caselaw discussion to the most prominent cases. With a few exceptions, I have not included philosophical, political, or religious tracts. I apologize to those who would have preferred that I include Hale or Locke or another writer or yet another opinion. Perhaps, if this book proves useful, there may be an opportunity for an expanded edition.

How To Use This Book

A book claiming accessibility should be easy to use, and I have made every effort to ensure that this volume is user-friendly. I have assigned a chapter for each clause of the Bill of Rights, with the exception of the criminal clauses of the Sixth Amendment, which are found together in Chapter 12. I have divided the materials relating to each clause into three sections: texts, that is, the texts of the drafts, proposals, and sources of the clause; discussion of the clause's drafts and proposals; and discussion of the rights that are protected by the clause.

Thus, in Chapter 1, all of the drafts, proposals, and sources for the Establishment and Free Exercise Clauses are found in the first section, designated 1.1. All discussion of these drafts and proposals are found in the second section, designated 1.2. All discussion of the rights protected by the clauses, for example in Blackstone or pertinent caselaw, were there such, would be found in a third section, designated 1.3. Within each section the reader will find subsections for drafts of the clauses, designated 1.1.1, proposals for the clauses, designated 1.1.2, state and Colonial sources for the clauses, designated 1.1.3, and so on. Numbering continues within each subsection; thus, Madison's proposal for the clauses is designated 1.1.1.1, Sherman's proposal to the House Committee of Eleven is designated 1.1.1.2, and so on. The full structure of the volume can be seen by consulting the table of contents, which begins on page ix.

Acknowledgments

I have many persons to thank for their assistance and support. I began the project that became this book in a civil rights seminar at Southern Methodist University School of Law. The students in that seminar were David Lindsay Adams, Cynthia Beatrice Asensio, Charla Hopkins Bradshaw, Janet Lee Ebanks Booker, Sharlee Ann Cole, Kathleen Denise Garcia, Ricky Donnell Green, Teresa Lynn Harvey, Christopher M. Joe, Karen Ann Holt, Charlotte Coleman Landry, Tonya Johnson Myck, Scarlett Dawn Orenstein, Courtney E. Pellegrino, Kathryn Ann Richardson, Gina Kay Robeen, Steven Dillon Roberts, and Stacy Holt Wadsworth. Two of those students, Mr. Adams and Ms. Harvey, continued work on the project as research assistants and deserve special recognition for their careful and devoted work.

I owe thanks also to Roy Mersky, librarian of the Tarlton Law Library of the University of Texas; Gail Daly, librarian of the Underwood Law Library of Southern Methodist University; and Bruce Muck, assistant librarian of Underwood.

In addition, I thank the typists and proofreaders, Pam Castellano, Susan M. Coassin, Jody DeStafanis, Rosanne Ferraro, Rosemary T. Golia, Shaun Jensen, Les Lane, Eileen Lennox, Laurie Mentz, Dana Mariano, Gillian Moses, Sue

Passander, June Stanton, Bonnie Trexler, Rita E. Watson, and Teresa Zajac. Ms. Watson is blessed with skill and good humor, as is Ms. Stanton, who is assisting with the preparation of my book collecting the drafts, debates, sources, and discussion of the amendments to the United States Constitution ratified during Reconstruction, as well as related statutes.

I thank the outstanding professionals of the Quinnipiac College School of Law Library, Ann Deveaux, director, Michael Hughes, associate director, and Christina DeLucia and Larry Raftery, reference librarians. Ms. DeLucia was especially helpful in locating rare materials, as were my colleague Stanton Krauss, and my son (and future professor), Jacob K. Cogan.

Two archivists at the National Archives, Charles E. Schamel and John Van Derweedt, gave me more time and attention than the equitable division of services should allow. They gave me the special privilege of reading original materials, including the amendment proposals and the Senate journals. They work under difficult conditions in a time of significant underfunding for the preservation of our nation's history.

Phil Lapsansky of the Library Company of Philadelphia was also more than generous with his time and attention. He allowed me the privilege of reading the Library Company's superb collection of pre-nineteenth-century American law books, including the special privilege of reading several books from the library of President Washington.

None of this work would have been possible without the support of two colleagues, President John L. Lahey and Provost John B. Bennett of Quinnipiac College. They have supported all of my efforts above and beyond any reasonable expectation. They have a profound understanding of the importance of scholarship, including scholarship by their deans.

I stand in the long line of persons who are indebted to Stanley N. Katz, professor in the Woodrow Wilson School, Princeton University, and president of the American Council of Learned Societies, who provided his very special encouragement and support for this project. We reconstruct the world by our own works and by the works we assist. Dr. Katz merits a special place on both grounds.

None of this work would have been possible, either, without the support, encouragement, and love of my spouse, Mannette Antill Dodge. She understands my drive to learn what is true and what is just.

Neil H. Cogan
Hamden, Connecticut
July 1997

Chapter 1

AMENDMENT I
ESTABLISHMENT AND FREE EXERCISE CLAUSES

1.1 TEXTS

1.1.1 DRAFTS IN FIRST CONGRESS

1.1.1.1 Proposal by Madison in House, June 8, 1789

1.1.1.1.a   Fourthly. That in article 1st, section 9, between clauses 3 and 4 [of the Constitution], be inserted these clauses, to wit, The civil rights of none shall be abridged on account of religious belief or worship, nor shall any national religion be established, nor shall the full and equal rights of conscience be in any manner, or on any pretext infringed.

Congressional Register, June 8, 1789, vol. 1, p. 427.

1.1.1.1.b   *Fourthly*. That in article 1st, section 9, between clauses 3 and 4 [of the Constitution], be inserted these clauses, to wit: The civil rights of none shall be abridged on account of religious belief or worship, nor shall any national religion be established, nor shall the full and equal rights of conscience be in any manner, or on any pretext infringed.

Daily Advertiser, June 12, 1789, p. 2, col. 1.

1.1.1.1.c   *Fourth*. That in article 1st, section 9, between clauses 3 and 4 [of the Constitution], be inserted these clauses, to wit: The civil rights of none shall be abridged on account of religious belief or worship, nor shall any national religion be established, nor shall the full and equal rights of conscience be in any manner, or on any pretext infringed.

New-York Daily Gazette, June 13, 1789, p. 574, col. 3.

1.1.1.2 Proposal by Sherman to House Committee of Eleven, July 21–28, 1789

[Amendment] 2 The people have certain natural rights which are retained by them when they enter into society, Such are the rights of conscience in matters of religion; of acquiring property, and of pursuing happiness & safety; of Speaking, writing and publishing their Sentiments with decency and freedom; of peaceably Assembling to consult their common good, and of applying to Government by petition or remonstrance for redress of grievances. Of these rights therefore they Shall not be deprived by the government of the united States.

Madison Papers, DLC.

1.1.1.3   Report of House Committee of Eleven, July 28, 1789

ART. I, SEC. 9 — Between PAR. 2 and 3 insert, "No religion shall be established by law, nor shall the equal rights of conscience be infringed."

Broadside Collection, DLC.

1.1.1.4   Motion by Madison in House, August 15, 1789

MR. MADISON

Thought, if the word national was inserted before religion, it would satisfy the minds of honorable gentlemen. He believed the people feared one sect might obtain a pre-eminence, or two combine together and establish a religion to which they would compel others to conform; he thought if the word national was introduced, it would point the amendment directly to the object it was intended to prevent.

Congressional Register, August 15, 1789, vol. 2, p. 196
(motion made and withdrawn).

1.1.1.5   Motion by Livermore in House, August 15, 1789

1.1.1.5.a   MR. LIVERMORE

Was not satisfied with that amendment, but he did not wish them to dwell long on the subject; he thought it would be better if it [the amendment] was altered, and made to read in this manner, that congress shall make no laws touching religion, or infringing the rights of conscience.

Congressional Register, August 15, 1789, vol. 2, p. 196
(motion made and "passed in the affirmative, 31 for, 20 against").

1.1.1.5.b   "The Congress shall make no laws touching religion or the rights of conscience."

Daily Advertiser, August 17, 1789, p. 2, col. 1
("The question on this motion was carried.").

1.1.1.5.c   "The Congress shall make no laws touching religion or the rights of conscience."

New-York Daily Gazette, August 18, 1789, p. 798, col. 4
("The question on this motion was carried.").

1.1.1.5.d   *"Congress shall make no laws touching religion or the rights of conscience.*

Gazette of the U.S., August 19, 1789, p. 147, col. 1
("The question on this motion was carried.").

1.1.1.6   Motion by Ames in House, August 20, 1789

1.1.1.6.a   "[C]ongress shall make no law establishing religion, or to prevent the free exercise thereof, or to infringe the rights of conscience."

Congressional Register, August 20, 1789, vol. 2,
p. 242, col. 2 ("This being adopted.").

1.1.1.6.b   "Congress shall make no law establishing religion, or to prevent the free exercise thereof; or to infringe the rights of conscience."

Gazette of the U.S., August 22, 1789, p. 150.
("This was adopted.").

1.1.1.7 Further House Consideration, August 21, 1789

Third. Congress shall make no law establishing religion, or prohibiting the free exercise thereof, nor shall the rights of conscience be infringed.

HJ, p. 107 ("read and debated . . . agreed to by the House, . . . two-thirds of the members present concurring").[1]

1.1.1.8 House Resolution, August 24, 1789

ARTICLE THE THIRD.

Congress shall make no law establishing religion or prohibiting the free exercise thereof, nor shall the rights of Conscience be infringed.

House Pamphlet, RG 46, DNA.

1.1.1.9 Senate Consideration, August 25, 1789

1.1.1.9.a   The Resolve of the House of Representatives of the 24th of August, upon certain "Articles to be proposed to the Legislatures of the several States as Amendments to the Constitution of the United States" was read as followeth:

. . .

Article the third

Congress shall make no law establishing Religion, or prohibiting the free exercise thereof, nor shall the rights of Conscience be infringed.   Rough SJ, p. 215.

1.1.1.9.b   The Resolve of the House of Representatives of the 24th of August, was read as followeth:

. . .

"Article the Third.

"Congress shall make no law establishing Religion, or prohibiting the free exercise thereof, nor shall the rights of conscience be infringed.   Smooth SJ, p. 194.

1.1.1.9.c   The Resolve of the House of Representatives of the 24th of August, was read as followeth:

. . .

"ARTICLE the THIRD.

"Congress shall make no law establishing Religion, or prohibiting the free exercise thereof, nor shall the rights of conscience be infringed.   Printed SJ, p. 104.

1.1.1.10 Further Senate Consideration, September 3, 1789

1.1.1.10.a   On Motion to amend Article third and to strike out these words, "<u>Religion or prohibiting the free exercise thereof,</u>"
and insert,
"One Religious Sect or Society in preference to others,"

Rough SJ, pp. 243–44 ("It passed in the negative.").

---

[1] On August 22, 1789, the following motion was agreed to:
ORDERED, That it be referred to a committee of three, to prepare and report a proper arrangement of, and introduction to the articles of amendment to the Constitution of the United States, as agreed to by the House; and that Mr. Benson, Mr. Sherman, and Mr. Sedgwick be of the said committee.

HJ, p. 112.

1.1.1.10.b   On motion, To amend Article third, and to strike out these words, "Religion or prohibiting the free Exercise thereof," and insert, "One Religious Sect or Society in preference to others," Smooth SJ, p. 217 ("It passed in the Negative.").

1.1.1.10.c   On motion, To amend Article third, and to strike out these words, "Religion or prohibiting the free Exercise thereof," and insert, "One Religious Sect or Society in preference to others," Printed SJ, p. 116 ("It passed in the Negative.").

1.1.1.11   Further Senate Consideration, September 3, 1789

1.1.1.11.a   On Motion that the Article third be stricken out
Rough SJ, p. 244 ("It passed in the negative.").

1.1.1.11.b   On motion, That Article the third be stricken out,
Smooth SJ, p. 218 ("It passed in the Negative.").

1.1.1.11.c   On motion, That Article the third be stricken out,
Printed SJ, p. 116 ("It passed in the Negative.").

1.1.1.12   Further Senate Consideration, September 3, 1789

1.1.1.12.a   On Motion to adopt the following, in lieu of the third Article
"Congress shall not make any law infringing the rights of conscience, or establishing any Religious Sect or Society," Rough SJ, p. 244 ("It passed in the negative.").

1.1.1.12.b   On motion, to adopt the following, in lieu of the third Article,
"Congress shall not make any law, infringing the rights of conscience, or establishing any Religious Sect or Society," Smooth SJ, p. 218 ("It passed in the Negative.").

1.1.1.12.c   On motion, To adopt the following, in lieu of the third Article,
"Congress shall not make any law, infringing the rights of conscience, or establishing any Religious Sect or Society," Printed SJ, p. 116 ("It passed in the Negative.").

1.1.1.13   Further Senate Consideration, September 3, 1789

1.1.1.13.a   On Motion to amend the third Article to read thus —
"Congress shall make no law establishing any particular denomination of religion in preference to another or prohibiting the free exercise thereof, nor shall the rights of Conscience be infringed." Rough SJ, p. 244 ("It passed in the negative.").

1.1.1.13.b   On motion, To amend the third Article, to read thus —
"Congress shall make no law establishing any particular denomination of Religion in preference to another, or prohibiting the free exercise thereof, nor shall the rights of conscience be infringed" — . . . .
Smooth SJ, p. 218 (" It passed in the Negative.").

1.1.1.13.c   On motion, To amend the third Article, to read thus —
"Congress shall make no law establishing any particular denomination of reli-

gion in preference to another, or prohibiting the free exercise thereof, nor shall the rights of conscience be infringed" —   Printed SJ, p. 117 ("It passed in the Negative.").

1.1.1.14   Further Senate Consideration, September 3, 1789

1.1.1.14.a   On the question upon the third Article as it came from the House of Representatives.
                                        Rough SJ, p. 244 ("It passed in the negative.").

1.1.1.14.b   On the question upon the third Article as it came from the House of Representatives — . . . .
                                        Smooth SJ, p. 218 ("It passed in the Negative.").

1.1.1.14.c   On the question upon the third Article as it came from the House of Representatives — . . . .
                                        Printed SJ, p. 117 ("It passed in the Negative.").

1.1.1.15   Further Senate Consideration, September 3, 1789

1.1.1.15.a   On Motion to adopt the third Article proposed in the Resolve of the House of Representatives amended by striking out these words.
          "Nor shall the rights of conscience be infringed"
                                        Rough SJ, p. 245 ("It passed in the affirmative.").

1.1.1.15.b   On motion, To adopt the third Article proposed in the Resolve of the House of Representatives, amended by striking out these words —
          "Nor shall the rights of conscience be infringed" —
                                        Smooth SJ, p. 218 ("It passed in the Affirmative.").

1.1.1.15.c   On motion, To adopt the third Article proposed in the Resolve of the House of Representatives, amended by striking out these words —
          "Nor shall the rights of conscience be infringed" —
                                        Printed SJ, p. 117 ("It passed in the Affirmative.").

1.1.1.15.d   that the Senate do
          Resolved ∧ to concur with the House of Representatives in Article Third, by striking out these words "Nor shall the rights of conscience be infringed."
                                        Senate MS, RG 46, p. 2.

1.1.1.16   Further Senate Consideration, September 9, 1789

1.1.1.16.a   And on Motion to amend article the third to read as follows:
          "Congress shall make no law establishing articles of faith or a mode of worship, or prohibiting the free exercise of Religion; or abridging the freedom of Speech, or the press, or the right of the People peaceably to assemble, and petition to the government for the redress of grievances."
                  . . .
          On motion, To strike out the fourth article,
                                        Rough SJ, p. 274 (As to each motion, "It passed in the Affirmative.").

1.1.1.16.b   On motion, To amend article the third, to read as follows:
          "Congress shall make no law establishing articles of faith or a mode of worship, or prohibiting the free exercise of religion, or abridging the freedom of speech, or

the press, or the right of the people peaceably to assemble, and petition to the Government for the redress of grievances" —

. . .

On motion, To strike out the fourth article, ...

Smooth SJ, p. 243 (As to each motion, "It passed in the Affirmative.").

1.1.1.16.c On motion, To amend Article the third, to read as follows:

"Congress shall make no law establishing articles of faith or a mode of worship, or prohibiting the free exercise of religion, or abridging the freedom of speech, or the press, or the right of the people peaceably to assemble, and petition to the Government for the redress of grievances" —

. . .

On motion, To strike out the fourth Article,

Printed SJ, p. 129 (As to each motion, "It passed in the Affirmative.").

1.1.1.16.d On the question to concur with the House of Representatives on their resolution of the 24th of Augt. proposing amendments to the constitution of the United States, with the following amendments viz:

. . .

To erase from the 3d. Article the word "Religion" & insert — Articles of faith or a mode of Worship. —

And to erase from the same article the words "thereof, nor shall the rights of Conscience be infringed" & insert — of Religion; or abridging the freedom of speech, or of the press, or of the right of the people peaceably to assemble, & to petition to the government for a redress of grievances

To erase the 4th. article, & the words "Article the fourth."

Ellsworth MS, pp. 1–2, RG 46, DNA.

1.1.1.17 **Senate Resolution, September 9, 1789**

ARTICLE THE THIRD.

Congress shall make no law establishing articles of faith, or a mode of worship, or prohibiting the free exercise of religion, or abridging the freedom of speech, or of the press, or the right of the people peaceably to assemble, and to petition to the government for a redress of grievances.

Senate Pamphlet, RG 46, DNA.

1.1.1.18 **Further House Consideration, September 21, 1789**

RESOLVED, That this House doth agree to the second, fourth, eighth, twelfth, thirteenth, sixteenth, eighteenth, nineteenth, twenty-fifth, and twenty-sixth amendments, and doth disagree to the first, third, fifth, sixth, seventh, ninth, tenth, eleventh, fourteenth, fifteenth, seventeenth, twentieth, twenty-first, twenty-second, twenty-third, and twenty-fourth amendments proposed by the Senate to the said articles, two thirds of the members present concurring on each vote.

RESOLVED, That a conference be desired with the Senate on the subject matter of the amendments disagreed to, and that Mr. Madison, Mr. Sherman, and Mr. Vining, be appointed managers at the same on the part of this House.

HJ, p. 146.

1.1.1.19   Further Senate Consideration, September 21, 1789

1.1.1.19.a   A message from the House of Representatives —
Mr. Beckley, their Clerk, brought up a Resolve of the House of this date, to agree to the 2nd, 4th, 8th, 12th, 13th, 16th, 18th, 19th, 25th, and 26th Amendments proposed by the Senate, "To articles of Amendment to be proposed to the Legislatures of the several States, as Amendments to the Constitution of the United States," and to disagree to the 1st, 3d, 5th, 6th, 7th, 9th, 10th, 11th, 14th, 15th, 17th, 20th, 21st, 22d, 23d, and 24th amendments: Two thirds of the members present concurring on each vote: And "That a conference be desired with the Senate on the subject matter of the amendments disagreed to," and that Mr. Madison, Mr. Sherman, and Mr. Vining, be appointed managers of the same, on the part of the House of Representatives —
And he withdrew.   Smooth SJ, pp. 265–66.

1.1.1.19.b   A message from the House of Representatives —
Mr. Beckley, their Clerk, brought up a Resolve of the House of this date, to agree to the 2d, 4th, 8th, 12th, 13th, 16th, 18th, 19th, 25th, and 26th Amendments proposed by the Senate, "To Articles of Amendment to be proposed to the Legislatures of the several States, as Amendments to the Constitution of the United States," and to disagree to the 1st, 3d, 5th, 6th, 7th, 9th, 10th, 11th, 14th, 15th, 17th, 20th, 21st, 22d, 23d, and 24th Amendments: Two thirds of the members present concurring on each vote: And "That a conference be desired with the Senate on the subject matter of the Amendments disagreed to," and that Mr. Madison, Mr. Sherman, and Mr. Vining, be appointed managers of the same, on the part of the House of Representatives —
And he withdrew.   Printed SJ, pp. 141–42.

1.1.1.20   Further Senate Consideration, September 21, 1789

1.1.1.20.a   The Senate proceeded to consider the Message of the House of Representatives disagreeing to the Amendments made by the Senate "To Articles to be proposed to the Legislatures of the several States, as Amendments to the Constitution of the United States" And
RESOLVED, That the Senate do recede from their third Amendment, and do insist on all the others.
RESOLVED, That the Senate do concur with the House of Representatives in a conference on the subject matter of disagreement on the said Articles of Amendment, and that Mr. Ellsworth Mr. Carroll and Mr. Paterson be managers of the conference on the part of the Senate.   Smooth SJ, p. 267.

1.1.1.20.b   The Senate proceeded to consider the message of the House of Representatives disagreeing to the Amendments made by the Senate "To Articles to be proposed to the Legislatures of the several States, as Amendments to the Constitution of the United States" — And
RESOLVED, That the Senate do recede from their third Amendment, and do insist on all the others.

RESOLVED, That the Senate do concur with the House of Representatives in a conference on the subject matter of disagreement on the said Articles of Amendment, and that Mr. Ellsworth, Mr. Carroll, and Mr. Paterson be managers of the conference on the part of the Senate.

Printed SJ, p. 142.

1.1.1.21 Conference Committee Report, September 24, 1789

[T]hat it will be proper for the House of Representatives to agree to the said Amendments proposed by the Senate, with an Amendment to their fifth Amendment, so that the third Article shall read as follows: "Congress shall make no Law <u>respecting an establishment of Religion</u>, or prohibiting the free exercise thereof; or abridging the freedom of Speech, or of the Press; or the right of the people peaceably to assemble and ~~to~~ petition the Government for a redress of grievances;" And with an Amendment to the fourteenth Amendment proposed by the Senate, so that the eighth Article, as numbered in the Amendments proposed by the Senate, shall read as follows "In all criminal prosecutions, the accused shall enjoy the right to a speedy & publick trial <u>by an impartial jury of the district wherein the crime shall have been committed, as the district shall have been previously ascertained by law</u>, and to be informed of the nature and cause of the accusation; to be confronted with the witnesses against him, and to have com-

pulsory process for obtaining witnesses ~~against him~~ in his favour, & $\wedge$ have the assistance of counsel for his defence."

to

Conference MS, RG 46, DNA (Ellsworth's handwriting).

1.1.1.22 House Consideration of Conference Committee Report, September 24 [25], 1789

RESOLVED, That this House doth recede from their disagreement to the first, third, fifth, sixth, seventh, ninth, tenth, eleventh, fourteenth, fifteenth, seventeenth, twentieth, twenty-first, twenty-second, twenty-third, and twenty-fourth amendments, insisted on by the Senate: PROVIDED, That the two articles which by the amendments of the Senate are now proposed to be inserted as the third and eighth articles, shall be amended to read as followeth;

Article the third. "Congress shall make no law respecting an establishment of religion, or prohibiting the free exercise thereof; or abridging the freedom of speech, or of the press; or the right of the people peaceably to assemble, and to petition the government for a redress of grievances."

Article the eighth. "In all criminal prosecutions, the accused shall enjoy the right to a speedy and public trial by an impartial jury of the state and district wherein the crime shall have been committed, which district shall have been previously ascertained by law, and to be informed of the nature and cause of the accusation, to be confronted with the witnesses against him, to have compulsory process for obtaining witnesses in his favor, and to have the assistance of council for his defence."

HJ, p. 152 ("On the question, that the House do agree to the alteration and amendment of the eighth article, in manner aforesaid, It was resolved in the affirmative. Ayes 37 Noes 14").

1.1.1.23   Senate Consideration of Conference Committee Report, September 24, 1789

1.1.1.23.a   Mr. Ellsworth, on behalf of the managers of the conference on "articles to be proposed to the several States as Amendments to the Constitution of the United States," reported as follows:

That it will be proper for the House of Representatives to agree to the said amendments proposed by the Senate, with an Amendment to their fifth Amendment, so that the third Article shall read as follows: "Congress shall make no law respecting an establishment of <u>Religion</u>, or prohibiting the free exercise thereof; or abridging the freedom of Speech, or of the Press; or the right of the people peaceably to assemble and petition the Government for a redress of Grievances;" And with an Amendment to the fourteenth Amendment proposed by the Senate, so that the eighth article, as numbered in the Amendments proposed by the Senate, shall read as follows; "In all criminal prosecutions, the accused shall enjoy the right to a speedy and public trial by an impartial <u>Jury</u> of the district wherein the <u>Crime</u> shall have been committed, as the district shall have been previously ascertained by law, and to be informed of the nature and cause of the accusation, to be confronted with the witnesses against him, and to have compulsory process for obtaining witnesses in his favor, and to have the assistance of Counsel for defence."

Smooth SJ, pp. 272–73.

1.1.1.23.b   Mr. Ellsworth, on behalf of the managers of the conference on "Articles to be proposed to the several States as Amendments to the Constitution of the United States," reported as follows:

That it will be proper for the House of Representatives to agree to the said Amendments proposed by the Senate, with an Amendment to their fifth Amendment, so that the third Article shall read as follows: "Congress shall make no Law RESPECTING AN ESTABLISHMENT OF RELIGION, or prohibiting the free exercise thereof; or abridging the freedom of Speech, or of the Press; or the right of the People peaceably to assemble and petition the Government for a redress of Grievances;" And with an Amendment to the fourteenth Amendment proposed by the Senate, so that the eighth Article, as numbered in the Amendments proposed by the Senate, shall read as follows; "In all criminal prosecutions, the accused shall enjoy the right to a speedy and public trial BY AN IMPARTIAL JURY OF THE DISTRICT WHEREIN THE CRIME SHALL HAVE BEEN COMMITTED, AS THE DISTRICT SHALL HAVE BEEN PREVIOUSLY ASCERTAINED BY LAW, and to be informed of the nature and cause of the accusation, to be confronted with the witnesses against him, and to have compulsory process for obtaining witnesses in his favor, and to have the assistance of Counsel for defence."

Printed SJ, p. 145.

1.1.1.24   Further Senate Consideration of Conference Committee Report, September 24, 1789

1.1.1.24.a   A Message from the House of Representatives —

Mr. Beckley, their Clerk, brought up the Amendments to the "Articles to be proposed to the Legislatures of the several States, as Amendments to the Constitution of the United States;" and informed the Senate, that the House of Representatives had receded from their disagreement to the 1st, 3d, 5th, 6th, 7th, 9th, 10th, 11th, 14th, 15th, 17th, 20th, 21st, 22d, 23d, and 24th Amendments, insisted on by the Senate: Provided that the "Two Articles, which by the Amendments of the Senate are now proposed to be inserted as the third and eighth Articles," shall be amended to read as followeth:

Article the Third. "Congress shall make no Law respecting an establishment of Religion, or prohibiting the free exercise thereof; or abridging the freedom of Speech, or of the Press; or the right of the people peaceably to assemble, and petition the Government for a redress of Grievances."

Article the Eighth. "In all criminal prosecutions the accused shall enjoy the right to a speedy and public trial by an impartial Jury of the State and District, wherein the crime shall have been committed, which District shall have been previously ascertained by law, and to be informed of the nature and cause of the accusation, to be confronted with the witnesses against him, and to have compulsory process for obtaining witnesses in his favor, and to have the assistance of Counsel for his defence."

Smooth SJ, pp. 278–79.

1.1.1.24.b A Message from the House of Representatives —

Mr. Beckley, their Clerk, brought up the Amendments to the "Articles to be proposed to the Legislatures of the several States, as Amendments to the Constitution of the United States;" and informed the Senate, that the House of Representatives had receded from their disagreement to the 1st, 3d, 5th, 6th, 7th, 9th, 10th, 11th, 14th, 15th, 17th, 20th, 21st, 22d, 23d, and 24th Amendments, insisted on by the Senate: Provided that the "Two Articles, which by the Amendments of the Senate are now proposed to be inserted as the third and eighth Articles," shall be amended to read as followeth:

Article the Third. "Congress shall make no Law respecting an establishment of Religion, or prohibiting the free exercise thereof; or abridging the freedom of Speech, or of the Press; or the right of the People peaceably to assemble, and petition the Government for a redress of Grievances."

Article the Eighth. "In all criminal prosecutions the accused shall enjoy the right to a speedy and public trial by an impartial Jury of the State and District, wherein the crime shall have been committed, which District shall have been previously ascertained by law, and to be informed of the nature and cause of the accusation, to be confronted with the witnesses against him, and to have compulsory process for obtaining witnesses in his favor, and to have the assistance of Counsel for his defence."

Printed SJ, p.148.

1.1.1.25 Further Senate Consideration of Conference Committee Report, September 25, 1789

1.1.1.25.a The Senate proceeded to consider the Message from the House of Representatives of the 24th, with Amendments to the Amendments of the Senate, to "Articles to be proposed to the Legislatures of the several States, as Amendments to the Constitution of the United States" — And

RESOLVED, That the Senate do concur in the Amendments proposed by the House of Representatives, to the Amendments of the Senate. Smooth SJ, p. 283.

1.1.1.25.b   The Senate proceeded to consider the Message from the House of Representatives of the 24th, with Amendments to the Amendments of the Senate, to "Articles to be proposed to the Legislatures of the several States, as Amendments to the Constitution of the United States" — And

RESOLVED, That the Senate do concur in the Amendments proposed by the House of Representatives, to the Amendments of the Senate.

Printed SJ, pp. 150–51.

1.1.1.26   Agreed Resolution, September 25, 1789

1.1.1.26.a   Article the Third.

Congress shall make no law respecting an establishment of religion, or prohibiting the free exercise thereof, or abridging the freedom of speech, or of the press, or the right of the people peaceably to assemble, and to petition the Government for a redress of grievances.

Smooth SJ, Appendix, p. 292.

1.1.1.26.b   ARTICLE THE THIRD.

Congress shall make no law respecting an establishment of religion, or prohibiting the free exercise thereof, or abridging the freedom of speech, or of the press, or the right of the people peaceably to assemble, and to petition the Government for a redress of grievances.

Printed SJ, Appendix, p. 163.

1.1.1.27   Enrolled Resolution, September 28, 1789

Article the third . . . Congress shall make no law respecting an establishment of religion, or prohibiting the free exercise thereof; or abridging the freedom of speech, or of the press, or the right of the people peaceably to assemble, and to petition the Government for a redress of grievances.

Enrolled Resolutions, RG 11, DNA.

1.1.1.28   Printed Versions

1.1.1.28.a   ART. I. Congress shall make no law respecting an establishment of religion, or prohibiting the free exercise thereof; or abridging the freedom of speech, or of the press; or the right of the people peaceably to assemble, and to petition the government for a redress of grievances.

Statutes at Large, vol. 1, p. 21.

1.1.1.28.b   ART. III. Congress shall make no law respecting an establishment of religion, or prohibiting the free exercise thereof; or abridging the freedom of speech, or of the press; or the right of the people peaceably to assemble, and to petition the government for a redress of grievances.

Statutes at Large, vol. 1, p. 97.

1.1.2 PROPOSALS FROM THE STATE CONVENTIONS

1.1.2.1   Maryland Minority, April 26, 1788

12. That there be no national religion established by law, but that all persons be equally entitled to protection in their religious liberty.

Maryland Gazette, May 1, 1788 (committee minority).

1.1.2.2 Massachusetts Minority, February 6, 1788

[T]hat the said Constitution be never construed to authorize Congress to infringe the just liberty of the press, or the rights of conscience; or to prevent the people of the United States, who are peaceable citizens, from keeping their own arms; or to raise standing armies, unless when necessary for the defence of the United States, or of some one or more of them; or to prevent the people from petitioning, in a peaceable and orderly manner, the federal legislature, for a redress of grievances; or to subject the people to unreasonable searches and seizures of their persons, papers or possessions.   Massachusetts Convention, pp. 86–87.

1.1.2.3 New Hampshire, June 21, 1788

Eleventh

Congress shall make no Laws touching Religion, or to infringe the rights of Conscience —   State Ratifications, RG 11, DNA.

1.1.2.4 New York, July 26, 1788

That the People have an equal, natural and unalienable right, freely and peaceably to Exercise their Religion according to the dictates of Conscience, and that no Religious Sect or Society ought to be favoured or established by Law in preference of others.   State Ratifications, RG 11, DNA.

1.1.2.5 North Carolina, August 1, 1788

19th. That any person religiously scrupulous of bearing arms ought to be exempted upon payment of an equivalent to employ another to bear arms in his stead.

10. [20th.] That religion, or the duty which we owe to our Creator, and the manner of discharging it, can be directed only by reason and conviction, not by force or violence, and therefore all men have an equal, natural and unalienable right, to the free exercise of religion according to the dictates of conscience, and that no particular religious sect or society ought to be favoured or established by law in preference to others.   State Ratifications, RG 11, DNA.

1.1.2.6 Pennsylvania Minority, December 12, 1787

1. The rights of conscience shall be held inviolable, and neither the legislative, executive, nor judicial powers of the United States shall have authority to alter, abrogate, or infringe any part of the constitutions of the several states, which provide for the preservation of liberty in matters of religion.
                    Pennsylvania Packet, December 18, 1787.

1.1.2.7 Rhode Island, May 29, 1790

4th. That religion, or the duty which we owe to our Creator, and the manner of discharging it, can be directed only by reason and conviction, and not by force or violence, and therefore all men, have an equal, natural and unalienable right to the free exercise of religion according to the dictates of conscience, and that no particular religious sect or society ought to be favoured, or established by law in preference to others.

State Ratifications, RG 11, DNA.

1.1.2.8 Virginia, June 27, 1788

That there be a Declaration or Bill of Rights asserting and securing from encroachment the essential and unalienable Rights of the People in some such manner as the following:

. . .

Twentieth, That religion or the duty which we owe to our Creator, and the manner of discharging it can be directed only by reason and conviction, not by force or violence, and therefore all men have an equal, natural and unalienable right to the free exercise of religion according to the dictates of conscience, and that no particular religious sect or society ought to be favored or established by Law in preference to others.

State Ratifications, RG 11, DNA.

1.1.3 STATE CONSTITUTIONS AND LAWS; COLONIAL CHARTERS AND LAWS

1.1.3.1 Connecticut

1.1.3.1.a Fundamental Orders of Connecticut, 1638–39

FORASMUCH as it hath pleased the Almighty God, by the wise disposition of his divine providence, so to order and dispose of things, that we the Inhabitants and residents of Windsor, Hartford and Weathersfield, are now cohabiting, and dwelling in and uppon the river of Connecticutt, and the lands thereunto adjoining, and well knowing when a people are gathered together, the word of God requires, that to meinteine the peace and union of such a people, there should bee an orderly and decent government established according to God, to order and dispose of the affaires of the people at all seasons, as occasion shall require; doe therefore associate and conjoine ourselves to bee as one publique STATE or COMMONWEALTH; and doe for ourselves and our successors, and such as shall bee adjoined to us at any time hereafter, enter into combination, and confederation together, to meinteine and preserve the libberty and purity of the Gospell of our Lord Jesus, which we now profess, as also the discipline of the churches, which, according to the truth of the said Gospell, is now practised amongst us; as allso in our civill affaires to be guided and governed according to such lawes, rules, orders, and decrees as shall bee made, ordered, and decreed. . . .

Connecticut Code, pp. 13–14.

1.1.3.1.b New Haven Code, 1655

That none shall be admitted Free-men, or free Burgesses within this Jurisdiction, or any part of it, but such Planters as are Members of some one, or other of the approved Churches of *New-England*; nor shall any but such be chosen to Magistracy, or to carry on any part of Civil Judicature, or as Deputies or Assistants to have power, or Vote in establishing Lawes, or in making or repealing Orders, or to any chief Military Office, or trust, nor shall any others, but such Church Members, have any Vote in any such Elections. Though all others admitted to be Planters, have right to their proper Inheritances, and doe and shall enjoy all other Civil liberties and priviledges, according to all Lawes, Orders, or grants, which are, or hereafter shall be made for this Colony. New Haven's Lawes, pp. 9–10.

1.1.3.1.c **Charter of Connecticut, 1662**

CHARLES the Second, by the Grace of GOD, KING OF *England, Scotland, France* and *Ireland,* Defender of the Faith &c., . . . And We do further of Our especial Grace, certain Knowledge, and meer Motion, Give, and Grant unto the said Governour and Company of the English Colony of *Connecticut,* in *New-England* in *America,* and their Successors, That it shall and may be Lawful to and for the Governour, or Deputy-Governour, . . . to Erect and Make such Judicatories, for the Hearing and Determining of all Actions, Causes, Matters and Things happening within the said Colony or Plantation, and which shall be in Dispute and Depending there, as they shall think Fit and Convenient, and also from Time to Time to Make, Ordain, and Establish all manner of Wholesome and Reasonable Laws, Statutes, Ordinances, Directions and Instructions, not Contrary to the Laws of this Realm of *England,* as well for Settling the Forms, and Ceremonies of Government and Magistracy, Fit and Necessary for the said Plantation and the Inhabitants there, as for Naming and Stiling all Sorts of Officers, both Superiour and Inferiour, which they shall Find Needful for the Government and Plantation of the said Colony, and the Distinguishing and settling forth of the several Duties, Powers and Limits of every such Office and Place, and the Forms of such Oaths, not being Contrary to the Laws and Statutes of this Our Realm of *England,* to be Administered for the Execution of the said several Offices and Places, as also for the Disposing and Ordering of the Election of such of the said Officers as are to be Annually Chosen, and of such others as shall Succeed in case of Death or Removal, and Administring the said Oath to the New-Elected Officers, and Granting Necessary Commissions, and for Imposition of Lawful Fines, Mulcts, Imprisonment or other Punishment upon Offenders and Delinquents according to the Course of other Corporations within this Our Kingdom of *England,* and the same Laws, Fines, Mulcts and Executions, to Alter, Change, Revoke, Annul, Release, or Pardon under their Common Seal, as by the said General Assembly, or the major Part of them shall be thought Fit, and for the Directing, Ruling and Disposing of all other Matters and Things, whereby Our said People Inhabitants there, may be so Religiously, Peaceably and Civilly Governed, as their Good Life and Orderly Conversation, may Win and Invite the Natives of the Country, to the Knowledge and Obedience of the Only True God, and the Saviour of Mankind and the Christian Faith, which in Our Royal Intentions, and the Adventurers Free Profession is the Only and Principal End of this Plantation. . . . Connecticut Charter, pp. 1, 4–5.

1.1.3.2   **Delaware**

1.1.3.2.a   **Charter of Delaware, 1701**

WILLIAM PENN, Proprietary and Governor of the province of Pennsylvania and territories thereunto belonging, to all whom these presents shall come, sendeth greeting. . . .

. . .

I. *Because* no people can be truly happy, though under the greatest enjoyment of civil liberties, if abridged of the freedom of their consciences, as to their religious profession and worship: And Almighty God being the only Lord of conscience, Father of lights and spirits; and the Author as well as Object of all divine knowledge, faith and worship, who only doth enlighten the minds, and persuade and convince the understandings of people, I do hereby grant and declare, That no person or persons, inhabiting in this province or territories, who shall confess and acknowledge One Almighty God, the Creator, Upholder and Ruler of the world; and professes him or themselves obliged to live quietly under the civil government, shall be in any case molested or prejudiced, in his or their person or estate, because of his or their consciencious persuasion or practice, nor be compelled to frequent or maintain any religious worship, place or ministry, contrary to his or their mind, or to do or suffer any other act or thing, contrary to their religious persuasion.

And that all persons who also profess to believe in Jesus Christ, the Saviour of the world, shall be capable (notwithstanding their other persuasions and practices in point of conscience and religion) to serve this government in any capacity, both Legislatively and Executively, he or they solemnly promising, when lawfully required, allegiance to the King as Sovereign, and fidelity to the Proprietary and Governor. . . .

. . .

But, because the happiness of mankind depends so much upon the enjoying of liberty of their consciences, as aforesaid, I do hereby solemnly declare, promise and grant, for me, my heirs and assigns, That the first article of this charter relating to liberty of conscience, and every part and clause therein, according to the true intent and meaning thereof, shall be kept and remain, without any alteration, inviolably for ever.

Delaware Laws, vol. 1, App., pp. 37, 39, 42.

1.1.3.2.b   **Declaration of Rights, 1776**

SECT. 2. That all men have a natural and unalienable right to worship Almighty God according to the dictates of their own consciences and understandings; and that no man ought or of right can be compelled to attend any religious worship or maintain any ministry contrary to or against his own free will and consent, and that no authority can or ought to be vested in, or assumed by any power whatever that shall in any case interfere with, or in any manner controul the right of conscience in the free exercise of religious worship.

SECT. 3. That all persons professing the Christian religion ought forever to enjoy equal rights and privileges in this state, unless, under colour of religion, any man disturb the peace, the happiness or safety of society.

Delaware Laws, vol. 1, App., p. 79.

1.1.3.2.c **Constitution, 1776**

ART. 29. There shall be no establishment of any one religious sect in this state in preference to another; and no Clergyman or Preacher of the Gospel of any denomination shall be capable of holding any civil office in this state, or of being a Member of either of the branches of the Legislature while they continue in the exercise of the pastoral function. *Delaware Laws, vol. 1, App., pp. 90–91.*

1.1.3.3 **Georgia**

1.1.3.3.a **Constitution, 1777**

LVI. All persons whatever shall have the free exercise of their religion; provided it be not repugnant to the peace and safety of the State; and shall not, unless by consent, support any teacher, or teachers, except those of their own profession.

. . .

LXII. No clergyman, of any denomination, shall be allowed a seat in the legislature. *Georgia Laws, pp. 15–16.*

1.1.3.3.b **Constitution, 1789**

ARTICLE I.

. . .

Sect. 18. No clergyman of any denomination shall be a member of the general assembly.

. . .

ARTICLE IV.

. . .

Sect. 5. All persons shall have the free exercise of religion; without being obliged to contribute to the support of any religious profession but their own.

Georgia Laws, pp. 27, 29.

1.1.3.4 **Maine: Grant of the Province of Maine, 1639**

CHARLES by the grace of God King of England Scotland Fraunce and Ireland Defender of the faith, &c. . . . And for the better government of such our Subjectes and others as at any tyme shall happen to dwell or reside within the said Province and premisses or passe to or from the same, Our Will and pleasure is That the Religion nowe professed in the Church of England and Ecclesiasticall Governement nowe used in the same shalbee forever hereafter professed and with asmuch convenient speede as may bee setled and established in and throughout the said Province and premisses and every of them. . . . *Maine Historical Society.*

1.1.3.5 **Maryland**

1.1.3.5.a **Charter of Maryland, 1632**

CHARLES By the Grace of God, King of *England, Scotland, France and Ireland*, Defender of the Faith, &c. . . .

We do also grant and confirm . . . the Patronages and Advowsons of all Churches, which (as Christian Religion shall encrease within the Countrey, Isles,

Ilets, and limits aforesaid) shall happen hereafter to be erected: together with license and power to build & found Churches, Chappels, & Oratories, in convenient & fit places within the premises, and to cause them to be dedicated, and consecrated according to the Ecclesiastical Laws of our Kingdom of *England.* . . .

Maryland Charter, pp. 1, 3–4.

1.1.3.5.b   Act Concerning Religion, 1649

Be it Therefore also by the Lo: Proprietary . . . that noe person or psons whatsoever within this Province, . . . professing to beleive in Jesus Christ, shall from henceforth bee any waies troubled, Molested or discountenanced for or in respect of his or her religion nor in the free exercise thereof within this Province or the Islands thereunto belonging nor any way compelled to the beleife or exercise of any other Religion against his or her consent, soe as they be not unfaithfull to the Lord Proprietary, or molest or conspire against the civill Governemt, established or to bee established in this Province vnder him or his heires. . . .

Archives of Maryland: Proceedings and Acts of the General Assembly
of Maryland (Baltimore: Maryland Historical Society, 1883),
vol. 1, pp. 246–47.

1.1.3.5.c   Declaration of Rights, 1776

33. That as it is the duty of every man to worship God in such manner as he thinks most acceptable to him, all persons professing the christian religion are equally entitled to protection in their religious liberty, wherefore no person ought by any law to be molested in his person or estate on account of his religious persuasion or profession, or for his religious practice, unless under colour of religion any man shall disturb the good order, peace or safety of the state, or shall infringe the laws of morality, or injure others, in their natural, civil or religious rights; nor ought any person to be compelled to frequent or maintain, or contribute, unless on contract, to maintain, any particular place of worship, or any particular ministry; yet the legislature may, in their discretion, lay a general and equal tax for the support of the christian religion, leaving to each individual the power of appointing the payment over of the money collected from him, to the support of any particular place of worship or minister, or for the benefit of the poor of his own denomination, or the poor in general of any particular county; but the churches, chapels, glebes, and all other property now belonging to the church of England, ought to remain to the church of England for ever. . . .

34. That every gift, sale, or devise of lands, to any minister, public teacher, or preacher of the gospel, as such, or to any religious sect, order or denomination, or to or for the support, use or benefit of, or in trust for, any minister, public teacher, or preacher of the gospel, as such, or any religious sect, order or denomination; and also every devise of goods or chattels to, or to or for the support, use or benefit of any minister, public teacher, or preacher of the gospel, as such, or any religious sect, order or denomination, without the leave of the legislature, shall be void; except always any sale, gift, lease or devise of any quantity of land not exceeding two acres, for a church, meeting, or other house of worship, and for a burying

ground, which shall be improved, enjoyed or used only for such purpose, or such sale, gift, lease or devise, shall be void.

35. That no other test or qualification ought to be required on admission to any office of trust or profit, than such oath of support and fidelity to this state, and such oath of office, as shall be directed by this convention, or the legislature of this state, and a declaration of a belief in the christian religion.

36. That the manner of administering an oath to any person ought to be such as those of the religious persuasion, profession or denomination of which such person is one, generally esteem the most effectual confirmation, by the attestation of the Divine Being. And that the people called quakers, those called dunkers, and those called menonists, holding it unlawful to take an oath on any occasion, ought to be allowed to make their solemn affirmation in the manner that quakers have been heretofore allowed to affirm, and to be of the same avail as an oath, in all such cases as the affirmation of quakers hath been allowed and accepted within this state instead of an oath. And further, on such affirmation warrants to search for stolen goods, or the apprehension or commitment of offenders, ought to be granted, or security for the peace awarded; and quakers, dunkers, or menonists ought also, on their solemn affirmation as aforesaid, to be admitted as witnesses in all criminal cases not capital.

Maryland Laws, November 3, 1776.

1.1.3.5.d Constitution, 1776

55. That every person appointed to any office of profit or trust shall, before he enters on the execution thereof, take the following oath; to wit: "I, A.B. do swear, that I do not hold myself bound in allegiance to the king of Great-Britain, and that I will be faithful and bear true allegiance to the state of Maryland." And shall also subscribe a declaration of his belief in the christian religion.

Maryland Laws, November 8, 1776.

1.1.3.6 Massachusetts

1.1.3.6.a Charter of New England, 1620

JAMES, by the Grace of God, King of *England, Scotland, France,* and *Ireland,* Defender of the Faith, &c. to all whom these Presents shall come, *Greeting,* Whereas, upon the humble Petition of divers of our well disposed Subjects, that intended to make several Plantations in the Parts of *America,* between the Degrees of thirty-ffoure and ffourty-five; We according to our princely Inclination, favouring much their worthy Disposition, in Hope thereby to advance the in Largement of Christian Religion, to the Glory of God Almighty, as also by that Meanes to streatch out the Bounds of our Domininions, and to replenish those Deserts with People governed by Lawes and Magistrates, for the peaceable Commerce of all, . . . Now forasmuch as We have been in like Manner humbly petitioned unto by our trusty and well beloved Servant, Sir *fferdinando Gorges,* Knight, Captain of our ffort and Island by Plymouth, and by certain the principal Knights and Gentleman Adventurers of the said Second Collonye, and by divers other Persons of Quality, who now intend to be their Associates, divers of which have been at great and extraordinary Charge, and sustained many Losses in seeking and discovering a Place fitt and convenient to lay the Foundation of a hopeful Plantation, and have divers Years past by God's Assistance, and their own endeavours, taken actual Possession of the Continent hereafter mentioned, in our Name and to our Use, as Sovereign Lord thereof, and have settled already some of our People in Places agreeable to their Desires in those Parts, and in Confidence of prosperous Success therein, by the Continuance of God's Devine Blessing, and our Royall Permission, have resolved in a more plentifull and effectual Manner to prosecute the same, and to that Purpose and Intent have desired of Us, for their better Encouragement and Satisfaction herein, and that they may avoide all Confusion, Questions, or Differences between themselves, and those of the said first Collonye, . . . And also for that We have been further given certainly to knowe, that within these late Years there hath been by God's Visitation raigned a wonderfull Plague, together with many horrible Slaugthers, and Murthers, committed amoungst the Sauages and brutish People there, heertofore inhabiting, in a Manner to the utter Destruction, Deuastacion, and Depopulacion of that whole Territorye, so that there is not left for many Leagues together in a Manner, any that doe claime or challenge any Kind of Interests therein, nor any other Superious Lord or Souveraigne to make Claime thereunto, whereby We in our Judgment are persuaded and satisfied that the appointed Time is come in which Almighty God in his great Goodness and Bountie towards Us and our People hath thought fitt and determined, that those large and goodly Territoryes, deserted as it were by their naturall Inhabitants, should be possessed and enjoyed by such of our Subjects and People as heertofore have and hereafter shall by his Mercie and Favour, and by his Powerfull Arme, be directed and conducted thither. In Contemplacion and serious Consideracion whereof, Wee have thougt it fitt according to our Kingly Duty, soe much as in Us lyeth, to second and followe God's sacred Will, rendering reverend Thanks to his Divine Majestie for his gracious favour in laying open and revealing the same unto us, before any other Christian Prince or State, by which Meanes without Offence, and as We trust to his Glory, Wee may with Boldness goe on to the settling of soe hopefull a Work, which tendeth to the reducing and Conversion of such Sauages as remaine wandering in Desolacion and Distress, to Civil Societie and Christian Religion, to the Inlargement of our own Dominions, and the Aduancement of the Fortunes of such of our good Subjects as shall willingly intresse themselves in the said Imployment, to whom We cannot but give singular Commendations for their soe worthy Intention and Enterprize. . . . And lastly, because the principall Effect which we can desire to expect of this Action, is the Conversion and Reduction of the People in those Parts unto the true Worship of God and Christian Religion, in which Respect, Wee would be loath that any person should be permitted to pass that Wee suspected to affect the Superstition of the Chh of Rome, Wee do hereby declare that it is our Will and Pleasure that noe be permitted to pass, in any Voyage from time to time to be made in the said Country, but such as shall first have taken the Oathe of Supremacy. . . .   New Plymouth Laws, pp. 1, 3, 17.

1.1.3.6.b Warwicke Patent (Charter of New Plymouth)

. . . And for as much as they have noe conveniente place either of tradinge or ffishinge within their own precints whereby (after soe longe travell and great paines,) so hopefull a plantačon may subsiste, as alsoe that they may bee incouraged the better to proceed in soe pious a worke which may especially tend to the propagation of religion and the great increase of trade to his Ma^{ts} realme. . . .

New Plymouth Laws, p. 23.

1.1.3.6.c Charter of Massachusetts Bay, 1628

. . . And, wee do of our further grace, certaine knowledge and meere motion give and grant to the said Governor and Companie, and their successors, that it shall and may be lawfull to and for the Governor or deputy Governor and such of the Assistants and Freemen of the said Company . . . to make, ordaine and establish all manner of wholesome and reasonable orders, lawes, statutes, and ordinances, directions, and instructions . . . for the directing, ruleing, and disposeing of all other matters and things whereby our said people inhabiting there may be so religiously, peaceably and civilly governed, as theire good life and orderly conversation, may winne and invite the natives of that country to the knowledge and obedience of the onely true God and saviour of mankind, and the christian faith, which in our royall intention, and the adventurers free profession is the principal end of this plantation. . . . Massachusetts Bay First Charter, pp. 26–27.

1.1.3.6.d Body of Liberties, 1641

[58] Civill Authoritie hath power and libertie to see the peace, ordinances and Rules of Christ observed in every church according to his word. so it be done in a Civill and not in an Ecclesiastical way.

[59] Civill Authoritie hath power and libertie to deale with any Church member in a way of Civill Justice, notwithstanding any Church relation, office or interest.

Massachusetts Colonial Laws, p. 47.

1.1.3.6.e Charter of Massachusetts Bay, 1692

. . . And for the greater Ease and Encouragement of Our loving Subjects, inhabiting Our said Province or Territory of the *Massachusetts-Bay,* and of such as shall come to inhabit there, We do by these Presents, for Us, our Heirs and Successors, grant, establish and ordain, that for ever hereafter there shall be a Liberty of Conscience allowed in the Worship of GOD to all Christians (except Papists) inhabiting or which shall inhabit or be resident within Our said Province or Territory. . . .

Massachusetts Bay Charter, p. 9.

1.1.3.6.f Constitution, 1780

PART I.

. . .

ARTICLE

. . .

II. It is the right as well as the duty of all men in society, publickly, and at stated seasons, to worship the **SUPREME BEING**, the Great Creator and Preserver of the Universe. And no subject shall be hurt, molested, or restrained, in his person, liberty, or estate, for worshipping **GOD** in the manner and season most agreeable to the dictates of his own conscience; or for his religious profession or sentiments; provided he doth not disturb the publick peace, or obstruct others in their religious worship.

III. As the happiness of a people, and the good order and preservation of civil government, essentially depend upon piety, religion and morality, and as these cannot be generally diffused through a community, but by the institution of the publick worship of **GOD**, and of publick instructions in piety, religion and morality: Therefore, to promote their happiness, and to secure the good order and preservation of their government, the people of this Commonwealth, have a right to invest their legislature with power to authorize and require, and the legislature shall, from time to time, authorize and require, the several towns, parishes, precincts, and other bodies politick, or religious societies, to make suitable provision, at their own expence, for the institution of the publick worship of **GOD**, and for the support and maintenance of publick protestant teachers of piety, religion and morality, in all cases where such provision shall not be made voluntarily.

And the people of this commonwealth have also a right to, and do, invest their legislature with authority to enjoin upon all the subjects, an attendance upon the instructions of the publick teachers aforesaid, at stated times and seasons, if there be any on whose instructions they can conscientiously and conveniently attend.

Provided notwithstanding, that the several towns, parishes, precincts, and other bodies politick, or religious societies, shall, at all times, have the exclusive right of electing their publick teachers, and of contracting with them for their support and maintenance.

And all monies paid by the subject to the support of publick worship, and of the publick teachers aforesaid, shall, if he require it, be uniformly applied to the support of the publick teacher or teachers of his own religious sect or denomination, provided there be any on whose instructions he attends; otherwise it may be paid towards the support of the teacher or teachers of the parish or precinct in which the said monies are raised.

And every denomination of christians, demeaning themselves peaceably, and as good subjects of the Commonwealth, shall be equally under the protection of the law: And no subordination of any one sect or denomination to another shall ever be established by law.

PART II.

. . .

CHAPTER VI.

. . .

[ARTICLE] I. ANY person chosen Governour, Lieutenant Governour, Counsellor, Senator, or Representative, and accepting the trust, shall, before he proceed to execute the duties of his place or office, make and subscribe the following declaration, viz.:

21

"I, A.B., do declare, that I believe the christian religion, and have a firm persuasion of its truth; and that I am seized and possessed, in my own right, of the property required by the Constitution, as one qualification for the office or place to which I am elected."

. . .

Provided always, that when any person chosen or appointed as aforesaid, shall be of the denomination of the people called Quakers, and shall decline taking the said oaths, he shall make his affirmation in the foregoing form, and subscribe the same, omitting the words *"I do swear," "and abjure," "oath or," "and abjuration,"* in the first oath; and in the second oath, the words *"swear and;"* and in each of them the words *"So help me, GOD;"* subjoining instead thereof, *"This I do under the pains and penalties of perjury."*

Massachusetts Perpetual Laws, pp. 5–6, 18.

1.1.3.7 New Hampshire

1.1.3.7.a Agreement of Settlers at Exeter, 1639

whereas it hath pleased the lord to moue the heart of our Dread Soveraigne Charles by the grace of god, king of England, Scotland, France & Ireland, to grant license and liberty to sundry of his subjects to plant them selves in the westerne partes of America; Wee, his loyall subjects, brethern of the church of Exeter, situate & lying upon the river Pascataquacke wth other inhabitants there, considering wth our selves the holy will of god and our owne necessity, that we should not live wthout wholesome lawes and civil governement amongst us, of wch we are altogether destitute; doe in the name of christ & in the sight of god, combine our selves together, to erect & set up among us such governement, as shall be to our best discerning agreeable to the will of god: professing our selves subjects to our Soveraigne Lord King Charles according to the libertys of our English Colony of Massachusets & binding of our selves solemnely by the grace & helpe of christ & in his name, & fear to submit our selves to such godly & christian laws as are established in the Realme of England to our best knowledge; & to all other such Laws wch shall upon good grounds, be made & enacted amongst us according to god, yt we may live quietly and peaceablely together in all godlyness & honesty.

New Hampshire Division of Records Management and Archives,
Old Town Papers, Exeter, 876161.

1.1.3.7.b Constitution, 1783

. . .

[Part I, Article] IV. Among the natural rights, some are in their very nature unalienable, because no equivalent can be given or received for them. Of this kind are the RIGHTS OF CONSCIENCE.

V. Every individual has a natural and unalienable right to worship GOD according to the dictates of his own conscience, and reason; and no subject shall be hurt, molested, or restrained in his person, liberty or estate for worshipping GOD in the manner and season most agreeable to the dictates of his own conscience, or for his religious profession, sentiments or persuasion; provided he doth not disturb the public peace, or disturb others in their religious worship.

VI. As morality and piety, rightly grounded on evangelical principles, will give the best and greatest security to government, and will lay in the hearts of men the strongest obligations to due subjection; and as the knowledge of these, is most likely to be propagated through a society by the institution of the public worship of the DEITY, and of public instruction in morality and religion; therefore, to promote those important purposes, the people of this State have a right to empower, and do hereby fully empower the legislature to authorize from time to time, the several towns, parishes, bodies-corporate, or religious societies within this State, to make adequate provision at their own expence, for the support and maintenance of public protestant teachers of piety, religion and morality:

Provided notwithstanding, That the several towns, parishes, bodies-corporate, or religious societies, shall at all times have the exclusive right of electing their own public teachers, and of contracting with them for their support and maintenance. And no portion of any one particular religious sect or denomination, shall ever be compelled to pay towards the support of the teacher or teachers of another persuasion, sect or denomination.

And every denomination of christians demeaning themselves quietly, and as good subjects of the state, shall be equally under the protection of the law: and no subordination of any one sect or denomination to another, shall ever be established by law.

And nothing herein shall be understood to affect any former contracts made for the support of the ministry; but all such contracts shall remain, and be in the same state as if this constitution had not been made.   New Hampshire Laws, p. 23.

1.1.3.8   New Jersey

1.1.3.8.a   Concession and Agreement of the Lords Proprietors of the Province of New Caesarea, or New-Jersey, 1664

ITEM. That no Person qualified as aforesaid within the said Province, at any Time shall be any ways molested, punished, disquieted or called in question for any Difference in Opinion or Practice in matter of Religious Concernments, who do not actually disturb the civil Peace of the said Province; but that all and every such Person and Persons may from Time to Time, and at all Times, freely and fully have and enjoy his and their Judgments and Consciences in matters of Religion throughout the said Province, they behaving themselves peaceably and quietly, and not using this Liberty to Licentiousness, nor to the civil Injury or outward disturbance of others; any Law, Statute or Clause contained, or to be contained, usage or custom of this Realm of *England,* to the contrary thereof in any wise notwithstanding.

ITEM. That no pretence may be taken by our Heirs or Assigns for or by reason of our right of Patronage and Power of Advouson, granted by his Majesty's Letter's Patents, unto his Royal Highness James Duke of *York,* and by his said Royal Highness unto us, thereby to Infringe the general Clause of Liberty of Conscience, aforementioned: WE do hereby grant unto the General Assembly of the said

Province, Power by Act to constitute and appoint such and so many Ministers or Preachers as they shall think fit, and to establish their Maintenance, giving liberty beside to any Person or Persons to keep and maintain what Preachers or Ministers they please.

New Jersey Grants, p. 14.

1.1.3.8.b Concessions and Agreements of West New-Jersey, 1676

CHAPTER XVI

That no Men, nor number of Men upon Earth, hath Power or Authority to rule over Men's Consciences in religious Matters, therefore it is consented, agreed and ordained, that no Person or Persons whatsoever within the said Province, at any Time or Times hereafter, shall be any ways upon any pretence whatsoever, called in Question, or in the least punished or hurt, either in Person, Estate, or Priviledge, for the sake of his Opinion, Judgment, Faith or Worship towards God in Matters of Religion. But that all and every such Person, and Persons, may from Time to Time, and at all Times, freely and fully have, and enjoy his and their Judgments, and the exercise of their Consciences in Matters of religious Worship throughout all the said Province.

New Jersey Grants, p. 394.

1.1.3.8.c Laws of West New-Jersey, 1681

X. That Liberty of Conscience in Matters of Faith and Worship towards God, shall be granted to all People within the Province aforesaid; who shall live peaceably and quietly therein; and that none of the free People of the said Province, shall be rendered uncapable of Office in respect of their Faith and Worship.

New Jersey Grants, p. 425.

1.1.3.8.d Fundamental Constitutions for East New-Jersey, 1683

XVI. All Persons living in the Province who confess and acknowledge the one Almighty and Eternal God, and holds themselves obliged in Conscience to live peaceably and quietly in a civil Society, shall in no way be molested or prejudged for their Religious Perswasions and Exercise in matters of Faith and Worship; nor shall they be compelled to frequent and maintain any Religious Worship, Place or Ministry whatsoever: Yet it is also hereby provided, that no Man shall be admitted a member of the Great or Common Council, or any other Place of publick Trust, who shall not profess Faith in *Christ-Jesus,* and solemnly declare that he doth no ways hold himself obliged in Conscience to endeavour alteration in the Government, or seeks the turning out of any in it or their ruin or prejudice, either in Person or Estate, because they are in his Opinion Hereticks, or differ in their Judgment from him: Nor by this Article is it intended, that any under the Notion of the Liberty shall allow themselves to avow Atheism, Irreligiousness, or to practice Cursing, Swearing, Drunkenness, Prophaness, Whoring, Adultery, Murdering or any kind of violence, or indulging themselves in Stage Plays, Masks, Revells or such like abuses; for restraining such and preserving of the People in Deligence and in good Order, the great Council is to make more particular Laws, which are punctually to be put in Execution.

. . .

XX. That all Marriages not forbidden in the Law of God, shall be esteemed lawful, where the Parents or Guardians being first acquainted, the Marriage is publickly intimated in such Places and Manner as is agreeable to Mens different Perswasions in Religion, being afterwards still solemnized before creditable Witnesses, by taking one another as Husband and Wife, and a certificate of the whole, under the Parties and Witnesses Hands, being brought to the proper Register for that End, under a Penalty if neglected.

New Jersey Grants, pp. 162, 164.

1.1.3.8.e   Constitution, 1776

XVIII. THAT no Person shall ever within this Colony be deprived of the inestimable Privilege of worshipping Almighty GOD in a Manner agreeable to the Dictates of his own Conscience; nor under any Pretence whatsoever compelled to attend any Place of Worship contrary to his own Faith and Judgment; nor shall any Person within this Colony ever be obliged to pay Tithes, Taxes or any other Rates, for the Purpose of building or repairing any Church or Churches, Place or Places of Worship, or for the Maintenance of any Minister or Ministry, contrary to what he believes to be Right, or has deliberately or voluntarily engaged himself to perform.

XIX. THAT there shall be no Establishment of any one religious Sect in this Province in Preference to another; and that no Protestant Inhabitant of this Colony shall be denied the Enjoyment of any civil Right merely on Account of his religious Principles; but that all Persons, professing a Belief in the Faith of any Protestant Sect, who shall demean themselves peaceably under the Government as hereby established, shall be capable of being elected into any Office of Profit or Trust, or being a Member of either Branch of the Legislature, and shall fully and freely enjoy every Privilege and Immunity enjoyed by others their Fellow-Subjects.

New Jersey Acts, p. viii.

1.1.3.9   New York, 1691

1.1.3.9.a   Act Declaring . . . Rights & Priviledges, 1691

That no Person or Persons which profess Faith in God by Jesus Christ his only Son, shall at any time be any way molested, punished, disturbed, disquieted or called in question for any Difference in Opinion, or matter of Religious Concernment, who do not under that pretence disturb the Civil Peace of the Province, &c. And that all and every such Person and Persons may from time to time and at all times hereafter, freely have and fully enjoy his or their Opinion, Perswasions and Judgments in matters of Conscience and Religion, throughout all this Province; and freely meeet at convenient Places within this Province, and there Worship according to their respective Perswasions, without being hindered or molested, they behaving themselves peaceably, quietly, modestly and Religiously, and not using this Liberty to Licentiousness, nor to the civil Injury or outward Disturbance of others. Always provided, That nothing herein mentoined [*sic*] or contained shall extend to give Liberty to any Persons of the *Romish Religion* to exercise their manner of Worship, contrary to the Laws and Statutes of their Majesties Kingdom of *England*.

New York Acts, p. 19.

1.1.3.9.b **Constitution, 1777**

XXXVIII. AND WHEREAS we are required, by the benevolent Principles of rational Liberty, not only to expel civil Tyranny, but also to guard against that spiritual Oppression and Intolerance, wherewith the Bigotry and Ambition of weak and wicked Priests and Princes have scourged Mankind: This Convention doth further, in the Name and by the Authority of the good People of this State, ORDAIN, DETERMINE, AND DECLARE, That the free Exercise and Enjoyment of religious Profession and Worship, without Discrimination or Preference, shall forever hereafter be allowed within this State to all Mankind. *Provided*, That the Liberty of Conscience hereby granted, shall not be so construed, as to excuse Acts of Licentiousness, or justify Practices inconsistent with the Peace or Safety of this State.

XXXIX. AND WHEREAS the Ministers of the Gospel are, by their Profession, dedicated to the Service of God and the Cure of Souls, and ought not be diverted from the great Duties of their Function; therefore no Minister of the Gospel, or Priest of any Denomination whatsoever, shall at any Time hereafter, under any Pretence or Description whatever, be eligible to, or capable of holding any civil or military Office or Place, within this State.   New York Laws, vol. 1, p. 13.

1.1.3.10 **North Carolina**

1.1.3.10.a **First Charter of Carolina, 1663**

I. **Whereas** our right trusty and right well beloved Cousins and Counsellors . . . being excited with a laudable and pious Zeal for the Propagation of the Christian Faith, and the Enlargement of our Empire and Dominions, have humbly besought leave of us, by their Industry and Charge, to transport and make an ample Colony of our Subjects, Natives of our Kingdom of *England*, and elsewhere within our Dominions, unto a certain Country hereafter described, in the Parts of *America*, not yet cultivated or planted, and only inhabited by some barbarous People who have no Knowledge of Almighty God.

. . .

III. And furthermore, the Patronage and Avowsons of all the Churches and Chappels, which as Christian Religion shall increase within the Country, Isles, Islets and Limits aforesaid, shall happen hereafter to be erected, together with License and Power to build and found Churches, Chappels and Oratories, in convenient and fit Places, within the said Bounds and Limits, and to cause them to be dedicated and consecrated according to the Ecclesiastical Laws of our Kingdom of *England*, together with all and singular the like, and as ample Rights, Jurisdictions, Priviledges, Prerogatives, Royalties, Liberties, Immunities and Franchises of what kind soever, within the Countries, Isles, Islets and Limits aforesaid.

. . .

XVIII. AND because it may happen, that some of the People and Inhabitants of the said *Province*, cannot in their private Opinions conform to the publick Exercise of *Religion*, according to the Liturgy, Form and Ceremonies of the Church of *England*, or take and subscribe the Oaths and Articles made and established in that behalf, and for that the same, by reason of the remote Distances of these

Places, will, we hope, be no Breach of the Unity and Uniformity establish'd in this Nation, Our Will and Pleasure therefore is, and we do by these Presents, for us, our Heirs and Successors, give and grant unto the said *Edward* Earl of *Clarendon*, *George* Duke of *Albemarle*, *William* Lord *Craven*, *John* Lord *Berkley*, *Anthony* Lord *Ashley*, Sir *George Carteret*, Sir *William Berkley*, and Sir *John Colleton*, their Heirs and Assigns, full and free Licence, Liberty and Authority, by such legal Ways and Means as they shall think fit, to give and grant unto such person and persons inhabiting and being within the said Province, or any part thereof, who really in their Judgments, and for Conscience sake, cannot or shall not conform to the said Liturgy and Ceremonies, and take and subscribe the Oaths and Articles aforesaid, or any of them, such Indulgencies and Dispensations in that behalf, for and during such Time and Times, and with such Limitations and Restrictions, as they the said *Edward* Earl of *Clarendon*, *George* Duke of *Albemarle*, *William* Lord *Craven*, *John* Lord *Berkley*, *Anthony* Lord *Ashley*, Sir *George Carteret*, Sir *William Berkley*, and Sir *John Colleton*, their Heirs or Assigns shall in their Discretion think fit and reasonable; and with this express *Proviso* and *Limitation* also, That such person and persons, to whom such Indulgences and Dispensations shall be granted as aforesaid, do and shall, from Time to Time, declare and continue all Fidelity, Loyalty and Obedience to us, our Heirs and Successors, and be subject and obedient to all other the Laws, Ordinances and Constitutions of the said *Province,* in all Matters whatsoever, as well Ecclesiastical as Civil, and do not in any wise disturb the Peace and Safety thereof, or scandalize or reproach the said Liturgy, Forms and Ceremonies, or any thing relating thereunto, or any person or persons whatsoever, for or in respect of his or their Use or Exercise thereof, or his or their Obedience or Conformity thereunto.

South Carolina Provincial Laws, pp. xxi–xxii, xxxi–xxxii.

1.1.3.10.b Declaration and Proposals of Lord Proprietor of Carolina, 1663

His majesty having been graciously pleased, by his charter bearing date the 24th of March, in the 15th year of his reign, out of a pious and good intention for the propagation of the Christian faith amongst the barbarous and ignorant Indians, the enlargement of his empire and dominions, and enriching of his subjects, to grant and confirm to us . . . we do hereby declare and propose to all his majesty's loving subjects wheresoever abiding or residing, and do hereby engage inviolably to perform and make good those ensuing proposals in such manner as the first undertakers of the first settlement shall reasonable desire.

. . .

5. We will grant, in as ample manner as the undertakers shall desire, freedom and liberty of conscience in all religious or spiritual things, and to be kept inviolably with them, we having power in our charter so to do.

Colonial Records of North Carolina, William L. Saunders, ed.
(Raleigh: P. M. Hale, 1886), vol. 1, pp. 43, 45.

1.1.3.10.c Second Charter of Carolina, 1665

. . .

NOW Know ye, That We, at the humble Request of the said Grantees, in the aforesaid Letters Patents named, and as a further Mark of our especial Favour to them, we are graciously pleased to enlarge our said Grant unto them, according to the Bounds and Limits hereafter specified, and in Favour to the pious and noble Purpose of the said *Edward* Earl of *Clarendon, George* Duke of *Albemarle, William* Earl of *Craven, John* Lord *Berkeley, Anthony* Lord *Ashley,* Sir *George Carteret,* Sir *John Colleton,* and Sir *William Berkeley,* their Heirs and Assigns, all that Province, Territory, or Tract of Land, situate, lying and being within our Dominions of *America* aforesaid. . . . And further more, the Patronage and Advowsons of all the Churches and Chapels, which, as Christian Religion shall increase within the Province, Territory, Isles, and Limits aforesaid, shall happen hereafter to be erected; together with License and Power to build and found Churches, Chapels, and Oratories, in convenient and fit Places, within the said Bounds and Limits; and to cause them to be dedicated and consecrated, according to the Ecclesiastical Laws of our Kingdom of *England;* together with all and singular the like and as ample Rights, Jurisdictions, Privileges, Prerogatives, Royalties, Liberties, Immunities, and Franchises, of what Kind soever, within the Territory, Isles, Islets, and Limits aforesaid: To have, hold, use, exercise, and enjoy the same, as amply, fully, and in as ample Manner, as any Bishop of *Durham,* in our Kingdom of *England,* ever heretofore, had, held, used, or enjoyed, or of Right ought or could have, use, or enjoy. . . .

. . .

AND because it may happen that some of the People and Inhabitants of the said Province, cannot, in their private Opinions, conform to the Public Exercise of Religion, according to the Liturgy, Forms, and Ceremonies of the Church of *England,* or take and subscribe the Oaths and Articles made and Established in that Behalf; and for that the same, by Reason of the remote Distances of those Places, will, as we hope, be no Breach of the Unity and Conformity established in this Nation; our Will and Pleasure therefore is, and we do, by these Presents, for us, our Heirs and Successors, give and grant unto the said *Edward* Earl of *Clarendon, George* Duke of *Albemarle, William* Earl of *Craven, John* Lord *Berkeley, Anthony* Lord *Ashley,* Sir *George Carteret,* Sir *John Colleton,* and Sir *William Berkeley,* their Heirs and Assigns, full and free Licence, Liberty, and Authority, by such Ways and Means as they shall think fit, to give and grant unto such Person or Persons, inhabiting and being within the said Province or Territory, hereby, or by the said recited Letters Patents mentioned to be granted as aforesaid, or any Part thereof, such Indulgences and Dispensations, in that Behalf, for and during such Time and Times, and with such Limitations and Restrictions, as they . . . shall, in their Discretion, think fit and reasonable: And that no Person or Persons unto whom such Liberty shall be given, shall be in any way molested, punished, disquieted, or called in Question, for any Differences in Opinion, or Practice in Matters of religious Concernments, who do not actually disturb the Civil Peace of the Province, County or Colony, that they shall make their Abode in: But all and every such Person and Persons may, from Time to Time, and at all Times, freely and quietly have and enjoy his and their Judgments and Consciences, in Matters of Religion, throughout all the said Province or Colony, they behaving themselves peaceably, and not using this Liberty to Licentiousness, nor to the Civil Injury, or outward Disturbance of others: Any Law, Statute, or Clause, contained or to be contained, Usage or Custom of our Realm of *England,* to the contrray [*sic*] hereof, in any-wise, notwithstanding.

North Carolina Acts, p. i–ii, xi.

1.1.3.10.d   **Fundamental Constitutions of Carolina, 1669**

95th. No man shall be permitted to be a freeman of Carolina, or to have any estate or habitation within it, that doth not acknowledge a God, and that God is publicly and solemnly to be worshipped.

96th. (As the country comes to be sufficiently planted, and distributed in fit divisions, it shall belong to the Parliament to take care for the building of churches and the public maintenance of divines, to be employed in the exercise of religion, according to the Church of England; which being the only true and orthodox, and the national religion of all the king's dominions, is so also of Carolina, and therefore it alone shall be allowed to receive public maintenance by grant of parliament.)

97th. But since the natives of that place, who will be concerned in our plantation, are utterly strangers to Christianity, whose idolatry, ignorance or mistake gives us no right to expell or treat them ill, and those who remove from other parts to plant there will unavoidably be of different opinions, concerning matters of religion, the liberty whereof they will expect to have allowed them, and it will not be reasonable for us on this account to keep them out; that civil peace may be obtained amidst diversity of opinions, and our agreement and compact with all men, may be duly and faithfully observed, the violation whereof, upon what pretence soever, cannot be without offence to Almighty God, and great scandal to the true religion which we profess; and also that Jews, Heathens and other dissenters from the purity of the Christian religion, may not be scared and kept at a distance from it, but by having an opportunity of acquainting themselves with the truth and reasonableness of its doctrines, and the peaceableness and inoffensiveness of its professors, may be good usage and persuasion, and all those convincing methods of gentleness and meekness, suitable to the rules and design of the gospel, be won over to embrace and unfeignedly receive the truth; therefore any seven or more persons agreeing in any religion, shall constitute a church or profession, to which they shall give some name, to distinguish it from others.

98th. The terms of admittance and communion with any church or profession shall be written in a book, and therein be subscribed by all the members of the said church or profession; which book shall be kept by the public Register of the Precinct wherein they reside.

99th. The time of every one, subscription admittance, shall be dated in the said book or religious record.

100th. In the terms of communion of every church or profession, these following shall be three, without which no agreement or assembly of men upon pretence of religion, shall be accounted a church or profession within these rules:

1st. "That there is a God."

2nd. "That God is publickly to be worshipped."

3rd. "That it is lawful and the duty of every man being thereunto called by those that govern, to bear witness to truth; and that every church or profession shall in their terms of communion, set down the eternal way whereby they witness a truth as in the presence of God whether it be by laying hands on or kissing the Bible, as in the Church of England, or by holding up the hand, or any other sensible way."

101st. No person above seventeen years of age, shall have any benefit or protection of the law, or be capable of any place of profit or honor who is not a member of some church or profession, having his name recorded in some one, and but one religious record at once.

102nd. No person of any other church or profession shall disturb or molest any religious assembly.

103rd. No person whatsoever, shall speak anything in their religious assembly irreverently or seditiously of the government or governors, or of state matters.

104th. Any person subscribing the terms of communion, in the record of the said church or profession, before the precinct register and any five members of the said church or profession, shall be thereby made a member of the said church or profession.

105th. Any person striking out his own name out of any religious record, or his name being struck out by any officer thereunto authorized by such church or profession respectively, shall cease to be a member of that church or profession.

106th. No man shall use any reproachful, reviling, or abusive language against any religion of any church or profession; that being the certain way of disturbing the peace, and of hindering the conversion of any to the truth, by engaging them in quarrels and animosities, to the hatred of the professors and that profession which otherwise they might be brought to assent.

107th. Since charity obliges us to wish well to the souls of all men, and religion ought to alter nothing in any man's civil estate or right, it shall be lawful for slaves as well as others, to enter themselves and be of what church or profession any of them shall think best, and thereof be as fully members as any freemen. But yet no slave shall hereby be exempted from that civil dominion his master hath over him, but be in all things in the same state and condition he was in before.

108th. Assemblies upon what pretence soever of religion, not observing and performing the above said rules, shall not be esteemed as churches, but unlawful meetings, and be punished as riots.

109th. No person whatsoever shall disturb, molest, or persecute another, for his speculative opinions in religion, or his way of worship.

110th. Every freeman of Carolina, shall have absolute power and authority over his negro slaves, of what opinion or religion soever.

North Carolina State Records, pp. 147–49 (John Locke).

1.1.3.10.e **Declaration of Rights, 1776**

Sect. XIX. That all Men have a natural and unalienable Right to worship Almighty God according to the Dictates of their own Conscience.

North Carolina Laws, p. 276.

1.1.3.10.f **Constitution, 1776**

Sect. XXXIV. That there shall be no Establishment of any one Religious Church in this State in Preference to any other; neither shall any Person, on any Pretence whatsoever, be compelled to attend any Place of Worship, contrary to his own Faith or Judgment; nor be obliged to pay for the purchase of any Glebe, or the building of any House of Worship, or for the Maintenance of any building of any house of worship, or for the Maintenance of any Minister or Ministry, contrary to what he believes right, or has voluntarily and personally engaged to perform; but all Persons shall be at Liberty to exercise their own Mode of Worship. *Provided,* That nothing herein contained, shall be construed to exempt Preachers of treasonable or seditious Discourses from legal Trial and Punishment.

North Carolina Laws, p. 280.

1.1.3.11   Pennsylvania

1.1.3.11.a   Charter of Province of Pennsylvania, 1682

SECT. XXII.

AND Our farther Pleasure is, And We do hereby, for Us, our Heirs and Successors, charge and require, That if any of the Inhabitants of the said Province, to the Number of Twenty, shall at any Time hereafter be desirous, and shall by any Writing or by any Person deputed for them, signify such their Desire to the Bishop of *London* for the Time being, That any Preacher or Preachers, to be approved of by the said Bishop, may be sent unto them for their Instruction; that then such Preacher or Preachers shall and may reside within the said Province, without any Denial or Molestation whatsoever.

Pennsylvania Charters, pp. 12–13.

1.1.3.11.b   Laws Agreed Upon in England, 1682

LAWS AGREED UPON IN ENGLAND.

XXXV. That all Persons living in this Province, who confess and acknowledge the One Almighty and Eternal God, to be the Creator, Upholder and Ruler of the World and that hold themselves obliged in Conscience to live peaceably and justly in *Civil Society,* shall, in no wayes be molested or prejudiced for their Religious Perswasion or Practice in matters of *Faith* and *Worship,* nor shall they be compelled, at any time, to frequent or maintain any Religious **Worship,** Place or **Ministry** whatever.

XXXVI. That according to the good Example of the Primitive Christians, and for the ease of the Creation, every *First Day* of the Week, called the *Lords Day,* People shall abstain from their common daily Labour, that they may the better dispose themselves to Worship God according to their Understandings.

Pennsylvania Frame, p. 11.

1.1.3.11.c   Charter of Privileges Granted by William Penn, 1701

FIRST.

BECAUSE no People can be truly happy, though under the greatest Enjoyment of Civil Liberties, if abridged of the Freedom of their Consciences, as to their Religious Profession and Worship: And Almighty God being the only Lord of Conscience, Father of Lights and Spirits; and the Author as well as Object of all divine Knowledge, Faith and Worship, who only doth enlighten the Minds, and persuade and convince the Understandings of People, I do hereby grant and declare, That no Person or Persons, inhabiting in this Province or Territories, who shall confess and acknowledge *One* almighty God, the Creator, Upholder and Ruler of the World; and profess him or themselves obliged to live quietly under the Civil Government, shall be in any Case molested or prejudiced, in his or their Person or Estate, because of his or their consciencious [*sic*] Persuasion or Practice, nor be compelled to frequent or maintain any religious Worship, Place or Ministry, contrary to his or their Mind, or to do or suffer any other Act or Thing, contrary to their religious Persuasion.

AND that all Persons who also profess to believe in *Jesus Christ,* the Saviour of the World, shall be capable (notwithstanding their other Persuasions and Practices in Point of Conscience and Religion) to serve this Government in any Capacity, both legislatively and executively, he or they solemnly promising, when lawfully required, Allegiance to the King as Sovereign, and Fidelity to the Proprietary and Governor, and taking the Attests as now established by the Law made at *New-Castle,* in the Year *One Thousand and Seven Hundred,* entitled, *An Act directing the Attests of several Officers and Ministers,* as now amended and confirmed this present Assembly.

. . .

VIII.

. . .

BUT because the Happiness of Mankind depends so much upon the Enjoying of Liberty of their Consciences as aforesaid, I do hereby solemnly declare, promise and grant, for me, my Heirs and Assigns, That the *First* Article of this Charter relating to Liberty of Conscience, and every Part and Clause therein, according to the true Intent and Meaning thereof, shall be kept and remain, without any Alteration, inviolably for ever.

Penn Charter, pp. 4, 7.

1.1.3.11.d **Constitution, 1776**

CHAPTER I.
A DECLARATION of the RIGHTS of the Inhabitants of the State of Pennsylvania.

. . .

II. That all men have a natural and unalienable right to worship Almighty God according to the dictates of their own consciences and understanding: And that no man ought to or of right can be compelled to attend any religious worship, or erect or support any place of worship, or maintain any ministry, contrary to, or against, his own free will and consent: Nor can any man, who acknowledges the being of a God, be justly deprived or abridged of any civil right as a citizen, on account of his religious sentiments or peculiar mode of religious worship: And that no authority can or ought to be vested in, or assumed by any power whatever, that shall in any case interfere with, or in any manner controul, the right of conscience in the free exercise of religious worship.

CHAPTER II.
PLAN *or* FRAME *of* GOVERNMENT.

. . .

Sect. 10. . . .

. . .

And each member, before he takes his seat, shall make and subscribe the following declaration, viz.

I do believe in one God, the Creator and governor of the universe, the rewarder of the good and the punisher of the wicked. And I do acknowledge the Scriptures of the Old and New Testament to be given by Divine inspiration.

And no further or other religious test shall ever hereafter be required of any civil officer of magistrate in this state.

. . .

Sect. 45. Laws for the encouragement of virtue, and prevention of vice and immorality, shall be made and constantly kept in force, and provision shall be made for their due execution: And all religious societies or bodies of men heretofore united or incorporated for the advancement of religion or learning, or for other pious and charitable purposes, shall be encouraged and protected in the enjoyment of the privileges, immunities and estates which they were accustomed to enjoy, or could of right have enjoyed under the laws and former constitution of this state.

Pennsylvania Acts, M'Kean, pp. ix, xii, xx.

1.1.3.11.e Constitution, 1790

ARTICLE IX.

. . .

Sᴇᴄᴛ. III. That all men have a natural and indefeasible right to worship Almighty God according to the dictates of their own consciences; that no man can, of right, be compelled to attend, erect or support any place of worship, or to maintain any ministry against his consent; that no human authority can, in any case whatever, controul or interfere with the rights of conscience; and that no preference shall ever be given, by law, to any religious establishments or modes of worship.

Sᴇᴄᴛ. IV. That no person, who acknowledges the being of a God and a future state of rewards and punishments, shall, on account of his religious sentiments, be disqualified to hold any office or place of trust or profit under this commonwealth.

Pennsylvania Acts, Dallas, p. xxxiii.

1.1.3.12 Rhode Island

1.1.3.12.a Plantation Agreement at Providence, 1640

2. . . .

Wee agree, as formerly hath bin the liberties of the town, so still, to hould forth liberty of Conscience.

Rhode Island Records, vol. 1, p. 28.

1.1.3.12.b **Charter of Rhode Island and Providence Plantations, 1663**

CHARLES THE SECOND, . . . Whereas We have been informed by the Humble Petition of our Trusty and well-beloved Subject[s] . . . That they pursuing with Peaceable and Loyal Minds, their Sober, Serious and Religious intentions, of Godly edifying themselves, and one another in the Holy Christian Faith and Worship, as they were perswaded . . . AND Whereas in their Humble Address, They have Freely Declared, that it is much on their Heart, if they my be permitted to Hold forth a Lively Experiment, That a most Flourishing Civil State, may stand and best be Maintained, and that amongst our English Subjects, With a full Liberty in Religious Concernements; and that true Piety, Rightly Grounded upon Gospel Principles, will Give the Best and Greatest Security to soveraignty; And will lay in the Hearts of Men the Strongest Obligations to true Loyalty. NOW KNOW YEE, That we being Willing to Encourage the Hopeful Undertakings of our said Loyal and Loving Subjects, And to Secure them in the Free Exercise and Enjoyment of all their Civil and Religious Rights Appertaining to them, as our Loving Subjects; and to Preserve unto them that Liberty in the true Christian Faith and Worship of GOD, Which They have sought with so much Travel, And with Peaceable Minds and Loyal Subjection to Our Royal Progenitors and Our Selves to Enjoy. AND because some of the People and Inhabitants of the same Colony, cannot in their private Opinions, Conform to the publick Exercise of Religion, according to the Liturgy, Forms and Ceremonies of the *Church of England,* or take or Subscribe the Oathes and Articles made and Established in that behalfe. AND for that the same by reason of the Remote Distances of those Places will (as we Hope) be no Breach of the Unity and Uniformity Established in this Nation. HAVE THEREFORE Thought fit, AND DO HEREBY Publish, Grant, Ordain, and Declare. That Our Royal Will and Pleasure is, That no Person within the said *Colony,* at any Time hereafter, shall be any ways Molested, Punished, Disquieted, or called in Question for any Differences in Opinion, in matters of Religion, And do not Actually disturb the Civil Peace of Our said *Colony.* But that all and Every Person and Persons, may from time to time, and at all times hereafter, Freely, and Fully Have and Enjoy, His and Their own Judgments, and Conscience in matters of Religious Concernments, Throughout the Tract of Land hereafter Mentioned; They Behaving themselves Peaceably and Quietly, *And not Using This Liberty to Licentiousness and Prophaneness;* nor to the Civil Injury, or outward Disturbance of others. Any *Law, Statute, or Clause, therein contained, or to be Contained; Any Usage or Custome of this Realm to the Contrary thereof in any wise notwithstanding.* And that they may be in the better Capacity to Defend themselves in their Just Rights and Liberties, against all the Enemys of the Christian Faith, and others in all Respects. WEE Have further thought Fit; And at the Humble Petition of the Persons aforesaid, Are Graciously pleased to Declare, That they shall Have, an Enjoy, the Benefit of Our Late Act of Indemnity, and Free Pardon, as the rest of our Subjects in other Our Dominions and Territorys have. AND TO CREATE, and make Them a Body Politick and Corporate, with the Powers, and Priviledges herein after-mentioned.

Rhode Island Acts, pp. 1–2.

1.1.3.13   South Carolina

1.1.3.13.a   First Charter of Carolina, 1663

I. **Whereas** our right trusty and right well beloved Cousins and Counsellors . . . being excited with a laudable and pious Zeal for the Propagation of the Christian Faith, and the Enlargement of our Empire and Dominions, have humbly besought leave of us, by their Industry and Charge, to transport and make an ample Colony of our Subjects, Natives of our Kingdom of *England,* and elsewhere within our Dominions, unto a certain Country hereafter described, in the Parts of *America,* not yet cultivated or planted, and only inhabited by some barbarous People who have no Knowledge of Almighty God.

. . .

III. And furthermore, the Patronage and Avowsons of all the Churches and Chappels, which as Christian Religion shall increase within the Country, Isles, Islets and Limits aforesaid, shall happen hereafter to be erected, together with License and Power to build and found Churches, Chappels and Oratories, in convenient and fit Places, within the said Bounds and Limits, and to cause them to be dedicated and consecrated according to the Ecclesiastical Laws of our Kingdom of *England,* together with all and singular the like, and as ample Rights, Jurisdictions, Priviledges, Prerogatives, Royalties, Liberties, Immunities and Franchises of what kind soever, within the Countries, Isles, Islets and Limits aforesaid.

. . .

XVIII. AND because it may happen, that some of the People and Inhabitants of the said *Province,* cannot in their private Opinions conform to the publick Exercise of *Religion,* according to the Liturgy, Form and Ceremonies of the Church of *England,* or take and subscribe the Oaths and Articles made and established in that behalf, and for that the same, by reason of the remote Distanes of these Places, will, we hope, be no Breach of the Unity and Uniformity establish'd in this Nation, Our Will and Pleasure therefore is, and we do by these Presents, for us, our Heirs and Successors, give and grant unto the said *Edward* Earl of *Clarendon, George* Duke of *Albemarle, William* Lord *Craven, John* Lord *Berkley, Anthony* Lord *Ashley,* Sir *George Carteret,* Sir *William Berkley,* and Sir *John Colleton,* their Heirs and Assigns, full and free Licence, Liberty and Authority, by such legal Ways and Means as they shall think fit, to give and grant unto such person and persons inhabiting and being within the said Province, or any part thereof, who really in their Judgments, and for Conscience sake, cannot or shall not conform to the said Liturgy and Ceremonies, and take and subscribe the Oaths and Articles aforesaid, or any of them, such Indulgencies and Dispensations in that behalf, for and during such Time and Times, and with such Limitations and Restrictions, as they the said *Edward* Earl of *Clarendon, George* Duke of *Albemarle, William* Lord *Craven, John* Lord *Berkley, Anthony* Lord *Ashley,* Sir *George Carteret,* Sir *William Berkley,* and Sir *John Colleton,* their Heirs or Assigns shall in their Discretion think fit and reasonable; and with this express *Proviso* and *Limitation* also, That such person and persons, to whom such Indulgences and Dispensations shall be granted as aforesaid, do and shall, from Time to Time, declare and continue all Fidelity, Loyalty and Obedience to us, our Heirs and Successors, and be subject and obedient to all other the Laws, Ordinances and Constitutions of the said *Province,* in all Matters whatsoever, as well Ecclesiastical as Civil, and do not in any wise disturb the Peace and Safety thereof, or scandalize or reproach the said Liturgy, Forms and Ceremonies, or any thing relating thereunto, or any person or persons whatsoever, for or in respect of his or their Use or Exercise thereof, or his or their Obedience or Conformity thereunto.

South Carolina Provincial Laws, pp. xxi–xxii, xxxi–xxxii.

1.1.3.13.b   Declaration and Proposals of Lord Proprietor of Carolina, 1663

His majesty having been graciously pleased, by his charter bearing date the 24th of March, in the 15th year of his reign, out of a pious and good intention for the propagation of the Christian faith amongst the barbarous and ignorant Indians, the enlargement of his empire and dominions, and enriching of his subjects, to grant and confirm to us . . . we do hereby declare and propose to all his majesty's loving subjects wheresoever abiding or residing, and do hereby engage inviolably to perform and make good those ensuing proposals in such manner as the first undertakers of the first settlement shall reasonable desire.

. . .

5. We grant, in as ample manner as the undertakers shall desire, freedom and liberty of conscience in all religious or spiritual things, and to be kept inviolably with them, we having power in our charter so to do.

Colonial Records of North Carolina, William L. Saunders, ed.
(Raleigh: P. M. Hale, 1886), vol. 1, pp. 43, 45.

1.1.3.13.c   Second Charter of Carolina, 1665[2]

. . .

NOW KNOW YE, That We, at the humble Request of the said *Grantees* in the aforesaid Letters Patents named, and as a further Mark of our especial Favour towards them, we are graciously pleased to enlarge our said Grant unto them, according to the Bounds and Limits hereafter specified, and in Favour to the pious and noble Purpose of the said *Edward* Earl of *Clarendon, George* Duke of *Albemarle, William* Earl of *Craven, John* Lord *Berkley, Anthony* Lord *Ashley,* Sir *George Carteret,* Sir *John Colleton,* and Sir *William Berkley,* their Heirs and Assigns, all that Province, Territory or Tract of Ground, scituate [*sic*], lying and being within our Dominions of *America* aforesaid. . . .

III. AND furthermore the Patronage and Avowsons of all the Churches and Chappels, which, as Christian Religion shall increase within the Province, Territory, Isles, and Limits aforesaid, shall happen hereafter to be erected; together with License and Power to build and found Churches, Chappels, and Oratories in convenient and fit Places, within the said Bounds and Limits; and to cause them to be dedicated and consecrated, according to the Ecclesiastical Laws of our Kingdom of *England;* together with all and singular the like, and as ample Rights, Jurisdictions, Privileges, Prerogatives, Royalties, Liberties, Immunities and Franchises of what kind soever, within the Territory, Isles, Islets, and Limits aforesaid: **To have,** hold, use, exercise and enjoy the same, as amply, fully, and in as ample

---

[2]This version of the charter, printed in South Carolina, differs in several instances from that in 1.1.3.10.c, printed in North Carolina.

Manner as any Bishop of *Durham* in our Kingdom of *England,* ever heretofore had, held, used or enjoyed, or of Right ought or could have, use, or enjoy. . . .

. . .

XVIII. AND because it may happen, that some of the People and Inhabitants of the said *Province,* cannot in their private Opinions conform to the publick Exercise of *Religion,* according to the Liturgy, Form and Ceremonies of the Church of *England,* or take and subscribe the Oaths and Articles made and established in that behalf, and for that the same, by reason of the remote Distances of those Places, will, as we hope, be no Breach of the Unity and Conformity established in this Nation, Our Will and Pleasure therefore is, and we do by these Presents, for us, our Heirs and Successors, give and grant unto the said *Edward* Earl of *Clarendon, George* Duke of *Albemarle, William* Earl of *Craven, John* Lord *Berkley, Anthony* Lord *Ashley,* Sir *George Carteret,* Sir *John Colleton,* and Sir *William Berkley,* their Heirs and Assigns, full and free Licence, Liberty and Authority, by such Ways and Means as they shall think fit, to give and grant unto such Person and Persons, inhabiting and being within the said *Province* or *Territory,* hereby, or by the said recited Letters Patents, mentioned to be granted as aforesaid, or any Part thereof, such *Indulgencies* and *Dispensations,* in that behalf, for and during such *Time* and *Times,* and with such *Limitations* and *Restrictions* as the said *Edward* Earl of *Clarendon, George* Duke of *Albemarle, William* Earl of *Craven, John* Lord *Berkley, Anthony* Lord *Ashley,* Sir *George Carteret,* Sir *John Colleton,* and Sir *William Berkley,* their Heirs or Assigns, shall in their Discretion think fit and reasonable, and that no Person or Persons unto whom such Liberty shall be given, shall be any way molested, punished, disquieted, or called in question, for any difference in Opinion or Practice, in Matters of religious Concernment, who do not actually disturb the civil Peace of the Province, County or Colony that they shall make their abode in; but all and every such Person and Persons, may from Time to Time, and at all Times, freely and quietly have and enjoy his or their Judgments and Consciences in Matters of Religion, throughout all the said *Province* or Colony, they behaving peaceably, and not using this Liberty to Licentiousness, nor to the civil Injury or outward Disturbance of others; any Law, Statute or Clause, contained or to be contained, Usage or Customs of our Realm of *England,* to the contrary hereof, in in [*sic*] any wise notwithstanding.

South Carolina Provincial Laws, pp. xxiii–xv, xliii–xliv.

1.1.3.13.d   Fundamental Constitutions of Carolina, 1669

95th. No man shall be permitted to be a freeman of Carolina, or to have any estate or habitation within it, that doth not acknowledge a God, and that God is publicly and solemnly to be worshipped.

96th. (As the country comes to be sufficiently planted, and distributed in fit divisions, it shall belong to the Parliament to take care for the building of churches and the public maintenance of divines, to be employed in the exercise of religion, according to the Church of England; which being the only true and orthodox, and the national religion of all the king's dominions, is so also of Carolina, and therefore it alone shall be allowed to receive public maintenance by grant of parliament.)

97th. But since the natives of that place, who will be concerned in our plantation, are utterly strangers to Christianity, whose idolatry, ignorance or mistake gives us no right to expell or treat them ill, and those who remove from other parts to plant there will unavoidably be of different opinions, concerning matters of religion, the liberty whereof they will expect to have allowed them, and it will not be reasonable for us on this account to keep them out; that civil peace may be obtained amidst diversity of opinions, and our agreement and compact with all men, may be duly and faithfully observed, the violation whereof, upon what pretence soever, cannot be without offence to Almighty God, and great scandal to the true religion which we profess; and also that Jews, Heathens and other dissenters from the purity of the Christian religion, may not be scared and kept at a distance from it, but by having an opportunity of acquainting themselves with the truth and reasonableness of its doctrines, and the peaceableness and inoffensiveness of its professors, may be good usage and persuasion, and all those convincing methods of gentleness and meekness, suitable to the rules and design of the gospel, be won over to embrace and unfeignedly receive the truth; therefore any seven or more persons agreeing in any religion, shall constitute a church or profession, to which they shall give some name, to distinguish it from others.

98th. The terms of admittance and communion with any church or profession shall be written in a book, and therein be subscribed by all the members of the said church or profession; which book shall be kept by the public Register of the Precinct wherein they reside.

99th. The time of every one, subscription admittance, shall be dated in the said book or religious record.

100th. In the terms of communion of every church or profession, these following shall be three, without which no agreement or assembly of men upon pretence of religion, shall be accounted a church or profession within these rules:

1st. "That there is a God."

2nd. "That God is publickly to be worshipped."

3rd. "That it is lawful and the duty of every man being thereunto called by those that govern, to bear witness to truth; and that every church or profession shall in their terms of communion, set down the eternal way whereby they witness a truth as in the presence of God whether it be by laying hands on or kissing the Bible, as in the Church of England, or by holding up the hand, or any other sensible way."

101st. No person above seventeen years of age, shall have any benefit or protection of the law, or be capable of any place of profit or honor who is not a member of some church or profession, having his name recorded in some one, and but one religious record at once.

102nd. No person of any other church or profession shall disturb or molest any religious assembly.

103rd. No person whatsoever, shall speak anything in their religious assembly irreverently or seditiously of the government or governors, or of state matters.

104th. Any person subscribing the terms of communion, in the record of the said church or profession, before the precinct register and any five members of the said church or profession, shall be thereby made a member of the said church or profession.

105th. Any person striking out his own name out of any religious record, or his name being struck out by any officer thereunto authorized by such church or profession respectively, shall cease to be a member of that church or profession.

106th. No man shall use any reproachful, reviling, or abusive language against any religion of any church or profession; that being the certain way of disturbing the peace, and of hindering the conversion of any to the truth, by engaging them in quarrels and animosities, to the hatred of the professors and that profession which otherwise they might be brought to assent.

107th. Since charity obliges us to wish well to the souls of all men, and religion ought to alter nothing in any man's civil estate or right, it shall be lawful for slaves as well as others, to enter themselves and be of what church or profession any of them shall think best, and thereof be as fully members as any freemen. But yet no slave shall hereby be exempted from that civil dominion his master hath over him, but be in all things in the same state and condition he was in before.

108th. Assemblies upon what pretence soever of religion, not observing and performing the above said rules, shall not be esteemed as churches, but unlawful meetings, and be punished as riots.

109th. No person whatsoever shall disturb, molest, or persecute another, for his speculative opinions in religion, or his way of worship.

110th. Every freeman of Carolina, shall have absolute power and authority over his negro slaves, of what opinion or religion soever.

North Carolina State Records, pp. 147–49 (John Locke).

1.1.3.13.e   Constitution, 1778

XXI. And whereas the Ministers of the Gospel are, by their Profession, dedicated to the Service of God, and the Cure of Souls, and ought not to be diverted from the great Duties of their Function; therefore, no Minister of the Gospel, or public Preacher, of any religious Persuasion, while he continues in the Exercise of his pastoral Function, and for *two* Years after, shall be eligible either as Governor, Lieutenant Governor, a Member of the Senate, House of Representatives, or Privy Council in this State.

   . . .

XXXVIII. That all Persons and religious Societies, who acknowledge that there is one God, and a future state of Rewards and Punishments, and that God is publickly to be worshipped, shall be freely tolerated. The Christian Protestant Religion, shall be deemed, and is hereby constituted and declared to be, the established Religion of this State. That all Denominations of Christian Protestants in this State, demeaning themselves peaceably and faithfully, shall enjoy equal religious and civil Privileges. To accomplish this desirable Purpose, without injury to the religious Property of those Societies of Christians, which are by Law already incorporated for the Purpose of religious Worship; and to put it fully into the Power of every other Society of Christian Protestants, either already formed or hereafter to be formed, to obtain the like Incorporation, *It is hereby constituted, appointed, and declared,* That the respective Societies of the Church of England, that are already formed in this State for the Purposes of religious Worship, shall still continue incorporate, and hold the religious Property now in their Possession.

And that, whenever *fifteen* or more male Persons, not under *twenty-one* Years of Age, professing the Christian Protestant Religion, and agreeing to unite themselves in a Society, for the Purposes of religious Worship, they shall, (on complying with the Terms hereinafter mentioned,) be, and be constituted, a Church, and be esteemed and regarded in Law as of the established Religion of the State, and on a Petition to the Legislature, shall be intitled to be incorporated, and to enjoy equal Privileges. That every Society of Christians, so formed, shall give themselves a Name or Denomination, by which they shall be called and known in Law; and all that associate with them for the Purposes of Worship, shall be esteemed as belonging to the Society so called: But that, previous to the Establishment and Incorporation of the respective Societies of every Denomination as aforesaid, and in order to intitle them thereto, each Society so petitioning, shall have agreed to, and subscribed, in a Book, the following *Five* Articles, without which, no Agreement or Union of Men, upon Pretence of Religion, shall intitle them to be incorporated, and esteemed as a Church of the established Religionof this State:

First, *That there is one eternal God, and a future State of Rewards and Punishments.*

Second, *That God is publickly to be worshipped.*

Third, *That the Christian Religion is the true Religion.*

Fourth, *That the Holy Scriptures of the Old and New Testaments are of Divine Inspiration, and are of the Rule of Faith and Practice.*

Fifth, *That it is lawful, and the Duty of every Man, being thereunto called by those that govern, to bear witness to the Truth.*

And that every Inhabitant of this State, when called to make an Appeal to God, as a Witness to Truth, shall be permitted to do it in that Way which is most agreeable to the Dictates of his own Conscience. And, that the People of this State may forever enjoy the Right of electing their own Pastors or Clergy; and, at the same Time, that the State may have sufficient Security, for the due Discharge of the Pastoral Office, by those who shall be admitted to be Clergymen; no Person shall officiate as Minister of any established Church, who shall not have been chosen by a Majority of the Society to which he shall minister, or by Persons appointed by the said Majority to chuse and procure a Minister for them, nor until the Minister so chosen and appointed, shall have made and subscribed to the following Declaration, over and above the aforesaid *five* Articles, *viz.*

That he is determined, by God's Grace, out of the Holy Scriptures, to instruct the People committed to his Charge, and to teach nothing (as required of Necessity to Eternal Salvation) but that which he shall be persuaded may be concluded and proved from the Scripture; that he will use both public and private Admonitions, as well to the Sick as to the Whole, within his Cure, as Need shall require and Occasion shall be given; and that he will be diligent in Prayers, and in reading of the Holy Scriptures, and in such Studies as help to the Knowledge of the same; that he will be diligent to frame and fashion his own self, and his Family, according to the Doctrine of Christ, and to make both himself and them, as much as in him lieth, wholesome Examples and Patterns to the Flock of Christ; that he will maintain and set forwards, as much as he can, Quietness, Peace, and Love, among all People; and especially among those that are or shall be committed to his Charge.

No Person shall disturb or molest any religious Assembly, nor shall use any reproachful, reviling, or abusive Language, against any Church; that being the certain Way of disturbing the Peace, and of hindering the Conversion of any to the Truth, by engaging them in Quarrels and Animosities, to the Hatred of the Professors, and that Profession which otherwise they might be brought to assent to. No Person whatsoever shall speak any Thing, in their religious Assembly, irreverently, or seditiously, of the Government of this State. No Person shall, by Law, be obliged to pay towards the Maintenance and Support of a religious Worship that he does not freely join in, or has not voluntarily engaged to support: But, the Churches, Chapels, Parsonages, Glebes, and all other Property, now belonging to any Societies of the Church of England, or any other religious Societies, shall remain, and be secured, to them for ever. The Poor shall be supported, and Elections managed, in the accustomed Manner, until Laws shall be provided, to adjust those Matters in the most equitable Way.

South Carolina Constitution, pp. 10, 12–14.

1.1.3.13.f **Constitution, 1790**

ARTICLE VIII.

Section 1. The free exercise and enjoyment of religious profession and worship, without discrimination or preference, shall, forever hereafter, be allowed within this state to all mankind; provided that the liberty of conscience thereby declared shall not be so construed as to excuse acts of licentiousness, or justify practices inconsistent with the peace or safety of this state.

Section 2. The rights, privileges, immunities and estates of both civil and religious societies, and of corporate bodies, shall remain as if the constitution of this state had not been altered or amended.

South Carolina Laws, App., p. 41.

1.1.3.14 **Vermont: Constitution, 1777**

CHAPTER I.

. . .

3. THAT all Men have a natural and unalienable Right to worship ALMIGHTY GOD according to the Dictates of their own Consciences and Understanding, regulated by the Word of GOD; and that no Man ought or of Right can be compelled to attend any religious Worship, or erect, or support any Place of Worship, or maintain any Minister contrary to the Dictates of his Conscience; nor can any Man who professes the Protestant Religion, be justly deprived or abridged of any civil Right, as a Citizen, on Account of his religious Sentiment, or peculiar Mode of religious Worship, and that no Authority can, or ought to be vested in, or assumed by any Power whatsoever, that shall in any Case interfere with, or in any Manner control the Rights of Conscience, in the free Exercise of religious Worship; nevertheless, every Sect or Denomination of People ought to observe the Sabbath, or Lord's Day, and keep up and support some Sort of reli-

gious Worship, which to them shall seem most agreeable to the revealed Will of GOD.

CHAPTER II.

. . .

SECTION VI.

EVERY Man, of the full Age of twenty-one Years, having resided in this State for the Space of one whole Year next before the Election of Representatives, and is of a quiet and peaceable Behaviour, and will take the following Oath (or Affirmation) shall be entitled to all the Privileges of a Freeman of this State.

I —— —— solemnly swear, by the ever-living God, (or affirm, in Presence of Almighty God,) that whenever I am called to give my Vote or Suffrage, touching any Matter that concerns the State of Vermont, I will do it so, as in my Conscience I shall judge will most conduce to the best Good of the same, as established by the Constitution, without Fear or Favor of any Man.

. . .

SECTION IX.

A QUORUM of the House of Representatives shall consist of Two-thirds of the whole Number of Members elected; and having met and chosen their Speaker, shall each of them, before they proceed to Business, take and subscribe as well the Oath of Fidelity and Allegiance, herein after directed, as the following Oath or Affirmation, viz.

I —— —— do solemnly swear by the ever-living God, (or I do solemnly affirm in the Presence of Almighty God) that as a Member of this Assembly, I will not propose or assent to any Bill, Vote, or Resolution, which shall appear to me injurious to the People; nor do or consent to any Act or Thing whatever, that shall have a Tendency to lessen or abridge their Rights and Privileges, as declared in the Constitution of this State; but will in all Things, conduct myself as a faithful, honest Representative and Guardian of the People, according to the best of my Judgment and Abilities,

And each Member, before he takes his Seat, shall make and subscribe the following Declaration, viz.

I do believe in one God, the Creator and Governor of the Universe, the Rewarder of the good, and Punisher of the wicked. And I do acknowledge the Scriptures of the Old and New Testament, to be given by Divine Inspiration, and own and profess the Protestant Religion.

And no further or other religious Test shall ever hereafter, be required of any civil Officer or Magistrate of this State.

. . .

SECTION XXXVI.

EVERY Officer, whether judicial, executive, or military, in Authority under this State, shall take the following Oath or Affirmation of Allegiance, and general Oath of Office, before he enter on the Execution of his Office.

The Oath Or Affirmation Of Allegiance.

"I —— —— do solemnly swear by the ever-living God, (or affirm in the presence of Almighty God) that I will be true and faithful to the State of Vermont; and that I will not, directly or indirectly, do any Act or Thing prejudicial or

injurious, to the Constitution or Government therof, as established by Convention."

The Oath Or Affirmation Of Office

"I —— —— do solemnly swear by the ever-living God, (or affirm in the presence of Almighty God) that I will faithfully execute the Office of   for the   of   and will do equal Right and Justice to all Men, to the best of my Judgment and Abilities, according to Law."   Vermont Acts, pp. 3, 5, 6, 10.

1.1.3.15   Virginia

1.1.3.15.a   First Charter of Virginia, 1606

. . .

III. We greatly commending, and graciously accepting of, their desires for the furtherance of so noble a work, which may, by the providence of Almighty God, hereafter tend to the glory of his divine Majesty, in propagating of Christian religion to such people, as yet live in Darkness and miserable ignorance of the true knowledge and worship of God, and may in time bring the infidels and savages, living in those parts, to human civility, and to a settled and quiet government: Do, by theses our letters Pattents, graciously accept of, and agree to, their humble and well-intended desires. . . .

Virginia Laws, p. 58.

1.1.3.15.b   Second Charter of Virginia, 1609

XXIII. And forasmuch, as it shall be necessary for all such our loving subjects, as shall inhabit within the said precincts of Virginia, aforesaid, to determine to live together, in the fear and true worship of Almighty God, Christian peace, and civil quietness, each with other, whereby every one may, with more safety, pleasure, and profit, enjoy that, whereunto they shall attain with great pain, and peril; we, for us, our heirs, and successors, are likewise pleased and contented, and by these presents, do give and grant unto the said treasurer and company, and their successors, and to such governors, officers, and ministers, as shall be, by our said council, constituted and appointed, according to the natures and limits of their offices and places respectively, that they shall and may, from time to time forever hereafter, within the said precincts, of Virginia, or in the way by sea thither and from thence, have full and absolute power and authority, to correct, punish, pardon, govern and rule, all such the subjects of us, our heirs and successors, as shall, from time to time, adventure themselves in any voyage thither, or that shall, at any hereafter, inhabit in the precincts and territories of the said colony, as aforesaid, according to such orders, ordinances, constitutions, directions, and instructions, as by our said council, as aforesaid, shall be established; and in defect thereof, in case of necessity, according to the good discretions of the said governor and officers, respectively, as well in cases capital and Criminal as civil, both marine and other; So always, as the said statutes, ordinances and proceedings, as near as conveniently may be, be agreeable to the laws, statutes, government, and policy of our realm of this England.

Virginia Laws, pp. 95–96 (footnotes omitted).

1.1.3.15.c **Declaration of Rights, 1776**

XVI. THAT religion, or the duty which we owe to our Creator, and the manner of discharging it, can be directed only by reason and conviction, not by force or violence, and therefore all men are equally entitled to the free exercise of religion, according to the dictates of conscience; and that it is the mutual duty of all to practise Christian forbearance, love, and charity, towards each other.

Virginia Acts, p. 33.

1.1.3.15.d **An Act, October 7, 1776**

CHAP. II

An act for exempting the different societies of Dissenters from contributing to the support and maintenance of the Church as by law established, and its Ministers, and for other purposes therein mentioned.

I. WHEREAS several oppressive acts of Parliament respecting religion have been formerly enacted, and doubts have arisen, and may hereafter arise, whether the same are in force within this commonwealth or not: For prevention whereof, *Be it enacted by the General Assembly of the commonwealth of* Virginia, *and it is hereby enacted by the authority of the same,* that all and every act of Parliament, by whatever title known or distinguished, which renders criminal the maintaining any opinions in matters of religion, forbearing to repair to church, or the exercising any mode of worship whatsoever, or which prescribes punishments for the same, shall henceforth be of no validity or force within this commonwealth.

II. AND whereas there are within this commonwealth great numbers of dissenters from the church established by law who have been heretofore taxed for its support, and it is contrary to the principles of reason and justice that any should be compelled to contribute to the maintenance of a church with which their consciences will not permit them to join, and from which they can therefore receive no benefit: For remedy whereof, and that equal liberty, as well religious as civil, may be universally extended to all the good people of this commonwealth, *Be it enacted by the General Assembly of the commonwealth of* Virginia, *and it is hereby enacted by the authority of the same,* that all dissenters, of whatever denomination, from the said church, shall, from and after the passing this act, be totally free and exempt from all levies, taxes, and impositions whatever, towards supporting and maintaining the said church, as it now is or hereafter may be established, and its ministers.

III. *PROVIDED nevertheless, and it is further enacted, by the authority aforesaid,* that the vestries of the several parishes, where the same hath not been already done, shall and may, and they are hereby authorized and required, at such time as they shall appoint, to levy and assess on all tithables within their respective parishes, as well as dissenters as others, all such salaries and arrears of salaries as are or may be due to the ministers or incumbents of their parishes for services to the first day of *January* next; moreover to make such assessments on all tithables as will enable the said vestries to comply with their legal parochial engagements already entered into; and lastly, to continue such future provision for the poor in their respective parishes as they have hitherto by law been accustomed to make.

IV. *AND be it further enacted, by the authority aforesaid,* that there shall in all time coming be saved and reserved to the use of the church by law established the several tracts of glebe land already purchased, the chuches and chapels already built, and such as were begun or contracted for before the passing of this act for the use of the parishes, all books, plate, and ornaments, belonging or appropriated to the use of the said church, and all arrears of money or tobacco arising from former assessments or otherwise; and that there shall moreover be saved and reserved to the use of such parishes as may have received private donations, for the better support of the said church and its ministers, the perpetual benefit and enjoyment of all such donations.

V. AND whereas great variety of opinions hath arisen, touching the propriety of a general assessment, or whether every religious society should be left to voluntary contributions for the support and maintenance of the several ministers and teachers of the Gospel who are of different persuasions and denominations, and this difference of sentiments cannot now be well accommodated, so that it is thought most prudent to defer this matter to the discussion and final determination of a future Assembly, when the opinions of the country in general may be better known: To the end, therefore, that so important a subject may in no sort be prejudged, *Be it enacted, by the authority aforesaid,* that nothing in this act contained shall be construed to affect or influence the said question of a general assessment, or voluntary contribution, in any respect whatever.

VI. AND whereas, by the exemptions allowed dissenters, it may be too burthensome in some parishes to the members of the established church if they are still compelled to support the clergy by certain fixed salaries, and it is judged best that this should be done for the present by voluntary contributions: *Be it therefore enacted, by the authority aforesaid,* that so much of an act of the General Assembly made in the twenty-second year of the reign of King *George* the Second, entitled *An act for the support of the clergy, and for the regular collecting and paying the parish levies,* or any other act as provides salaries for the ministers, and authorizes the vestries to levy the same, except in the cases before directed, shall be, and the same is hereby suspended, until the end of the next session of Assembly.

VII. AND whereas it is represented that in some counties lists of tithables have been omitted to be taken: For remedy whereof, and for the regular listing all tithable persons, *Be it further enacted,* that the court of every county where lists of the tithables, agreeable to the directions of the laws now in force, are not already taken, it shall and may be lawful for the courts of such counties, and they are hereby required, at the first or second court after the end of this session of Assembly, to divide their counties into convenient precincts, and appoint one of the Justices for each precinct to take a list of all the tithables therein; and every such Justice so to be appointed, shall give public notice of his being so appointed, and at what place or places he intends to receive the lists, by advertisements thereof affixed to the doors of churches and meeting-houses in the parish where the precinct lies, and shall accordingly attend on the said day by him to be appointed and at the second court next following shall deliver a fair list of the names and number of the tithables by him taken, to the clerk of the court who on the next court day shall set up fair copies of such lists in his courthouse, there to remain during the sitting of that court, for the better discovery of such as shall be concealed.

VIII. AND if the Justices of any county, where lists of tithables have not been already taken, shall fail to appoint some of their members to take the list of tithables in the manner directed by this act, every such Justice so failing shall forfeit and pay ten pounds; to be recovered in the General Court with costs, by action of debt or information against such Justices jointly. And if any Justice so appointed shall refuse or fail to give notice as aforesaid, and to take and return such list as aforesaid, he shall forfeit and pay two thousand pounds of tobacco, or ten pounds; to be recovered with costs, in any court of record in this commonwealth. And every master or owner of a family, or in his absence or non-residence at the plantation, his or her agent, attorney, or overseer, shall, on the said time appointed by the Justice for taking in the lists, deliver, or cause to be delivered, under his or her hand, to the Justice appointed for that precinct, a list of the names and number of all tithable persons who were abiding in or belonging to his or her family on the ninth day of *June* last. Every master or owner, or in his or her absence or non-residence, every overseer, failing herein, shall be adjudged a concealer of such and so many tithables as shall not be listed and given in, and for every tithable person so concealed shall forfeit and pay five hundred pounds of tobacco, or fifty shillings; to be recovered by action of debt or information, in any court of record. And when any overseer shall fail to list the tithables upon the plantation whereof he is overseer, the master or owner shall be subject to the payment of his levies, in the same manner as he would have been if they had been listed. Every person, at the time of giving in lists of tithables, shall also give in a list of his or her wheel carriages subject to a tax, to the several Justices appointed to take the list of tithables, under the like penalty for each failure, and to be recovered in the same manner as herein directed for concealing tithables. All the penalties hereby imposed shall be, one moiety to the informer, and the other moiety to the use of the county where the offence shall be committed, towards lessening the county levy.

Virginia Acts, pp. 39–40.

1.1.3.15.e **Memorial and Remonstrance Against Religious Assessments, 1786**

WE, the subscribers, citizens of the said Commonwealth, having taken into serious consideration, a bill printed by order of the last session of General Assembly, entitled 'A Bill establishing a Provision for Teachers of the Christian Religion,' and conceiving that the same, if finally armed with the sanctions of a law, will be a dangerous abuse of power, are bound as faithful members of a free state, to remonstrate against it; and to declare the reasons by which we are determined. We remonstrate against the said Bill,

BECAUSE, We hold it for a fundamental and undeniable truth, "That religion, or the duty which we owe to our Creator, and the manner of discharging it, can be directed only by reason and conviction, not by force or violence." The religion then of every man must be left to the conviction and conscience of every man; and it is the right of every man to exercise it as these may dictate. This right is in its nature an unalienable right. It is unalienable; because the opinions of men, depending only on the evidence contemplated by their own minds, cannot follow the dictates of other men: It is unalienable also; because what is here a right towards men, is a duty towards the Creator. It is the duty of every man to render to the Creator such homage, and such only, as he believes to be acceptable to him; this duty is predecent, both in order of time, and degree of obligation, to the claims of civil society. Before any man can be considered as a member of civil society, he must be considered as a subject of the Governour of the Universe: And if a member of civil society, who enters into any subordinate association, must always do it with a reservation of his duty to the general authority, much more must every man who becomes a member of any particular civil society, do it with a saving of his allegiance to the Universal Sovereign. We maintain therefore, that in matters of religion, no man's right is abridged by the institution of civil society; and that religion is wholly exempt from its cognizance. True it is, that no other rule exists, by which any question which may divide a society, can be ultimately determined, but the will of the majority; but it is also true, that the majority may trespass on the rights of the minority.

Because, If religion be exempt from the authority of the society at large, still less can it be subject to that of the legislative body. The latter are but the creatures and vicegerents of the former. Their jurisdiction is both derivative and limited: it is limited with regard to the co-ordinate departments, more necessarily is it limited with regard to the constituents. The preservation of a free government requires, not merely that the metes and bounds which separate each department of power may be invariably maintained, but more especially, that neither of them be suffered to overleap the great barrier which defends the rights of the people. The rulers who are guilty of such an encroachment, exceed the commission from which they derive their authority, and are tyrants. The people who submit to it are governed by laws made neither by themselves, nor by an authority derived from them, and are slaves.

Because, It is proper to take alarm at the first experiment on our liberties. We hold this prudent jealousy to be the first duty of citizens, and one of the noblest characteristicks of the late revolution. The freemen of America did not wait till usurped power had strengthened itself by exercise, and entangled the question in precedents. They saw all the consequences in the principle, and they avoided the consequences by denying the principle. We revere this lesson too much soon to forget it. Who does not see that the same authority which can establish Christianity, in exclusion of all other religions, may establish, with the same ease, any particular sect of Christians, in exclusion of all other sects? That the same authority which can force a citizen to contribute three-pence only of his property for the support of any one establishment, may force him to conform to any other establishment in all cases whatsoever.

Because, The bill violates that equality which ought to be the basis of every law; and which is more indispensable, in proportion as the validity or expediency of any law is more liable to be impeached. If "all men are by nature equally free and independent," all men are to be considered as entering into society on equal conditions, as relinquishing no more, and therefore retaining no less, one than another, of their rights. Above all are they to be considered as retaining an *"equal title to the free exercise of religion according to the dictates of conscience."* Whilst we assert for ourselves a freedom to embrace, to profess and to observe the religion which we believe to be of divine origin, we cannot deny an equal freedom to those, whose minds have not yet yielded to the evidence which has convinced us. If this freedom be abused, it is an offence against God, not against man: To God, therefore, not to men, must an account of it be rendered. As the bill violates equality by subjecting some to peculiar burdens, so it violates the same principle, by granting to others peculiar exemptions. Are the Quakers and Menonists the only sects who think a compulsive support of their religions unnecessary and unwarrantable? Can their piety alone be intrusted with the care of publick worship? Ought their religions to be endowed, above all others, with extraordinary privileges, by which proselytes may be enticed from all others? We think too favourably of the justice and good sense of these denominations, to believe, that they either covet pre-eminencies over their fellow citizens, or that they will be seduced by them, from the common opposition to the measure.

Because, The bill implies, either that the civil magistrate is a competent judge of religious truth; or that he may employ religion as an engine of civil policy. The first is an arrogant pretension, falsified by the contradictory opinions of rulers in all ages, and throughout the world: The second an unhallowed perversion of the means of salvation.

Because, The establishment proposed by the bill is not requisite for the support of the Christian religion. To say that it is, is a contradiction to the Christian religion itself; for every page of it disavows a dependence on the powers of this world: It is a contradiction to fact; for it is known that this religion both existed and flourished, not only without the support of human laws, but in spite of every opposition from them; and not only during the period of miraculous aid, but long after it had been left to its own evidence, and the ordinary care of Providence: Nay, it is a contradiction in terms; for a religion not invented by human policy, must have pre-existed and been supported, before it was established by human policy. It is moreover to weaken in those who profess this religion, a pious confidence in its innate excellence, and the patronage of its author; and to foster in those who still reject it, a suspicion, that its friends are too conscious of its fallacies, to trust it to its own merits.

Because, Experience witnesseth, that ecclesiastical establishments, instead of maintaining the purity and efficacy of religion, have had a contrary operation. During almost fifteen centuries, has the legal establishment of Christianity been on trial. What have been its fruits? More or less in all places, pride and indolence in the clergy; ignorance and servility in the laity; in both, superstition, bigotry and persecution. Inquire of the teachers of Christianity for the ages in which it appeared in its greatest lustre; those of every sect point to the ages prior to its incorporation with civil policy. Propose a restoration of this primitive state, in which its teachers depended on the voluntary rewards of their flocks; many of them predict its downfall. On which side ought their testimony to have greatest weight, when for, or when against their interest?

Because, The establishment in question is not necessary for the support of civil government. If it be urged as necessary for the support of civil government, only as it is a means of supporting religion; and it be not necessary for the latter purpose, it cannot be necessary for the former. If religion be not within the cognizance of civil government, how can its legal establishment be said to be necessary to civil government? What influence, in fact [*sic*] have ecclesiastical establishments had on civil society? In some instances they have been seen to erect a spiritual tyranny on the ruins of civil authority; in many instances they have been seen upholding the thrones of political tyranny; in no instance have they been seen the guardians of the liberties of the people. Rulers who wished to subvert the publick liberty, may have found an established clergy, convenient auxiliaries. A just government, instituted to secure and perpetuate it, needs them not. Such a government will be best supported by protecting every citizen in the enjoyment of his religion, with the same equal hand, which protects his person, and his property; by neither invading the equal rights by any sect; nor suffering any sect to invade those of another.

Because, The proposed establishment is a departure from that generous policy; which, offering an asylum to the persecuted and oppressed of every nation and religion, promised a lustre to our country, and an accession to the number of its citizens. What a melancholy mark is the Bill of sudden degeneracy? Instead of holding forth an asylum to the persecuted, it is itself a signal of persecution. It degrades from the equal rank of citizens all those whose opinions in religion do not bend to those of the Legislative Authority. Distant as it may be, in its present form, from the Inquisition, it differs from it only in degree. The one is the first step, the other the last, in the career of intolerance. The magnanimous sufferer under this cruel scourge in foreign regions, must view the Bill as a beacon on our coast, warning him to seek some other haven, where liberty and philanthropy, in their due extent, may offer a more certain repose from his troubles.

Because, It will have a like tendency to banish our citizens. The allurements presented by other situations are every day thinning their number. To superadd a fresh motive to emigration, by revoking the liberty which they now enjoy, would be the same species of folly, which has dishonoured and depopulated flourishing kingdoms.

Because, It will destroy that moderation and harmony which the forbearance of our laws to intermeddle with religion, has produced amongst its several sects. Torrents of blood have been spilt in the old world, by vain attempts of the secular arm to extinguish religious discord, by proscribing all differences in religious opinion. Time has at length revealed the true remedy. Every relaxation of narrow and rigorous policy, wherever it has been tried, has been found to assuage the disease. The American theatre has exhibited proofs, that equal and complete liberty, if it does not wholly eradicate it, sufficiently destroys its malignant influence on the health and prosperity of the State. If, with the salutary effects of this system under our own eyes, we begin to contract the bounds of religious freedom, we know no name that will too severely reproach our folly. At least let warning be taken at the first fruit of the threatened innovation. The very appearance of the Bill has transformed that "Christian forbearance, love and charity," which of late mutually prevailed, into animosities and jealousies, which may not soon be appeased. What mischiefs may not be dreaded, should this enemy to the publick quiet be armed with the force of a law?

Because, The policy of the Bill is adverse to the diffusion of the light of Christianity. The first wish of those who enjoy this precious gift, ought to be that it may be imparted to the whole race of mankind. Compare the number of those who have as yet received it, with the number still remaining under the dominion of false religions; and how small is the former? Does the policy of the Bill tend to lessen the disproportion? No: It at once discourages those, who are strangers to the light of revelation from coming into the region of it; and countenances, by example, the nations who continue in darkness, in shutting out those who might convey it to them. Instead of levelling as far as possible, every obstacle to the victorious progress of truth, the Bill, with an ignoble and unchristian timidity, would circumscribe it, with a wall of defence, against the encroachments of errour.

Because, Attempts to enforce by legal sanctions, acts obnoxious to so great a proportion of citizens, tend to enervate the laws in general, and to slacken the bands of society. If it be difficult to execute any law which is not generally deemed necessary or salutary, what must be the case, where it is deemed invalid and dangerous? And what may be the effect of so striking an example of impotency in the government, on its general authority?

Because, A measure of such singular magnitude and delicacy ought not to be imposed, without the clearest evidence that it is called for by a majority of citizens: And no satisfactory method is yet proposed, by which the voice of the majority in this case may be determined, or its influence secured. "The people of the respective counties are indeed requested to signify their opinion respecting the adoption of the Bill to the next session of Assembly." But the representation must be made equal, before the voice either of the Representatives, or of the counties, will be that of the people. Our hope is that neither of the former will, after due consideration, espouse the dangerous principle of the Bill. Should the event disappoint us, it will still leave us in full confidence, that a fair appeal to the latter will reverse the sentence against our liberties.

Because, Finally, "The equal right of every citizen to the free exercise of his religion according to the dictates of conscience," is held by the same tenure with all our other rights. If we recur to its origin, it is equally the gift of nature; if we weigh its importance, it cannot be less dear to us; if we consult the "declaration of those rights which pertain to the good people of Virginia, as the basis and foundation of government," it is enumerated with equal solemnity, or rather studied emphasis. Either then we must say, that the will of the Legislature is the only measure of their authority, and that in the plenitude of this authority, they may sweep away all our fundamental rights; or that they are bound to leave this particular right untouched and sacred: Either we must say, that they may controul the freedom of the press, may abolish the trial by jury, may swallow up the Executive and Judiciary Powers of the State; nay, that they may despoil us of our very right of suffrage, and erect themselves into an independent and hereditary Assembly: or we must say, that they have no authority to enact into law the Bill under consideration. We the subscribers say, that the General Assembly of this Commonwealth have no such Authority: And that no effort may be omitted on our part against so dangerous an usurpation, we oppose to it, this remonstrance; earnestly praying, as we are in duty bound, that the Supreme Lawgiver of the Universe, by illuminating those to whom it is addressed, may on the one hand, turn their councils from every act which would affront his holy prerogative, or violate the trust committed to them: And on the other, guide them into every measure which may be worthy of his blessing, may redound to their own praise, and may establish more firmly the liberties, the prosperity and the happiness of the Commonwealth.

Virginia Memorial & Remonstrance, pp. 3–12.

1.1.3.15.f Bill for Religious Freedom, 1786

Well aware that Almighty God hath created the mind free; that all attempts to influence it by temporal punishments or burdens, or by civil incapacitations, tend only to beget habits of hypocrisy and meanness, and are a departure from the plan of the Holy Author of our religion, who, being Lord both of body and mind, yet chose not to propagate it by coercions on either, as was in his Almighty power to do; that the impious presumption of legislators and rulers, civil as well as ecclesiastical, who, being themselves but fallible and uninspired men have assumed dominion over the faith of others, setting up their own opinions and modes of thinking as the only true and infallible, and as such endeavoring to impose them on others, hath established and maintained false religions over the greatest part of the world, and through all time; That to compel a man to furnish contributions of money for the propagation of opinions which he disbelieves, is sinful and tyrannical; that even the forcing him to support this or that teacher of his own religious persuasion, is depriving him of the comfortable liberty of giving his contributions to the particular pastor whose morals he would make his pattern, and whose powers he feels most persuasive to righteousness, and is withdrawing from the ministry those temporal rewards, which proceeding from an approbation of their personal conduct, are an additional incitement to earnest and unremitting labors for the instruction of mankind; that our civil rights have no dependence on our religious opinions, more than our opinions in physics or geometry; that therefore the proscribing any citizen as unworthy the public confidence by laying upon him an incapacity of being called to the offices of trust and emolument, unless he profess or renounce this or that religious opinion, is depriving him injuriously of those privileges and advantages to which in common with his fellow citizens he has a natural right; that it intends also to corrupt the principles of that very religion it is meant to encourage, by bribing, with a monopoly of worldly honors and emoluments, those who will externally profess and conform to it; that though indeed these are criminal who do not withstand such temptation, yet neither are those innocent who lay the bait in their way; that to suffer the civil magistrate to intrude his powers into the field of opinion, and to restrain the profession or propagation of principles, on supposition of their ill tendency, is a dangerous fallacy, which at once destroys all religious liberty, because he being of course judge of that tendency, will make his opinions the rule of judgment, and approve or condemn the sentiments of others only as they shall square with or differ from his own; that it is time enough for the rightful purposes of civil government for its offices to interfere when principles break out into overt acts against peace and good order; and finally, that truth is great and will prevail if left to herself, that she is the proper and sufficient antagonist to error, and has nothing to fear from the conflict, unless by human interposition disarmed of her natural weapons, free argument and debate, errors ceasing to be dangerous when it is permitted freely to contradict them.

Be it therefore enacted by the General Assembly, That no man shall be compelled to frequent or support any religious worship, place or ministry whatsoever, nor shall be enforced, restrained, molested, or burthened in his body or goods, nor shall otherwise suffer on account of his religious opinions or belief; but that all men shall be free to profess, and by argument to maintain, their opinions in matters of religion, and that the same shall in nowise diminish, enlarge, or affect their civil capacities.

And though we well know that this Assembly, elected by the people for the ordinary purposes of legislation only, have no power to restrain the acts of succeeding Assemblies, constituted with powers equal to our own, and that therefore to declare this act irrevocable, would be of no effect in law, yet we are free to declare, and do declare, that the rights hereby asserted are the natural rights of mankind, and that if any act shall be hereafter passed to repeal the present or to narrow its operation, such act will be an infringement of natural right.

Virginia Religious Freedom Art, pp. 3, 5, 7.

1.1.4 OTHER TEXTS

1.1.4.1 Mayflower Compact, 1620

. . . Having undertaken for the glory of God, and advancement of the christian faith, and the honour of our King and country, a voyage to plant the first colony in the northern parts of Virginia. . . .

New Plymouth Laws, p. 19.

1.1.4.2 English Bill of Rights, 1689

. . . That the commission for erecting the late court of commissioners of ecclesiastical causes and all other commissions and courts of like nature are illegal and pernicious.

1 Will. & Mar. sess. 2, c. 2.

1.1.4.3 Northwest Territory Ordinance, 1787

Article the First. No person demeaning himself in a peaceable and orderly manner shall ever be molested on account of his mode of worship or religious sentiments in the said territory.

Continental Congress Papers, DNA.

1.1.4.4 Richard Henry Lee to Edmund Randolph, Proposed Amendments, October 16, 1787

. . . That the rights of conscience in matters of religion shall not be violated. . . .

Virginia Gazette, December 22, 1787.

1.2 DISCUSSION OF DRAFTS AND PROPOSALS
1.2.1 THE FIRST CONGRESS

1.2.1.1 **June 8, 1789**

1.2.1.1.a   Mr. MADISON.

. . .

. . . The first of these amendments, relates to what may be called a bill of rights; I will own that I never considered this provision so essential to the federal constitution, as to make it improper to ratify it, until such an amendment was added; at the same time, I always conceived, that in a certain form and to a certain extent, such a provision was neither improper nor altogether useless. I am aware, that a great number of the most respectable friends to the government and champions for republican liberty, have thought such a provision, not only unneccessary, but even improper, nay, I believe some have gone so far as to think it even dangerous. Some policy has been made use of perhaps by gentlemen on both sides of the question: I acknowledge the ingenuity of those arguments which were drawn against the constitution, by a comparison with the policy of Great Britain, in establishing a declaration of rights; but there is too great a difference in the case to warrant the comparison: therefore the arguments drawn from that source, were in a great measure inapplicable. In the declaration of rights which that country has established, the truth is, they have gone no farther, than to raise a barrier against the power of the Crown, the power of the legislature is left altogether indefinite. Altho' I know whenever the great rights, the trial by jury, freedom of the press, or liberty of conscience, came in question in that body [Great Britain], the invasion of them is resisted by able advocates, yet their Magna Charta does not contain any one provision for the security of those rights, respecting which, the people of America are most alarmed. The freedom of the press and rights of conscience, those choicest privileges of the people, are unguarded in the British constitution.

But altho' the case may be widely different, and it may not be thought necessary to provide limits for the legislative power in that country, yet a different opinion prevails in the United States. The people of many states, have thought it necessary to raise barriers against power in all forms and departments of government, and I am inclined to believe, if once bills of rights are established in all the states as well as the federal constitution, we shall find that altho' some of them are rather unimportant, yet, upon the whole, they will have a salutary tendency.

It may be said, in some instances they do no more than state the perfect equality of mankind, this to be sure is an absolute truth, yet it is not absolutely necessary to be inserted at the head of a constitution.

In some instances they assert those rights which are exercised by the people in forming and establishing a plan of government. In other instances, they specify those rights which are retained when particular powers are given up to be exercised by the legislature. In other instances, they specify positive rights, which may seem to result from the nature of the compact. Trial by jury cannot be considered as natural right, but a right resulting from the social compact which regulates the action of the community, but is essential to secure the liberty of the people as any one of the pre-existent rights of nature. In other instances they lay down dogmatic maxims with respect to the construction of the government; declaring that the legislative, executive, and judicial branches shall be kept separate and distinct: Perhaps the best way of securing this in practice is to provide such checks, as will prevent the encroachment of the one upon the another.

But whatever may be form which the several states have adopted in making declaration in favor of particular rights, the great object in view is to limit and qualify the powers of government, by excepting out of the grant of power those cases in which the government ought not to act, or to act only in a particular mode. They point these exceptions sometimes against the abuse of the executive power, sometimes against the legislative, and in some cases, against the community itself; or, in other words, against the majority in favor of the minority.

In our government it is, perhaps, less necessary to guard against the abuse in the executive department than any other; because it is not the stronger branch of the system, but the weaker: It therefore must be levelled against the legislative, for it is the most powerful, and most likely to be abused, because it is under the least controul; hence, so far as a declaration of rights can tend to prevent the exercise of undue power, it cannot be doubted but such declaration is proper. But I confess that I do conceive, that in a government modified like this of the United States, the great danger lies rather in the abuse of the community than in the legislative body. The prescriptions in favor of liberty, ought to be levelled against that quarter where the greatest danger lies, namely, that which possesses the highest perogative [*sic*] of power: But this not found in either the executive or legislative departments of government, but in the body of the people, operating by the majority against the minority.

It may be thought all paper barriers against the power of the community, are too weak to be worthy of attention. I am sensible they are not so strong as to satisfy gentlemen of every descripton who have seen and examined thoroughly the texture of such a defence; yet, as they have a tendency to impress some degree of respect for them, to establish the public opinion in their favor, and rouse the attention of the whole community, it may be one mean to controul the majority from those acts to which they might be otherwise inclined.

It has been said by way of objection to a bill of rights, by many respectable gentlemen out of doors, and I find opposition on the same principles likely to be made by gentlemen on this floor, that they are unnecessary articles of a republican government, upon the presumption that the people have those rights in their own hands, and that is the proper place for them to rest. It would be a sufficient answer to say that this objection lies against such provisions under the state governments as well as under the general government; and there are, I believe, but few gentlemen who are inclined to push their theory so far as to say that a declaration of rights in those cases is either ineffectual or improper. It has been said that in the federal government they are unnecessary, because the powers are enumerated, and it follows that all that are not granted by the constitution are retained: that the constitution is a bill or powers, the great residuum being the rights of the people; and therefore a bill of rights cannot be so necessary as if the residuum was thrown into the hands of the government. I admit that these arguments are not entirely without foundation; but they are not conclusive to the extent which has been supposed. It is true the powers of the general government are circumscribed, they are directed to particular objects; but even if government keeps within those limits, it has certain discretionary powers with respect to the means, which may admit of abuse to a certain extent, in the same manner as the powers of the state governments under their constitutions may to an indefinite extent; because in the constitution of the United States there is a clause granting to Congress the power to make all laws which shall be necessary and proper for carrying into execution all the powers vested in the government of the United States, or in any department or officer thereof; this enables them to fulfil every purpose for which the government was established. Now, may not laws be considered necessary and proper by Congress, for it is them who are to judge of the necessity and propriety to accomplish those special purposes which they may have in contemplation, which laws in themselves are neither necessary or proper; as well as improper laws could be enacted by the state legislatures, for fulfilling the more extended objects of those governments. I will state an instance which I think in point, and proves that this might be the case. The general government has a right to pass all laws which shall be necessary to collect its revenue; the means for enforcing the collection are within the direction of the legislature: may not general warrants be considered necessary for this purpose, as well as for some purposes which it was supposed at the framing of their constitutions the state governments had in view. If there was reason for restraining the state governments from exercising this power, there is like reason for restraining the federal government.

It may be said, because it has been said, that a bill of rights is not necessary, because the establishment of this government has not repealed those declarations of rights which are added to the several state constitutions; that those rights of the people, which had been established by the most solemn act, could not be annihilated by a subsequent act of that people, who meant, and declared at the head of the instrument, that they ordained and established a new system, for the express purpose of securing to themselves and posterity the liberties they had gained by an arduous conflict.

I admit the force of this observation, but I do not look upon it to be conclusive. In the first place, it is too uncertain ground to leave this provision upon, if a provision is at all necessary to secure rights so important as many of those I have mentioned are conceived to be, by the public in general, as well as those in particular who opposed the adoption of this constitution. Beside some states have no bills of rights, there are others provided with very defective ones, and there are others whose bills of rights are not only defective, but absolutely improper; instead of securing some in the full extent which republican principles would require, they limit them too much to agree with the common ideas of liberty.

It has been objected also against a bill of rights, that, by enumerating particular exceptions to the grant of power, it would disparage those rights which were not placed in that enumeration, and it might follow by implication, that those rights which were not singled out, were intended to be assigned into the hands of the general government, and were consequently insecure. This is one of the most plausible arguments I have ever heard urged against the admission of a bill of rights into this system; but, I conceive, it may be guarded against. I have attempted it, as gentlemen may see by turning to the last clause of the 4th resolution.

It has been said, that it is unnecessary to load the constitution with this provision, because it was not found effectual in the constitution of the particular states. It is true, there are a few particular states in which some of the most valuable articles have not, at one time or other, been violated, but it does not follow but they may have, to a certain degree, a salutary effect against the abuse of power. If they are incorporated into the constitution, independent tribunals of justice will consider themselves in a peculiar manner the guardians of those rights; they will be an impenetrable bulwark against every assumption of power in the legislative or executive; they will be naturally led to resist every encroachment upon rights expressly stipulated for in the constitution by the declaration of rights. Beside this security, there is a great probability that such a declaration in the federal system would be inforced; because the state legislatures will jealously and closely watch the operations of this government, and be able to resist with more effect every assumption of power than any other power on earth can do; and the greatest opponents to a federal government admit the state legislatures to be sure guardians of the people's liberty. I conclude from this view of the subject, that it will be proper in itself, and highly politic, for the tranquility of the public mind, and the stability of the government, that we should offer something, in the form I have proposed, to be incorporated in the system of government, as a declaration of the rights of the people.

. . .

I wish also, in revising the constitution, we may throw into the section, which interdicts the abuse of certain powers in the state legislatures, some other provisions of equal if not greater importance than those already made. The words, "No state shall pass any bill of attainder, ex post facto law, &c." were wise and proper restrictions in the constitution. I think there is more danger of those powers being abused by the state governments than by the government of the United States. The same may be said of other powers which they possess, if not controued by the general principle, that laws are unconstitutional which infringe the rights of the community. I should therefore wish to extend this interdiction, and add, as I have stated in the 5th resolution, that no state shall violate the equal right of conscience, freedom of the press, or trial by jury in criminal cases; because it is proper that every government should be disarmed of powers which trench upon those particular rights. I know in some of the state constitutions the power of the government is controued by such a declaration, but others are not. I cannot see any reason against obtaining even a double security on those points; and nothing can give a more sincere proof of the atachment [sic] of those who opposed this constitution to those great and important rights, than to see them join in obtaining the security I have now proposed; because it must be admitted, on all hands, that the state governments are as liable to attack those invaluable privileges as the general government is, and therefore ought to be as cautiously guarded against.

I think it will be proper, with respect to the judiciary powers, to satisfy the public mind on those points which I have mentioned. Great inconvenience has been apprehended to suitors from the distance they would be dragged to obtain justice in the supreme court of the United States, upon an appeal on an action for a final debt. To remedy this, declare, that no appeal shall be made unless the matter in controversy amounts to a particular sum: This, with the regulations respecting jury trials in criminal cases, and suits at common law, it is to be hoped will quiet and reconcile the minds of the people to that part of the constitution.

I find, from looking into the amendments proposed by the state conventions, that several are particularly anxious that it should be declared in the constitution, that the powers not therein delegated, should be reserved to the several states. Perhaps words which may define this more precisely, than the whole of the instrument now does, may be considered as superfluous. I admit they may be deemed unnecessary; but there can be no harm in making such a declaration, if gentlemen will allow that the fact is as stated, I am sure I understand it so, and do therefore propose it.

These are the points on which I wish to see a revision of the constitution take place. How far they will accord with the sense of this body, I cannot take upon me absolutely to determine; but I believe every gentleman will readily admit that nothing is in contemplation, so far as I have mentioned, that can endanger the beauty of government in any one important feature, even in the eyes of its most sanguine admirers. I have proposed nothing that does not appear to me as proper in itself, or eligible as patronised by a respectable number of our fellow citizens; and if we can make the constitution better in the opinion of those who are opposed to it, without weakening its frame, or abridging its usefulness, in the judgment of those who are attached to it, we act the part of wise and liberal men to make such alterations as shall produce that effect.

Congressional Register, June 8, 1789, vol. 1, pp. 429–36.

1.2.1.1.b   Mr. MADISON replied in a long and able speech, in which he enforced the propriety of entering, at an early period, into the subject of amendments. He had no design to propose any alterations which in the view of the most sanguine friends to the constitution could affect its main structure or principles, or do it any possible injury — His object was to quiet the mind of the people by giving them some early assurance of a disposition in the house to provide expressly against all encroachments on their liberties, and against the abuses to which the principles of the constitution were liable.

He then stated a number of amendments which he thought should be incorporated in the constitution, and enforced the propriety of each by various explanations and arguments.

The opposition the original motion received, induced him at last to withdraw it in order to propose, that a special committee should be appointed to consider and report what amendments it would be proper to adopt.

He afterwards waved this proposition; and offered to the house a resolution comprehending the amendments at large, together with a bill of rights, which he moved might be referred to the committee of the whole, when fitting on the state of the Union. This was carried.

Daily Advertiser, June 9, 1789, p. 2.

1.2.1.1.c   . . . He then observed, That he thought it would be attended with salutary effects, should Congress devote, at the present time, so much at least as one day to this business, to convince the world, that the friends of the Constitution were as firm friends to liberty as those who had opposed it: The advocates for amendments are numerous and respectable — some alteration of the Constitution lays with great weight upon their minds — they merit consideration. — He urged the expediency of the measure, from the situation of Rhode-Island and North-Carolina — He had no doubt that it would conciliate them towards the Union, and induce them to unite, and again become branches of the great American Family. — He was, he observed, in favour of sundry alterations, or amendments, to the Constitution — he supposed that they could be made without injury to the system — He did not wish a re-consideration of the whole — but supposed that alterations might be made, without effecting the essential principles of the Constitution, which would meet with universal approbation; — those he would propose should be incorporated in the body of the Constitution. — He then mentioned the several objections which had been made by several of the States, and by people at large: — A bill of rights has been the great object contended for — but this was one of those amendments which he had not supposed very essential. — The freedom of the press, and the rights of conscience, those choicest flowers in the prerogative of the people, are not guarded by the British Constitution: — With respect to these, apprehensions had been entertained of their insecurity under the new Constitution; a bill of rights, therefore, to quiet the minds of people upon these points, may be salutary. — He then adverted to the several bills of rights, which were annexed to the Constitutions of individual States; — the great object of these was, to limit and qualify the powers of Government — to guard against the encroachments of the Executive. — In the Federal Government, the Executive is the weakest — the great danger lies not in the Executive, but in the great body of the people — in the disposition which the majority always discovers, to bear down, and depress the minority.

In stating objections which had been made to affixing a bill of rights to the constitution, Mr. MADISON observed, that objections to a continental bill of rights applied equally to their adoption by the States — The objection to a bill of rights, from the powers delegated by the Constitution, being defined and limited, has weight, while the Government confines itself to those specified limits; but instances may occur, in which those limits may be exceeded, by virtue of a construction of that clause empowering Congress to make all necessary laws to carry the Constitution into execution — The article of general warrants may be instanced. — It has been observed, that the Constitution does not repeal the State bills of rights; — to this it may be replied, that some of the States are without any — and that articles contained in those that have them, are very improper, and infringe upon the rights of human nature, in several respects. — It has been said, that bills of rights have been violated — but does it follow from thence that they do not produce salutary effects: This objection may be urged against every regulation whatever. — From these, and other considerations, Mr. Madison inferred the expediency of a declaration of rights, to be incorporated in the Constitution.

Mr. MADISON further observed, That the proportion of Representatives had been objected to — and particularly the discretionary power of diminishing the number. — There is an impropriety in the Legislatures' determining their own compensation, with a power to vary its amount. — The rights of conscience; liberty of the press; and trial by jury, should be so secured, as to put it out of the power of the Legislature to infringe them. — Fears respecting the judiciary system, should be entirely done away — and an express declaration made, that all rights not expressly given up, are retained. — He wished, that a declaration upon these points might be attended to — and if the Constitution can be made better in the view of its most sanguine supporters, by making some alterations in it, we shall not act the part of wise men not to do it — He therefore moved for the appointment of a committee to propose amendments, which should be laid before the Legislatures of the several States, agreeably to the 5th article of the Constitution.

Gazette of the U.S., June 10, 1789, p. 67, cols. 2–3.

1.2.1.2   August 15, 1789

1.2.1.2.a   The house resolved itself into a committee of the whole, and resumed the consideration of the report of the committee on the subject of amendments.

Mr. BOUDINOT in the chair.

The fourth proposition under consideration being as follows:

Article 1. Sect. 9. Between paragraph 2 and 3 insert "no religion shall be established by law, nor shall the equal rights of conscience be infringed."

Mr. SYLVESTER

Had some doubts of the propriety of the mode of expression used in this paragraph; he apprehended that it was liable to a construction different from what had been made by the committee, he feared it might be thought to have a tendency to abolish religion altogether.

Mr. VINING

Suggested the propriety of transposing the two members of the sentence.

Mr. GERRY

Said it would read better if it was, that no religious doctrine shall be established by law.

Mr. SHERMAN

Thought the amendment altogether unnecessary, inasmuch as congress had no authority whatever delegated to them by the constitution, to make religious establishments, he would therefore move to have it struck out.

Mr. CARROLL

As the rights of conscience are in their nature of peculiar delicacy, and will little bear the gentlest touch of the governmental hand; and as many sects have concurred in opinion that they are not well secured under the present constitution, he said he was much in favor of adopting the words; he thought it would tend more toward conciliating the minds of the people to the government than almost any other amendment he had heard proposed. He would not contend with gentlemen about the phraseology, his object was to secure the substance in such a manner as to satisfy the wishes of the honest part of the community.

Mr. MADISON

Said, he apprehended the meaning of the words to be, that congress should not establish a religion, and enforce the legal observation of it by law, nor compel men to worship God in any manner contrary to their conscience; whether the words are necessary or not he did not mean to say, but they had been required by some of the state conventions, who seemed to entertain an opinion that under the clause of the constitution, which gave power to congress to make all laws necessary and proper to carry into execution the constitution, and the laws made under it, enabled them to make laws of such a nature as might infringe the rights of conscience, or establish a national religion, to prevent these effects he presumed the amendment was intended, and he thought it as well expressed as the nature of the language would admit.

Mr. HUNTINGTON

Said that he feared with the gentleman first up on this subject, that the words might be taken in such latitude as to be extremely hurtful to the cause of religion: He understood the amendment to mean what had been expressed by the gentleman from Virginia but others might find it convenient to put another construction upon it. The ministers of their congregations to the eastward, were maintained by the contributions of those who belonged to their society; the expense of building meeting-houses was contributed in the same manner, these things were regulated by bye laws: If an action was brought before a federal court on any of these cases, the person who had neglected to perform his engagements could not be compelled to do it; for a support of ministers, or building places of worship might be construed into a religious establishment.

By the charter of Rhode-Island, no religion could be established by law, he could give a history of the effects of such a regulation; indeed the people were now enjoying the blessed fruits of it: He hoped therefore the amendment would be made in such a way as to secure the rights of conscience, and a free exercise of the rights of religion, but not to patronize those who professed no religion at all.

Mr. MADISON

Thought, if the word national was inserted before religion, it would satisfy the minds of honorable gentlemen. He believed that the people feared one sect might obtain a pre-eminence, or two combine together, and establish a religion to which they would compel others to conform; he thought if the word national was introduced, it would point the amendment directly to the object it was intended to prevent.

Mr. LIVERMORE

Was not satisfied with that amendment, but he did not wish them to dwell long on the subject; he thought it would be better if it was altered, and made to read in this manner, that congress shall make no laws touching religion, or infringing the rights of conscience.

Mr. GERRY

Did not like the term national, proposed by the gentleman from Virginia, and he hoped it would not be adopted by the house. It brought to his mind some observations that had taken place in the conventions at the time they were considering the present constitution; it had been insisted upon by those who were called antifederalists, that this form of government consolidated the union; the honorable gentleman's motion shews that he considers it in the same light; those who were called antifederalists at that time complained that they had injustice done them by the title, because they were in favor of a federal government, and the others were in favor of a national one; the federalists were for ratifying the constitution as it stood, and the others not until amendments were made. Their names then ought not to have been distinguished by federalists and antifederalists, but rats and antirats.

Mr. MADISON

Withdrew his motion, but observed that the words "no national religion shall be established by law," did not imply that the government was a national one; the question was then taken on Mr. Livermore's motion, and passed in the affirmative, 31 for, 20 against it.   *Congressional Register, August 15, 1789, vol. 2, pp. 194–97.*

1.2.1.2.b   The House went into a committee on the amendments to the Constitution. Mr. BOUDINOT in the chair.

The committee took up the fourth amendment. — "Art. I. Sec. 9. Between par. 2 and 3 insert, "no religion shall be established by law, nor shall the equal rights of conscience be infringed."

Mr. LIVERMORE moved to strike out this clause and to substitute one to the following effect — "The Congress shall make no laws touching religion or the rights of conscience." He observed that tho' the sense of both provisions was the same, yet the former might seem to wear an ill face and was subject to misconstruction.   *Daily Advertiser, August 17, 1789, p. 2, col. 1.*
("The question on this motion was carried.").

1.2.1.2.c   The House went into a committee on the amendments to the Constitution. Mr. Boudinot in the chair.

The committee took up the fourth amendment.

"Art. I. Sec. 9. Between par. 2 and 3 insert, no religion shall be established by law, nor shall the equal rights of conscience be infringed."

Mr. Livermore moved to strike out this clause and to substitute one to the following effect — "The Congress shall make no laws touching religion or the rights of conscience." He observed tho' the sense of both provisions was the same, yet the former might seem to wear an ill face and was subject to misconstruction.   *New-York Daily Gazette, August 18, 1789, p. 798, col. 4.*
("The question on this motion was carried.").

1.2.1.2.d   In committee of the whole, on amendments to the constitution — the fourth amendment under consideration; viz. Art. I. Sec. 9, between Par. 2 and 3 insert *"no religion shall be established by law, nor shall the equal rights of conscience be infringed."*

Mr. SYLVESTER said he doubted the propriety of the mode of expression used in this paragraph; he thought it was liable to a construction different from what was intended by the committee.

Mr. SHERMAN. It appears to me best that this article should be omitted intirely: Congress has no power to make any religious establishments, it is therefore unnecessary.

Mr. CARROLL, Mr. HUNTINGTON, Mr. MADISON, and Mr. LIVERMORE made some observations: The last proposed that the words should be struck out to substitute these words, *"Congress shall make no laws touching religion or the rights of conscience."*

Gazette of the U.S., August 19, 1789, p. 147, col. 1.
("The question on this motion was carried.").

1.2.1.3 August 20, 1789

On motion of Mr. Ames, the fourth amendment was altered so as to read "congress shall make no law establishing religion, or to prevent the free exercise thereof, or to infringe the rights of conscience." This being adopted.

Congressional Register, August 20, 1789, vol. 2, p. 242.

1.2.2 STATE CONVENTIONS

1.2.2.1 Connecticut, January 9, 1788

Hon. OLIVER WOLCOTT. . . .

. . . Knowledge and liberty are so prevalent in this country, that I do not believe that the United States would ever be disposed to establish one religious sect, and lay all others under legal disabilities.

Elliot, vol. 2, p. 202.

1.2.2.2 New York, July 2, 1788

Mr. TREDWELL. . . .

. . . I could have wished also that sufficient caution had been used to secure to us our religious liberties, and to have prevented the general government from tyrannizing over our consciences by a religious establishment — a tyranny of all others most dreadful, and which will assuredly be exercised whenever it shall be thought necessary for the promotion and support of their political measures.

Elliot, vol. 2, p. 399.

1.2.2.3 North Carolina, July 30, 1788

The last clause of the 6th article read.

Mr. HENRY ABBOT, after a short exordium, which was not distinctly heard, proceeded thus: Some are afraid, Mr. Chairman, that, should the Constitution be received, they would be deprived of the privilege of worshipping God according to their consciences, which would be taking from them a benefit they enjoy under the present constitution. They wish to know if their religious and civil liberties be secured under this system, or whether the general government may not make laws infringing their religious liberties. The worthy member from Edenton mentioned sundry political reasons why treaties should be the supreme law of the land. It is feared, by some people, that, by the power of making treaties, they might make a treaty engaging with foreign powers to adopt the Roman Catholic religion in the United States, which would prevent the people from worshipping God according to their own consciences. The worthy member from Halifax has in some measure satisfied my mind on this subject. But others may be dissatisfied. Many wish to know what *religion* shall be established. I believe a majority of the community are Presbyterians. I am, for my part, against any exclusive establishment; but if there were any, I would prefer the Episcopal. The exclusion of religious tests is by many thought dangerous and impolitic. They suppose that if there be no religious test required, pagans, deists, and Mahometans might obtain offices among us, and that the senators and representatives might all be pagans. Every person employed by the general and state governments is to take an oath to support the former. Some are desirous to know how and by whom they are to swear, since no religious tests are required — whether they are to swear by Jupiter, Juno, Minerva, Proserpine, or Pluto. We ought to be suspicious of our liberties. We have felt the effects of oppressive measures, and know the happy consequences of being jealous of our rights. I would be glad some gentleman would endeavor to obviate these objections, in order to satisfy the religious part of the society. Could I be convinced that the objections were well founded, I would then declare my opinion against the Constitution. [Mr. Abbot added several other observations, but spoke too low to be heard.]

Mr. IREDELL. Mr. Chairman, nothing is more desirable than to remove the scruples of any gentleman on this interesting subject. Those concerning religion are entitled to particular respect. I did not expect any objection to this particular regulation, which, in my opinion, is calculated to prevent evils of the most pernicious consequences to society. Every person in the least conversant in the history of mankind, knows what dreadful mischiefs have been committed by religious persecutions. Under the color of religious tests, the utmost cruelties have been exercised. Those in power have generally considered all wisdom centred in themselves; that they alone had a right to dictate to the rest of mankind; and that all opposition to their tenets was profane and impious. The consequence of this intolerant spirit had been, that each church has in turn set itself up against every other; and persecutions and wars of the most implacable and bloody nature have taken place in every part of the world. America has set an example to mankind to think more modestly and reasonably — that a man may be of different religious sentiments from our own, without being a bad member of society. The principles of toleration, to the honor of this age, are doing away those errors and prejudices which have so long prevailed, even in the most intolerant countries. In the Roman Catholic countries, principles of moderation are adopted which would have been spurned at a century or two ago. I should be sorry to find, when examples of toleration are set even by arbitrary governments, that this country, so impressed with the highest sense of liberty, should adopt principles on this subject that were narrow and illiberal.

I consider the clause under consideration as one of the strongest proofs that could be adduced, that it was the intention of those who formed this system to establish a general religious liberty in America. Were we to judge from the examples of religious tests in other countries, we should be persuaded that they do not answer the purpose for which they are intended. What is the consequence of such in England? In that country no man can be a member in the House of Commons, or hold any office under the crown, without taking the sacrament according to the rites of the Church. This, in the first instance, must degrade and profane a rite which never ought to be taken but from a sincere principle of devotion. To a man of base principles, it is made a mere instrument of civil policy. The intention was, to exclude all persons from offices but the members of the Church of England. Yet it is notorious that dissenters qualify themselves for offices in this manner, though they never conform to the Church on any other occasion; and men of no religion at all have no scruple to make use of this qualification. It never was known that a man who had no principles of religion hesitated to perform any rite when it was convenient for his private interest. No test can bind such a one. I am therefore clearly of opinion that such a discrimination would neither be effectual for its own purposes, nor, if it could, ought it by any means to be made. Upon the principles I have stated, I confess the restriction on the power of Congress, in this particular, has my hearty approbation. They certainly have no authority to interfere in the establishment of any religion whatsoever; and I am astonished that any gentlemen should conceive they have. Is there any power given to Congress in matters of religion? Can they pass a single act to impair our religious liberties? If they could, it would be a just cause of alarm. If they could, sir, no man would have more horror against it than myself. Happily, no sect here is superior to another. As long as this is the case, we shall be free from those persecutions and distractions with which other countries have been torn. If any future Congress should pass an act concerning the religion of the country, it would be an act which they are not authorized to pass, by the Constitution, and which the people would not obey. Every one would ask, "Who authorized the government to pass such an act? It is not warranted by the Constitution, and is barefaced usurpation." The power to make treaties can never be supposed to include a right to establish a foreign religion among ourselves, though it might authorize a toleration of others.

But it is objected that the people of America may, perhaps, choose representatives who have no religion at all, and that pagans and Mahometans may be admitted into offices. But how is it possible to exclude any set of men, without taking away that principle of religious freedom which we ourselves so warmly contend for? This is the foundation on which persecution has been raised in every part of the world. The people in power were always right, and every body else wrong. If you admit the least difference, the door to persecution is opened. Nor would it answer the purpose, for the worst part of the excluded sects would comply with the test, and the best men only be kept out of our counsels. But it is never to be supposed that the people of America will trust their dearest rights to persons who have no religion at all, or a religion materially different from their own. I would be happy for mankind if religion was permitted to take its own course, and maintain itself by the excellence of its own doctrines. The divine Author of our religion never wished for its support by worldly authority. Has he not said that the gates of hell shall not prevail against it? It made much greater progress for itself, than when supported by the greatest authority upon earth.

It has been asked by that respectable gentleman (Mr. Abbot) what is the meaning of that part, where it is said that the United States shall *guaranty* to every state in the Union a republican form of government, and why a *guaranty* of religious freedom was not included. The meaning of the guaranty provided was this: There being thirteen governments confederated upon a republican principle, it was essential to the existence and harmony of the confederacy that each should be a republican government, and that no state should have a right to establish an aristocracy or monarchy. That clause was therefore inserted to prevent any state from establishing any government but a republican one. Every one must be convinced of the mischief that would ensue, if any state had a right to change its government to a monarchy. If a monarchy was established in any one state, it would endeavor to subvert the freedom of the others, and would, probably, by degrees succeed in it. This must strike the mind of every person here, who recollects the history of Greece, when she had confederated governments. The king of Macedon, by his arts and intrigues, got himself admitted a member of the Amphictyonic council, which was the superintending government of the Grecian republics; and in a short time he became master of them all. It is, then, necessary that the members of a confederacy should have similar governments. But consistently with this restriction, the states may make what change in their own governments they think proper. Had Congress undertaken to guaranty religious freedom, or any particular species of it, they would then have had a pretence to interfere in a subject they have nothing to do with. Each state, so far as the clause in question does not interfere, must be left to the operation of its own principles.

There is a degree of jealousy which it is impossible to satisfy. Jealousy in a free government ought to be respected; but it may be carried to too great an extent. It is impracticable to guard against all possible danger of people's choosing their officers indiscreetly. If they have a right to choose, they may make a bad choice.

I met, by accident, with a pamphlet, this morning, in which the author states, as a very serious danger, that the pope of Rome might be elected President. I confess this never struck me before; and if the author had read all the qualifications of a President, perhaps his fears might have been quieted. No man but a native, or who has resided fourteen years in America, can be chosen President. I know not all the qualifications for pope, but I believe he must be taken from the college of cardinals; and probably there are many previous steps necessary before he arrives at this dignity. A native of America must have very singular good fortune, who, after residing fourteen years in his own country, should go to Europe, enter into Romish orders, obtain the promotion of cardinal, afterwards that of pope, and at length be so much in the confidence of his own country as to be elected President. It would be still more extraordinary if he should give up his popedom for our presidency. Sir, it is impossible to treat such idle fears with any degree of gravity. Why is it not objected, that there is no provision in the Constitution against electing one of the kings of Europe President? It would be a clause equally rational and judicious.

I hope that I have in some degree satisfied the doubts of the gentleman. This article is calculated to secure universal religious liberty, by putting all sects on a level — the only way to prevent persecution. I thought nobody would have objected to this clause, which deserves, in my opinion, the highest approbation. This country has already had the honor of setting an example of civil freedom, and I trust it will likewise have the honor of teaching the rest of the world the way to religious freedom also. God grant both may be perpetuated to the end of time!

Mr. ABBOT, after expressing his obligations for the explanation which had been given, observed that no answer had been given to the question he put concerning the form of an *oath*.

Mr. IREDELL. Mr. Chairman, I beg pardon for having omitted to take notice of that part which the worthy gentleman has mentioned. It was by no means from design, but from its having escaped my memory, as I have not the conveniency of taking notes. I shall now satisfy him in that particular in the best manner in my power.

According to the modern definition of an oath, it is considered a "solemn appeal to the Supreme Being, for the truth of what is said, by a person who believes in the existence of a Supreme Being and in a future state of rewards and punishments, according to that form which will bind his conscience most." It was long held that no oath could be administered but upon the New Testament, except to a Jew, who was allowed to swear upon the Old. According to this notion, none but Jews and Christians could take an oath; and heathens were altogether excluded. At length, by the operation of principles of toleration, these narrow notions were done away. Men at length considered that there were many virtuous men in the world who had not had an opportunity of being instructed either in the Old or New Testament, who yet very sincerely believed in a Supreme Being, and in a future state of rewards and punishments. It is well known that many nations entertain this belief who do not believe either in the Jewish or Christian religion. Indeed, there are few people so grossly ignorant or barbarous as to have no religion at all. And if none but Christians or Jews could be examined upon oath, many innocent persons might suffer for want of the testimony of others. In regard to the form of an oath, that ought to be governed by the religion of the person taking it. I remember to have read an instance which happened in England, I believe in the time of Charles II. A man who was a material witness in a cause, refused to swear upon the book, and was admitted to swear with his uplifted hand. The jury had a difficulty in crediting him; but the chief justice told them, he had, in his opinion, taken as strong an oath as any of the other witnesses, though, had he been to swear himself, he should have kissed the book. A very remarkable instance also happened in England, about forty years ago, of a person who was admitted to take an oath according to the rites of his own country, though he was a heathen. He was an East Indian, who had a great suit in chancery, and his answer upon oath to a bill filed against him was absolutely necessary. Not believing either in the Old or New Testament, he could not be sworn in the accustomed manner, but was sworn according to the form of the Gentoo religion, which he professed, by touching the foot of a priest. It appeared that, according to the tenets of this religion, its members believed in a Supreme Being, and in a future state of rewards and punishments. It was accordingly held by the judges, upon great consideration, that the oath ought to be received; they considering that it was probable those of that religion were equally bound in conscience by an oath according to their form of swearing, as they themselves were by one of theirs; and that it would be a reproach to the justice of the country, if a man, merely because he was of a different religion from their own, should be denied redress of an injury he had sustained. Ever since this great case, it has been universally considered that, in administering an oath, it is only necessary to inquire if the person who is to take it, believes in a Supreme Being, and in a future state of rewards and punishments. If he does, the oath is to be administered according to that form which it is supposed will bind his conscience most. It is, however, necessary that such a belief should be entertained, because otherwise there would be nothing to bind his conscience that could be relied on; since there are many cases where the terror of punishment in this world for perjury could not be dreaded. I have endeavored to satisfy the committee. We may, I think, very safely leave religion to itself; and as to the form of the oath, I think this may well be trusted to the general government, to be applied on the principles I have mentioned.

Gov. JOHNSTON expressed great astonishment that the people were alarmed on the subject of religion. This, he said, must have arisen from the great pains which had been taken to prejudice men's minds against the Constitution. He begged leave to add the following few observations to what had been so ably said by the gentleman last up.

I read the Constitution over and over, but could not see one cause of apprehension or jealousy on this subject. When I heard there were apprehensions that the pope of Rome could be the President of the United States, I was greatly astonished. It might as well be said that the king of England or France, or the Grand Turk, could be chosen to that office. It would have been as good an argument. It appears to me that it would have been dangerous, if Congress could intermeddle with the subject of religion. True religion is derived from a much higher source than human laws. When any attempt is made, by any government, to restrain men's consciences, no good consequence can possibly follow. It is apprehended that Jews, Mahometans, pagans, &c., may be elected to high offices under the government of the United States. Those who are Mahometans, or any others who are not professors of the Christian religion, can never be elected to the office of President, or other high office, but in one of two cases. First, if the people of America lay aside the Christian religion altogether, it may happen. Should this unfortunately take place, the people will choose such men as think as they do themselves. Another case is, if any persons of such descriptions should, notwithstanding their religion, acquire the confidence and esteem of the people of America by their good conduct and practice of virtue, they may be chosen. I leave it to gentlemen's candor to judge what probability there is of the people's choosing men of different sentiments from themselves.

But great apprehensions have been raised as to the influence of the Eastern States. When you attend to circumstances, this will have no weight. I know but two or three states where there is the least chance of establishing any particular religion. The people of Massachusetts and Connecticut are mostly Presbyterians. In every other state, the people are divided into a great number of sects. In Rhode Island, the tenets of the Baptists, I believe, prevail. In New York, they are divided very much: the most numerous are the Episcopalians and the Baptists. In New Jersey, they are as much divided as we are. In Pennsylvania, if any sect prevails more than others, it is that of the Quakers. In Maryland, the Episcopalians are most numerous, though there are other sects. In Virginia, there are many sects; you all know what their religious sentiments are. So in all the Southern States they differ; as also in New Hampshire. I hope, therefore, that gentlemen will see there is no cause of fear that any one religion shall be exclusively established.

Mr. CALDWELL thought that some danger might arise. He imagined it might be objected to in a political as well as in a religious view. In the first place, he said, there was an invitation for Jews and pagans of every kind to come among us. At some future period, said he, this might endanger the character of the United States. Moreover, even those who do not regard religion, acknowledge that the Christian religion is best calculated, of all religions, to make good members of society, on account of its morality. I think, then, added he, that, in a political view, those gentlemen who formed this Constitution should not have given this invitation to Jews and heathens. All those who have any religion are against the emigration of those people from the eastern hemisphere.

Mr. SPENCER was an advocate for securing every unalienable right, and that of worshipping God according to the dictates of conscience in particular. He therefore thought that no one particular religion should be established. Religious tests, said he, have been the foundation of persecutions in all countries. Persons who are conscientious will not take the oath required by religious tests, and will therefore be excluded from offices, though equally capable of discharging them as any member of the society. It is feared, continued he, that persons of bad principles, deists, atheists, &c., may come into this country; and there is nothing to restrain them from being eligible to offices. He asked if it was reasonable to suppose that the people would choose men without regarding their characters. Mr. Spencer then continued thus: Gentlemen urge that the want of a test admits the most vicious characters to offices. I desire to know what test could bind them. If they were of such principles, it would not keep them from enjoying those offices. On the other hand, it would exclude from offices conscientious and truly religious people, though equally capable as others. Conscientious persons would not take such an oath, and would be therefore excluded. This would be a great cause of objection to a religious test. But in this case, as there is not a religious test required, it leaves religion on the solid foundation of its own inherent validity, without any connection with temporal authority; and no kind of oppression can take place. I confess it strikes me so. I am sorry to differ from the worthy gentleman. I cannot object to this part of the Constitution. I wish every other part was as good and proper.

Gov. JOHNSTON approved of the worthy member's candor. He admitted a possibility of Jews, pagans, &c., emigrating to the United States; yet, he said, they could not be in proportion to the emigration of Christians who should come from other countries; that, in all probability, the children even of such people would be Christians; and that this, with the rapid population of the United States, their zeal for religion, and love of liberty, would, he trusted, add to the progress of the Christian religion among us.

Elliot, vol. 4, pp. 191–200.

1.2.2.4 South Carolina, January 18, 1788

Hon. PATRICK CALHOUN, of *Ninety-six,* made some observations on the too great latitude allowed in religion.

Elliot, vol. 4, p. 312.

1.2.2.5 Virginia

1.2.2.5.a June 4, 1788

Gov. RANDOLPH. Mr. Chairman, had the most enlightened statesman whom America has yet seen, foretold, but a year ago, the crisis which has now called us together, he would have been confronted by the universal testimony of history; for never was it yet known, that, in so short a space, by the peaceable working of events, without a war, or even the menace of the smallest force, a nation has been brought to agitate a question, an error in the issue of which may blast their happiness. It is, therefore, to be feared, lest to this trying exigency the best wisdom should be unequal; and here (if it were allowable to lament any ordinance of nature) might it be deplored that, in proportion to the magnitude of a subject, is the mind intemperate. Religion, the dearest of all interests, has too often sought proselytes by fire rather than by reason; and politics, the next in rank, is too often nourished by passion, at the expense of the understanding. Pardon me, however, for expecting one exception to the tendency of mankind from the dignity of this Convention — a mutual toleration, and a persuasion that no man has a right to impose his opinions on others. . . .

Elliot, vol. 3, pp. 23–24.

1.2.2.5.b June 6, 1788

Mr. MADISON. . . .

I confess to you, sir, were uniformity of religion to be introduced by this system, it would, in my opinion, be ineligible; but I have no reason to conclude that uniformity of government will produce that of religion. This subject is, for the honor of America, perfectly free and unshackled. The government has no jurisdiction over it: the least reflection will convince us there is no danger to be feared on this ground.

Elliot, vol. 3, p. 93.

1.2.2.5.c June 10, 1788

Gov. RANDOLPH. . . .

Freedom of religion is said to be in danger. I will candidly say, I once thought that it was, and felt great repugnance to the Constitution for that reason. I am willing to acknowledge my apprehensions removed; and I will inform you by what process of reasoning I did remove them. The Constitution provides that "the senators and representatives before mentioned, and the members of the several state legislatures, and all executive and judicial officers, both of the United States and of the several states, shall be bound, by oath or affirmation, to support this Constitution; but no religious test shall ever be required as a qualification to any office or public trust under the United States." It has been said that, if the exclusion of the religious test were an exception from the general power of Congress, the power over religion would remain. I inform those who are of this opinion, that no power is given expressly to Congress over religion. The senators and representatives, members of the state legislatures, and executive and judicial officers, are bound, by oath or affirmation, to support this Constitution. This only binds them to support it in the exercise of the powers constitutionally given it. The exclusion of religious tests is an exception from this general provision, with respect to oaths or affirmations. Although officers, &c., are to swear that they will support this Constitution, yet they are not bound to support one mode of worship, or to adhere to one particular sect. It puts all sects on the same footing. A man of abilities and character, of any sect whatever, may be admitted to any office or public trust under the United States. I am a friend to a variety of sects, because they keep one another in order. How many different sects are we composed of throughout the United States! How many different sects will be in Congress! We cannot enumerate the sects that may be in Congress! And there are now so many in the United States, that they will prevent the establishment of any one sect, in prejudice to the rest, and will forever oppose all attempts to infringe religious liberty. If such an attempt be made, will not the alarm be sounded throughout America? If Congress should be as wicked as we are foretold they will be, they would not run the risk of exciting the resentment of all, or most, of the religious sects in America.

Elliot, vol. 3, pp. 204–05.

1.2.2.5.d **June 12, 1788**

Mr. HENRY. . . .

. . . His amendments go to that despised thing, called *a bill of rights*, and all the rights which are dear to human nature — trial by jury, the liberty of religion and the press, &c. Do not gentlemen see that, if we adopt, under the idea of following Mr. Jefferson's opinion, we amuse ourselves with the shadow, while the substance is given away? . . .

. . .

. . . Even the advocates for the plan do not all concur in the certainty of its security. Wherefore is religious liberty not secured? One honorable gentleman, who favors adoption, said that he had his fears on the subject. If I can well recollect, he informed us that he was perfectly satisfied, by the powers of reasoning, (with which he is so happily endowed,) that those fears were not well grounded. There is many a religious man who knows nothing of argumentative reasoning; there are many of our most worthy citizens who cannot go through all the labyrinths of syllogistic, argumentative deductions, when they think that the rights of conscience are invaded. This sacred right ought not to depend on constructive, logical reasoning.

When we see men of such talents and learning compelled to use their utmost abilities to convince themselves that there is no danger, is it not sufficient to make us tremble? Is it not sufficient to fill the minds of the ignorant part of men with fear? If gentlemen believe that the apprehensions of men will be quieted, they are mistaken, since our best-informed men are in doubt with respect to the security of our rights. Those who are not so well informed will spurn at the government. When our common citizens, who are not possessed with such extensive knowledge and abilities, are called upon to change their bill of rights (which, in plain, unequivocal terms, secures their most valuable rights and privileges) for construction and implication, will they implicitly acquiesce? Our declaration of rights tells us that "all men are by nature free and independent," &c. [Here Mr. Henry read the declaration of rights.] Will they exchange these rights for logical reasons? If you

70

had a thousand acres of land dependent on this, would you be satisfied with logical construction? Would you depend upon a title of so disputable a nature? The present opinions of individuals will be buried in entire oblivion when those rights will be thought of. That sacred and lovely thing, religion, ought not to rest on the ingenuity of logical deduction. Holy religion, sir, will be prostituted to the lowest purposes of human policy. What has been more productive of mischief among mankind than religious disputes? Then here, sir, is a foundation for such disputes, when it requires learning and logical deduction to perceive that religious liberty is secure.

. . .

Mr. MADISON. . . .

The honorable member has introduced the subject of religion. Religion is not guarded; there is no bill of rights declaring that religion should be secure. Is a bill of rights a security for religion? Would the bill of rights, in this state, exempt the people from paying for the support of one particular sect, if such sect were exclusively established by law? If there were a majority of one sect, a bill of rights would be a poor protection for liberty. Happily for the states, they enjoy the upmost [*sic*] freedom of religion. This freedom arises from that multiplicity of sects which pervades America, and which is the best and only security for religious liberty in any society; for where there is such a variety of sects, there cannot be a majority of any one sect to oppress and persecute the rest. Fortunately for this commonwealth, a majority of the people are decidedly against any exclusive establishment. I believe it to be so in the other states. There is not a shadow of right in the general government to intermeddle with religion. Its least interference with it would be a most flagrant usurpation. I can appeal to my uniform conduct on this subject, that I have warmly supported religious freedom. It is better that this security should be depended upon from the general legislature, than from one particular state. A particular state might concur in one religious project. But the United States abound in such a variety of sects, that it is a strong security against religious persecution; and it is sufficient to authorize a conclusion, that no one sect will ever be able to outnumber or depress the rest.

Elliot, vol. 3, pp. 314, 317–18, 330.

1.2.2.5.e **June 15, 1788**

Gov. RANDOLPH. . . .

He has added religion to the objects endangered, in his conception. Is there any power given over it? Let it be pointed out. Will he not be contented with the answer that has been frequently given to that objection? The variety of sects which abounds in the United States is the best security for the freedom of religion. No part of the Constitution, even if strictly construed, will justify a conclusion that the general government can take away or impair the freedom of religion.

The gentleman asks, with triumph, Shall we be deprived of these valuable rights? Had there been an exception, or an express infringement of those rights, he might object; but I conceive every fair reasoner will agree that there is no just cause to suspect that they will be violated.

But he objects that the common law is not established by the Constitution. The wisdom of the Convention is displayed by its omission, because the common law ought not to be immutably fixed. Is it established in our own Constitution, or the bill of rights, which has been resounded through the house? It is established only by an act of the legislature, and can therefore be changed as circumstances may require it. Let the honorable gentleman consider what would be the destructive consequences of its establishment in the Constitution. Even in England, where the firmest opposition has been made to encroachments upon it, it has been frequently changed. What would have been our dilemma if it had been established? Virginia has declared that children shall have equal portions of the real estate of their intestate parents, and it is consistent with the principles of a republican government.

Elliot, vol. 3, p. 469.

1.2.3 PHILADELPHIA CONVENTION

1.2.3.1 Proposal by Pinckney, May 29, 1787

"ART. VI. . . . The legislature of the United States shall pass no law on the subject of religion; nor touching or abridging the liberty of the press; [n]or shall the privilege of the writ of habeas corpus ever be suspended, except in case of rebellion or invasion.

Elliot, vol. 5, p. 131–32.

1.2.4 NEWSPAPERS AND PAMPHLETS

1.2.4.1 An American Citizen, No. 1, September 26, 1787

It is impossible for an honest and feeling mind, of any nation or country whatever, to be insensible to the present circumstances of America. Were I an East Indian, or a Turk, I should consider this singular situation of a part of my fellow creatures, as most curious and interesting. Intimately connected with the country, as a citizen of the union, I confess it entirely engrosses my mind and feelings.

To take a proper view of the ground on which we stand, it may be necessary to recollect the manner in which the United States were originally settled and established. — Want of charity in the religious systems of Europe and of justice in their political governments were the principal moving causes, which drove the emigrants of various countries to the American continent. The Congregationalists, Quakers, Presbyterians, and other British dissenters, the Catholics of England and Ireland, the Hugonots of France, the German Lutherans, Calvinists, and Moravians, with several other societies, established themselves in the different colonies, thereby laying the ground of that catholicism in ecclesiastical affairs, which has been observable since the late revolution: Religious liberty naturally promotes corresponding dispositions in matters of government. The Constitution of England, as it stood on paper, was one of the freest at that time existing in the world, and the American colonies considered themselves as entitled to the fullest enjoyment of it. . . .

. . .

In America our President will not only be *without* these influencing advantages, *but they will be in the possession of the people at large, to strengthen their hands in the event of a contest with him.* All religious funds, honors and powers, are in the gift of numberless, unconnected, disunited, and contending corporations, wherein the principle of perfect equality universally prevails. In short, danger from ecclesiastical tyranny, that long standing and still remaining curse of the people — that sacrilegious engine of royal power in some countries, can be feared by no man in the United States. . . .

[Philadelphia] Independent Gazetteer, Kaminski & Saladino, vol. 13, pp. 247–49.

1.2.4.2 A Meeting of Philadelphia Association of Baptist Churches, October 12, 1787

Last week the BAPTIST Churches belonging to the middle States, convened in association in this city. After finishing the particular business on which they met as a *religious* body, it was agreed to incorporate with their general circular letter, the following recommendation to their people of the proposed plan of the *Foederal Government* — which has been handed to the Printers by a correspondent, and redounds much to their honor as a society.

After congratulating their brethren on the great increase of their churches the year past — they proceed, "we also congratulate you on the kind interposition of Divine Providence visible in that happy unanimity which obtained among the members of the late Foederal Convention, to agree upon, and report to the States in this union, a form of Foederal Government, which promises, on its adoption, to rescue our dear country from that national dishonor, injustice, anarchy, confusion and bloodshed, which have already resulted from the weakness and inefficiency of the *present* form, and which we have the greatest reason to fear is but the beginning of sorrows, unless the people lay hold on this favourable opportunity offered to establish an EFFICIENT government; which, we hope may, under God, secure our invaluable rights, both civil and religious, and which it will be in the power of the great body of the people, if hereafter found necessary, to controul and amend."

New York Packet, Kaminski & Saladino, vol. 13, pp. 374–75.

1.2.4.3 An Old Whig, No. 1, October 12, 1787

. . . Should the freedom of the press be restrained on the subject of politics, there is no doubt it will soon after be restrained on all other subjects, religious as civil. . . .

[Philadelphia] Independent Gazetteer, Kaminski & Saladino, vol. 13, p. 378.

1.2.4.4 An American Citizen, No. 4, October 21, 1787

. . .

No *religious* test is ever to be required of any officer or servant of the United States. The people may employ *any wise and good citizen* in the execution of the various duties of the government. In Italy, Spain and Portugal, *no protestant* can hold a public trust. In England, *every presbyterian, and other person not of their established church,* is incapable of holding an office. No such *impious* deprivation of the rights of men can take place under the new foederal constitution. The convention has the honor of proposing the *first public act,* by which any nation has ever *divested itself* of a power, every exercise of which is a *trespass on the Majesty of Heaven.*

Pennsylvania Gazette, Kaminski & Saladino, vol. 13, p. 432.

1.2.4.5 Centinel, No. 2, October 24, 1787

. . .

The new plan, it is true, does propose to secure the people of the benefit of personal liberty by the *habeas corpus*; and trial by jury for all crimes, except in case of impeachment: but there is no declaration, that all men have a natural and unalienable right to worship Almighty God, according to the dictates of their own consciences and understanding; and that no man ought, or of right can be compelled to attend any religious worship, or erect or support any place of worship, or maintain any ministry, contrary to, or against his own free will and consent; and that no authority can or ought to be vested in, or assumed by any power whatever, that shall in any case interfere with, or in any manner controul, the right of conscience in the free exercise of religious worship: . . . .

[Philadelphia] Freeman's Journal, Kaminski & Saladino, vol. 13, p. 466.

1.2.4.6 Timoleon, November 1, 1787

. . .

After some judicious reflections on this subject, which tended to shew the necessity of the most plain and unequivocal language in the all important business of constituting government, which necessarily conveying great powers, is always liable (from the natural tendency of power to corrupt the human heart and deprave the head) to great abuse; by perverse and subtle arguments calculated to extend dominion over all things and all men. One of the club supposed the following case: — A gentleman, *in the line of his profession* is appointed a *judge* of the supreme court under the new Constitution, and the *rulers,* finding that the rights of conscience and the freedom of the press were exercised in such a manner, by *preaching* and *printing* as to be troublesome to the new government — which event would probably happen, if the rulers finding themselves possessed of great power, should so use it as to oppress and injure the community. — In this state of things the *judge* is called upon, *in the line of his profession,* to give his opinion — whether the *new Constitution* admitted of a legislative act to *suppress the rights of conscience, and violate the liberty of the press?* The answer of the learned *judge* is conceived in didactic mode, and expressed in learned phrase; thus, — In the 8th section of the first article of the *new Constitution,* the Congress have power given to *lay and collect taxes for the general welfare of the United States.* By this power, the right of taxing is co-extensive with the *general welfare,* and the *general welfare* is as unlimitted as actions and things are that may disturb or benefit that general welfare. A right being given to *tax* for the general welfare, necessarily includes the right of judging what is for the general welfare, and a right of judging what is for the general welfare, as *necessarily* includes a power of protecting, defending, and promoting it by all such laws and means as are fitted to that end; for, qui dat finem dat media ad finem necessaria, who gives the end gives the means necessary to obtain the end. The Constitution must be so construed as not to involve an absurdity, which would clearly follow from allowing the end and denying the means. A right of *taxing* for the general welfare being the highest and most important mode of providing for it, cannot be supposed to exclude inferior modes of effecting the same purpose, because the rule of law is, that, omne majus continct in se minus.

From hence it clearly results, that, if *preachers* and *printers* are troublesome to the new government; and that in the opinion of its rulers, it shall be for the general welfare to restrain or suppress both the one and the other, it may be done consistently with the new Constitution. And that this was the opinion of the community when they consented to it, is evident from this consideration; that although the all comprehending power of the new legislature is fixed, by its acts being made the *supreme law* of the land, any thing in the *Constitutions* or laws of any state to the contrary notwithstanding: Yet no *express* declaration in favor of the *rights of conscience* or *liberty* of the *press* is to be found in the new Constitution, as we see was carefully done in the Constitutions of the states composing this union — Shewing clearly, that what was *then* thought necessary to be specially reserved from the pleasure of power, is *now* designed to be yielded to its will.

A grave old gentleman of the club, who had sat with his head reclined on his hand, listening in pensive mood to the argument of the *judge,* said, "I verily believe, that neither the logic or the law of that opinion will be hereafter doubted by the professors of power, who, through the history of human nature, have been for enlarging the sphere of their authority. And thus the dearest rights of men and the best security of civil liberty may be sacrificed by the sophism of a lawyer, who, Carneades like, can to day shew that to be necessary, before the people, which tomorrow he can likewise shew to be unnecessary and useless — For which reason the sagacious Cato advised, that such a man should immediately be sent from the city, as a person dangerous to the morals of the people and to society." The old gentleman continued, "I now plainly see the necessity of express declarations and reservations in favor of the great, unalienable rights of mankind, to prevent the oppressive and wicked extention of power to the ruin of human liberty. For the opinion above stated, absolutely refutes the sophistry of "that being retained which is not given," where the words conveying power admit of the most extensive construction that language can reach to, or the mind conceive, as is the case in this new Constitution. By which we have already seen how logically it may be proved, that both *religion* and the *press* can be made to bend before the views of power. . . .

New York Journal, Kaminski & Saladino, vol. 13, pp. 535–36.

1.2.4.7 An Old Whig, No. 5, November 1, 1787

Mr. Printer, In order that people may be sufficiently impressed, with the necessity of establishing a BILL OF RIGHTS in the forming of a new constitution, it is very proper to take a short view of some of those liberties, which it is of the greatest importance for Freemen to retain to themselves, when they surrender up a part of their natural rights for the good of society.

The first of these, which it is of the utmost importance for the people to retain to themselves, which indeed they have not even the right to surrender, and which at the same time it is of no kind of advantages to government to strip them of, is the LIBERTY OF CONSCIENCE. I know that a ready answer is at hand, to any objections upon this head. We shall be told that in this enlightened age, the rights of conscience are perfectly secure: There is no necessity of guarding them; for no man has the remotest thoughts of invading them. If this be the case, I beg leave to reply that now is the very time to secure them. — Wise and prudent men always take care to guard against danger beforehand, and to make themselves safe whilst it is yet in their power to do it without inconvenience or risk. — who shall answer for the ebbings and flowings of opinion, or be able to say what will be the fashionable frenzy of the next generation? It would have been treated as a very ridiculous supposition, a year ago, that the charge of witchcraft would cost a person her life in the city of Philadelphia; yet the fate of the unhappy old woman called *Corbmaker,* who was beaten — repeatedly wounded with knives — mangled and at last killed in our streets, in obedience to the commandment which requires "that we shall not suffer a witch to live," without a possibility of punishing or even of detecting the authors of this inhuman folly, should be an example to warn us how little we ought to trust to the unrestrained discretion of human nature.

Uniformity of opinion in science, morality, politics or religion, is undoubtedly a very great happiness to mankind; and there have not been wanting zealous champions in every age, to promote the means of securing so invaluable a blessing. If in America we have not lighted up fires to consume Heretics in religion, if we have not persecuted unbelievers to promote the unity of the faith, in matters which pertain to our final salvation in a future world, I think we have all of us been witness to something very like the same spirit, in matters which are supposed to regard our political salvation in this world. In Boston it seems at this very moment, that no man is permitted to publish a doubt of the infalibility [*sic*] of the late convention, without giving up his name to the people, that he may be delivered over to speedy destruction; and it is but a short time since the case was little better in this city. Now this is a portion of the very same spirit, which has so often kindled the fires of the inquisition: and the same Zealot who would hunt a man down for a difference of opinion upon a political question which is the subject of public enquiry, if he should happen to be fired with zeal for a particular species of religion, would be equally intolerant. The fact is, that human nature is still the same that ever it was: the fashion indeed changes; but the seeds of superstition, bigotry and enthusiasm, are too deeply implanted in our minds, ever to be eradicated; and fifty years hence, the French may renew the persecution of the Huguenots, whilst the Spaniards in their turn may become indifferent to their forms of religion. They are idiots who trust their future security to the whim of the present hour. One extreme is always apt to produce the contrary, and these countries, which are now the most lax in their religious notions, may in a few years become the most rigid, just as the people of this country from not being able to bear any continental government at all, are now flying into the opposite extreme of surrendering up all the powers of the different states, to one continental government.

The more I reflect upon the history of mankind, the more I am disposed to think that it is our duty to secure the essential rights of the people, by every precaution;

for not an avenue has been left unguarded, through which oppression could possibly enter in any government; without some enemy of the public peace and happiness improving the opportunity to break in upon the liberties of the people; and none have been more frequently successful in the attempt, than those who have covered their ambitious designs under the garb of a fiery zeal for religious orthodoxy. What has happened in other countries and in other ages, may very possibly happen again in our own country, and for aught we know, before the present generation quits the stage of life. We ought therefore in a *bill of rights* to secure, in the first place, by the most express stipulations, the sacred rights of conscience. Has this been done in the constitution, which is now proposed for the consideration of the people of the country? — Not a word on this subject has been mentioned in any part of it; but we are left in this important article, as well as many others, entirely to the mercy of our future rulers.

But supposing our future rulers to be wicked enough to attempt to invade the rights of conscience; I may be asked how will they be able to effect so horrible a design? I will tell you my friends — *The unlimited power of taxation* will give them the command of all the treasures of the continent; *a standing army* will be wholly at their devotion, and the authority which is given them over the *militia*, by virtue of which they may, if they please, change all the officers of the militia on the continent in one day, and put in new officers whom they can better trust; by which they can subject all the militia to strict military laws, and punish the disobedient with death, or otherwise, as they shall think right; by which they can march the militia back and forward from one end of the continent to the other, at their discretion; these powers, if they should ever fall into bad hands, may be abused to the worst of purposes. Let us instance one thing arising from this right of organizing and governing the militia. Suppose a man alledges that he is conscientiously scrupulous of bearing Arms. — By the bill of rights of Pennsylvania he is bound only to pay an equivalent for this personal service. — What is there in the new proposed constitution to prevent his being dragged like a Prussian soldier to the camp and there compelled to bear arms? — This will depend wholly upon the wisdom and discretion of the future legislature of the continent in the framing their militia laws; and I have lived long enough to hear the practice *of commuting personal service for a paltry fine* in time of war and foreign invasion most severely reprobated by some persons who ought to have judged more rightly on the subject — Such flagrant oppressions as these I dare say will not happen at the beginning of the new government; probably not till the powers of government shall be firmly fixed; but it is a duty we owe to ourselves and our posterity if possible to prevent their ever happening. I hope and trust that there are few persons at present hardy enough to entertain thoughts of creating any religious establishment for this country; although I have lately read a piece in the newspaper, which speaks of *religious* as well as civil and military *offices,* as being hereafter to be disposed of by the new government; but if a majority of the continental legislature should at any time think fit to establish a form of religion, for the good people of this continent, with all the pains and penalties which in other countries are annexed to the establishment of a national church, what is there in the proposed constitution to hinder their doing so? Nothing; for we have no bill of rights, and every thing therefore is in their power and at their discretion. And at whose discretion? We know not any more than we know the fates of those generations which are yet unborn.

It is needless to repeat the necessity of securing other personal rights in the forming a new government. The same argument which proves the necessity of securing one of them shews also the necessity of securing others. Without a bill of rights we are totally insecure in all of them; and no man can promise himself with any degree of certainty that his posterity will enjoy the inestimable blessings of liberty of conscience, of freedom of speech and of writing and publishing their thoughts on public matters, of trial by jury, of holding themselves, their houses and papers free from seizure and search upon general suspicion or general warrants; or in short, that they will be secured in the enjoyment of life, liberty and property without depending on the will and pleasure of their rulers.

[Philadelphia] Independent Gazetteer, Kaminski & Saladino, vol. 13, pp. 538–41.

1.2.4.8 A Landholder, No. 7, December 17, 1787

But while I assert the right of religious liberty; I would not deny that the civil power has a right, in some cases, to interfere in matters of religion. It has a right to prohibit and punish gross immoralities and impieties; because the open practice of these is of evil example and public detriment. For this reason, I heartily approve of our laws against drunkenness, profane swearing, blasphemy, and professed atheism. But in this state, we have never thought it expedient to adopt a test-law; and yet I sincerely believe we have as great a proportion of religion and morality, as they have in England, where every person who holds a public office, must be either a saint by law, or a hypocrite by practice. A test-law is the parent of hypocrisy, and the offspring of error and the spirit of persecution. Legislatures have no right to set up an inquisition, and examine into the private opinions of men. Test-laws are useless and ineffectual, unjust and tyrannical; therefore the Convention have done wisely in excluding this engine of persecution, and providing that no religious test shall ever be required. Connecticut Courant, Kaminski & Saladino, vol. 14, pp. 451–52.

1.2.5 LETTERS AND DIARIES

1.2.5.1 James Madison to Thomas Jefferson, October 4, 1787

. . . 3. Religion. The inefficacy of this restraint on individuals is well known. The conduct of every popular Assembly, acting on oath, the strongest of religious ties, shews that individuals join without remorse in acts agst. which their consciences would revolt, if proposed to them separately in their closets. When Indeed [*sic*] Religion is kindled into enthusiasm, its force like that of other passions is increased by the sympathy of a multitude. But enthusiasm is only a temporary state of Religion, and whilst it lasts will hardly be seen with pleasure at the helm. Even in its coolest state, it has been much oftener a motive to oppression than a restraint from it. If then there must be different interests and parties in Society; and a majority when united by a common interest or passion can not be restrained from oppressing the minority, what remedy can be found in a republican Government, where the majority must ultimately decide, but that of giving such an extent to its sphere, that no common interest or passion will be likely to unite a majority of the whole number in an unjust pursuit. In a large Society, the people are broken into so many interests and parties, that a common sentiment is less likely to be felt, and the requisite concert less likely to be formed, by a majority of the whole. The same security seems requisite for the civil as for the religious rights of individuals. If the same sect form a majority and have the power, other sects will be sure to be depressed. Divide et impera, the reprobated axiom of tyranny, is under certain qualifications, the only policy, by which a republic can be administered on just principles. It must be observed however that this doctrine can only hold within a sphere of a mean extent. As in too small a sphere oppressive combinations may be too easily formed agst. the weaker party; so in too extensive a one, a defensive concert may be rendered too difficult against the oppression of those entrusted with the administration. The great desideratum in Government is, so to modify the sovereignty as that it may be sufficiently neutral between different parts of the Society to controul one part from invading the rights of another, and at the same time sufficiently controulled itself, from setting up an interest adverse to that of the entire Society. In absolute monarchies, the Prince may be tolerably neutral towards different classes of his subjects; but may sacrifice the happiness of all to his personal ambition or avarice. In small republics, the sovereign will is controuled from such a sacrifice of the entire Society, but is not sufficiently neutral towards the parts composing it. In the extended Republic of the United States, The General Government would hold a pretty even balance between the parties of particular States, and be at the same time sufficiently restrained by its dependence on the community, from betraying its general interests.

Kaminski & Saladino, vol. 13, pp. 448–49.

1.2.5.2 Thomas Jefferson to James Madison, December 20, 1787

. . . There are other good things of less moment. I will now add what I do not like. First the omission of a bill of rights providing clearly and without the aid of sophisms for freedom of religion, freedom of the press, protection against standing armies, restriction against monopolies, the eternal and unremitting force of the habeas corpus laws, and trials by jury in all matters of fact triable by the laws of the land and not by the law of Nations.

Boyd, vol. 12, p. 440.

1.2.5.3 Thomas Jefferson to William Stephens Smith, February 2, 1788

. . . But I own it astonishes me to find such a change wrought in the opinions of our countrymen since I left them, as that threefourths of them should be contented to live under a system which leaves to their governors the power of taking from them the trial by jury in civil cases, freedom of religion, freedom of the press, freedom of commerce, the habeas corpus laws, and of yoking them with a standing army. This is a degeneracy in the principles of liberty to which I had given four centuries instead of four years.

Boyd, vol. 12, p. 558.

1.2.5.4   Thomas Jefferson to Alexander Donald, February 7, 1788

. . . By a declaration of rights I mean one which shall stipulate freedom of religion, freedom of the press, freedom of commerce against monopolies, trial by juries in all cases, no suspensions of the habeas corpus, no standing armies. These are fetters against doing evil which no honest government should decline.

Boyd, vol. 12, p. 571.

1.2.5.5   Tench Coxe to George Thatcher, March 12, 1789

If due attention be paid to removing the jealosies & fears of the honest part of the Opposition we may gain strength & respectability without impairing one essential power of the constitution. Some declaration concerning the liberty of the press, of conscience &ca. ought perhaps to be frankly made parts of the constitution.

Veit, pp. 217–18.

1.2.5.6   Thomas Jefferson to Francis Hopkinson, March 13, 1789

. . . What I disapproved from the first moment also was the want of a bill of rights to guard liberty against the legislative as well as executive branches of the government, that is to say to secure freedom in religion, freedom of the press, freedom from monopolies, freedom from unlawful imprisonment, freedom from a permanent military, and a trial by jury in all cases determinable by the laws of the land.

Boyd, vol. 14, p. 650.

1.2.5.7   Jeremy Belknap to Paine Wingate, May 29, 1789

. . . You will see in the speech wh. our *new* Lieut. Governor [*Samuel Adams*] made at his investiture that he has not thrown off the old idea of "*independence*" as an attribute of each individual State in the "confederated Republic" — & you will know in what light to regard his "devout & fervent wish" that the "people may enjoy well grounded confidence that their *personal & domestic* rights are *secure*." This is the same Language or nearly the same which he used in the Convention when he moved for an addition to the proposed Amendments — by inserting a clause to provide for the Liberty of the press — the right to keep arms — Protection from seizure of person & property & the *Rights of Conscience*. By which motion he gave an alarm to both sides of the house & had nearly overset the whole business which the Friends of the Constitution had been labouring for several Weeks to obtain. . . .

Veit, p. 241.

1.2.5.8   George Clymer to Richard Peters, June 8, 1789

Madison this morning is to make an essay towards amendments — but whether he means merely a tub to the whale, or declarations about the press liberty of conscience &c. or will suffer himself to be so far frightened with the antifederalism of his own state as to attempt to lop off essentials I do not know — I hope however we shall be strong enough to postpone. . . .

Afternoon — Madison's has proved a tub on a number of Ad. but Gerry is not content with them alone, and proposes to treat us with all the amendments of all the antifederalists in America.

Veit, p. 245.

1.2.5.9   William R. Davie to James Madison, June 10, 1789

You are well acquainted with the political situation of this State [*North Carolina*], . . . that wild scepticism which has prevailed in it since the publication of the Constitution. It has been the uniform cant of the enemies of the Government, that Congress would exert all their influence to prevent the calling of a Convention, and would never propose an amendment themselves, or consent to an alteration that would in any manner diminish their powers. The people whose fears had been already alarmed, have received this opinion as fact, and become confirmed in their opposition; your notification however of the 4th. of May has dispersed almost universal pleasure, we hold it up as a refutation of the gloomy profecies of the leaders of the opposition, and the honest part of our antifederalists have publickly expressed great satisfaction on this event. . . .

That farago of Amendments borrowed from Virginia is by no means to be considered as the sense of this Country; they were proposed amidst the violence and confusion of party heat, at a critical moment in our convention, and adopted by the opposition without one moment's consideration. I have collected with some attention the objections of the honest and serious — they are but few & perhaps necessary — They require some explanations rather than alteration of power of Congress over elections — an abridgment of the Jurisdiction of the federal Court in a few instances, and some fixed regulations respecting appeals — They also insist on the trial by jury being expressly secured to them in all cases — and a constitutional guarantee for the free exercise of their religious rights and priveledges. . . .

Veit, pp. 245–46.

1.2.5.10   Fisher Ames to Thomas Dwight, June 11, 1789

Mr. Madison has introduced his long expected Amendments. They are the fruit of much labour and research. He has hunted up all the grievances and complaints of newspapers — all the articles of Conventions — and the small talk of their debates. It contains a Bill of Rights — the right of enjoying property — of changing the govt. at pleasure — freedom of the press — of conscience — of juries — exemption from general Warrants gradual increase of representatives till the whole number at the rate of one to every 30,000 shall amount to   and allowing two to every State, at least this is the substance. There is too much of it — O. I had forgot the right of the people to bear Arms.

Risum teneatis amici —

Upon the whole, it may do good towards quieting men who attend to sounds only, and may get the mover some popularity — which he wishes. Veit, p. 247.

1.2.5.11   Fisher Ames to George R. Minot, June 12, 1789

. . . The civil departments will employ us next, and the judiciary the Senate. They will finish their stint, as the boys say, before the House has done. Their number is less, and they have matured the business in committee. Yet Mr. Madison has inserted, in his amendments, the increase of representatives, each State having two at least. The rights of conscience, of bearing arms, of changing the government, are declared to be inherent in the people. Freedom of the press, too. There is a prodigious great dose for a medicine. But it will stimulate the stomach as little as hasty-pudding. It is rather food than physic. An immense mass of sweet and other herbs and roots for a diet drink.

Veit, p. 247.

1.2.5.12 Tench Coxe to James Madison, June 18, 1789

I observe you have brought forward the amendments you proposed to the federal Constitution. I have given them a very careful perusal, and have attended particularly to their reception by the public. The most decided friends of the constitution admit (generally) that they will meliorate the government by removing some points of litigation and jealousy, and by heightening and strengthening the barriers between necessary power and indispensible liberty. . . . Those who are honest are well pleased at the footing on which the press, liberty of conscience, original right & power, trial by jury &ca. are rested. . . .

Veit, p. 252.

1.2.5.13 Henry Gibbs to Roger Sherman, July 16, 1789

. . . All Ambiguity of Expression certainly ought to be remov'd; Liberty of Conscience in religious matters, right of trial by Jury, Liberty of the Press &c. may perhaps be more explicitly secur'd to the Subject & a general reservation made to the States respectively of all the powers not expressly delegated to the general Government. . . .

Veit, p. 263.

1.2.5.14 Pierce Butler to James Iredell, August 11, 1789

. . . If you wait for substantial amendments, you will wait longer than I wish you to do, speaking *interestedly*. A few *milk-and-water* amendments have been proposed by Mr. M[adison]., such as liberty of conscience, a free press, and one or two general things already well secured. I suppose it was done to keep his promise with his constituents, to move for alterations; but, if I am not greatly mistaken, he is not hearty in the cause of amendments.

Veit, p. 274.

1.2.5.15 Richard Henry Lee to Samuel Adams, October 27, 1789

. . . Because Independent States are in the same relation to each other as Individuals are with respect to uncreated government. So that if reservations were necessary in one case, they are equally necessary in the other. But the futility of this distinction appears from the conduct of the Convention itself, for they have made several reservations — every one of which proves the Rule in Conventional ideas to be, that what was not reserved was given — for example, they have reserved from their Legislature a power to prevent the importation of Slaves for 20 years, and also from Creating Titles. But they have no reservation in favor of the Press, Rights of Conscience, Trial by Jury in Civil Cases or Common Law securities.

As if these were of less importance to the happiness of Mankind than the making of Lords, or the importations of Slaves! . . .

Kaminski & Saladino, vol. 13, pp. 484–85.

Chapter 2

AMENDMENT I
FREE SPEECH AND FREE PRESS CLAUSES

2.1 TEXTS

2.1.1 DRAFTS IN FIRST CONGRESS

2.1.1.1 **Proposal by Madison in House, June 8, 1789**

2.1.1.1.a   Fourthly. That in article 1st, section 9, between clauses 3 and 4 [of the Constitution], be inserted these clauses, to wit, . . .

The people shall not be deprived or abridged of their right to speak, to write, or to publish their sentiments; and the freedom of the press, as one of the great bulwarks of liberty, shall be inviolable.

Congressional Register, June 8, 1789, vol. 1, p. 427.

2.1.1.1.b   *Fourthly.* That in article 1st, section 9, between clauses 3 and 4 [of the Constitution], be inserted these clauses, to wit: . . .

The people shall not be deprived or abridged of their right to speak, to write, or to publish their sentiments; and the freedom of the press, as one of the great bulwarks of liberty, shall be inviolable.

Daily Advertiser, June 12, 1789, p. 2, col. 1.

2.1.1.1.c   *Fourth.* That in article 1st, section 9, between clauses 3 and 4 [of the Constitution], be inserted these clauses, to wit: . . .

The people shall not be deprived or abridged of their right to speak, to write, or to publish their sentiments; and the freedom of the press, as one of the great bulwarks of liberty, shall be inviolable.

New-York Daily Gazette, June 13, 1789, p. 574, col. 3.

2.1.1.2 **Proposal by Sherman to House Committee of Eleven, July 21–28, 1789**

[Amendment] 2 The people have certain natural rights which are retained by them when they enter into society, Such are the rights of conscience in matters of religion; of acquiring property, and of pursuing happiness & safety; of Speaking, writing and publishing their Sentiments with decency and freedom; of peaceably Assembling to consult their common good, and of applying to Government by petition or remonstrance for redress of grievances. Of these rights therefore they Shall not be deprived by the government of the united States.

. . .

[Amendment] 8 Congress shall not have power to grant any monopoly or exclusive advantages of Commerce to any person or Company; nor to restrain the liberty of the Press.

Madison Papers, DLC.

2.1.1.3 House Committee of Eleven Report, July 28, 1789

ART. I, SEC. 9 — Between PAR. 2 and 3 insert, . . .
"The freedom of speech, and of the press, and the right of the people peaceably to assemble and consult for their common good, and to apply to the government for redress of grievances, shall not be infringed."

Broadside Collection, DLC.

2.1.1.4 House Consideration, August 15, 1789

2.1.1.4.a   The next clause of the 4th proposition was taken into consideration, and was as follows: "The freedom of speech and of the press, and the right of the people peaceably to assemble and consult for their common good, and to apply to the government for redress of grievances shall not be infringed."

Congressional Register, August 15, 1789, vol. 2, p. 197 ("agreed to").

2.1.1.4.b   Fifth amendment — "The freedom of speech, and of the press, and of the right of the people peaceably to assemble and consult for their common good, and to apply to the government for redress of grievances, shall not be infringed."

Daily Advertiser, August 17, 1789, p. 2, col. 1
("carried in the affirmative.").

2.1.1.4.c   Fifth amendment — "The freedom of speech, and of the press, and of the right of the people peaceably to assemble and consult for their common good, and to apply to the government for redress of grievances, shall not be infringed."

New-York Daily Gazette, August 18, 1789, p. 798, col. 3
("carried in the affirmative").

2.1.1.4.d   Fifth Amendment. *The freedom of speech, and of the press, and of the rights of the people peaceably to assemble and consult for their common good, and to apply to government for the redress of grievances shall not be infringed.*

Gazette of the U.S., August 19, 1789, p. 147, col. 1 ("agreed to").

2.1.1.5 Further House Consideration, August 21, 1789

Fourth. The freedom of speech, and of the press, and the right of the people peaceably to assemble and consult for their common good, and to apply to the government for redress of grievances, shall not be infringed.

HJ, p. 107 ("read and debated . . . agreed to by the House,
. . . two-thirds of the members present concurring").[1]

---

[1] On August 22, 1789, the following motion was agreed to:
ORDERED, That it be referred to a committee of three, to prepare and report a proper arrangement of, and introduction to the articles of amendment to the Constitution of the United States, as agreed to by the House; and that Mr. Benson, Mr. Sherman, and Mr. Sedgwick be of the said committee.

HJ, p. 112.

2.1.1.6   House Resolution, August 24, 1789

ARTICLE the FOURTH.

The Freedom of Speech, and of the Press, and the right of the People peaceably to assemble, and consult for their common good, and to apply to the Government for a redress of grievances, shall not be infringed.   House Pamphlet, RG 46, DNA.

2.1.1.7   Senate Consideration, August 25, 1789

2.1.1.7.a   The Resolve of the House of Representatives of the 24th of August, upon certain "Articles to be proposed to the Legislatures of the several States as Amendments to the Constitution of the United States" was read as followeth:

Article the fourth

. . .

The freedom of speech, and of the press, and the right of the People peaceably to assemble and consult for their common good and to apply to the Government for redress of grievances shall not be infringed.   Rough SJ, p. 215.

2.1.1.7.b   The Resolve of the House of Representatives of the 24th of August, was read as followeth:

. . .

Article the Fourth.

The freedom of speech, and of the press, and the right of the people peaceably to assemble, and consult for their common good, and to apply to the Government for redress of grievances, shall not be infringed.   Smooth SJ, p. 194.

2.1.1.7.c   The Resolve of the House of Representatives of the 24th of August, was read as followeth:

. . .   "ARTICLE the FOURTH.

"The freedom of speech, and of the press, and the right of the people peaceably to assemble, and consult for their common good, and to apply to the Government for redress of grievances, shall not be infringed.   Printed SJ, p. 104.

2.1.1.8   Further Senate Consideration, September 3, 1789

2.1.1.8.a   On Motion to insert these words after "Press," "In as ample a manner as hath at any time been secured by the common law."

Rough SJ, p. 246 ("It passed in the negative.").

2.1.1.8.b   On motion, To insert these words after "Press," — "In as ample a manner as hath at any time been secured by the common law" —

Smooth SJ, p. 219 ("It passed in the Negative.").

2.1.1.8.c   On motion, To insert these words after "Press," — "In as ample a manner as hath at any time been secured by the common law" —

Printed SJ, p. 117 ("It passed in the Negative.").

2.1.1.9   Further Senate Consideration, September 4, 1789

2.1.1.9.a   On Motion to adopt the fourth Article proposed by the House of Representatives to read as followeth,

"That Congress shall make no law, abridging the freedom of speech or of the press, or the right of the People peaceably to assemble <u>and consult for their common good</u>, and to petition the Government for a redress of grievances,"

Rough SJ, September 4, 1789, p. 247 ("It passed in the affirmative.").

2.1.1.9.b   On motion, To adopt the fourth Article proposed by the Resolve of the House of Representatives, to read as followeth,

"That Congress shall make no law, abridging the freedom of Speech, or of the Press, or the right of the People peaceably to assemble and consult for their common good, and to petition the Government for a redress of grievances,"

Smooth SJ, September 4, 1789, pp. 220–21
("It passed in the Affirmative.").

2.1.1.9.c   On motion, To adopt the fourth Article proposed by the Resolve of the House of Representatives, to read as followeth,

"That Congress shall make no law, abridging the freedom of Speech, or of the Press, or the right of the People peaceably to assemble and consult for their common good, and to petition the Government for a redress of grievances,"

Printed SJ, September 4, 1789, p. 118
(" It passed in the Affirmative.").

2.1.1.9.d   that the Senate do

Resolved ~~to~~ ∧ concur with the House of Representatives in
Article fourth.

To read as follows, to wit:

"That Congress shall make no law, abridging the freedom of Speech or of the press, or the right of the people peaceably to assemble and consult for their common good, and to petition the government for a redress of grievances,"

Senate MS, RG 46, p. 2.

2.1.1.10   Further Senate Consideration, September 9, 1789

2.1.1.10.a   And on Motion to amend article the third to read as follows:

"Congress shall make no law establishing articles of faith or a mode of worship, or prohibiting the free exercise of Religion; or abridging the freedom of Speech, or the press, or the right of the People peaceably to assemble, and petition to the government for the redress of grievances."

. . .

On motion, To strike out the fourth article,

Rough SJ, p. 274 (As to each motion, "It passed in the affirmative.").

2.1.1.10.b   On motion, To amend article the third, to read as follows:

"Congress shall make no law establishing articles of faith or a mode of worship, or prohibiting the free exercise of religion, or abridging the freedom of speech, or

the press, or the right of the people peaceably to assemble, and petition to the Government for the redress of grievances" —

. . .

On motion, To strike out the fourth article,

Smooth SJ, p. 243 (As to each motion, "It passed in the Affirmative.").

2.1.1.10.c   On motion, To amend Article the third, to read as follows:

"Congress shall make no law establishing articles of faith or a mode of worship, or prohibiting the free exercise of religion, or abridging the freedom of speech, or the press, or the right of the people peaceably to assemble, and petition to the Government for the redress of grievances" —

On motion, To strike out the fourth Article,

Printed SJ, p. 129 (As to each motion, "It passed in the Affirmative.").

2.1.1.10.d   On the question to concur with the House of Representatives on their resolution of the 24th of Augt. proposing amendments to the constitution of the United States, with the following amendments viz:

. . .

To erase from the 3d. Article the word "Religion" & insert — Articles of faith or a mode of Worship. —

And to erase from the same article the words "thereof, nor shall the rights of Conscience be infringed" & insert — of Religion, or abridging the freedom of speech, or of the press, or ~~of~~ the right of the people peaceably to assemble, & to petition to the government for a redress of grievances

To erase the 4th. article, & the words "Article the fourth."

Ellsworth MS, pp. 1–2, RG 46, DNA.

2.1.1.11   Senate Resolution, September 9, 1789

ARTICLE THE THIRD.

Congress shall make no law establishing articles of faith, or a mode of worship, or prohibiting the free exercise of religion, or abridging the freedom of speech, or of the press, or the right of the people peaceably to assemble, and to petition to the government for a redress of grievances.

Senate Pamphlet, RG 46, DNA.

2.1.1.12.   Further House Consideration, September 21, 1789

RESOLVED, That this House doth agree to the second, fourth, eighth, twelfth, thirteenth, sixteenth, eighteenth, nineteenth, twenty-fifth, and twenty-sixth amendments, and doth disagree to the first, third, fifth, sixth, seventh, ninth, tenth, eleventh, fourteenth, fifteenth, seventeenth, twentieth, twenty-first, twenty-second, twenty-third, and twenty-fourth amendments proposed by the Senate to the said articles, two thirds of the members present concurring on each vote.

RESOLVED, That a conference be desired with the Senate on the subject matter of the amendments disagreed to, and that Mr. Madison, Mr. Sherman, and Mr. Vining, be appointed managers at the same on the part of this House.

HJ, p. 146.

2.1.1.13 Further Senate Consideration, September 21, 1789

2.1.1.13.a   A message from the House of Representatives —
Mr. Beckley, their Clerk, brought up a Resolve of the House of this date, to agree to the 2nd, 4th, 8th, 12th, 13th, 16th, 18th, 19th, 25th, and 26th Amendments proposed by the Senate, "To articles of Amendment to be proposed to the Legislatures of the several States, as Amendments to the Constitution of the United States," and to disagree to the 1st, 3d, 5th, 6th, 7th, 9th, 10th, 11th, 14th, 15th, 17th, 20th, 21st, 22d, 23d, and 24th amendments: Two thirds of the members present concurring on each vote: And "That a conference be desired with the Senate on the subject matter of the amendments disagreed to," and that Mr. Madison, Mr. Sherman, and Mr. Vining, be appointed managers of the same, on the part of the House of Representatives —
And he withdrew.
Smooth SJ, pp. 265–66.

2.1.1.13.b   A message from the House of Representatives —
Mr. Beckley, their Clerk, brought up a Resolve of the House of this date, to agree to the 2d, 4th, 8th, 12th, 13th, 16th, 18th, 19th, 25th, and 26th Amendments proposed by the Senate, "To Articles of Amendment to be proposed to the Legislatures of the several States, as Amendments to the Constitution of the United States," and to disagree to the 1st, 3d, 5th, 6th, 7th, 9th, 10th, 11th, 14th, 15th, 17th, 20th, 21st, 22d, 23d, and 24th Amendments: Two thirds of the members present concurring on each vote: And "That a conference be desired with the Senate on the subject matter of the Amendments disagreed to," and that Mr. Madison, Mr. Sherman, and Mr. Vining, be appointed managers of the same, on the part of the House of Representatives —
And he withdrew.
Printed SJ, pp. 141–42.

2.1.1.14 Further Senate Consideration, September 21, 1789

2.1.1.14.a   The Senate proceeded to consider the Message of the House of Representatives disagreeing to the Amendments made by the Senate "To Articles to be proposed to the Legislatures of the several States, as Amendments to the Constitution of the United States" And
RESOLVED, That the Senate do recede from their third Amendment, and do insist on all the others.
RESOLVED, That the Senate do concur with the House of Representatives in a conference on the subject matter of disagreement on the said Articles of Amendment, and that Mr. Ellsworth, Mr. Carroll and Mr. Paterson be managers of the conference on the part of the Senate.
Smooth SJ, p. 267.

2.1.1.14.b   The Senate proceeded to consider the message of the House of Representatives disagreeing to the Amendments made by the Senate "To Articles to be proposed to the Legislatures of the several States, as Amendments to the Constitution of the United States" — And
RESOLVED, That the Senate do recede from their third Amendment, and do insist on all the others.

RESOLVED, That the Senate do concur with the House of Representatives in a conference on the subject matter of disagreement on the said Articles of Amendment, and that Mr. Ellsworth, Mr. Carroll, and Mr. Paterson be managers of the conference on the part of the Senate.

Printed SJ, p. 142.

2.1.1.15 Conference Committee Report, September 24, 1789

[T]hat it will be proper for the House of Representatives to agree to the said Amendments proposed by the Senate, with an Amendment to their fifth Amendment, so that the third Article shall read as follows: "Congress shall make no Law <u>respecting an establishment of Religion</u>, or prohibiting the free exercise thereof; or abridging the freedom of Speech, or of the Press; or the right of the people peaceably to assemble and to petition the Government for a redress of grievances;" And with an Amendment to the fourteenth Amendment proposed by the Senate, so that the eighth Article, as numbered in the Amendments proposed by the Senate, shall read as follows "In all criminal prosecutions, the accused shall enjoy the right to a speedy & publick trial <u>by an impartial jury of the district wherein the crime shall have been committed, as the district shall have been previously ascertained by law</u>, and to be informed of the nature and cause of the accusation; to be confronted with the witnesses against him, and to have com-

to

pulsory process for obtaining witnesses ~~against him~~ in his favour, & /\ have the assistance of counsel for his defence."

Conference MS, RG 46, DNA (Ellsworth's handwriting).

2.1.1.16 House Consideration of Conference Committee Report, September 24 [25], 1789

RESOLVED, That this House doth recede from their disagreement to the first, third, fifth, sixth, seventh, ninth, tenth, eleventh, fourteenth, fifteenth, seventeenth, twentieth, twenty-first, twenty-second, twenty-third, and twenty-fourth amendments, insisted on by the Senate: PROVIDED, That the two articles which by the amendments of the Senate are now proposed to be inserted as the third and eighth articles, shall be amended to read as followeth;

Article the third. "Congress shall make no law respecting an establishment of religion, or prohibiting the free exercise thereof; or abridging the freedom of speech, or of the press; or the right of the people peaceably to assemble, and to petition the government for a redress of grievances."

Article the eighth. "In all criminal prosecutions, the accused shall enjoy the right to a speedy and public trial by an impartial jury of the state and district wherein the crime shall have been committed, which district shall have been previously ascertained by law, and to be informed of the nature and cause of the accusation, to be confronted with the witnesses against him, to have compulsory process for obtaining witnesses in his favor, and to have the assistance of council for his defence."

HJ, p. 152 ("On the question, that the House do agree to the
alteration and amendment of the eighth article, in manner
aforesaid, It was resolved in the affirmative.
Ayes 37 Noes 14").

2.1.1.17 Senate Consideration of Conference Committee Report, September 24, 1789

2.1.1.17.a   Mr. Ellsworth, on behalf of the managers of the conference on "articles to be proposed to the several States as Amendments to the Constitution of the United States," reported as follows:

That it will be proper for the House of Representatives to agree to the said amendments proposed by the Senate, with an Amendment to their fifth Amendment, so that the third Article shall read as follows: "Congress shall make no law respecting an establishment of <u>Religion</u>, or prohibiting the free exercise thereof; or abridging the freedom of Speech, or of the Press; or the right of the people peaceably to assemble and petition the Government for a redress of Grievances;" And with an Amendment to the fourteenth Amendment proposed by the Senate, so that the eighth article, as numbered in the Amendments proposed by the Senate, shall read as follows; "In all criminal prosecutions, the accused shall enjoy the right to a speedy and public trial by an impartial <u>Jury</u> of the district wherein the <u>Crime</u> shall have been committed, as the district shall have been previously ascertained by law, and to be informed of the nature and cause of the accusation, to be confronted with the witnesses against him, and to have compulsory process for obtaining witnesses in his favor, and to have the assistance of Counsel for defence."

Smooth SJ, pp. 272–73.

2.1.1.17.b   Mr. Ellsworth, on behalf of the managers of the conference on "Articles to be proposed to the several States as Amendments to the Constitution of the United States," reported as follows:

That it will be proper for the House of Representatives to agree to the said Amendments proposed by the Senate, with an Amendment to their fifth Amendment, so that the third Article shall read as follows: "Congress shall make no Law RESPECTING AN ESTABLISHMENT OF RELIGION, or prohibiting the free exercise thereof; or abridging the freedom of Speech, or of the Press; or the right of the People peaceably to assemble and petition the Government for a redress of Grievances;" And with an Amendment to the fourteenth Amendment proposed by the Senate, so that the eighth Article, as numbered in the Amendments proposed by the Senate, shall read as follows; "In all criminal prosecutions, the accused shall enjoy the right to a speedy and public trial BY AN IMPARTIAL JURY OF THE DISTRICT WHEREIN THE CRIME SHALL HAVE BEEN COMMITTED, AS THE DISTRICT SHALL HAVE BEEN PREVIOUSLY ASCERTAINED BY LAW, and to be informed of the nature and cause of the accusation, to be confronted with the witnesses against him, and to have compulsory process for obtaining witnesses in his favor, and to have the assistance of Counsel for defence."

Printed SJ, p. 145.

2.1.1.18 Further Senate Consideration of Conference Committee Report, September 24, 1789

2.1.1.18.a   A Message from the House of Representatives —

Mr. Beckley, their Clerk, brought up the Amendments to the "Articles to be proposed to the Legislatures of the several States, as Amendments to the Constitution of the United States;" and informed the Senate, that the House of Representatives had receded from their disagreement to the 1st, 3d, 5th, 6th, 7th, 9th, 10th,

11th, 14th, 15th, 17th, 20th, 21st, 22d, 23d, and 24th Amendments, insisted on by the Senate: Provided that the "Two Articles, which by the Amendments of the Senate are now proposed to be inserted as the third and eighth Articles," shall be amended to read as followeth:

Article the Third. "Congress shall make no Law respecting an establishment of Religion, or prohibiting the free exercise thereof; or abridging the freedom of Speech, or of the Press; or the right of the people peaceably to assemble, and petition the Government for a redress of Grievances."

Article the Eighth. "In all criminal prosecutions the accused shall enjoy the right to a speedy and public trial by an impartial Jury of the State and District, wherein the crime shall have been committed, which District shall have been previously ascertained by law, and to be informed of the nature and cause of the accusation, to be confronted with the witnesses against him, and to have compulsory process for obtaining witnesses in his favor, and to have the assistance of Counsel for his defence."

Smooth SJ, pp. 278–79.

2.1.1.18.b   A Message from the House of Representatives —

Mr. Beckley, their Clerk, brought up the Amendments to the "Articles to be proposed to the Legislatures of the several States, as Amendments to the Constitution of the United States;" and informed the Senate, that the House of Representatives had receded from their disagreement to the 1st, 3d, 5th, 6th, 7th, 9th, 10th, 11th, 14th, 15th, 17th, 20th, 21st, 22d, 23d, and 24th Amendments, insisted on by the Senate: Provided that the "Two Articles, which by the Amendments of the Senate are now proposed to be inserted as the third and eighth Articles," shall be amended to read as followeth:

Article the Third. "Congress shall make no Law respecting an establishment of Religion, or prohibiting the free exercise thereof; or abridging the freedom of Speech, or of the Press; or the right of the People peaceably to assemble, and petition the Government for a redress of Grievances."

Article the Eighth. "In all criminal prosecutions the accused shall enjoy the right to a speedy and public trial by an impartial Jury of the State and District, wherein the crime shall have been committed, which District shall have been previously ascertained by law, and to be informed of the nature and cause of the accusation, to be confronted with the witnesses against him, and to have compulsory process for obtaining witnesses in his favor, and to have the assistance of Counsel for his defence."

Printed SJ, p.148.

2.1.1.19   Further Senate Consideration of Conference Committee Report, September 25, 1789

2.1.1.19.a   The Senate proceeded to consider the Message from the House of Representatives of the 24th, with Amendments to the Amendments of the Senate, to "Articles to be proposed to the Legislatures of the several States, as Amendments to the Constitution of the United States" — And

RESOLVED, That the Senate do concur in the Amendments proposed by the House of Representatives, to the Amendments of the Senate. Smooth SJ, p. 283.

2.1.1.19.b   The Senate proceeded to consider the Message from the House of Representatives of the 24th, with Amendments to the Amendments of the Senate, to "Articles to be proposed to the Legislatures of the several States, as Amendments to the Constitution of the United States" — And

RESOLVED, That the Senate do concur in the Amendments proposed by the House of Representatives, to the Amendments of the Senate.

Printed SJ, pp. 150–51.

2.1.1.20 Agreed Resolution, September 25, 1789

2.1.1.20.a   Article the Third.

Congress shall make no law respecting an establishment of religion, or prohibiting the free exercise thereof, or abridging the freedom of speech, or of the press, or the right of the people peaceably to assemble, and to petition the Government for a redress of grievances.

Smooth SJ, Appendix, p. 292.

2.1.1.20.b   ARTICLE the THIRD.

Congress shall make no law respecting an establishment of religion, or prohibiting the free exercise thereof, or abridging the freedom of speech, or of the press, or the right of the people peaceably to assemble, and to petition the Government for a redress of grievances.

Printed SJ, Appendix, p. 163.

2.1.1.21 Enrolled Resolution, September 28, 1789

Article The Third . . . Congress shall make no law respecting an establishment of religion, or prohibiting the free exercise thereof; or abridging the freedom of speech, or of the press, or the right of the people peaceably to assemble, and to petition the Government for a redress of grievances.

Enrolled Resolutions, RG 11, DNA.

2.1.1.22 Printed Versions

2.1.1.22.a   ART. I. Congress shall make no law respecting an establishment of religion, or prohibiting the free exercise thereof; or abridging the freedom of speech, or of the press; or the right of the people peaceably to assemble, and to petition the government for a redress of grievances.

Statutes at Large, vol. 1, p. 21.

2.1.1.22.b   ART. III. Congress shall make no law respecting an establishment of religion, or prohibiting the free exercise thereof; or abridging the freedom of speech, or of the press; or the right of the people peaceably to assemble, and to petition the government for a redress of grievances.

Statutes at Large, vol. 1, p. 97.

2.1.2 PROPOSALS FROM THE STATE CONVENTIONS

2.1.2.1 Maryland Minority, April 26, 1788

12. That the freedom of the press be inviolably preserved.

Maryland Gazette, May 1, 1788 (committee majority).

2.1.2.2 Massachusetts Minority, February 6, 1788

[T]hat the said Constitution be never construed to authorize Congress to infringe the just liberty of the press, or the rights of conscience; or to prevent the people of the United States, who are peaceable citizens, from keeping their own arms; or to raise standing armies, unless when necessary for the defence of the United States, or of some one or more of them; or to prevent the people from petitioning, in a peaceable and orderly manner, the federal legislature, for a redress of grievances; or to subject the people to unreasonable searches and seizures of their persons, papers or possessions.

Massachusetts Convention, pp. 86–87.

2.1.2.3 New York, July 26, 1788

That the people have a right peaceably to assemble together to consult for their common good, or to instruct their Representatives; and that every person has a right to Petition or apply to the Legislature for redress of Grievances. — That the Freedom of the Press ought not to be violated or restrained.

State Ratifications, RG 11, DNA.

2.1.2.4 North Carolina, August 1, 1788

16th. That the people have a right to freedom of speech, and of writing and publishing their sentiments; that the freedom of the press is one of the greatest bulwarks of Liberty, and ought not to be violated.

State Ratifications, RG 11, DNA.

2.1.2.5 Pennsylvania Minority, December 12, 1787

6. That the people have a right to the freedom of speech, of writing, and of publishing their sentiments, therefore, the freedom of the press shall not be restrained by any law of the United States.

Pennsylvania Packet, December 18, 1787.

2.1.2.6 Rhode Island, May 29, 1790

16th. That the people have a right to freedom of speech and of writing and publishing their sentiments, that freedom of the press is one of the greatest bulwarks of liberty, and ought not to be violated.

State Ratifications, RG 11, DNA.

2.1.2.7 Virginia, June 27, 1788

Sixteenth, That the people have a right to freedom of speech, and of writing and publishing their Sentiments; that the freedom of the press is one of the greatest bulwarks of liberty and ought not to be violated.

State Ratifications, RG 11, DNA.

2.1.3 STATE CONSTITUTIONS AND LAWS; COLONIAL CHARTERS AND LAWS

2.1.3.1 Delaware: Declaration of Rights, 1776

Sect. 23. That the liberty of the press ought to be inviolably preserved.

Delaware Laws, vol. 1, App., p. 81.

2.1.3.2 **Georgia**

2.1.3.2.a **Constitution, 1777**

LXI. Freedom of the press, and trial by jury, to remain inviolate *forever.*

Georgia Laws, p. 16.

2.1.3.2.b **Constitution, 1789**

ARTICLE IV.

. . .

Sect. 3. Freedom of the press, and trial by jury, shall remain inviolate.

Georgia Laws, p. 29.

2.1.3.3 **Maryland: Declaration of Rights, 1776**

38. That the liberty of the press ought to be inviolably preserved.

Maryland Laws, November 3, 1776.

2.1.3.4 **Massachusetts**

2.1.3.4.a **Body of Liberties, 1641**

[12] Every man whether Inhabitant or fforreiner, free or not free shall have libertie to come to any publique Court, Councel, or Towne meeting, and either by speech or writing to move any lawfull, seasonable, and materiall question, or to present any necessary motion, complaint, petition, Bill or information, whereof that meeting hath proper cognizance, so it be done in convenient time, due order, and respective manner.

Massachusetts Colonial Laws, p. 35.

2.1.3.4.b **Constitution, 1780**

PART I

. . .

ARTICLE

. . .

XVI. The Liberty of the Press is essential to the security of freedom in a State, it ought not, therefore, to be restrained in this Commonwealth.

Massachusetts Perpetual Laws, p. 7.

2.1.3.5 **New Hampshire: Constitution, 1783**

[Part I, Article] XXII. The Liberty of the press is essential to the security of freedom in a State; it ought, therefore, to be inviolably preserved.

. . .

XXX. The freedom of deliberation, speech, and debate, in either house of the legislature, is so essential to the rights of the people, that it cannot be the foundation of any action, complaint, or prosecution, in any other court or place whatsoever.

New Hampshire Laws, pp. 26, 27.

2.1.3.6   North Carolina

2.1.3.6.a   Fundamental Constitutions of Carolina, 1669

80th. Since multiplicity of comments, as well as of laws, have great inconveniences, and serve only to obscure and perplex; all manner of comments or expositions, or [*sic;* on] any part of these Fundamental Constitutions, or on any part of the common or statute laws of Carolina are absolutely prohibited.

North Carolina State Records, p. 146.

2.1.3.6.b   Declaration of Rights, 1776

Sect. XV. That the Freedom of the Press is one of the great Bulwarks of Liberty, and therefore ought never to be restrained.

North Carolina Laws, p. 275.

2.1.3.7   Pennsylvania

2.1.3.7.a   Constitution, 1776

CHAPTER I.

A DECLARATION of the RIGHTS of the Inhabitants
of the State of Pennsylvania.

. . .

XII[.] That the people have a right to freedom of speech, and of writing, and publishing their sentiments; therefore the freedom of the press ought not to be restrained.

Pennsylvania Acts, M'Kean, p. x.

2.1.3.7.b   Constitution, 1790

ARTICLE IX.

. . .

Sect. VII. That the printing presses shall be free to every person who undertakes to examine the proceedings of the legislature, or any branch of government: And no law shall ever be made to restrain the right thereof. The free communication of thoughts and opinions is one of the invaluable rights of man; and every citizen may freely speak, write and print on any subject, being responsible for the abuse of that liberty. In prosecutions for the publication of papers, investigating the official conduct of officers, or men in a public capacity, or where the matter published is proper for public information, the truth thereof may be given in evidence: And, in all indictments for libels, the jury shall have a right to determine the law and the facts, under the direction of the court, as in other cases.

Pennsylvania Acts, Dallas, p. xxxiv.

2.1.3.8   South Carolina

2.1.3.8.a   Constitution, 1778

XLIII. That the Liberty of the Press be inviolably preserved.

South Carolina Constitution, p. 15.

2.1.3.8.b **Constitution, 1790**

ARTICLE IX.

. . .

Section 6. The trial by jury as heretofore used in this state, and the liberty of the press, shall be for ever inviolably preserved.   South Carolina Laws, App., p. 42.

2.1.3.9 **Vermont: Constitution, 1777**

CHAPTER I.

. . .

14. THAT the People have a Right to Freedom of Speech, and of writing and publishing their Sentiments; therefore the Freedom of the Press ought not to be restrained.   Vermont Acts, p. 4.

2.1.3.10 **Virginia: Declaration of Rights, 1776**

XII. THAT the freedom of the press is one of the great bulwarks of liberty, and can never be restrained but by despotick governments.   Virginia Acts, p. 33.

2.1.4 OTHER TEXTS

2.1.4.1 **English Bill of Rights, 1689**

. . . That the freedome of speech and debates or proceedings in Parlyament ought not to be impeached or questioned in any court or place out of Parlyament.
                                                         1 Will. & Mar. sess. 2, c. 2.

2.1.4.2 **Richard Henry Lee to Edmund Randolph, Proposed Amendments, October 16, 1787**

. . . That the freedom of the press shall be secured. . . .
                                                 Virginia Gazette, December 22, 1787.

2.2 DISCUSSION OF DRAFTS AND PROPOSALS
2.2.1 THE FIRST CONGRESS

2.2.1.1 **June 8, 1789[2]**

2.2.1.1.a   MR. JACKSON

. . .

The gentleman endeavours to secure the liberty of the press; pray how is this in danger. There is no power given to congress to regulate this subject as they can commerce, or peace, or war. Has any transactions taken place to make us suppose such an amendment necessary? An honorable gentleman, a member of this house, has been attacked in the public news-papers, on account of sentiments delivered on this floor. Have congress taken any notice of it? Have they ordered the writer before them, even for a breach of privilege, altho' the constitution provides that a member shall not be questioned in any place for any speech or debate in the house? No, these things are suffered to public view, and held up to the inspection

[2] For the reports of Madison's speech in support of his proposals, *see* 1.2.1.1.a–c.

of the world. These are principles which will always prevail; I am not afraid, nor are other members I believe, our conduct should meet the severest scrutiny. Where then is the necessity of taking measures to secure what neither is nor can be in danger?

Congressional Register, June 8, 1789, vol. 1, pp. 437–38.

2.2.1.1.b The press, Mr. Jackson observed, is unboundedly free — a recent instance of which the House had witnessed in an attack upon one of its members — A bill of rights is a mere *ignis fatuus,* amusing by appearances, and leading often to dangerous conclusions. —

Gazette of the U.S., June 10, 1789, p. 67, col. 2.

2.2.1.2 **August 15, 1789**[3]

2.2.2 STATE CONVENTIONS

2.2.2.1 **North Carolina, July 30, 1788**

Mr. SPAIGHT. . . .

. . . The gentleman advises such amendments as would satisfy him, and proposes a mode of amending before ratifying. If we do not adopt first, we are no more a part of the Union than any foreign power. It will be also throwing away the influence of our state to propose amendments as the condition of our ratification. If we adopt first, our representatives will have a proportionable weight in bringing about amendments, which will not be the case if we do not adopt. It is adopted by ten states already. The question, then, is, not whether the Constitution be good, but whether we will or will not confederate with the other states. The gentleman supposes that the liberty of the press is not secured. The Constitution does not take it away. It says nothing of it, and can do nothing to injure it. But it is secured by the constitution of every state in the Union in the most ample manner.

He objects to giving the government exclusive legislation in a district not exceeding ten miles square, although the previous consent and cession of the state within which it may be, is required. Is it to be supposed that the representatives of the people will make regulations therein dangerous to liberty? Is there the least color or pretext for saying that the militia will be carried and kept there for life? Where is there any power to do this? The power of calling forth the militia is given for the common defence; and can we suppose that our own representatives, chosen for so short a period, will dare to pervert a power, given for the general protection, to an absolute oppression? But the gentleman has gone farther, and says, that any man who will complain of their oppressions, or write against their usurpation, may be deemed a traitor, and tried as such in the ten miles square, without a jury. What an astonishing misrepresentation! Why did not the gentleman look at the Constitution, and see their powers? Treason is there defined. It says, expressly, that treason against the United States shall consist only in levying war against them, or in adhering to their enemies, giving them aid and comfort. Complaining, therefore, or writing, cannot be treason. [Here Mr. Lenoir rose, and

---

[3] For the reports of the debate, *see* 3.2.1.2.a–d.

said he meant misprision of treason.] The same reasons hold against that too. The liberty of the press being secured, creates an additional security.

Elliot, vol. 4, pp. 208–09.

2.2.2.2 South Carolina, January 18, 1788

Hon. JAMES LINCOLN. . . .

He would be glad to know why, in this Constitution, there is a total silence with regard to the liberty of the press. Was it forgotten? Impossible! Then it must have been purposely omitted; and with what design, good or bad, he left the world to judge. The liberty of the press was the tyrant's scourge — it was the true friend and firmest supporter of civil liberty; therefore why pass it by in silence? He perceived that not till almost the very end of the Constitution was there any provision made for the nature or form of government we were to live under: he contended it should have been the very first article; it should have been, as it were, the groundwork or foundation on which it should have been built. But how is it? At the very end of the Constitution, there is a clause which says, — "The Congress of the United States shall guaranty to each state a republican form of government." But pray, who are the United States? — A President and four or five senators? Pray, sir, what security have we for a republican form of government, when it depends on the mere will and pleasure of a few men, who, with an army, navy, and rich treasury at their back, may change and alter it as they please? It may be said they will be sworn. Sir, the king of Great Britain, at his coronation, swore to govern his subjects with justice and mercy. We were then his subjects, and continued so for a long time after. He would be glad to know how he observed his oath. If, then, the king of Great Britain forswore himself, what security have we that a future President and four or five senators — men like himself — will think more solemnly of so sacred an obligation than he did?

Why was not this Constitution ushered in with the bill of rights? Are the people to have no rights? Perhaps this same President and Senate would, by and by, declare them. He much feared they would. He concluded by returning his hearty thanks to the gentleman who had so nobly opposed this Constitution: it was supporting the cause of the people; and if ever any one deserved the title of man of the people, he, on this occasion, most certainly did.

Gen. CHARLES COTESWORTH PINCKNEY answered Mr. Lincoln on his objections. . . . With regard to the liberty of the press, the discussion of that matter was not forgotten by the members of the Convention. It was fully debated, and the impropriety of saying any thing about it in the Constitution clearly evinced. The general government has no powers but what are expressly granted to it; it therefore has no power to take away the liberty of the press. That invaluable blessing, which deserves all the encomiums the gentleman has justly bestowed upon it, is secured by all our state constitutions; and to have mentioned it in our general Constitution would perhaps furnish an argument, hereafter, that the general government had a right to exercise powers not expressly delegated to it. For the same reason, we had no bill of rights inserted in our Constitution; for, as we might perhaps have omitted the enumeration of some of our rights, it might hereafter be said we had delegated to the general government a power to take away such of our rights as we had not enumerated; but by delegating express powers, we certainly reserve to ourselves every power and right not mentioned in the Constitution.

Elliot, vol. 4, pp. 314–16.

2.2.2.3 Pennsylvania, December 1, 1787

Mr. WILSON. . . .

. . . In answer to the gentlemen from Fayette, (Mr. Smilie,) on the subject of the press, I beg leave to make an observation. It is very true, sir, that this Constitution says nothing with regard to that subject, nor was it necessary; because it will be found that there is given to the general government no power whatsoever concerning it; and no law, in pursuance of the Constitution, can possibly be enacted to destroy that liberty.

I heard the honorable gentleman make this general assertion, that the Congress was certainly vested with power to make such a law; but I would be glad to know by what part of this Constitution such a power is given? Until that is done, I shall not enter into a minute investigation of the matter, but shall at present satisfy myself with giving an answer to a question that has been put. It has been asked, If a law should be made to punish libels, and the judges should proceed under that law, what chance would the printer have of an acquittal? And it has been said he would drop into a den of devouring monsters!

I presume it was not in the view of the honorable gentleman to say there is no such thing as a libel, or that the writers of such ought not to be punished. The idea of the liberty of the press is not carried so far as this in any country. What is meant by the liberty of the press is, that there should be no antecedent restraint upon it; but that every author is responsible when he attacks the security or welfare of the government, or the safety, character, and property of the individual.

With regard to attacks upon the public, the mode of proceeding is by a prosecution. Now, if a libel is written, it must be within some one of the United States, or the district of Congress. With regard to that district, I hope it will take care to preserve this as well as the other rights of freemen; for, whatever district Congress may choose, the cession of it cannot be completed without the consent of its inhabitants. Now, sir, if this *libel* is to be tried, it must be tried where the offence was committed; for, under this Consitition, as declared in the 2d section of the 3d article, the trial must be held in the state; therefore, on this occasion, it must be tried where it was published, if the indictment is for publishing; and it must be tried likewise by a jury of that state. Now, I would ask, is the person prosecuted in a worse situation under the general government, even if it had the power to make laws on this subject, than he is at present under the state government? It is true, there is no particular regulation made, to have the jury come from the body of the county in which the offence was committed; but there are some states in which this mode of collecting juries is contrary to their established custom, and gentlemen ought to consider that this Constitution was not meant merely for Pennsylvania. In some states, the juries are not taken from a single county. In Virginia, the sheriff, I believe, is not confined even to the inhabitants of the state, but is at liberty to take any man he pleases, and put him on the jury. In Maryland, I think, a set of jurors serve for the whole western shore, and another for the eastern shore.

Elliot, vol. 2, pp. 449–50.

2.2.2.4 Virginia

2.2.2.4.a June 14, 1788

Mr. HENRY. . . .

A bill of rights may be summed up in a few words. What do they tell us? — That our rights are reserved. Why not say so? Is it because it will consume too much paper? Gentlemen's reasoning against a bill of rights does not satisfy me. Without saying which has the right side, it remains doubtful. A bill of rights is a favorite thing with the Virginians and the people of the other states likewise. It may be their prejudice, but the government ought to suit their geniuses; otherwise, its operation will be unhappy. A bill of rights, even if its necessity be doubtful, will exclude the possibility of dispute; and, with great submission, I think the best way is to have no dispute. In the present Constitution, they are restrained from issuing general warrants to search suspected places, or seize persons not named, without evidence of the commission of a fact, &c. There was certainly some celestial influence governing those who deliberated on that Constitution; for they have, with the most cautious and enlightened circumspection, guarded those indefeasible rights which ought ever to be held sacred! The officers of Congress may come upon you now, fortified with all the terrors of paramount federal authority. Excisemen may come in multitudes; for the limitation of their numbers no man knows. They may, unless the general government be restrained by a bill of rights, or some similar restriction, go into your cellars and rooms, and search, ransack, and measure, every thing you eat, drink, and wear. They ought to be restrained within proper bounds. With respect to the freedom of the press, I need say nothing; for it is hoped that the gentlemen who shall compose Congress will take care to infringe as little as possible the rights of human nature. This will result from their integrity. They should, from prudence, abstain from violating the rights of their constituents. They are not, however, expressly restrained. But whether they will intermeddle with that palladium of our liberties or not, I leave you to determine.

Elliot, vol. 3, pp. 448–49.

2.2.2.4.b June 15, 1788

Gov. RANDOLPH. . . .

Then, sir, the freedom of the press is said to be insecure. God forbid that I should give my voice against the freedom of the press. But I ask, (and with confidence that it cannot be answered,) Where is the page where it is restrained? If there had been any regulation about it, leaving it insecure, then there might have been reason for clamors. But this is not the case. If it be, I again ask for the particular clause which gives liberty to destroy the freedom of the press.

Elliot, vol. 3, p. 469.

2.2.2.4.c **June 24, 1788**

Mr. DAWSON. . . .

That sacred palladium of liberty, the freedom of the press, (the influence of which is so great that it is the opinion of the ablest writers that no country can remain long in slavery where it is unrestrained,) has not been expressed; nor are the liberties of the people ascertained and protected by any declaration of rights; that inestimable privilege, (the most important which freemen can enjoy,) the trial by jury in all civil cases, has not been guarded by the system; — and while they have been inattentive to these all-important considerations, they have made provision for the introduction of standing armies in time of peace. These, sir, ever have been used as the grand machines to suppress the liberties of the people, and will ever awaken the jealousy of republicans, so long as liberty is dear, and tyranny odious, to mankind.

Elliot, vol. 3, pp. 610–11.

2.2.3 PHILADELPHIA CONVENTION

2.2.3.1 **Proposal by Pinckney, May 29, 1787**

"Art. VI. . . . The legislature of the United States shall pass no law on the subject of religion; nor touching or abridging the liberty of the press; [n]or shall the privilege of the writ of habeas corpus ever be suspended, except in case of rebellion or invasion.

Elliot, vol. 5, pp. 130–31.

2.2.3.2 **Proposal by Pinckney, August 20, 1787**

In Convention. — Mr. PINCKNEY submitted to the House, in order to be referred to the committee of detail, the following propositions: —

. . .

"The liberty of the press shall be inviolably preserved.

Elliot, vol. 5, p. 445.

2.2.3.3 **Proposal by Pinckney & Gerry, September 14, 1787**

Mr. PINCKNEY and Mr. GERRY moved to insert a declaration, "that the liberty of the press should be inviolably observed."

Mr. SHERMAN. It is unnecessary. The power of the Congress does not extend to the press.

On the question, it passed in the negative.

Elliot, vol. 5, p. 545.

2.2.4 NEWSPAPERS AND PAMPHLETS

2.2.4.1 **A Citizen of New-York: An Address to the People of the State of New York, April 15, 1787**

We are told, among other strange things, that the liberty of the press is left insecure by the proposed Constitution, and yet that Constitution says neither more nor less about it, than the Constitution of the State of New York does. We are told that it deprives us of trial by jury, whereas the fact is, that it expressly securesit in certain cases, and takes it away in none — it is absurd to construe the silenceof this, or of our own Constitution, relative to a great number of our rights, into a total extinction of them — silence and blank paper neither grant nor take away anything. Complaints are also made that the proposed Constitution is not accompanied by a bill of rights; and yet they who would make these complaints, know and are content that no bill of rights accompanied the Constitution of this State. In days and countries, where Monarchs and their subjects were frequently disputing about prerogative and privileges, the latter often found it necessary, as it were to run out the line between them, and oblige the former to admit by solemn acts, called bills of rights, that certain enumerated rights belonged to the people, and were not comprehended in the royal prerogative. But thank God we have no such disputes — we have no Monarchs to contend with, or demand admission from — the proposed Government is to be the government of the people — all its officers are to be their officers, and to exercise no rights but such as the people commit to them. The Constitution only serves to point out that part of the people's business, which they think proper by it to refer to the management of the persons therein designated — those persons are to receive that business to manage, not for themselves, and as their own, but as agents and overseers for the people to whom they are constantly responsible, and by whom only they are to be appointed.

Kaminski & Saladino, vol. 17, pp. 112–13.

2.2.4.2 George Mason, Objections to the Constitution, October 4, 1787

Under their own construction of the general Clause at the End of the enumerated powers, the Congress may grant Monopolies in Trade and Commerce, constitute new Crimes, inflict unusual and severe Punishments, and extend their power as far as they shall think proper; so that the State Legislatures have no Security for the Powers now presumed to remain to them; or the People for their Rights.

There is no declaration of any kind for preserving the Liberty of the Press, the Tryal by Jury in civil Causes; nor against the Danger of standing Armys in time of Peace.

Storing, vol. 2, p. 13.

2.2.4.3 James Wilson, Speech at a Meeting in Philadelphia, October 6, 1787

. . . This distinction being recognized, will furnish an answer to those who think the omission of a bill of rights, a defect in the proposed constitution: for it would have been superfluous and absurd, to have stipulated with a foederal body of our own creation, that we should enjoy those privileges, of which we are not divested either by the intention or the act that has brought that body into existence. For instance, the liberty of the press, which has been a copious subject of declamation and opposition: what controul can proceed from the foederal government, to shackle or destroy that sacred palladium of national freedom? If, indeed, a power similar to that which has been granted for the regulation of commerce, had been granted to regulate literary publications, it would have been as necessary to stipulate that the liberty of the press should be preserved inviolate, as that the impost should be general in its operation.

Kaminski & Saladino, vol. 13, pp. 339–40.

2.2.4.4 The Federal Farmer, No. 4, October 12, 1787

I confess I do not see in what cases the congress can, with any pretence of right, make a law to suppress the freedom of the press; though I am not clear, that congress is restrained from laying any duties whatever on printing, and from laying duties particularly heavy on certain pieces printed, and perhaps congress may require large bonds for the payment of these duties. Should the printer say, the freedom of the press was secured by the constitution of the state in which he lived, congress might, and perhaps, with great propriety, answer, that the federal constitution is the only compact existing between them and the people; in this compact the people have named no others, and therefore congress, in exercising the powers assigned them, and in making laws to carry them into execution, are restrained by nothing beside the federal constitution, any more than a state legislature is restrained by a compact between the magistrates and people of a county, city, or town of which the people, in forming the state constitution, have taken no notice.

It is not my object to enumerate rights of inconsiderable importance; but there are others, no doubt, which ought to be established as a fundamental part of the national system.

Storing, vol. 2, p. 250.

2.2.4.5   An Old Whig, No. 1, October 12, 1787

. . . Should the freedom of the press be restrained on the subject of politics, there is no doubt it will soon after be restrained on all other subjects, religious as well as civil. . . .

[Philadelphia] Independent Gazetteer, Kaminski & Saladino,
vol. 13, p. 378.

2.2.4.6   Centinel, No. 2, October 24, 1787

FRIENDS, COUNTRYMEN, *and* FELLOW-CITIZENS, As long as the liberty of the press continues unviolated, and the people have the right of expressing and publishing their sentiments upon every public measure, it is next to impossible to enslave a free nation. The state of society must be very corrupt and base indeed, when the people in possession of such a monitor as the press, can be induced to exchange the heavenborn blessings of liberty for the galling chains of despotism. — Men of an aspiring and tyrannical disposition, sensible of this truth, have ever been inimical to the press, and have considered the shackling of it, as the first step towards the accomplishment of their hateful dominaton, and the entire suppression of all liberty of public discussion, as necessary to its support. — For even a standing army, that grand engine of oppression, if it were as numerous as the abilities of any nation could maintain, would not be equal to the purposes of despotism over an enlightenend [*sic*] people.

The abolition of that grand palladium of freedom, the liberty of the press, in the proposed plan of government, and the conduct of its authors, and patrons, is a striking exemplification of these observations. The reason assigned for the omission of a *bill of rights,* securing the *liberty of the press,* and *other invaluable personal rights,* is an insult on the understanding of the people.

. . .

Mr. *Wilson* asks, "What controul can proceed from the federal government to shackle or destroy that *sacred palladium* of national freedom, the *liberty of the press?*" What! — Cannot Congress, when possessed of the immense authority

proposed to be devolved, restrain the printers, and put them under regulation. —
Recollect that the omnipotence of the federal legislature over the State establishments is recognized by a special article, viz. — "that this Constitution, and the
laws of the United States which shall be made in pursuance thereof, and all treaties
made, or which shall be made, under the authority of the United States, shall be
the *supreme law* of the land; and the judges in every State shall be bound thereby,
any thing in the *Constitutions* or laws of any State to the contrary notwithstanding." — After such a declaration, what security does the *Constitutions* of the
several States afford for the *liberty of the press and other invaluable personal
rights,* not provided for by the new plan? — Does not this sweeping clause subject
every thing to the controul of Congress?

. . .

The new plan, it is true, does propose to secure the people of the benefit of
personal liberty by the *habeas corpus*; and trial by jury for all crimes, except in
case of impeachment: but there is no declaration, . . . that *the liberty of the press
be held sacred;* . . . .
[Philadelphia] Freeman's Journal, Kaminski & Saladino,
vol. 13, pp. 457, 460, 466.

2.2.4.7 Timoleon, November 1, 1787

. . .

After some judicious reflections on this subject, which tended to shew the necessity of the most plain and unequivocal language in the all important business of
constituting government, which necessarily conveying great powers, is always
liable (from the natural tendency of power to corrupt the human heart and deprave the head) to great abuse; by perverse and subtle arguments calculated to
extend dominion over all things and all men. One of the club supposed the
following case: — A gentleman, *in the line of his profession* is appointed a *judge* of
the supreme court under the new Constitution, and the *rulers,* finding that the
rights of conscience and the freedom of the press were exercised in such a manner,
by *preaching* and *printing* as to be troublesome to the new government — which
event would probably happen, if the rulers finding themselves possessed of great
power, should so use it as to oppress and injure the community. — In this state of
things the *judge* is called upon, *in the line of his profession,* to give his opinion —
whether the *new Constitution* admitted of a legislative act to *suppress the rights of
conscience,* and *violate the liberty of the press?* The answer of the learned *judge* is
conceived in didactic mode, and expressed in learned phrase; thus, — In the 8th
section of the first article of the *new Constitution,* the Congress have power given
to lay and collect taxes for the general welfare of the United States. By this power,
the right of taxing is co-extensive with the *general welfare,* and the *general welfare*
is as unlimitted as actions and things are that may disturb or benefit that general
welfare. A right being given to *tax* for the general welfare, necessarily includes the
right of judging what is for the general welfare, and a right of judging what is for
the general welfare, as *necessarily* includes a power of protecting, defending, and
promoting it by all such laws and means as are fitted to that end; for, qui dat finem
dat media ad finem necessaria, who gives the end gives the means necessary to

obtain the end. The Constitution must be so construed as not to involve an absurdity, which would clearly follow from allowing the end and denying the means. A right of *taxing* for the general welfare being the highest and most important mode of providing for it, cannot be supposed to exclude inferior modes of effecting the same purpose, because the rule of law is, that, omne majus contint in se minus.

From hence it clearly results, that, if *preachers* and *printers* are troublesome to the new government; and that in the opinion of its rulers, it shall be for the general welfare to restrain or suppress both the one and the other, it may be done consistently with the new Constitution. And that this was the opinion of the community when they consented to it, is evident from this consideration; that although the all comprehending power of the new legislature is fixed, by its acts being made the *supreme law* of the land, any thing in the *Constitutions* or laws of any state to the contrary notwithstanding: Yet no *express* declaration in favor of the *rights of conscience* or *liberty* of the *press* is to be found in the new Constitution, as we see was carefully done in the *Constitutions* of the states composing this union — Shewing clearly, that what was *then* thought necessary to be specially reserved from the pleasure of power, is *now* designed to be yielded to its will.

A grave old gentleman of the club, who had sat with his head reclined on his hand, listening in pensive mood to the argument of the *judge,* said, "I verily believe, that neither the logic or the law of that opinion will be hereafter doubted by the professors of power, who, through the history of human nature, have been for enlarging the sphere of their authority. And thus the dearest rights of men and the best security of civil liberty may be sacrificed by the sophism of a lawyer, who, Carneades like, can to day shew that to be necessary, before the people, which to-morrow he can likewise shew to be unnecessary and useless — For which reason the sagacious Cato advised, that such a man should immediately be sent from the city, as a person dangerous to the morals of the people and to society." The old gentleman continued, "I now plainly see the necessity of express declarations and reservations in favor of the great, unalienable rights of mankind, to prevent the oppressive and wicked extention of power to the ruin of human liberty. For the opinion above stated, absolutely refutes the sophistry of 'that being retained which is not given,' where the words conveying power admit of the most extensive construction that language can reach to, or the mind conceive, as is the case in this new Constitution. By which we have already seen how logically it may be proved, that both *religion* and the *press* can be made to bend before the views of power. . . .

New York Journal, Kaminski & Saladino, vol. 13, pp. 534–36.

2.2.4.8 An Old Whig, No. 5, November 1, 1787

It is needless to repeat the necessity of securing other personal rights in the forming a new government. The same argument which proves the necessity of securing one of them shews also the necessity of securing others. Without a bill of rights we are totally insecure in all of them; and no man can promise himself with any degree of certainty that his posterity will enjoy the inestimable blessings of liberty of conscience, of freedom of speech and of writing and publishing their thoughts on public matters, of trial by jury, of holding themselves, their houses and papers free from seizure and search upon general suspicion or general warrants; or in short that they will be secured in the enjoyment of life, liberty and property without depending on the will and pleasure of their rulers.

[Philadelphia] Independent Gazetteer, Kaminski & Saladino, vol. 13, p. 541.

2.2.4.9 Cincinnatus, No. 1, November 1, 1787

You instance, Sir, the liberty of the press; which you would persuade us, is in *no* danger, though not secured, because there is no express power granted to regulate literary publications. But you surely know, Sir, that where general powers are expressly granted, the particular ones comprehended within them, must also be granted. For instance, the proposed Congress are empowered — to define and punish offences against the law of the nations — mark well, Sir, if you please — to *define* and punish. Will you, will any one say, can any one even think that does not comprehend a power to define and declare all publications from the press against the conduct of government, in making treaties, or in any other foreign transactions, an offence against the law of nations? If there should ever be an influential president, or arbitrary senate, who do not choose that their transactions with foreign powers should be discussed or examined in the public prints, they will easily find pretexts to prevail upon the other branch to concur with them, in restraining what it may please them to call — the licentiousness of the press. And this may be, even without the concurrence of the representative of the people; because the president and senate are empowered to make treaties, and these treaties are declared the supreme law of the land.

What use they will make of this power, is not now the question. Certain it is, that such power is given, and that power is not restrained by any declaration — that the liberty of the press, which even you term, the sacred palladium of national freedom, shall be forever free and inviolable. I have proved that the power of restraining the press, is necessarily involved in the unlimited power of defining offences, or of making treaties, which are to be the supreme law of the land. You acknowledge, that it is not expressly excepted, and consequently it is at the mercy of the powers to be created by this constitution.

New York Journal, Storing, vol. 6, pp. 8–9.

2.2.4.10 Cincinnatus, No. 2, November 8, 1787

I have proved, sir, that not only some power is given in the constitution to restrain, and even to subject the press, but that it is a power totally unlimited; and may certainly annihilate the freedom of the press, and convert it from being the palladium of liberty to become an engine of imposition and tyranny. It is an easy step from restraining the press to making it place the worst actions of government in so favorable a light, that we may groan under tyranny and oppression without knowing from whence it comes.

But you comfort us, by saying, — "there is no reason to suspect so popular a privilege will be neglected." The wolf, in the fable, said as much to the sheep, when he was persuading them to trust him as their protector, and to dismiss their guardian dogs. Do you indeed suppose, Mr. Wilson, that if the people give up their privileges to these new rulers they will render them back again to the people? Indeed, sir, you should not trifle upon a question so serious — You would not have us to suspect any ill. If we throw away suspicion — to be sure, the thing will go smoothly enough, and we shall deserve to continue a free, respectable, and happy people. Suspicion shackles rulers and prevents good government. All great and honest politicians, *like yourself*, have reprobated it. Lord Mansfield is a great authority against it, and has often treated it as the worst of libels. But such men as Milton, Sidney, Locke, Montesquieu, and Trenchard, have thought it essential to the preservation of liberty against the artful and persevering encroachments of those with whom power is trusted. You will pardon me, sir, if I pay some respect to these opinions, and wish that the freedom of the press may be *previously* secured as a *constitutional and unalienable right*, and not left to the precarious care of popular privileges which may or may not influence our new rulers. You are fond of, and happy at, quaint expressions of this kind in your observation — that a formal declaration would have done harm, by implying, that some degree of power was given when we undertook to define its extent. This thought has really a brilliancy in it of the first water. But permit me, sir, to ask, why any saving clause was admitted into this constitution, when you tell us, every thing is reserved that is not expressly given? Why is it said in sec. 9th, "The migration or importation of such persons as any of the states now existing shall think proper to admit, shall not be prohibited by Congress, prior to the year, 1808." There is no power expressly given to the Congress to prohibit migrations and importations. By your doctrine then they could have none, and it was, according to your own position, nugatory to declare they should not do it. Which are we to believe, sir, — you or the constitution? The text, or the comment. If the former, we must be persuaded, that in the contemplation of the framers of the constitution implied powers were given, otherwise the exception would have been an absurdity. If we listen to you we must affirm it to be a distinctive characteristic of the constitution, that — "what is not expressly given is reserved." Such are the inconsistencies into which men over ingenuous, like yourself, are betrayed in advocating a bad cause. Perhaps four months more consideration of the subject, would have rendered you more guarded.

New York Journal, Storing, vol. 6, pp. 10–11.

2.2.4.11 A Countryman, No. 2, November 22, 1787

Of a very different nature, tho' only one degree better than the other reasoning, is all that sublimity of *nonsense* and *alarm*, that has been thundered against it in every shape of *metaphoric terror*, on the subject of a *bill* of *rights*, the *liberty* of the *press, rights of conscience, rights of taxation and election, trials in the vicinity, freedom of speech, trial by jury,* and a *standing army*. These last are undoubtedly important points, much too important to depend on mere paper protection. For, guard such privileges by the strongest expressions, still if you leave the legislative and executive power in the hands of those who are or may be disposed to deprive you of them — you are but slaves. Make an absolute monarch — give him the supreme authority, and guard as much as you will by bills of rights, your liberty of the press, and trial by jury; — he will find means either to take them from you, or to render them useless.

. . .

On examining the new proposed constitution, there can not be a question, but that there is authority enough lodged in the proposed federal Congress, if abused, to do the greatest injury. And it is perfectly idle to object to it, that there is no bill of rights, or to propose to add to it a provision that a trial by jury shall in no case be omitted, or to patch it up by adding a stipulation in favor of the press, or to guard it by removing the paltry objection to the right of Congress to regulate the time and manner of elections.

New Haven Gazette, Kaminski & Saladino, vol. 14, pp. 172–74.

2.2.4.12 Landholder, No. 6, December 10, 1787

There is no declaration of any kind to preserve the liberty of the press, &c. Nor is liberty of conscience, or of matrimony, or of burial of the dead; it is enough that congress have no power to prohibit either, and can have no temptation. This objection is answered in that the states have all the power originally, and congress have only what the states grant them.

Connecticut Courant, Kaminski & Saladino, vol. 14, p. 401.

2.2.4.13 The Federal Farmer, No. 6, December 25, 1787

The following, I think, will be allowed to be unalienable or fundamental rights in the United States: —

No man, demeaning himself peaceably, shall be molested on account of his religion or mode of worship — The people have a right to hold and enjoy their property according to known standing laws, and which cannot be taken from them without their consent, or the consent of their representatives; and whenever taken in the pressing urgencies of government, they are to receive a reasonable compensation for it — Individual security consists in having free recourse to the laws — The people are subject to no laws or taxes not assented to by their representatives constitutionally assembled — They are at all times intitled to the benefits of the writ of habeas corpus, the trial by jury in criminal and civil causes — They have a right, when charged, to a speedy trial in the vicinage; to be heard by themselves or counsel, not to be compelled to furnish evidence against themselves, to have witnesses face to face, and to confront their adversaries before the judge — No man is held to answer a crime charged upon him till it be substantially described to him; and he is subject to no unreasonable searches or seizures of his person, papers or effects — The people have a right to assemble in an orderly manner, and petition the government for a redress of wrongs — The freedom of the press ought not to be restrained — No emoluments, except for actual service — No hereditary honors, or orders of nobility, ought to be allowed — The military ought to be subordinate to the civil authority, and no soldier be quartered on the citizens without their consent — The militia ought always to be armed and disciplined, and the usual defence of the country — The supreme power is in the people, and power delegated ought to return to them at stated periods, and frequently — The legislative, executive, and judicial powers, ought always to be kept distinct — others perhaps might be added.   Storing, vol. 2, p. 262.

2.2.4.14. The Federal Farmer, No. 16, January 20, 1788

All parties apparently agree, that the freedom of the press is a fundamental right, and ought not to be restrained by any taxes, duties, or in any manner whatever. Why should not the people, in adopting a federal constitution, declare this, even if there are only doubts about it. But, say the advocates, all powers not given are reserved: — true; but the great question is, are not powers given, in the exercise of which this right may be destroyed? The people's or the printers claim to a free press, is founded on the fundamental laws, that is, compacts, and state constitutions, made by the people. The people, who can annihilate or alter those constitutions, can annihilate or limit this right. This may be done by giving general powers, as well as by using particular words. No right claimed under a state constitution, will avail against a law of the union, made in pursuance of the federal constitution: therefore the question is, what laws will congress have a right to make by the constitution of the union, and particularly touching the press? By art. 1. sect. 8. congress will have power to lay and collect taxes, duties, imposts and excise. By this congress will clearly have power to lay and collect all kind of taxes whatever — taxes on houses, lands, polls, industry, merchandize, &c. — taxes on deeds, bonds, and all written instruments — on writs, pleas, and all judicial proceedings, on licences, naval officers papers, &c. on newspapers, advertisements, &c. and to require bonds of the naval officers, clerks, printers, &c. to account for the taxes that may become due on papers that go through their hands. Printing, like all other business, must cease when taxed beyond its profits; and it appears to me, that a power to tax the press at discretion, is a power to destroy or restrain the freedom of it. There may be other powers given, in the exercise of which this freedom may be effected; and certainly it is of too much importance to be left thus liable to be taxed, and constantly to constructions and inferences. A free press is the channel of communication as to mercantile and public affairs; by means of it the people in large countries ascertain each others sentiments; are enabled to unite, and become formidable to those rulers who adopt improper measures. Newspapers may sometimes be the vehicles of abuse, and of many things not true; but these are but small inconveniences, in my mind, among many advantages. A celebrated writer, I have several times quoted, speaking in high terms of the English liberties, says, "lastly the key stone was put to the arch, by the final establishment of the freedom of the press."   Storing, vol. 2, pp. 329–30.

2.2.4.15 Aristides' Remarks on the Proposed Plan, January 31, 1788

By their scheme, however, thus deeply concerted, the house of representatives is to be chosen by the people once in two years; and if they have acted so as to warrant any reasonable apprehension of their designs, it will be easy, at any time, to prevent their election. The truth is, that very few of them either wish to be elected, or would consent to serve, either in that house, or in the senate. I have exercised my imagination to devise in what manner they, or any other men, supposing them to bear full sway in both houses, could erect this imaginary fabric of power. I request any person to point out any law, or system of laws, that could be possibly contrived for that purpose, obtain the final assent of each branch, and be carried into effect, contrary to the interests and wishes of a free, intelligent, prying people, accustomed to the most unbounded freedom of inquiry. To begin by an attempt to restrain the press, instead of promoting their designs, would be the most effectual thing to prevent them.

. . .

Whilst mankind shall believe freedom to be better than slavery; whilst our lands shall be generally distributed, and not held by a few insolent barons, on the debasing terms of vassallage; whilst we shall teach our children to read and write; whilst the liberty of the press, that grand palladium, which tyrants are compelled to respect, shall remain; whilst a spark of public love shall animate even a small part of the people; whilst even self-love shall be the general ruling principle; so long will it be impossible for an aristocracy to arise from the proposed plan. — Should Heaven, in its wrath, inflict blindness on the people of America; should they reject this fair offer of permanent safety and happiness; — to predict, what species of government shall at last spring from disorder, is beyond the short reach of political foresight.

Kaminski & Saladino, vol. 15, pp. 522–23, 548.

2.2.4.16 A Columbian Patriot, February 1788

2. There is no security in the profered system, either for the rights of conscience, or the liberty of the Press: Despotism usually while it is gaining ground, will suffer men to think, say, or write what they please; but when once established, if it is thought necessary to subserve the purposes of arbitrary power, the most unjust restrictions may take place in the first instance, and an *imprimator* [*sic*] on the Press in the next, may silence the complaints, and forbid the most decent remonstrances of an injured and oppressed people.

Kaminski & Saladino, vol. 16, p. 279.

2.2.4.17 Hugh Williamson, February 25–27, 1788

We have been told that the Liberty of the Press is not secured by the New Constitution. Be pleased to examine the plan, and you will find that the Liberty of the Press and the laws of Mahomet are equally affected by it. The New Government is to have the power of protecting literary property; the very power which you have by a special act delegated to the present Congress. There was a time in England, when neither book, pamphlet, nor paper could be published without a license from Government. That restraint was finally removed in the year 1694 and by such removal, their press became perfectly free, for it is not under the restraint of any license. Certainly the new Government can have no power to impose restraints. The citizens of the United States have no more occasion for a second Declaration of Rights, than they have for a section in favor of the press. Their rights, in the several States, have long since been explained and secured by particular declarations, which make a part of their several Constitutions. It is granted, and perfectly understood, that under the Government of the Assemblies of the

States, and under the Government of the Congress, every right is reserved to the individual, which he has not expressly delegated to this, or that Legislature. . . .

[New York] *Daily Advertiser*, Kaminski & Saladino, vol. 16, p. 202.

2.2.4.18   A Plebeian, Spring 1788

"We are told, (says he [John Jay]) among other strange things, that the liberty of the press is left insecure by the proposed constitution, and yet that constitution says neither more nor less about it, than the constitution of the state of New-York does. We are told it deprives us of trial by jury, whereas the fact is, that it expressly secures it in certain cases, and takes it away in none, &c. it is absurd to construe the silence of this, or of our own constitution relative to a great number of our rights into a total extinction of them; silence and a blank paper neither grant nor take away anything."

It may be a strange thing to this author to hear the people of America anxious for the preservation of their rights, but those who understand the true principles of liberty, are no strangers to their importance. The man who supposes the constitution, in any part of it, is like a blank piece of paper, has very erroneous ideas of it. He may be assured every clause has a meaning, and many of them such extensive meaning, as would take a volume to unfold. The suggestion, that the liberty of the press is secure, because it is not in express words spoken of in the constitution, and that the trial by jury is not taken away, because it is not said in so many words and letters it is so, is puerile and unworthy of a man who pretends to reason. We contend, that by the indefinite powers granted to the general government, the liberty of the press may be restricted by duties, &c. and therefore the constitution ought to have stipulated for its freedom. The trial by jury, in all civil cases is left at the discretion of the general government, except in the supreme court on the appellate jurisdiction, and in this I affirm it is taken away, not by express words, but by fair and legitimate construction and inference; for the supreme court have expressly given them an appellate jurisdiction, in every case to which their powers extend (with two or three exceptions) both as to *law and fact*. The court are the judges; every man in the country, who has served as a juror, knows, that there is a distinction between the court and the jury, and that the lawyers in their pleading, make the distinction. If the court, upon appeals, are to determine both the law and the fact, there is no room for a jury, and the right of trial in this mode is taken away.

The author manifests equal levity in referring to the constitution of this state, to shew that it was useless to stipulate for the liberty of the press, or to insert a bill of rights in the constitution. With regard to the first, it is perhaps an imperfection in our constitution that the liberty of the press is not expressly reserved; but still there was not equal necessity of making this reservation in our State as in the general Constitution, for the common and statute law of England, and the laws of the colony are established, in which this privilege is fully defined and secured. It is true, a bill of rights is not prefixed to our constitution, as it is in that of some of the states; but still this author knows, that many essential rights are reserved in the body of it; and I will promise, that every opposer of this system will be satisfied, if the stipulations that they contend for are agreed to, whether they are prefixed, affixed, or inserted in the body of the constitution, and that they will not contend which way this is done, if it be but done.

Storing, vol. 6, pp. 144–45.

2.2.4.19 Marcus, No. 4, March 12, 1788

VIIIth Objection.

"Under their own construction of the general clause at the end of the enumerated powers, the Congress may grant monopolies in trade and commerce, constitute new crimes, inflict unusual and severe punishments, and extend their power as far as they shall think proper; so that the State Legislatures have no security for the powers now presumed to remain to them: or the people for their rights. There is no declaration of any kind for preserving the liberty of the press, the trial by jury in civil causes, nor against the danger of standing armies in time of peace."

. . .

Answer.

The Liberty of the Press is always a grand topic for declamation, but the future Congress will have no other authority over this than to secure to authors for a limited time an exclusive privilege of publishing their works. This authority has been long exercised in England, where the press is as free as among ourselves or in any country in the world, and surely such an encouragement to genius is no, restraint on the liberty of the press, since men are allowed to publish what they please of their own; and so far as this may be deemed a restraint upon others it is certainly a reasonable one, and can be attended with no danger of copies not being sufficiently multiplied, because the interest of the proprietor will always induce him to publish a quantity fully equal to the demand — besides that such encouragement may give birth to many excellent writings which would otherwise have never appeared. If the Congress should exercise any other power over the press than this, they will do it without any warrant from this Constitution, and must answer for it as for any other act of tyranny.

Norfolk and Portsmouth Journal, Kaminski & Saladino, vol. 16, pp. 379–82.

2.2.4.20 Benjamin Franklin, An Account of the Supremest Court of Judicature in Pennsylvania, viz., the Court of the Press, September 12, 1789

Power of this Court.

IT may receive and promulgate accusations of all kinds, against all persons and characters among the citizens of the State, and even against all inferior courts; and may judge, sentence, and condemn to infamy, not only private individuals, but public bodies, &c., with or without inquiry or hearing, *at the court's discretion.*

In whose Favour and for whose Emolument this Court is established.

In favour of about one citizen in five hundred, who, by education or practice in scribbling, has acquired a tolerable style as to grammar and construction, so as to bear printing; or who is possessed of a press and a few types. This five hundredth part of the citizens have the privilege of accusing and abusing the other four hundred and ninety-nine parts at their pleasure; or they may hire out their pens and press to others for that purpose.

Practice of the Court.

It is not governed by any of the rules of common courts of law. The accused is allowed no grand jury to judge of the truth of the accusation before it is publicly made, nor is the Name of the Accuser made known to him nor has he an Opportunity of confronting the Witnesses against him; for they are kept in the dark, as in the Spanish Court of Inquisition. Nor is there any petty Jury of his Peers, sworn to try the Truth of the Charges. The Proceedings are also sometimes so rapid, that an honest, good Citizen may find himself suddenly and unexpectedly accus'd, and in the same Morning judg'd and condemn'd, and sentence pronounc'd against him, that he is a *Rogue* and a *Villain*. Yet, if an officer of this court receives the slightest check for misconduct in this his office, he claims immediately the rights of a free citizen by the constitution, and demands to know his accuser, to confront the witnesses, and to have a fair trial of his peers.

The Foundation of its Authority.

It is said to be founded on an Article of the Constitution of the State, which established *the Liberty of the Press*; a Liberty which every Pennsylvanian would fight and die for; tho' few of us, I believe, have distinct Ideas of its Nature and Extent. It seems indeed somewhat like the *Liberty of the Press* that Felons have, by the Common Law of England, before Conviction, that is, to be Press'd to death or hanged. If by the *Liberty of the Press* were understood merely the Liberty of discussing the Propriety of Public Measures and political opinions, let us have as much of it as you please: But if it means the Liberty of affronting, calumniating, and defaming one another, I, for my part, own myself willing to part with my Share of it when our Legislators shall please so to alter the Law, and shall cheerfully consent to exchange my *Liberty* of Abusing others for the *Privilege* of not being abus'd myself.

By Whom this Court is commissioned or constituted.

It is not by any Commission from the Supreme Executive Council, who might previously judge of the Abilities, Integrity, Knowledge, &c. of the Persons to be appointed to this great Trust, of deciding upon the Characters and good Fame of the Citizens; for this Court is above that Council, and may *accuse, judge,* and *condemn* it, at pleasure. Nor is it hereditary, as in the Court of *Dernier Resort,* in the Peerage of England. But any Man who can procure Pen, Ink, and Paper, with a Press, and a huge pair of BLACKING BALLS, may commissionate himself; and his court is immediately established in the plenary Possession and exercise of its rights. For, if you make the least complaint of the *judge's* conduct, he daubs his blacking balls in your face wherever he meets you; and, besides tearing your private character to flitters, marks you out for the odium of the public, as an *enemy to the liberty of the press.*

Of the natural Support of these Courts.

Their support is founded in the depravity of such minds, as have not been mended by religion, nor improved by good education;

"There is a Lust in Man no Charm can tame,
Of loudly publishing his Neighbour's Shame."

113

Hence;

> "On Eagle's Wings immortal Scandals fly,
> While virtuous Actions are but born and die."
>
> DRYDEN

Whoever feels pain in hearing a good character of his neighbour, will feel a pleasure in the reverse. And of those who, despairing to rise into distinction by their virtues, are happy if others can be depressed to a level with themselves, there are a number sufficient in every great town to maintain one of these courts by their subscriptions. A shrewd observer once said, that, in walking the streets in a slippery morning, one might see where the good-natured people lived by the ashes thrown on the ice before their doors; probably he would have formed a different conjecture of the temper of those whom he might find engaged in such a subscription.

Of the Checks proper to be established against the Abuse of Power in these Courts.

Hitherto there are none. But since so much has been written and published on the federal Constitution, and the necessity of checks in all other parts of good government has been so clearly and learnedly explained, I find myself so far enlightened as to suspect some check may be proper in this part also; but I have been at a loss to imagine any that may not be construed an infringement of the sacred *liberty of the press.* At length, however, I think I have found one that, instead of diminishing general liberty, shall augment it; which is, by restoring to the people a species of liberty, of which they have been deprived by our laws, I mean the *liberty of cudgel.* In the rude state of society prior to the existence of laws, if one man gave another ill language, the affronted person would return it by a box on the ear, and, if repeated, by a good drubbing; and this without offending against any law. But now the right of making such returns is denied, and they are punished as breaches of the peace; while the right of abusing seems to remain in full force, the laws made against it being rendered ineffectual by the *liberty of the press.*

My proposal then is, to leave the liberty of the press untouched, to be exercised in its full extent, force, and vigor; but to permit the *liberty of the cudgel* to go with it *pari passu.* Thus, my fellow-citizens, if an impudent writer attacks your reputation, dearer to you perhaps than your life, and puts his name to the charge, you may go to him as openly and break his head. If he conceals himself behind the printer, and you can nevertheless discover who he is, you may in like manner way-lay him in the night, attack him behind, and give him a good drubbing. Thus far goes my project as to *private* resentment and retribution. But if the public should ever happen to be affronted, *as it ought to be,* with the conduct of such writers, I would not advise proceeding immediately to these extremities; but that we should in moderation content ourselves with tarring and feathering, and tossing them in a blanket.

If, however, it should be thought that this proposal of mine may disturb the public peace, I would then humbly recommend to our legislators to take up the consideration of both liberties, that of the *press,* and that of the *cudgel,* and by an explicit law mark their extent and limits; and, at the same time that they secure the person of a citizen from *assaults,* they would likewise provide for the security of his *reputation.*

Writings of Benjamin Franklin, Albert Henry Smith, ed.
(New York: Macmillan, 1907), vol. 10, pp. 36–40.

2.2.5 LETTERS AND DIARIES

2.2.5.1 Thomas Jefferson to Edward Carrington, January 16, 1787

The tumults in America, I expected would have produced in Europe an unfavorable opinion of our political state. But it has not. On the contrary, the small effect of those tumults seems to have given more confidence in the firmness of our governments. The interposition of the people themselves on the side of government has had a great effect on the opinion here. I am persuaded myself that the good sense of the people will always be found to be the best army. They may be led astray for a moment, but will soon correct themselves. The people are the only censors of their governors: and even their errors will tend to keep these to the true principles of their institution. To punish these errors too severely would be to suppress the only safeguard of the public liberty. The way to prevent these irregular interpositions of the people is to give them full information of their affairs thro' the channel of the public papers, and to contrive that those papers should penetrate the whole mass of the people. The basis of our governments being the opinion of the people, the very first object should be to keep that right; and were it left to me to decide whether we should have a government without newspapers, or newspapers without a government, I should not hesitate a moment to prefer the latter. But I should mean that every man should receive these papers and be capable of reading them. I am convinced that those societies (as the Indians) which live without government enjoy in their general mass an infinitely greater degree of happiness than those who live under European governments. Among the former, public opinion is in the place of law, and restrains morals as powerfully as laws ever did any where. Among the latter, under pretence of governing they have divided their nations into two classes, wolves and sheep. I do not exaggerate. This is a true picture of Europe. Cherish therefore the spirit of our people, and keep alive their attention. Do not be too severe upon their errors, but reclaim them by enlightening them. If once they become inattentive to the public affairs, you and I, and Congress, and Assemblies, judges and governors shall all become wolves. It seems to be the law of our general nature, in spite of individual exceptions; and experience declares that man is the only animal which devours his own kind, for I can apply no milder term to the governments of Europe, and to the general prey of the rich on the poor.

Boyd, vol. 11, pp. 48–49.

2.2.5.2 Richard Henry Lee to Samuel Adams, October 27, 1787

. . . Because Independent States are in the same relation to each other as Individuals are with respect to uncreated government. So that if reservations were necessary in one case, they are equally necessary in the other. But the futility of this distinction appears from the conduct of the Convention itself, for they have made several reservations — every one of which proves the Rule in Conventional ideas to be, that what was not reserved was given — For example, they have reserved from their Legislature a power to prevent the importation of Slaves for 20 years, and also from Creating Titles. But they have no reservation in favor of the Press, Rights of Conscience, Trial by Jury in Civil Cases, or Common Law securities.

As if these were of less importance to the happiness of Mankind than the making of Lords, or the importations of Slaves! . . .

Kaminski & Saladino, vol. 13, pp. 484–85.

2.2.5.3 Thomas Jefferson to James Madison, December 20, 1787

. . . There are other good things of less moment. I will now add what I do not like. First the omission of a bill of rights providing clearly and without the aid of sophisms for freedom of religion, freedom of the press, protection against standing armies, restriction against monopolies, the eternal and unremitting force of the habeas corpus laws, and trials by jury in all matters of fact triable by the laws of the land and not by the law of Nations.

Boyd, vol. 12, p. 440.

2.2.5.4 Thomas Jefferson to William Stephens Smith, February 2, 1788

. . . But I own it astonishes me to find such a change wrought in the opinions of our countrymen since I left them, as that threefourths of them should be contented to live under a system which leaves to their governors the power of taking from them the trial by jury in civil cases, freedom of religion, freedom of the press, freedom of commerce, the habeas corpus laws, and of yoking them with a standing army. This is a degeneracy in the principles of liberty to which I had given four centuries instead of four years.

Boyd, vol. 12, p. 558.

2.2.5.5 Thomas Jefferson to Alexander Donald, February 7, 1788

. . . By a declaration of rights I mean one which shall stipulate freedom of religion, freedom of the press, freedom of commerce against monopolies, trial by juries in all cases, no suspensions of the habeas corpus, no standing armies. These are fetters against doing evil which no honest government should decline.

Boyd, vol. 12, p. 571.

2.2.5.6 Thomas Jefferson to C. W. F. Dumas, February 12, 1788

. . . Besides other objections of less moment, she will insist on annexing a bill of rights to the new constitution, i.e. a bill wherein the government shall declare that . . . 2. Printing presses free.

Boyd, vol. 12, p. 583.

2.2.5.7 Thomas Jefferson to Francis Hopkinson, March 13, 1789

. . . What I disapproved from the first moment also was the want of a bill of rights to guard liberty against the legislative as well as executive branches of the government, that is to say to secure freedom in religion, freedom of the press, freedom from monopolies, freedom from unlawful imprisonment, freedom from a permanent military, and a trial by jury in all cases determinable by the laws of the land.

Boyd, vol. 14, p. 650.

2.2.5.8 Edmund Randolph to James Madison, March 27, 1789

. . . The liberty of the press is indeed a blessing, which ought not to be surrendered but with blood; and yet it is not an illfounded expectation in those, who deserve well of their country, that they should be assailed by an enemy in disguise, and have their characters deeply wounded, before they can prepare for defence. I apply not this to any particular person.

Veit, pp. 223–24.

2.2.5.9 Jeremy Belknap to Paine Wingate, May 29, 1789

. . . You will see in the speech wh. our *new* Lieut. Governor [*Samuel Adams*] made at his investiture that he has not thrown off the old idea of *"independence"* as an attribute of each individual State in the "confederated Republic" — & you will know in what light to regard his "devout & fervent wish" that the "people may enjoy well grounded confidence that their *personal & domestic* rights are *secure.*" This is the same Language or nearly the same which he used in the Convention when he moved for an addition to the proposed Amendments — by inserting a clause to provide for the Liberty of the press — the right to keep arms — Protection from seizure of person & property & the *Rights of Conscience.* By which motion he gave an alarm to both sides of the house & had nearly overset the whole business which the Friends of the Constitution had been labouring for several Weeks to obtain. . . .

Veit, p. 241.

2.2.5.10 George Clymer to Richard Peters, June 8, 1789

Madison this morning is to make an essay towards amendments — but whether he means merely a tub to the whale, or declarations about the press liberty of conscience &c. or will suffer himself to be so far frightened with the antifederalism of his own state as to attempt to lop off essentials I do not know — I hope however we shall be strong enough to postpone. . . .

Afternoon — Madison's has proved a tub on a number of Ad. but Gerry is not content with them alone, and proposes to treat us with all the amendments of all the antifederalists in America.

Veit, p. 245.

2.2.5.11 Fisher Ames to Thomas Dwight, June 11, 1789

Mr. Madison has introduced his long expected Amendments. They are the fruit of much labour and research. He has hunted up all the grievances and complaints of newspapers — all the articles of Conventions — and the small talk of their debates. It contains a Bill of Rights — the right of enjoying property — of changing the govt. at pleasure — freedom of the press — of conscience — of juries — exemption from general Warrants gradual increase of representatives till the whole number at the rate of one to every 30,000 shall amount to and allowing two to every State, at least this is the substance. There is too much of it — O. I had forgot the right of the people to bear Arms.

Risum teneatis amici —

Upon the whole, it may do good towards quieting men who attend to sounds only, and may get the mover some popularity — which he wishes.

Veit, p. 247.

2.2.5.12 Fisher Ames to George R. Minot, June 12, 1789

. . . The civil departments will employ us next, and the judiciary the Senate. They will finish their stint, as the boys say, before the House has done. Their number is less, and they have matured the business in committee. Yet Mr. Madison has inserted, in his amendments, the increase of representatives, each State having two at least. The rights of conscience, of bearing arms, of changing the government, are declared to be inherent in the people. Freedom of the press, too. There is a prodigious great dose for a medicine. But it will stimulate the stomach as little as hasty-pudding. It is rather food than physic. An immense mass of sweet and other herbs and roots for a diet drink.

Veit, pp. 247–48.

2.2.5.13 Abraham Baldwin to Joel Barlow, June 14, 1789

A few days since, Madison brought before us propositions of amendment agreeable to his promise to his constituents. Such as he supposed would tranquillize the minds of honest opposers without injuring the system. viz. "That what is not given is reserved, that liberty of the press & trial by jury shall remain *inviolable*. that the representation shall never be less than one for every 30,000 &c. ordered to lie on the table.["] We are too busy at present in cutting away at the whole cloth, to stop to do any body's patching. There is no such thing as antifederalism heard of. R[hode] I[sland] and N[orth] C[arolina] had local reasons for their conduct, and will come right before long.

Veit, p. 250.

2.2.5.14 Henry Gibbs to Roger Sherman, July 17, 1789

. . . All Ambiguity of Expression certainly ought to be remov'd; Liberty of Conscience in religious matters, right of trial by Jury, Liberty of the Press &c. may perhaps be more explicitly secur'd to the Subject & a general reservation made to the States respectively of all the powers not expressly delegated to the general Government.

Veit, p. 263.

2.2.5.15 Pierce Butler to James Iredell, August 11, 1789

. . . If you wait for substantial amendments, you will wait longer than I wish you to do, speaking *interestedly*. A few *milk-and-water* amendments have been proposed by Mr. M[adison]., such as liberty of conscience, a free press, and one or two general things already well secured. I suppose it was done to keep his promise with his constituents, to move for alterations; but, if I am not greatly mistaken, he is not hearty in the cause of amendments.

Veit, p. 274.

2.2.5.16 Thomas Jefferson to James Madison, August 28, 1789

[T]he following alterations & additions would have pleased me. Art 4. "The people shall not be deprived or abridged of their right to speak to write or *otherwise* to publish any thing but false facts affecting injuriously the life, liberty, property, or reputation of others or affecting the peace of the confederacy with foreign nations.

Hobson & Rutland, vol. 12, p. 363.

2.2.5.17   Theodorick Bland Randolph to St. George Tucker, September 9, 1789

. . . The house of Representatives have been for some time past engaged on the subject of amendments to the constitution, though in my opinion they have not made one single material one. The senate are at present engaged on the subject; Mr. Richd. H. Lee told me that he proposed to strike out the standing army in time of peace but could not carry it. He also said that it has been proposed, and warmly favoured that, liberty of Speach [*sic*] and of the press may be stricken out, as they only tend to promote licenciousness. If this takes place god knows what will follow.

Veit, p. 293.

2.3 DISCUSSION OF RIGHTS

2.3.1 TREATISES

2.3.1.1   Blackstone, 1765

5. THE security of his reputation or good name from the arts of detraction and slander, are rights to which every man is intitled, by reason and natural justice; since without these it is impossible to have the perfect enjoyment of any other advantage or right. But these three last articles (being of much less importance than those which have gone before, and those which are yet to come) it will suffice to have barely mentioned among the rights of person; referring the more minute discussion of their several branches, to those parts of our commentaries which treat of the infringement of these rights, under the head of personal wrongs.

Commentaries, bk. 1, ch. 1, sec. 1; vol. 1, p. 130.

2.3.2 CASELAW

2.3.2.1   Respublica v. Oswald, 1788

On the 12th of *July, Lewis* moved for a rule to shew cause why an attachment should not issue against *Eleazer Oswald,* the printer and publisher of the *Independent Gazetteer.*

The case was this: *Oswald* having inserted in his newspapers several anonymous pieces against the character of *Andrew Browne,* the master of a female academy, in the city of *Philadephia, Browne* applied to him to give up the authors of those pieces; but being refused that satisfaction, he brought an action for the libel against *Oswald,* returnable into the Supreme Court, *on the 2d day of July;* and therein demanded bail for £1,000. Previously to the return day of the writ, the question of bail being brought by citation before Mr. *Justice* BRYAN, at his chambers, the Judge, on a full hearing of the cause of action, in the presence of both the parties, ordered the Defendant to be discharged on common bail; and the Plaintiff appealed from this order to the court. Afterwards, *on the 1st of July, Oswald* published under his own signature, an address to the public, which contained a narrative of these proceedings, and the following passages, which, I conceive, to have been the material grounds of the present motion.

"When violent attacks are made upon a person under pretext of justice, and legal steps are taken on the occasion, not perhaps to redress the supposed injury, but to feed and gratify partisaning and temporising resentments, it is not unwarrantable in such person to represent the real statement of his case, and appeal to the world for their sentiments and countenance.

"Upon these considerations, principally, I am now emboldened to trespass on the public patience, and must solicit the indulgence of my friends and customers, while I present to their notice, an account of the steps lately exercised with me; from which it will appear that my situation *as a printer,* and the *rights of the press* and of *freemen,* are fundamentally struck at; and an earnest endeavour is on the carpet to involve me in difficulties to please the malicious dispositions of old and permanent enemies."

"But until the news had arrived last *Thursday,* that the *ninth* state had acceded to the new federal government, I was not called upon; and Mr. *Page* in the afternoon of that day visited me in due form of law with a writ. Had Mr. *Browne* pursued me in this line, "without loss of time," agreeably to his lawyer's letter, I should not have supposed it extraordinary — but to arrest me the moment the *federal* intelligence came to hand, indicated that the commencement of this suit was not so much the child of his own fancy, as it has been probably dictated to and urged on him by others, whose sentiments upon the new constitution have not in every respect coincided with mine. In fact, it was my idea, in the first progress of the business, that Mr. *Browne* was merely the *hand-maid* of some of my enemies among the federalists; and in this class I must rank, his great patron Doctor *Rush* (whose brother is a judge of the *Supreme Court*). I think Mr. *Brown's* conduct has since confirmed the idea beyond a doubt."

"Enemies I have had in the legal profession, and it may perhaps add to the hopes of *malignity,* that this action is instituted in the *Supreme Court* of *Pennsylvania.* However, if former prejudices should be found to operate against me on the bench, it is with a jury of my country, properly elected and empannelled, a jury of freemen and independent citizens, I must rest the suit. I have escaped the jaws of persecution through this channel on certain memorable occasions, and hope I shall never be a sufferer, let the blast of faction blow with all its furies!"

"The doctrine of libels being a doctrine incompatible with law and liberty, and at once destructive of the privileges of a free country in the communication of our thoughts, has not hitherto gained any footing in *Pennsylvania:* and the vile measures formerly taken to lay me by the heels on this subject only brought down obloquy upon the conductors themselves. I may well suppose the same love of liberty yet pervades my fellow citizens, and that they will not allow the freedom of the press to be violated upon any refined pretence, which oppressive ingenuity or courtly study can invent."

"Upon trial of the cause, the public will decide for themselves, whether Mr. *Browne's* motives have been laudable and dignified; whether his conduct in declining an acquittal of his character in the paper, and suing me in the manner he did, was decent and consistent; and, in a word, whether he is not actuated by some of my inveterate foes and opponents, to lend his name in their service for the purpose of harrassing and injuring me."

A transcript from the records was read to shew that the action between *Browne* and *Oswald* was depending in the court; *James Martin* proved that the paper containing *Oswald's* address was bought at his printing office, fresh and damp from the press; and a deposition, made by *Browne*, was read to prove the preceding facts relative to the cause of action, the hearing before Mr. *Justice* BRYAN, and the appeal from his order.

Lewis then adverted to the various pieces, which were charged as libellous in the depending action; and argued, that, though the liberty of the press was invaluable in its nature, and ought not to be infringed: yet, that its value did not consist in a boundless licentiousness of slander and defamation. He contended, that the profession of *Browne*, to whom the education of more than a hundred children was sometimes entrusted, exposed him, in a peculiar manner, to be injured by wanton aspersions of his character; and he inferred the necessity of the action, which had been instituted, from this consideration, that if *Browne* were really the monster which the papers in question described him to be, he ought to be hunted from society; but, that if he had been falsely accused, if he had been maliciously traduced, it was a duty that he owed to himself and to the public to vindicate his reputation, and to call upon the justice of the laws, to punish so gross a violation of truth and decency. For this purpose, he continued, a writ had been issued, and bail was required. The defendant, if not before, was certainly, on the hearing at the Judge's chambers, apprized of the cause of action: The order of Mr. *Justice* BRYAN on that occasion, and the appeal to the court, were circumstances perfectly within his knowledge; and yet, while the whole merits of the cause were thus in suspense, he thought proper to address the public in language evidently calculated to excite the popular resentment against *Browne;* to create doubts and suspicions of the integrity and impartiality of the Judges, who must preside upon the trial; and to promote an unmerited compassion in his own favour. He has described himself as the object of former persecutions upon similar principles; he has asserted that, in this instance, an individual is made the instrument of a party to destroy him; and he artfully calls upon his fellow citizens to interest themselves to preserve the freedom of the press, which he considers as attacked in his person. Nay, in order to cast an odium upon the new government of the *United States*, he insinuates, that his arrest was purposely protracted 'till the ratification of nine states had given stability to that system: a falsehood, as unwarrantable as it is insidious; for, it will be proved that this delay took place at his own request, communicated by Col. *Proctor*.

Col. *Proctor*, being examined on this point, said, that he, at first, desired the action might not be brought, in hopes of accomplishing a compromise between the parties; that, afterwards, he requested Mr. *Lewis* to defer issuing the writ 'till as near the term as it was possible: but that all this interference was of his own accord, and not at the instance of the defendant. He acknowledged, however, that he had informed *Oswald*, that the commencement of the action would be postponed as long as possible, after having obtained a promise to that effect from Mr. *Lewis*.

Lewis said he was very much mistaken, indeed, if Col. *Proctor* had not mentioned the request as coming from the defendant; and Col. *Proctor* answered, "if ever I told you so, he certainly sent me; but I cannot remember that ever he asked me to do a thing of the kind."

Lewis then added, that the address to the public manifestly tended to interrupt the course of justice; it was an attempt to prejudice the minds of the people in a cause then depending, and, by that means, to defeat the plaintiff's claim to justice, and to stigmatize the Judges, whose duty it was to administer the laws. There could be no doubt, therefore, that it amounted to a contempt of the court; and it only remained, in support of his motion, to shew that an attachment was the legal mode of proceeding against the offender. For this he cited 4 *Black. Com.* 280. 2 *Atk.* 469.

BY THE COURT: — Take a rule to shew cause on *Monday* next, at 9 o'clock in the morning.

The defendant appearing on *Monday* the 14th, agreeably to the rule to shew cause, obtained on *Saturday*, prayed that the rule might be enlarged, as he had not had a reasonable time to prepare for the argument. But *Lewis* opposed the enlargement of the rule, observing that the defendant would be heard in extenuation, or excuse, of the contempt, after the attachment had issued.

By M'KEAN, C. J. — I know not of any instance where a delay of a term has been allowed in the case of an attachment: one reason for such a summary proceeding is to prevent delay. Let cause be now shewn.

Sergeant, in shewing cause against the attachment, contended, that the doctrine, in 4 *Black. Com.* 280. was laid down much too wide; that in 2 *Atk.* 469. the Chancellor expressly assigns this reason, for his determining without a jury, that he was a judge of *fact;* and in 1 *Burr.* 510. 513. an information is granted on this principle, that courts of common law will not decide upon facts without the intervention of a jury.

M'KEAN, C. J. — This was not the reason that influenced the court in their decision.

But, whatever the law might be in *England, Sergeant* insisted, that it could not avail in *Pennsylvania.* Even in *England,* indeed, though it is said to be a contempt to report the decisions of the courts, unless under the *imprimatur* of the judges; yet, we find *Burrow,* and all the subsequent reporters, proceeding without that sanction. But the constitution of *Pennsylvania* authorizes many things to be done which in *England* are prohibited. Here the press is laid open to the inspection of every citizen, who wishes to examine the proceedings of the government; of which the judicial authority is certainly to be considered as a branch. *Const. Penn. Sect.* 35.

M'KEAN, C. J. — Could not this be done in *England?* Certainly it could: for, in short, there is nothing in the constitution of this state, respecting the liberty of the press, that has not been authorized by the constitution of that kingdom for near a century past.

Sergeant. The 9th *section of the Bill of Rights,* however, puts this supposed offence into such a form, as must entitle the defendant to a trial by jury; and precludes every attempt to compel him to give evidence against himself. It declares, "that, in all prosecutions for *criminal offences,* a man has a right to be heard by himself and his council, to demand the cause and nature of his accusation, to be confronted with the witnesses, to call for evidence in his favour, and a speedy public trial, *by an impartial jury of the country,* without the *unanimous* consent of which jury he cannot be found guilty; *nor can he be compelled to give evidence against himself;* nor can any man be justly deprived of his liberty except by the laws of the land, or the judgment of his peers." — Now, the present proceeding against the defendant is for a *criminal offence;* and, yet, if the attachment issues, the essential parts of this section must be defeated: for, in that case, the defendant *cannot be tried by a jury;* and, according to the practice upon attachments, he will *be compelled to answer interrogatories;* in doing which, he must either be guilty of perjury, or *give evidence against himself.* The proceeding by attachment is, indeed, a novelty in this country, except for the purpose of enforcing the attendance of witnesses. Those contempts which are committed in the face of a court stand upon a very different ground. Even the court of *Admiralty* (which is not a court of record) possesses a power to punish them; and the reason arises from the necessity that every jurisdiction should be competent to protect itself from immediate violence and interruption. But contempts which are alledged to have been committed out of doors, are not within this reason; they come properly within the class of *criminal offences;* and, as such, by the 9th *Sect.* of the bill of rights, they can only be tried by a jury.

M'KEAN, C. J. Do you then apprehend that the 9th *Sect.* of the bill of rights introduced something new on the subject of *trials?* I have always understood it to be the law, independent of this section, that the twelve jurors must be *unanimous* in their verdict, and yet this section makes this express provision.

Sergeant said, that he had discussed the subject as well as the little opportunity afforded him would admit. He pressed the court to give further time for the argument, or, at once, to direct a trial. This he contended was, at least, discretionary; and, considering the Defendant's protestation of innocence,[*] his readiness to give ample security for his future appearance, the magnitude of the question as arising from the constitution, and its immense consequences to the public, he thought a delay, that was essential to deliberation and justice, ought not to be refused.

Heatly and *Lewis*, in support of the motion, contended, that under the circumstances of the case, *Oswald's* publication, whether true or false, amounted to a contempt of the court, as it respected a cause then depending in judgment, and reflected upon one of the Judges in his official capacity; that the argument of the adverse counsel went so far as to assert, that there could be no such offence as a contempt even in *England,* since the very words inserted in the constitution of *Pennsylvania,* were used in the *Magna Charta* of that kingdom; that, in truth, neither the bill of rights nor the constitution extended to the case of *contempts,* for they mean only to secure to every citizen the right of expressing his sentiments with a manly freedom, but not to authorize wanton attacks upon private reputation, or to deprive the court of a power essential to its own existence, and to the due administration of justice; that the court were as competent to judge of the fact and the law, upon the inspection of the publication in question, as *the Chancellor* was in the authority cited from *Atkins;* and that although the prosecutor could, perhaps, proceed either by indictment or information, yet that the abuses of the

---

[*] Mr. *Oswald* repeatedly declared that he meant no contempt of the court in what he had published.

Star Chamber had rendered the process by information odious, and an attachment, which was sanctified by immemorial usage, was the most expeditious, and, therefore, the most proper remedy for the evil complained of.

THE CHIEF JUSTICE delivered the opinion of the Court to the following effect, Judge BRYAN having shortly before taken his seat.

M'KEAN, C. J. — This is a motion for an attachment against *Eleazer Oswald,* the printer and publisher of the *Independent Gazetteer,* of the 1st of *July* last, No. 796. As a ground for granting the attachment, it is proved, that an action for a libel had been instituted in this court, in which *Andrew Browne* is the plaintiff, and *Eleazer Oswald* the defendant; that a question with respect to bail in that action, had been agitated before one of the Judges, from whose order, discharging the defendant on common bail, the plaintiff had appealed to the court; and that Mr. *Oswald's* address to the public, which is the immediate subject of complaint, relates to the action thus depending before us.

The counsel in support of their motion, have argued, that this address was intended to prejudice the public mind upon the merits of the cause, by propagating an opinion that *Browne* was the instrument of a party to persecute and destroy the defendant; that he acted under the particular influence of Dr. *Rush,* whose brother is a judge of this court; and, in short, that from the ancient prejudices of all the judges, the defendant did not stand a chance of a fair trial.

Assertions and imputations of this kind are certainly calculated to defeat and discredit the administration of justice. Let us, therefore, enquire, *first,* whether they ought to be considered as a contempt of the court; and, *secondly,* whether, if so, the offender is punishable by attachment.

And here, I must be allowed to observe, that libelling is a great crime, whatever sentiments may be entertained by those who live by it. With respect to the heart of the libeller, it is more dark and base than that of the assassin, or than his who commits a midnight arson. It is true, that I may never discover the wretch who has burned my house, or set fire to my barn; but these losses are easily repaired, and bring with them no portion of ignominy or reproach. But the attacks of the libeller admit not of this consolation: the injuries which are done to character and reputation seldom can be cured, and the most innocent man may in a moment be deprived of his good name, upon which, perhaps, he depends for all the prosperity, and all the happiness of his life. To what tribunal can he then resort? how shall he be tried, and by whom shall he be acquitted? It is in vain to object, that those who know him will disregard the slander, since the wide circulation of public prints must render it impracticable to apply the antedote as far as the poison has been extended. Nor can it be fairly said, that the same opportunity is given to *vindicate,* which has been employed to *defame* him; for, many will read the charge, who may never see the answer; and while the object of accusation is publicly pointed at, the malicious and malignant author, rests in the dishonorable security of an anonymous signature. Where much has been said, something will be believed; and it is one of the many artifices of the libeller, to give to his charges an aspect of general support, by changing and multiplying the style and name of his performances. But shall such things be transacted with impunity in a free country, and among an enlightened people? Let every honest man make this appeal to his heart and understanding, and the answer must be — no!

What then is the meaning of *the Bill of rights,* and *the Constitution of Pennsylvania,* when they declare, "That the freedom of the press shall not be restrained,"* and "that the printing presses shall be free to every person who undertakes to examine the proceedings of the legislature, or any part of the government?" † However ingenuity may torture the expressions, there can be little doubt of the just sense of these sections: they give to every citizen a right of investigating the conduct of those who are entrusted with the public business; and they effectually preclude any attempt to fetter the press by the institution of a *licenser.* The same principles were settled in *England,* so far back as the reign of *William the Third,* and since that time, we all know, there has been the freest animadversion upon the conduct of the ministers of that nation. But is there any thing in the language of the constitution (much less in its spirit and intention) which authorizes one man to impute crimes to another, for which the law has provided the mode of trial, and the degree of punishment? Can it be presumed that the slanderous words, which, when spoken to a few individuals, would expose the speaker to punishment, become sacred, by the authority of the constitution, when delivered to the public through the more permanent and diffusive medium of the press? Or, will it be said, that the constitutional right to examine the proceedings of government, extends to warrant an anticipation of the acts of the legislature, or the judgments of the court? and not only to authorize a candid commentary upon what has been done, but to permit every endeavour to biass [*sic*] and intimidate with respect to matters still in suspense? The futility of any attempt to establish a construction of this sort, must be obvious to every intelligent mind. The true liberty of the press is amply secured by permitting every man to publish his opinions; but it is due to the peace and dignity of society to enquire into the motives of such publications, and to distinguish between those which are meant for use and reformation, and with an eye solely to the public good, and those which are intended merely to delude and defame. To the latter description, it is impossible that any good government should afford protection and impunity.

If, then, the liberty of the press is regulated by any just principle, there can be little doubt, that he, who attempts to raise a prejudice against his antagonist, in the minds of those that must ultimately determine the dispute between them; who, for that purpose, represents himself as a persecuted man, and asserts that his judges are influenced by passion and prejudice, — wilfully seeks to corrupt the source, and to dishonor the administration of justice.

Such is evidently the object and tendency of Mr. *Oswald's* address to the public. Nor can that artifice prevail, which insinuates that the decision of this court will be the effect of personal resentment; for, if it could, every man might evade the punishment due to his offences, by first pouring a torrent of abuse upon his judges, and then asserting that they act from passion, because their treatment has been such as would naturally excite resentment in the human disposition. But it must be

*Declar. of Rights, s. 12.
†Constit. of Penn., s. 35.

remembered, that judges discharge their functions under the solemn obligations of an oath: and, if their virtue entitles them to their station, they can neither be corrupted by favour to swerve from, nor influenced by fear to desert, their duty. That judge, indeed, who courts popularity by unworthy means, while he weakens his pretensions, diminishes, likewise, the chance of attaining his object; and he will eventually find that he has sacrificed the substantial blessing of a good conscience, in an idle and visionary pursuit.

Upon the whole, we consider the publication in question, as having the tendency which has been ascribed to it, that of prejudicing the public (a part of whom must hereafter be summoned as jurors) with respect to the merits of a cause depending in this court, and of corrupting the administration of justice: We are, therefore, unanimously of opinion, on the *first* point, that it amounts to a contempt.

It only remains then to consider, whether the offence is punishable in the way that the present motion has proposed.

It is certain that the proceeding by *attachment* is as old as the law itself, and no act of the legislature, or section of the constitution, has interposed to alter or suspend it. Besides the sections which have been already read from the constitution, there is another section which declares, that "trials by jury shall be as *heretofore;*" and surely it cannot be contended, that the offence, with which the defendant is now charged, was *heretofore* tried by that tribunal. If a man commits an outrage in the face of the court, what is there to be tried? — what further evidence can be necessary to convict him of the offence, than the actual view of the Judges? A man has been compelled to enter into security for his good behaviour, for giving the lie in the presence of the Judges in *Westminster-Hall.*

On the present occasion, is not the proof, from the inspection of the paper, as full and satisfactory as any that can be offered? And whether the publication amounts to a contempt, or not, is a point of law, which, after all, it is the province of the judges, and not of the jury, to determine. Being a contempt, if it is not punished immediately, how shall the mischief be corrected? Leave it to the customary forms of trial by jury, and the cause may be continued long in suspense, while the party perseveres in this misconduct. The injurious consequences might then be justly imputed to the court, for refusing to exercise their legal power in preventing them.

For these reasons we have no doubt of the competency of our gu-jurisdiction [sic]; and we think, that justice and propriety call upon us to proceed by *attachment.*

BRYAN, *Justice,* observed, that he did not mean to give an opinion as to the mode of proceeding; but added, that he had always entertained a doubt with respect to the legality of the process by attachment, in such cases, under the constitution of Pennsylvania.

M'KEAN, C. J. Will the defendant enter into a recognizance to answer interrogatories, or will he answer *gratis?*

Oswald. I will not answer interrogatories. Let the attachment issue.

M'KEAN, C. J. His counsel had better advise him to consider of it.

Sergeant said that the defendant had not had time, even to peruse what had been sworn against him; for only *Sunday* had intervened since the obtaining the rule to shew cause, and that was an improper day for applying to the records of the court.

M'KEAN, *C. J.* In criminal matters *Sunday* has always been deemed a legal day. There has been as ample time for consideration as could well be allowed; the term will end to-morrow. Will he answer, or not?

Sergeant prayed the court would grant 'till to-morrow morning to form a determination on the subject, and offered bail for the defendant's appearance at that time.

M'KEAN, *C. J.* Be it so. Let the bail be taken, himself in £200 and one surety in the like sum, for his appearance to-morrow morning.

The Defendant appearing on the 15th of *July,* in discharge of his recognizance; the CHIEF JUSTICE again asked, whether he would answer interrogatories or not?

Bankson, for the defendant, requested, that the interrogatories might be reduced to writing before he was called upon to determine.

M'KEAN, *C. J.* Is that your advice to him? He must *now* say whether he will answer them or not; they will be filed according to the usage of the court, and all just exceptions to them will be allowed.

Bankson. He instructs me to declare that he will not answer interrogatories; and he then began to urge, that there was no contempt committed, but was told by the CHIEF JUSTICE, that, as that point had been determined by an unanimous opinion of the four judges yesterday, it was not now open for argument.

Lewis said, that as a misrepresentation had been industriously spread abroad respecting the conduct of the court, he thought it proper, at this time, concisely to state the real nature of the present proceedings. It has been asserted that the court were about to compel Mr. *Oswald* to convict himself of the offence with which he is charged: but the fact is this, that it is incumbent upon the person who suggests the contempt to prove it by disinterested witnesses; and then, indeed, the defendant is allowed by his own oath to purge and acquit himself, in spite of all the testimony which can possibly be produced against him. It appears clearly, therefore, that Mr. *Oswald's* being called upon to answer interrogatories, is not meant to establish his guilt (for that has been already done) but to enable him to avoid the punishment which is the consequence of it. The court employ no compulsion in this respect. He may either answer, or not, as he pleases: if he does answer, his single oath, in his own favour, will countervail the oaths of a thousand witnesses; and if he does not answer, his silence corroborates the evidence which has been offered of the contempt, and the judgment of the court must necessarily follow.

M'KEAN, *C. J.* Your statement is certainly right, and the misrepresentation, which is attempted, must either be the effect of wickedness, or ignorance.

Lewis now prayed, that the rule might be made absolute; but remarked, that, according to the authorities, the court might either do that; or, as the defendant was present, they might proceed at once to pass sentence upon him.

M'KEAN, *C. J.* There can be no occasion, when the party is present, to make the rule for the attachment absolute: the court will proceed to give judgment.

BRYAN, *Justice.* I was not here when the complaint was made to the court, when the evidence in support of the motion was produced, or the arguments against it were delivered: I consider myself therefore totally incapacitated for taking any part in this business.

Lewis. We can immediately furnish the court with the proofs.

BRYAN, *Justice.* Can you furnish me, likewise, with Mr. *Sergeant's* arguments?

Lewis said, that he had not penetration enough to discover any argument in what had been said for the defendant; and having again read all the evidence which had been produced, he recapitulated what he had before said in support of the motion.

Page, the under-sheriff, was then called upon to prove, that the writ in the action of *Browne* vs. *Oswald* had been in his possession, at least twelve days before it was served; and that the delay in sering [sic] it arose at first, from the defendant's being at *Baltimore;* and, afterwards, from his not being at home when the witness had repeatedly called upon him.

BRYAN, *Justice.* I still say, that not having heard what has been offered in extenuation of the offence, I am incompetent to join in any opinion respecting the punishment. I cannot surely be suspected of partiality to libellers: I have had my share of their malevolence. But, it is true, I have not suffered much; for these trifles do not wrankle in my mind.

The CHIEF JUSTICE pronounced the judgment of the court in the following words:

M'KEAN, *C. J.* — *Eleazer Oswald:* Having yesterday considered the charge against you, we were unanimously of opinion, that it amounted to a contempt of the court. Some doubts were suggested, whether, even a contempt of the court, was punishable by attachment: but, not only my brethren and myself, but, likewise, all the judges of *England,* think, that without this power no court could possibly exist; — nay, that no *contempt* could, indeed, be committed against us, we should be *so truly contemptible.* The law upon the subject is of immemorial antiquity; and there is not any period when it can be said to have ceased, or discontinued. On this point, therefore, we entertain no doubt.

But some difficulty has arisen with respect to our sentence; for, on the one hand, we have been informed of your circumstances, and on the other, we have seen your conduct: your circumstances are small, but your offence is great and persisted in. Since, however, the question seems to resolve itself into this, whether you shall bend to the law, or the law shall bend to you, it is our duty to determine that the former shall be the case.

Upon the whole, therefore, THE COURT pronounce this sentence: — That you pay a fine of 10£. to the *Commonwealth;* that you be imprisoned for the space of one month, that is, from the 15th day of July to the 15th day of August next; and, afterwards, till the fine and costs are paid. — Sheriff he is in your custody.

1 Dall. 319 (Pa.)

Chapter 3

AMENDMENT I
ASSEMBLY AND PETITION CLAUSES

3.1 TEXTS

3.1.1 DRAFTS IN FIRST CONGRESS

3.1.1.1 Proposal by Madison in House, June 8, 1789

3.1.1.1.a   Fourthly. That in article 1st, section 9, between clauses 3 and 4 [of the Constitution], be inserted these clauses, to wit, . . .

. . .

The people shall not be restrained from peaceably assembling and consulting for their common good; nor from applying to the legislature by petitions, or remonstrances for redress of their grievances.

Congressional Register, June 8, 1789, vol. 1, p. 427.

3.1.1.1.b   *Fourthly.* That in article 1st, section 9, between clauses 3 and 4 [of the Constitution], be inserted these clauses, to wit: . . .

. . .

The people shall not be restrained from peaceably assembling and consulting for their common good; nor from applying to the legislature by petitions, or remonstrances for redress of their grievances.

Daily Advertiser, June 12, 1789, p. 2, col. 1.

3.1.1.1.c   *Fourth.* That in article 1st, section 9, between clauses 3 and 4 [of the Constitution], be inserted these clauses, to wit: . . .

. . .

The people shall not be restrained from peaceably assembling and consulting for their common good; nor from applying to the legislature by petitions, or remonstrances for redress of their grievances.

New-York Daily Gazette, June 13, 1789, p. 574, col. 3.

3.1.1.2 Proposal by Sherman to House Committee of Eleven, July 21–28, 1789

[Amendment] 2 The people have certain natural rights which are retained by them when they enter into society, Such are the rights of conscience in matters of religion; of acquiring property, and of pursuing happiness & safety; of Speaking, writing and publishing their Sentiments with decency and freedom; of peaceably Assembling to consult their common good, and of applying to Government by petition or remonstrance for redress of grievances. Of these rights therefore they Shall not be deprived by the government of the united States.

Madison Papers, DLC.

3.1.1.3 House Committee of Eleven Report, July 28, 1789

ART. I, SEC. 9 — Between PAR. 2 and 3 insert, . . .

"The freedom of speech, and of the press, and the right of the people peaceably to assemble and consult for their common good, and to apply to the government for redress of grievances, shall not be infringed."

Broadside Collection, DLC.

3.1.1.4 House Consideration, August 15, 1789

3.1.1.4.a   The next clause of the 4th proposition was taken into consideration, and was as follows: "The freedom of speech and of the press, and the right of the people peaceably to assemble and consult for their common good, and to apply to the government for redress of grievances shall not be infringed."

Congressional Register, August 15, 1789, vol. 2, p. 197 ("agreed to").

3.1.1.4.b   Fifth amendment — "The freedom of speech, and of the press, and of the right of the people peaceably to assemble and consult for their common good, and to apply to the government for redress of grievances, shall not be infringed."

Daily Advertiser, August 17, 1789, p. 2, col. 1 ("carried in the affirmative").

3.1.1.4.c   Fifth amendment — "The freedom of speech, and of the press, and of the right of the people peaceably to assemble and consult for their common good, and to apply to the government for redress of grievances, shall not be infringed."

New-York Daily Gazette, August 18, 1789, p. 798, col. 3 ("carried in the affirmative").

3.1.1.4.d   Fifth amendment. *The freedom of speech, and of the press, and of the rights of the people peaceably to assemble and consult for their common good, and to apply to government for the redress of grievances shall not be infringed.*

Gazette of the U.S., August 19, 1789, p. 147, col. 1 ("agreed to").

3.1.1.5 Motion by Sedgwick in House, August 15, 1789

3.1.1.5.a   Mr. SEDGWICK

. . . therefore moved to strike out "assemble and."

Congressional Register, August 15, 1789, vol. 2, p. 197
(motion "lost by a considerable majority").

3.1.1.5.b   Mr. SEDGWICK moved to strike out the words "assemble and."

Gazette of the U.S., August 19, 1789, p. 147, col. 1 ("[I]t was negatived.").

3.1.1.6 Motion by Tucker in House, August 15, 1789

3.1.1.6.a   Mr. TUCKER

[H]e noticed that the most material part proposed by those states [namely, Virginia and North Carolina] was omitted, which was, a declaration that the people should have a right to instruct their representatives; he would move to have those words inserted as soon as the motion [by Mr. Sedgwick] for striking out was decided.

> Congressional Register, August 15, 1789, vol. 2, p. 198
> ("determined in the negative, 10 in favor and 41 against it.").

3.1.1.6.b   Mr. Tucker moved to insert between the words "common good," "and to" in this paragraph, these words "to instruct their representatives."

> Daily Advertiser, August 17, 1787, p. 2, col. 1
> ("the motion was negatived by a great majority").

3.1.1.6.c   Mr. Tucker moved to insert between the words "common good," "and to" in this paragraph, these words "to instruct their representatives."

> New-York Daily Gazette, August 18, 1789, p. 798, col. 4.
> ("was negatived by a great majority").

3.1.1.6.d   Mr. Tucker moved to insert these words, *to instruct their representatives.*

> Gazette of the U.S., August 19, 1789, p. 147, col. 1
> ("[I]t was negatived by a large majority").

3.1.1.7   Further House Consideration, August 21, 1789

Fourth. The freedom of speech, and of the press, and the right of the people peaceably to assemble and consult for their common good, and to apply to the government for redress of grievances, shall not be infringed.

> HJ, p. 107 ("read and debated . . . , agreed to by House, . . .
> two-thirds of the members present concurring").[1]

3.1.1.8   House Resolution, August 24, 1789

ARTICLE THE FOURTH.

The Freedom of Speech, and of the Press, and the right of the People peaceably to assemble, and consult for their common good, and apply to the Government for a redress of grievances, shall not be infringed.   House Pamphlet, RG 46, DNA.

3.1.1.9   Senate Consideration, August 25, 1789

3.1.1.9.a   The Resolve of the House of Representatives of the 24th of August, upon certain "Articles to be proposed to the Legislatures of the several States as Amendments to the Constitution of the United States" was read as followeth:

. . .

Article the fourth

The freedom of speech, and of the press, and the right of the People peaceably to assemble and consult for their common good and to apply to the Government for redress of grievances shall not be infringed.   Rough SJ, p. 215.

---

[1] On August 22, 1789, the following motion was agreed to:
ORDERED, That it be referred to a committee of three, to prepare and report a proper arrangement of, and introduction to the articles of amendment to the Constitution of the United States, as agreed to by the House; and that Mr. Benson, Mr. Sherman, and Mr. Sedgwick be of the said committee.

> HJ, p. 112.

3.1.1.9.b   The Resolve of the House of Representatives of the 24th of August, was read as followeth:

. . .

Article the Fourth.

"The freedom of speech, and of the press, and the right of the people peaceably to assemble, and consult for their common good, and to apply to the Government for redress of grievances, shall not be infringed.   Smooth SJ, p. 194.

3.1.1.9.c   The Resolve of the House of Representatives of the 24th of August, was read as followeth:

"ARTICLE THE FOURTH.

. . .

"The freedom of speech, and of the press, and the right of the people peaceably to assemble, and consult for their common good, and to apply to the Government for redress of grievances, shall not be infringed.   Printed SJ, p. 104.

3.1.1.10   Further Senate Consideration, September 3, 1789

3.1.1.10.a   On the fourth Article it was moved to insert these words "To instruct their Representatives" after the words "Common good."
                                    Rough SJ, p. 245 ("it passed in the Negative.").

3.1.1.10.b   On the fourth Article it was moved to insert these words, — "To instruct their Representatives," after the words "Common good" — . . .
                                    Smooth SJ, p. 218 ("it passed in the Negative.").

3.1.1.10.c   On the fourth Article it was moved to insert these words, — "To instruct their Representatives," after the words "Common good" — . . .
                                    Printed SJ, p. 117 ("it passed in the Negative.").

3.1.1.11   Further Senate Consideration, September 3, 1789

3.1.1.11.a   On Motion, To strike out the words "And consult for their common good and,"
                                    Rough SJ, p. 246 ("It passed in the negative.").

3.1.1.11.b   On motion, To strike out the words "And to consult for their common good and,"
                                    Smooth SJ, p. 219 ("It passed in the Negative.").

3.1.1.11.c   On motion, To strike out the words "And consult for their common good and,"
                                    Printed SJ, p. 117 ("It passed in the Negative.").

3.1.1.12   Further Senate Consideration, September 4, 1789

3.1.1.12.a   On Motion to adopt the fourth Article proposed by Resolve of the House of Representatives to read as followeth,

"That Congress shall make no law, abridging the freedom of speech, or of the press, or the right of the People peaceably to assemble and consult for their common good, and to petition the Government for a redress of grievances,"
                                    Rough SJ, p. 247 ("It passed in the affirmative.").

3.1.1.12.b   On motion, To adopt the fourth Article proposed by the Resolve of the House of Representatives, to read as followeth,

"That Congress shall make no law, abridging the freedom of Speech, or of the Press, or the right of the People peaceably to assemble and consult for their common good, and to petition the Government for a redress of grievances,"

Smooth SJ, pp. 220–21 ("It passed in the Affirmative.").

3.1.1.12.c   On motion, To adopt the fourth Article proposed by the Resolve of the House of Representatives, to read as followeth,

"That Congress shall make no law, abridging the freedom of Speech, or of the Press, or the right of the People peaceably to assemble and consult for their common good, and to petition the Government for a redress of grievances,"

Printed SJ, p. 118 ("It passed in the Affirmative.").

3.1.1.12.d   that the Senate do
Resolved ~~to~~ /\ concur with the House of Representatives in
Article fourth.

To read as follows, to wit:

"That Congress shall make no law, abridging the freedom of Speech or of the press, or the right of the people peaceably to assemble and consult for their common good, and to petition the government for a redress of grievances,"

Senate MS, RG 46, p. 3.

3.1.1.13   Further Senate Consideration, September 9, 1789

3.1.1.13.a   And on Motion to amend article the third to read as follows:

"Congress shall make no law establishing articles of faith or a mode of worship, or prohibiting the free exercise of Religion; or abridging the freedom of Speech, or the press, or the right of the People peaceably to assemble, and petition to the government for the redress of grievances."

. . .

On motion, To strike out the fourth article,

Rough SJ, p. 274 (As to each motion, "It passed in the Affirmative.").

3.1.1.13.b   On motion, To amend article the third, to read as follows:

"Congress shall make no law establishing articles of faith or a mode of worship, or prohibiting the free exercise of religion, or abridging the freedom of speech, or the press, or the right of the people peaceably to assemble, and petition to the Government for the redress of grievances" —

. . .

On motion, To strike out the fourth article, ...

Smooth SJ, p. 243 (As to each motion, "It passed in the Affirmative.").

3.1.1.13.c   On motion, To amend Article the third, to read as follows:

"Congress shall make no law establishing articles of faith or a mode of worship, or prohibiting the free exercise of religion, or abridging the freedom of speech, or

the press, or the right of the people peaceably to assemble, and petition to the Government for the redress of grievances" —

. . .

On motion, To strike out the fourth Article,

Printed SJ, p. 129 (As to each motion, "It passed in the Affirmative.").

3.1.1.13.d   On the question to concur with the House of Representatives on their resolution of the 24th of Augt. proposing amendments to the constitution of the United States, with the following amendments viz:

. . .

To erase from the 3d. Article the word "Religion" & insert — Articles of faith or a mode of Worship. —

And to erase from the same article the words "thereof, nor shall the rights of Conscience be infringed" & insert — of Religion; or abridging the freedom of speech, or of the press, or of the right of the people peaceably to assemble, & to petition to the government for a redress of grievances

To erase the 4th. article, & the words "Article the fourth."

Ellsworth MS, pp. 1–2, RG 46, DNA.

3.1.1.14   Senate Resolution, September 9, 1789

ARTICLE THE THIRD.

Congress shall make no law establishing articles of faith, or a mode of worship, or prohibiting the free exercise of religion, or abridging the freedom of speech, or of the press, or the right of the people peaceably to assemble, and to petition to the government for a redress of grievances.

Senate Pamphlet, RG 46, DNA.

3.1.1.15   Further House Consideration, September 21, 1789

RESOLVED, That this House doth agree to the second, fourth, eighth, twelfth, thirteenth, sixteenth, eighteenth, nineteenth, twenty-fifth, and twenty-sixth amendments, and doth disagree to the first, third, fifth, sixth, seventh, ninth, tenth, eleventh, fourteenth, fifteenth, seventeenth, twentieth, twenty-first, twenty-second, twenty-third, and twenty-fourth amendments proposed by the Senate to the said articles, two thirds of the members present concurring on each vote.

RESOLVED, That a conference be desired with the Senate on the subject matter of the amendments disagreed to, and that Mr. Madison, Mr. Sherman, and Mr. Vining, be appointed managers at the same on the part of this House.

HJ, p. 146.

3.1.1.16   Further Senate Consideration, September 21, 1789

3.1.1.16.a   A message from the House of Representatives —

Mr. Beckley, their Clerk, brought up a Resolve of the House of this date, to agree to the 2nd, 4th, 8th, 12th, 13th, 16th, 18th, 19th, 25th, and 26th Amendments proposed by the Senate, "To articles of Amendment to be proposed to the Legislatures of the several States, as Amendments to the Constitution of the United States," and to disagree to the 1st, 3d, 5th, 6th, 7th, 9th, 10th, 11th, 14th, 15th, 17th, 20th, 21st, 22d, 23d, and 24th amendments: Two thirds of the members present concurring on each vote: And "That a conference be desired with the Senate on the subject matter of the amendments disagreed to," and that Mr. Madison, Mr. Sherman, and Mr. Vining, be appointed managers of the same, on the part of the House of Representatives —

And he withdrew.

Smooth SJ, pp. 265–66.

3.1.1.16.b   A message from the House of Representatives —

Mr. Beckley, their Clerk, brought up a Resolve of the House of this date, to agree to the 2d, 4th, 8th, 12th, 13th, 16th, 18th, 19th, 25th, and 26th Amendments proposed by the Senate, "To Articles of Amendment to be proposed to the Legislatures of the several States, as Amendments to the Constitution of the United States," and to disagree to the 1st, 3d, 5th, 6th, 7th, 9th, 10th, 11th, 14th, 15th, 17th, 20th, 21st, 22d, 23d, and 24th Amendments: Two thirds of the members present concurring on each vote: And "That a conference be desired with the Senate on the subject matter of the Amendments disagreed to," and that Mr. Madison, Mr. Sherman, and Mr. Vining, be appointed managers of the same, on the part of the House of Representatives —

And he withdrew.

Printed SJ, pp. 141–42.

3.1.1.17   Further Senate Consideration, September 21, 1789

3.1.1.17.a   The Senate proceeded to consider the Message of the House of Representatives disagreeing to the Amendments made by the Senate "To Articles to be proposed to the Legislatures of the several States, as Amendments to the Constitution of the United States" And

RESOLVED, That the Senate do recede from their third Amendment, and do insist on all the others.

RESOLVED, That the Senate do concur with the House of Representatives in a conference on the subject matter of disagreement on the said Articles of Amendment, and that Mr. Ellsworth, Mr. Carroll and Mr. Paterson be managers of the conference on the part of the Senate.

Smooth SJ, p. 267.

3.1.1.17.b   The Senate proceeded to consider the message of the House of Representatives disagreeing to the Amendments made by the Senate "To Articles to be proposed to the Legislatures of the several States, as Amendments to the Constitution of the United States" — And

RESOLVED, That the Senate do recede from their third Amendment, and do insist on all the others.

RESOLVED, That the Senate do concur with the House of Representatives in a conference on the subject matter of disagreement on the said Articles of Amendment, and that Mr. Ellsworth, Mr. Carroll, and Mr. Paterson be managers of the conference on the part of the Senate.

Printed SJ, p. 142.

3.1.1.18   Conference Committee Report, September 24, 1789

[T]hat it will be proper for the House of Representatives to agree to the said Amendments proposed by the Senate, with an Amendment to their fifth Amendment, so that the third Article shall read as follows: "Congress shall make no Law <u>respecting an establishment of Religion</u>, or prohibiting the free exercise thereof; or abridging the freedom of Speech, or of the Press; or the right of the people peaceably to assemble and ~~to~~ petition the Government for a redress of grievances;" And with an Amendment to the fourteenth Amendment proposed by the Senate, so that the eighth Article, as numbered in the Amendments proposed by the Senate, shall read as follows "In all criminal prosecutions, the accused shall enjoy the right to a speedy & publick trial <u>by an impartial jury of the district wherein the crime shall have been committed, as the district shall have been previously ascertained by law</u>, and to be informed of the nature and cause of the accusation; to be confronted with the witnesses against him, and to have com

pulsory process for obtaining witnesses ~~against him~~ in his favour, & ∧ have the ^{to} assistance of counsel for his defence."

Conference MS, RG 46, DNA (Ellsworth's handwriting).

3.1.1.19 House Consideration of Conference Committee Report, September 24 [25], 1789

RESOLVED, That this House doth recede from their disagreement to the first, third, fifth, sixth, seventh, ninth, tenth, eleventh, fourteenth, fifteenth, seventeenth, twentieth, twenty-first, twenty-second, twenty-third, and twenty-fourth amendments, insisted on by the Senate: PROVIDED, That the two articles which by the amendments of the Senate are now proposed to be inserted as the third and eighth articles, shall be amended to read as followeth;

Article the third. "Congress shall make no law respecting an establishment of religion, or prohibiting the free exercise thereof; or abridging the freedom of speech, or of the press; or the right of the people peaceably to assemble, and to petition the government for a redress of grievances."

Article the eighth. "In all criminal prosecutions, the accused shall enjoy the right to a speedy and public trial by an impartial jury of the state and district wherein the crime shall have been committed, which district shall have been previously ascertained by law, and to be informed of the nature and cause of the accusation, to be confronted with the witnesses against him, to have compulsory process for obtaining witnesses in his favor, and to have the assistance of council for his defence."

HJ, p. 152 ("On the question, that the House do agree to the alteration
and amendment of the eighth article, in manner aforesaid,
It was resolved in the affirmative. Ayes 37 Noes 14").

3.1.1.20 Senate Consideration of Conference Committee Report, September 24, 1789

3.1.1.20.a   Mr. Ellsworth, on behalf of the managers of the conference on "articles to be proposed to the several States as Amendments to the Constitution of the United States," reported as follows:

That it will be proper for the House of Representatives to agree to the said amendments proposed by the Senate, with an Amendment to their fifth Amendment, so that the third Article shall read as follows: "Congress shall make no law respecting an establishment of <u>Religion</u>, or prohibiting the free exercise thereof; or abridging the freedom of Speech, or of the Press; or the right of the people peaceably to assemble and petition the Government for a redress of Grievances;" And with an Amendment to the fourteenth Amendment proposed by the Senate, so that the eighth article, as numbered in the Amendments proposed by the Senate, shall read as follows; "In all criminal prosecutions, the accused shall enjoy the right to a speedy and public trial by an impartial <u>Jury</u> of the district wherein the <u>Crime</u> shall have been committed, as the district shall have been previously ascertained by law, and to be informed of the nature and cause of the accusation, to be confronted with the witnesses against him, and to have compulsory process for obtaining witnesses in his favor, and to have the assistance of Counsel for defence."

Smooth SJ, pp. 272–73.

3.1.1.20.b   Mr. Ellsworth, on behalf of the managers of the conference on "Articles to be proposed to the several States as Amendments to the Constitution of the United States," reported as follows:

That it will be proper for the House of Representatives to agree to the said Amendments proposed by the Senate, with an Amendment to their fifth Amendment, so that the third Article shall read as follows: "Congress shall make no Law RESPECTING AN ESTABLISHMENT OF RELIGION, or prohibiting the free exercise thereof; or abridging the freedom of Speech, or of the Press; or the right of the People peaceably to assemble and petition the Government for a redress of Grievances;" And with an Amendment to the fourteenth Amendment proposed by the Senate, so that the eighth Article, as numbered in the Amendments proposed by the Senate, shall read as follows; "In all criminal prosecutions, the accused shall enjoy the right to a speedy and public trial BY AN IMPARTIAL JURY OF THE DISTRICT WHEREIN THE CRIME SHALL HAVE BEEN COMMITTED, AS THE DISTRICT SHALL HAVE BEEN PREVIOUSLY ASCERTAINED BY LAW, and to be informed of the nature and cause of the accusation, to be confronted with the witnesses against him, and to have compulsory process for obtaining witnesses in his favor, and to have the assistance of Counsel for defence."

Printed SJ, p. 145.

3.1.1.21   Further Senate Consideration of Conference Committee Report, September 24, 1789

3.1.1.21.a   A Message from the House of Representatives —

Mr. Beckley, their Clerk, brought up the Amendments to the "Articles to be proposed to the Legislatures of the several States, as Amendments to the Constitution of the United States;" and informed the Senate, that the House of Representatives had receded from their disagreement to the 1st, 3d, 5th, 6th, 7th, 9th, 10th, 11th, 14th, 15th, 17th, 20th, 21st, 22d, 23d, and 24th Amendments, insisted on by the Senate: Provided that the "Two Articles, which by the Amendments of the Senate are now proposed to be inserted as the third and eighth Articles," shall be amended to read as followeth:

Article the Third. "Congress shall make no Law respecting an establishment of Religion, or prohibiting the free exercise thereof; or abridging the freedom of Speech, or of the Press; or the right of the people peaceably to assemble, and petition the Government for a redress of Grievances."

Article the Eighth. "In all criminal prosecutions the accused shall enjoy the right to a speedy and public trial by an impartial Jury of the State and District, wherein the crime shall have been committed, which District shall have been previously ascertained by law, and to be informed of the nature and cause of the accusation, to be confronted with the witnesses against him, and to have compulsory process for obtaining witnesses in his favor, and to have the assistance of Counsel for his defence."

Smooth SJ, pp. 278–79.

3.1.1.21.b   A Message from the House of Representatives —

Mr. Beckley, their Clerk, brought up the Amendments to the "Articles to be proposed to the Legislatures of the several States, as Amendments to the Constitution of the United States;" and informed the Senate, that the House of Representatives had receded from their disagreement to the 1st, 3d, 5th, 6th, 7th, 9th, 10th, 11th, 14th, 15th, 17th, 20th, 21st, 22d, 23d, and 24th Amendments, insisted on by the Senate: Provided that the "Two Articles, which by the Amendments of the Senate are now proposed to be inserted as the third and eighth Articles," shall be amended to read as followeth:

Article the Third. "Congress shall make no Law respecting an establishment of Religion, or prohibiting the free exercise thereof; or abridging the freedom of Speech, or of the Press; or the right of the People peaceably to assemble, and petition the Government for a redress of Grievances."

Article the Eighth. "In all criminal prosecutions the accused shall enjoy the right to a speedy and public trial by an impartial Jury of the State and District, wherein the crime shall have been committed, which District shall have been previously ascertained by law, and to be informed of the nature and cause of the accusation, to be confronted with the witnesses against him, and to have compulsory process for obtaining witnesses in his favor, and to have the assistance of Counsel for his defence."

Printed SJ, p.148.

3.1.1.22   Further Senate Consideration of Conference Committee Report, September 25, 1789

3.1.1.22.a   The Senate proceeded to consider the Message from the House of Representatives of the 24th, with Amendments to the Amendments of the Senate, to "Articles to be proposed to the Legislatures of the several States, as Amendments to the Constitution of the United States" — And

RESOLVED, That the Senate do concur in the Amendments proposed by the House of Representatives, to the Amendments of the Senate.   Smooth SJ, p. 283.

3.1.1.22.b   The Senate proceeded to consider the Message from the House of Representatives of the 24th, with Amendments to the Amendments of the Senate, to "Articles to be proposed to the Legislatures of the several States, as Amendments to the Constitution of the United States" — And

RESOLVED, That the Senate do concur in the Amendments proposed by the House of Representatives, to the Amendments of the Senate.

Printed SJ, pp. 150–51.

3.1.1.23   Agreed Resolution, September 25, 1789

3.1.1.23.a

Article the Third.

Congress shall make no law respecting an establishment of religion, or prohibiting the free exercise thereof, or abridging the freedom of speech, or of the press, or the right of the people peaceably to assemble, and to petition the Government for a redress of grievances.

Smooth SJ, Appendix, p. 292.

3.1.1.23.b

ARTICLE THE THIRD.

Congress shall make no law respecting an establishment of religion, or prohibiting the free exercise thereof, or abridging the freedom of speech, or of the press, or the right of the people peaceably to assemble, and to petition the Government for a redress of grievances.

Printed SJ, Appendix, p. 163.

3.1.1.24   Enrolled Resolution, September 28, 1789

Article the third . . . Congress shall make no law respecting an establishment of religion, or prohibiting the free exercise thereof; or abridging the freedom of speech, or of the press; or the right of the people peaceably to assemble, and to petition the Government for a redress of grievances.

Enrolled Resolutions, RG 11, DNA.

3.1.1.25   Printed Versions

3.1.1.25.a   ART. I. Congress shall make no law respecting an establishment of religion, or prohibiting the free exercise thereof; or abridging the freedom of speech, or of the press; or the right of the people peaceably to assemble, and to petition the government for a redress of grievances.

Statutes at Large, vol. 1, p. 21.

3.1.1.25.b   ART. III. Congress shall make no law respecting an establishment of religion, or prohibiting the free exercise thereof; or abridging the freedom of speech, or of the press; or the right of the people peaceably to assemble, and to petition the government for a redress of grievances.

Statutes at Large, vol. 1, p. 97.

3.1.2 PROPOSALS FROM THE STATE CONVENTIONS

3.1.2.1   Maryland Minority, April 26, 1788

14. That every man hath a right to petition the legislature for the redress of grievances in a peaceable and orderly manner.

Maryland Gazette, May 1, 1788 (Committee minority).

3.1.2.2   Massachusetts Minority, February 6, 1788

[T]hat the said Constitution be never construed to authorize Congress to infringe the just liberty of the press, or the rights of conscience; or to prevent the people of the United States, who are peaceable citizens, from keeping their own arms; or to raise standing armies, unless when necessary for the defence of the United States, or of some one or more of them; or to prevent the people from petitioning, in a peaceable and orderly manner, the federal legislature, for a redress of grievances; or to subject the people to unreasonable searches and seizures of their persons, papers or possessions.

Massachusetts Convention, pp. 86–87.

3.1.2.3 New York, July 26, 1788

That the People have a right peaceably to assemble together to consult for their common good, or to instruct their Representatives; and that every person has a right to Petition or apply to the Legislature for redress of Grievances. — That the Freedom of the Press ought not to be violated or restrained.

State Ratifications, RG 11, DNA.

3.1.2.4 North Carolina, August 1, 1788

15th. That the people have a right peaceably to assemble together to consult for the common good, or to instruct their representatives; and that every freeman has a right to petition or apply to the Legislature for redress of grievances.

State Ratifications, RG 11, DNA.

3.1.2.5 Rhode Island, May 29, 1790

15th. That the people have a right peaceably to assemble together, to consult for their common good, or to instruct their representatives; and that every person has a right to petition or apply to the legislature for redress of grievances.

State Ratifications, RG 11, DNA.

3.1.2.6 Virginia, June 27, 1788

Fifteenth. That the people have a right peaceably to assemble together to consult for the common good, or to instruct their Representatives; and that every freeman has a right to petition or apply to the legislature for redress of grievances.

State Ratifications, RG 11, DNA.

3.1.3 STATE CONSTITUTIONS AND LAWS; COLONIAL CHARTERS AND LAWS

3.1.3.1 Delaware: Declaration of Rights, 1776

SECT. 9. That every man hath a right to petition the Legislature for the redress of grievances in a peaceable and orderly manner.

Delaware Laws, vol. 1, App., p. 80.

3.1.3.2 Maryland: Constitution, 1776

11. That every man hath a right to petition the legislature for the redress of grievances, in a peaceable and orderly manner.

Maryland Laws, November 3, 1776.

3.1.3.3 Massachusetts

3.1.3.3.a Body of Liberties, 1641

[12] Every man whether Inhabitant or fforreiner, free or not free shall have libertie to come to any publique Court, Councel, or Towne meeting, and either by speech or writeing to move any lawfull, seasonable, and materiall question, or to present any necessary motion, complaint, petition, Bill or information, whereof

that meeting hath proper cognizance, so it be done in convenient time, due order, and respective manner.

Massachusetts Colonial Laws, p. 35.

3.1.3.3.b   Constitution, 1780

[Part I, Article] XIX. The people have a right, in an orderly and peaceable manner, to assemble to consult upon the common good: Give instructions to their representatives; and to request of the legislative body, by the way of addresses, petitions, or remonstrances, redress of the wrongs done them, and of the grievances they suffer.

Massachusetts Perpetual Laws, p. 7.

3.1.3.4   New Hampshire: Constitution, 1783

[Part I, Article] XXXII. The people have a right in an orderly and peaceable manner, to assemble and consult upon the common good, give instructions to their representatives; and to request of the legislative body, by way of petition or remonstrance, redress of the wrongs done them, and of the grievances they suffer.

New Hampshire Laws, p. 27.

3.1.3.5   New York: Bill of Rights, 1787

Tenth, That it is the Right of the Citizens of this State to petition the Person administering the Government of this State for the Time being, or either House of the Legislature; and all Commitments and Prosecutions for such petitioning, are illegal.

New York Laws, vol. 2, p. 2.

3.1.3.6   North Carolina: Declaration of Rights, 1776

Sect. XVIII. That the People have a Right to assemble together to consult for their common good, to instruct their Representatives, and to apply to the Legislature for Redress of Grievances.

North Carolina Laws, p. 276.

3.1.3.7   Pennsylvania

3.1.3.7.a   Constitution, 1776

CHAPTER I.

A DECLARATION of the RIGHTS of the Inhabitants
of the State of Pennsylvania.

. . .

XVI. That the people have a right to assemble together, to consult for their common good, to instruct their representatives, and to apply to the legislature for redress of grievances, by address, petition, or remonstrance.

Pennsylvania Acts, M'Kean, pp. x–xi.

3.1.3.7.b   Constitution, 1790

ARTICLE IX.

. . .

Sect. XX. That the citizens have right [*sic*], in a peaceable manner, to assemble together for their common good, and to apply to those invested with the powers of government for redress of grievances, or other proper purposes, by petition, address, or remonstrance.

Pennsylvania Acts, Dallas, pp. xxxv–xxxvi.

3.1.3.8 Vermont: Constitution, 1777

CHAPTER I.

. . .

18. THAT the People have a Right to assemble together, to consult for their common Good — to instruct their Representatives, and to apply to the Legislature for Redress of Grievances, by Address, Petition or Remonstrance.

Vermont Acts, p. 5.

3.1.4 OTHER TEXTS

3.1.4.1 Tumultuous Petition Act, 1661

[N]o person or persons whatsoever shall repaire to his Majesty or both or either of the Houses of Parliament upon p[re]tense of presenting or delivering any peticion complaint remonstrance or declaration or other addresses accompanied with excessive number of people not att any one time with abouve the number of ten persons upon pain of incurring a penalty not exceeding the sum of one hundred pounds in money and three months imprisonment . . . for every offence which offence to be prosecuted at the Court of King's Bench or att the assizes or generall quarter sessions within six months after the offence committed and proved by two or more credible witnesses.

2. PROVIDED alwaies that this Act or any thing therein contained shall not be construed to extend or debar or hinder any person or persons not exceeding the number or ten aforesaid to present any publique or private grievance or complaint to any member or members of Parliament after his election and during the continuance of the Parliament or to the King's Majesty for any remedy to bee thereupon had nor to extend to any address whatsoever to his Majesty by all or any the members of both or either Houses of Parliament during the sitting of Parliament but that they may enjoye theire freedome of accesse to his Majesty as heretofore hath beene used.

13 Chas. 2, st. 1, c. 5.

3.1.4.2 English Bill of Rights, 1689

. . . That it is the right of the subjects to petition the King and all commitments and prosecutions for such petitioning are illegal.

. . .

And that for redresse of all grievances, and for the amending strengthening and preserving of the lawes Parlyaments ought to be held frequently.

1 Will. & Mar. sess. 2, c. 2.

3.1.4.3 Resolutions of the Stamp Act Congress, October 19, 1765

13th. That it is the right of the British subjects in these colonies, to petition the king or either house of parliament.

First Congress Journal, p. 29.

3.1.4.4   Declaration and Resolves of the First Continental Congress, October 14, 1774

Resolved, N.C.D.8. That they have a right peaceably to assemble, consider of their grievances, and petition the king; and that all prosecutions, prohibitory proclamations, and committments for the same, are illegal.

Tansill, p. 3.

3.1.4.5   Declaration of Independence, July 4, 1776

. . . In every stage of these Oppressions We have Petitioned for Redress in the most humble terms: Our repeated Petitions have been answered only by repeated injury. A Prince, whose character is thus marked by every act which may define a Tyrant, is unfit to be the ruler of a free people. Nor have We been wanting in attentions to our British brethren. We have warned them from time to time of attempts by their legislature to extend an unwarrantable jurisdiction over us. We have reminded them of the circumstances of our emigration and settlement here. We have appealed to their native justice and magnanimity, and we have conjured them by the ties of our common kindred to disavow these usurpations, which, would inevitably interrupt our connections and correspondence. They too have been deaf to the voice of justice and of consanguinity. We must, therefore, acquiesce in the necessity, which denounces our Separation, and hold them, as we hold the rest of mankind, Enemies in War, in Peace Friends. —

Continental Congress Papers, DNA.

3.1.4.6   Richard Henry Lee to Edmund Randolph, Proposed Amendments, October 16, 1787

. . . That the right of the people to assemble peaceably for the purpose of petitioning the legislature shall not be prevented. . . .

Virginia Gazette, December 22, 1787.

3.2 DISCUSSION OF DRAFTS AND PROPOSALS
3.2.1 THE FIRST CONGRESS

3.2.1.1   June 8, 1789[2]

3.2.1.2   August 15, 1789

3.2.1.2.a   The next clause of the 4th proposition was taken into consideration, and was as follows: "The freedom of speech and of the press, and the right of the people peaceably to assemble and consult for their common good, and to apply to the government for redress of grievances shall not be infringed."

Mr. SEDGWICK

Submitted to those gentlemen who had contemplated the subject, what effect such an amendment as this would have; he feared it would tend to make them appear trifling in the eyes of their constituents; what, said he, shall we secure the freedom of speech, and think it necessary at the same time to allow the right of assembling? If people freely converse together, they must assemble for that purpose; it is a self-evident, unalienable right which the people possess; it is certainly a thing that never would be called in question; it is derogatory to the dignity of the

---

[2] For reports of Madison's speech in support of his proposals, *see* 1.2.1.1.a–c.

House to descend to such minutiae — he therefore moved to strike out "assemble and."

Mr. BENSON.

The committee who framed this report, proceeded on the principle that these rights belonged to the people; they conceived them to be inherent, and all that they meant to provide against, was their being infringed by the government.

Mr. SEDGWICK

Replied, that if the committee were governed by that general principle, they might have gone into a very lengthy enumeration of rights; they might have declared that a man should have a right to wear his hat if he pleased, that he might get up when he pleased, and go to bed when he thought proper; but he would ask the gentleman whether he thought it necessary to enter these trifles in a declaration of rights, under a government where none of them were intended to be infringed.

Mr. TUCKER

Hoped the words would not be struck out, for he considered them of importance; beside, they were recommended by the states of Virginia and North-Carolina, though he noticed that the most material part proposed by those states was omitted, which was, a declaration that the people should have a right to instruct their representatives; he would move to have those words inserted as soon as the motion for striking out was decided.

Mr. GERRY

Was also against the words being struck out, because he conceived it to be an essential right; it was inserted in the constitutions of several states, and though it had been abused in the year 1786 in Massachusetts, yet that abuse ought not to operate as an argument against the use of it; the people ought to be secure in the peaceable enjoyment of this privilege, and that can only be done by making a declaration to that effect in the constitution.

Mr. PAGE.

The gentleman from Massachusetts, (mr. Sedgwick) who has made this motion, objects to the clause; because the right is of so trivial a nature; he supposes it no more essential than whether a man has a right to wear his hat or not, but let me observe to him that such rights have been opposed, and a man has been obliged to pull off his hat when he appeared before the face of authority; people have also been prevented from assembling together on their lawful occasions, therefore it is well to guard against such stretches of authority, by inserting the privilege in the declaration of rights; if the people could be deprived of the power of assembling under any pretext whatsoever, they might be deprived of every other privilege contained in the clause.

Mr. VINING

Said, if the thing was harmless, and it would tend to gratify the states that had proposed amendments, he should agree to it.

Mr. HARTLEY

Observed that it had been asserted in the convention of Pennsylvania, by the friends of the constitution, that all the rights and powers that were not given to the government, were retained by the states and the people thereof; this was also his own opinion, but as four or five states had required to be secured in those rights by an express declaration in the constitution, he was disposed to gratify them; he thought every thing that was not incompatible with the general good ought to be granted, if it would tend to obtain the confidence of the people in the government, and upon the whole, he thought these words were as necessary to be inserted in the declaration of rights as most in the clause.

Mr. GERRY

Said that his colleague contended for nothing, if he supposed that the people had a right to consult for the common good, because they could not consult unless they met for that purpose.

Mr. SEDGWICK

Replied that if they were understood or implied in the word consult, they were utterly unnecessary, and upon that ground he moved to have them struck out.

The question was now put upon mr. Sedgwick's motion, and lost by a considerable majority.

Mr. TUCKER then moved to insert these words, "to instruct their representatives."

Mr. HARTLEY

Wished the motion had not been made, for gentlemen acquainted with the circumstances of this country, and the history of the country from which we separated, differed exceedingly on this point; the members of the house of representatives, said he, are chosen for two years, the members of the senate for six.

According to the principles laid down in the constitution, it is presumable that the persons elected know the interests and the circumstances of their constituents, and being checked in their determinations by a division of the legislative power into two branches, there is little danger of error, at least it ought to be supposed that they have the confidence of the people during the period for which they are elected; and if, by misconduct, they forfeit it, their constituents have the power of leaving them out at the expiration of that time; thus they are answerable for the part they have taken in measures that may be contrary to the general wish.

Representation is the principle of our government; the people ought to have confidence in the honor and integrity of those they send forward to transact their business; their right to instruct them is a problematical subject. We have seen it attended with bad consequences, both in England and in America. When the passions of the people were excited, instructions have been resorted to and obtained, to answer party purposes; and although the public opinion is generally respectable, yet at such moments it has been known to be often wrong; and happy is that government composed of men of firmness and wisdom to discover and resist the popular error.

If, in a small community, where the interests, habits, and manners are neither so numerous or deversified [*sic*], instructions bind not: — What shall we say of instructions to this body; can it be supposed that the inhabitants of a single district in a state, are better informed with respect to the general interests of the union than a select body assembled from every part? Can it be supposed that a part will be more desirous of promoting the good of the whole than the whole will of the part? I apprehend, sir, that congress will be judges of proper measures, and that instructions will never be resorted to but for party purposes, when they will generally contain the prejudices and acrimony of the party rather than the dictates of honest reason and sound policy.

In England this question has been considerably agitated, the representatives of some towns in parliament, have acknowledged, and submitted to the binding force of instructions, while the majority have thrown off the shackles with disdain. I would not have this precedent influence our decision; but let the doctrine be tried upon its own merits, and stand or fall as it shall be found to deserve.

It appears to my mind, that the principle of representation is distinct from an agency, which may require written instructions. The great end of meeting is to consult for the common good; but can the common good be discerned without the object is reflected and shewn in every light. A local or partial view does not necessarily enable any man to comprehend it clearly; this can only result from an inspection into the aggregate. Instructions viewed in this light, will be found to embarrass the best and wisest men. And were all the members to take their seats in order to obey instructions, and those instructions were as various as it is probable they would be, what possibility would there exist of so many accommodating each to the other, as to produce any act whatever? Perhaps a majority of the whole might not be instructed to agree to any one point; and is it thus the people of the United States propose to form a more perfect union, provide for the common defence, and promote the general welfare?

Sir, I have known within my own time so many inconveniences and real evils arise from adopting the popular opinions on the moment, that although I respect them as much as any man, I hope this government will particularly guard against them, at least that they will not bind themselves by a constitutional act, and by oath to submit to their influence, if they do, the great object which this government has been established to attain, will inevitably elude our grasp on the uncertain and veering winds of popular commotion.

MR. PAGE.

The gentleman from Pennsylvania tells you, that in England this principle is doubted; how far this is consonant with the nature of the government I will not pretend to say, but I am not astonished to find that the administrators of a monarchical government are unassailable by the weak voice of the people, but under a democracy whose great end is, to form a code of laws congenial with the public sentiment, the popular opinion ought to be collected and attended to. Our present object is, I presume, to secure to our constituents and to posterity these inestimable rights. Our government is derived from the people, of consequence the people have a right to consult for the common good; but to what end will this be done, if they have not the power of instructing their representatives? Instruction and representation in a republic, appear to me to be inseparably connected; but was I the subject of a monarch, I should doubt whether the public good did not depend more upon the prince's will than the will of the people. I should dread a popular assembly consulting for the public good, because under its influence, commotions and tumults might arise that would shake the foundation of the monarch's throne, and make the empire tremble in expectation. The people of

England have submitted the crown to the Hanover family, and have rejected the Stuarts, if instructions upon such a revolution were considered as binding, it is difficult to know what would have been the effects, it might be well therefore to have the doctrine exploded from that kingdom; but it will not be advanced as a substantial reason in favor of our treading in the same steps.

The honorable gentleman has said, that when once the people have chosen a representative, they must rely on his integrity and judgment during the period for which he is elected. I think, sir, that to doubt the authority of the people to instruct their representatives, will give them just cause to be alarmed for their fate: I look upon it as a dangerous doctrine, subversive of the great end for which the United States have confederated. Every friend of mankind, every well-wisher of his country will be desirous of obtaining the sense of the people on every occasion of magnitude; but how can this be so well expressed as in instructions to their representatives; I hope, therefore, that gentlemen will not oppose the insertion of it in this part of the report.

MR. CLYMER.

I hope the amendment will not be adopted, but if our constituents chuse to instruct us, that they may be left at liberty to do so; do gentlemen foresee the extent of these words? If they have a constitutional right to instruct us, it infers that we are bound by those instructions, and as we ought not to decide constitutional questions by implication, I presume we shall be called upon to go further, and expressly declare the members of the legislature bound by the instruction of their constituents; this is a most dangerous principle, utterly destructive of all ideas of an independent and deliberative body, which are essential requisites in the legislatures of free governments, they prevent men of abilities and experience from rendering those services to the community that are in their power, destroying the object contemplated by establishing an efficient general government, and rendering congress a mere passive machine.

MR. SHERMAN.

It appears to me, that the words are calculated to mislead the people by conveying an idea, that they have a right to control the debates of the legislature; this cannot be admitted to be just, because it would destroy the object of their meeting. I think, when the people have chosen a representative, it is his duty to meet others from the different parts of the union, and consult, and agree with them to such acts as are for the general benefit of the whole community; if they were to be guided by instructions, there would be no use in deliberations, all that a man would have to do, would be to produce his instructions and lay them on the table, and let them speak for him, from hence I think it may be fairly inferred, that the right of the people to consult for their common good can go no further than to petition the legislature or apply for a redress of grievances. It is the duty of a good representative to enquire what measures are most likely to promote the general welfare, and after he has discovered them to give them his support; should his instructions therefore coincide with his ideas on any measure, they would be unnecessary; if they were contrary to the conviction of his own mind, he must be bound by every principle of justice to disregard them.

Mr. Jackson

Was in favor of the right of the people, to assemble and consult for the common good, it had been used in this country as one of the best checks on the British legislature in their unjustifiable attempts to tax the colonies without their consent. America had no representatives in the British parliament, therefore they could instruct none, yet they exercised the power of consultation to a good effect. He begged gentlemen to consider the dangerous tendency of establishing such a doctrine, it would necessarily drive the house into a number of factions, there might be different instructions from every state, and the representation from each state would be a faction to support its own measures.

If we establish this as a right, we shall be bound by those instructions; now, I am willing to leave both the people and the representatives to their own discretion on this subject, let the people consult and give their opinion, let the representative judge of it, and if it is just, let him govern himself by it as a good member ought to do, but if it is otherwise, let him have it in his power to reject their advice.

What may be the consequence of binding a man to vote in all cases according to the will of others? He is to decide upon a constitutional point, and on this question his conscience is bound by the obligation of a solemn oath; you now involve him in a serious dilemma, if he votes according to his conscience, he decides against his instructions, but in deciding against his instructions he commits a breach of the constitution, by infringing the prerogative of the people, secured to them by this declaration. In short, it will give rise to such a variety of absurdities and inconsistencies as no prudent legislature would wish to involve themselves in.

Mr. Gerry.

By the checks provided in the constitution, we have good grounds to believe that the very framers of it conceived that the government would be liable to maladministration, and I presume that the gentlemen of this house do not mean to arrogate themselves more perfection than human nature has as yet been found to be capable of; if they do not, they will admit an additional check against abuses which this, like every other government, is subject to. Instructions from the people will furnish this in a considerable degree.

It has been said that the amendment proposed by the honorable gentleman from South-Carolina, (mr. Tucker) determines this point, "that the people can bind their representatives to follow their instructions;" I do not conceive that this necessarily follows: I think the representative, notwithstanding the insertion of these words, would be at liberty to act as he pleased; if he declined to pursue such measures as he was directed to attain, the people would have a right to refuse him their suffrages at a future election.

Now, though I do not believe the amendment would bind the representatives to obey the instructions, yet I think the people have a right both to instruct and bind them. Do gentlemen conceive that on any occasion instructions would be so general as to proceed from all our constituents? If they do it is the sovereign will, for gentlemen will not contend that the sovereign will, presides in the legislature; the friends and patrons of this constitution have always declared that the sovereignty resides in the people, and that they do not part with it on any occasion; to say the sovereignty vests in the people, and that they have not a right to instruct and control their representatives, is absurd to the last degree; they must either give up their principle, or grant that the people have a right to exercise their sovereignty to control the whole government, as well as this branch of it; but the amendment does not carry the principle to such an extent, it only declares the right of the people to send instructions; the representative will, if he thinks proper, communicate his instructions to the house, but how far they shall operate on his conduct, he will judge for himself.

The honorable gentleman from Georgia (mr. Jackson) supposes that instructions will tend to generate factions in this house, but he did not see how it could have that effect, any more than the freedom of debate had. If the representative entertains the same opinion with his constituents, he will decide with them in favor of the measure; if other gentlemen, who are not instructed on the point, are convinced by argument that the measure is proper, they will also vote with them, consequently the influence of debate and of instruction is the same.

The gentleman says further, that the people have the right of instructing their representatives; if so, why not declare it? Does he mean that it shall lay dormant and never be exercised? If so, it will be a right of no utility. But much good may result from a declaration in the constitution that they possess this privilege; the people will be encouraged to come forward with their instructions, which will form a fund of useful information for the legislature; we cannot, I apprehend, be too well informed of the true state, condition, and sentiment of our constituents, and perhaps this is the best mode in our power of obtaining information. I hope we shall never shut our ears against that information which is to be derived from the petitions and instructions of our constituents. I hope we shall never presume to think that all the wisdom of this country is concentred within the walls of this house. Men, unambitious of distinctions from their fellow citizens, remain within their own domestic walk, unheard of and unseen, possessing all the advantages resulting from a watchful observance of public men and public measures, whose voice, if we would descend to listen to it, would give us knowledge superior to what could be acquired amidst the cares and bustles of a public life; let us then adopt the amendment, and encourage the diffident to enrich our stock of knowledge with the treasure of their remarks and observations.

Mr. MADISON.

I think the committee acted prudently in omitting to insert these words in the report they have brought forward; if unfortunately the attempt of proposing amendments should prove abortive, it will not arise from the want of a disposition in the friends of the constitution to do what is right with respect to securing the rights and privileges of the people of America; but from the difficulties arising from discussing and proposing abstract propositions, of which the judgment may not be convinced. I venture to say that if we confine ourselves to an enumeration of simple acknowledged principles, the ratification will meet with but little difficulty. Amendments of a doubtful nature will have a tendency to prejudice the whole system; the proposition now suggested, partakes highly of this nature; it is doubted by many gentlemen here; it has been objected to in intelligent publications throughout the union; it is doubted by many members of the state legislatures: In one sense this declaration is true, in many others it is certainly not true; in the sense in which it is true, we have asserted the right sufficiently in what we have done; if we mean nothing more than this, that the people have a right to express and communicate their sentiments and wishes, we have provided for it already. The right of freedom of speech is secured; the liberty of the press is expressly declared to be beyond the reach of this government; the people may therefore publicly address their representatives; may privately advise them, or declare their sentiments by petition to the whole body; in all these ways they may communicate their will. If gentlemen mean to go further, and to say that the people have a right to instruct their representatives in such a sense as that the delegates were obliged to conform to those instructions, the declaration is not true. Suppose they instruct a representative by his vote to violate the constitution, is he at liberty to obey such instructions? Suppose he is instructed to patronize certain measures, and from circumstances known to him, but not to his constituents, he is convinced that they will endanger the public good, is he obliged to sacrifice his own judgment to them? Is he absolutely bound to perform what he is instructed to do? Suppose he refuses, will his vote be the less valid, or the community be disengaged from that obedience which is due from the laws of the union? If his vote must inevitably have the same effect, what sort of a right is this in the constitution to instruct a representative who has a right to disregard the order, if he pleases? In this sense the right does not exist, in the other sense it does exist, and is provided largely for.

The honorable gentleman from Massachusetts, asks if the sovereignty is not with the people at large; does he infer that the people can, in detached bodies, contravene an act established by the whole people? My idea of the sovereignty of the people is, that the people can change the constitution if they please, but while the constitution exists, they must conform themselves to its dictates: But I do not believe the inhabitants of any district can speak the voice of the people, so far from it, their ideas may contradict the sense of the whole people; hence the consequence that instructions are binding on the representative is of a doubtful, if not of a dangerous nature. I do not conceive, therefore, that it is necessary to agree to the proposition now made; so far as any real good is to arise from it, so far that real good is provided for; so far as it is of a doubtful nature, so far it obliges us to run the risk of losing the whole system.

Mr. SMITH (of S.C.)

I am opposed to this motion, because I conceive it will operate as a partial inconvenience to the more distant states; if every member is to be bound by instructions how to vote, what are gentlemen from the extremeties of the continent to do?

Members from the neighbouring states can obtain their instructions earlier than those from the southern ones, and I presume that particular instructions will be necessary for particular measures, of consequence we vote perhaps against instructions on their way to us, or we must decline voting at all; but what is the necessity of having a numerous representation; one member from a state can receive the instructions, and by his vote answer all the purposes of many, provided his vote is allowed to count for the proportion the state ought to send; in this way the business might be done at a less expence than having one or two hundred members in the house, which had been strongly contended for yesterday.

Mr. STONE.

I think the clause would change the government entirely, instead of being a government founded upon representation, it would be a democracy of singular properties.

I differ from the gentleman from Virginia (mr. Madison) if he thinks this clause would not bind the representative; in my opinion it would bind him effectually, and I venture to assert, without diffidence, that any law passed by the legislature, would be of no force, if a majority of the members of this house were instructed to the contrary, provided the amendment become part of the constitution. What would follow from this? Instead of looking in the code of laws passed by congress, your judiciary would have to collect and examine the instructions from the various parts of the union. It follows very clearly from hence, that the government would be altered from a representative one to a democracy, wherein all laws are made immediately by the voice of the people.

This is a power not to be found in any part of the earth except among the Swiss Cantons; there the body of the people vote upon the laws, and give instructions to their delegates. But here we have a different form of government, the people at large are not authorised under it to vote upon the law, nor did I ever hear that any man required it. Why then are we called upon to propose amendments subversive of the principles of the constitution which were never desired.

Several members now called for the question, and the chairman being about to put the same.

Mr. GERRY.

Gentlemen seem in a great hurry to get this business through, I think, mr. chairman, it requires a further discussion; for my part I had rather do less business and do it well, than precipitate measures before they are fully understood.

The honorable gentleman from Virginia (mr. Madison) stated, that if the proposed amendments are defeated, it will be by the delay attending the discussion of doubtful propositions; and he declares this to partake of that quality. It is natural, sir, for us to be fond of our own work, we do not like to see it disfigured by other hands. That honorable gentleman brought forward a string of propositions; among them was the clause now proposed to be amended, he is no doubt ready for the question and determined not to admit what we think an improvement. The gentlemen who were on the committee, and brought in the report, have considered the subject, and are also ripe for a decision. But other gentlemen may crave a like indulgence, is not the report before us for deliberation and discussion and to obtain the sense of the house upon it, and will not gentlemen allow us a day or two for these purposes, after they have forced us to proceed upon them at this time? I appeal to their candor and good sense on the occasion, and am sure not to be refused; and I must inform them now, that they may not be surprized hereafter, that I wish all the amendments, proposed by the respective states to be considered. Gentlemen say it is necessary to finish the subject, in order to reconcile a number of our fellow citizens to the government. If this is their principle, they ought to consider the wishes and intentions which the conventions have expressed for them; if they do this, they will find that they expect and wish for the declaration proposed by the honorable gentleman over the way (mr. Tucker) and of consequence they ought to agree to it, and why it, with others recommended in the same way, were not reported, I cannot pretend to say; the committee know this best themselves.

The honorable gentleman near me (mr. Stone) says, that the laws passed contrary to instruction will be nugatory. And other gentlemen ask, if their constituents instruct them to violate the constitution, whether they must do it? Sir, does not the constitution declare that all laws passed by congress are paramount to the laws and constitutions of the several states; if our decrees are of such force as to set aside the state laws and constitutions, certainly they may be repugnant to any instructions whatever without being injured thereby. But can we conceive that our constituents would be so absurd to instruct us to violate our oath, and act directly contrary to the principles of a government ordained by themselves. We must look upon them to be absolutely abandoned and false to their own interests to suppose them capable of giving such instructions.

If this amendment is introduced into the constitution, I do not think we shall be much troubled with instructions; a knowledge of the right will operate to check a spirit that would render instruction necessary.

The honorable gentleman from Virginia asked, will not the affirmative of a member who votes repugnant to his instructions, bind the community as much as the votes of those who conform? There is no doubt, sir, but it will; but does this tend to shew that the constituent has no right to instruct? Surely not. I admit, sir, that instructions contrary to the constitution, ought not to bind, though the sovereignty resides in the people. The honorable gentleman acknowledges that the sovereignty vests there, if so, it may exercise its will in any case not inconsistent with a previous contract. The same honorable gentlemen asks if we are to give the power to the people in detached bodies to contravene the government while it exists? Certainly not, nor does the proposed proposition extend to that point, it is only intended to open for them a convenient mode in which they may convey their sense to their agents. The gentleman therefore takes for granted what is inadmissible, that congress will always be doing illegal things, and make it necessary for the sovereign to declare its pleasure.

He says the people have a right to alter the constitution, but they have no right to oppose the government. If, while the government exists, they have no right to control it, it appears they have divested themselves of the sovereignty over the constitution. Therefore, our language, with our principles, must change, and we ought to say that the sovereignty existed in the people previous to the establishment of this government. This will be ground for alarm indeed if it is true, but I trust, sir, too much to the good sense of my fellow citizens ever to believe, that the doctrine will generally obtain in this country of freedom.

Mr. VINING.

If, mr. chairman, there appears on one side too great an urgency to dispatch this business, there appears on the other an unnecessary delay and procrastination equally improper and unpardonable. I think this business has been already well considered by the house, and every gentleman in it; however, I am not for an unseemly expedition.

The gentleman last up, has insinuated a reflection upon the committee for not reporting all the amendments proposed by some of the state conventions. I can assign him a reason for this, the committee conceived some of them superfluous or dangerous, and found many of them so contradictory that it was impossible to make any thing of them, and this is a circumstance the gentleman cannot pretend ignorance of.

It is not inconsistent in that honorable member to complain of hurry, when he comes day after day reiterating the same train of arguments, and demanding the attention of this body by rising six or seven times on a question. I wish, sir, this subject discussed coolly and dispassionately, but I hope we shall have no more reiterations or tedious discussions; let gentlemen try to expedite public business, and their arguments will be conducted in a laconic and consistent manner. As to the business of instruction, I look upon it inconsistent with the general good. Suppose our constituents were to instruct us to make paper money, no gentleman pretends to say it would be unconstitutional, yet every honest mind must shudder at the thought. How can we then assert that instructions ought to bind us in all cases not contrary to the constitution?

Mr. LIVERMORE

Was not very anxious whether the words were inserted or not, but he had a great deal of doubt about the meaning of this whole amendment, it provides that the people may meet and consult for the common good; does this mean a part of the people in a township or district, or does it mean the representatives in the state legislatures? If it means the latter, there is no occasion for a provision that the legislature may instruct the members of this body.

In some states the representatives were chosen by districts, in this case, perhaps, the instructions may be considered as coming from the districts, but in other states, each representative was chosen by the whole people; in New-Hampshire it was the case there, the instructions of any particular place would have but little weight, but a legislative instruction would have considerable influence upon each representative. If, therefore, the words mean that the legislature may instruct, he presumed it would have considerable effect, though he did not believe it binding. Indeed he was inclined to pay a deference to any information, he might receive from any number of gentlemen, even by a private letter, but as for full binding force, no instructions contained that quality. They could not, nor ought not to have it, because different parties pursue different measures, and it might be expedient, nay absolutely necessary, to sacrifice them in mutual concessions.

The doctrine of instructions would hold better in England than here, because the boroughs and corporations might have an interest to pursue, totally immaterial to the rest of the kingdom, in this case it would be prudent to instruct their members in parliament.

Mr. GERRY

Wished the constitution amended without his having any hand in it, but if he must interfere he would do his duty. The honorable gentleman from Delaware, had given him an example of moderation and laconic and consistent debate that he meant to follow, and would just observe to the worthy gentleman last up, that several states had proposed the amendment, and among the rest New-Hampshire.

There was one remark which escaped him, when he was up before, the gentleman from Maryland (mr. Stone) had said that the amendment would change the nature of the government and make it a democracy; now he had always heard that it was a democracy, but perhaps he was mislead, and the honorable gentleman was right in distinguishing it by some other appellation, perhaps an aristocracy was a term better adapted to it.

Mr. SEDGWICK

Opposed the idea of the gentleman from New-Hampshire, that the state legislatures had the power of instructing the members of this house; he looked upon it as a subordination of the rights of the people to admit such an authority. We stand not here, said he, the representatives of the state legislatures as under the former congress, but as the representatives of the great body of the people. The sovereignty, the independence, and the rights of the states, are intended to be guarded by the senate; if we are to be viewed in any other light, the greatest security the people have for their rights and privileges is destroyed.

But with respect to instructions, it is well worthy of consideration how they are to be procured, it is not the opinion of an individual that is to control my conduct; I consider myself a representative of the whole union. An individual may give me information, but his sentiments may be in opposition to the sense of the majority of the people: If instructions are to be of any efficacy they must speak the sense of the majority of the people, at least of a state. In a state so large as Massachusetts it will behoove gentlemen to consider how the sense of the majority of the freemen is to be obtained and communicated. Let us take care to avoid the insertion of crude and undigested propositions, more likely to produce acrimony, than that spirit of harmony which we ought to cultivate.

Mr. LIVERMORE

Said that he did not understand the honorable gentleman, or was not understood by him; he did not presume peremptorily to say what degree of influence the legislative instructions would have on a representative, he knew it was not the thing in contemplation here; and what he had said respected only the influence it would have on his private judgments.

Mr. AMES

Said there would be a very great inconvenience attending the establishment of the doctrine contended for by his colleague, those states who had selected their members by districts would have no right to give them instructions, consequently the members ought to withdraw, in which case the house might be reduced below a majority, and not be able, according to the constitution, to do any business at all.

According to the doctrine of the gentleman from New-Hampshire, one part of the government would be annihilated, for of what avail is it that the people have the appointment of a representative, if he is to pay obedience to the dictates of another body.

Several members now rose and called for the question.

Mr. PAGE

Was sorry to see gentlemen so impatient, the more so as he saw there was very little attention paid to any thing that was said, but he would express his sentiments if he was only heard by the chair; — he discovered clearly, notwithstanding what had been observed by the most ingenious supporters of the opposition, that there was an absolute necessity for adopting the amendment, it was strictly compatible with the spirit and the nature of the government, all power vests in the people of the United States, it is therefore a government of the people, a democracy; if it was consistent with the peace and tranquility of the inhabitants, every freeman would have a right to come and give his vote upon the law, but inasmuch as this cannot be done, by reason of the extent of territory, and some other causes, the people have agreed that their representatives shall exercise a part of their authority; to pretend to refuse them the power of instructing their agents, appears to me to deny them a right. One gentleman asks how the instructions are to be collected. many [*sic*] parts of this country have been in the practice of instructing their representatives; they found no difficulty in communicating their sense: Another gentleman asks if they were to instruct us to make paper money, what we would do? I would tell them, said he, it was unconstitutional, alter that, and we will consider on the point; unless laws are made satisfactory to the people, they will lose their support, they will be abused or done away; this tends to destroy the efficiency of the government.

It is the sense of several of the conventions that this amendment should take place; I think it my duty to support it, and fear it will spread an alarm among our constituents if we decline to do it.

Mr. WADSWORTH.

Instructions have frequently been given to the representatives throughout the United States, but the people did not claim as a right that they should have any obligation upon the representative; it is not right that they should: In troublesome times designing men have drawn the people to instruct the representatives to their harm; the representatives have, on such occasions, refused to comply with their instructions. I have known, myself, that they have been disobeyed, and yet the representative was not brought to account for it, on the contrary, he was carressed and re-elected, while those who have obeyed them, contrary to their private sentiments, have ever after been despised for it: Now, if the people considered it an inherent right in them to instruct their representatives, they would have undoubtedly punished the violation of them. I have no idea of instructions, unless they are obeyed; a discretionary power is incompatible with them.

The honorable gentleman who was up last says, if he was instructed to make paper money, he would tell his constituents it was unconstitutional; I believe that is not the case, for this body would have a right to make paper money, but if my constituents were to instruct me to vote for such a measure, I would disobey them let the consequence be what it would.

Mr. SUMPTER.

The honorable gentlemen who are opposed to the motion of my colleague, do not treat it fairly; they suppose that it is meant to bind the representative to conform to his instructions, the mover of this question, I presume to say, has no such thing in idea; that they shall notice them and obey them as far as is consistent and proper, may be very just; perhaps they ought to produce them to the house, and let them have as much influence as they deserve; but nothing further, I believe, is contended for.

I rose on this occasion, not so much to make any observations upon the point immediately under consideration, as to beg the committee to consider the consequences that may result from an undue precipitancy and hurry; nothing can distress me more than to be obliged to notice what I conceive to be somewhat improper in the conduct of so respectable a body. Gentlemen will reflect how difficult it is to remove error when once the passions are engaged in the discussion, temper and coolness are necessary to complete what must be the work of time; it cannot be denied but what the present constitution is imperfect, we must therefore take time to improve it. If gentlemen are pressed for want of time, and are disposed to adjourn the sessions of congress at a very early period, we had better drop the subject of amendments, and leave it until we have more leisure to consider and do the business effectually; for my part I would rather sit till this day twelve month, than have this all-important subject inconsiderately passed over; the people have already complained that the adoption of the constitution was done in too hasty a manner, what will they say of us if we press the amendments with so much haste.

Mr. BURKE.

It has been asserted, mr. chairman, that the people of America do not require this right; I beg leave to ask the gentleman from Massachusetts, whether the constitution of that state does not recognize that right, and the gentlemen from Maryland, whether their declaration of rights does not expressly secure it to the inhabitants of that state? These circumstances, added to what has been proposed by the state conventions as amendments to this constitution, pretty plainly declares the sense of the people to be in favor of securing to themselves and their posterity, a right of this nature.

Mr. SENEY

Said that the declaration of rights prefixed to the constitution of Maryland, secured to every man a right of petitioning the legislature for a redress of grievances, in a peaceable and orderly manner.

Mr. BURKE.

I am not positive with respect to the particular expression in the declaration of the rights of the people of Maryland, but the constitutions of Massachusetts, Pennsylvania and North-Carolina, all of them recognize, in express terms, the right of the people to give instruction to their representatives. — I do not mean to insist particularly upon this amendment, but I am very well satisfied that those that are reported and likely to be adopted by this house, are very far from giving satisfaction to our constituents; they are not those solid and substantial amendments which the people expect; they are little better than whip-syllabub, frothy and full of wind, formed only to please the palate, or they are like a tub thrown out to a whale, to secure the freight of the ship and its peaceable voyage; in my judgment they will not be gratified by the mode we have pursued in bringing them forward; there was a committee of eleven appointed, and out of them I think there were five who were members of the convention that formed the constitution, such gentlemen having already given their opinion with respect to the perfection of the work, may be thought improper agents to bring forward amendments; upon the whole, I think it will be found that we have done nothing but lose our time, and that it will be better to drop the subject now, and to proceed to the organization of the government.

Mr. Sinnickson

Enquired of mr. chairman, what was the question before the committee, for really debate had become so desultory, as to induce him to think it was lost sight of altogether.

Mr. Lawrance

Was averse to entering on the business at first, but since they had proceeded so far, he hoped they would finish it; he said, if gentlemen would confine themselves to the question, when they were speaking, that the business might be done in a more agreeable manner; he said he was against the amendmentproposed by-thegentleman [*sic*] from S. Carolina (mr. Tucker,) because every member on this floor ought to consider himself the representative of the whole union, and not of the particular district which had chosen him, as their decisions were to bind every individual of the confederated states, it was wrong to be guided by the voice of a single district, whose interests might happen to clash with that of the general good, and unless instructions were to be considered as binding, they were altogether superfluous.

Mr. Madison

Was unwilling to take up any more of the time of the committee, but on the other hand, he was not willing to be silent after the charges that had been brought against the committee, and the gentleman who introduced the amendments, by the honorable members on each side of him, (mr. Sumpter and mr. Burke.) Those gentlemen say we are precipitating the business, and insinuate that we are not acting with candor; I appeal to the gentlemen who have heard the voice of their country, to those who have attended the debates of the state conventions, whether the amendments now proposed are not those most strenuously required by the opponents to the constitution? It was wished that some security should be given for those great and essential rights which they had been taught to believe were in danger. I concurred, in the convention of Virginia, with those gentlemen, so far as to agree to a declaration of those rights which corresponded with my own judgment, and the other alterations which I had the honor to bring forward before the present congress. I appeal to the gentlemen on this floor who are desirous of amending the constitution, whether these proposed are not compatible with what are required by our constituents; have not the people been told that the rights of conscience, the freedom of speech, the liberty of the press, and trial by jury, were in jeopardy; that they ought not to adopt the constitution until those important rights were secured to them.

But while I approve of these amendments, I should oppose the consideration at this time, of such as are likely to change the principles of the government, or that are of a doubtful nature; because I apprehend there is little prospect of obtaining the consent of two-thirds of both houses of congress, and three-fourths of the state legislatures, to ratify propositions of this kind; therefore, as a friend to what is attainable, I would limit it to the plain, simple, and important security that has been required. If I was inclined to make no alteration in the constitution I would bring forward such amendments as were of a dubious cast, in order to have the whole rejected.

Mr. Burke

Never entertained an idea of charging gentlemen with the want of candor; but he would appeal to any man of sense and candor, whether the amendments contained in the report were any thing like the amendments required by the states of New-York, Virginia, New-Hampshire and Carolina, and having these amendments in his hand, he turned to them to shew the difference, concluding that all the important amendments were omitted in the report.

Mr. Smith (of S.C.)

Understood his colleague, who has just sat down, to have asserted that the amendment under consideration was contained in the constitution of the state of South-Carolina, this was not the fact.

Mr. Burke

Said he mentioned the state of North-Carolina, and there it was inserted in express terms.

The question was now called for from several parts of the house, but a desultory conversation took place before the conversation was put; at length the call becoming very general, it was stated from the chair, and determined in the negative, 10 rising in favor of it, and 41 against it.

Congressional Register, August 15, 1789, vol. 2, pp. 197– 217.

3.2.1.2.b Fifth amendment — "The freedom of speech, and of the press, and of the right of the people peaceably to assemble and consult for their common good, and to apply to the government for redress of grievances, shall not be infringed."

Mr. Tucker moved to insert between the words "common good," "and to" in this paragraph, these words "to instruct their representatives."

On this motion a long debate ensued. —

Mr. Hartley said it was a problematical subject — The practice on this principle might be attended with danger. There were periods when from various causes the popular mind was in a state of fermentation and incapable of acting wisely — This had frequently been experienced in the mother country, and once in a sister State. — In such cases it was a happiness to obtain representatives who might be free to exert their abilities against the popular errors and passions. The power of instructing might be liable to great abuses; it would generally be exercised in times of public disturbance, and would express rather the prejudices of faction, than the voice of policy; thus it would convey improper influences into the government. — He said he had seen so many unhappy examples of the influence of the popular humours in public bodies, that he hoped they would be provided against in this government.

Mr. Page was in favor of the motion.

Mr. Clymer remarked that the principle of the motion was a dangerous one. It would take away all the freedom and independence of the representatives, it would destroy the very spirit of representation itself, by rendering Congress a passive machine instead of a deliberative body.

Mr. SHERMAN insisted that instructions were not a proper rule for the representative, since they were not adequate to the purposes for which he was delegated. He was to consult the common good of the whole, and was the servant of the people at large. If they should coincide with his ideas of the common good, they would be unnecessary; if they contradicted them, he would be bound by every principle of justice to disregard them.

Mr. JACKSON also opposed the motion.

Mr. GERRY advocated the proposition — he said the power of instructing was essential in order to check an administration which should be guilty of abuses. Such things would probably happen. He hoped gentlemen would not arrogate to themselves more perfection, than any other government had been found to possess, or more at all times than the body of the people. — It had he said been always contended by the friends of this government that the sovereignty resided in the people. That principle seemed inconsistent with what gentlemen now asserted; if the people were the sovereign, he could not conceive why they had not the right to instruct and direct their agents at their pleasure.

Mr. MADISON observed that the existence of this right of instructing was at least a doubtful right. He wished that the amendments which were to go to the people should consist of an enumeration of simple and acknowledged principles. Such rights only ought to be expressly secured as were certain and fixed. The insertion of propositions that were of a doubtful nature, would have a tendency to prejudice the whole system of amendments, and render their adoption difficult. The right suggested was doubtful, and would be so considered by many of the states. In some degree the declaration of this right might be true; in other respects false. If by instructions were meant a given advice, or expressing the wishes of the people, the proposition was true; but still was unnecessary, since that right was provided for already. The amendments already passed had declared that the press should be free, and that the people should have the freedom of speech and petitioning: therefore the people might speak to their representatives, might address them through the medium of the press, or by petition to the whole body. They might freely express their wills by these several modes. But if it was meant that they had any obligatory force, the principle was certainly false. Suppose the representatives were instructed to do any act incompatible with the constitution, would he be bound to obey those instructions? Suppose he was directed to do what he knew was contrary to the public good, would be bound [*sic*] to sacrifice his own opinion? Would not the vote of a representative contrary to his instructions be as binding on the people as a different one? If these things then be true, where is the right of the constituent? or where is the advantage to result from. It must either supercede all the other obligations, the most sacred, or it could be of no benefit to the people. The gentleman says, the people are the sovereign — True. But who are the people? Is every small district, the PEOPLE? and do the inhabitants of this district express the voice of the people, when they may not be a thousandth part, and although their instructions may contradict the sense of the whole people besides? Have the people in detached assemblies a right to violate the constitution or controul the actions of the whole sovereign power? This would be setting up a hundred sovereignties in the place of one.

Mr. SMITH (S.C.) was opposed to the motion — He said the doctrine of Instructions in practice would operate partially. The States who were near the seat of government would have an advantage over those more distant. — Particular instructions might be necessary for a particular measure; such could not be obtained by the members of the distant states. He said there was no need of a large representation, if in all important matters they were to be guided by express instructions — One member from each state would serve every purpose. It was inconsistent with the principle of the amendment which had been adopted the preceding day.

Mr. STONE differed with Mr. Madison, that the members would not be bound by instructions — He said when this principle was inserted in the constitution, it would render instructions sacred and obligatory in all cases; but he looked on this as one of the greatest of evils. He believed this would change the nature of the constitution — Instead of being a representative government, it would be a singular kind of democracy, and whenever a question arose what was the law, it would not properly be decided by recurring to the codes and institutions of Congress, but by collecting and examining the various instructions of different parts of the Union.

Several of the members spoke, and the debate was continued in a desultory manner — and at last the motion was negatived by a great majority — The question on the amendment was then put, and carried in the affirmative.

Daily Advertiser, August 17, 1789, p. 2, cols. 1–2.

3.2.1.2.c   Fifth amendment — "The freedom of speech, and of the press, and of the right of the people peaceably to assemble and consult for their common good, and to apply to the government for redress of grievances, shall not be infringed."

Mr. Tucker moved to insert between the words "common good," "and to" in this paragraph, these words "to instruct their representatives."

On this motion a long debate ensued. —

Mr. Hartley said it was a problematical subject, — The practice on this principle might be attended with danger. There were periods when from various causes the popular mind was in a state of fermentation and incapable of acting wisely — This had frequently been experienced in the mother country, and once in a sister state. — In such cases it was a happiness to obtain representatives who might be free to exert their abilities against the popular errors and passions. The power of instructing might be liable to great abuses; it would generally be exercised in times of public disturbance, and would express rather the prejudices of faction, than the voice of policy; thus it would convey improper influence into the government. — He said he had seen so many unhappy examples of the influence of the popular humours in public bodies, that he hoped they would be provided against in this government.

Mr. Clymer remarked that the principle of the motion was a dangerous one. It would take away all the freedom and independence of the representatives, it would destroy the very spirit of representation itself, by rendering Congress a passive machine instead of a deliberative body.

Mr. Sherman insisted that instructions were not adequate to the purposes for which he was delegated. He was to consult the common good of the whole, and was the servant of the people at large. If they would coincide with the ideas of the common good, they would be unnecessary; if they contradicted them, he would be bound by every principle of justice to disregard them.

Mr. Gerry advocated the proposition — he said the power of instructing was essential in order to check an administration which should be guilty of abuses. Such things would probably happen. He hoped gentlemen would not arrogate to themselves more perfection, than any other government had been found to possess, or more at all times than the body of the people. — It had he said been always contended by the friends of this government that the sovereignty resided in the people. That principle seemed inconsistent with what gentlemen now asserted; if the people were the sovereign, he could not conceive why they had not the right to instruct and direct their agents at their pleasure.

Mr. Madison observed that the existence of this right of instructing was at least a doubtful right. He wished that the amendments which were to go to the people should consist of an enumeration of simple and acknowledged principles. Such rights only ought to be expressly secured as were certain and fixed. The insertion of propositions that were of a doubtful nature, would have a tendency to prejudice the whole system of amendments, and render their adoption difficult. The right suggested was doubtful, and would be so considered by many of the states. In some degree the declaration of this right might be true; in other respects false. If by instructions were meant a given advice, or expressing the wishes of the people, the proposition was true; but still was unnecessary, since that right was provided for already. The amendments already passed had declared that the press should be free, and that the people should have the freedom of speech and petitioning: therefore the people might speak to their representatives, might address them through the medium of the press, or by petition to the whole body. They might freely express their wills by these several modes. But if it was meant that they had any obligatory force, the principle was certainly false. Suppose the representatives were instructed to do any act incompatible with the constitution, would be bound to obey those instructions? Suppose he was directed to do what he knew was contrary to the public good, would be bound [*sic*] to sacrifice his own opinion? Would not the vote of a representative contrary to his instructions be as binding on the people as a different one? If these things be true, where is the rights of the constituent? Or where is the advantage to result from. It must either supercede all the other obligations the most sacred, or it could be of no benefit to the people. The gentleman says, the people are the sovereign — True. But who are the people? Is every small district, the the [*sic*] *people?* and do the inhabitants of this district express the voice of the people, when they may not be a thousandth part, and although their instructions may contradict the sense of the whole people besides? Have the people in detached assemblies a right to violate the constitution or controul the actions of the whole sovereign power? This would be setting up a hundred sovereignties in the place of one.

Mr. Smith (S.C.) was opposed to the motion — He said the doctrine of instructions in practice would operate partially. The States who were near the seat of government would have an advantage over those more distant. Particular instructions might be necessary for a particular measure; such could not be obtained by the members of the distant states. He said there was no need of a large representation, If in all important matters they were to be guided by express instructions — One member from each state would serve every purpose. It was inconsistent with the principle of the amendment which had been adopted the preceding day.

Mr. Stone differed with Mr. Madison, that the members would not be bound by instructions — He said when this principle was inserted in the constitution, it would render instructions sacred and obligatory in all cases; but he looked on this as one of the greatest of evils: it would change the nature of the constitution — Instead of being a representative government, it would be a singular kind of democracy, and whenever a question arose what was the law, it would not properly be decided by recurring to the codes and institutions of Congress, by collecting and examining the various instructions of different parts of the Union.

Several of the members spoke, and the debate was continued in a desultory manner — and at last the motion was negatived by a great majority — The question on the amendment was then put, and carried in the affirmative.

Committee rose. —

Mr. Ames moved that all questions on the subject of the amendments, should be decided in committee by two thirds of the members. This was laid on the table.

The house was then adjourned.

New-York Daily Gazette, August 18, 1789, p. 798, col. 3, and p. 799, col. 1.

3.2.1.2.d In committee of the whole, on amendments to the constitution — . . . .

. . . Fifth amendment. *The freedom of speech, and of the press, and of the rights of the people peaceably to assemble and consult for their common good, and to apply to government for the redress of grievances shall not be infringed.*

Mr. SEDGWICK moved to strike out the words "assemble and." This is a self evident unalienable right of the people, said he, and it does appear to me below the dignity of this house, to insert such things in the constitution. The right will be as fully recognized if the words are struck out, as if they were retained: For if the people may converse, they must meet *for* the purpose.

This motion was opposed by Mr. GERRY, Mr. PAGE, Mr. VINING and Mr. HARTLY; [sic] and the question being taken it was negatived.

Mr. TUCKER moved to insert these words, *to instruct their representatives*. This produced a long debate.

Mr. HARTLEY. I could wish, Mr. chairman, that these words had not been proposed. Representatives ought to possess the confidence of their constituents; they ought to rely on their honour and integrity. The practice of instructing representatives may be attended with danger; we have seen it attended with bad consequences; it is commonly resorted to for party purposes, and when the passions are up. It is a right, which even in England is considered a problematical [sic]. The right of instructing is liable to great abuses; it will generally be exercised in times of popular commotion; and these instructions will rather express the prejudices of party, than the dictates of reason and policy. I have known, Sir, so many evils arise from adopting the popular opinion of the moment, that I hope this government will be guarded against such an influence; and wish the words may not be inserted.

Mr. PAGE was in favour of the motion — He said, that the right may well be doubted in a monarchy; but in a government instituted for the sole purpose of guarding the rights of the people, it appears to me to be proper.

Mr. CLYMER: I hope, Sir, the clause will not be adopted, for if it is, we must go further, and say, that the representatives are *bound* by the instructions, which is a most dangerous principle, and is destructive of all ideas of an independent and deliberative body.

Mr. SHERMAN said, these words had a tendency to mislead the people, by conveying an idea that they had a right to controul the debates of the federal legislature. Instructions cannot be considered as a proper rule for a representative to form his conduct by; they cannot be adequate to the purpose for which he is delegated. He is to consult the good of the whole: Should instructions therefore coincide with his ideas of the common good, they would be unnecessary: If they were contrary, he would be bound by every principle of justice to disregard them.

Mr. JACKSON opposed the motion: He said this was a dangerous article, as its natural tendency is to divide the house into factions: He then adverted to the absurdities and inconsistencies which would be involved in adopting the measure.

Mr. GERRY supported the motion: He observed, that to suppose we cannot be instructed, is to suppose that we are perfect: The power of instruction is in my opinion essential to check an administration which should be guilty of abuses: No one will deny that these may not happen: To deny the people this right is to arrogate to ourselves more wisdom than the whole body of the people possess. — I contend, Sir, that our constituents have not only a right to instruct, but to *bind* this legislature — It has been contended by the friends to the constitution, that the people are sovereign: if so it involves an absurdity to suppose that they cannot, not only instruct, but controul the house: Debates may create factions, as well as instructions: We cannot be too well informed; this is the best method of obtaining information, and I hope we shall never shut our ears against that information which is to be derived from the voice of the people.

Mr. MADISON observed, that the existence of this right is at least doubtful. — I wish that the amendments may consist of an enumeration of simple and acknowledged principles: The insertion of propositions that are of a doubtful nature, will have a tendency to prejudice the whole system of amendments: The right now suggested is doubtful, and will be so considered by many of the States: In some respects the declaration of this right may be true, in others it is false: If we mean nothing more by it than this, that the people have a right to give advice or express their sentiments and wishes it is true; but still unnecessary, as such a right is already recognized: The press shall be free, and the people shall have the same freedom of speech and petitioning: but if it is meant that the representatives are to be bound by these instructions, the principle is false: Suppose a representative is instructed to do what is contrary to the public good? Would he be bound to sacrifice his own opinion? Or will not the vote of a representative contrary to his instruction be as binding on the people as a different one? If these things are true, where is the right of the constituent to instruct? or where is the advantage to result from it? It must either supercede all other obligations, the most sacred; or it can be of no benefit to the people. The gentleman says, the people are the sovereign; but who are the people? Is every small district the PEOPLE? And can the inhabitants of this district express the voice of the people, when they may not be a thousandth part, and all their instructions may contradict the sense of the whole people besides? Have the people in detached assemblies a right to violate the constitution or controul the whole sovereign power? This would be setting up an hundred sovereignties in the place of one.

Mr. SMITH (S.C.) was opposed to the motion: The doctrine of instructions would, in practice, operate partially: The States near the seat of government will have an obvious advantage over those remote from it: There is no necessity for so large a representation as had been determined on, if the members are to be guided in all their deliberations by positive instructions; one member from a State will serve every purpose; but then the nature of the assembly will be changed from a legislative to a diplomatic body: It would in fact be turning all our representatives into ambassadors.

Mr. STONE observed that to adopt this motion would change the nature of the constitution; instead of being a representative government, it would be a singular kind of democracy; in which, whenever a question arises, what is the law? It will not be determined by recurring to the codes and institutions of Congress, but by collecting the various instructions from different parts of the Union.

Mr. GERRY observed that several of the States had proposed this amendment, which rendered it proper to be attended to: In answer to Mr. Madison's query he said, he meant that instructions should be consistent with the laws and the constitution.

Mr. LIVERMORE said that though no particular districts could instruct, yet the Legislatures of the States most undoubtedly possessed this right.

This assertion of Mr. LIVERMORE was controverted by several gentlemen — by Mr. SEDGWICK, Mr. SMITH, Mr. AMES, and Mr. WADSWORTH: The last, speaking on the subject of instructions in general, said, I never knew merely political instructions to be observed; and I never knew a representative brought to an account for it: But I have known representatives follow instructions, contrary to their private sentiments, and they have even been despised for it. Others have disregarded their instructions, and have been re-elected, and caressed. Now if the *people* consider it as an inherent right in *them* to instruct their representatives, they would undoubtedly have punished the violation of such instructions; but this I believe has never been the case. I consider the measure as having a mischievous tendency.

The debate was continued much longer, but in a desultory way, as the speakers appeared to take it for granted, that they might touch upon collateral circumstances. The question on the motion being at length taken, it was negatived by a large majority; and then the committee agreed to the amendment in its original form.

Gazette of the U.S., August 19, 1789, p. 147, cols. 1–2.

3.2.2 STATE CONVENTIONS

None.

3.2.3 PHILADELPHIA CONVENTION

None.

3.2.4 NEWSPAPERS AND PAMPHLETS

3.2.4.1   Centinel, No. 2, October 24, 1787

. . . The new plan, it is true, does propose to secure the people of the benefit of personal liberty by the *habeas corpus;* and trial by jury for all crimes, except in case of impeachment: but there is no declaration, . . . that the right of the people to assemble peaceably for the purpose of consulting about public matters, and petitioning or remonstrating to the federal legislature ought not to be prevented;

. . . .
                    [Philadelphia] Freeman's Journal, Kaminski & Saladino, vol. 13, p. 466.

3.2.4.2   The Federal Farmer, No. 6, December 25, 1787

The following, I think, will be allowed to be unalienable or fundamental rights in the United States: —

No man demeaning himself peaceably, shall be molested on account of his religion or mode of worship — The people have a right to hold and enjoy their property according to known standing laws, and which cannot be taken from them without their consent, or the consent of their representatives; and whenever taken in the pressing urgencies of government, they are to receive a reasonable compensation for it — Individual security consists in having free recourse to the laws — The people are subject to no laws or taxes not assented to by their representatives constitutionally assembled — They are at all times intitled to the benefits of the writ of habeas corpus, the trial by jury in criminal and civil causes — They have the right, when charged, to a speedy trial in the vicinage; to be heard by themselves or counsel, not to be compelled to furnish evidence against themselves, to have witnesses face to face, and to confront their adversaries before the judge — No man is held to answer a crime charged upon him till it be substantially described to him; and he is subject to no unreasonable searches or seizures of his person, papers or effects — The people have a right to assemble in an orderly manner, and petition the government for a redress of wrongs — The freedom of the press ought not to be restrained — No emoluments, except for actual service — No hereditary honors, or orders of nobility, ought to be allowed — The military ought to be subordinate to the civil authority, and no soldier be quartered on the citizens without their consent — The militia ought always to be armed and disciplined, and the usual defence of the country — The supreme power is in the people, and power delegated ought to return to them at stated periods, and frequently — The legislative, executive, and judicial powers, ought always to be kept distinct — others perhaps might be added.
                                                        Storing, vol. 2, p. 262.

3.2.4.3 Samuel, January 10, 1788

And the whole of the purse, and of the sword, is put into the hands of the President, and a Congress so unequal, and which also may consist, of men of no principle or property. For no religion or property is required, as any qualification, to fill any and every seat in the Legislative, Judicial and Executive departments, in the whole nation. That a Pagan, a Mahometan, a Bankrupt, may fill the highest seat, and any and every seat; nothing but age and residence, are required, as qualifications, for the most important trusts. And there is nothing to hinder their keeping a standing army, at all times, peace or war. Nor is there any provision made for the people or States, to petition or remonstrate, let their grievances be what they will. . . .

[Boston] Independent Chronicle and Universal Advertiser, Storing, vol. 4, p. 193.

3.2.5 LETTERS AND DIARIES

None.

3.3 DISCUSSION OF RIGHTS

3.3.1 TREATISES

3.3.1.1 William Blackstone, 1765

4. I<small>F</small> there should happen any uncommon injury, or infringement of the rights beforementioned, which the ordinary course of law is too defective to reach, there still remains a fourth subordinate right appertaining to every individual, namely, the right of petitioning the king, or either house of parliamnet, for the redress of grievances. In Russia we are told that the czar Peter established a law, that no subject might petition the throne, till he had first petitioned two different ministers of state. In case he obtained justice from neither, he might then present a third petition to the prince; but upon pain of death, if found to be in the wrong. The consequence of which was, that no one dared to offer such third petition; and grievances seldom falling under the notice of the sovereign, he had little opportunity to redress them. The restrictions, for some there are, which are laid upon petitioning in England, are of a nature extremely different; and while they promote the spirit of peace, they are no check upon that of liberty. Care only must be taken, lest, under the pretence of petitioning, the subject be guilty of any riot or tumult; as happened in the opening of the memorable parliament in 1640: and, to prevent this, it is provided by the statute 13 Car. II. st. 1. c. 5. that no petition to the king, or either house of parliament, for any alterations in church or state, shall be signed by above twenty persons, unless the matter thereof be approved by three justices of the peace or the major part of the grand jury, in the country; and in London by the lord mayor, aldermen, and common council; nor shall any petition be presented by more than two persons at a time. But under these regulations, it is declared by the statute 1 W. & M. st. 2 c. 2. that the subject hath a right to petition; and that all committments and prosecutions for such petitioning are illegal.

Commentaries, bk. 1, ch. 1, sec. 3; vol. 1, pp. 138–39.

3.3.1.2 William Blackstone, 1769

6. RIOTS, *routs,* and *unlawful assemblies* must have *three* persons at least to constitute them. An *unlawful assembly* is when three, or more, do assemble themselves together to do an unlawful act, as to pull down inclosures, to destroy a warren or the game therein; and part without doing it, or making any motion towards it. A *rout* is where three or more meet to do an unlawful act upon a common quarrel, as forcibly breaking down fences upon a right claimed of common, or of way; and make some advances towards it. A *riot* is where three or more actually do an unlawful act of violence, either with or without a common cause or quarrel; as if they beat a man; or hunt and kill game in another's park, chase, warren, or liberty; or do any other unlawful act with force and violence; or even do a lawful act, as removing a nusance, in a violent and tumultuous manner. The punishment of unlawful assemblies, if to the number of twelve, we have just now seen may be capital, according to the circumstances that attend it; but, from the number of three to eleven, is by fine and imprisonment only. The same is the case in riots and routs by the common law; to which the pillory in very enormous cases has been sometimes superadded. And by the statute 13 Hen. IV. c. 7. any two justices, together with the sheriff or under-sheriff of the county, may come with the *posse comitatus,* if need be, and suppress any such riot, assembly, or rout, arrest the rioters, and record upon the spot the nature and circumstances of the whole transaction; which record alone shall be sufficient conviction of the offenders. In the interpretation of which statute it hath been holden, that all persons, noblemen and others, except women, clergymen, persons decrepit, and infants under fifteen, are bound to attend the justices in suppressing a riot, upon pain of fine and imprisonment; and that any battery, wounding, or killing the rioters, that may happen in suppressing the riot, is justifiable. So that our ancient law, previous to the modern riot act, seems pretty well to have guarded against any breach of the public peace; especially as any riotous assembly on a public or general account, as to redress grievances or pull down all enclosures, and also resisting the king's forces if sent to keep the peace, may amount to overt acts of high treason, by levying war against the king.

7. NEARLY related to this head of riots is the offence of *tumultuous petitioning;* which was carried on to an enormous height in the times preceding the grand rebellion. Wherefore by statute 13 Car. II. st. 1. c. 5. it is enacted, that not more than twenty names shall be signed to any petition to the king or either house of parliament, for any alteration of matters established by law in church or state; unless the contents thereof be previously approved, in the country, by three justices, or the majority of the grand jury at the assises or quarter sessions; and, in London, by the lord mayor, aldermen, and common council: and that no petition shall be delivered by a company of more than ten persons; on pain in either case of incurring a penalty not exceeding 100 *l,* and three months imprisonment.

Commentaries, bk. 4, ch. 11; vol. 4, pp. 146–47 (footnotes omitted).

3.3.2 CASELAW

None.

Chapter 4

AMENDMENT II
KEEP AND BEAR ARMS CLAUSE

4.1 TEXTS

4.1.1 DRAFTS IN FIRST CONGRESS

4.1.1.1 Proposal by Madison in House, June 8, 1789

4.1.1.1.a   Fourthly. That in article 1st, section 9, between clauses 3 and 4 [of the Constitution], be inserted these clauses, to wit,

. . .

The right of the people to keep and bear arms shall not be infringed; a well armed, and well regulated militia being the best security of a free country: but no person religiously scrupulous of bearing arms, shall be compelled to render military service in person.   *Congressional Register, June 8, 1789, vol. 1, p. 427.*

4.1.1.1.b   *Fourthly.* That in article 1st, section 9, between clauses 3 and 4 [of the Constitution], be inserted these clauses, to wit: . . .

. . .

The right of the people to keep and bear arms shall not be infringed; a well armed, and well regulated militia being the best security of a free country: but no person religiously scrupulous of bearing arms, shall be compelled to render military service in person.

Daily Advertiser, June 12, 1789, p. 2, col. 1.

4.1.1.1.c   *Fourth.* That in article 1st, section 9, between clauses 3 and 4 [of the Constitution], be inserted these clauses, to wit: . . . .

. . .

The right of the people to keep and bear arms shall not be infringed; a well armed, and well regulated militia being the best security of a free country: but no person religiously scrupulous of bearing arms, shall be compelled to render military service in person.   *New-York Daily Gazette, June 13, 1789, p. 574, col. 3.*

4.1.1.2 Proposal by Sherman to House Committee of Eleven, July 21–28, 1789

[Amendment] 5 The Militia shall be under the government of the laws of the respective States, when not in the actual Service of the united States, but Such rules as may be prescribed by Congress for their uniform organisation & discipline shall be observed in officering and training them. but military Service Shall not be required of persons religiously Scrupulous of bearing arms. Madison Papers, DLC.

4.1.1.3 House Committee of Eleven Report, July 28, 1789

ART. I, SEC. 9 — Between PAR. 2 and 3 insert, . . .

. . .

"A well regulated militia, composed of the body of the people, being the best security of a free State, the right of the people to keep and bear arms shall not be infringed, but no person religiously scrupulous shall be compelled to bear arms." Broadside Collection, DLC.

4.1.1.4 House Consideration, August 17, 1789

4.1.1.4.a The 3d clause of the 4th proposition in the report was taken into consideration, being as follows; "A well regulated militia, composed of the body of the people, being the best security of a free state; the right of the people to keep and bear arms shall not be infringed, but no person, religiously scrupulous, shall be compelled to bear arms." Congressional Register, August 17, 1789, vol. 2, p. 219 (reported); *id.*, p. 222 (adopted, after motions 4.1.1.5–4.1.1.8).

4.1.1.4.b The House resolved itself into a committee of the whole on the subject of amendments to the constitution.

Sixth Amendment: — "A well regulated militia, composed of the body of the people, being the best security of a free state, the right of the people to keep and bear arms shall not be infringed, but no person religiously scrupulous shall be compelled to bear arms." Daily Advertiser, August 18, 1789, p. 2, col. 4.

4.1.1.4.c The house resolved itself into a committee of the whole on the subject of amendments to the constitution.

Sixth amendment — "A well regulated militia, composed of the body of the people, being the best security of a free state, the right of the people to keep and bear arms shall not be infringed, but no person religiously scrupulous shall be compelled to bear arms." New-York Daily Gazette, August 19, 1789, p. 802, col. 3.

4.1.1.4.d SIXTH AMENDMENT — "A well regulated militia, composed of the body of the people, being the best security of a free state, the right of the people to keep and bear arms shall not be infringed, but no person religiously scrupulous shall be compelled to bear arms." Gazette of the U.S., August 22, 1789, p. 249, col. 3.

4.1.1.5 Motion by Gerry in House, August 17, 1789

Mr. GERRY

[W]ished the words to be altered so as to be confined to persons belonging to a religious sect, scrupulous of bearing arms.
Congressional Register, August 17, 1789, vol. 2, p. 220
(motion failed for want of a second).

4.1.1.6   Motion by Jackson in House, August 17, 1789

Mr. JACKSON

[M]oved to amend the clause, by inserting at the end of it "upon paying an equivalent to be established by law."

. . .

Mr. JACKSON

Was willing to accommodate [a suggestion of Mr. Smith of South Carolina]; he thought the expression was, "No one, religiously scrupulous of bearing arms, shall be compelled to render military service in person, upon paying an equivalent."

Congressional Register, August 17, 1789, vol. 2, p. 221 (not voted upon).

4.1.1.7   Motion by Benson in House, August 17, 1789

4.1.1.7.a

Mr. BENSON,

Moved to have the words "But no person religiously scrupulous shall be compelled to bear arms" struck out.

Congressional Register, August 17, 1789, vol. 2, pp. 221–222
(decided in the negative, 22 for, 24 against).

4.1.1.7.b   Mr. BENSON moved that the words "but no person religiously scrupulous shall be compelled to bear arms," be struck out. He wished that this humane provision should be left to the wisdom and benevolence of the government. It was improper to make it a fundamental in the constitution.

Daily Advertiser, August 18, 1789, p. 2, col. 4
("The motion was negatived, and the amendment agreed to.").

4.1.1.7.c   Mr. Benson moved that the words "but no person religiously scrupulous shall be compelled to bear arms," be struck out. He wished that this humane provision should be left to the wisdom and benevolence of the government. It was improper to make it a fundamental in the constitution.

New-York Daily Gazette, August 19, 1789, p. 802, col. 3
("The motion was negatived, and the amendment agreed to.").

4.1.1.7.d   Mr. BENSON moved that the words "but no person religiously scrupulous shall be compelled to bear arms," be struck out. He wished that this humane provision should be left to the wisdom and benevolence of the government. It was improper to make it a fundamental in the constitution.

Gazette of the U.S., August 22, 1789, p. 249, col. 3
("The motion was negatived, and the amendment agreed to.").

4.1.1.8   Motion by Gerry in House, August 17, 1789

Mr. GERRY

Objected to the first part of the clause, ... : A well-regulated militia being the best security of a free state, ... It ought to read "a well regulated militia, trained to arms," . . . .

Congressional Register, August 17, 1789, vol. 2, p. 222
(not seconded).

4.1.1.9   Motion by Burke in House, August 17, 1789

4.1.1.9.a

Mr. BURKE

Proposed to add to the clause just agreed to, an amendment to the following effect: "A standing army of regular troops in time of peace, is dangerous to public liberty, and such shall not be raised or kept up in time of peace but from necessity, and for the security of the people, nor then without the consent of two-thirds of the members present of both houses, and in all cases the military shall be subordinate to the civil authority."   Congressional Register, August 17, 1789, vol. 2, p. 222
(lost by a majority of 13).

4.1.1.9.b   Mr. BURKE moved to add a clause to the last paragraph to this effect: That a standing army of regular troops in time of peace is dangerous to public liberty, and should not be supported in time of peace, except by the consent of two thirds of each house of the legislature."   Daily Advertiser, August 18, 1789, p. 2, col. 4
("This amendment was negatived.").

4.1.1.9.c   Mr. Burke moved to add a clause to the last paragraph to this effect: That a standing army of regular troops in time of peace is dangerous to public liberty, and should not be supported in time of peace, except by the consent of two thirds of each house of the legislature."   New-York Daily Gazette, August 19, 1789, p. 802, col. 3
("This amendment was negatived.").

4.1.1.9.d   Mr. BURKE moved to add a clause to the last paragraph to this effect: That *a standing army of regular troops in time of peace is dangerous to public liberty, and should not be supported in time of peace, except by the consent of two thirds of both houses.*   Gazette of the U.S., August 22, 1789, p. 249, col. 3
("This amendment was negatived.").

4.1.1.10   Further House Consideration, August 20, 1789

The words *in person* were added after the word "arms," . . . .
Gazette of the U.S., August 22, 1789, p. 250.

4.1.1.11   Further House Consideration, August 21, 1789

Fifth. A well regulated militia, composed of the body of the people, being the best security of a free state, the right of the people to keep and bear arms, shall not be infringed; but no one religiously scrupulous of bearing arms, shall be compelled to render military service in person.
HJ, p. 107 ("read and debated . . . agreed to by the House,
. . . two-thirds of the members present concurring").[1]

---

[1] On August 22, 1789, the following motion was agreed to:
ORDERED, That it be referred to a committee of three, to prepare and report a proper arrangement of, and introduction to the articles of amendment to the Constitution of the United States, as agreed to by the House; and that Mr. Benson, Mr. Sherman, and Mr. Sedgwick be of the said committee.
HJ, p. 112.

4.1.1.12   House Resolution, August 24, 1789

ARTICLE THE FIFTH.

A well regulated militia, composed of the body of the People, being the best security of a free State, the right of the People to keep and bear arms, shall not be infringed, but no one religiously scrupulous of bearing arms, shall be compelled to render military service in person.

House Pamphlet, RG 46, DNA.

4.1.1.13   Senate Consideration, August 25, 1789

4.1.1.13.a   The Resolve of the House of Representatives of the 24th of August, upon certain "Articles to be proposed to the Legislatures of the several States as Amendments to the Constitution of the United States" was read as followeth:

. . .

Article the fifth

"A well regulated militia, composed of the body of the People, being the best security of a free State, the right of the People to keep and bear arms, shall not be infringed, but no one religiously scrupulous of bearing arms, shall be compelled to render military service in person.

Rough SJ, p. 216.

4.1.1.13.b   The Resolve of the House of Representatives of the 24th of August, was read as followeth:

. . .

"Article the Fifth.

"A well regulated militia, composed of the body of the people, being the best security of a free State, the right of the people to keep and bear arms, shall not be infringed, but no one religiously scrupulous of bearing arms, shall be compelled to render military service in person.

Smooth SJ, p. 194.

4.1.1.13.c   The Resolve of the House of Representatives of the 24th of August, was read as followeth:

. . .

"ARTICLE THE FIFTH.

"A well regulated militia, composed of the body of the people, being the best security of a free State, the right of the people to keep and bear arms, shall not be infringed, but no one religiously scrupulous of bearing arms, shall be compelled to render military service in person.

Printed SJ, p. 104.

4.1.1.14   Further Senate Consideration, September 4, 1789

4.1.1.14.a   [On motion, Upon the fifth Article, to subjoin the following proposition, to wit: "That standing armies, in time of peace, being dangerous to Liberty, should be avoided as far as the circumstances and protection of the community will admit; and that in all cases the military should be under strict subordination to, and governed by the civil Power. — That no standing army or regular] troops shall be raised in time of peace, without the consent of two thirds of the Members present in both Houses, and that no soldier shall be inlisted for any longer term than the continuance of the war."

Rough SJ, pp. 247–48 ("it passed in the Negative.")
[material in brackets not legible].

4.1.1.14.b On motion, Upon the fifth Article, to subjoin the following proposition, to wit: "That standing armies, in time of peace, being dangerous to Liberty, should be avoided as far as the circumstances and protection of the community will admit; and that in all cases the military should be under strict subordination to, and governed by the civil Power. — That no standing army or regular troops shall be raised in time of peace, without the consent of two thirds of the Members present in both Houses, and that no Soldier shall be enlisted for any longer term than the continuance of the war."

Smooth SJ, p. 221 ("It passed in the Negative.").

4.1.1.14.c On motion, Upon the fifth Article, to subjoin the following proposition, to wit: "That standing armies, in time of peace, being dangerous to Liberty, should be avoided as far as the circumstances and protection of the community will admit; and that in all cases the military should be under strict subordination to, and governed by the civil Power. — That no standing army or regular troops shall be raised in time of peace, without the consent of two thirds of the Members present in both Houses, and that no soldier shall be inlisted for any longer term than the continuance of the war."

Printed SJ, p. 118 ("it passed in the Negative.").

4.1.1.15 Further Senate Consideration, September 4, 1789

4.1.1.15.a On Motion to adopt the fifth article of the amendment proposed by the House of Representatives, amended to read as followeth — "A well regulated militia, being the best security of a free state, the right of the People to keep and bear Arms, shall not be infringed."

Rough SJ, p. 248 ("It passed in the Affirmative.").

4.1.1.15.b On motion, To adopt the fifth article of the Amendment proposed by the House of Representatives, amended to read as followeth — "A well regulated militia, being the best security of a free State, the right of the people to keep and bear arms, shall not be infringed —

Smooth SJ, p. 222 ("It passed in the affirmative.").

4.1.1.15.c On motion, To adopt the fifth Article of the Amendment proposed by the House of Representatives, amended to read as followeth — "A well regulated militia, being the best security of a free State, the right of the people to keep and bear arms, shall not be infringed —

Printed SJ, p. 119 ("It passed in the Affirmative.").

4.1.1.16 Further Senate Consideration, September 9, 1789

4.1.1.16.a On Motion to amend Article the fifth, by inserting these words, "For the common defence," next to the words "bear arms" —

Rough SJ, p. 274 ("It passed in the Negative.").

4.1.1.16.b   On motion, To amend Article the fifth, by inserting these words, "For the common defence," next to the words "Bear arms" —

Smooth SJ, p. 243 ("It passed in the Negative.").

4.1.1.16.c   On motion, To amend Article the fifth, by inserting these words, "For the common defence," next to the words "Bear arms" —

Printed SJ, p. 129 ("It passed in the Negative.").

4.1.1.17 Further Senate Consideration, September 9, 1789

4.1.1.17.a   On motion, To strike out of the Article, line the second, these words, "The best," and insert in lieu thereof "Necesary to the."

Rough SJ, p. 274 ("It passed in the Affirmative.").

4.1.1.17.b   On motion, To strike out of this Article, line the second, these words, "The best," and insert in lieu thereof "Necesary to the"

Smooth SJ, p. 243 ("It passed in the Affirmative.").

4.1.1.17.c   On motion, To strike out of this Article, line the second, these words, "The best," and insert in lieu thereof "Necesary to the"

Printed SJ, p. 129 ("It passed in the Affirmative.").

4.1.1.17.d   that the Senate do

Resolved ∧ ~~to~~ concur with the House of Representatives in

Article fifth

amended to read as follows

necessary to the

"A well regulated Militia, being ~~the best~~ ∧ security of a free State the right of the People to keep and bear Arms shall not be infringed."

Senate MS, pp. 2–3, RG 46, DNA.

4.1.1.18 Further Senate Consideration, September 9, 1789

4.1.1.18.a   On motion, on article the fifth, to strike out the word "fifth," after "Article the," and insert "fourth" —

And to amend the Article to read as follows "A well regulated Militia being the security of a free State, the right of the people to keep and bear arms, shall not be infringed."

Rough SJ, pp. 274–75 ("It passed in the affirmative.").

4.1.1.18.b   On motion, On article the fifth, to strike out the word "Fifth," after "article the," and insert "Fourth" —

And to amend the article to read as follows,

"A well regulated militia being the security of a free State, the right of the people to keep and bear arms, shall not be infringed" —

Smooth SJ, pp. 243–44 ("It passed in the Affirmative.").

4.1.1.18.c   On motion, On Article the fifth, to strike out the word "Fifth," after "Article the," and insert "Fourth" —

And to amend the Article to read as follows,

"A well regulated militia being the security of a free State, the right of the people to keep and bear arms, shall not be infringed" —

Printed SJ, p. 129 ("It passed in the Affirmative.").

4.1.1.18.d   To erase the word "fifth" — & insert — fourth — & to erase from the fifth article the words, "composed of the body of the people" — the word "best" — & the words "but no one religiously scrupulous of bearing arms shall be compelled

"being"

to render military service in person" — & insert after the word ~~the~~ /\ in the first line — necessary to.

Ellsworth MS, p. 2, RG 46, DNA.

4.1.1.19   Senate Resolution, September 9, 1789

ARTICLE THE FOURTH.

A well regulated militia, being necessary to the security of a free State, the right of the people to keep and bear arms, shall not be infringed.

Senate Pamphlet, RG 46, DNA.

4.1.1.20   Further House Consideration, September 21, 1789

RESOLVED, That this House doth agree to the second, fourth, eighth, twelfth, thirteenth, sixteenth, eighteenth, nineteenth, twenty-fifth, and twenty-sixth amendments, and doth disagree to the first, third, fifth, sixth, seventh, ninth, tenth, eleventh, fourteenth, fifteenth, seventeenth, twentieth, twenty-first, twenty-second, twenty-third, and twenty-fourth amendments proposed by the Senate to the said articles, two thirds of the members present concurring on each vote.

RESOLVED, That a conference be desired with the Senate on the subject matter of the amendments disagreed to, and that Mr. Madison, Mr. Sherman, and Mr. Vining, be appointed managers at the same on the part of this House.

HJ, p. 146.

4.1.1.21   Further Senate Consideration, September 21, 1789

4.1.1.21.a   A message from the House of Representatives —

Mr. Beckley, their Clerk, brought up a Resolve of the House of this date, to agree to the 2nd, 4th, 8th, 12th, 13th, 16th, 18th, 19th, 25th, and 26th Amendments proposed by the Senate, "To articles of Amendment to be proposed to the Legislatures of the several States, as Amendments to the Constitution of the United States," and to disagree to the 1st, 3d, 5th, 6th, 7th, 9th, 10th, 11th, 14th, 15th, 17th, 20th, 21st, 22d, 23d, and 24th amendments: Two thirds of the members present concurring on each vote: And "That a conference be desired with the Senate on the subject matter of the amendments disagreed to," and that Mr. Madison, Mr. Sherman, and Mr. Vining, be appointed managers of the same, on the part of the House of Representatives —

And he withdrew.

Smooth SJ, pp. 265–66.

4.1.1.21.b   A message from the House of Representatives —

Mr. Beckley, their Clerk, brought up a Resolve of the House of this date, to agree to the 2d, 4th, 8th, 12th, 13th, 16th, 18th, 19th, 25th, and 26th Amend-

176

ments proposed by the Senate, "To Articles of Amendment to be proposed to the Legislatures of the several States, as Amendments to the Constitution of the United States," and to disagree to the 1st, 3d, 5th, 6th, 7th, 9th, 10th, 11th, 14th, 15th, 17th, 20th, 21st, 22d, 23d, and 24th Amendments: Two thirds of the members present concurring on each vote: And "That a conference be desired with the Senate on the subject matter of the Amendments disagreed to," and that Mr. Madison, Mr. Sherman, and Mr. Vining, be appointed managers of the same, on the part of the House of Representatives —

And he withdrew.

Printed SJ, pp. 141–42.

4.1.1.22   Further Senate Consideration, September 21, 1789

4.1.1.22.a   The Senate proceeded to consider the Message of the House of Representatives disagreeing to the Amendments made by the Senate "To Articles to be proposed to the Legislatures of the several States, as Amendments to the Constitution of the United States" And

RESOLVED, That the Senate do recede from their third Amendment, and do insist on all the others.

RESOLVED, That the Senate do concur with the House of Representatives in a conference on the subject matter of disagreement on the said Articles of Amendment, and that Mr. Ellsworth, Mr. Carroll and Mr. Paterson be managers of the conference on the part of the Senate.

Smooth SJ, p. 267.

4.1.1.22.b   The Senate proceeded to consider the message of the House of Representatives disagreeing to the Amendments made by the Senate "To Articles to be proposed to the Legislatures of the several States, as Amendments to the Constitution of the United States" — And

RESOLVED, That the Senate do recede from their third Amendment, and do insist on all the others.

RESOLVED, That the Senate do concur with the House of Representatives in a conference on the subject matter of disagreement on the said Articles of Amendment, and that Mr. Ellsworth, Mr. Carroll, and Mr. Paterson be managers of the conference on the part of the Senate.

Printed SJ, p. 142.

4.1.1.23   Conference Committee Report, September 24, 1789

[T]hat it will be proper for the House of Representatives to agree to the said Amendments proposed by the Senate, with an Amendment to their fifth Amendment, so that the third Article shall read as follows: "Congress shall make no Law respecting an establishment of Religion, or prohibiting the free exercise thereof; or abridging the freedom of Speech, or of the Press; or the right of the people peaceably to assemble and to petition the Government for a redress of grievances; "And with an Amendment to the fourteenth Amendment proposed by the Senate, so that the eighth Article, as numbered in the Amendments proposed by the Senate, shall read as follows "In all criminal prosecutions, the accused shall enjoy the right to a speedy & publick trial by an impartial jury of the district wherein the crime shall have been committed, as the district shall have been previously ascertained by law, and to be informed of the nature and cause of the accusation; to be confronted with the witnesses against him, and to have compulsory process for

to

obtaining witnesses ~~against him~~ in his favour, & /\ have the assistance of counsel for his defence."

Conference MS, RG 46, DNA (Ellsworth's handwriting).

4.1.1.24 **House Consideration of Conference Committee Report, September 24 [25], 1789**

RESOLVED, That this House doth recede from their disagreement to the first, third, fifth, sixth, seventh, ninth, tenth, eleventh, fourteenth, fifteenth, seventeenth, twentieth, twenty-first, twenty-second, twenty-third, and twenty-fourth amendments, insisted on by the Senate: PROVIDED, That the two articles which by the amendments of the Senate are now proposed to be inserted as the third and eighth articles, shall be amended to read as followeth;

Article the third. "Congress shall make no law respecting an establishment of religion, or prohibiting the free exercise thereof; or abridging the freedom of speech, or of the press; or the right of the people peaceably to assemble, and to petition the government for a redress of grievances."

Article the eighth. "In all criminal prosecutions, the accused shall enjoy the right to a speedy and public trial by an impartial jury of the state and district wherein the crime shall have been committed, which district shall have been previously ascertained by law, and to be informed of the nature and cause of the accusation, to be confronted with the witnesses against him, to have compulsory process for obtaining witnesses in his favor, and to have the assistance of council for his defence."

HJ, p. 152 ("On the question, that the House do agree to the
alteration and amendment of the eighth article, in manner aforesaid,
It was resolved in the affirmative. Ayes 37 Noes 14").

4.1.1.25 **Senate Consideration of Conference Committee Report, September 24, 1789**

4.1.1.25.a   Mr. Ellsworth, on behalf of the managers of the conference on "articles to be proposed to the several States as Amendments to the Constitution of the United States," reported as follows:

That it will be proper for the House of Representatives to agree to the said amendments proposed by the Senate, with an Amendment to their fifth Amendment, so that the third Article shall read as follows: "Congress shall make no law respecting an establishment of Religion, or prohibiting the free exercise thereof; or abridging the freedom of Speech, or of the Press; or the right of the people peaceably to assemble and petition the Government for a redress of Grievances;" And with an Amendment to the fourteenth Amendment proposed by the Senate, so that the eighth article, as numbered in the Amendments proposed by the Senate, shall read as follows; "In all criminal prosecutions, the accused shall enjoy the right to a speedy and public trial by an impartial Jury of the district wherein the Crime shall have been committed, as the district shall have been previously ascertained by law, and to be informed of the nature and cause of the accusation, to be confronted with the witnesses against him, and to have compulsory process for obtaining witnesses in his favor, and to have the assistance of Council for defence."

Smooth SJ, pp. 272–73.

4.1.1.25.b   Mr. Ellsworth, on behalf of the managers of the conference on "Articles to be proposed to the several States as Amendments to the Constitution of the United States," reported as follows:

That it will be proper for the House of Representatives to agree to the said Amendments proposed by the Senate, with an Amendment to their fifth Amendment, so that the third Article shall read as follows: "Congress shall make no Law RESPECTING AN ESTABLISHMENT OF RELIGION, or prohibiting the free exercise thereof; or abridging the freedom of Speech, or of the Press; or the right of the People peaceably to assemble and petition the Government for a redress of Grievances;" And with an Amendment to the fourteenth Amendment proposed by the Senate, so that the eighth Article, as numbered in the Amendments proposed by the Senate, shall read as follows; "In all criminal prosecutions, the accused shall enjoy the right to a speedy and public trial BY AN IMPARTIAL JURY OF THE DISTRICT WHEREIN THE CRIME SHALL HAVE BEEN COMMITTED, AS THE DISTRICT SHALL HAVE BEEN PREVIOUSLY ASCERTAINED BY LAW, and to be informed of the nature and cause of the accusation, to be confronted with the witnesses against him, and to have compulsory process for obtaining witnesses in his favor, and to have the assistance of Counsel for defence."

Printed SJ, p. 145.

4.1.1.26   Further Senate Consideration of Conference Committee Report, September 24, 1789

4.1.1.26.a   A Message from the House of Representatives —

Mr. Beckley, their Clerk, brought up the Amendments to the "Articles to be proposed to the Legislatures of the several States, as Amendments to the Constitution of the United States;" and informed the Senate, that the House of Representatives had receded from their disagreement to the 1st, 3d, 5th, 6th, 7th, 9th, 10th, 11th, 14th, 15th, 17th, 20th, 21st, 22d, 23d, and 24th Amendments, insisted on by the Senate: Provided that the "Two Articles, which by the Amendments of the Senate are now proposed to be inserted as the third and eighth Articles," shall be amended to read as followeth:

Article the Third. "Congress shall make no Law respecting an establishment of Religion, or prohibiting the free exercise thereof; or abridging the freedom of Speech, or of the Press; or the right of the people peaceably to assemble, and petition the Government for a redress of Grievances."

Article the Eighth. "In all criminal prosecutions the accused shall enjoy the right to a speedy and public trial by an impartial Jury of the State and District, wherein the crime shall have been committed, which District shall have been previously ascertained by law, and to be informed of the nature and cause of the accusation, to be confronted with the witnesses against him, and to have compulsory process for obtaining witnesses in his favor, and to have the assistance of Counsel for his defence."

Smooth SJ, pp. 278–79.

4.1.1.26.b   A Message from the House of Representatives —

Mr. Beckley, their Clerk, brought up the Amendments to the "Articles to be proposed to the Legislatures of the several States, as Amendments to the Constitution of the United States;" and informed the Senate, that the House of Representatives had receded from their disagreement to the 1st, 3d, 5th, 6th, 7th, 9th, 10th, 11th, 14th, 15th, 17th, 20th, 21st, 22d, 23d, and 24th Amendments, insisted on by the Senate: Provided that the "Two Articles, which by the Amendments of the Senate are now proposed to be inserted as the third and eighth Articles," shall be amended to read as followeth:

Article the Third. "Congress shall make no Law respecting an establishment of Religion, or prohibiting the free exercise thereof; or abridging the freedom of Speech, or of the Press; or the right of the People peaceably to assemble, and petition the Government for a redress of Grievances."

Article the Eighth. "In all criminal prosecutions the accused shall enjoy the right to a speedy and public trial by an impartial Jury of the State and District, wherein the crime shall have been committed, which District shall have been previously ascertained by law, and to be informed of the nature and cause of the accusation, to be confronted with the witnesses against him, and to have compulsory process for obtaining witnesses in his favor, and to have the assistance of Counsel for his defence."

Printed SJ, p.148.

4.1.1.27 Further Senate Consideration of Conference Committee Report, September 25, 1789

4.1.1.27.a   The Senate proceeded to consider the Message from the House of Representatives of the 24th, with Amendments to the Amendments of the Senate, to "Articles to be proposed to the Legislatures of the several States, as Amendments to the Constitution of the United States" — And

RESOLVED, That the Senate do concur in the Amendments proposed by the House of Representatives, to the Amendments of the Senate.   Smooth SJ, p. 283.

4.1.1.27.b   The Senate proceeded to consider the Message from the House of Representatives of the 24th, with Amendments to the Amendments of the Senate, to "Articles to be proposed to the Legislatures of the several States, as Amendments to the Constitution of the United States" — And

RESOLVED, That the Senate do concur in the Amendments proposed by the House of Representatives, to the Amendments of the Senate.

Printed SJ, pp. 150–51.

4.1.1.28 Agreed Resolution, September 25, 1789

Article the Fourth.

A well regulated militia, being necessary to the security of a free State, the right of the people to keep and bear arms, shall not be infringed.

Smooth SJ, Appendix, p. 293.

ARTICLE THE FOURTH.

A well regulated militia, being necessary to the security of a free State, the right of the people to keep and bear arms, shall not be infringed.

Printed SJ, Appendix, p. 163.

4.1.1.29   Enrolled Resolution, September 28, 1789

Article the fourth . . . A well regulated militia, being necessary to the security of a free State, the right of the people to keep and bear arms, shall not be infringed.

Enrolled Resolutions, RG 11, DNA.

4.1.1.30   Printed Versions

4.1.1.30.a   ART. II. A well regulated militia being necessary to the security of a free State, the right of the people to keep and bear arms shall not be infringed.

Statutes at Large, vol. 1, p. 21.

4.1.1.30.b   ART. IV. A well regulated militia being necessary to the security of a free state, the right of the people to keep and bear arms shall not be infringed.

Statutes at Large, vol. 1, p. 97.

4.1.2 PROPOSALS FROM THE STATE CONVENTIONS

4.1.2.1   Maryland Minority, April 26, 1788

4. That no standing army shall be kept up *in time of peace,* unless with the consent of two thirds of the members present of each branch of congress.

. . .

10. That no person, conscientiously scrupulous of bearing arms in any case, shall be compelled *personally* to serve as a soldier.

Maryland Gazette, May 1, 1788 (committee minority).

4.1.2.2   Massachusetts Minority, February 6, 1788

[T]hat the said Constitution be never construed to authorize Congress to infringe the just liberty of the press, or the rights of conscience; or to prevent the people of the United States, who are peaceable citizens, from keeping their own arms; or to raise standing armies, unless when necessary for the defence of the United States, or of some one or more of them; or to prevent the people from petitioning, in a peaceable and orderly manner, the federal legislature, for a redress of grievances; or to subject the people to unreasonable searches and seizures of their persons, papers or possessions.   Massachusetts Convention, pp. 86–87.

4.1.2.3   New Hampshire, June 21, 1788

Twelfth

Congress shall never disarm any Citizen unless such as are or have been in Actual Rebellion. —

State Ratifications, RG 11, DNA.

4.1.2.4   New York, July 26, 1788

That the People have a right to keep and bear Arms; that a well regulated Militia, including the body of the People capable of bearing Arms, is the proper, natural and safe defence of a free State.

That the Militia should not be subject to Martial Law except in time of War, Rebellion or Insurrection.

That standing Armies in time of Peace are dangerous to Liberty, and ought not to be kept up, except in Cases of necessity; and that at all times, the Military should be under strict Subordination to the civil Power.

State Ratifications, RG 11, DNA.

4.1.2.5 North Carolina, August 1, 1788

17th. That the people have a right to keep and bear arms; that a well regulated militia composed of the body of the people, trained to arms, is the proper, natural and safe defence of a free state. That standing armies in time of peace are dangerous to Liberty, and therefore ought to be avoided, as far as the circumstances and protection of the community will admit; and that in all cases, the military should be under strict subordination to, and governed by the civil power.

. . .

19th. That any person religiously scrupulous of bearing arms ought to be exempted upon payment of an equivalent to employ another to bear arms in his stead.

State Ratifications, RG 11, DNA.

4.1.2.6 Pennsylvania Minority, December 12, 1787

7. That the people have a right to bear arms for the defense of themselves and their own state, or the United States, or for the purpose of killing game; and no law shall be passed for disarming the people or any of them, unless for crimes committed, or real danger of public injury from individuals; and as standing armies in the time of peace are dangerous to liberty, they ought not to be kept up; and that the military shall be kept under strict subordination to and governed by the civil power.

Pennsylvania Packet, December 18, 1787.

4.1.2.7 Rhode Island, May 29, 1790

17th. That the people have a right to keep and bear arms, that a well regulated militia, including the body of the people capable of bearing arms, is the proper, natural and safe defence of a free state; that the militia shall not be subject to martial law except in time of war, rebellion or insurrection; that standing armies in time of peace, are dangerous to liberty, and ought not be kept up, except in cases of necessity; and that at all times the military should be under strict subordination to the civil power; that in time of peace no soldier ought to be quartered in any house without the consent of the owner, and in time of war, only by the civil magistrate, in such manner as the law directs.

State Ratifications, RG 11, DNA.

4.1.2.8 Virginia, June 27, 1788

Seventeenth, That the people have a right to keep and bear arms; that a well regulated Militia composed of the body of the people trained to arms is the proper, natural and safe defence of a free State. That standing armies in time of peace are dangerous to liberty, and therefore ought to be avoided, as far as the circumstances and protection of the Community will admit; and that in all cases the military should be under strict subordination to and governed by the Civil power.

State Ratifications, RG 11, DNA.

4.1.3 STATE CONSTITUTIONS AND LAWS; COLONIAL CHARTERS AND LAWS

4.1.3.1 Delaware: Declaration of Rights, 1776

SECT. 18. That a well regulated militia is the proper, natural and safe defence of a free government.

SECT. 19. That standing armies are dangerous to liberty, and ought not to be raised or kept up without the consent of the Legislature.

SECT. 20. That in all cases and at all times the military ought to be under strict subordination to and governed by the civil power.

Delaware Laws, vol. 1, App., p. 81.

4.1.3.2 Georgia: Constitution, 1777

XXXV. Every county in this State that has, or hereafter may have, two hundred and fifty men, and upwards, liable to bear arms, shall be formed into a battalion; and when they become too numerous for one battalion, they shall be formed into more, by bill of the legislature; and those counties that have a less number than two hundred and fifty, shall be formed into independent companies.

Georgia Laws, p. 13.

4.1.3.3 Massachusetts: Constitution, 1780

[Part I, Article] XVII. The people have a right to keep and to bear arms for the common defence. And as in time of peace armies are dangerous to liberty, they ought not to be maintained without the consent of the legislature; and the military power shall always be held in an exact subordination to the civil authority, and be governed by it.

Massachusetts Perpetual Laws, p. 7.

4.1.3.4 New Hampshire: Constitution, 1783

[Part I, Article] XIII. No person who is conscientiously scrupulous about the lawfulness of bearing arms, shall be compelled thereto, provided he will pay an equivalent.

New Hampshire Laws, p. 24.

4.1.3.5 New York: Constitution, 1777

XL. AND WHEREAS it is of the utmost Importance to the Safety of every State, that it should always be in a Condition of Defence; and it is the Duty of every Man who enjoys the Protection of Society, to be prepared and willing to defend it: This Convention therefore, in the Name and by the Authority of the good People of this State, doth ORDAIN, DETERMINE, AND DECLARE, That the Militia of the State, at all Times hereafter, as well in Peace as in War, shall be armed and disciplined, and in Readiness for Service. That all such of the Inhabitants of this State, being of the People called Quakers, as from Scruples of Conscience may be averse to the bearing of Arms, be therefrom excused by the Legislature; and do pay to the State such Sums of Money in Lieu of their personal Service, as the same may, in the Judgment of the Legislature, be worth: And that a proper Magazine of warlike Stores, proportionate to the Number of Inhabitants, be for ever hereafter at the Expence of this State, and by the Acts of the Legislature, established, maintained, and continued in every County of this State.

New York Laws, vol. 1, pp. 13–14.

4.1.3.6 North Carolina: Declaration of Rights, 1776

Sect. XVII. That the People have a Right to bear Arms for the Defense of the State; and, as standing Armies in Time of Peace are dangerous to liberty, they ought not to be kept up; and that the military should be kept under strict subordination to, and governed by, the civil Power.
North Carolina Laws, p. 276.

4.1.3.7 Pennsylvania

4.1.3.7.a Constitution, 1776

CHAPTER I.
A DECLARATION of the RIGHTS of the Inhabitants of the State of Pennsylvania.

. . .

VIII. That every member of society hath a right to be protected in the enjoyment of life, liberty and property, and therefore is bound to contribute his proportion towards the expence of that protection, and yield his personal service when necessary, or an equivalent thereto: But no part of a man's property can be justly taken from him, or applied to public uses, without his own consent, or that of his legal representatives: Nor can any man who is conscientiously scrupulous of bearing arms, be justly compelled thereto, if he will pay such equivalent; nor are the people bound by any laws, but such as they have in like manner assented to, for their common good.

. . .

XIII. That the people have a right to bear arms for the defence of themselves and the state; and as standing armies in the time of peace are dangerous to liberty, they ought not to be kept up: And that the military should be kept under strict subordination to, and governed by, the civil power.
Pennsylvania Acts, M'Kean, pp. ix–x.

4.1.3.7.b Constitution, 1790

ARTICLE IX.

. . .

Sect. XXI. That the right of citizens to bear arms, in defence of themselves and the state, shall not be questioned.
Pennsylvania Acts, Dallas, p. xxxvi.

4.1.3.8 Vermont: Constitution, 1777

CHAPTER I.

. . .

15. That that [*sic*] the People have a Right to bear Arms, for the Defence of themselves and the State: — And, as standing Armies, in the Time of Peace, are

dangerous to Liberty, they ought not to be kept up; and that the military should be kept under strict Subordination to, and governed by, the civil Power.

Vermont Acts, p. 4.

4.1.3.9 Virginia: Declaration of Rights, 1777

XIII. THAT a well regulated militia, composed of the body of the people, trained to arms, is the proper, natural and safe defence of a free state; that standing armies, in time of peace, should be avoided, as dangerous to liberty; and that in all cases, the military should be under strict subordination to, and governed by, the civil power.

Virginia Acts, p. 33.

4.1.4 OTHER TEXTS

4.1.4.1 English Bill of Rights, 1689

. . . By causing severall good subjects being protestants to be disarmed at the same time when papists were both armed and imployed contrary to law.

. . .

That the subjects which are protestants may have arms for their defence suitable to their conditions and as allowed by law.

1 Will. & Mar. sess. 2, c. 2.

4.1.4.2 Declaration of Independence, 1776

. . . He has kept among us, in times of Peace, Standing Armies without the Consent of our legislatures. — He has affected to render the Military independent of and superior to the Civil power. . . .

Engrossed Manuscripts, DNA.

4.1.4.3 Richard Henry Lee to Edmund Randolph, Proposed Amendments, October 16, 1787

. . . That standing armies in times of peace are dangerous to liberty, and ought not to be permitted unless assented to by two thirds of the members composing each house of the legislature under the new constitution. . . .

Virginia Gazette, December 22, 1787.

4.2 DISCUSSION OF DRAFTS AND PROPOSALS
4.2.1 THE FIRST CONGRESS

4.2.1.1 June 8, 1789[2]

4.2.1.2 August 17, 1789

4.2.1.2.a   The house went into a committeee of the whole, on the subject of amendments. The 3rd clause of the 4th proposition in the report was taken into consideration, being as follows; "A well regulated militia, composed of the body of the people, being the best security of a free state; the right of the people to keep and bear arms

---

[2] For the reports of Madison's speech in support of his proposals, *see* 1.2.1.a–c.

shall not be infringed, but no person, religiously scrupulous, shall be compelled to bear arms."

Mr. GERRY.

This declaration of rights, I take it, is intended to secure the people against the mal-administration of the government; if we could suppose that in all cases the rights of the people would be attended to, the occasion for guards of this kind would be removed. Now I am apprehensive, sir, that this clause would give an opportunity to the people in power to destroy the constitution itself. They can declare who are those religiously scrupulous, and prevent them from bearing arms.

What, sir, is the use of a militia? It is to prevent the establishment of a standing army, the bane of liberty. Now it must be evident, that under this provision, together with their other powers, Congress could take such measures with respect to a militia, as make a standing army necessary. Whenever government mean to invade the rights and liberties of the people, they always attempt to destroy the militia, in order to raise an army upon their ruins. This was actually done by Great Britain at the commencement of the late revolution. They used every means in their power to prevent the establishment of an effective militia to the eastward. The assembly of Massachusetts, seeing the rapid progress that administration were making, to divest them of their inherent privileges, endeavored to counteract them by the organization of the militia, but they were always defeated by the influence of the crown.

Mr. SENEY

Wished to know what question there was before the committee, in order to ascertain the point upon which the gentleman was speaking?

Mr. GERRY

Replied that he meant to make a motion, as he disapproved of the words as they stood. He then proceeded, No attempts that they made, were successful, until they engaged in the struggle which emancipated them at once from their thraldom. Now, if we give a discretionary power to exclude those from militia duty who have religious scruples, we may as well make no provision on this head; for this reason he wished the words to be altered so as to be confined to persons belonging to a religious sect, scrupulous of bearing arms.

Mr. JACKSON

Did not expect that all the people of the United States would turn Quakers or Moravians, consequently one part would have to defend the other, in case of invasion; now this, in his opinion, was unjust, unless the constitution secured an equivalent, for this reason he moved to amend the clause, by inserting at the end of it "upon paying an equivalent to be established by law."

Mr. SMITH, (of S.C.)

Enquired what were the words used by the conventions respecting this amendment; if the gentleman would conform to what was proposed by Virginia and Carolina, he would second him: He thought they were to be excused provided they found a substitute.

Mr. Jackson

Was willing to accommodate; he thought the expression was, "No one, religiously scrupulous of bearing arms, shall be compelled to render military service in person, upon paying an equivalent."

Mr. Sherman

Conceived it difficult to modify the clause and make it better. It is well-known that those who are religiously scrupulous of bearing arms, are equally scrupulous of getting substitutes or paying an equivalent; many of them would rather die than do either one or the other — but he did not see an absolute necessity for a clause of this kind. We do not live under an arbitrary government, said he, and the states respectively will have the government of the militia, unless when called into actual service; beside, it would not do to alter it so as to exclude the whole of any sect, because there are men amongst the quakers who will turn out, notwithstanding the religious principles of the society, and defend the cause of their country. Certainly it will be improper to prevent the exercise of such favorable dispositions, at least whilst it is the practice of nations to determine their contests by the slaughter of their citizens and subjects.

Mr. Vining

Hoped the clause would be suffered to remain as it stood, because he saw no use in it if it was amended so as to compel a man to find a substitute, which, with respect to the government, was the same as if the person himself turned out to fight.

Mr. Stone

Enquired what the words "Religiously scrupulous" had reference to, was it of bearing arms? If it was, it ought so be expressed.

Mr. Benson,

Moved to have the words "But no person religiously scrupulous shall be compelled to bear arms" struck out. He would always leave it to the benevolence of the legislature — for, modify it, said he, as you please, it will be impossible to express it in such a manner as to clear it from ambiguity. No man can claim this indulgence of right. It may be a religious persuasion, but it is no natural right, and therefore ought to be left to the discretion of the government. If this stands part of the constitution, it will be a question before the judiciary, on every regulation you make with respect to the organization of the militia, whether it comports with this declaration or not? It is extremely injudicious to intermix matters of doubt with fundamentals.

I have no reason to believe but the legislature will always possess humanity enough to indulge this class of citizens in a matter they are so desirous of, but they ought to be left to their discretion.

The motion for striking out the whole clause being seconded, was put, and decided in the negative, 22 members voting for it, and 24 against it.

Mr. Gerry

Objected to the first part of the clause, an account of the uncertainty with which it is expressed: A well-regulated militia being the best security of a free state, admitted an idea that a standing army was a secondary one. It ought to read "a well regulated militia, trained to arms," in which case it would become the duty of the government to provide this security and furnish a greater certainty of its being done.

Mr. GERRY's motion not being seconded, the question was put on the clause as reported, which being adopted,

Mr. BURKE

Proposed to add to the clause just agreed to, an amendment to the following effect: "A standing army of regular troops in time of peace, is dangerous to public liberty, and such shall not be raised or kept up in time of peace but from necessity, and for the security of the people, nor then without the consent of two-thirds of the members present of both houses, and in all cases the military shall be subordinate to the civil authority." This being seconded,

Mr. VINING

Asked whether, this was be considered as an addition to the last clause, or an amendment by itself? If the former, he would remind the gentleman the clause was decided; if the latter, it was improper to introduce new matter, as the house had referred the report specially to the committee of the whole.

Mr. BURKE

Feared that what with being trammelled in rules, and the apparent disposition of the committee, he should not be able to get them to consider any amendment; he submitted to such proceeding because he could not help himself.

Mr. HATLEY [*sic;* Hartley]

Thought the amendment in order, and was ready to give his opinion of it. He hoped the people of America would always be satisfied with having a majority to govern. He never wished to see two-thirds or three-forths required, because it might put it in the power of a small minority to govern the whole union.

The question on mr. Burke's motion was put, and lost by a majority of 13.

Congressional Register, August 17, 1789, vol. 2, pp. 219–23.

4.2.1.2.b   The House resolved itself into a committee of the whole on the subject of amendments to the constitution.

Sixth Amendment: — "A well regulated militia, composed of the body of the people, being the best security of a free state, the right of the people to keep and bear arms shall not be infringed, but no person religiously scrupulous shall be compelled to bear arms."

Mr. BENSON moved that the words "but no person religiously scrupulous shall be compelled to bear arms," be struck out. He wished that this humane provision should be left to the wisdom and benevolence of the government. It was improper to make it a fundamental in the constitution.

The motion was negatived, and the amendment agreed to.

Mr. BURKE moved to add a clause to the last paragraph to this effect: That a standing army of regular troops in time of peace is dangerous to public liberty, and should not be supported in time of peace, except by the consent of two thirds of each house of the legislature."

This amendment was negatived.

Daily Advertiser, August 18, 1789, p. 2, col. 4.

4.2.1.2.c   The house resolved itself into a committee of the whole on the subject of amendments to the constitution.

Sixth amendment — "A well regulated militia, composed of the body of the people, being the best security of a free state, the right of the people to keep and bear arms shall not be infringed, but no person religiously scrupulous shall be compelled to bear arms."

Mr. Benson moved that the words "but no person religiously scrupulous shall be compelled to bear arms," be struck out. He wished that this humane provision should be left to the wisdom and benevolence of the government. It was improper to make it a fundamental in the constitution.

The motion was negatived, and the amendment agreed to.

Mr. Burke moved to add a clause to the last paragraph to this effect: "That a standing army of regular troops in time of peace is dangerous to public liberty, and should not be supported in time of peace, except by the consent of two thirds of each house of the legislature."

This amendment was negatived.

New-York Daily Gazette, August 19, 1789, p. 802, col.3.

4.2.1.2.d   SIXTH AMENDMENT — "A well regulated militia, composed of the body of the people, being the best security of a free state, the right of the people to keep and bear arms shall not be infringed, but no person religiously scrupulous shall be compelled to bear arms."

Mr. BENSON moved that the words "but no person religiously scrupulous shall be compelled to bear arms," be struck out. He wished that this humane provision should be left to the wisdom and benevolence of the government. It was improper to make it a fundamental in the constitution.

The motion was negatived, and the amendment agreed to.

Mr. BURKE moved to add a clause to the last paragraph to this effect: That *a standing army of regular troops in time of peace is dangerous to public liberty, and should not be supported in time of peace, except by the consent of two thirds of both houses.*

This amendment was negatived.   Gazette of the U.S., August 22, 1789, p. 249, col. 3.

4.2.1.3 August 20, 1789

4.2.1.3.a

Mr. SCOTT

Objected to the clause in the sixth amendment, "No person religiously scrupulous, shall be compelled to bear arms." He observed that if this becomes part of the constitution, such persons can neither be called upon for their services, nor can an equivalent be demanded; it is also attended with still further difficulties, for a militia can never be depended upon. This would lead to the violation of another article in the Constitution, which secures to the people the right of keeping arms, and in this case recourse must be had to a standing army. I conceive it said he to be a legislative right altogether. There are many sects I know, who are religiously scrupulous in this respect; I do not mean to deprive them of any indulgence the law affords; my design is to guard against those who are of no religion. It has been urged that religion is on the decline; if so the argument is more strong in my favor, for when the time comes that religion shall be discarded, the generality of persons will have recourse to these pretexts, to get excused from bearing arms.

Mr. BOUDINOT

Thought the provision in the clause, or something similar to it, was necessary. Can any dependence said he, be placed in men who are conscientious in this respect; or what justice can there be in compelling them to bear arms, when, according to their religious principles, they would rather die than use them. He adverted to several instances of oppression in this point, that occurred during the war. In forming a militia, an effectual defence ought to be calculated, and no characters of this religious description ought to be compelled to take up arms. I hope that in establishing this government, we may show the world that proper care is taken that the government may not interfere with the religious sentiments of any person. Now, by striking out the clause, people may be led to believe that there is an intention in the general government to compel all its citizens to bear arms.

Some further desultory conversation arose and it was agreed to insert the words "in person" to the end of the clause; after which, it was adopted, as was the 4th, 5th, 6th, 7th, and 8th clauses of the 4th proposition; then the 5th, 6th, and 7th propositions was agreed to, and the house adjourned.

Congressional Register, August 20, 1789, vol. 2, pp. 242–43.

4.2.1.3.b   Mr. SCOT objected to the clause in the sixth amendment, "No person religiously scrupulous shall be compelled to bear arms." He said, if this becomes part of the constitution, we can neither call upon such persons for services nor an equivalent; it is attended with still further difficulties, for you can never depend on your militia. This will lead to the violation of another article in the constitution, which secures to the people the right of keeping arms, as in this case you must have recourse to a standing army. I conceive it is a matter of legislative right altogether. I know there are many sects religiously scrupulous in this respect: I am not for abridging them of any indulgence by law; my design is to guard against those who are of no religion. It is a said that religion is on the decline; if this is the case, it is an argument in my favour; for when the time comes that there is no religion, persons will more generally have recourse to these pretexts to get excused.

Mr. BOUDINOT said that the provision in the clause or something like it appeared to be necessary. What dependence can be placed in men who are conscientious in the respect? Or what justice can there be in compelling them to bear arm [sic], when, it they are honest men they would rather die than use them. He then adverted to several instances of oppression in the case which occurred during the war. In forming a militia we ought to calculate for an effectual defence, and not compel characters of this description to bear arms. I wish that in establishing the government we may be careful to let every person know that we will not interfere with any person's particular religious profession. If we strike out this clause, we shall lead such persons to conclude that we mean to compel them to bear arms.

Mr. VINING and Mr. JACKSON spoke upon the question. The words *in person* were added after the word "arms," and the amendement was adopted.

Adjourned.
Gazette of the U.S., August 22, 1789, p. 250, col. 2.

4.2.2 STATE CONVENTIONS

4.2.2.1 Massachusetts, January 24, 1788

The Hon. Mr. SEDGWICK. . . . Is it possible, he asked, that an army could be raised for the purpose of enslaving themselves and their brethren? or, if raised, whether they could subdue a nation of freemen, who know how to prize liberty, and who have arms in their hands?
Elliot, vol. 2, pp. 96–97.

4.2.2.2 North Carolina, July 30, 1788

Mr. LENOIR. . . .

. . .

[Congress] can disarm the militia. If they were armed, they would be a resource against the great oppressions. The laws of a great empire are difficult to be executed. If the laws of the Union were oppressive, they could not carry them into effect, if the people were possessed of proper means of defence.
Elliot, vol. 4, p. 203.

4.2.2.3 Pennsylvania, December 6, 1787

JOHN SMILIE: (113) I object to the power of Congress over the militia and to keep a standing army.

. . .

(123) In a free government there never will be need of standing armies; for it depends on the confidence of the people. If it does not so depend, it is not free.

(124) The Convention, in framing this government, knew it was not a free one; otherwise they would not have asked the power of the purse and the sword.

(125) The last resource of a free people is taken away; for Congress are to have the command of the militia.

(126) The laws of Pennsylvania have hitherto been executed without the aid of the militia.

(127) The governor of each state will be only the drill sergeant of Congress.

(128) The militia officers will be obliged by oath to support the general government against that of their own state.

(129) Congress may give us a select militia which will, in fact, be a standing army — or Congress, afraid of a general militia, may say there shall be no militia at all.

(130) When a selected militia is formed; the people in general may be disarmed.

(131) Will the states give up to Congress their last resource — the command of the militia?

(132) Will the militia laws be as mild under the general government as under the state governments? Militia men may be punished with whipping or death. They may [be] dragged from one state to any other.

(133) "Congress guarantees to each State a *Republican* Form of Government." Is this a security for a *free* government?

(134) Can even the shadow of state governments be continued if Congress please to take it away?

(134) [*sic*] The Senate and President may dismiss the Representatives, when once a standing army is established with funds; and there this government will terminate.

. . .

WILLIAM FINDLEY: (135) The objections of the member from Fayette [John Smilie] are founded, important, and of extensive practical influence. Tax and militia laws are of universal operation.

(136) The militia will be taken from home; and when the militia of one state has quelled insurrections and destroyed the liberties, the militia of the last state may, at another time, be employed in retaliation on the first.

(137) No provision in behalf of those who are conscientiously scrupulous of bearing arms.

Jensen, vol. 2, pp. 508–09 (references omittted).

4.2.2.4 Virginia, June 14, 1788

Mr. CLAY wished to be informed why the Congress were to have power to provide for calling forth the militia, to put the laws of the Union into execution.

Mr. MADISON supposed the reasons of this power to be so obvious that they would occur to most gentlemen. If resistance should be made to the execution of the laws, he said, it ought to be overcome. This could be done only in two ways — either by regular forces or by the people. By one or the other it must unquestionably be done. If insurrections should arise, or invasions should take place, the people ought unquestionably to be employed, to suppress and repel them, rather than a standing army. The best way to do these things was to put the militia on a good and sure footing, and enable the government to make use of their services when necessary.

Mr. GEORGE MASON. Mr. Chairman, unless there be some restrictions on the power of calling forth the militia, to execute the laws of the Union, suppress insurrections, and repel invasions, we may very easily see that it will produce dreadful oppressions. It is extremely unsafe, without some alterations. It would be to use the militia to a very bad purpose, if any disturbance happened in New Hampshire, to call them from Georgia. This would harass the people so much that they would agree to abolish the use of the militia, and establish a standing army. I conceive the general government ought to have power over the militia, but it ought to have some bounds. If gentlemen say that the militia of a neighboring state is not sufficient, the government ought to have power to call forth those of other states, the most convenient and contiguous. But in this case, the consent of the state legislatures ought to be had. On *real* emergencies, this consent will never be denied, each state being concerned in the safety of the rest. This power may be restricted without any danger. I wish such an amendment as this — that the militia of any state should not be marched beyond the limits of the adjoining state; and if it be necessary to draw them from one end of the continent to the other, I wish such a check, as the consent of the state legislature, to be provided. Gentlemen may say that this would impede the government, and that the state legislatures would counteract it by refusing their consent. This argument may be applied to all objections whatsoever. How is this compared to the British constitution? Though the king may declare war, the Parliament has the means of carrying it on. It is not so here. Congress can do both. Were it not for that check in the British government, the monarch would be a despot. When a war is necessary for the benefit of the nation, the means of carrying it on are never denied. If any unjust requisition be made on Parliament, it will be, as it ought to be, refused. The same principle ought to be observed in our government. In times of real danger, the states will have the same enthusiasm in aiding the general government, and granting its demands, which is seen in England, when the king is engaged in a war apparently for the interest of the nation. This power is necessary; but we ought to guard against danger. If ever they attempt to harass and abuse the militia, they may abolish them, and raise a standing army in their stead. There are various ways of destroying the militia. A standing army may be perpetually established in their stead. I abominate and detest the idea of a government, where there is a standing army. The militia may be here destroyed by that method which has been practised in other parts of the world before; that is, by rendering them useless — by disarming them. Under various pretenses, Congress may neglect to provide for arming and disciplining the militia; and the state governments cannot do it, for Congress has an exclusive right to arm them, &c. Here is a line of division drawn between them — the state and general governments. The power over the militia is divided between them. The national government has an exclusive right to provide for arming, organizing, and disciplining the militia, and for governing such part of them as may be employed in the service of the United States. The state governments have the power of appointing the officers, and of training the militia, according to the discipline prescibed by Congress, if they should think proper to prescribe any. Should the national government wish to render the militia useless, they may neglect them, and let them perish, in order to have a pretence of establishing a standing army.

No man has a greater regard for the military gentlemen than I have. I admire their intrepidity, perseverance, and valor. But when once a standing army is established in any country, the people lose their liberty. When, against a regular and disciplined army, yeomanry are the only defence, — yeomanry, unskillful and unarmed, — what chance is there for preserving freedom? Give me leave to recur to the page of history, to warn you of your present danger. Recollect the history of most nations of the world. What havoc, desolation, and destruction, have been perpetrated by standing armies! An instance within the memory of some of this house will show us how our militia may be destroyed. Forty years ago, when the resolution of enslaving America was formed in Great Britain, the British Parliament was advised by an artful man, who was governor of Pennsylvania, to disarm the people; that it was the best and most effectual way to enslave them; but that they should not do it openly, but weaken them, and let them sink gradually, by totally disusing and neglecting the militia. [Here Mr. Mason quoted sundry passages to this effect.] This was a most iniquitous project. Why should we not provide against the danger of having our militia, our real and natural strength, destroyed? The general government ought, at the same time, to have some such power. But we need not give them power to abolish our militia. If they neglect to arm them, and prescribe proper discipline, they will be of no use. I am not acquainted with the military profession. I beg to be excused for any errors I may commit with respect to it. But I stand on the general principles of freedom, whereon I dare to meet anyone. I wish that, in case the general government should neglect to arm and discipline the militia, there should be an express declaration that the state governments might arm and discipline them. With this single exception, I would agree to this part, as I am conscious the government ought to have the power.

They may effect the destruction of the militia, by rendering the service odious to the people themselves, by harassing them from one end of the continent to the other, and by keeping them under martial law.

The English Parliament never pass a mutiny bill but for one year. This is necessary; for otherwise the soldiers would be on the same footing with the officers, and the army would be dissolved. One mutiny bill has been here in force since the revolution. I humbly conceive there is extreme danger of establishing cruel martial regulations. If, at any time, our rulers should have unjust and iniquitous designs against our liberties, and should wish to establish a standing army, the first attempt would be to render the service and use of militia odious to the people themselves — subjecting them to unnecessary severity of discipline in time of peace, confining them under martial law, and disgusting them so much as to make them cry out, "Give us a standing army!" I would wish to have some check to exclude this danger; as, that the militia should never be subject to martial law but in time of war. I consider and fear the natural propensity of rulers to oppress the people. I wish only to prevent them from doing evil. By these amendments I would give necessary powers, but no unnecessary power[.] If the clause stands as it is now, it will take from the state legislatures what divine Providence has given to every individual — the means of self-defence. Unless it be moderated in some degree, it will ruin us, and introduce a standing army.

Mr. MADISON. Mr. Chairman, I most cordially agree, with the honorable member last up, that a standing army is one of the greatest mischiefs that can possibly happen. It is a great recommendation for this system, that it provides against this evil more than any other system known to us, and, particularly, more than the old system of confederation. The most effectual way to guard against a standing army, is to render it unnecessary. The most effectual way to render it unnecessary, is to give the general government full power to call forth the militia, and exert the whole natural strength of the Union, when necessary. Thus you will furnish the people with sure and certain protection, without recurring to this evil; and the certainty of this protection from the whole will be a strong inducement to individual exertion. Does the organization of the government warrant a belief that this power will be abused? Can we believe that a government of a federal nature, consisting of many coëqual sovereignties, and particularly having one branch chosen from the people, would drag the militia unnecessarily to an immense distance? This, sir, would be unworthy the most arbitrary despot. They have no temptation whatever to abuse this power; such abuse could only answer the purpose of exciting the universal indignation of the people, drawing on themselves the general hatred and detestation of their country.

I cannot help thinking that the honorable gentleman has not considered, in all its consequences, the amendment he has proposed. Would this be an equal protection, sir, or would it not be a most partial provision? Some states have three or four states in contact. Were this state invaded, as it is bounded by several states, the militia of three or four states would, by this proposition, be obliged to come to our aid; and those from some of the states would come a far greater distance than those of others. There are other states, which, if invaded, could be assisted by the militia of one state only, there being several states which border but on one state. Georgia and New Hampshire would be infinitely less safe than the other states. Were we to adopt this amendment, we should set up those states as butts for invasions, invite foreign enemies to attack them, and expose them to peculiar hardships and dangers. Were the militia confined to any limited distance from their respective places of abode, it would produce equal, nay, more inconveniences. The principles of equality and reciprocal aid would be destroyed in either case.

I cannot conceive that this Constitution, by giving the general government the power of arming the militia, takes it away from the state governments. The power is concurrent, and not exclusive. Have we not found, from experience, that, while the power of arming and governing the militia has been solely vested in state legislatures, they were neglected and rendered unfit for immediate service? Every state neglected too much this most essential object. But the general government can do it more effectually. Have we not also found that the militia of one state were almost always insufficient to succor its harassed neighbor? Did all the states furnish their quotas of militia with sufficient promptitude? The assistance of one state will be of little avail to repel invasion. But the general head of the whole Union can do it with effect, if it be vested with power to use the aggregate strength of the Union. If the regualtion of the militia were to be committed to the executive authority alone, there might be reason for providing restrictions. But, sir, it is the legislative authority that has this power. They must make a law for the purpose.

The honorable member is under another mistake. He wishes martial law to be exercised only in time of war, under an idea that Congress can establish it in time of peace. The states are to have the authority of training the militia according to the congressional discipline; and of governing them at all times when not in the service of the Union. Congress is to govern such part of them as may be employed in the actual service of the United States; and such part only can be subject to martial law. The gentlemen in opposition have drawn a most tremendous picture of the Constitution in this respect. Without considering that the power was absolutely indispensable, they have alarmed us with the possible abuse of it, but have shown no inducement or motive to tempt them to such abuse. Would the legislature of the state drag the militia of the eastern shore to the western frontiers, or those of the western frontiers to the eastern shore, if the local militia were sufficient to effect the intended purpose? There is something so preposterous, and so full of mischief, in the idea of dragging the militia unnecessarily from one end of the continent to the other, that I think there can be no ground of apprehension. If you limit their power over the militia, you give them a pretext for substituting a standing army. If you put it in the power of the state governments to refuse the militia, by requiring their consent, you destroy the general government, and sacrifice particular states. The same principles and motives which produce disobedience to requisitions, will produce refusal in this case.

The restrictions which the honorable gentleman mentioned to be in the British constitution are all provisions against the power of the executive magistrate; but the House of Commons may, if they be so disposed, sacrifice the interest of their constituents in all those cases. They may prolong the duration of mutiny bills, and grant supplies to the king to carry on an impolitic war. But they have no motives to do so; for they have strong motives to do their duty. We have more ample security than the people of Great Britain. The powers of the government are more limited and guarded, and our representatives are more responsible than the members of the British House of Commons.

Mr. CLAY apprehended that, by this power, our militia might be sent to the Mississippi. He observed that the sheriff might raise the *posse comitatus* to execute the laws. He feared it would lead to the establishment of a military government, as the militia were to be called forth to put the laws into execution. He asked why this mode was preferred to the old, established custom of executing the laws.

Mr. MADISON answered, that the power existed in all countries; that the militia might be called forth, for that purpose, under the laws of this state and every other state in the Union; that public force must be used when resistance to the laws required it, otherwise society itself must be destroyed; that the mode referred to by the gentleman might not be sufficient on every occasion, as the sheriff must be necessarily restricted to the *posse* of his own county. If the *posse* of one county were insufficient to overcome the resistance to the execution of the laws, this power must be resorted to. He did not, by any means, admit that the old mode was superseded by the introduction of the new one. And it was obvious to him, that, when the civil power was sufficient, this mode would never be put in practice.

Mr. HENRY. Mr. Chairman, in my judgment the friends of the opposition have to act cautiously. We must make a firm stand before we decide. I was heard to say, a few days ago, that the sword and purse were the two great instruments of government; and I professed great repugnance at parting with the purse, without any control, to the proposed system of government. And now, when we proceed in this formidable compact, and come to the national defence, the sword, I am persuaded we ought to be still more cautious and circumspect; for I feel still more reluctance to surrender this most valuable of rights.

The honorable member who has risen to explain several parts of the system was pleased to say, that the best way of avoiding the danger of a standing army, was, to have the militia in such a way as to render it unnecessary; and that, as the new government would have power over the militia, we should have no standing army — it being unnecessary. This argument destroys itself. It demands a power and denies the probability of its exercise. There are suspicions of power on one hand,

and absolute and unlimited confidence on the other. I hope to be one of those who have a large share of suspicion. I leave it to this house, if there be not too small a portion on the other side, by giving up too much to that government. You can easily see which is the worst of two extremes. Too much suspicion may be corrected. If you give too little power to-day, you may give more to-morrow. But the reverse of the proposition will not hold. If you give too much power to-day, you cannot retake it to-morrow: for to-morrow will never come for that purpose. If you have the fate of other nations, you will never see it. It is easier to supply deficiencies of power than to take back excess of power. This no man can deny.

But, says the honorable member, Congress will keep the militia armed; or, in other words, they will do their duty. Pardon me if I am too jealous and suspicious to confide in this remote possibility. My honorable friend went on a supposition that the American rulers, like all others, will depart from their duty without bars and checks. No government can be safe without checks. Then he told us they had no temptation to violate their duty, and that it would be their interest to perform it. Does he think you are to trust men who cannot have separate interests from the people? It is a novelty in the political world (as great a novelty as the system itself) to find rulers without private interests, and views of personal emoluments, and ambition. His supposition, that they will not depart from their duty, as having no interest to do so, is no satisfactory answer to my mind. This is no check. The government may be most intolerable and destructive, if this be our only security.

My honorable friend attacked the honorable gentleman with universal principles — that, in all nations and ages, rulers have been actuated by motives of individual interest and private emoluments, and that in America it would be so also. I hope, before we part with this great bulwark, this noble palladium of safety, we shall have such checks interposed as will render us secure. The militia, sir, is our ultimate safety. We can have no security without it. But then, he says that the power of arming and organizing the militia is concurrent, and to be equally exercised by the general and state governments. I am sure, and I trust in the candor of that gentleman, that he will recede from that opinion, when his recollection will be called to the particular clause which relates it to.

As my worthy friend said, there is a positive partition of power between the two governments. To Congress is given the power of "arming, organizing, and disciplining the militia, and governing such part of them as may be employed in the service of the United States." To the state legislatures is given the power of "appointing the officers, and training the militia according to the discipline prescribed by Congress." I observed before, that, if the power be concurrent as to arming them, it is concurrent in other respects. If the states have the right of arming them, &c., concurrently, Congress has a concurrent power of appointing the officers, and training the militia. If Congress have that power, it is absurd. To admit this mutual concurrence of powers will carry you into endless absurdity — that Congress has nothing exclusive on the one hand, nor the states on the other. The rational explanation is, that Congress shall have exclusive power of arming them, &c., and that the state governments shall have exclusive power of appointing the officers, &c. Let me put it in another light.

May we not discipline and arm them, as well as Congress, if the power be concurrent? so that our militia shall have two sets of arms, double sets of regimentals, &c.; and thus, at a very great cost, we shall be doubly armed. The great object is, that every man be armed. But can the people afford to pay for double sets of arms &c.? Every one who is able may have a gun. But we have learned, by experience, that necessary as it is to have arms, and though our Assembly has, by a succession of laws for many years, endeavored to have the militia completely armed, it is still far from being the case. When this power is given up to Congress without limitation or bounds, how will your militia be armed? You trust to chance; for sure I am that nation which shall trust its liberties in other hands cannot long exist. If gentlemen are serious when they suppose a concurrent power, where can be the impolicy to amend it? Or, in other words, to say that Congress shall not arm or discipline them, till the states shall have refused or neglected to do it? This is my object. I only wish to bring it to what they themselves say is implied. Implication is to be the foundation of our civil liberties, and when you speak of arming the militia by a concurrence of power, you use implication. But implication will not save you, when a strong army of veterans comes upon you. You would be laughed at by the whole world for trusting your safety implicitly to implication.

The argument of my honorable friend was, that rulers might tyrannize. The answer he received was, that they will not. In saying that they would not, he admitted they might. In this great, this essential part of the Constitution, if you are safe, it is not from the Constitution, but from the virtues of the men in government. If gentlemen are willing to trust themselves and posterity to so slender and improbable a chance, they have greater strength of nerves than I have.

The honorable gentleman, in endeavoring to answer the question why the militia were to be called forth to execute the laws, said that the civil power would probably do it. He is driven to say, that the civil power may do it instead of the militia. Sir, the military power ought not to interpose till the civil power refuse. If this be the spirit of your new Constitution, that the laws are to be enforced by military coercion, we may easily divine the happy consequences which will result from it. The civil power is not to be employed at all. If it be, show me it. I read it attentively, and could see nothing to warrant a belief that the civil power can be called for. I shall be glad to see the power that authorizes Congress to do so. The sheriff will be aided by military force. The most wanton excesses may be committed under color of this; for every man in office, in the states, is to take an oath to support it in all its operations. The honorable gentleman said, in answer to the objection that the militia might be marched from New Hampshire to Georgia, that the members of the government would not attempt to excite the indignation of the people. Here, again, we have the general unsatisfactory answer, that they will be virtuous, and that there is no danger.

Will gentlemen be satisfied with an answer which admits of dangers and abuses if they be wicked? Let us put it out of their power to do mischief. I am convinced there is no safety in the paper on the table as it stands now. I am sorry to have an occasion to pass a eulogium on the British government, as gentlemen may object to it. But how natural it is, when comparing deformities to beauty, to be struck with the superiority of the British government to that system! In England, self-love — self-interest — powerfully stimulates the executive magistrate to advance the posterity of the nation. In the most distant part, he feels the loss of his subjects. He will see the great advantage of his prosperity inseparable from the felicity of his people. Man is a fallen creature, a fallible being, and cannot be depended on without self-love. Your President will not have the same motives of self-love to impel him to favor your interests. His political character is but transient, and he will promote, as much as possible, his own private interests. He will conclude, the constant observation has been that he will abuse his power, and that it is expected. The king of England has a more permanent interest. His stock, his family, is to continue in possession of the same emolument. The more flourishing his nation, the more formidable and powerful is he. The sword and purse are not united, in that government, in the same hands, as in this system. Does not infinite security result from a separation?

But it is said that our Congress are more responsible than the British Parliament. It appears to me that there is no real, but there may be some specious responsibility. If Congress, in the execution of their unbounded powers, shall have done wrong, how will you come at them to punish them, if they are at the distance of five hundred miles? At such a great distance, they will evade responsibility altogether. If you have given up your militia, and Congress shall refuse to arm them, you have lost every thing. Your existence will be precarious, because you depend on others, whose interests are not affected by your infelicity. If Congress are to arm us exclusively, the man of New Hampshire may vote for or against it, as well as the Virginian. The great distance and difference between the two places render it impossible that the people of that country can know or pursue what will promote our convenience. I therefore contend that, if Congress do not arm the militia, we ought to provide for it ourselves.[3]

Elliot, vol. 3, pp. 378–88.

4.2.3 PHILADELPHIA CONVENTION

4.2.3.1 June 8, 1787

In Committee of the Whole. — On a reconsideration of the clause giving the national legislature a negative on such laws of the states as might be contrary to the Articles of Union, or treaties with foreign nations, —

Mr. PINCKNEY moved, "that the national legislature should have authority to negative all laws which they should judge to be improper." He urged that such a universality of the power was indispensibly necessary to render it effectual; that the states must be kept in due subordination to the nation; that, if the states were left to act of themselves in any case, it would be impossible to defend the national prerogatives, however extensive they might be, on paper. . . .

Mr. MADISON seconded the motion. He could not but regard an indefinite power to negative legislative acts of the states as absolutely necessary to a perfect system. . . . Was such a remedy eligible? Was it practicable? Could the national resources, if exerted to the upmost, enforce a national decree against Massachusetts, abetted, perhaps, by several of her neighbors? It would not be possible. A

---

[3] For further reports of the debate, *see* Elliot, vol. 3, pp. 388 *et seq.*

small proportion of the community, in a compact situation, acting on the defensive, and at one of its extremities, might at any time bid defiance to the national authority. Any government for the United States, formed on the supposed practicability of using force against the unconstitutional proceedings of the states, would prove as visionary and fallacious as the government of Congress. The negative would render the use of force unnecessary. The states could of themselves pass no operative act, any more than one branch of a legislature, where there are two branches, can proceed without the other. But, in order to give the negative this efficacy, it must extend to all cases. . . .

Mr. WILLIAMSON was against giving a power that might restrain the states from regulating their internal police.

Mr. GERRY could not see the extent of such a power, and was against every power that was not necessary. He thought a remonstrance against unreasonable acts of the states would restrain them. If it should not, force might be resorted to. He had no objection to authorize a negative to paper money, and similar measures. When the Confederation was depending before Congress, Massachusetts was then for inserting the power of emitting paper money among the exclusive powers of Congress. He observed, that the proposed negative would extend to the regulations of the militia — a matter on which the existence of the state might depend. The national legislature, with such a power, may enslave the states. Such an idea as this will never be acceded to. It has never been suggested or conceived among the people.

Elliot, vol. 5, pp. 170–72.

4.2.4 NEWSPAPERS AND PAMPHLETS

4.2.4.1 The Federal Farmer, No. 3, October 10, 1787

. . . By the constitution it is proposed that congress shall have power "to raise and support armies, but no appropriation of money to that use shall be for a longer term than two years; to provide and maintain a navy; to provide for calling forth the militia to execute the laws of the union, suppress insurrections, and repel invasions: to provide for organizing, arming, and disciplining the militia: reserving to the states the right to appoint the officers, and to train the militia according to the discipline prescribed by congress; congress will have unlimited power to raise armies, and to engage officers and men for any number of years; but a legislative act applying money for their support can have operation for no longer term than two years, and if a subsequent congress do not within two years renew the appropriation, or further appropriate monies for the use of the army, the army will be left to take care of itself. When an army shall once be raised for a number of years, it is not probable that it will find much difficulty in getting congress to pass laws for applying monies to its support. I see so many men in America fond of a standing army, and especially among those who probably will have a large share in administering the federal system; it is very evident to me, that we shall have a large standing army as soon as the monies to support them can be possibly found. An army is a very agreeable place of employment for the young gentlemen of many families. A power to raise armies must be lodged some where; still this will not justify the lodging this power in a bare majority of so few men without any checks;

or in the government in which the great body of the people, in the nature of things, will be only nominally represented. In the state governments the great body of the people, the yeomanry, etc. of the country, are represented: It is true they will chuse the members of congress, and may now and then chuse a man of their own way of thinking; but it is impossible for forty, or thirty thousand people in this country, one time in ten to find a man who can possess similar feelings, views, and interests with themselves: Powers to lay and collect taxes and to raise armies are of the greatest moment; for carrying them into effect, laws need not be frequently made, and the yeomanry, etc of the country ought substantially to have a check upon the passing of these laws; this check ought to be placed in the legislatures, or at least, in the few men the common people of the country, will, probably, have in congress, in the true sense of the word, "from among themselves." It is true, the yeomanry of the country possess the lands, the weight of property, possess arms, and are too strong a body of men to be openly offended — and, therefore, it is urged, they will take care of themselves, that men who shall govern will not dare pay any disrespect to their opinions. It is easily perceived, that if they have not their proper negative upon passing laws in congress, or on the passage of laws relative to taxes and armies, they may in twenty or thirty years be by means imperceptible them, totally deprived of that boasted weight and strength: This may be done in a great measure by congress, if disposed to do it, by modelling the militia. Should one fifth, or one eighth part of the men capable of bearing arms, be made a select militia, as has been proposed, and those the young and ardent part of the community, possessed of but little or no property, and all the others put upon a plan that will render them of no importance, the former will answer all the purposes of an army, while the latter will be defenceless. The state must train the militia in such form and according to such systems and rules as congress shall prescribe: and the only actual influence the respective states will have respecting the milita will be in appointing the officers. I see no provision made for calling out the *posse commitatus* [*sic*] for executing the laws of the union, but provision is made for congress to call forth the militia for the execution of them — and the militia in general, or any select part of it, may be called out under military officers, instead of the sheriff to enforce an execution of federal laws, in the first instance and thereby introduce an entire military execution of the laws. I know that powers to raise taxes, to regulate the military strength of the community on some uniform plan, to provide for its defence and internal order, and for duly executing the laws, must be lodged somewhere; but still we ought not so to lodge them, as evidently to give one order of men in the community, undue advantages over others; or commit the many to the mercy, prudence, and moderation of the few. And so far as it may be necessary to lodge any of the peculiar powers in the general government, a more safe exercise of them ought to be secured, by requiring the consent of two-thirds or three-fourths of congress thereto — until the federal representation can be increased, so that the democratic members in congress may stand some tolerable chance of a reasonable negative, in behalf of the numerous, important, and democratic part of the community.

Storing, vol. 2, pp. 241–43.

4.2.4.2 The Federal Farmer, No. 6, December 25, 1787

The following, I think, will be allowed to be unalienable or fundamental rights in the United States: —

No man, demeaning himself peaceably, shall be molested on account of his religion or mode or worship — The people have a right to hold and enjoy their property according to known standing laws, and which cannot be taken from them without their consent, or the consent of their representatives; and whenever taken in the pressing urgencies of government, they are to receive a reasonable compensation for it — Individual security consists in having free recourse to the laws — The people are subject to no laws or taxes not assented to by their representatives constitutionally assembled — They are at all times intitled to the benefits of the writ of habeas corpus, the trial by jury in criminal and civil causes — They have a right, when charged, to a speedy trial in the vicinage; to be heard by themselves or counsel, not to be compelled to furnish evidence against themselves, to have witnesses face to face, and to confront their adversaries before the judge — No man is held to answer a crime charged upon him till it be substantially described to him; and he is subject to no unreasonable searches or seizures of his person, papers or effects — The people have a right to assemble in an orderly manner, and petition the government for a redress of wrongs — The freedom of the press ought not to be restrained — No emoluments, except for actual service — No hereditary honors, or orders of nobility, ought to be allowed — The military ought to be subordinate to the civil authority, and no soldier be quartered on the citizens without their consent — The militia ought always to be armed and disciplined, and the usual defence of the country — The supreme power is in the people, and power delegated ought to return to them at stated periods, and frequently — The legislative, executive, and judicial powers, ought always to be kept distinct — others perhaps might be added.

Storing, vol. 2, p. 262.

4.2.4.3 The Federalist, No. 29, January 9, 1788

The power of regulating the militia and of commanding its services in times of insurrection and invasion are natural incidents to the duties of superintending the commmon defence, and of watching over the internal peace of the confederacy.

It requires no skill in the science of war to discern that uniformity in the organization and discipline of the militia would be attended with the most beneficial effects, whenever they were called into service for the public defence. It would enable them to discharge the duties of the camp and of the field with mutual intelligence and concert; an advantage of peculiar moment in the operations of an army: And it would fit them much sooner to acquire the degree of proficiency in military functions, which would be essential to their usefulness. This desirable uniformity can only be accomplished by confiding the regulation of the militia to the direction of the national authority.

. . .

Of the different grounds which have been taken in opposition to the plan of the Convention, there is none that was so little to have been expected, or so untenable in itself, as the one which from this particular provision has been attacked. If a well regulated militia be the most natural defence of a free country, it ought certainly to be under the regulation and at the disposal of that body which is constituted the guardian of the national security. If standing armies are dangerous to liberty, an efficacious power over the militia, in the body to whose care the protection of the State is committed, ought as far as possible to take away the inducement and the pretext to such unfriendly institutions. If the foederal government can command the aid of the militia in those emergencies which call for the military arm in support of the civil magistrate, it can the better dispense with the employment of a different kind of force. If it cannot avail itself of the former, it will be obliged to recur to the latter. To render an army unnecessary will be a more certain method of preventing its existence than a thousand prohibitions upon paper.

. . .

. . . Where in the name of common sense are our fears to end if we may not trust our sons, our brothers, our neighbours, our fellow-citizens? What shadow of danger can there be from men who are daily mingling with the rest of their countrymen; and who participate with them in the same feelings, sentiments, habits and interests? What reasonable cause of apprehension can be inferred from a power in the Union to prescribe regulations for the militia and to command its services when necessary; while the particular States are to have the *sole and exclusive appointment of the officers?* If it were possible seriously to indulge a jealousy of the militia upon any conceivable establishment under the Foederal Government, the circumstance of the officers being in the appointment of the States ought at once to extinguish it. There can be no doubt that this circumstance will always secure to them a preponderating influence over the militia.

Kaminski & Saladino, vol. 15, pp. 318–19, 321.

4.2.4.4 A Pennsylvanian, June 18, 1789

As civil rulers, not having their duty to the people duly before them, may attempt to tyrannize, and as the military forces which must be occasionally raised to defend our country, might pervert their power to the injury of their fellow citizens, the people are confirmed by the next article in their right to keep and bear their private arms.

[Philadelphia] Federal Gazette, p. 2, col. 1.

4.2.5 LETTERS AND DIARIES

4.2.5.1 Jeremy Belknap to Paine Wingate, May 29, 1789

. . . You will see in the speech wh. our *new* Lieut. Governor [*Samuel Adams*] made at his investiture that he has not thrown off the old idea of *"independence"* as an attribute of each individual State in the "confederated Republic" — & you will know in what light to regard his "devout & fervent wish" that the "people may enjoy well grounded confidence that their *personal & domestic* rights are *secure."* This is the same Language or nearly the same which he used in the Convention when he moved for an addition to the proposed Amendments — by inserting a clause to provide for the Liberty of the press — the right to keep arms

— Protection from seizure of person & property & the *Rights of Conscience*. By which motion he gave an alarm to both sides of the house & had nearly overset the whole business which the Friends of the Constitution had been labouring for several Weeks to obtain. . . .

Veit, p. 241.

4.2.5.2 Samuel Nasson to George Thatcher, July 9, 1789

. . . I find that Ammendments are once again on the Carpet. I hope that such may take place as will be for the Best Interest of the whole A Bill of rights well secured that we the people may know how far we may Proceade in Every Department then their will be no Dispute Between the people and rulers in that may be secured the right to keep arms for Common and Extraordinary occasions such as to secure ourselves against the wild Beast and also to amuse us by fowling and for our Defence against a common Enemy you know to learn the Use of arms is all that can Save us from a forighn foe that may attempt to subdue us for if we keep up the Use of arms and become well acquainted with them we Shall allway be able to look them in the face that arise up against us for it is impossible to Support a Standing armey large Enough to Guard our Lengthy Sea Coast and now Spare me on the subject of Standing armeys in a time of Peace they allway was first or last the downfall of all free Governments it was by their help Caesar made proud Rome Own a Tyrant and a Traytor for a Master.

Veit, pp. 260–61.

4.2.5.3 John Randolph to St. George Tucker, September 11, 1789

. . . A majority of the Senate were for not allowing the militia arms & if two thirds had agreed it would have been an amendment to the Constitution. They are afraid that the Citizens will stop their full Career to Tyranny & Oppression.

Veit, p. 293.

4.3 DISCUSSION OF RIGHTS

4.3.1 TREATISES

4.3.1.1 William Blackstone, 1765

5. THE fifth and last auxiliary right of the subject, that I shall at present mention, is that of having arms for their defence, suitable to their condition and degree, and such as are allowed by law. Which is also declared by the same statute 1 W. & M. st. 2 c. 2 and is indeed a public allowance, under due restrictions, of the natural right of resistance and self-preservation, when the sanctions of society and laws are found insufficient to restrain the violence of oppression.

Commentaries, bk. 1, ch.1, sec. 3; vol. 1, p. 139.

4.3.2 CASELAW

4.3.2.1 Sir John Knight's Case, 1686

An information was exhibited against him by the Attorney General, upon the statute of 2 Edw. 3, c. 3, which prohibits "all persons from coming with force and arms before the King's Justices, &c., and from going or riding armed in affray of peace, on pain to forfeit his armour, and suffer imprisonment at the King's pleasure.'' This statute is confirmed by that of 20 Rich. 2, c. 1, with an addition of a further punishment, which is to make a fine to the King.

The information sets forth, that the defendant did walk about the streets armed with guns, and that he went into the church of St. Michael, in Bristol, in the time of divine service, with a gun, to terrify the King's subjects, *contra formam statuti.*

This case was tried at the Bar, and the defendant was acquitted.

The Chief Justice said, that the meaning of the statute of 2 Edw. 3, c. 3, was to punish people who go armed to terrify the King's subjects. It is likewise a great offence at the *common law,* as if the King were not able or willing to protect his subjects; and therefore this Act is but an affirmance of that law; and it having appointed a penalty, this Court can inflict no other punishment than what is therein directed.

87 Eng. Rep. 75 (K. B.).

Chapter 5

AMENDMENT III
QUARTERING SOLDIERS CLAUSE

5.1 TEXTS

5.1.1 DRAFTS IN FIRST CONGRESS

5.1.1.1 Proposal by Madison in House, June 8, 1789

5.1.1.1.a   Fourthly. That in article 1st, section 9, between clauses 3 and 4 [of the Constitution], be inserted these clauses, to wit, . . .

. . .

No soldier shall in time of peace be quartered in any house without the consent of the owner; nor at any time, but in a manner warranted by law.

Congressional Register, June 8, 1789, vol. 1, p. 427.

5.1.1.1.b   *Fourthly.* That in article 1st, section 9, between clauses 3 and 4 [of the Constitution], be inserted these clauses, to wit: . . .

. . .

No soldier shall in time of peace be quartered in any house, without consent of the owner; nor at any time, but in a manner warranted by law.

Daily Advertiser, June 12, 1789, p. 2, col. 1.

5.1.1.1.c   *Fourth.* That in article 1st, section 9, between clauses 3 and 4 [of the Constitution], be inserted these clauses, to wit: . . .

. . .

No soldier shall in time of peace be quartered in any house, without consent of the owner; nor at any time but in a manner warranted by law.

New-York Daily Gazette, June 13, 1789, p. 574, col. 3.

5.1.1.2 Proposal by Sherman to House Committee of Eleven, July 21–28, 1789

[Amendment] 6 No Soldier Shall be quartered in any private house, in time of Peace, nor at any time, but by authority of law.   *Madison Papers, DLC.*

5.1.1.3 House Committee of Eleven Report, July 28, 1789

Art. I, Sec. 9 — Between Par. 2 and 3 insert, . . .

. . .

"No soldier shall in time of peace be quartered in any house without the consent of the owner, nor in time of war but in a manner to be prescribed by law."

Broadside Collection, DLC.

5.1.1.4 House Consideration, August 17, 1789

5.1.1.4.a   The 4th clause of the 4th proposition was taken up as follows: "No soldier shall in time of peace, be quartered in any house, without the consent of the owner, nor in time of war but in a manner to be prescribed by law."

Congressional Register, August 17, 1789, vol. 2, p. 223 (reported);
id. (carried, after motions 5.1.5–5.1.6).

5.1.1.4.b   Seventh amendment — "No soldier shall in time of peace be quartered in any house without the consent of the owner, nor in time of war, but in a manner to be prescribed by law."

Daily Advertiser, August 18, 1789, p. 2, col. 4.

5.1.1.4.c   Seventh amendment — "No soldier shall in time of peace be quartered in any house without the consent of the owner, nor in time of war, but in a manner to be prescribed by law."

New-York Daily Gazette, August 19, 1789, p. 802, col. 3.

5.1.1.4.d   7th Amendment. "No soldier shall in time of peace be quartered in any house without the consent of the owner, nor in time of war, but in a manner to be prescribed by law."

Gazette of the U.S., August 22, 1789, p. 249, col. 3.

5.1.1.5 Motion by Sumpter in House, August 17, 1789

5.1.1.5.a   He [Mr. Sumpter] moved to strike out all the words from the clause but "No soldier shall be quartered in any house without the consent of the owner."

Congressional Register, August 17, 1789, vol. 2, p. 223
(motion lost by a majority of 16).

5.1.1.5.b   Mr. SUMPTER moved to strike out the words "in time of peace" and also all the last words of the paragraph from the word "owner."

Daily Advertiser, August 18, 1789, p. 2, col. 4 ("This was negatived").

5.1.1.5.c   Mr. Sumpter moved to strike out the words "in time of peace" and also all the last words of the paragraph from the word "owner."

New-York Daily Gazette, August 19, 1789,
p. 802, col. 4 ("This was negatived.").

5.1.1.5.d   Mr. SUMPTER moved to strike out the words "in time of peace" and also the last words of the paragraph from the word "owner."

Gazette of the U.S., August 22, 1789, p. 249, col. 3 (motion negatived).

5.1.1.6 Motion by Gerry in House, August 17, 1789

5.1.1.6.a

Mr. GERRY

Moved to insert between "but" and "in a manner" the words "by a civil magistrate." . . .

Congressional Register, August 17, 1789, vol. 2, p. 223
(failed, 13 in favor, 35 against).

5.1.1.6.b   Mr. GERRY then moved to insert between the words "but" and "in a manner," the words "by a civil magistrate"

Daily Advertiser, August 18, 1789, p. 2, col. 4 ("Negatived").

5.1.1.6.c   Mr. Gerry then moved to insert between the words "but" and "in a manner," the words "by a civil magistrate."

        New-York Daily Gazette, August 19, 1789, p. 802, col. 4 ("Negatived").

5.1.1.6.d   Mr. GERRY . . . moved to insert between the words "but" and "in a manner," the words *by a civil magistrate.*   *Gazette of the U.S.*, August 22, 1789, p. 249, col. 3.

5.1.1.7   Further Consideration by House, August 21, 1789

Sixth. No soldier shall in time of peace be quartered in any house, without the consent of the owner; nor in time of war but in a manner to be prescribed by law.

        HJ, p. 107 ("read and debated . . . agreed to by the House, two-thirds of the members present concurring").[1]

5.1.1.8   House Resolution, August 24, 1789

ARTICLE THE SIXTH.

No soldier shall, in time of peace, be quartered in any house without the consent of the owner, nor in time of war, but in a manner to be prescribed by law.

        House Pamphlet, RG 46, DNA.

5.1.1.9   Senate Consideration, August 25, 1789

5.1.1.9.a   The Resolve of the House of Representatives of the 24th of August, upon certain "Articles to be proposed to the Legislatures of the several States as Amendments to the Constitution of the United States" was read as followeth: . . .

Article the sixth

No soldier shall in time of Peace be quartered in any house, without the consent of the owner, nor in time of War, but in a manner to be prescribed by law.

        Rough SJ, p. 216.

5.1.1.9.b   The Resolve of the House of Representatives of the 24th of August, was read as followeth:

"Article the Sixth.

"No Soldier shall, in time of peace, be quartered in any house without the consent of the owner, nor in time of war, but in a manner to be prescribed by law.

        Smooth SJ, p. 194.

5.1.1.9.c   The Resolve of the House of Representatives of the 24th of August, was read as followeth:

"ARTICLE THE SIXTH.

"No soldier shall, in time of peace, be quartered in any house without the consent of the owner, nor in time of war, but in a manner to be prescribed by law.

        Printed SJ, p. 104.

---

[1] On August 22, 1789, the following motion was agreed to:

ORDERED, That it be referred to a committee of three, to prepare and report a proper arrangement of, and introduction to the articles of amendment to the Constitution of the United States, as agreed to by the House; and that Mr. Benson, Mr. Sherman, and Mr. Sedgwick be of the said committee.

        HJ, p. 112.

5.1.1.10 Further Senate Consideration, September 4, 1789

5.1.1.10.a On motion to adopt the sixth Article of Amendments proposed by the House of Representatives — Rough SJ, p. 248 ("It passed in the affirmative.").

5.1.1.10.b On motion, To adopt the sixth article of Amendments proposed by the House of Representatives — Smooth SJ, p. 222 ("It passed in the affirmative.").

5.1.1.10.c On motion, To adopt the sixth Article of Amendments proposed by the House of Representatives — Printed SJ, p. 119 ("It passed in the Affirmative.").

5.1.1.10.d that the Senate do
Resolved to ∧ concur with the House of Representatives in Articles Sixth and Seventh Senate MS, p. 3, RG 46, DNA.

5.1.1.11 Further Senate Consideration, September 9, 1789

5.1.1.11.a On motion, To alter Article 6th so as to stand Article 5th, and Article 7th so as to stand Article 6th, and Article 8th so as to stand Article 7th Rough SJ, p. 275 ("It passed in the Affirmative.").

5.1.1.11.b On motion, To alter article the sixth so as to stand article the fifth, and article the seventh so as to stand article the sixth, and article the eighth so as to stand article the seventh — Smooth SJ, p. 244 ("It passed in the affirmative.").

5.1.1.11.c On motion, To alter Article the sixth so as to stand Article the fifth, and Article the seventh so as to stand Article the sixth, and Article the eighth so as to stand Article the seventh — Printed SJ, p. 129 ("It passed in the Affirmative.").

5.1.1.11.d To erase the word "Sixth" & insert Fifth. — Ellsworth MS, p. 2, RG 46, DNA.

5.1.1.12 Senate Resolution, September 9, 1789

ARTICLE THE FIFTH.

No soldier shall, in time of peace, be quartered in any house, without the consent of the owner, nor in time of war, but in a manner to be prescribed by law.
Senate Pamphlet, RG 46, DNA.

5.1.1.13 Further House Consideration, September 21, 1789

RESOLVED, That this House doth agree to the second, fourth, eighth, twelfth, thirteenth, sixteenth, eighteenth, nineteenth, twenty-fifth, and twenty-sixth amendments, and doth disagree to the first, third, fifth, sixth, seventh, ninth, tenth, eleventh, fourteenth, fifteenth, seventeenth, twentieth, twenty-first, twenty-second, twenty-third, and twenty-fourth amendments proposed by the Senate to the said articles, two thirds of the members present concurring on each vote.

RESOLVED, That a conference be desired with the Senate on the subject matter of the amendments disagreed to, and that Mr. Madison, Mr. Sherman, and Mr. Vining, be appointed managers at the same on the part of this House.
HJ, p. 146.

5.1.1.14 Further Senate Consideration, September 21, 1789

5.1.1.14.a   A message from the House of Representatives —

Mr. Beckley, their Clerk, brought up a Resolve of the House of this date, to agree to the 2nd, 4th, 8th, 12th, 13th, 16th, 18th, 19th, 25th, and 26th Amendments proposed by the Senate, "To articles of Amendment to be proposed to the Legislatures of the several States, as Amendments to the Constitution of the United States," and to disagree to the 1st, 3d, 5th, 6th, 7th, 9th, 10th, 11th, 14th, 15th, 17th, 20th, 21st, 22d, 23d, and 24th amendments: Two thirds of the members present concurring on each vote: And "That a conference be desired with the Senate on the subject matter of the amendments disagreed to," and that Mr. Madison, Mr. Sherman, and Mr. Vining, be appointed managers of the same, on the part of the House of Representatives —

And he withdrew.

Smooth SJ, pp. 265–66.

5.1.1.14.b   A message from the House of Representatives —

Mr. Beckley, their Clerk, brought up a Resolve of the House of this date, to agree to the 2d, 4th, 8th, 12th, 13th, 16th, 18th, 19th, 25th, and 26th Amendments proposed by the Senate, "To Articles of Amendment to be proposed to the Legislatures of the several States, as Amendments to the Constitution of the United States," and to disagree to the 1st, 3d, 5th, 6th, 7th, 9th, 10th, 11th, 14th, 15th, 17th, 20th, 21st, 22d, 23d, and 24th Amendments: Two thirds of the members present concurring on each vote: And "That a conference be desired with the Senate on the subject matter of the Amendments disagreed to," and that Mr. Madison, Mr. Sherman, and Mr. Vining, be appointed managers of the same, on the part of the House of Representatives —

And he withdrew.

Printed SJ, pp. 141–42.

5.1.1.15 Further Senate Consideration, September 21, 1789

5.1.1.15.a   The Senate proceeded to consider the Message of the House of Representatives disagreeing to the Amendments made by the Senate "To Articles to be proposed to the Legislatures of the several States, as Amendments to the Constitution of the United States" And

RESOLVED, That the Senate do recede from their third Amendment, and do insist on all the others.

RESOLVED, That the Senate do concur with the House of Representatives in a conference on the subject matter of disagreement on the said Articles of Amendment, and that Mr. Ellsworth, Mr. Carroll and Mr. Paterson be managers of the conference on the part of the Senate.

Smooth SJ, p. 267.

5.1.1.15.b   The Senate proceeded to consider the message of the House of Representatives disagreeing to the Amendments made by the Senate "To Articles to be proposed to the Legislatures of the several States, as Amendments to the Constitution of the United States" — And

RESOLVED, That the Senate do recede from their third Amendment, and do insist on all the others.

RESOLVED, That the Senate do concur with the House of Representatives in a conference on the subject matter of disagreement on the said Articles of Amendment, and that Mr. Ellsworth, Mr. Carroll, and Mr. Paterson be managers of the conference on the part of the Senate.

Printed SJ, p. 142.

5.1.1.16 Conference Committee Report, September 24, 1789

[T]hat it will be proper for the House of Representatives to agree to the said Amendments proposed by the Senate, with an Amendment to their fifth Amendment, so that the third Article shall read as follows: "Congress shall make no Law <u>respecting an establishment of Religion</u>, or prohibiting the free exercise thereof; or abridging the freedom of Speech, or of the Press; or the right of the people peaceably to assemble and ~~to~~ petition the Government for a redress of grievances;" And with an Amendment to the fourteenth Amendment proposed by the Senate, so that the eighth Article, as numbered in the Amendments proposed by the Senate, shall read as follows "In all criminal prosecutions, the accused shall enjoy the right to a speedy & publick trial <u>by an impartial jury of the district wherein the crime shall have been committed, as the district shall have been previously ascertained by law</u>, and to be informed of the nature and cause of the accusation; to be confronted with the witnesses against him, and to have com-

pulsory process for obtaining witnesses ~~against him~~ in his favour, & /\\ have the assistance of counsel for his defence."

Conference MS, RG 46, DNA (Ellsworth's handwriting).

5.1.1.17 House Consideration of Conference Committee Report, September 24 [25], 1789

RESOLVED, That this House doth recede from their disagreement to the first, third, fifth, sixth, seventh, ninth, tenth, eleventh, fourteenth, fifteenth, seventeenth, twentieth, twenty-first, twenty-second, twenty-third, and twenty-fourth amendments, insisted on by the Senate: PROVIDED, That the two articles which by the amendments of the Senate are now proposed to be inserted as the third and eighth articles, shall be amended to read as followeth;

Article the third. "Congress shall make no law respecting an establishment of religion, or prohibiting the free exercise thereof; or abridging the freedom of speech, or of the press; or the right of the people peaceably to assemble, and to petition the government for a redress of grievances."

Article the eighth. "In all criminal prosecutions, the accused shall enjoy the right to a speedy and public trial by an impartial jury of the state and district wherein the crime shall have been committed, which district shall have been previously ascertained by law, and to be informed of the nature and cause of the accusation, to be confronted with the witnesses against him, to have compulsory process for obtaining witnesses in his favor, and to have the assistance of council for his defence."

HJ, p. 152 ("On the question, that the House do agree to the
alteration and amendment of the eighth article, in manner
aforesaid, It was resolved in the affirmative. Ayes 37 Noes 14").

5.1.1.18 Senate Consideration of Conference Committee Report, September 24, 1789

5.1.1.18.a   Mr. Ellsworth, on behalf of the managers of the conference on "articles to be proposed to the several States as Amendments to the Constitution of the United States," reported as follows:

That it will be proper for the House of Representatives to agree to the said amendments proposed by the Senate, with an Amendment to their fifth Amendment, so that the third Article shall read as follows: "Congress shall make no law respecting an establishment of <u>Religion</u>, or prohibiting the free exercise thereof; or abridging the freedom of Speech, or of the Press; or the right of the people peaceably to assemble and petition the Government for a redress of Grievances;" And with an Amendment to the fourteenth Amendment proposed by the Senate, so that the eighth article, as numbered in the Amendments proposed by the Senate, shall read as follows; "In all criminal prosecutions, the accused shall enjoy the right to a speedy and public trial by an impartial <u>Jury</u> of the district wherein the <u>Crime</u> shall have been committed, as the district shall have been previously ascertained by law, and to be informed of the nature and cause of the accusation, to be confronted with the witnesses against him, and to have compulsory process for obtaining witnesses in his favor, and to have the assistance of Counsel for defence."

Smooth SJ, pp. 272–73.

5.1.1.18.b   Mr. Ellsworth, on behalf of the managers of the conference on "Articles to be proposed to the several States as Amendments to the Constitution of the United States," reported as follows:

That it will be proper for the House of Representatives to agree to the said Amendments proposed by the Senate, with an Amendment to their fifth Amendment, so that the third Article shall read as follows: "Congress shall make no Law RESPECTING AN ESTABLISHMENT OF RELIGION, or prohibiting the free exercise thereof; or abridging the freedom of Speech, or of the Press; or the right of the People peaceably to assemble and petition the Government for a redress of Grievances;" And with an Amendment to the fourteenth Amendment proposed by the Senate, so that the eighth Article, as numbered in the Amendments proposed by the Senate, shall read as follows; "In all criminal prosecutions, the accused shall enjoy the right to a speedy and public trial BY AN IMPARTIAL JURY OF THE DISTRICT WHEREIN THE CRIME SHALL HAVE BEEN COMMITTED, AS THE DISTRICT SHALL HAVE BEEN PREVIOUSLY ASCERTAINED BY LAW, and to be informed of the nature and cause of the accusation, to be confronted with the witnesses against him, and to have compulsory process for obtaining witnesses in his favor, and to have the assistance of Counsel for defence."

Printed SJ, p. 145.

5.1.1.19 Further Senate Consideration of Conference Committee Report, September 24, 1789

5.1.1.19.a   A Message from the House of Representatives —

Mr. Beckley, their Clerk, brought up the Amendments to the "Articles to be proposed to the Legislatures of the several States, as Amendments to the Constitution of the United States;" and informed the Senate, that the House of Representatives had receded from their disagreement to the 1st, 3d, 5th, 6th, 7th, 9th, 10th,

11th, 14th, 15th, 17th, 20th, 21st, 22d, 23d, and 24th Amendments, insisted on by the Senate: Provided that the "Two Articles, which by the Amendments of the Senate are now proposed to be inserted as the third and eighth Articles," shall be amended to read as followeth:

Article the Third. "Congress shall make no Law respecting an establishment of Religion, or prohibiting the free exercise thereof; or abridging the freedom of Speech, or of the Press; or the right of the people peaceably to assemble, and petition the Government for a redress of Grievances."

Article the Eighth. "In all criminal prosecutions the accused shall enjoy the right to a speedy and public trial by an impartial Jury of the State and District, wherein the crime shall have been committed, which District shall have been previously ascertained by law, and to be informed of the nature and cause of the accusation, to be confronted with the witnesses against him, and to have compulsory process for obtaining witnesses in his favor, and to have the assistance of Counsel for his defence."

Smooth SJ, pp. 278–79.

5.1.1.19.b   A Message from the House of Representatives —

Mr. Beckley, their Clerk, brought up the Amendments to the "Articles to be proposed to the Legislatures of the several States, as Amendments to the Constitution of the United States;" and informed the Senate, that the House of Representatives had receded from their disagreement to the 1st, 3d, 5th, 6th, 7th, 9th, 10th, 11th, 14th, 15th, 17th, 20th, 21st, 22d, 23d, and 24th Amendments, insisted on by the Senate: Provided that the "Two Articles, which by the Amendments of the Senate are now proposed to be inserted as the third and eighth Articles," shall be amended to read as followeth:

Article the Third. "Congress shall make no Law respecting an establishment of Religion, or prohibiting the free exercise thereof; or abridging the freedom of Speech, or of the Press; or the right of the People peaceably to assemble, and petition the Government for a redress of Grievances."

Article the Eighth. "In all criminal prosecutions the accused shall enjoy the right to a speedy and public trial by an impartial Jury of the State and District, wherein the crime shall have been committed, which District shall have been previously ascertained by law, and to be informed of the nature and cause of the accusation, to be confronted with the witnesses against him, and to have compulsory process for obtaining witnesses in his favor, and to have the assistance of Counsel for his defence."

Printed SJ, p.148.

5.1.1.20 Further Senate Consideration of Conference Committee Report, September 25, 1789

5.1.1.20.a   The Senate proceeded to consider the Message from the House of Representatives of the 24th, with Amendments to the Amendments of the Senate, to "Articles to be proposed to the Legislatures of the several States, as Amendments to the Constitution of the United States" — And

RESOLVED, That the Senate do concur in the Amendments proposed by the House of Representatives, to the Amendments of the Senate.   Smooth SJ, p. 283.

5.1.1.20.b   The Senate proceeded to consider the Message from the House of Representatives of the 24th, with Amendments to the Amendments of the Senate, to "Articles to be proposed to the Legislatures of the several States, as Amendments to the Constitution of the United States" — And

RESOLVED, That the Senate do concur in the Amendments proposed by the House of Representatives, to the Amendments of the Senate.

Printed SJ, pp. 150–51.

5.1.1.21   Agreed Resolution, September 25, 1789

5.1.1.21.a   Article the Fifth.

No Soldier shall, in time of peace, be quartered in any house, without the consent of the owner, nor in time of war, but in a manner to be prescribed by law.

Smooth SJ, Appendix, p. 293.

5.1.1.21.b   ARTICLE THE FIFTH.

No soldier shall, in time of peace, be quartered in any house, without the consent of the owner, nor in time of war, but in a manner to be prescribed by law.

Printed SJ, Appendix, p. 163.

5.1.1.22   Enrolled Resolution, September 28, 1789

Article the fifth . . . No Soldier shall, in time of peace be quartered in any house, without the consent of the owner, nor in time of war, but in a manner to be prescribed by law.

Enrolled Resolutions, RG 11, DNA.

5.1.1.23   Printed Versions

5.1.1.23.a   ART. III. No soldier shall, in time of peace, be quartered in any house without the consent of the owner; nor in time of war, but in a manner to be prescribed by law.

Statutes at Large, vol. 1, p. 21.

5.1.1.23.b   ART. V. No soldier shall in time of peace be quartered in any house without the consent of the owner; nor in time of war, but in a mannner to be prescribed by law.

Statutes at Large, vol. 1, p. 97.

5.1.2 PROPOSALS FROM THE STATE CONVENTIONS

5.1.2.1   Maryland Minority, April 26, 1788

10. That soldiers be not quartered in time of peace upon private houses, without the consent of the owners.

Maryland Gazette, May 1, 1788 (committee majority).

5.1.2.2   New Hampshire, June 21, 1788

Tenth,

That no standing Army shall be Kept up in time of Peace unless with the consent of three fourths of the Members of each branch of Congress, nor shall Soldiers in Time of Peace be quartered upon private Houses without the consent of Owners.

State Ratifications, RG 11, DNA.

5.1.2.3 New York, July 26, 1788

That in time of Peace no Soldier ought be quartered in any House without the consent of the Owner, and in time of War only by the Civil Magistrate in such manner as the Laws may direct.

State Ratifications, RG 11, DNA.

5.1.2.4 North Carolina, August 1, 1788

18th. That no soldier in time of peace ought to be quartered in any house without the consent of the owner, and in time of war in such manner only as the Laws direct.

State Ratifications, RG 11, DNA.

5.1.2.5 Rhode Island, May 29, 1790

17th. That the people have a right to keep and bear arms, that a well regulated militia, including the body of the people capable of bearing arms, is the proper, natural and safe defence of a free state; that the militia shall not be subject to martial law except in time of war, rebellion or insurrection; that standing armies in time of peace, are dangerous to liberty, and ought not be kept up, except in cases of necessity; and that at all times the military should be under strict subordination to the civil power; that in time of peace no soldier ought to be quartered in any house without the consent of the owner, and in time of war, only by the civil magistrate, in such manner as the law directs.

State Ratifications, RG 11, DNA.

5.1.2.6 Virginia, June 27, 1788

Eighteenth. That no Soldier in time of peace ought to be quartered in any house without the consent of the owner, and in time of war in such manner only as the laws direct.

State Ratifications, RG 11, DNA.

5.1.3 STATE CONSTITUTIONS AND LAWS; COLONIAL CHARTERS AND LAWS

5.1.3.1 Delaware: Declaration of Rights, 1776

SECT. 21. That no soldier ought to be quartered in any house in time of peace without the consent of the owner; and in time of war in such manner only as the Legislature shall direct.

Delaware Laws, vol. 1, App., p. 81.

5.1.3.2 Maryland: Declaration of Rights, 1776

28. That no soldier ought to be quartered in any house in time of peace without the consent of the owner, and in time of war in such manner only as the legislature shall direct.

Maryland Laws, November 3, 1776.

5.1.3.3 Massachusetts: Constitution, 1780

[Part I, Article] XXVII. In time of peace no soldier ought to be quartered in any house without the consent of the owner; and in time of war such quarters ought not to be made but by the civil magistrate, in a manner ordained by the legislature.

Massachusetts Perpetual Laws, p. 7.

5.1.3.4   New Hampshire: Bill of Rights, 1783

[Part I, Article] XXVII. No soldier in time of peace, shall be quartered in any house without the consent of the owner; and in time of war, such quarters ought not to be made but by the civil magistrate, in a manner ordained by the legislature.

New Hampshire Laws, pp. 26–27.

5.1.3.5   New York

5.1.3.5.a   Act Declaring . . . Rights & Priviledges, 1691

That no Free-man shall be compelled to receive any Souldiers or Marriners, except Inholders, and other Houses of publick Entertainment, who are to quarter for ready Money into his House, and there suffer them to sojourn again their Wills; provided it be not in time of actual War within this Province.

New York Acts, p. 18.

5.1.3.5.b   Bill of Rights, 1787

Thirteenth, That by the Laws and Customs of this State, the Citizens and Inhabitants thereof cannot be compelled, against their Wills, to receive Soldiers into their Houses, and to sojourn them there; and therefore no Officer, military or civil, nor any other Person whatsoever, shall, from henceforth, presume to place, quarter or billet any Soldier or Soldiers, upon any Citizen or Inhabitant of this State, of any Degree or Profession whatever, without his or her Consent; and that it shall and may be lawful for every such Citizen and Inhabitant, to refuse to sojourn or quarter any Soldier or Soldiers, notwithstanding any Command, Order, Warrant, or billetting whatever.

New York Laws, vol. 2, p. 2.

5.1.3.6   Pennsylvania: Constitution, 1790

ARTICLE IX.

. . .

SECT. XXIII. That no soldier shall, in time of peace, be quartered in any house without the consent of the owner, nor in time of war, but in a manner to be prescribed by law.

Pennsylvania Acts, Dallas, p. xxxvi.

5.1.4 OTHER TEXTS

5.1.4.1   Petition of Right, 1627

6. And whereas of late great companies of souldiers and marriners have been dispersed into divers counties of the realme, and the inhabitants against their wille have been compelled to receive them into their houses, and there to suffer them to sojourne against the lawes and customes of this realme and to the great greivance and vexacion of the people.

3 Chas. 1, c. 1.

5.1.4.2   English Bill of Rights, 1689

. . . By raising and keeping a standing army within this kingdome in time of peace without consent of Parlyament and quartering soldiers contrary to law. . . .

. . .

That the raising or keeping a standing army within the kingdome in time of peace unlesse it be with consent of Parlyament is against law.

1 Will. & Mar. sess. 2, c. 2.

5.1.4.3 Declaration and Resolves of the First Continental Congress, 1774

Resolved, N.C.D. That the following acts of parliament are infringements and violations of the rights of the colonists; and that the repeal of them is essentially necessary, in order to restore harmony between Great-Britain and the American colonies, viz.

. . .

Also the act passed in the same session, for the better providing suitable quarters for officers and soldiers in his majesty's service, in North-America.

Tansill, pp. 4–5.

5.1.4.4 Declaration of Independence, 1776

. . . For Quartering large bodies of armed troops among us. . . .

Continental Congress Papers, DNA.

5.2 DISCUSSION OF DRAFTS AND PROPOSALS
5.2.1 THE FIRST CONGRESS

5.2.1.1 June 8, 1789[2]

5.2.1.2 August 17, 1789

5.2.1.2.a The house went into a committee of the whole on the subject of amendments.

. . .

The 4th clause of the 4th proposition was taken as follows: "No soldier shall in time of peace, be quartered in any house, without the consent of the owner, nor in time of war but in a manner to be prescribed by law."

MR. SUMPTER

Hoped soldiers would never be quartered on the inhabitants, either in time of peace or war, without the consent of the owner: It was a burthen, and very oppressive, even in cases where the owner gave his consent; but where this was wanting, it would be a hardship indeed! Their property would lie at the mercy of men irritated by a refusal, and well disposed to destroy the peace of the family.

He moved to strike out all the words from the clause but "No soldier shall be quartered in any house without the consent of the owner."

MR. SHERMAN

Observed that it was absolutely necessary that marching troops should have quarters, whether in time of peace or war, and that it ought not to be put in the power of an individual to obstruct the public service; if quarters were not be obtained in public barracks, they must be procured elsewhere. In England, where

---

[2] For reports of Madison's speech in support of his proposals, *see* 1.2.1.1.a–c.

they paid considerable attention to private rights, they billeted the troops upon the keepers of public houses also, with the consent of the magistracy. Mr. Sumpter's motion being put, was lost by a majority of sixteen.

Mr. Gerry

Moved to insert between "but" and "in a manner" the words "by a civil magistrate," observing that there was no part of the Union but what they could have access to such authority.

Mr. Hartley

Said those things ought to be entrusted to the legislature; that cases might arise where the public safety would be endangered by putting it in the power of one person to keep a division of troops standing in the inclemency of the weather for many hours, therefore he was against inserting the words.

Mr. Gerry said either his amendment was essential, or the whole clause was unnecessary.

On putting the question 13 rose in favor of the motion, 35 against it, and then the clause was carried on as reported.

Congressional Register, August 17, 1789, vol. 2, pp. 219, 223–24.

5.2.1.2.b   Seventh amendment — "No soldier shall in time of peace be quartered in any house without the consent of the owner, nor in time of war, but in a manner to be prescribed by law."

Mr. Sumpter moved to strike out the words "in time of peace" and also all the last words of the paragraph from the word "owner." This was negatived.

Mr. Gerry then moved to insert between the words "but" and "in a manner," the words "by a civil magistrate" — Negatived.

The amendment was agreed to.   *Daily Advertiser, August 18, 1789, p. 2, col. 4.*

5.2.1.2.c   Seventh amendment — "No soldier shall in time of peace be quartered in any house without the consent of the owner, nor in time of war, but in a manner to be prescribed by law."

Mr. Sumpter moved to strike out the words "in time of peace" and also all the last words of the paragraph from the word "owner." This was negatived.

Mr. Gerry then moved to insert between the words "but" and "in a manner," the words "by a civil magistrate." Negatived.

The amendment was agreed to.

New-York Daily Gazette, August 19, 1789, p. 802, cols. 3–4.

5.2.1.2.d   7th Amendment. "No soldier shall in time of peace be quartered in any house without the consent of the owner, nor in time of war, but in a manner to be prescribed by law."

Mr. Sumpter moved to strike out the words "in time of peace" and also the last words of the paragraph from the word "owner."

Mr. Sherman said he thought this was going too far; occasion might arise in which it would be extremely injurious to put it in the power of any man to obstruct the public service: He adverted to the British regulations in this case, of quartering soldiers in public houses. This motion was negatived.

Mr. GERRY said, that he conceived the article might be so altered as to relieve the minds of the citizens of the United States. It is said, government will take care of the rights of the people; but these amendments are designed to prevent the arbitrary exercise of power. He then moved to insert between the words "but" and "in a manner," the words *by a civil magistrate*. Negatived.

The amendment was agreed to.   Gazette of the U.S., August 22, 1789, p. 249, col. 3.

5.2.2 STATE CONVENTIONS

5.2.2.1 Maryland, April 1788

I am opposed to the new Government; —

. . .

3. Because Congress will have a right to quarter soldiers in our *private* houses, not only in time of war, but also in time of *peace*. Bill of Rights 28.

Samuel Chase, Storing, vol. 5, pp. 85–86.

5.2.2.2 Virginia, June 16, 1788

Mr. HENRY. . . .

. . . One of our first complaints, under the former government, was the quartering of troops upon us. This was one of the principal reasons for dissolving the connection with Great Britain. Here we may have troops in time of peace. They may be billeted in any manner — to tyrannize, oppress, and crush us.

Mr. MADISON. . . .

He says that one ground of complaint, at the beginning of the revolution, was, that a standing army was quartered upon us. This was not the whole complaint. We complained because it was done without the local authority of this country — without the consent of the people of America.   Elliot, vol. 3, p. 411–13.

5.2.3 PHILADELPHIA CONVENTION

None.

5.2.4 NEWSPAPERS AND PAMPHLETS

5.2.4.1 The Federal Farmer, No. 6, December 25, 1787

The following, I think, will be allowed to be unalienable or fundamental rights in the United States: —

No man, demeaning himself peaceably, shall be molested on account of his religion or mode or [*sic*] worship — The people have a right to hold and enjoy their property according to known standing laws, and which cannot be taken from them without their consent, or the consent of their representatives; and whenever taken in the pressing urgencies of government, they are to receive a reasonable compensation for it — Individual security consists in having free recourse to the laws — The people are subject to no laws or taxes not assented to by their representatives constitutionally assembled — They are at all times intitled to the benefits of the writ of habeas corpus, the trial by jury in criminal and civil causes — They have a right, when charged, to a speedy trial in the vicinage; to be heard by themselves or counsel, not to be compelled to furnish evidence against themselves, to have witnesses face to face, and to confront their adversaries before the judge — No man is held to answer a crime charged upon him till it be substantially described to him; and he is subject to no unreasonable searches or seizures of his person, papers or effects — The people have a right to assemble in an orderly manner, and petition the government for a redress of wrongs — The freedom of the press ought not to be restrained — No emoluments, except for actual service — No hereditary honors, or orders of nobility, ought to be allowed — The military ought to be subordinate to the civil authority, and no soldier be quartered on the citizens without their consent — The militia ought always to be armed and disciplined, and the usual defence of the country — The supreme power is in the people, and power delegated ought to return to them at stated periods, and frequently — The legislative, executive, and judicial powers, ought always to be kept distinct — others perhaps might be added. Storing, vol. 2, p. 262.

5.2.4.2 The Federal Farmer, No. 16, January 20, 1788

The constitution will give congress general powers to raise and support armies. General powers carry with them incidental ones, and the means necessary to the end. In the exercise of these powers, is there any provision in the constitution to prevent the quartering of soldiers on the inhabitants? you will answer, there is not. This may sometimes be deemed a necessary measure in the support of armies; on what principle can the people claim the right to be exempt from this burden? they will urge, perhaps, the practice of the country, and the provisions made in some of the state constitutions — they will be answered, that their claim thus to be exempt is not founded in nature, but only in custom and opinion, or at best, in stipulations in some of the state constitutions, which are local, and inferior in their operation, and can have no controul over the general government — that they had adopted a federal constitution — had noticed several rights, but had been totally silent about this exemption — that they had given general powers relative to the subject, which, in their operation, regularly destroyed the claim. Though it is not to be presumed, that we are in immediate danger from this quarter, yet it is fit and proper to establish, beyond dispute, those rights which are particularly valuable to individuals, and essential to the permanency and duration of free government. An excellent writer observes, that the English, always in possession of their freedom, are frequently unmindful of the value of it: we, at this period, do not seem to be so well off, having, in some instances abused ours; many of us are quite disposed to barter it away for what we call energy, coercion, and some other terms we use as vaguely as that of liberty — There is often as great a rage for change and novelty in politics, as in amusements and fashions. Storing, vol. 2, p. 329.

5.2.5 LETTERS AND DIARIES

None.

5.3 DISCUSSION OF RIGHTS

5.3.1 TREATISES

None.

5.3.2 CASELAW

None.

Chapter 6

AMENDMENT IV
SEARCH AND SEIZURE CLAUSE

6.1 TEXTS

6.1.1 DRAFTS IN FIRST CONGRESS

6.1.1.1 Proposal by Madison in House, June 8, 1789

6.1.1.1.a   Fourthly. That in article 1st, section 9, between clauses 3 and 4 [of the Constitution], be inserted these clauses, to wit, . . .

. . .

The rights of the people to be secured in their persons, their houses, their papers. [*sic*] and their other property from all unreasonable searches and seizures, shall not be violated by warrants issued without probable cause, supported by oath or affirmation, or not particularly describing the places to be searched, or the persons or things to be seized.   Congressional Register, June 8, 1789, vol. 1, p. 428.

6.1.1.1.b   *Fourthly.* That in article 1st, section 9, between clauses 3 and 4 [of the Constitution], be inserted these clauses, to wit: . . .

. . .

The rights of the people to be secured in their persons, their houses, their papers, and their other property from all unreasonable searches and seizures, shall not be violated by warrants issued without probable cause, supported by oath or affirmation, or not particularly describing the places to be searched, or the persons or things to be seized.   Daily Advertiser, June 12, 1789, p. 2, col. 2.

6.1.1.1.c   *Fourth.* That in article 1st, section 9, between clauses 3 and 4 [of the Constitution], be inserted these clauses, to wit: . . .

. . .

The rights of the people to be secured in their persons, their houses, their papers, and their other property, from all unreasonable searches and seizures, shall not be violated by warrants issued without probable cause, supported by oath or affirmation, or not particularly describing the places to be searched, or the persons or things to be seized.   New-York Daily Gazette, June 13, 1789, p. 574, col. 3.

6.1.1.2 House Committee of Eleven Report, July 28, 1789

Art. I, Sec. 9 — Between Par. 2 and 3 insert, . . .

. . .

"The right of the people to be secure in their person, houses, papers and effects, shall not be violated by warrants issuing, without probable cause supported by oath or affirmation, and not particularly describing the places to be searched, and the persons or things to be seized."

Broadside Collection, DLC.

6.1.1.3 House Consideration, August 17, 1789

6.1.1.3.a The committee went on to the consideration of the 7th clause of the 4th proposition, being as follows; "the right of the people to be secured in their person, houses, papers and effects, shall not be violated by warrants issuing without probable cause, supported by oath or affirmation, and not particularly describing the place to be searched, and the persons or things to be seized."

Congressional Register, August 17, 1789, vol. 2, p. 226 (reported).

6.1.1.3.b 10th Amendment. "The rights of the people to be secure in their persons, houses, papers and effects, shall not be violated[1] without probable cause, supported by oath or affirmation, and not particularly describing the places to be searched, and the persons or things to be seized."

Daily Advertiser, August 18, 1789, p. 2, col. 4.

6.1.1.3.c Tenth amendment. — "The rights of the people to be secure in their persons, houses, papers and effects, shall not be violated by warrants issuing without probable cause, supported by oath or affirmation, and not particularly describing the places to be searched, and the persons or things to be seized."

New-York Daily Gazette, August 19, 1789, p. 802, col. 4.

6.1.1.3.d 10th Amendment. "The rights of the people to be secure in their persons, houses, papers and effects, shall not be violated [by warrants issuing] without probable cause, supported by oath or affirmation, and not particularly describing the places to be searched, and the persons or things to be seized."

Gazette of the U.S., August 22, 1789, p. 249, col. 3.

6.1.1.4 Motion by Gerry or Benson in House, August 17, 1789

6.1.1.4.a Mr. GERRY

Said he presumed there was a mistake in the wording of this clause, it ought to be "the right of the people to be secure in their persons, houses, papers and effects, against unreasonable seizures and searches," . . . .

Congressional Register, August 17, 1789, vol. 2, p. 226 (adopted);
id., p. 226 (agreed to, following motions 6.1.5–6.1.6).

6.1.1.4.b Mr. BENSON moved to insert after the words "and effects," these words "against unreasonable searches and seizures."

Daily Advertiser, August 18, 1789, p. 2, col. 4 ("This was carried.
The question was then put on the amendment and carried.").

6.1.1.4.c Mr. Benson moved to insert after the words "and effects," these words, "against unreasonable searches and seizures."

New-York Daily Gazette, August 19, 1789, p. 802, col. 4.
("This was carried.").

6.1.1.4.d   Mr. BENSON moved to insert after the words "and effects," these words *against unreasonable seizures, and searches.*

> Gazette of the U.S., August 22, 1789, p. 249, col. 3
> ("This was carried.").

6.1.1.5   Motion by Benson or Gerry in House, August 17, 1789

6.1.1.5.a   Mr. BENSON

Objected to the words "by warrants issuing," . . . he therefore proposed to alter it so as to read "and no warrant shall issue."

> Congressional Register, August 17, 1789, vol. 2, p. 226
> (motion "lost by a considerable majority").

6.1.1.5.b   Mr. GERRY objected to the words, "by warrants issuing" — He said the provision was good, as far as it went; but he thought it was not sufficient: He moved that it be altered to *and no warrant shall issue.*

> Gazette of the U.S., August 22, 1789, p. 249, col. 3
> ("This was negatived.").

6.1.1.6   Motion by Livermore in House, August 17, 1789

Mr. LIVERMORE objected to the words "and not" between "affirmative and particularly." He moved to strike them out. . . .

> Congressional Register, August 17, 1789, vol. 2, p. 226
> ("the motion passed in the negative.").

6.1.1.7   Further House Consideration, August 21, 1789

Ninth. The right of the people to be secure in their persons, houses, papers and effects, against unreasonable searches and seizures, shall not be violated; and no warrants shall issue, but upon probable cause, supported by oath or affirmation, and particularly describing the place to be searched, and the persons or things to be seized.

> HJ, p. 108 ("read and debated . . . agreed to by the House, . . .
> two-thirds of the members present concurring").[1]

6.1.1.8   House Resolution, August 24, 1789

ARTICLE the SEVENTH.

The right of the People to be secure in their persons, houses, papers and effects, against unreasonable searches and seizures, shall not be violated, and no warrants shall issue, but upon probable cause supported by oath or affirmation, and particularly describing the place to be searched, and the persons or things to be seized.

> House Pamphlet, RG 46, DNA.

---

[1]On August 22, 1789, the following motion was agreed to:

ORDERED, That it be referred to a committee of three, to prepare and report a proper arrangement of, and introduction to the articles of amendment to the Constitution of the United States, as agreed to by the House; and that Mr. Benson, Mr. Sherman, and Mr. Sedgwick be of the said committee.

> HJ, p. 112.

6.1.1.9   Senate Consideration, August 25, 1789

6.1.1.9.a   The Resolve of the House of Representatives of the 24th of August, upon certain "Articles to be proposed to the Legislatures of the several States as Amendments to the Constitution of the United States" was read as followeth:

. . .

Article the seventh

["The right of the people to be secure in their persons, houses, papers and effects, against unreasonable searches and seizures, shall not be violated, and no warrants shall issue, but upon probable cause, supported by oath or affirmation, and particularly describing the place to be searched, and the persons or things to be seized.]

Rough SJ, p. 216 [matter in brackets not legible].

6.1.1.9.b   The Resolve of the House of Representatives of the 24th of August, was read as followeth:

. . .

"Article the Seventh.

"The right of the people to be secure in their persons, houses, papers and effects, against unreasonable searches and seizures, shall not be violated, and no warrants shall issue, but upon probable cause, supported by oath or affirmation, and particularly describing the place to be searched, and the persons or things to be seized.

Smooth SJ, pp. 194–95.

6.1.1.9.c   The Resolve of the House of Representatives of the 24th of August, was read as followeth:

. . .

"ARTICLE THE SEVENTH.

"The right of the people to be secure in their persons, houses, papers and effects, against unreasonable searches and seizures, shall not be violated, and no warrants shall issue, but upon probable cause, supported by oath or affirmation, and particularly describing the place to be searched, and the persons or things to be seized.

Printed SJ, pp. 104–05.

6.1.1.10   Further Senate Consideration, September 4, 1789

6.1.1.10.a   On Motion to adopt the seventh article of amendments proposed by the House of Representatives.

Rough SJ, p. 249 ("It passed in the affirmative.").

6.1.1.10.b   On motion, To adopt the seventh article of Amendments proposed by the House of Representatives —

Smooth SJ, p. 222 ("It passed in the Affirmative.").

6.1.1.10.c   On motion, To adopt the seventh Article of Amendments proposed by the House of Representatives —

Printed SJ, p. 119 ("It passed in the Affirmative.").

6.1.1.10.d   that the Senate do
Resolved t̶o̶ /\ concur with the House of Representatives in Articles Sixth and Seventh

Senate MS, p. 3, RG 46, DNA.

6.1.1.11   Further Senate Consideration, September 9, 1789

6.1.1.11.a   On motion, To alter Article 6th so as to stand Article 5th, and Article 7th so as to stand Article 6th, and Article 8th so as to stand Article 7th

Rough SJ, p. 275 ("It passed in the Affirmative.").

6.1.1.11.b   On motion, To alter article the sixth so as to stand article the fifth, and article the seventh so as to stand article the sixth, and article the eighth so as to stand article the seventh —

Smooth SJ, p. 244 ("It passed in the affirmative.").

6.1.1.11.c   On motion, To alter Article the sixth so as to stand Article the fifth, and Article the seventh so as to stand Article the sixth, and Article the eighth so as to stand Article the seventh —

Printed SJ, p. 129 ("It passed in the Affirmative.").

6.1.1.11.d   To erase the word "Seventh" & insert Sixth. —   Ellsworth MS, p. 2, RG 46, DNA.

6.1.1.12   Senate Resolution, September 9, 1789

ARTICLE THE SIXTH.

The right of the people to be secure in their persons, houses, papers, and effects, against unreasonable searches and seizures, shall not be violated, and no warrants shall issue, but upon probable cause, supported by oath or affirmation, and particularly describing the place to be searched, and the persons or things to be seized.

Senate Pamphlet, RG 46, DNA.

6.1.1.13   Further Consideration by House, September 21, 1789

RESOLVED, That this House doth agree to the second, fourth, eighth, twelfth, thirteenth, sixteenth, eighteenth, nineteenth, twenty-fifth, and twenty-sixth amendments, and doth disagree to the first, third, fifth, sixth, seventh, ninth, tenth, eleventh, fourteenth, fifteenth, seventeenth, twentieth, twenty-first, twenty-second, twenty-third, and twenty-fourth amendments proposed by the Senate to the said articles, two thirds of the members present concurring on each vote.

RESOLVED, That a conference be desired with the Senate on the subject matter of the amendments disagreed to, and that Mr. Madison, Mr. Sherman, and Mr. Vining, be appointed managers at the same on the part of this House.

HJ, p. 146.

6.1.1.14   Further Senate Consideration, September 21, 1789

6.1.1.14.a   A message from the House of Representatives —

Mr. Beckley, their Clerk, brought up a Resolve of the House of this date, to agree to the 2nd, 4th, 8th, 12th, 13th, 16th, 18th, 19th, 25th, and 26th Amendments proposed by the Senate, "To articles of Amendment to be proposed to the Legislatures of the several States, as Amendments to the Constitution of the United States," and to disagree to the 1st, 3d, 5th, 6th, 7th, 9th, 10th, 11th, 14th, 15th, 17th, 20th, 21st, 22d, 23d, and 24th amendments: Two thirds of the members present concurring on each vote: And "That a conference be desired with the Senate on the subject matter of the amendments disagreed to," and that Mr.

Madison, Mr. Sherman, and Mr. Vining, be appointed managers of the same, on the part of the House of Representatives —
And he withdrew.

Smooth SJ, pp. 265–66.

6.1.1.14.b   A message from the House of Representatives —
Mr. Beckley, their Clerk, brought up a Resolve of the House of this date, to agree to the 2d, 4th, 8th, 12th, 13th, 16th, 18th, 19th, 25th, and 26th Amendments proposed by the Senate, "To Articles of Amendment to be proposed to the Legislatures of the several States, as Amendments to the Constitution of the United States," and to disagree to the 1st, 3d, 5th, 6th, 7th, 9th, 10th, 11th, 14th, 15th, 17th, 20th, 21st, 22d, 23d, and 24th Amendments: Two thirds of the members present concurring on each vote: And "That a conference be desired with the Senate on the subject matter of the Amendments disagreed to," and that Mr. Madison, Mr. Sherman, and Mr. Vining, be appointed managers of the same, on the part of the House of Representatives —
And he withdrew.

Printed SJ, pp. 141–42.

6.1.1.15 Further Senate Consideration, September 21, 1789

6.1.1.15.a   The Senate proceeded to consider the Message of the House of Representatives disagreeing to the Amendments made by the Senate "To Articles to be proposed to the Legislatures of the several States, as Amendments to the Constitution of the United States" And
RESOLVED, That the Senate do recede from their third Amendment, and do insist on all the others.
RESOLVED, That the Senate do concur with the House of Representatives in a conference on the subject matter of disagreement on the said Articles of Amendment, and that Mr. Ellsworth Mr. Carroll and Mr. Paterson be managers of the conference on the part of the Senate.

Smooth SJ, p. 267.

6.1.1.15.b   The Senate proceeded to consider the message of the House of Representatives disagreeing to the Amendments made by the Senate "To Articles to be proposed to the Legislatures of the several States, as Amendments to the Constitution of the United States" — And
RESOLVED, That the Senate do recede from their third Amendment, and do insist on all the others.
RESOLVED, That the Senate do concur with the House of Representatives in a conference on the subject matter of disagreement on the said Articles of Amendment, and that Mr. Ellsworth, Mr. Carroll, and Mr. Paterson be managers of the conference on the part of the Senate.

Printed SJ, p. 142.

6.1.1.16 Conference Committee Report, September 24, 1789

[T]hat it will be proper for the House of Representatives to agree to the said Amendments proposed by the Senate, with an Amendment to their fifth Amendment, so that the third Article shall read as follows: "Congress shall make no Law respecting an establishment of Religion, or prohibiting the free exercise thereof; or abridging the freedom of Speech, or of the Press; or the right of the people peaceably to assemble and ~~to~~ petition the Government for a redress of grievances;" And with an Amendment to the fourteenth Amendment proposed by the Senate, so that the eighth Article, as numbered in the Amendments proposed by the Senate, shall read as follows "In all criminal prosecutions, the accused shall enjoy the right to a speedy & publick trial <u>by an impartial jury of the district wherein the crime shall have been committed, as the district shall have been previously ascertained by law</u>, and to be informed of the nature and cause of the accusation; to be confronted with the witnesses against him, and to have com-

pulsory process for obtaining witnesses ~~against him~~ in his favour, & $\wedge^{\text{to}}$ have the assistance of counsel for his defence."

Conference MS, RG 46, DNA (Ellsworth's handwriting).

6.1.1.17 House Consideration of Conference Committee Report, September 24 [25], 1789

RESOLVED, That this House doth recede from their disagreement to the first, third, fifth, sixth, seventh, ninth, tenth, eleventh, fourteenth, fifteenth, seventeenth, twentieth, twenty-first, twenty-second, twenty-third, and twenty-fourth amendments, insisted on by the Senate: PROVIDED, That the two articles which by the amendments of the Senate are now proposed to be inserted as the third and eighth articles, shall be amended to read as followeth;

Article the third. "Congress shall make no law respecting an establishment of religion, or prohibiting the free exercise thereof; or abridging the freedom of speech, or of the press; or the right of the people peaceably to assemble, and to petition the government for a redress of grievances."

Article the eighth. "In all criminal prosecutions, the accused shall enjoy the right to a speedy and public trial by an impartial jury of the state and district wherein the crime shall have been committed, which district shall have been previously ascertained by law, and to be informed of the nature and cause of the accusation, to be confronted with the witnesses against him, to have compulsory process for obtaining witnesses in his favor, and to have the assistance of council for his defence."

HJ, p. 152 ("On the question, that the House do agree to the alteration
and amendment of the eighth article, in manner aforesaid,
It was resolved in the affirmative. Ayes 37 Noes 14").

6.1.1.18 Senate Consideration of Conference Committee Report, September 24, 1789

6.1.1.18.a   Mr. Ellsworth, on behalf of the managers of the conference on "articles to be proposed to the several States as Amendments to the Constitution of the United States," reported as follows:

That it will be proper for the House of Representatives to agree to the said amendments proposed by the Senate, with an Amendment to their fifth Amendment, so that the third Article shall read as follows: "Congress shall make no law respecting an establishment of <u>Religion</u>, or prohibiting the free exercise thereof; or abridging the freedom of Speech, or of the Press; or the right of the people peaceably to assemble and petition the Government for a redress of Grievances;" And with an Amendment to the fourteenth Amendment proposed by the Senate, so that the eighth article, as numbered in the Amendments proposed by the Senate, shall read as follows; "In all criminal prosecutions, the accused shall enjoy the right to a speedy and public trial by an impartial <u>Jury</u> of the district wherein the <u>Crime</u> shall have been committed, as the district shall have been previously ascertained by law, and to be informed of the nature and cause of the accusation, to be confronted with the witnesses against him, and to have compulsory process for obtaining witnesses in his favor, and to have the assistance of Counsel for defence."

Smooth SJ, pp. 272–73.

6.1.1.18.b Mr. Ellsworth, on behalf of the managers of the conference on "Articles to be proposed to the several States as Amendments to the Constitution of the United States," reported as follows:

That it will be proper for the House of Representatives to agree to the said Amendments proposed by the Senate, with an Amendment to their fifth Amendment, so that the third Article shall read as follows: "Congress shall make no Law RESPECTING AN ESTABLISHMENT OF RELIGION, or prohibiting the free exercise thereof; or abridging the freedom of Speech, or of the Press; or the right of the People peaceably to assemble and petition the Government for a redress of Grievances;" And with an Amendment to the fourteenth Amendment proposed by the Senate, so that the eighth Article, as numbered in the Amendments proposed by the Senate, shall read as follows; "In all criminal prosecutions, the accused shall enjoy the right to a speedy and public trial BY AN IMPARTIAL JURY OF THE DISTRICT WHEREIN THE CRIME SHALL HAVE BEEN COMMITTED, AS THE DISTRICT SHALL HAVE BEEN PREVIOUSLY ASCERTAINED BY LAW, and to be informed of the nature and cause of the accusation, to be confronted with the witnesses against him, and to have compulsory process for obtaining witnesses in his favor, and to have the assistance of Counsel for defence."

Printed SJ, p. 145.

6.1.1.19 Further Senate Consideration of Conference Committee Report, September 24, 1789

6.1.1.19.a A Message from the House of Representatives —

Mr. Beckley, their Clerk, brought up the Amendments to the "Articles to be proposed to the Legislatures of the several States, as Amendments to the Constitution of the United States;" and informed the Senate, that the House of Representatives had receded from their disagreement to the 1st, 3d, 5th, 6th, 7th, 9th, 10th, 11th, 14th, 15th, 17th, 20th, 21st, 22d, 23d, and 24th Amendments, insisted on by the Senate: Provided that the "Two Articles, which by the Amendments of the Senate are now proposed to be inserted as the third and eighth Articles," shall be amended to read as followeth:

Article the Third. "Congress shall make no Law respecting an establishment of Religion, or prohibiting the free exercise thereof; or abridging the freedom of Speech, or of the Press; or the right of the people peaceably to assemble, and petition the Government for a redress of Grievances."

Article the Eighth. "In all criminal prosecutions the accused shall enjoy the right to a speedy and public trial by an impartial Jury of the State and District, wherein the crime shall have been committed, which District shall have been previously ascertained by law, and to be informed of the nature and cause of the accusation, to be confronted with the witnesses against him, and to have compulsory process for obtaining witnesses in his favor, and to have the assistance of Counsel for his defence."

Smooth SJ, pp. 278–79.

6.1.1.19.b   A Message from the House of Representatives —

Mr. Beckley, their Clerk, brought up the Amendments to the "Articles to be proposed to the Legislatures of the several States, as Amendments to the Constitution of the United States;" and informed the Senate, that the House of Representatives had receded from their disagreement to the 1st, 3d, 5th, 6th, 7th, 9th, 10th, 11th, 14th, 15th, 17th, 20th, 21st, 22d, 23d, and 24th Amendments, insisted on by the Senate: Provided that the "Two Articles, which by the Amendments of the Senate are now proposed to be inserted as the third and eighth Articles," shall be amended to read as followeth:

Article the Third. "Congress shall make no Law respecting an establishment of Religion, or prohibiting the free exercise thereof; or abridging the freedom of Speech, or of the Press; or the right of the People peaceably to assemble, and petition the Government for a redress of Grievances."

Article the Eighth. "In all criminal prosecutions the accused shall enjoy the right to a speedy and public trial by an impartial Jury of the State and District, wherein the crime shall have been committed, which District shall have been previously ascertained by law, and to be informed of the nature and cause of the accusation, to be confronted with the witnesses against him, and to have compulsory process for obtaining witnesses in his favor, and to have the assistance of Counsel for his defence."

Printed SJ, p.148.

6.1.1.20   Further Senate Consideration of Conference Committee Report, September 25, 1789

6.1.1.20.a   The Senate proceeded to consider the Message from the House of Representatives of the 24th, with Amendments to the Amendments of the Senate, to "Articles to be proposed to the Legislatures of the several States, as Amendments to the Constitution of the United States" — And

RESOLVED, That the Senate do concur in the Amendments proposed by the House of Representatives, to the Amendments of the Senate.

Smooth SJ, p. 283.

6.1.1.20.b   The Senate proceeded to consider the Message from the House of Representatives of the 24th, with Amendments to the Amendments of the Senate, to "Articles to be proposed to the Legislatures of the several States, as Amendments to the Constitution of the United States" — And

RESOLVED, That the Senate do concur in the Amendments proposed by the House of Representatives, to the Amendments of the Senate.

Printed SJ, pp. 150–51.

6.1.1.21   Agreed Resolution, September 25, 1789

6.1.1.21.a   Article the Sixth.

The right of the people to be secure in their persons, houses, papers, and effects, against unreasonable searches and seizures, shall not be violated, and no warrants shall issue, but upon probable cause, supported by oath or affirmation, and particularly describing the place to be searched, and the persons or things to be seized.

Smooth SJ, Appendix, p. 293.

6.1.1.21.b   ARTICLE THE SIXTH.

The right of the people to be secure in their persons, houses, papers, and effects, against unreasonable searches and seizures, shall not be violated, and no warrants shall issue, but upon probable cause, supported by oath or affirmation, and particularly describing the place to be searched, and the persons or things to be seized.

Printed SJ, Appendix, p. 164.

6.1.1.22   Enrolled Resolution, September 28, 1789

Article the sixth . . . The right of the people to be secure in their persons, houses, papers, and effects, against unreasonable searches and seizures, shall not be violated, and no warrants shall issue, but upon probable cause, supported by oath or affirmation, and particularly describing the place to be searched, and the persons or things to be seized.

Enrolled Resolutions, RG 11, DNA.

6.1.1.23   Printed Versions

6.1.1.23.a   ART. IV. The right of the people to be secure in their persons, houses, papers, and effects, against unreasonable searches and seizures, shall not be violated; and no warrants shall issue, but upon probable cause, supported by oath or affirmation, and particularly describing the place to be searched, and the persons or things to be seized.

Statutes at Large, vol. 1, p. 21.

6.1.1.23.b   ART. VI. The right of the people to be secure in their persons, houses, papers, and effects, against unreasonable searches and seizures, shall not be violated; and no warrants shall issue, but upon probable cause, supported by oath or affirmation, and particularly describing the place to be searched, and the persons or things to be seized.

Statutes at Large, vol. 1, pp. 97–98.

6.1.2 PROPOSALS FROM THE STATE CONVENTIONS

6.1.2.1   Maryland Minority, April 26, 1788

8. That all warrants without oath, or affirmation of a person conscientiously scrupulous of taking an oath, to search suspected places, or seize any person or his property, are grievous and oppressive; and all general warrants to search suspected places, or to apprehend any person suspected, without naming or describing the place or person in special, are dangerous, and ought not to be granted.

Maryland Gazette, May 1, 1788 (committee majority).

6.1.2.2   Massachusetts Minority, February 6, 1788

[T]hat the said Constitution be never construed to authorize Congress to infringe the just liberty of the press, or the rights of conscience; or to prevent the people of the United States, who are peaceable citizens, from keeping their own arms; or to raise standing armies, unless when necessary for the defence of the United States, or of some one or more of them; or to prevent the people from petitioning, in a peaceable and orderly manner, the federal legislature, for a redress of grievances; or to subject the people to unreasonable searches and seizures of their persons, papers or possessions.

Massachusetts Convention, pp. 86–87.

6.1.2.3 New York, July 26, 1788

That every Freeman has a right to be secure from all unreasonable searches and seizures of his person his papers or his property, and therefore, that all Warrants to search suspected places or seize any Freeman his papers or property, without information upon Oath or Affirmation of sufficient cause, are grievous and oppressive; and that all general Warrants (or such in which the place or person suspected are not particularly designated) are dangerous and ought not to be granted.

State Ratifications, RG 11, DNA.

6.1.2.4 North Carolina, August 1, 1788

14. That every freeman has a right to be secure from all unreasonable searches, and seizures of his person, his papers, and property: all warrants therefore to search suspected places, or seize any freeman, his papers or property, without information upon oath (or affirmation of a person religiously scrupulous of taking an oath) of legal and sufficient cause, are grievous and oppressive, and all general warrants to search suspected places, or to apprehend any suspected person without specially naming or describing the place or person, are dangerous and ought not to be granted.

State Ratifications, RG 11, DNA.

6.1.2.5 Pennsylvania Minority, December 12, 1787

5. That warrants unsupported by evidence, whereby any officer or messenger may be commanded or required to search suspected places, or to seize any person or persons, his or their property, not particularly described, are grievous and oppressive, and shall not be granted either by the magistrates of the federal government or others.

Pennsylvania Packet, December 18, 1787.

6.1.2.6 Virginia, June 27, 1788

Fourteenth, That every freeman has a right to be secure from all unreasonable searches and siezures [*sic*] of his person, his papers and his property; all warrants, therefore, to search suspected places, or sieze [*sic*] any freeman, his papers or property, without information upon Oath (or affirmation of a person religiously scrupulous of taking an oath) of legal and sufficient cause, are grievous and oppressive; and all general Warrants to search suspected places, or to apprehend any suspected person, without specially naming or describing the place or person, are dangerous and ought not to be granted.

State Ratifications, RG 11, DNA.

6.1.3 STATE CONSTITUTIONS AND LAWS; COLONIAL CHARTERS AND LAWS

6.1.3.1 Delaware: Declaration of Rights, 1776

SECT. 17. That all warrants without oath to search suspected places, or to seize any person or his property, are grievous and oppressive; and all general warrants to search suspected places, or to apprehend all persons suspected, without naming or describing the place or any person in special, are illegal and ought not to be granted.

Delaware Laws, vol. 1, App., p. 81.

6.1.3.2 Maryland: Declaration of Rights, 1776

23. That all warrants without oath, or affirmation, to search suspected places, or to seize any person, or property, are grievous and oppressive; and all general warrants to search suspected places, or to apprehend suspected persons, without naming or describing the place, or the person in special, are illegal, and ought not to be granted.

Maryland Laws, November 3, 1776.

6.1.3.3 Massachusetts: Constitution, 1780

[Part I, Article] XIV. Every subject has a right to be secure from all unreasonable searches and seizures, of his person, his houses, his papers, and all his possessions. All warrants, therefore, are contrary to this right, if the cause or foundation of them be not previously supported by oath or affirmation; and if the order in the warrant to a civil officer, to make search in suspected places, or to arrest one or more suspected persons, or to seize their property, be not accompanied with a special designation of the persons or objects of search, arrest, or seizure: And no warrant ought to be issued, but in cases, and with the formalities, prescribed by the laws.

Massachusetts Perpetual Laws, p. 7.

6.1.3.4 New Hampshire: Constitution, 1783

[Part I, Article] XIX. Every subject hath a right to be secure from all unreasonable searches and seizures of his person, his houses, his papers, and all his possessions. All warrants, therefore, are contrary to this right, if the cause or foundation of them be not previously supported by oath, or affirmation; and if the order in the warrant to a civil officer, to make search in suspected places, or to arrest one or more suspected persons, or to seize their property, be not accompanied with a special designation of the persons or objects of search, arrest or seizure; and no warrant ought to be issued but in cases, and with the formalities prescribed by the laws.

New Hampshire Laws, p. 26.

6.1.3.5 North Carolina: Declaration of Rights, 1776

Sect. XI. That General Warrants whereby an Officer or Messenger may be commanded to search suspected Places, without Evidence of the Fact committed, or to seize any Person or Persons not named, whose Offence is not particularly described and supported by Evidence, are dangerous to Liberty, and ought not to be granted.

North Carolina Laws, p. 275.

6.1.3.6   Pennsylvania

6.1.3.6.a   Constitution, 1776

CHAPTER I.

*A DECLARATION of the RIGHTS of the Inhabitants
of the State of* Pennsylvania.

. . .

X. That the people have a right to hold themselves, their houses, papers, and possessions free from search or seizure; and therefore warrants without oaths or affirmations first made, affording a sufficient foundation for them, and whereby any officer or messenger may be commanded or required to search suspected places, or to seize any person or persons, his or their property, not particularly described, are contrary to that right, and ought not to be granted.

Pennsylvania Acts, M'Kean, pp. x.

6.1.3.6.b   Constitution, 1790

ARTICLE IX.

. . .

SECT. VIII. That the people shall be secure in their persons, houses, papers and possessions, from unreasonable searches and seizures: And that no warrant to search any place, or to seize any person or things, shall issue, without describing them as nearly as may be, nor without probable cause supported by oath or affirmation.

Pennsylvania Acts, Dallas, p. xxxiv.

6.1.3.7   Vermont: Constitution, 1777

CHAPTER I.

. . .

11. THAT the People have a Right to hold themselves, their Houses, Papers and Possessions free from Search or Seizure; and therefore Warrants, without Oaths or Affirmations first made, affording a sufficient Foundation for them, and whereby any Officer or Messenger may be commanded or required to search Suspected Places, or to seize any Person or Persons, his, her or their Property, not particularly described, are contrary to that Right, and ought not to be granted.

Vermont Acts, p. 4.

6.1.3.8   Virginia: Declaration of Rights, May 6, 1776

X. THAT general warrants, whereby an officer or messenger may be commanded to search suspected places without evidence of a fact committed, or to seize any person or persons not named, or whose offence is not particularly described and supported by evidence, are grievous and oppressive, and ought not to be granted.

Virginia Acts, p. 33.

6.1.4 OTHER TEXTS

6.1.4.1 **Richard Henry Lee to Edmund Randolph, Proposed Amendments, October 16, 1787**

. . . That the citizens shall not be exposed to unreasonable searches, seizure of their persons, houses, papers or property; and it is necessary for the good of society, that the administration of government be conducted with all possible maturity of judgment, for which reason it hath been the practice of civilized nations and so determined by every state in the Union. . . .

Virginia Gazette, December 22, 1787.

6.2 DISCUSSION OF DRAFTS AND PROPOSALS

6.2.1 THE FIRST CONGRESS

6.2.1.1 **June 8, 1789[2]**

6.2.1.2 **August 17, 1789**

6.2.1.2.a   The committee went on to the consideration of the 7th clause of the 4th proposition, being as follows; "the right of the people to be secured in their persons, houses, papers and effects, shall not be violated by warrants issuing without probable cause, supported by oath or affirmation, and not particularly describing the place to be searched, and the persons or things to be seized."

Mr. GERRY

Said he presumed there was a mistake in the wording of this clause, it ought to be "the right of the people to be secure in their persons, houses, papers and effects, against unreasonable seizures and searches," and therefore moved that amendment.

This was adopted by the committee.

Mr. BENSON

Objected to the words "by warrants issuing," this declaratory provision was good as far as it went, but he thought it was not sufficient, he therefore proposed to alter it so as to read "and no warrant shall issue."

The question was put on this motion, and lost by a considerable majority.

Mr. LIVERMORE objected to the words "and not" between "affirmative and particularly." He moved to strike them out, in order to make it an affirmative proposition.

But the motion passed in the negative.

The clause as amended being now agreed to, ...

Congressional Register, August 17, 1789, vol. 2, p. 226.

6.2.1.2.b   Tenth Amendment — "The rights of the people to be secure in their persons, houses, papers and effects, shall not be violated by warrants issuing without probable cause, supported by oath or affirmation, and not particularly describing the place to be searched, and the persons or things to be seized."

Mr. BENSON moved to insert after the words "and effects," these words "against unreasonable searches and seizures." This was carried.

The question was then put on the amendment and carried.

Daily Advertiser, August 18, 1789, p. 2, col. 4.

[2]For the reports of Madison's speech in support of his proposals, *see* 1.2.1.1.a–c.

6.2.1.2.c   Tenth amendment — "The rights of the people to be secure in their persons, houses, papers and effects, shall not be violated by warrants issuing without probable cause, supported by oath or affirmation, and not describing the places to be searched, and the persons or things to be seized."

Mr. Benson moved to insert after the words "and effects," these words, "against unreasonable searches and seizures." This was carried.

The question was then put on the amendment and carried.

New-York Daily Gazette, August 19, 1789, p. 802, col. 4.

6.2.1.2.d   10th Amendment. "The rights of the people to be secure in their persons, houses, papers and effects, shall not be violated without probable cause, supported by oath or affirmation, and not particularly describing the places to be searched, and the persons or things to be seized."

Mr. BENSON moved to insert after the words "and effects," these words *against unreasonable seizures, and searches.*

This was carried.

Mr. GERRY objected to the words, "by warrants issuing" — He said the provision was good, as far as it went; but he thought it was not sufficient: He moved that it be altered to *and no warrant shall issue.* This was negatived.

The question was then put on the amendment and carried.

Gazette of the U.S., August 22, 1789, p. 249, col. 3.

6.2.2 STATE CONVENTIONS

6.2.2.1 Maryland, April 26, 1788

This amendment[3] was considered indispensable by many of the committee, for congress having the power of laying excises, the horror of a free people, by which our dwelling-houses, those castles considered so sacred by the English law will be laid open to the insolence and oppression of office, there could be no constitutional check provided, that would prove so effectual a safeguard to our citizens. General warrants too, the great engine by which power may destroy those individuals who resist usurpation, are also hereby forbid to those magistrates who are to administer the general government.

Maryland Gazette, May 1, 1788.

6.2.2.2 Massachusetts, January 30, 1788

Mr. HOLMES.

. . .

The framers of our state constitution took particular care to prevent the General Court from authorizing the judicial authority to issue a warrant against a man for a crime, unless his being guilty of the crime was supported by oath or affirmation, prior to the warrant being granted; why it should be esteemed so much more safe to intrust Congress with the power of enacting laws, which it was deemed so unsafe to intrust our state legislature with, I am unable to conceive.

Elliot, vol. 2, pp. 111–12.

[3]*See 6.1.2.1.*

6.2.2.3 Virginia, June 24, 1788

Mr. HENRY. . . .

. . .

A bill of rights may be summed up in a few words. What do they tell us? — That our rights are reserved. Why not say so? Is it because it will consume too much paper? Gentlemen's reasoning against a bill of rights does not satisfy me. Without saying which has the right side, it remains doubtful. A bill of rights is a favorite thing with the Virginians and the people of the other states likewise. It may be their prejudice, but the government ought to suit their geniuses; otherwise, its operation will be unhappy. A bill of rights, even if its necessity be doubtful, will exclude the possibility of dispute; and, with great submission, I think the best way is to have no dispute. In the present Constitution, they are restrained from issuing general warrants to search suspected places, or seize persons not named, without evidence of the commission of a fact, &c. There was certainly some celestial influence governing those who deliberated on that Constitution; for they have, with the most cautious and enlightened circumspection, guarded those indefeasible rights which ought ever to be held sacred! The officers of Congress may come upon you now, fortified with all the terrors of paramount federal authority. Excisemen may come in multitudes; for the limitation of their numbers no man knows. They may, unless the general government be restrained by a bill of rights, or some similar restriction, go into your cellars and rooms, and search, ransack, and measure, every thing you eat, drink, and wear. They ought to be restrained within proper bounds. . . .

. . .

I feel myself distressed, because the necessity of securing our *personal rights* seems not to have pervaded the minds of men; for many other valuable things are omitted: — for instance general warrants, by which an officer may search suspected places, without evidence of the commission of a fact, or seize any person without evidence of his crime, ought to be prohibited. As these are admitted, any man may be seized, any property may be taken, in the most arbitrary manner, without any evidence or reason. Every thing the most sacred may be searched and ransacked by the strong hand of power. We have infinitely more reason to dread general warrants here than they have in England, because there, if a person be confined, liberty may be quickly obtained by the writ of *habeas corpus*. But here a man living many hundred miles from the judges may get in prison before he can get that writ.

Elliot, vol. 3, pp. 448–49, 588.

6.2.3 PHILADELPHIA CONVENTION

None.

6.2.4 NEWSPAPERS AND PAMPHLETS

6.2.4.1 Centinel, No. 1, October 5, 1787

. . . Permit one of yourselves to put you in mind of certain *liberties* and *privileges* secured to you by the constitution of this commonwealth, and to beg your serious attention to his uninterested opinion upon the plan of federal government submitted to your consideration, before you surrender these great and valuable privileges up forever. Your present frame of government, secures you to a right to hold yourselves, houses, papers and possessions free from search and seizure, and therefore warrants granted without oaths or affirmations first made, affording sufficient foundation for them, whereby any officer or messenger may be commanded or required to search your house or seize your persons or property, not particularly described in such warrant, shall not be granted. . . . The constitution of Pennsylvania is *yet* in existence, *as yet* you have the right to *freedom of speech,* and of *publishing your sentiments.* How long those rights will appertain to you, you yourselves are called upon to say, whether your *houses* shall continue to be your *castles*; whether your *papers,* your *persons,* and your *property,* are to be held sacred and free from *general warrants,* you are now to determine.

> [Philadelphia] Independent Gazetteer, Kaminski & Saladino,
> vol. 13, pp. 328–29.

6.2.4.2   The Federal Farmer, No. 4, October 12, 1787

. . . There are other essential rights, which we have justly understood to be the rights of freemen; as freedom from hasty and unreasonable search warrants, warrants not founded on oath, and not issued with due caution, for searching and seizing men's papers, property, and persons.

> Storing, vol. 2, p. 249.

6.2.4.3   Centinel, No. 2, October 24, 1787

. . .

The new plan, it is true, does propose to secure the people of the benefit of personal liberty by the *habeas corpus;* and trial by jury for all crimes, except in case of impeachment: but there is no declaration, . . . that the people have a right to hold themselves, their houses, papers and possessions free from search or seizure; and that therefore warrants without oaths or affirmations first made, affording a sufficient foundation for them, and whereby any officer or messenger may be commanded or required to search suspected places, or to seize any person or his property, not particularly described, are contrary to that right and ought not to be granted; . . .

> [Philadelphia] Freeman's Journal, Kaminski & Saladino,
> vol. 13, pp. 466–67.

6.2.4.4   Brutus, No. 2, November 1, 1787

For the security of liberty it has been declared, "that excessive bail should not be required, nor excessive fines imposed, nor cruel or unusual punishments inflicted — That all warrants, without oath or affirmation, to search suspected places, or seize any person, his papers or property, are grievous and oppressive."

These provisions are as necessary under the general government as under that of the individual states; for the power of the former is as complete to the purpose of requiring bail, imposing fines, inflicting punishments, granting search warrants, and seizing persons, papers, or property, in certain cases, as the other.

> New York Journal, Kaminski & Saladino, vol. 13, p. 527.

6.2.4.5 An Old Whig, No. 5, November 1, 1787

It is needless to repeat the necessity of securing other personal rights in the forming a new government. The same argument which proves the necessity of securing one of them shews also the necessity of securing others. Without a bill of rights we are totally insecure in all of them; and no man can promise himself with any degree of certainty that his posterity will enjoy the inestimable blessings of liberty of conscience, of freedom of speech and of writing and publishing their thoughts on public matters, of trial by jury, of holding themselves, their houses and papers free from seizure and search upon general suspicion or general warrants; or in short that they will be secured in the enjoyment of life, liberty and property without depending on the will and pleasure of their rulers.

[Philadelphia] Independent Gazetteer, Kaminski & Saladino, vol. 13, p. 541.

6.2.4.6 A Son of Liberty, November 8, 1787

. . . Having observed in your paper of the 25th ult. that a writer under the signature of *A Slave,* has pointed out a number of advantages or blessings, which, he says, will result from an adoption of the new government, proposed by the Convention: — I have taken the liberty to request, that you will give the following a place in your next paper, it being an enumeration of a *few* of the *curses* which will be entailed on the people of America, by this preposterous and newfangled system, if they are ever so infatuated as to receive it.

. . .

4th. Men of all ranks and conditions, subject to have their houses searched by officers, acting under the sanction of *general warrants,* their private papers seized, and themselves dragged to prison, under various pretences, whenever the fear of their lordly masters shall suggest, that they are plotting mischief against their arbitrary conduct.

5th. Excise laws established, by which our bed chambers will be subjected to be searched by brutal tools of power, under pretence, that they contain contraband or smuggled merchandize, and the most delicate part of our families, liable to every species of rude or indecent treatment, without the least prospect, or shadow of redress, from those by whom they are commissioned.

New York Journal, Kaminski & Saladino, vol. 13, p. 481–82.

6.2.4.7 The Federal Farmer, No. 6, December 25, 1787

The following, I think, will be allowed to be unalienable or fundamental rights in the United States: —

No man, demeaning himself peaceably, shall be molested on account of his religion or mode of worship — The people have a right to hold and enjoy their property according to known standing laws, and which cannot be taken from them without their consent, or the consent of their representatives; and whenever taken in the pressing urgencies of government, they are to receive a reasonable compensation for it — Individual security consists in having free recourse to the laws — The people are subject to no laws or taxes not assented to by their representatives constitutionally assembled — They are at all times intitled to the benefits of the writ of habeas corpus, the trial by jury in criminal and civil causes — They have a right, when charged, to a speedy trial in the vicinage; to be heard by themselves or counsel, not to be compelled to furnish evidence against themselves, to have witnesses face to face, and to confront their adversaries before the judge — No man is held to answer a crime charged upon him till it be substantially described to him; and he is subject to no unreasonable searches or seizures of his person, papers or effects — The people have a right to assemble in an orderly manner, and petition the government for a redress of wrongs — The freedom of the press ought not to be restrained — No emoluments, except for actual service — No hereditary honors, or orders of nobility, ought to be allowed — The military ought to be subordinate to the civil authority, and no soldier be quartered on the citizens without their consent — The militia ought always to be armed and disciplined, and the usual defence of the country — The supreme power is in the people, and power delegated ought to return to them at stated periods, and frequently — The legislative, executive, and judicial powers, ought always to be kept distinct — others perhaps might be added.

Storing, vol. 2, p. 262.

6.2.4.8 A Columbian Patriot, February 1788

14. There is no provision by a bill of rights to guard against the dangerous encroachments of power in too many instances to be named: but I cannot pass over in silence the insecurity with which we are left with regard to warrants unsupported by evidence — the daring experiment of granting *writs of assistance* in a former arbitrary administration is not yet forgotten in the Massachusetts; nor can we be so ungrateful to the memory of the patriots who counteracted their operation, as so soon after their manly exertions to save us from such a detestable instrument of arbitrary power, to subject ourselves to the insolence of any petty revenue officer to enter our houses, search, insult, and seize at pleasure. We are told by a gentleman of too much virtue and real probity to suspect he has a design to deceive — "that the whole constitution is a declaration of rights" — but mankind must think for themselves, and to many judicious and discerning characters, the whole constitution with very few exceptions appears a perversion of the rights of particular states, and of private citizens.

Kaminski & Saladino, vol. 16, p. 281.

6.2.4.9 A Farmer and Planter, April 1, 1788

. . . The excise-officers have power to enter your houses at all times, by night or day, and if you refuse them entrance, they can, under pretence of searching for exciseable goods, that the duty has not been paid on, break open your doors, chests, trunks, desks, boxes, and rummage your houses from bottom to top; nay, they often search the cloaths, petticoats and pockets of ladies or gentlemen, (particularly when they are coming from on board an East-India ship) and if they find any the least article that you cannot prove the duty to be paid on, seize it and carry it away with them; who are the very scurf and refuse of mankind, who value not their oaths, and will break them for a shilling. This is their true character in England, and I speak from experience, for I have had the opportunity of putting their virtue to the test; and saw two of them break their oath for one guinea, and a third for one shilling's worth of punch. What do you think of a law to let loose such a set of vile officers among you! Do you expect the Congress excise-officers will be any better, if God, in his anger, should think it proper to punish us for our ignorance, and sins of ingratitude to him, after carrying us through the late war, and giving us liberty, and now so tamely to give it up by adopting this aristocratical government?

Maryland Journal, Storing, vol. 5, pp. 75–76.

6.2.5 LETTERS AND DIARIES

6.2.5.1 Jeremy Belknap to Paine Wingate, May 29, 1789

. . . You will see in the speech wh. our *new* Lieut. Governor [*Samuel Adams*] made at his investiture that he has not thrown off the old idea of *"independence"* as an attribute of each individual State in the "confederated Republic" — & you will know in what light to regard his "devout & fervent wish" that the "people may enjoy well grounded confidence that their *personal & domestic* rights are *secure*." This is the same Language or nearly the same which he used in the Convention when he moved for an addition to the proposed Amendments — by inserting a clause to provide for the Liberty of the press — the right to keep arms — Protection from seizure of person & property & the *Rights of Conscience*. By which motion he gave an alarm to both sides of the house & had nearly overset the whole business which the Friends of the Constitution had been labouring for several Weeks to obtain. . . .

Veit, p. 241.

6.2.5.2 Fisher Ames to Thomas Dwight, June 11, 1789

Mr. Madison has introduced his long expected Amendments. They are the fruit of much labour and research. He has hunted up all the grievances and complaints of newspapers — all the articles of Conventions — and the small talk of their debates. It contains a Bill of Rights — the right of enjoying property — of changing the govt. at pleasure — freedom of the press — of conscience — of juries — exemption from general Warrants gradual increase of representatives till the whole number at the rate of one to every 30,000 shall amount to — and allowing two to every State, at least this is the substance. There is too much of it — O. I had forgot the right of the people to bear Arms.

Risum teneatis amici —

Upon the whole, it may do good towards quieting men who attend to sounds only, and may get the mover some popularity — which he wishes.

Veit, p. 247.

6.3 DISCUSSION OF RIGHTS

6.3.1 TREATISES

6.3.1.1 William Blackstone, 1768, 1769

An *arrest* must be by corporal seising or touching the defendant's body; after which the bailiff may justify breaking open the house in which he is, to take him:

otherwise he has no such power; but must watch his opportunity to arrest him. For every man's house is looked upon by the law to be his castle of defence and asylum, wherein he should suffer no violence. Which principle is carried so far in the civil law, that for the most part not so much as a common citation or summons, much less an arrest, can be executed upon a man within his own walls. Peers of the realm, members of parliament, and corporations, are privileged from arrests. . . .

    . . .

FIRST then, of an *arrest:* which is the apprehending or restraining of one's person, in order to be forthcoming to answer an alleged or suspected crime. To this arrest all persons whatsoever are, without distinction, equally liable to all criminal cases: but no man is to be arrested, unless charged with such a crime, as will at least justify holding him to bail, when taken. And, in general, an arrest may be made in four ways: 1. By warrant: 2. By an officer without warrant: 3. By a private person also without warrant: 4. By an hue and cry.

1. A WARRANT may be granted in extraordinary cases by the privy council, or secretaries of state; but ordinarily by justices of the peace. This they may do in any cases where they have a jurisdiction over the offence; in order to compel the person accused to appear before them: for it would be absurd to give them power to examine an offender, unless they had also a power to compel him to attend, and submit to such examination. And this extends undoubtedly to all treasons, felonies, and breaches of the peace; and also to all such offences as they have power to punish by statute. Sir Edward Coke indeed hath laid it down, that a justice of the peace cannot issue a warrant to apprehend a felon upon bare suspicion; no, not even till an indictment be actually found; and the contrary practice is by others held to be grounded rather upon connivance, than the express rule of law; though now by long custom established. A doctrine, which would in most cases give a loose to felons to escape without punishment; and therefore sir Matthew Hale hath combated it with invincible authority, and strength of reason: maintaining, 1. That a justice of peace hath power to issue a warrant to apprehend a person *accused* of a felony, though not yet *indicted*; and 2. That he may also issue a warrant to apprehend a person *suspected* of a felony, though the original suspicion be not in himself, but in the party that prays his warrant; because he is a competent judge of the probability offered to him of such suspicion. But in both cases it is fitting to examine upon oath the party requiring a warrant, as well as to ascertain that there *is* a felony or other crime actually committed, without which no warrant should be granted; as also to *prove* the cause and probability of suspecting the party, against whom the warrant is prayed. This warrant ought to be under the hand and seal of justice, should set forth the time and place of making, and the cause for which it is made, and should be directed to the constable, or other peace officer, requiring him to bring the party either generally before *any* justice of the peace for the county, or only before the justice who granted it; the warrant in the latter case being called a *special* warrant. A *general* warrant to apprehend all persons suspected, without naming or particularly describing any person in special, is illegal and void for it's [*sic*] uncertainty; for it is the duty of the

magistrate, and ought not to be left to the officer, to judge of the ground of suspicion. And a warrant to apprehend all persons guilty of a crime therein specified, is no legal warrant: for the point, upon which it's [*sic*] authority rests, is a fact to be decided on a subsequent trial; namely whether the person apprehended thereupon be really guilty or not. It is therefore in fact no warrant at all: for it will not justify the officer who acts under it; whereas a lawful warrant will at all events indemnify the officer, who executes the same ministerially. When a warrant is received by the officer, he is bound to execute it, so far as the jurisdiction of the magistrate and himself extends. A warrant from the chief, or other, justice of the court of king's bench extends all over the kingdom: and is *teste*'d, or dated, *England;* but not Oxfordshire, Berks, or other particular county. But the warrant of a justice of the peace in one county, as Yorkshire, must be backed, that is, signed by a justice of the peace in another, as Middlesex, before it can be executed there. Formerly, regularly speaking, there ought to have been a fresh warrant in every fresh county; but the practice of backing warrants had long prevailed without law, and was at last authorized by statutes 23 Geo. II. c. 26. and 24 Geo. II. c. 55.

2. ARRESTS by *officers, without warrant,* may be executed, 1. By a justice of the peace; who may himself apprehend, or cause to be apprehended, by word only, any person committing a felony or breach of the peace in his presence. 2. The sheriff, and 3. The coroner, may apprehend any felon within the county without warrant. 4. The constable, of whose office we formerly spoke, hath great original and inherent authority with regard to arrests. He may, without warrant, arrest anyone for a breach of the peace, and carry him before a justice of the peace. And, in case of a felony actually committed, or a dangerous wounding whereby felony is likely to ensue, he may upon probable suspicion arrest the felon; and for that purpose is authorized (as upon a justice's warrant) to break open doors, and even to kill the felon if he cannot otherwise be taken; and, if he or his assistants be killed in attempting such arrest, it is murder in all concerned. 5. Watchmen, either those appointed by the statute of Winchester, 13 Edw. I. c. 4. to keep watch and ward in all towns from sunsetting to sunrising, or such as are mere assistants to the constable, may *virtute officii* arrest all offenders, and particularly nightwalkers, and commit them to custody till the morning.

3. ANY private person (and *a fortiori* a peace officer) that is present when any felony is committed, is bound by the law to arrest the felon; on pain of fine and imprisonment, if he escapes through the negligence of the standers by. And they may justify breaking open doors upon following such felon: and if *they kill him,* provided he cannot be otherwise taken, it is justifiable; though if *they are killed* in endeavouring to make such an arrest, it is murder. Upon probable suspicion also a private person may arrest the felon, or other person so suspected, but he cannot justify breaking open doors to do it; and if either party kill the other in the attempt, it is manslaughter, and no more. It is no more, because there is no malicious design to kill: but it amounts to so much, because it would be of most pernicious consequence, if, under pretence of suspecting felony, any private person might break open a house, or kill another; and also because such arrest upon

suspicion is barely *permitted* by the law, and not *enjoined,* as in the case of those who are present when a felony is committed.

4. THERE is yet another species of arrest, wherein both officers and private men are concerned, and that is upon an *hue* and *cry* raised upon a felony committed. An hue (from *huer,* to shout) and cry, *hutesium et clamor,* is the old common law process of pursuing, with horn and with voice, all felons, and such as have dangerously wounded another. It is also mentioned by statute Westm. I. 3 Edw. I. c. 9. and 4 Edw. I. *de officio coronatoris.* But the principal statue [*sic*], relative to this matter, is that of Winchester, 13 Edw. I. c. I & 4. which directs, that from thenceforth every country shall be so well kept, that, immediately upon robberies and felonies committed, fresh suit shall be made from town to town, and from county to county; and that hue and cry shall be raised upon the felons, and they that keep the town shall follow with hue and cry, with all the town and the towns near; and so hue and cry shall be made from town to town, until they be taken and delivered to the sheriff. . . .

> Commentaries, vol. 3, pp. 288–89; bk. 4, ch. 21,
> vol. 4, pp. 286–90 (footnotes omitted).

6.3.2 CASELAW

6.3.2.1 The King v. Dr. Purnell, 1748

The defendant was vice chancellor of Oxford; and the Attorney-General had ex officio exhibited against him an information, for not taking the deposition of Blacow the evidence [*sic*], and for neglect of his duty both as vice chancellor and justice of the peace, in not punishing Whitmore and Dawes, who had spoken treasonable words in the streets of Oxford. The defendant appeared to the first information, upon which a noli prosequi was entered, and a second filed, to which also the defendant appeared and pleaded; and a trial at Bar was appointed November 21, but it was countermanded, and a new day, viz. February 6th was afterwards appointed. And now the last day of the term, the attorney, without any affidavit, moved for a rule directed to the proper officers of the university to permit their books, records and archives to be inspected, in order to furnish evidence against the vice chancellor. This was moved as a motion of course for a preemptory rule, on a suggestion that the King, being visitor of the university, had a right to inspect their books whenever he thought proper. Notice of the motion was however given the night before at nine o'clock, and it was opposed by Henley and Evans. And the Court, being of opinion it was not a preemptory motion, only granted a rule to shew cause.

In the next term, Mr. Wilbraham, standing counsel for the university, shewed cause. That the rule was made on no affidavit: that it was drawn in very general terms, (to inspect books, records, and archives). — Records, if any, may be seen elsewhere. Archives cannot be inspected but by a figure, continens pro contenta. But this is a case of too much concern, to stand upon form. The principal case is, whether on a prosecution of a public officer for a supposed misdemeanor, the Court ought to grant inspection of the public books of a corporation. The rule is on Dr. Purnell himself. Nemo tenetur seipsum accusare. The law will not tempt a man to make shipwreck of his conscience, in order to disculpate himself. In

Chancery, a man may demur, if on the face of the bill it appears, that the matter to be discovered will affect the defendant in a criminal way. It will be said, the Court usually grants rules to inspect public books. True, but then it is usually when franchises are contested, and the like; when inspection of those books are the only evidence, and the corporation are considered only as trustees, just as lords of manors are, of the public evidences belonging to the manor. But in no case has the Court ever interposed in a criminal prosecution to grant such a rule, and force such inspection. Many indeed have been granted to inspect poor's rates; but those are public evidences which every body has a right to do. Was there never any prosecution carried on with the same spirit as this? Why then are no examples produced? By the same reason every person indicted might be obliged to shew, whether he had any evidence against himself. In *Bradshaw qui tam* v. *Philips,* A.D. 1735, in an action for bribery, motion was, to inspect the books of a corporation, to prove the defendant a freeman. Hardwick, C.J., denied the rule, because the plaintiff was a stranger. This case is much stronger. It is a precedent of the first impression. There seems to be a general want of evidence; but it is to be hoped, there is no other view than for evidence in this particular case. A hundred cases may be shewn where such rules have been granted in quo warranto's, &c. but none in criminal cases. [The Attorney "mentioned *K. and Burkins,* 7 Geo. 1, which was an indictment at a borough sessions, removed into B. R. by certiorari. Court said, the defendant might have a rule on the clerk of the peace, to have a copy of the names on the back of the indictment."] This is by no means a case. The indictment is a public record; he might have had it without a rule. . . .

Mr. Henley on the same side. — This is a rule of the greatest importance to the most respectable body in the nation. It gives authority to the lowest agent of the Crown to rummage the MSS. of the university. One rule, in applications of this kind, is, that the person applying has an interest in the books and papers, so that in justice he is at all times entitled to have recourse to them. Another, that the person in possession is a trustee for the person applying (as a lord of a manor &c.), and then the trust must be the subject in dispute; the suit must be about land in the manor, and averred by affidavit so to be. So corporations are the trustees and repository of the common franchise has been disputed, as on a mandamus or quo warranto. The present rule is on an information against an individual of the university, and therefore desires to inspect the records of the university. By the parity of reason, on an indictment against a citizen of London, they might inspect the records of the city. But it is suggested, that the King is visitor, and therefore entitled to a rule. I question the fact. The Court will require to be well satisfied of that. But if so, 'tis a strong reason against granting the rule, for then the Crown may enforce its demand in a visitatorial way. Suppose the Crown has a general interest in the books of a corporation; that will not entitle them to an inspection, except the books are the subject of the dispute. *Crew qui tam and Blackburn,* H. 8 G. 2, an action for interfering in elections of members of Parliament, being a clerk of the post-office: the Court would not grant a rule to inspect the post-office books (though public books), because the cause did not concern them. *Benson and Cole,* M. 22 G. 2; motion to inspect Custom-House books, to prove the plaintiff in an insurance cause had no interest: urged that they were public books: refused, because they were not the subject of dispute. These were civil actions; the present otherwise. The avowed design of this motion being to furnish evidence, some precedent will be necessary; especially as a very bad use may be made of such a rule, when the university is much out of favour with some people.

Mr. Ford, on the same side. — *The College of Physicians* v. *Dr. West*, H. 2 G. 1; action for practising sans license; motion to inspect the public books of the college; denied, because the defendant is a stranger to the college. *Cox and Copping*, 5 Mod. 395; dispute about the glebe: Court would not grant rule to inspect the churchwardens' books; because it was a private dispute. There is no reason to grant this inspection, because the vice-chancellor is a justice. Is it because he is a vice-chancellor? Why? Not on account of his supposed visitatorial power; for in *Dr. Walker's case*, the Court quashed a rule because they would not take upon themselves to act the part of visitors. The Court will not assist visitors, but only in support of their visitatorial authority. The visitatorial authority is not now in question; the vice-chancellor is prosecuted for a supposed offence at common law. If a witness has a question put him that may affect himself, the Court will not oblige him to answer it. *Qu. and Mead*, 2 Lord Raym. 927; defendant was an attorney, and with others incorporated by Act of Parliament as surveyors of highways, &c. Action against him, for not talking the oaths to qualify. Motion to inspect the corporation books; but denied, because they would not force a man to produce evidence against himself. *K. and Lee*, M. 17 G. 2; information against defendant as overseer, for making rate without churchwardens. Rule obtained by surprise, to inspect papers: not obeyed. Motion against Lee for attachment. Lee C.J., cited *Bradshaw and Philips;* Court refused to grant attachment, enlarged the rule, and it was dropped. The *K. and Burkins* only shews the tenderness which the Court always shews for persons under prosecution, and was to let him know his accusers. If the present defendant has evidence in his custody, and refuses to obey the rule, an attachment must issue; which would be as strange, as to grant one against a man, for not confessing his crime.

Mr. Evans on the same side. — Had this been an information for exercising the office of vice-chancellor, motion might have been regular. In ecclesiastical jurisdictions, they used to compel a man to furnish evidence against him: but by Stat. Car. 2. oaths ex officio are taken away. On indictment for coining, the attorney might as well move, to have a prisoner discover all his correspondence. 'Tis true, the crimes are less, and the punishment less; but the barrier of liberty is the same. If this rule be granted, the Court of K. B. would be no longer a Court of Justice, but an aid to an inquisition of State. This Court sits to hear, not to furnish evidence.

Mr. Morton, on the same would not repeat.

Ryder, Attorney General, in support of the rule. This prosecution is out of favour to the university; to keep up a spirit of religion and loyalty there. Hard, that the university should interest themselves, to vindicate a member of their body that is under prosecution. If the prosecution be just, or unjust, it cannot hurt the university. Motion relates only to the public records, not the MSS. letters, &c. therefore cannot be so prejudicial as is represented. The intent is to see the statutes of the university, to which the motion shall be confined. The information is for not taking depositions against an enormous crime, as vice-chancellor. The Court grants motions of course to inspect public books. It is as reasonable that public records should be produced for public justice, as private papers for private justice. It is not desired that the vice-chancellor but the public officer should produce them: should he prove to be the public officer, that is no reason against the motion; for it does not respect him as defendant, but as public officer. The public is interested in the university statutes. We do not apply on behalf of the King as visitor, but as guardian of the public peace. In *K. and Blackburn,* there was a rule of this kind made in a penal prosecution; a rule on a public officer, keeping a public record, for an inspection in a criminal prosecution. Informations in nature of quo warranto are public and criminal suits. There, rules of this sort are frequent. The case of *Bradshaw and Philips* was not of a public nature. *K. and Blackburn*; post-office books are not public, but the King's private books. *Benson and Cole*; same answer. As to the case of *College of Physicians,* that was the case of plaintiffs, and the Court will not compel the plaintiff to produce evidence against himself. In *The Qu. and Mead,* the books were of a private nature, and it appeared that the defendant was the person who kept the books. In *The K. and Lee,* it was plain, that the defendant was himself the person against whom the rule is to be made. Not so here; the vice-chancellor is not the person on whom the rule is to be made.

[Hereupon Mr. Henley suggested, that the vice-chancellor had the custody of the original statutes.]

Sir John Strange for the Crown. — Affidavits are not usual in such cases. In the case of *The Skinners' Company,* the clerk refused to grant inspection, and an attachment was granted; but it was argued, whether the papers required were proper to be seen, and the Court held that they were. So here, if any thing improper be demanded, the inspection may be refused. Strange, that the university should conceal their statutes; since they are of so public a nature, that all the youth there entered, take oaths to observe them, and yet they are secreted from them. The Crown is the founder and lawgiver of the university, and such has a right to inspect those laws.

[Lee, C.J. — I apprehend this case is argued to differ from all others (as qui tam actions, &c.) because in those the party applying is a stranger; but that in the present case the King is no stranger, because he is founder. But how does that appear? Another question; is there any instance of an information against an officer of a corporation for breach of by-laws, and a rule granted to inspect those by-laws?]

Murray, Solicitor-General for the Crown. — Four necessary requisites for inspections of this kind. First, that they be public books. Second, that the party applying has an interest in them. Third, that they be material in a suit in this Court. Fourth, that the person in possession be forced to discover nothing to charge himself criminally. — First, these are of a public nature, given by the King, and open to all members of university. The very youngest have a copy given them at their matriculation. Second, the King has an interest; he gave them, and has an interest in seeing them obeyed; and may enforce that obedience two ways; as visitor, and as King, where an offence at common law is mixed with the breach of them. Third, there is a suit in this Court, and the statutes may be material; and, if it is suggested that they will be so, the Court will grant the rule. Fourth, the objection is, that in criminal suits no one is bound to furnish evidence against himself. Agreed, but a distinction may be made. When a man is magistrate, and as such has books in his custody; his having the office shall not secrete those books, which another vice-chancellor must have produced. Besides, the statutes are not in the vice-chancellor's custody only, but also in the hands of the custos archivorum.

Sir R. Lloyd, on the same side. — The university is not accused; the university may therefore very safely produce their books. The King is as much related to the Corporation of the University of Oxford, as to that of the City of York, and no more a stranger to one than the other. It is hoped, that the King is no stranger to either university. If a man were to be indicted for burning the records of a corporation; no doubt but such rule would then be granted, and why not now? Per Lee, C.J. — This is quite a new case. There is no precedent to warrant it, I therefore chuse to consider of it.

Afterwards, Lee C.J., delivered the opinion of the Court. This rule has been much narrowed, since it was first moved by Mr. Attorney. But still we are all of opinion, that we cannot, consistently with the rules of this Court, make such a rule. We ground ourselves on what has been done in similar cases, though none so strong as this. No case has been cited to support this application, but *The K. and Burkin*, which is not apposite. The clerk of the peace ought ex officio to have given a copy of the indictment, and the Court would have granted a rule on him to do it. The cases which we apprehend to be close to this are 1st. *Qu. and Mead*, 2 Ann. Ld. Raym. 927. The reasons for denying the motion were, because, 1. The books were of a private nature. 2. Granting such rule would be to make a man produce evidence against himself, in a criminal prosecution. The second case is *The K. and Cornelius and Others, Justices of Ipswich*, T. 17 & 18 Geo. 2, an information for exacting money from persons for licensing ale houses: a motion to inspect the corporation-books; cause was shewn against it by Sir J. Strange and Sir R. Lloyd. The Court on consideration were of opinion, that the rule could not be granted; as it was in a criminal proceeding, and it tended to make the defendants furnish evidence against themselves. These cases are very similar, only the present is rather stronger; because the information here is for a breach of and crime against the laws of the land, and this is an application to search books, which relate to the defendant's behaviour, as a nature of quo warranto; because these; [*sic*] concern franchises, whereof the corporation books are the proper and only evidence, and they concern the Crown and the defendants equally. We know no instance, wherein this Court has granted a rule to inspect books in a criminal prosecution nakedly considered.

The rule was discharged per totam Curiam.

"N.B. As the university statute-book really contains nothing which could affect the merits of this case in any degree; and as (if it had) printed copies of it are very numerous and easy to be met with; and the custos archivorum, in whose keeping the original is, might have been compelled to have attended with it at the trial: this extraordinary motion seemed only to have been intended, as an excuse for dropping a prosecution, which could not be maintained: and it was accordingly dropped immediately after, having cost the defendant to the amount of several hundred pounds."

96 Eng. Rep. 20 (K.B. 1748).

6.3.2.2 Writs of Assistance

6.3.2.2.a Charles Paxton's Plea for Writ of Assistance, 1755

To the Honourable Majestys Justices of his Superior Court for said Province to be held at York in and for the County of York on the third Tuesday of June 1755.

HUMBLEY SHEWS Charles Paxton Esqr: That he is lawfully authorized to Execute the Office of Surveyor of all Rates Duties and Impositions arising and growing due to his Majesty at Boston in this Province & cannot fully Exercise said Office in such Manner as his Majestys Service and the Laws in such Cases Require Unless Your Honours who are vested with the Power of a Court of Exchequer for this Province will please to Grant him a Writ of Assistants under the Seal of this Superior Court in Legal form & according to Usage in his Majestys Court of Exchequer & in Great Britain, & your Petitioner &Ca: 'CHAS PAXTON'

. . .

UPON READING the petition of Charles Paxton Esquire wherein he shewed that he is lawfully authorized to execute the office of Surveyor of all Rates Duties and Impositions arising & growing due to his majesty at Boston in this Province, and could not fully exercise said office in such manner as his Majestys Service and the Laws in such cases require, unless said Court who are vested with the power of a Court of Exchequer for this province would grant him a writ of Assistants, he therefore prayed that he and his Deputies might be aided in the Execution of said office with his District by a writ of Assistants under the Seal of Said Court in Legal form and according to Usage in his Majestys Court of Exchequer & in Great Britain. ALLOWED, AND TIS ORDERED BY SAID COURT that a writ be issued as prayed for.

1761–72 Quincy's Reports (Mass.), pp. 402–03.

6.3.2.2.b John Adams' Report of Argument, 1761

GRIDLEY. — The Constables distraining for Rates. more inconsistent with Eng. Rts.& liberties than Writts of assistance. And Necessity, authorizes both.

Thatcher. I have searched, in all the ancient Repertories, of Precedents, in Fitzherberts Natura Brevium, and in the Register (Q. w^t ye Reg. is) and have found no such Writt of assistance as this Petition prays. — I have found two Writts of ass. in the Reg. But they are very difft, from ye Writt prayd for. —

In a Book, intitled the Modern Practice of the Court of Exchequer there is indeed one such Writt, and but one.

By ye Act of Pal^t . any other private Person, may as well as a Custom House Officer, take an officer, a Sheriff, or Constable, &c and go into any Shop, Store &c & seize: any Person authorized by such a Writt, under the Seal of the Court of Exchequer, may, not Custom House Officers only. — Strange. — Only a temporary thing.

The most material Question is, whether the Practice of the Exchequer, will warrant this Court in granting the same.

The Act impowers all the officers of yᵉ Revenue to enter and seise in the Plantations, as well as in England. 7. & 8 Wᵐ 3, C. 22, § 6, gives the same as 13. & 14. Of C. Gives in England. The Ground of Mʳ Gridleys argᵗ is this, that this Court has the Power of the Court of Exchequer. — But This Court has renounced the Chancery Jurisdiction, wʰ the Exchequer has in Cases where either Party, is yᵉ Kings Debtor. — Q. Into yᵗ Case.

In Eng. all Informations of uncusted or prohibited Importations, are in yᵉ Exchequer. — So yᵗ yᵉ Custom House officers are the officers of yᵗ Court. — under the Eye, and Direction of the Barons.

The Writ of Assistance is not returnable. — If such seisure were brot before your Honours, youd often find a wanton Exercise of their Power.

At home, yᵉ officers, seise at their Peril, even with Probable Cause. —

Otis. This Writ is against the fundamental Principles of Law. — The Priviledge of House. A Man, who is quiet, is as secure in his House, as a Prince in his Castle — notwithstanding all his Debts, & civil processes of any Kind. — But

For flagrant Crimes, and in Cases of great public Necessity, the Priviledge may be incrohd on. — For Felonies an officer may break, upon Proscess, and oath. — i.e. by a Special Warrant to search such an House, ~~susp~~ sworn to be suspected, and good Grounds of suspicion appearing.

Make oath corᵐ Ld. Treaᵉʳ or Exchequer, in Engᵈ or a Magistrate here, and get a Special Warrant, for yᵉ public good, to infringe the Priviledge of House.

Genˡ Warrant to search for Felonies. Hawk. Pleas Crown. — every petty officer from the highest to yᵉ lowest, and if some of 'em are ~~com, others~~ uncom others are uncomm. Gouvᵗ Justices used to issue such perpetual Edicts. (Q. with wᵗ particular Reference?)

But one Precedent, and yᵗ in yᵉ Reign of C. 2 when Star Chamber Powers, and all Powers but lawful & useful Powers were pushed to Extremity. —

The authority of this Modern Practice of the Court of Exchequer. — it has an Imprimatur. — But wᵗ may not have? — It may be owing to some ignorant Clerk of yᵉ Exchequer.

But all Precedents and this am'g yᵉ Rest are under yᵉ Control of yᵉ Principles of Law. Ld. Talbot. better to observe the Known Principles of Law yⁿ any one Precedent, tho in the House of Lords. —

As to acts of Parliament. an Act against the Constitution is void: an Act against natural Equity is void: and if any Act of Parliament should be made, in the very Words of this Petition, it would be void. The Executive Courts must pass such Acts into disuse — 8. Rep. 118. from Viner. — Reason of yᵉ Com Law to control an Act of Parliament. — Iron Manufacture. noble Lord's Proposal, yᵗ we should send our Horses to Eng. To be shod. —

If an officer will justify under a Writ he must return it. 12ᵗʰ Mod. 396. — perpetual Writ.

Stat. C. 2. We have all as good Rt to inform as Custom House officers — & every Man may have a general, irreturnable ~~Writ~~ Commission to break Houses. —

By 12. Of C. on oath before Lᵈ Treasurer, Barons of Exchequer, or Chief Magistrate to break with an officer. — 14ᵗʰ C. to issue a Warrant requiring sheriffs

&c to assist the officers to search for Goods not entrd, or prohibitd; 7 & 8th W. & M. gives Officers in Plantations same Powers with officers in England. —

Continuance of Writts and Proscesses, proves no more nor so much as I grant a special Writ of ass. On special oath, for specl Purpose. —

Pew indorsd Warrant to Ware. — Justice Walley fearc'd House. Law Prov. Bill in Chancery. — this Court confined their Chancery Power to Revenue &c.

Gridley. By the 7. & 8 of Wm C. 22. § 6th — This authority, of breaking and entering Ships, Warehouses Cellars &c given to the Custom House officers in England by the Statutes of the 12th and 14th of Charl. 2^d, is extended to the Custom House officers in ye Plantations: — and by the Statute of the 6th of Anne, ~~this~~ Writts of Assistance are continued, in Company with all other legal Proscesses for 6 months after the Demise of the Crown. — Now what this Writ of assistance is, we can know only by Books of Precedents. — And we have produced, in a Book intituld the modern Practice of the Court of Exchequer, a form of such a Writ of assistance to the officers of the Customs. The Book has the Imprimatur of Wright C. J. of the K.'s B. w^h is as great a sanction as any Books of Precedents ever have. altho Books of Reports are usually approved by all the Judges — and I take Brown the author of this Book to have been a very good Collector of Precedents. — I have two Volumes of Precedents of his Collection, w^h I look upon as good as any, except Coke & Rastal.

And the Power given in this Writ is no greater Infringement of our Liberty than the Method of collecting Taxes in this Province. —

Every Body knows that the Subject has the Priviledge of House only against his fellow Subjects, not vs ye K. either in matters of Crime or fine.

1761–72 Quincy's Reports (Mass.), pp. 469–77.

6.3.2.3 Huckle v. Money, 1763

. . .

Lord Chief Justice. — In all motions for new trials, it is as absolutely necessary for the Court to enter into the nature of the cause, the evidence, facts, and circumstances of the case, as for a jury; the law has not laid down what shall be the measure in damages in actions of tort; the measure is vague and uncertain, depending upon a vast variety of causes, facts, and cicumstances; torts or injuries which may be done by one man to another are infinite; in cases of criminal conversation, battery, imprisonment, slander, malicious prosecutions, &c. the state, degree, quality, trade or profession of the party injured, as well as of the person who did the injury, must be, and generally are, considered by a jury in giving damages. The few cases to be found in the books of new trials for torts, shews that Courts of Justice have most commonly set their faces against them; and the Courts interfering in these cases would be laying aside juries. Before the time of granting new trials, there is no instance that the Judges ever intermeddled with the damages.

I shall now state the nature of this case, as it appeared upon the evidence at the trial: a warrant was granted by Lord Halifax, Secretary of State, directed to four messengers, to apprehend and seize the printers and publishers of a paper called the *North Briton,* Number 45, without any information or charge laid before the

Secretary of State, previous to the granting thereof, and without naming any person whatsoever in the warrant; Carrington, the first of the messengers to whom the warrant was directed, from some private intelligence he had got that Leech was the printer of the *North Briton,* Number 45, directed the defendant to execute the warrant upon the plaintiff, (one of Leech's journeymen,) and took him into custody for about six hours, and during that time treated him well; the personal injury done to him was very small, so that if the jury had been confined by their oath to consider the mere personal injury only, perhaps 20l damages would have been thought damages sufficient; but the small injury done to the plaintiff, or the inconsiderableness of his station and rank in life did not appear to the jury in that striking light in which the great point of law touching the liberty of the subject appeared to them at the trial; they saw a magistrate over all the King's subjects, exercising arbitrary power, violating Magna Charta, and attempting to destroy the liberty of the kingdom, by insisting upon the legality of this general warrant before them; they heard the King's Counsel, and saw the solicitor of the Treasury endeavouring to support and maintain the legality of the warrant in a tyrannical and severe manner. These are the ideas which struck the jury on the trial; and I think they have done right in giving exemplary damages. To enter a man's house by virtue of a nameless warrant, in order to procure evidence, is worse than the Spanish Inquisition; a law under which no Englishman would wish to live an hour; it was a most daring public attack made upon the liberty of the subject. I thought that the 29th chapter of Magna Charta, Nullus liber homo capiatur vel imprisonetur, &c. nec super eum ibimus, &c. nisi per legale judicium parium suorum vel per legem terrae, &c. which is pointed against arbitrary power, was violated. I cannot say what damages I should have given if I had been upon the jury; but I directed and told them they were not bound to any certain damages against the Solicitor-General's argument. Upon the whole, I am of opinion the damages are not excessive; and that it is very dangerous for the Judges to intermeddle in damages for torts; it must be a glaring case indeed of outrageous damages in a tort, and which all mankind at first blush must think so, to induce a Court to grant a new trial for excessive damages.

Bathurst J. — I am of my Lord's opinion, and particularly in the matter of damages, wherein he directed the jury that they were not bound to certain damages. This is a motion to set aside 15 verdicts in effect; for all the other persons who have brought actions against these messengers have had verdicts for 200l in each cause by consent, after two of the actions were fully heard and tried. Clive J. absent.

Per Curiam. — New trial refused.

95 Eng. Rep. 768 (C.P. 1763).

6.3.2.4   Wilkes v. Wood, 1763

. . . His Lordship then went upon the warrant, which he declared was a point of the greatest consequence he had ever met with in his whole practice. The defendants claimed a right, under precedents, to force persons houses, break open escrutores, seize their papers, &c. upon a general warrant, where no inventory is made of the things thus taken away, and where no offenders names are specified in the warrant, and therefore a discretionary power given to messengers to search wherever their suspicions may chance to fall. If such a power is truly invested in a Secretary of State, and he can delegate this power, it certainly may affect the person and property of every man in this kingdom, and is totally subversive of the liberty of the subject.

And as for the precedents, will that be esteemed law in a Secretary of State which is not law in any other magistrate of this kingdom? If they should be found to be legal, they are certainly of the most dangerous consequences; if not legal, must aggravate damages. Notwithstanding what Mr. Solicitor-General has said, I have formerly delivered it as my opinion on another occasion, and I still continue of the same mind, that a jury have it in their power to give damages for more than the injury received. Damages are designed not only as a satisfaction to the injured person, but likewise as a punishment to the guilty, to deter from any such proceeding for the future, and as a proof of the detestation of the jury to the action itself.

As to the proof of what papers were taken away, the plaintiff could have no account of them; and those who were able to have given an account (which might have been an extenuation of their guilt) have produced none. It lays upon the jury to allow what weight they think proper to that part of the evidence. It is my opinion the office precedents, which had been produced since the revolution, are no justification of a practice in itself illegal, and contrary to the fundamental principles of the constitution; though its having been the constant practice of the office, might fairly be pleaded in mitigation of damages.

He then told the jury they had a very material affair to determine upon, and recommended it to them to be particularly cautious in bringing in their verdict. Observed, that if the jury found Mr. Wilkes the author or publisher of No. 45, it will be filed, and stand upon record in the Court of Common Pleas, and of course be produced as proof, upon the criminal cause depending, in barr of any future more ample discussion of that matter on both sides; that on the other side they should be equally careful to do justice, according to the evidence; he therefore left it to their consideration.

The jury, after withdrawing for near half an hour, returned, and found a general verdict upon both issues for the plaintiff, with a thousand pounds damages.

After the verdict was recorded, the Solicitor-General offered to prefer a bill of exceptions, which the Lord Chief Justice refused to accept, saying it was out of time.

The Court sat at nine o'clock in the morning, and the verdict was brought in at twenty minutes past eleven o'clock at night. 98 Eng. Rep. 489, 498–99 (C.P. 1763).

6.3.2.5 Rex v. Wilkes, 1763

. . .

Lord Chief Justice Pratt, after stating the warrant of commitment, said, there are two objections taken to the legality of this warrant, and a third matter insisted on for the defendant, is privilege of Parliament.

The first objection is, that it does not appear to the Court that Mr. Wilkes was charged by any evidence before the Secretaries of State, that he was the author or publisher of the *North Briton,* Number XLV. In answer to this, we are all of the opinion, that it is not necessary to state in the warrant that Mr. Wilkes was charged by any evidence before the Secretaries of State, and that this objection has no weight. Whether a justice of peace can, ex officio, without any evidence or information, issue a warrant for apprehending for a crime, is a different question: if a crime be done in his sight, he may commit the criminal upon the spot; but where he is not present, he ought not to commit upon discretion. Suppose a magistrate hath notice, or a particular knowledge that a person has been guilty of an offence, yet I do not think it is a sufficient ground for him to commit the criminal; but in that case he is rather a witness than a magistrate, and ought to make oath of the fact before some other magistrate, who should thereupon act the official part, by granting a warrant to apprehend the offender, it being more fit that the accuser should appear as a witness than act as a magistrate. But that is not the question upon this warrant; the question here is, whether it is an essential part of the warrant that the information, evidence, or grounds of the charge before the Secretaries of State, should be set forth in the warrant? And we think it is not. *Thomas Rudyard's case,* 2 Vent. 22, cannot be applied to this case, for in the case of a conviction it is otherwise. It was said that a charge by witness was the ground of a warrant; but we think it not requisite to set out more than the offence, and the particular species of it. It may be objected, if this be good every man's liberty will be in the power of a justice of peace. But Hale, Coke, and Hawkins take no notice that a charge is necessary to be set out in the warrant. In the case of *The Seven Bishops* their counsel did not take this objection, which no doubt but they would have done if they had thought there had been any weight in it. I do not rely upon the determination of the Judges who then presided in the King's Bench. I have been attended with many precedents of warrants returned into the King's Bench; they are almost universally like this; and in *Sir William Wyndham's case,* 1 Stra. 2, 3, this very point before us is determined. And Hawkins, in his 2 Pl. Coron. 120, sect. 17, says, "It is safe to set forth that the party is charged upon oath; but this is not necessary; for it hath been resolved that a commitment for treason, or for suspicion of it, without setting forth any particular accusation, or ground of suspicion, is good;" and cites *Sir William Wyndham's case,* Trin. 2 Geo. Dalt. cap. 125. Cromp. 233 b.

The second objection is, that the libel ought to be set forth in the warrant in haec verba, or at least so much thereof as the Secretaries of State deemed infamous, seditious, &c. that the Court may judge whether any such paper ever existed, or if it does exist, whether it be an infamous and seditious libel or not. But we are all of a contrary opinion: a warrant of commitment for felony must contain the species of felony briefly, "as for felony for the death of J. S., or for burglary in breaking the house of J. S. &c.; and the reason is, because it may appear to the Judges upon the return of an habeas corpus, whether it be felony or not." The magistrate forms his judgment upon the writing, whether it be an infamous and seditious libel or not, at his peril, and perhaps the paper itself may not contain the whole of the libel; inuendoes may be necessary to make the whole out; there is no other word in the law but libel whereby to express the true idea of an infamous writing; we understand the nature of a libel as well as a species of felony; it is said the libel ought to be stated, because the Court cannot judge whether it is a libel or not without it; but that is a matter for the Judge and jury to determine at the trial. If the paper was here, I should be afraid to read it. We might perhaps be able to determine that it was a libel, but we could not judge that it was not a libel, because of inuendoes, &c. It may be said, that without seeing the libel we are not able to fix the quantum of the bail; but in answer to this, the nature of the offence is known by us; it is said to be an infamous and seditious libel, &c.: it is such a misdemeanor as we should require good bail for, (moderation to be observed,) and such as the party may be able to procure.

The third matter insisted upon for Mr. Wilkes is, that he is a member of Parliament, (which has been admitted by the King's Serjeants,) and entitled to privilege to be free from arrests in all cases except treason, felony, and actual breach of the peace, and therefore ought to be discharged from imprisonment without bail; and we are all of opinion that he is entitled to that privilege, and must be discharged without bail. In the case of *The Seven Bishops* the Court took notice of the privilege of Parliament, and thought the bishops would have been entitled to it if they had not judged them to have been guilty of a breach of the peace; for three of them, Wright, Holloway, and Allybone, deemed a seditious libel to be an actual breach of the peace, and therefore they were ousted of their privilege most unjustly. If Mr. Wilkes had been described as a member of Parliament in the return, we must have taken notice of the law of privilege of Parliament, otherwise the members would be without remedy where they are wrongfully arrested against the law of Parliament; we are bound to take notice of their privileges, as being part of the law of the land. 4 Inst. 25 says, the privilege of Parliament holds unless it be in three cases, viz. treason, felony, and the peace; these are the words of Coke. In the trial of *The Seven Bishops* the word peace, in this case of privilege, is explained to mean where surety of the peace is required. Privilege of Parliament holds in informations for the King, unless in the cases before excepted; the case of an information against Lord Tankerville for bribery, 4 Annae, was within the privilege of Parliament. See the resolution of the Lords and Commons, anno 1675. We are all of opinion that a libel is not a breach of the peace: it tends to the breach of the peace, and that is the utmost. 1 Lev. 139. But that which only tends to the breach of the peace cannot be a breach of it. Suppose a libel be a breach of the peace, yet I think it cannot exclude privilege, because I cannot find that a libeller is bound to find surety of the peace, in any book whatever, nor ever was, in any case, except one, viz. the case of *The Seven Bishops,* where three Judges said, that surety of the peace was required in the case of a libel: Judge Powell, the only honest man of the four Judges, dissented, and I am bold to be of his opinion, and to say that case is not law; but it shews the miserable condition of the State at that time. Upon the whole, it is absurd to require surety of the peace or bail in the case of a libeller, and therefore Mr. Wilkes must be discharged from his imprisonment: whereupon there was a loud huzza in Westminster-Hall. He was discharged accordingly. 95 Eng. Rep. 737 (C.P. 1763).

6.3.2.6 Entick v. Carrington, 1765

Lord Chief Justice. — I shall not give any opinion at present, because this case, which is of the utmost consequence to the public, is to be argued again; I shall only just mention a matter which has slipped the sagacity of the counsel on both sides, that it may be taken notice of upon the next argument. Suppose a warrant which is against law be granted, such as no justice of peace, or other magistrate high or low whomsoever, has power to issue, whether that magistrate or justice who grants such warrant, or the officer who executes it, are within the stat. 24 Geo. 2, c. 44? To put one case (among an hundred that might happen); suppose a justice of peace issues a warrant to search a house for stolen goods, and directs it to four of his servants, who search and find no stolen goods, but seize all the books and papers of the owners of the house, whether in such a case would the justice of peace, his officers or servants, be within the Stat. 24 Geo. 2? I desire that every point of this case may be argued to the bottom; for I shall think myself bound, when I come to give judgment, to give my opinion upon every point in the case.

. . . [Counsel made their arguments.]

Curia. — The defendants make two defences; first, that they are within the stat. 24 Geo. 2, c. 44; 2dly, that such warrants have frequently been granted by Secretaries of State ever since the Revolution, and have never been controverted, and that they are legal; upon both which defences the defendants rely.

A Secretary of State, who is a Privy Counsellor, if he be a conservator of the peace, whatever power he has to commit is by the common law: if he be considered only as a Privy Counsellor, he is the only one at the board who has exercised this authority of late years; if as a conservator, he never binds to the peace; no other conservator ever did that we can find: he has no power to administer an oath, or take bail; but yet it must be admitted that he is in the full exercise of this power to commit, for treason and seditious libels against the Government, whatever was the original source of that power; as appears from the cases of *The Queen and Derby, The King and Earbury,* and *Kendale and Roe's case.*

We must know what a Secretary of State is, before we can tell whether he is within the stat. 24 Geo. 2, c. 44. He is the keeper of the King's signet wherewith the King's private letters are signed. 2 Inst. 556. Coke upon Articuli Super Chartas, 28 Ed. 1. Lord Coke's silence is a strong presumption that no such power as he now exercises was in him at that time; formerly he was not a Privy Counsellor, or considered as a magistrate; he began to be significant about the time of the Revolution, and he grew great when the princes of Europe sent ambassadors hither; it seems inconsistent that a Secretary of State should have power to commit, and no power to administer an oath, or take bail; who can commit and not have power to examine? the House of Commons indeed commit without oath, but that is nothing to the present case; there is no account in our law-books of Secretaries of State except in the few cases mentioned; he is not to be found among the old conservators; in Lambert, Crompton, Fitzherbert, &c. nor is a Privy Counsellor to be found among our old books till *Kendall and Roe's case,* and 1 Leon. 70, 71, 29 Eliz. is the first case that takes notice of a commitment by a Secretary of State; but in 2 Leon. 175 the Judges knew no such committing magistrate as the Secretary of State. It appears by the Petition of Right, that the King and Council claimed a power to commit; if the Secretary of State had claimed any such power, then certainly the Petition of Right would have taken notice of it; but from its silence on that head we may fairly conclude he neither claimed nor had any such power; the Stat. 16 Car. 1, for regulating the Privy Council, and taking away the Court of Star-Chamber, binds the King not to commit, and in such case gives a habeas corpus; it is strange that House of Commons should take no notice of the Secretary of State, if he then had claimed power to commit. This power of a Secretary of State to commit was derivative from the commitment per mandatum Regis: Ephemeris Parliamentaria. Coke says in his speech to the House, "If I do my duty to the King, I must commit without shewing the cause;" 1 Leon. 70, 71, shews that a commitment by a single Privy Counsellor was not warranted. By the Licensing Statute of 13 & 14 Car. 2, cap. 33, sec. 15, licence is given to a messenger under a warrant of the Secretary of State to search for books unlicensed, and if they find any against the religion of the Church of England, to bring them before the Secretary of State; the warrant in that case expressed that it was by the King's command. See Stamford's comments on the mandate of the King, and Lambert, cap. Bailment. All the Judges temp. Eliz. held that in a warrant or commitment by one Privy Counsellor he must shew it was by the mandate of the King in Council. See And. 297, the opinion of all the Judges; they remonstrated to the King that no subject ought to be committed by a Privy Counsellor against the law of the realm. Before the 3 Car. 1 all the Privy Counsellors exercised this power to commit; from that aera they disused this power, but then they prescribed still to commit per mandatum Regis. Journal of the House of Commons 195. 16 Car. 1. Coke, Selden, &c. argued that the King's power to commit, meant that he had such power by his Courts of Justice. In the case of *The Seven Bishops* all the Court and King's Council admit, that supposing the warrant had been signed out of the Council, that it would have been bad, but the Court presumed it to be signed at the board; Pollexfen in his argument says, we do not deny but the Council board have power to commit, but not out of Council; this is a very strong authority; the whole body of the law seem not to know that Privy Counsellors out of Council had any power to commit, if there had been any such power they could not have been ignorant of it; and this power was only in cases of high treason, they never claimed it in any other case. It was argued that if a Secretary of State hath power to commit in high treason, he hath it in cases of lesser crimes: but this we deny, for if it appears that he hath power to commit in one case only, how can we then without authority say he has that power in other cases? He is not a conservator of the peace; Justice Rokeby only says he is in the nature of a conservator of the peace: we are now bound by the cases of *The Queen and Derby,* and *The King and Earbury.*

The Secretary of State is no conservator nor a justice of the peace, quasi secretary, within the words or equity of Stat. 24 Geo. 2, admitting him (for arguments sake) to be a conservator, the preamble of the statute shews why it was made, and for what purpose; the only grantor of a warrant therein mentioned, is a justice of the peace; justice of peace and conservator are not convertible terms; the cases of construction upon old statutes, in regard to the warden of the Fleet, the Bishop of Norwich, &c. are not to be applied to cases upon modern statutes. The best way to construe modern statutes is to follow the words thereof; let us compare a justice of peace and a conservator; the justice is liable to actions, as the statute takes notice, it is applicable to him who acts by warrant directed to constables; a conservator is not intrusted with the execution of the laws, which by this Act is meant statutes, which gives justices jurisdiction; a conservator is not liable to actions; he never acts: he is almost forgotten; there never was an action against a conservator of the peace as such; he is antiquated, and could never be thought of when this Act was made; and ad ea quae frequenter accidunt jura adaptantur. There is no act of a constable or tithingman as conservator taken notice of in the statute; will the Secretary of State be ranked with the highest or lowest of these conservators? the Statute of Jac. 1, for officers acting by authority to plead the general issue, and give the special matter in evidence, when considered with this Statute of 24 Geo. 2, the latter seems to be a second part of the Act of Jac. 1, and we are all clearly of the opinion that neither the Secretary of State, nor the messengers, are within the Stat. 24 Geo. 2, but if the messengers had been within it, as they did not take a constable with them according to the warrant, that alone would have been fatal to them, nor did they pursue the warrant in the execution thereof, when they carried the plaintiff and his books, &c. before Lovel Stanhope, and not before Lord Halifax; that was wrong, because a Secretary of State cannot delegate his power, but ought to act in this part of his office personally.

The defendants having failed in their defence under the Statute 24 Geo. 2; we shall now consider the special justification, whether it can be supported in law, and this depends upon the jurisdiction of the Secretary of State; for if he has no jurisdiction to grant a warrant to break open doors, locks, boxes, and to seize a man and all his books, &c. in the first instance upon an information of his being guilty of publishing a libel, the warrant will not justify the defendants: it was resolved by B. R. in the case of *Shergold v. Holloway,* that a justice's warrant expressly to arrest the party will not justify the officer, there being no jurisdiction. 2 Stran. 1002. The warrant in our case was an execution in the first instance, without any previous summons, examination, hearing the plaintiff, or proof that he was the author of the supposed libels; a power claimed by no other magistrate whatever (Scroggs C. J. always excepted); it was left to the discretion of these defendants to execute the warrant in the absence or presence of the plaintiff, when he might have no witness present to see what they did; for they were to seize all papers, bank bills, or any other valuable papers they might take away if they were so disposed; there might be nobody to detect them. If this be lawful, both Houses of Parliament are involved in it, for they have both ruled, that privilege doth not extend to this case. In the case of *Wilkes,* a member of the Commons House, all his books and papers were seized and taken away; we were told by one of these messengers that he was obliged by his oath to sweep away all papers whatsoever; if this was law it would be found in our books, but no such law ever existed in this country; our law holds the property of every man so sacred, that no man can set his foot upon his neighbours close without his leave; if he does he is a trespasser, though he does no damage at all; if he will tread upon his neighbor's ground, he must justify it by law. The defendants have no right to avail themselves of the usage of these warrants since the Revolution, and if that would have justified them they have not averred it in their plea, so it could not be put, nor was in issue at the trial; we can safely say there is no law in this country to justify the defendants in what they have done; if there was, it would destroy all the comforts of society; for papers are often the dearest property a man can have. This case was compared to that of stolen goods; Lord Coke denied the lawfulness of granting warrants to search for stolen goods, 4 Inst. 176, 177, though now it prevails to be law; but in that case the justice and the informer must proceed with great caution; there must be an oath that the party has had his goods stolen, and his strong reason to believe they are concealed in such a place; but if the goods are not found there, he is a trespasser; the officer in that case is a witness; there are none in this case, no inventory taken; if it had been legal many guards of property would have attended it. We shall now consider the usage of these warrants since the Revolution; if it began then, it is too modern to be law; the common law did not begin with the Revolution; the ancient constitution which had been almost overthrown and destroyed, was then repaired and revived; the Revolution added a new buttress to the ancient venerable edifice: the K.B. lately said that no objection had ever been taken to general warrants, they have passed sub silentio: this is the first instance of an attempt to prove a modern practice of a private office to make and execute warrants to enter a man's house, search for and take away all his books and papers in the first instance, to be law, which is not found in our books. It must have been the guilt or poverty of those upon whom such warrants have been executed, that deterred or hindered them from contending against the power of a Secretary of State and the Solicitor of the Treasury, or such warrants could never have passed for lawful till this time. We are inclined to think the present warrant took its first rise from the Licensing Act, 13 & 14 Car. 2, c. 33, and are all of the opinion that it cannot be justified by law, notwithstanding the resolution of the Judges in the time of Cha. 2, and Jac. 2, that such search warrants are lawful. State Trials, vol. 3, 58, the trial of Carr for a libel. There is no authority but of the Judges of that time that a house may be searched for a libel, but the twelve Judges cannot make law; and if a man is punishable for having a libel in his private custody, as many cases say he is, half the kingdom would be guilty in the case of a favourable libel, if libels may be searched for and seized by whomsoever and wheresoever the Secretary of State thinks fit. It is said it is better for the Government and the public to seize the libel before it is published; if the Legislature be of that opinion they will make it lawful. Sir Samuel Astry was committed to the Tower, for asserting there was a law of State distinct from the common law. The law never forces evidence from the party in whose power it is; when an adversary has got your deeds, there is no lawful way of getting them again but by an action. 2 Stran. 1210, *The King and Cornelius. The King and Dr. Purnell*, Hil. 22 Geo. B.R. Our law is wise and merciful, and supposes every man accused is innocent before he is tried by his peers; upon the whole, we are all of the opinion that this warrant is wholly illegal and void. One word more for ourselves; we are no advocates for libels, all Governments must set their faces against them, and whenever they come before us and a jury we shall set our faces against them; and if juries do not prevent them they may prove fatal to liberty, destroy Government and introduce anarchy; but tyranny is better than anarchy, and the worst government better than none at all.

Judgment for the plaintiff.

95 Eng. Rep. 807 (K.B. 1765).

6.3.2.7 Money v. Leach, 1765

[Lord Mansfield]. . . . The last point is, "whether this general warrant be good." —

One part of it may be laid out for the case: for, as to what relates to the seizing of his papers, that part of it was never executed; and therefore it is out of the case.

It is not material to determine, "whether the warrant be good or bad;" except in the event of the case being within 7 J. 1, but not within 24 G. 2.

At present — As to the validity of the warrant, upon the single objection of the incertainty of the person, being neither named nor described — The common law, in many cases, gives authority to arrest without warrant; more especially, where taken in the very act: and there are many cases where particular Acts of Parliament have given authority to apprehend, under general warrants; as in the case of writs of assistance, or warrants to take up loose, idle and disorderly people. But here it is not contended, that the common law gave the officer authority to apprehend; nor that there is any act of Parliament which warrants this case.

Therefore it must stand upon principles of common law.

It is not fit, that the receiving or judging of the information should be left to the discretion of the officer. The magistrate ought to judge; and should give certain directions to the officer. This is so, upon reason and convenience.

Then as to authorities — Hale and all others hold such an uncertain warrant void: and there is no case or book to the contrary.

It is said, "that the usage has been so; and that many such have been issued, since the revolution, down to this time."

But a usage, to grow into law, ought to be a general usage, *communiter usitata et approbata*; and which, after a long continuance, it would be mischievous to overturn.

This is only the usage of a particular office, and contrary to the usage of all other justices and conservators of the peace.

There is the less reason for regarding this usage; because the form of the warrant probably took its rise from a positive statute; and the former precedents were inadvertently followed, after that law was expired.

Mr. Justice Wilmot declared, that he had no doubt, nor ever had, upon these warrants: he thought them illegal and void.

Neither had the two other Judges, Mr. Justice Yates, and Mr. Justice Aston, any doubt (upon this first argument) of the illegality of them: for, no degree of antiquity can give sanction to a usage bad in itself. And they esteemed this usage to be so. They were clear and unanimous in opinion that "this warrant was illegal and bad."

97 Eng. Rep. 1075, 1088 (K.B. 1765).

6.3.2.8 Frisbie v. Butler, 1787

ERROR from the judgment of a justice of the peace. On the application of Butler, to George Catlin, a justice of the peace, the following warrant was issued, viz. "Whereas Josiah Butler hath made complaint, under oath, that he lost, on or about the 11th day of March, in Torrington, about twenty pounds of good pork, out of the cellar of Daniel Winchel, of the value of ten shillings, lawful money; it being taken by some evil-minded person: And said Butler suspects one Benjamin Frisbie, of Harwinton, to be the person that hath taken said pork, and prays for a writ, or search warrant, to search for his lost meat, etc. — To John Birge, an indifferent person, lawfully to serve this writ, there being no proper officer, without cost and charge, greeting: By authority of the state of Connecticut, you are commanded forthwith to search all suspected places and persons that the complainant thinks proper, to find his lost pork, and to cause the same, and the person with whom it shall be found, or suspected to have taken the same, and have him to appear before some proper authority, to be examined according to law."

By virtue of this warrant, Frisbie was arrested, brought before the justice who issued it, and upon the plea, not guilty, judgment was rendered, that "he was guilty of stealing said pork; and that he pay eighteen shillings as treble damages, to the complainant, and a fine of six shillings to the town treasurer."

The errors assigned, were,

1. That the warrant issued upon a verbal complaint only being exhibited.

2. That the warrant for searching and arresting was illegal, the facts alleged being of civil nature, and not such as would justify such a process.

3. The warrant is a general search warrant, commanding all persons and places throughout the world to be searched, at the discretion of the complainant; — therefore, illegal and void.

4. The judgment was for the gross sum of eighteen shillings as treble damages, for the loss of said pork, without ascertaining the real value.

5. That the process is not founded on any statute of this state; and the common law does not empower a justice to adjudge treble damages to the complainant, as was done in this case.

6. That said justice adjudged that said Frisbie should pay a fine to the treasurer of the town of Harwinton, without complaint or prosecution by any public officer, or any other person, on the part of the public.

Without argument, the judgment of the justice was reversed,

By the whole COURT. The complaint on which the arraignment and conviction was had, contained no direct charge of the theft, but only an averment that the defendant was suspected to be guilty; nor, indeed, does it appear to have been theft that he was even suspected of, but only a taking away of the plantiff's property, which might amount to no more than a trespass; — and his being found guilty of the matters alleged against him in the complaint, could be no ground for sentencing and punishing him as for theft.

With regard to the warrant — Although it is the duty of a justice of the peace granting a search warrant (in doing which he acts judicially) to limit the search to such particular place or places, as he, from the circumstances, shall judge there is reason to suspect; and the arrest of such person or persons as the goods shall be found with: And the warrant in the present case, being general, to search all places, and arrest all persons, the complainant should suspect, is clearly illegal; yet, how far this vitiates the proceedings upon the arraignment, may be a question, which is not necessary now to determine; as also the sufficiency of several of the other matters assigned in error.

Kirby 213 (Conn. 1787).

Chapter 7

AMENDMENT V
GRAND JURY CLAUSE

7.1 TEXTS

7.1.1 DRAFTS IN FIRST CONGRESS

7.1.1.1 **Proposal by Madison in House, June 8, 1789**

7.1.1.1.a   Seventhly. That in article 3d, section 2 [of the Constitution], the third clause be struck out, and in its place be inserted the clauses following, to wit:

The trial of all crimes (except in cases of impeachments, and cases arising in the land or naval forces, or the militia when on actual service in time of war or public danger) shall be by an impartial jury of freeholders of the vicinage, with the requisite of unanimity for conviction, of the right of challenge, and other accustomed requisites; and in all crimes punishable with loss of life or member, presentment or indictment by a grand jury, shall be an essential preliminary, provided that in cases of crimes committed within any county which may be in possession of an enemy, or in which a general insurrection may prevail, the trial may by law be authorised in some other county of the same state, as near as may be to the seat of the offence.

In cases of crimes committed not within any county, the trial may by law be in such county as the laws shall have prescribed. In suits at common law, between man and man, the trial by jury, as one of the best securities to the rights of the people, ought to remain inviolate.

Congressional Register, June 8, 1789, vol. 1, pp. 428–29.

7.1.1.1.b   *Seventhly.* That in article 3d, section 2 [of the Constitution], the third clause be struck out, and in its place be inserted the clauses following, to wit: . . .

The trial of all crimes (except in cases of impeachments, and cases arising in the land and naval forces, or the militia when on actual service in time of war, or public danger,) shall be by an impartial jury of freeholders of the vicinage, with the requisite of unanimity for conviction, of the right of challenge, and other accustomed requisites; and in all crimes punishable with loss of life or member, presentment or indictment by a grand jury, shall be an essential preliminary, provided that in cases of crimes committed within any county which may be in possession of an enemy, or in which a general insurrection may prevail, the trial may by law be authorised in some other county of the same state, as near as may be to the seat of the offence.

In cases of crimes committed not within any county, the trial may by law be in such county as the laws shall have prescribed. In suits at common law between man and man, the trial by jury as one of the best securities to the rights of the people, ought to remain inviolate.

Daily Advertiser, June 12, 1789, p. 2, col. 2.

7.1.1.1.c   *Seventh.* That in article 3d, section 1 [of the Constitution], the third clause be struck out, and in its place be inserted the clauses following, to wit,

The trial of all crimes (except in cases of impeachments, and cases arising in the land or naval forces, or the militia when on actual service in time of war, or public danger) shall be by an impartial jury of freeholders of the vicinage, with the requisite of unanimity for conviction, of the right of challenge, and other accustomed requisites; and in all crimes punishable with loss of life or member, presentment or indictment by a grand jury shall be an essential preliminary, provided that in cases of crimes committed within any county which may be in possession of an enemy, or in which a general insurrection may prevail, the trial may be authorised in some other county of the same state, as near as may be to the seat of the offence.

In cases of crimes committed not within any county, the trial may be in such county as the laws shall have prescribed. In suits at common law between man and man, the trial by jury, as one of the best securities to the rights of the people, ought to remain inviolate.

New-York Daily Gazette, June 13, 1789, p. 574, col. 4.

7.1.1.2 Proposal by Sherman to House Committee of Eleven, July 21–28, 1789

[Amendment] 3 No person shall be tried for any crime whereby he may incur loss of life or any infamous punishment, without Indictment by a grand Jury, nor be convicted but by the unanimous verdict of a Petit Jury of good and lawful men Freeholders of the vicinage or district where the trial shall be had.

Madison Papers, DLC.

7.1.1.3 House Committee of Eleven Report, July 28, 1789

ART. 3, SEC. 2 — Strike out the whole of the 3d paragraph, and insert — . . .

"The trial of all crimes (except in cases of impeachment, and in cases arising in the land or naval forces, or in the militia, when in actual service in time of war or public danger) shall be by an impartial jury of freeholders of the vicinage, with the requisite of unanimity for conviction, the right of challenge and other accustomed requisites; and no person shall be held to answer for a capital, or otherwise infamous crime, unless on a presentment or indictment by a Grand Jury; but if a crime be committed in a place in the possession of an enemy, or in which an insurrection may prevail, the indictment and trial may by law be authorized in some other place within the same State; and if it be committed in a place not within a State, the indictment and trial may be at such place or places as the law may have directed."

Broadside Collection, DLC.

7.1.1.4   House Consideration, August 18, 1789

7.1.1.4.a   The house now resolved itself into a committee of the whole on the subject of amendments, and took into consideration the 2d clause of the 7th proposition, in the words following, "The trial of all crimes (except in cases of impeachment, and in cases arising in the land or naval forces, or in the militia when in actual service in time of war, or public danger) shall be by an impartial jury of freeholders of the vicinage, with the requisite of unanimity for conviction, the right of challenge, and other accustomed requisites; and no person shall be held to answer for a capital, or otherwise infamous crime, unless on a presentment, or indictment, by a grand jury; but if a crime be committed in a place in the possession of an enemy, or in which an insurrection may prevail, the indictment and trial may by law be authorised in some other place within the same state; and if it be committed in a place not within a state, the indictment and trial may be at such place or places as the law may have directed."

Congressional Register, August 18, 1789, vol. 2, p. 233 (after the motions noted below, "The clause was now adopted without amendment." *Id.*).

7.1.1.4.b   The committee took up the fifteenth amendment which is as follows:

"The trial of all crimes (except in cases of impeachment, and in cases arising in the land or naval forces, or in the militia, when in actual service in time of war or public danger) shall be by an impartial jury of freeholders of the vicinage, with the requisite of unanimity for conviction, the right of challenge, and other accustomed requisites; and no person shall be held to answer for a capital, or otherwise infamous crime, unless on a presentment or indictment by a grand jury; but if a crime be committed in a place in the possession of an enemy, or in which an insurrection may prevail, the indictment and trial may by law be authorized in some other place within the same state; and if it be committed in a place not within a state, the indictment and trial may be at such place or places as the law may have directed."

Daily Advertiser, August 19, 1789, p. 2, col. 2 ("Some inconsiderable amendments to this amendment were moved and lost, and the main question was carried.").

7.1.1.4.c   The committee took up the fifteenth amendment, which is

"The trial of all crimes (except in cases of impeachment, and in cases arising in the land or naval forces, or in the militia, when in actual service in time of war or public danger) shall be by an impartial jury of freeholders of the vicinage, with the requisite of unanimity for conviction, the right of challenge, and other accustomed requisites; and no person shall be held to answer for a capital, or otherwise infamous crime, unless on a presentment or indictment by a grand jury; but if a crime be committed in a place in the possession of an enemy, or in which an insurrection may prevail, the indictment and trial may by law be authorized in some other place within the same state; and if it be committed in a place not within a state, the indictment and trial may be at such place or places as the law may have directed."

Gazette of the U.S., August 22, 1789, p. 250, col. 1 (reported as August 19, 1789; after the motions noted below, "And then the paragraph was adopted. *Id.*).

7.1.1.5 Motion by Burke in House, August 18, 1789

7.1.1.5.a   Mr. BURKE
Moved to change the word "vicinage" into "district or county in which the
offence has been committed," . . .
Congressional Register, August 18, 1789, vol. 2, p. 233 ("[t]he question
on mr. Burke's motion being put was negatived").

7.1.1.5.b Mr. BURKE moved to strike out "vicinage," and to insert *county or district in
which the offence has been committed.*"
Gazette of the U.S., August 22, 1789, p. 250, col. 1
("The motion was negatived.").

7.1.1.6 Motion by Burke in House, August 18, 1789

7.1.1.6.a Mr. BURKE then revived his motion for preventing prosecutions upon information. . . .
Congressional Register, August 18, 1789, vol. 2, p. 233
("on the question this was also lost").[1]

7.1.1.6.b Mr. BURKEth n [*sic;* then] proposed to add a clause to prevent prosecutions
upon informations: . . .
Gazette of the U.S., August 22, 1789, p. 250, col. 1
("This motion was lost.").

7.1.1.7 Motion by Gerry in House, August 21, 1789

7.1.1.7.a   Mr. GERRY
Then proposed to amend it by striking out these words, "public danger" and to
insert foreign invasion. . . .
Congressional Register, August 21, 1789, vol. 2, p. 243
("this being negatived").

7.1.1.7.b Mr. Gerry moved to strike out these words, "public danger," to insert *foreign
invasion.*
New-York Daly Gazette, August 24, 1789, p. 818, col. 3
("This was negatived.").

7.1.1.8 Motion by Gerry in House, August 21, 1789

[I]t was then moved to strike out the last clause, "and if it be committed, &c." to
the end.
Congressional Register, August 21, 1789, vol. 2, p. 243 ("This motion
was carried, and the amendment was adopted."); New-York Daily
Gazette, August 24, 1789, p. 818, col. 3 ("This motion obtained,
and the amendment as it then stood was adopted.").

7.1.1.9 Further House Consideration, August 21, 1789

Fourteenth. The trial of all crimes, (except in cases of impeachment, and in cases
arising in the land or naval forces, or in the militia when in actual service in time of

---

[1]On August 17, 1789, Mr. Burke made an identical motion to amend the proposed amendment.
After being referred to the proposed grand jury clause and after "[a] desultory conversation . . . Mr.
Burke withdrew [the motion] for the present."
Congressional Register, August 17, 1789, vol. 2, pp. 228–29.

war or public danger) shall be by an impartial jury of the vicinage, with the requisite of unanimity for conviction, the right of challenge and other accustomed requisites; and no person shall be held to answer for a capital or otherwise infamous crime, unless on a presentment or indictment by a grand jury; but if a crime be committed in a place in the possession of an enemy, or in which an insurrection may prevail, the indictment and trial may by law be authorised in some other place within the same state.

HJ, p. 108 ("read and debated . . . agreed to by the House, . . . two-thirds of the members present concurring").[2]

7.1.1.10   House Resolution, August 24, 1789

ARTICLE THE TENTH.

The trial of all crimes (except in cases of impeachment, and in cases arising in the land or naval forces, or in the militia when in actual service in time of War or public danger) shall be by an Impartial Jury of the Vicinage, with the requisite of unanimity for conviction, the right of challenge, and other accostomed [*sic*] requisites; and no person shall be held to answer for a capital, or oterways infamous crime, unless on a presentment or indictment by a Grand Jury; but if a crime be committed in a place in the possession of an enemy, or in which an insurrection may prevail, the indictment and trial may by law be authorised in some other place within the same State.

House Pamphlet, RG 46, DNA.

7.1.1.11   Senate Consideration, August 25, 1789

7.1.1.11.a   The Resolve of the House of Representatives of the 24th of August, upon certain "Articles to be proposed to the Legislatures of the several States as Amendments to the Constitution of the United States" was read as followeth:

. . .

Article the tenth

[The trial of all crimes (except in cases of impeachment, and in cases arising in the land or naval forces, or in the militia when in actual service in time of war or public danger) shall be by] an impartial jury of the Vicinage, with the requisite of unanimity for conviction, the right of Challenge, and other accustomed requisites; and no person shall be held to answer for a capital or otherwise infamous crime, unless on a presentment or indictment by a Grand Jury; but if a crime be committed in a place in the possession of an Enemy, or in which an insurrection may prevail, the indictment and trial may by law be authorised in some other place within the same State.

Rough SJ, pp. 217–18 [material in brackets not legible].

7.1.1.11.b   The Resolve of the House of Representatives of the 24th of August, was read as followeth:

[2]On August 22, 1789, the following motion was agreed to:
ORDERED, That it be referred to a committtee of three, to prepare and report a proper arrangement of, and introduction to the articles of amendment to the Constitution of the United States, as agreed to by the House; and that Mr. Benson, Mr. Sherman, and Mr. Sedgwick be of the said committee.

HJ, p. 112.

. . .

"Article the Tenth.

"The trial of all crimes (except in cases of impeachment, and in cases arising in the land or naval forces, or in the militia when in actual service in time of war or public danger) shall be by an impartial Jury of the vicinage, with the requisite of unanimity for conviction, the right of challenge, and other accustomed requisites; and no person shall be held to answer for a capital, or otherwise infamous crime, unless on a presentment or indictment by a Grand Jury; but if a crime be committed in a place in the possession of an enemy, or in which an insurrection may prevail, the indictment and trial may by law be authorised in some other place within the same State.

Smooth SJ, pp. 195–96.

7.1.1.11.c   The Resolve of the House of Representatives of the 24th of August, was read as followeth:

. . .

"ARTICLE THE TENTH.

"The trial of all crimes (except in cases of impeachment, and in cases arising in the land or naval forces, or in the militia when in actual service in time of war or public danger) shall be by an impartial Jury of the vicinage, with the requisite of unanimity for conviction, the right of challenge, and other accustomed requisites; and no person shall be held to answer for a capital, or otherways infamous crime, unless on a presentment or indictment by a Grand Jury; but if a crime be committed in a place in the possession of an enemy, or in which an insurrection may prevail, the indictment and trial may by law be authorised in some other place within the same State.

Printed SJ, p. 105.

7.1.1.12   Further Senate Consideration, September 4, 1789

7.1.1.12.a   On Motion to adopt the tenth Article amended to read thus To strike out all the clauses in the Article, except the following:

"No person shall be held to answer for a capital, or otherwise infamous crime, unless on a presentment or indictment by a Grand Jury."

Rough SJ, p. 249 ("It passed in the affirmative.").

7.1.1.12.b   On motion, To adopt the tenth Article amended by striking out all the clauses in the Article, except the following:

"No person shall be held to answer for a capital, or otherwise infamous crime, unless on a presentment or indictment by a Grand Jury."

Smooth SJ, pp. 222–23 ("It passed in the Affirmative.").

7.1.1.12.c   On motion, To adopt the tenth Article amended by striking out all the clauses in the Article, except the following:

"No person shall be held to answer for a capital, or otherwise infamous crime, unless on a presentment or indictment by a Grand Jury."

Printed SJ, p. 119 ("It passed in the Affirmative.").

7.1.1.12.d   that the Senate do

Resolved ~~to~~ ∧ concur with the House of Representatives in

Article tenth

with the following amendment, to wit:

To Strike out all the clauses in the Article, except the following:

"no person shall be held to answer for a capital, or otherwise infamous crime, unless on a presentment or indictment by a grand jury."

Senate MS, p. 3, RG 46, DNA.

7.1.1.13   Further Senate Consideration, September 9, 1789

7.1.1.13.a   On motion, To alter Article 6th so as to stand Article 5th, and Article 7th so as to stand Article 6th, and Article 8th so as to stand Article 7th

. . .

On motion, That this last mentioned Article[3] be amended to read as follows: "No person shall be held to answer for a capital or otherwise infamous crime, unless on a presentment or indictment of a grand Jury, except in cases arising in the land or naval forces, or in the Militia, when in actual service, in time of war or public danger, nor shall any person be subject to be put in jeopardy of life or limb, for the same offence, nor shall be compelled in any criminal case to be a witness against himself, nor be deprived of life, liberty or property, without due process of law; Nor shall private property be taken for public use without just compensation."

Rough SJ, p. 275 ("It passed in the affirmative.").

7.1.1.13.b   On motion, To alter article the sixth so as to stand article the fifth, and article the seventh so as to stand article the sixth, and article the eighth so as to stand article the seventh —

. . .

On motion, That this last mentioned article[4] be amended to read as follows: "No person shall be held to answer for a capital or otherwise infamous crime, unless on a presentment or indictment of a Grand Jury, except in cases arising in the land or naval forces, or in the militia, when in actual service, in time of war or public danger, nor shall any person be subject to be put in jeopardy of life or limb, for the same offence, nor shall be compelled in any criminal case to be a witness against himself, nor be deprived of life, liberty or property, without due process of law: Nor shall private property be taken for public use without just compensation" —

Smooth SJ, p. 244 ("It passed in the Affirmative.").

7.1.1.13.c   On motion, To alter Article the sixth so as to stand Article the fifth, and Article the seventh so as to stand Article the sixth, and Article the eighth so as to stand Article the seventh —

. . .

On motion, That this last mentioned Article[5] be amended to read as follows: "No person shall be held to answer for a capital or otherwise infamous crime,

---

[3]"Article the 7th," the prior textual history of which is found in Chapters 8, 9 and 10.
[4]"Article the seventh," the prior textual history of which is found in Chapters 8, 9 and 10.
[5]"Article the seventh," the prior textual history of which is found in Chapters 8, 9 and 10.

unless on a presentment or indictment of a Grand Jury, except in cases arising in the land or naval forces, or in the militia, when in actual service, in time of war or public danger, nor shall any person be subject to be put in jeopardy of life or limb, for the same offence, nor shall be compelled in any criminal case to be a witness against himself, nor be deprived of life, liberty or property, without due process of law: Nor shall private property be taken for public use without just compensation" —

Printed SJ, pp. 129–30 ("It passed in the Affirmative.").

7.1.1.13.d   To erase the word "Eighth" & insert Seventh —

To insert in the ~~Eighth~~ 8th [7th] article ~~as~~ after the word "shall" in the "1" line — be held to answer for a capital or otherwise infamous crime, unless on a presentment or indictment of a grand Jury, except in cases arising in the land or naval forces, or in the militia when in actual Service in time of War or publick danger, nor shall any person — &

To erase from the same article the words "except in case of impeachment, to more than one trial or one punishment" & insert — to be twice put in jeopardy of life or limb —

Ellsworth MS, p. 3, RG 46, DNA.

7.1.1.14   Senate Resolution, September 9, 1789

ARTICLE THE SEVENTH.

No person shall be held to answer for a capital, or otherwise infamous crime, unless on a presentment or indictment of a Grand Jury, except in cases arising in the land or naval forces, or in the militia, when in actual service in time of war or public danger; nor shall any person be subject for the same offence to be twice put in jeopardy of life or limb; nor shall be compelled in any criminal case, to be a witness against himself, nor be deprived of life, liberty or property, without due process of law; nor shall private property be taken for public use without just compensation.

Senate Pamphlet, RG 46, DNA.

7.1.1.15   Further House Consideration, September 21, 1789

RESOLVED, That this House doth agree to the second, fourth, eighth, twelfth, thirteenth, sixteenth, eighteenth, nineteenth, twenty-fifth, and twenty-sixth amendments, and doth disagree to the first, third, fifth, sixth, seventh, ninth, tenth, eleventh, fourteenth, fifteenth, seventeenth, twentieth, twenty-first, twenty-second, twenty-third, and twenty-fourth amendments proposed by the Senate to the said articles, two thirds of the members present concurring on each vote.

RESOLVED, That a conference be desired with the Senate on the subject matter of the amendments disagreed to, and that Mr. Madison, Mr. Sherman, and Mr. Vining, be appointed managers at the same on the part of this House.

HJ, p. 146.

7.1.1.16   Further Senate Consideration, September 21, 1789

7.1.1.16.a   A message from the House of Representatives —

Mr. Beckley, their Clerk, brought up a Resolve of the House of this date, to agree to the 2nd, 4th, 8th, 12th, 13th, 16th, 18th, 19th, 25th, and 26th Amend-

ments proposed by the Senate, "To articles of Amendment to be proposed to the Legislatures of the several States, as Amendments to the Constitution of the United States," and to disagree to the 1st, 3d, 5th, 6th, 7th, 9th, 10th, 11th, 14th, 15th, 17th, 20th, 21st, 22d, 23d, and 24th amendments: Two thirds of the members present concurring on each vote: And "That a conference be desired with the Senate on the subject matter of the amendments disagreed to," and that Mr. Madison, Mr. Sherman, and Mr. Vining, be appointed managers of the same, on the part of the House of Representatives —

And he withdrew.

Smooth SJ, pp. 265–66.

7.1.1.16.b   A message from the House of Representatives —

Mr. Beckley, their Clerk, brought up a Resolve of the House of this date, to agree to the 2d, 4th, 8th, 12th, 13th, 16th, 18th, 19th, 25th, and 26th Amendments proposed by the Senate, "To Articles of Amendment to be proposed to the Legislatures of the several States, as Amendments to the Constitution of the United States," and to disagree to the 1st, 3d, 5th, 6th, 7th, 9th, 10th, 11th, 14th, 15th, 17th, 20th, 21st, 22d, 23d, and 24th Amendments: Two thirds of the members present concurring on each vote: And "That a conference be desired with the Senate on the subject matter of the Amendments disagreed to," and that Mr. Madison, Mr. Sherman, and Mr. Vining, be appointed managers of the same, on the part of the House of Representatives —

And he withdrew.

Printed SJ, pp. 141–42.

7.1.1.17 Further Senate Consideration, September 21, 1789

7.1.1.17.a   The Senate proceeded to consider the Message of the House of Representatives disagreeing to the Amendments made by the Senate "To Articles to be proposed to the Legislatures of the several States, as Amendments to the Constitution of the United States" And

RESOLVED, That the Senate do recede from their third Amendment, and do insist on all the others.

RESOLVED, That the Senate do concur with the House of Representatives in a conference on the subject matter of disagreement on the said Articles of Amendment, and that Mr. Ellsworth Mr. Carroll and Mr. Paterson be managers of the conference on the part of the Senate.

Smooth SJ, p. 267.

7.1.1.17.b   The Senate proceeded to consider the message of the House of Representatives disagreeing to the Amendments made by the Senate "To Articles to be proposed to the Legislatures of the several States, as Amendments to the Constitution of the United States" — And

RESOLVED, That the Senate do recede from their third Amendment, and do insist on all the others.

RESOLVED, That the Senate do concur with the House of Representatives in a conference on the subject matter of disagreement on the said Articles of Amendment, and that Mr. Ellsworth, Mr. Carroll, and Mr. Paterson be managers of the conference on the part of the Senate.

Printed SJ, p. 142.

7.1.1.18 Conference Committee Report, September 24, 1789

[T]hat it will be proper for the House of Representatives to agree to the said Amendments proposed by the Senate, with an Amendment to their fifth Amendment, so that the third Article shall read as follows: "Congress shall make no Law respecting an establishment of Religion, or prohibiting the free exercise thereof; or abridging the freedom of Speech, or of the Press; or the right of the people peaceably to assemble and to petition the Government for a redress of grievances;" And with an Amendment to the fourteenth Amendment proposed by the Senate, so that the eighth Article, as numbered in the Amendments proposed by the Senate, shall read as follows "In all criminal prosecutions, the accused shall enjoy the right to a speedy & publick trial by an impartial jury of the district wherein the crime shall have been committed, as the district shall have been previously ascertained by law, and to be informed of the nature and cause of the accusation; to be confronted with the witnesses against him, and to have com-

pulsory process for obtaining witnesses ~~against him~~ in his favour, & /\ have the assistance of counsel for his defence."

to

Conference MS, RG 46, DNA (Ellsworth's handwriting).

7.1.1.19 House Consideration of Conference Committee Report, September 24 [25], 1789

RESOLVED, That this House doth recede from their disagreement to the first, third, fifth, sixth, seventh, ninth, tenth, eleventh, fourteenth, fifteenth, seventeenth, twentieth, twenty-first, twenty-second, twenty-third, and twenty-fourth amendments, insisted on by the Senate: PROVIDED, That the two articles which by the amendments of the Senate are now proposed to be inserted as the third and eighth articles, shall be amended to read as followeth;

Article the third. "Congress shall make no law respecting an establishment of religion, or prohibiting the free exercise thereof; or abridging the freedom of speech, or of the press; or the right of the people peaceably to assemble, and to petition the government for a redress of grievances."

Article the eighth. "In all criminal prosecutions, the accused shall enjoy the right to a speedy and public trial by an impartial jury of the state and district wherein the crime shall have been committed, which district shall have been previously ascertained by law, and to be informed of the nature and cause of the accusation, to be confronted with the witnesses against him, to have compulsory process for obtaining witnesses in his favor, and to have the assistance of council for his defence."

HJ, p. 152 ("On the question, that the House do agree to the alteration
and amendment of the eighth article, in manner aforesaid, It was resolved
in the affirmative. Ayes 37 Noes 14").

7.1.1.20 Senate Consideration of Conference Committee Report, September 24, 1789

7.1.1.20.a   Mr. Ellsworth, on behalf of the managers of the conference on "articles to be proposed to the several States as Amendments to the Constitution of the United States," reported as follows:

That it will be proper for the House of Representatives to agree to the said amendments proposed by the Senate, with an Amendment to their fifth Amend-

274

ment, so that the third Article shall read as follows: "Congress shall make no law respecting an establishment of <u>Religion</u>, or prohibiting the free exercise thereof; or abridging the freedom of Speech, or of the Press; or the right of the people peaceably to assemble and petition the Government for a redress of Grievances;" And with an Amendment to the fourteenth Amendment proposed by the Senate, so that the eighth article, as numbered in the Amendments proposed by the Senate, shall read as follows; "In all criminal prosecutions, the accused shall enjoy the right to a speedy and public trial by an impartial <u>Jury</u> of the district wherein the <u>Crime</u> shall have been committed, as the district shall have been previously ascertained by law, and to be informed of the nature and cause of the accusation, to be confronted with the witnesses against him, and to have compulsory process for obtaining witnesses in his favor, and to have the assistance of Counsel for defence."

Smooth SJ, pp. 272–73.

7.1.1.20.b   Mr. Ellsworth, on behalf of the managers of the conference on "Articles to be proposed to the several States as Amendments to the Constitution of the United States," reported as follows:

That it will be proper for the House of Representatives to agree to the said Amendments proposed by the Senate, with an Amendment to their fifth Amendment, so that the third Article shall read as follows: "Congress shall make no Law RESPECTING AN ESTABLISHMENT OF RELIGION, or prohibiting the free exercise thereof; or abridging the freedom of Speech, or of the Press; or the right of the People peaceably to assemble and petition the Government for a redress of Grievances;" And with an Amendment to the fourteenth Amendment proposed by the Senate, so that the eighth Article, as numbered in the Amendments proposed by the Senate, shall read as follows; "In all criminal prosecutions, the accused shall enjoy the right to a speedy and public trial by AN IMPARTIAL JURY OF THE DISTRICT WHEREIN THE CRIME SHALL HAVE BEEN COMMITTED, AS THE DISTRICT SHALL HAVE BEEN PREVIOUSLY ASCERTAINED BY LAW, and to be informed of the nature and cause of the accusation, to be confronted with the witnesses against him, and to have compulsory process for obtaining witnesses in his favor, and to have the assistance of Counsel for defence."

Printed SJ, p. 145.

7.1.1.21   Further Senate Consideration of Conference Committee Report, September 24, 1789

7.1.1.21.a   A Message from the House of Representatives —

Mr. Beckley, their Clerk, brought up the Amendments to the "Articles to be proposed to the Legislatures of the several States, as Amendments to the Constitution of the United States;" and informed the Senate, that the House of Representatives had receded from their disagreement to the 1st, 3d, 5th, 6th, 7th, 9th, 10th, 11th, 14th, 15th, 17th, 20th, 21st, 22d, 23d, and 24th Amendments, insisted on by the Senate: Provided that the "Two Articles, which by the Amendments of the Senate are now proposed to be inserted as the third and eighth Articles," shall be amended to read as followeth:

Article the Third. "Congress shall make no Law respecting an establishment of Religion, or prohibiting the free exercise thereof; or abridging the freedom of

Speech, or of the Press; or the right of the people peaceably to assemble, and petition the Government for a redress of Grievances."

Article the Eighth. "In all criminal prosecutions the accused shall enjoy the right to a speedy and public trial by an impartial Jury of the State and District, wherein the crime shall have been committed, which District shall have been previously ascertained by law, and to be informed of the nature and cause of the accusation, to be confronted with the witnesses against him, and to have compulsory process for obtaining witnesses in his favor, and to have the assistance of Counsel for his defence."

Smooth SJ, pp. 278–79.

7.1.1.21.b   A Message from the House of Representatives —

Mr. Beckley, their Clerk, brought up the Amendments to the "Articles to be proposed to the Legislatures of the several States, as Amendments to the Constitution of the United States;" and informed the Senate, that the House of Representatives had receded from their disagreement to the 1st, 3d, 5th, 6th, 7th, 9th, 10th, 11th, 14th, 15th, 17th, 20th, 21st, 22d, 23d, and 24th Amendments, insisted on by the Senate: Provided that the "Two Articles, which by the Amendments of the Senate are now proposed to be inserted as the third and eighth Articles," shall be amended to read as followeth:

Article the Third. "Congress shall make no Law respecting an establishment of Religion, or prohibiting the free exercise thereof; or abridging the freedom of Speech, or of the Press; or the right of the People peaceably to assemble, and petition the Government for a redress of Grievances."

Article the Eighth. "In all criminal prosecutions the accused shall enjoy the right to a speedy and public trial by an impartial Jury of the State and District, wherein the crime shall have been committed, which District shall have been previously ascertained by law, and to be informed of the nature and cause of the accusation, to be confronted with the witnesses against him, and to have compulsory process for obtaining witnesses in his favor, and to have the assistance of Counsel for his defence."

Printed SJ, p.148.

7.1.1.22   Further Senate Consideration of Conference Committee Report, September 25, 1789

7.1.1.22.a   The Senate proceeded to consider the Message from the House of Representatives of the 24th, with Amendments to the Amendments of the Senate, to "Articles to be proposed to the Legislatures of the several States, as Amendments to the Constitution of the United States" — And

RESOLVED, That the Senate do concur in the Amendments proposed by the House of Representatives, to the Amendments of the Senate.   Smooth SJ, p. 283.

7.1.1.22.b   The Senate proceeded to consider the Message from the House of Representatives of the 24th, with Amendments to the Amendments of the Senate, to "Articles to be proposed to the Legislatures of the several States, as Amendments to the Constitution of the United States" — And

RESOLVED, That the Senate do concur in the Amendments proposed by the House of Representatives, to the Amendments of the Senate.

Printed SJ, pp. 150–51.

7.1.1.23 Agreed Resolution, September 25, 1789

7.1.1.23.a   Article the Seventh.

No person shall be held to answer for a capital, or otherwise infamous crime, unless on a presentment or indictment of a Grand Jury, except in cases arising in the land or naval forces, or in the militia, when in actual service in time of war or public danger; nor shall any person be subject for the same offence to be twice put in jeopardy of life or limb; nor shall be compelled in any criminal case, to be a witness against himself, nor be deprived of life, liberty or property, without due process of law; nor shall private property be taken for public use without just compensation.

Smooth SJ, Appendix, p. 293.

7.1.1.23.b   ARTICLE THE SEVENTH.

No person shall be held to answer for a capital, or otherwise infamous crime, unless on a presentment or indictment of a Grand Jury, except in cases arising in the land or naval forces, or in the militia, when in actual service in time of war or public danger; nor shall any person be subject for the same offence to be twice put in jeopardy of life or limb; nor shall be compelled in any criminal case, to be a witness against himself, nor be deprived of life, liberty or property, without due process of law; nor shall private property be taken for public use without just compensation.

Printed SJ, Appendix, p. 164.

7.1.1.24 Enrolled Resolution, September 28, 1789

Article the seventh. . . . No person shall be held to answer for a capital, or otherwise infamous crime, unless on a presentment or indictment of a Grand Jury, except in cases arising in the land or naval forces, or in the militia, when in actual service in time of war or public danger; nor shall any person be subject for the same offence to be twice put in jeopardy of life or limb, nor shall be compelled in any criminal case to be a witness against himself, nor be deprived of life, liberty, or property, without due process of law; nor shall private property be taken for public use without just compensation.

Enrolled Resolutions, RG 11, DNA.

7.1.1.25 Printed Versions

7.1.1.25.a   ART. V. No person shall be held to answer for a capital or otherwise infamous crime, unless on a presentment or indictment of a grand jury, except in cases arising in the land or naval forces, or in the militia, when in actual service, in time of war or public danger; nor shall any person be subject for the same offence to be twice put in jeopardy of life or limb; nor shall be compelled, in any criminal case, to be witness against himself; nor be deprived of life, liberty, or property, without due process of law; nor shall private property be taken for public use without just compensation.

Statutes at Large, vol.1, p. 21.

7.1.1.25.b ART. VII. No person shall be held to answer for a capital, or otherwise infamous crime, unless on a presentment or indictment of a grand jury, except in cases arising in the land or naval forces, or in the militia when in actual service in time of war or public danger; nor shall any person be subject for the same offence to be twice put in jeopardy of life or limb; nor shall be compelled in any criminal case to be a witness against himself, nor be deprived of life, liberty or property, without due process of law; nor shall private property be taken for public use without just compensation.

Statutes at Large, vol. 1, p. 98.

7.1.2 PROPOSALS FROM THE STATE CONVENTIONS

7.1.2.1 New Hampshire, June 21, 1788

Sixthly That no Person shall be Tryed for any Crime by which he may incur an Infamous Punishment, or loss of Life, untill he first be indicted by a Grand Jury except in such Cases as may arise in the Government and regulation of the Land & Naval Forces. —

State Ratifications, RG 11, DNA.

7.1.2.2 Massachusetts, February 6, 1788

Sixthly, That no person Shall be tried for any Crime by which he may incur an infamous punishment or loss of life until he be first indicted by a Grand Jury, except in such cases as may arise in the Government & regulation of the Land & Naval forces

State Ratifications, RG 11, DNA.

7.1.2.3 New York, July 26, 1788

That (except in the Government of the Land and Naval Forces, and of the Militia when in actual Service, and in cases of Impeachment) a Presentment or Indictment by a Grand Jury ought to be observed as a necessary preliminary to the trial of all Crimes cognizable by the Judiciary of the United States, and such Trial should be speedy, public, and by an impartial Jury of the County where the Crime was committed; and that no person can be found Guilty without the unanimous consent of such Jury. But in cases of Crimes not committed within any County of the United States, and in Cases of Crimes committed within any County in which a general Insurrection may prevail, or which may be in the possession of a foreign Enemy, the enquiry and trial may be in such County as /\ Congress shall by Law direct; which County in the two Cases last mentioned should be as near as conveniently may be to that County in which the Crime may have been committed. And that in all Criminal Prosecutions, the Accused ought to be informed of the cause and nature of his Accusation, to be confronted with his accusers and the Witnesses against him, to have the means of producing his Witnesses, and the assistance of Council for his defence, and should not be compelled to give Evidence against himself.

That the trial by Jury in the extent that it obtains by the Common Law of England is one of the greatest securities to the rights of a free People, and ought to remain inviolate.

State Ratifications, RG 11, DNA.

7.1.3 STATE CONSTITUTIONS AND LAWS; COLONIAL CHARTERS AND LAWS

7.1.3.1 Georgia: Constitution, 1777

XLV. No grand jury shall consist of less than eighteen, and twelve may find a bill.

Georgia Laws, p. 14.

7.1.3.2 New Jersey: Fundamental Constitutions for East New Jersey, 1683

That no Person or Persons within the said Province shall be taken and imprisoned, or be devised of his Freehold, free Custom or Liberty, or be outlawed or exiled, or any other Way destroyed; nor shall they be condemn'd or Judgment pass'd upon them, but by lawful Judgment of their Peers: Neither shall Justice nor Right be bought or sold, defered or delayed, to any Person whatsoever: In order to which by the Laws of the Land, all Tryals shall be by twelve Men, and as near as it may be, Peers and Equals, and of the Neighbourhood, and Men without just Exception. In Cases of Life there shall be at first Twenty four returned by the Sherriff for a Grand Inquest, of whom twelve at least shall be to find the Complaint to be true; and then the Twelve Men or Peers to be likewise returned, shall have the final Judgment; but reasonable Challenges shall be always admitted against the Twelve Men, or any of them: But the Manner of returning Juries shall be thus, the Names of all the Freemen above five and Twenty Years of Age, within the District or Boroughs out of which the Jury is to be returned, shall be written on equal Pieces of Parchment and put into a Box, and then the Number of the Jury shall be drawn out by a Child under Ten Years of Age. And in all Courts Persons of all Perswasions may freely appear in their own Way, and according to their own Manner, and there personally plead their own Causes themselves, or if unable, by their Friends, no Person being allowed to take Money for pleading or advice in such Casas [*sic*]: And the first Process shall be the Exhibition of the Complaint in Court fourteen Days before the Tryal, and the Party complain'd against may be fitted for the same, he or she shall be summoned ten Days before, and a Copy of the Complaint delivered at their dwelling House: But before the Complaint of any Person be received, he shall solemnly declare in Court, that he believes in his Conscience his Cause is just. Moreover, every Man shall be first cited before the Court for the Place where he dwells, nor shall the Cause be brought before any other Court but by way of Appeal from Sentence of the first Court, for receiving of which Appeals, there shall be a Court consisting of eight Persons, and the Governor (protempore) President thereof, (*to wit*) four Proprietors and four Freemen, to be chosen out of the great Council in the following Manner, *viz.* the Names of Sixteen of the Proprietors shall be written on small pieces of Parchment and put into a Box, out of which by a Lad under Ten Years of Age, shall be drawn eight of them, the eight remaining in the Box shall choose four; and in like Manner shall be done for the choosing of four of the Freemen.

New Jersey Grants, pp. 163–64.

7.1.3.3   New York

7.1.3.3.a   Act Declaring . . . Rights & Priviledges, 1691

That In all Cases Capital and Criminal, there shall be a grand Inquest, who shall first present the Offence, and then Twelve Good Men of the Neighbourhood to Try the Offender, who, after his Plea to the Indictment, shall be allowed his reasonable Challenges.

New York Acts, p. 18.

7.1.3.3.b   Constitution, 1777

XXXIV. AND IT IS FURTHER ORDAINED, That in every Trial on Impeachment or Indictment for Crimes or Misdemeanors, the Party impeached or indicted, shall be allowed Counsel, as in civil Actions.

New York Laws, vol. 1, p. 12.

7.1.3.3.c   Bill of Rights, 1787

Third, That no Citizen of this State shall be taken or imprisoned for any Offence upon Petition or Suggestion, unless it be by Indictment or Presentment of good and lawful Men of the same Neighbourhood where such Deeds be done, in due Manner, or by due Process of Law.

New York Laws, vol. 2, p. 1.

7.1.3.4   North Carolina

7.1.3.4.a   Fundamental Constitutions of Carolina, 1669

66th. The Grand Jury at the several assizes, shall upon their oaths and under their hands and seals, deliver into their itinerant Judges, a presentment of such grievances, misdemeanors, exigencies, or defects, which they think necessary for the public good of the country; which presentments shall by the itinerant Judges, at the end of their circuit, be delivered in to the grand council, at their next sitting. And whatsoever therein concerns the execution of laws already made, the several Proprietor's courts, in the matters belonging to each of them respectively, shall take cognizance of it, and give such order about it, as shall be effectual for the due execution of the laws. . . .

North Carolina State Records, pp. 144–45.

7.1.3.4.b   Declaration of Rights, 1776

Sect. VIII. That no Freeman shall be put to answer any criminal Charge, but by Indictment, Presentment, Impeachment.

North Carolina Laws, p. 275.

7.1.3.5   Pennsylvania

7.1.3.5.a   Laws Agreed Upon in England, 1682

VIII. That all **Tryals** shall be by **Twelve Men,** and as near as may be, *Peers* or *Equals,* and of the *Neighbourhood,* and men without just Exception. In cases of *Life* there shall be first **Twenty Four** returned by the Sheriffs for a **Grand Inquest,** of whom *Twelve,* at least, shall find the Complaint to be true, and then the **Twelve Men** or *Peers,* to be likewise returned by the Sheriff, shall have the *final Judg-*

ment: But reasonable Challenges shall be alwayes admitted against the said *Twelve Men,* or any of them.

Pennsylvania Frame, p. 8.

7.1.3.5.b Constitution, 1790

ARTICLE IX.

. . .

SECT. X. That no person shall, for any indictable offence, be proceeded against criminally by information, except in cases arising in the land or naval forces, or in the militia, when in actual service in time of war or public danger, or, by leave of the court, for oppression and misdemeanor in office. No person shall, for the same offence, be twice put in jeopardy of life or limb; nor shall any man's property be taken or applied to public use, without the consent of his representatives, and without just compensation being made.

Pennsylvania Acts, Dallas, p. xxxiv–xxxv.

7.1.4 OTHER TEXTS

7.1.4.1 Assize of Clarendon, 1166

Chapter I

First the aforesaid King Henry established by the counsel of all his barons for the maintenance of peace and justice, that inquiry shall be made in every county and in every hundred by the twelve most lawful men of the hundred and by the four most lawful men of every vill, upon oath that they shall speak the truth, whether in their hundred or vill there be any man who is accused or believed to be a robber, murderer, thief, or a receiver of robbers, murderers or thieves since the King's accession. And this the justices and sheriffs shall enquire before themselves.

Chapter II

And he who shall be found, by the oath of the aforesaid, accused or believed to be a robber, murderer, thief, or receiver of such since the King's accession shall be taken and put to the ordeal of water and made to swear that he was no robber, murderer, thief, or receiver of such up to the value of five shillings, as far as he knows, since the King's accession. . . .

. . .

Chapter IV

And when a robber, murderer, thief, or receiver of such is captured as a result of the oath, the sheriff shall send to the nearest justice (if there are no justices shortly visiting the county wherein he was captured) by an intelligent man saying that he has captured so many men. And the justices shall reply telling the sheriff where prisoners are to be brought before them. And the sheriff shall bring them before the justices together with two lawful men from the hundred and the vill where they were captured to bring the record of the county and the hundred as to why they were captured; and there they shall make their law before the justices.

Theodore F. T. Plucknett, A Concise History of the Common Law, 5th ed.
(Boston: Little, Brown & Co., 1956), pp. 112–13.

7.2 DISCUSSION OF DRAFTS AND PROPOSALS
7.2.1 THE FIRST CONGRESS

7.2.1.1 June 8, 1789[6]

7.2.1.2 August 18, 1789

7.2.1.2.a   The house now resolved itself into a committee of the whole on the subject of amendments, and took into consideration the 2d clause of the 7th proposition, in the words following, "The trial of all crimes (except in cases of impeachment, and in cases arising in the land or naval forces, or in the militia when in actual service in time of war, or public danger) shall be by an impartial jury of freeholders of the vicinage, with the requisitie of unanimity for conviction, the right of challenge, and other accustomed requisites; and no person shall be held to answer for a capital, or otherwise infamous crime, unless on a presentment, or indictment, by a grand jury; but if a crime be committed in a place in the possession of an enemy, or in which an insurrection may prevail, the indictment and trial may by law be authorised in some other place within the same state; and if it be committed in a place not within a state, the indictment and trial may be at such place or places as the law may have directed."

Mr. Burke

Moved to change the word "vicinage" into "district or county in which the offence has been committed," he said this was conformable to the practice of the state of South Carolina, and he believed to most of the states in the union, it would have a tendency also to quiet the alarm entertained by the good citizens of many of the states for their personal security, they would no longer fear being dragged from one extremity of the state to the other for trial, at the distance of 3 or 400 miles.

Mr. Lee

Thought the word "vicinage" was more applicable than that of "district, or county," it being a term well understand by every gentleman of legal knowledge.

The question of mr. Burke's motion being put was negatived.

Mr. Burke then revived his motion for preventing prosecutions upon information, but on the question this was also lost.

The clause was now adopted without amendment.

Congressional Register, August 18, 1789, vol. 2, p. 233.

7.2.1.2.b   The house then resolved itself into a committee of the whole on the subject of amendments.

Mr. Boudinot in the chair.

The committee took up the fifteenth amendment which is as follows:

"The trial of all crimes (except in cases of impeachment, and in cases arising in the land or naval forces, or in the militia, when in actual service in time of war or public danger) shall be by an impartial jury of freeholders of the vicinage, with the

---

[6]For the reports of Madison's speech in support of his proposals, *see* 1.2.1.1.a–c.

requisite of unanimity for conviction, the right of challenge, and other accustomed requisites; and no person shall be held to answer for a capital, or otherwise infamous crime, unless on a presentment or indictment by a grand jury; but if a crime be committed in a place in the possession of an enemy, or in which an insurrection may prevail, the indictment and trial may by law be authorized in some other place within the same state; and if it be committed in a place not within a state, the indictment and trial may be at such place or places as the law may have directed."

Some inconsiderable amendments to this amendment were moved and lost, and the main question was carried.   Daily Advertiser, August 19, 1789, p. 2, col. 2.

7.2.1.2.c   Committee of the whole on the subject of amendments.
                            Mr. BOUDINOT in the chair.
The committee took up the fifteenth amendment, which is

"The trial of all crimes (except in cases of impeachment, and in cases arising in the land or naval forces, or in the militia, when in actual service in time of war or public danger) shall be by an impartial jury of freeholders of the vicinage, with the requisite of unanimity for conviction, the right of challenge, and other accustomed requisites; and no person shall be held to answer for a capital or otherwise infamous crime, unless on a presentment or indictment by a grand jury; but if a crime be committed in a place in the possession of an enemy, or in which an insurrection may prevail, the indictment and trial may by law be authorized in some other place within the same state; and if it be committed in a place not within a state, the indictment and trial may be at such place or places as the law may have directed."

Mr. Burke moved to strike out "vicinage," and to insert *county or district in which the offence has been committed.*" The gentleman enforced the motion by a variety of observations; and among others said that it was agreeable to the practice of the state he represented, and would give the constitution a more easy operation; that it was a matter of serious alarm to the good citizens of many of the States, the idea that they might be dragged from one part of the State perhaps 2 or 300 miles to the other for trial.

Mr. GERRY objected to the word "district" as too indefinite.

Mr. SEDGWICK said, that he conceived that the proposed amendment is not so adequate to the gentleman's object as the word "vicinage" — the latter part of the clause is sufficient for the gentleman's purpose.

The motion was negatived.

Mr. BURKEth n [*sic;* then] proposed to add a clause to prevent prosecutions upon informations: This was objected to, as the object of the clause was to provide that high crimes, &c. should be by presentment of a grand jury; but that other things should take the course heretofore practised. This motion was lost.

And then the paragraph was adopted.

Gazette of the U.S., August 22, 1789, p. 250, col. 1
(reported as August 19).

7.2.1.3   August 21, 1789

7.2.1.3.a   The house proceeded in the consideration of the amendments to the constitution reported by the committee of the whole, and took up the 2nd clause of the 4th proposition.

Mr. GERRY

Then proposed to amend it by striking out these words ,"public danger" and to insert foreign invasion; this being negatived, it was then moved to strike out the last clause, "and if it be committed, &c." to the end. This motion was carried, and the amendment was adopted.   Congressional Register, August 21, 1789, vol. 2, p. 243.

7.2.1.3.b   The order of the day, on amendments to the constitution. 15th amendment under consideration.

Mr. Gerry moved to strike out these words, "public danger," to insert *foreign invasion*. This was negatived. It was then moved to strike out the last clause, "and if it be committed, &c." to the end. This motion obtained, and the amendment as it then stood was adopted.   New-York Daily Gazette, August 24, 1789, p. 818, col. 3.

7.2.2 STATE CONVENTIONS

7.2.2.1   Massachusetts

7.2.2.1.a   January 30, 1788

. . . Mr. HOLMES. Mr. President, I rise to make some remarks on the paragraph under consideration, which treats of the judiciary power.

It is a maxim universally admitted, that the safety of the subject consists in having a right to a trial as free and impartial as the lot of humanity will admit of. Does the Constitution make provision for such a trial? I think not; for in a criminal process, a person shall not have a right to insist on a trial in the vicinity where the fact was committed, where a jury of the peers would, from their local situation, have an opportunity to form a judgment of the *character* of the person charged with the crime, and also to judge of the *credibility* of the witnesses. There a person must be tried by a jury of strangers; a jury who *may be* interested in his conviction; and where he *may,* by reason of the distance of his residence from the place of trial, be incapable of making such a defence as he is, in justice, entitled to, and which he could avail himself of, if his trial was in the same county where the crime is said to have been committed.

These circumstances, as horrid as they are, are rendered still more dark and gloomy, as there is no provision made in the Constitution to prevent the attorney-general from filing information against any person, whether he is indicted by the grand jury or not; in consequence of which the most innocent person in the commonwealth may be taken by virtue of a warrant issued in consequence of such information, and dragged from his home, his friends, his acquaintance, and confined in prison, until the next session of the court, which has jurisdiction of the crime with which he is charged, (and how frequent those sessions are to be we are not yet informed of,) and after long, tedious, and painful imprisonment, though acquitted on trial, may have no possibility to obtain any kind of satisfaction for the loss of his liberty, the loss of his time, great expenses, and perhaps cruel sufferings.

But what makes the matter still more alarming is, that the mode of criminal process is to be pointed out by Congress, and they have no constitutional check on them, except that the trial is to be by a *jury:* but who this jury is to be, how qualified, where to live, how appointed, or by what rules to regulate their procedure, we are ignorant as of yet: whether they are to live in the county where the trial is; whether they are to be chosen by certain districts, or whether they are to be appointed by the sheriff *ex officio;* whether they are to be for one session of the court only, or for a certain term of time, or for good behavior, or during pleasure, are matters which we are entirely ignorant of as yet.

The mode of trial is altogether indetermined; whether the criminal is to be allowed the benefit of counsel; whether he is to be allowed to meet his accuser face to face; whether he is to be allowed to confront the witnesses, and have the advantage of cross-examination, we are not yet told.

These are matters of by no means small consequence; yet we have not the smallest consitutional security that we shall be allowed the exercise of these privileges, neither is it made certain, in the Consitution, that a person charged with the crime shall have the privilege of appearing before the court or jury which is to try him.

On the whole, when we fully consider this matter, and fully investigate the powers granted, explicitly given, and specially delegated, we shall find Congress possessed of powers enabling them to institute judicatories little less inauspicious than a certain tribunal in Spain, which has long been the disgrace of Christendom: I mean that diabolical institution, the *Inquisition*.

What gives an additional glare of horror to these gloomy circumstances is the consideration, that Congress have to ascertain, point out, and determine, what kind of punishments shall be inflicted on persons convicted of crimes. They are nowhere restrained from inventing the most cruel and unheard-of punishments, and annexing them to crimes; and there is no constitutional check on them, but that *racks* and *gibbets* may be amongst the most mild instruments of their discipline.

There is nothing to prevent Congress from passing laws which shall compel a man, who is accused or suspected of a crime, to furnish evidence against himself, and even from establishing laws which shall order the court to take the charge exhibited against a man for truth, unless he can furnish evidence of his innocence.

I do not pretend to say Congress *will* do this; but, sir, I undertake to say that Congress (according to the powers proposed to be given them by the Constitution) *may* do it; and if they do not, it will be owing *entirely* — I repeat it, it will be owing *entirely* — to the goodness of the men and not in the *least degree* owing to the goodness of the Constitution.

The framers of our state constitution took particular care to prevent the General Court from authorizing the judicial authority to issue a warrant against a man for a crime, unless his being guilty of the crime was supported by oath or affirmation, prior to the warrant being granted; why it should be esteemed so much more safe to intrust Congress with the power of enacting laws, which it was deemed so unsafe to intrust our state legislature with, I am unable to conceive.

MR. GORE observed, in reply to Mr. Holmes, that it had been the uniform conduct of those in opposition to the proposed form of government, to determine, in every case where it was possible that the administrators thereof could do wrong, that they would do so, although it were demonstrable that such wrong would be against their own honor and interest, and productive of no advantage to themselves. On this principle alone have they determined that the trial by jury would be taken away in civil cases; when it had been clearly shown, that no words could be adopted, apt to the situation and customs of each state in this particular. Jurors are differently chosen in different states, and in point of qualification the laws of the several states are very diverse; not less so in the causes and disputes which are entitled to trial by jury. What is the result of this? That the laws of Congress may and will be conformable to the local laws in this particular, although the Constitution could not make a universal rule equally applying to the customs and statutes of the different states. Very few governments (certainly not this) can be interested in depriving the people of trial by jury, in questions of *meum et tuum*. In criminal cases alone are they interested to have the trial under their own control; and, in such cases, the Constitution expressly stipulates for trial by jury; but then, says the gentleman from Rochester, (Mr. Holmes,) to the safety of life it is indispensably necessary the trial of crimes should be in the vicinity; and the vicinity is construed to mean county; this is very incorrect, and gentlemen will see the impropriety, by referring themselves to the different local divisions and districts of the several states. But further, said the gentleman, the idea that the jury coming from the neighborhood, and knowing the character and circumstances of the party in trial, is promotive of justice, on reflection will appear not founded in truth. If the jury judge from any other circumstances but what are part of the cause in question, they are not impartial. The great object is to determine on the real merits of the cause, uninfluenced by any personal considerations; if, therefore, the jury could be perfectly ignorant of the person in trial, a just decision would be more probable. From such motives did the wise Athenians so constitute the famed Areopagus, that, when in judgment, this court should sit at midnight, and in total darkness, that the decision might be on the thing, and not on the person. Further, said the gentleman, it has been said, because the Constitution does not expressly provide for an indictment by grand jury in criminal cases, therefore some officer under this government will be authorized to file informations, and bring any man to jeopardy of his life, and indictment by grand jury will be disused. If gentlemen who pretend such fears will look into the constitution of Massachusetts, they will see that no provision is therein made for an indictment by grand jury, or to oppose the danger of an attorney-general filing informations; yet no difficulty or danger has arisen to the people of this commonwealth from this defect, if gentlemen please to call it so. If gentlemen would be candid, and not consider that, wherever Congress may possibly abuse power, they certainly will, there would be no difficulty in the minds of any in adopting the proposed Constitution.

Elliot, vol. 2, pp. 109–13.

7.2.2.1.b February 1, 1788

Hon. Mr. ADAMS. As your Excellency was pleased yesterday to offer, for the consideration of this Convention, certain propositions intended to accompany the ratification of the Constitution before us, I did myself the honor to bring them forward by a regular motion, not only from the respect due to your excellency, but from a clear conviction, in my own mind, that they would tend to effect the salutary and important purposes which you had in view — "the removing the fears and quieting the apprehensions of many of the good people of this commonwealth, and the more effectually guarding against an undue administration of the federal government."

. . .

Your excellency's next proposition is, to introduce the indictment of a grand jury, before any person shall be tried for any crime, by which he may incur infamous punishment, or loss of life; and it is followed by another, which recommends a trial by jury in civil actions between citizens of different states, if either of the parties shall request it. These, and several others which I have mentioned, are so evidently beneficial as to need no comment of mine. And they are all, in every particular, of so general a nature, and so equally interesting to every state, that I cannot but persuade myself to think they would all readily join with us in the measure proposed by your excellency, if we should now adopt it.

Elliot, vol. 2, pp. 130, 132–33.

7.2.3 PHILADELPHIA CONVENTION

None.

7.2.4 NEWSPAPERS AND PAMPHLETS

7.2.4.1 Federal Farmer, No. 16, January 20, 1788

Security against expost [*sic*] facto laws, the trial by jury, and the benefits of the writ of habeas corpus, are but a part of those inestimable rights the people of the United States are entitled to, even in judicial proceedings, by the course of the common law. These may be secured in general words, as in New-York, the Western Territory, &c. by declaring the people of the United States shall always be entitled to judicial proceedings according to the course of the common law, as used and established in the said states. Perhaps it would be better to enumerate the particular essential rights the people are entitled to in these proceedings, as has been done in many of the states, and as has been done in England. In this case, the people may proceed to declare, that no man shall be held to answer to any offence, till the same be fully described to him; nor to furnish evidence against himself: that, except in the government of the army and navy, no person shall be tried for any offence, whereby he may incur loss of life, or an infamous punishment, until he be first indicted by a grand jury: that every person shall have a right to produce all proofs that may be favourable to him, and to meet the witnesses against him face to face: that every person shall be entitled to obtain right and justice freely and without delay; that all persons shall have a right to be secure from all unreasonable searches and seizures of their persons, houses, papers, or possessions; and that all warrants shall be deemed contrary to this right, if the foundation of them be not previously supported by oath, and there be not in them a special designation of persons or objects of search, arrest, or seizure: and that no person shall be exiled or molested in his person or effects, otherwise than by the judgment of his peers, or according to the law of the land. A celebrated writer observes upon this last article, that in itself it may be said to comprehend the whole end of political society. These rights are not necessarily reserved, they are established, or enjoyed but in few countries: they are stipulated rights, almost peculiar to British and American laws. In the execution of those laws, individuals, by long custom, by magna charta, bills of rights &c. have become entitled to them. A man, at first, by act of parliament, became entitled to the benefits of the writ of habeas corpus — men are entitled to these rights and benefits in the judicial proceedings of our state courts generally: but it will by no means follow, that they will be entitled to them in the federal courts, and have a right to assert them, unless secured and established by the constitution or federal laws. We certainly, in federal processes, might as well claim the benefits of the writ of habeas corpus, as to claim trial by a jury — the right to have council — to have witnesses face to face — to be secure against unreasonable search warrants, &c. was the constitution silent as to the whole of them: — but the establishment of the former, will evince that we could not claim them without it; and the omission of the latter, implies they are relinquished, or deemed of no importance. These are rights and benefits individuals acquire by compact; they must claim them under compacts, or immemorial usage — it is doubtful, at least, whether they can be claimed under immemorial usage in this country; and it is, therefore, we generally claim them under compacts, as charters and constitutions.

Storing, vol. 2, pp. 327–28.

7.2.4.2 Hampden, January 26, 1788

I have had no hand in the productions respecting the proposal plan of government — but I feel interested as a citizen. I have waited to see if any motion might be made, or any disposition appear in the Convention, to prevent one of two evils taking place; the first is, *that of rejecting the Constitution;* the second is, *that of adopting it by a bare majority.*

I am not contented with it as it now stands, my reasons are assigned: —

I am not satisfied with the provision for amendments, as it stands in that system, because the amendments I propose, are such as two thirds of the Senate will perhaps never agree to — the indictment by grand jury, and trial of fact by jury, is not so much set by in the southern States, as in the northern — the great men there, are too rich and important to serve on the juries, and the smaller are considered as not having consequence enough to try the others; in short, there can be no trial by peers there: — The middle States gain advantages by having the legal business done in one of them, which may prevent their leading men, from engaging seriously in amendments: — I therefore propose the adopting the Constitution, in the following manner, in which I conceive there will be great unanimity.

THAT this Convention do adopt and ratify the Constitution, or frame of government for the United States of America, proposed by the Federal Convention, lately holden at Philadelphia; upon the following conditions, viz.

That the first Congress which shall be holden under the same, shall before they proceed to exercise any powers possessed under the Constitution, excepting those of organising themselves, and of establishing rules of procedure, take into consideration all amendments proposed by the Convention of this or any other State, and to make such amendments therein proposed as aforesaid, as any seven of the States shall agree to; and which amendments shall be considered as part of the Constitution.

And that the Senators and Representatives of the several States, shall set together in one body, and vote by States, in considering such amendments; — but the President or Vice-President elect, shall have no vote therein.

. . .

5th. In the second clause of the same section, strike out the words, "Both as to law and fact," *and add to that clause these words* — Provided nevertheless, that all issues of fact shall be tried by a jury to be appointed according to standing laws made by Congress.

This will preserve the inestimable right of a trial by jury — This right is the democratical balance in the Judiary [*sic*] power; without it, in civil actions, no relief can be had against the High Officers of State, for abuse of private citizens; without this the English Constitution would be a tyranny — See Judge Blackstone's excellent Commentary on this privilege, in his third volume, page 2.

6th. In the last clause in the same section next after the word State, insert these words, In, or near the County.

This keeps up the idea of trial in the vicinity. See the Massachusetts declaration of rights on this point — Also, that of other States, &c.

7th. At the end of the same clause, add these words — Provided that no person shall be held to answer to any charge of a criminal nature, unless it be upon indictment of a Grand Jury, appointed, sworn and charged according to known and standing laws.

This is the greatest security against arbitrary power; without this, every person who opposes the violation of the constitutional right of the people, may be dragged to the bar, and tried upon a bare information of an Attorney-General. — The loss of this privilege carries with it the loss of every friend to the people. — There is no instance yet, in England, or in America, excepting in the Stuart's reign, of a person's being tried for his life, otherwise than upon indictment. It was attempted before the Revolution, but successfully opposed.

Massachusetts Centinel, Storing, vol. 4, pp. 198–200.

7.2.5 LETTERS AND DIARIES

7.2.5.1 William Pierce to St. George Tucker, September 28, 1787

. . .

"As to trial by jury in criminal cases, it is right, it is just, perhaps it is indispensable, — the life of a citizen ought not to depend on the fiat of a single person. Prejudice, resentment, and partiality, are among the weaknesses of human nature, and are apt to pervert the judgment of the greatest and best of men. The solemnity of trial by jury is suited to nature of criminal cases, because, before a man is brought to answer the indictment, the fact or truth of every accusation is inquired into by the Grand Jury, composed of his fellow citizens, and the same truth or fact afterwards (should the Grand Jury find the accusation well founded) is to be confirmed by the unanimous suffrage of twelve good men, 'superior to all suspicion.' I do not think there can be a greater guard to the liberties of a people than such a mode of trial on the affairs of life and death. . . . ["]

Gazette of the State of Georgia, Kaminski & Saladino, vol. 16, p. 445.

7.3 DISCUSSION OF RIGHTS

7.3.1 TREATISES

7.3.1.1 William Blackstone, 1769

THE next step towards the punishment of offenders is their prosecution, or the manner of their formal accusation. And this is either upon a previous finding of the fact by an inquest or grand jury; or without such previous finding. The former way is either by *presentment,* or *indictment.*

I. A presentment, *generally* taken, is a very comprehensive term; including not only presentments properly so called, but also inquisitions of office, and indictments by a grand jury. A presentment, *properly* speaking, is the notice taken by a grand jury of any offence from their own knowledge or observation, without any bill of indictment laid before them at the suit of the king. As, the presentment of a nusance, a libel, and the like; upon which the officer of the court must afterwards frame an indictment, before the party presented as the author can be put to answer it. An inquisition of office is the act of a jury, summoned by the proper officer to enquire of matters relating to the crown, upon evidence laid before them. Some of these are in themselves convictions, and cannot afterwards be traversed or denied; and therefore the inquest, or jury, ought to hear all that can be alleged on both sides. Of this nature are all inquisitions of *felo de se*; of flight in persons accused of felony; of deodands, and the like; and presentments of petty offences in the sheriff's tourn or court-leet, whereupon the presiding officer may set a fine. Other inquisitions may be afterwards traversed and examined; as particularly the coroner's inquisition of the death of a man, when it finds any one guilty of homicide: for in such cases the offender so presented must be arraigned upon this inquisition, and may dispute the truth of it; which brings it to a kind of indictment, the most usual and effectual means of prosecution, and into which we will therefore enquire a little more minutely.

II. AN *indictment* is a written accusation of one or more persons of a crime or misdemesnor, preferred to, and presented upon oath by, a grand jury. To this end the sheriff of every county is bound to return to every session of the peace, and every commission of *oyer* and *terminer,* and of general gaol delivery, twenty four good and lawful men of the county, some out of every hundred, to enquire, present, do, and execute all those things, which on the part of our lord the king shall then and there be commanded them. They ought to be freeholders, but to what amount is uncertain: which seems to be *casus omissus,* and as proper to be supplied by the legislature as the qualifications of the petit jury; which were formerly equally vague and uncertain, but are now settled by several acts of parliament. However, they are usually gentlemen of the best figure in the county. As many as appear upon this panel, are sworn upon the grand jury, to the amount of twelve at the least, and not more than twenty three; that twelve may be a majority. Which number, as well as the constitution itself, we find exactly described, so early as the laws of king Ethelred. "*Exeant seniores duodecim thani, et praefectus cum eis, et jurent super sanctuarium quod eis in manus datur, quod nolint ullum innocentem accusare, nec aliquem noxium celare.*" In the time of king Richard the first (according to Hoveden) the process of electing the grand jury, ordained by that prince, was as follows: four knights were to be taken from the county at large, who chose two more out of every hundred; which two associated to themselves ten other principal freemen, and those twelve were to answer concerning all particulars relating to their own district. This number was probably found too large and inconvenient; but the traces of this institution still remain, in that some of the jury must be summoned out of every hundred. This grand jury are previously instructed in the articles of the enquiry, by a charge from the judge who presides upon the bench. They then withdraw, to sit and receive indictments, which are preferred to them in the name of the king, but at the suit of any private prosecutor; and they are only to hear evidence on behalf of the prosecution: for the finding of an indictment is only in the nature of an enquiry or accusation, which is afterwards to be tried and determined; and the grand jury are only to enquire upon their oaths, whether there be sufficient cause to call upon the party to answer it. A grand jury however ought to be thoroughly persuaded of the truth of an indictment, so far as their evidence goes; and not to rest satisfied merely with remote probabilities: a doctrine, that might be applied to very oppressive purposes.

THE grand jury are sworn to enquire, only for the body of the county, *pro corpore comitatus;* and therefore they cannot regularly enquire of a fact done out of that county for which they are sworn, unless particularly enabled by act of parliament. And to so high a nicety was this matter antiently carried, that where a man was wounded in one county, and died in antoher, the offender was at common law indictable in neither, because no complete act of felony was done in any one of them: but by statute 2 & 3 Edw. VI. c. 24. he is now indictable in the county where the party died. And so in some other cases: as particularly, where treason is committed out of the realm, it may be enquired of in any county within the realm, as the king shall direct, in pursuance of statutes 26 Hen. VIII. c.13. 35 Hen. VIII. c. 2. and 5 & 6 Edw. VI. c. 11. But, in general, all offences must be enquired into as well as tried in the county where the fact is committed.

WHEN the grand jury have heard the evidence, if they think it a groundless accusation, they used formerly to endorse on the back of the bill, *ignoramus;*" or, we know nothing of it; intimating, that though the facts might possibly be true, that truth did not appear to them: but now, they assert in English, more absolutely, "not a true bill;" and then the party is discharged without farther answer. But a fresh bill may afterwards be preferred to a subsequent grand jury. If they are satisfied of the truth of the accusation, they then endorse upon it, "a true bill;" antiently, *"billa vera."* The indictment is then said to be found and the party stands indicted. But, to find a bill, there must at least twelve of the jury agree: for so tender is the law of England of the lives of the subjects, that no man can be convicted at the suit of the king of any capital offence, unless by the unanimous voice of twenty four of his equals and neighbours: that is, by twelve at least of the grand jury, in the first place, assenting to the accusation; and afterwards, by the whole petit jury, of twelve more, finding him guilty upon his trial. But, if twelve of the grand jury assent, it is a good presentment, though some of the rest disagree. And the indictment, when so found, is publicly delivered into court.

INDICTMENTS must have a precise and sufficient certainty. By statute 1 Hen. V. c. 5. all indictments must set forth the christian name, sirname, and addition of the state and degree, mystery, town, or place, and the county of the offender: and all this to identify his *person*. The *time,* and *place,* are also to be ascertained, by naming the day, and township, in which the fact was committed: though a mistake in these points is in general not held to be material, provided the *time* be laid previous to the finding of indictment, and the *place* to be within the jurisdiction of the court. But sometimes the *time* may be very material, where there is any limitation in point of time assigned for the prosecution of offenders; as by the statute 7 Will. III. c. 3. which enacts, that no prosecution shall be had for any of the treasons or misprisions therein mentioned (except an assassination designed or attempted on the person of the king) unless the bill of indictment be found within three years after the offence committed; and, in case of murder, the time of the death must be laid within a year and a day after the mortal stroke was given. The *offence* itself must also be set forth with clearness and certainty: and in some crimes particular words of art must be used which are so appropriated by the law to express the precise idea which it entertains of the offence, that no other words, however synonymous they may seem, are capable of doing it. Thus in treasons, the facts must be laid to be done, "treasonably, and against his allegiance;" antiently "*proditorie et contra ligeantiae suae debitum:*" else the indictment is void. In indictments for murder, it is necessary to say that the party indicted "murdered," not "killed" or "slew," the other; which till the late statute was expressed in Latin by the word "*murdravit*["]. In all indictments for felonies, the adverb "feloniously, *felonice,*" must be used; and for burglaries also, "*burglariter,*" or in English, "burglariously:" and all these to ascertain the intent. In rapes, the word "*rapuit,*" or "ravished," is necessary, and must not be expressed by any periphrasis; in order to render the crime certain. So in larcinies also, the words "*felonice cepit et asportavit,* feloniously took and carried away," are necessary to every indictment; for these only can express the very offence. Also in indictments for murder, the length and depth of the wound should in general be expressed, in order that it may appear to the court to have been of a mortal nature: but if it goes through the body, then it's dimensions are immaterial, for that is apparently sufficient to have been the cause of the death. Also where a limb, or the like, is absolutely cut off, there such description is impossible. Lastly, in indictments the *value* of the thing, which is the subject or instrument of the offence, must sometimes be expressed. In indictments for larcinies this is necessary, that it may appear whether it be grand or petit larciny; and whether entitled or not to the benefit of clergy: in homicide of all sorts it is necessary; as the weapon, with which it is committed, is forfeited to the king as a deodand.

Commentaries, bk. 4, c. 23; vol. 4, pp. 298–303 (footnotes omitted).

7.3.2 CASELAW

7.3.2.1 Earl of Shaftesbury's Case, 1681

[Then a Bill of High-Treason was offered against the Earl of Shaftesbury; and Sir Francis Withins moved, That the evidence might be heard in court.]

Foreman. My Lord Chief Justice, it is the opinion of the jury, that they ought to examine the witnesses in private, and it hath been the constant practice of our ancestors and predecessors to do it; and they insist upon it as their right to examine in private, because they are bound to keep the king's secrets, which they cannot do, if it be done in court.

[PEMBERTON,] L.C.J. Look ye, gentlemen of the jury, it may very probably be, that some late usage has brought you into this error, that it is your right, but it is not your right in truth. . . . What you say concerning keeping your counsels, that is quite of another nature, that is, your debates, and those things, there you shall be in private, for to consider of what you hear publicly. But certainly it is the best way, both for the king, and for you, that there should, in a case of this nature, be an open and plain examination of the witnesses, that all the world may see what they say.

Foreman. My lord, if your lordship pleases, I must beg your lordship's pardon, if I mistake in anything, it is contrary to the sense of what the jury apprehend. First, they apprehend that the very words of the oath doth bind them, it says, "That they shall keep the counsel's, and their own secrets:" Now, my lord, there can be no secret in public; the very intimation of that doth imply, that the examination should be secret; besides, my lord, I beg your lordship's pardon if we mistake, we do not understand any thing of law.

Mr. *Papillon* [a juror]. . . . If it be the ancient usage and custom of England, that hath never been altered from time to time, and hath continued so, we desire your lordship's opinion upon that; as we would not do any that may be prejudicial to the king, so we would not do the least that should be prejudicial to the liberties of the people; if it be the ancient custom of the kingdom to examine in private, then there is something may be very prejudicial to the king in this public examination; for sometimes in examining witnesses in private, there come to be discovered some persons guilty of treason, and misprision of treason, that were not known, nor thought on before. Then the jury sends down to the court, and gives them intimation, and these men are presently secured; whereas, my lord, in case they be examined in open court publicly, then presently there is intimation given and these men are gone away. Another thing that may be prejudicial to the king, is, that all the evidences here, will be foreknown before they come to the main trial upon issue by the petty jury; then if there be not a very great deal of care, these witnesses may be confronted by raising up witnesses to prejudice them, as in some cases it has been: Then besides, the jury do apprehend, that in private they are more free to examine things in particular, for the satisfying their own consciences, and that without favour or affection; and we hope we shall do our duty.

[PEMBERTON,] L.C.J. . . . [T]he king's counsel have examined whether he hath cause to accuse these persons, or not; and, gentlemen, they understand very well, that it will be no prejudice to the king to have the evidence heard openly in court; or else the king would never desire it.

Foreman. My lord, the gentlemen of the jury desire that it may be recorded, that we insisted upon it as our right; but if the court over-rule, we must submit to it.

Howell's State Trials, vol. 8, pp. 759, 771–74.

7.3.2.2 Respublica v. Shaffer, 1788

AFTER some conversation with the Grand Inquest, the Attorney General informed the court, that a list of eleven persons had been presented to him by the Foreman, with a request, that they might be qualified and sent to the jury, as witnesses upon a bill then depending before them. He stated that the list had been made out by the defendant's bail: that the persons named were intended to furnish testimony in favor of the party charged, upon facts with which the Inquest, of their own knowledge, were unacquainted; and he concluded with requesting, that the opinion of the court might be given upon this application. THE CHIEF JUSTICE, accordingly, addressed the Grand Jury to the following effect:

MCKEAN, *Chief Justice.* — Were the proposed examination of witnesses, on the part of the Defendant, to be allowed, the long-established rules of law and justice would be at an end. It is a matter well known, and well understood, that by the laws of our country, every question which affects a man's life, reputation, or property, must be tried by *twelve* of his peers; and that their *unanimous* verdict is, alone, competent to determine the fact in issue. If, then, you undertake to inquire, not only upon what foundation the charge is made, but, likewise, upon what foundation it is denied, you will, in effect, usurp the jurisdiction of the Petit Jury, you will supersede the legal authority of the court, in judging of the competency and admissibility of witnesses, and, having thus undertaken to try the question, that question may be determined by a bare majority, or by a much greater number of your body, than the twelve peers prescribed by the law of the land. This point has, I believe, excited some doubts upon former occasions; but those doubts have never arisen in the mind of any lawyer, and they may easily be removed by a proper consideration of the subject. For, the bills, or presentments, found by a grand Jury, amount to nothing more than an official accusation, in order to put the party accused upon his trial; 'till the bill is returned, there is, therefore, no charge from which he can be required to exculpate himself; and we know that many persons, against whom bills were returned, have been afterwards acquitted by a verdict of their country. Here, then, is the just line of discrimination: It is the duty of the Grand-Jury to enquire into the nature and probable grounds of the charge; but it is the exclusive province of the Petit Jury, to hear and determine, with the assistance, and under the direction of the court, upon points of law, whether the Defendant is, or is not guilty, on the whole evidence, for, as well as against, him. —— You will therefore, readily perceive, that if you examine the witnesses on both sides, you do not confine your consideration to the probable grounds of charge, but engage completely in the trial of the cause; and your return must, consequently, be tantamount to a verdict of acquittal or condemnation. But this would involve us in another difficulty; for, by the law, it is declared, that no man shall be twice put in jeopardy for the same offence: and, yet, it is certain, that the enquiry now proposed by the Grand Jury, would necessarily introduce the oppression of a double trial. Nor is it merely upon maxims of law, but, I think, likewise, upon principles of humanity, that this innovation should be opposed. Considering the bill as an accusation grounded entirely upon the testimony in support of the prosecution, the Petit Jury receive no biass [*sic*] from the sanction which the indorsement of the Grand Jury has conferred upon it.—But, on the other hand, would it not, in some degree, prejudice the most upright mind against the Defendant, that on a full hearing of his defence, another tribunal had pronounced it insufficient? — which would then be the natural inference from every *true bill*. Upon the whole, the court is of opinion, that it would be improper and illegal to examine the witnesses, on behalf of the Defendant, while the charge against him lies before the Grand-Jury.

One of the Grand Inquest then observed to the court, that "there was a clause in the qualifications of the Jurors, upon which he, and some of his brethren, wished to hear the interpretation of the Judges—to wit—what is the legal acceptation of the words *"diligently to enquire?"* To this the CHIEF JUSTICE replied, that "the expression meant, *diligently to enquire* into the circumstances of the charge, the credibility of the witnesses who support it, and, from the whole, to judge whether the person accused ought to be put upon his trial. For, (he added), though it would be improper to determine the merits of the cause, it is incumbent upon the Grand Jury to satisfy their minds, by a *diligent enquiry,* that there is a probable ground for the accusation, before they give it their authority, and call upon the Defendant to make a public defence."

1 Dall. 236 (Pa. O. & T., 1788).

Chapter 8

AMENDMENT V
DOUBLE JEOPARDY CLAUSE

8.1 TEXTS

8.1.1 DRAFTS IN FIRST CONGRESS

8.1.1.1 Proposal by Madison in House, June 8, 1789

8.1.1.1.a   Fourthly. That in article 1st, section 9, between clauses 3 and 4 [of the Constitution], be inserted these clauses, to wit, . . .

. . .

No person shall be subject, except in cases of impeachment, to more than one punishment, or one trial for the same offence; nor shall be compelled to be a witness against himself; nor be deprived of life, liberty, or property without due process of law; nor be obliged to relinquish his property, where it may be necessary for public use, without a just compensation.

Congressional Register, June 8, 1789, vol. 1, pp. 427–28.

8.1.1.1.b   *Fourthly*. That in article 1st, section 9, between clauses 3 and 4 [of the Constitution], be inserted these clauses, to wit: . . .

. . .

No person shall be subject, except in cases of impeachment, to more than one punishment, or one trial for the same offence; nor shall be compelled to be a witness against himself; nor be deprived of life, liberty, or property without due process of law; nor be obliged to relinquish his property, where it may be necessary for public use, without a just compensation.   Daily Advertiser, June 12, 1789, p. 2, col. 1.

8.1.1.1.c   *Fourth*. That in article 1st, section 9, between clauses 3 and 4 [of the Constitution], be inserted these clauses, to wit: . . .

. . .

No person shall be subject, except in cases of impeachment, to more than one punishment, or one trial for the same offence; nor shall be compelled to be a witness against himself; nor be deprived of life, liberty, or property without due process of law; nor be obliged to relinquish his property, where it may be necessary for public use, without a just compensation.

New-York Daily Gazette, June 13, 1789, p. 574, col. 3.

8.1.1.2 House Committee of Eleven Report, July 28, 1789

ART. I, SEC. 9 — Between PAR. 2 and 3 insert,
. . .

"No person shall be subject, except in case of impeachment, to more than one trial or one punishment for the same offence, nor shall be compelled to be a witness against himself, nor be deprived of life, liberty, or property without due process of law; nor shall private property be taken for public use without just compensation."

Broadside Collection, DLC.

8.1.1.3 House Consideration, August 17, 1789

8.1.1.3.a   The 5th clause of the 4th proposition was taken up, viz. "no person shall be subject, [*sic; except*] in case of impeachment, to more than one trial or one punishment for the same offence, nor shall be compelled to be a witness against himself, nor be deprived of life, liberty or property, without due process of law, nor shall private property be taken for public use without just compensation."

Congressional Register, August 17, 1789, vol. 2, p. 224.

8.1.1.3.b   Eighth Amendment — "No person shall be subject, except in case of impeachment, to more than one trial or one punishment for the same offence, nor shall be compelled to be a witness against himself, nor be deprived of life, liberty or property, without due process of law, nor shall private property be taken for public use without just compensation."

Daily Advertiser, August 18, 1789, p. 2, col. 4.

8.1.1.3.c   Eighth Amendment — "No person shall be subject, except in case of impeachment, to more than one trial or one punishment for the same offence, nor shall be compelled to be a witness against himself, nor be deprived of life, liberty or property, without due process of law, nor shall private property be taken for public use without just compensation."

New-York Daily Gazette, August 19, 1789, p. 802, col. 4.

8.1.1.3.d   8th Amendment. "No person shall be subject, except in case of impeachment, to more than one trial for the same offence, nor shall be compelled to be a witness against himself, nor be deprived of life, liberty or property, without due process of law, nor shall private property be taken for public use without just compensation."

Gazette of the U.S., August 22, 1789, p. 249, col. 3.

8.1.1.4 Motion by Benson in House, August 17, 1789

8.1.1.4.a   Mr. BENSON
[H]e would move to amend it by striking out the words "one trial or."

Congressional Register, August 17, 1789, vol. 2, p. 224
("was lost by a considerable majority").

8.1.1.4.b   Mr. BENSON moved to strike out the words "One trial or"

Daily Advertiser, August 18, 1789, p. 2, col. 4.
("This was negatived.").

8.1.1.4.c   Mr. Benson moved to strike out the words "one trial or."

New-York Daily Gazette, August 19, 1789, p. 802, col. 4.
("This was negatived").

8.1.1.4.d   Mr. BENSON . . . moved to strike out the words "one trial or"

Gazette of the U.S., August 22, 1789, p. 249, col. 3
("This was negatived.").

8.1.1.5   Motion by Partridge in House, August 17, 1789

8.1.1.5.a   Mr. PARTRIDGE moved to insert after "same offence," the words, "by any law of the United States;" . . .

Congressional Register, August 17, 1789, vol. 2, p. 225
("this amendment was lost also").

8.1.1.5.b   Mr. PARTRIDGE moved to insert after the words "same offence," the words "by any law of the United States," Resolved in the negative.

Daily Advertiser, August 18, 1789, p. 2, col. 4.

8.1.1.5.c   Mr. Partridge moved to insert after the words "same offence," the words "by any law of the United States." New-York Daily Gazette, August 19, 1789, p. 802, col. 4
("Resolved in the negative.").

8.1.1.5.d   Mr. PARTRIDGE moved to insert after the words "same offence," the words *by any law of the United States,* . . .

Gazette of the U.S., August 22, 1789, p. 249,
col. 3 ("Negatived").

8.1.1.6   Motion by Lawrance in House, August 17, 1789

8.1.1.6.a   Mr. LAWRANCE

[H]e thought it [the clause] ought to be confined to criminal cases, and moved an amendment for that purpose, . . .

Congressional Register, August 17, 1789, vol. 2, p. 225
("which amendment being adopted, the clause as amended
was unanimously agreed to by the committee").

8.1.1.6.b   Mr. LAWRANCE moved to insert after the words "nor shall" these words "in any criminal case."

Daily Advertiser, August 18, 1789, p. 2, col. 4
("This amendment was agreed to.").

8.1.1.6.c   Mr. Lawrance moved to insert after the words "nor shall," these words, "in any criminal case."

New-York Daily Gazette, August 19, 1789, p. 802, col. 4
("This amendment was agreed to").

8.1.1.6.d   Mr. LAURANCE moved to insert after the words "nor shall" these words *in any criminal case.*

Gazette of the U.S., August 22, 1789, p. 249, col. 3
("This amendment was agreed to").

8.1.1.7   Further House Consideration, August 21, 1789

Seventh. No person shall be subject, except in case of impeachment, to more than one trial or one punishment for the same offence; nor shall he be compelled

in any criminal case to be a witness against himself; nor be deprived to life, liberty or property, without due process of law; nor shall private property be taken for public use, without just compensation.

HJ, p. 107 ("read and debated . . . agreed to by the House, . . . two-thirds of the members present concurring").[1]

8.1.1.8 House Resolution, August 24, 1789

ARTICLE THE EIGHTH.

No person shall be subject, except in case of impeachment, to more than one trial, or one punishment for the same offence, nor shall be compelled in any criminal case, to be a witness against himself, nor be deprived to life, liberty or property, without due process of law; nor shall private property be taken for public use without just compensation.

House Pamphlet, RG 46, DNA.

8.1.1.9 Senate Consideration, August 25, 1789

8.1.1.9.a   The Resolve of the House of Representatives of the 24th of August, upon certain "Articles to be proposed to the Legislatures of the several States as Amendments to the Constitution of the United States" was read as followeth:

. . .

Article the Eighth

"No person shall be subject, except in case of Impeachment, to more than one Trial, or one punishment for the same offence, nor shall be compelled in any Criminal case, to be a witness against himself, nor be deprived to life, liberty, or property, without due process of law; nor shall private property be taken for public use without just compensation.

Rough SJ, p. 217.

8.1.1.9.b   The Resolve of the House of Representatives of the 24th of August, was read as followeth:

. . .

"Article the Eighth.

No person shall be subject, except in case of impeachment, to more than one trial, or one punishment for the same offence, nor shall be compelled in any criminal case, to be a witness against himself, nor be deprived to life, liberty or property, without due process of law; nor shall private property be taken for public use without just compensation.

Smooth SJ, p. 195.

"ARTICLE THE EIGHTH.

8.1.1.9.c   The Resolve of the House of Representatives of the 24th of August, was read as followeth:

. . .

---

[1]On August 22, 1789, the following motion was agreed to:
ORDERED, That it be referred to a committee of three, to prepare and report a proper arrangement of, and introduction to the articles of amendment to the Constitution of the United States, as agreed to by the House; and that Mr. Benson, Mr. Sherman, and Mr. Sedgwick be of the said committee.

HJ, p. 112.

"No person shall be subject, except in case of impeachment, to more than one trial, or one punishment for the same offence, nor shall be compelled in any criminal case, to be a witness against himself, nor be deprived to life, liberty or property, without due process of law; nor shall private property be taken for public use without just compensation.   Printed SJ, p. 105.

8.1.1.10   Further Senate Consideration, September 4, 1789

8.1.1.10.a   On Motion to adopt the eighth Article of amendments proposed by the House of Representatives, striking out these words "Except in case of impeachment to more than one trial or one punishment" and substitute the following words.
"Be twice put in jeopardy of life or limb by any public prosecution."
                    Rough SJ, p. 249 ("It passed in the affirmative.").

8.1.1.10.b   On motion, To adopt the eighth article of Amendments proposed by the House of Representatives, striking out these words, — "Except in case of impeachment to more than one trial or one punishment," and substitute the following words —
"Be twice put in jeopardy of life or limb by any public prosecution" —
                    Smooth SJ, p. 222 ("It passed in the Affirmative.").

8.1.1.10.c   On motion, To adopt the eighth Article of Amendments proposed by the House of Representatives, striking out these words, — "Except in case of impeachment to more than one trial or one punishment," and substitute the following words —
"Be twice put in jeopardy of life or limb by any public prosecution" —
                    Printed SJ, p. 119 ("It passed in the Affirmative.").

8.1.1.10.d   that the Senate do
          Resolved ~~to~~ /\ concur with the House of Representatives in
                          Article eighth
          ~~by~~ striking out these words. "Except in cases of impeachment to more than one
                                ing
          trial or one punishment," and substitute /\ the following words;
          "Be twice put in jeopardy of life or limb by any public prosecution."
                    Senate MS, p. 3, RG 46, DNA.

8.1.1.11   Further Senate Consideration, September 9, 1789

8.1.1.11.a   On motion, To alter Article 6th so as to stand Article 5th, and Article 7th so as to stand Article 6th, and Article 8th so as to stand Article 7th

          . . .

On motion, That this last mentioned Article be amended to read as follows: "No person shall be held to answer for a capital or otherwise infamous crime, unless on a presentment or indictment of a grand Jury, except in cases arising in the land or naval forces, or in the Militia, when in actual service, in time of war or public danger, nor shall any person be subject to be put in jeopardy of life or limb, for the same offence, nor shall be compelled in any criminal case to be a witness against himself, nor be deprived of life, liberty or property, without due process of law; Nor shall private property be taken for public use without just compensation."

Rough SJ, p. 275 ("It passed in the affirmative.").

8.1.1.11.b On motion, To alter article the sixth so as to stand article the fifth, and article the seventh so as to stand article the sixth, and article the eighth so as to stand article the seventh —

. . .

On motion, That this last mentioned article be amended to read as follows: "No person shall be held to answer for a capital or otherwise infamous crime, unless on a presentment or indictment of a Grand Jury, except in cases arising in the land or naval forces, or in the militia, when in actual service, in time of war or public danger, nor shall any person be subject to be put in jeopardy of life or limb, for the same offence, nor shall be compelled in any criminal case to be a witness against himself, nor be deprived of life, liberty or property, without due process of law: Nor shall private property be taken for public use without just compensation" —

Smooth SJ, p. 244 ("It passed in the Affirmative.").

8.1.1.11.c On motion, To alter Article the sixth so as to stand Article the fifth, and Article the seventh so as to stand Article the sixth, and Article the eighth so as to stand Article the seventh —

. . .

On motion, That this last mentioned Article be amended to read as follows: "No person shall be held to answer for a capital or otherwise infamous crime, unless on a presentment or indictment of a Grand Jury, except in cases arising in the land or naval forces, or in the militia, when in actual service, in time of war or public danger, nor shall any person be subject to be put in jeopardy of life or limb, for the same offence, nor shall be compelled in any criminal case to be a witness against himself, nor be deprived of life, liberty or property, without due process of law: Nor shall private property be taken for public use without just compensation" —

Printed SJ, pp. 129–30 ("It passed in the Affirmative.").

8.1.1.11.d To erase the word "Eighth" & insert Seventh —
To insert in the ~~Eighth~~ 8th [7th] article ~~as~~ after the word "shall" in the "1" line — be held to answer for a capital or otherwise infamous crime, unless on a presentment or indictment of a grand Jury, except in cases arising in the land or naval forces, or in the militia when in actual Service in time of War or publick danger, nor shall any person — &
To erase from the same article the words "except in case of impeachment, to more than one trial or one punishment" & insert — to be twice put in jeopardy of life or limb —

Ellsworth MS, p. 3, RG 46, DNA.

8.1.1.12 **Senate Resolution, September 9, 1789**

ARTICLE THE SEVENTH.

No person shall be held to answer for a capital, or otherwise infamous crime, unless on a presentment or indictment of a Grand Jury, except in cases arising in the land or naval forces, or in the militia, when in actual service in time of war or public danger; nor shall any person be subject for the same offence to be twice put in jeopardy of life or limb; nor shall be compelled in any criminal case, to be a witness against himself, nor be deprived of life, liberty or property, without due process of law; nor shall private property be taken for public use without just compensation.

Senate Pamphlet, RG 46, DNA.

8.1.1.13　Further House Consideration, September 21, 1789

RESOLVED, That this House doth agree to the second, fourth, eighth, twelfth, thirteenth, sixteenth, eighteenth, nineteenth, twenty-fifth, and twenty-sixth amendments, and doth disagree to the first, third, fifth, sixth, seventh, ninth, tenth, eleventh, fourteenth, fifteenth, seventeenth, twentieth, twenty-first, twenty-second, twenty-third, and twenty-fourth amendments proposed by the Senate to the said articles, two thirds of the members present concurring on each vote.

RESOLVED, That a conference be desired with the Senate on the subject matter of the amendments disagreed to, and that Mr. Madison, Mr. Sherman, and Mr. Vining, be appointed managers at the same on the part of this House.

HJ, p. 146.

8.1.1.14　Further Senate Consideration, September 21, 1789

8.1.1.14.a　A message from the House of Representatives —

Mr. Beckley, their Clerk, brought up a Resolve of the House of this date, to agree to the 2nd, 4th, 8th, 12th, 13th, 16th, 18th, 19th, 25th, and 26th Amendments proposed by the Senate, "To articles of Amendment to be proposed to the Legislatures of the several States, as Amendments to the Constitution of the United States," and to disagree to the 1st, 3d, 5th, 6th, 7th, 9th, 10th, 11th, 14th, 15th, 17th, 20th, 21st, 22d, 23d, and 24th amendments: Two thirds of the members present concurring on each vote: And "That a conference be desired with the Senate on the subject matter of the amendments disagreed to," and that Mr. Madison, Mr. Sherman, and Mr. Vining, be appointed managers of the same, on the part of the House of Representatives —

And he withdrew.

Smooth SJ, pp. 265–66.

8.1.1.14.b　A message from the House of Representatives —

Mr. Beckley, their Clerk, brought up a Resolve of the House of this date, to agree to the 2d, 4th, 8th, 12th, 13th, 16th, 18th, 19th, 25th, and 26th Amendments proposed by the Senate, "To Articles of Amendment to be proposed to the Legislatures of the several States, as Amendments to the Constitution of the United States," and to disagree to the 1st, 3d, 5th, 6th, 7th, 9th, 10th, 11th, 14th, 15th, 17th, 20th, 21st, 22d, 23d, and 24th Amendments: Two thirds of the members present concurring on each vote: And "That a conference be desired with the Senate on the subject matter of the Amendments disagreed to," and that Mr. Madison, Mr. Sherman, and Mr. Vining, be appointed managers of the same, on the part of the House of Representatives —

And he withdrew.

Printed SJ, pp. 141–42.

8.1.1.15 Further Senate Consideration, September 21, 1789

8.1.1.15.a   The Senate proceeded to consider the Message of the House of Representatives disagreeing to the Amendments made by the Senate "To Articles to be proposed to the Legislatures of the several States, as Amendments to the Constitution of the United States" And

RESOLVED, That the Senate do recede from their third Amendment, and do insist on all the others.

RESOLVED, That the Senate do concur with the House of Representatives in a conference on the subject matter of disagreement on the said Articles of Amendment, and that Mr. Ellsworth Mr. Carroll and Mr. Paterson be managers of the conference on the part of the Senate.
Smooth SJ, p. 267.

8.1.1.15.b   The Senate proceeded to consider the message of the House of Representatives disagreeing to the Amendments made by the Senate "To Articles to be proposed to the Legislatures of the several States, as Amendments to the Constitution of the United States" — And

RESOLVED, That the Senate do recede from their third Amendment, and do insist on all the others.

RESOLVED, That the Senate do concur with the House of Representatives in a conference on the subject matter of disagreement on the said Articles of Amendment, and that Mr. Ellsworth, Mr. Carroll, and Mr. Paterson be managers of the conference on the part of the Senate.
Printed SJ, p. 142.

8.1.1.16 Conference Committee Report, September 24, 1789

[T]hat it will be proper for the House of Representatives to agree to the said Amendments proposed by the Senate, with an Amendment to their fifth Amendment, so that the third Article shall read as follows: "Congress shall make no Law respecting an establishment of Religion, or prohibiting the free exercise thereof; or abridging the freedom of Speech, or of the Press; or the right of the people peaceably to assemble and to petition the Government for a redress of grievances;" And with an Amendment to the fourteenth Amendment proposed by the Senate, so that the eighth Article, as numbered in the Amendments proposed by the Senate, shall read as follows "In all criminal prosecutions, the accused shall enjoy the right to a speedy & publick trial by an impartial jury of the district wherein the crime shall have been committed, as the district shall have been previously ascertained by law, and to be informed of the nature and cause of the accusation; to be confronted with the witnesses against him, and to have com

to

pulsory process for obtaining witnesses against him in his favour, & /\ have the assistance of counsel for his defence."
Conference MS, RG 46, DNA (Ellsworth's handwriting).

8.1.1.17 House Consideration of Conference Committee Report, September 24 [25], 1789

RESOLVED, That this House doth recede from their disagreement to the first, third, fifth, sixth, seventh, ninth, tenth, eleventh, fourteenth, fifteenth, seven-

teenth, twentieth, twenty-first, twenty-second, twenty-third, and twenty-fourth amendments, insisted on by the Senate: PROVIDED, That the two articles which by the amendments of the Senate are now proposed to be inserted as the third and eighth articles, shall be amended to read as followeth;

Article the third. "Congress shall make no law respecting an establishment of religion, or prohibiting the free exercise thereof; or abridging the freedom of speech, or of the press; or the right of the people peaceably to assemble, and to petition the government for a redress of grievances."

Article the eighth. "In all criminal prosecutions, the accused shall enjoy the right to a speedy and public trial by an impartial jury of the state and district wherein the crime shall have been committed, which district shall have been previously ascertained by law, and to be informed of the nature and cause of the accusation, to be confronted with the witnesses against him, to have compulsory process for obtaining witnesses in his favor, and to have the assistance of council for his defence."

HJ, p. 152 ("On the question, that the House do agree to the alteration and amendment of the eighth article, in manner aforesaid, It was resolved in the affirmative. Ayes 37 Noes 14").

8.1.1.18   Senate Consideration of Conference Committee Report, September 24, 1789

8.1.1.18.a   Mr. Ellsworth, on behalf of the managers of the conference on "articles to be proposed to the several States as Amendments to the Constitution of the United States," reported as follows:

That it will be proper for the House of Representatives to agree to the said amendments proposed by the Senate, with an Amendment to their fifth Amendment, so that the third Article shall read as follows: "Congress shall make no law respecting an establishment of <u>Religion</u>, or prohibiting the free exercise thereof; or abridging the freedom of <u>Speech</u>, or of the <u>Press</u>; or the right of the people peaceably to assemble and petition the Government for a redress of <u>Grievances</u>;" And with an Amendment to the fourteenth Amendment proposed by the Senate, so that the eighth article, as numbered in the Amendments proposed by the Senate, shall read as follows; "In all criminal prosecutions, the accused shall enjoy the right to a speedy and public trial by an impartial <u>Jury</u> of the district wherein the <u>Crime</u> shall have been committed, as the district shall have been previously ascertained by law, and to be informed of the nature and cause of the accusation, to be confronted with the witnesses against him, and to have compulsory process for obtaining witnesses in his favor, and to have the assistance of Counsel for defence."

Smooth SJ, pp. 272–73.

8.1.1.18.b   Mr. Ellsworth, on behalf of the managers of the conference on "Articles to be proposed to the several States as Amendments to the Constitution of the United States," reported as follows:

That it will be proper for the House of Representatives to agree to the said Amendments proposed by the Senate, with an Amendment to their fifth Amendment, so that the third Article shall read as follows: "Congress shall make no Law RESPECTING AN ESTABLISHMENT OF RELIGION, or prohibiting the free exercise thereof; or abridging the freedom of Speech, or of the Press; or the right of the

People peaceably to assemble and petition the Government for a redress of Grievances;" And with an Amendment to the fourteenth Amendment proposed by the Senate, so that the eighth Article, as numbered in the Amendments proposed by the Senate, shall read as follows; "In all criminal prosecutions, the accused shall enjoy the right to a speedy and public trial BY AN IMPARTIAL JURY OF THE DISTRICT WHEREIN THE CRIME SHALL HAVE BEEN COMMITTED, AS THE DISTRICT SHALL HAVE BEEN PREVIOUSLY ASCERTAINED BY LAW, and to be informed of the nature and cause of the accusation, to be confronted with the witnesses against him, and to have compulsory process for obtaining witnesses in his favor, and to have the assistance of Counsel for defence."

Printed SJ, p. 145.

8.1.1.19 Further Senate Consideration of Conference Committee Report, September 24, 1789

8.1.1.19.a   A Message from the House of Representatives —

Mr. Beckley, their Clerk, brought up the Amendments to the "Articles to be proposed to the Legislatures of the several States, as Amendments to the Constitution of the United States;" and informed the Senate, that the House of Representatives had receded from their disagreement to the 1st, 3d, 5th, 6th, 7th, 9th, 10th, 11th, 14th, 15th, 17th, 20th, 21st, 22d, 23d, and 24th Amendments, insisted on by the Senate: Provided that the "Two Articles, which by the Amendments of the Senate are now proposed to be inserted as the third and eighth Articles," shall be amended to read as followeth:

Article the Third. "Congress shall make no Law respecting an establishment of Religion, or prohibiting the free exercise thereof; or abridging the freedom of Speech, or of the Press; or the right of the people peaceably to assemble, and petition the Government for a redress of Grievances."

Article the Eighth. "In all criminal prosecutions the accused shall enjoy the right to a speedy and public trial by an impartial Jury of the State and District, wherein the crime shall have been committed, which District shall have been previously ascertained by law, and to be informed of the nature and cause of the accusation, to be confronted with the witnesses against him, and to have compulsory process for obtaining witnesses in his favor, and to have the assistance of Counsel for his defence."

Smooth SJ, pp. 278–79.

8.1.1.19.b   A Message from the House of Representatives —

Mr. Beckley, their Clerk, brought up the Amendments to the "Articles to be proposed to the Legislatures of the several States, as Amendments to the Constitution of the United States;" and informed the Senate, that the House of Representatives had receded from their disagreement to the 1st, 3d, 5th, 6th, 7th, 9th, 10th, 11th, 14th, 15th, 17th, 20th, 21st, 22d, 23d, and 24th Amendments, insisted on by the Senate: Provided that the "Two Articles, which by the Amendments of the Senate are now proposed to be inserted as the third and eighth Articles," shall be amended to read as followeth:

Article the Third. "Congress shall make no Law respecting an establishment of Religion, or prohibiting the free exercise thereof; or abridging the freedom of

Speech, or of the Press; or the right of the People peaceably to assemble, and petition the Government for a redress of Grievances."

Article the Eighth. "In all criminal prosecutions the accused shall enjoy the right to a speedy and public trial by an impartial Jury of the State and District, wherein the crime shall have been committed, which District shall have been previously ascertained by law, and to be informed of the nature and cause of the accusation, to be confronted with the witnesses against him, and to have compulsory process for obtaining witnesses in his favor, and to have the assistance of Counsel for his defence."

Printed SJ, p.148.

8.1.1.20   Further Senate Consideration of Conference Committee Report, September 25, 1789

8.1.1.20.a   The Senate proceeded to consider the Message from the House of Representatives of the 24th, with Amendments to the Amendments of the Senate, to "Articles to be proposed to the Legislatures of the several States, as Amendments to the Constitution of the United States" — And

RESOLVED, That the Senate do concur in the Amendments proposed by the House of Representatives, to the Amendments of the Senate.

Smooth SJ, p. 283.

8.1.1.20.b   The Senate proceeded to consider the Message from the House of Representatives of the 24th, with Amendments to the Amendments of the Senate, to "Articles to be proposed to the Legislatures of the several States, as Amendments to the Constitution of the United States" — And

RESOLVED, That the Senate do concur in the Amendments proposed by the House of Representatives, to the Amendments of the Senate.

Printed SJ, pp. 150–51.

8.1.1.21   Agreed Resolution, September 25, 1789

8.1.1.21.a   Article the Seventh.

No person shall be held to answer for a capital, or otherwise infamous crime, unless on a presentment or indictment of a Grand Jury, except in cases arising in the land or naval forces, or in the militia, when in actual service in time of war or public danger; nor shall any person be subject for the same offence to be twice put in jeopardy of life or limb; nor shall be compelled in any criminal case, to be a witness against himself, nor be deprived of life, liberty or property, without due process of law; nor shall private property be taken for public use without just compensation.

Smooth SJ, Appendix, p. 293.

8.1.1.21.b   ARTICLE THE SEVENTH.

No person shall be held to answer for a capital, or otherwise infamous crime, unless on a presentment or indictment of a Grand Jury, except in cases arising in the land or naval forces, or in the militia, when in actual service in time of war or public danger; nor shall any person be subject for the same offence to be twice put in jeopardy of life or limb; nor shall be compelled in any criminal case, to be a witness against himself, nor be deprived of life, liberty or property, without due

process of law; nor shall private property be taken for public use without just compensation.

Printed SJ, Appendix, p. 164.

8.1.1.22 Enrolled Resolution, September 28, 1789

Article the seventh . . . No person shall be held to answer for a capital, or otherwise infamous crime, unless on a presentment or indictment of a Grand Jury, except in cases arising in the land or naval forces, or in the militia, when in actual service in time of war or public danger; nor shall any person be subject for the same offence to be twice put in jeopardy of life or limb, nor shall be compelled in any criminal case, to be a witness against himself, nor be deprived of life, liberty, or property, without due process of law; nor shall private property be taken for public use without just compensation.

Enrolled Resolutions, RG 11, DNA.

8.1.1.23 Printed Versions

8.1.1.23.a   ART. V. No person shall be held to answer for a capital or otherwise infamous crime, unless on a presentment or indictment of a grand jury, except in cases arising in the land or naval forces, or in the militia, when in actual service, in time of war or public danger; nor shall any person be subject for the same offence to be twice put in jeopardy of life or limb; nor shall be compelled, in any criminal case, to be witness against himself; nor be deprived of life, liberty, or property, without due process of law; nor shall private property be taken for public use without just compensation.

Statutes at Large, vol. 1, p. 21.

8.1.1.23.b   ART. VII. No person shall be held to answer for a capital, or otherwise infamous crime, unless on a presentment or indictment of a grand jury, except in cases arising in the land or naval forces, or in the militia when in actual service in time of war or public danger; nor shall any person be subject for the same offence to be twice put in jeopardy of life or limb; nor shall be compelled in any criminal case to be a witness against himself, nor be deprived of life, liberty or property, without due process of law; nor shall private property be taken for public use without just compensation.

Statutes at Large, vol. 1, p. 98.

8.1.2 PROPOSALS FROM THE STATE CONVENTIONS

8.1.2.1 Maryland Minority, April 26, 1788

2. That there shall be a trial by jury in all criminal cases, according to the course of proceeding in the state where the offence is committed; and that there be no appeal from matter of fact, or second trial after acquittal; but that this provision shall not extend to such cases as may arise in the government of the land or naval forces.

Maryland Gazette, May 1, 1788 (committee majority).

8.1.2.2 New York, July 26, 1788

That no Person ought to be put twice in Jeopardy of Life or Limb for one and the same Offence, nor, unless in case of impeachment, be punished more than once for the same Offence.

State Ratifications, RG 11, DNA.

8.1.3 STATE CONSTITUTIONS AND LAWS; COLONIAL CHARTERS AND LAWS

8.1.3.1 **Massachusetts: Body of Liberties, 1641**

[42] No man shall be twise sentenced by Civill Justice for one and the same Crime, offence, or Trespasse.

Massachusetts Colonial Laws, p. 43.

8.1.3.2 **New Hampshire: Constitution, 1783**

[Part I, Article] XVI. No subject shall be liable to be tried, after an acquittal, for the same crime or offence. — Nor shall the legislature make any law that shall subject any person to a capital punishment, excepting for the government of the army and navy, and the militia in actual service, without trial by jury.

New Hampshire Laws, p. 25.

8.1.3.3 **North Carolina: Fundamental Constitutions of Carolina, 1669**

64th. No cause shall be twice tried in any one court, upon any reason or pretence whatsoever.

North Carolina State Records, p. 144.

8.1.3.4 **Pennsylvania: Constitution, 1790**

ARTICLE IX

. . .

Sect. X. That no person shall, for any indictable offence, be proceeded against criminally by information, except in cases arising in the land or naval forces, or in the militia, when in actual service in time of war or public danger, or, by leave of the court, for oppression and misdemeanor in office. No person shall, for the same offence, be twice put in jeopardy of life or limb; nor shall any man's property be taken or applied to public use, without the consent of his representatives, and without just compensation being made.

Pennsylvania Acts, Dallas, pp. xxiv–xxxv.

8.1.4 OTHER TEXTS

None.

8.2 DISCUSSION OF DRAFTS AND PROPOSALS

8.2.1 THE FIRST CONGRESS

8.2.1.1 **June 8, 1789**[2]

8.2.1.2 **August 17, 1789**

8.2.1.2.a The 5th clause of the 4th proposition was taken up, viz. "no person shall be subject, in case of impeachment, to more than one trial or one punishment for the same offence, nor shall be compelled to be a witness against himself, nor be deprived of life, liberty or property, without due process of law, nor shall private property be taken for public use without just compensation."

[2]For the reports of Madison's speech in support of his proposals, *see* 1.2.1.1.a–c.

MR. BENSON

Thought the committee could not agree to the amendment in the manner it stood, because its meaning, appeared rather doubtful, it says that no person shall be tried more than once for the same offence, this is contrary to the right heretofore established, he presumed it was intended to express what was secured by our former constitution, that no man's life should be more than once put in jeopardy for the same offence, yet it was well known, that they were intitled to more than one trial; the humane intention of the clause was to prevent more than one punishment, for which reason he would move to amend it by striking out the words "one trial or."

MR. SHERMAN

Approved of the motion, he said, that as the clause now stood, a person found guilty could not arrest the judgment, and obtain a second trial in his own favor, he thought that the courts of justice would never think of trying and punishing twice for the same offence, if the person was acquitted on the first trial, he ought not to be tried a second time, but if he was convicted on the first, and anything should appear to set the judgement aside, he was intitled to a second, which was certainly favorable to him. Now the clause as it stands would deprive him of this advantage.

MR. LIVERMORE

Thought the clause very essential, it was declaratory of the law as it now stood, striking out the words, would seem as if they meant to change the law by implication, and expose a man to the danger of more than one trial; many persons may be brought to trial for crimes they are guilty of, but for want of evidence may be acquitted; in such cases it is the universal practice in Great-Britain, and in this country, that persons shall not be brought to a second trial for the same offence, therefore the clause is proper as it stands.

Mr. SEDGWICK thought, instead of securing the liberty of the subject, it would be abridging the privileges of those who were prosecuted.

The question on Mr. Benson's motion being put, was lost by a considerable majority.

Mr. PARTRIDGE moved to insert after "same offence," the words, "by any law of the United States;" this amendment was lost also.

Congressional Register, August 17, 1789, vol. 2, pp. 224–25.

8.2.1.2.b   Eighth Amendment — "No person shall be subject, except in case of impeachment, to more than one trial or one punishment for the same offence, nor shall be compelled to be a witness against himself, nor be deprived of life, liberty or property, without due process of law, nor shall private property be taken for public use without just compensation."

Mr. BENSON moved to strike out the words "One trial or"

This was negatived.

Mr. PARTRIDGE moved to insert after the words "same offence," the words "by any law of the United States," Resolved in the negative.

Mr. LAWRANCE moved to insert after the words "nor shall" these words "in any criminal case." This amendment was agreed to.

Daily Advertiser, August 18, 1789, p. 2, col. 4.

8.2.1.2.c   Eighth amendment — "No person shall be subject, except in case of impeachment, to more than one trial or one punishment for the same offence, nor shall be compelled to be a witness against himself, nor be deprived of life, liberty or property, without due process of law, nor shall private property be taken for public use without just compensation."

Mr. Benson moved to strike out the words "one trial or."

This was negatived.

Mr. Partridge moved to insert after the words "same offence," the words "by any law of the United States." Resolved in the negative.

Mr. Lawrance moved to insert after the words "nor shall," these words, "in any criminal case."

This amendment was agreed to.

New-York Daily Gazette, August 19, 1789, p. 802, col. 4.

8.2.1.2.d   8th Amendment. "No person shall be subject, except in case of impeachment, to more than one trial for the same offence, nor shall be compelled to be a witness against himself, nor be deprived of life, liberty or property, without due process of law, nor shall private property be taken for public use without just compensation."

Mr. BENSON observed, that it was certainly a fact, that a person might be tried more than once for the same offence: Instances of this kind frequently occured. He therefore moved to strike out the words "one trial or" This was negatived.

Mr. SHERMAN was in favor of the motion.

Mr. LIVERMORE was opposed to it: He said: The clause appears to me essential; if it is struck out, it will hold up the idea that a person may be tried more than once for the same offence. Some instances of this kind have taken place; but they have caused great uneasiness: It is contrary to the usages of law and practice among us; and so it is to those of that country from which we have adopted our laws. I hope the clause will not be struck out.

Mr. PARTRIDGE moved to insert after the words "same offence," the words *by any law of the United States,"* Negatived.

Mr. LAURANCE moved to insert after the words "nor shall" these words *in any criminal case.* This amendment was agreed to.

Gazette of the U.S., August 22, 1789, p. 249, col. 3.

8.2.2 STATE CONVENTIONS

None.

8.2.3 PHILADELPHIA CONVENTION

None.

8.2.4 NEWSPAPERS AND PAMPHLETS

None.

8.2.5 LETTERS AND DIARIES

None.

8.3 DISCUSSION OF RIGHTS
8.3.1 TREATISES

8.3.1.1 William Blackstone, 1769

IV. SPECIAL pleas in *bar;* which go to the merits of the indictment, and give a reason why the prisoner ought not to answer it at all, nor put himself upon his trial for the crime alleged. These are of four kinds: a former acquittal, a former conviction, a former attainder, or a pardon. There are many other pleas, which may be pleaded in bar of an appeal: but these are applicable to both appeals and indictments.

1. FIRST, the plea of *auterfoits acquit,* or a former acquittal, is grounded on this universal maxim of the common law of England, that no man is to be brought into jeopardy of his life, more than once, for the same offence. And hence it is allowed as a consequence, that when a man is once fairly found not guilty upon any indictment, or other prosecution, he may plead such acquittal in bar of any subsequent accusation for the same crime. Therefore an acquittal on an appeal is a good bar to an indictment of the same offence. And so also was an acquittal on an indictment a good bar to an appeal, by the common law: and therefore, in favour of appeals, a general practice was introduced, not to try any person on an indictment of homicide, till after the year and day, within which appeals may be brought, were past; by which time it often happened that the witnesses died, or the whole was forgotten. To remedy which inconvenience, the statute 3 Hen. VII. c. 1. enacts, that indictments shall be proceeded on, immediately, at the king's suit, for the death of a man, without waiting for bringing an appeal; and that the plea, of *auterfoits acquit* on an indictment, shall be no bar to the prosecuting of any appeal.

2. SECONDLY, the plea of *auterfoits convict,* or a former conviction for the same identical crime, though no judgment was ever given, or perhaps will be, (being suspended by the benefit of clergy or other causes) is a good plea in bar to an indictment. And this depends upon the same principle as the former, that no man ought to be twice brought in danger of his life for one and the same crime. Hereupon it has been held, that a conviction of manslaughter, on an appeal, is a bar even in another appeal, and much more in an indictment, of murder; for the fact prosecuted is the same in both, though the offences differ in colouring and in degree. It is to be observed, that the pleas of *auterfoits acquit,* and *auterfoits convict,* or a former acquittal, and former conviction, must be upon a prosecution for the same identical act and crime. But the case is otherwise, in

3. THIRDLY, the plea of *auterfoits attaint,* or former attainder; which is a good plea in bar, whether it be for the same or any other felony. For wherever a man is attainted of felony, by judgment of death either upon a verdict or confession, by outlawry, or heretofore by abjuration; and whether upon an appeal or an indictment; he may plead such attainder in bar to any subsequent indictment or appeal, for the same or for any other felony. And this because, generally, such proceeding on a second prosecution cannot be to any purpose; for the prisoner is dead in law by the first attainder, his blood is already corrupted, and he hath forfeited all that he had: so that it is absurd and superfluous to endeavour to attaint him a second

time. But to this general rule however, as to all others, there are some exceptions; wherein, *cessante ratione, cessat et ipsa lex*. As, 1. Where the former attainder is reversed for error, for then it is the same as if it had never been. And the same reason holds, where the attainder is reversed by parliament, or the judgment vacated by the king's pardon, with regard to felonies committed afterwards. 2. Where the attainder was upon indictment, such attainder is no bar to an appeal: for the prior sentence is pardonable by the king; and if that might be pleaded in bar of the appeal, the king might in the end defeat the suit of the subject, by suffering the prior sentence to stop the prosecution of a second, and then, when the time of appealing is elapsed, granting the delinquent a pardon. 3. An attainder in felony is no bar to an indictment of treason: because not only the judgment and manner of death are different, but the forfeiture is more extensive, and the land goes to different persons. 4. Where a person attainted of one felony, as robbery, is afterwards indicted as principal in another, as murder, to which there are also accessories, prosecuted at the same time; in this case it is held, that the plea of *auterfoit attaint* is no bar, but he shall be compelled to take his trial, for the sake of public justice: because the accessories to such second felony cannot be convicted till after the conviction of the principal. And from these instances we may collect that the plea of *auterfoits attaint* is never good, but when a second trial would be quite superfluous.

Commentaries, bk. 4, ch. 26, sec. 4; vol. 4, pp. 329–31
(footnotes omitted).

8.3.2 CASELAW

8.3.2.1 Respublica v. Shaffer, 1788

AFTER some conversation with the Grand Inquest, the Attorney General informed the court, that a list of eleven persons had been presented to him by the Foreman, with a request, that they might be qualified and sent to the jury, as witnesses upon a bill then depending before them. He stated that the list had been made out by the defendant's bail: that the persons named were intended to furnish testimony in favor of the party charged, upon facts with which the Inquest, of their own knowledge, were unacquainted; and he concluded with requesting, that the opinion of the court might be given upon this application. THE CHIEF JUSTICE, accordingly, addressed the Grand Jury to the following effect:

McKEAN, *Chief Justice*. — Were the proposed examination of witnesses, on the part of the Defendant, to be allowed, the long-established rules of law and justice would be at an end. It is a matter well known, and well understood, that by the laws of our country, every question which affects a man's life, reputation, or property, must be tried by *twelve* of his peers; and that their *unanimous* verdict is, alone, competent to determine the fact in issue. If, then, you undertake to inquire, not only upon what foundation the charge is made, but, likewise, upon what foundation it is denied, you will, in effect, usurp the jurisdiction of the Petit Jury, you will supersede the legal authority of the court, in judging of the competency and admissibility of witnesses, and, having thus undertaken to try the question, that question may be determined by a bare majority, or by a much greater number of your body, than the twelve peers prescribed by the law of the land. This point has, I believe, excited some doubts upon former occasions; but those doubts have never arisen in the mind of any lawyer, and they may easily be removed by a proper consideration of the subject. For, the bills, or presentments, found by a grand Jury, amount to nothing more than an official accusation, in order to put the party accused upon his trial; 'till the bill is returned, there is, therefore, no charge from which he can be required to exculpate himself; and we know that many persons, against whom bills were returned, have been afterwards acquitted by a verdict of their country. Here, then, is the just line of discrimination: It is the duty of the Grand-Jury to enquire into the nature and probable grounds of the charge; but it is the exclusive province of the Petit Jury, to hear and determine, with the assistance, and under the direction of the court, upon points of law, whether the Defendant is, or is not guilty, on the whole evidence, for, as well as against, him. —— You will therefore, readily perceive, that if you examine the witnesses on both sides, you do not confine your consideration to the probable grounds of charge, but engage completely in the trial of the cause; and your return must, consequently, be tantamount to a verdict of acquittal or condemnation. But this would involve us in another difficulty; for, by the law, it is declared, that no man shall be twice put in jeopardy for the same offence: and, yet, it is certain, that the enquiry now proposed by the Grand Jury, would necessarily introduce the oppression of a double trial. Nor is it merely upon maxims of law, but, I think, likewise, upon principles of humanity, that this innovation should be opposed. Considering the bill as an accusation grounded entirely upon the testimony in support of the prosecution, the Petit Jury receive no biass [*sic*] from the sanction which the indorsement of the Grand Jury has conferred upon it.—But, on the other hand, would it not, in some degree, prejudice the most upright mind against the Defendant, that on a full hearing of his defence, another tribunal had pronounced it insufficient? — which would then be the natural inference from every *true bill*. Upon the whole, the court is of opinion, that it would be improper and illegal to examine the witnesses, on behalf of the Defendant, while the charge against him lies before the Grand-Jury.

One of the Grand Inquest then observed to the court, that "there was a clause in the qualifications of the Jurors, upon which he, and some of his brethren, wished to hear the interpretation of the Judges—to wit—what is the legal acceptation of the words *"diligently to enquire?"* To this the CHIEF JUSTICE replied, that "the expression meant, *diligently to enquire* into the circumstances of the charge, the credibility of the witnesses who support it, and, from the whole, to judge whether the person accused ought to be put upon his trial. For, (he added), though it would be improper to determine the merits of the cause, it is incumbent upon the Grand Jury to satisfy their minds, by a *diligent enquiry,* that there is a probable ground for the accusation, before they give it their authority, and call upon the Defendant to make a public defence."

1 Dall. 236 (Pa. O. & T., 1788).

Chapter 9

AMENDMENT V
SELF-INCRIMINATION CLAUSE

9.1 TEXTS

9.1.1 DRAFTS IN FIRST CONGRESS

9.1.1.1 Proposal by Madison in House, June 8, 1789

9.1.1.1.a   Fourthly. That in article 1st, section 9, between clauses 3 and 4 [of the Constitution], be inserted these clauses, to wit, . . .

. . .

No person shall be subject, except in cases of impeachment, to more than one punishment, or one trial for the same offence; nor shall be compelled to be a witness against himself; nor be deprived of life, liberty, or property without due process of law; nor be obliged to relinquish his property, where it may be necessary for public use, without a just compensation.

Congressional Register, June 8, 1789, vol. 1, pp. 427–28.

9.1.1.1.b   *Fourthly.* That in article 1st, section 9, between clauses 3 and 4 [of the Constitution], be inserted these clauses, to wit: . . .

. . .

No person shall be subject, except in cases of impeachment, to more than one punishment, or one trial for the same offence; nor shall be compelled to be a witness against himself; nor be deprived of life, liberty, or property without due process of law; nor be obliged to relinquish his property, where it may be necessary for public use, without a just compensation.   Daily Advertiser, June 12, 1789, p. 2, col. 1.

9.1.1.1.c   *Fourth.* That in article 1st, section 9, between clauses 3 and 4, be inserted these clauses, to wit: . . .

. . .

No person shall be subject, except in cases of impeachment, to more than one punishment, or one trial for the same offence; nor shall be compelled to be a witness against himself; nor be deprived of life, liberty, or property without due process of law; nor be obliged to relinquish his property, where it may be necessary for public use, without a just compensation.

New-York Daily Gazette, June 13, 1789, p. 574, col. 3.

9.1.1.2 House Committee of Eleven Report, July 28, 1789

Art. i, Sec. 9 — Between Par. 2 and 3 insert,

. . .

"No person shall be subject, except in case of impeachment, to more than one trial or one punishment for the same offence, nor shall be compelled to be a witness against himself, nor be deprived of life, liberty, or property without due process of law; nor shall private property be taken for public use without just compensation."

Broadside Collection, DLC.

9.1.1.3 House Consideration, August 17, 1789

9.1.1.3.a   The 5th clause of the 4th proposition was taken up, viz. "no person shall be subject, [*sic;* except] in case of impeachment, to more than one trial or one punishment for the same offence, nor shall be compelled to be a witness against himself, nor be deprived of life, liberty or property, without due process of law, nor shall private property be taken for public use without just compensation."

Congressional Register, August 17, 1789, vol. 2, p. 224.

9.1.1.3.b   Eighth Amendment. "No person shall be subject, except in case of impeachment, to more than one trial or one punishment for the same offence, nor shall be compelled to be a witness against himself, nor be deprived of life, liberty or property, without due process of law, nor shall private property be taken for public use without just compensation."   Daily Advertiser, August 18, 1789, p. 2, col. 4.

9.1.1.3.c   Eighth Amendment — "No person shall be subject, except in case of impeachment, to more than one trial or one punishment for the same offence, nor shall be compelled to be a witness against himself, nor be deprived of life, liberty or property, without due process of law, nor shall private property be taken for public use without just compensation."

New-York Daily Gazette, August 19, 1789, p. 802, col. 4.

9.1.1.3.d   8th Amendment. "No person shall be subject, except in case of impeachment, to more than one trial for the same offence, nor shall be compelled to be a witness against himself, nor be deprived of life, liberty or property, without due process of law, nor shall private property be taken for public use without just compensation."

Gazette of the U.S., August 22, 1789, p. 249, col. 3.

9.1.1.4 Motion by Benson in House, August 17, 1789

9.1.1.4.a   Mr. Benson

[H]e would move to amend it by striking out the words "one trial or."

Congressional Register, August 17, 1789, vol. 2, p. 224
("was lost by a considerable majority").

9.1.1.4.b   Mr. Benson moved to strike out the words "One trial or."

Daily Advertiser, August 18, 1789, p. 2, col. 4
("This was negatived.").

9.1.1.4.c   Mr. Benson moved to strike out the words "one trial or."

New-York Daily Gazette, August 19, 1789, p. 802, col. 4
("This was negatived").

9.1.1.4.d   Mr. Benson . . . moved to strike out the words "one trial or."

Gazette of the U.S., August 22, 1789, p. 249, col. 3
("This was negatived.").

9.1.1.5 Motion by Partridge in House, August 17, 1789

9.1.1.5.a   Mr. Partridge moved to insert after "same offence," the words, "by any law of the United States;" . . . .

Congressional Register, August 17, 1789, vol. 2,
p. 225 ("this amendment was lost also").

9.1.1.5.b   Mr. Partridge moved to insert after the words "same offence," the words, "by any law of the United States," . . .

Daily Advertiser, August 18, 1789, p. 2, col. 4
("Resolved in the negative.").

9.1.1.5.c   Mr. Partridge moved to insert after the words "same offence," the words "by any law of the United States."

New-York Daily Gazette, August 19, 1789, p. 802, col. 4
("Resolved in the negative").

9.1.1.5.d   Mr. Partridge moved to insert after the words "same offence," the words *"by any law of the United States,"* . . .

Gazette of the U.S., August 22, 1789, p. 249, col. 3
("Negatived").

9.1.1.6 Motion by Lawrance in House, August 17, 1789

9.1.1.6.a   Mr. Lawrance

[H]e thought it [the clause] ought to be confined to criminal cases, and moved an amendment for that purpose. . . .

Congressional Register, August 17, 1789, vol. 2, p. 225
("which amendment being adopted, the clause as amended
was unanimously agreed to by the committee").

9.1.1.6.b   Mr. Lawrance moved to insert after the words "nor shall" these words "in any criminal case."

Daily Advertiser, August 18, 1789, p. 2, col. 4
("This amendment was agreed to.").

9.1.1.6.c   Mr. Lawrance moved to insert after the words "nor shall," these words, "in any criminal case."

New-York Daily Gazette, August 19, 1789, p. 802, col. 4
("This amendment was agreed to").

9.1.1.6.d   Mr. Laurance moved to insert after the words "nor shall" these words *in any criminal case.*

Gazette of the U.S., August 22, 1789, p. 249, col. 3
("This amendment was agreed to").

9.1.1.7 Further House Consideration, August 21, 1789

Seventh. No person shall be subject, except in case of impeachment, to more than one trial or one punishment for the same offence; nor shall he be compelled in any criminal case to be a witness against himself; nor be deprived to life, liberty or property, without due process of law; nor shall private property be taken for public use, without just compensation.

HJ, p. 107 ("read and debated . . . agreed to by the House, . . . two-thirds of the members present concurring").[1]

9.1.1.8 House Resolution, August 24, 1789

ARTICLE the EIGHTH.

No person shall be subject, except in case of impeachment, to more than one trial, or one punishment for the same offence, nor shall be compelled in any criminal case, to be a witness against himself, nor be deprived to life, liberty or property, without due process of law; nor shall private property be taken for public use without just compensation.

House Pamphlet, RG 46, DNA.

9.1.1.9 Senate Consideration, August 25, 1789

9.1.1.9.a   The Resolve of the House of Representatives of the 24th of August, upon certain "Articles to be proposed to the Legislatures of the several States as Amendments to the Constitution of the United States" was read as followeth:

. . .

Article the Eighth

No person shall be subject, except in case of Impeachment, to more than one Trial, or one punishment for the same offence, nor shall be compelled in any Criminal case, to be a witness against himself, nor be deprived to life, liberty, or property, without due process of law; nor shall private property be taken for public use without just compensation.

Rough SJ, p. 217.

9.1.1.9.b   The Resolve of the House of Representatives of the 24th of August, was read as followeth:

. . .

"Article the Eighth.

"No person shall be subject, except in case of impeachment, to more than one trial, or one punishment for the same offence, nor shall be compelled in any criminal case, to be a witness against himself, nor be deprived to life, liberty or property, without due process of law; nor shall private property be taken for public use without just compensation.

Smooth SJ, p. 195.

[1]On August 22, 1789, the following motion was agreed to:
ORDERED, That it be referred to a committee of three, to prepare and report a proper arrangement of, and introduction to the articles of amendment to the Constitution of the United States, as agreed to by the House; and that Mr. Benson, Mr. Sherman, and Mr. Sedgwick be of the said committee.

HJ, p. 112.

9.1.1.9.c   The Resolve of the House of Representatives of the 24th of August, was read as followeth:

. . .

"ARTICLE the EIGHTH.

"No person shall be subject, except in case of impeachment, to more than one trial, or one punishment for the same offence, nor shall be compelled in any criminal case, to be a witness against himself, nor be deprived to life, liberty or property, without due process of law; nor shall private property be taken for public use without just compensation.

Printed SJ, p. 105.

9.1.1.10   Further Senate Consideration, September 4, 1789

9.1.1.10.a   On Motion to adopt the eighth Article of amendments proposed by the House of Representatives, striking out these words "Except in case of impeachment to more than one trial or one punishment" and substitute the following words.
"Be twice put in jeopardy of life or limb by any public prosecution."

Rough SJ, p. 249 ("It passed in the affirmative.").

9.1.1.10.b   On motion, To adopt the eighth article of Amendments proposed by the House of Representatives, striking out these words, — "Except in case of impeachment to more than one trial or one punishment," and substitute the following words —
"Be twice put in jeopardy of life or limb by any public prosecution" —

Smooth SJ, p. 222 ("It passed in the Affirmative.").

9.1.1.10.c   On motion, To adopt the eighth Article of Amendments proposed by the House of Representatives, striking out these words, — "Except in case of impeachment to more than one trial or one punishment," and substitute the following words —
"Be twice put in jeopardy of life or limb by any public prosecution" —

Printed SJ, p. 119 ("It passed in the Affirmative.").

9.1.1.10.d   that the Senate do
Resolved ~~to~~ ∧ concur with the House of Representatives in
Article eighth
~~by~~ striking out these words. "Except in cases of impeachment to more than one
ing
trial or one punishment," and substitute ∧ the following words;
"Be twice put in jeopardy of life or limb by any public prosecution."

Senate MS, p. 3, RG 46, DNA.

9.1.1.11   Further Senate Consideration, September 9, 1789

9.1.1.11.a   On motion, To alter Article 6th so as to stand Article 5th, and Article 7th so as to stand Article 6th, and Article 8th so as to stand Article 7th.

. . .

On motion, That this last mentioned Article be amended to read as follows:
"No person shall be held to answer for a capital or otherwise infamous crime, unless on a presentment or indictment of a grand Jury, except in cases arising in the land or naval forces, or in the Militia, when in actual service, in time of war or public danger, nor shall any person be subject to be put in jeopardy of life or limb,

for the same offence, nor shall be compelled in any criminal case to be a witness against himself, nor be deprived of life, liberty or property, without due process of law; Nor shall private property be taken for public use without just compensation."

Rough SJ, p. 275 ("It passed in the affirmative.").

9.1.1.11.b   On motion, To alter article the sixth so as to stand article the fifth, and article the seventh so as to stand article the sixth, and article the eighth so as to stand article the seventh —

. . .

On motion, That this last mentioned article be amended to read as follows: "No person shall be held to answer for a capital or otherwise infamous crime, unless on a presentment or indictment of a Grand Jury, except in cases arising in the land or naval forces, or in the militia, when in actual service, in time of war or public danger, nor shall any person be subject to be put in jeopardy of life or limb, for the same offence, nor shall be compelled in any criminal case to be a witness against himself, nor be deprived of life, liberty or property, without due process of law: Nor shall private property be taken for public use without just compensation" —

Smooth SJ, p. 244 ("It passed in the Affirmative.").

9.1.1.11.c   On motion, To alter Article the sixth so as to stand Article the fifth, and Article the seventh so as to stand Article the sixth, and Article the eighth so as to stand Article the seventh —

. . .

On motion, That this last mentioned Article be amended to read as follows: "No person shall be held to answer for a capital or otherwise infamous crime, unless on a presentment or indictment of a Grand Jury, except in cases arising in the land or naval forces, or in the militia, when in actual service, in time of war or public danger, nor shall any person be subject to be put in jeopardy of life or limb, for the same offence, nor shall be compelled in any criminal case to be a witness against himself, nor be deprived of life, liberty or property, without due process of law: Nor shall private property be taken for public use without just compensation" —

Printed SJ, pp. 129–30 ("It passed in the Affirmative.").

9.1.1.11.d   To erase the word "Eighth" & insert Seventh —
To insert in the ~~Eighth~~ 8th [7th] article ~~as~~ after the word "shall" in the "1" line — be held to answer for a capital or otherwise infamous crime, unless on a presentment or indictment of a grand Jury, except in cases arising in the land or naval forces, or in the militia when in actual Service in time of War or publick danger, nor shall any person — &
To erase from the same article the words "except in case of impeachment, to more than one trial or one punishment" & insert — to be twice put in jeopardy of life or limb —

Ellsworth MS, p. 3, RG 46, DNA.

9.1.1.12   Senate Resolution, September 9, 1789

ARTICLE THE SEVENTH.

No person shall be held to answer for a capital, or otherwise infamous crime, unless on a presentment or indictment of a Grand Jury, except in cases arising in the land or naval forces, or in the militia, when in actual service in time of war or public danger; nor shall any person be subject for the same offence to be twice put in jeopardy of life or limb; nor shall be compelled in any criminal case, to be a witness against himself, nor be deprived of life, liberty or property, without due process of law; nor shall private property be taken for public use without just compensation.

Senate Pamphlet, RG 46, DNA.

9.1.1.13   Further House Consideration, September 21, 1789

RESOLVED, That this House doth agree to the second, fourth, eighth, twelfth, thirteenth, sixteenth, eighteenth, nineteenth, twenty-fifth, and twenty-sixth amendments, and doth disagree to the first, third, fifth, sixth, seventh, ninth, tenth, eleventh, fourteenth, fifteenth, seventeenth, twentieth, twenty-first, twenty-second, twenty-third, and twenty-fourth amendments proposed by the Senate to the said articles, two thirds of the members present concurring on each vote.

RESOLVED, That a conference be desired with the Senate on the subject matter of the amendments disagreed to, and that Mr. Madison, Mr. Sherman, and Mr. Vining, be appointed managers at the same on the part of this House.

HJ, p. 146.

9.1.1.14   Further Senate Consideration, September 21, 1789

9.1.1.14.a   A message from the House of Representatives —

Mr. Beckley, their Clerk, brought up a Resolve of the House of this date, to agree to the 2nd, 4th, 8th, 12th, 13th, 16th, 18th, 19th, 25th, and 26th Amendments proposed by the Senate, "To articles of Amendment to be proposed to the Legislatures of the several States, as Amendments to the Constitution of the United States," and to disagree to the 1st, 3d, 5th, 6th, 7th, 9th, 10th, 11th, 14th, 15th, 17th, 20th, 21st, 22d, 23d, and 24th amendments: Two thirds of the members present concurring on each vote: And "That a conference be desired with the Senate on the subject matter of the amendments disagreed to," and that Mr. Madison, Mr. Sherman, and Mr. Vining, be appointed managers of the same, on the part of the House of Representatives —

And he withdrew.

Smooth SJ, pp. 265–66.

9.1.1.14.b   A message from the House of Representatives —

Mr. Beckley, their Clerk, brought up a Resolve of the House of this date, to agree to the 2d, 4th, 8th, 12th, 13th, 16th, 18th, 19th, 25th, and 26th Amendments proposed by the Senate, "To Articles of Amendment to be proposed to the Legislatures of the several States, as Amendments to the Constitution of the United States," and to disagree to the 1st, 3d, 5th, 6th, 7th, 9th, 10th, 11th, 14th, 15th, 17th, 20th, 21st, 22d, 23d, and 24th Amendments: Two thirds of the members present concurring on each vote: And "That a conference be desired with the Senate on the subject matter of the Amendments disagreed to," and that Mr. Madison, Mr. Sherman, and Mr. Vining, be appointed managers of the same, on the part of the House of Representatives —

And he withdrew.

Printed SJ, pp. 141–42.

9.1.1.15 Further Senate Consideration, September 21, 1789

9.1.1.15.a   The Senate proceeded to consider the Message of the House of Representatives disagreeing to the Amendments made by the Senate "To Articles to be proposed to the Legislatures of the several States, as Amendments to the Constitution of the United States" And

RESOLVED, That the Senate do recede from their third Amendment, and do insist on all the others.

RESOLVED, That the Senate do concur with the House of Representatives in a conference on the subject matter of disagreement on the said Articles of Amendment, and that Mr. Ellsworth Mr. Carroll and Mr. Paterson be managers of the conference on the part of the Senate.

Smooth SJ, p. 267.

9.1.1.15.b   The Senate proceeded to consider the message of the House of Representatives disagreeing to the Amendments made by the Senate "To Articles to be proposed to the Legislatures of the several States, as Amendments to the Constitution of the United States" — And

RESOLVED, That the Senate do recede from their third Amendment, and do insist on all the others.

RESOLVED, That the Senate do concur with the House of Representatives in a conference on the subject matter of disagreement on the said Articles of Amendment, and that Mr. Ellsworth, Mr. Carroll, and Mr. Paterson be managers of the conference on the part of the Senate.

Printed SJ, p. 142.

9.1.1.16 Conference Committee Report, September 24, 1789

[T]hat it will be proper for the House of Representatives to agree to the said Amendments proposed by the Senate, with an Amendment to their fifth Amendment, so that the third Article shall read as follows: "Congress shall make no Law respecting an establishment of Religion, or prohibiting the free exercise thereof; or abridging the freedom of Speech, or of the Press; or the right of the people peaceably to assemble and to petition the Government for a redress of grievances;" And with an Amendment to the fourteenth Amendment proposed by the Senate, so that the eighth Article, as numbered in the Amendments proposed by the Senate, shall read as follows "In all criminal prosecutions, the accused shall enjoy the right to a speedy & publick trial by an impartial jury of the district wherein the crime shall have been committed, as the district shall have been previously ascertained by law, and to be informed of the nature and cause of the accusation; to be confronted with the witnesses against him, and to have com

                                                                    to
pulsory process for obtaining witnesses ~~against him~~ in his favour, & ∧ have the
assistance of counsel for his defence."

Conference MS, RG 46, DNA (Ellsworth's handwriting).

9.1.1.17   House Consideration of Conference Committee Report, September 24 [25], 1789

RESOLVED, That this House doth recede from their disagreement to the first,
third, fifth, sixth, seventh, ninth, tenth, eleventh, fourteenth, fifteenth, seventeenth, twentieth, twenty-first, twenty-second, twenty-third, and twenty-fourth
amendments, insisted on by the Senate: PROVIDED, That the two articles which by
the amendments of the Senate are now proposed to be inserted as the third and
eighth articles, shall be amended to read as followeth;

Article the third. "Congress shall make no law respecting an establishment of
religion, or prohibiting the free exercise thereof; or abridging the freedom of
speech, or of the press; or the right of the people peaceably to assemble, and to
petition the government for a redress of grievances."

Article the eighth. "In all criminal prosecutions, the accused shall enjoy the right
to a speedy and public trial by an impartial jury of the state and district wherein
the crime shall have been committed, which district shall have been previously
ascertained by law, and to be informed of the nature and cause of the accusation,
to be confronted with the witnesses against him, to have compulsory process for
obtaining witnesses in his favor, and to have the assistance of council for his
defence."

HJ, p. 152 ("On the question, that the House do agree to the alteration
and amendment of the eighth article, in manner aforesaid, It was resolved
in the affirmative. Ayes 37 Noes 14").

9.1.1.18   Senate Consideration of Conference Committee Report, September 24, 1789

9.1.1.18.a   Mr. Ellsworth, on behalf of the managers of the conference on "articles to be
proposed to the several States as Amendments to the Constitution of the United
States," reported as follows:

That it will be proper for the House of Representatives to agree to the said
amendments proposed by the Senate, with an Amendment to their fifth Amendment, so that the third Article shall read as follows: "Congress shall make no law
respecting an establishment of <u>Religion</u>, or prohibiting the free exercise thereof; or
abridging the freedom of Speech, or of the Press; or the right of the people
peaceably to assemble and petition the Government for a redress of Grievances;"
And with an Amendment to the fourteenth Amendment proposed by the Senate,
so that the eighth article, as numbered in the Amendments proposed by the Senate,
shall read as follows; "In all criminal prosecutions, the accused shall enjoy the
right to a speedy and public trial by an impartial <u>Jury</u> of the district wherein the
<u>Crime</u> shall have been committed, as the district shall have been previously ascer-
tained by law, and to be informed of the nature and cause of the accusation, to be
confronted with the witnesses against him, and to have compulsory process for
obtaining witnesses in his favor, and to have the assistance of Counsel for defence."

Smooth SJ, pp. 272–73.

9.1.1.18.b   Mr. Ellsworth, on behalf of the managers of the conference on "Articles to be proposed to the several States as Amendments to the Constitution of the United States," reported as follows:

That it will be proper for the House of Representatives to agree to the said Amendments proposed by the Senate, with an Amendment to their fifth Amendment, so that the third Article shall read as follows: "Congress shall make no Law RESPECTING AN ESTABLISHMENT OF RELIGION, or prohibiting the free exercise thereof; or abridging the freedom of Speech, or of the Press; or the right of the People peaceably to assemble and petition the Government for a redress of Grievances;" And with an Amendment to the fourteenth Amendment proposed by the Senate, so that the eighth Article, as numbered in the Amendments proposed by the Senate, shall read as follows; "In all criminal prosecutions, the accused shall enjoy the right to a speedy and public trial by AN IMPARTIAL JURY OF THE DISTRICT WHEREIN THE CRIME SHALL HAVE BEEN COMMITTED, AS THE DISTRICT SHALL HAVE BEEN PREVIOUSLY ASCERTAINED BY LAW, and to be informed of the nature and cause of the accusation, to be confronted with the witnesses against him, and to have compulsory process for obtaining witnesses in his favor, and to have the assistance of Counsel for defence."

Printed SJ, p. 145.

9.1.1.19   Further Senate Consideration of Conference Committee Report, September 24, 1789

9.1.1.19.a   A Message from the House of Representatives —

Mr. Beckley, their Clerk, brought up the Amendments to the "Articles to be proposed to the Legislatures of the several States, as Amendments to the Constitution of the United States;" and informed the Senate, that the House of Representatives had receded from their disagreement to the 1st, 3d, 5th, 6th, 7th, 9th, 10th, 11th, 14th, 15th, 17th, 20th, 21st, 22d, 23d, and 24th Amendments, insisted on by the Senate: Provided that the "Two Articles, which by the Amendments of the Senate are now proposed to be inserted as the third and eighth Articles," shall be amended to read as followeth:

Article the Third. "Congress shall make no Law respecting an establishment of Religion, or prohibiting the free exercise thereof; or abridging the freedom of Speech, or of the Press; or the right of the people peaceably to assemble, and petition the Government for a redress of Grievances."

Article the Eighth. "In all criminal prosecutions the accused shall enjoy the right to a speedy and public trial by an impartial Jury of the State and District, wherein the crime shall have been committed, which District shall have been previously ascertained by law, and to be informed of the nature and cause of the accusation, to be confronted with the witnesses against him, and to have compulsory process for obtaining witnesses in his favor, and to have the assistance of Counsel for his defence."

Smooth SJ, pp. 278–79.

9.1.1.19.b   A Message from the House of Representatives —

Mr. Beckley, their Clerk, brought up the Amendments to the "Articles to be proposed to the Legislatures of the several States, as Amendments to the Constitution of the United States;" and informed the Senate, that the House of Representatives had receded from their disagreement to the 1st, 3d, 5th, 6th, 7th, 9th, 10th, 11th, 14th, 15th, 17th, 20th, 21st, 22d, 23d, and 24th Amendments, insisted on by the Senate: Provided that the "Two Articles, which by the Amendments of the Senate are now proposed to be inserted as the third and eighth Articles," shall be amended to read as followeth:

Article the Third. "Congress shall make no Law respecting an establishment of Religion, or prohibiting the free exercise thereof; or abridging the freedom of Speech, or of the Press; or the right of the People peaceably to assemble, and petition the Government for a redress of Grievances."

Article the Eighth. "In all criminal prosecutions the accused shall enjoy the right to a speedy and public trial by an impartial Jury of the State and District, wherein the crime shall have been committed, which District shall have been previously ascertained by law, and to be informed of the nature and cause of the accusation, to be confronted with the witnesses against him, and to have compulsory process for obtaining witnesses in his favor, and to have the assistance of Counsel for his defence."

Printed SJ, p.148.

9.1.1.20 Further Senate Consideration of Conference Committee Report, September 25, 1789

9.1.1.20.a The Senate proceeded to consider the Message from the House of Representatives of the 24th, with Amendments to the Amendments of the Senate, to "Articles to be proposed to the Legislatures of the several States, as Amendments to the Constitution of the United States" — And

RESOLVED, That the Senate do concur in the Amendments proposed by the House of Representatives, to the Amendments of the Senate.

Smooth SJ, p. 283.

9.1.1.20.b The Senate proceeded to consider the Message from the House of Representatives of the 24th, with Amendments to the Amendments of the Senate, to "Articles to be proposed to the Legislatures of the several States, as Amendments to the Constitution of the United States" — And

RESOLVED, That the Senate do concur in the Amendments proposed by the House of Representatives, to the Amendments of the Senate.

Printed SJ, pp. 150–51.

9.1.1.21 Agreed Resolution, September 25, 1789

9.1.1.21.a Article the Seventh.

No person shall be held to answer for a capital, or otherwise infamous crime, unless on a presentment or indictment of a Grand Jury, except in cases arising in the land or naval forces, or in the militia, when in actual service in time of war or public danger; nor shall any person be subject for the same offence to be twice put in jeopardy of life or limb; nor shall be compelled in any criminal case, to be a witness against himself, nor be deprived of life, liberty or property, without due process of law; nor shall private property be taken for public use without just compensation.

Smooth SJ, Appendix, p. 293.

9.1.1.21.b   ARTICLE THE SEVENTH.

No person shall be held to answer for a capital, or otherwise infamous crime, unless on a presentment or indictment of a Grand Jury, except in cases arising in the land or naval forces, or in the militia, when in actual service in time of war or public danger; nor shall any person be subject for the same offence to be twice put in jeopardy of life or limb; nor shall be compelled in any criminal case, to be a witness against himself, nor be deprived of life, liberty or property, without due process of law; nor shall private property be taken for public use without just compensation.

Printed SJ, Appendix, p. 164.

9.1.1.22 Enrolled Resolution, September 28, 1789

Article the seventh . . . No person shall be held to answer for a capital, or otherwise infamous crime, unless on a presentment or indictment of a Grand Jury, except in cases arising in the land or naval forces, or in the militia, when in actual service in time of war or public danger; nor shall any person be subject for the same offence to be twice put in jeopardy of life or limb, nor shall be compelled in any criminal case, to be a witness against himself, nor be deprived of life, liberty, or property, without due process of law; nor shall private property be taken for public use without just compensation.

Enrolled Resolutions, RG 11, DNA.

9.1.1.23 Printed Versions

9.1.1.23.a   ART. V. No person shall be held to answer for a capital or otherwise infamous crime, unless on a presentment or indictment of a grand jury, except in cases arising in the land or naval forces, or in the militia, when in actual service, in time of war or public danger; nor shall any person be subject for the same offence to be twice put in jeopardy of life or limb; nor shall be compelled, in any criminal case, to be witness against himself; nor be deprived of life, liberty, or property, without due process of law; nor shall private property be taken for public use without just compensation.

Statutes at Large, vol. 1, p. 21.

9.1.1.23.b   ART. VII. No person shall be held to answer for a capital, or otherwise infamous crime, unless on a presentment or indictment of a grand jury, except in cases arising in the land or naval forces, or in the militia when in actual service in time of war or public danger; nor shall any person be subject for the same offence to be twice put in jeopardy of life or limb; nor shall be compelled in any criminal case to be a witness against himself, nor be deprived of life, liberty or property, without due process of law; nor shall private proprty be taken for public use without just compensation.

Statutes at Large, vol. 1, p. 98.

9.1.2 PROPOSALS FROM THE STATE CONVENTIONS

9.1.2.1 New York, July 26, 1788

That (except in the Government of the Land and Naval Forces, and of the Militia when in actual Service, and in cases of Impeachment) a Presentment or

Indictment by a Grand Jury ought to be observed as a necessary preliminary to the trial of all Crimes cognizable by the Judiciary of the United States, and such Trial should be speedy, public, and by an impartial Jury of the County where the Crime was committed; and that no person can be found Guilty without the unanimous consent of such Jury. But in cases of Crimes not committed within any County of any of the United States, and in Cases of Crimes committed within any County in which a general Insurrection may prevail, or which may be in the possession of a
the
foreign Enemy, the enquiry and trial may be in such County as ∧ Congress shall by Law direct; which County in the two Cases last mentioned should be as near as conveniently may be to that County in which the Crime may have been committed. And that in all Criminal Prosecutions, the Accused ought to be informed of the cause and nature of his Accusation, to be confronted with his accusers and the Witnesses against him, to have the means of producing his Witnesses, and the assistance of Council for his defence, and should not be compelled to give Evidence against himself.

State Ratifications, RG 11, DNA.

9.1.2.2 North Carolina, August 1, 1788

8th. That, in all capital and criminal prosecutions, a man hath a right to demand the cause and nature of his accusation, to be confronted with the accusers and witnesses, to call for evidence and be allowed counsel in his favor, and to a fair and speedy trial by an impartial jury of his vicinage, without whose unanimous consent he cannot be found guilty (except in the government of the land and naval forces) nor can he be compelled to give evidence against himself.

State Ratifications, RG 11, DNA.

9.1.2.3 Pennsylvania Minority, December 12, 1787

3. That in all capital and criminal prosecutions, a man has a right to demand the cause and nature of his accusations, as well in the federal courts, as in those of the several states; to be heard by himself or his counsel; to be confronted with the accusers and witnesses; to call for evidence in his favor, and a speedy trial, by an impartial jury of the vicinage, without whose unanimous consent, he cannot be found guilty, nor can he be compelled to give evidence against himself; that no man be deprived of his liberty, except by the law of the land or the judgment of his peers.

Pennsylvania Packet, December 18, 1787.

9.1.2.4 Rhode Island, May 29, 1790

8th. That in all capital and criminal prosecutions, a man hath a right to demand the cause and nature of his accusation, to be confronted with the accusers and witnesses, to call for evidence and be allowed counsel in his favour, and to a fair and speedy trial by an impartial jury of his vicinage, without whose unanimous consent he cannot be found guilty; (except in the government of the land and naval forces) nor can he be compelled to give evidence against himself.

State Ratifications, RG 11, DNA.

9.1.2.5   Virginia, June 27, 1788

Eighth, That in all capital and criminal prosecutions, a man hath a right to demand the cause and nature of his accusation, to be confronted with the accusers and witnesses, to call for evidence and be allowed counsel in his favor, and to a fair and speedy trial by an impartial Jury of his vicinage, without whose unanimous consent he cannot be found guilty, (except in the government of the land and naval forces) nor can he be compelled to give evidence against himself.

State Ratifications, RG 11, DNA.

9.1.3 STATE CONSTITUTIONS AND LAWS; COLONIAL CHARTERS AND LAWS

9.1.3.1   Delaware: Declaration of Rights, 1776

Sect. 15. That no man in the Courts of Common Law ought to be compelled to give evidence against himself.

Delaware Laws, vol. 1, App., p. 81.

9.1.3.2   Maryland: Declaration of Rights, 1776

20. That no man ought to be compelled to give evidence against himself in a court of common law, or in any other court, but in such cases as have been usually practised in this state, or may hereafter be directed by the legislature.

Maryland Laws, November 3, 1776

9.1.3.3   Massachusetts

9.1.3.3.a   Body of Liberties, 1641

[45] No man shall be forced by Torture to confesse any Crime against himselfe nor any other unlesse it be in some Capitall case where he is first fullie convicted by cleare and suffitient evidence to be guilty, After which if the cause be that of nature, That it is very apparent there be other conspiratours, or confederates with him, Then he may be tortured, yet not with such Tortures as be Barbarous and inhumane.

Massachusetts Colonial Laws, p. 43.

9.1.3.3.b   Constitution, 1780

[Part I, Article] XII. No subject shall be held to answer for any crime or offence until the same is fully and plainly, substantially and formally, described to him; or be compelled to accuse, or furnish evidence against himself. And every subject shall have a right to produce all proofs, that may be favourable to him; to meet the witnesses against him, face to face, and to be fully heard in his defence by himself, or his counsel, at his election. And no subject shall be arrested, imprisoned, despoiled, or deprived of his property, immunities, or privileges, put out of the protection of the law, exiled, or deprived of his life, liberty, or estate, but by the judgment of his peers, or the law of the land.

And the legislature shall not make any law, that shall subject any person to a capital or infamous punishment, excepting for the government of the army and navy, without trial by jury.

Massachusetts Perpetual Laws, pp. 6–7.

9.1.3.4 New Hampshire: Constitution, 1783

[Part I, Article] XV. No subject shall be held to answer for any crime, or offence, until the same is fully and plainly, substantially and formally described to him; or be compelled to accuse or furnish evidence against himself. And every subject shall have a right to produce all proofs that may be favorable to himself: To meet the witnesses against him face to face, and to be fully heard in his defence by himself and counsel. And no subject shall be arrested, imprisoned, despoiled, or deprived of his property, immunities, or priviliges, put out of the protection of the law, exiled or deprived of his life, liberty, or estate, but by the judgment of his peers or the law of the land.

New Hampshire Laws, p. 25.

9.1.3.5 North Carolina: A Declaration of Rights, 1776

Sect. VII. That in all criminal Prosecutions every Man has a Right to be informed of the Accusation against him, and to confront the Accusers and Witnesses with other Testimony, and shall not be compelled to give Evidence against himself.

North Carolina Laws, p. 275.

9.1.3.6 Pennsylvania

9.1.3.6.a Constitution, 1776

CHAPTER I.

. . .

IX. That in all prosecutions for criminal offences, a man hath a right to be heard by himself and his council, to demand the cause and nature of his accusation, to be confronted with the witnesses, to call for evidence in his favour, and a speedy public trial, by an impartial jury of the country, without the unanimous consent of which jury he cannot be found guilty; nor can he be compelled to give evidence against himself; nor can any man be justly deprived of his liberty except by the laws of the land, or the judgment of his peers.

Pennsylvania Acts, M'Kean, pp. ix–x.

9.1.3.6.b Constitution, 1790

ARTICLE IX.

. . .

Sᴇᴄᴛ. IX. That, in all criminal prosecutions, the accused hath a right to be heard by himself and his council, to demand the nature and cause of the accusation against him, to meet the witnesses face to face, to have compulsory process for obtaining witnesses in his favour, and, in prosecutions by indictment or information, a speedy public trial by an impartial jury of the vicinage: That he cannot be compelled to give evidence against himself, nor can he be deprived of his life, liberty, or property, unless by the judgment of his peers, or the law of the land.

Pennsylvania Acts, Dallas, p. xxxiv.

9.1.3.7 Vermont: Constitution, 1777

CHAPTER I.

. . .

10. THAT, in all Prosecutions for criminal Offences, a Man hath a Right to be heard by himself and his Counsel, — to demand the Cause and Nature of his Accusation, — to be confronted with the Witnesses, — to call for Evidence in his Favor, and a speedy public Trial, by an impartial Jury of the Country, without the unanimous Consent of which Jury, he cannot be [fo]und guilty; nor can he be compelled to give Evidence against himself; nor can any man be justly deprived of his Liberty, except by the Laws of the Land, or the Judgment of his Peers.

Vermont Acts, p. 4.

9.1.3.8 Virginia: Declaration of Rights, 1776

VIII. THAT in all capital or criminal prosecutions a man hath a right to demand the cause and nature of his accusation, to be confronted with the accusers and witnesses, to call for evidence in his favour, and to a speedy trial by an impartial jury of his vicinage, without whose unanimous consent he cannot be found guilty, nor can he be compelled to give evidence against himself; that no man be deprived of his liberty except by the law of the land, or the judgment of his peers.

Virginia Acts, p. 33.

9.1.4 OTHER TEXTS

None.

9.2 DISCUSSION OF DRAFTS AND PROPOSALS

9.2.1 THE FIRST CONGRESS

9.2.1.1 June 8, 1789[2]

9.2.1.2 August 17, 1789[3]

9.2.1.2.a

Mr. LAWRANCE

Said this clause contained a general declaration, in some degree contrary to laws passed, he alluded to that part where a person shall not be compelled to give evidence against himself; he thought it ought to be confined to criminal cases, and moved an amendment for that purpose, which amendment being adopted, the clause as amended was unanimously agreed to by the committee. . . .

Congressional Register, August 17, 1789, vol. 2, p. 225.

9.2.1.2.b   Mr. LAWRANCE moved to insert after the words "nor shall" these words "in any criminal case." This amendment was agreed to.

Daily Advertiser, August 18, 1789, p. 2, col. 4.

---

[2]For the reports of Madison's speech in support of his proposals, *see* 1.2.1.1.a–c.
[3]For the full reports of the House's discussion of its Eighth Amendment, *see* 8.2.1.2.a–d.

9.2.1.2.c   Mr. Lawrance moved to insert after the words "nor shall," these words, "in any criminal case."

This amendment was agreed to.

New-York Daily Gazette, August 19, 1789, p. 802, col. 4.

9.2.1.2.d   Mr. LAURANCE moved to insert after the words "nor shall" these words *in any criminal case.* This amendment was agreed to.

Gazette of the U.S., August 22, 1789, p. 249, col. 3.

9.2.2 STATE CONVENTIONS

9.2.2.1   **Massachusetts, January 30, 1788**

. . . Mr. HOLMES. Mr. President, I rise to make some remarks on the paragraph under consideration, which treats of the judiciary power.

. . .

On the whole, when we fully consider this matter, and fully investigate the powers granted, explicitly given, and specially delegated, we shall find Congress possessed of powers enabling them to institute judicatories little less inauspicious than a certain tribunal in Spain, which has long been the disgrace of Christendom: I mean that diabolical institution, the *Inquisition.*

What gives an additional glare of horror to these gloomy circumstances is the consideration, that Congress have to ascertain, point out, and determine, what kind of punishments shall be inflicted on persons convicted of crimes. They are nowhere restrained from inventing the most cruel and unheard-of punishments, and annexing them to crimes; and there is no constitutional check on them, but that *racks* and *gibbets* may be amongst the most mild instruments of their discipline.

There is nothing to prevent Congress from passing laws which shall compel a man, who is accused or suspected of a crime, to furnish evidence against himself, and even from establishing laws which shall order the court to take the charge exhibited against a man for truth, unless he can furnish evidence of his innocence.

I do not pretend to say that Congress *will* do this; but, sir, I undertake to say that Congress (according to the powers proposed to be given them by the Constitution) *may* do it; and if they do not, it will be owing *entirely* — I repeat it, it will be owing *entirely* — to the goodness of the men, and not in the *least degree* owing to the goodness of the Constitution.

Elliot, vol. 2, pp. 109, 111.

9.2.2.2   **Virginia, June 14, 1788**

Mr. GEORGE NICHOLAS, in answer to the two gentlemen last up, observed that, though there was a declaration of rights in the government of Virginia, it was no conclusive reason that there should be one in this Constitution; for, if it was unnecessary in the former, its omission in the latter could be no defect.

. . .

But sir, this Constitution is defective because the common law is not declared to be in force! What would have been the consequence if it had? It would be immutable. But now it can be changed or modified as the legislative body may find necessary for the community. But the common law is not excluded. There is nothing in that paper to warrant the assertion. As to the exclusion of a jury from the vicinage, he has mistaken the fact. The legislature may direct a jury to come from the vicinage. But the gentleman says that, by this Constitution, they have power to make laws to define crimes and prescribe punishments; and that, consequently, we are not free from torture. Treason against the United States is defined in the Constitution, and the forfeiture limited to the life of the person attainted. Congress have power to define and punish piracies and felonies committed on the high seas, and offences against the laws of nations; but they cannot define or prescribe the punishment of any other crime whatever, without violating the Constitution. If we had no security against torture but our declaration of rights, we might be tortured to-morrow; for it has been repeatedly infringed and disregarded. A bill of rights is only an acknowledgment of the preëxisting claim to rights in the people. They belong to us as much as if they had been inserted in the Constitution. But it is said that, if it be doubtful, the possiblity of dispute ought to be precluded. Admitting it was proper for the Convention to have inserted a bill of rights, it is not proper here to propose it as the condition of our accession to the Union. Would you reject this government for its omission, dissolve the Union, and bring miseries on yourselves and posterity? I hope the gentleman does not oppose it on this ground solely. Is there another reason? He said that it is not only the general wish of this state, but all the states, to have a bill of rights. If it be so, where is the difficulty of having this done by way of subsequent amendment? We shall find the other states willing to accord with their own favorite wish. The gentleman last up says that the power of legislation includes every special power of legislation. Therefore, it does not contain that plenitude of power which he imagines. They cannot legislate in any case but those particularly enumerated. No gentleman, who is a friend to the government, ought to withhold his assent from it for this reason.

Mr. GEORGE MASON replied that the worthy gentleman was mistaken in his assertion that the bill of rights did not prohibit torture; for that one clause expressly provided that no man can give evidence against himself; and that the worthy gentleman must know that, in those countries where torture is used, evidence was extorted from the criminal himself. Another clause of the bill of rights provided that no cruel and unusual punishments shall be inflicted; therefore, torture was included in the prohibition.

Mr. NICHOLAS acknowledged the bill of rights to contain that prohibition, and that the gentleman was right with respect to the practice of extorting confession from the criminal in those countries where torture is used; but still he saw no security arising from the bill of rights as separate from the Constitution, for that it had been frequently violated with impunity.

Elliot, vol. 3, pp. 449–52.

9.2.3 PHILADELPHIA CONVENTION

None.

9.2.4 NEWSPAPERS AND PAMPHLETS

9.2.4.1 Brutus, No. 2, November 1, 1787

For the security of life, in criminal prosecutions, the bill of rights of most of the States have declared, that no man shall be held to answer for a crime until he is made fully acquainted with the charge brought against him; he shall not be held to accuse, or furnish evidence against himself — The witnesses against him shall be brought face to face, and he shall be fully heard by himself and counsel. That it is essential to the security of life and liberty that trial of facts be in the vicinity where they happen. Are not provisions of this kind as necessary in the general government, as in that of a particular state? The powers vested in the new Congress extend in many cases to life; they are authorised to provide for the punishment of a variety of capital crimes, and no restraint is laid upon them in its exercise, save only, that "the trial of all crimes, except incases of impeachment, shall be by jury; and such trial shall be in the state where the said crimes shall have been committed."

New York Journal, Storing, vol. 2, pp. 374–75.

9.2.4.2 The Federal Farmer, No. 6, December 25, 1787

The following, I think, will be allowed to be unalienable or fundamental rights in the United States: —

No man, demeaning himself peaceably, shall be molested on account of his religion or mode of worship — The people have a right to hold and enjoy their property according to known standing laws, and which cannot be taken from them without their consent, or the consent of their representatives; and whenever taken in the pressing urgencies of government, they are to receive a reasonable compensation for it — Individual security consists in having free recourse to the laws — The people are subject to no laws or taxes not assented to by their representatives constitutionally assembled — They are at all times intitled to the benefits of the writ of habeas corpus, the trial by jury in criminal and civil causes — They have a right, when charged, to a speedy trial in the vicinage; to be heard by themselves or counsel, not to be compelled to furnish evidence against themselves, to have witnesses face to face, and to confront their adversaries before the judge — No man is held to answer a crime charged upon him till it be substantially described to him; and he is subject to no unreasonable searches or seizures of his person, papers or effects — The people have a right to assemble in an orderly manner, and petition the government for a redress of wrongs — The freedom of the press ought not to be restrained — No emoluments, except for actual service — No hereditary honors, or orders of nobility, ought to be allowed — The military ought to be subordinate to the civil authority, and no soldier be quartered on the citizens without their consent — The militia ought always to be armed and disciplined, and the usual defence of the country — The supreme power is in the people, and power delegated ought to return to them at stated periods, and frequently — The legislative, executive, and judicial powers, ought always to be kept distinct — others perhaps might be added.

Storing, vol. 2, p. 262.

9.2.5 LETTERS AND DIARIES

None.

9.3 DISCUSSION OF RIGHTS

9.3.1 TREATISES

None.

9.3.2 CASELAW

9.3.2.1 **The King v. Dr. Purnell, 1748[4]**

9.3.2.2 **Brownsword v. Edwards, 1751**

Lord Chancellor, This appears a very plain case, in which defendant may protect herself from making a discovery of her marriage; and I am afraid, if the court should over-rule such a plea, it would be setting up the oath *ex officio;* which then the parliament in the time of *Charles* I. would in vain have taken away, if the party might come into this court for it. The general rule is, that no one is bound to answer so as to subject himself to punishment, whether that punishment arises by the ecclesiastical law of the land. (2 Ves. Sen. 389, 451; 1 Atk. 539; 2 Atk. 393; 1 Brown 97. In case of a bankrupt smuggler, the commissioners may examine him, but he may demur to the interrogatories, and have the opinion of the court. 2 Atk. 200; 1 vol. 247; 3 Wms. 376; 1 Vern. 109.) Incest is undoubtedly punishable in ecclesiastical court; and such a crime is generally excepted out of the acts of pardon. The ecclesiastical court has conusance of incest in two respects, *diverso intuitu:* first to judge of the legality of the marriage, and to pronounce sentence of nullity; and if they do so, proceeding lawfully and rightfully, it binds all parties, being the judgment of a court having proper jurisdiction of the cause. The other is to censure and punish persons guilty by ecclesiastical censure, as for fornication, adultery, &c. Nor is it material what the nature of the punishment is. It is a punishment which must be performed or got rid of by commutation, which is like a fine. Then consider the present case. The discovery whether lawfully married takes in the whole, whether married in fact, and whether that marriage was lawful. Defendant has pleaded to it; which she may do; and in the plea it is proper to bring in facts and averments to support that plea; whereas a demurrer can be to nothing but what appears on the face of the bill, otherwise it would be a speaking demurrer. (Averments are necessary to exclude intendments which would be made against the pleader, for the court will always intend the matters charged against the pleader unless fully denied. 2 Atk. 241; Gilb. 185.) But here it was necessary to bring in such an averment, that testator was lawfully married before to her sister, and had issue; which is a fact necessary to shew; and that fact she has taken on herself to prove: the plea therefore is regular in form, and good in substance. The objection to the plea is, that one of the parties to the incestuous marriage being dead, there can be no proceeding afterward. I always took the distinction to be what is laid down in *Hicks v. Harris,* that by the law of the land the ecclesiastical court cannot proceed to judge of the marriage and to pronounce sentence of nullity after death of one of the married parties, especially where there is issue,

[4]*See* 6.3.2.1.

because it tends to bastardise the issue; and none after death of one of the parties to that marriage is to be bastardised: but there is no rule of law standing to prevent either of the parties from punishment after death of the other. Suppose it was an offence of adultery or fornication, there is no rule of the civil or ecclesiastical law, that after death of one of the parties the survivor may not be punished for the offence: undoubtedly they may, either proceeding *ex officio,* by office of the ecclesiastical judge, or by promotion of a proper informant. Then why may not the ecclesiastical court do it in the case of incest, whether without the formality of marriage or attended with it? But it is said, *Hicks v. Harris* is no judicial determination in the point, and that all that was material before the court, was the joint jurisdiction; which is true: but there was a plain difference. If the court held, that the proceeding (and this is an answer to one part of the objection) even for the censure against the surviving party would have tended to affect the legitimacy of the marriage or the issue, the court of *B.R.* would have stopped there: but they went on this, that it could not be given in evidence against the issue or the plaintiff claiming under that issue: as was determined solemnly in *B.R.* on a long trial at bar, directed out of this court in *Hillyard v. Grantham,* in which I was counsel. (See 3 Wooddeson, 318.) In that cause during life of the father and mother there had been a proceeding against both of them in the consistory court of *Lincoln* for living together in fornication, and sentence given against them. On the trial that sentence was offered in evidence to prove, that they were not married: the whole court were of opinion that it could not be given in evidence; because first, it was a criminal matter, and could not be given in evidence in a civil cause; next that it was *res inter alios acta,* and could not affect the issue: but they held, that if it had been a sentence on the point of the marriage on a question of the lawfulness of the marriage, it being a sentence of a court having proper jurisdiction, might have been given in evidence. If indeed there had been collusion that might be shewn on the part of the child to take off the force of it; because collusion affects every thing: but if no collusion, it binds all the world: but in a proceeding in a criminal way that could not be given in evidence: and that was the distinction the court went on in *Hicks v. Harris.* But if there had not been the authority, I should not have doubted on the nature of the thing, but that the ecclesiastical court might have proceeded after death of one of the party as well for incest as fornication; in which case there is no doubt they may. Thus far as to the merits of the plea. Some collateral arguments have been used, that it is not in every case the party shall protect himself against relief in this court upon an allegation, that it will subject him to a supposed crime. It is true, it never creates a defence against relief in this court, therefore in case of usury of forgery, if a proof can be made of it, the court will let the cause go on still to a hearing, but will not force the party by his own oath to subject himself to punishment for it (if plaintiff waves [*sic*] the penalty, defendant shall be obliged to discover, 1 Vern. 60, or whether the penalty arises from defendant's own particular agreement, he is obliged to discover. 2 Ver. [*sic*] 244. Or where the discovery sought is not of a fact which can subject defendant to any penalty, but connected with some other fact which may, 2 Ves. sen. 493). In a bill to inquire into the reality of deeds on suggestion of forgery, the court has entertained jurisdiction of the cause; though it does not oblige the party to a discovery, but directs an issue to try whether forged. I remember a case where there was a deed of rent-charge suggested to be forged: it was tried twice at law, and found for the deed: a bill was afterward brought to set it aside for forgery, and to have it delivered up to be cancelled. Lord *King,* notwithstanding the two trials, which has been in *Avowry* and *Replevin,* directed an issue: wherein it was found forged, and, I remember, was cancelled and cut to pieces in court. There are several instances of that: so that the relief the party may have is no objection. As to the objection from the consequence of allowing this plea if the defendant should fail in the proof of it, that would be an objection to the allowing any plea to a discovery: though it would be no objection to a demurrer, because that must abide by the bill: but all pleas must suggest a fact (which fact must conduce to one single point, per Lord *Thurlow,* 1 Brown, 417. 1 Atk. 54): it must go to a hearing; and if the party does not prove that fact which is necessary to support the plea, the plaintiff is not to lose the benefit of his discovery: but the court may direct an examination on interrogatories in order to supply that. The plea therefore ought to be allowed.

28 Eng. Rep. 157 (Ch. 1751).

Chapter 10

AMENDMENT V
DUE PROCESS CLAUSE

10.1 TEXTS

10.1.1 DRAFTS IN FIRST CONGRESS

10.1.1.1 Proposal by Madison in House, June 8, 1789

10.1.1.1.a   Fourthly. That in article 1st, section 9, between clauses 3 and 4 [of the Constitution], be inserted these clauses, to wit, . . .

. . .

No person shall be subject, except in cases of impeachment, to more than one punishment, or one trial for the same offence; nor shall be compelled to be a witness against himself; nor be deprived of life, liberty, or property without due process of law; nor be obliged to relinquish his property, where it may be necessary for public use, without a just compensation.

Congressional Register, June 8, 1789, vol. 1, pp. 427–28.

10.1.1.1.b   *Fourthly.* That in article 1st, section 9, between clauses 3 and 4 [of the Constitution], be inserted these clauses, to wit: . . .

. . .

No person shall be subject, except in cases of impeachment, to more than one punishment, or one trial for the same offence; nor shall be compelled to be a witness against himself; nor be deprived of life, liberty, or property without due process of law; nor be obliged to relinquish his property, where it may be necessary for public use, without a just compensation.   Daily Advertiser, June 12, 1789, p. 2, col. 1.

10.1.1.1.c   *Fourth.* That in article 1st, section 9, between clauses 3 and 4, be inserted these clauses, to wit: . . .

. . .

No person shall be subject, except in cases of impeachment, to more than one punishment, or one trial for the same offence; nor shall be compelled to be a witness against himself; nor be deprived of life, liberty, or property without due process of law; nor be obliged to relinquish his property, where it may be necessary for public use, without a just compensation.

New-York Daily Gazette, June 13, 1789, p. 574, col. 3.

10.1.1.2 House Committee of Eleven Report, July 28, 1789

ART. I, SEC. 9 — Between PAR. 2 and 3 insert,

. . .

"No person shall be subject, except in case of impeachment, to more than one trial or one punishment for the same offence, nor shall be compelled to be a witness against himself, nor be deprived of life, liberty, or property without due process of law; nor shall private property be taken for public use without just compensation."

Broadside Collection, DLC.

10.1.1.3 House Consideration, August 17, 1789

10.1.1.3.a The 5th clause of the 4th proposition was taken up, viz. "no person shall be subject, [*sic; except*] in case of impeachment, to more than one trial or one punishment for the same offence, nor shall be compelled to be a witness against himself, nor be deprived of life, liberty or property, without due process of law, nor shall private property be taken for public use without just compensation."

Congressional Register, August 17, 1789, vol. 2, p. 224.

10.1.1.3.b Eighth Amendment — "No person shall be subject except in case of impeachment, to more than one trial or one punishment for the same offence, nor shall be compelled to be a witness against himself, nor be deprived of life, liberty or property, without due process of law, nor shall private property be taken for public use without just compensation."

Daily Advertiser, August 18, 1789, p. 2, col. 4.

10.1.1.3.c Eighth Amendment — "No person shall be subject, except in case of impeachment, to more than one trial or one punishment for the same offence, nor shall be compelled to be a witness against himself, nor be deprived of life, liberty or property, without due process of law, nor shall private property be taken for public use without just compensation."

New-York Daily Gazette, August 19, 1789, p. 802, col. 4.

10.1.1.3.d 8th Amendment. "No person shall be subject, except in case of impeachment, to more than one trial for the same offence, nor shall be compelled to be a witness against himself, nor be deprived of life, liberty or property, without due process of law, nor shall private property be taken for public use without just compensation."

Gazette of the U.S., August 22, 1789, p. 249, col. 3.

10.1.1.4 Motion by Benson in House, August 17, 1789

10.1.1.4.a Mr. BENSON

[H]e would move to amend it by striking out the words "one trial or."

Congressional Register, August 17, 1789, vol. 2, p. 224
("was lost by a considerable majority").

10.1.1.4.b Mr. BENSON moved to strike out the words "One trial or"

Daily Advertiser, August 18, 1789, p. 2, col. 4
("This was negatived").

10.1.1.4.c   Mr. Benson moved to strike out the words "one trial or."
New-York Daily Gazette, August 19, 1789, p. 802, col. 4
("This was negatived").

10.1.1.4.d   Mr. BENSON . . . moved to strike out the words "one trial or"
Gazette of the U.S., August 22, 1789, p. 249, col. 1
("This was negatived.").

10.1.1.5   Motion by Partridge in House, August 17, 1789

10.1.1.5.a   Mr. PARTRIDGE moved to insert after "same offence," the words, "by any law of the United States;" . . . .
Congressional Register, August 17, 1789, vol. 2,
p. 225 ("this amendment was lost also").

10.1.1.5.b   Mr. PARTRIDGE moved to insert after the words "same offence," the words "by any law of the United States,"
Daily Advertiser, August 18, 1789, p. 2, col. 3
("Resolved in the negative").

10.1.1.5.c   Mr. Partridge moved to insert after the words "same offence," the words "by any law of the United States."
New-York Daily Gazette, August 19, 1789, p. 802, col. 4
("Resolved in the negative").

10.1.1.5.d   Mr. PARTRIDGE moved to insert after the words "same offence," the words *"by any law of the United States,"* . . . .
Gazette of the U.S., August 22, 1789, p. 249, col. 3 ("Negatived").

10.1.1.6   Motion by Lawrance in House, August 17, 1789

10.1.1.6.a   Mr. LAWRANCE
[H]e thought it [the clause] ought to be confined to criminal cases, and moved an amendment for that purpose, . . .
Congressional Register, August 17, 1789, vol. 2, p. 225
("which amendment being adopted, the clause as amended
was unanimously agreed to by the committee").

10.1.1.6.b   Mr. LAWRANCE moved to insert after the words "nor shall" these words "in any criminal case."
Daily Advertiser, August 18, 1789, p. 2, col. 4
("This amendment was agreed to").

10.1.1.6.c   Mr. Lawrance moved to insert after the words "nor shall," these words, "in any criminal case."
New-York Daily Gazette, August 19, 1789, p. 802, col. 4
("This amendment was agreed to").

10.1.1.6.d   Mr. LAURANCE moved to insert after the words "nor shall" these words *in any criminal case.*
Gazette of the U.S., August 22, 1789, p. 249, col. 3
("This amendment was agreed to").

10.1.1.7   Further House Consideration, August 21, 1789

Seventh. No person shall be subject, except in case of impeachment, to more than one trial or one punishment for the same offence; nor shall he be compelled

in any criminal case to be a witness against himself; nor be deprived to life, liberty or property, without due process of law; nor shall private property be taken for public use, without just compensation.

HJ, p. 107 ("read and debated . . . agreed to by the House, . . . two-thirds of the members present concurring").[1]

10.1.1.8 House Resolution, August 24, 1789

ARTICLE THE EIGHTH.

No person shall be subject, except in case of impeachment, to more than one trial, or one punishment for the same offence, nor shall be compelled in any criminal case, to be a witness against himself, nor be deprived to life, liberty or property, without due process of law; nor shall private property be taken for public use without just compensation.

House Pamphlet, RG 46, DNA.

10.1.1.9 Senate Consideration, August 25, 1789

10.1.1.9.a The Resolve of the House of Representatives of the 24th of August, upon certain "Articles to be proposed to the Legislatures of the several States as Amendments to the Constitution of the United States" was read as followeth: . . .

Article the Eighth

"No person shall be subject, except in case of Impeachment, to more than one Trial, or one punishment for the same offence, nor shall be compelled in any Criminal case, to be a witness against himself, nor be deprived to life, liberty, or property, without due process of law; nor shall private property be taken for public use without just compensation.

Rough SJ, p. 217.

10.1.1.9.b The Resolve of the House of Representatives of the 24th of August, was read as followeth:

. . .

"Article the Eighth.

No person shall be subject, except in case of impeachment, to more than one trial, or one punishment for the same offence, nor shall be compelled in any criminal case, to be a witness against himself, nor be deprived to life, liberty or property, without due process of law; nor shall private property be taken for public use without just compensation.

Smooth SJ, p. 195.

10.1.1.9.c The Resolve of the House of Representatives of the 24th of August, was read as followeth:

. . .

"ARTICLE THE EIGHTH.

"No person shall be subject, except in case of impeachment, to more than one trial, or one punishment for the same offence, nor shall be compelled in any

---

[1]On August 22, 1789, the following motion was agreed to:
ORDERED, That it be referred to a committee of three, to prepare and report a proper arrangement of, and introduction to the articles of amendment to the Constitution of the United States, as agreed to by the House; and that Mr. Benson, Mr. Sherman, and Mr. Sedgwick be of the said committee.
HJ, p. 112.

criminal case, to be a witness against himself, nor be deprived to life, liberty or property, without due process of law; nor shall private property be taken for public use without just compensation.
Printed SJ, p. 105.

10.1.1.10 Further Senate Consideration, September 4, 1789

10.1.1.10.a On Motion to adopt the eighth Article of amendments proposed by the House of Representatives, striking out these words "Except in case of impeachment to more than one trial or one punishment" and substitute the following words.
"Be twice put in jeopardy of life or limb by any public prosecution."
Rough SJ, p. 249 ("It passed in the affirmative.").

10.1.1.10.b On motion, To adopt the eighth article of Amendments proposed by the House of Representatives, striking out these words, — "Except in case of impeachment to more than one trial or one punishment," and substitute the following words —
"Be twice put in jeopardy of life or limb by any public prosecution" —
Smooth SJ, p. 222 ("It passed in the Affirmative.").

10.1.1.10.c On motion, To adopt the eighth Article of Amendments proposed by the House of Representatives, striking out these words, — "Except in case of impeachment to more than one trial or one punishment," and substitute the following words —
"Be twice put in jeopardy of life or limb by any public prosecution" —
Printed SJ, p. 119 ("It passed in the Affirmative.").

10.1.1.10.d that the Senate do
Resolved ~~to~~ ∧ concur with the House of Representatives in
Article eighth
~~by~~ striking out these words. "Except in cases of impeachment to more than one
ing
trial or one punishment," and substitute ∧ the following words;
"Be twice put in jeopardy of life or limb by any public prosecution."
Senate MS, p. 3, RG 46, DNA.

10.1.1.11 Further Senate Consideration, September 9, 1789

10.1.1.11.a On motion, To alter Article 6th so as to stand Article 5th, and Article 7th so as to stand Article 6th, and Article 8th so as to stand Article 7th

. . .

On motion, That this last mentioned Article be amended to read as follows: "No person shall be held to answer for a capital or otherwise infamous crime, unless on a presentment or indictment of a grand Jury, except in cases arising in the land or naval forces, or in the Militia, when in actual service, in time of war or public danger, nor shall any person be subject to be put in jeopardy of life or limb, for the same offence, nor shall be compelled in any criminal case to be a witness against himself, nor be deprived of life, liberty or property, without due process of law; Nor shall private property be taken for public use without just compensation."
Rough SJ, p. 275 ("It passed in the affirmative.").

10.1.1.11.b   On motion, To alter article the sixth so as to stand article the fifth, and article the seventh so as to stand article the sixth, and article the eighth so as to stand article the seventh —

. . .

On motion, That this last mentioned article be amended to read as follows: "No person shall be held to answer for a capital or otherwise infamous crime, unless on a presentment or indictment of a Grand Jury, except in cases arising in the land or naval forces, or in the militia, when in actual service, in time of war or public danger, nor shall any person be subject to be put in jeopardy of life or limb, for the same offence, nor shall be compelled in any criminal case to be a witness against himself, nor be deprived of life, liberty or property, without due process of law: Nor shall private property be taken for public use without just compensation" —

Smooth SJ, p. 244 ("It passed in the Affirmative.").

10.1.1.11.c   On motion, To alter Article the sixth so as to stand Article the fifth, and Article the seventh so as to stand Article the sixth, and Article the eighth so as to stand Article the seventh —

. . .

On motion, That this last mentioned Article be amended to read as follows: "No person shall be held to answer for a capital or otherwise infamous crime, unless on a presentment or indictment of a Grand Jury, except in cases arising in the land or naval forces, or in the militia, when in actual service, in time of war or public danger, nor shall any person be subject to be put in jeopardy of life or limb, for the same offence, nor shall be compelled in any criminal case to be a witness against himself, nor be deprived of life, liberty or property, without due process of law: Nor shall private property be taken for public use without just compensation" —

Printed SJ, pp. 129–30 ("It passed in the Affirmative.").

10.1.1.11.d   To erase the word "Eighth" & insert Seventh —

To insert in the ~~Eighth~~ 8th [7th] article ~~as~~ after the word "shall" in the "1" line — be held to answer for a capital or otherwise infamous crime, unless on a presentment or indictment of a grand Jury, except in cases arising in the land or naval forces, or in the militia when in actual Service in time of War or publick danger, nor shall any person — &

To erase from the same article the words "except in case of impeachment, to more than one trial or one punishment" & insert — to be twice put in jeopardy of life or limb —

Ellsworth MS, p. 3, RG 46, DNA.

10.1.1.12   **Senate Resolution, September 9, 1789**

ARTICLE THE SEVENTH.

No person shall be held to answer for a capital, or otherwise infamous crime, unless on a presentment or indictment of a Grand Jury, except in cases arising in the land or naval forces, or in the militia, when in actual service in time of war or public danger; nor shall any person be subject for the same offence to be twice put in jeopardy of life or limb; nor shall be compelled in any criminal case, to be a witness against himself, nor be deprived of life, liberty or property, without due process of law; nor shall private property be taken for public use without just compensation.

Senate Pamphlet, RG 46, DNA.

10.1.1.13   Further House Consideration, September 21, 1789

RESOLVED, That this House doth agree to the second, fourth, eighth, twelfth, thirteenth, sixteenth, eighteenth, nineteenth, twenty-fifth, and twenty-sixth amendments, and doth disagree to the first, third, fifth, sixth, seventh, ninth, tenth, eleventh, fourteenth, fifteenth, seventeenth, twentieth, twenty-first, twenty-second, twenty-third, and twenty-fourth amendments proposed by the Senate to the said articles, two thirds of the members present concurring on each vote.

RESOLVED, That a conference be desired with the Senate on the subject matter of the amendments disagreed to, and that Mr. Madison, Mr. Sherman, and Mr. Vining, be appointed managers at the same on the part of this House.

HJ, p. 146.

10.1.1.14   Further Senate Consideration, September 21, 1789

10.1.1.14.a   A message from the House of Representatives —

Mr. Beckley, their Clerk, brought up a Resolve of the House of this date, to agree to the 2nd, 4th, 8th, 12th, 13th, 16th, 18th, 19th, 25th, and 26th Amendments proposed by the Senate, "To articles of Amendment to be proposed to the Legislatures of the several States, as Amendments to the Constitution of the United States," and to disagree to the 1st, 3d, 5th, 6th, 7th, 9th, 10th, 11th, 14th, 15th, 17th, 20th, 21st, 22d, 23d, and 24th amendments: Two thirds of the members present concurring on each vote: And "That a conference be desired with the Senate on the subject matter of the amendments disagreed to," and that Mr. Madison, Mr. Sherman, and Mr. Vining, be appointed managers of the same, on the part of the House of Representatives —

And he withdrew.

Smooth SJ, pp. 265–66.

10.1.1.14.b   A message from the House of Representatives —

Mr. Beckley, their Clerk, brought up a Resolve of the House of this date, to agree to the 2d, 4th, 8th, 12th, 13th, 16th, 18th, 19th, 25th, and 26th Amendments proposed by the Senate, "To Articles of Amendment to be proposed to the Legislatures of the several States, as Amendments to the Constitution of the United States," and to disagree to the 1st, 3d, 5th, 6th, 7th, 9th, 10th, 11th, 14th, 15th, 17th, 20th, 21st, 22d, 23d, and 24th Amendments: Two thirds of the members present concurring on each vote: And "That a conference be desired with the Senate on the subject matter of the Amendments disagreed to," and that Mr. Madison, Mr. Sherman, and Mr. Vining, be appointed managers of the same, on the part of the House of Representatives —

And he withdrew.

Printed SJ, pp. 141–42.

10.1.1.15 **Further Senate Consideration, September 21, 1789**

10.1.1.15.a   The Senate proceeded to consider the Message of the House of Representatives disagreeing to the Amendments made by the Senate "To Articles to be proposed to the Legislatures of the several States, as Amendments to the Constitution of the United States" And

RESOLVED, That the Senate do recede from their third Amendment, and do insist on all the others.

RESOLVED, That the Senate do concur with the House of Representatives in a conference on the subject matter of disagreement on the said Articles of Amendment, and that Mr. Ellsworth Mr. Carroll and Mr. Paterson be managers of the conference on the part of the Senate.   Smooth SJ, p. 267.

10.1.1.15.b   The Senate proceeded to consider the message of the House of Representatives disagreeing to the Amendments made by the Senate "To Articles to be proposed to the Legislatures of the several States, as Amendments to the Constitution of the United States" — And

RESOLVED, That the Senate do recede from their third Amendment, and do insist on all the others.

RESOLVED, That the Senate do concur with the House of Representatives in a conference on the subject matter of disagreement on the said Articles of Amendment, and that Mr. Ellsworth, Mr. Carroll, and Mr. Paterson be managers of the conference on the part of the Senate.   Printed SJ, p. 142.

10.1.1.16 **Conference Committee Report, September 24, 1789**

[T]hat it will be proper for the House of Representatives to agree to the said Amendments proposed by the Senate, with an Amendment to their fifth Amendment, so that the third Article shall read as follows: "Congress shall make no Law respecting an establishment of Religion, or prohibiting the free exercise thereof; or abridging the freedom of Speech, or of the Press; or the right of the people peaceably to assemble and to petition the Government for a redress of grievances;" And with an Amendment to the fourteenth Amendment proposed by the Senate, so that the eighth Article, as numbered in the Amendments proposed by the Senate, shall read as follows "In all criminal prosecutions, the accused shall enjoy the right to a speedy & publick trial by an impartial jury of the district wherein the crime shall have been committed, as the district shall have been previously ascertained by law, and to be informed of the nature and cause of the accusation; to be confronted with the witnesses against him, and to have com-

to
pulsory process for obtaining witnesses against him in his favour, & /\ have the assistance of counsel for his defence."

Conference MS, RG 46, DNA (Ellsworth's handwriting).

10.1.1.17 **House Consideration of Conference Committee Report, September 24 [25], 1789**

RESOLVED, That this House doth recede from their disagreement to the first, third, fifth, sixth, seventh, ninth, tenth, eleventh, fourteenth, fifteenth, seven-

teenth, twentieth, twenty-first, twenty-second, twenty-third, and twenty-fourth amendments, insisted on by the Senate: PROVIDED, That the two articles which by the amendments of the Senate are now proposed to be inserted as the third and eighth articles, shall be amended to read as followeth;

Article the third. "Congress shall make no law respecting an establishment of religion, or prohibiting the free exercise thereof; or abridging the freedom of speech, or of the press; or the right of the people peaceably to assemble, and to petition the government for a redress of grievances."

Article the eighth. "In all criminal prosecutions, the accused shall enjoy the right to a speedy and public trial by an impartial jury of the state and district wherein the crime shall have been committed, which district shall have been previously ascertained by law, and to be informed of the nature and cause of the accusation, to be confronted with the witnesses against him, to have compulsory process for obtaining witnesses in his favor, and to have the assistance of council for his defence."

HJ, p. 152 ("On the question, that the House do agree to the alteration and amendment of the eighth article, in manner aforesaid, It was resolved in the affirmative. Ayes 37 Noes 14").

10.1.1.18   Senate Consideration of Conference Committee Report, September 24, 1789

10.1.1.18.a   Mr. Ellsworth, on behalf of the managers of the conference on "articles to be proposed to the several States as Amendments to the Constitution of the United States," reported as follows:

That it will be proper for the House of Representatives to agree to the said amendments proposed by the Senate, with an Amendment to their fifth Amendment, so that the third Article shall read as follows: "Congress shall make no law respecting an establishment of <u>Religion</u>, or prohibiting the free exercise thereof; or abridging the freedom of Speech, or of the Press; or the right of the people peaceably to assemble and petition the Government for a redress of Grievances;" And with an Amendment to the fourteenth Amendment proposed by the Senate, so that the eighth article, as numbered in the Amendments proposed by the Senate, shall read as follows; "In all criminal prosecutions, the accused shall enjoy the right to a speedy and public trial by an impartial <u>Jury</u> of the district wherein the <u>Crime</u> shall have been committed, as the district shall have been previously ascertained by law, and to be informed of the nature and cause of the accusation, to be confronted with the witnesses against him, and to have compulsory process for obtaining witnesses in his favor, and to have the assistance of Counsel for defence."

Smooth SJ, pp. 272–73.

10.1.1.18.b   Mr. Ellsworth, on behalf of the managers of the conference on "Articles to be proposed to the several States as Amendments to the Constitution of the United States," reported as follows:

That it will be proper for the House of Representatives to agree to the said Amendments proposed by the Senate, with an Amendment to their fifth Amendment, so that the third Article shall read as follows: "Congress shall make no Law RESPECTING AN ESTABLISHMENT OF RELIGION, or prohibiting the free exercise thereof; or abridging the freedom of Speech, or of the Press; or the right of the

People peaceably to assemble and petition the Government for a redress of Grievances;" And with an Amendment to the fourteenth Amendment proposed by the
Senate, so that the eighth Article, as numbered in the Amendments proposed by
the Senate, shall read as follows; "In all criminal prosecutions, the accused shall
enjoy the right to a speedy and public trial BY AN IMPARTIAL JURY OF THE DIS-
TRICT WHEREIN THE CRIME SHALL HAVE BEEN COMMITTED, AS THE DISTRICT
SHALL HAVE BEEN PREVIOUSLY ASCERTAINED BY LAW, and to be informed of the
nature and cause of the accusation, to be confronted with the witnesses against
him, and to have compulsory process for obtaining witnesses in his favor, and to
have the assistance of Counsel for defence."

Printed SJ, p. 145.

10.1.1.19 Further Senate Consideration of Conference Committee Report, September 24, 1789

10.1.1.19.a   A Message from the House of Representatives —
Mr. Beckley, their Clerk, brought up the Amendments to the "Articles to be
proposed to the Legislatures of the several States, as Amendments to the Constitution of the United States;" and informed the Senate, that the House of Representatives had receded from their disagreement to the 1st, 3d, 5th, 6th, 7th, 9th, 10th,
11th, 14th, 15th, 17th, 20th, 21st, 22d, 23d, and 24th Amendments, insisted on
by the Senate: Provided that the "Two Articles, which by the Amendments of the
Senate are now proposed to be inserted as the third and eighth Articles," shall be
amended to read as followeth:
Article the Third. "Congress shall make no Law respecting an establishment of
Religion, or prohibiting the free exercise thereof; or abridging the freedom of
Speech, or of the Press; or the right of the people peaceably to assemble, and
petition the Government for a redress of Grievances."
Article the Eighth. "In all criminal prosecutions the accused shall enjoy the right
to a speedy and public trial by an impartial Jury of the State and District, wherein
the crime shall have been committed, which District shall have been previously
ascertained by law, and to be informed of the nature and cause of the accusation, to
be confronted with the witnesses against him, and to have compulsory process for
obtaining witnesses in his favor, and to have the assistance of Counsel for his
defence."

Smooth SJ, pp. 278–79.

10.1.1.19.b   A Message from the House of Representatives —
Mr. Beckley, their Clerk, brought up the Amendments to the "Articles to be
proposed to the Legislatures of the several States, as Amendments to the Constitution of the United States;" and informed the Senate, that the House of Representatives had receded from their disagreement to the 1st, 3d, 5th, 6th, 7th, 9th, 10th,
11th, 14th, 15th, 17th, 20th, 21st, 22d, 23d, and 24th Amendments, insisted on
by the Senate: Provided that the "Two Articles, which by the Amendments of the
Senate are now proposed to be inserted as the third and eighth Articles," shall be
amended to read as followeth:
Article the Third. "Congress shall make no Law respecting an establishment of
Religion, or prohibiting the free exercise thereof; or abridging the freedom of

Speech, or of the Press; or the right of the People peaceably to assemble, and petition the Government for a redress of Grievances."

Article the Eighth. "In all criminal prosecutions the accused shall enjoy the right to a speedy and public trial by an impartial Jury of the State and District, wherein the crime shall have been committed, which District shall have been previously ascertained by law, and to be informed of the nature and cause of the accusation, to be confronted with the witnesses against him, and to have compulsory process for obtaining witnesses in his favor, and to have the assistance of Counsel for his defence."

Printed SJ, p.148.

10.1.1.20 Further Senate Consideration of Conference Committee Report, September 25, 1789

10.1.1.20.a   The Senate proceeded to consider the Message from the House of Representatives of the 24th, with Amendments to the Amendments of the Senate, to "Articles to be proposed to the Legislatures of the several States, as Amendments to the Constitution of the United States" — And

RESOLVED, That the Senate do concur in the Amendments proposed by the House of Representatives, to the Amendments of the Senate.   Smooth SJ, p. 283.

10.1.1.20.b   The Senate proceeded to consider the Message from the House of Representatives of the 24th, with Amendments to the Amendments of the Senate, to "Articles to be proposed to the Legislatures of the several States, as Amendments to the Constitution of the United States" — And

RESOLVED, That the Senate do concur in the Amendments proposed by the House of Representatives, to the Amendments of the Senate.

Printed SJ, pp. 150–51.

10.1.1.21 Agreed Resolution, September 25, 1789

10.1.1.21.a   Article the Seventh.

No person shall be held to answer for a capital, or otherwise infamous crime, unless on a presentment or indictment of a Grand Jury, except in cases arising in the land or naval forces, or in the militia, when in actual service in time of war or public danger; nor shall any person be subject for the same offence to be twice put in jeopardy of life or limb; nor shall be compelled in any criminal case, to be a witness against himself, nor be deprived of life, liberty or property, without due process of law; nor shall private property be taken for public use without just compensation.

Smooth SJ, Appendix, p. 293.

10.1.1.21.b   ARTICLE the SEVENTH.

No person shall be held to answer for a capital, or otherwise infamous crime, unless on a presentment or indictment of a Grand Jury, except in cases arising in the land or naval forces, or in the militia, when in actual service in time of war or public danger; nor shall any person be subject for the same offence to be twice put in jeopardy of life or limb; nor shall be compelled in any criminal case, to be a witness against himself, nor be deprived of life, liberty or property, without due

process of law; nor shall private property be taken for public use without just compensation.

Printed SJ, Appendix, p. 164.

10.1.1.22 Enrolled Resolution, September 28, 1789

Article the seventh . . . No person shall be held to answer for a capital, or otherwise infamous crime, unless on a presentment or indictment of a Grand Jury, except in cases arising in the land or naval forces, or in the militia, when in actual service in time of war or public danger; nor shall any person be subject for the same offence to be twice put in jeopardy of life or limb, nor shall be compelled in any criminal case, to be a witness against himself, nor be deprived of life, liberty, or property, without due process of law; nor shall private property be taken for public use without just compensation.

Enrolled Resolutions, RG 11, DNA.

10.1.1.23 Printed Versions

10.1.1.23.a ART. V. No person shall be held to answer for a capital or otherwise infamous crime, unless on a presentment or indictment of a grand jury, except in cases arising in the land or naval forces, or in the militia, when in actual service, in time of war or public danger; nor shall any person be subject for the same offence to be twice put in jeopardy of life or limb; nor shall be compelled, in any criminal case, to be witness against himself; nor be deprived of life, liberty, or property, without due process of law; nor shall private property be taken for public use without just compensation.

Statutes at Large, vol. 1, p. 21.

10.1.1.23.b ART. VII. No person shall be held to answer for a capital, or otherwise infamous crime, unless on a presentment or indictment of a grand jury, except in cases arising in the land or naval forces, or in the militia when in actual service in time of war or public danger; nor shall any person be subject for the same offence to be twice put in jeopardy of life or limb; nor shall be compelled in any criminal case to be a witness against himself, nor be deprived of life, liberty or property, without due process of law; nor shall private property be taken for public use without just compensation.

Statutes at Large, vol. 1, p. 98.

10.1.2 PROPOSALS FROM THE STATE CONVENTIONS

10.1.2.1 New York, July 26, 1788

That no Person ought to be taken imprisoned, or disseised of his freehold, or be exiled or deprived of his Privileges, Franchises, Life, Liberty or Property but by due process of Law.

State Ratifications, RG 11, DNA.

10.1.2.2 North Carolina, August 1, 1788

9th. That no freeman ought to be taken, imprisoned, or disseized of his freehold, liberties, privileges or franchises, or outlawed or exiled, or in any manner destroyed or deprived of his life, liberty, or property but by the law of the land.

State Ratifications, RG 11, DNA.

10.1.2.3 Pennsylvania Minority, December 12, 1787

3. That in all capital and criminal prosecutions, a man has a right to demand the cause and nature of his accusation, as well in the federal courts, as in those of the several states; to be heard by himself or his counsel; to be confronted with the accusers and witnesses; to call for evidence in his favor, and a speedy trial, by an impartial jury of the vicinage, without whose unanimous consent, he cannot be found guilty, nor can he be compelled to give evidence against himself; that no man be deprived of his liberty, except by the law of the land or the judgment of his peers.

Pennsylvania Packet, December 18, 1787.

10.1.2.4 Virginia, June 27, 1788

Ninth, That no freeman ought to be taken, imprisoned, or disseised of his freehold, liberties, privileges or franchises, or outlawed or exiled, or in any manner destroyed or deprived of his life, liberty or property but by the law of the land.

State Ratifications, RG 11, DNA.

10.1.3 STATE CONSTITUTIONS AND LAWS; COLONIAL CHARTERS AND LAWS

10.1.3.1 Connecticut

10.1.3.1.a New Haven Code, 1655

It is Ordered by this Court, and the Authority thereof, that no mans life, shall be taken away, no mans honour, or good name, shall be stained, no mans person shall be imprisoned, banished, or otherwise punished, no man shall be deprived of his wife, or children, no mans goods, or estate shall be taken from him, under colour of Law, or Countenance of Authority, unlesse it be by vertue, or equity of some expresse Law of this Jurisdiction, established by the Generall Court, and sufficiently published, or for want of a Law in any particular case, by the word of God, either in the Court of Magistrates, or some Plantation Court, according to the weight and valew of the cause, onely all Capitall causes, concerning life or banishment; where there is no expresse Law, shall be judged according to the word and Law of God, by the Generall Court.

New Haven's Lawes, pp. 16–17.

10.1.3.1.b Declaration of Rights, 1776

[2] *And be it further Enacted and Declared, by the Authority aforesaid,* That no Man's Life shall be taken away: No Man's Honor or good Name shall be stained: No Man's Person shall be arrested, restrained, banished, dismembered, nor any ways punished: No Man shall be deprived of his Wife or Children: No Man's Goods or Estate shall be taken away from him, nor any ways indamaged under the colour of Law, or countenance of Authority; unless clearly warranted by the Laws of this State.

Connecticut Acts, pp. 1–2.

10.1.3.2 Maryland

10.1.3.2.a Act for the Liberties of the People, 1639

Be it Enacted By the Lord Proprietarie of this Province of and with the advice and approbation of the ffreemen of the same that all the Inhabitants of this Province being Christians (Slaves excepted[)] Shall have and enjoy all such rights liberties immunities priviledges and free customs within this Province as any naturall born subject of England hath or ought to have or enjoy in the Realm of England by force or vertue of the common law or Statute Law of England (saveing in such Cases as the same are or may be altered or changed by the Laws and ordinances of this Province)

And Shall not be imprisoned nor disseissd or dispossessed of their freehold goods or Chattels or be out Lawed Exiled or otherwise destroyed fore judged or punished then according to the Laws of this province saveing to the Lord proprietarie and his heirs all his rights and prerogatives by reason of his domination and Seigniory over this Province and the people of the same This Act to Continue till the end of the next Generall Assembly

Liber C.K.W.H., p. 2, Archives of the State of Maryland
(read twice, not passed).

10.1.3.2.b Declaration of Rights, 1776

21. That no freeman ought to be taken or imprisoned, or disseized of his freehold, liberties or privileges, or outlawed, or exiled, or in any manner destroyed, or deprived of his life, liberty or property, but by the judgment of his peers, or by the law of the land.

Maryland Laws, November 3, 1776.

10.1.3.3 Massachusetts

10.1.3.3.a Body of Liberties, 1641

[1] No mans life shall be taken away, no mans honour or good name shall be stayned, no mans person shall be arested, restrayned, banished, dismembred, nor any wayes punished, no man shall be deprived of his wife or children, no mans goods or estaite shall be taken away from him, nor any way indammaged under coulor of law or Countenance of Authoritie, unlesse it be by vertue or equitie of some expresse law of the Country waranting the same, established by a generall Court and sufficiently published, or in case of the defect of a law in any parteculer case by the word of god. And in Capitall cases, or in cases concerning dismembring or banishment, according to that word to be judged by the Generall Court.

[2] Every person within this Jurisdiction, whether Inhabitant or forreiner shall enjoy the same justice and law, that is generall for the plantation, which we constitute and execute one towards another without partialitie or delay.

Massachusetts Colonial Laws, p. 33.

10.1.3.3.b General Laws of New-Plimouth, 1671 [1636]

4. It is also Enacted, that no person in this Government shall be endamaged in respect of Life, Limb, Liberty, Good name or Estate, under colour of Law, or

countenance of Authority, but by virtue or equity of some express Law of the General Court of this Colony, the known Law of God, or the good and equitable Laws of our Nation suitable for us, being brought to Answer by due process thereof.

New-Plimouth Laws, p. 2.

10.1.3.3.c Constitution, 1780

[Part I, Article] XII. No subject shall be held to answer for any crime or offence until the same is fully and plainly, substantially and formally, described to him; or be compelled to accuse, or furnish evidence against himself. And every subject shall have a right to produce all proofs, that may be favourable to him; to meet the witnesses against him, face to face, and to be fully heard in his defence by himself, or his counsel, at his election. And no subject shall be arrested, imprisoned, despoiled, or deprived of his property, immunities, or privileges, put out of the protection of the law, exiled, or deprived of his life, liberty, or estate, but by the judgment of his peers, or the law of the land.

And the legislature shall not make any law, that shall subject any person to a capital or infamous punishment, excepting for the government of the army and navy, without trial by jury.

Massachusetts Perpetual Laws, pp. 6–7.

10.1.3.4 New Hampshire: Constitution, 1783

[Part I, Article] XV. No subject shall be held to answer for any crime, or offence, until the same is fully and plainly, substantially and formally described to him; or be compelled to accuse or furnish evidence against himself. And every subject shall have a right to produce all proofs that may be favorable to himself: To meet the witnesses against him face to face, and to be fully heard in his defence by himself and counsel. And no subject shall be arrested, imprisoned, despoiled, or deprived of his property, immunities, or priviliges, put out of the protection of the law, exiled or deprived of his life, liberty, or estate, but by the judgment of his peers or the law of the land.

New Hampshire Laws, p. 25.

10.1.3.5 New Jersey

10.1.3.5.a Concessions and Agreements of West New Jersey, 1676

Chapter XVII.

THAT no Proprietor, Freeholder or Inhabitant of the said Province of *West New-Jersey,* shall be deprived or condemned of Life, Limb, Liberty, Estate, Property or any ways hurt in his or their Privileges, Freedoms or Franchises, upon any account whatsoever, without a due Tryal, and Judgment passed by Twelve good and lawful Men of his Neighbourhood first had: And that in all Causes to be tryed, and in all Tryals, the Person or Persons, arraigned may except against any of the said Neighbourhood, without any Reason rendered, (not exceeding Thirty five) and in case of any valid reason alleged, against every Person nominated for that Service.

New Jersey Grants, p. 395.

10.1.3.5.b Fundamental Constitutions for East New Jersey, 1683

XIX. That no Person or Persons within the said Province shall be taken and imprisoned, or be devised of his Freehold, free Custom or Liberty, or be outlawed or exiled, or any other Way destroyed; nor shall they be condemn'd or Judgment pass'd upon them, but by lawful Judgment of their Peers: Neither shall Justice nor Right be bought or sold, defered or delayed, to any Person whatsoever: In order to which by the Laws of the Land, all Tryals shall be by twelve Men, and as near as it may be, Peers and Equals, and of the Neighbourhood, and Men without just Exception. In Cases of Life there shall be at first Twenty four returned by the Sherriff for a Grand Inquest, of whom twelve at least shall be to find the Complaint to be true; and then the Twelve Men or Peers to be likewise returned, shall have the final Judgment; but reasonable Challenges shall be always admitted against the Twelve Men, or any of them: But the Manner of returning Juries shall be thus, the Names of all the Freemen above five and Twenty Years of Age, within the District or Boroughs out of which the Jury is to be returned, shall be written on equal Pieces of Parchment and put into a Box, and then the Number of the Jury shall be drawn out by a Child under Ten Years of Age. And in all Courts Persons of all Perswasions may freely appear in their own Way, and according to their own Manner, and there personally plead their own Causes themselves, or if unable, by their Friends, no Person being allowed to take Money for pleading or advice in such Casas [sic]: And the first Process shall be the Exhibition of the Complaint in Court fourteen Days before the Tryal, and the Party complain'd against may be fitted for the same, he or she shall be summoned ten Days before, and a Copy of the Complaint delivered at their dwelling House: But before the Complaint of any Person be received, he shall solemnly declare in Court, that he believes in his Conscience his Cause is just. Moreover, every Man shall be first cited before the Court for the Place where he dwells, nor shall the Cause be brought before any other Court but by way of Appeal from Sentence of the first Court, for receiving of which Appeals, there shall be a Court consisting of eight Persons, and the Governor (protempore) President thereof, (*to wit*) four Proprietors and four Freemen, to be chosen out of the great Council in the following Manner, *viz.* the Names of Sixteen of the Proprietors shall be written on small pieces of Parchment and put into a Box, out of which by a Lad under Ten Years of Age, shall be drawn eight of them, the eight remaining in the Box shall choose four; and in like Manner shall be done for the choosing of four of the Freemen.   New Jersey Grants, pp. 163–64.

10.1.3.6 New York

10.1.3.6.a Act Declaring . . . Rights & Priviledges, 1691

That no Free-man shall be taken or imprisoned, or be deprived of his Free-hold or Liberty, or free Customs, or Out-Lawed, or Exiled, or any other wayes destroyed; nor shall be passed upon, adjudged or condemned, but by the lawful Judgment of his Peers, and by the Laws of this Province.

Justice nor Right shall be neither Sold, Denyed or Delayed to any Person within this Province.

. . .

That no Man, of what Estate or Condition soever, shall be put out of his Lands, Tenements, nor taken, nor imprisoned, nor disinherited, nor banished, nor any ways destroyed or molested, without first being brought to answer by due course of Law.

New York Acts, p. 17.

10.1.3.6.b Constitution, 1777

XIII. And this Convention doth further, in the Name, and by the Authority of the good People of this State, ORDAIN, DETERMINE, AND DECLARE, That no Member of this State shall be disfranchised, or deprived of any of the Rights or Privileges secured to the Subjects of this State by this Constitution, unless by the Law of the Land, or the Judgment of his Peers.

New York Laws, vol. 1, p. 8.

10.1.3.6.c Bill of Rights, 1787

Second, That no Citizen of this State shall be taken or imprisoned, or be disseised of his or her Freehold, or Liberties, or Free-Customs; or outlawed, or exiled, or condemned, or otherwise destroyed, but by lawful Judgment of his or her Peers, or by due Process of Law.

Third, That no Citizen of this State shall be taken or imprisoned for any Offence, upon Petition or Suggestion, unless it be by indictment or Presentment of good and lawful Men of the same Neighbourhood where such Deeds be done, in due Manner, or by due Process of Law.

Fourth, That no Person shall be put to answer without Presentment before Justices, or Matter of Record, or due Process of Law, according to the Law of the Land; and if any Thing be done to the Contrary, it shall be void in Law, and holden for Error.

Fifth, That no Person, of what Estate or Condition soever, shall be taken, or imprisoned, or disinherited, or put to death, without being brought to answer by due Process of Law; and that no Person shall be put out of his or her Franchise or Freehold, or lose his or her Life or Limb, or Goods and Chattels, unless he or she be duly brought to answer, and be fore-judged of the same, by due Course of Law; and if any Thing be done contrary to the same, it shall be void in Law, and holden for none.

New York Laws, vol. 2, p. 1.

10.1.3.7 North Carolina: Declaration of Rights, 1776

Sect. XII. That no Freeman ought to be taken, imprisoned or disseissed of his Freehold, Liberties or Privileges, or outlawed or exiled, or in any manner destroyed or deprived of his Life, Liberty or Property, but by the Law of the Land.

North Carolina Laws, p. 275.

10.1.3.8 Pennsylvania

10.1.3.8.a Constitution, 1776

CHAPTER I.

. . .

IX. That in all prosecutions for criminal offences, a man hath a right to be heard by himself and his council, to demand the cause and nature of his accusation, to be confronted with the witnesses, to call for evidence in his favour, and a speedy public trial, by an impartial jury of the country, without the unanimous consent of which jury he cannot be found guilty; nor can he be compelled to give evidence against himself; nor can any man be justly deprived of his liberty except by the laws of the land, or the judgment of his peers.   Pennsylvania Acts, M'Kean, pp. ix–x.

10.1.3.8.b   **Constitution, 1790**

ARTICLE IX.

. . .

SECT. IX. That, in all criminal prosecutions, the accused hath a right to be heard by himself and his council, to demand the nature and cause of the accusation against him, to meet the witnesses face to face, to have compulsory process for obtaining witnesses in his favour, and, in prosecutions by indictment or information, a speedy public trial by an impartial jury of the vicinage: That he cannot be compelled to give evidence against himself, nor can he be deprived of his life, liberty, or property, unless by the judgment of his peers, or the law of the land.
Pennsylvania Acts, Dallas, p. xxxiv.

10.1.3.9   **Rhode Island: Code of Laws, 1647**

1. That no person, in this Colony, shall be taken or imprisoned, or be disseized of his lands or liberties, or be exiled, or any otherwise molested or destroyed, but by the lawful judgment of his peers, or by some known law, and according to the letter of it, ratified and confirmed by the major part of the General Assembly, lawfully met and orderly managed.   Rhode Island Code, p. 12.

10.1.3.10   **South Carolina**

10.1.3.10.a   **Constitution, 1778**

XLI. That no Freeman of this State be taken, or imprisoned, or disseized of his Freehold, Liberties or Privileges, or out-lawed, or exiled, or in any Manner destroyed, or deprived of his Life, Liberty, or Property, but by the Judgment of his Peers, or by the Law of the Land.   South Carolina Constitution, p. 15.

10.1.3.10.b   **Constitution, 1790**

ARTICLE IX.

. . .

Section 2. No freeman of this state shall be taken, or imprisoned, or disseised of his freehold, liberties, or privileges, or outlawed or exiled, or in any manner destroyed, or deprived of his life, liberty or property, but by the judgment of his peers, or by the law of the land; nor shall any bill of the attainder, ex post facto law or law impairing the obligation of contracts ever be passed by the legislature of this state.

. . .

Section 6. The trial by jury as heretofore used in this state, and the liberty of the press, shall be for ever inviolably preserved.   South Carolina Laws, App., pp. 41–42.

10.1.3.11 Vermont: Declaration of Rights, 1777

CHAPTER I.

. . .

10. THAT, in all Prosecutions for criminal Offences, a Man hath a Right to be heard by himself and his Counsel, — to demand the Cause and Nature of his Accusation, — to be confronted with the Witnesses, — to call for Evidence in his Favor, and a speedy public Trial, by an impartial Jury of the Country, without the unanimous Consent of which Jury, he cannot be [fo]und guilty; nor can he be compelled to give Evidence against himself; nor can any man be justly deprived of his Liberty, except by the Laws of the Land, or the Judgment of his Peers.

Vermont Acts, p. 4.

10.1.3.12 Virginia: Declaration of Rights, May 6, 1776

VIII. THAT in all capital or criminal prosecutions a man hath a right to demand the cause and nature of his accusation, to be confronted with the accusers and witnesses, to call for evidence in his favour, and to a speedy trial by an impartial jury of his vicinage, without whose unanimous consent he cannot be found guilty, nor can he be compelled to give evidence against himself; that no man be deprived of his liberty except by the law of the land, or the judgment of his peers.

Virginia Acts, p. 33.

10.1.4 OTHER TEXTS

10.1.4.1 Magna Carta, 1297

No freeman shall be taken or imprisoned, or be disseised of his freehold, or liberties, or free customs, or be outlawed, or exiled, or any other wise destroyed; nor will we not pass upon him, nor condemn him, but by lawful judgment of his peers, or by the law of the land. We will sell to no man, we will not deny or defer to any man either justice or right.   25 Edw. 1, c. 29.

10.1.4.2 Petition of Right, 1627

3. And where alsoe by the Statute called the Great Charter of the liberties of England, it is declared and enacted, that no freeman may be taken or imprisoned or be disseised of his freehold or liberties or his free customes or be outlawed or exiled or in any manner destroyed, but by the lawfull judgment of his peeres or by the law of the land.

4. And in the eight and twentith yeere of the raigne of King Edward the Third it was declared and enacted by authoritie of Parliament, that no man of what estate or condicion that he be, should be put out of his land or tenemente nor taken nor imprisoned nor disherited nor put to death without being brought to aunswere by due pcesse of lawe.   3 Car. 1, c. 1.

10.1.4.3 Declaration and Resolves of the First Continental Congress, October 14, 1774

Resolved, N.C.D. 1. That they are entitled to life, liberty and property: and they have never ceded to any foreign power whatever, a right to dispose of either without their consent.

Tansill, p. 2.

10.1.4.4 Northwest Territory Ordinance, 1787

Article the Second. The inhabitants of the said territory shall always be entitled to the benefits of the writ of habeas corpus, and of the trial by jury; of a proportionate representation of the people in the legislature, and of judicial proceedings according to the course of the common law; all persons shall be bailable unless for Capital Offences, where the proof shall be evident, or the presumption great; all fines shall be moderate, and no cruel or unusual punishments shall be inflicted; no man shall be deprived of his liberty or property but by the judgment of his peers, or the law of the land; and should the public exigencies make it Necessary for the common preservation to take any persons property, or to demand his particular services, full compensation shall be made for the same; and in the just preservation of rights and property it is understood and declared, that no law ought ever to be made, or have force in the said territory, that shall in any manner whatever interfere with, or affect private contracts or engagements bona fide and without fraud, previously formed.

Continental Congress Papers, DNA.

10.2 DISCUSSION OF DRAFTS AND PROPOSALS

10.2.1 THE FIRST CONGRESS

10.2.1.1 June 8, 1789[2]

10.2.1.2 August 17, 1789

Discussion was limited to self-incrimination and double jeopardy issues.[3]

10.2.2 STATE CONVENTIONS

None.

10.2.3 PHILADELPHIA CONVENTION

None.

10.2.4 NEWSPAPERS AND PAMPHLETS

10.2.4.1 The Federal Farmer, No. 16, January 20, 1788

Security against expost facto laws, the trial by jury, and the benefits of the writ of habeas corpus, are but a part of those inestimable rights the people of the United States are entitled to, even in judicial proceedings, by the course of the common law. These may be secured in general words, as in New-York, the Western Territory, &c. by declaring the people of the United States shall always be

---

[2]For the reports of Madison's speech in support of his proposals, *see* 1.2.1.1.a–c.
[3]For the reports of the House's discussion of its Eighth Amendment, *see* 8.2.1.2.a–d.

entitled to judicial proceedings according to the course of the common law, as used and established in the said states. Perhaps it would be better to enumerate the particular essential rights the people are entitled to in these proceedings, as has been done in many of the states, and as has been done in England. In this case, the people may proceed to declare, that no man shall be held to answer to any offence, till the same be fully described to him; nor to furnish evidence against himself: that, except in the government of the army and navy, no person shall be tried for any offence, whereby he may incur loss of life, or an infamous punishment, until he be first indicted by a grand jury: that every person shall have a right to produce all proofs that may be favourable to him, and to meet the witnesses against him face to face: that every person shall be entitled to obtain right and justice freely and without delay; that all persons shall have a right to be secure from all unreasonable searches and seizures of their persons, houses, papers, or possessions; and that all warrants shall be deemed contrary to this right, if the foundation of them be not previously supported by oath, and there be not in them a special designation of persons or objects of search, arrest, or seizure: and that no person shall be exiled or molested in his person or effects, otherwise than by the judgment of his peers, or according to the law of the land. A celebrated writer observes upon this last article, that in itself it may be said to comprehend the whole end of political society. These rights are not necessarily reserved, they are established, or enjoyed but in few countries: they are stipulated rights, almost peculiar to British and American laws. In the execution of those laws, individuals by long custom, by magna charta, bills of rights &c. have become entitled to them. A man, at first, by act of parliament, became entitled to the benefits of the writ of habeas corpus — men are entitled to these rights and benefits in the judicial proceedings of our state courts generally: but it will by no means follow, that they will be entitled to them in the federal courts, and have a right to assert them, unless secured and established by the constitution or federal laws. We certainly, in federal processes, might as well claim the benefits of the writ of habeas corpus, as to claim trial by a jury — the right to have council — to have witnesses face to face — to be secure against unreasonable search warrants, &c. was the constitution silent as to the whole of them: — but the establishment of the former, will evince that we could not claim them without it; and the omission of the latter, implies they are relinquished, or deemed of no importance. These are rights and benefits individuals acquire by compact; they must claim them under compacts, or immemorial usage — it is doubtful, at least, whether they can be claimed under immemorial usage in this country; and it is, therefore, we generally claim them under compacts, as charters and constitutions.

Storing, vol. 2, pp. 327–28.

10.2.4.2   The Impartial Examiner, No. 1, March 5, 1788

. . . For a system, which is to supersede the present different governments of the states, by ordaining that "laws made in pursuance thereof shall be supreme, and shall bind the judges in every state, any thing in the constitution or laws of any state to the contrary notwithstanding," must be alarming indeed! What cannot this omnipotence of power effect? How will your bill of rights avail you any thing?

By this authority the Congress can make laws, which shall bind all, repugnant to your present constitution — repugnant to every article of your right; for they are a part of your constitution, — they are the basis of it. So that if you pass this new constitution, you will have a naked plan of government unlimited in its jurisdiction, which not only expunges your bill of rights by rendering ineffectual, all the state governments; but is proposed without any kind of stipulation for any of those natural rights, the security whereof ought to be the end of all governments. Such a stipulaton is so necessary, that it is an absurdity to suppose any civil liberty can exist without it. Because it cannot be alledged in any case whatsoever, that a breach has been committed — that a right has been violated; as there will be no standard to resort to — no criterion to ascertain the breach, or even to find whether there has been any violation at all. Hence it is evident that the most flagrant acts of oppression may be inflicted; yet, still there will be no apparent object injured: there will be no unconstitutional infringement. For instance, if Congress should pass a law that persons charged with capital crimes shall not have a *right to demand the cause or nature of the accusation,* shall not be *confronted with the accusers or witnesses, or call for evidence in their own favor;* and a question should arise respecting their authority therein, — can it be said that they have exceeded the limits of their jurisdiction, when *that* has no limits; when no provision has been made for such a right? — When no responsibility on the part of Congress has been required by the constitution? The same observation may be made on any arbitrary or capricious imprisonments *contrary to the law of the land.* The same may be made, if *excessive bail should be required;* if *excessive fines should be imposed;* if *cruel and unusual punishments should be inflicted;* if *the liberty of the press should be restrained;* in a word — if laws should be made totally derogatory to the whole catalogue of rights, which are now secure under your present form of government.

Virginia Independent Chronicle, Kaminski & Saladino, vol. 8, p. 462.

10.2.5 LETTERS AND DIARIES

None.

10.3 DISCUSSION OF RIGHTS

10.3.1 TREATISES

10.3.1.1 William Blackstone, 1765

THE absolute rights of every Englishman (which, taken in a political and extensive sense, are usually called their liberties) as they are founded on nature and reason, so they are coeval with our form of government; though subject at times to fluctuate and change: their establishment (excellent as it is) being still human. At some times we have seen them depressed by overbearing and tyrannical princes; at others so luxuriant as even to tend to anarchy, a worse state than tyranny itself, as any government is better than none at all. But the vigour of our free constitution has always delivered the nation from these embarassments, and, as soon as the convulsions consequent on the struggle have been over, the ballance of our rights and liberties has settled to it's [*sic*] proper level; and their fundamental articles have been from time to time asserted in parliament, as often as they were thought to be in danger.

FIRST, by the great charter of liberties, which was obtained, sword in hand, from king John; and afterwards, with some alterations, confirmed in parliament by king Henry the third, his son. Which charter contained very few new grants; but, as sir Edward Coke observes, was for the most part declaratory of the principal grounds of the fundamental laws of England. Afterwards by the statute called *confirmatio cartarum*, whereby the great charter is directed to be allowed as the common law; all judgments contrary to it are declared void; copies of it are ordered to be sent to all cathedral churches, and read twice a year to the people; and sentence of excommunication is directed to be as constantly denounced against all those that by word, deed, or counsel act contrary thereto, or in any degree infringe it. Next by a multitude of subsequent corroborating statutes, (sir Edward Coke, I think, reckons thirty two,) from the first Edward to Henry the fourth. Then, after a long interval, by *the petition of right;* which was a parliamentary declaration of the liberties of the people, assented to by king Charles the first in the beginning of his reign. Which was closely followed by the still more ample concessions made by that unhappy prince to his parliament, before the fatal rupture between them; and by the many salutary laws, particularly the *habeas corpus* act, passed under Charles the second. To these succeeded *the bill of rights,* or declaration delivered by the lords and commons to the prince and princess of Orange 13 February 1688; and afterwards enacted in parliament, when they became king and queen: which declaration concludes in these remarkable words; "and they do claim, demand, and insist upon all singular the premises, as their undoubted rights and liberties." And the act of parliament itself recognizes "all and singular the rights and liberties asserted and claimed in the said declaration to be the true, antient, and indubitable rights of the people of this kingdom." Lastly, these liberties were again asserted at the commencement of the present century, in the *act of settlement,* whereby the crown is limited to his present majesty's illustrious house, and some new provisions were added at the same fortunate aera [*sic*] for better securing our religion, laws, and liberties; which the statute declares to be "the birthright of the people of England;" according to the antient doctrine of the common law.

. . .

THIS natural life being, as was before observed, the immediate donation of the great creator, cannot legally be disposed of or destroyed by any individual, neither by the person himself nor by any other of his fellow creatures, merely upon their own authority. Yet nevertheless it may, by the divine permission, be frequently forfeited for the breach of those laws of society, which are enforced by the sanction of capital punishments; of the nature, restrictions, expedience, and legality of which, we may hereafter more conveniently enquire in the concluding book of these commentaries. At present, I shall only observe, that whenever the *constitution* of a state vests in any man, or body of men, a power of destroying at pleasure, without the direction of laws, the lives or members of the subject, such constitution is in the highest degree tyrannical: and that whenever any *laws* direct such destruction for light and trivial causes, such laws are likewise tyrannical, though in an inferior degree; because here the subject is aware of the danger he is exposed to, and may by prudent caution provide against it. The statute law of England does therefore very seldom, and the common law does never, inflict any punishment extending to life or limb, unless upon the highest necessity: and the constitution is an utter stranger to any arbitrary power of killing or maiming the subject without the express warrant of law. *"Nullus liber homo,* says the great charter, *aliquo modo destruatur, nisi per legale judicium parium suorum aut per legem terrae."* Which words, *"aliquo modo destruatur,"* according to sir Edward Coke, include a prohibition not only of *killing,* and *maiming,* but also of *torturing* (to which our laws are strangers) and of every oppression by colour of an illegal authority. And it is enacted by the statute 5 Edw. III. c. 9. that no man shall be forejudged of life or limb, contrary to the great charter and the law of the land: and again, by statute 28 Ed. III. c. 3. that no man shall be put to death, without being brought to answer by due process of law.

Commentaries, bk. 1, ch. 1; vol. 1, pp. 123–24, 129–30
(footnotes omitted).

10.3.2 CASELAW

10.3.2.1 Ham v. M'Claws, 1789

It is clear, that statutes passed against the plain and obvious principles of common right, and common reason, are absolutely null and void, as *far as they are calculated to operate against those principles.*

1 S.C. (1 Bay) 93, 98 (C.P.).

Chapter 11

AMENDMENT V
TAKINGS CLAUSE

11.1 TEXTS

11.1.1 DRAFTS IN FIRST CONGRESS

11.1.1.1 Proposal by Madison in House, June 8, 1789

11.1.1.1.a Fourthly. That in article 1st, section 9, between clauses 3 and 4 [of the Constitution], be inserted these clauses, to wit, . . .

. . .

No person shall be subject, except in cases of impeachment, to more than one punishment, or one trial for the same offence; nor shall be compelled to be a witness against himself; nor be deprived of life, liberty, or property without due process of law; nor be obliged to relinquish his property, where it may be necessary for public use, without a just compensation.

Congressional Register, June 8, 1789, vol. 1, pp. 427–28.

11.1.1.1.b *Fourthly.* That in article 1st, section 9, between clauses 3 and 4 [of the Constitution], be inserted these clauses, to wit: . . .

. . .

No person shall be subject, except in cases of impeachment, to more than one punishment, or one trial for the same offence; nor shall be compelled to be a witness against himself; nor be deprived of life, liberty, or property without due process of law; nor be obliged to relinquish his property, where it may be necessary for public use, without a just compensation. Daily Advertiser, June 12, 1789, p. 2, col. 1.

11.1.1.1.c *Fourth.* That in article 1st, section 9, between clauses 3 and 4 [of the Constitution], be inserted these clauses, to wit: . . .

. . .

No person shall be subject, except in cases of impeachment, to more than one punishment, or one trial for the same offence; nor shall be compelled to be a witness against himself; nor be deprived of life, liberty, or property without due process of law; nor be obliged to relinquish his property, where it may be necessary for public use, without a just compensation.

New-York Daily Gazette, June 13, 1789, p. 574, col. 3.

11.1.1.2 House Committee of Eleven Report, July 28, 1789

ART. I, SEC. 9 — Between PAR. 2 and 3 insert,

. . .

"No person shall be subject, except in case of impeachment, to more than one trial or one punishment for the same offence, nor shall be compelled to be a witness against himself, nor be deprived of life, liberty, or property without due process of law; nor shall private property be taken for public use without just compensation."

Broadside Collection, DLC.

11.1.1.3 Consideration by House, August 17, 1789

11.1.1.3.a The 5th clause of the 4th proposition was taken up, viz. "no person shall be subject, [*sic;* except] in case of impeachment, to more than one trial or one punishment for the same offence, nor shall be compelled to be a witness against himself, nor be deprived of life, liberty or property, without due process of law, nor shall private property be taken for public use without just compensation."

Congressional Register, August 17, 1789, vol. 2, p. 224.

11.1.1.3.b Eighth Amendment — "No person shall be subject, except in case of impeachment, to more than one trial or one punishment for the same offence, nor shall be compelled to be a witness against himself, nor be deprived of life, liberty or property, without due process of law, nor shall private property be taken for public use without just compensation."

Daily Advertiser, August 18, 1789, p. 2, col. 4.

11.1.1.3.c Eighth Amendment — "No person shall be subject, except in case of impeachment, to more than one trial or one punishment for the same offence, nor shall be compelled to be a witness against himself, nor be deprived of life, liberty or property, without due process of law, nor shall private property be taken for public use without just compensation."

New-York Daily Gazette, August 19, 1789, p. 802, col. 4.

11.1.1.3.d 8th Amendment. "No person shall be subject, except in case of impeachment, to more than one trial for the same offence, nor shall be compelled to be a witness against himself, nor be deprived of life, liberty or property, without due process of law, nor shall private property be taken for public use without just compensation."

Gazette of the U.S., August 22, 1789, p. 249, col. 3.

11.1.1.4 Motion by Benson in House, August 17, 1789

11.1.1.4.a Mr. BENSON

[H]e would move to amend it by striking out the words "one trial or."

Congressional Register, August 17, 1789, vol. 2, p. 224
("was lost by a considerable majority").

11.1.1.4.b Mr. BENSON moved to strike out the words "One trial or"

Daily Advertiser, August 18, 1789, p. 2, col. 4.

11.1.1.4.c   Mr. Benson moved to strike out the words "one trial or."
New-York Daily Gazette, August 19, 1789,
p. 802, col. 4 ("This was negatived").

11.1.1.4.d   Mr. BENSON . . . moved to strike out the words "one trial or"
Gazette of the U.S., August 22, 1789,
p. 249, col. 3 ("This was negatived.").

11.1.1.5   Motion by Partridge in House, August 17, 1789

11.1.1.5.a   Mr. PARTRIDGE moved to insert after "same offence," the words, "by any law of the United States;". . . .
Congressional Register, August 17, 1789, vol. 2,
p. 225 ("this amendment was lost also").

11.1.1.5.b   Mr. PARTRIDGE moved to insert after the words "same offence," the words "by any law of the United States," . . .
Daily Advertiser, August 18, 1789, p. 2, col. 4
("Resolved in the negative.").

11.1.1.5.c   Mr. Partridge moved to insert after the words "same offence," the words "by any law of the United States."
New-York Daily Gazette, August 19, 1789,
p. 802, col. 4 ("Resolved in the negative").

11.1.1.5.d   Mr. PARTRIDGE moved to insert after the words "same offence," the words *by any law of the United States,"*. . . .
Gazette of the U.S., August 22, 1789, p. 249, col. 3 ("Negatived").

11.1.1.6   Motion by Lawrance in House, August 17, 1789

11.1.1.6.a   Mr. LAWRANCE
[H]e thought it [the clause] ought to be confined to criminal cases, and moved an amendment for that purpose. . . .
Congressional Register, August 17, 1789, vol. 2, p. 225
("which amendment being adopted, the clause as amended
was unanimously agreed to by the committee").

11.1.1.6.b   Mr. LAWRANCE moved to insert after the words "nor shall" these words "in any criminal case."
Daily Advertiser, August 18, 1789, p. 2, col. 4
("This amendment was agreed to.").

11.1.1.6.c   Mr. Lawrance moved to insert after the words "nor shall," these words, "in any criminal case."
New-York Daily Gazette, August 19, 1789, p. 802, col. 4
("This amendment was agreed to").

11.1.1.6.d   Mr. LAURANCE moved to insert after the words "nor shall" these words *in any criminal case.*
Gazette of the U.S., August 22, 1789, p. 249, col. 3
("This amendment was agreed to").

11.1.1.7   Further House Consideration, August 21, 1789

Seventh. No person shall be subject, except in case of impeachment, to more than one trial or one punishment for the same offence; nor shall he be compelled

in any criminal case to be a witness against himself; nor be deprived to life, liberty or property, without due process of law; nor shall private property be taken for public use, without just compensation.

HJ, p. 107 ("read and debated . . . agreed to by the House, . . . two-thirds of the members present concurring").[1]

11.1.1.8 House Resolution, August 24, 1789

ARTICLE THE EIGHTH.

No person shall be subject, except in case of impeachment, to more than one trial, or one punishment for the same offence, nor shall be compelled in any criminal case, to be a witness against himself, nor be deprived to life, liberty or property, without due process of law; nor shall private property be taken for public use without just compensation.

House Pamphlet, RG 46, DNA.

11.1.1.9 Senate Consideration, August 25, 1789

11.1.1.9.a   The Resolve of the House of Representatives of the 24th of August, upon certain "Articles to be proposed to the Legislatures of the several States as Amendments to the Constitution of the United States" was read as followeth:

. . .

Article the Eighth

"No person shall be subject, except in case of Impeachment, to more than one Trial, or one punishment for the same offence, nor shall be compelled in any Criminal case, to be a witness against himself, nor be deprived to life, liberty, or property, without due process of law; nor shall private property be taken for public use without just compensation.

Rough SJ, p. 217.

11.1.1.9.b   The Resolve of the House of Representatives of the 24th of August, was read as followeth:

. . .

"Article the Eighth.

No person shall be subject, except in case of impeachment, to more than one trial, or one punishment for the same offence, nor shall be compelled in any criminal case, to be a witness against himself, nor be deprived to life, liberty or property, without due process of law; nor shall private property be taken for public use without just compensation.

Smooth SJ, p. 195.

"ARTICLE THE EIGHTH.

11.1.1.9.c   The Resolve of the House of Representatives of the 24th of August, was read as followeth:

---

[1]On August 22, 1789, the following motion was agreed to:
ORDERED, That it be referred to a committee of three, to prepare and report a proper arrangement of, and introduction to the articles of amendment to the Constitution of the United States, as agreed to by the House; and that Mr. Benson, Mr. Sherman, and Mr. Sedgwick be of the said committee.

HJ, p. 112.

. . .

"No person shall be subject, except in case of impeachment, to more than one trial, or one punishment for the same offence, nor shall be compelled in any criminal case, to be a witness against himself, nor be deprived to life, liberty or property, without due process of law; nor shall private property be taken for public use without just compensation.

Printed SJ, p. 105.

11.1.1.10   **Further Consideration by Senate, September 4, 1789**

11.1.1.10.a   On Motion to adopt the eighth Article of amendments proposed by the House of Representatives, striking out these words "Except in case of impeachment to more than one trial or one punishment" and substitute the following words.
"Be twice put in jeopardy of life or limb by any public prosecution."

Rough SJ, p. 249 ("It passed in the affirmative.").

11.1.1.10.b   On motion, To adopt the eighth article of Amendments proposed by the House of Representatives, striking out these words, — "Except in case of impeachment to more than one trial or one punishment," and substitute the following words —
"Be twice put in jeopardy of life or limb by any public prosecution" —

Smooth SJ, p. 222 ("It passed in the Affirmative.").

11.1.1.10.c   On motion, To adopt the eighth Article of Amendments proposed by the House of Representatives, striking out these words, — "Except in case of impeachment to more than one trial or one punishment," and substitute the following words —
"Be twice put in jeopardy of life or limb by any public prosecution" —

Printed SJ, p. 119 ("It passed in the Affirmative.").

11.1.1.10.d   that the Senate do
Resolved ~~to~~ /\ concur with the House of Representatives in
Article eighth
~~by~~ striking out these words. "Except in cases of impeachment to more than one
ing
trial or one punishment," and substitute /\ the following words;
"Be twice put in jeopardy of life or limb by any public prosecution."

Senate MS, p. 3, RG 46, DNA.

11.1.1.11   **Further Senate Consideration, September 9, 1789**

11.1.1.11.a   On motion, To alter Article 6th so as to stand Article 5th, and Article 7th so as to stand Article 6th, and Article 8th so as to stand Article 7th

. . .

On motion, That this last mentioned Article be amended to read as follows: "No person shall be held to answer for a capital or otherwise infamous crime, unless on a presentment or indictment of a grand Jury, except in cases arising in the land or naval forces, or in the Militia, when in actual service, in time of war or public danger, nor shall any person be subject to be put in jeopardy of life or limb, for the same offence, nor shall be compelled in any criminal case to be a witness against himself, nor be deprived of life, liberty or property, without due process of law; Nor shall private property be taken for public use without just compensation."

Rough SJ, p. 275 ("It passed in the affirmative.").

11.1.1.11.b   On motion, To alter article the sixth so as to stand article the fifth, and article the seventh so as to stand article the sixth, and article the eighth so as to stand article the seventh —

. . .

On motion, That this last mentioned article be amended to read as follows: "No person shall be held to answer for a capital or otherwise infamous crime, unless on a presentment or indictment of a Grand Jury, except in cases arising in the land or naval forces, or in the militia, when in actual service, in time of war or public danger, nor shall any person be subject to be put in jeopardy of life or limb, for the same offence, nor shall be compelled in any criminal case to be a witness against himself, nor be deprived of life, liberty or property, without due process of law: Nor shall private property be taken for public use without just compensation" —

Smooth SJ, p. 244 ("It passed in the Affirmative.").

11.1.1.11.c   On motion, To alter Article the sixth so as to stand Article the fifth, and Article the seventh so as to stand Article the sixth, and Article the eighth so as to stand Article the seventh —

. . .

On motion, That this last mentioned Article be amended to read as follows: "No person shall be held to answer for a capital or otherwise infamous crime, unless on a presentment or indictment of a Grand Jury, except in cases arising in the land or naval forces, or in the militia, when in actual service, in time of war or public danger, nor shall any person be subject to be put in jeopardy of life or limb, for the same offence, nor shall be compelled in any criminal case to be a witness against himself, nor be deprived of life, liberty or property, without due process of law: Nor shall private property be taken for public use without just compensation" —

Printed SJ, pp. 129–30 ("It passed in the Affirmative.").

11.1.1.11.d   To erase the word "Eighth" & insert Seventh —

To insert in the ~~Eighth~~ 8th [7th] article ~~as~~ after the word "shall" in the "1" line — be held to answer for a capital or otherwise infamous crime, unless on a presentment or indictment of a grand Jury, except in cases arising in the land or naval forces, or in the militia when in actual Service in time of War or publick danger, nor shall any person — &

To erase from the same article the words "except in case of impeachment, to more than one trial or one punishment" & insert — to be twice put in jeopardy of life or limb —

Ellsworth MS, p. 3, RG 46, DNA.

11.1.1.12 Senate Resolution, September 9, 1789

ARTICLE THE SEVENTH.

No person shall be held to answer for a capital, or otherwise infamous crime, unless on a presentment or indictment of a Grand Jury, except in cases arising in the land or naval forces, or in the militia, when in actual service in time of war or public danger; nor shall any person be subject for the same offence to be twice put in jeopardy of life or limb; nor shall be compelled in any criminal case, to be a witness against himself, nor be deprived of life, liberty or property, without due process of law; nor shall private property be taken for public use without just compensation.

Senate Pamphlet, RG 46, DNA.

11.1.1.13   Further House Consideration, September 21, 1789

RESOLVED, That this House doth agree to the second, fourth, eighth, twelfth, thirteenth, sixteenth, eighteenth, nineteenth, twenty-fifth, and twenty-sixth amendments, and doth disagree to the first, third, fifth, sixth, seventh, ninth, tenth, eleventh, fourteenth, fifteenth, seventeenth, twentieth, twenty-first, twenty-second, twenty-third, and twenty-fourth amendments proposed by the Senate to the said articles, two thirds of the members present concurring on each vote.

RESOLVED, That a conference be desired with the Senate on the subject matter of the amendments disagreed to, and that Mr. Madison, Mr. Sherman, and Mr. Vining, be appointed managers at the same on the part of this House.

HJ, p. 146.

11.1.1.14   Further Senate Consideration, September 21, 1789

11.1.1.14.a   A message from the House of Representatives —

Mr. Beckley, their Clerk, brought up a Resolve of the House of this date, to agree to the 2nd, 4th, 8th, 12th, 13th, 16th, 18th, 19th, 25th, and 26th Amendments proposed by the Senate, "To articles of Amendment to be proposed to the Legislatures of the several States, as Amendments to the Constitution of the United States," and to disagree to the 1st, 3d, 5th, 6th, 7th, 9th, 10th, 11th, 14th, 15th, 17th, 20th, 21st, 22d, 23d, and 24th amendments: Two thirds of the members present concurring on each vote: And "That a conference be desired with the Senate on the subject matter of the amendments disagreed to," and that Mr. Madison, Mr. Sherman, and Mr. Vining, be appointed managers of the same, on the part of the House of Representatives —

And he withdrew.

Smooth SJ, pp. 265–66.

11.1.1.14.b   A message from the House of Representatives —

Mr. Beckley, their Clerk, brought up a Resolve of the House of this date, to agree to the 2d, 4th, 8th, 12th, 13th, 16th, 18th, 19th, 25th, and 26th Amendments proposed by the Senate, "To Articles of Amendment to be proposed to the Legislatures of the several States, as Amendments to the Constitution of the United States," and to disagree to the 1st, 3d, 5th, 6th, 7th, 9th, 10th, 11th, 14th, 15th, 17th, 20th, 21st, 22d, 23d, and 24th Amendments: Two thirds of the members present concurring on each vote: And "That a conference be desired with the Senate on the subject matter of the Amendments disagreed to," and that Mr. Madison, Mr. Sherman, and Mr. Vining, be appointed managers of the same, on the part of the House of Representatives —

And he withdrew.

Printed SJ, pp. 141–42.

11.1.1.15 Further Senate Consideration, September 21, 1789

11.1.1.15.a   The Senate proceeded to consider the Message of the House of Representatives disagreeing to the Amendments made by the Senate "To Articles to be proposed to the Legislatures of the several States, as Amendments to the Constitution of the United States" And

RESOLVED, That the Senate do recede from their third Amendment, and do insist on all the others.

RESOLVED, That the Senate do concur with the House of Representatives in a conference on the subject matter of disagreement on the said Articles of Amendment, and that Mr. Ellsworth Mr. Carroll and Mr. Paterson be managers of the conference on the part of the Senate.

Smooth SJ, p. 267.

11.1.1.15.b   The Senate proceeded to consider the message of the House of Representatives disagreeing to the Amendments made by the Senate "To Articles to be proposed to the Legislatures of the several States, as Amendments to the Constitution of the United States" — And

RESOLVED, That the Senate do recede from their third Amendment, and do insist on all the others.

RESOLVED, That the Senate do concur with the House of Representatives in a conference on the subject matter of disagreement on the said Articles of Amendment, and that Mr. Ellsworth, Mr. Carroll, and Mr. Paterson be managers of the conference on the part of the Senate.

Printed SJ, p. 142.

11.1.1.16 Conference Committee Report, September 24, 1789

[T]hat it will be proper for the House of Representatives to agree to the said Amendments proposed by the Senate, with an Amendment to their fifth Amendment, so that the third Article shall read as follows: "Congress shall make no Law respecting an establishment of Religion, or prohibiting the free exercise thereof; or abridging the freedom of Speech, or of the Press; or the right of the people peaceably to assemble and ~~to~~ petition the Government for a redress of grievances;" And with an Amendment to the fourteenth Amendment proposed by the Senate, so that the eighth Article, as numbered in the Amendments proposed by the Senate, shall read as follows "In all criminal prosecutions, the accused shall enjoy the right to a speedy & publick trial by an impartial jury of the district wherein the crime shall have been committed, as the district shall have been previously ascertained by law, and to be informed of the nature and cause of the accusation; to be confronted with the witnesses against him, and to have com-

to

pulsory process for obtaining witnesses ~~against him~~ in his favour, & /\ have the assistance of counsel for his defence."

Conference MS, RG 46, DNA (Ellsworth's handwriting).

11.1.1.17 House Consideration of Conference Committee Report, September 24 [25], 1789

RESOLVED, That this House doth recede from their disagreement to the first, third, fifth, sixth, seventh, ninth, tenth, eleventh, fourteenth, fifteenth, seven-

teenth, twentieth, twenty-first, twenty-second, twenty-third, and twenty-fourth amendments, insisted on by the Senate: PROVIDED, That the two articles which by the amendments of the Senate are now proposed to be inserted as the third and eighth articles, shall be amended to read as followeth;

Article the third. "Congress shall make no law respecting an establishment of religion, or prohibiting the free exercise thereof; or abridging the freedom of speech, or of the press; or the right of the people peaceably to assemble, and to petition the government for a redress of grievances."

Article the eighth. "In all criminal prosecutions, the accused shall enjoy the right to a speedy and public trial by an impartial jury of the state and district wherein the crime shall have been committed, which district shall have been previously ascertained by law, and to be informed of the nature and cause of the accusation, to be confronted with the witnesses against him, to have compulsory process for obtaining witnesses in his favor, and to have the assistance of council for his defence."

> HJ, p. 152 ("On the question, that the House do agree to the alteration and amendment of the eighth article, in manner aforesaid, It was resolved in the affirmative. Ayes 37 Noes 14").

11.1.1.18　Senate Consideration of Conference Committee Report, September 24, 1789

11.1.1.18.a　Mr. Ellsworth, on behalf of the managers of the conference on "articles to be proposed to the several States as Amendments to the Constitution of the United States," reported as follows:

That it will be proper for the House of Representatives to agree to the said amendments proposed by the Senate, with an Amendment to their fifth Amendment, so that the third Article shall read as follows: "Congress shall make no law respecting an establishment of Religion, or prohibiting the free exercise thereof; or abridging the freedom of Speech, or of the Press; or the right of the people peaceably to assemble and petition the Government for a redress of Grievances;" And with an Amendment to the fourteenth Amendment proposed by the Senate, so that the eighth article, as numbered in the Amendments proposed by the Senate, shall read as follows; "In all criminal prosecutions, the accused shall enjoy the right to a speedy and public trial by an impartial Jury of the district wherein the Crime shall have been committed, as the district shall have been previously ascertained by law, and to be informed of the nature and cause of the accusation, to be confronted with the witnesses against him, and to have compulsory process for obtaining witnesses in his favor, and to have the assistance of Counsel for defence."

> Smooth SJ, pp. 272–73.

11.1.1.18.b　Mr. Ellsworth, on behalf of the managers of the conference on "Articles to be proposed to the several States as Amendments to the Constitution of the United States," reported as follows:

That it will be proper for the House of Representatives to agree to the said Amendments proposed by the Senate, with an Amendment to their fifth Amendment, so that the third Article shall read as follows: "Congress shall make no Law RESPECTING AN ESTABLISHMENT OF RELIGION, or prohibiting the free exercise thereof; or abridging the freedom of Speech, or of the Press; or the right of the

People peaceably to assemble and petition the Government for a redress of Griev-ances;" And with an Amendment to the fourteenth Amendment proposed by the Senate, so that the eighth Article, as numbered in the Amendments proposed by the Senate, shall read as follows; "In all criminal prosecutions, the accused shall enjoy the right to a speedy and public trial BY AN IMPARTIAL JURY OF THE DIS-TRICT WHEREIN THE CRIME SHALL HAVE BEEN COMMITTED, AS THE DISTRICT SHALL HAVE BEEN PREVIOUSLY ASCERTAINED BY LAW, and to be informed of the nature and cause of the accusation, to be confronted with the witnesses against him, and to have compulsory process for obtaining witnesses in his favor, and to have the assistance of Counsel for defence."

Printed SJ, p. 145.

11.1.1.19 Further Senate Consideration of Conference Committee Report, September 24, 1789

11.1.1.19.a   A Message from the House of Representatives —

Mr. Beckley, their Clerk, brought up the Amendments to the "Articles to be proposed to the Legislatures of the several States, as Amendments to the Constitu-tion of the United States;" and informed the Senate, that the House of Representa-tives had receded from their disagreement to the 1st, 3d, 5th, 6th, 7th, 9th, 10th, 11th, 14th, 15th, 17th, 20th, 21st, 22d, 23d, and 24th Amendments, insisted on by the Senate: Provided that the "Two Articles, which by the Amendments of the Senate are now proposed to be inserted as the third and eighth Articles," shall be amended to read as followeth:

Article the Third. "Congress shall make no Law respecting an establishment of Religion, or prohibiting the free exercise thereof; or abridging the freedom of Speech, or of the Press; or the right of the people peaceably to assemble, and petition the Government for a redress of Grievances."

Article the Eighth. "In all criminal prosecutions the accused shall enjoy the right to a speedy and public trial by an impartial Jury of the State and District, wherein the crime shall have been committed, which District shall have been previously ascertained by law, and to be informed of the nature and cause of the accusation, to be confronted with the witnesses against him, and to have compulsory process for obtaining witnesses in his favor, and to have the assistance of Counsel for his defence."

Smooth SJ, pp. 278–79.

11.1.1.19.b   A Message from the House of Representatives —

Mr. Beckley, their Clerk, brought up the Amendments to the "Articles to be proposed to the Legislatures of the several States, as Amendments to the Constitu-tion of the United States;" and informed the Senate, that the House of Representa-tives had receded from their disagreement to the 1st, 3d, 5th, 6th, 7th, 9th, 10th, 11th, 14th, 15th, 17th, 20th, 21st, 22d, 23d, and 24th Amendments, insisted on by the Senate: Provided that the "Two Articles, which by the Amendments of the Senate are now proposed to be inserted as the third and eighth Articles," shall be amended to read as followeth:

Article the Third. "Congress shall make no Law respecting an establishment of Religion, or prohibiting the free exercise thereof; or abridging the freedom of

Speech, or of the Press; or the right of the People peaceably to assemble, and petition the Government for a redress of Grievances."

Article the Eighth. "In all criminal prosecutions the accused shall enjoy the right to a speedy and public trial by an impartial Jury of the State and District, wherein the crime shall have been committed, which District shall have been previously ascertained by law, and to be informed of the nature and cause of the accusation, to be confronted with the witnesses against him, and to have compulsory process for obtaining witnesses in his favor, and to have the assistance of Counsel for his defence."

Printed SJ, p.148.

11.1.1.20 Further Senate Consideration of Conference Committee Report, September 25, 1789

11.1.1.20.a The Senate proceeded to consider the Message from the House of Representatives of the 24th, with Amendments to the Amendments of the Senate, to "Articles to be proposed to the Legislatures of the several States, as Amendments to the Constitution of the United States" — And

RESOLVED, That the Senate do concur in the Amendments proposed by the House of Representatives, to the Amendments of the Senate. Smooth SJ, p. 283.

11.1.1.20.b The Senate proceeded to consider the Message from the House of Representatives of the 24th, with Amendments to the Amendments of the Senate, to "Articles to be proposed to the Legislatures of the several States, as Amendments to the Constitution of the United States" — And

RESOLVED, That the Senate do concur in the Amendments proposed by the House of Representatives, to the Amendments of the Senate.

Printed SJ, pp. 150–51.

11.1.1.21 Agreed Resolution, September 25, 1789

11.1.1.21.a Article the Seventh.

No person shall be held to answer for a capital, or otherwise infamous crime, unless on a presentment or indictment of a Grand Jury, except in cases arising in the land or naval forces, or in the militia, when in actual service in time of war or public danger; nor shall any person be subject for the same offence to be twice put in jeopardy of life or limb; nor shall be compelled in any criminal case, to be a witness against himself, nor be deprived of life, liberty or property, without due process of law; nor shall private property be taken for public use without just compensation.

Smooth SJ, Appendix, p. 293.

11.1.1.21.b ARTICLE THE SEVENTH.

No person shall be held to answer for a capital, or otherwise infamous crime, unless on a presentment or indictment of a Grand Jury, except in cases arising in the land or naval forces, or in the militia, when in actual service in time of war or public danger; nor shall any person be subject for the same offence to be twice put in jeopardy of life or limb; nor shall be compelled in any criminal case, to be a witness against himself, nor be deprived of life, liberty or property, without due

process of law; nor shall private property be taken for public use without just compensation.

Printed SJ, Appendix, p. 164.

11.1.1.22 Enrolled Resolution, September 28, 1789

Article the seventh . . . No person shall be held to answer for a capital, or otherwise infamous crime, unless on a presentment or indictment of a Grand Jury, except in cases arising in the land or naval forces, or in the militia, when in actual service in time of war or public danger; nor shall any person be subject for the same offence to be twice put in jeopardy of life or limb, nor shall be compelled in any criminal case, to be a witness against himself, nor be deprived of life, liberty, or property, without due process of law; nor shall private property be taken for public use without just compensation.

Enrolled Resolutions, RG 11, DNA.

11.1.1.23 Printed Versions

11.1.1.23.a   ART. V. No person shall be held to answer for a capital or otherwise infamous crime, unless on a presentment or indictment of a grand jury, except in cases arising in the land or naval forces, or in the militia, when in actual service, in time of war or public danger; nor shall any person be subject for the same offence to be twice put in jeopardy of life or limb; nor shall be compelled, in any criminal case, to be witness against himself; nor be deprived of life, liberty, or property, without due process of law; nor shall private property be taken for public use without just compensation.

Statutes at Large, vol. 1, p. 21.

11.1.1.23.b   ART. VII. No person shall be held to answer for a capital, or otherwise infamous crime, unless on a presentment or indictment of a grand jury, except in cases arising in the land or naval forces, or in the militia when in actual service in time of war or public danger; nor shall any person be subject for the same offence to be twice put in jeopardy of life or limb; nor shall be compelled in any criminal case to be a witness against himself, nor be deprived of life, liberty or property, without due process of law; nor shall private property be taken for public use without just compensation.

Statutes at Large, vol. 1, p. 98.

11.1.2 PROPOSALS FROM THE STATE CONVENTIONS

None.

11.1.3 STATE CONSTITUTIONS AND LAWS; COLONIAL CHARTERS AND LAWS

11.1.3.1 Massachusetts

11.1.3.1.a Body of Liberties, 1641

[8] No mans Cattel [*sic*]or goods of what kinde soever shall be pressed or taken for any publique use or service, unlesse it be by warrant grounded upon some act of the generall Court, nor without such reasonable prices and hire as the ordinarie

rates of the Countrie do afford. And if his Cattle or goods shall perish or suffer damage in such service, the owner shall be suffitiently recompenced.

Massachusetts Colonial Laws, p. 35.

11.1.3.1.b   Constitution, 1780

[Part I, Article] X. Each individual of the society, has a right to be protected by it, in the enjoyment of his life, liberty and property, according to standing laws. He is obliged consequently, to contribute his share to the expence of this protection; to give his personal service, or an equivalent, when necessary: But no part of the property of any individual, can, with justice, be taken from him, or applied to publick uses, without his own consent, or that of the representative body of the people: In fine, the people of this Commonwealth, are not controulable by any other laws, than those to which their constitutional representative body have given their consent. And whenever the publick exigencies require, that the property of any individual should be appropriated to publick uses, he shall receive a reasonable compensation therefor.

Massachusetts Perpetual Laws, p. 6.

11.1.3.2   Pennsylvania

11.1.3.2.a   Constitution, 1776

CHAPTER I.

. . .

VIII. That every member of society hath a right to be protected in the enjoyment of life, liberty and property, and therefore is bound to contribute his proportion towards the expence of that protection, and yield his personal service when necessary, or an equivalent thereto: But no part of a man's property can be justly taken from him, or applied to public uses, without his own consent, or that of his legal representatives: Nor can any man who is conscientiously scrupulous of bearing arms, be justly compelled thereto, if he will pay such equivalent; nor are the people bound by any laws, but such as they have in like manner assented to, for their common good.

Pennsylvania Acts, p. ix.

11.1.3.2.b   Constitution, 1790

ARTICLE IX.

Sect. X. That no person shall, for any indictable offence, be proceeded against criminally by information, except in cases arising in the land or naval forces, or in the militia, when in actual service in time of war or public danger, or, by leave of the court, for oppression and misdemeanor in office. No person shall, for the same offence, be twice put in jeopardy of life or limb; nor shall any man's property be taken or applied to public use, without the consent of his representatives, and without just compensation being made.

Pennsylvania Acts, Dallas, p. xxxiv–xxxv.

11.1.3.3 Vermont: Constitution, 1777

CHAPTER I.

. . .

2. THAT private Property ought to be subservient to public Uses when Necessity requires it; nevertheless, whenever any particular Man's Property is taken for the Use of the Public, the Owner ought to receive an Equivalent in Money.

. . .

9. THAT every Member of Society hath a Right to be protected in the Enjoyment of Life, Liberty and Property, and therefore is bound to Contribute his Proportion towards the Expence of that Protection, and yield his Personal Service, when necessary, or an Equivalent thereto; but no Part of a Man's Property can be justly taken from him, or applied to public Uses, without his own Consent, or that of his legal Representatives: Nor can any Man, who is conscientiously scrupulous of bearing Arms, be justly compelled thereto, if he will pay such Equivalent: Nor are the People bound by any Law, but such as they have in like Manner assented to, for their common Good.

Vermont Acts, pp. 3, 4.

11.1.3.4 Virginia: Declaration of Rights, 1776

VI. THAT elections of members to serve as representatives of the people, in Assembly, ought to be free; and that all men, having sufficient evidence of permanent common interest with, and attachment to, the community, have the right of suffrage, and cannot be taxed or deprived of their property for public uses without their own consent, or that of their representatives so elected, nor bound by any law to which they have not, in like manner, assented, for the public good.

Virginia Acts, p. 33.

11.1.4 OTHER TEXTS

11.1.4.1 Northwest Territory Ordinance, 1787

Article the Second. The inhabitants of the said territory shall always be entitled to the benefits of the writ of habeas corpus, and of the trial by jury; of a proportionate representation of the people in the legislature, and of judicial proceedings according to the course of the common law; all persons shall be bailable unless for Capital Offences, where the proof shall be evident, or the presumption great; all fines shall be moderate, and no cruel or unusual punishments shall be inflicted; no man shall be deprived of his liberty or property but by the judgment of his peers, or the law of the land; and should the public exigencies make it Necessary for the common preservation to take any persons property, or to demand his particular services, full compensation shall be made for the same; and in the just preservation of rights and property it is understood and declared, that no law ought ever to be made, or have force in the said territory, that shall in any manner whatever interfere with, or affect private contracts or engagements bona fide and without fraud, previously formed.

Continental Congress Papers, DNA.

11.2 DISCUSSION OF DRAFTS AND PROPOSALS

11.2.1 THE FIRST CONGRESS

11.2.1.1   June 8, 1789[2]

11.2.1.2   August 17, 1789

Discussion was limited to self-incrimination and double jeopardy issues.[3]

11.2.2 STATE CONVENTIONS

None.

11.2.3 PHILADELPHIA CONVENTION

None.

11.2.4 NEWSPAPERS AND PAMPHLETS

11.2.4.1   The Federal Farmer, No. 6, December 25, 1787

The following, I think, will be allowed to be unalienable or fundamental rights in the United States: —

No man, demeaning himself peaceably, shall be molested on account of his religion or mode of worship — The people have a right to hold and enjoy their property according to known standing laws, and which cannot be taken from them without their consent, or the consent of their representatives; and whenever taken in the pressing urgencies of government, they are to receive a reasonable compensation for it — Individual security consists in having free recourse to the laws — The people are subject to no laws or taxes not assented to by their representatives constitutionally assembled — They are at all times intitled to the benefits of the writ of habeas corpus, the trial by jury in criminal and civil causes — They have a right, when charged, to a speedy trial in the vincinage; to be heard by themselves or counsel, not to be compelled to furnish evidence against themselves, to have witnesses face to face, and to confront their adversaries before the judge — No man is held to answer a crime charged upon him till it be substantially described to him; and he is subject to no unreasonable searches or seizures of his person, papers or effects — The people have a right to assemble in an orderly manner, and petition the government for a redress of wrongs — The freedom of the press ought not to be restrained — No emoluments, except for actual service — No hereditary honors, or orders of nobility, ought to be allowed — The military ought to be subordinate to the civil authority, and no soldier be quartered on the citizens without their consent — The militia ought always to be armed and disciplined, and the usual defence of the country — The supreme power is in the people, and power delegated ought to return to them at stated periods, and frequently — The legislative, executive, and judicial powers, ought always to be kept distinct — others perhaps might be added.

         Storing, vol. 2, p. 262.

---

[2]For the reports of Madison's speech in support of his proposals, *see* 1.2.1.1.a–c.

[3]For the reports of the House's discussion of its Eighth Amendment, *see* 8.2.1.2.a–d.

11.2.4.2 Luther Martin, Genuine Information, No. 8, January 22, 1788

I considered, Sir, that there might be times of such *great public calamities* and *distress,* and of such *extreme scarcity* of *specie* as should render it the *duty* of a government for the *preservation* of even the *most valuable part* of its citizens in some measure to interfere in their favour, by passing laws *totally* or *partially stopping* the courts of justice — or authorising the debtor to pay by *instalments,* or by delivering up his property to his creditors at a *reasonable* and *honest* valuation. — The times have been such as to render regulations of this kind necessary in most, or all of the States, to prevent the *wealthy creditor* and the *monied* man from *totally* destroying the *poor* though even *industrious* debtor — *Such times* may *again* arrive. — I therefore, voted against depriving the States of this power, a power which I am decided they ought to possess, but which I admit ought only to be exercised on very important and urgent occasions. — I apprehended, Sir, the principal cause of complaint among the people at large is, the public and private debt with which they are oppressed, and which, in the present scarcity of cash, threatens them with destruction, unless thay can obtain so much indulgence in point of time that by industry and frugality they may extricate themselves.

This *government proposed,* I apprehend so *far from removing* will greatly *encrease* those complaints, since grasping in its all powerful hand the citizens of the respective States, it will buy the imposition of the variety of *taxes, imposts, stamps, excises* and *other duties, squeeze* from them the little money they may acquire, the hard earnings of their industry, as you would squeeze the juice from an orange, till not a drop more can be extracted, and then let *loose* upon them, their *private creditors,* to whose *mercy* it *consigns* them, by *whom* their property is to be *seized upon* and *sold* in this *scarcity* of *specie at a sheriffs sale,* where nothing but *ready cash* can be received for a *tenth part* of its *value,* and *themselve*s and their *families* to be consigned to *indigence* and *distress,* without *their governments* having a *power* to *give them a moment's indulgence,* however *necessary* it might be, and however *desirous* to grant them aid.

[Baltimore] Maryland Gazette, Kaminski & Saladino, vol. 15, p. 436.

11.2.5 LETTERS AND DIARIES

None.

11.3 DISCUSSION OF RIGHTS
11.3.1 TREATISES

11.3.1.1 William Blackstone, 1765

III. THE third absolute right, inherent in every Englishman, is that of property: which consists in the free use, enjoyment, and disposal of all his acquisitions, without any control or diminution, save only by the laws of the land. The original of private property is probably founded in nature, as will be more fully explained in the second book of ensuing commentaries: but certainly the modifications under which we at present find it, the method of conserving it in its present owner, and of translating it from man to man, are entirely derived from society; and are some of those civil advantages, in exchange for which every individual has resigned a part of his natural liberty. The laws of England are therefore, in point of honor and justice, extremely watchful in ascertaining and protecting this right. Upon this principle the great charter has declared that no freeman shall be disseised or divested, of his freehold, or of his liberties, or free customs, but by the judgment of his peers, or by the law of the land. And by a variety of antient statutes it is enacted, that no man's lands or goods shall be seised into the king's hands, against the great charter, and the law of the land; and that no man shall be disinherited, nor put out of his franchises or freehold, unless he be duly brought to answer, and be forejudged by course of law; and if any thing be done to the contrary, it shall be redressed, and holden for none.

So great moreover is the regard of the law for private property, that it will not authorize the least violation of it; no, not even for the general good of the whole community. If a new road, for instance, were to be made through the grounds of a private person, it might be perhaps be extensively beneficial to the public; but the law permits no man, or set of men, to do this without the consent of the owner of the land. In vain may it be urged, that the good of the individual ought to yield to that of the community; for it would be dangerous to allow any private man, or even any public tribunal, to be the judge of this common good, and to decide whether it be expedient or no. Besides, the public good is in nothing more essentially interested, than in the protection of every individual's private rights, as modelled by the municipal law. In this, and similar cases the legislature alone can, and indeed frequently does, interpose and compel the individual to acquiesce. But how does it interpose and compel? Not by absolutely stripping the subject of his property in an arbitrary manner; but by giving him a full indemnification and equivalent for the injury thereby sustained. The public is now considered an individual, treating with an individual for an exchange. All that the legislature does is to oblige the owner to alienate his possessions for a reasonable price; and even this is an exertion of power, which the legislature indulge with caution, and which nothing but the legislature can perform.

Commentaries, bk. 1, ch.1; vol. 1, pp. 134–35 (footnotes omitted).

11.3.2 CASELAW

11.3.2.1 Respublica v. Sparhawk, 1788

THIS was an appeal from the *Comptroller General's* decision, on the trial of which, by consent of the *Attorney General, Sparhawk* was considered as Plaintiff.

There was a verdict and judgment *nisi* for the Commonwealth, when *Ingersol* obtained a rule to shew cause why a new trial should not be granted.

The case was this: — Congress, perceiving that it was the intention of the *British* army to possess themselves of *Philadelphia,* and being informed that considerable deposits of provisions &c. were made in that city, entered into a resolution on the 11th of *April,* 1777, thats "a Committee should be appointed to examine into the truth of their information; and, if it was found true, to take effectual measures, in conjunction with the *Pennsylvania* Board of War, to prevent such provisions from falling into the hands of the enemy," [*sic*]

On the 13th of the same month, the *Pennsylvania* Board of War, in aid of this resolution, addressed a circular letter to a number of citizens in each ward of the city, requesting them "to obtain from every family a return of the provisions &c. then in possession, and the number of persons that composed the families respectively, in order that proper measures might be pursued for removing any unnecessary quantity of supplies to a place of security." At the same time, it was mentioned, that "this proceeding was not intended to alter or divest the property in the articles removed: but, on the contrary, that the same should be at all times liable to the order of the respective owners, provided they were not exposed to be taken by the enemy."

That no precaution might be omitted upon this occasion, the *Pennsylvania* Board of War, on the succeeding day, desired General *Schuyler* to prevent the introduction of further supplies, and to adopt the most effectual means for preventing the departure of the waggons which were then in the city, and for procuring as many more as would be necessary to transport, not only the public stores, but also such private effects, as it might be thought expedient to remove.

Several intercepted letters having encreased the apprehensions of Congress, on the 16th of *April,* 1777, they resolved, "that it be recommended to the President and Members of the executive authority of this State, to request the commanding officer of the continental forces in this city, to take the most effectual means, that all provisions, and every other article, which, by falling into the hands of the enemy, may aid them in their operations of war against the *United States,* or the loss of which might distress the continental army, be immediately removed to such places, as shall be deemed most convenient and secure."

This recommendation was transmitted by the Executive Council to the *Pennsylvania* Board of War, who, on the 18th of *April,* passed an order, that "houses, barns, stores, &c. should be hired or seized, for the reception of such articles, as should be sent out of the city by their direction or that of Congress;" and, accordingly, a very considerable quantity of property was soon removed to *Chestnut-Hill,* and placed under the care of Messrs. *Loughead* and *Barnhill*; who gave receipts to the owners, promising "to restore what belonged to them respectively, or to deliver the same to their respective orders."

The enemy, not approaching so rapidly as was expected, a considerable part of this property had, accordingly, been re-delivered to the order of the owners, before the city was entered by the *British* troops; when, however, the depot at *Chestnut-Hill* fell, likewise, into their hands, and, with it, 227 barrels of flour, belonging to *Sparhawk*; being the remainder of 323 barrels that had been originally removed thither, in consequence of the above mentioned proceedings.

For the price of these 227 barrels of flour, with interest from the time of their being taken, *Sparhawk* exhibited an account, amounting to £919 6 6 against the public; upon which the *Comptroller-General* reported to the *Executive Council,* that "neither the principal, the interest, nor any part of either, could be allowed;" and against this decision the present appeal was entered.

The question, therefore, on the motion for a new trial, was, whether this claim, under all the circumstances, ought to be admitted? and it was argued on the 28th of *April,* by *Ingersol,* for the Appellant; and the *Attorney General,* for the Commonwealth.

On the part of the *Appellant,* it was premised, that, in a season of *peace,* the law had so great a regard for private property, that it would not authorize the least violation of it; no, not even for the general good of the whole community. 1 *Black. Com.* 139 [135?]. And, it was contended, that, although a state of *war* entitled one nation to seize and lay waste the property of another, and their respective subjects to molest the persons, and to seize the effects of their opponents, yet, as between a state and its own citizens, the principle, with respect to the rights or property, is immutably the same, in war as well as peace. Sometimes, indeed, the welfare of the public may be allowed to interfere with the immediate possessions of an individual; but these must be cases of absolute necessity, in which every good citizen ought chearfully [*sic*] to acquiesce: Yet, even then, justice requires, and the law declares, that an adequate compensation should be made for the wrong that is done. For, the burthen of the war ought to be equally borne by all who are interested in it, and not fall disproportionately heavy upon a few. These general principles are fortified by the explicit language of the *Declaration of Rights, Sect.* 8. which provides, that "no part of a man's property can be justly taken from him, or applied to public uses, without his own consent, or that of his legal Representatives." In the present case the Appellant did not voluntarily surrender his property, nor was it taken from him by any legislative sanction.

That there are, however, some instances where an individual is not entitled to redress for injuries committed on his property in the prosecution of public objects, must be admitted; but these instances are carefully distinguished by the writers on the law of nations; *Vatt. B.* 3. *Sect* 232. and are in no degree analogous to the foundation of the Appellant's claim. If, indeed, the property in question had remained in *Philadelphia,* and had there been seized by the enemy, there could have been no reason to claim an indemnification from the public; but, when it was taken out of the possession of the owner by the executive authority of the State, and removed to a distant place, with a promise of restoring it on demand, the subsequent capture being clearly a consequence of this interference, the government is bound to indemnify the Appellant for his loss.

It is unnecessary to travel into an investigation of the various modes, by which an individual may seek for redress and compensation, where his property has been divested for the use of the public. The right is clear, and that every right must have a remedy, is a principle of general law, which the Legislature of *Pennsylvania* has expressly recognized; directing, by an early Act of Assembly, the settlement of the accounts of the Committee and Council of Safety; and prescribing in what manner the claims of individuals should be settled and discharged. 2 *State Laws* 144. To these bodies, the *Pennsylvania* Board of War succeeded; the business of the Board was transacted in the same way; and there can be no good reason, why the obligations which they incurred, should not be as fairly and fully adjusted and satisfied. The Legislature, indeed, must have regarded the matter in the same light; for, finding that the former law was inadequate to its objects, another was enacted to appoint a *Comptroller General,* and to authorize him "to liquidate and settle, according to law and equity, all claims against *the Commonwealth,* for services performed, monies advanced, or articles furnished, by order of the legislative, or executive powers for the use of the same, or for any other purpose whatever." — This authority embraced the Appellant's claim, and the Comptroller General has erred in deciding against it.

The *Attorney General,* for the *Commonwealth,* stated the case to be breifly this; that the *Pennsylvania* Board of War, acting under the recommendations of *Congress,* removed, among other things, a quantity of flour belonging to the Appellant, in order to prevent its falling into the hands of the enemy: declaring, however, that the removal was not intended to divest the property, but that the flour should still be subject to the order of the owner, provided it was not exposed to a capture. The flour being afterwards seized by the *British* troops at the place where the *Pennsylvania* Board of War had deposed it, two questions arise: — 1st. Whether this Court has power to grant relief to the Appellant, if any ought to be granted. And 2dly. Whether, on principles of the law and equity, he is entitled to be relieved.

I. Considering this as a case immediately between *Sparhawk* and the *Commonwealth,* it is clear, that a sovereign is not amenable in any Court, unless by his own consent; I *Black. Com.* 242. And, therefore, unless the Commonwealth has expressly consented, there is nothing in the constitution of this Court, which can warrant their sustaining the present proceeding. What then is the evidence of consent? We are refered [*sic*] to the law appointing the *Comptroller General.* Let us examine this law; and as the case comes by appeal from the Comptroller, if it appears that he had no authority to liquidate and settle *Sparhawk's* claim, it follows, as a necessary consequence, that this Court, also, has no jurisdiction for the purpose.

By the Act of Assembly which gives the appeal from the *Comptroller General's* decision to the *Supreme Court,* 3 *State Laws* 444. this in restricted to such accounts as he shall settle in *pursuance* of the preceding Act, by which he was appointed; 3 *State Laws* 57. and there, we find, the specific object of his authority to be, the liquidation and settlement of all claims against the *Commonwealth,* "for services performed, monies advanced, or articles furnished, by order of the legislative, or executive powers, &c." In order, therefore, to found the jurisdiction of the Comptroller, two thing must concur — 1st. that the claim be for services performed, movies advanced, or articles furnished; and 2dly. that the debt has been incurred by order of the legislative or executive power.

Now, in the present case, the Appellant makes no claim for services performed, or money advanced, and it is impossible for the most ingenious fancy to bring his demand within the description of articles furnished. It is conceded, indeed, that the law does not, *in peace,* acknowledge any authority to violate the rights of property, or to interfere with the possessions of individuals; but there is *in war* a transcendant power, which is connected with the fundamental principle of all governments, the preservation of the whole; and the interest of private persons may certainly, in that season, be sacrificed, *ne quid respublica detrimenti capiat.* The loss, of which the Appellant complains, was occasioned by the exercise of this power. As a *tort* it cannot be charged against the *Commonwealth*; for, a declaration stating it so would be cause of demurrer: And, therefore, as it is only in cases of contract, either express or implied, that the *Comptroller General* is authorized to act, there is no jurisdiction which can relieve him, but that of the Legislative.

But, in the next place, the claim does not originate upon any order of the legislative, or executive, power, agreeably to the terms of the act. The order for the removal of the provision, &c. to *Chestnut-Hill* was issued by the *Pennsylvania Board of war,* not in obedience to the Executive Council, but in pursuance of a recommendation from Congress, which the Executive Council merely transmitted to the Board. Even, indeed, if the Executive Council had undertaken to direct this proceeding, a question would still arise, whether they had a right to do so? for, the act of Assembly, providing for the settlement of claims against the public by order of the Executive Council, though not in express words, yet, by a necessary implication, must intend a legitimate order, founded upon the constitutional powers of that department, or issued under the authority of some law. The Executive Council cannot otherwise charge the public; without the legislative sanction they cannot erect magazines, or any other public building; nor enter into the most trifling contract; of which, indeed, a recent proof apears, in the refusal of the General Assembly to pay for the arms of the State, that had been placed in the Supreme Court, or to discharge the additional expence of the Triumphal Arch, which had been incurred by the direction and upon the faith of the Executive Council.

II. But, it is further to be shewn; that, even supposing the *Comptroller General,* or this Court upon appeal, had the power of granting *Sparhawk's* claim, yet, that the claim itself is not founded in law or equity, and ought, therefore, to be rejected. — If the Appellant's claim is just, he ought either to urge it against the immediate agent in the wrong which he has sustained, or travel to the source, and demand reparation from Congress. The *Commonwealth* of *Pennsylvania* cannot be liable; for, the persons who took and kept the provisions, &c. at *Chestnut-Hill,* acted under the authority of the Board of war, who, it is true, were appointed by the Executive Council; but, in this instance, proceeded entirely upon the recommendation of Congress, which the Executive Council did not, and could not legally, enjoin or enforce. It is possible, however, that, in strict law, Messers. *Loughead* and *Barnhill* would have been liable as trespassers, had not the Legislature interfered to protect persons in their situation from vexatious prosecutions: 3 *State Laws.* 178. And this act, although it relates immediately to individuals, shews, generally, that the temporary bodies, by whose orders such individuals were governed, are, likewise, to be exempted from suits, on account of their conduct in the service of their country.

But, on what ground can redress be at all expected on this occasion? The removal of the Appellant's property arose from the necessity of the war; it was not done to convert the flour to the public use, nor to deprive the owner of the advantages of it, any farther than the paramount consideration of the public welfare required. The object was to secure it from the depredations of the enemy; and, that it, afterwards, fell into their hands, was an event involuntary, and merely accidental, in which case *Vattel* expressly says, no compensation shall be made. *Vatt. lib.* 3. *sect.* 232. If the Appellant is entitled to relief, every farmer whose cattle have been driven from his plantation to avoid the enemy; every man whose liquors have been staved, or provisions destroyed, upon the approach of the

British troops; all the owners of *Tynicum* island, which was deluged by a military mandate; and, in short, every one whose interests have been affected by the chance of war, must also, in an equal distribution of justice, be effectually indemnified. — What nation could sustain the enormous load of debt which so ruinous a doctrine would create!

Ingersoll, in reply. — With respect to the *first* point made on the part of the Commonwealth, it is not contended, for the Appellant, that, generally speaking, citizens may sue the State; but only that every Government, which is not absolutely despotic, has provided some means (in *England,* for instance, by petition in Chancery) to obtain a redress of injuries from the Sovereign.

As to the *second* point; — The Pennsylvania Board of war acted under the authority of the Executive Council; and the principal is responsible for the agent. When the Appellant's property was taken out of his own custody, the Government stood in his place, and undertook all the consequent risques. The individuals, who were charged with the care of it, are protected by the act of Assembly; but the State, upon every principle of justice, is still liable for the loss; and the authority of the *Comptroller General* was intended and has always been understood, to be competent for granting the satisfaction which is now claimed.

The CHIEF JUSTICE, after stating the case, delivered the opinion of the Court as follows:

MCKEAN, *Chief Justice.* — On the circumstances of this case, two points arise: 1st, Whether the Appellant ought to receive any compensation, or not? And 2dly, Whether this Court can grant the relief which is claimed?

Upon the *first* point we are to be governed by reason, by the law of nations, and by precedents analogous to the subject before us. The transaction, it must be remembered, happened *flagrante bello*; and many things are lawful in that season, which would not be permitted in a time of peace. The seizure of the property in question, can, indeed, only be justified under this distinction; for, otherwise, it would clearly have been a *trespass*; which, from the very nature of the term, *transgressio,* imports *to go beyond* what is right. 5 *Bac. Abr.* 150. It is a rule, however, that it is better to suffer a private mischief, than a public inconvenience; and *the rights of necessity,* form a part of our law.

Of this principle, there are many striking illustrations. If a road be out of repair, a passenger may lawfully go through a private enclosure 2 *Black. Com.* 36. So, if a man is assaulted, he may fly through another's close. 5 *Bac. Abr.* 173. In time of war, bulwarks may be built on private ground. *Dyer.* 8. *Brook. trespass.* 213. 5 *Bac. Abr.* 175. and the reason assigned is particularly applicable to the present case, because it is for the *public safety.* 20 *Vin. Abr.* (*treaspass*) B. a. sec. 4. fo. 476. Thus, also, every man may, of common right, justify the going of his servants, or horses, upon the banks of navigable rivers, for towing barges, &c. to whomsoever the right of the soil belongs. I *Ld. Raym.* 725. The pursuit of *Foxes* through another's ground is allowed, because the destruction of such animals is for the *public good,* 2 *Buls.* 62. *Cro. I.* 321. And, as the safety of the people is a law above all others, it is lawful to part affrayers in the house of another man. *Keyl.* 46. 5 *Bac. Abr.* 177. 20 *Vin Abr. fo.* 407. *sec.* 14. Houses may be razed to prevent the spreading of fire, because for the public good. *Dyer.* 36. *Rud. L. and E.* 312. See

Puff. lib. 2. c. 6. sec. 8. Hutch. Mor. Philos. lib. 2. c. 16. We find, indeed, a memorable instance of folly recorded in the 3 *Vol. of Clarendon's History,* where it is mentioned, that the *Lord Mayor* of *London,* in 1666, when that city was on fire, would not give directions for, or consent to, the pulling down forty wooden houses, or to the removing the furniture, &c. belonging to the Lawyers of the Temple, then on the Circuit, for fear he should be answerable for a trespass; and in consequence of this conduct half that great city was burnt.

We are clearly of opinion, that Congress might lawfully direct the removal of any articles that were necessary to the maintenance of the Continental army, or useful to the enemy, and in danger of falling into their hands; for they were vested with the powers of peace and war, to which this was a natural and necessary incident: And, having done it lawfully, there is nothing in the circumstances of the case, which, we think, entitles the Appellant to a compensation for the consequent loss.

With respect to the *second* point; — This Court has authority to confirm, or alter, any proceedings, that come properly before the *Comptroller General;* but if he had no jurisdiction, we can have none. It appears then, that his power is expressly limited to claims "for services performed, monies advanced, or articles furnished," by order of the Legislature, or the Executive Council. And, as he has no right to adjudge a compensation from the State *for damages,* which individuals may have suffered in the course of our military operations, we are of opinion, that we could grant no relief, even if the Appellant was entitled to it.

By the Court: — Let the rule be discharged; and the Judgment for the Commonwealth be made absolute.

1 Dall. 357 (Pa.).

Chapter 12

AMENDMENT VI
CRIMINAL TRIAL CLAUSES

12.1 TEXTS

12.1.1 DRAFTS IN FIRST CONGRESS

12.1.1.1 **Proposal by Madison in House, June 8, 1789**

12.1.1.1.a Fourthly. That in article 1st, section 9, between clauses 3 and 4 [of the Constitution], be inserted these clauses, to wit, . . .
. . .

In all criminal prosecutions, the accused shall enjoy the right to a speedy and public trial, to be informed of the cause and nature of the accusation, to be confronted with his accusers, and the witnesses against him; to have a compulsory process for obtaining witnesses in his favor; and to have the assistance of counsel for his defence.
. . .

Seventhly. That in article 3d, section 2, the third clause be struck out, and in its place be inserted the clauses following, to wit:
The trial of all crimes (except in cases of impeachments, and cases arising in the land or naval forces, or the militia when on actual service in time of war or public danger) shall be by an impartial jury of freeholders of the vicinage, with the requisite of unanimity for conviction, of the right of challenge, and other accustomed requisites; and in all crimes punishable with loss of life or member, presentment or indictment by a grand jury, shall be an essential preliminary, provided that in cases of crimes committed within any county which may be in possession of an enemy, or in which a general insurrection may prevail, the trial may by law be authorised in some other county of the same state, as near as may be to the seat of the offence.

In cases of crimes committed not within any county, the trial may by law be in such county as the laws shall have prescribed. In suits at common law, between man and man, the trial by jury, as one of the best securities to the rights of the people, ought to remain inviolate.

Congressional Register, June 8, 1789, vol. 1, pp. 427–29.

12.1.1.1.b *Fourthly*. That in article 1st, section 9, between clauses 3 and 4 [of the Constitution], be inserted these clauses, to wit: . . .
. . .

In all criminal prosecutions, the accused shall enjoy the right to a speedy and public trial, to be informed of the cause and nature of the accusation, to be confronted with his accusers, and the witnesses against him; to have a compulsory process for obtaining witnesses in his favor; and to have the assistance of counsel for his defence.

. . .

Seventhly. That in article 3d, section 2 [of the Constitution], the third clause be struck out, and in its place be inserted the clauses following, to wit:

The trial of all crimes (except in cases of impeachments, and cases arising in the land or naval forces, or the militia when on actual service in time of war, or public danger,) shall be by an impartial jury of freeholders of the vicinage, with the requisite of unanimity for conviction, of the right of challenge, and other accustomed requisites; and in all crimes punishable with loss of life or member, presentment or indictment by a grand jury, shall be an essential preliminary, provided that in cases of crimes committed within any county which may be in possession of an enemy, or in which a general insurrection may prevail, the trial may by law be authorised in some other county of the same state, as near as may be to the seat of the offence.

In cases of crimes committed not within any county, the trial may by law be in such county as the laws shall have prescribed. In suits at common law between man and man, the trial by jury, as one of the best securities to the rights of the people, ought to remain inviolate.

Daily Advertiser, June 12, 1789, p. 2, cols. 1–2.

12.1.1.1.c   *Fourth.* That in article 1st, section 9, between clauses 3 and 4, be inserted these clauses, to wit: . . .

. . .

Seventh. In all criminal prosecutions, the accused shall enjoy the right to a speedy and public trial, to be informed of the cause and nature of the accusation, to be confronted with his accusers, and the witnesses against him; to have a compulsory process for obtaining witnesses in his favour; and to have the assistance of counsel for his defence.

The trial of all crimes (except in cases of impeachments, and cases arising in the land or naval forces, or the militia when on actual service in time of war, or public danger,) shall be by an impartial jury of freeholders of the vicinage, with the requisite of unanimity for conviction, of the right of challenge, and other accustomed requisites; and in all crimes punishable with loss of life or member, presentment or indictment by a grand jury shall be an essential preliminary, provided that in cases of crimes committed within any county which may be in possession of an enemy, or in which a general insurrection may prevail, the trial may by law be authorised in some other county of the same state, as near as may be to the seat of the offence.

In cases of crimes committed not within any county, the trial may by law be in such county as the laws shall have prescribed. In suits at common law between man and man, the trial by jury, as one of the best securities to the rights of the people, ought to remain inviolate.

New-York Daily Gazette, June 13, 1789, p. 575, cols. 3–4.

12.1.1.2 Proposal by Sherman to House Committee of Eleven, July 21–28, 1789

[Amendment] 3 No person shall be tried for any crime whereby he may incur loss of life or any infamous punishment, without Indictment by a grand Jury, nor be convicted but by the unanimous verdict of a Petit Jury of good and lawful men Freeholders of the vicinage or district where the trial shall be had.

Madison Papers, DLC.

12.1.1.3 House Committee of Eleven Report, July 28, 1789

ART. 3, SEC. 2 — Strike out the whole of the 3d paragraph, and insert — "In all criminal prosecutions the accused shall enjoy the right to a speedy and public trial, to be informed of the nature and cause of the accusation, to be confronted with the witnesses against him, to have compulsory process for obtaining witnesses in his favor, and to have the assistance of counsel for his defence."

"The trial of all crimes (except in cases of impeachment, and in cases arising in the land or naval forces, or in the militia, when in actual service in time of war or public danger) shall be by an impartial jury of freeholders of the vicinage, with the requisite of unanimity for conviction, the right of challenge and other accustomed requisites; and no person shall be held to answer for a capital, or otherwise infamous crime, unless on a presentment or indictment by a Grand Jury; but if a crime be committed in a place in the possession of an enemy, or in which an insurrection may prevail, the indictment and trial may by law be authorized in some other place within the same State; and if it be committed in a place not within a State, the indictment and trial may be at such place or places as the law may have directed."

"In suits at common law the right of trial by jury shall be preserved."

Broadside Collection, DLC.

12.1.1.4 House Consideration, August 17, 1789

12.1.1.4.a Art. 3, Sect. 2. Strike out the whole of the 3d paragraph, and insert, "In all criminal prosecutions, the accused, shall enjoy the right to a speedy and public trial, to be informed of the nature and cause of the accusation, to be confronted with the witnesses against him, to have compulsory process for obtaining witnesses in his favor, and to have the assistance of counsel for his defence."

Congressional Register, August 17, 1789, vol. 2, p. 228 ("adopted").

12.1.1.4.b Fourteenth Amendment — Art. 2. Sec. 3 [*sic;* article 3, section 2], Strike out the whole of the 3d par. And insert — "In all criminal prosecutions the accused shall enjoy the right to a speedy and public trial, to be informed of the nature of the nature and cause of the accusation, to be confronted with the witnesses against him, to have compulsory process for obtaining witnesses in his favor, and to have the assistance of counsel for his defence."

Daily Advertiser, August 18, 1789, p. 2, col. 4 ("passed").

12.1.1.4.c   Fourteenth amendment — Art. II, Sec. 3 [*sic*; article 3, section 2], strike out the whole of the 3d par. and insert — "In all criminal prosecutions the accused shall enjoy the right to a speedy and public trial, to be informed of the nature and cause of the accusation, to be confronted with the witnesses against him, to have compulsory process for obtaining witnesses in his favor, and to have the assistance of counsel for his defence."

New-York Daily Gazette, August 19, 1789, p. 802, col. 4 ("passed").

12.1.1.4.d   14th Amendment. Art. II Sec. 3d [*sic*; article 3, section 2], Strike out the whole of the 3d par. And insert: "In all criminal prosecutions the accused shall enjoy the right to a speedy and public trial, to be informed of the nature and cause of the accusation, to be confronted with the witness against him, to have compulsory process for obtaining witnesses in his favour, and to have the assistance of counsel for his defence."   Gazette of the U.S., August 22, 1789, p. 250, col. 1 ("adopted").

12.1.1.5   Motion by Burke in House, August 17, 1789

12.1.1.5.a   Mr. Burke

Moved to amend this proposition in such a manner, as to leave it in the power of the accused to put off their trial to the next session, provided he made appear to the court, that the evidence of the witnesses, for whom process was granted, but not served, was material to his defence.

Congressional Register, August 17, 1789, vol. 2, p. 228 ("The question on mr. Burke's motion was taken, and lost. Affirmative 9, negative 41.").

12.1.1.5.b   Several amendments to this article were proposed, some of them were withdrawn and others negatived; and one only obtained, which respected the place of trial, which was to be in the State where the supposed crime was committed.

This amendment was adopted.   Gazette of the U.S., August 22, 1789, p. 250, col. 1.

12.1.1.6   Motion by Livermore in House, August 17, 1789

Mr. Livermore moved to alter the clause, so as to secure to the criminal the right of being tried in the state where the offence was committed.

Congressional Register, August 17, 1789, vol. 2, p. 228 ("On the question, Mr. Livermore's motion was adopted.").

12.1.1.7   Motion by Burke in House, August 17, 1789

Mr. Burke

. . . proposed to add to the clause, that no criminal prosecution should be had by way of information.   Congressional Register, August 17, 1789, vol. 2, p. 228 ("Mr. Burke withdrew it for the present.").

12.1.1.8   House Consideration, August 18, 1789

12.1.1.8.a   The house now resolved itself into a committee of the whole on the subject of amendments, and took into consideration the 2d clause of the 7th proposition, in the words following, "The trial of all crimes (except in cases of impeachment, and in cases arising in the land or naval forces, or in the militia when in actual service in time of war, or public danger) shall be by an impartial jury of freeholders of the vicinage, with the requisite of unanimity for conviction, the right of challenge, and other accustomed requisites; and no person shall be held to answer for a capital, or otherwise infamous crime, unless on a presentment, or indictment, by a grand jury; but if a crime be committed in a place in the possession of an enemy, or in which an insurrection may prevail, the indictment and trial may by law be authorised in some other place within the same state; and if it be committed in a place not within a state, the indictment and trial may be at such place or places as the law may have directed."

Congressional Register, August 18, 1789, vol. 2, p. 233
(after the motions noted below, "[t]he clause was now
adopted without amendment." *Id.*).

12.1.1.8.b   The committee took up the fifteenth amendment which is as follows:

"The trial of all crimes (except in cases of impeachment, and in cases arising in the land or naval forces, or in the militia, when in actual service in time of war or public danger) shall be by an impartial jury of freeholders of the vicinage, with the requisite of unanimity for conviction, the right of challenge, and other accustomed requisites; and no person shall be held to answer for a capital, or otherwise infamous crime, unless on a presentment or indictment by a grand jury; but if a crime be committed in a place in the possession of an enemy, or in which an insurrection may prevail, the indictment and trial may by law be authorized in some other place within the same state; and if it be committed in a place not within a state, the indictment and trial may be at such place or places as the law may have directed."

Daily Advertiser, August 19, 1789, p. 2, cols. 2–3
("Some inconsiderable amendments to this amendment were
moved and lost, and the main question was carried.").

12.1.1.8.c   The committee took up the fifteenth amendment, which is

"The trial of all crimes (except in cases of impeachment, and in cases arising in the land or naval forces, or in the militia, when in actual service in time of war or public danger) shall be by an impartial jury of freeholders of the vicinage, with the requisite of unanimity for conviction, the right of challenge, and other accustomed requisites; and no person shall be held to answer for a capital, or otherwise infamous crime, unless on a presentment or indictment by a grand jury; but if a crime be committed in a place in the possession of an enemy, or in which an insurrection may prevail, the indictment and trial may by law be authorized in some other place within the same state; and if it be committed in a place not within a state, the indictment and trial may be at such place or places as the law may have directed."

Gazette of the U.S., August 22, 1789, p. 250, col. 1
(reported as August 19, 1789); after the motions noted below,
"And then the paragraph was adopted. *Id.*).

12.1.1.9   Motion by Burke in House, August 18, 1789

12.1.1.9.a   Mr. Burke

Moved to change the word "vicinage" into "district or county in which the offence has been committed," . . .

Congressional Register, August 18, 1789, vol. 2, p. 233
("[t]he question on Mr. Burke's motion being put was negatived").

12.1.1.9.b   Mr. Burke moved to strike out "vicinage," and to insert *county or district in which the offence has been committed.*"

Gazette of the U.S., August 22, 1789, p. 250, col. 1
("The motion was negatived.").

12.1.1.10   Motion by Burke in House, August 18, 1789

12.1.1.10.a   Mr. Burke then revived his motion for preventing prosecutions upon information, . . .

Congressional Register, August 18, 1789, vol. 2, p. 233
("on the question this was also lost").

12.1.1.10.b   Mr. Burketh n [*sic;* Burke then] proposed to add a clause to prevent prosecutions upon informations. . . .

Gazette of the U.S., August 22, 1789, p. 250, col. 1
("This motion was lost.").

12.1.1.11   Motion by Gerry in House, August 21, 1789

12.1.1.11.a   Mr. Gerry

Then proposed to amend it by striking out these words, "public danger" and to insert foreign invasion, . . .

Congressional Register, August 21, 1789, vol. 2, p. 243
("this being negatived").

12.1.1.11.b   Mr. Gerry moved to strike out these words, "public danger," to insert *foreign invasion,*

New-York Daily Gazette, August 24, 1789, p. 818, col. 3
("negatived").

12.1.1.11.c   Mr. Gerry moved to strike out these words "public danger" to insert *foreign invasion.*

Gazette of the U. S., August 22, 1789, p. 250, col. 3
("This was negatived.").

12.1.1.12   Motion by Gerry in House, August 21, 1789

12.1.1.12.a   [I]t was then moved to strike out the last clause, "and if it be committed, &c." to the end.

Congressional Register, August 21, 1789, vol. 2, p. 243
("This motion was carried, and the amendment was adopted.").

12.1.1.12.b   It was then moved to strike out the last clause, "and if it be committed, &c," to the end.

New-York Daily Gazette, August 24, 1789, p. 818, col. 3
("This motion obtained, and the amendment as it then stood was adopted.").

12.1.1.12.c   It was then moved to strike out the last clause "and if it be committed, &c." to the end.

Gazette of the U. S., August 22, 1789, p. 250, col. 3
("This motion obtained, and the amendment
as it then stood adopted.").

12.1.1.13 Further House Consideration, August 21, 1789

Thirteenth. In all criminal prosecutions, the accused shall enjoy the right to a speedy and public trial; to be informed of the nature and cause of the accusation; to be confronted with the witnesses against him; to have compulsory process for obtaining witnesses in his favour; and to have the assistance of counsel for his defence.

Fourteenth. The trial of all crimes, (except in cases of impeachment, and in cases arising in the land or naval forces, or in the militia when in actual service in time of war or public danger) shall be by an impartial jury of the vicinage, with the requisite of unanimity for conviction, the right of challenge and other accustomed requisites; and no person shall be held to answer for a capital or otherwise infamous crime, unless on a presentment or indictment by a grand jury; but if a crime be committed in a place in the possession of an enemy, or in which an insurrection may prevail, the indictment and trial may by law be authorised in some other place within the same state.

HJ, p. 108 ("read and debated . . . agreed to by the House,
. . . two-thirds of the members present concurring").[1]

12.1.1.14 House Resolution, August 24, 1789

ARTICLE THE NINTH.

In all criminal prosecutions, the accused shall enjoy the right to a speedy and public trial, to be informed of the nature and cause of the accusation, to be confronted with the witnesses against him, to have compulsory process for obtaining witnesses in his favor, and to have the assistance of counsel for his defence.

ARTICLE THE TENTH.

The trial of all crimes (except in cases of impeachment, and in cases arising in the land or naval forces, or in the militia when in actual service in time of War or public danger) shall be by an Impartial Jury of the Vicinage, with the requisite of unanimity for conviction, the right of challenge, and other accostomed requisites; and no person shall be held to answer for a capital, or otherways infamous crime, unless on a presentment or indictment by a Grand Jury; but if a crime be committed in a place in the possession of an enemy, or in which an insurrection may prevail, the indictment and trial may by law be authorised in some other place within the same State.

House Pamphlet, RG 46, DNA.

[1]On August 22, 1789, the following motion was agreed to:

ORDERED, That it be referred to a committee of three, to prepare and report a proper arrangement of, and introduction to the articles of amendment to the Constitution of the United States, as agreed to by the House; and that Mr. Benson, Mr. Sherman, and Mr. Sedgwick be of the said committee.

HJ, p. 112.

12.1.1.15 Senate Consideration, August 25, 1789

12.1.1.15.a   The Resolve of the House of Representatives of the 24th of August, upon certain "Articles to be proposed to the Legislatures of the several States as Amendments to the Constitution of the United States" was read as followeth:

. . .

"Article the Ninth

In all criminal prosecutions, the accused shall enjoy the right to a speedy and public trial, to be informed of the nature and cause of the accusation, to be confronted with the witnesses against him, to have compulsory process for obtaining witnesses in his favor, and to have the assistance of counsel for his defence.

"Article the Tenth

[The trial of all crimes (except in cases of impeachment, and in cases arising in the land or naval forces, or in the militia when in actual service in time of war or public danger) shall be by] an impartial jury of the Vicinage, with the requisite of unanimity for conviction, the right of Challenge, and other accustomed requisites; and no person shall be held to answer for a capital or otherwise infamous crime, unless on a presentment or indictment by a Grand Jury; but if a crime be committed in a place in the possession of an Enemy, or in which an insurrection may prevail, the indictment and trial may by law be authorised in some other place within the same State.   Rough SJ, pp. 217–18 [material in brackets not legible].

12.1.1.15.b   The Resolve of the House of Representatives of the 24th of August, was read as followeth:

. . .

"Article the Ninth.

"In all criminal prosecutions, the accused shall enjoy the right to a speedy and public trial, to be informed of the nature and cause of the accusation, to be confronted with the witnesses against him, to have compulsory process for obtaining witnesses in his favor, and to have the assistance of counsel for his defence.

"Article the Tenth.

"The trial of all crimes (except in cases of impeachment, and in cases arising in the land or naval forces, or in the militia when in actual service in time of war or public danger) shall be by an impartial Jury of the vicinage, with the requisite of unanimity for conviction, the right of challenge, and other accustomed requisites; and no person shall be held to answer for a capital, or otherwise infamous crime, unless on a presentment or indictment by a Grand Jury; but if a crime be committed in a place in the possession of an enemy, or in which an insurrection may prevail, the indictment and trial may by law be authorised in some other place within the same State.   Smooth SJ, pp. 195–96.

12.1.1.15.c   The Resolve of the House of Representatives of the 24th of August, was read as followeth:

. . .

"ARTICLE the NINTH.

"In all criminal prosecutions, the accused shall enjoy the right to a speedy trial, to be informed of the nature and cause of the accusation, to be confronted with the witnesses against him, to have compulsory process for obtaining witnesses in his favor, and to have the assistance of counsel for his defence.

"ARTICLE the TENTH.

"The trial of all crimes (except in cases of impeachment, and in cases arising in the land or naval forces, or in the militia when in actual service in time of war or public danger) shall be by an impartial Jury of the vicinage, with the requisite of unanimity for conviction, the right of challenge, and other accustomed requisites; and no person shall be held to answer for a capital, or otherways infamous crime, unless on a presentment or indictment by a Grand Jury; but if a crime be committed in a place in the possession of an enemy, or in which an insurrection may prevail, the indictment and trial may by law be authorised in some other place within the same State.

Printed SJ, p. 105.

12.1.1.16   Further Senate Consideration, September 4, 1789

12.1.1.16.a   On Motion to adopt the ninth article of amendments proposed by the House of Representatives.

. . .

On Motion to adopt the tenth Article amended to read thus To strike out all the clauses in the Article, except the following:

"No person shall be held to answer for a capital, or otherwise infamous crime, unless on a presentment or indictment by a Grand Jury,"
Rough SJ, p. 249 (As to each motion, "It passed in the affirmative.").

12.1.1.16.b   On motion, To adopt the ninth article of Amendments proposed by the House of Representatives —

. . .

On motion, To adopt the tenth article amended by striking out all the clauses in the Article, except the following;

"No person shall be held to answer for a capital, or otherwise infamous crime, unless on a presentment or indictment by a Grand Jury,"
Smooth SJ, pp. 222–23 (As to each motion, "It passed in the Affirmative.").

12.1.1.16.c   On motion, To adopt the ninth Article of Amendments proposed by the House of Representatives —

. . .

On motion, To adopt the tenth Article amended by striking out all the clauses in the Article, except the following;

"No person shall be held to answer for a capital, or otherwise infamous crime, unless on a presentment or indictment by a Grand Jury,"
Printed SJ, p. 119 (As to each motion, "It passed in the Affirmative.").

12.1.1.16.d   that the Senate do

Resolved ~~to~~ /\ concur with the House of Representatives in
Article ninth

     that the Senate do

Resolved ~~to~~ /\ concur with the House of Representatives in
Article tenth

with the following amendment, to wit:

To Strike out all the clauses in the Article, except the following:

"no person shall be held to answer for a capital, or otherwise infamous crime, unless on a presentment or indictment by a grand jury."

Senate MS, p. 3, RG 46, DNA.

12.1.1.17   Further Senate Consideration, September 9, 1789

12.1.1.17.a   On motion, To strike out from the ninth Article the word "<u>Ninth</u>," and insert "eighth"

. . .

On motion, to strike out the tenth and eleventh Articles

Rough SJ, p. 275 (As to each motion, "It passed in the Affirmative.").[2]

12.1.1.17.b   On motion, To strike out from the ninth article the word "Ninth," and insert "Eighth" —

. . .

On motion, To strike out the tenth and eleventh articles —

Smooth SJ, pp. 244–45 (As to each motion, "It passed in the affirmative.").

12.1.1.17.c   On motion, To strike out from the ninth Article the word "Ninth," and insert eighth —

. . .

On motion, To strike out the tenth and eleventh articles —

Printed SJ, p. 130 (As to each motion, "It passed in the Affirmative.").

12.1.1.17.d   To erase the word "<u>Ninth</u>," and insert ~~the word~~ <u>Eighth</u>

To erase the 10th article, & the words "<u>article the tenth</u>" —

To erase the 11th article & the words "<u>Article the Eleventh</u>."

Ellsworth MS, p. 3, RG 46, DNA.

12.1.1.18   Further Senate Consideration, September 9, 1789

12.1.1.18.a   On motion, To reconsider Article the tenth, and to restore these words, to wit:

"The trial of all crimes (except in case of impeachment, and in cases arising in the land or naval forces, or in the Militia when in actual service in time of war or public danger) shall be by an [impartial Jury] of the vicinage, with the [requisite of unanimity for conviction, the right of challenge, and other accustomed requisites" —]

Rough SJ, p. 276 ("Yeas . . . 8, Nays . . . 8,
So the question was lost.") [material in brackets not legible].

---

[2]Earlier, on September 9, the Senate took the following language from the tenth Article and added it to the seventh Article; *see* 7.1.1.13, "No person shall be held to answer for a capital or otherwise infamous crime, unless on a presentment or indictment of a Grand Jury. . . .

12.1.1.18.b On motion, To reconsider Article the tenth, and to restore these words, to wit: "The trial of all crimes (except in case of impeachment, and in cases arising in the land or naval forces, or in the militia, when in actual service in time of war of public danger) shall be by an impartial Jury of the vicinage, with the requisite of unanimity for conviction, the right of challenge, and other accustomed requisites" —

Smooth SJ, p. 245 ("Yeas . . . 8, Nays . . . 8, So the question was lost.")

12.1.1.18.c On motion, To reconsider Article the tenth, and to restore these words, to wit: "The trial of all crimes (except in case of impeachment, and in cases arising in the land or naval forces, or in the militia, when in actual service in time of war or public danger) shall be by an impartial Jury of the vicinage, with the requisite of unanimity for conviction, the right of challenge, and other accustomed requisites" —

Printed SJ, p. 130 ("Yeas . . . 8, Nays . . . 8, So the question was lost.")

12.1.1.19 Senate Resolution, September 9, 1789

ARTICLE the EIGHTH.

In all criminal prosecutions, the accused shall enjoy the right to a speedy and public trial, to be informed of the nature and cause of the accusation, to be confronted with the witnesses against him, to have compulsory process for obtaining witnesses in his favour, and to have the assistance of counsel for his defence.

Senate Pamphlet, RG 46, DNA.

12.1.1.20 Further House Consideration, September 21, 1789

RESOLVED, That this House doth agree to the second, fourth, eighth, twelfth, thirteenth, sixteenth, eighteenth, nineteenth, twenty-fifth, and twenty-sixth amendments, and doth disagree to the first, third, fifth, sixth, seventh, ninth, tenth, eleventh, fourteenth, fifteenth, seventeenth, twentieth, twenty-first, twenty-second, twenty-third, and twenty-fourth amendments proposed by the Senate to the said articles, two thirds of the members present concurring on each vote.

RESOLVED, That a conference be desired with the Senate on the subject matter of the amendments disagreed to, and that Mr. Madison, Mr. Sherman, and Mr. Vining, be appointed managers at the same on the part of this House.

HJ, p. 146.

12.1.1.21 Further Senate Consideration, September 21, 1789

12.1.1.21.a A message from the House of Representatives —

Mr. Beckley, their Clerk, brought up a Resolve of the House of this date, to agree to the 2nd, 4th, 8th, 12th, 13th, 16th, 18th, 19th, 25th, and 26th Amendments proposed by the Senate, "To articles of Amendment to be proposed to the Legislatures of the several States, as Amendments to the Constitution of the United States," and to disagree to the 1st, 3d, 5th, 6th, 7th, 9th, 10th, 11th, 14th, 15th, 17th, 20th, 21st, 22d, 23d, and 24th amendments: Two thirds of the members present concurring on each vote: And "That a conference be desired with the Senate on the subject matter of the amendments disagreed to," and that Mr.

Madison, Mr. Sherman, and Mr. Vining, be appointed managers of the same, on the part of the House of Representatives —

And he withdrew.

Smooth SJ, pp. 265–66.

12.1.1.21.b   A message from the House of Representatives —

Mr. Beckley, their Clerk, brought up a Resolve of the House of this date, to agree to the 2d, 4th, 8th, 12th, 13th, 16th, 18th, 19th, 25th, and 26th Amendments proposed by the Senate, "To Articles of Amendment to be proposed to the Legislatures of the several States, as Amendments to the Constitution of the United States," and to disagree to the 1st, 3d, 5th, 6th, 7th, 9th, 10th, 11th, 14th, 15th, 17th, 20th, 21st, 22d, 23d, and 24th Amendments: Two thirds of the members present concurring on each vote: And "That a conference be desired with the Senate on the subject matter of the Amendments disagreed to," and that Mr. Madison, Mr. Sherman, and Mr. Vining, be appointed managers of the same, on the part of the House of Representatives —

And he withdrew.

Printed SJ, pp. 141–42.

12.1.1.22   Further Senate Consideration, September 21, 1789

12.1.1.22.a   The Senate proceeded to consider the Message of the House of Representatives disagreeing to the Amendments made by the Senate "To Articles to be proposed to the Legislatures of the several States, as Amendments to the Constitution of the United States" And

RESOLVED, That the Senate do recede from their third Amendment, and do insist on all the others.

RESOLVED, That the Senate do concur with the House of Representatives in a conference on the subject matter of disagreement on the said Articles of Amendment, and that Mr. Ellsworth Mr. Carroll and Mr. Paterson be managers of the conference on the part of the Senate.

Smooth SJ, p. 267.

12.1.1.22.b   The Senate proceeded to consider the message of the House of Representatives disagreeing to the Amendments made by the Senate "To Articles to be proposed to the Legislatures of the several States, as Amendments to the Constitution of the United States" — And

RESOLVED, That the Senate do recede from their third Amendment, and do insist on all the others.

RESOLVED, That the Senate do concur with the House of Representatives in a conference on the subject matter of disagreement on the said Articles of Amendment, and that Mr. Ellsworth, Mr. Carroll, and Mr. Paterson be managers of the conference on the part of the Senate.

Printed SJ, p. 142.

12.1.1.23   Conference Committee Report, September 24, 1789

[T]hat it will be proper for the House of Representatives to agree to the said Amendments proposed by the Senate, with an Amendment to their fifth Amendment, so that the third Article shall read as follows: "Congress shall make no Law <u>respecting an establishment of Religion</u>, or prohibiting the free exercise thereof; or

abridging the freedom of Speech, or of the Press; or the right of the people peaceably to assemble and ~~to~~ petition the Government for a redress of grievances;" And with an Amendment to the fourteenth Amendment proposed by the Senate, so that the eighth Article, as numbered in the Amendments proposed by the Senate, shall read as follows "In all criminal prosecutions, the accused shall enjoy the right to a speedy & publick trial <u>by an impartial jury of the district wherein the crime shall have been committed, as the district shall have been previously ascertained by law</u>, and to be informed of the nature and cause of the accusation; to be confronted with the witnesses against him, and to have com
                                                                               to
pulsory process for obtaining witnesses ~~against him~~ in his favour, & ∧ have the assistance of counsel for his defence."

Conference MS, RG 46, DNA (Ellsworth's handwriting).

12.1.1.24 House Consideration of Conference Committee Report, September 24 [25], 1789

RESOLVED, That this House doth recede from their disagreement to the first, third, fifth, sixth, seventh, ninth, tenth, eleventh, fourteenth, fifteenth, seventeenth, twentieth, twenty-first, twenty-second, twenty-third, and twenty-fourth amendments, insisted on by the Senate: PROVIDED, That the two articles which by the amendments of the Senate are now proposed to be inserted as the third and eighth articles, shall be amended to read as followeth;

Article the third. "Congress shall make no law respecting an establishment of religion, or prohibiting the free exercise thereof; or abridging the freedom of speech, or of the press; or the right of the people peaceably to assemble, and to petition the government for a redress of grievances."

Article the eighth. "In all criminal prosecutions, the accused shall enjoy the right to a speedy and public trial by an impartial jury of the state and district wherein the crime shall have been committed, which district shall have been previously ascertained by law, and to be informed of the nature and cause of the accusation, to be confronted with the witnesses against him, to have compulsory process for obtaining witnesses in his favor, and to have the assistance of council for his defence."

HJ, p. 152 ("On the question, that the House do agree to the alteration and amendment of the eighth article, in manner aforesaid, It was resolved in the affirmative. Ayes 37 Noes 14").

12.1.1.25 Senate Consideration of Conference Committee Report, September 24, 1789

12.1.1.25.a   Mr. Ellsworth, on behalf of the managers of the conference on "articles to be proposed to the several States as Amendments to the Constitution of the United States," reported as follows:

That it will be proper for the House of Representatives to agree to the said amendments proposed by the Senate, with an Amendment to their fifth Amendment, so that the third Article shall read as follows: "Congress shall make no law respecting an establishment of <u>Religion</u>, or prohibiting the free exercise thereof; or abridging the freedom of Speech, or of the Press; or the right of the people peaceably to assemble and petition the Government for a redress of Grievances;"

And with an Amendment to the fourteenth Amendment proposed by the Senate, so that the eighth article, as numbered in the Amendments proposed by the Senate, shall read as follows; "In all criminal prosecutions, the accused shall enjoy the right to a speedy and public trial by an impartial <u>Jury</u> of the district wherein the <u>Crime</u> shall have been committed, as the district shall have been previously ascertained by law, and to be informed of the nature and cause of the accusation, to be confronted with the witnesses against him, and to have compulsory process for obtaining witnesses in his favor, and to have the assistance of Counsel for defence."

Smooth SJ, pp. 272–73

12.1.1.25.b   Mr. Ellsworth, on behalf of the managers of the conference on "Articles to be proposed to the several States as Amendments to the Constitution of the United States," reported as follows:

That it will be proper for the House of Representatives to agree to the said Amendments proposed by the Senate, with an Amendment to their fifth Amendment, so that the third Article shall read as follows: "Congress shall make no Law RESPECTING AN ESTABLISHMENT OF RELIGION, or prohibiting the free exercise thereof; or abridging the freedom of Speech, or of the Press; or the right of the People peaceably to assemble and petition the Government for a redress of Grievances;" And with an Amendment to the fourteenth Amendment proposed by the Senate, so that the eighth Article, as numbered in the Amendments proposed by the Senate, shall read as follows; "In all criminal prosecutions, the accused shall enjoy the right to a speedy and public trial BY AN IMPARTIAL JURY OF THE DISTRICT WHEREIN THE CRIME SHALL HAVE BEEN COMMITTED, AS THE DISTRICT SHALL HAVE BEEN PREVIOUSLY ASCERTAINED BY LAW, and to be informed of the nature and cause of the accusation, to be confronted with the witnesses against him, and to have compulsory process for obtaining witnesses in his favor, and to have the assistance of Counsel for defence."

Printed SJ, p. 145.

12.1.1.26   Further Senate Consideration of Conference Committee Report, September 24, 1789

12.1.1.26.a   A Message from the House of Representatives —

Mr. Beckley, their Clerk, brought up the Amendments to the "Articles to be proposed to the Legislatures of the several States, as Amendments to the Constitution of the United States;" and informed the Senate, that the House of Representatives had receded from their disagreement to the 1st, 3d, 5th, 6th, 7th, 9th, 10th, 11th, 14th, 15th, 17th, 20th, 21st, 22d, 23d, and 24th Amendments, insisted on by the Senate: Provided that the "Two Articles, which by the Amendments of the Senate are now proposed to be inserted as the third and eighth Articles," shall be amended to read as followeth:

Article the Third. "Congress shall make no Law respecting an establishment of Religion, or prohibiting the free exercise thereof; or abridging the freedom of Speech, or of the Press; or the right of the people peaceably to assemble, and petition the Government for a redress of Grievances."

Article the Eighth. "In all criminal prosecutions the accused shall enjoy the right to a speedy and public trial by an impartial Jury of the State and District, wherein the crime shall have been committed, which District shall have been previously ascertained by law, and to be informed of the nature and cause of the accusation, to be confronted with the witnesses against him, and to have compulsory process for obtaining witnesses in his favor, and to have the assistance of Counsel for his defence."

Smooth SJ, pp. 278–79.

12.1.1.26.b   A Message from the House of Representatives —

Mr. Beckley, their Clerk, brought up the Amendments to the "Articles to be proposed to the Legislatures of the several States, as Amendments to the Constitution of the United States;" and informed the Senate, that the House of Representatives had receded from their disagreement to the 1st, 3d, 5th, 6th, 7th, 9th, 10th, 11th, 14th, 15th, 17th, 20th, 21st, 22d, 23d, and 24th Amendments, insisted on by the Senate: Provided that the "Two Articles, which by the Amendments of the Senate are now proposed to be inserted as the third and eighth Articles," shall be amended to read as followeth:

Article the Third. "Congress shall make no Law respecting an establishment of Religion, or prohibiting the free exercise thereof; or abridging the freedom of Speech, or of the Press; or the right of the People peaceably to assemble, and petition the Government for a redress of Grievances."

Article the Eighth. "In all criminal prosecutions the accused shall enjoy the right to a speedy and public trial by an impartial Jury of the State and District, wherein the crime shall have been committed, which District shall have been previously ascertained by law, and to be informed of the nature and cause of the accusation, to be confronted with the witnesses against him, and to have compulsory process for obtaining witnesses in his favor, and to have the assistance of Counsel for his defence."

Printed SJ, p. 148.

12.1.1.27 Further Senate Consideration of Conference Committee Report, September 25, 1789

12.1.1.27.a   The Senate proceeded to consider the Message from the House of Representatives of the 24th, with Amendments to the Amendments of the Senate, to "Articles to be proposed to the Legislatures of the several States, as Amendments to the Constitution of the United States" — And

RESOLVED, That the Senate do concur in the Amendments proposed by the House of Representatives, to the Amendments of the Senate.

Smooth SJ, p. 283.

12.1.1.27.b   The Senate proceeded to consider the Message from the House of Representatives of the 24th, with Amendments to the Amendments of the Senate, to "Articles to be proposed to the Legislatures of the several States, as Amendments to the Constitution of the United States" — And

RESOLVED, That the Senate do concur in the Amendments proposed by the House of Representatives, to the Amendments of the Senate.

Printed SJ, pp. 150–51.

12.1.1.28   Agreed Resolution, September 25, 1789

Article the Eighth.

12.1.1.28.a   In all criminal prosecutions the accused shall enjoy the right to a speedy and public trial by an impartial Jury of the State and District wherein the crime shall have been committed, which District shall have been previously ascertained by law; and to be informed of the nature and cause of the accusation, to be confronted with the witnesses against him, to have compulsory process for obtaining witnesses in his favor, and to have the assistance of Counsel for his defence.

Smooth SJ, Appendix, p. 294.

ARTICLE THE EIGHTH.

12.1.1.28.b   In all criminal prosecutions the accused shall enjoy the right to a speedy and public trial by an impartial Jury of the State and District wherein the crime shall have been committed, which District shall have been previously ascertained by law; and to be informed of the nature and cause of the accusation, to be confronted with the witnesses against him, to have compulsory process for obtaining witnesses in his favor, and to have the assistance of counsel for his defence.

Printed SJ, Appendix, p. 164.

12.1.1.29   Enrolled Resolution, September 28, 1789

Article the eighth . . . In all criminal prosecutions, the accused shall enjoy the right to a speedy and public trial, by an impartial jury of the State and district wherein the crime shall have been committed, which district shall have been previously ascertained by law, and to be informed of the nature and cause of the accusation; to be confronted with the witnesses against him; to have compulsory process for obtaining witnesses in his favor, and to have the assistance of counsel for his defence.

Enrolled Resolutions, RG 11, DNA.

12.1.1.30   Printed Versions

12.1.1.30.a   ART. VI. In all criminal prosecutions the accused shall enjoy the right to a speedy and public trial, by an impartial jury of the State and district wherein the crime shall have been committed, which district shall have been previously ascertained by law, and to be informed of the nature and cause of the accusation; to be confronted with the witnesses against him; to have compulsory process for obtaining witnesses in his favour; and to have the assistance of counsel for his defence.

Statutes at Large, vol. 1, p. 21

12.1.1.30.b   ART. VIII. In all criminal prosecutions the accused shall enjoy the right to a speedy and public trial, by an impartial jury of the state and district wherein the crime shall have been committed, which district shall have been previously ascertained by law, and to be informed of the nature and cause of the accusation; to be confronted with the witnesses against him; to have compulsory process for obtaining witnesses in his favour, and to have the assistance of counsel for his defence.

Statutes at Large, vol. 1, p. 98.

12.1.2 PROPOSALS FROM THE STATE CONVENTIONS

12.1.2.1 Maryland Minority, April 26, 1788

2. That there shall be a trial by jury in all criminal cases, according to the course of proceeding in the state where the offence is committed; and that there be no appeal from matter of fact, or second trial after acquittal; but this provision shall not extend to such cases as may arise in the government of the land or naval forces.

Maryland Gazette, May 1, 1788 (committee majority).

12.1.2.2 New York, July 26, 1788

That (except in the Government of the Land and Naval Forces, and of the Militia when in actual Service, and in cases of Impeachment) a Presentment or Indictment by a Grand Jury ought to be observed as a necessary preliminary to the trial of all Crimes cognizable by the Judiciary of the United States, and such Trial should be speedy, public, and by an impartial Jury of the County where the Crime was committed; and that no person can be found Guilty without the unanimous consent of such Jury. But in cases of Crimes not committed within any County of the United States, and in Cases of Crimes committed within any County in which a general Insurrection may prevail, or which may be in the possession of a foreign Enemy, the enquiry and trial may be in such County as /\ Congress shall by Law direct; which County in the two Cases last mentioned should be as near as conveniently may be to that County in which the Crime may have been committed. And that in all Criminal Prosecutions, the Accused ought to be informed of the cause and nature of his Accusations, to be confronted with his accusers and the Witnesses against him, to have the means of producing his Witnesses, and the assistance of Council for his defence, and should not be compelled to give Evidence against himself.

That the trial by Jury in the extent that it obtains by the Common Law of England is one of the greatest securities to the rights of a free People, and ought to remain inviolate.

State Ratifications, RG 11, DNA.

12.1.2.3 North Carolina, August 1, 1788

8th. That in all capital and criminal prosecutions, a man hath a right to demand the cause and nature of his accusation, to be confronted with the accusers and witnesses, to call for evidence and be allowed counsel in his favor, and to a fair and speedy trial by an impartial jury of his vicinage, without whose unanimous consent he cannot be found guilty (except in the government of the land and naval forces) nor can he be compelled to give evidence against himself.

. . .

Amendments to the [Body of the] Constitution.

. . .

XVI That in criminal prosecutions, no man shall be restrained in the exercise of the usual and accustomed right of challenging or excepting to the jury.

State Ratifications, RG 11, DNA.

12.1.2.4 Pennsylvania Minority, December 12, 1787

3. That in all capital and criminal prosecutions, a man has the right to demand the cause and nature of the accusation, as well in the federal courts, as those of the several states; to be heard by himself or his counsel; to be confronted with the accusers and witnesses; to call for evidence in his favor, and a speedy trial, by an impartial jury of the vicinage, without whose unanimous consent, he cannot be found guilty, nor can he be compelled to give evidence against himself; that no man be deprived of his liberty, except by the law of the land or the judgment of his peers.

Pennsylvania Packet, December 18, 1787

12.1.2.5 Rhode Island, May 29, 1790

8th. That in all capital and criminal prosecutions, a man hath a right to demand the cause and nature of the accusation, to be confronted with the accusers and witnesses, to call for evidence and be allowed counsel in his favour, and to a fair and speedy trial by an impartial jury of his vicinage, without whose unanimous consent he cannot be found guilty; (except in the government of the land and naval forces) nor can he be compelled to give evidence against himself.

State Ratifications, RG 11, DNA.

12.1.2.6 Virginia, June 27, 1788

Eighth, That in all capital and criminal prosecutions, a man hath a right to demand the cause and nature of his accusation, to be confronted with the accusers and witnesses, to call for evidence and be allowed counsel in his favor, and to a fair and speedy trial by an impartial Jury of his vicinage, without whose unanimous consent he cannot be found guilty, (except in the government of the land and naval forces) nor can he be compelled to give evidence against himself.

. . .

Amendments to the Body of the Constitution.

. . .

Fifteenth, that in criminal prosecutions no man shall be restrained in the exercise of the usual and accustomed right of challenging or excepting to the Jury.

State Ratifications, RG 11, DNA.

12.1.3 STATE CONSTITUTIONS AND LAWS; COLONIAL CHARTERS AND LAWS

12.1.3.1 Delaware: Declaration of Rights, 1776

SECT. 14. That in all prosecutions for criminal offences, every man hath a right to be informed of the accusation against him, to be allowed counsel, to be confronted with the accusers or witnesses, to examine evidence on oath in his favour, and to a speedy trial by an impartial jury, without whose unanimous consent he ought not be found guilty.

Delaware Laws, vol. 1, App., p. 81.

12.1.3.2   **Georgia**

12.1.3.2.a   **Constitution, 1777**

LXI. Freedom of the press, and trial by jury, to remain inviolate *forever*.

Georgia Laws, p. 16.

12.1.3.2.b   **Constitution, 1789**

ARTICLE IV.

. . .

Sect. 3. Freedom of the press, and trial by jury, shall remain inviolate.

Georgia Laws, p. 29.

12.1.3.3   **Maryland, Declaration of Rights, 1776**

3. That the inhabitants of Maryland are entitled to the common law of England, and the trial by jury, according to the course of that law, and to the benefit of such of the English statutes as existed at the time of their first emigration, and which by experience have been found applicable to their local and other circumstances, and of such others as have been since made in England or Great-Britain, and have been introduced, used, and practised by the courts of law or equity; and also to all acts of assembly in force on the first of June seventeen hundred and seventy-four, except such as may have since expired, or have been, or may be altered by acts of convention, or this declaration of rights; subject nevertheless to the revision of, and amendment or repeal by, the legislature of this state; and the inhabitants of Maryland are also entitled to all property derived to them from or under the charter granted by his majesty Charles the first, to Caecilius Calvert, baron of Baltimore.

. . .

19. That in all criminal prosecutions, every man hath a right to be informed of the accusation against him, to have a copy of the indictment or charge in due time (if required) to prepare for his defence, to be allowed council, to be confronted with the witnesses against him, to have process for his witnesses, to examine the witnesses for and against him on oath, and to a speedy trial by an impartial jury, without whose unanimous consent he ought not to be found guilty.

Maryland Laws, November 3, 1776.

12.1.3.4   **Massachusetts**

12.1.3.4.a   **Body of Liberties, 1641**

[26] Every man that findeth himselfe unfit to plead his owne cause in any Court shall have Libertie to imploy any man against whom the Court doth not except, to helpe him, Provided he give him noe fee or reward for his paines. This shall not exempt the partie him selfe from Answering such Questions in person as the Court shall thinke meete to demand of him.

. . .

[29] In all Actions at law it shall be the libertie of the plantife and defendant by mutual consent to choose whether they will be tryed by the Bench or by a Jurie, unlesse it be where the law upon just reason hath otherwise determined. The like libertie shall be granted to all persons in Criminall cases.

. . .

[36] It shall be in the libertie of every man cast condemed or sentenced in any cause in any Inferior Court, to make their Appeale to the Court of Assistants, provided they tender their appeale and put in securitie to prosecute it before the Court be ended wherein they were condemned, And within six dayes next ensuing put in good securitie before some Assistant to satisfie what his Adversarie shall recover against him; And if the cause be of a Criminall nature, for his good behaviour, and appearance, And everie man shall have libertie to complaine to the Generall Court of any Injustice done him in any Court of Assistants or other.

Massachusetts Colonial Laws, pp. 39–41.

12.1.3.4.b General Laws of New-Plimouth, 1671 [1636]

4. It is also Enacted, that no person in this Government shall be endamaged in respect of Life, Limb, Liberty, Good name or Estate, under colour of Law, or countenance of Authority, but by virtue or equity of some express law of the General Court of this Colony, the known Law of God, or the good and equitable Laws of our Nation suitable for us, being brought to Answer by due process thereof.

5. That all Trials, whether Capital, Criminal, or between Man and Man, be tried by Jury of twelve good and lawful Men, according to the commendable custome of England; except the party or parties concerned, do refer it to the Bench, or some express Law doth refer it to their Judgement and Tryal, or the Tryal of some other Court where Jury is not, in which case any party aggrieved, may appeal, and shall have Tryal by a Jury.

And it shall be in the liberty of both Plaintiffe and Defendant or any Delinquent, that is to be tryed by a Jury, to chalenge any of the Jurors, and if the chalenge be found just and reasonable by the Bench, it shall be allowed him, and others without just exception shall be impannelled in their room; And if it be in case of Life and Death, the Prisoner shall have liberty to except against six or eight of the Jury, without giving any reason for his exception.

6. That no Man be sentenced to Death without Testimony of two witnesses at least, or that which is equivalent thereunto, and that two or three Witnesses being of competent Age, Understanding and good Reputation, Testifying to the Case in question, shall be accounted and accepted as full Testimony in any Case, though they did not together see or hear, and so Witness to the same individual Act, in reference to circumstances of time and place; Provided and Bench and Jury be Satisfied with such Testimony.

New-Plimouth Laws, p. 2.

12.1.3.4.c Constitution, 1780

[Part I, Article] XII. No subject shall be held to answer for any crimes or offence until the same is fully and plainly, substantially and formally, described to him; or be compelled to accuse, or furnish evidence against himself. And every subject shall have a right to produce all proofs, that may be favourable to him; to meet the witnesses against him face to face, and to be fully heard in his defence by himself, or counsel, at his election. And no subject shall be arrested, imprisoned, despoiled, or deprived of his property, immunities, or privileges, put out of the protection of the law, exiled, or deprived of his life, liberty, or estate, but by the judgment of his peers, or the law of the land.

And the legislature shall not make any law, that shall subject any person to a capital or infamous punishment, excepting for the government of the army and navy, without trial by jury.

XIII. In criminal prosecutions, the verification of facts in the vicinity where they happen, is one of the greatest securities of the life, liberty and property of the citizen.

Massachusetts Perpetual Laws, pp. 6–7.

12.1.3.5 New Hampshire: Constitution, 1783

[Part I, Article] XV. No subject shall be held to answer for any crime, or offence, until the same is fully and plainly, substantially and formally described to him; or be compelled to accuse or furnish evidence against himself. And every subject shall have a right to produce all proofs that may be favorable to himself: To meet the witnesses against him face to face, and to be fully heard in his defence by himself and counsel. And no subject shall be arrested, imprisoned, despoiled, or deprived of his property, immunities, or priviliges, put out of the protection of the law, exiled or deprived of his life, liberty, or estate, but by the judgment of his peers or the law of the land.

New Hampshire Laws, p. 25.

12.1.3.6 New Jersey
12.1.3.6.a Concessions and Agreements of West New Jersey, 1676

Chapter XVII.

THAT no Proprietor, Freeholder or Inhabitant of the said Province of *West New-Jersey,* shall be deprived or condemned of Life, Limb, Liberty, Estate, Property or any ways hurt in his or their Privileges, Freedoms or Franchises, upon any account whatsoever, without a due Tryal, and Judgment passed by Twelve good and lawful Men of his Neighbourhood first had: And that in all Causes to be tryed, and in all Tryals, the Person or Persons, arrained may except against any of the said Neighbourhood, without any Reason rendered, (not exceeding Thirty five) and in case of any valid reason alledged, against every Person nominated for that Service.

Chapter XVIII.

AND that no Proprietor, Freeholder, Freedenison, or Inhabitant in the said Province, shall be attached, arrested, or imprisoned, for or by reason of a Debt, Duty, or other Thing whatsoever (Cases Felonious, Criminal and Treasonable excepted) before he or she have personal Summon, or Summons, left at his or her last dwelling Place, if in the said Province, by some legal authorized Officer, constituted and appointed for that Purpose, to appear in some Court of Judicature for the said Province, with a full and plain account of the Cause or Thing in demand, as also the Name or Names of the Person or Persons at whose suit, and the Court where he is to appear, and that he hath at least Fourteen Days Time to appear and answer the said suit, if he or she live or inhabit within Forty Miles *English* of the said Court, and if at a further distance, to have for every Twenty

Miles, two Days more, for his and their appearance, and so proportionably for a larger distance of space.

That upon the Recording of the Summons, and non appearance of such Person and Persons, a Writ or attachment shall or may be issued out to arrest, or attach the Person or Persons of such defaulters, to cause his or their Appearance in such Court, returnable at a Day certain, to answer the Penalty or Penalties, in such Suit or Suits; and if he or they shall be condemned by legal Tryal and Judgment, the Penalty or Penalties shall be paid and satisfied out of his or their real or personal Estate so condemned, or cause the Person or Persons so condemned, to lie in execution till Satisfaction of the Debt and Damages be made. PROVIDED AL- WAYS, if such Person or Persons so condemned, shall pay and deliver such Estate, Goods and Chattles which he or any other Person hath for his or their use, and shall solemnly declare and aver, that he or they have not any further Estate, Goods, or Chattles wheresoever, to satisfy the Person or Persons, (at whose Suit, he or they are condemned) their respective Judgments, and shall also bring and produce three other Persons as compurgators, who are well known and of honest Reputation, and approved of by the Commissioners of that Division, where they dwell or inhabit, which shall in such open Court, likewise solemnly declare and aver, that they believe in their Consciences, such Person and Persons so con- demned, have not werewith [sic] further to pay the said Condemnation or Con- demnations, he or they shall be thence forthwith discharged from their said im- prisonment, any Law or Custom to the contrary thereof, heretofore in the said Province, notwithstanding. And upon such Summons and Default of appearance, recorded as aforesaid, and such Person and Persons not appearing within Forty Days after, it shall and may be lawful for such Court of Judicature to proceed to tryal, of twelve lawful Men to Judgment, against such Defaulters, and issue forth Execution against his or their Estate, real and personal, to satisfy such Penalty or Penalties, to such Debt and Damages so Recorded, as far as it shall or may extend.

Chapter XIX.

THAT there shall be in every Court, three Justices or Commissioners, who shall sit with the twelve Men of the Neighbourhood, with them to hear all Causes, and to assist the said Twelve Men of the Neighbourhood in Case of Law; and that they the said Justices shall pronounce such Judgment as they shall receive from, and be directed by the said Twelve Men, in whom only the Judgment resides, and not otherwise.

And in Case of their neglect and refusal, that then one of the Twelve, by con- sent of the rest, pronounce their own Judgment as the Justices should have done.

And if any Judgment shall be past, in any Case Civil or Criminal, by any other Person or Persons, or any other way, then according to this Agreement and Appointment, it shall be held null and void, and such Person or Persons so pre- suming to give Judgment, shall be severely Fin'd, and upon complaint made to the General Assembly, by them be declared incapable of any Office or Trust within this Province.

Chapter XX.

THAT in all Matters and Causes, Civil and Criminal, Proof is to be made by the solemn and plain averment, of at least two honest and reputable Persons; and in Case that any Person or Persons shall bear false Witness, and bring in his or their Evidence, contrary to the Truth of the Matter as shall be made plainly to appear, that then every such Person or Persons, shall in Civil Causes, suffer the Penalty which would be due to the Person or Persons he or they bear Witness against. And in Case any Witness or Witnesses, on the behalf of any Person or Persons, Indicted in a Criminal Cause, shall be found to have born False Witness for Fear, Gain, Malice, or Favour, and thereby hinder the due Execution of the Law, and deprive the suffering Person or Persons of their due Satisfaction, that then and in all other Cases of false Evidence, such Person or Persons, shall be first severely Fined, and next that he or they shall forever be disabled from being admitted in evidence, or into any Publick Office, Employment, or Service within this Province.

Chapter XXI.

THAT all and every Person and Persons whatsoever, who shall prosecute or prefer any Indictment or Information against others for any personal Injuries, or Matter Criminal, or shall Prosecute for any other Criminal Cause, (Treason, Murther, and Felony, only excepted) shall and may be Master of his own Process, and have full Power to forgive and remit the Person or Persons offending against him or herself only, as well before as after Judgment, and Condemnation, and Pardon and Remit the Sentence, Fine, and Punishment of the Person or Persons Offending, be it personal or other whatsoever.

Chapter XXII.

THAT the Tryals of all Causes, Civil and Criminal, shall be heard and decided by the Virdict or Judgment of Twelve honest Men of the Neighbourhood, only to be summoned and presented by the Sheriff of that Division, or Propriety where the Fact or Trespass is committed; and that no Person or Persons shall be compelled to Fee any Attorney or Counciller to plead his Cause, but that all Persons have free Liberty to plead his own Cause, if he please: And that no Person nor Persons imprisoned upon any account whatsoever within this Province, shall be obliged to pay any Fees to the Officer or Officers of the said Prison, either when committed or discharged.

Chapter XXIII.

THAT in all publick Courts of Justice for Tryals of Causes, Civil or Criminal, any Person or Persons, Inhabitants of the said Province, may freely come into, and attend the said Courts, and hear and be present, at all or any such Tryals as shall be there had or passed, that Justice may not be done in a Corner nor in any covert manner, being intended and resolved, by the help of the Lord, and by these our Concessions and Fundamentals, that all and every Person and Persons Inhabiting the said Province, shall, as far as in us lies, be free from Oppression and Slavery.

New Jersey Grants, pp. 395–98.

12.1.3.6.b   Fundamental Constitutions for East New Jersey, 1683

XIX. That no Person or Persons within the said Province shall be taken and imprisoned, or be devised of his Freehold, free Custom or Liberty, or be outlawed or exiled, or any other Way destroyed; nor shall they be condemn'd or Judgment pass'd upon them, but by lawful Judgment of their Peers: Neither shall Justice nor Right be bought or sold, defered or delayed, to any Person whatsoever: In order to which by the Laws of the Land, all Tryals shall be by twelve Men, and as near as it may be, Peers and Equals, and of the Neighbourhood, and Men without just Exception. In Cases of Life there shall be at first Twenty four returned by the Sherriff for a Grand Inquest, of whom twelve at least shall be to find the Complaint to be true; and then the Twelve Men or Peers to be likewise returned, shall have the final Judgment; but reasonable Challenges shall be always admitted against the Twelve Men, or any of them: But the Manner of returning Juries shall be thus, the Names of all the Freemen above five and Twenty Years of Age, within the District or Boroughs out of which the Jury is to be returned, shall be written on equal Pieces of Parchment and put into a Box, and then the Number of the Jury shall be drawn out by a Child under Ten Years of Age. And in all Courts Persons of all Perswasions may freely appear in their own Way, and according to their own Manner, and there personally plead their own Causes themselves, or if unable, by their Friends, no Person being allowed to take Money for pleading or advice in such Casas [sic]: And the first Process shall be the Exhibition of the Complaint in Court fourteen Days before the Tryal, and the Party complain'd against may be fitted for the same, he or she shall be summoned ten Days before, and a Copy of the Complaint delivered at their dwelling House: But before the Complaint of any Person be received, he shall solemnly declare in Court, that he believes in his Conscience his Cause is just. Moreover, every Man shall be first cited before the Court for the Place where he dwells, nor shall the Cause be brought before any other Court but by way of Appeal from Sentence of the first Court, for receiving of which Appeals, there shall be a Court consisting of eight Persons, and the Governor (protempore) President thereof, (to wit) four Proprietors and four Freemen, to be chosen out of the great Council in the following Manner, viz. the Names of Sixteen of the Proprietors shall be written on small pieces of Parchment and put into a Box, out of which by a Lad under Ten Years of Age, shall be drawn eight of them, the eight remaining in the Box shall choose four; and in like Manner shall be done for the choosing of four of the Freemen.   New Jersey Grants, pp. 163–64.

12.1.3.6.c Constitution, 1776

XVI. THAT all criminals shall be admitted to the same Privileges of Witnesses and Council, as their Prosecutors are or shall be entitled to.

. . .

XXII. THAT the Common Law of *England*, as well as so much of the Statute Law, as have been heretofore practised in this Colony, shall still remain in Force, until they shall be altered by a future Law of the Legislature, such Parts only excepted as are repugnant to the Rights and Privileges contained in this Charter; and that of Trial by Jury shall remain confirmed, as a Part of the Law of this Colony, without Repeal for-ever.   New Jersey Acts, pp. viii–ix.

12.1.3.7 New York

12.1.3.7.a Act Declaring . . . Rights & Priviledges, 1691

That no Free-man shall be taken or imprisoned, or be deprived of his Free-hold or Liberty, or free Customs, or Out-Lawed, or Exiled, or any other wayes destroyed; nor shall be passed upon, adjudged or condemned, but by the lawful Judgment of his Peers, and by the Laws of this Province.

Justice nor Right shall be neither Sold, Denyed or Delayed to any Person within this Province.

. . .

That no Man, of what Estate or Condition soever, shall be put out of his Lands, Tenements, nor taken, nor imprisoned, nor disinherited, nor banished, nor any ways destroyed or molested, without first being brought to answer by due course of Law.

. . .

That in all Cases Capital and Criminal, there shall be a grand Inquest who shall first present the Offence, and then Twelve Good Men of the Neighbourhood to Try the Offender; who, after his Plea to the Indictment, shall be allowed his reasonable Challanges.

New York Acts, pp. 17–18.

12.1.3.7.b Constitution, 1777

XIII. AND this Convention doth further, in the Name, and by the Authority of the good People of this State, ORDAIN, DETERMINE, AND DECLARE, That no Member of this State shall be disfranchised, or deprived of any the Rights or Privileges secured to the Subjects of this State by this Constitution, unless by the Law of the Land, or the Judgment of his Peers.

. . .

XXXIV. AND IT IS FURTHER ORDAINED, That in every Trial on Impeachment or Indictment for Crimes or Misdemeanors, the Party impeached or indicted, shall be allowed Counsel, as in civil Actions.

. . .

XLI. And this Convention doth further ORDAIN, DETERMINE, AND DECLARE, in the Name and by the Authority of the good People of this State, That Trial by Jury, in all Cases in which it hath heretofore been used in the Colony of *New-York,* shall be established, and remain inviolate for ever. And that no Acts of Attainder shall be passed by the Legislature of this State, for Crimes other than those committed before the Termination of the present War; and that such Acts shall not work a Corruption of Blood. And further, that the Legislature of this State shall at no Time hereafter, Institute any new Court or Courts, but such as shall proceed according to the Course of the Common Law.

New York Laws, vol. 1, pp. 8, 12, 14.

12.1.3.7.c Bill of Rights, 1787

Second, That no Citizen of this State shall be taken or imprisoned, or be disseised of his or her Freehold, or Liberties, or Free-Customs: or outlawed, or exiled, or condemned, or otherwise destroyed, but by lawful Judgment of his or her Peers, or by due Process of Law.

Third, That no Citizen of this State shall be taken or imprisoned for any Offence, upon Petition or Suggestion, unless it be by indictment or Presentment of good and lawful Men of the same Neighbourhood where such Deeds be done, in due Manner, or by due Process of Law.

Fourth, That no Person shall be put to answer without Presentment before Justices, or Matter of Record, or due Process of Law, according to the Law of the Land; and if any Thing be done to the Contrary, it shall be void in Law, and holden for Error.

Fifth, That no Person, of what Estate or Condition soever, shall be taken, or imprisoned, or disinherited, or put to death, without being brought to answer by due Process of Law; and that no Person shall be put out of his or her Franchise or Freehold, or lose his or her Life or Limb, or Goods and Chattels, unless he or she be duly brought to answer, and be fore-judged of the same, by due Course of Law; and if any Thing be done contrary to the same, it shall be void in Law, and holden for none.

Sixth, That neither Justice nor Right shall be sold to any Person, nor denied, nor deferred; and that Writs and Process shall be granted freely and without Delay, to all Persons requiring the same; and nothing from henceforth shall be paid or taken for any Writ or Process, but the accustomed Fees for writing, and for the Seal of the same Writ or Process; and all Fines, Duties and Impositions whatsoever, heretofore taken or demanded, under what Name or Description soever, for, or upon granting any Writs, Inquests, Commissions, or Process to Suitors in their Causes, shall be, and hereby are abolished.

Seventh, That no Citizens of this State shall be fined or amerced without reasonable Cause, and such Fine or Amerciament shall always be according to the Quantity of his or her Trespass or Offence, and saving to him or her his or her Contenement; *That is to say,* Every Freeholder saving his Freehold, a Merchant saving his Merchandize, and a mechanic saving the Implements of his Trade.

New York Laws, vol. 2, pp. 1–2.

12.1.3.8 North Carolina
12.1.3.8.a Fundamental Constitutions of Carolina, 1669

69th. Every jury shall consist of twelve men; and it shall not be necessary they should all agree, but the verdict shall be according to the consent of the majority.

. . .

111th. No cause whether civil or ciminal, of any freeman, shall be tried in any court of judicature, without a jury of his peers.

North Carolina State Records, pp. 145, 149.

12.1.3.8.b Declaration of Rights, 1776

Sect. VII. That in all criminal Prosecutions every Man has a Right to be informed of the Accusation against him, and to confront the Accusers and Witnesses with other Testimony, and shall not be compelled to give Evidence against himself.

Sect. VIII. That no Freeman shall be put to answer any criminal Charge, but by Indictment, Presentment, Impeachment.

Sect. IX. That no Freeman shall be convicted of any Crime, but by the unanimous Verdict of a Jury of good and lawful Men, in open Court as heretofore used.

North Carolina Laws, p. 275.

12.1.3.9   Pennsylvania

12.1.3.9.a   Laws Agreed Upon in England, 1682

VIII. That all **Tryals** shall be by **Twelve Men,** and as near as may be, *Peers* or *Equals,* and of the *Neighborhood,* and men without just Exception. In cases of *Life,* there shall be first **Twenty Four** returned by the Sheriff for a **Grand Inquest,** of whom *Twelve* at least shall find the Complaint to be true, and then the **Twelve Men** or *Peers,* to be likewise returned by the Sheriff, shall have the *final Judgment.* But reasonable *Challenges* shall be always admitted against the said *Twelve Men,* or any of them.

Pennsylvania Frame, p. 8.

12.1.3.9.b   Provincial Laws, 1700

19. Noe *Freeman* to be *Imprisoned,* or Disseized, Outlaw'd or Exiled, or otherwise hurt, T*ryed,* or C*ondemned,* but by the *Judgement* of his *Twelve* Equalls, or *Laws* of this *Province.*

Pennsylvania Abstract, p. 5.

12.1.3.9.c   Constitution, 1776

CHAPTER I.

A DECLARATION of the RIGHTS of the Inhabitants of the State of Pennsylvania.

. . .

IX. That in all prosecutions for criminal offences, a man hath a right to be heard by himself and his council, to demand the cause and nature of his accusation, to be confronted with the witnesses, to call for evidence in his favour, and a speedy public trial, by an impartial jury of the country, without the unanimous consent of which jury he cannot be found guilty; nor can be compelled to give evidence against himself; nor can any man be justly deprived of his liberty except by the laws of the land, or the judgment of his peers.

. . .

CHAPTER II.

PLAN *or* FRAME *of* GOVERNMENT.

. . .

Sᴇᴄᴛ. 25. Trial shall be by jury as heretofore: And it is recommended to the legislature of this state, to provide by law against every corruption or partiality in the choice, return, or appointment of juries. Pennsylvania Acts, McKean, pp. ix–x, xvii.

12.1.3.9.d **Constitution, 1790**

ARTICLE IX.

. . . Sect. IX. That, in all criminal prosecutions, the accused hath a right to be heard by himself and his council, to demand the nature and cause of the accusation against him, to meet the witnesses face to face, to have compulsory process for obtaining witnesses in his favour, and, in prosecutions by indictment or information, a speedy public trial by an impartial jury of the vicinage: That he cannot be compelled to give evidence against himself, nor can he be deprived of his life, liberty, or property, unless by the judgment of his peers, or the law of the land.

Pennsylvania Acts, Dallas, p. xxxiv.

12.1.3.10 **Rhode Island: Code of Laws, 1647**

1. That no person, in this Colony, shall be taken or imprisoned, or be disseized of his lands or liberties, or be exiled, or any otherwise molested or destroyed, but by the lawful judgment of his peers, or by some known law, and according to the letter of it, ratified and confirmed by the major part of the General Assembly, lawfully met and orderly managed.

Rhode Island Code, p. 12.

12.1.3.11 **South Carolina**

12.1.3.11.a **Fundamental Constitutions of Carolina, 1669**

69th. Every jury shall consist of twelve men; and it shall not be necessary they should all agree, but the verdict shall be according to the consent of the majority.

. . .

111th. No cause whether civil or criminal, of any freeman, shall be tried in any court of judicature, without a jury of his peers.

North Carolina State Records, pp. 145, 149.

12.1.3.11.b **Constitution, 1778**

XLI. That no Freeman of this State be taken, or imprisoned or desseized of his Freehold, Liberties or Privileges, or out-lawed, or exiled, or in any Manner destroyed, or deprived of his Life, Liberty, or Property, but by the Judgment of his Peers, or by the Law of the Land.

South Carolina Constitution, p. 15.

12.1.3.11.c **Constitution, 1790**

ARTICLE IX.

. . .

Section 2. No freeman of this state shall be taken, or imprisoned, or disseised of his freehold, liberties, or privileges, or outlawed or exiled, or in any manner destroyed, or deprived of his life, liberty or property, but by the judgment of his peers, or by the law of the land; nor shall any bill of the attainder, ex post facto law or law impairing the obligation of contracts ever be passed by the legislature of this state.

. . .

Section 6. The trial by jury as heretofore used in this state, and the liberty of the press, shall be for ever inviolably preserved.   South Carolina Laws, App., pp. 41–42.

12.1.3.12   Vermont: Constitution, 1777

CHAPTER I

. . .

10. THAT in all Prosecutions for criminal offences, a Man hath a Right to be heard by himself and his Counsel, — to demand the Cause and Nature of his Accusation, — to be confronted with the Witnesses, — to call for Evidence in his Favor, and a speedy public Trial, by an impartial Jury of the Country, without the unanimous Consent of which Jury, he cannot be [fo]und guilty; nor can he be compelled to give Evidence against himself; nor can any man be justly deprived of his Liberty, except by the Laws of the Land, or the Judgment of his Peers.

Vermont Acts, p. 4.

12.1.3.13   Virginia: Declaration of Rights, 1776

VIII. THAT in all capital or criminal prosecutions a man hath a right to demand the cause and nature of his accusation, to be confronted with the accusers and witnesses, to call for evidence in his favour, and to a speedy trial by an impartial jury of his vicinage, without whose unanimous consent he cannot be found guilty, nor can he be compelled to give evidence against himself; that no man be deprived of his liberty except by the law of the land, or the judgment of his peers.

Virginia Acts, p. 33.

12.1.4 OTHER TEXTS

12.1.4.1   Statute of Westminster I, 1275

That notorious felons who are openly of evil fame and who refuse to put themselves upon inquests of felony at the suit of the King before his justices, shall be remanded to a hard and strong prison as befits those who refuse to abide by the common law of the land; but this is not to be understood of persons who are taken upon light suspicion.

3 Edw. 1, c. 12.

12.1.4.2   Magna Carta, 1297

No freeman shall be taken or imprisoned, or be disseised of his freehold, or liberties, or free customs, or be outlawed, or exiled, or any other wise destroyed; nor will we not pass upon him, nor condemn him, but by lawful judgment of his peers, or by the law of the land. We will sell to no man, we will not deny or defer to any man either justice or right.

25 Edw. 1, c. 29.

12.1.4.3   Petition of Right, 1627

3. And where alsoe by the Statute called the Great Charter of the liberties of England, it is declared and enacted, that no freeman may be taken or imprisoned or be disseised of his freehold or liberties or his free customes or be outlawed or

exiled or in any manner destroyed, but by the lawfull judgment of his peeres or by the law of the land.

4. And in the eight and twentith yeere of the raigne of King Edward the Third it was declared and enacted by authoritie of Parliament, that no man of what estate or condicion that he be, should be put out of his land or tenemente nor taken nor imprisoned nor disherited nor put to death without being brought to aunswere by due pcesse of lawe.

5. Neverthelesse against the tenor of the said statutes and other the good lawes and statutes of your realme to that end pvided, divers of your subjecte have of late been imprisoned without any cause shewed: And when for their deliverance they were brought before your justices by your Majesties writte of habeas corpus there to undergoe and receive as the court should order, and their keepers cōmaunded to certifie the causes of their detayner, no cause was certified, but that they were deteined by your Majesties speciall cōmaund signified by the lorde of your privie councell, and yet were returned backe to severall prisons without being charged with any thing to which they might make aunswere according to the lawe.

.   .   .

8. They doe therefore humblie pray your most excellent Majestie . . . that no freeman in any such manner as is before mencioned be imprisoned or de-teined. . . .

3 Chas. 1, c. 1 (1628).

12.1.4.4 English Bill of Rights, 1689

11. That jurors ought to be duly impanelled and returned, and jurors which pass upon men in trials for high treason ought to be freeholders.

1 Will. & Mar., 2d sess., c. 2.

12.1.4.5 Resolutions of the Stamp Act Congress, October 19, 1765

7th. That trial by jury is the inherent and invaluable right of every British subject in these colonies.

First Congress Journal, p. 28.

12.1.4.6 Declaration and Resolves of the First Continental Congress, October 14, 1774

Resolved, N.C.D. 5. That the respective colonies are entitled to the common law of England, and more especially to the great and inestimable privilege of being tried by their peers of the vicinage, according to the course of that law.

Tansill, p. 3.

12.1.4.7 Declaration of Independence, 1776

.   . . For depriving us in many cases, of the benefits of Trial by Jury: For transporting us beyond Seas to be tried for pretended offences. . . .

Continental Congress Papers, DNA.

12.1.4.8 Northwest Territory Ordinance, 1787

Article the Second. The inhabitants of the said territory shall always be entitled to the benefits of the writ of habeas corpus, and of the trial by jury; of a proportionate representation of the people in the legislature, and of judicial proceedings according to the course of the common law; all persons shall be bailable unless for Capital Offences, where the proof shall be evident, or the presumption great; all fines shall be moderate, and no cruel or unusual punishments shall be inflicted; no man shall be deprived of his liberty or property but by the judgment of his peers, or the law of the land; and should the public exigencies make it Necessary for the common preservation to take any persons property, or to demand his particular services, full compensation shall be made for the same; and in the just preservation of rights and property it is understood and declared, that no law ought ever to be made, or have force in the said territory, that shall in any manner whatever interfere with, or affect private contracts or engagements bona fide and without fraud, previously formed.

Continental Congress Papers, DNA.

12.1.4.9 **Richard Henry Lee to Edmund Randolph, Proposed Amendments, October 16, 1787**
. . . That the trial by jury in criminal and civil cases, and the modes prescribed by the common law for safety of life in criminal prosecutions shall be held sacred — . . . That such parts of the new consitution be amended as provide imperfectly for the trial of criminals by a jury of the vicinage, and to supply the omission of a jury trial in civil causes or disputes about property between individuals where by the common law is directed, and as generally it is secured by the several State constitutions. That such parts of the new constitution be amended, as permit the vexatious and oppressive calling of citizens from their own country, and all controversies between citizens of different states and between citizens and foreigners, to be tried in a far distant court, and as it may be without a jury, whereby in a multitude of cases, the circumstances of distance and expence may compel numbers to submit to the most unjust and ill-founded demand . . . .

Virginia Gazette, December 22, 1787.

12.2 DISCUSSION OF DRAFTS AND PROPOSALS

12.2.1 THE FIRST CONGRESS

12.2.1.1 **June 8, 1789**[3]

12.2.1.2 **August 15, 1789**

MR. MADISON.

[H]ave not the people been told that the rights of conscience, the freedom of speech, the liberty of the press, and trial by jury, were in jeopardy. That they ought not to adopt the constitution until those important rights were secured to them.

Congressional Register, August 15, 1789, vol. 1, p. 216.

12.2.1.3 **August 17, 1789**

12.2.1.3.a The committee then proceeded to consider the 7th proposition in the words following:
Art. 3, Sect. 2. Strike out the whole of the 3d paragraph, and insert, "In all criminal prosecutions, the accused, shall enjoy the right to a speedy and public

---

[3]For the reports of Madison's speech in support of his proposals, *see* 1.2.1.1.a–c.

trial, to be informed of the nature and cause of the accusation, to be confronted with the witnesses against him, to have compulsory process for obtaining witnesses in his favor, and to have the assistance of counsel for his defence.''

Mr. BURKE

Moved to amend this proposition in such a manner, as to leave it in the power of the accused to put off their trial to the next session, provided he made appear to the court, that the evidence of the witnesses, for whom process was granted, but not served, was material to his defence.

Mr. HARTLEY

Said that in securing him the right of compulsatory process, the government did all it could, the remainder must lay in the discretion of the court.

Mr. SMITH (of S.C.) Thought the regulation would come properly in, as part of the judicial system.

The question on mr. Burke's motion was taken, and lost. Affirmative 9, negative 41.

Mr. LIVERMORE moved to alter the clause, so as to secure to the criminal the right of being tried in the state where the offence was committed.

Mr. STONE observed, that full provision was made on the subject in the subsequent clause.

On the question, mr. Livermore's motion was adopted.

Mr. BURKE

Said he was not so much discouraged by the fate of his former motions, but what he would venture upon another, he therefore proposed to add to the clause, that no criminal prosecution should be had by way of information.

Mr. HARTLEY only requested the gentleman to look to the clause, and he would see the impropriety of inserting it in this place.

A desultory conversation rose, respecting the foregoing motion, and after some time mr. Burke withdrew it for the present.

The committee then arose, and reported progress, after which the house adjourned.

Congressional Register, August 17, 1789, vol. 2, pp. 228–29.

12.2.1.3.b   Fourteenth Amendment — Art. 2 [3]. Sec. 3 [2], Strike out the whole of the 3d par. And insert — "In all criminal prosecutions the accused shall enjoy the right to a speedy and public trial, to be informed of the nature and cause of the accusation, to be confronted with the witnesses against him, to have compulsory process for obtaining witnesses in his favor, and to have the assistance of counsel for his defence."

This amendment passed.

The committee then rose and the house adjourned.

Daily Advertiser, August 18, 1789, p. 2, col. 4.

12.2.1.3.c   Fourteenth amendment — Art, II [III]. Sec. 3 [2], strike out the whole of the 3d par. and insert — "In all criminal prosecutions the accused shall enjoy the right to a speedy and public trial, to be informed of the nature and cause of the accusation, to be confronted with the witnesses against him; to have compulsory process for obtaining witnesses in his favor, and to have the assistance of counsel for his defence."

This amendment passed.

The committee then rose and the house adjourned.

New-York Daily Gazette, August 19, 1789, p. 802, col. 4.

12.2.1.3.d   14th Amendment. Art. II [III]. Sec. 3d [2d], Strike out the whole of the 3d par. and insert: "In all criminal prosecutions the accused shall enjoy the right to a speedy and public trial, to be informed of the nature and cause of the accusation, to be confronted with the witnesses against him, to have compulsory process for obtaining witnesses in his favour, and to have the assistance of counsel for his defence."

Several amendments to this article were proposed, some of them were withdrawn and others negatived; and one only obtained, which respected the place of trial, which was to be in the State where the supposed crime was committed.

This amendment was then adopted.

The committee then arose and the house adjourned.

Gazette of the U.S., August 22, 1789, p. 250, col. 1.

12.2.1.4   August 18, 1789

12.2.1.4.a   The house again resolved itself into a committee of the whole on the subject of amendments, and took into consideration the 2d clause of the 7th proposition, in the words following, "The trial of all crimes (except in cases of impeachment, and in cases arising in the land or naval forces, or in the militia when in actual service in time of war or public danger) shall be by an impartial jury of freeholders of the vicinage, with the requisite of unanimity for conviction, the right of challenge, and other accustomed requisites; and no person shall be held to answer for a capital, or otherwise infamous crime, unless on a presentment, or indictment, by a grand jury; but if a crime be committed in a place in the possession of an enemy, or in which an insurrection may prevail, the indictment and trial may by law be authorised in some other place within the same state; and if it be committed in a place not within a state, the indictment and trial may be at such place or places as the law may have directed."

MR. BURKE

Moved to change the word "vicinage" into "district or county in which the offence has been committed," he said this was conformable to the practice of the state of South Carolina, and he believed to most of the states in the union, it would have a tendency also to quiet the alarm entertained by the good citizens of many of the states for their personal security, they would no longer fear being dragged from one extremity of the state to the other for trial, at the distance of 3 or 400 miles.

MR. LEE

Thought the word "vicinage" was more applicable than that of "district, or county," it being a term well understood by every gentleman of legal knowledge.

The question on mr. Burke's motion being put was negatived.

417

MR. BURKE then revived his motion for preventing prosecutions upon information, but on the question this was also lost.

The clause was now adopted without amendment.

Congressional Register, August 18, 1789, vol. 2, p. 233.

12.2.1.4.b The house then resolved inself into a committee of the whole on the subject of amendments.

Mr. BOUDINOT in the chair.

The committee took up the fifteenth amendment which is as follows.

"The trial of all crimes (except in cases of impeachment, and in cases arising in the land or naval forces, or in the militia, when in actual service in time of war or public danger) shall be by an impartial jury of freeholders of the vicinage, with the requisite of unanimity for conviction, the right of challenge, and other accustomed requisites; and no person shall be held to answer for a capital, or otherwise infamous crime, unless on a presentment or indictment by a grand jury; but if a crime be committed in a place in the possession of an enemy, or in which an insurrection may prevail, the indictment and trial may by law be authorized in some other place within the same state; and if it be committed in a place not within a state, the indictment and trial may be at such place or places as the law may have directed."

Some inconsiderable amendments to this amendment were moved and lost, and the main question was carried.

Daily Advertiser, August 19, 1789, p. 2, cols. 2–3.

12.2.1.4.c Committee of the whole on the subject of amendments.

The committee took up the fifteenth amendment, which is

"The trial of all crimes (except in cases of impeachment, and in cases arising in the land or naval forces, or in the militia when in actual service in time of war or public danger) shall be by an impartial jury of freeholders of the vicinage, with the requisite of unanimity for conviction, the right of challenge, and other accustomed requisites; and no person shall be held to answer for a capital, or otherwise infamous crime, unless on a presentment or indictment by a grand jury; but if a crime be committed in a place in the possession of an enemy, or in which an insurrection may prevail, the indictment and trial may by law be authorized in some other place within the same state; and if it be committed in a place not within a state, the indictment and trial may be at such place or places as the law may have directed."

MR. BURKE moved to strike out "vicinage," and to insert *county or district in which the offence has been committed.* The gentleman enforced this motion by a variety of observations; and among others said that it was agreeable to the practice of the state he represented, and would give the constitution a more easy operation; that it was a matter of serious alarm to the good citizens of many of the States, the idea that they may be dragged from one part of the State perhaps 2 or 300 miles to the other for trial.

MR. GERRY objected to the word "district" as too indefinite.

MR. SEDGWICK said, that he conceived that the proposed amendment is not so adequate to the gentleman's object as the word "vicinage" — the latter part of the clause is sufficient for the gentleman's purpose.

The motion was negatived.

Mr. BURKEth [*sic;* then] proposed to add a clause to prevent prosecutions upon informations: This was objected to, as the object of the clause was to provide that high crime, &c. should be by presentment of a grand jury; but that other things should take the course heretofore practised. This motion was lost.

And then the paragraph was adopted.

Gazette of the U.S., August 22, 1789, p. 250, col. 1.

12.2.1.5   August 21, 1789

12.2.1.5.a   The house proceeded in its consideration of the amendments to the constitution reported by the committee of the whole, and took up the 2d clause of the 4th proposition.

Mr. GERRY

Then proposed to amend it by striking out these words, "public danger" and to insert foreign invasion; this being negatived, it was then moved to strike out the last clause, "and if it be committed, &c." to the end. This motion was carried, and the amendment was adopted.

Congressional Register, August 21, 1789, vol. 2, p. 243.

12.2.1.5.b   Mr. Gerry moved to strike out these words, "public danger," to insert foreign invasion. This was negatived. It was then moved to strike out the last clause, "and if it be committed, &c." to the end. This motion obtained, and the amendment as it then stood was adopted.

New-York Daily Gazette, August 24, 1789, p. 818, col. 3.

12.2.1.5.c   15th Amendment under consideration.

Mr. GERRY moved to strike out these words "public danger" to insert *foreign invasion*. This was negatived. It was then moved to strike out the last clause "and if it be committed, &c." to the end. This motion obtained, and the amendment as it then stood adopted.

Gazette of the U.S., August 22, 1789, p. 250, col. 3.

12.2.2 STATE CONVENTIONS

12.2.2.1 Massachusetts, January 30, 1788

Mr. HOLMES. . . . It is a maxim universally admitted, that the safety of the subject consists in having a right to a trial as free and impartial as the lot of humanity will admit of. Does the Constitution make provision for such a trial? I think not; for in a criminal process, a person shall not have a right to insist on a trial in the vicinity where the fact was committed, where a jury of the peers would, from their local situation, have an opportunity to form a judgment of the *character* of the person charged with the crime, and also to judge of the *credibility* of the witnesses. There a person must be tried by a jury of strangers; a jury who *may be* interested in his conviction; and where he *may*, by reason of the distance of his residence from the place of trial, be incapable of making such a defence, as he is, in justice, entitled to, and which he could avail himself of, if his trial was in the same county where the crime is said to have been committed.

. . .

But what makes the matter still more alarming is, that the mode of criminal process is to be pointed out by Congress, and they have no constitutional check on them, except that the trial is to be by *a jury:* but who this jury is to be, how qualified, where to live, how appointed, or by what rules to regulate their procedure, we are ignorant of as yet: whether they are to live in the county where the trial is; whether they are to be chosen by certain districts, or whether they are to be appointed by the sheriff *ex officio;* whether they are to be for one session of the court only, or for a certain term of time, or for good behavior, or during pleasure, are matters which we are entirely ignorant of as yet.

The mode of trial is altogether indetermined; whether the criminal is to be allowed the benefit of counsel; whether he is to be allowed to meet with his accuser face to face; whether he is to be allowed to confront the witnesses, and have the advantage of cross-examination, we are not yet told.

These are matters of by no means small consequence; yet we have not the smallest constitutional security that we shall be allowed the exercise of these privileges, neither is it made certain, in the Constitution, that a person charged with the crime shall have the privilege of appearing before the court or jury which is to try him.

. . .

Mr. GORE observed, in reply to Mr. Holmes, that it had been the uniform conduct of those in opposition to the proposed form of government, to determine, in every case where it is possible that the administrators thereof could do wrong, that they would do so, although it were demonstrable that such wrong would be against their own honor and interest, and productive of no advantage to themselves. On this principle alone have they determined that the trial by jury would be taken away in civil cases; when it had been clearly shown, that no words could be adopted, apt to the situation and customs of each state in this particular. Jurors are differently chosen in different states, and in point of qualification the laws of the several states are very diverse; not less so in the causes and disputes which are entitled to trial by jury. What is the result of this? That the laws of Congress may and will be conformable to the local laws in this particular, although the Constitution could not make a universal rule equally applying to the customs and statutes of the different states. Very few governments (certainly not this) can be interested in depriving the people of trial by jury, in questions of *meum et tuum.* In criminal cases alone are they interested to have the trial under their own control; and, in such cases, the Constitution expressly stipulates for trial by jury; but then, says the gentleman from Rochester, (Mr. Holmes,) to the safety of life it is indispensably necessary the trial of crimes should be in the vicinity; and the vicinity is construed to mean county; this is very incorrect, and gentlemen will see the impropriety, by referring themselves to the different local divisions and districts of the several states. But further, said the gentleman, the idea that the jury coming from the neighborhood, and knowing the character and circumstances of the party in trial, is promotive of justice, on reflection will appear not founded in truth. If the jury judge from any other circumstances but what are part of the cause in question, they are not impartial. The great object is to determine on the real merits of the cause, uninfluenced by any personal considerations; if, therefore, the jury could be perfectly ignorant of the person in trial, a just decision would be more probable. From such motives did the wise Athenians so constitute the famed Areopagus, that, when in judgment, this court should sit at midnight, and in total darkness, that the decision might be on the thing, and not on the person. . . .

Mr. DAWES said, he did not see that the right of trial by jury was taken away by the article. The word *court* does not, either by a popular or technical construction, exclude the use of a jury to try facts. When people, in common language, talk of a trial at the *Court* of Common Pleas, or the Supreme Judicial *Court,* do they not include all the branches and members of such court — the *jurors* as well as the judges? They certainly do, whether they mention the jurors expressly or not. Our state legislators have construed the word *cour*t in the same way; for they have given appeals from a justice of peace to the Court of Common Pleas, and from thence to the Supreme Court, without saying any thing of the jury; but in cases which, almost time out of mind, have been tried without jury, there the jurisdiction is given expressly to the justices of a particular court, as may be instanced by suits upon the absconding act, so called.

Gentlemen have compared the article under consideration to that power which the British claimed, and we resisted, at the revolution; namely, the power of trying the Americans without a jury. But surely there was no parallel in the cases; it was criminal cases in which they attempted to make this abuse of power. Mr. D. mentioned one example of this, which, though young, he well remembered; and that was the case of Nickerson, the pirate, who was tried without a jury, and whose judges were the governors of Massachusetts and of some neighboring provinces, together with Admiral Montague, and some gentlemen of distinction. Although this trial was without a jury, yet, as it was a trial upon the civil law, there was not so much clamor about it as otherwise there might have been; but still it was disagreeable to the people, and was one of the then complaints. But the trial by jury was not attempted to be taken from civil causes. It was no object of power, whether one subject's property was lessened, while another's was increased; nor can it be now an object with the federal legislature. What interest can they have in constituting a judiciary, to proceed in civil causes without a trial by jury? In criminal causes, by the proposed government, there must be a jury. It is asked, Why is not the Constitution as explicit in securing the right of jury in civil as in criminal cases? The answer is, Because it was out of the power of the Convention. The several states differ so widely in their modes of trial, some states using a jury in causes wherein other states employ only their judges, that the Convention have very wisely left it to the federal legislature to make such regulations as shall, as far as possible, accommodate the whole. Thus our own state constitution authorizes the General Court to erect judicatories, but leaves the nature, number, and extent of them, wholly to the discretion of the legislature. . . .   Elliot, vol. 2, pp. 109–14.

12.2.2.2   New York, July 2, 1788

Mr. TREDWELL. . . . I could have wished, sir, that a greater caution had been used to secure to us the freedom of election, a sufficient and responsible representation, the freedom of the press, and the trial by jury both in civil and criminal cases.

. . . What better provisions have we made for mercy, when a man, for ignorantly passing a counterfeit continental note, or bill of credit, is liable to be dragged to a distant county, two or three hundred miles from home, deprived of the support and assistance of friends, to be tried by a strange jury, ignorant of his character, ignorant of the character of the witnesses, unable to contradict any false testimony brought against him by their own knowledge of facts, and with whom the prisoner being unacquainted, he must be deprived totally of the benefit of his challenge? and besides all that, he may be exposed to lose his life, merely for want of property to carry his witnesses to such a distance; and after all this solemn farce and mockery of a trial by jury, if they should acquit him, it will require more ingenuity than I am master of, to show that he does not hold his life at the will and pleasure of the Supreme Court, to which an appeal lies, and consequently depend on the tender mercies, perhaps, of the wicked, (for judges may be wicked;) and what those tender mercies are, I need not tell you. You may read them in the history of the Star Chamber Court in England, and in the courts of Philip, and in your Bible.

Elliot, vol. 2, pp. 399–400.

12.2.2.3   North Carolina

12.2.2.3.a   July 28, 1788

Mr. IREDELL. . . . The greatest danger from ambition is in criminal cases. But here they have no option. The trial must be by jury, in the state wherein the offence is committed; and the writ of *habeas corpus* will in the mean time secure the citizen against arbitrary imprisonment, which has been the principal source of tyranny in all ages.

. . .

Mr. J. M'DOWALL. Mr. Chairman, the learned gentleman made use of several arguments to induce us to believe that the trial by jury, in civil cases, was not in danger, and observed that, in criminal cases, it is provided that the trial is to be in the state where the crime was committed. Suppose a crime is committed at the Mississippi; the man may be tried at Edenton. They ought to be tried by the people of the vicinage; for when the trial is at such an immense distance, the principal privilege attending the trial by jury is taken away; therefore the trial ought to be limited to a district or certain part of the state. It has been said, by the gentleman from Edenton, that our representatives will have virtue and wisdom to regulate all these things. But it would give me much satisfaction, in a matter of this importance, to see it absolutely secured. The depravity of mankind militates against such a degree of confidence. I wish to see every thing fixed.

Gov. JOHNSTON. Mr. Chairman, the observations of the gentleman last up confirm what the other gentleman said. I mean that, as there are dissimilar modes with respect to the trial by jury in different states, there could be no general rule fixed to accommodate all. He says that this clause is defective, because the trial is not to be by a jury of the vicinage. Let us look at the state of Virginia, where, as long as I have known it, the laws have been executed so as to satisfy the inhabitants, and, I believe, as well as in any part of the Union. In that country, juries are summoned every day from the by-standers. We may expect less partiality when the trial is by strangers; and were I to be tried for my property or life, I would rather be tried by disinterested men, who were not biased, than by men who were perhaps intimate friends of my opponent. Our mode is different from theirs; but whether theirs be better than ours or not, is not the question. It would be improper for our delegates to impose our mode upon them, or for theirs to impose their mode upon us. The trial will probably be, in each state, as it has been hitherto used in such state, or otherwise regulated as conveniently as possible for the people. The delegates who are to meet in Congress will, I hope, be men of virtue and wisdom. If not, it will be our own fault. They will have it in their power to make necessary regulations to accommodate the inhabitants of each state. In the Constitution, the general principles only are laid down. It will be the object of the future legislation to Congress to make such laws as will be most convenient for the people. . . .

Mr. BLOODWORTH. Mr. Chairman, the footing on which the trial by jury is, in the Constitution, does not satisfy me. Perhaps I am mistaken; but if I understand the thing right, the trial by jury is taken away. If the Supreme Federal Court has jurisdiction both as to law and fact, it appears to me to be taken away. The honorable gentleman who was in the Convention told us that the clause, as it now stands, resulted from the difficulty of fixing the mode of trial. I think it was easy to have put it on a secure footing. But, if the genius of the people of the United States is so dissimilar that our liberties cannot be secured, we can never hang long together. Interest is the band of social union; and when this is taken away, the Union itself must dissolve.

Mr. MACLAINE. Mr. Chairman, I do not take the interest of the states to be so dissimilar; I take them to be all nearly alike, and inseparably connected. It is impossible to lay down any constitutional rule for the government of all the different states in each particular. But it will be easy for the legislature to make laws to accommodate the people in every part of the Union, as circumstances may arise. Jury trial is not taken away in such cases where it may be found necessary. Although the Supreme Court has cognizance of the appeal, it does not follow but that the trial by jury may be had in the court below, and the testimony transmitted to the Supreme Court, who will then finally determine, on a review of all the circumstances. This is well known to be the practice in some of the states. In our own state, indeed, when a cause is instituted in the county court, and afterwards there is an appeal upon it, a new trial is had in the superior court, as if no trial had been before. In other countries, however, when a trial is had in an inferior court, and an appeal is taken, no testimony can be given in the court above, but the court determines upon the circumstances appearing upon the record. If I am right, the plain inference is, that there may be a trial in the inferior courts, and that the record, including the testimony, may be sent to the Supreme Court. But if there is a necessity for a jury in the Supreme Court, it will be a very easy matter to empanel a jury at the bar of the Supreme Court, which may save great expense, and be very convenient to the people. It is impossible to make every regulation at once. Congress, who are our own representatives, will undoubtedly make such regulations as will suit the convenience and secure the liberty of the people.

Mr. IREDELL declared it as his opinion that there might be juries in the Superior Court as well as in the inferior courts, and that it was in the power of Congress to regulate it so.

Elliot, vol. 4, pp. 145, 149–52.

12.2.2.3.b July 29, 1788

Mr. SPENCER. . . . The trial by jury has been also spoken of. Every person who is acquainted with the nature of liberty need not be informed of the importance of this trial. Juries are called the bulwarks of our rights and liberty; and no country can ever be enslaved as long as those cases which affect their lives and property are to be decided, in a great measure, by the consent of twelve honest, disinterested men, taken from the respectable body of yeomanry. It is highly improper that any clause which regards the security of the trial by jury should be any way doubtful. In the clause that has been read, it is ascertained that criminal cases are to be tried by jury in the states where they are committed. It has been objected to that clause, that it is not sufficiently explicit. I think that it is not. It was observed that one may be taken to a great distance. One reason of the resistance to the British government was, because they required that we should be carried to the country of Great Britain, to be tried by juries of that country. But we insisted on being tried by juries of the vicinage, in our own country. I think it therefore proper that something explicit should be said with respect to the vicinage.

With regard to that part, that the Supreme Court shall have appellate jurisdiction both as to law and fact, it has been observed that, though the federal court might decide without a jury, yet the court below, which tried it, might have a jury. I ask the gentleman what benefit would be received in the suit by having a jury trial in the court below, when the verdict is set aside in the Supreme Court. It was intended by this clause that the trial by jury should be suppressed in the superior and inferior courts. It has been said, in defence of the omission concerning the trial by jury in civil cases, that one general regulation could not be made; that in several cases the constitution of several states did not require a trial by jury, — for instance, in cases of equity and admiralty, — whereas in others it did, and that, therefore, it was proper to leave this subject at large. I am sure that, for the security of liberty, they ought to have been at the pains of drawing some line. I think that the respectable body who formed the Constitution should have gone so far as to put matters on such a footing as that there should be no danger. They might have provided that all those cases which are now triable by a jury should be tried in each state by a jury, according to the mode usually practiced in such state. This would have been easily done, if they had been at the trouble of writing five or six lines. Had it been done, we should have been entitled to say that our rights and liberties were not endangered. If we adopt this clause as it is, I think, notwithstanding what gentlemen have said, that there will be danger. There ought to be some amendments to it, to put this matter on a sure footing. There does not appear to me to be any kind of necessity that the federal court should have jurisdiction in the body of the country. I am ready to give up that, in the cases expressly enumerated, an appellate jurisdiction (except in one or two instances) might be given. I wish them also to have jurisdiction in maritime affairs, and to try offences committed on the high seas. . . .

. . .

Mr. MACLAINE. . . . But the gentleman seems to be most tenacious of the judicial power of the states. The honorable gentleman must know, that the doctrine of reservation of power not relinquished, clearly demonstrates that the judicial power of the states is not impaired. He asks, with respect to the trial by jury, "When the cause has gone up to the superior court, and the verdict is set aside, what benefit arises from having had a jury trial in the inferior court?" I would ask the gentleman, "What is the reason, that, on a special verdict or case agreed, the decision is left to the court?" There are a number of cases where juries cannot decide. When a jury finds the fact specially, or when it is agreed upon by the parties, the decision is referred to the court. If the law be against the party, the court decides against him; if the law be for him, the court judges accordingly. He, as well as every gentleman here, must know that, under the Confederation, Congress set aside juries. There was an appeal given to Congress: did Congress determine by a jury? Every party carried his testimony in writing to the judges of appeal, and Congress determined upon it.

. . .

Mr. SPENCER. . . . I contend that there should be a bill of rights, ascertaining and securing the great rights of the states and people. Besides my objection to the revision of facts by the federal court, and the insecurity of jury trial, I consider the concurrent jurisdiction of those courts with the state courts as extremely dangerous. . . .

. . .

Mr. IREDELL. . . . In criminal cases, however, no latitude ought to be allowed. In these the greatest danger from any government subsists, and accordingly it is provided that there shall be a trial by jury, in all such cases, in the state wherein the offence is committed. I thought the objection against the want of a bill of rights had been obviated unanswerably. It appears to me most extraordinary. Shall we give up anything but what is positively granted by that instrument? It would be the greatest absurdity for any man to pretend that, when a legislature is formed for a particular purpose, it can have any authority but what is so expressly given to it, any more than a man acting under a power of attorney could depart from the authority it conveyed to him, according to an instance which I stated when speaking on the subject before. As for example: — if I had three tracts of land, one in Orange, another in Caswell, and another in Chatham, and I gave a power of attorney to a man to sell the two tracts in Orange and Caswell, and he should attempt to sell my land in Chatham, would any man of common sense suppose he had authority to do so? In like manner, I say, the future Congress can have no right to exercise any power but what is contained in that paper. Negative words, in my opinion, could make the matter no plainer than it was before. The gentleman says that unalienable rights ought not to be given up. Those rights which are unalienable are not alienated. They still remain with the great body of the people. If any right be given up that ought not to be, let it be shown. Say it is a thing which affects your country, and that it ought not to be surrendered: this would be reasonable. But when it is evident that the exercise of any power not given up would be a usurpation, it would be not only useless, but dangerous, to enumerate a number of rights which are not intended to be given up; because it would be implying, in the strongest manner, that every right not included in the exception might be impaired by the government without usurpation; and it would be impossible to enumerate every one. Let any one make what collection or enumeration of rights he pleases, I will immediately mention twenty or thirty more rights not contained in it.

Mr. BLOODWORTH. Mr. Chairman, I have listened with attention to the gentleman's arguments; but whether it be for want of sufficient attention, or from the grossness of my ideas, I cannot be satisfied with his defence of the omission, with respect to the trial by jury. He says that it would be impossible to fall on any satisfactory mode of regulating the trial by jury, because there are various customs relative to it in the different states. Is this a satisfactory cause for the omission? Why did it not provide that the trial by jury should be preserved in civil cases? It has said that the trial should be by jury in criminal cases; and yet this trial is different in its manner in criminal cases in the different states. If it has been possible to secure it in criminal cases, notwithstanding the diversity concerning it, why has it not been possible to secure it in civil cases? I wish this to be cleared up. . . .

. . .

Mr. IREDELL. Mr. Chairman, I hope some other gentleman will answer what has been said by the gentlemen who have spoken last. I only rise to answer the question of the member from New Hanover — which was, if there was such a difficulty, in establishing the trial by jury in civil cases, that the Convention could not concur in any mode, why the difficulty did not extend to criminal cases? I beg leave to say, that the difficulty, in this case, does not depend so much on the mode of proceeding, as on the difference of the subjects of controversy, and the laws relative to them. . . .

We have been told, and I believe this was the real reason, why they could not concur in any general rule. I have great respect for the characters of those gentlemen who formed the Convention, and I believe they were not capable of overlooking the importance of the trial by jury, much less of designedly plotting against it. But I fully believe that the real difficulty of the thing was the cause of the omission. I trust sufficient reasons have been offered, to show that it is in no danger. As to criminal cases, I must observe that the great instrument of arbitrary power is criminal prosecutions. By the privileges of *habeas corpus*, no man can be confined without inquiry; and if it should appear that he has been committed contrary to law, he must be discharged. That diversity which is to be found in civil controversies, does not exist in criminal cases. That diversity which contributes to the security of property in civil cases, would have pernicious effects in criminal ones. There is no other safe mode to try these but by a jury. If any man had the means of trying another his own way, or were it left to the control of arbitrary judges, no man would have that security for life and liberty which every freeman ought to have. I presume that in no state on the continent is a man tried on a criminal accusation but by a jury. It was necessary, therefore, that it should be fixed, in the Constitution, that the trial should be by jury in criminal cases; and such difficulties did not occur in this as in the other case. . . .

Elliot, vol. 4, pp. 154–55, 162, 163–64, 166–67, 170–71.

12.2.2.4 Pennsylvania

12.2.2.4.a November 30, 1787

Mr. Hartley. . . . Even on that principle, however, it has occasionally been found necessary to make laws for the security of the subject — a necessity that has produced the writ of habeas corpus, which affords an easy and immediate redress for the unjust imprisonment of the person, and the trial by jury, which is the fundamental security for every enjoyment that is valuable in the contemplation of a freeman. These advantages have not been obtained by the influence of a bill of rights, which after all we find is an instrument that derives its validity only from the sanction and ratification of the prince. How different then is our situation from the circumstances of the British nation?

McMaster & Stone, p. 290.

12.2.2.4.b December 11, 1787

Mr. WILSON. . . . We have been told, sir, by the honorable member from Fayette, (Mr. Smilie,) "that the trial by jury was intended to be given up, and the civil law was intended to be introduced into its place, in civil cases."

Before a sentiment of this kind was hazarded, I think, sir, the gentleman ought to be prepared with better proof in its support than any he has yet attempted to produce. It is a charge, sir, not only unwarrantable, but cruel: the idea of such a thing, I believe, never entered into the mind of a single member of that Convention; and I believe further, that they never suspected there would be found, within the United States, a single person that was capable of making such a charge. If it should be well founded, sir, they must abide by the consequences; but if (as I trust it will fully appear) it is ill founded, then he or they who make it ought to abide by the consequences.

Trial by jury forms a large field for investigation, and numerous volumes are written on the subject; those who are well acquainted with it may employ much time in its discussion; but in a country where its excellences are so well understood, it may not be necessary to be very prolix in pointing them out. For my part, I shall confine myself to a few observations in reply to the objections that have been suggested.

The member from Fayette (Mr. Smilie) has labored to infer that, under the Articles of Confederation, the Congress possessed no appellate jurisdiction; but this being decided against him by the words of that instrument, by which is granted to Congress the power of "establishing courts for receiving, and determining finally, appeals in all cases of capture, he next attempts a distinction, and allows the power of appealing from the decisions of the judges, but not from the verdict of a jury; but this is determined against him also by the practice of the states; for, in every instance which has occurred, this power has been claimed by

Congress, and exercised by the Courts of Appeals. But what would be the consequence of allowing the doctrine for which he contends? Would it not be in the power of a jury, by their verdict, to involve the whole Union in a war? They may condemn the property of a neutral, or otherwise infringe the law of nations, in this case, ought their verdict to be without revisal? Nothing can be inferred from this to prove that trials by jury were intended to be given up. In Massachusetts, and all the Eastern States, their causes are tried by juries, though they acknowledge the appellate jurisdiction of Congress.

I think I am not now to learn the advantages of a trial by jury. It has excellences that entitle it to a superiority over any other mode, in cases to which it is applicable.

Where jurors can be acquainted with the characters of the parties and the witnesses, — where the whole cause can be brought within their knowledge and their view, — I know no mode of investigation equal to that by a jury: they hear every thing that is alleged; they not only hear the words, but they see and mark the features of the countenance; they can judge of weight due to such testimony; and moreover, it is a cheap and expeditious manner of distributing justice. There is another advantage annexed to the trial by jury; the jurors may indeed return a mistaken or ill-founded verdict, but their errors cannot be systematical.

Let us apply these observations to the objects of the judicial department, under this Constitution. I think it has been shown, already, that they all extend beyond the bounds of any particular state; but further, a great number of the civil causes there enumerated depend either upon the law of nations, or the marine law, that is, the general law of mercantile countries. Now, sir, in such cases, I presume it will not be pretended that this mode of decision ought to be adopted; for the law with regard to them is the same here as in every other country, and ought to be administered in the same manner. There are instances in which I think it highly probable that the trial by jury will be found proper; and if it is highly probable that it will be found proper, is it not equally probable that it will be adopted? There may be causes depending between citizens of different states; and as trial by jury is known and regarded in all the states, they will certainly prefer that mode of trial before any other. The Congress will have the power of making proper regulations on this subject, but it was impossible for the Convention to have gone minutely into it; but if they could, it must have been very improper, because alterations, as I observed before, might have been necessary; and whatever the Convention might have done would have continued unaltered, unless by an alteration of the Constitution. Besides, there was another difficulty with regard to this subject. In some of the states they have courts of chancery, and other appellate jurisdictions, and those states are as attached to that mode of distributing justice as those that have none are to theirs.

I have desired, repeatedly, that honorable gentlemen, who find fault, would be good enough to point out what they deem to be an improvement. The member from Westmoreland (Mr. Findley) tells us that the trial between citizens of different states ought to be by a jury of that state in which the cause of action rose. Now, it is easy to see that, in many instances, this would be very improper and very partial; for, besides the different manner of collecting and forming juries in the several states, the plaintiff comes from another state; he comes a stranger, unknown as to his character or mode of life, while the other party is in the midst of his friends, or perhaps his dependents. Would a trial by jury, in such a case, insure justice to the stranger? But again: I would ask that gentleman whether, if a great part of his fortune was in the hands of some person in Rhode Island, he would wish that his action to recover it should be determined by a jury of that country, under its present circumstances.

The gentleman from Fayette (Mr. Smilie) says that, if the Convention found themselves embarrassed, at least they might have done thus much — they should have declared that the substance should be secured by Congress. This would be saying nothing unless the cases were particularized.

Mr. SMILIE. I said the Convention ought to have declared that the legislature should establish the trial by jury by proper regulations.

Mr. WILSON. The legislature shall establish it by proper regulations! So, after all, the gentleman has landed us at the very point from which we set out. He wishes them to do the very thing they have done — to leave it to the discretion of Congress. The fact, sir, is nothing more could be done.

It is well known that there are some cases that should not come before juries; there are others, that, in some of the states, never come before juries, and in those states where they do come before them, appeals are found necessary, the facts reëxamined, and the verdict of the jury sometimes is set aside; but I think, in all cases where the cause has come originally before a jury, that the last examination ought to be before a jury likewise.

The power of having appellate jurisdiction, as to facts, has been insisted upon as a proof, "that the Convention *intended* to give up the trial by jury in civil cases, and to introduce the civil law." I have already declared my own opinion on this point, and have shown not merely that it is founded on reason and authority; — the express declaration of Congress (*Journals of Congress*, March 6, 1779) is to the same purpose. They insist upon this power, as requisite to preserve the peace of the Union; certainly, therefore, it ought always to be possessed by the head of the Confederacy. We are told, as an additional proof, that the trial by jury was intended to be given up; "that appeals are unknown to the common law; that the term is a civil-law term, and with it the civil law is intended to be introduced." I confess I was a good deal surprised at this observation being made; for Blackstone, in the very volume which the honorable member (Mr. Smilie) had in his hand, and read us several extracts from, has a chapter entitled "Of Proceeding in the Nature of Appeals," — and in that chapter says, that the principal method of redress for erroneous judgments, in the king's courts of record, is by writ of error to some superior *"court of appeal."* (3 *Blackstone*, 406.) Now, it is well known that his book is a commentary upon the common law. Here, then, is a strong refutation of the assertion, "that appeals are unknown to the common law."

I think these were all the circumstances adduced to show the truth of the assertion, that, in this Constitution, the trial by jury was *intended* to be given up by the late Convention in framing it. Has the assertion been proved? I say not: and the allegations offered, if they apply at all, apply in a contrary direction. I am glad that this objection has been stated, because it is a subject upon which the enemies of this Constitution have much insisted. We have now had an opportunity of investigating it fully; and the result is, that there is no foundation for the charge, but it must proceed from ignorance, or something worse. Elliot, vol. 2, pp. 515–19.

12.2.2.4.c December 12, 1787

. . . Mr. Whitehill then read, and offered as the ground of a motion for adjourning to some remote day the consideration of the following articles, which, he said, might either be taken collectively, as a bill of rights, or, separately, as amendments to the general form of government proposed . . .

. . .

3. That in all capital and criminal prosecutions, a man has a right to demand the cause and nature of his accusation, as well in the federal courts, as in those of the several States; to be heard by himself or his counsel; to be confronted with the accusers and witnesses; to call for evidence in his favor, and a speedy trial, by an impartial jury of the vicinage, without whose unanimous consent he cannot be found guilty, nor can he be compelled to give evidence against himself; that no man be deprived of his liberty, except by the law of the land or the judgment of his peers. McMaster & Stone, p. 421.

12.2.2.4.d Address and Reasons of Dissent of the Minority of the Pennsylvania Convention, December 12, 1787

The first consideration that this review suggests, is the omission of a BILL of RIGHTS, ascertaining and fundamentally establishing those unalienable and personal rights of men, without the full, free, and secure enjoyment of which there can be no liberty, and over which it is not necessary for a good government to have the controul. The principal of which are the rights of conscience, personal liberty by the clear and unequivocal establishment of the writ of *habeas corpus,* jury trial in criminal and civil cases, by an impartial jury of the vicinage or county, with the common-law proceedings, for the safety of the accused in criminal prosecutions; and the liberty of the press, that scourge of tyrants, and the grand bulwark of every other liberty and privilege. The stipulations heretofore made in favor of them in the state constitutions, are entirely superseded by this constitution.

. . .

The judicial power, under the proposed constitution, is founded on well-known principles of the *civil law,* by which the judge determines both on law and fact, and appeals are allowed from the inferior tribunals to the superior, upon the whole question; so that *facts* as well as *law,* would be re-examined, and even new facts brought forward in the court of appeals; and to use the words of a very eminent Civilian — "The cause is many times another thing before the court of appeals, than it was at the time of the first sentence."

That this mode of proceeding is the one which must be adopted under this constitution, is evident from the following circumstances: 1st. That the trial by jury, which is the grand characteristic of the common law, is secured by the constitution only in criminal cases. — 2d. That the appeal from both *law* and *fact* is expressly established, which is utterly inconsistent with the principles of the common law, and trials by jury. The only mode in which an appeal from law and fact can be established, is, by adopting the principles and practice of the civil law; unless the United States should be drawn into the absurdity of calling and swearing juries, merely for the purpose of contradicting their verdicts, which would render juries contemptible and worse than useless. . . .

Not to enlarge upon the loss of the invaluable right of trial by an unbiased jury, so dear to every friend of liberty, the monstrous expence and inconveniences of the mode of proceedings to be adopted, are such as will prove intolerable to the people of this country. The lengthy proceedings of the civil law courts in the chancery of England, and in the courts of Scotland and France, are such that few men of moderate fortune can endure the expence of; the poor man must therefore submit to the wealthy. Length of purse will too often prevail against right and justice. For instance, we are told by the learned judge *Blackstone*, that a question only on the property of an ox, of the value of *three* guineas, orginating under the civil law proceedings in Scotland, after many interlocutory orders and sentences below, was carried at length from the court of sessions, the highest court in that part of Great Britain, by way of *appeal* to the house of lords, *where* the question of law and fact was finally determined. He adds, that no pique or spirit could in the court of king's bench common pleas Westminster, have given continuance to such a cause for a tenth part of the time, nor have cost a twentieth part of the expence. Yet the costs in the courts of king's bench and common pleas in England, are infinitely greater than those which the people of this country have ever experienced. We abhor the idea of losing the transcendant privilege of trial by jury, with the loss of which, it is remarked by the same learned author, that in Sweden, the liberties of the commons were extinguished by an aristocratic senate: and that *trial by jury* and the liberty of the people went out together. At the same time we regret the intolerable delay, the enormous expences and infinite vexation to which the people of this country will be exposed from the voluminous proceedings of the courts of civil law, and especially from the appellate jurisdiction, by means of which a man may be drawn from the utmost boundaries of this extensive country to the seat of the supreme court of the nation to contend, perhaps with a wealthy and powerful adversary. The consequence of this establishment will be an absolute confirmation of the power of aristocratical influence in the courts of justice: for the common people will not be able to contend or struggle against it.

Trial by jury in criminal cases may also be excluded by declaring that the libeller for instance shall be liable to an action of debt for a specified sum; thus evading the common law prosecution by indictment and trial by jury. And the common course of proceeding against a ship for breach of revenue laws by information (which will be classed among civil causes) will at the civil law be within the resort of a court, where no jury intervenes. Besides, the benefit of jury trial, in cases of a criminal nature, which cannot be evaded, will be rendered of little value, by calling the accused to answer far from home; there being no provision that the trial be by a jury of the neighbourhood or country. Thus an inhabitant of Pittsburgh, on a charge of crime committed on the banks of the Ohio, may be obliged to defend himself at the side of the Delaware, and so *vice versa*. To conclude this head: we observe that the judges of the courts of Congress would not be independent, as they are not debarred from holding other offices, during the pleasure of the president and senate, and as they may derive their support in part from fees, alterable by the legislature.

Storing, vol. 3, pp. 157, 159–61.

12.2.2.5 South Carolina, January 17, 1788

Hon. RAWLINS LOWNDES. . . . It was true, no article of the Constitution declared there should not be jury trials in civil cases; yet this must be implied, because it stated that all crimes, except in cases of impeachment, shall be tried by a jury. But even if trials by jury were allowed, could any person rest satisfied with a mode of trial which prevents the parties from being obliged to bring a cause for discussion before a jury of men chosen from the vicinage, in a manner conformable to the present administration of justice, which had stood the test of time and experience, and ever been highly approved of? . . .

. . .

Hon. ROBERT BARNWELL. . . . The honorable gentleman asks why the trial by jury was not established in every instance. Mr. Barnwell considered this right of trial as the birthright of every American, and the basis of our civil liberty; but still most certainly particular circumstances may arise, which would induce even the greatest advocates for this right to yield it for a time. In his opinion, the circumstances that would lead to this point were those which are specified by the Constitution. Mr. Barnwell said, Suffer me to state a case, and let every gentleman determine whether, in particular instances, he would not rather resign than retain this right of trial. A suit is depending between a citizen of Carolina and Georgia, and it becomes necessary to try it in Georgia. What is the consequence? Why, the citizen of this state must rest his cause upon the jury of his opponent's vicinage, where, unknown and unrelated, he stands a very poor chance for justice against one whose neighbors, whose friends and relations, compose the greater part of his judges. It is in this case, and only in cases of a similar nature with this, that the right of trial by jury is not established; and judging from myself, it is in this instance only that every man would wish to resign it, not to a jury with whom he is unacquainted, but to an impartial and responsible individual.

Elliot, vol. 4, pp. 290, 294–95.

12.2.2.6 Virginia

12.2.2.6.a June 5, 1788

Mr. HENRY. . . . Here is a resolution as radical as that which separated us from Great Britain. It is radical in this transition; our rights and privileges are endangered, and the sovereignty of the states will be relinquished: and cannot we plainly see that this is actually the case? The rights of conscience, trial by jury, liberty of the press, all your immunities and franchises, all pretensions to human rights and privileges, are rendered insecure, if not lost, by this change, so loudly talked of by some, and inconsiderately by others. Is this tame relinquishment of rights worthy of freemen? Is it worthy of that manly fortitude that ought to characterize republicans? . . .

Having premised these things, I shall, with the aid of my judgment and information, which, I confess, are not extensive, go into the discussion of this system more minutely. Is it necessary for your liberty that you should abandon those great rights by the adoption of this system? Is the relinquishment of the trial by jury and the liberty of the press necessary for your liberty? . . .

. . . In some parts of the plan before you, the great rights of freemen are endangered; in other parts, absolutely taken away. How does your trial by jury stand? In civil cases gone — not sufficiently secured in criminal — this best privilege is gone. But we are told that we need not fear; because those in power, being our representatives, will not abuse the powers we put in their hands. I am not well versed in history, but I will submit to your recollection, whether liberty has been destroyed most often by the licentiousness of the people, or by the tyranny of rulers. . . . My great objection to this government is, that it does not leave us the means of defending our rights. . . .

Elliot, vol. 3, pp. 44, 45, 47.

12.2.2.6.b **June 7, 1788**

Mr. HENRY. . . . If we are to have one representative for every thirty thousand souls, it must be by implication. The Constitution does not positively secure it. Even say it is a natural implication, — why not give us a right to that proportion in express terms, in language that could not admit of evasions or subterfuges? If they can use implication for us, they can also use implication against us. We are giving power; they are getting power; judge, then, on which side the implication will be used! When we once put it in their option to assume constructive power, danger will follow. Trial by jury, and liberty of the press, are also on this foundation of implication. If they encroach on these rights, and you give your implication for a plea, you are cast; for they will be justified by the last part of it, which gives them full power "to make all laws which shall be necessary and proper to carry their power into execution." Implication is dangerous, because it is unbounded: if it be admitted at all, and no limits be prescribed, it admits of the utmost extension. . . .

Elliot, vol. 3, p. 149.

12.2.2.6.c **June 9, 1788**

Gov. RANDOLPH. . . . Why have we been told that maxims can alone save nations; that our maxims are our bill of rights; and that the liberty of the press, trial by jury, and religion, are destroyed? Give me leave to say, that the maxims of Virginia are union and justice.

Elliot, vol. 3, p. 190.

12.2.2.6.d **June 10, 1788**

Gov. RANDOLPH. . . . It is also objected that the trial by jury, the writ of *habeas corpus,* and the liberty of the press, are insecure. But I contend that the *habeas corpus* is at least on as secure and good a footing as it is in England. In that country, it depends on the will of the legislature. That privilege is secured here by the Constitution, and is only to be suspended in cases of extreme emergency. Is this not a fair footing? After agreeing that the government of England secures liberty, how do we distrust this government? Why distrust ourselves? The liberty of the press is supposed to be in danger. If this were the case, it would produce extreme repugnancy in my mind. If it ever will be suppressed in this country, the liberty of the people will not be far from being sacrificed. Where is the danger of it? He says that every power is given to the general government that is not reserved to the states. Pardon me if I say the reverse of the proposition is true. I defy any one to prove the contrary. Every power not given it by this system is left with the states. This being the principle, from what part of the Constitution can the liberty of the press be said to be in danger?

[Here his excellency read the 8th section of the 1st article, containing all the powers given to Congress.]

Go through these powers, examine every one, and tell me if the most exalted genius can prove that the liberty of the press is in danger. The trial by jury is supposed to be in danger also. It is secured in criminal cases, but supposed to be taken away in civil cases. It is not relinquished by the Constitution; it is only not provided for. Look at the interest of Congress to suppress it. Can it be in any manner advantageous for them to suppress it? In equitable cases, it ought not to prevail, nor with respect to admiralty causes; because there will be an undue leaning against those characters, of whose business courts of admiralty will have cognizance. I will rest myself secure under this reflection — that it is impossible for the most suspicious or malignant mind to show that it is the interest of Congress to infringe on this trial by jury.

Elliot, vol. 3, pp. 203–04.

12.2.2.6.e **June 12, 1788**

Mr. HENRY. . . . His amendments go to that despised thing, called *a bill of rights,* and all the rights which are dear to human nature — trial by jury, the liberty of religion and the press, &c. Do not gentlemen see that, if we adopt, under the idea of following Mr. Jefferson's opinion, we amuse ourselves with the shadow, while the substance is given away?

Elliot, vol. 3, p. 314.

12.2.2.6.f **June 14, 1788**

Mr. HENRY. . . . By this Constitution, some of the best barriers of human rights are thrown away. Is there not an additional reason to have a bill of rights? By the ancient common law, the trial of all facts is decided by a jury of impartial men from the immediate vicinage. This paper speaks of different juries from the common law in criminal cases; and in civil controversies excludes trial by jury altogether. There is, therefore, more occasion for the supplementary check of a bill of rights now than then. Congress, from their general powers, may fully go into business of human legislation. They may legislate, in criminal cases, from treason to the lowest offence — petty larceny. They may define crimes and prescribe punishments. In the definition of crimes, I trust they will be directed by what wise representatives ought to be governed by. But when we come to punishments, no latitude ought to be left, nor dependence put on the virtue of representatives. What says our bill of rights? — "that excessive bail ought not to be required, nor excessive fines imposed, nor cruel and unusual punishments inflicted." Are you not, therefore, now calling on those gentlemen who are to compose Congress, to prescribe trials and define punishments without this control? Will they find sentiments there similar to this bill of rights? You let them loose; you do more — you depart from the genius of your country. That paper tells you that the trial of crimes shall be by jury, and held in the state where the crime shall have been committed. Under this extensive provision, they may proceed in a manner extremely dangerous to liberty: a person accused may be carried from one extremity of the state to another, and be tried, not by an impartial jury of the vicinage, acquainted with his character and the circumstances of the fact, but by a jury unacquainted with both, and who may be biased against him. Is this not sufficient to alarm men? How different is this from the immemorial practice of your British ancestors, and your own! I need not tell you that, by the common law, a number of hundredors were required on a jury, and that afterwards it was sufficient if the jurors came from the same county. With less than this the people of England have never been satisfied. That paper ought to have declared the common law in force.

Elliot, vol. 3, pp. 446–47.

12.2.2.6.g **June 15, 1788**

Gov. RANDOLPH. . . . But let me ask the gentleman where his favorite rights are violated. . . . Are they violated by the enumerated powers? [Here his excellency read from the 8th to the 12th article of the bill of rights.] Is there not provision made, in this Constitution, for the trial by jury in criminal cases? Does not the 3d article provide that the trial of all crimes shall be by jury, and held where the said crimes shall have been committed? Does it not follow that the cause and nature of the accusation must be produced? — because, otherwise, they cannot proceed on the cause. Every one knows that the witnesses must be brought before the jury, or else the prisoner will be discharged. Calling of evidence in his favor is coincident to his trial. There is no suspicion that less than twelve jurors will be thought sufficient. The only defect is, that there is no speedy trial. Consider how this could have been amended. We have heard complaints against it because it is supposed the jury is to come from the state at large. It will be in their power to have juries from the vicinage. And would not the complaints have been louder if they had appointed a federal court to be had in every county in the state? Criminals are brought, in this state, from every part of the country to the general court, and jurors from the vicinage are summoned to the trials. There can be no reason to prevent the general government from adopting a similar regulation.

. . .

Gentlemen have been misled, to a certain degree, by a general declaration that the trial by jury was gone. We see that, in the most valuable cases, it is reserved. Is it abolished in civil cases? Let him put his finger on the part where it is abolished. The Constitution is silent on it. . . .

Elliot, vol. 3, pp. 467–68.

12.2.2.6.h **June 20, 1788**

Mr. MADISON. . . . It was objected, yesterday, that there was no provision for a jury from the vicinage. If it could have been done with safety, it would not have been opposed. It might happen that a trial would be impracticable in the country. Suppose a rebellion in a whole district; would it not be impossible to get a

435

jury? The *trial by jury* is held as sacred in England as in America. There are deviations from it in England; yet greater deviations have happened here, since we established our independence, than have taken place there for a long time, though it be left to the legislative discretion. It is a misfortune in any case that this trial should be departed from; yet in some cases it is necessary. It must be, therefore, left to the discretion of the legislature to modify it according to circumstances. This is a complete and satisfactory answer.

. . .

Mr. HENRY. . . . "In all cases affecting ambassadors, other public ministers, and consuls, and those in which a state shall be a party, the Supreme Court shall have original jurisdiction. In all the other cases before mentioned, the Supreme Court shall have appellate jurisdiction, both as to law and fact. . . ." This will, in its operation, destroy the trial by jury. The verdict of an impartial jury will be reversed by judges unacquainted with the circumstances. But we are told that Congress are to make regulations to remedy this. . . . If Congress alter this part, they will repeal the Constitution. . . . When Congress, by virtue of this sweeping clause, will organize these courts, they cannot depart from the Constitution; and their laws in opposition to the Constitution would be void. . . . What then, Mr. Chairman? We are told that, if this does not satisfy every mind, they will yield. It is not satisfactory to my mind, whatever it may be to others. . . .

We are told of certain difficulties. I acknowledge it is difficult to form a constitution. But I have seen difficulties conquered which were as unconquerable as this. We are told that trial by jury is difficult to be had in certain cases. Do we not know the meaning of the term? We are also told it is a technical term. I see one thing in this Constitution; I made the observation before, and I am still of the same opinion, that everything with respect to privileges is so involved in darkness, it makes me suspicious — not of those gentlemen who formed it, but of its operations in its present form. Could not precise terms have been used? You find, by the observations of the gentleman last up, that, when there is a plentitude of power, there is no difficulty; but when you come to a plain thing, understood by all America, there are contradictions, ambiguities, difficulties, and what not. Trial by jury is attended, it seems, with insuperable difficulties, and therefore omitted altogether in civil cases. But an idea is held out that it is secured in criminal cases. I had rather it had been left out altogether than have it so vaguely and equivocally provided for. Poor people do not understand technical terms. Their rights ought to be secured in language of which they know the meaning. As they do not know the meaning of such terms, they may be injured with impunity. If they dare oppose the hands of tyrannical power, you will see what has been practised elsewhere. They may be tried by the most partial powers, by their most implacable enemies, and be sentenced and put to death, with all the forms of a fair trial. I would rather be left to the judges. An abandoned juror would not dread the loss of character like a judge. From these, and a thousand other considerations, I would rather the trial by jury were struck out altogether. There is no right of challenging partial jurors. There is no common law of America, (as has been said,) nor constitution, but that on your table. If there be neither common law nor constitution, there can be no right to challenge partial jurors. Yet the right is as valuable as the trial by jury itself.

. . .

Mr. HENRY. . . . To hear gentlemen of such penetration make use of such arguments, to persuade us to part with that trial by jury, is very astonishing. We are told that we are to part with that trial by jury which our ancestors secured their lives and property with, and we are to build castles in the air, and substitute visionary modes of decision for that noble palladium. I hope we shall never be induced, by such arguments, to part with that excellent mode of trial. No appeal can now be made as to fact in common-law suits. The unanimous verdict of twelve impartial men cannot be reversed. I shall take the liberty of reading to the committee the sentiments of the learned Judge Blackstone, so often quoted, on the subject.

[Here Mr. Henry read the eulogium of that writer on this trial, *Blackstone's Commentaries,* iii. 319.]

The opinion of this learned writer is more forcible and cogent than any thing I could say. Notwithstanding the transcendent excellency of this trial, its essentiality to the preservation of liberty, and the extreme danger of substituting any other mode, yet we are now about to alienate it.

But on this occasion, as on all others, we are admonished to rely on the wisdom and virtue of our rulers. We are told that the members from Georgia, New Hampshire, &c., will not dare to infringe this privilege; that, as it would excite the indignation of the people, they would not attempt it: that is, the enormity of the offence is urged as a security against its commission. It is so abominable that Congress will not exercise it. Shall we listen to arguments like these, when trial by jury is about to be relinquished? I beseech you to consider before you decide. I ask you, What is the value of that privilege? When Congress, in all the plentitude of their arrogance, magnificence, and power, can take it from you, will you be satisfied? Are we to go so far as to concede every thing to the virtue of Congress? Throw yourselves at once on their mercy; be no longer free than their virtue will predominate: if this will satisfy republican minds, there is an end of every thing. I disdain to hold any thing of any man. We ought to cherish that disdain. America viewed with indignation the idea of holding her rights in England. The Parliament gave you the most solemn assurances that they would not exercise this power. Were you satisfied with their promises? No. Did you trust any man on earth? No. You answered that you disdained to hold your innate, indefeasible rights of any one. Now, you are called upon to give an exorbitant and most alarming power. The genius of my countrymen is the same now that it was then. They have the same feelings. They are equally martial and bold. Will not their answer therefore be the same? I hope that gentlemen will, on a fair investigation, be candid, and not on every occasion recur to the virtue of our representatives.

When deliberating on the relinquishment of the sword and purse, we have a right to some other reason than the possible virtue of our rulers. We are informed that the strength and energy of the government call for the surrender of this right. Are we to make our country strong by giving up our privileges? I tell you that, if you judge from reason, or the experience of other nations, you will find that your country will be great and respectable according as you will preserve this great privilege. It is prostrated by that paper. Juries from the vicinage being not secured, this right is in reality sacrificed. All is gone. And why? Because a rebellion may arise. Resistance will come from certain countries, and juries will come from the same countries.

I trust the honorable gentleman, on a better recollection, will be sorry for this observation. Why do we love this trial by jury? Because it prevents the hand of oppression from cutting you off. They may call any thing rebellion, and deprive you of a fair trial by an impartial jury of your neighbors. Has not your mother country magnanimously preserved this noble privilege upwards of a thousand years? Did she relinquish a jury of the vicinage because there was a possibility of resistance to oppression? She has been magnanimous enough to resist every attempt to take away this privilege. She has had magnanimity enough to rebel when her rights were infringed. That country had juries of hundredors for many generations. And shall Americans give up that which nothing could induce the English people to relinquish? The idea is abhorrent to my mind. There was a time when we should have spurned at it. This gives me comfort — that, as long as I have existence, my neighbors will protect me. Old as I am, it is probable I may yet have the appellation of *rebel*. I trust that I shall see congressional oppression crushed in embryo. As this government stands, I despise and abhor it. Gentlemen demand it, though it takes away the trial by jury in civil cases, and does worse than take it away in criminal cases. It is gone unless you preserve it now. I beg pardon for speaking so long. Many more observations will present themselves to the minds of gentlemen when they analyze this part. We find enough, from what has been said, to come to this conclusion — that it was not intended to have jury trials at all; because, difficult as it was, the name was known, and it might have been inserted. Seeing that appeals are given, in matters of fact, to the Supreme Court, we are led to believe that you must carry your witnesses an immense distance to the seat of government, or decide appeals according to the Roman law. I shall add no more, but that I hope that gentlemen will recollect what they are about to do, and consider that they are going to give up this last and best privilege.

Mr. PENDLETON. Mr. Chairman, before I enter upon the objections made to this part, I will observe that I should suppose, if there were any person in this audience who had not read this Constitution, or who had not heard what has been said, and should have been told that the trial by jury was intended to be taken away, he would be surprised to find, on examination, that there was no exclusion of it in civil cases, and that it was expressly provided for in criminal cases. I never could see such intention, or any tendency towards it. I have not heard any arguments of that kind used in favor of the Constitution. If there were any words in it which said that trial by jury should not be used, it would be dangerous. I find it secured in criminal cases, and that the trial is to be had in the state where the crime shall have been committed. It is strongly insisted that the privilege of challenging, or excepting to the jury, is not secured. When the Constitution says that the trial shall be by jury, does it not say that every incident will go along with it? I think the honorable gentleman was mistaken yesterday in his reasoning on the propriety of a jury from the vicinage.

He supposed that a jury from the neighborhood is had from this view — that they should be acquainted with the personal character of the person accused. I thought it was with another view — that the jury should have some personal knowledge of the fact, and acquaintance with the witnesses, who will come from the neighborhood. How is it understood in this state? Suppose a man, who lives in Winchester, commits a crime at Norfolk; the jury to try him must come, not from Winchester, but from the neighborhood of Norfolk. *Trial by jury* is secured by this system in criminal cases, as are all the incidental circumstances relative to it. The honorable gentleman yesterday made an objection to that clause which says that the judicial power shall be vested in one Supreme Court, and such inferior courts as Congress may ordain and establish. He objects that there is an unlimited power of appointing inferior courts. I refer to that gentleman, whether it would have been proper to limit this power. Could those gentlemen who framed that instrument have extended their ideas to all the necessities of the United States, and seen every case in which it would be necessary to have an inferior tribunal? By the regulations of Congress, they may be accommodated to public convenience and utility. We may expect that there will be an inferior court in each state; each state will insist on it; and each, for that reason, will agree to it.

. . .

Mr. JOHN MARSHALL. . . . The exclusion of trial by jury, in this case, he [Patrick Henry] urged to prostrate our rights. Does the word *court* only mean the judges? Does not the determination of a jury necessarily lead to the judgment of the court? Is there any thing here which gives the judges exclusive jurisdiction of matters of fact? What is the object of a jury trial? To inform the court of the facts. When a court has cognizance of facts does it not follow that they can make inquiry by a jury? It is impossible to be otherwise. I hope that in this country, where impartiality is so much admired, the laws will direct facts to be ascertained by a jury. But, says the honorable gentleman, the juries in the ten miles square will be mere tools of parties, with which he would not trust his person or property; which, he says, he would rather leave to the court. Because the government may have a district of ten miles square, will no man stay there but the tools and officers of the government? Will nobody else be found there? Is it so in any other part of the world, where a government has legislative power? Are there none but officers, and tools of the government of Virginia, in Richmond? Will there not be independent merchants, and respectable gentlemen of fortune, within the ten miles square? Will there not be worthy farmers and mechanics? Will not a good jury be found there, as well as anywhere else? Will the officers of the government become improper to be on a jury? What is it to the government whether this man or that man succeeds? It is all one thing. Does the Constitution say that juries shall consist of officers, or that the Supreme Court shall be held in the ten miles square? It was acknowledged, by the honorable member, that it was secure in England. What makes it secure there? Is it their constitution? What part of their constitution is there that the Parliament cannot change? As the preservation of this right is in the hands of Parliament, and it has ever been held sacred by them, will the government of America be less honest than that of Great Britain? Here a restriction is to be found. The jury is not to be brought out of the state. There is no such restriction in that government; for the laws of Parliament decide every thing respecting it. Yet gentlemen tell us that there is safety there, and nothing here but danger. It seems to me that the laws of the United States will generally secure trials by a jury of the vicinage, or in such manner as will be most safe and convenient for the people.

But it seems that the right of challenging the jurors is not secured in this Constitution. Is this done by our own Constitution, or by any provision of the English government? Is it done by their Magna Charta, or bill of rights? This privilege is founded on their laws. If so, why should it be objected to the American Constitution, that it is not inserted in it? If we are secure in Virginia without mentioning it in our Constitution, why should not this security be found in the federal court?

The honorable gentleman said much about the quitrents in the Northern Neck. I will refer it to the honorable gentleman himself. Has he not acknowledged that there was no complete title? Was he not satisfied that the right of the legal representatives of the proprietor did not exist at the time he mentioned? If so, it cannot exist now. I will leave it to those gentlemen who come from that quarter. I trust they will not be intimidated, on this account, in voting on this question. A law passed in 1782, which secures this. He says that many poor men may be harassed and injured by the representatives of Lord Fairfax. If he has no right, this cannot be done. If he has this right, and comes to Virginia, what laws will his claims be determined by? By those of the state. By what tribunals will they be determined? By our state courts. Would not the poor man, who was oppressed by an unjust prosecution, be abundantly protected and satisfied by the temper of his neighbors, and would he not find ample justice? What reason has the honorable member to apprehend partiality or injustice? He supposes that, if the judges be judges of both the federal and state courts, they will incline in favor of one government. If such contests should arise, who could more properly decide them than those who are to swear to do justice? If we can expect a fair decision any where, may we not expect justice to be done by the judges of both the federal and state governments? But, says the honorable member, laws may be executed tyrannically. Where is the independency of your judges? If a law be exercised tyrannically in Virginia, to what can you trust? To your judiciary. What security have you for justice? Their independence. Will it not be so in the federal court?

Gentlemen ask, What is meant by law cases, and if they be not distinct from facts? Is there no law arising on cases of equity and admiralty? Look at the acts of Assembly. Have you not many cases where law and fact are blended? Does not the jurisdiction in point of law as well as fact, find itself completely satisfied in law and fact? The honorable gentleman says that no law of Congress can make any exception to the federal appellate jurisdiction of facts as well as law. He has frequently spoken of technical terms, and the meaning of them. What is the meaning of the term *exception*? Does it not mean alteration and diminution? Congress is empowered to make exceptions to the appellate jurisdiction, as to law and fact, of the Supreme Court. These exceptions certainly go as far as the legislature may think proper for the interest and liberty of the people. Who can understand this word, *exception,* to extend to one case as well as the other? I am persuaded that a reconsideration of this case will convince the gentlemen that he was mistaken. This may go to the cure of the mischief apprehended. Gentlemen must be satisfied that this power will not be so much abused as they have said.

The honorable member says that he derives no consolation from the wisdom and integrity of the legislature, because we call them to rectify defects which it is our duty to remove. We ought well to weigh the good and evil before we determine. We ought to be well convinced that the evil will be really produced before we decide against it. If we be convinced that the good greatly preponderates, though there be small defects in it, shall we give up that which is really good, when we can remove the little mischief it may contain, in the plain, easy method pointed out in the system itself?

I was astonished when I heard the honorable gentleman say that he wished the trial by jury to be struck out entirely. Is there no justice to be expected by a jury of our fellow citizens? Will any man prefer to be tried by a court, when the jury is to be of his countrymen, and probably of his vicinage? We have reason to believe the regulations with respect to juries will be such as shall be satisfactory. Because it does not contain all, does it contain nothing? But I conceive that this committee will see there is safety in the case, and that there is no mischief to be apprehended.

He states a case, that a man may be carried from a federal to an anti-federal corner, (and *vice versa*) where men are ready to destroy him. Is this probable? Is it presumable that they will make a law to punish men who are of different opinions in politics from themselves? Is it presumable that they will do it in one single case, unless it be such a case as must satisfy the people at large? The good opinion of the people at large must be consulted by their representatives; otherwise, mischiefs would be produced which would shake the government to its foundation. As it is late, I shall not mention all the gentleman's argument, but some parts of it are so glaring that I cannot pass them over in silence. He says that the establishment of these tribunals, and more particularly in their jurisdiction of controversies between citizens of these states and foreign citizens and subjects, is like a retrospective law. Is there no difference between a tribunal which shall give justice and effect to an existing right, and creating a right that did not exist before? The debt or claim is created by the individual. He has bound himself to comply with it. Does the creation of a new court amount to a retrospective law?

We are satisfied with the provision made in this country on the subject of trial by jury. Does our Constitution direct trials to be by jury? It is required in our bill of rights, which is not a part of the Constitution. Does any security arise from hence? Have you a jury when a judgment is obtained on a replevin bond, or by default? Have you a jury when a motion is made for the commonwealth against an individual; or when a motion is made by one joint obligor against another, to recover sums paid as security? Our courts decide in all these cases, without the intervention of a jury; yet they are all civil cases. The bill of rights is merely recommendatory. Were it otherwise, the consequence would be that many laws which are found convenient would be unconstitutional. What does the government before you say? Does it exclude the legislature from giving a trial by jury in civil cases? If it does not forbid its exclusion, it is on the same footing on which your state government stands now. The legislature of Virginia does not give a trial by jury where it is not necessary, but gives it wherever it is thought expedient. The federal legislature will do so too, as it is formed on the same principles.

The honorable gentleman says that unjust claims will be made, and the defendant had better pay them than go to the Supreme Court. Can you suppose such a disposition in one of your citizens, as that, to oppress another man, he will incur great expenses? What will he gain by an unjust demand? Does a claim establish a right? He must bring his witnesses to prove his claim. If he does not bring his witnesses, the expenses must fall upon him. Will he go on a calculation that the defendant will not defend it, or cannot produce a witness? Will he incur a great deal of expense, from a dependence on such a chance? Those who know human nature, black as it is, must know that mankind are too well attached to their interest to run such a risk. I conceive that this power is absolutely necessary, and not dangerous; that, should it be attended by little inconveniences, they will be altered, and that they can have no interest in not altering them. Is there any real danger? When I compare it to the exercise of the same power in the government of Virginia, I am persuaded there is not. The federal government has no other motive, and has every reason for doing right which the members of our state legislature have. Will a man on the eastern shore be sent to be tried in Kentucky, or a man from Kentucky be brought to the eastern shore to have his trial? A government, by doing this, would destroy itself. I am convinced the trial by jury will be regulated in the manner most advantageous to the community.

Elliot, vol. 3, pp. 537, 540–42, 544–47, 557–62.

12.2.2.6.i **June 23, 1788**

He [MR. HENRY] then proceeded to state the appellate jurisdiction of the judicial power, both as to law and fact, with such exceptions and under such regulations as Congress shall make. He observed, that, as Congress had a right to organize the federal judiciary, they might or might not have recourse to a jury, as they pleased. He left it to the candor of the honorable gentleman to say whether those persons who were at the expense of taking witnesses to Philadelphia, or wherever the federal judiciary may sit, could be certain whether they were to be heard before a jury or not. An honorable gentleman (Mr. Marshall) the other day observed, that he conceived the trial by jury better secured under the plan on the table than in the British government, or even in our bill of rights. I have the highest veneration and respect for the honorable gentleman, and I have experienced his candor on all occasions; but, Mr. Chairman, in this instance, he is so materially mistaken that I cannot but observe, he is much in error. I beg the clerk to read that part of the Constitution which relates to trial by jury. [*The clerk then read the 8th article of the bill of rights.*]

Mr. MARSHALL rose to explain what he had before said on this subject: he informed the committee that the honorable gentleman (Mr. Henry) must have misunderstood him. He said that he conceived the trial by jury was as well secured, and not better secured, in the proposed new Constitution as in our bill of rights. [*The clerk then read the 11th article of the bill of rights.*]

Mr. HENRY. Mr. Chairman: The gentleman's candor, sir, as I informed you before, I have the highest opinion of, and am happy to find he has so far explained what he meant; but, sir, has he mended the matter? Is not the ancient trial by jury preserved in the Virginia bill of rights? and is that the case in the new plan? No, sir; they can do it if they please. Will gentlemen tell me the trial by jury of the vicinage where the party resides is preserved? True, sir, there is to be a trial by the jury in the state where the fact was committed; but, sir, this state, for instance, is so large that your juries may be collected five hundred miles from where the party resides — no neighbors who are acquainted with their characters, their good or bad conduct in life, to judge of the unfortunate man who may be thus exposed to the rigor of that government. Compare this security, then, sir, in our bill of rights with that in the new plan of government; and in the first you have it, and in the other, in my opinion, not at all. But, sir, in what situation will our citizens be, who have made large contracts under our present government? They will be called to a federal court, and tried under the retrospective laws; for it is evident, to me at least, that the federal court must look back, and give better remedies, to compel individuals to fulfill them.

The whole history of human nature cannot produce a government like that before you. The manner in which the judiciary and other branches of the government are formed, seems to me calculated to lay prostrate the states, and the liberties of the people. But, sir, another circumstance ought totally to reject that plan, in my opinion; which is, that it cannot be understood, in many parts, even by the supporters of it. A constitution, sir, ought to be, like a beacon, held up to the public eye, so as to be understood by every man. Some gentlemen have observed that the word *jury* implies a jury of the vicinage. There are so many inconsistencies in this, that, for my part, I cannot understand it. By the bill of rights of England, a subject has a right to a trial by his peers. What is meant by his peers? Those who reside near him, his neighbors, and who are well acquainted with his character and situation in life. Is this secured in the proposed plan before you? No, sir. As I have observed before, what is to become of the *purchases of the Indians?* — those unhappy nations who have given up their lands to private purchasers; who, by being made drunk, have given a thousand, nay, I might say, ten thousand acres, for the trifling sum of sixpence! It is with true concern, with grief, I tell you that I have waited with pain to come to this part of the plan; because I observed gentlemen admitted its being defective, and, I had my hopes, would have proposed amendments. But this part they have defended; and this convinces me of the necessity of obtaining amendments before it is adopted. They have defended it with ingenuity and perseverance, but by no means satisfactorily. If previous amendments are not obtained, the trial by jury is gone. British debtors will be ruined by being dragged to the federal court, and the liberty and happiness of our citizens gone, never again to be recovered.   Elliot, vol. 3, pp. 578–79.

12.2.2.6.j   June 24, 1788

Mr. HENRY. . . . The honorable member must forgive me for declaring my dissent from it; because, if I understand it rightly, it admits that the new system is defective, and most capitally; for, immediately after the proposed ratification, there comes a declaration that the paper before you is not intended to violate any of these three great rights — the liberty of religion, liberty of the press, and the trial by jury. What is the inference when you enumerate the rights which you are to enjoy? That those not enumerated are relinquished. There are only three things to be retained — religion, freedom of the press, and jury trial. Will not the ratification carry every thing, without excepting these three things? Will not all the world pronounce that we intended to give up all the rest? Every thing it speaks of, by way of rights, is comprised in these things. Your subsequent amendments only go to these three amendments.

. . .

. . . In my weak judgment, a government is strong when it applies to the most important end of all governments — the rights and privileges of the people. In the honorable member's proposal, jury trial, the press and religion, and other essential rights, are not to be given up. Other essential rights — what are they? The world will say that you intended to give them up. When you go into an enumeration of your rights, and stop that enumeration, the inevitable conclusion is, that what is omitted is intended to be surrendered.

Elliot, vol. 3, pp. 587–88, 594.

12.2.3 PHILADELPHIA CONVENTION

None.

12.2.4 NEWSPAPERS AND PAMPHLETS

12.2.4.1 Centinel, No. 1, October 5, 1787

Friends Countrymen and *Fellow Citizens*: Permit one of yourselves to put you in mind of certain *liberties* and *privileges* secured to you by the constitution of this commonwealth, and to beg your serious attention to his uninterested opinion upon the plan of federal government submitted to your consideration, before you surrender these great and valuable privileges up forever. . . . Whether the *trial by jury* is to continue as your birth-right, the freemen of Pennsylvania, nay, of all America, are now called upon to declare.

[Philadelphia] Independent Gazetteer, Kaminski & Saladino, pp. 328–29.

12.2.4.2 The Federal Farmer, No. 2, October 9, 1787

The essential parts of a free and good government are a full and equal representation of the people in the legislature, and the jury trial of the vicinage in the administration of justice — a full and equal representation, is that which possesses the same interests, feelings, opinions, and views the people themselves would were they all assembled — a fair representation, therefore, should be so regulated, that every order of men in the community, according to the common course of elections, can have a share in it — in order to allow professional men, merchants, traders, farmers, mechanics, &c. to bring a just proportion of their best informed men respectively into the legislature, the representation must be considerably numerous — We have about 200 state senators in the United States, and a less number than that of federal representatives cannot, clearly, be a full representation of this people, in the affairs of internal taxation and police, were there but one legislature for the whole union. The representation cannot be equal, or the situation of the people proper for one government only — if the extreme parts of the society cannot be represented as fully as the central — It is apparently impracticable that this should be the case in this extensive country — it would be impossible to collect a representation of the parts of the country five, six, and seven hundred miles from the seat of government.

Under one general government alone, there could be but one judiciary, one supreme and a proper number of inferior courts. I think it would be totally impracticable in this case to preserve a due administration of justice, and the real benefits of the jury trial of the vicinage — there are now supreme courts in each state in the union, and a great number of county and other courts, subordinate to each supreme court — most of these supreme and inferior courts are itinerant, and hold their sessions in different parts every year of their respective states, counties and districts — with all these moving courts, our citizens, from the vast extent of the country, must travel very considerable distances from home to find the place where justice is administered. I am not for bringing justice to individuals as to afford them any temptation to engage in law suits; though I think it one of the greatest benefits in a good government, that each citizen should find a court of justice within a reasonable distance, perhaps, within a day's travel of his home; so that without great inconveniences and enormous expense, he may have the advantages of his witnesses and jury — it would be impracticable to derive these advantages from one judiciary — the one supreme court at most could only set in the centre of the union, and move once a year into the centre of the eastern and southern extremes of it — and, in this case, each citizen, on an average, would travel 150 or 200 miles to find this court — that, however, inferior courts might be properly placed in the different counties, and districts of the union, the appellate jurisdiction would be intolerable and expensive.

If it were possible to consolidate the states, and preserve the features of a free government, still it is evident that the middle states, the parts of the union, about the seat of government, would enjoy great advantages, while the remote states would experience the many inconveniences of remote provinces. Wealth, offices, and the benefits of government would collect in the centre: and the extreme states; and their principal towns, become much less important.

There are other considerations which tend to prove that the idea of one consolidated whole, on free principles, is ill founded — the laws of a free government rest on the confidence of the people, and operate gently — and never can extend the influence very far — if they are executed on free principles, about the centre, where benefits of the government induce the people to support it voluntarily; yet they must be executed on the principles of fear and force in the extremes — This has been the case with every extensive republic of which we have any accurate account.

There are certain unalienable and fundamental rights, which in forming the social compact, ought to be explicitly ascertained and fixed — a free and enlightened people, in forming this compact, will not resign all their rights to those who govern, and they will fix limits to their legislators and rulers, which will soon be plainly seen by those who are governed, as well as by those who govern: and the latter will know they cannot be passed unperceived by the former, and without giving a general alarm — These rights should be made the basis of every constitution; and if a people be so situated, or have such different opinions that they cannot agree in ascertaining and fixing them, it is a very strong argument against their attempting to form one entire society, to live under one system of laws only. — I confess, I never thought the people of these states differed essentially in these respects; they having derived all these rights from one common source, the British systems; and having in the formation of their state constitutions, discovered that their ideas relative to these rights are very similar. However, it is now said that the states differ so essentially in these respects, and even in the important article of the trial by jury, that when assembled in convention, they can agree to no words by which to establish that trial, or by which to ascertain and establish many other of these rights, as fundamental articles in the social compact. If so, we proceed to consolidate the states on no solid basis whatever.

Kaminski & Saladino, vol. 14, pp. 25–27.

12.2.4.3 The Federal Farmer, No. 3, October 10, 1787

. . . There are some powers proposed to be lodged in the general government in the judicial department, I think very unnecessarily, I mean powers respecting questions arising upon the internal laws of the respective states. . . . In almost all these cases, either party may have the trial by jury in the state courts; . . . justice may be obtained in these courts on reasonable terms; they must be more competent to proper decisions on the laws of their respective states, than the federal courts can possibly be. . . . It is true, those courts may be so organized by a wise and prudent legislature, as to make the obtaining of justice in them tolerably easy; they may in general be organized on the common law principles of the country: But this benefit is by no means secured by the constitution. The trial by jury is secured only in those few criminal cases, to which the federal laws will extend — as crimes committed on the seas against the law of nations, treason and counterfeiting the federal securities and coin: But even in these cases, the jury trial of the vicinage is not secured, particularly in the large states, a citizen may be tried for a crime committed in the state, and yet tried in some states 500 miles from the place where it was committed; but the jury trial is not secured at all in civil causes. Though the convention have not established this trial, it is to be hoped that congress, in putting the new system into execution, will do it by a legislative act, in all cases in which it can be done with propriety. Whether the jury trial is not excluded [in] the supreme judicial court, is an important question. . . .

Kaminski & Saladino, vol. 14, pp. 40–41.

12.2.4.4 The Federal Farmer, No. 4, October 12, 1787

. . . If the federal constitution is to be construed so far in connection with the state constitutions, as to leave the trial by jury in civil causes, for instance, secured; on the same principles it would have left the trial by jury in criminal causes, the benefits of the writ of habeas corpus, &c. secured; they all stand on the same footing; they are the common rights of Americans, and have been recognized by the state constitutions: But the convention found it necessary to recognize or reestablish the benefits of that writ, and the jury trial in criminal cases. . . . The establishing of one right implies the necessity of establishing another and similar one.

On the whole, the position appears to me to be undeniable, that this bill of rights ought to be carried farther, and some other principles established, as a part of this fundamental compact between the people of the United States and their federal rulers.

. . . There are other essential rights, which we have justly understood to be the rights of freemen. . . . The trials by jury in civil causes, it is said, varies [*sic*] so much in the several states, that no words could be found for the uniform establishment of it. If so the federal legislation will not be able to establish it by any general laws. I confess I am of opinion it may be established, but not in that beneficial manner in which we may enjoy it, for the reasons beforementioned. When I speak of the jury trial of the vicinage, or the trial of the fact in the neighbourhood, — I do not lay so much stress upon the circumstance of our being tried by our neighbors: in this enlightened country men may be probably impartially tried by those who do not live very near them: but the trial of facts in the neighborhood is of great importance in other respects. Nothing can be more essential than the cross examining witnesses, and generally before the triers of the facts in question. The common people can establish facts with much more ease with oral than written evidence; when trials of fact are removed to a distance from the homes of the parties and witnesses, oral evidence becomes intolerably expensive, and the parties must depend on written evidence, which to the common people is expensive and almost useless; it must be frequently taken ex-parte, and but very seldom leads to the proper discovery of truth.

The trial by jury is very important in another point of view. It is essential in every free country, that common people should have a part and share of influence, in the judicial as well as in the legislative department. To hold open to them the offices of senators, judges, and offices to fill which an expensive education is required, cannot answer any valuable purposes for them; they are not in a situation to be brought forward and to fill those offices; these, and most other offices of any considerable importance, will be occupied by the few. The few, the well born, &c. as Mr. Adams calls them, in judicial decisions as well as in legislation, are generally disposed, and very naturally too, to favour those of their own description.

The trial by jury in the judicial department, and the collection of the people by their representatives in the legislature, are those fortunate inventions which have procured for them, in this country, their true proportion of influence, and the wisest and most fit means of protecting themselves in the community. Their situation, as jurors and representatives, enables them to acquire information and knowledge in the affairs and government of the society; and to come forward, in turn, as the centinels and guardians of each other. I am very sorry that even a few of our countrymen should consider jurors and representatives in a different point of view, as ignorant, troublesome bodies, which ought not to have any share in the concerns of government.

Kaminski & Saladino, vol. 14, pp. 45–47.

12.2.4.5 One of the People, October 17, 1787

The . . . trials by jury are not infringed on. The Constitution is silent, and with propriety too, on these and every other subject relative to the internal government of the states. These are secured by the different state constitutions.

Pennsylvania Gazette, Jensen, vol. 2, p. 190.

12.2.4.6 An Old Whig, No. 3, October 20, 1787

. . . As to the trial by jury, the question may be decided in a few words. Any future Congress sitting under the authority of the proposed new constitution, may, if they chuse, enact that there shall be no more trial by jury, in any of the United States; except in the trial of crimes; and this "SUPREME LAW" will at once annul the trial by jury, in all other cases. The author of the speech supposes that no danger "can possibly ensue, since the proceedings of the supreme court are to be regulated by the Congress, which is a faithful representation of the people; and the oppression of government is effectually barred; by declaring that in all criminal cases the trial by jury shall be preserved." Let us examine the last clause of this sentence first. — I know that an affected indifference to the trial by jury has been expressed, by some persons high in the confidence of the present ruling party in some of the states; — and yet for my own part I cannot change the opinion I had early formed of the excellence of this mode of trial even in civil causes. On the other hand I have no doubt that whenever a settled plan shall be formed for the extirpation of liberty, the banishment of jury trials will be one of the means adopted for the purpose. — But how is it that "the oppression of government is effectually barred by declaring that in all criminal cases the trial by jury shall be preserved?" —Are there not a thousand civil cases in which the government is a party? — In all actions for penalties, forfeitures and public debts, as well as many others, the government is a party and the whole weight of government is thrown into the scale of the prosecution[,] yet there are all of them civil causes. — These penalties, forfeitures and demands of public debts may be multiplied at the will and pleasure of government. — These modes of harassing the subject have perhaps been more effectual than direct criminal prosecutions. . . . No, Mr. Printer, we ought not to part with the trial by jury; we ought to guard this and many other privileges by a bill of rights, which cannot be invaded. The reason that is pretended in the speech why such a declaration; as a bill of rights requires, cannot be made for the protection of the trial by jury; — "that we cannot with any propriety say 'that the trial by jury shall be as heretofore'" in the case of a federal system of jurisprudence, is almost too contemptible to merit notice. — Is this the only form of words that language could afford on such an important occasion? Or if it were to what did these words refer when adopted in the constitutions of the states? — Plainly sir, to the trial by juries as established by the common law of England in the state of its purity; — That common law for which we contended so eagerly at the time of the revolution, and which now after the interval of a very few years, by the proposed new constitution we seem ready to abandon forever; at least in that article which is the most invaluable part of it; the trial by jury.

[Philadelphia] Independent Gazetteer, Kaminski & Saladino,
vol. 13, pp. 427–28.

12.2.4.7 An American Citizen, No. 4, October 21, 1787

. . . Both the old and new foederal constitutions, and indeed *the constitution of Pennsylvania*, admit of courts in which no use is made of a jury. The board of property, the court of admiralty, and the high court of errors and appeals, in the state of Pennsylvania, as also the court of appeals under the old confederation, exclude juries. *Tryal by jury will therefore be in the express words of the Pennsylvania constitution, "as heretofore,"* — almost always used, though sometimes omitted. Trials for lands lying in any state between persons residing in such state, for bonds, notes, book debts, contracts, trespasses, assumptions, and all other matters between two or more citizens of any state, will be held in the state courts by juries, *as now.* In these cases, the foederal courts *cannot interfere.* But when a dispute arises between the citizens of any state about lands lying out of the bounds *thereof,* or when a trial is to be had between the citizens of any state and those of another, or the government of another, the private citizen will not be obliged to go into a court *constituted by the state,* with which, or with the citizens of which, *his dispute is. He can appeal to a disinterested foederal court.* This is surely a *great advantage,* and promises a *fair trial,* and an *impartial judgement.* The trial by jury is *not excluded* in these foederal courts. In all *criminal* cases, where the property or life of the citizen is at stake, he has the benefit of a jury. If convicted on impeachment, which is never done by a jury in any country, he cannot be fined, imprisoned or punished, but only may be *disqualified* from doing public mischief by losing his office, and his capacity to hold another. If the nature of his offence, besides its danger to his country, should be *criminal* in itself — should involve a charge of fraud, murder or treason — he may be tried for such crime, but cannot be convicted *without a jury.* In trials about property in the foederal courts, which can only be *as above stated,* there is nothing in the new constitution *to prevent a trial by jury.* No doubt it will be the mode in every case, wherein it is practicable. This will be adjusted by law, and it could not be done otherwise. In short, the sphere of jurisdiction for the foederal courts *is limited,* and that sphere only is subject to the regulations of our foederal government. The known principles of justice, the attachment to trial by jury whenever it can be used, the instructions of the state legislatures, the instructions of the people at large, the operation of the foederal regulations on the property of a president, a senator, a representative, a judge, as well as on that of a private citizen, will certainly render those regulations as favorable as possible to *property; for life and liberty are put more than ever into the hands of the juries.* Under the *present* constitution of all the states, a public officer may be condemned *to imprisonment or death* on impeachment, *without a jury;* but the new foederal constitution protects the accused, till he shall be convicted, from the hands of power, by rendering *a jury the indispensible judges of all crimes.*

Pennsylvania Gazette (October 24),
Kaminski & Saladino, vol. 13, pp. 434–35.

12.2.4.8   Centinel, No. 2, October 24, 1787

Mr. *Wilson* says, that it would have been impracticable to have made a general rule for jury trial in the civil cases assigned to the federal judiciary, because of the want of uniformity in the mode of jury trial, as practiced by the several states. This objection proves too much, and therefore amounts to nothing. If it precludes the mode of common law in civil cases, it certainly does in criminal. Yet in these we are told "the oppression of government is effectually barred by declaring that in all criminal cases *trial by jury* shall be preserved." Astonishing, that provision could not be made for a jury in civil controversies, of 12 men, whose verdict should be unanimous, *to be taken from the vicinage*; a precaution which is omitted as to trial of crimes, which may be any where in the state within which they have been committed. So that an inhabitant of *Kentucky* may be tried for treason at *Richmond.*

[Philadelphia] Freeman's Journal, Kaminski & Saladino, vol. 13, p. 462.

12.2.4.9 Timothy Meanwell, October 29, 1787

. . . I was informed that the trial by jury, which was guaranteed to us by the constitution of Pennsylvania, was in many instances abolished; this I did not believe when I heard it — I could not entertain an opinion that men so enlightened as those of the convention, among whose names I saw friend — and friend — , could be inattentive to the preservation of the trial by jury. I immediately took the constitution in my hand, and began to search it from end to end, and was in hopes of finding some clause like that in the Bill of Rights in the constitution of Pennsylvania, that would secure the trial by juries in all cases whatsoever, but I was disappointed.

[Philadelphia] Independent Gazetteer, Kaminski & Saladino, vol. 14, p. 512.

12.2.4.10 Cincinnatus, No. 1, November 1, 1787

Let us suppose then, that what has happened, may happen again: That a patriotic printer, like Peter Zenger, should incur the resentment of our new rulers, by publishing to the world, transactions which they wish to conceal. If he should be prosecuted, if his judges should be as desirous of punishing him, *at all events*, as the judges were to punish Peter Zenger, what would his innocence or his virtue avail him? This constitution is so admirably framed for tyranny, that, by clear construction, the judges might put the verdict of a jury out of the question. Among the cases in which the court is to have appellate jurisdiction, are — controversies, to which the United States are a party: — In this appellate jurisdiction, the judges are to determine, *both law and fact*. That is, the court is both judge and jury. The attorney general then would have only to move a question of law in the court below, to ground an appeal to the supreme judicature, and the printer would be delivered up to the mercy of his judges. Peter Zenger's case will teach us, what mercy he might expect. Thus, if the president, vice-president, or any other officer, or favorite of state, should be censured in print, he might effectually deprive the printer, or author, of his trial by jury, and subject him to something, that will probably very much resemble the Star Chamber of former times. The freedom of the press, the sacred palladium of public liberty, would be pulled down; — all useful knowledge on the conduct of government would be withheld from the people — the press would become subservient to the purposes of bad and arbitrary rulers, and imposition, not information, would be its object.

. . . Yet it was the jury only, that saved Zenger, it was a jury only, that saved Woodfall, it can only be a jury that will save any future printer from the fangs of power.

New York Journal, Kaminski & Saladino, vol. 13, pp. 532–33.

12.2.4.11   Timoleon, November 1, 1787

". . . With as little ceremony, and similar constructive doctrine, the inestimable trial by jury can likewise be depraved and destroyed — because the Constitution in the 2d section of the 3d article, by expressly assuming the trial by jury in *criminal cases,* and being silent about it in *civil causes,* evidently declares it to be unnecessary in the latter. And more strongly so, by giving the supreme court jurisdiction in appeals, *'both as to law and fact.'* If this be added, that the trial by jury in criminal cases is only stipulated to be *'in the state,'* not in the county where the crime is supposed to have been committed; one excellent part of the jury trial, from the vicinage, or at least from the county, is even in criminal cases rendered precarious, and at the mercy of rulers under the new Constitution. — Yet the danger to liberty, peace, and property, from restraining and injuring this excellent mode of trial, will clearly appear from the following observations of the learned Dr. Blackstone, in his commentaries on the laws of England, Art. Jury Trial Book 3. chap. 33. — 'The establishment of jury trial was always so highly esteemed and valued by the people, that no conquest, *no change of government,* could ever prevail to abolish it. In the magna charta it is more than once insisted upon *as the principle bulwark of our liberties* — And this is a species of knowledge most absolutely necessary for every gentleman; as well, because he may be frequently called upon to determine in this capacity the rights of others, his fellow subjects; as, *because his own property, his liberty, and his life, depend upon maintaining in its legal force the trial by jury* . . . And in every country as the trial by jury has been *gradually disused,* so the great have increased in power, until the state has been torn to pieces by rival factions, and oligarchy in effect has been established, though under the shadow of regal government; unless where the miserable people have taken shelter under absolute monarchy, as the lighter evil of the two. . . . *It is therefore upon the whole, a duty which every man owes to his country, his friends, his posterity, and himself, to maintain, to the utmost of his power, this valuable trial by jury in all its rights'.*" Thus far the learned Dr. Blackstone, — "Could the Doctor, if he were here, at this moment," . . . "have condemned those parts of the new Constitution in stronger terms, which give the supreme court jurisdiction both as to law and *fact;* which have weakened the jury trial in criminal cases and which have discountenanced it in all civil causes? At first I wondered at the complaint that some people made of this new Constitution, because it led to the government of a few; but it is fairly to be concluded, from this injury to the trial by jury, that *some* who framed this new system, saw with Dr. Blackstone, how operative jury trial was in preventing the tyranny of the great ones, and therefore frowned upon it, as this new Constitution does. . . ."

New York Journal, Extraordinary, Kaminski & Saladino, vol. 13, pp. 536–38.

12.2.4.12   Brutus, No. 2, November 1, 1787

For the security of life, in criminal prosecutions, the bill of rights of most of the states have declared, that no man shall be held to answer for a crime until he is made fully acquainted with the charge brought against him; he shall not be compelled to accuse, or furnish evidence against himself — The witnesses against him shall be brought face to face, and he shall be fully heard by himself or counsel. That it is essential to the security of life and liberty, that trial of facts be in the vicinity where they happen. Are not provisions of this kind as necessary in the general government, as in that of a particular state? The powers vested in the new Congress extend in many cases to life; they are authorised to provide for the punishment of a variety of capital crimes, and no restraint is laid upon them in its exercise, save only, that "the trial of all crimes, except in cases of impeachment, shall be by jury; and such trial shall be in the state where the said crimes shall have been committed." No man is secure of a trial in the county where he is charged to have committed a crime; he may be brought from Niagara to New-York, or carried from Kentucky to Richmond for trial for an offence, supposed to be committed. What security is there, that a man shall be furnished with a full and plain description of the charges against him? That he shall be allowed to produce all proof he can in his favor? That he shall see the witnesses against him face to face, or that he shall be fully heard in his own defence by himself or counsel?

New York Journal, Kaminski & Saladino, vol. 13, p. 527.

12.2.4.13 An Old Whig, No. 5, November 1, 1787

. . . It is needless to repeat the necessity of securing other personal rights in the forming a new government. The same argument which proves the necessity of securing one of them shews also the necessity of securing others. Without a bill of rights we are totally insecure in all of them; and no man can promise himself with any degree of certainty that his posterity will enjoy the inestimable blessings of liberty of conscience, of freedom of speech and of writing and publishing their thoughts on public matters, of trial by jury, of holding themselves, their houses and papers free from seizure and search upon general suspicion or general warrants; or in short that they will be secured in the enjoyment of life, liberty and property without depending on the will and pleasure of their rulers.

[Philadelphia] *Independent Gazetteer*, Kaminski & Saladino, vol. 13, p. 541.

12.2.4.14 A Son of Liberty, November 8, 1787

MR. GREENLEAF, Having observed in your paper of the 25th ult. that a writer under the signature of *A Slave,* has pointed out a number of advantages or blessings, which, he says, will result from an adoption of the new government, proposed by the Convention: — I have taken the liberty to request, that you will give the following a place in your next paper, it being an enumeration of a *few* of the *curses* which will be entailed on the people of America, by this preposterous and newfangled system, if they are ever so infatuated as to receive it. . . . 3d. A suppression of trial by jury of your peers, in all civil cases, and even in criminal cases, the loss of the trial in the vicinage, where the fact and the credibility of your witnesses are known, and where you can command their attendance without insupportable expence, or inconveniences.

New York Journal, Kaminski & Saladino, vol. 13, p. 481.

12.2.4.15 Uncus, November 9, 1787

Mr. GODDARD, When you began publishing the *Centinel* in numbers, I expected we should have had one in each of your papers for some weeks, hoping, that after he had done finding fault with the doings of the late convention, the members of which were either too designing, — of too aristocratic principles, — too old, — or too ignorant, "inexperienced and fallible," for business of such magnitude; *he* would, by the *perfect rule* existing in his own mind, by which he has tried and condemned the proposed constitution, exhibit to the world a perfect model; which these States would have only to read, and invite "those who are competent to the task of developing the principles of government," to come forward, approve and adopt.

. . .

I believe, there is not a single article, wherein the *new plan* has proposed any amendment to the *old*, but what would be objected to by *Centinel*. To some he has objected, where they have made no amendment; as the power of Congress to try causes without a jury, which they have ever possessed.

Maryland Journal, Kaminski & Saladino, vol. 14, pp. 76, 79.

12.2.4.16 Gentleman in New-York, November 14, 1787

". . . I have not only no objection to, but am extremely desirous of, a strong and general government, provided the fundamental principles of liberty be well secured. These I take to be, trial by jury as has been and is practised. . . . In all these great points the proposed constitution requires amendment, before it can be adopted even with safety.

"In the constitution of the fœderal court, where its jurisdiction is original, the securing jury trial in criminal, is, according to all legal reasoning, an exclusion of it in civil matters — and in its appellant function it is expressly said the court shall judge both of *law* and *fact*. This of course renders the finding of a jury below, totally nugatory.   Virginia Independent Chronicle, Kaminski & Saladino, vol. 14, p. 103.

12.2.4.17 A Georgian, November 15, 1787

And now we come to the point which at once teems with numberless enormous innovations by introducing strange and new courts of almost any denomination into any of the states whereby our own courts will soon be annihilated, and abolishing the only pledge of liberty, the trial by jury, to tyrants only formidable, in all civil cases, countenancing the greatest injustice to be lawfully, nay constitutionally, committed by the rich against their brave fellow citizens whose only misfortune is to be, perhaps, not so rich as they, by dragging their lawsuits of any denomination and of any sum, however small, if they choose, before the GRAND TRIBUNAL OF APPEAL to which the poor will be unable to follow with their evidences and witnesses, and on account of the great expenses. Therefore, fellow citizens, pray restrain this encroachment so destructive to the inestimable rights the more numerous part of middle-circumstanced citizens now enjoy. With horror beware of the precipice before you; and, if you will, please join me in amending the third Article in the Federal Constitution thus:

. . .

"The trial of all civil and criminal causes, except in cases of impeachment (as provided for in Article I, section 3) shall be by jury, drawn by lot out of a box from among the freeholders of that state where Congress shall reside, and within five miles thereof; and, when a crime against the United States has been committed within no state, the Supreme Court of Congress shall have the trial of the same where Congress then resides.

Gazette of the State of Georgia, Kaminski & Saladino, vol. 3, pp. 241–42.

12.2.4.18   A Countryman, No. 2, November 22, 1787

Of a very different nature, tho' only one degree better than the other reasoning, is all that sublimity of *nonsense* and *alarm*, that has been thundered against it in every shape of *metaphoric terror*, on the subject of a *bill of rights*, the *liberty of the press, rights of conscience, rights of taxation and election, trials in the vicinity, freedom of speech, trial by jury,* and a *standing army*. These last are undoubtedly important points, much too important to depend on mere paper protection. For, guard such privileges by the strongest expressions, still if you leave the legislative and executive power in the hands of those who are or may be disposed to deprive you of them — you are but slaves. Make an absolute monarch — give him the supreme authority, and guard as much as you will by bills of right, your liberty of the press, and trial by jury; — he will find means either to take them from you, or to render them useless.

Your General Assembly under your present constitution are supreme. They may keep troops on foot in the most profound peace, if they think proper. They have heretofore abridged the trial by jury in some cases, and they can again in all. They can restrain the press, and may lay the most burdensome taxes if they please, and who can forbid? But still the people are perfectly safe that not one of these events shall take place so long as the members of the General Assembly are as much interested, and interested in the same manner, as the other subjects.

On examining the new proposed constitution, there can not be a question, but that there is authority enough lodged in the proposed federal Congress, if abused, to do the greatest injury. And it is perfectly idle to object to it, that there is no bill of rights, or to propose to add to it a provision that a trial by jury shall in no case be omitted, or to patch it up by adding a stipulation in favor of the press, or to guard it by removing the paltry objection to the right of Congress to regulate the time and manner of elections.

New Haven Gazette, Kaminski & Saladino, vol. 14, pp. 172–74.

12.2.4.19   A Well-Informed Correspondent, November 28, 1787

. . . "The judicial powers of the Fœderal Courts have, also, been grossly misrepresented. It is said 'that the trial by jury is to be abolished, and that the courts of the several states are to be annihilated.' But these, Sir, are mistaken notions, scandalous perversions of truth. The courts of judicature in each state will still continue in their present situation. The trial by jury in all disputes between man and man in each state will still remain inviolate, and in all cases of this description, there can be no appeal to the Fœderal Courts. It is only in particular specified cases, of which each state cannot properly take cognizance, that the judicial authority of the Fœderal Courts can be exercised. Even in the congressional courts of judicature, the trial of all crimes except in cases of impeachment, shall be by jury. How then can any man say that the trial by jury will be abolished, and that the courts of the several states will be annihilated by the adoption of the Fœderal Government? Must not the man who makes this assertion be either consummately imprudent, or consummately ignorant? My God! what can he mean by such bareface representations? Can he be a friend to his country? Can he be the friend to the happiness of mankind? Is he not some insidious foe? Some emissary, hired by *British Gold* — plotting the ruin of both, by disseminating the seeds of suspicion and discontent among us?

Virginia Independent Chronicle, Kaminski & Saladino,
vol. 14, pp. 244–45.

12.2.4.20 James McHenry, Speech to the Maryland House, November 29, 1787

. . . 1st. The judicial power of the United States underwent a full investigation — it is impossible for me to Detail the observations that were delivered on that subject — The right of tryal by Jury was left open and undefined from the difficulty attending any limitation to so valuable a priviledge, and from the persuasion that Congress might hereafter make provision more suitable to each respective State — To suppose that mode of Tryal intended to be abolished would be to suppose the Representatives in Convention to act contrary to the Will of their Constituents, and Contrary to their own Interest. — . . .

Kaminski & Saladino, vol. 14, p. 284.

12.2.4.21 A Countryman, No. 3, November 29, 1787

. . . Last week I endeavored to evince, that the only surety you could have for your liberties must be in the nature of your government; that you could derive no security from bills of rights, or stipulations, on the subject of a standing army, the liberty of the press, trial by jury, or on any other subject. Did you ever hear of an absolute monarchy, where those rights which are proposed by the pigmy politicians of this day, to be secured by stipulation, were ever preserved? Would it not be mere trifling to make any such stipulations, in any absolute monarchy?

On the other hand, if your interest and that of your rulers are the same, your liberties are abundantly secure. . . .

No people can be more secure against tyranny and oppression in their rulers than you are at present; and no rulers can have more supreme and unlimited authority than your general assembly have.

New Haven Gazette, Kaminski & Saladino, vol. 4, p. 296.

12.2.4.22 Philadelphiensis, No. 3, December 5, 1787

. . . The only thing in which a government should be efficient, is to protect the *liberties, lives,* and *property* of the people governed, from foreign and domestic violence. This, and this only is what every government should do effectually. For any government to do more than this is impossible, and every one that falls short of it is defective. Let us now compare the new constitution with this legitimate definition of an efficient government, and we shall find that it has scarce a particle of an efficient government in its whole composition.

In the first place then it does not protect the people in those liberties and privileges that all freemen should hold sacred — The *liberty of conscience,* the *liberty of the press,* the *liberty of trial by jury, &c.* are all unprotected by this constitution. . . . [Philadelphia] Freeman's Journal, Kaminski & Saladino, vol. 14, p. 351.

12.2.4.23 Agrippa, No. 5, December 11, 1787

There is another sense in which the clause relating to causes between the state and individuals is to be understood, and it is more probable than the other, as it will be eternal in its duration, and increasing in its extent. This is the whole branch of the law relating to criminal prosecutions. In all such cases the state is plaintiff, and the person accused is defendant. The process, therefore, will be, for the attorney-general of the state to commence his suit before a continental court. Considering the state as a party, the cause must be tried in another, and all of the expense of transporting witnesses incurred. The individual is to take his trial among strangers, friendless and unsupported, without its being known whether he is habitually a good or a bad man; and consequently with one essential circumstance wanting by which to determine whether the action was performed maliciously or accidentally. All these inconveniences are avoided by the present important restriction, that the cause shall be tried by a jury of the vicinity, and tried in the county where the offence was commited [*sic*]. But by the proposed *derangement,* I can call it by no softer name, a man must be ruined to prove his innocence. This is far from being a forced construction of the proposed form. The words appear to me not intelligible, upon the idea that it is to be a *system* of government, unless the construction now given, both for civil and criminal process, be admitted. Massachusetts Gazette, Storing, vol. 4, pp. 78–79.

12.2.4.24 Address and Reasons of Dissent of the Minority of the Pennsylvania Convention, December 12, 1787

The first consideration that this review suggests, is the omission of a BILL OF RIGHTS ascertaining and fundamentally establishing those unalienable and personal rights of men, without the full, free, and secure enjoyment of which there can be no liberty, and over which it is not necessary for a good government to have the controul. The principal of which are the rights of conscience, personal liberty by the clear and unequivocal establishment of the writ of *habeas corpus,* jury trial in criminal and civil cases, by an impartial jury of the vicinage or county; with the common law proceedings, for the safety of the accused in criminal prosecutions and the liberty of the press, that scourge of tyrants; and the grand bulwark of every other liberty and, privilege; the stipulations heretofore made in favor of them in the state constitutions, are entirely superceded by this constitution.

. . .

We have before noticed the judicial power as it would effect a consolidation of the states into one government; we will now examine it, as it would affect the liberties and welfare of the people, supposing such a government were practicable and proper.

The judicial power, under the proposed constitution, is founded on the well-known principles of the *civil law*, by which the judge determines both on law and fact, and appeals are allowed from the inferior tribunals to the superior, upon the whole question; so that facts as well as law, would be re-examined, and even new facts brought forward in the court of appeals. . . .

That this mode of proceeding is the one which must be adopted under this constitution, is evident from the following circumstances: — 1st. That the trial by jury, which is the grand characteristic of the common law, is secured by the constitution, only in criminal cases. — 2d. That the appeal from both *law* and *fact* is expressly established, which is utterly inconsistent with the principles of the common law, and trials by jury. The only mode in which an appeal from law and fact can be established, is, by adopting the principles and practice of the civil law; unless the United States should be drawn into the absurdity of calling and swearing juries, merely for the purpose of contradicting their verdicts, which would render juries contemptible and worse than useless. — 3d. That the courts to be established would decide on all cases *of law and equity*, which is a well known characteristic of the civil law, . . .

Not to enlarge upon the loss of the invaluable right of trial by an unbiassed jury, so dear to every friend of liberty, the monstrous expence and inconveniences of the mode of proceeding to be adopted, are such as will prove intolerable to the people of this country. . . . We abhor the idea of losing the transcendent privilege of trial by jury, with the loss of which, it is remarked by the same learned author, that in Sweden, the liberties of the commons were extinguished by an aristocratic senate: and that *trial by jury* and the liberty of the people went out together.

Kaminski & Saladino, vol. 15, pp. 25, 27–28.

12.2.4.25 A Countryman, No. 5, December 20, 1787

The great power and influence of an hereditary monarch of Britain has spread many alarms, from an apprehension that the commons would sacrifice the liberties of the people to the money or influence of the crown: But the influence of a powerful *hereditary monarch*, with the national Treasury — Army — and fleet at his command — and the whole executive government — and one third of the legislative in his hands, — constantly operating on a house of commons, whose duration is never less than *seven years*, unless the same monarch should *end* it, (which he can do in an hour) has never yet been sufficient to obtain one vote of the house of commons which has taken from the people the *liberty of the press, — trial by jury, — the rights of conscience, or of private property*. — Can you then apprehend danger of oppression and tyranny from the too great duration of the power of *your* rulers.

New Haven Gazette, Kaminski & Saladino, vol. 15, p. 55.

12.2.4.26 Richard Henry Lee to Edmund Randolph, December 22, 1787

. . . The rights of conscience, the freedom of the press, and the trial by jury are at mercy. It is there stated that in criminal cases, the trial shall be by jury. But how?

In the state. What then becomes of the jury of the vicinage or at least from the county in the first instance, the states being from 50 to 700 miles in extent? This mode of trial even in criminal cases may be greatly impaired, and in civil cases the inference is strong, that it may be altogether omitted as the constitution positively assumes it in criminal, and is silent about it in civil causes. Nay it is more strongly discountenanced in civil cases by giving the supreme court in appeals, jurisdiction both as to law and fact.

Judge Blackstone in his learned commentaries (Art. Jury Trial) says, ["it] is the most transcendent privilege which any subject can enjoy or wish for, that he cannot be affected either in his property, his liberty, his person, but by the unanimous consent of twelve of his neighbors and equals. A constitution, that I may venture to affirm, has under providence, secured the just liberties of this nation for a long succession of ages. The impartial administration of justice, which secures both our persons and our properties, is the great end of civil society. But if that be entirely entrusted to the magistracy, a select body of men, and those generally selected by the prince, or such as enjoy the highest offices of the state, these decisions, in spite of their own natural integrity, will have frequently an involuntary bias towards those of their own rank and dignity. It is not to be expected from human nature, that the few should always be attentive to the good of the many.["] The learned judge further says, that ["]every tribunal selected for the decision of facts is a step towards establishing aristocracy; the most oppressive of all governments.["] The answer to these objections is, that the new legislature may provide remedies! but as they may, so they may not, and if they did, a succeeding assembly may repeal the provisions. The evil is found resting upon constitutional bottom, and the remedy upon the mutable ground of legislation, revocable at any annual meeting. It is the more unfortunate that this great security of human rights, the trial by jury, should be weakened in this system, as power is unnecessarily given in the second section of the third article, to call people from their own country in all cases of controversy about property between citizens of different states and foreigners, with citizens of the United States, to be tried in a distant court where the congress meets. For although inferior congressional courts may for the above parties be instituted in the different states, yet this is a matter altogether in the pleasure of the new legislature, so that if they please not to institute them, or if they do not regulate the right of appeal reasonably, the people will be exposed to endless oppression, and the necessity of submitting in multitudes of cases, to pay unjust demands, rather than follow suitors, through great expence, to far distant tribunals, and to be determined upon there, as it may be, without a jury. In this congressional legislature a bare majority of votes, can enact commercial laws, so that the representatives of the seven northern states, as they will have a majority, can by law create the most oppressive monopoly upon the five southern states, whose circumstances and productions are essentially different from theirs, although not a single man of these voters are the representatives of, or amenable to the people of the southern states. Can such a set of men be, with the least colour of truth, called a representative of those they make laws for? It is supposed that the policy of the northern states, will prevent such abuses.

Virginia Gazette, Storing, vol. 5, pp. 114–15.

12.2.4.27 The Federal Farmer, No. 6, December 25, 1787

Of rights, some are natural and unalienable, of which even the people cannot deprive individuals: Some are constitutional or fundamental; these cannot be altered or abolished by the ordinary laws; but the people, by express acts, may alter or abolish them — These, such as the trial by jury, the benefits of the writ of habeas corpus, &c. individuals claim under the solemn compacts of the people, as constitutions, or at least under laws so strengthened by long usage as not to be repealable by the ordinary legislature — and some are common or mere legal rights, that is, such as individuals claim under laws which the ordinary legislature may alter or abolish at pleasure.

. . .

The following, I think, will be allowed to be unalienable or fundamental rights in the United States: — . . . The people . . . are at all times intitled to the benefits of the writ of habeas corpus, the trial by jury in criminal and civil causes — They have a right, when charged, to a speedy trial in the vicinage; to be heard by themselves or counsel, not to be compelled to furnish evidence against themselves, to have witnesses face to face, and to confront their adversaries before the judge — No man is held to answer a crime charged upon him till it be substantially described to him. . . .

Storing, vol. 2, pp. 261–62.

12.2.4.28 America, December 31, 1787

. . . But you will say, that trial by jury, is an unalienable right, that ought not to be trusted with our rulers. Why not? If it is such a darling privilege, will not Congress be as fond of it, as their constituents? An elevation into that Council, does not render a man insensible to his privileges, nor place him beyond the necessity of securing them. A member of Congress is liable to all the operations of law, except during his attendance on public business; and should he consent to a law, annihilating any right whatever, he deprives himself, his family and estate, of the benefit resulting from that right, as well as his constituents. This circumstance alone, is a sufficient security.

But, why this outcry about juries? If the people esteem them so highly, why do they ever neglect them, and suffer the trial by them to go into disuse? In some States, *Courts of Admiralty* have no juries — nor Courts of Chancery at all. In the City-Courts of some States, juries are rarely or never called, altho' the parties may demand them; and one State, at least, has lately passed an act, empowering the parties to submit both *law* and *fact* to the Court. It is found, that the judgment of a Court, gives as much satisfaction, as the verdict of a jury, as the Court are as good judges of fact, as juries, and much better judges of law. I have no desire to abolish trials by jury, although the original design and excellence of them, is in many cases superseded. — While the people remain attached to this mode of deciding causes, I am confident, that no Congress can wrest the privilege from them.

[New York] Daily Advertiser, Kaminski & Saladino, vol. 15, p. 197.

12.2.4.29 A Countryman, December 1787–January 1788

There is another thing our Congress told the people of Canada, in their letter, and I believe they were in earnest, "That the trial by jury, was one of the best securities in the world, for the life, liberty and property of the people." — Now to be sure, I am very much of their opinion in this; for I would rather trust my life, liberty and property to a verdict of twelve of my honest neighbors, than to the opinion of any great man in the world, for great men are not always honest men, and they may be too proud, and not care to give themselves the trouble to enquire very narrowly into common people's disputes; and if an honest farmer should happen to say any thing against a great man, tho' it was ever so true, it would be in the power of the judge to punish him for it very severely — and I don't doubt, but what he would do it; but I am sure a good honest jury of his neighbors would never punish him for speaking the truth; I know it is said that truth is not to be spoken at all times, but the best of us may be guilty of little acts of imprudence, for which however, we should not be too severely handled: I find the writers disagree about this matter; the one says this right of trial by jury is taken away by the new constitution, and the other says it is not. — Now, as they differ, I have been trying to find out the truth myself, and, it appears to me middling clear, that if it is not absolutely taken away; yet that this new General Congress, that we read of, may take it away whenever they please — now, if it is so good a thing that it never ought to be taken away, I think we ought not to give them power to do it; for I can't see the reason of giving them power, which they never can make use of, without doing us a great deal of hurt: Now all parties may mean what is honest at present, but notwithstanding, there may be a time, when we have bad men to rule us, and I think it would be imprudent to give power, which every one allows there is no necessity for, and with which bad men, if so disposed, might do us a great deal of harm, and I am more confirmed in this belief, when I think of what the said Mr. Beccaria says about this desire, which has always prevailed in men of increasing their power. This is all I can say about the matter at present. . . .

New York Journal, Storing, vol. 6, p. 73

12.2.4.30 Agrippa, No. 10, January 1, 1788

. . . For a more concise view of my proposal, I have thrown it into the form of a resolve to be passed by the [Massachusetts] convention which is shortly to set in this town.

"Commonwealth of Massachusetts

Resolved. . . .

"XIV. The United States shall have power to regulate the intercou[r]se between these states and foreign dominions, under the following restrictions. . . . [T]he United S[t]ates shall have authority to constitute judicatories, whether supreme or subordinate, with power to try all piracies and felonies done on the high seas. . . . They shall also have authority to try all causes in which ambassadours shall be concerned. All these trials shall be by jury and in some sea-port town. . . .

Massachusettes Gazette, Storing, vol. 4, p. 89.

12.2.4.31 The Federal Farmer, No. 15, January 18, 1788

. . . By the same section [article 3, section 2 of the Constitution], the jury trial, in criminal causes, except in cases of impeachment, is established; but not in civil causes, and the whole state may be considered as the vicinage in cases of crimes. These clauses present to view the constitutional features of the federal judiciary: this has been called a monster by some of the opponents, and some, even of the able advocates, have confessed they do not comprehend it. For myself, I confess, I see some good things in it, and some very extraordinary ones. . . . [T]he legislature will have full power to form and arrange judicial courts in the federal cases enumerated, at pleasure, with these eight exceptions only. . . . 6. There must be a jury trial in criminal causes. 7. The trial of crimes must be in the state where committed — . . . .

. . .

[T]he supreme court shall have jurisdiction both as to law and fact. What is meant by court? Is the jury included in the term, or is it not? I conceive it is not included: and so do the members of the convention, I am very sure, understand it.

Storing, vol. 2, pp. 316–17, 319.

12.2.4.32 Curtiopolis, January 18, 1788

Fathers, Friends, Countrymen, Brethren and Fellow Citizens, The happiness and existence of America being now suspended upon your wise deliberations; three or four sly Aristocrats having lashed the public passions, like wild horses, to the car of Legislation, and driving us all in the midst of political clouds of error, into that ditch of despotism lately dug by the Convention: Such dismal circumstances have induced a private citizen to lay before you, in as concise a manner as possible, the objections that have been made, by the Pennsylvania Secession, Brutus, Cato, Cincinnatus, Farmer, An Officer, &c. &c. our best men.

. . .

26. It allows of other modes of trial besides that by jury, and of course this is *abolished:* such modes will be instituted under the direction of Congress, as will leave offenders, traitors, *malcontents,* or such of us as fall under the lash, *no chance at all.*

[New York] Daily Advertiser, Kaminski & Saladino, vol. 15, pp. 399–400, 402.

12.2.4.33 The Federalist, No. 41, January 19, 1788

Had no other enumeration or definition of the powers of the Congress been found in the Constitution than the general expressions just cited, the authors of the objection might have had some color for it; though it would have been difficult to find a reason for so awkward a form of describing an authority to legislate in all possible cases. A power to destroy the freedom of the press, the trial by jury, or even to regulate the course of descents, or the forms of conveyances, must be very singularly expressed by the terms "to raise money for the general welfare."

Kaminski & Saladino, vol. 15, p. 424.

12.2.4.34 The Federal Farmer, No. 16, January 20, 1788

The trial by jury in criminal as well as in civil causes, has long been considered as one of our fundamental rights, and has been repeatedly recognized and confirmed by most of the state conventions. But the constitution expressly establishes this trial in criminal, and wholly omits it in civil causes. The jury trial in criminal causes, and the benefit of the writ of habeas corpus, are already as effectually established as any of the fundamental or essential rights of the people in the United States. . . . [I]nstead of establishing it in criminal causes only; we ought to establish it generally; — instead of the clause of forty or fifty words relative to this subject, why not use the language that has always been used in this country, and say, "the people of the United States shall always be entitled to the trial by jury." This would shew the people still hold the right sacred, and enjoin it upon congress substantially to preserve the jury trial in all cases, according to the usage and custom of the country. I have observed before, that it is *the jury trial* we want; the little different appendages and modifications tacked to it in the different states, are no more than a drop in the ocean: the jury trial is a solid uniform feature in a free government; it is the substance we would save, not the little articles of form.

Security against expost [*sic*] facto laws, the trial by jury, and the benefits of the writs of habeas corpus, are but a part of those inestimable rights the people of the United States are entitled to, even in judicial proceedings, by the course of the common law. These may be secured in general words, as in New-York, the Western Territory, &c. by declaring the people of the United States shall always be entitled to judicial proceedings according to the course of the common law, as used and established in the said states. Perhaps it would be better to enumerate the particular essential rights the people are entitled to in these proceedings, as has been done in many of the states, and as has been done in England. . . . We certainly, in federal processes, might as well claim the benefits of the writ of habeas corpus, as to claim trial by a jury — the right to have council — to have witnesses face to face — to be secure against unreasonable search warrrants, &c. was the constitution silent as to the whole of them: — but the establishment of the former, will evince that we could not claim them without it; and the omission of the latter, implies they are relinquished, or deemed of no importance. These are rights and benefits individuals acquire by compact; they must claim them under compacts, or immemorial usage — it is doubtful, at least, whether they can be claimed under immemorial usage in this country; and it is, therefore, we generally claim them under compacts, as charters and constitutions.

Storing, vol. 2, pp. 326–28.

12.2.4.35 A Countryman, No. 5, January 22, 1788

. . . I could very easily imagine, that a gentleman of far less understanding than "Alexander Hamilton," is said to be, would have had modesty enough to wait for further authority, before he set his name to an instrument of such immense importance to the state which entrusted him, and honored him with its interests and commands.

What was this but setting the state and his colleagues at open defiance, and, tacitly, telling the legislature and them, "I want none of your instructions, advice, nor assistance. I better know than you or they what ought to be done, and how to do it. Yes, I know what will suit you all, much better than any body else in the state. I know, that trial by jury, of the vicinage, is a foolish custom, besides frequently embarrassing the judges, it often disappoints the lawyers, and therefore, as I may never have it in my power again, I will now contribute all I can to the abolition of it." If it be true, that actions may speak plainer than words, which, I believe, is a maxim pretty well established, must not the foregoing, or something like it, have been the language or ideas held by the gentleman?

New York Journal, Storing, vol. 6, pp. 61–62.

12.2.4.36 **Philadelphiensis, No. 8, January 23, 1788**

. . . But the matter now in debate has no relation to that: the men opposed to the new constitution have the same cause to defend, that the people of America had during the period of a seven years war. Who is he so base, that will peaceably submit to a government that will eventually destroy his sacred *rights and privileges*? The liberty of conscience, the liberty of the press, the liberty of trial by jury, &c. must lie at the mercy of a few despots — an infernal junto, that are for changing our *free republican government* into a tyrannical and absolute monarchy. These are what roused the sons of America to oppose Britain, and from the nature of things, they must have a similar effect now.

[Philadelphia] Freeman's Journal, Kaminski & Saladino, vol. 15, p. 461.

12.2.4.37 **Hampden, January 26, 1788**

Mr. Russell, . . . I am not contented with it [the proposed plan of government] as it now stands, my reasons are assigned: —

I am not satisfied with the provision for amendments, as it stands in that system, because the amendments I propose, are such as two thirds of the Senate will perhaps never agree to — the indictment by grand jury, and trial of fact by jury, is not so much set by in the southern States, as in the northern — the great men there, are too rich and important to serve on the juries, and the smaller are considered as not having consequence enough to try the others; in short, there can be no trial by peers there. . . .

. . .

THE AMENDMENTS PROPOSED.

. . .

5th. In the second clause of the same section, strike out the words, "Both as to law and fact," *and add to that clause these words* — Provided nevertheless, that all issues of fact shall be tried by a jury to be appointed according to standing laws made by Congress.

This will preserve the inestimable right of a trial by jury — This right is the democratical balance in the Judciary power; without it, in civil actions, no relief can be had against the High Officers of State, for abuse of private citizens; without this the English Constitution would be a tyranny — See Judge Blackstone"'s excellent Commentary on this privilege, in his third volume, page [section 23].

6th. In the last clause in the same section next after the word State, insert these words, In, or near the County.

This keeps up the idea of trial in the vicinity. See the Massachusetts declaration of rights on this point — Also, that of other States, &c.

Massachusetts Centinel, Storing, vol. 4, pp. 198–200.

12.2.4.38 Aristides, January 31, 1788

The institution of the trial by jury has been sanctified by the experience of ages. It has been recognised by the constitution of every state in the union. It is deemed the birthright of Americans; and it is imagined, that liberty cannot subsist without it. The proposed plan expressly adopts it, for the decision of all criminal accusations, except impeachment; and is silent with respect to the determination of facts in civil causes.

The inference, hence drawn by many, is not warranted by the premises. By recognising the jury trial in criminal cases, the constitution effectually provides, that it shall prevail, so long as the constitution itself shall remain unimpaired and unchanged. But, from the great variety of civil cases, arising under this plan of government, it would be unwise and impolitic to say ought [sic] about it, in regard to these. Is there not a great variety of cases, in which this trial is taken away in each of the states? Are there not many more cases, where it is denied in England? For the convention to ascertain in what cases it shall prevail, and in what others it may be expedient to prefer other modes, was impracticable. On this subject, a future congress is to decide; and I see no foundation under Heaven for the opinion, that congress will despise the known prejudices and inclination of their countrymen. A very ingenious writer of Philadelphia has mentioned the objections without deigning to refute that, which he conceives to have originated "in sheer malice." —

I proceed to attack the whole body of anti-federalists in their strong hold. The proposed constitution contains no *bill of rights.* Kaminski & Saladino, vol. 15, p. 536.

12.2.4.39 A Farmer, No. 2, February 1, 1788

My friends and fellow farmers, I intended here to have made an end, and left Alfredus, with all his impudence to return peaceably to his cell, where I sent him in the first paragraph — But when I came to read over his piece a second time couched in such language, it made me shudder to see how abusively he has treated our juries, the grand palladium of liberty. I will for your observation copy his sentiment, it appears to be written with blood. These are his words — "*What are the advantages of this* boasted Trial by Jury, *and on which side do they lie, not certainly on the side of justice, for one unprincipled juror, secured in the interest of the opposite party, will frequently divert her course, and in four cases out of five, when injustice is done, it is by the ignorance or knavery of the jury.*" — This is a bold stroke, my friends, and shows you at once the disposition of Mr. Alfredus, that he is no friend to your liberties. I shall make no further observation on this particular, but when a leisure hour offers, I will give him a further combing for his insolence to the juries. . . . New Hampshire Freeman's Oracle, Storing, vol. 4, p. 211.

12.2.4.40 Luther Martin, Genuine Information, No. 10, February 1, 1788

Thus, Sir, *jury trials*, which have ever been the *boast* of the English constitution, which have been by our several *State constitutions* so *cautiously secured* to us, — jury trials which have so long been considered the *surest barrier* against *arbitrary power*, and the *palladium* of *liberty*, — with the *loss* of *which* the *loss* of our *freedom* may be dated, are *taken away* by the proposed form of government, not *only* in a *great variety* of questions between *individual* and *individual*, but in *every case* whether *civil* or *criminal* arising *under the laws* of the United States or the *execution* of those laws. — It is *taken away* in *those very cases* where of *all others* it is *most essential for our liberty*, to have it *sacredly guarded* and *preserved* — in *every case* whether *civil* or *criminal*, between *government* and *its officers* on the one part and the *subject or citizen* on the other. — Nor was this the effect of inattention, nor did it arise from any real difficulty in establishing and securing jury trials by the proposed constitution, if the convention had wished so to do — But the *same reason* influenced *here* as in the case of the establishment of inferior courts; — as they could not trust *State judges*, so would they not confide in *State juries*. — They alleged that the general government and the State governments would always be at variance — that the citizens of the different States would enter into the views and interests of their respective States, and therefore ought not to be trusted in determining causes in which the general government was any way interested, without giving the general government an opportunity, if it disapproved the verdict of the jury, to appeal, and to have the *facts examined* into *again* and *decided upon* by *its own judges*, on whom it was thought a reliance might be had by the general government, they being appointed under its authority.

Maryland Gazette, Kaminski & Saladino, vol. 16, pp. 9–10.

12.2.4.41 Agrippa, No. 16, February 5, 1788

. . . If the new constitution means no more than the friends of it acknowledge, they certainly can have no objection to affixing a declaration of rights of states and of citizens, especially as a majority of the states have not yet voted upon it —

. . .

"14. In all those causes which are triable before the continental courts, the trial by jury shall be held sacred."

These at present appear to me the most important points to be guarded. . . .

Massachusetts Gazette, Storing, vol. 4, pp. 110, 112.

12.2.4.42 Philadelphiensis, No. 9, February 6, 1788

To such lengths have these bold conspirators carried their scheme of despotism, that your most sacred rights and privileges are surrendered at discretion. When government thinks proper, under the pretence of writing a libel, &c. it may imprison, inflict the most cruel and unusual punishment, seize property, carry on prosecutions, &c. and the unfortunate citizen has no *magna charta*, no *bill of rights*, to protect him; nay, the prosecution may be carried on in such a manner that even a *jury* will not be allowed him. . . .

[Philadelphia] Freeman's Journal, Kaminski & Saladino, vol. 16, p. 59.

12.2.4.43 An Old Whig, No. 8, February 6, 1788

First then, the general expectation seems to be that our future rulers will rectify all that is amiss. If a bill of rights is wanting, they will frame a bill of rights. If too much power is vested in them, they will not abuse it; nay, they will divest themselves of it. The very first thing they will do, will be to establish the liberties of the people by good and wholesome ordinances, on so solid a foundation as to baffle all future encroachments from themselves or their successors. Much good no doubt might be done in this way; if Congress should possess the most virtuous inclinations, yet there are some things which it will not be in their power to rectify. For instance; *the appellate jurisdiction as to law and fact,* which is given to the supreme court of the continent, and which annihilates the trial by jury in all civil causes, the Congress can only modify: — They cannot extinguish this power, so destructive of the principles of real liberty. It would not be by any means extravagant to say, that a new continental convention ought to be called, if it were only for the sake of preserving the sacred palladium — THE INESTIMABLE RIGHT OF TRIAL BY JURY.

. . .

. . . Again; how could the stripping people of the right of trial by jury conduce to the strength of the state? Do we find the government in England at all weakened by the people retaining the right of trial by jury? Far from it. Yet these things which merely tend to oppress the people, without conducing at all to the strength of the state, are the last which aristocratic rulers would consent to restore to the people; because they encrease the personal power and importance of the rulers. Judges, unincumbered by juries, have ever been found much better friends to government than to the people. Such judges will always be more desireable than juries to a self-created senate, upon the same principle that a large standing army, and the entire command of the militia and of the purse, is ever desireable to those who wish to enslave the people, and upon the same principle that a bill of rights is their aversion.

[Philadelphia] Independent Gazetteer, Kaminski & Saladino, vol. 16, pp. 53, 55.

12.2.4.44 Deliberator, February 20, 1788

9. Congress may, in their courts of judicature, abolish trial by a jury, in civil cases, altogether; and even in criminal cases, trial by a jury of the vicinage is not secured by the constitution — A crime committed at Fort-Pitt may be tried by a jury of the citizens of Philadelphia.

[Philadelphia] Freeman's Journal, Storing, vol. 3, p. 179.

12.2.4.45 Hugh Williamson, Speech, February 25, 1788

It seems to be generally admitted, that the system of Government which has been proposed by the late Convention, is well calculated to relieve us from many of the grievances under which we have been laboring. If I might express my particular sentiments on this subject, I should describe it as more free and more perfect than any form of government that ever has been adopted by any nation; but I would not say it has no faults. Imperfection is inseparable from every human device. Several objections were made to this system by two or three very respectable characters in the Convention, which have been the subject of much conversation; and other objections, by citizens of this State, have lately reached our ears. It is proper that you should consider of these objections. They are of two kinds; they respect the things that are in the system, and the things that are not in it. We are told that there . . . should also have been a Declaration of Rights. In the new system it is provided, that "*the Trial of all crimes,* except in cases of Impeachment," *shall be by Jury,* but this provision could not possibly be extended to all *Civil* cases. For it is well known that the Trial by Jury is not general and uniform throughout the United States, . . . hence it became necessary to submit the question to the General Legislature, who might accommodate their laws on this occasion to the desires and habits of the nation. Surely there is no prohibition in a case that is untouched.   [New York] Daily Advertiser, Kaminski & Saladino, vol. 16, p. 202.

12.2.4.46 The Impartial Examiner, No. 1, February 27 and March 5, 1788

I believe, it is acknowledged that the establishment of excises has been one of the greatest grievances, under which the English nation has labored for almost a century and an half. . . . If this branch of revenue takes place, all the consequent rigour of excise laws will necessarily be introduced in order to enforce a due collection. On any charges or offence in this instance you will see yourselves deprived of your boasted trial by jury. The much admired common law process will give way to some quick and summary mode, by which the unhappy defendant will find himself reduced, perhaps to ruin, in less time than a charge could be exhibited against him in the usual course. . . .

And what is that "appellate jurisdiction both as to law and fact," but an establishment, which may in effect operate as original jurisdiction? — Or what is an appeal to enquire into facts after a solemn adjudication in any court below, but a trial *de novo?* . . . Add to all, that this high prerogative court establishes no fundamental rule of proceeding, except that the trial by jury is allowed in some criminal cases. All other cases are left open — and subject "to such regulations as the Congress shall make." — Under these circumstances I beseech you all, as citizens of Virginia, to consider seriously whether you will not endanger the solemn trial by jury, which you have long revered, as a sacred barrier against injustice — which has been established by your ancestors many centuries ago, and transmitted to you, as one of the greatest bulwarks of civil liberty — which you have to this day maintained inviolate: — I beseech you, I say, as members of this commonwealth, to consider whether you will not be in danger of losing this inestimable mode of trial in all those cases, wherein the constitution does not provide for its security. Nay, does not that very provision, which is made, by being confined to a few particular cases, almost imply a total exclusion of the rest? Let it, then, be a reflection deeply impressed on your minds — that if this noble privilege, which by long experience has been found the most exquisite method of determining controversies according to the scale of equal liberty, should once be taken away, it is unknown what new species of trial may be substituted in its room. Perhaps you may be surprised with some strange piece of judicial polity, — some arbitrary method, perhaps confining all trials to the entire decision of the magistracy, and totally excluding the great body of the people from any share in the administration of public justice.

. . . For instance, if Congress should pass a law that persons charged with capital crimes shall not have a *right to demand the cause or nature of the accusation*, shall not be *confronted with the accusers or witnesses, or call for evidence in their favor*; and a question should arise respecting their authority therein, — can it be said that they have exceeded the limits of their jurisdiction, when *that* has no limits; when no provision has been made for such a right?

Virginia Independent Chronicle, Storing, vol. 5, pp. 181–83, 185.

12.2.4.47 Brutus, No. 14, February 28, 1788

I believe it is a new and unusual thing to allow appeals in criminal matters. It is contrary to the sense of our laws, and dangerous to the lives and liberties of the citizen. As our law now stands, a person charged with a crime has a right to a fair and impartial trial by a jury of his country, and their verdict is final. If he is acquitted no other court can call upon him to answer for the same crime. But by this system, a man may have had ever so fair a trial, have been acquitted by ever so respectable a jury of his country; and still the officer of the government who prosecutes, may appeal to the supreme court. The whole matter may have a second hearing. By this means, persons who may have disobliged those who execute the general government, may be subjected to intolerable oppression. They may be kept in long and ruinous confinement, and exposed to heavy and insupportable charges, to procure the attendance of witnesses, and provide the means of their defence, at a great distance from their places of residence.

I can scarcely believe there can be a considerate citizen of the United States, that will approve of this appellate jurisdiction, as extending to criminal cases, if they will give themselves time for reflection.

New York Journal, Storing, vol. 2, p. 432.

12.2.4.48 The Landholder, No. 10, February 29, 1788

To the Honourable LUTHER MARTIN, Esq;

. . . Since the publication of the Constitution, every topic of vulgar declamation has been employed to persuade the people, that it will destroy the *trial by jury*, and is defective for being without a *bill of rights*. You, Sir, had more candour in the Convention than we can allow to those declaimers out of it; there you never signified by any motion or expression whatever, that it stood in need of a bill of rights, or in anywise endangered the trial by jury. In these respects the Constitution met your entire approbation: for had you believed it defective in these essentials, you ought to have mentioned it in the Convention, or had you thought it wanted further guards, it was your *indispensable duty to have proposed them*. I hope to hear that the same candour that influenced you on this occasion, has induced you to obviate any improper impressions such publications may have excited in your constituents, when you had the honour to appear before the General Assembly.

Maryland Journal, Kaminski & Saladino, vol. 16, pp. 267–68.

12.2.4.49   Publicola, March 20, 1788

. . . The constitution of the respective states, and the rights of the people, are to remain as under the confederation, excepting such parts as interfere with the express powers given to Congress by the new constitution. All the clamour therefore, which has been raised about the trial by jury, and the liberty of the press, might have been spared, as altogether unfounded. To those who wish to trust themselves under separate state governments, which may, as they have hitherto done, disregard the recommendations and requisitions of the union, I would recommend an attentive perusal of history, and as they do not seem to place any dependance on the reasoning of their fellow citizens, learn to be wise from the experience of past ages. They will find that in all countries, a strict union among the people, has been the only means of preserving liberty. . . .

> State Gazette of North Carolina, Kaminski & Saladino,
> vol. 16, pp. 436–37.

12.2.4.50   A Farmer, No. 4, March 21, 1788

. . . But moreover does not *Aristedes,* and every lawyer, know that in the interpretation of all political as well as civil laws, this fundamental maxim must be observed, *That where there are two objects in contemplation of any legislature, the express adoption of one, is the total exclusion of the other;* and that the adoption of juries in civil *criminal* cases, in every legal interpretation, amounts to be an absolute rejection in *civil* cases: — If the right of establishing juries, by a *Congressional* law is admitted at all, it must be admitted, as an *inherent legislative right,* paramount to the constitution, as it is not derived from it, and then the power that can make, can by law unmake; so that referring this power to a source of authority *superior* to the act of government, would leave us without any juries at all (even in *criminal* cases) if Congress should so please; which position can never be the object of either friends or enemies to the system at present. — If it is defective, it is still bad policy to make it worse; but still in every view, we must reflect, that the establishment of trials by jury, belongs to *political,* not to *civil* legislation. It includes the right of organizing government, not of regulating the conduct of individuals, as the following enquiry will prove; we must never give an assembly the power of giving itself power.

As the worth and excellence of this mode of trial, preserved and handed down from generation to generation for near two thousand years, has drawn down the enthusiastic encomiums of the most enlightened lawyers and statesmen of every age; as it has taken deep root in the breast of every freeman, encompassed by the defences of affection and veneration, a repetition of its praises would be as tedious as useless: Some remarks however, still remain to be made, which will place this subject in a more important and conspicuous view.

The trial by jury, is the only remaining power which the Commons of England have retained in their own hands, of all that plentitude of authority and freedom, which rendered their northern progenitors irresistible in war, and flourishing in peace. — The usurpations of *the few,* gradually effected by artifice and force, have robbed *the many,* of that power which once formed the basis of those governments, so celebrated by mankind. — The government of Sparta, the form of which, it is said, has continued from the days of Lycurgus to our age, preserving its model amidst those overwheming tides of revolution and shipwrecks of governments, which Greece has sustained for near three thousand years; the same form of government among the Saxons and other Germans, consisting of King, Lords and Commons, applauded by Tacitus and Machiavelli, were thus distinguished from the present government of England — The power of the Commons resided with them, not in representatives but in the body of the people. — *De minoribus rebus, principes consultant; de majoribus omnes,* are either the words of Tacitus or Caesar. The administration of *ordinary* affairs was committed to the select men; but all important subjects were deliberated on by the whole body of the people. — Such was the constitution of Sparta, and of England, when Machiavelli gives them as a model, for there can be no doubt but that the *folk-motes* of the Saxons were not formed by representation — The venerable remembrance of which assemblies, hung long about the affections of Englishmen, and it was to restore them that they offered such frequent libations of their noblest blood; but the usurpations of *the few* have been unwearied and irresistible, and the trial by jury is all that now remains to *the many.*

The trial by jury is — *the democratic branch of the judiciary power* — more necessary than representatives in the legislature; for those usurpations, which silently undermine the spirit of liberty, under the sanction of law, are more dangerous than direct and open legislative attacks; in the one case the treason is never discovered until liberty, and with it the power of defence is lost; the other is an open summons to arms, and then if the people will not defend their rights, they do not deserve to enjoy them.

The *judiciary* power, has generally been considered as a *branch* of the *executive,* because these two powers, have been so frequently united; — but where united, there is no liberty. — In every *free* State, the judiciary is kept separate, independent, and considered as an intermediate power; — and it certainly partakes more of a *legislative,* than an *executive* nature — The sound definition which Delolme applied to one branch may be justly extended to the whole judiciary, — *That it is a subordinate legislation in most instances, supplying by analogy, and precedent in each particular case, the defects of general legislative acts,* — [W]ithout then the check of the *democratic branch* — *the jury,* to ascertain those facts, to which the judge is to apply the law, and even in many cases to determine the cause by a *general* verdict — the latitude of judicial power, combined with the various and uncertain nature of evidence, will render it impossible to convict a judge of corruption, and ascertain his guilt. — Remove the fear of punishment, give hopes of impunity, and vice and tyranny come scowling from their dark abodes in the human heart. — Destroy juries and every thing is prostrated to judges, who may easily disguise law, by suppressing and varying fact: — Whenever therefore the trial by juries has been abolished, the liberties of the people were soon lost — The judiciary power is immediately absorbed, or placed under the direction of the executive, as example teaches in most of the States of Europe. — So formidable an engine of power, defended only by the gown and the robe, is soon seized and engrossed by the power that wields the sword. — Thus we find the judiciary and executive branches united, or the *former* totally dependent on the *latter* in most of the governments in the world. — It is true, where the judges will put on the sword and wield it with success, they will subject both princes and legislature to their despotism, as was the case in the memorable usurpation of the Justizia of Arragon, where the judiciary erected themselves into a frightful tyranny.

Why then shall we risque this important check to judiciary usurpation, provided by the wisdom of antiquity? Why shall we rob the Commons of the only remaining power they have been able to preserve, for their personal exercise? Have they ever abused it? — I know it has and will be said — they have — that they are too ignorant — that they cannot distinguish between right and wrong — that decisions on property are submitted to chance; and that the last word, commonly determines the cause: — There is some truth in these allegations — but whence comes it — The Commons are much degraded in the powers of the mind: — They were deprived of the use of understanding, when they were robbed of the power of employing it. — Men no longer cultivate, what is no longer useful, — should every opportunity be taken away, of exercising their reason, you will reduce them to that state of mental baseness, in which they appear in nine-tenths of this globe — distinguished from brutes, only by form and the articulation of sound — *Give them power and they will find understanding to use it* — But taking juries with all their real and attributed defects, it is not better to submit a cause to an impartial tribunal, who would at least, as soon do you right as wrong — than for every man to become subservient to government and those in power? — Would any man oppose government, where his property would be wholly at the mercy and decision of those that govern? — We know the influence that property has over the minds of men — they will risque their lives rather than their property; and a government, where there is no trial by jury, has an unlimited command over every man who has any thing to loose. — It is by the attacks on private property through the judiciary, that despotism becomes as irresistible as terrible. I could relate numerous examples of the greatest and best men in all countries, who have been driven to despair, by vexatious lawsuits, commenced at the instigation of the court, of favorites and of minions, and all *from the loss of juries.* — France was reduced to the brink of destruction in one instance. — The Queen mother Louise of Savoy, piqued at the constable of Bourbon, a young and amiable man, who refused to marry her, commenced a suit against him for all his estate — The judges were ready at the beck of the court, and without a shadow of justice deprived him by law of every shilling he was worth; and drove from this country an unfortunate hero, whose mad revenge carried desolation into her bosom. — In Denmark a despicable minion, who came in rags to the court, after the establishment of their new government, which they solicited Frederick the IIId to make for them, acquired an immense fortune by plunder, sheltered by the favour of the Sovereign. At last he fixed his eyes on a most delightful estate, and offered to buy it — The owner did not want money, and could not think of selling the patrimony of an ancient family; this wretch then spirited up law-suits against him, and after the most cruel vexations obliged him to sell the estate for much less than he at first offered him. This unfortunate gentleman was driven from the country which gave him birth, and a once happy society of relations and friends. — Such would have been the fate of England, from those courts without juries, which took cognizance of causes arising in the revenues and imports in Charles the first's time, the court fortunately for the liberties of England, seized the bull by the horns, when they attacked that wonderful man John Hampden. He spent 20,000 *l.* rather than pay an illegal tax of twenty shillings, brought the case before the Parliament, roused the spirit of the nation, and finally overturned courts, King, and even the constitution for many years. These dreadful examples may teach us the importance of juries in *civil* cases — they may recal [*sic*] to my countrymen a maxim which their ancestors, as wise, and more virtuous than their posterity, held ever in view — *That if the people creep like tortoises, they will still find themselves too fast in giving away power.*

[Baltimore] Maryland Gazette, Storing, vol. 5, pp. 37–40.

12.2.4.51 Luther Martin, Speech to Maryland General Assembly, March 30, 1788

[N]or is *trial by jury secured in criminal cases*; it is true, that in the first instance, in the inferior court the trial is to be by jury, in this and in this only, is the difference between criminal and civil cases; but, Sir, the *appellate jurisdiction extends,* as I have observed, to cases *criminal* as well as to civil, and on the *appeal* the *court* is to *decide not only* on the law but on the *fact*, if, therefore, *even in criminal* cases the general government is not satisfied with the verdict of the jury, its officer may remove the prosecution to the supreme court; and *there* the *verdict of the jury is to be of no effect,* but the *judges of this court* are to *decide upon the fact* as well as the law, the *same as in civil cases.*

Thus, Sir, *jury trials,* which have ever been the *boast* of the English constitution, which have been by our several *State constitutions* so *cautiously secured* to us — *jury trials* which have so long been considered the *surest barrier* against *arbitrary power,* and the *palladium* of *liberty,* — with the *loss* of *which* the *loss* of our *freedom* may be dated, are *taken away* by the proposed form of government, not *only* in a *great variety* of questions between *individual* and *individual,* but in *every case* whether *civil* or *criminal* arising *under the laws* of the United States, or the *execution* of those laws. — It is *taken away* in *those very cases* where of *all others* it is *most essential for our liberty,* to have it *sacredly guarded* and *preserved,* in *every case,* whether *civil* or *criminal,* between *government* and *its officers* on the one part, and the *subject* or *citizen* on the other. — Nor was this the effect of inattention, nor did it arise from any real difficulty in establishing and securing jury trials by the proposed constitution, if the convention had wished so to do: but the *same reason* influenced *here* as in the case of the establishment of inferior courts; as they could not trust *State Judges,* so would they not confide in *State juries.* — They alleged that the general government and the State governments would always be at variance; that the citizens of the different States would enter into the views and interests of their respective States, and therefore ought not to be trusted in determining causes in which the general government was any way interested, without giving the general government an opportunity, if it disapproved the verdict of the jury, to appeal, and to have the *facts examined into again* and *decided upon* by *its own judges,* on whom it was thought a reliance might be had by the general government, they being appointed under its authority.

Storing, vol. 2, pp. 70–71.

12.2.4.52 A Citizen of New-York, April 15, 1788

We are told, among other strange things, that the liberty of the press is left insecure by the proposed Constitution, and yet that Constitution says neither more nor less about it, than the Constitution of the State of New-York does. We are told that it deprives us of trial by jury, whereas the fact is, that it expresly [*sic*] secures it in certain cases, and takes it away in none — it is absurd to construe the silence of this, or of our own Constitution, relative to a great number of our rights, into a total extinction of them — silence and blank paper neither grant nor take away any thing. Complaints are also made that the proposed Constitution is not accompanied by a bill of rights; and yet they who make these complaints, know and are content that no bill of rights accompanied the Constitution of this State. In days and countries where Monarchs and their subjects were frequently disputing about prerogative and privileges, the latter often found it necessary, as it were to run out the line between them, and oblige the former to admit by solemn acts, called bills of rights, that certain enumerated rights belonged to the people, and were not comprehended in the royal prerogative. But thank God we have no such disputes — we have no Monarchs to contend with, or demand admissions from — the proposed Government is to be the government of the people — all its officers are to be their officers, and to exercise no rights but such as the people commit to them. The Constitution only serves to point out that part of the people's business, which they think proper by it to refer to the management of the persons therein designated — those persons are to receive that business to manage, not for themselves, and as their own, but as agents and overseers for the people to whom they are constantly responsible, and by whom only they are to be appointed.

Kaminski & Saladino, vol. 17, pp. 112–13.

12.2.4.53 Fabius, No. 4, April 19, 1788

It seems highly probable, that those who would reject this labour of public love, would also have rejected the Heaven-taught institution of *trial by jury,* had they been consulted upon its establishment. Would they not have cried out, that there never was framed so detestable, so paltry, and so tyrannical a device for extinguishing freedom, and throwing unbounded domination into the hands of the king and barons, under a contemptible pretence of preserving it? What! Can *freedom* be preserved by *imprisoning* its *guardians*? Can *freedom* be preserved, by keeping *twelve* men *closely confined* without *meat, drink, fire,* or *candle,* until they *unanimously agree,* and this to be infinitely repeated? Can *freedom* be preserved, by thus delivering up *a number of freemen* to a monarch and an aristocracy, fortified by dependant and obedient judges and officers, to be shut up, *until under duress they speak as they are ordered*? Why can't the twelve jurors *separate,* after hearing the evidence, return to their *respective homes,* and there *take time,* and *think* of the matter *at their ease*? Is there not *a variety of ways,* in which causes have been, and can be tried, without this tremendous, *unprecedented inquisition*? Why then is it insisted on; but because the fabricators of it *know* that it *will,* and *intend* that it *shall* reduce the people to slavery? Away with it — Freemen will never be enthralled by so insolent, so execrable, so pitiful a contrivance.

. . .

Trial by jury and the dependance of taxation upon representation, those corner stones of liberty, were not obtained by a *bill* of *rights,* or any other records, and have not been and cannot be preserved by them. They and all other rights must be preserved, by soundness of sense and honesty of heart. Compared with *these,* what are a bill of rights, or any characters drawn upon paper or parchment, those frail remembrances? Do we want to be reminded, that the sun enlightens, warms, invigorates, and cheers? or how horrid it would be, to have his blessed beams intercepted, by our being thrust into mines or dungeons? Liberty is the sun of freemen, and the beams are their rights.

. . . Trial by Jury is our birth-right; and tempted to his own ruin, by some seducing spirit, must be the man, who in opposition to the genius of United *America,* shall dare to attempt its subversion.

In the proposed confederation, it is preserved inviolable in criminal cases, and cannot be altered in other respects, but when United *America* demands it.

Pennsylvania Mercury, Kaminski & Saladino, vol. 17, p. 182–84.

12.2.4.54 Aristocrotis, April 1788

. . . Another privilege which the people possesses at present, and which the new congress will find it their interest to deprive them of, is trial by jury — for of all the powers which the people have wrested from government, this is the most absurd; it is even a gross violation of common sense, and most destructive to energy. In the first place it is absurd, that twelve ignorant plebians, should be constituted judges of a law, which passed through so many learned hands; — first a learned legislature after many learned animadversions and criticisms have enacted it — Second, learned writers have explained and commented on it. — Third, lawyers twisted, turned and new modeled it — and lastly, a learned judge opened up and explained it. Yet after all these learned discussions, an illiterate jury (who have scarce a right to think for themselves instead of judging for others) must determine whether it applies to the fact or not; and by their verdict the learned judge must be governed in passing sentence; and perhaps a learned gentleman be cast in an action with an insignificant cottager.

Secondly. Common sense recoils at the very idea of such a pernicious practice as this, because it makes no difference between the virtuous and the vicious, the precious and the vile; between those of noble birth, and illustrious descent, and those of base blood, and ignoble obscure pedigree — for an ignorant stupid jury, cannot discern the merit of persons — it is the merits of the cause they examine; which is just reversing the question, and beginning at the wrong end. Thirdly. This custom is fatal to energy, for tho' a law should be expressed in the most pointed terms, a jury may soften and mitigate, and in a great measure destroy the spirit of it. . . .

Storing, vol. 3, pp. 204–05.

12.2.4.55 Address of a Minority of the Maryland Convention, May 1, 1788

The great objects of these amendments were, 1st. To secure the trial by jury in all cases, the boasted birth-right of Englishmen, and their descendants, and the palladium of civil liberty; and to prevent the *appeal from fact,* which not only destroys that trial in civil cases, but by *construction*, may also elude it in criminal cases; a mode of proceeding both expensive and burthensome; and also by blending law with fact, will destroy all check on the judiciary authority, render it almost impossible to convict judges of corruption, and may lay the foundation of that gradual and silent attack on individuals, by which the approaches of tyranny become irresistable.   [Baltimore] Maryland Gazette, Kaminski & Saladino, vol. 17, p. 243.

12.2.4.56 The Federalist, No. 81, May 28, 1788

. . . To avoid all inconveniences, it will be safest to declare generally that the Supreme Court shall possess appellate jurisdiction both as to law and *fact*, and that this jurisdiction shall be subject to such *exceptions* and regulations as the national legislature may prescribe. This will enable the government to modify it in such a manner as will best answer the ends of public justice and security.

This view of the matter, at any rate puts it out of all doubt that the supposed abolition of the trial by jury by the operation of this provision is fallacious and untrue. The legislature of the United States would certainly have full power to provide that in appeals to the Supreme Court there should be no reexamination of facts where they had been tried in the original causes by juries. This would certainly be an authorised exception; but if for the reason already intimated it should be thought too extensive, it might be qualified with a limitation to such causes only as are determinable at common law in that mode of trial.

The amount of the observations hitherto made on the authority of the judicial department is this — . . . that this appellate jurisdiction does, in no case, *abolish* the trial by jury; and that an ordinary degree of prudence and integrity in the national councils will insure us solid advantages from the establishment of the proposed judiciary, without exposing us to any of the inconveniences which have been predicted from that source.   Kaminski & Saladino, vol. 18, p. 110.

12.2.4.57 The Federalist, No. 83, May 28, 1788

. . . The mere silence of the Constitution in regard to civil causes is represented as an abolition of the trial by jury, and the declamations to which it has afforded a pretext are artfully calculated to induce a persuasion that this pretended abolition is complete and universal, extending not only to every species of civil, but even to *criminal causes*. To argue with respect to the latter would be as vain and fruitless as to attempt the serious proof of the *existence* of *matter*, or to demonstrate any of those propositions which by their own internal evidence force conviction, when expressed in language adapted to convey their meaning.   Kaminski & Saladino, vol. 18, p. 115.

12.2.4.58 The Federalist, No. 84, May 28, 1788

[T]he Constitution proposed by the convention contains, as well as the constitution of this state, a number of such provisions [in favor of rights and privileges].

Independent of those which relate to the structure of the government, we find the following: . . . Article 3, section 2, clause 3 "The trial of all crimes, except in cases of impeachment, shall be by jury; and such trial shall be held in the State where the said crimes shall have been committed; but when not committed within any State, the trial shall be at such place or places as the Congress may by law have directed."

Kaminski & Saladino, vol. 18, p. 128.

12.2.4.59 A [New Hampshire] Farmer, No. 3, June 6, 1788

I shall now make some observations on the unjust and illiberal sarcasms, passed by Mr. Alfredus, on our jurors: — And, as he has such a peculiar nack of leaping over important things, by saying "they are nothing to the purpose," or by stigmatizing them, "as impertinent observations, groundless assertions," etc. I shall copy his own words, and then follow, with the sentiments of the Hon. Justice Blackstone, who is one of the most celebrated Authors now extant.

Sir, in your publication of Friday, January 18th, ult. you say, "What are the advantages of this boasted trial by jury, and on which side do they lie? *Not certainly on the side of justice,* for one unprincipled juror, secured in the interest of the opposite party, will frequently divert her course, and in four cases out of five where injustice is done, it is by *the ignorance or knavery of the jury."* This, I may venture to affirm, is an impudent and bold stroke; it attacks the whole community at once, and has a tendency to sap and undermine the best preservative of liberty, and therefore ought to be held in abhorrence by every freeman; it is totally repugnant to the sense of the best writers on the subject, and especially to the ideas of the renowned author above mentioned, whose sentiments I shall now quote, vol. 3, page 378. *"When the jury have delivered in their verdict, and it is recorded in court, that ends the trial by jury; a trial which besides the other vast advantages which we have occasionally observed in its progress, is also as expeditious and cheap as it is convenient, equitable and certain: upon these accounts — the trial by jury has been, as I trust ever will be looked upon as the glory of the English law; and if it has so great an advantage over individuals in regulating civil property, how much must that advantage be heightened, when it is applied* to criminal cases; *it is the most transcendant privilege which any subject can enjoy or wish for; he cannot be affected either in his property, his liberty or his person, but by the unanimous consent of twelve of his neighbors and equals; a Constitution that I may venture to affirm has, under Providence, secured the just liberties of the English nation for a long succession of ages; and therefore a celebrated French writer (Montesque) who concludes, that because Rome, Sparta, and Carthage have lost their liberties, therefore those of England in time must perish, should have recollected that Rome, Sparta and Carthage, at the time when their liberties were lost, were strangers to the trial by jury.*

Great as this eulogium may seem, it is no more than this admirable Constitution, when traced to its principles, will be found, in sober reason, to deserve. The impartial administration of justice, which secures both our persons and properties, is the great end of civil society; but if that be entirely entrusted to the magistracy of a select body of men, and those generally selected by the Prince, or those who enjoy the highest offices in the state, their decision, in spite of their own natural integrity, will have frequently an involuntary bias toward those of their own rank and dignity; here therefore, a competent number of sensible and upright jurymen, chosen by lot from among those of the middle rank, will be found the best investigators of truth, and the surest guardians of public justice; for the most powerful individual in the state, will be cautious of committing any flagrant invasion of another's right, when he knows that the fact of his oppression, must be examined, and decided by twelve indifferent men, not appointed till near the hour of trial: and that, when once the fact is ascertained, the law must of course redress it — This therefore preserves, in the hands of the people, that share which they ought to have, in the administration of public justice; and prevents the encroachments of the more powerful and wealthy citizens.

Every new tribunal erected for the decision of facts, without the intervention of a jury, whether composed of justices of the peace; commissioners of the revenue; judges of a court of conscience; or any other standing magistrate, is a step towards establishing aristocracy, the most oppressive of absolute government. It is, therefore, upon the whole, the duty which every man owes to his country, his friends, his posterity, and himself, to maintain to the utmost of his power, this valuable Constitution in all its rights, and above all to guard with the most jealous circumspection against the introduction of new, and arbitrary methods of trial, which, under a variety of plausible pretenses, may in time, imperceptibly undermine this best preservative of LIBERTY," — Added to this, there is a late law of this state, which puts the pay, and travel of our jurors upon a very respectable footing — And lest Mr. Alfredus should say, this is nothing to the purpose, because the trial, by jury, under the English Constitution, — may be very different from what it is in ours, I will just mention, wherein they differ, under the English Constitution, — The jurors are returned by the sheriff. — under ours they are draughted by lot, from each town, which, I think, is the most equitable method, and as to the modes of process through the trials, they are nearly the same, both endeavor to do justice to the parties. [New Hampshire] Freeman's Oracle and New Hampshire Advertiser, Storing, vol. 4, pp. 213–14.

12.2.4.60 Sydney, Address, June 13 & 14, 1788

By the 13th paragraph "no member of this State shall be disfranchised, or deprived of any of the rights or privileges secured to the subjects of the State by this constitution, unless by the law of the land, or judgment of its peers."

. . .

The 41st provides "that the trial by jury remain inviolate forever; that no acts of attainder shall be passed by the legislature of this State for crimes other than those committed before the termination of the present war. . . ."

There can be no doubt that if the new government be adopted in all its latitude, every one of these paragraphs will become a dead letter. . . .

New York Journal, Storing, vol. 6, p. 116.

12.2.5 LETTERS AND DIARIES

12.2.5.1 Thomas Jefferson to James Madison, December 20, 1787

. . . I will now add what I do not like. First the omission of a bill of rights providing clearly and without the aid of sophisms for . . . the eternal and unremitting force of the habeas corpus laws, and trials by jury in all matters of fact triable by the laws of the land and not by the law of Nations. To say, as Mr. Wilson does that a bill of rights was not necessary because all is reserved in the case of the general government which is not given, while in the particular ones all is given which is not reserved might do for the Audience to whom it was addressed, but is surely gratis dictum, opposed by strong inferences from the body of the instrument, as well as from the omission of the clause of our present confederation which had declared that in express terms. It was a hard conclusion to say because there has been no uniformity among the states as to the cases triable by jury, because some have been so incautious as to abandon this mode of trial, therefore the more prudent states shall be reduced to the same level of calamity. It would have been much more just and wise to have concluded the other way that as most of the states had judiciously preserved this palladium, those who had wandered should be brought back to it, and to have established general right instead of general wrong.

Boyd, vol. 12, p. 440.

12.2.5.2 Thomas Jefferson to Alexander Donald, February 7, 1788

I wish with all my soul that the nine first Conventions may accept the new Constitution, because this will secure to us the good it contains, which I think great and important. But I equally wish that the four latest conventions, whichever they be, may refuse to accede to it till a declaration of rights be annexed. . . . By a declaration of rights. . . . I mean one which shall stipulate . . . trials by juries in all cases. . . .

Boyd, vol. 12, p. 571.

12.2.5.3 Thomas Jefferson to C. W. F. Dumas, February 12, 1788

. . . With respect to the new government, 9. or 10. states will probably have accepted it by the end of this month. The others may oppose it. . . . Besides other objections of less moment, she [Virginia] will insist on annexing a bill of rights to the new constitution, i.e. a bill wherein the government shall declare that . . . 3. Trials by jury preserved in all cases.

Boyd, vol. 12, pp. 583–84.

12.2.5.4 George Washington to Marquis de Lafayette, April 28, 1788

. . . For example, there was not a member of the convention, I believe, who had the least objection to what is contended for by the Advocates for a *Bill of Rights* and *Tryal by Jury*. . . . [A]s to the second, it was only the difficulty of establishing a mode which should not interfere with the fixed modes of any of the States, that induced the Convention to leave it, as a matter of future adjustment.

Writings of George Washington, John C. Fitzpatrick, ed.
(Washington: G.P.O.), vol. 29, pp. 478–79.

12.2.5.5 James Madison to George Eve, January 2, 1789

[I]t is my sincere opinion that the Constitution ought to be revised, and that the first Congress meeting under it, ought to prepare and recommend to the States for ratification, the most satisfactory provisions for all essential rights, particularly the rights of Conscience in the fullest latitude, the freedom of the press, trials by jury, security against general warrants &c. Rutland & Hobson, vol. 11, p. 405.

12.2.5.6 Thomas Jefferson to Francis Hopkinson, March 13, 1789

. . . What I disapproved from the first moment also was the want of the bill of rights to guard liberty against the legislative as well as the executive branches of the government, that is to say to secure freedom in religion, freedom of the press, freedom from monopolies, freedom from unlawful imprisonment, freedom from a permanent military, and a trial by jury in all cases determinable by the laws of the land. Boyd, vol. 14, p. 650.

12.2.5.7 William R. Davie to James Madison, June 10, 1789

That farago of Amendments borrowed from Virginia is by no means to be considered as the sense of this Country; they were proposed amidst the violence and confusion of party heat, at a critical moment in our convention, and adopted by the opposition without one moment's consideration. I have collected with some attention the objections of the honest and serious . . . they also insist on the trial by jury being expressly secured to them in all cases. . . . Veit, p. 246.

12.2.5.8 Fisher Ames to Thomas Dwight, June 11, 1789

Mr. Madison has introduced his long expected Amendments. They are the fruit of much labour and research. He has hunted up all the grievances and complaints of newspapers — all the articles of Conventions — and the small talk of their debates. It contains a Bill of Rights — the right of enjoying property — of changing the govt. at pleasure — freedom of the press — of conscience — of juries — exemption from general Warrants gradual increase of representatives till the whole number at the rate of one to every 30,000 shall amount to   and allowing two to every State, at least this is the substance. There is too much of it — O. I had forgot the right of the people to bear Arms.

Risum teneatis amici —

Upon the whole, it may do good towards quieting men who attend to sounds only, and may get the mover some popularity — which he wishes. Veit, p. 247.

12.2.5.9 Abraham Baldwin to Joel Barlow, June 14, 1789

A few days since, Madison brought before us propositions of amendment agreeably to his promise to his constituents. . . . "That what is not given is reserved, that liberty of the press & trial by jury shall remain *inviolable*. . . . ["] Veit, p. 250.

12.2.5.10 Tench Coxe to James Madison, June 18, 1789

I observe you have brought forward the amendments you proposed to the federal Constitution. . . . Those who are honest are well pleased at the footing on which the press, liberty of conscience, original right and power, trial by jury &c. are rested.

Hobson & Rutland, vol. 12, p. 239.

12.2.5.11 Samuel Nasson to George Thatcher, July 9, 1789

I find that Ammendments are once again on the Carpet . . . anoather [*sic*] that I hope will be Established in the bill is tryals by Juryes in all Causes Excepting where the parties agree to be without. . . .

Veit, pp. 260–61.

12.2.5.12 Henry Gibbs to Roger Sherman, July 16, 1789

. . . All Ambiguity of Expression certainly ought to be remov'd; Liberty of Conscience in religious matters, right of trial by Jury, Liberty of the Press &c. may perhaps be more explicitly secur'd to the Subject & a general reservation made to the States respectively of all the powers not expressly delegated to the general Government.

Veit, p. 263.

12.2.5.13 Benjamin Goodhue to Samuel Phillips, September 13, 1789

. . . The Amendments have come from the Senate with amendments, such as striking out the word *vicinage* as applied to Jurors, and have struck out the limitations of sums for an appeal to the federal Court &c. Those two have been the darling objects with the Virginians who have been the great movers on amendments, and I am suspicious, it may mar the whole business, at least so far as to refer it to the next session.

Veit, p. 294.

12.2.5.14 James Madison to Edmund Pendleton, September 14, 1789

The Senate have sent back the plan of amendments with some alterations which strike in my opinion at the most salutary articles. In many of the States juries even in criminal cases are taken from the State at large — in others from districts of conside[rable] extent — in very few from the County alone. Hence a [dis]like to the restraint with respect to *vicinage*, which has produced a negative on that clause. . . . Several others have had a similar fate. The difficulty of uniting the minds of men accustomed to think and act differently can only be conceived by those who have witnessed it.

Hobson & Rutland, vol 12, pp. 402–03.

12.2.5.15 James Madison to Edmund Pendleton, September 23, 1789

The pressure of unfinished business has suspended the adjournment of Congs. till saturday next. Among the articles which required it was the plan of amendments, on which the two Houses so far disagreed as to require conferences. It will be impossible I find to prevail on the Senate to concur in the limitation on the *value* of appeals to the Supreme Court . . . They are equally inflexible in opposing a definition of the *locality* of Juries. The vicinage they contend is either too vague or too strict a term: too vague if depending on limits to be fixed by the pleasure of the law, too strict if limited to the County. It was proposed to insert after the word juries — 'with the accustomed requisites' — leaving the definition to be construed according to the judgment of professional men. Even this could not be obtained. The truth is that in most of the States the practice is different, and hence the irreconcilable difference of ideas on the subject. In some States, jurors are drawn from the whole body of the community indiscrim[in]ately; In others, from large districts comprehending a number of Counties; and in a few only from a single County. The Senate suppose also that the provision for vicinage in the Judiciary bill, will sufficiently quiet the fears which called for an amendment on this point. . . .

Hobson & Rutland, vol. 12, pp. 418–19.

12.3 DISCUSSION OF RIGHTS

12.3.1 TREATISES

12.3.1.1 William Blackstone, 1769

V. THE trial by jury, or the country, *per patriam,* is also that trial by the peers of every Englishman, which, as the grand bulwark of his liberties, is secured to him by the great charter, *"nullus liber homo capiatur, vel imprisonetur, aut exulet, aut aliquo alio modo destruatur, nisi per legale judicium parium suorum, vel per legem terrae."*

THE antiquity and excellence of this trial, for the settling of civil property, has before been explained at large. And it will hold much stronger in criminal cases; since, in times of difficulty and danger, more is to be apprehended from the violence and partiality of judges appointed by the crown, in suits between the king and the subject, than in disputes between one individual and another, to settle the metes and boundaries of private property. Our law has therefore wisely placed this strong and two-fold barrier, of a presentment and a trial by jury, between the liberties of the people, and the prerogative of the crown. It was necessary, for preserving the admirable ballance [*sic*] of our constitution, to vest the executive power of the laws in the prince: and yet this power might be dangerous and destructive to that very constitution, if exerted without check or control, by justices of *oyer* and *terminer* occasionally named by the crown; who might then, as in France or Turkey, imprison, dispatch, or exile any man that was obnoxious to the government, by an instant declaration, that such is their will and pleasure. But the founders of the English laws have with excellent forecast contrived, that no man should be called to answer to the king for any capital crime, unless upon the preparatory accusation of twelve or more of his fellow subjects, the grand jury: and that the truth of every accusation, whether preferred in the shape of indictment, information, or appeal, should afterwards be confirmed by the unanimous suffrage of twelve of his equals and neighbours, indifferently chosen, and superior to all suspicion. So that the liberties of England cannot but subsist, so long as this *palladium* remains sacred and inviolate, not only from all open attacks, (which none will be so hardy as to make) but also from all secret machinations, which may sap and undermine it; by introducing new and arbitrary methods of trial, by justices of the peace, commissioners of the revenue, and courts of conscience. And however *convenient* these may appear at first, (as doubtless all arbitrary powers, well executed, are the most *convenient*) yet let it be again remembered, that delays, and little inconveniences in the forms of justice, are the price that all free nations must pay for their liberty in more substantial matters; that these inroads upon this sacred bulwark of the nation are fundamentally opposite to the spirit of our constitution; and that, though begun in trifles, the precedent may gradually increase and spread, to the utter disuse of juries in questions of the most momentous concern.

WHAT was said of juries in general, and the trial thereby, in *civil* cases, will greatly shorten our present remarks, with regard to the trial of *criminal* suits; indictments, informations, and appeals: which trial I shall consider in the same method that I did the former; by following the order and course of the proceedings themselves, as the most clear and perspicuous way to treating it.

WHEN therefore a prisoner on this arraignment has pleaded *not guilty,* and for his trial hath put himself upon the country, which country the jury are, the sheriff of the county must return a panel of jurors, *liberos et legales homines, de vicineto;* that is, freeholders, without just exception, and of the *visne* or neighbourhood; which is interpreted to be of the county where the fact is committed. If the proceedings are before the court of king's bench, there is time allowed, between the arraignment and the trial, for a jury to be impanelled by writ of *venire facias* to the sheriff, as in civil causes: and the trial in case of a misdemesnor is had at *nisi prius,* unless it be of such consequence as to merit a trial at bar; which is always invariably had when the prisoner is tried for any capital offence. But, before commissioners of *oyer* and *terminer* and gaol delivery, the sheriff by virtue of a general precept directed to him beforehand, returns to the court a panel of forty eight jurors, to try all felons that may be called upon their trial at that session: and therefore it is there usual to try all felons immediately, or soon, after their arraignment. But it is not customary, nor agreeable to the general course of proceedings, unless by consent of parties, to try persons indicted of smaller misdemesnors at the same court in which they have pleaded *not guilty,* or *traversed* the indictment. But they usually give security to the court, to appear at the next assises or sessions, and then and there to try the traverse, giving notice to the prosecutor of the same.

IN cases of high treason, whereby corruption of blood may ensue, or misprision of such treason, it is enacted by statute 7 W. III. c. 3. First, that no person shall be tried for any such treason, except an attempt to assassinate the king, unless the indictment be found within three years after the offence committed: next, that the prisoner shall have a copy of the indictment, but not the names of the witnesses, five days at least before the trial; that is, upon the true construction of the act, before his arraignment; for then is his time to take any exceptions thereto, by way of pleas or demurrer: thirdly, that he shall also have a copy of the panel of jurors two days before his trial: and, lastly, that he shall have the same compulsive process to bring in his witnesses *for* him. And, by statute 7 Ann. c. 21. (which did not take place till after the decease of the late pretender) all persons, indicted for high treason or misprision thereof, shall have not only a copy of the indictment, but a list of all the witnesses to be produced, and of the jurors impanelled, with their professions and places of abode, delivered to him ten days before the trial, and in the presence of two witnesses; the better to prepare him to make his challenges and defence. But this last act, so far as it affected indictments for the inferior species of high treason, respecting the coin and the royal seals, is repealed by the statute 6 Geo. III. c. 53. Else it had been impossible to have tried those offences in the same circuit in which they are indicted: for ten clear days, between the finding and the trial of the indictment, will exceed the time usually allotted for any session of *oyer* and *terminer*. And no person indicted for felony is, or (as the law stands) ever can be, entitled to such copies, before the time of this trial.

WHEN the trial is called on, the jurors are to be sworn, as they appear, to the number of twelve, unless they are challenged by the party.

CHALLENGES may here be made, either on the part of the king, or on that of the prisoner; and either to the whole array, or to the separate polls, for the very same reasons that they may be made in civil causes. For it is here at least as necessary, as there, that the sheriff or returning officer be totally indifferent; that where an alien is indicted, the jury should be *de medietate*, or half foreigners; (which does not indeed hold in treasons, aliens being very improper judges of the breach of allegiance to the king) that on every panel there should be a competent number of hundredors; and that the particular jurors should be *omni exceptione majores*; not liable to objection either *propter honoris respectum, propter defectum, propter affectum*, or *propter delictum*.

CHALLENGES upon any of the foregoing accounts are stiled [*sic*] challenges *for cause;* which may be without stint in both criminal and civil trials. But in criminal cases, or at least in capital ones, there is, *in favorem vitæ*, allowed to the prisoner an arbitrary and capricious species of challenge to a certain number of jurors, without shewing any cause at all; which is called a *peremptory* challenge: a provision full of that tenderness and humanity to prisoners, for which our English laws are justly famous. This is grounded on two reasons. 1. As every one must be sensible, what sudden impressions and unaccountable prejudices we are apt to conceive upon the bare looks and gestures of another; and how necessary it is, that a prisoner (when put to defend his life) should have a good opinion of his jury, the want of which might totally disconcert him; the law wills not that he should be tried by any one man against whom he had conceived a prejudice, even without being able to assign a reason for such his dislike. 2. Because, upon challenges for cause shewn, if the reason assigned prove insufficient to set aside the juror, perhaps the bare questioning his indifference may sometimes provoke a resentment; to prevent all ill consequences from which, the prisoner is still at liberty, if he pleases, peremptorily to set him aside.

THIS privilege, of peremptory challenges, though granted to the prisoner, is denied to the king by the statute 33 Edw. I. st. 4. which enacts, that the king shall challenge no jurors without assigning a cause certain, to be tried and approved by the court. However it is held, that the king need not assign his cause of challenge, till all the panel is gone through, and unless there cannot be a full jury without the persons so challenged. And then, and not sooner, the king's counsel must shew the cause: otherwise the juror shall be sworn.

THE peremptory challenges of the prisoner must however have some reasonable boundary; otherwise he might never be tried. This reasonable boundary is settled by the common law to be the number of thirty five; that is, one under the number of three full juries. For the law judges that five and thirty are fully sufficient to allow the most timorous man to challenge through mere caprice; and that he who peremptorily challenges a greater number, or three full juries, has not intention to be tried at all. And therefore it dealt with one, who peremptorily challenges above thirty five, and will not retract his challenge, as with one who stands mute or refuses his trial; by sentencing him to the *peine forte et dure* in felony, and by attainting him in treason. And so the law stands at this day with regard to treason, of any kind.

But by statute 22 Hen. VIII. c. 14. (which, with regard to felonies, stands unrepealed by statute 1 & 2 Ph. & Mar. c. 10.) by this statute, I say, no person, arraigned for felony, can be admitted to make any more than *twenty* peremptory challenges. But how if the prisoner will peremptorily challenge twenty one? What shall be done? The old opinion was, that judgments of *peine forte et dure* should be given, as where he challenged thirty six at the common law: but the better opinion seems to be, that such challenge shall only be disregarded and overruled. Because, first, the common law doth not inflict the judgment of penance for challenging twenty one, neither doth the statute inflict it; and so heavy a judgment shall not be imposed by implication. Secondly, the words of the statute are, "that he be not *admitted* to challenge more than twenty;" the evident construction of which is, that any farther challenge shall be disallowed or prevented: and therefore, being null from the beginning, and never in fact a challenge, it can subject the prisoner to no punishment; but the juror shall be regularly sworn.

If, by reason of challenges or the default of the jurors, a sufficient number cannot be had of the original panel, a *tales* may be awarded as in civil causes, till the number of twelve is sworn, "well and truly to try, and true deliverance make, between our sovereign lord the king, and the prisoner whom they have in charge; and a true verdict to give, according to their evidence."

When the jury is sworn, if it be a cause of any consequence, the indictment is usually opened, and the evidence marshalled, examined, and enforced by the counsel for the crown, or prosecution. But it is a settled rule at common law, that no counsel shall be allowed a prisoner upon his trial, upon the general issue, in any capital crime, unless some point of law shall arise proper to be debated. A rule, which (however it may be palliated under cover of that noble declaration of the law, when rightly understood, that the judge shall be counsel for the prisoner; that is, shall see that the proccedings against him are legal and strictly regular) seems to be not at all of a piece with the rest of the humane treatment of prisoners by the English law. For upon what face of reason can that assistance be denied to save the life of a man, which yet is allowed him in prosecutions for every petty trespass? Nor indeed is it strictly speaking a part of our antient law: for the mirror, having observed the necessity of counsel in civil suits, "who know how to forward and defend the cause, by the rules of law and customs of the realm," immediately afterwards subjoins; "and more necessary are they for defence upon indictments and appeals of felony, than upon other venial causes." And, to say that truth, the judges themselves are so sensible of this defect in our modern practice, that they seldom scruple to allow a prisoner counsel to stand by him at the bar, and instruct him what questions to ask, or even to ask questions for him, and with respect to matters of fact: for as to matters of law, arising on the trial, they are *intitled* to the assistance of counsel. But still this is a matter of too much importance to be left to the good pleasure of any judge, and is worthy the interposition of the legislature; which has shewn it's [*sic*] inclination to indulge prisoners with this reasonable assistance, by enacting in statute 7W. III. c. 3. that persons *indicted* for such high treason, as works a corruption of the blood, or misprision thereof, may make their full defence by counsel, not exceeding two, to be named by the prisoner and assigned by the court or judge: and this indulgence, by statute 20 Geo. II. c. 30. is extended to parliamentary *impeachments* for high treason, which were excepted in the former act.

THE doctrine of evidence upon pleas of the crown is, in most respects, the same as that upon civil actions. There are however a few leading points, wherein, by several statutes and resolutions, a difference is made between civil and criminal evidence.

FIRST, in all cases of high treason, petit treason, and misprision of treason, by statutes 1 Edw. VI. c. 12. 5 &6 Edw. VI. c. 11. and 1 & 2 Ph. & Mar. c. 10. *two* lawful witnesses are required to convict a prisoner; except in cases of coining, and counterfeiting the seals; or unless the party shall willingly and without violence confess the same. By statute 7 W. III. c. 3. in prosecutions for those treasons to which that act extends, the same rule is again enforced, with this addition, that the confessions of the prisoner, which shall countervail the necessity of such proof, must be in open court; and it is declared that both witnesses must be to the same overt act of treason, or one to one overt act, and the other to another overt act of the same species of treason, and not of distinct heads or kinds: and no evidence shall be admitted to prove any overt act not expressly laid in the indictment. And therefore in sir John Fenwick's case, in king William's time, where there was but one witness, an act of parliament was made on purpose to attaint him of treason, and he was executed. But in almost every other accusation one positive witness is sufficient. Baron Montesquieu lays it down for a rule, that those laws which condemn a man to death *in any case* on the deposition of a single witness, are fatal to liberty: and he adds this reason, that the witness who affirms, and the accused who denies, makes an equal ballance; there is a necessity therefore to call in a third man to incline the scale. But this seems to be carrying matters too far: for there are some crimes, in which the very privacy of their nature excludes the possibility of having more than one witness: must these therefore escape unpunished? Neither indeed is the bare denial of the person accused equivalent to the positive oath of a disinterested witness. In cases of indictments for perjury, this doctrine is better founded; and there our law adopts it: for one witness is not allowed to convict a man indicted for perjury; because then there is only one oath against another. In cases of treason also there is the accused's oath of allegiance, to counterpoise the information of a single witness; and that may perhaps be one reason why the law requires a double testimony to convict him: though the principal reason, undoubtedly, is to secure the subject from being sacrificed to fictitious conspiracies, which have been the engines of profligate and crafty politicians in all ages.

SECONDLY, though from the reversal of colonel Sidney's attainder by act of parliament in 1689 it may be collected, that the mere similitude of hand-writing in two papers shewn to a jury, without other concurrent testimony, is no evidence that both were written by the same person; yet undoubtedly the testimony of witnesses, well acquainted with the party's hand, that they believe the paper in question to have been written by him, is evidence to be left to a jury.

THIRDLY, by the statute 21 Jac. I. c. 27. a mother of a bastard child, concealing it's death, must prove by one witness that the child was born dead; otherwise such concealment shall be evidence of her having murdered it.

FOURTHLY, all presumptive evidence of felony should be admitted cautiously: for the law holds, that it is better that ten guilty persons escape, than that one innocent suffer. And sir Matthew Hale in particular lays down two rules, most prudent and necessary to be observed: 1. Never to convict a man for stealing the goods of a person unknown, merely because he will give no account how he came by them, unless an actual felony be proved of such goods: and, 2. Never to convict any person of murder or manslaughter, till at least the body be found dead; on account of two instances he mentions, where persons were executed for the murder of others, who were then alive, but missing.

LASTLY, it was an antient [sic] and commonly received practice, (derived from the civil law, and which also to this day obtains in the kingdom of France) that, as counsel was not allowed to any prisoner accused of a capital crime, so neither should he be suffered to exculpate himself by the testimony of any witnesses. And therefore it deserves to be remembered, to the honour of Mary I, (whose early sentiments, till her marriage with Philip of Spain, seem to have been humane and generous) that when she appointed sir Richard Morgan chief justice of the common-pleas, she injoined him, "that notwithstanding the old error, which did not admit any witness to speak, or any other matter to be heard, in favour of the adversary, her majesty being party; her highness' pleasure was, that whatsoever could be brought in favour of the subject should be admitted to be heard: and moreover, that the justices should not persuade themselves to sit in judgment otherwise for her highness than for her subject." Afterwards, in one particular instance (when embezzling the queen's military stores was made felony by statute 31 Eliz. c. 4.) it was provided that any person, impeached for such felony, "should be received and admitted to make any lawful proof that he could, by lawful witness or otherwise, for his discharge and defence:" and in general the courts grew so heartily ashamed of a doctrine so unreasonable and oppressive, that a practice was gradually introduced of examining witnesses for the prisoner, but not upon oath: the consequence of which still was, that the jury gave less credit to the prisoner's evidence, than to that produced by the crown. Sir Edward Coke protests very strongly against this tyrannical practice: declaring that he never read in any act of parliament, book-case, or record, that in criminal cases the party accused should not have witnesses sworn for him; and therefore there was not so much as *scintilla juris* against it. And the house of commons were so sensible of this absurdity, that, in the bill for abolishing hostilities between England and Scotland, when felonies committed by Englishmen in Scotland were ordered to be tried in one of the three northern counties, they insisted on a clause, and carried it against the efforts of both the crown and the house of lords, against the practice of the courts in England, and the express law of Scotland, "that in all such trials, for the better discovery of the truth, and the better information of the consciences of the jury and justices, there shall be allowed to the party arraigned the benefit of such credible witnesses, to be examined upon oath, as can be produced for his clearing and justification." At length by the statute 7 W. III. c. 3. the same measure of justice was established throughout all the realm, in cases of treason within the act: and it was afterwards declared by statute 1 Ann. st. 2. c. 9. that in all cases of treason and felony, all witnesses *for* the prisoner should be examined upon oath, in like manner as the witnesses *against* him.

WHEN the evidence on both sides is closed, the jury cannot be discharged till they have given in their verdict; but are to consider of it, and deliver it in, with the same forms, as upon civil causes: only they cannot, in a criminal case, give a *privy* verdict. But an open verdict may be either general, guilty, or not guilty; of special, setting forth all the circumstances of the case, and praying the judgment of the court, whether, for instance, on the facts stated, it be murder, manslaughter, or no crime at all. This is where they *doubt* the matter of law, and therefore *chuse* to leave it to the determination of the court; though they have an unquestionable right of determining upon all the circumstances, and finding a general verdict, if they think proper so to hazard a breach of their oaths: and, if their verdict be notoriously wrong, they may be punished and the verdict set aside by attaint at the suit of the king; but not at the suit of the prisoner. But the practice, heretofore in use, of fining, inprisoning [*sic*], or otherwise punishing jurors, merely at the discretion of the court, for finding their verdict contrary to the direction of the judge, was arbitrary, unconstitutional and illegal: and is treated as such by sir Thomas Smith, two hundred years ago; who accounted "such doings to be very violent, tyrannical, and contrary to the liberty and custom of the realm of England." For, as sir Matthew Hale well observes, it would be a most unhappy case for the judge himself, if the prisoner's fate depended upon his directions: — unhappy also for the prisoner; for, if the judge's opinion must rule the verdict, the trial by jury would be useless. Yet in many instances, where contrary to evidence the jury have found the prisoner guilty, their verdict hath been mercifully set aside, and a new trial granted by the court of king's bench; for in such case, as hath been said, it cannot be set right by attaint. But there hath yet been no instance of granting a new trial, where the prisoner was *acquitted* upon the first.

IF the jury therefore find the prisoner not guilty, he is then for ever quit and discharged of the accusation; except he be appealed of felony within the time limited by law. But if the jury find him guilty, he is then said to be *convicted* of the crime whereof he stands indicted. Which conviction may accrue two ways; either by his confessing the offence and pleading guilty, or by his being found so by the verdict of this country.

WHEN the offender is thus convicted, there are two collateral circumstances that immediately arise. 1. On a conviction, in general, for any felony, the reasonable expenses of prosecution are by statute 25 Geo. II. c. 36. to be allowed to the prosecutor out of the county stock, if he petitions the judge for that purpose; and by statute 27 Geo. II. c. 3. poor persons, bound over to give evidence, are likewise entitled to be paid their charges, as well without conviction as with it. 2. On a conviction of larciny [*sic*] in particular, the prosecutor shall have restitution of his goods, by virtue of the statute 21 Hen. VIII. c. 11. For by the common law there was no restitution of goods upon an indictment, because it is at the suit of the king only; and therefore the party was enforced to bring an appeal of robbery, in order to have his goods again. But, it being considered that the party, prosecuting the offender by indictment, deserves to the full as much encouragement as he who prosecutes by appeal, this statute was made, which enacts, that if any person be convicted of larciny by the evidence of the party robbed, he shall have a full restitution of his money, goods, and chattels; or the value of them out of the offender's goods, if [he] has any, by a writ to be granted by the justices. And this writ of restitution shall reach the goods so stolen, notwithstanding the property of them is endeavoured to be altered by sale in market overt. And, though this may seem somewhat hard upon the buyer, yet the rule of law is that "*spoliatus debet, ante omnia, restitui;*" especially when he has used all the diligence in his power to convict the felon. And, since the case is reduced to this hard necessity, that either the owner or the buyer must suffer; the law prefers the right of the owner, who has done a meritorious act by pursuing a felon to condign punishment, to the right of the buyer, whose merit is only negative, that he has been guilty of no unfair transaction. Or else, secondly, without such writ of restitution, the party may peaceably retake his goods, wherever he happens to find them, unless a new property be fairly acquired therein. Or, lastly, if the felon be convicted and pardoned, or be allowed his clergy, the party robbed may bring his action of trover against him for his goods; and recover a satisfaction in damages. But such action lies not, before prosecution; for so felonies would be made up and healed: and also recaption is unlawful, if it be done with intention to smother or compound the larciny; it then becoming the heinous offence of theft-bote, as was mentioned in a former chapter.

IT is not uncommon, when a person is convicted of a misdemesnor, which principally and more immeediately affects some individual, as a battery, imprisonment, or the like, for the court to permit the defendant to *speak with the prosecutor,* before any judgment is pronounced; and, if the prosecutor declares himself satisfied, to inflict but a trivial punishment. This is done, to reimburse the prosecutor his expenses, and make him some private amends, without the trouble and circuity of a civil action. But it surely is a dangerous practice: and, though it may be intrusted [*sic*] to the prudence and discretion of the judges in the superior courts of record, it ought never to be allowed in local or inferior jurisdictions, such as the quarter-sessions; where prosecutions for assaults are by this means too frequently commenced, rather for private lucre than for the great ends of public justice. Above all, it should never be suffered, where the testimony of the prosecutor himself is necessary to convict the defendant: for by this means, the rules of evidence are intirely [*sic*] subverted; the prosecutor becomes in effect a plaintiff, and yet is suffered to bear witness for himself. Nay even a voluntary forgiveness, by the party injured, ought not in true policy to intercept the stroke of justice. "This," says an elegant writer, (who pleads with equal strength for the *certainty* as for the *lenity* of punishment) "may be an act of good-nature and humanity, but it is contrary to the good of the public. For, although a private citizen may dispense with satisfaction for his private injury, he cannot remove the necessity of public example. The right of punishing belongs not to any one individual in particular, but to the society in general, or the sovereign who represents that society: and a man may renounce his own portion of this right, but he cannot give up that of others."

Commentaries, bk. 4, ch. 27; vol. 4, pp. 342–57 (footnotes omitted).

12.3.2 CASELAW

12.3.2.1 Earl of Shaftesbury's Trial, 1681

[Then a Bill of High-Treason was offered against the Earl of Shaftesbury; and Sir Francis Withins moved, That the evidence might be heard in court.]

Foreman. My Lord Chief Justice, it is the opinion of the jury, that they ought to examine the witnesses in private, and it hath been the constant practice of our ancestors and predecessors to do it; and they insist upon it as their right to examine in private, because they are bound to keep the king's secrets, which they cannot do, if it be done in court.

[PEMBERTON,] L.C.J. Look ye, gentlemen of the jury, it may very probably be, that some late usage has brought you into this error, that it is your right, but it is not your right in truth. . . . What you say concerning keeping your counsels, that is quite of another nature, that is, your debates, and those things, there you shall be in private, for to consider of what you hear publicly. But certainly it is the best way, both for the king, and for you, that there should, in a case of this nature, be an open and plain examination of the witnesses, that all the world may see what they say.

Foreman. My lord, if your lordship pleases, I must beg your lordship's pardon, if I mistake in anything, it is contrary to the sense of what the jury apprehend. First, they apprehend that the very words of the oath doth bind them, it says, "That they shall keep the counsel's, and their own secrets:" Now, my lord, there can be no secret in public; the very intimation of that doth imply, that the examination should be secret; besides, my lord, I beg your lordship's pardon if we mistake, we do not understand any thing of law.

Mr. *Papillon* [a juror]. . . . If it be the ancient usage and custom of England, that hath never been altered from time to time, and hath continued so, we desire your lordship's opinion upon that; as we would not do any that may be prejudicial to the king, so we would not do the least that should be prejudicial to the liberties of the people; if it be the ancient custom of the kingdom to examine in private, then there is something may be very prejudicial to the king in this public examination; for sometimes in examining witnesses in private, there come to be discovered some persons guilty of treason, and misprision of treason, that were not known, nor thought on before. Then the jury sends down to the court, and gives them intimation, and these men are presently secured; whereas, my lord, in case they be examined in open court publicly, then presently there is intimation given and these men are gone away. Another thing that may be prejudicial to the king, is, that all the evidences here, will be foreknown before they come to the main trial upon issue by the petty jury; then if there be not a very great deal of care, these witnesses may be confronted by raising up witnesses to prejudice them, as in some cases it has been: Then besides, the jury do apprehend, that in private they are more free to examine things in particular, for the satisfying their own consciences, and that without favour or affection; and we hope we shall do our duty.

[PEMBERTON,] L.C.J. . . . [T]he king's counsel have examined whether he hath cause to accuse these persons, or not; and, gentlemen, they understand very well, that it will be no prejudice to the king to have the evidence heard openly in court; or else the king would never desire it.

Foreman. My lord, the gentlemen of the jury desire that it may be recorded, that we insisted upon it as our right; but if the court over-rule, we must submit to it.

Howell's State Trials, vol. 8, pp. 759, 771–74.

12.3.2.2 Respublica v. Shaffer, 1788

AFTER some conversation with the Grand Inquest, the Attorney General informed the court, that a list of eleven persons had been presented to him by the Foreman, with a request, that they might be qualified and sent to the jury, as witnesses upon a bill then depending before them. He stated that the list had been made out by the defendant's bail: that the persons named were intended to furnish testimony in favor of the party charged, upon facts with which the Inquest, of their own knowledge, were unacquainted; and he concluded with requesting, that the opinion of the court might be given upon this application. THE CHIEF JUSTICE, accordingly, addressed the Grand Jury to the following effect:

McKEAN, *Chief Justice.* — Were the proposed examination of witnesses, on the part of the Defendant, to be allowed, the long-established rules of law and justice would be at an end. It is a matter well known, and well understood, that by the laws of our country, every question which affects a man's life, reputation, or property, must be tried by *twelve* of his peers; and that their *unanimous* verdict is, alone, competent to determine the fact in issue. If, then, you undertake to inquire, not only upon what foundation the charge is made, but, likewise, upon what foundation it is denied, you will, in effect, usurp the jurisdiction of the Petit Jury, you will supersede the legal authority of the court, in judging of the competency and admissibility of witnesses, and, having thus undertaken to try the question, that question may be determined by a bare majority, or by a much greater number of your body, than the twelve peers prescribed by the law of the land. This point has, I believe, excited some doubts upon former occasions; but those doubts have never arisen in the mind of any lawyer, and they may easily be removed by a proper consideration of the subject. For, the bills, or presentments, found by a grand Jury, amount to nothing more than an official accusation, in order to put the party accused upon his trial; 'till the bill is returned, there is, therefore, no charge from which he can be required to exculpate himself; and we know that many persons, against whom bills were returned, have been afterwards acquitted by a verdict of their country. Here, then, is the just line of discrimination: It is the duty of the Grand-Jury to enquire into the nature and probable grounds of the charge; but it is the exclusive province of the Petit Jury, to hear and determine, with the assistance, and under the direction of the court, upon points of law, whether the Defendant is, or is not guilty, on the whole evidence, for, as well as against, him. —— You will therefore, readily perceive, that if you examine the witnesses on both sides, you do not confine your consideration to the probable grounds of charge, but engage completely in the trial of the cause; and your return must, consequently, be tantamount to a verdict of acquittal or condemnation. But this would involve us in another difficulty; for, by the law, it is declared, that no man shall be twice put in jeopardy for the same offence: and, yet, it is certain, that the enquiry now proposed by the Grand Jury, would necessarily introduce the oppression of a double trial. Nor is it merely upon maxims of law, but, I think, likewise, upon principles of humanity, that this innovation should be opposed. Considering the bill as an accusation grounded entirely upon the testimony in support of the prosecution, the Petit Jury receive no biass [*sic*] from the sanction which the indorsement of the Grand Jury has conferred upon it.—But, on the other hand, would it not, in some degree, prejudice the most upright mind against the Defendant, that on a full hearing of his defence, another tribunal had pronounced it insufficient? — which would then be the natural inference from every *true bill*. Upon the whole, the court is of opinion, that it would be improper and illegal to examine the witnesses, on behalf of the Defendant, while the charge against him lies before the Grand-Jury.

One of the Grand Inquest then observed to the court, that "there was a clause in the qualifications of the Jurors, upon which he, and some of his brethren, wished to hear the interpretation of the Judges—to wit—what is the legal acceptation of the words *"diligently to enquire?"* To this the CHIEF JUSTICE replied, that "the expression meant, *diligently to enquire* into the circumstances of the charge, the credibility of the witnesses who support it, and, from the whole, to judge whether the person accused ought to be put upon his trial. For, (he added), though it would be improper to determine the merits of the cause, it is incumbent upon the Grand Jury to satisfy their minds, by a *diligent enquiry,* that there is a probable ground for the accusation, before they give it their authority, and call upon the Defendant to make a public defence."

1 Dall. 236 (Pa. O. & T., 1788).

12.3.2.3 Holmes v. Comegys, 1789

. . . SHIPPEN, *President:* — It would be of very dangerous consequence, if it was established, that a commercial agent was not amenable as a witness in a Court of Justice, in a cause against his constituent. It is straining the matter of privilege too far. And, if the law makes him a witness, we are too fond of getting at the truth, to permit him to excuse himself from declaring it, because he conceives, that, in point of delicacy, it would be a breach of confidence.

1 Dall. 439 (Pa. C.P. 1789)

Chapter 13

AMENDMENT VII
CIVIL JURY TRIAL CLAUSES

13.1 TEXTS

13.1.1 DRAFTS IN FIRST CONGRESS

13.1.1.1 Proposal by Madison in House, June 8, 1789

13.1.1.1.a   Sixthly. That article 3d, section 2 [of the Constitution], be annexed to the end of clause 2d, these words to wit: but no appeal to such court shall be allowed where the value in controversy shall not amount to   dollars: nor shall any fact triable by jury, according to the course of common law, be otherwise re-examinable than may consist with the principles of common law.

Seventhly. That in article 3d, section 2 [of the Constitution], the third clause be struck out, and in its place be inserted the clauses following, to wit:

The trial of all crimes (except in cases of impeachments, and cases arising in the land or naval forces, or the militia when on actual service in time of war or public danger) shall be by an impartial jury of freeholders of the vicinage, with the requisite of unanimity for conviction, of the right of challenge, and other accustomed requisites; and in all crimes punishable with loss of life or member, presentment or indictment by a grand jury, shall be an essential preliminary, provided that in cases of crimes committed within any county which may be in possession of an enemy, or in which a general insurrection may prevail, the trial may by law be authorised in some other county of the same state, as near as may be to the seat of the offence.

In cases of crimes committed not within any county, the trial may by law be in such county as the laws shall have prescribed. In suits at common law, between man and man, the trial by jury, as one of the best securities to the rights of the people, ought to remain inviolate. Congressional Register, June 8, 1789, vol. 1, pp. 428–29.

13.1.1.1.b   *Sixthly.* That article 3d, section 2 [of the Constitution], be annexed to the end of clause 2d, these words, to wit: but no appeal to such court shall be allowed where the value in controversy shall not amount to   dollars: nor shall any fact triable by jury, according to the course of common law, be otherwise re-examinable than may consist with the principles of common law.

493

Seventhly. That in article 3d, section 2 [of the Constitution], the third clause be struck out, and in its place be inserted the clauses following, to wit:

The trial of all crimes (except in cases of impeachments, and cases arising in the land or naval forces, or the militia when on actual service in time of war, or public danger,) shall be by an impartial jury of freeholders of the vicinage, with the requisite of unanimity for conviction, of the right of challenge, and other accustomed requisites; and in all crimes punishable with loss of life or member, presentment or indictment by a grand jury, shall be an essential preliminary, provided that in cases of crimes committed within any county which may be in possession of an enemy, or in which a general insurrection may prevail, the trial may by law be authorised in some other county of the same state, as near as may be to the seat of the offence.

In cases of crimes committed not within any county, the trial may by law be in such county as the laws shall have prescribed. In suits at common law between man and man, the trial by jury as one of the best securities to the rights of the people, ought to remain inviolate.

Daily Advertiser, June 12, 1789, p. 2, col. 2.

13.1.1.1.c   *Sixth.* That article 3d, section 2 [of the Constitution], be annexed to the end of clause 2d, these words, to wit, But no appeal to such court shall be allowed where the value in controversy shall not amount to   dollars: nor shall any fact triable by jury, according to the course of common law, be otherwise re-examinable than may consist with the principles of common law.

Seventh. That in article 3d, section 1[2] [of the Constitution], the third clause be struck out, and in its place be inserted the clauses following, to wit,

The trial of all crimes (except in cases of impeachments, and cases arising in the land or naval forces, or the militia when on actual service in time of war, or public danger) shall be by an impartial jury of freeholders of the vicinage, with the requisite of unanimity for conviction, of the right of challenge, and other accustomed requisites; and in all crimes punishable with loss of life or member, presentment or indictment by a grand jury shall be an essential preliminary, provided that in cases of crimes committed within any county which may be in possession of an enemy, or in which a general insurrection may prevail, the trial may by law be authorised in some other county of the same state, as near as may be to the seat of the offence.

In cases of crimes committed not within any county, the trial may by law be in such county as the laws shall have prescribed. In suits at common law between man and man, the trial by jury, as one of the best securities to the rights of the people, ought to remain inviolate.

New-York Daily Gazette, June 13, 1789, p. 575, col. 4.

13.1.1.2 Proposal by Sherman to House Committee of Eleven, July 21–28, 1789

[Amendment] 9 In Suits at common law in courts acting under the authority of the united States, issues of fact Shall be tried by a Jury if either party, request it.

Madison Papers, DLC.

13.1.1.3 House Committee of Eleven Report, July 28, 1789

Art. 3, Sec. 2, add to the 2d Par. "But no appeal to such court shall be allowed, where the value in controversy shall not amount to one thousand dollars; nor shall any fact, triable by a Jury according to the course of the common law, be otherwise re-examinable than according to the rules of the common law."

Art. 3, Sec. 2 — Strike out the whole of the 3d paragraph, and insert — "In all criminal prosecutions the accused shall enjoy the right to a speedy and public trial, to be informed of the nature and cause of the accusation, to be confronted with the witnesses against him, to have compulsory process for obtaining witnesses in his favor, and to have the assistance of counsel for his defence."

"The trial of all crimes (except in cases of impeachment, and in cases arising in the land or naval forces, or in the militia, when in actual service, in time of war or public danger) shall be by an impartial jury of freeholders of the vicinage, with the requisite of unanimity for conviction, the right of challenge and other accustomed requisites; and no person shall be held to answer for a capital, or otherwise infamous crime, unless on a presentment or indictment by a Grand Jury; but if a crime be committed in a place in the possession of an enemy, or in which an insurrection may prevail, the indictment and trial may by law be authorized in some other place within the same State; and if it be committed in a place not within a State, the indictment and trial may be at such place or places as the law may have directed."

"In suits at common law the right of trial by jury shall be preserved."

Broadside Collection, DLC.

13.1.1.4 House Consideration, August 17, 1789

13.1.1.4.a   The 6th proposition, art. 3, sect. 2. add to the 2d paragraph "But no appeal to such court shall be allowed, where the value in controversy shall not amount to one thouusand dollars; nor shall any fact, triable by a jury according to the course of the common law, be otherwise re-examinable than according to the rules of common law."

Congressional Register, August 17, 1789, vol. 2, p. 227.

13.1.1.4.b   Thirteenth Amendment — Art. 3. Sec. 2, add to the 2d par. "But no appeal to such court shall be allowed, where the value in controversy shall not amount to one thousand dollars; nor shall any fact triable by a jury, according to the course of the common law, be otherwise re examinable than according to the rules of common law."

Daily Advertiser, August 18, 1789, col. 4.

13.1.1.4.c   Thirteenth Amendment — "Art. III. Sec. 2, add to the 2d par. "But no appeal to such court shall be allowed, where the value in controversy shall not amount to one thousand dollars; nor shall any fact triable by a jury, according to the course of the common law, be otherwise re examinable than according to the rules of common law."

New-York Daily Gazette, August 19, 1789, p. 802, col. 4.

13.1.1.4.d   13th Amendment. Art. 3. Sec. 2, add to the 2d par. "But no appeal to such court shall be allowed, where the value in controversy shall not amount to one thousand dollars; nor shall any fact triable by jury, according to the course of common law, be otherwise re-examinable than according to the rules of common law."

Gazette of the U.S., August 22, 1789, p. 249, col. 3.

13.1.1.5 Motion by Benson in House, August 17, 1789

13.1.1.5.a   Mr. BENSON
Moved to strike out the first part of the paragraph respecting the limitations of appeals, because the question in controversy might be an important one, though the action was not to the amount of a thousand dollars.

Congressional Register, August 17, 1789, vol. 2, p. 227
(no recording of disposition).

13.1.1.5.b   Mr. BENSON moved to strike out the first part of the paragraph, respecting the limitation of appeals.

Daily Advertiser, August 18, 1789, p. 2, col. 4
("This motion was negatived.").

13.1.1.5.c   Mr Benson moved to strike out the first part of the paragraph, respecting the limitation of appeals.

New-York Daily Gazette, August 18, 1789, p. 802, col. 4
("This motion was negatived.").

13.1.1.5.d   Mr. BENSON moved to strike out the first part of the paragraph, respecting the limitation of appeals.

Gazette of the U.S., August 22, 1789, p. 249, col. 3,
and p. 250, col. 1 ("The motion was negatived.").

13.1.1.6 Motion by Sedgwick in House, August 17, 1789

13.1.1.6.a   Mr. SEDGWICK
Moved to insert 3,000 dollars, in lieu of 1,000. . . .

Congressional Register, August 17, 1789, vol. 2, p. 228
("On the question, this motion was rejected, and the
proposition accepted in its original form.").

13.1.1.6.b   Mr. SEDGWICK moved to strike out the words "one thousand" and inset "three thousand."

Daily Advertiser, August 18, 1789,
p. 2, col. 4 ("Negatived.").

13.1.1.6.c   Mr. Sedgwick moved to strike out the words "one thousand" and insert "three thousand."

New-York Daily Gazette, August 19, 1789,
p. 802, col. 4 ("Negatived.").

13.1.1.6.d Mr. SEDGWICK, to strengthen the clause, moved to strike out 1,000 dollars, and to insert 3,000.

> Gazette of U.S., August 22, 1789, p. 250, col. 1
> ("This motion was seconded and supported by Mr. Livermore,
> but was negatived, and the amendment accepted.").[1]

13.1.1.7 Further House Consideration, August 21, 1789

Twelfth. No appeal to the supreme court of the United States shall be allowed, where the value in controversy shall not amount to one thousand dollars; nor shall any fact, triable by a jury according to the course of the common law, be otherwise re-examinable than according to the rules of common law.

. . .

Fifteenth. In suits at common law, the right of trial by jury shall be preserved.

> HJ, p. 108 ("read and debated . . . agreed to by the House,
> . . . two-thirds of the members present concurring").[2]

13.1.1.8 House Resolution, August 24, 1789

ARTICLE THE ELEVENTH.

No appeal to the Supreme Court of the United States, shall be allowed, where the value in controversy shall not amount to one thousand dollars, nor shall any fact, triable by a Jury according to the course of the common law, be otherwise re-examinable, than according to the rules of common law.

ARTICLE THE TWELFTH.

In suits at common law, the right of trial by Jury shall be preserved.

> House Pamphlet, RG 46, DNA.

13.1.1.9 Senate Consideration, August 25, 1789

13.1.1.9.a Article the eleventh

No appeal to the Supreme Court of the United States, shall be allowed, where the value in controversy shall not amount to one thousand dollars, nor shall any fact, triable by a jury according to the course of the common law, be otherwise re-examinable, than according to the rules of common law.

Article the twelfth

In suits at common law, the right of trial by jury shall be preserved.

> Rough SJ, p. 218.

---

[1]For the history of the criminal prosecution clauses, *see* 12.1.1.

[2]On August 22, 1789, the following motion was agreed to:

ORDERED, That it be referred to a committee of three, to prepare and report a proper arrangement of, and introduction to the articles of amendment to the Constitution of the United States, as agreed to by the House; and that Mr. Benson, Mr. Sherman, and Mr. Sedgwick be of the said committee.

> HJ, p. 112.

13.1.1.9.b   "Article the Eleventh.

"No appeal to the Supreme Court of the United States, shall be allowed, where the value in controversy shall not amount to one thousand dollars, nor shall any fact, triable by a Jury according to the course of the common law, be otherwise re-examinable, than according to the rules of common law.

"Article the Twelfth.

"In suits at common law, the right of trial by Jury shall be preserved.

Smooth SJ, p. 196.

13.1.1.9.c   "ARTICLE THE ELEVENTH.

"No appeal to the Supreme Court of the United States, shall be allowed, where the value in controversy shall not amount to one thousand dollars, nor shall any fact, triable by a Jury according to the course of the common law, be otherwise re-examinable, than according to the rules of common law.

"ARTICLE THE TWELFTH.

"In suits at common law, the right of trial by Jury shall be preserved.

Printed SJ, p. 105.

13.1.1.10   Further Senate Consideration, September 4, 1789

13.1.1.10.a   On Motion to insert in lieu of the eleventh article

"The supreme judicial federal Court, shall have no jurisdiction of causes between Citizens of different States, unless the matter in dispute whether it concerns the realty or personalty, be of value of three thousand dollars, at the least: Nor shall the federal judicial powers extend to any actions between Citizens of different States, where the matter in dispute, whether it concerns the realty or personalty is not of the value of fifteen hundred dollars, at the least — And no part, triable by a jury according to the course of the common law, shall be otherwise reexaminable, than according to the rules of common law."

Rough SJ, p. 249 ("It passed in the Negative.").

13.1.1.10.b   On motion, To insert in lieu of the eleventh Article —

"The Supreme Judicial Federal Court, shall have no jurisdiction of causes between Citizens of different States, unless the matter in dispute, whether it concerns the realty or personalty, be of value of three thousand dollars, at the least: Nor shall the Federal Judicial Powers extend to any actions between Citizens of different States, where the matter in dispute, whether it concerns the realty or personalty, is not of the value of fifteen hundred dollars, at the least — And no part, triable by a Jury according to the course of the common law, shall be otherwise re-examinable, than according to the rules of common law" —

Smooth SJ, p. 223 ("It passed in the Negative.").

13.1.1.10.c   On motion, To insert in lieu of the eleventh Article —

"The Supreme Judicial Federal Court, shall have no jurisdiction of causes between citizens of different States, unless the matter in dispute, whether it concerns the realty or personalty, be of value of three thousand dollars, at the least: Nor shall the Federal Judicial Powers extend to any actions between citizens of different States, where the matter in dispute, whether it concerns the realty or personalty is not of the value of fifteen hundred dollars, at the least — And no part, triable by a Jury according to the course of the common law, shall be otherwise reexaminable, than according to the rules of common law" —

Printed SJ, p. 119 ("It passed in the Negative.").

13.1.1.11 Further Senate Consideration, September 4, 1789

13.1.1.11.a   On Motion to adopt the eleventh Article amended to read as follows
"No fact, triable by a jury according to the course of common law, shall be otherwise reexaminable in any Court of the United States, than according to the rules of common law."

Rough SJ, p. 249 ("It passed in the affirmative.").

13.1.1.11.b   On motion, To adopt the eleventh Article amended to read as follows —
"No fact, triable by a Jury according to the course of common law, shall be otherwise re-examinable in any Court of the United States, than according to the rules of common law" —

Smooth SJ, p. 223 ("It passed in the affirmative.").

13.1.1.11.c   On motion, To adopt the eleventh Article amended to read as follows —
"No fact, triable by a Jury according to the course of common law, shall be otherwise re-examinable in any Court of the United States, than according to the rules of common law" —

Printed SJ, p. 119 ("It passed in the Affirmative.").

13.1.1.12 Further Senate Consideration, September 7, 1789

13.1.1.12.a   On Motion to adopt the twelfth Article of the Amendments, proposed by the House of Representatives, amended by the addition of these words to the Article, to wit: "Where the consideration exceeds twenty dollars,"

Rough SJ, p. 256 ("It passed in the affirmative.").

13.1.1.12.b   On motion, To adopt the twelfth Article of the Amendments, proposed by the House of Representatives, amended by the addition of these words to the Article, to wit: "Where the consideration exceeds twenty dollars,"

Smooth SJ, p. 228 ("It passed in the Affirmative.").

13.1.1.12.c   On motion, To adopt the twelfth Article of the Amendments, proposed by the House of Representatives, amended by the addition of these words to the Article, to wit: "Where the consideration exceeds twenty dollars,"

Printed SJ, p. 121 ("It passed in the Affirmative.").

13.1.1.13 Further Senate Consideration, September 9, 1789

13.1.1.13.a   On motion, To strike out the tenth and the eleventh Articles.

Rough SJ, p. 275 ("It passed in the affirmative.").

13.1.1.13.b   On motion, To strike out the tenth and the eleventh articles —
> Smooth SJ, p. 245 ("It passed in the affirmative.").

13.1.1.13.c   On motion, To strike out the tenth and the eleventh Articles —
> Printed SJ, p. 130 ("It passed in the Affirmative.").

13.1.1.14   Further Senate Consideration, September 9, 1789

13.1.1.14.a   On motion, To strike out of the twelfth article the word "twelfth," and insert "ninth."
> Rough SJ, p. 275 ("It passed in the affirmative.").

13.1.1.14.b   On motion, To strike out of the twelfth article the word "Twelfth," and insert "ninth" —
> Smooth SJ, p. 245 ("It passed in the Affirmative.").

13.1.1.14.c   On motion, To strike out of the twelfth Article the word "Twelfth," and insert ninth —
> Printed SJ, p. 130 ("It passed in the Affirmative.").

13.1.1.15   Further Senate Consideration, September 9, 1789

13.1.1.15.a   And on motion to amend this article to read as follows:
"In suits at common law where the value in controversy shall exceed twenty dollars the right of trial by Jury shall be preserved, and no fact tried by a Jury, shall be otherwise reexamined in any Court of the United States, than according to the rules of the common law."
> Rough SJ, p. 276 ("It passed in the affirmative.").

13.1.1.15.b   And on motion, To amend this article, to read as follows:
"In suits at common law, where the value in controversy shall exceed twenty dollars, the right of trial by Jury shall be preserved, and no fact tried by a Jury, shall be otherwise re-examined in any Court of the United States, than according to the rules of the common law" —
> Smooth SJ, p. 245 ("It passed in the Affirmative.").

13.1.1.15.c   And on motion, To amend this Article, to read as follows:
"In suits at common law, where the value in controversy shall exceed twenty dollars, the right of trial by Jury shall be preserved, and no fact tried by a Jury, shall be otherwise re-examined in any Court of the United States, than according to the rules of the common law" —
> Printed SJ, p. 130 ("It passed in the Affirmative.").

13.1.1.15.d   [Fifteenth Amendment] To erase the 10th. article, & the words "article the Tenth."
[Sixteenth Amendment] To erase the 11th. article & the words "Article the Eleventh."
[Seventeenth Amendment] To ~~insert~~ erase the word "twelfth" & insert — Ninth.

[Eighteenth Amendment] To insert in the twelfth article after the word "<u>law</u>,"

shall

where the value in controversy $\wedge$ <s>exceeds</s> twenty dollars — &

[Nineteenth Amendment] To insert at the end of the same article — <u>And no fact tried by a Jury shall be otherwise reexamined, in any court of the United States, than according to the rules of the common law.</u>

Ellsworth MS, RG 46, DNA.

13.1.1.16   Senate Resolution, September 9, 1789

ARTICLE THE NINTH.

In suits at common law, where the value in controversy shall exceed twenty dollars, the right of trial by Jury shall be preserved, and no fact, tried by a Jury, shall be otherwise re-examined in any court of the United States, than according to the rules of the common law.

Senate Pamphlet, RG 46, DNA.

13.1.1.17   Further House Consideration, September 21, 1789

RESOLVED, That this House doth agree to the second, fourth, eighth, twelfth, thirteenth, sixteenth, eighteenth, nineteenth, twenty-fifth, and twenty-sixth amendments, and doth disagree to the first, third, fifth, sixth, seventh, ninth, tenth, eleventh, fourteenth, fifteenth, seventeenth, twentieth, twenty-first, twenty-second, twenty-third, and twenty-fourth amendments proposed by the Senate to the said articles, two thirds of the members present concurring on each vote.

RESOLVED, That a conference be desired with the Senate on the subject matter of the amendments disagreed to, and that Mr. Madison, Mr. Sherman, and Mr. Vining, be appointed managers at the same on the part of this House.

HJ, p. 146.

13.1.1.18   Further Senate Consideration, September 21, 1789

13.1.1.18.a   A message from the House of Representatives —

Mr. Beckley, their Clerk, brought up a Resolve of the House of this date, to agree to the 2nd, 4th, 8th, 12th, 13th, 16th, 18th, 19th, 25th, and 26th Amendments proposed by the Senate, "To articles of Amendment to be proposed to the Legislatures of the several States, as Amendments to the Constitution of the United States," and to disagree to the 1st, 3d, 5th, 6th, 7th, 9th, 10th, 11th, 14th, 15th, 17th, 20th, 21st, 22d, 23d, and 24th amendments: Two thirds of the members present concurring on each vote: And "That a conference be desired with the Senate on the subject matter of the amendments disagreed to," and that Mr. Madison, Mr. Sherman, and Mr. Vining, be appointed managers of the same, on the part of the House of Representatives —

And he withdrew.

Smooth SJ, pp. 265–66.

13.1.1.18.b   A message from the House of Representatives —

Mr. Beckley, their Clerk, brought up a Resolve of the House of this date, to agree to the 2d, 4th, 8th, 12th, 13th, 16th, 18th, 19th, 25th, and 26th Amend-

501

ments proposed by the Senate, "To Articles of Amendment to be proposed to the Legislatures of the several States, as Amendments to the Constitution of the United States," and to disagree to the 1st, 3d, 5th, 6th, 7th, 9th, 10th, 11th, 14th, 15th, 17th, 20th, 21st, 22d, 23d, and 24th Amendments: Two thirds of the members present concurring on each vote: And "That a conference be desired with the Senate on the subject matter of the Amendments disagreed to," and that Mr. Madison, Mr. Sherman, and Mr. Vining, be appointed managers of the same, on the part of the House of Representatives —

And he withdrew.

Printed SJ, pp. 141–42.

13.1.1.19 Further Senate Consideration, September 21, 1789

13.1.1.19.a The Senate proceeded to consider the Message of the House of Representatives disagreeing to the Amendments made by the Senate "To Articles to be proposed to the Legislatures of the several States, as Amendments to the Constitution of the United States" And

RESOLVED, That the Senate do recede from their third Amendment, and do insist on all the others.

RESOLVED, That the Senate do concur with the House of Representatives in a conference on the subject matter of disagreement on the said Articles of Amendment, and that Mr. Ellsworth Mr. Carroll and Mr. Paterson be managers of the conference on the part of the Senate.

Smooth SJ, p. 267.

13.1.1.19.b The Senate proceeded to consider the message of the House of Representatives disagreeing to the Amendments made by the Senate "To Articles to be proposed to the Legislatures of the several States, as Amendments to the Constitution of the United States" — And

RESOLVED, That the Senate do recede from their third Amendment, and do insist on all the others.

RESOLVED, That the Senate do concur with the House of Representatives in a conference on the subject matter of disagreement on the said Articles of Amendment, and that Mr. Ellsworth, Mr. Carroll, and Mr. Paterson be managers of the conference on the part of the Senate.

Printed SJ, p. 142.

13.1.1.20 Conference Committee Report, September 24, 1789

[T]hat it will be proper for the House of Representatives to agree to the said Amendments proposed by the Senate, with an Amendment to their fifth Amendment, so that the third Article shall read as follows: "Congress shall make no Law respecting an establishment of Religion, or prohibiting the free exercise thereof; or abridging the freedom of Speech, or of the Press; or the right of the people peaceably to assemble and to petition the Government for a redress of grievances;" And with an Amendment to the fourteenth Amendment proposed by the Senate, so that the eighth Article, as numbered in the Amendments proposed by the Senate, shall read as follows "In all criminal prosecutions, the accused shall enjoy the right to a speedy & publick trial <u>by an impartial jury of the district wherein the crime shall have been committed, as the district shall have been previously ascertained by law</u>, and to be informed of the nature and cause of the accusation; to be confronted with the witnesses against him, and to have com-

pulsory process for obtaining witnesses ~~against him~~ in his favour, & ∧ have the assistance of counsel for his defence."

to

Conference MS, RG 46, DNA (Ellsworth's handwriting).

13.1.1.21   House Consideration of Conference Committee Report, September 24 [25], 1789

RESOLVED, That this House doth recede from their disagreement to the first, third, fifth, sixth, seventh, ninth, tenth, eleventh, fourteenth, fifteenth, seventeenth, twentieth, twenty-first, twenty-second, twenty-third, and twenty-fourth amendments, insisted on by the Senate: PROVIDED, That the two articles which by the amendments of the Senate are now proposed to be inserted as the third and eighth articles, shall be amended to read as followeth;

Article the third. "Congress shall make no law respecting an establishment of religion, or prohibiting the free exercise thereof; or abridging the freedom of speech, or of the press; or the right of the people peaceably to assemble, and to petition the government for a redress of grievances."

Article the eighth. "In all criminal prosecutions, the accused shall enjoy the right to a speedy and public trial by an impartial jury of the state and district wherein the crime shall have been committed, which district shall have been previously ascertained by law, and to be informed of the nature and cause of the accusation, to be confronted with the witnesses against him, to have compulsory process for obtaining witnesses in his favor, and to have the assistance of council for his defence."

HJ, p. 152 ("On the question, that the House do agree to the alteration
and amendment of the eighth article, in manner aforesaid, It was resolved
in the affirmative. Ayes 37 Noes 14").

13.1.1.22   Senate Consideration of Conference Committee Report, September 24, 1789

13.1.1.22.a   Mr. Ellsworth, on behalf of the managers of the conference on "articles to be proposed to the several States as Amendments to the Constitution of the United States," reported as follows:

That it will be proper for the House of Representatives to agree to the said amendments proposed by the Senate, with an Amendment to their fifth Amendment, so that the third Article shall read as follows: "Congress shall make no law respecting an establishment of <u>Religion</u>, or prohibiting the free exercise thereof; or abridging the freedom of Speech, or of the Press; or the right of the people peaceably to assemble and petition the Government for a redress of Grievances;" And with an Amendment to the fourteenth Amendment proposed by the Senate, so that the eighth article, as numbered in the Amendments proposed by the Senate, shall read as follows; "In all criminal prosecutions, the accused shall enjoy the right to a speedy and public trial by an impartial <u>Jury</u> of the district wherein the

<u>Crime</u> shall have been committed, as the district shall have been previously ascertained by law, and to be informed of the nature and cause of the accusation, to be confronted with the witnesses against him, and to have compulsory process for obtaining witnesses in his favor, and to have the assistance of Counsel for defence."

Smooth SJ, pp. 272–73

13.1.1.22.b   Mr. Ellsworth, on behalf of the managers of the conference on "Articles to be proposed to the several States as Amendments to the Constitution of the United States," reported as follows:

That it will be proper for the House of Representatives to agree to the said Amendments proposed by the Senate, with an Amendment to their fifth Amendment, so that the third Article shall read as follows: "Congress shall make no Law RESPECTING AN ESTABLISHMENT OF RELIGION, or prohibiting the free exercise thereof; or abridging the freedom of Speech, or of the Press; or the right of the People peaceably to assemble and petition the Government for a redress of Grievances;" And with an Amendment to the fourteenth Amendment proposed by the Senate, so that the eighth Article, as numbered in the Amendments proposed by the Senate, shall read as follows; "In all criminal prosecutions, the accused shall enjoy the right to a speedy and public trial BY AN IMPARTIAL JURY OF THE DISTRICT WHEREIN THE CRIME SHALL HAVE BEEN COMMITTED, AS THE DISTRICT SHALL HAVE BEEN PREVIOUSLY ASCERTAINED BY LAW, and to be informed of the nature and cause of the accusation, to be confronted with the witnesses against him, and to have compulsory process for obtaining witnesses in his favor, and to have the assistance of Counsel for defence."

Printed SJ, p. 145.

13.1.1.23   Further Senate Consideration of Conference Committee Report, September 24, 1789

13.1.1.23.a   A Message from the House of Representatives —

Mr. Beckley, their Clerk, brought up the Amendments to the "Articles to be proposed to the Legislatures of the several States, as Amendments to the Constitution of the United States;" and informed the Senate, that the House of Representatives had receded from their disagreement to the 1st, 3d, 5th, 6th, 7th, 9th, 10th, 11th, 14th, 15th, 17th, 20th, 21st, 22d, 23d, and 24th Amendments, insisted on by the Senate: Provided that the "Two Articles, which by the Amendments of the Senate are now proposed to be inserted as the third and eighth Articles," shall be amended to read as followeth:

Article the Third. "Congress shall make no Law respecting an establishment of Religion, or prohibiting the free exercise thereof; or abridging the freedom of Speech, or of the Press; or the right of the people peaceably to assemble, and petition the Government for a redress of Grievances."

Article the Eighth. "In all criminal prosecutions the accused shall enjoy the right to a speedy and public trial by an impartial Jury of the State and District, wherein the crime shall have been committed, which District shall have been previously ascertained by law, and to be informed of the nature and cause of the accusation, to be confronted with the witnesses against him, and to have compulsory process for obtaining witnesses in his favor, and to have the assistance of Counsel for his defence."

Smooth SJ, pp. 278–79.

13.1.1.23.b   A Message from the House of Representatives —

Mr. Beckley, their Clerk, brought up the Amendments to the "Articles to be proposed to the Legislatures of the several States, as Amendments to the Constitution of the United States;" and informed the Senate, that the House of Representatives had receded from their disagreement to the 1st, 3d, 5th, 6th, 7th, 9th, 10th, 11th, 14th, 15th, 17th, 20th, 21st, 22d, 23d, and 24th Amendments, insisted on by the Senate: Provided that the "Two Articles, which by the Amendments of the Senate are now proposed to be inserted as the third and eighth Articles," shall be amended to read as followeth:

Article the Third. "Congress shall make no Law respecting an establishment of Religion, or prohibiting the free exercise thereof; or abridging the freedom of Speech, or of the Press; or the right of the People peaceably to assemble, and petition the Government for a redress of Grievances."

Article the Eighth. "In all criminal prosecutions the accused shall enjoy the right to a speedy and public trial by an impartial Jury of the State and District, wherein the crime shall have been committed, which District shall have been previously ascertained by law, and to be informed of the nature and cause of the accusation, to be confronted with the witnesses against him, and to have compulsory process for obtaining witnesses in his favor, and to have the assistance of Counsel for his defence."

Printed SJ, p.148.

13.1.1.24   Further Senate Consideration of Conference Committee Report, September 25, 1789

13.1.1.24.a   The Senate proceeded to consider the Message from the House of Representatives of the 24th, with Amendments to the Amendments of the Senate, to "Articles to be proposed to the Legislatures of the several States, as Amendments to the Constitution of the United States" — And

RESOLVED, That the Senate do concur in the Amendments proposed by the House of Representatives, to the Amendments of the Senate. Smooth SJ, p. 283.

13.1.1.24.b   The Senate proceeded to consider the Message from the House of Representatives of the 24th, with Amendments to the Amendments of the Senate, to "Articles to be proposed to the Legislatures of the several States, as Amendments to the Constitution of the United States" — And

RESOLVED, That the Senate do concur in the Amendments proposed by the House of Representatives, to the Amendments of the Senate.

Printed SJ, pp. 150–51.

13.1.1.25   Agreed Resolution, September 25, 1789

13.1.1.25.a   Article the Ninth.

In suits at common law, where the value in controversy shall exceed twenty dollars, the right of trial by Jury shall be preserved, and no fact, tried by a Jury, shall be otherwise re-examined in any Court of the United States, than according to the rules of the common law.   Smooth SJ, Appendix, p. 294, DNA.

13.1.1.25.b   ARTICLE the NINTH.

In suits at common law, where the value in controversy shall exceed twenty dollars, the right of trial by Jury shall be preserved, and no fact, tried by a Jury, shall be otherwise re-examined in any court of the United States, than according to the rules of the common law.   Printed SJ, Appendix, p. 164.

13.1.1.26   Enrolled Resolution, September 28, 1789

Article the Ninth . . . In suits at common law, where the value in controversy shall exceed twenty dollars, the right of trial by jury shall be preserved, and no fact tried by a jury shall be otherwise re-examined in any Court of the United States, than according to the rules of the common law.   Enrolled Resolutions, RG 11, DNA.

13.1.1.27   Printed Versions

13.1.1.27.a   ART. VII. In suits at common law, where the value in controversy shall exceed twenty dollars, the right of trial by jury shall be preserved; and no fact tried by a jury shall be otherwise re-examined in any court of the United States than according to the rules of the common law.   Statutes at Large, vol. 1, p. 21.

13.1.1.27.b   ART. IX. In suits at common law, where the value in controversy shall exceed twenty dollars, the right of trial by jury shall be preserved; and no fact, tried by a jury, shall be otherwise re-examined in any court of the United States, than according to the rules of the common law.   Statutes at Large, vol. 1, p. 98.

13.1.2 PROPOSALS FROM THE STATE CONVENTIONS

13.1.2.1   Maryland Minority, April 26, 1788

3. That in all actions on debts or contracts, and in all other controversies respecting property, of which the inferior federal courts have jurisdiction, the trial of facts shall be by jury, if required by either party; and that it be expressly declared, that the state courts, in such cases, have a concurrent jurisdiction with the federal courts, with an appeal from either, only as to matter of law, to the supreme federal court, if the matter in dispute be of the value of — dollars.

4. That the inferior federal courts shall not have jurisdiction of less than — dollars; and there may be an appeal in all cases of revenue, as well to matter of fact as law, and congress may give the state courts jurisdiction of revenue cases, for such sums, and in such manner, as they may think proper.

5. That in all cases of trespasses within the body of a county, and within the inferior federal jurisdiction, the party injured shall be entitled to trial by jury in the state where the injury shall be committed; and that it be expressly declared, that the state courts, in such cases, shall have concurrent jurisdiction with the federal courts; and there shall be no appeal from either, except on matter of law; and that no person be exempt from such jurisdiction and trial but ambassadors and ministers privileged by the law of nations.

Maryland Gazette, May 1, 1788
(committee majority).

13.1.2.2 Massachusetts, February 6, 1788

Seventhly, The Supreme Judicial Federal Court shall have no jurisdiction of Causes between Citizens of different States unless the matter in dispute whether it concerns the realty or personalty be of the value of three thousand dollars at the least. nor [*sic*] shall the Federal Judicial Powers extend to any actions between Citizens of different States where the matter in dispute whether it concerns the Realty or personalty is not of the value of Fifteen hundred dollars at the least.

Eighthly, In civil actions between Citizens of different States every issue of fact arising in Actions at common law shall be tried by a Jury if the parties or either of them request it.

State Ratifications, RG 11, DNA.

13.1.2.3 New Hampshire, June 21, 1788

Seventhly All Common Law Cases between Citizens of different States shall be commenced in the Common Law-Courts of the respective States & no appeal shall be allowed to the Federal Court in such Cases unless the sum or value of the thing in Controversy amount to three Thousand Dollars —

Eighthly In Civil Actions between Citizens of different States every Issue of Fact arising in Actions at Common Law shall be Tryed by Jury, if the Parties, or either of them request it —

State Ratifications, RG 11, DNA.

13.1.2.4 New York, July 26, 1788

That the trial by Jury in the extent that it obtains by the Common Law of England is one of the greatest securities to the rights of a free People, and ought to remain inviolate.

State Ratifications, RG 11, DNA.

13.1.2.5 North Carolina, August 1, 1788

11th. That in controversies respecting property, and in suits between man and man, the ancient trial by jury is one of the greatest securities to the rights of the people, and ought to remain sacred and inviolable.

State Ratifications, RG 11, DNA.

13.1.2.6 Pennsylvania Minority, December 12, 1787

2. That in controversies respecting property, and in suits between man and man, trial by jury shall remain as heretofore, as well in the federal courts, as in those of the several states.

Pennsylvania Packet, December 18, 1787

13.1.2.7 Rhode Island, May 29, 1790

11th. That in controversies respecting property, and in suits between man and man the antient trial by jury, as hath been exercised by us and our ancestors, from the time whereof the memory of man is not to the contrary, is one of the greatest securities to the rights of the people, and ought to remain sacred and inviolate.

State Ratifications, RG 11, DNA.

13.1.2.8 Virginia, June 27, 1788

Eleventh. That in controversies respecting property, and in suits between man and man, the ancient trial by Jury is one of the greatest Securities to the rights of the people, and ought to remain sacred and inviolable.

State Ratifications, RG 11, DNA.

13.1.3 STATE CONSTITUTIONS AND LAWS; COLONIAL CHARTERS AND LAWS

13.1.3.1 Delaware: Declaration of Rights, 1776

SECT. 13. That trial by jury of facts where they arise is one of the greatest securities of the lives, liberties and estates of the people.

Delaware Laws, vol. 1, App., p. 81.

13.1.3.2 Georgia

13.1.3.2.a Constitution, 1777

LXI. Freedom of the press, and trial by jury, to remain inviolate *forever*.

Georgia Laws, p. 16.

13.1.3.2.b Constitution, 1789

ARTICLE IV.

. . .

Sect. 3. Freedom of the press, and trial by jury, shall remain inviolate.

Georgia Laws, p. 29.

13.1.3.3 Maryland: Declaration of Rights, 1776

3. That the inhabitants of Maryland are entitled to the common law of England, and the trial by jury, according to the course of that law, and to the benefit of such of the English statutes as existed at the time of their first emigration, and which by experience have been found applicable to their local and other circumstances, and of such others as have been since made in England or Great-Britain, and have been introduced, used, and practised by the courts of law or equity; and also to all acts of assembly in force on the first of June seventeen hundred and seventy-four, except such as may have since expired, or have been, or may be altered by acts of convention, or this declaration of rights; subject nevertheless to the revision of, and amendment or repeal by, the legislature of this state; and the inhabitants of Maryland are also entitled to all property derived to them from or under the

charter granted by his majesty Charles the first, to Caecilius Calvert, baron of Baltimore.

. . .

18. That the trial of facts where they arise, is one of the greatest securities of the lives, liberties, and estate of the people.   Maryland Laws, November 3, 1776.

13.1.3.4   Massachusetts

13.1.3.4.a   Body of Liberties, 1641

[26] Every man that findeth himselfe unfit to plead his owne cause in any Court shall have Libertie to imploy any man against whom the Court doth not except, to helpe him, Provided he give him noe fee or reward for his paines. This shall not exempt the partie him selfe from Answering such Questions in person as the Court shall thinke meete to demand of him.

. . .

[29] In all Actions at law it shall be the libertie of the plantife and defendant by mutual consent to choose whether they will be tryed by the Bench or by a Jurie, unlesse it be where the law upon just reason hath otherwise determined. The like libertie shall be granted to all persons in Criminall cases.

Massachusetts Colonial Laws, p. 39.

13.1.3.4.b   General Laws of New-Plimouth, 1671 [1636]

4. It is also Enacted, that no person in this Government shall be endamaged in respect of Life, Limb, Liberty, Good name or Estate, under colour of Law, or countenance of Authority, but by virtue or equity of some express law of the General Court of this Colony, the known Law of God, or the good and equitable Laws of our Nation suitable for us, being brought to Answer by due process thereof.

5. That all Trials, whether Capital, Criminal, or between Man and Man, be tried by Jury of Twelve good and lawful Men, according to the commendable custome of England; except the party or parties concerned, do refer it to the Bench, or some express Law doth refer it to their Judgement and Tryal, or the Tryal of some other Court where Jury is not, in which case any party aggrieved, may appeal, and shall have Tryal by a Jury.

And it shall be in the liberty of both Plaintiffe and Defendant or any Delinquent, that is to be tryed by a Jury, to chalenge any of the Jurors, and if the chalenge be found just and reasonable by the Bench, it shall be allowed him, and others without just exception shall be impannelled in their room; And if it be incase of Life and Death, the Prisoner shall have liberty to except against six or eight of the Jury, without giving any reason for his exception.   New-Plimouth Laws, p. 2.

13.1.3.4.c   Constitution, 1780

[Part I, Article] XV. In all controversies concerning property, and in suits between two or more persons, except in cases in which it has heretofore been otherways used and practised, the parties have a right to a trial by a jury; and this method of procedure shall be held sacred, unless in causes arising on the high seas, and such as relate to mariner's wages, the legislature shall thereafter find it necessary to alter it.

Massachusetts Perpetual Laws, p. 7.

13.1.3.5 New Hampshire: Constitution, 1784

[Part I, Article] XX. In all controversies concerning property, and in all suits between two or more persons, except in cases in which it has been heretofore otherwise used and practised, the parties have a right to a trial by jury; and this method of procedure shall be held sacred, unless in causes on the high seas, and such as relate to mariners wages, the legislature shall think it necessary hereafter to alter it.

New Hampshire Laws, p. 26.

13.1.3.6 New Jersey

13.1.3.6.a Concessions and Agreements of West New Jersey, 1676

Chapter XVII.

THAT no Proprietor, Freeholder or Inhabitant of the said Province of *West New-Jersey,* shall be deprived or condemned of Life, Limb, Liberty, Estate, Property or any ways hurt in his or their Privileges, Freedoms or Franchises, upon any account whatsoever, without a due Tryal, and Judgment passed by Twelve good and lawful Men of his Neighbourhood first had: And that in all Causes to be tryed, and in all Tryals, the Person or Persons, arrained may except against any of the said Neighbourhood, without any Reason rendered, (not exceeding Thirty five) and in case of any valid reason alledged, against every Person nominated for that Service.

Chapter XVIII.

AND that no Proprietor, Freeholder, Freedenison, or Inhabitant in the said Province, shall be attached, arrested, or imprisoned, for or by reason of a Debt, Duty, or other Thing whatsoever (Cases Felonious, Criminal and Treasonable excepted) before he or she have personal Summon, or Summons, left at his or her last dwelling Place, if in the said Province, by some legal authorized Officer, constituted and appointed for that Purpose, to appear in some Court of Judicature for the said Province, with a full and plain account of the Cause or Thing in demand, as also the Name or Names of the Person or Persons at whose suit, and the Court where he is to appear, and that he hath at least Fourteen Days Time to appear and answer the said suit, if he or she live or inhabit within Forty Miles *English* of the said Court, and if at a further distance, to have for every Twenty Miles, two Days more, for his and their appearance, and so proportionably for a larger distance of space.

That upon the Recording of the Summons, and non appearance of such Person and Persons, a Writ or attachment shall or may be issued out to arrest, or attach the Person or Persons of such defaulters, to cause his or their Appearance in such

Court, returnable at a Day certain, to answer the Penalty or Penalties, in such Suit or Suits; and if he or they shall be condemned by legal Tryal and Judgment, the Penalty or Penalties shall be paid and satisfied out of his or their real or personal Estate so condemned, or cause the Person or Persons so condemned, to lie in execution till Satisfaction of the Debt and Damages be made, PROVIDED ALWAYS, if such Person or Persons so condemned, shall pay and deliver such Estate, Goods and Chattles which he or any other Person hath for his or their use, and shall solemnly declare and aver, that he or they have not any further Estate, Goods, or Chattles wheresoever, to satisfy the Person or Persons, (at whose Suit, he or they are condemned) their respective Judgments, and shall also bring and produce three other Persons as compurgators, who are well known and of honest Reputation, and approved of by the Commissioners of that Division, where they dwell or inhabit, which shall in such open Court, likewise solemnly declare and aver, that they believe in their Consciences, such Person and Persons so condemned, have not werewith [*sic*] further to pay the said Condemnation or Condemnations, he or they shall be thence forthwith discharged from their said imprisonment, any Law or Custom to the contrary thereof, heretofore in the said Province, notwithstanding. And upon such Summons and Default of appearance, recorded as aforesaid, and such Person and Persons not appearing within Forty Days after, it shall and may be lawful for such Court of Judicature to proceed to tryal, of twelve lawful Men to Judgment, against such Defaulters, and issue forth Execution against his or their Estate, real and personal, to satisfy such Penalty or Penalties, to such Debt and Damages so Recorded, as far as it shall or may extend.

Chapter XIX.

THAT there shall be in every Court, three Justices or Commissioners, who shall sit with the twelve Men of the Neighbourhood, with them to hear all Causes, and to assist the said Twelve Men of the Neighbourhood in Case of Law; and that they the said Justices shall pronounce such Judgment as they shall receive from, and be directed by the said Twelve Men, in whom only the Judgment resides, and not otherwise.

And in Case of their neglect and refusal, that then one of the Twelve, by consent of the rest, pronounce their own Judgment as the Justices should have done.

And if any Judgment shall be past, in any Case Civil or Criminal, by any other Person or Persons, or any other way, then according to this Agreement and Appointment, it shall be held null and void, and such Person or Persons so presuming to give Judgment, shall be severely Fin'd, and upon complaint made to the General Assembly, by them be declared incapable of any Office or Trust within this Province.

Chapter XX.

THAT in all Matters and Causes, Civil and Criminal, Proof is to be made by the solemn and plain averment, of at least two honest and reputable Persons; and in Case that any Person or Persons shall bear false Witness, and bring in his or their Evidence, contrary to the Truth of the Matter as shall be made plainly to appear, that then every such Person or Persons, shall in Civil Causes, suffer the Penalty which would be due to the Person or Persons he or they bear Witness against. And in Case any Witness or Witnesses, on the behalf of any Person or Persons, Indicted in a Criminal Cause, shall be found to have born False Witness for Fear, Gain, Malice, or Favour, and thereby hinder the due Execution of the Law, and deprive the suffering Person or Persons of their due Satisfaction, that then and in all other Cases of false Evidence, such Person or Persons, shall be first severely Fined, and next that he or they shall forever be disabled from being admitted in evidence, or into any Publick Office, Employment, or Service within this Province.

Chapter XXI.

THAT all and every Person and Persons whatsoever, who shall prosecute or prefer any Indictment or Information against others for any personal Injuries, or Matter Criminal, or shall Prosecute for any other Criminal Cause, (Treason, Murther, and Felony, only excepted) shall and may be Master of his own Process, and have full Power to forgive and remit the Person or Persons offending against him or herself only, as well before as after Judgment, and Condemnation, and Pardon and Remit the Sentence, Fine, and Punishment of the Person or Persons Offending, be it personal or other whatsoever.

Chapter XXII.

THAT the Tryals of all Causes, Civil and Criminal, shall be heard and decided by the Virdict or Judgment of Twelve honest Men of the Neighbourhood, only to be summoned and presented by the Sheriff of that Division, or Propriety where the Fact or Trespass is committed; and that no Person or Persons shall be compelled to Fee any Attorney or Counciller to plead his Cause, but that all Persons have free Liberty to plead his own Cause, if he please: And that no Person nor Persons imprisoned upon any account whatsoever within this Province, shall be obliged to pay any Fees to the Officer or Officers of the said Prison, either when committed or discharged.

Chapter XXIII.

That in all publick Courts of Justice for Tryals of Causes, Civil or Criminal, any Person or Persons, Inhabitants of the said Province, may freely come into, and attend the said Courts, and hear and be present, at all or any such Tryals as shall be there had or passed, that Justice may not be done in a Corner nor in any covert manner, being intended and resolved, by the help of the Lord, and by these our Concessions and Fundamentals, that all and every Person and Persons Inhabiting the said Province, shall, as far as in us lies, be free from Oppression and Slavery.

New Jersey Grants, pp. 395–98.

13.1.3.6.b **Fundamental Constitutions for East New Jersey, 1683**

XIX. That no Person or Persons within the said Province shall be taken and imprisoned, or be devised of his Freehold, free Custom or Liberty, or be outlawed or exiled, or any other Way destroyed; nor shall they be condemn'd or Judgment pass'd upon them, but by lawful Judgment of their Peers: Neither shall Justice nor Right be bought or sold, defered or delayed, to any Person whatsoever: In order to which by the Laws of the Land, all Tryals shall be by twelve Men, and as near as it may be, Peers and Equals, and of the Neighbourhood, and Men without just Exception. In Cases of Life there shall be at first Twenty four returned by the Sherriff for a Grand Inquest, of whom twelve at least shall be to find the Complaint to be true; and then the Twelve Men or Peers to be likewise returned, shall have the final Judgment; but reasonable Challenges shall be always admitted against the Twelve Men, or any of them: But the Manner of returning Juries shall be thus, the Names of all the Freemen above five and Twenty Years of Age, within the District or Boroughs out of which the Jury is to be returned, shall be written on equal Pieces of Parchment and put into a Box, and then the Number of the Jury shall be drawn out by a Child under Ten Years of Age. And in all Courts Persons of all Perswasions may freely appear in their own Way, and according to their own Manner, and there personally plead their own Causes themselves, or if unable, by their Friends, no Person being allowed to take Money for pleading or advice in such Casas: [*sic*] And the first Process shall be the Exhibition of the Complaint in Court fourteen Days before the Tryal, and the Party complain'd against may be fitted for the same, he or she shall be summoned ten Days before, and a Copy of the Complaint delivered at their dwelling House: But before the Complaint of any Person be received, he shall solemnly declare in Court, that he believes in his Conscience his Cause is just. Moreover, every Man shall be first cited before the Court for the Place where he dwells, nor shall the Cause be brought before any other Court but by way of Appeal from Sentence of the first Court, for receiving of which Appeals, there shall be a Court consisting of eight Persons, and the Governor (protempore) President thereof, *(to wit)* four Proprietors and four Freemen, to be chosen out of the great Council in the following Manner, *viz.* the Names of Sixteen of the Proprietors shall be written on small pieces of Parchment and put into a Box, out of which by a Lad under Ten Years of Age, shall be drawn eight of them, the eight remaining in the Box shall choose four; and in like Manner shall be done for the choosing of four of the Freemen.   New Jersey Grants, pp. 163–64.

13.1.3.6.c   **Constitution, 1776**

XXII. THAT the Common Law of *England,* as well as so much of the Statute Law, as have been heretofore practised in this Colony, shall still remain in Force, until they shall be altered by a future Law of the Legislature, such Parts only excepted as are repugnant to the Rights and Privileges contained in this Charter; and that the inestimable Right of Trial by Jury shall remain confirmed, as a Part of the Law of this Colony, without Repeal for-ever.   New Jersey Acts, p. ix.

13.1.3.7   **New York**

13.1.3.7.a   **Act Declaring . . . Rights & Priviledges, 1691**

That no Free-man shall be taken or imprisoned, or be deprived of his Free-hold or Liberty, or free Customs, or Out-Lawed, or Exiled, or any other wayes destroyed; nor shall be passed upon, adjudged or condemned, but by the lawful Judgment of his *Peers,* and by the Laws of this Province.

Justice nor Right shall be neither Sold, Denyed or Delayed to any Person within this Province.

. . .

That no Man , of what Estate or Condition soever, shall be put out of his Lands, Tenements, nor taken, nor imprisoned, nor disinherited, nor banished, nor any ways destroyed or molested, without first being brought to answer by due course of Law.

New York Acts, p. 17.

13.1.3.7.b **Constitution, 1777**

XIII. And this Convention doth further, in the Name, and by the Authority of the good People of this State, ORDAIN, DETERMINE, AND DECLARE, That no Member of this State shall be disfranchised, or deprived of any of the Rights or Privileges secured to the Subjects of this State by this Constitution, unless by the Law of the Land, or the Judgment of his Peers.

. . .

XLI. And this Convention doth further ORDAIN, DETERMINE, AND DE-CLARE, in the Name and by the Authority of the good People of this State, That Trial by Jury, in all Cases in which it hath heretofore been used in the Colony of *New-York,* shall be established, and remain inviolate for ever. And that no Acts of Attainder shall be passed by the Legislature of this State, for Crimes other than those committed before the Termination of the present War; and that such Acts shall not work a Corruption of Blood. And further, that the Legislature of this State shall at no Time hereafter, Institute any new Court or Courts, but such as shall proceed according to the Course of the Common Law.

New York Laws, vol. 1, pp. 8, 14.

13.1.3.7.c **Bill of Rights, 1787**

Second, That no Citizen of this State shall be taken or imprisoned, or be dis-seised of his or her Freehold, or Liberties, or Free-Customs: or outlawed, or exiled, or condemned, or otherwise destroyed, but by lawful Judgment of his or her Peers, or by due Process of Law.

. . .

Fourth, That no Person shall be put to answer without Presentment before Justices, or Matter of Record, or due Process of Law, according to the Law of the Land; and if any Thing be done to the Contrary, it shall be void in Law, and holden for Error.

Fifth, That no Person, of what Estate or Condition soever, shall be taken, or imprisoned, or disinherited, or put to death, without being brought to answer by due Process of Law; and that no Person shall be put out of his or her Franchise or Freehold, or lose his or her Life or Limb, or Goods and Chattels, unless he or she be duly brought to answer, and be fore-judged of the same, by due Course of Law; and if any Thing be done contrary to the same, it shall be void in Law, and holden for none.

Sixth, That neither Justice nor Right shall be sold to any Person, nor denied, nor deferred; and that Writs and Process shall be granted freely and without Delay, to all Persons requiring the same; and nothing from henceforth shall be paid or taken for any Writ or Process, but the accustomed Fees for writing, and for the Seal of the same Writ or Process; and all Fines Duties and Impositions whatsoever, heretofore taken or demanded, under what Name or Description soever, for, or upon granting any Writs, Inquests, Commissions, or Process to Suitors in their Causes, shall be, and hereby are abolished.

Seventh, That no Citizens of this State shall be fined or amerced without reasonable Cause, and such Fine or Amerciament shall always be according to the Quantity of his or her Trespass or Offence, and saving to him or her his or her Contenement; *That is to say,* Every Freeholder saving his Freehold, a Merchant saving his Merchandize, and a Mechanic saving the Implements of his Trade.

New York Laws, vol. 2, pp. 1–2.

13.1.3.8 North Carolina

13.1.3.8.a Fundamental Constitutions of Carolina, 1669

69th. Every jury shall consist of twelve men; and it shall not be necessary they should all agree, but the verdict shall be according to the consent of the majority.

. . .

111th. No cause whether civil or criminal, of any freeman, shall be tried in any court of judicature, without a jury of his peers.

North Carolina State Records, pp. 145, 149.

13.1.3.8.b Declaration of Rights, 1776

Sect. XIV. That in all Controversies at Law respecting Property, the ancient Mode of Trial by Jury is one of the best Securities of the Rights of the People, and ought to remain sacred and inviolable.

North Carolina Laws, p. 275.

13.1.3.9 Pennsylvania

13.1.3.9.a Laws Agreed Upon in England, 1682

VIII. That all **Tryals** shall be by **Twelve Men,** and as near as may be, *Peers* or *Equals,* and of the *Neighbourhood,* and men without just Exception. In cases of *Life,* there shall be first **Twenty Four** returned by the Sheriff for a **Grand Inquest,** of whom *Twelve* at least shall find the Complaint to be true, and then the **Twelve Men** or *Peers,* to be likewise returned by the Sheriff, shall have the *final Judgment:* But reasonable *Challenges* shall be alwayes admitted against the said *Twelve Men,* or any of them.

Pennsylvania Frame, p. 8.

13.1.3.9.b Provincial Laws, 1700

19 Noe *Freeman* to be *Imprisoned,* or Disseized, Outlaw'd, or Exiled, or otherwise hurt; Tryed, or *Condemned,* but by the *Judgement* of his *Twelve* Equalls, or *Laws* of this *Province.*

Penn Abstract, p. 5.

13.1.3.9.c **Constitution, 1776**

CHAPTER I.
A DECLARATION of the RIGHTS of the Inhabitants of the State of Pennsylvania.

. . .

XI. That in controversies respecting property, and in suits between man and man, the parties have a right to trial by jury, which ought to be held sacred.

. . .

CHAPTER II.
PLAN *or* FRAME *of* GOVERNMENT.

. . .

SECT. 25. Trial shall be by jury as heretofore: And it is recommended to the legislature of this state, to provide by law against every corruption or partiality in the choice, return, or appointment of juries. Pennsylvania Acts, McKean, pp. x, xvii.

13.1.3.9.d **Constitution, 1790**

ARTICLE IX.

Sect. VI. That trial by jury shall be as heretofore, and the right thereof remain inviolate. Pennsylvania Acts, Dallas, p. xxxiv.

13.1.3.10 **Rhode Island: Code of Laws, 1647**

1. That no person, in this Colony, shall be taken or imprisoned, or be disseized of his lands or liberties, or be exiled, or any otherwise molested or destroyed, but by the lawful judgment of his peers, or by some known law, and according to the letter of it, ratified and confirmed by the major part of the General Assembly, lawfully met and orderly managed. Rhode Island Code, p. 12.

13.1.3.11 **South Carolina**

13.1.3.11.a **Fundamental Constitutions of Carolina, 1669**

69th. Every jury shall consist of twelve men; and it shall not be necessary they should all agree, but the verdict shall be according to the consent of the majority.

. . .

111th. No cause whether civil or criminal, of any freeman, shall be tried in any court of judicature, without a jury of his peers. North Carolina State Records, pp. 145, 149.

13.1.3.11.b **Constitution, 1778**

XLI. That no Freeman of this State be taken, or imprisoned, or desseized of his Freehold, Liberties or Privileges, or out-lawed, or exiled, or in any Manner destroyed, or deprived of his Life, Liberty, or Property, but by the Judgement of his Peers, or by the Law of the Land. South Carolina Constitution, p. 15.

13.1.3.11.c **Constitution, 1790**

ARTICLE IX.

. . .

Section 2. No freeman of this state shall be taken, or imprisoned, or disseised of his freehold, liberties, or privileges, or outlawed or exiled, or in any manner destroyed, or deprived of his life, liberty or property, but by the judgment of his peers, or by the law of the land; nor shall any bill or the attainder, ex post facto law or law impairing the obligation of contracts ever be passed by the legislature of this state.

. . .

Section 6. The trial by jury as heretofore used in this state, and the liberty of the press, shall be for ever inviolably preserved.   South Carolina Laws, App., pp. 41–42.

13.1.3.12 **Vermont**

13.1.3.12.a **Constitution, 1777**

CHAPTER I.

. . .

13. THAT in Controversies respecting Property, and in Suits between Man and Man, the Parties have a Right to a Trial by Jury, which ought to be held sacred.

. . .

CHAPTER II.

. . .

SECTION XXII.

TRIALS shall be by Jury; and it is recommended to the Legislature of this State, to provide by Law against every Corruption or Partiality in the Choice, and Return, or Appointment of Juries.   Vermont Acts, pp. 4, 9.

13.1.3.12.b **Declaration of Rights, 1786**

IV: That when an issue in fact, proper for the cognizance of a jury, is joined in a court of law, the parties have a right to a trial by jury; which ought to be held sacred.

13.1.3.13 **Virginia: Declaration of Rights, 1776**

XI. THAT in controversies respecting property, and in suits between man and man, the ancient trial by jury is preferable to any other, and ought to be held sacred.
   Virginia Acts, p. 33.

13.1.4 OTHER TEXTS

13.1.4.1 **Magna Carta, 1297**

No freeman shall be taken or imprisoned, or be disseised of his freehold, or liberties, or free customs, or be outlawed, or exiled, or any other wise destroyed; nor will we not pass upon him, nor condemn him, but by lawful judgment of his peers, or by the law of the land. We will sell to no man, we will not deny or defer to any man either justice or right.   25 Edw. 1, c. 29.

13.1.4.2 Petition of Right, 1627

3. And where alsoe by the Statute called the Great Charter of the liberties of England, it is declared and enacted, that no freeman may be taken or imprisoned or be disseised of his freehold or liberties or his free customes or be outlawed or exiled or in any manner destroyed, but by the lawfull judgment of his peeres or by the law of the land.

4. And in the eight and twentith yeere of the raigne of King Edward the Third it was declared and enacted by authoritie of Parliament, that no man of what estate or condicion that he be, should be put out of his land or tenemente nor taken nor imprisoned nor disherited nor put to death without being brought to aunswere by due ꝑcesse of lawe.

5. Neverthelesse against the tenor of the said statutes and other the good lawes and statutes of your realme to that end ꝑvided, divers of your subjecte have of late been imprisoned without any cause shewed: And when for their deliverance they were brought before your justices by your Majesties writte of habeas corpus there to undergoe and receive as the court should order, and their keepers cōmaunded to certifie the causes of their detayner, no cause was certified, but that they were deteined by your Majesties speciall cōmaund signified by the lorde of your privie councell, and yet were returned backe to severall prisons without being charged with any thing to which they might make aunswere according to the lawe.

. . .

8. They doe therefore humblie pray your most excellent Majestie . . . that no freeman in any such manner as is before mencioned be imprisoned or deteined. . . .

3 Chas. 1, c. 1 (1628).

13.1.4.3 Declaration of Independence, 1776

. . . For depriving us in many cases, of the benefits of Trial by Jury. . . .

Continental Congress Papers, DNA.

13.1.4.4 Northwest Territory Ordinance, 1787

Article the Second. The inhabitants of the said territory shall always be entitled to the benefits of the writ of habeas corpus, and of the trial by jury; of a proportionate representation of the people in the legislature, and of judicial proceedings according to the course of the common law; all persons shall be bailable unless for Capital Offences, where the proof shall be evident, or the presumption great; all fines shall be moderate, and no cruel or unusual punishments shall be inflicted; no man shall be deprived of his liberty or property but by the judgment of his peers, or the law of the land; and should the public exigencies make it Necessary for the common preservation to take any persons property, or to demand his particular services, full compensation shall be made for the same; and in the just preservation of rights and property it is understood and declared, that no law ought ever to be made, or have force in the said territory, that shall in any manner whatever interfere with, or affect private contracts or engagements bona fide and without fraud, previously formed.

Continental Congress Papers, DNA.

13.1.4.5 Richard Henry Lee to Edmund Randolph, Proposed Amendments, October 16, 1787

. . . That the trial by jury in criminal and civil cases, and the modes prescribed by the common law for safety of life in criminal prosecutions shall be held sacred — . . . That such parts of the new constitution be amended as provide imperfectly for the trial of criminals by a jury of the vicinage, and to supply the omission of a jury trial in civil causes or disputes about property between individuals where by the common law is directed, and as generally it is secured by the several State constitutions. That such parts of the new constitution be amended, as permit the vexatious and oppressive calling of citizens from their own country, and all controversies between citizens of different states and between citizens and foreigners, to be tried in a far distant court, and as it may be without a jury, whereby in a multitude of cases, the circumstances of distance and expence may compel numbers to submit to the most unjust and ill-founded demand. . . .

Virginia Gazette, December 22, 1787.

13.2 DISCUSSION OF DRAFTS AND PROPOSALS
13.2.1 THE FIRST CONGRESS

13.2.1.1 June 8, 1789[3]

13.2.1.2 August 17, 1789

13.2.1.2.a   The 6th proposition, art. 3. sect. 2. add to the 2d paragraph "But no appeal to such court shall be allowed, where the value in controversy shall not amount to one thousand dollars; nor shall any fact, triable by jury according to the course of common law, be otherwise re-examinable than according to the rules of common law."

Mr. Benson

Moved to strike out the first part of the paragraph respecting the limitation of appeals, because the question in controversy might be an important one, though the action was not to the amount of a thousand dollars.

Mr. Madison.

If the gentleman will propose any restriction to answer his purpose, and for avoiding the inconvenience he apprehends, I am willing to agree to it, but it will be improper to strike out the clause without a substitute.

There is little danger that any court in the United States will admit an appeal where the matter in dispute does not amount to a thousand dollars, but as the possibility of such an event has excited in the minds of many citizens, the greatest apprehension that persons of opulence would carry a cause from the extremities of the union to the supreme court, and therefore prevent the due administration of justice, it ought to be guarded against.

Mr. Livermore thought the clause was objectionable, because it comprehended nothing more than the value.

---

[3]For the reports of Madison's speech in support of his proposals, *see* 1.2.1.1.a–c.

MR. SEDGWICK

Moved to insert 3,000 dollars, in lieu of 1,000, but on the question, this motion was rejected, and the proposition accepted in its original form.

Congressional Register, August 17, 1789, vol. 2, pp. 227–28.

13.2.1.2.b Thirteenth Amendment. — Art. 3. Sec. 2, add to the 2d par. "But no appeal to such court shall be allowed, where the value in controversy shall not amount to one thousand dollars; nor shall any fact triable by a jury, according to the course of the common law, be otherwise re examinable than according to the rules of common law."

MR. BENSON moved to strike out the first part of the paragraph, respecting the limitation of appeals. This motion was negatived.

MR. SEDGWICK moved to strike out the words "one thousand" and insert "three thousand." Negatived.

The amendment was accepted.

Daily Advertiser, August 18, 1789, p. 2, col. 4.

13.2.1.2.c Thirteenth amendmen: [*sic*] — "Art. III. Sec. 2, add to the 2d par. "But no appeal to such court shall be allowed, where the value in controversy shall not amount to one thousand dollars; nor shall any fact triable by a jury, according to the course of the common law, be otherwise re examinable than according to the rules of common law."

Mr Benson moved to strike out the first part of the paragraph, respecting the limitation of appeals. This motion was negatived.

Mr. Sedgwick moved to strike out the words "one thousand" and insert "three thousand." Negatived.

The amendment was accepted.

New-York Daily Gazette, August 19, 1789, p. 802, col. 4.

13.2.1.2.d 13th Amendment. Art. 3. Sec. 2, add to the 2d par. But no appeal to such court shall be allowed, where the value in controversy shall not amount to one thousand dollars; nor shall any fact triable by jury, according to the course of common law, be otherwise re-examinable than according to the rules of common law.

Mr. BENSON moved to strike out the first part of the paragraph, respecting the limitation of appeals.

MR. MADISON observed, that except some adequate substitute was proposed, he thought it would be necessary to retain the clause: There is, said he, perhaps no danger of any court in the United States, granting an appeal where the value in dispute does not amount to 1,000 dollars; still the possibility of such an event has excited the greatest apprehensions in the minds of many citizens of the United States: The idea that opulent persons might carry a cause from one end of the continent to another has caused serious fears in the minds of the people: I think it best to retain the clause.

The motion was negatived.

MR. SEDGWICK, to strengthen the clause, moved to strike out 1,000 dollars and to insert 3,000 dollars. — This motion was seconded and supported by Mr. Livermore, but was negatived, and the amendment accepted.

Gazette of the U.S., August 22, 1789, p. 249, col. 3, and p. 250, col. 1.

13.2.1.3 August 18, 1789

The 3d clause of the 7th proposition as follows, "In suits at common law, the right of trial by jury shall be preserved," was considered and adopted.

Congressional Register, August 18, 1789, vol. 2, p. 233.

13.2.1.4 August 21, 1789

The house then took into consideration the 3d clause of the 7th proposition, which was adopted without debate.

Congressional Register, August 21, 1789, vol. 2, p. 243.

13.2.1.5 Petition of John Fitch Read in the Senate, March 22, 1790

The petition of John Fitch, was read; praying that a clause, providing for the trial by jury, might be inserted in a Bill before Congress, "To promote the progress of useful arts."

ORDERED, That this petition be referred to the Committee who have under consideration the last mentioned Bill.

Senate Legislative Journal, Documentary History of the First Federal Congress, Linda Grant De Pauw, ed. (Baltimore: Johns Hopkins U. Pr., 1972), pp. 264–65.

13.2.2 STATE CONVENTIONS

13.2.2.1 Massachusetts

13.2.2.1.a January 30, 1788

Mr. GORE observed, . . . that it had been the uniform conduct of those in opposition to the proposed form of government, to determine, in every case where it was possible that the administrators thereof could do wrong, that they would do so, although it were demonstrable that such wrong would be against their own honor and interest, and productive of no advantage to themselves. On this principle alone have they determined that the trial by jury would be taken away in civil cases; when it had been clearly shown, that no words could be adopted, apt to the situation and customs of each state in this particular. Jurors are differently chosen in different states, and in point of qualification the laws of the several states are very diverse; not less so in causes and disputes which are entitled to trial by jury. What is the result of this? That the laws of Congress may and will be conformable to the local laws in this particular, although the Constitution could not make a universal rule equally applying to the customs and statutes of the different states. Very few governments (certainly not this) can be interested in depriving the people of trial by jury, in questions of *meum et tuum*. . . .

Mr. DAWES said, he did not see that the right of trial by jury was taken away by the article. The word *court* does not, either by popular or technical construction, exclude the use of a jury to try facts. When people, in common language, talk of a trial at the *Court* of Common Pleas, or the Supreme Judicial *Court*, do they not include all the branches and members of such court — the *jurors* as well as the judges? They certainly do, whether they mention the jurors expressly or not. Our state legislators have construed the word *court* in the same way; for they have given appeals from a justice of peace to the Court of Common Pleas, and from thence to the Supreme Court, without saying any thing of the jury; but in cases which, almost time out of mind, have been tried without jury, there the jurisdiction is given expressly to the justices of a particular court, as may be instanced by suits upon the absconding act, so called.

Gentlemen have compared the article under consideration to that power which the British claimed, and we resisted, at the revolution; namely, the power of trying the Americans without a jury. But surely there was no parallel in the cases; it was criminal cases in which they attempted to make this abuse of power. Mr. D. mentioned one example of this, which, though young, he well remembered; and that was the case of Nickerson, the pirate, who was tried without a jury, and whose judges were the governors of Massachusetts and of some neighboring provinces, together with Admiral Montague, and some gentlemen of distinction. Although this trial was without a jury, yet, as it was a trial upon the civil law, there was not so much clamor about it as otherwise there might have been; but still it was disagreeable to the people, and was one of the then complaints. But the trial by jury was not attempted to be taken from civil causes. It was no object of power, whether one subject's property was lessened, while another's was increased; nor can it be now an object with the federal legislature. What interest can they have in constituting a judiciary, to proceed in civil causes without a trial by jury? In criminal causes, by the proposed government, there must be a jury. It is asked, Why is not the Constitution as explicit in securing the right of jury in civil as in criminal cases? The answer is, Because it was out of the power of the Convention. The several states differ so widely in their modes of trial, some states using a jury in causes wherein other states employ only their judges, that the Convention have very wisely left it to the federal legislature to make such regulations as shall, as far as possible, accommodate the whole. Thus our own state constitution authorizes the General Court to erect judicatories, but leaves the nature, number, and extent of them, wholly to the discretion of the legislature. The bill of rights, indeed, secures the trial by jury, in civil causes, except in cases where a contrary practice has obtained. Such a clause as this some gentlemen wish were inserted in the proposed Constitution, but such a clause would be abused in that Constitution, as has been clearly been stated by the honorable gentleman from Charlestown, (Mr. Gorham,) because the "exception of all cases where a jury have not heretofore been used," would include almost all cases that could be mentioned, when applied to all the states, for they have severally differed in the kinds of causes where they have tried without a jury.

Elliot, vol. 2, pp. 112–14.

13.2.2.1.b February 1, 1788

Hon. Mr. ADAMS. . . . Your excellency's next proposition . . . recommends a trial by jury in civil actions between citizens of different states, if either of the parties shall request it. These, and several others which I have mentioned, are so evidently beneficial as to need no comment of mine. And they are all, in every particular, of so general a nature, and so equally interesting to every state, that I cannot but persuade myself to think they would all readily join with us in the measure proposed by your excellency, if we should now adopt it.

Elliot, vol. 2, pp. 132–33.

13.2.2.2 New York, July 2, 1788

Mr. TREDWELL. . . . I could have wished, sir, that a greater caution had been used to secure to us the freedom of election, a sufficient and responsible representation, the freedom of the press, and the trial by jury both in civil and criminal cases.

These, sir, are the rocks on which the Constitution should have rested . . . .

Elliot, vol. 2, p. 399.

13.2.2.3 North Carolina

13.2.2.3.a July 28, 1788

Mr. BLOODWORTH. . . . The honorable gentleman has said that the state courts and the courts of the United States would have concurrent jurisdiction. I beg the committee to reflect what would be the consequence of such measures. It has ever been considered that the trial by jury was one of the greatest rights of the people. I ask whether, if such causes go into the federal court, the trial by jury is not cut off, and whether there is any security that we shall have justice done us. I ask if there be any security that we shall have juries in civil causes. In criminal cases there are to be juries, but there is no provision made for having civil causes tried by jury. This concurrent jurisdiction is inconsistent with the security of that great right. If it be not, I would wish to hear how it is secured. I have listened with attention to what the learned gentlemen have said, and have endeavored to see whether their arguments had any weight; but I found none in them. Many words have been spoken, and long time taken up; but with me they have gone in at one ear, and out at the other. It would give me much pleasure to hear that the trial by jury was secured.

Mr. J. M'DOWALL. . . . We know that the trial by a jury of the vicinage is one of the greatest securities for property. If causes are to be decided at such a great distance, the poor will be oppressed; in land affairs, particularly, the wealthy suitor will prevail. A poor man, who has a just claim on a piece of land, has not substance to stand it. Can it be supposed that any man, of common circumstances, can stand the expense and trouble of going from Georgia to Philadelphia, there to have a suit tried? And can it be justly determined without the benefit of a trial by jury? These are things that have justly alarmed the people. What made the people revolt from Great Britain? The trial by jury, that great safeguard of liberty, was taken away, and a stamp duty was laid upon them. This alarmed them, and led them to fear that great oppressions would take place. We then resisted. It involved us in a war, and caused us to relinquish a government which made us happy in every thing else. The war as very bloody, but we got our independence. We are now giving away our dear-bought rights. We ought to consider what we are about to do before we determine.

Mr. SPAIGHT. Mr. Chairman, the trial by jury was not forgotten in the Convention; the subject took up a considerable time to investigate it. It was impossible to make any one uniform regulation for all the states, or that would include all cases where it would be necessary. It was impossible, by one expression, to embrace the whole. There are a number of equity and maritime cases, in some of the states, in which jury trials are not used. Had the Convention said that all causes should be tried by a jury, equity and maritime cases would have been included. It was therefore left to the legislature to say in what cases it should be used; and as the trial by jury is in full force in the state courts, we have the fullest security.

Mr. IREDELL. . . . I am by no means surprised at the anxiety which is expressed by gentlemen on this subject. Of all the trials that ever were instituted in the world, this, in my opinion, is the best, and that which I hope will continue the longest. . . . But I have been told that the omission of it arose from the difficulty of establishing one uniform, unexceptionable mode: this mode of trial being different, in many particulars, in the several states. Gentlemen will be pleased to consider that there is a material difference between an article fixed in the Constitution, and a regulation by law. An article in the Constitution, however inconvenient it may prove by experience, can only be altered by altering the Constitution itself, which manifestly is a thing that ought not to be done often. When regulated by law, it can easily be occasionally altered so as best to suit the conveniences of the people. Had there been an article in the Constitution taking away that trial, it would justly have excited the public indignation. It is not taken away by the Constitution. Though that does not provide expressly for a trial by jury in civil cases, it does not say that there shall not be such a trial. The reasons of the omission have been mentioned by a member of the late General Convention, (Mr. Spaight.) There are different practices in regard to this trial in different states. . . . I beg leave to say, that if any gentleman of ability and knowledge of the subject will only endeavor to fix upon any one rule that would be pleasing to all the states under the impression of their present different habits, he will be convinced that it is impracticable. . . . It is not to be presumed that the Congress would dare to deprive the people of this valuable privilege. . . .

. . .

. . . In respect to the trial by jury, its being taken away, in certain cases, was, to be sure, one of the causes assigned in the Declaration of Independence. . . . But this Constitution has not taken it away, and it is left to the discretion of our own legislature to act, in this respect, as their wisdom shall direct. In Great Britain, the people speak of the trial by jury with admiration. No monarch, or minister, however arbitrary in his principles, would dare to attack that noble palladium of liberty. The enthusiasm of the people in its favor would, in such a case, produce general resistance. That trial remains unimpaired there, although they have a considerable standing army, and their Parliament has authority to abolish it, if they please. But wo to those who should attempt it! If it be secure in that country, under these circumstances, can we believe that Congress either would or could take it away in this? Were they to attempt it, their authority would be instantly resisted. They would draw down on themselves the resentment and detestation of the people. They and their families, so long as any remained in being, would be held in eternal infamy, and the attempt prove as unsuccessful as it was wicked.

. . .

Gov. JOHNSTON. Mr. Chairman, the observations of the gentleman last up confirm what the other gentleman said. I mean that, as there are dissimilar modes with respect to the trial by jury in different states, there could be no general rule fixed to accommodate all. He says that this clause is defective, because the trial is not to be by a jury of the vicinage. Let us look at the state of Virginia, where, as long as I have known it, the laws have been executed so as to satisfy the inhabitants, and, I believe, as well as in any part of the Union. In that country, juries are summoned every day from the by-standers. We may expect less partiality when the trial is by strangers; and were I to be tried for my property or life, I would rather be tried by disinterested men, who were not biased, than by men who were perhaps intimate friends of my opponent. Our mode is different from theirs; but whether theirs be better than ours or not, is not the question. It would be improper for our delegates to impose our mode upon them, or for theirs to impose their mode upon us. The trial will probably be, in each state, as it has been hitherto used in such state, or otherwise regulated as conveniently as possible for the people. The delegates who are to meet in Congress will, I hope, be men of virtue and wisdom. If not, it will be our own fault. They will have it in their power to make necessary regulations to accommodate the inhabitants of each state. In the Constitution, the general principles only are laid down. It will be the object of the future legislation to Congress to make such laws as will be most convenient for the people. . . .

Mr. BLOODWORTH. Mr. Chairman, the footing on which the trial by jury is, in the Constitution, does not satisfy me. Perhaps I am mistaken; but if I understand the thing right, the trial by jury is taken away. If the Supreme Federal Court has jurisdiction both as to law and fact, it appears to me to be taken away. The honorable gentleman who was in the Convention told us that the clause, as it now stands, resulted from the difficulty of fixing the mode of trial. I think it was easy to have put it on a secure footing. But, if the genius of the people of the United States is so dissimilar that our liberties cannot be secured, we can never hang long together. Interest is the band of social union; and when this is taken away, the Union itself must dissolve.

Mr. MACLAINE. Mr. Chairman, I do not take the interest of the states to be so dissimilar; I take them to be all nearly alike, and inseparably connected. It is impossible to lay down any constitutional rule for the government of all the different states in each particular. But it will be easy for the legislature to make laws to accommodate the people in every part of the Union, as circumstances may arise. Jury trial is not taken away in such cases where it may be found necessary. Although the Supreme Court has cognizance of the appeal, it does not follow but that the trial by jury may be had in the court below, and the testimony transmitted to the Supreme Court, who will then finally determine, on a review of all the circumstances. This is well known to be the practice in some of the states. In our own state, indeed, when a cause is instituted in the county court, and afterwards there is an appeal upon it, a new trial is had in the superior court, as if no trial had been before. In other countries, however, when a trial is had in an inferior court, and an appeal is taken, no testimony can be given in the court above, but the court determines upon the circumstances appearing upon the record. If I am right, the plain inference is, that there may be a trial in the inferior courts, and that the record, including the testimony, may be sent to the Supreme Court. But if there is a necessity for a jury in the Supreme Court, it will be a very easy matter to empanel a jury at the bar of the Supreme Court, which may save great expense, and be very convenient to the people. It is impossible to make every regulation at once. Congress, who are our own representatives, will undoubtedly make such regulations as will suit the convenience and secure the liberty of the people.

Mr. IREDELL declared it as his opinion that there might be juries in the Superior Court as well as in the inferior courts, and that it was in the power of Congress to regulate it so.

Elliot, vol. 4, pp. 142–48, 150–52.

13.2.2.3.b July 29, 1788

Mr. SPENCER. . . . The trial by jury has been also spoken of. Every person who is acquainted with the nature of liberty need not be informed of the importance of this trial. Juries are called the bulwarks of our rights and liberty; and no country can ever be enslaved as long as those cases which affect their lives and property are to be decided, in a great measure, by the consent of twelve honest, disinterested men, taken from the respectable body of yeomanry. It is highly improper that any clause which regards the security of the trial by jury should be any way doubtful. In the clause that has been read, it is ascertained that criminal cases are to be tried by jury in the states where they are committed. It has been objected to that clause, that it is not sufficiently explicit. I think that it is not. It was observed that one may be taken to a great distance. One reason of the resistance to the British government was, because they required that we should be carried to the country of Great Britain, to be tried by juries of that country. But we insisted on being tried by juries of the vicinage, in our own country. I think it therefore proper that something explicit should be said with respect to the vicinage.

With regard to that part, that the Supreme Court shall have appellate jurisdiction both as to law and fact, it has been observed that, though the federal court might decide without a jury, yet the court below, which tried it, might have a jury. I ask the gentleman what benefit would be received in the suit by having a jury trial in the court below, when the verdict is set aside in the Supreme Court. It was intended by this clause that the trial by jury should be suppressed in the superior and inferior courts. It has been said, in defence of the omission concerning the trial by jury in civil cases, that one general regulation could not be made; that in several cases the constitution of several states did not require a trial by jury, — for instance, in cases of equity and admiralty, — whereas in others it did, and that, therefore, it was proper to leave this subject at large. I am sure that, for the security of liberty, they ought to have been at the pains of drawing some line. I think that the respectable body who formed the Constitution should have gone so far as to put matters on such a footing as that there should be no danger. They might have provided that all those cases which are now triable by a jury should be tried in each state by a jury, according to the mode usually practiced in such state. This would have been easily done, if they had been at the trouble of writing five or six lines. Had it been done, we should have been entitled to say that our rights and liberties were not endangered. If we adopt this clause as it is, I think, notwithstanding what gentlemen have said, that there will be danger. There ought to be some amendments to it, to put this matter on a sure footing. There does not appear to me to be any kind of necessity that the federal court should have jurisdiction in the body of the country. I am ready to give up that, in the cases expressly enumerated, an appellate jurisdiction (except in one or two instances) might be given. I wish them also to have jurisdiction in maritime affairs, and to try offences committed on the high seas. . . .

. . .

Mr. MACLAINE. . . . But the gentleman seems to be most tenacious of the judicial power of the states. The honorable gentleman must know, that the doctrine of reservation of power not relinquished, clearly demonstrates that the judicial power of the states is not impaired. He asks, with respect to the trial by jury, "When the cause has gone up to the superior court, and the verdict is set aside, what benefit arises from having had a jury trial in the inferior court?" I would ask the gentleman, "What is the reason, that, on a special verdict or case agreed, the decision is left to the court?" There are a number of cases where juries cannot decide. When a jury finds the fact specially, or when it is agreed upon by the parties, the decision is referred to the court. If the law be against the party, the court decides against him; if the law be for him, the court judges accordingly. He, as well as every gentleman here, must know that, under the Confederation, Congress set aside juries. There was an appeal given to Congress: did Congress determine by a jury? Every party carried his testimony in writing to the judges of appeal, and Congress determined upon it.

. . .

Mr. SPENCER. . . . I contend that there should be a bill of rights, ascertaining and securing the great rights of the states and people. Besides my objection to the revision of facts by the federal court, and the insecurity of jury trial, I consider the concurrent jurisdiction of those courts with the state courts as extremely dangerous. . . .

. . .

Mr. IREDELL. . . . In criminal cases, however, no latitude ought to be allowed. In these the greatest danger from any government subsists, and accordingly it is provided that there shall be a trial by jury, in all such cases, in the state wherein the offence is committed. I thought the objection against the want of a bill of rights had been obviated unanswerably. It appears to me most extraordinary. Shall we give up anything but what is positively granted by that instrument? It would be the greatest absurdity for any man to pretend that, when a legislature is formed for a particular purpose, it can have any authority but what is so expressly given to it, any more than a man acting under a power of attorney could depart from the authority it conveyed to him, according to an instance which I stated when speaking on the subject before. As for example: — if I had three tracts of land, one in Orange, another in Caswell, and another in Chatham, and I gave a power of attorney to a man to sell the two tracts in Orange and Caswell, and he should attempt to sell my land in Chatham, would any man of common sense suppose he had authority to do so? In like manner, I say, the future Congress can have no right to exercise any power but what is contained in that paper. Negative words, in my opinion, could make the matter no plainer than it was before. The gentleman says that unalienable rights ought not to be given up. Those rights which are unalienable are not alienated. They still remain with the great body of the people. If any right be given up that ought not to be, let it be shown. Say it is a thing which affects your country, and that it ought not to be surrendered: this would be reasonable. But when it is evident that the exercise of any power not given up would be a usurpation, it would be not only useless, but dangerous, to enumerate a number of rights which are not intended to be given up; because it would be implying, in the strongest manner, that every right not included in the exception might be impaired by the government without usurpation; and it would be impossible to enumerate every one. Let any one make what collection or enumeration of rights he pleases, I will immediately mention twenty or thirty more rights not contained in it.

Mr. BLOODWORTH. Mr. Chairman, I have listened with attention to the gentleman's arguments; but whether it be for want of sufficient attention, or from the grossness of my ideas, I cannot be satisfied with his defence of the omission, with respect to the trial by jury. He says that it would be impossible to fall on any satisfactory mode of regulating the trial by jury, because there are various customs relative to it in the different states. Is this a satisfactory cause for the omission? Why did it not provide that the trial by jury should be preserved in civil cases? It has said that the trial should be by jury in criminal cases; and yet this trial is different in its manner in criminal cases in the different states. If it has been possible to secure it in criminal cases, notwithstanding the diversity concerning it, why has it not been possible to secure it in civil cases? I wish this to be cleared up. . . .

. . .

Mr. IREDELL. Mr. Chairman, I hope some other gentleman will answer what has been said by the gentlemen who have spoken last. I only rise to answer the question of the member from New Hanover — which was, if there was such a difficulty, in establishing the trial by jury in civil cases, that the Convention could not concur in any mode, why the difficulty did not extend to criminal cases? I beg leave to say, that the difficulty, in this case, does not depend so much on the mode of proceeding, as on the difference of the subjects of controversy, and the laws relative to them. . . .

We have been told, and I believe this was the real reason, why they could not concur in any general rule. I have great respect for the characters of those gentlemen who formed the Convention, and I believe they were not capable of overlooking the importance of the trial by jury, much less of designedly plotting against it. But I fully believe that the real difficulty of the thing was the cause of the omission. I trust sufficient reasons have been offered, to show that it is in no danger. As to criminal cases, I must observe that the great instrument of arbitrary power is criminal prosecutions. By the privileges of *habeas corpus*, no man can be confined without inquiry; and if it should appear that he has been committed contrary to law, he must be discharged. That diversity which is to be found in civil controversies, does not exist in criminal cases. That diversity which contributes to the security of property in civil cases, would have pernicious effects in criminal ones. There is no other safe mode to try these but by a jury. If any man had the means of trying another his own way, or were it left to the control of arbitrary judges, no man would have that security for life and liberty which every freeman ought to have. I presume that in no state on the continent is a man tried on a criminal accusation but by a jury. It was necessary, therefore, that it should be fixed, in the Constitution, that the trial should be by jury in criminal cases; and such difficulties did not occur in this as in the other case. . . .

Elliot, vol. 4, pp. 154–55, 162, 163–64, 166–67, 170–71.

13.2.2.3.c   July 30, 1788

Mr. SPAIGHT. . . . The gentleman has again brought on the trial by jury. The Federal Convention, sir, had no wish to destroy the trial by jury. It was three or four days before them. There were a variety of objections to any one mode. It was thought impossible to fall upon any one mode but what would produce some inconveniences. . . . I should suppose that, if the representatives of twelve states, with many able lawyers among them, could not form any unexceptionable mode, this Convention could hardly be able to do it. . . .

. . .

Mr. J. M'DOWALL. . . . Trial by jury is not secured. The objections against this want of security have not been cleared up in a satisfactory manner. It is neither secured in civil nor criminal cases. The federal appellate cognizance of law and fact puts it in the power of the wealthy to recover unjustly of the poor man, who is not able to attend at such extreme distance, and bear such enormous expense as it must produce.

Elliot, vol. 4, pp. 208, 211.

13.2.2.4   Pennsylvania

13.2.2.4.a   September 29, 1787

Address of the Seceding Assemblymen
Gentlemen: When in consequence of your suffrages at the last election we were chosen to represent you in the General Assembly of this Commonwealth, we accepted of the important trust, with a determination to execute it in the best manner we were able, and we flatter ourselves we acted in such a manner as to convince you, that your interests with that of the good of the state has been the object of our measures.

. . .

. . . You will be able likewise to determine, whether in a free government there ought or ought not to be any provision . . . whether the trial by jury in civil causes is become dangerous and ought to be abolished and whether the judiciary of the United States is not so constructed as to absorb and destroy the judiciaries of the several states?

Jensen, vol. 2, pp. 112, 116.

13.2.2.4.b   December 5, 1787

. . . Findley: Contends for a bill of rights, the liberty of the *press*, trial by *jury*. When I was proposed as a member of the late Convention, I declined it as I thought it too great an undertaking *for me* to *represent* and *guard* all the rights and liberties of the people of Pennsylvania.

Jensen, vol. 2, p. 504.

13.2.2.4.c **December 7, 1787**

Mr. WILSON. . . . It is very true that trial by jury is not mentioned in civil cases; but I take it that it is very improper to infer from hence that it was not meant to exist under this government. Where the people are represented, where the interest of government cannot be separate from that of the people, (and this is the case in trial between citizen and citizen,) the power of making regulations with respect to the mode of trial may certainly be placed in the legislature; for I apprehend that the legislature will not do wrong in an instance from which they can derive no advantage. These were not all the reasons that influenced the Convention to leave it to the future Congress to make regulations on this head.

By the Constitution of the different states, it will be found that no particular mode of trial by jury could be discovered that would suit them all. The manner of summoning jurors, their qualifications, of whom they should consist, and the course of their proceedings, are all different in the different states; and I presume it will be allowed a good general principle, that, in carrying into effect the laws of the general government by the judicial department, it will be proper to make the regulations as agreeable to the habits and wishes of the particular states as possible; and it is easily discovered that it would have been impracticable, by any general regulation, to give satisfaction to all. We must have thwarted the custom of eleven or twelve to have accommodated any one. Why do this when there was no danger to be apprehended from the omission? We could not go into a particular detail of the manner that would have suited each state.

Time, reflection, and experience, will be necessary to suggest and mature the proper regulations on the subject; time and experience were not possessed by the Convention; they left it therefore to be particularly organized by the legislature — the representatives of the United States — from time to time, as should be most eligible and proper. Could they have done better?

I know, in every part where opposition has risen, what a handle has been made to this objection; but I trust, upon examination, it will be seen that more could not have been done with propriety. Gentlemen talk of bills of rights. What is the meaning of this continual clamor, after what has been urged? Though it may be proper, in a single state, whose legislature calls itself the sovereign and supreme power, yet it would be absurd in the body of the people, when they are delegating from among themselves persons to transact certain business, to add an enumeration of those things which they are not to do. "But trial by jury is secured in the bill of rights of Pennsylvania; the parties have a right to trials by jury, which *ought* to be held sacred." And what is the consequence? There have been more violations of this right in Pennsylvania, since the revolution, than are to be found in England in the course of a century.

*   *   *

ROBERT WHITEHILL . . .

(171) The trial of *crimes* is to be by jury; therefore the trial of civil causes is supposed not to be by jury.

(172) We preserved the trial by jury against the attempts of the British Crown.
(173) I wish, for the honor of the Convention, this had not been omitted.

. . .

JOHN SMILIE: (179) In common law cases there ought not to be an appeal as to facts. Facts found by a jury should never be re-examined.

. . .

Jury trials may be superseded in civil cases. Appellate jurisdiction is a civil law term. There can be no appeal after jury trials. I fear there is an intention to substitute the civil law in the room of the common law. Think of the expense of the different courts and of the federal system at large.

. . .

WILLIAM FINDLEY: . . .

(185) The judges are better for the guard of juries in all possible cases. The mistakes of juries are never systematical. The laws can never be so enacted as to prevent the judge's from doing wrong.

(186) I admit that it would have been impossible to accommodate the trial by jury to all the states; but power ought not to have been given applying to such *internal* objects.

(187) There might have been a declaration that the trial by jury in civil cases as it hath hitherto been in the several states; or in the state, where the cause arose.

(188) The jurisdiction will, I believe, be chiefly appellate; and therefore, chiefly without jury.

. . .

JOHN SMILIE: (193) I cannot see the great difficulty of securing at least the substance of jury [trial] in civil cases. It might have been said that the legislature should make regulations for the trial by jury in them.

(194) Whatever is not given is reserved. The trial by jury is given in criminal cases therefore reserved in civil cases.

Elliot, vol. 2, pp. 488–89; Jensen, vol. 2, pp. 513, 521–23.

13.2.2.4.d **December 8, 1787**

JOHN SMILIE: . . .

(198) It was the design and intention of the Convention to divest us of the liberty of trial by jury in civil cases; and to deprive us of the benefits of the common law.

(199) The word "appeal" is a civil law term; and therefore the Convention meant to introduce the *civil* law.

(200) On an appeal the judges may set aside the verdict of a jury.

(201) Appeals are not admitted in the common law.

(202) If a jury give a false verdict, a writ of attaint lies or the verdict may be set aside. A writ of error lies as to matters of law; but on that writ the fact are not reexamined.

. . .

(212) The Convention might have said, that Congress should establish trials by jury in civil cases.

. . .

ROBERT WHITEHILL: (213) Are we to trust to all judges, who will have their favorites?

. . .

(226) Our greatest liberties will, by this Constitution, be sacrificed to the will of men.

(227) The trial by jury is given up to the will of Congress.

. . .

WILLIAM FINDLEY: . . .

(229) Trial by jury is not secured in civil cases as in criminal ones. It is at the mercy of the legislature.

(230) By the appellate clause, an appeal lies from the verdict of a jury, a thing hitherto unknown.

(231) Personal liberty cannot be enjoyed without trial by jury.

(232) All the northern countries have been zealous of freedom. Sweden till lately had trials by jury — and certainly a free government well-balanced, consisting of four branches.

FINDLEY: On Saturday last, in the course of an argument to prove the dissolution of the trial by jury, if the proposed system was adopted, and the consequent sacrifice of the liberties of the people, Mr. Findley observed, that when the trial by jury, which was known in Sweden so late as the middle of the last century, fell into disuse, the commons of that nation lost their freedom and a tyrannical aristocracy prevailed.

JAMES WILSON and THOMAS MCKEAN interrupted Mr. Findley and called warmly for his authority to prove that the trial by jury existed in Sweden, Mr. Wilson declaring that he had never met with such an idea in the course of his reading; and Mr. M'Kean asserting that the trial by jury was never known in any other country than England and the governments descended from that kingdom. Mr. Findley answered that he did not, at that moment, recollect his authority, but having formerly read histories of Sweden, he had received and retained the opinion which he now advanced, and would on a future occasion, perhaps, refer immediately to the book.

WILLIAM FINDLEY: (233) Trial by jury is inconsistent with a complete aristocracy.

(234) The lower class of people will be oppressed without trial by jury.

(235) This part is explanatory of other parts of the plan.

(236) The people never expressed a wish to give up the trial by jury.

(237) In Pennsylvania the trial by jury must be by a jury of the proper county.

Jensen, vol. 2, pp. 525–28.

13.2.2.4.e **December 10, 1787**

FINDLEY: . . . Trials by jury are in disuse in Sweden except in the lower courts. . . . Every new tribunal without a jury is an introduction of aristocracy, the worst of all tyrannies. Trials by jury in Sweden have been in disuse for near a century past.

Jensen, vol. 2, p. 532.

December 11, 1787

Mr. WILSON. I shall now proceed, Mr. President, to notice the remainder of the objections that have been suggested by the honorable gentlemen who oppose the system now before you.

We have been told, sir, by the honorable member from Fayette (Mr. Smilie,) "that the trial by jury was intended to be given up, and the civil law was intended to be introduced into its place, in civil cases."

Before a sentiment of this kind was hazarded, I think, sir, the gentleman ought to be prepared with better proof in its support than any he has yet attempted to produce. It is a charge, sir, not only unwarrantable, but cruel: the idea of such a thing, I believe, never entered into the mind of a single member of that Convention; and I believe further, that they never suspected there would be found, within the United States, a single person that was capable of making such a charge. If it should be well founded, sir, they must abide by the consequences; but if (as I trust it will fully appear) it is ill founded, then he or they who make it ought to abide by the consequences.

Trial by jury forms a large field for investigation, and numerous volumes are written on the subject; those who are well acquainted with it may employ much time in its discussion; but in a country where its excellences are so well understood, it may not be necessary to be very prolix in pointing them out. For my part, I shall confine myself to a few observations in reply to the objections that have been suggested.

The member from Fayette (Mr. Smilie) has labored to infer that, under the Articles of Confederation, the Congress possessed no appellate jurisdiction; but this being decided against him by the words of that instrument, by which is granted to Congress the power of "establishing courts for receiving, and determining finally, appeals in all cases of capture, he next attempts a distinction, and allows the power of appealing from the decisions of the judges, but not from the verdict of a jury; but this is determined against him also by the practice of the states; for, in every instance which has occurred, this power has been claimed by Congress, and exercised by the Courts of Appeals. But what would be the consequence of allowing the doctrine for which he contends? Would it not be in the power of a jury, by their verdict, to involve the whole Union in a war? They may condemn the property of a neutral, or otherwise infringe the law of nations, in this case, ought their verdict to be without revisal? Nothing can be inferred from this to prove that trials by jury were intended to be given up. In Massachusetts, and all the Eastern States, their causes are tried by juries, though they acknowledge the appellate jurisdiction of Congress.

I think I am not now to learn the advantages of a trial by jury. It has excellences that entitle it to a superiority over any other mode, in cases to which it is applicable.

Where jurors can be acquainted with the characters of the parties and the witnesses, — where the whole cause can be brought within their knowledge and their view, — I know no mode of investigation equal to that by a jury: they hear everything that is alleged; they not only hear the words, but they see and mark the features of the countenance; they can judge of weight due to such testimony; and moreover, it is a cheap and expeditious manner of distributing justice. There is another advantage annexed to the trial by jury; the jurors may indeed return a mistaken or ill-founded verdict, but their errors cannot be systematical.

Let us apply these observations to the objects of the judicial department, under this Constitution. I think it has been shown, already, that they all extend beyond the bounds of any particular state; but further, a great number of the civil causes there enumerated depend either upon the law of nations, or the marine law, that is, the general law of mercantile countries. Now, sir, in such cases, I presume it will not be pretended that this mode of decision ought to be adopted; for the law with regard to them is the same here as in every other country, and ought to be administered in the same manner. There are instances in which I think it highly probable that the trial by jury will be found proper; and if it is highly probable that it will be found proper, is it not equally probable that it will be adopted? There may be causes depending between citizens of different states; and as trial by jury is known and regarded in all the states, they will certainly prefer that mode of trial before any other. The Congress will have the power of making proper regulations on this subject, but it was impossible for the Convention to have gone minutely into it; but if they could, it must have been very improper, because alterations, as I observed before, might have been necessary; and whatever Convention might have done would have continued unaltered, unless by an alteration of the Constitution. Besides, there was another difficulty with regard to this subject. In some of the states they have courts of chancery, and other appellate jurisdictions, and those states are as attached to that mode of distributing justice as those that have none are to theirs.

I have desired, repeatedly, that honorable gentlemen, who find fault, would be good enough to point out what they deem to be an improvement. The member from Westmoreland (Mr. Findley) tells us that the trial between citizens of different states ought to be by a jury of that state in which the cause of action arose. Now, it is easy to see that, in many instances, this would be very improper and very partial; for, besides the different manner of collecting and forming juries in the several states, the plaintiff comes from another state; he comes a stranger, unknown as to his character or mode of life, while the other party is in the midst of his friends, or perhaps his dependents. Would a trial by jury, in such a case, insure justice to the stranger? But again: I would ask that gentleman whether, if a great part of his fortune was in the hands of some person in Rhode Island, he would wish that his action to recover it should be determined by a jury of that country, under its present circumstances.

The gentleman from Fayette (Mr. Smilie) says that, if the Convention found themselves embarrassed, at least they might have done thus much — they should have declared that the substance should be secured by Congress. This would be saying nothing unless the cases were particularized.

Mr. SMILIE. I said the Convention ought to have declared that the legislature should establish the trial by jury by proper regulations.

Mr. WILSON. The legislature shall establish it by proper regulations! . . . He wishes them to do the very thing that they have done — to leave it to the discretion of Congress. The fact, sir, is, nothing more could be done.

It is well known that there are some cases that should not come before juries; there are others, that, in some of the states, never come before juries, and in those states where they do come before them, appeals are found necessary, the facts re-examined, and the verdict of the jury sometimes is set aside; but I think, in all cases where the cause has come originally before a jury, that the last examination ought to be before a jury likewise.

The power of having appellate jurisdiction, as to facts, has been insisted upon as a proof, "that the Convention *intended* to give up the trial by jury in civil cases, and to introduce the civil law." I have already declared my own opinion on this point, and have shown that not merely that it is founded on reason and authority; — the express declaration of Congress (*Journals of Congress*, March 6, 1779) is to the same purpose. They insist upon this power, as requisite to preserve the peace of the Union; certainly, therefore, it ought always to be possessed by the head of the confederacy. We are told, as an additional proof, that the trial by jury was intended to be given up; "that appeals are unknown to the common law; that the term is a civil-law term, and with it the civil law is intended to be introduced." I confess I was a good deal surprised at this observation being made; for Blackstone, . . . has a chapter entitled "Of Proceeding in the Nature of Appeals," — and in that chapter says, that the principal method of redress for erroneous judgements, in the king's courts of record, is by writ of error to some superior "*court of appeal*." (3 *Blackstone*, 406.) Now, it is well known that his book is a commentary upon the common law. Here, then, is a strong refutation of the assertion, "that appeals are unknown to the common law."

I think these were all the circumstances adduced to show the truth of the assertion, that, in this Constitution, the trial by jury was *intended* to be given up by the late Convention in framing it. Has the assertion been proved? I say not; and the allegations offered, if they apply at all, apply in a contrary direction. I am glad that this objection has been stated, because it is a subject upon which the enemies of this Constitution have much insisted. We have now had an opportunity of investigating it fully; and the result is, that there is no foundation for the charge, but it must proceed from ignorance, or something worse. Elliot, vol. 2, pp. 515–19.

13.2.2.4.g **December 12, 1787**

Thomas McKean: . . . Mr. M'Kean pronounced an animated eulogism on the character, information and abilities of Mr. George Mason, but concluded that the exclusion of juries in civil causes was not among the objections which had governed his [Mason's] conduct.

Robert Whitehill: On this assertion Mr. Whitehill quoted the following passage from Mr. Mason's objections: "There is no declaration of any kind for preserving the liberty of the press, *the trial by jury in civil causes*, nor against the danger of standing armies in time of peace."

Mr. Whitehill then read, and offered as the ground of a motion . . . the consideration of the following articles, . . .

2. That in controversies respecting property, and in suits between man and man, trial by jury shall remain as heretofore, as well in the federal courts, and in those of the several states.

Jensen, vol. 2, pp. 596–97.

13.2.2.5   South Carolina

13.2.2.5.a   January 16, 1788

Hon. CHARLES PINCKNEY. . . . Though at first he considered some declaration on the subject of trial by jury in civil causes, and the freedom of the press, necessary, and still thinks it would have been as well to have had it inserted, yet he fully acquiesced in the reasoning which was used to show that the insertion of them was not essential. . . .

On the subject of juries, in civil cases, the Convention were anxious to make some declaration; but when they reflected that all courts of admiralty and appeals, being governed in their propriety by the civil law and the laws of nations, never had, or ought to have, juries, they found it impossible to make any precise declaration upon the subject; they therefore left it as it was, trusting that the good sense of their constituents would never induce them to suppose that it could be the interest or intention of the general government to abuse one of the most invaluable privileges a free country can boast; in the loss of which, themselves, their fortunes and connections, must be so materially involved, and to the deprivation of which, except in the cases alluded to, the people of this country would never submit.

Elliot, vol. 4, p. 259.

13.2.2.5.b   January 17, 1788

Hon. RAWLINS LOWNDES. . . . It was true, no article of the Constitution declared there should not be jury trials in civil cases; yet this must be implied, because it stated that all crimes, except in cases of impeachment, shall be tried by a jury. But even if trials by jury were allowed, could any person rest satisfied with a mode of trial which prevents the parties from being obliged to bring a cause for discussion before a jury of men chosen from the vicinage, in a manner conformable to the present administration of justice, which had stood the test of time and experience, and ever been highly approved of? . . .

. . .

Hon. ROBERT BARNWELL. . . . The honorable gentleman asks why the trial by jury was not established in every instance. Mr. Barnwell considered this right of trial as the birthright of every American, and the basis of our civil liberty; but still most certainly particular circumstances may arise, which would induce even the greatest advocates for this right to yield it for a time. In his opinion, the circumstances that would lead to this point were those which are specified by the Constitution. Mr. Barnwell said, Suffer me to state a case, and let every gentleman determine whether, in particular instances, he would not rather resign than retain this right of trial. A suit is depending between a citizen of Carolina and Georgia, and it becomes necessary to try it in Georgia. What is the consequence? Why, the citizen of this state must rest his cause upon the jury of his opponent's vicinage, where, unknown and unrelated, he stands a very poor chance for justice against one whose neighbors, whose friends and relations, compose the greater part of his judges. It is in this case, and only in cases of a similar nature with this, that the right of trial by jury is not established; and judging from myself, it is in this instance only that every man would wish to resign it, not to a jury with whom he is unacquainted, but to an impartial and responsible individual.

Elliot, vol. 4, pp. 290, 294–95.

13.2.2.6 Virginia

13.2.2.6.a June 5, 1788

Mr. HENRY. . . . Here is a resolution as radical as that which separated us from Great Britain. It is radical in this transition; our rights and privileges are endangered, and the sovereignty of the states will be relinquished: and cannot we plainly see that this is actually the case? The rights of conscience, trial by jury, liberty of the press, all your immunities and franchises, all pretensions to human rights and privileges, are rendered insecure, if not lost, by this change, so loudly talked of by some, and inconsiderately by others. Is this tame relinquishment of rights worthy of freemen? Is it worthy of that manly fortitude that ought to characterize republicans? . . .

Having premised these things, I shall, with the aid of my judgment and information, which, I confess, are not extensive, go into the discussion of this system more minutely. Is it necessary for your liberty that you should abandon those great rights by the adoption of this system? Is the relinquishment of the trial by jury and the liberty of the press necessary for your liberty? . . .

. . . In some parts of the plan before you, the great rights of freemen are endangered; in other parts, absolutely taken away. How does your trial by jury stand? In civil cases gone — not sufficiently secured in criminal — this best privilege is gone. But we are told that we need not fear; because those in power, being our representatives, will not abuse the powers we put in their hands. I am not well versed in history, but I will submit to your recollection, whether liberty has been destroyed most often by the licentiousness of the people, or by the tyranny of rulers. . . . My great objection to this government is, that it does not leave us the means of defending our rights. . . .

Elliot, vol. 3, pp. 44, 45, 47.

13.2.2.6.b June 6, 1788

Gov. RANDOLPH. . . . Let us argue with unprejudiced minds. They say that the trial by jury is gone. Is this so? Although I have declared my determination to give my vote for it, yet I shall freely censure those parts which appear to me reprehensible.

The trial by jury in criminal cases is secured; in civil cases it is not so expressly secured as I should wish it; but it does not follow that Congress has the power of taking away this privilege, which is secured by the constitution of each state, and not given away by this Constitution. I have no fear on this subject. Congress must regulate it so as to suit every state. I will risk my property on the certainty that they will institute the trial by jury in such manner as shall accommodate the conveniences of the inhabitants in every state. The difficulty of ascertaining this accommodation was the principal cause of its not being provided for. It will be the interest of the individuals composing Congress to put it on this convenient footing.

Elliot, vol. 3, p. 68 [mistakenly dated June 16].

13.2.2.6.c **June 7, 1788**

Mr. HENRY. . . . If we are to have one representative for every thirty thousand souls, it must be by implication. The Constitution does not positively secure it. Even say it is a natural implication, — why not give us a right to that proportion in express terms, in language that could not admit of evasions or subterfuges? If they can use implication for us, they can also use implication against us. We are giving power; they are getting power; judge, then, on which side the implication will be used! When we once put it in their option to assume constructive power, danger will follow. Trial by jury, and liberty of the press, are also on this foundation of implication. If they encroach on these rights, and you give your implication for a plea, you are cast; for they will be justified by the last part of it, which gives them full power "to make all laws which shall be necessary and proper to carry their power into execution." Implication is dangerous, because it is unbounded: if it be admitted at all, and no limits be prescribed, it admits of the utmost extension. . . .

Elliot, vol. 3, p. 149.

13.2.2.6.d **June 9, 1788**

Gov. RANDOLPH. . . . Why have we been told that maxims can alone save nations; that our maxims are our bill of rights; and that the liberty of the press, trial by jury, and religion, are destroyed? Give me leave to say, that the maxims of Virginia are union and justice.

Elliot, vol. 3, p. 190.

13.2.2.6.e **June 10, 1788**

Gov. RANDOLPH. . . . It is also objected that the trial by jury, the writ of *habeas corpus,* and the liberty of the press, are insecure. But I contend that the *habeas corpus* is at least on as secure and good a footing as it is in England. In that country, it depends on the will of the legislature. That privilege is secured here by the Constitution, and is only to be suspended in cases of extreme emergency. Is this not a fair footing? After agreeing that the government of England secures liberty, how do we distrust this government? Why distrust ourselves? The liberty of the press is supposed to be in danger. If this were the case, it would produce extreme repugnancy in my mind. If it ever will be suppressed in this country, the liberty of the people will not be far from being sacrificed. Where is the danger of it? He says that every power is given to the general government that is not reserved to the states. Pardon me if I say the reverse of the proposition is true. I defy any one to prove the contrary. Every power not given it by this system is left with the states. This being the principle, from what part of the Constitution can the liberty of the press be said to be in danger?

[Here his excellency read the 8th section of the 1st article, containing all the powers given to Congress.]

Go through these powers, examine every one, and tell me if the most exalted genius can prove that the liberty of the press is in danger. The trial by jury is supposed to be in danger also. It is secured in criminal cases, but supposed to be taken away in civil cases. It is not relinquished by the Constitution; it is only not provided for. Look at the interest of Congress to suppress it. Can it be in any manner advantageous for them to suppress it? In equitable cases, it ought not to prevail, nor with respect to admiralty causes; because there will be an undue leaning against those characters, of whose business courts of admiralty will have cognizance. I will rest myself secure under this reflection — that it is impossible for the most suspicious or malignant mind to show that it is the interest of Congress to infringe on this trial by jury.

Elliot, vol. 3, pp. 203–04.

13.2.2.6.f June 12, 1788

Mr. HENRY. . . . His amendments go to that despised thing, called *a bill of rights,* and all the rights which are dear to human nature — trial by jury, the liberty of religion and the press, &c. Do not gentlemen see that, if we adopt, under the idea of following Mr. Jefferson's opinion, we amuse ourselves with the shadow, while the substance is given away?

Elliot, vol. 3, p. 314.

13.2.2.6.g June 14, 1788

Mr. HENRY. . . . By this Constitution, some of the best barriers of human rights are thrown away. Is there not an additional reason to have a bill of rights? By the ancient common law, the trial of all facts is decided by a jury of impartial men from the immediate vicinage. This paper speaks of different juries from the common law in criminal cases; and in civil controversies excludes trial by jury altogether. There is, therefore, more occasion for the supplementary check of a bill of rights now than then.

Elliot, vol. 3, pp. 446–47.

13.2.2.6.h June 15, 1788

Gov. RANDOLPH. . . . Gentlemen have been misled, to a certain degree, by a general declaration that the trial by jury was gone. We see that, in the most valuable cases, it is reserved. Is it abolished in civil cases? Let him put his finger on the part where it is abolished. The Constitution is silent on it. What expression would you wish the Constitution to use, to establish it? Remember we are not making a constitution for Virginia alone, or we might have taken Virginia for our directory. But we were forming a constitution for thirteen states. The trial by jury is different in the different states. In some states it is excluded in cases in which it is admitted to others. In admiralty causes it is not used. Would you have a jury to determine the case of a capture? The Virginia legislature thought proper to make an exception of that case. These depend on the law of nations, and no twelve men that could be picked up could be equal to the decision of such a matter.

Elliot, vol. 3, pp. 468–69.

June 20, 1788

Mr. MADISON. . . . It was objected, yesterday, that there was no provision for a jury from the vicinage. If it could have been done with safety, it would not have been opposed. It might happen that a trial would be impracticable in the country. Suppose a rebellion in a whole district; would it not be impossible to get a jury? The *trial by jury* is held as sacred in England as in America. There are deviations from it in England; yet greater deviations have happened here, since we established our independence, than have taken place there for a long time, though it be left to the legislative discretion. It is a misfortune in any case that this trial should be departed from; yet in some cases it is necessary. It must be, therefore, left to the discretion of the legislature to modify it according to circumstances. This is a complete and satisfactory answer.

. . .

Mr. HENRY. . . . "In all cases affecting ambassadors, other public ministers, and consuls, and those in which a state shall be a party, the Supreme Court shall have original jurisdiction. In all the other cases before mentioned, the Supreme Court shall have appellate jurisdiction, both as to law and fact. . . ." This will, in its operation, destroy the trial by jury. The verdict of an impartial jury will be reversed by judges unacquainted with the circumstances. But we are told that Congress are to make regulations to remedy this. . . . If Congress alter this part, they will repeal the Constitution. . . . When Congress, by virtue of this sweeping clause, will organize these courts, they cannot depart from the Constitution; and their laws in opposition to the Constitution would be void. . . . What then, Mr. Chairman? We are told that, if this does not satisfy every mind, they will yield. It is not satisfactory to my mind, whatever it may be to others. . . .

We are told of certain difficulties. I acknowledge it is difficult to form a constitution. But I have seen difficulties conquered which were as unconquerable as this. We are told that trial by jury is difficult to be had in certain cases. Do we not know the meaning of the term? We are also told it is a technical term. I see one thing in this Constitution; I made the observation before, and I am still of the same opinion, that everything with respect to privileges is so involved in darkness, it makes me suspicious — not of those gentlemen who formed it, but of its operations in its present form. Could not precise terms have been used? You find, by the observations of the gentleman last up, that, when there is a plentitude of power, there is no difficulty; but when you come to a plain thing, understood by all America, there are contradictions, ambiguities, difficulties, and what not. Trial by jury is attended, it seems, with insuperable difficulties, and therefore omitted altogether in civil cases. But an idea is held out that it is secured in criminal cases. I had rather it had been left out altogether than have it so vaguely and equivocally provided for. Poor people do not understand technical terms. Their rights ought to be secured in language of which they know the meaning. As they do not know the meaning of such terms, they may be injured with impunity. If they dare oppose the hands of tyrannical power, you will see what has been practised elsewhere. They may be tried by the most partial powers, by their most implacable enemies, and be sentenced and put to death, with all the forms of a fair trial. I would rather be left to the judges. An abandoned juror would not dread the loss of character like a judge. From these, and a thousand other considerations, I would rather the trial by jury were struck out altogether. There is no right of challenging partial jurors. There is no common law of America, (as has been said,) nor constitution, but that on your table. If there be neither common law nor constitution, there can be no right to challenge partial jurors. Yet the right is as valuable as the trial by jury itself.

. . .

Mr. HENRY. . . . To hear gentlemen of such penetration make use of such arguments, to persuade us to part with that trial by jury, is very astonishing. We are told that we are to part with that trial by jury which our ancestors secured their lives and property with, and we are to build castles in the air, and substitute visionary modes of decision for that noble palladium. I hope we shall never be induced, by such arguments, to part with that excellent mode of trial. No appeal can now be made as to fact in common-law suits. The unanimous verdict of twelve impartial men cannot be reversed. I shall take the liberty of reading to the committee the sentiments of the learned Judge Blackstone, so often quoted, on the subject.

[Here Mr. Henry read the eulogium of that writer on this trial, *Blackstone's Commentaries,* iii. 319.]

The opinion of this learned writer is more forcible and cogent than any thing I could say. Notwithstanding the transcendent excellency of this trial, its essentiality to the preservation of liberty, and the extreme danger of substituting any other mode, yet we are now about to alienate it.

But on this occasion, as on all others, we are admonished to rely on the wisdom and virtue of our rulers. We are told that the members from Georgia, New Hampshire, &c., will not dare to infringe this privilege; that, as it would excite the indignation of the people, they would not attempt it: that is, the enormity of the offence is urged as a security against its commission. It is so abominable that Congress will not exercise it. Shall we listen to arguments like these, when trial by jury is about to be relinquished? I beseech you to consider before you decide. I ask you, What is the value of that privilege? When Congress, in all the plentitude of their arrogance, magnificence, and power, can take it from you, will you be satisfied? Are we to go so far as to concede every thing to the virtue of Congress? Throw yourselves at once on their mercy; be no longer free than their virtue will predominate: if this will satisfy republican minds, there is an end of every thing. I disdain to hold any thing of any man. We ought to cherish that disdain. America viewed with indignation the idea of holding her rights in England. The Parliament gave you the most solemn assurances that they would not exercise this power. Were you satisfied with their promises? No. Did you trust any man on earth? No. You answered that you disdained to hold your innate, indefeasible rights of any one. Now, you are called upon to give an exorbitant and most alarming power. The genius of my countrymen is the same now that it was then. They have the same feelings. They are equally martial and bold. Will not their answer therefore be the same? I hope that gentlemen will, on a fair investigation, be candid, and not on every occasion recur to the virtue of our representatives.

When deliberating on the relinquishment of the sword and purse, we have a right to some other reason than the possible virtue of our rulers. We are informed that the strength and energy of the government call for the surrender of this right. Are we to make our country strong by giving up our privileges? I tell you that, if you judge from reason, or the experience of other nations, you will find that your country will be great and respectable according as you will preserve this great privilege. It is prostrated by that paper. Juries from the vicinage being not secured, this right is in reality sacrificed. All is gone. And why? Because a rebellion may arise. Resistance will come from certain countries, and juries will come from the same countries.

I trust the honorable gentleman, on a better recollection, will be sorry for this observation. Why do we love this trial by jury? Because it prevents the hand of oppression from cutting you off. They may call any thing rebellion, and deprive you of a fair trial by an impartial jury of your neighbors. Has not your mother country magnanimously preserved this noble privilege upwards of a thousand years? Did she relinquish a jury of the vicinage because there was a possibility of resistance to oppression? She has been magnanimous enough to resist every attempt to take away this privilege. She has had magnanimity enough to rebel when her rights were infringed. That country had juries of hundredors for many generations. And shall Americans give up that which nothing could induce the English people to relinquish? The idea is abhorrent to my mind. There was a time when we should have spurned at it. This gives me comfort — that, as long as I have existence, my neighbors will protect me. Old as I am, it is probable I may yet have the appellation of *rebel*. I trust that I shall see congressional oppression crushed in embryo. As this government stands, I despise and abhor it. Gentlemen demand it, though it takes away the trial by jury in civil cases, and does worse than take it away in criminal cases. It is gone unless you preserve it now. I beg pardon for speaking so long. Many more observations will present themselves to the minds of gentlemen when they analyze this part. We find enough, from what has been said, to come to this conclusion — that it was not intended to have jury trials at all; because, difficult as it was, the name was known, and it might have been inserted. Seeing that appeals are given, in matters of fact, to the Supreme Court, we are led to believe that you must carry your witnesses an immense distance to the seat of government, or decide appeals according to the Roman law. I shall add no more, but that I hope that gentlemen will recollect what they are about to do, and consider that they are going to give up this last and best privilege.

Mr. PENDLETON. Mr. Chairman, before I enter upon the objections made to this part, I will observe that I should suppose, if there were any person in this audience who had not read this Constitution, or who had not heard what has been said, and should have been told that the trial by jury was intended to be taken away, he would be surprised to find, on examination, that there was no exclusion of it in civil cases, and that it was expressly provided for in criminal cases. I never could see such intention, or any tendency towards it. I have not heard any arguments of that kind used in favor of the Constitution. If there were any words in it which said that trial by jury should not be used, it would be dangerous. I find it secured in criminal cases, and that the trial is to be had in the state where the crime shall have been committed. It is strongly insisted that the privilege of challenging, or excepting to the jury, is not secured. When the Constitution says that the trial shall be by jury, does it not say that every incident will go along with it? I think the honorable gentleman was mistaken yesterday in his reasoning on the propriety of a jury from the vicinage.

He supposed that a jury from the neighborhood is had from this view — that they should be acquainted with the personal character of the person accused. I thought it was with another view — that the jury should have some personal knowledge of the fact, and acquaintance with the witnesses, who will come from the neighborhood. How is it understood in this state? Suppose a man, who lives in Winchester, commits a crime at Norfolk; the jury to try him must come, not from Winchester, but from the neighborhood of Norfolk. *Trial by jury* is secured by this system in criminal cases, as are all the incidental circumstances relative to it. The honorable gentleman yesterday made an objection to that clause which says that the judicial power shall be vested in one Supreme Court, and such inferior courts as Congress may ordain and establish. He objects that there is an unlimited power of appointing inferior courts. I refer to that gentleman, whether it would have been proper to limit this power. Could those gentlemen who framed that instrument have extended their ideas to all the necessities of the United States, and seen every case in which it would be necessary to have an inferior tribunal? By the regulations of Congress, they may be accommodated to public convenience and utility. We may expect that there will be an inferior court in each state; each state will insist on it; and each, for that reason, will agree to it.

. . .

Mr. JOHN MARSHALL. . . . The exclusion of trial by jury, in this case, he [Patrick Henry] urged to prostrate our rights. Does the word *court* only mean the judges? Does not the determination of a jury necessarily lead to the judgment of the court? Is there any thing here which gives the judges exclusive jurisdiction of matters of fact? What is the object of a jury trial? To inform the court of the facts. When a court has cognizance of facts does it not follow that they can make inquiry by a jury? It is impossible to be otherwise. I hope that in this country, where impartiality is so much admired, the laws will direct facts to be ascertained by a jury. But, says the honorable gentleman, the juries in the ten miles square will be mere tools of parties, with which he would not trust his person or property; which, he says, he would rather leave to the court. Because the government may have a district of ten miles square, will no man stay there but the tools and officers of the government? Will nobody else be found there? Is it so in any other part of the world, where a government has legislative power? Are there none but officers, and tools of the government of Virginia, in Richmond? Will there not be independent merchants, and respectable gentlemen of fortune, within the ten miles square? Will there not be worthy farmers and mechanics? Will not a good jury be found there, as well as anywhere else? Will the officers of the government become improper to be on a jury? What is it to the government whether this man or that man succeeds? It is all one thing. Does the Constitution say that juries shall consist of officers, or that the Supreme Court shall be held in the ten miles square? It was acknowledged, by the honorable member, that it was secure in England. What makes it secure there? Is it their constitution? What part of their constitution is there that the Parliament cannot change? As the preservation of this right is in the hands of Parliament, and it has ever been held sacred by them, will the government of America be less honest than that of Great Britain? Here a restriction is to be found. The jury is not to be brought out of the state. There is no such restriction in that government; for the laws of Parliament decide every thing respecting it. Yet gentlemen tell us that there is safety there, and nothing here but danger. It seems to me that the laws of the United States will generally secure trials by a jury of the vicinage, or in such manner as will be most safe and convenient for the people.

But it seems that the right of challenging the jurors is not secured in this Constitution. Is this done by our own Constitution, or by any provision of the English government? Is it done by their Magna Charta, or bill of rights? This privilege is founded on their laws. If so, why should it be objected to the American Constitution, that it is not inserted in it? If we are secure in Virginia without mentioning it in our Constitution, why should not this security be found in the federal court?

The honorable gentleman said much about the quitrents in the Northern Neck. I will refer it to the honorable gentleman himself. Has he not acknowledged that there was no complete title? Was he not satisfied that the right of the legal representatives of the proprietor did not exist at the time he mentioned? If so, it cannot exist now. I will leave it to those gentlemen who come from that quarter. I trust they will not be intimidated, on this account, in voting on this question. A law passed in 1782, which secures this. He says that many poor men may be harassed and injured by the representatives of Lord Fairfax. If he has no right, this cannot be done. If he has this right, and comes to Virginia, what laws will his claims be determined by? By those of the state. By what tribunals will they be determined? By our state courts. Would not the poor man, who was oppressed by an unjust prosecution, be abundantly protected and satisfied by the temper of his neighbors, and would he not find ample justice? What reason has the honorable member to apprehend partiality or injustice? He supposes that, if the judges be judges of both the federal and state courts, they will incline in favor of one government. If such contests should arise, who could more properly decide them than those who are to swear to do justice? If we can expect a fair decision any where, may we not expect justice to be done by the judges of both the federal and state governments? But, says the honorable member, laws may be executed tyrannically. Where is the independency of your judges? If a law be exercised tyrannically in Virginia, to what can you trust? To your judiciary. What security have you for justice? Their independence. Will it not be so in the federal court?

Gentlemen ask, What is meant by law cases, and if they be not distinct from facts? Is there no law arising on cases of equity and admiralty? Look at the acts of Assembly. Have you not many cases where law and fact are blended? Does not the jurisdiction in point of law as well as fact, find itself completely satisfied in law and fact? The honorable gentleman says that no law of Congress can make any exception to the federal appellate jurisdiction of facts as well as law. He has frequently spoken of technical terms, and the meaning of them. What is the meaning of the term *exception*? Does it not mean alteration and diminution? Congress is empowered to make exceptions to the appellate jurisdiction, as to law and fact, of the Supreme Court. These exceptions certainly go as far as the legislature may think proper for the interest and liberty of the people. Who can understand this word, *exception,* to extend to one case as well as the other? I am persuaded that a reconsideration of this case will convince the gentlemen that he was mistaken. This may go to the cure of the mischief apprehended. Gentlemen must be satisfied that this power will not be so much abused as they have said.

The honorable member says that he derives no consolation from the wisdom and integrity of the legislature, because we call them to rectify defects which it is our duty to remove. We ought well to weigh the good and evil before we determine. We ought to be well convinced that the evil will be really produced before we decide against it. If we be convinced that the good greatly preponderates, though there be small defects in it, shall we give up that which is really good, when we can remove the little mischief it may contain, in the plain, easy method pointed out in the system itself?

I was astonished when I heard the honorable gentleman say that he wished the trial by jury to be struck out entirely. Is there no justice to be expected by a jury of our fellow citizens? Will any man prefer to be tried by a court, when the jury is to be of his countrymen, and probably of his vicinage? We have reason to believe the regulations with respect to juries will be such as shall be satisfactory. Because it does not contain all, does it contain nothing? But I conceive that this committee will see there is safety in the case, and that there is no mischief to be apprehended.

He states a case, that a man may be carried from a federal to an anti-federal corner, (and *vice versa*) where men are ready to destroy him. Is this probable? Is it presumable that they will make a law to punish men who are of different opinions in politics from themselves? Is it presumable that they will do it in one single case, unless it be such a case as must satisfy the people at large? The good opinion of the people at large must be consulted by their representatives; otherwise, mischiefs would be produced which would shake the government to its foundation. As it is late, I shall not mention all the gentleman's argument, but some parts of it are so glaring that I cannot pass them over in silence. He says that the establishment of these tribunals, and more particularly in their jurisdiction of controversies between citizens of these states and foreign citizens and subjects, is like a retrospective law. Is there no difference between a tribunal which shall give justice and effect to an existing right, and creating a right that did not exist before? The debt or claim is created by the individual. He has bound himself to comply with it. Does the creation of a new court amount to a retrospective law?

We are satisfied with the provision made in this country on the subject of trial by jury. Does our Constitution direct trials to be by jury? It is required in our bill of rights, which is not a part of the Constitution. Does any security arise from hence? Have you a jury when a judgment is obtained on a replevin bond, or by default? Have you a jury when a motion is made for the commonwealth against an individual; or when a motion is made by one joint obligor against another, to recover sums paid as security? Our courts decide in all these cases, without the intervention of a jury; yet they are all civil cases. The bill of rights is merely recommendatory. Were it otherwise, the consequence would be that many laws which are found convenient would be unconstitutional. What does the government before you say? Does it exclude the legislature from giving a trial by jury in civil cases? If it does not forbid its exclusion, it is on the same footing on which your state government stands now. The legislature of Virginia does not give a trial by jury where it is not necessary, but gives it wherever it is thought expedient. The federal legislature will do so too, as it is formed on the same principles.

The honorable gentleman says that unjust claims will be made, and the defendant had better pay them than go to the Supreme Court. Can you suppose such a disposition in one of your citizens, as that, to oppress another man, he will incur great expenses? What will he gain by an unjust demand? Does a claim establish a right? He must bring his witnesses to prove his claim. If he does not bring his witnesses, the expenses must fall upon him. Will he go on a calculation that the defendant will not defend it, or cannot produce a witness? Will he incur a great deal of expense, from a dependence on such a chance? Those who know human nature, black as it is, must know that mankind are too well attached to their interest to run such a risk. I conceive that this power is absolutely necessary, and not dangerous; that, should it be attended by little inconveniences, they will be altered, and that they can have no interest in not altering them. Is there any real danger? When I compare it to the exercise of the same power in the government of Virginia, I am persuaded there is not. The federal government has no other motive, and has every reason for doing right which the members of our state legislature have. Will a man on the eastern shore be sent to be tried in Kentucky, or a man from Kentucky be brought to the eastern shore to have his trial? A government, by doing this, would destroy itself. I am convinced the trial by jury will be regulated in the manner most advantageous to the community.

Elliot, vol. 3, pp. 537, 540–42, 544–47, 557–62.

13.2.2.6.j **June 23, 1788**

He [MR. HENRY] then proceeded to state the appellate jurisdiction of the judicial power, both as to law and fact, with such exceptions and under such regulations as Congress shall make. He observed, that, as Congress had a right to organize the federal judiciary, they might or might not have recourse to a jury, as they pleased. He left it to the candor of the honorable gentleman to say whether those persons who were at the expense of taking witnesses to Philadelphia, or wherever the federal judiciary may sit, could be certain whether they were to be heard before a jury or not. An honorable gentleman (Mr. Marshall) the other day observed, that he conceived the trial by jury better secured under the plan on the table than in the British government, or even in our bill of rights. I have the highest veneration and respect for the honorable gentleman, and I have experienced his candor on all occasions; but, Mr. Chairman, in this instance, he is so materially mistaken that I cannot but observe, he is much in error. I beg the clerk to read that part of the Constitution which relates to trial by jury. [*The clerk then read the 8th article of the bill of rights.*]

Mr. MARSHALL rose to explain what he had before said on this subject: he informed the committee that the honorable gentleman (Mr. Henry) must have misunderstood him. He said that he conceived the trial by jury was as well secured, and not better secured, in the proposed new Constitution as in our bill of rights. [*The clerk then read the* 11*th article of the bill of rights.*]

Mr. HENRY. Mr. Chairman: The gentleman's candor, sir, as I informed you before, I have the highest opinion of, and am happy to find he has so far explained what he meant; but, sir, has he mended the matter? Is not the ancient trial by jury preserved in the Virginia bill of rights? and is that the case in the new plan? No, sir; they can do it if they please. Will gentlemen tell me the trial by jury of the vicinage where the party resides is preserved? True, sir, there is to be a trial by the jury in the state where the fact was committed; but, sir, this state, for instance, is so large that your juries may be collected five hundred miles from where the party resides — no neighbors who are acquainted with their characters, their good or bad conduct in life, to judge of the unfortunate man who may be thus exposed to the rigor of that government. Compare this security, then, sir, in our bill of rights with that in the new plan of government; and in the first you have it, and in the other, in my opinion, not at all. But, sir, in what situation will our citizens be, who have made large contracts under our present government? They will be called to a federal court, and tried under the retrospective laws; for it is evident, to me at least, that the federal court must look back, and give better remedies, to compel individuals to fulfill them.

The whole history of human nature cannot produce a government like that before you. The manner in which the judiciary and other branches of the government are formed, seems to me calculated to lay prostrate the states, and the liberties of the people. But, sir, another circumstance ought totally to reject that plan, in my opinion; which is, that it cannot be understood, in many parts, even by the supporters of it. A constitution, sir, ought to be, like a beacon, held up to the public eye, so as to be understood by every man. Some gentlemen have observed that the word *jury* implies a jury of the vicinage. There are so many inconsistencies in this, that, for my part, I cannot understand it. By the bill of rights of England, a subject has a right to a trial by his peers. What is meant by his peers? Those who reside near him, his neighbors, and who are well acquainted with his character and situation in life. Is this secured in the proposed plan before you? No, sir. As I have observed before, what is to become of the *purchases of the Indians?* — those unhappy nations who have given up their lands to private purchasers; who, by being made drunk, have given a thousand, nay, I might say, ten thousand acres, for the trifling sum of sixpence! It is with true concern, with grief, I tell you that I have waited with pain to come to this part of the plan; because I observed gentlemen admitted its being defective, and, I had my hopes, would have proposed amendments. But this part they have defended; and this convinces me of the necessity of obtaining amendments before it is adopted. They have defended it with ingenuity and perseverance, but by no means satisfactorily. If previous amendments are not obtained, the trial by jury is gone. British debtors will be ruined by being dragged to the federal court, and the liberty and happiness of our citizens gone, never again to be recovered.

Elliot, vol. 3, pp. 578–79.

13.2.2.6.k June 24, 1788

Mr. HENRY. . . . The honorable member must forgive me for declaring my dissent from it; because, if I understand it rightly, it admits that the new system is defective, and most capitally; for, immediately after the proposed ratification, there comes a declaration that the paper before you is not intended to violate any of these three great rights — the liberty of religion, liberty of the press, and the trial by jury. What is the inference when you enumerate the rights which you are to enjoy? That those not enumerated are relinquished. There are only three things to be retained — religion, freedom of the press, and jury trial. Will not the ratification carry every thing, without excepting these three things? Will not all the world pronounce that we intended to give up all the rest? Every thing it speaks of, by way of rights, is comprised in these things. Your subsequent amendments only go to these three amendments.

. . .

. . . In my weak judgment, a government is strong when it applies to the most important end of all governments — the rights and privileges of the people. In the honorable member's proposal, jury trial, the press and religion, and other essential rights, are not to be given up. Other essential rights — what are they? The world will say that you intended to give them up. When you go into an enumeration of your rights, and stop that enumeration, the inevitable conclusion is, that what is omitted is intended to be surrendered.
Elliot, vol. 3, pp. 587–88, 594.

13.2.3 PHILADELPHIA CONVENTION

13.2.3.1 September 12, 1787

Mr. WILLIAMSON observed to the House, that no provision was yet made for juries in civil cases, and suggested the necessity of it.

Mr. GORHAM. It is not possible to discriminate equity cases from those in which juries are proper. The representatives of the people may be safely trusted in this matter.

Mr. GERRY urged the necessity of juries to guard against corrupt judges. He proposed that the committee last appointed should be directed to provide a clause for securing the trial by juries.

Col. MASON perceived the difficulty mentioned by Mr. Gorham. The jury cases cannot be specified. A general principle laid down, on this and some other points, would be sufficient. . . .

Mr. SHERMAN . . . There are many cases, where juries are proper, which cannot be discriminated. The Legislature may be safely trusted.
Elliot, vol. 5, p. 538.

13.2.3.2 September 15, 1787

Article 3, sect. 2, (the third paragraph,) Mr. PINCKNEY and Mr. GERRY moved to annex to the end, "and a trial by jury shall be preserved as usual in civil cases."

Mr. GORHAM. The constitution of juries is different in different states, and the trial itself is *usual* in different cases, in different states.

Mr. KING urged the same objections.

Gen. PINCKNEY also. He thought such a clause in the Constitution would be pregnant with embarrassments.

The motion was disagreed to, *nem. con.*

*   *   *

Mr. Gerry. Stated the objections which determined him to withhold his name from the Constitution. . . . He could however he said get over all these, if the rights of the Citizens were not rendered insecure . . . to establish a tribunal without juries, which will be a Star- Chamber as to Civil cases. Under such a view of the Constitution, the best that could be done he conceived was to provide for a second general Convention.   Elliot, vol. 5, p. 550; Kaminski & Saladino, vol. 13, p. 199.

13.2.4 NEWSPAPERS AND PAMPHLETS

13.2.4.1 Address of the Seceding Assemblymen, October 2, 1787

. . . You will be able likewise to determine, whether in a free government there ought or ought not to be any provision against a standing army in time of peace? or whether the trial by jury in civil causes is become dangerous and ought to be abolished? . . .

[Philadelphia] Independent Gazetteer, Kaminski & Saladino,
vol. 13, p. 296.

13.2.4.2 Centinel, No. 1, October 5, 1787

Friends, Countrymen and Fellow Citizens, Permit one of yourselves to put you in mind of certain *liberties* and *privileges* secured to you by the constitution of this commonwealth, and to beg your serious attention to his uninterested opinion upon the plan of federal government submitted to your consideration, before you surrender these great and valuable privileges up forever. . . . Your constitution further provides "that in controversies respecting property, and in suits between man and man, the parties have a right *to trial by jury, which ought to be held sacred.*" . . . Whether the *trial by jury* is to continue as your birth-right, the freemen of Pennsylvania, nay, of all America, are now called upon to declare.

. . .

. . . And it is worthy of remark, that there is no declaration of personal rights, premised in most free constitutions; and that trial by *jury* in *civil* cases is taken away; for what other construction can be put on the following, viz. Article III. Sect. 2d. "In all cases affecting ambassadors, other public ministers and consuls, and those in which a State shall be a party, the Supreme Court shall have *original* jurisdiction. In all other cases above mentioned, the Supreme Court shall have *appellate* jurisdiction, both as to *law and fact?*" It would be a novelty in jurisprudence, as well as evidently improper to allow an appeal from the verdict of a jury, on the matter of fact; therefore, it implies and allows of a dismission of the jury in civil cases, and especially when it is considered, that the jury trial in criminal cases is expresly [*sic*] stipulated for, but not in civil cases.

[Philadelphia] Independent Gazetteer, Kaminski & Saladino,
vol. 13, pp. 328–29, 336.

13.2.4.3 Blessings of the New Government, October 6, 1787

Another correspondent observes, that although the tide seems to run so high at present in favor of the new constitution, there is no doubt but the people will soon change their minds, when they have time to examine it with coolness and impartiality.

Among the *blessings* of the new-proposed government our correspondent enumerates the following:—. . . 6. No trial by jury in civil cases. . . . 13. And *death* if we dare to complain.   [Philadelphia] Independent Gazetteer, Kaminski & Saladino, vol. 13, pp. 345.

13.2.4.4 James Wilson, Address to the Citizens of Philadelphia, October 6, 1787

. . . Another objection that has been fabricated against the new Constitution, is expressed in disingenuous form — "the trial by jury is abolished in civil cases." . . . Let it be remembered then, that the business of the Fœderal Convention was not local, but general; not limited to the views and establishments of a single state, but co-extensive with the continent, and comprehending the views and establishments of thirteen independent sovereignties. When therefore, this subject was in discussion, we were involved in difficulties which pressed on all sides, and no precedent could be discovered to direct our course. The cases open to a trial by jury, differed in the different states, it was therefore impracticable on that ground to have made a general rule. The want of uniformity would have rendered any reference to the practice of the states idle and useless; and it could not, with any propriety, be said that "the trial by jury shall be as heretofore," since there has never existed any federal system of jurisprudence, to which the declaration could relate. Besides, it is not in all civil cases that the trial by jury is adopted in civil questions, for causes depending in courts of admiralty, such as relate to maritime captures, and such as are agitated in courts of equity, do not require the intervention of that tribunal. How then, was the line of discrimination to be drawn? The convention found the task too difficult for them, and they left the business as it stands, in the fullest confidence that no danger could possibly ensue, since the proceedings of the supreme court are to be regulated by the congress, which is a faithful representation of the people; . . .

Pennsylvania Herald, October 9, 1787, Kaminski & Saladino, vol. 13, pp. 340–41.

13.2.4.5 George Mason, Objections to the Constitution, October 7, 1787

There is no Declaration of Rights; and the Laws of the general Government being paramount to the Laws & Constitutions of the several States, the Declarations of Rights in the separate States are no Security.

. . .

There is no Declaration of any kind for preserving the Liberty of the Press, the Tryal by jury in civil Causes; nor against the Danger of standing Armys in time of peace.

. . .

This Government will commence in a moderate Aristocracy; it is at present impossible to foresee whether it will, in it's Operation, produce a Monarchy, or a corrupt oppressive Aristocracy; it will most probably vibrate some years between the two, and then terminate in the one or the other.

Kaminski & Saladino, vol. 13, pp. 348–50.

13.2.4.6 The Federal Farmer, No. 2, October 9, 1787

The essential parts of a free and good government are a full and equal representation of the people in the legislature, and the jury trial of the vicinage in the administration of justice — a full and equal representation, is that which possesses the same interests, feelings, opinions, and views the people themselves would were they all assembled — a fair representation, therefore, should be so regulated, that every order of men in the community, according to the common course of elections, can have a share in it — in order to allow professional men, merchants, traders, farmers, mechanics, &c. to bring a just proportion of their best informed men respectively into the legislature, the representation must be considerably numerous — We have about 200 state senators in the United States, and a less number than that of federal representatives cannot, clearly, be a full representation of this people, in the affairs of internal taxation and police, were there but one legislature for the whole union. The representation cannot be equal, or the situation of the people proper for one government only — if the extreme parts of the society cannot be represented as fully as the central — It is apparently impracticable that this should be the case in this extensive country — it would be impossible to collect a representation of the parts of the country five, six, and seven hundred miles from the seat of government.

Under one general government alone, there could be but one judiciary, one supreme and a proper number of inferior courts. I think it would be totally impracticable in this case to preserve a due administration of justice, and the real benefits of the jury trial of the vicinage — there are now supreme courts in each state in the union, and a great number of county and other courts, subordinate to each supreme court — most of these supreme and inferior courts are itinerant, and hold their sessions in different parts every year of their respective states, counties and districts — with all these moving courts, our citizens, from the vast extent of the country, must travel very considerable distances from home to find the place where justice is administered. I am not for bringing justice to individuals as to afford them any temptation to engage in law suits; though I think it one of the greatest benefits in a good government, that each citizen should find a court of justice within a reasonable distance, perhaps, within a day's travel of his home; so that without great inconveniences and enormous expense, he may have the advantages of his witnesses and jury — it would be impracticable to derive these advantages from one judiciary — the one supreme court at most could only set in the centre of the union, and move once a year into the centre of the eastern and southern extremes of it — and, in this case, each citizen, on an average, would travel 150 or 200 miles to find this court — that, however, inferior courts might be properly placed in the different counties, and districts of the union, the appellate jurisdiction would be intolerable and expensive.

If it were possible to consolidate the states, and preserve the features of a free government, still it is evident that the middle states, the parts of the union, about the seat of government, would enjoy great advantages, while the remote states would experience the many inconveniences of remote provinces. Wealth, offices, and the benefits of government would collect in the centre: and the extreme states; and their principal towns, become much less important.

There are other considerations which tend to prove that the idea of one consolidated whole, on free principles, is ill founded — the laws of a free government rest on the confidence of the people, and operate gently — and never can extend the influence very far — if they are executed on free principles, about the centre, where benefits of the government induce the people to support it voluntarily; yet they must be executed on the principles of fear and force in the extremes — This has been the case with every extensive republic of which we have any accurate account.

There are certain unalienable and fundamental rights, which in forming the social compact, ought to be explicitly ascertained and fixed — a free and enlightened people, in forming this compact, will not resign all their rights to those who govern, and they will fix limits to their legislators and rulers, which will soon be plainly seen by those who are governed, as well as by those who govern: and the latter will know they cannot be passed unperceived by the former, and without giving a general alarm — These rights should be made the basis of every constitution; and if a people be so situated, or have such different opinions that they cannot agree in ascertaining and fixing them, it is a very strong argument against their attempting to form one entire society, to live under one system of laws only. — I confess, I never thought the people of these states differed essentially in these respects; they having derived all these rights from one common source, the British systems; and having in the formation of their state constitutions, discovered that their ideas relative to these rights are very similar. However, it is now said that the states differ so essentially in these respects, and even in the important article of the trial by jury, that when assembled in convention, they can agree to no words by which to establish that trial, or by which to ascertain and establish many other of these rights, as fundamental articles in the social compact. If so, we proceed to consolidate the states on no solid basis whatever.

Kaminski & Saladino, vol. 14, pp. 25–27.

13.2.4.7 The Federal Farmer, No. 3, October 10, 1787

. . . There are some powers proposed to be lodged in the general government in the judicial department, I think very unnecessarily, I mean powers respecting questions arising upon the internal laws of the respective states. . . . In almost all these cases, either party may have the trial by jury in the state courts; . . . justice may be obtained in these courts on reasonable terms; they must be more competent to proper decisions on the laws of their respective states, than the federal courts can possibly be. . . . It is true, those courts may be so organized by a wise and prudent legislature, as to make the obtaining of justice in them tolerably easy; they may in general be organized on the common law principles of the country: But this benefit is by no means secured by the constitution. The trial by jury is secured only in those few criminal cases, to which the federal laws will extend — as crimes committed on the seas against the law of nations, treason and counterfeiting the federal securities and coin: But even in these cases, the jury trial of the vicinage is not secured, particularly in the large states, a citizen may be tried for a crime committed in the state, and yet tried in some states 500 miles from the place where it was committed; but the jury trial is not secured at all in civil causes. Though the convention have not established this trial, it is to be hoped that congress, in putting the new system into execution, will do it by a legislative act, in all cases in which it can be done with propriety. Whether the jury trial is not excluded [in] the supreme judicial court, is an important question. . . .

Kaminski & Saladino, vol. 14, pp. 40–41.

13.2.4.8   The Federal Farmer, No. 4, October 12, 1787

. . . If the federal constitution is to be construed so far in connection with the state constitutions, as to leave the trial by jury in civil causes, for instance, secured; on the same principles it would have left the trial by jury in criminal causes, the benefits of the writ of habeas corpus, &c. secured; they all stand on the same footing; they are the common rights of Americans, and have been recognized by the state constitutions: But the convention found it necessary to recognize or re-establish the benefits of that writ, and the jury trial in criminal cases. . . . The establishing of one right implies the necessity of establishing another and similar one.

On the whole, the position appears to me to be undeniable, that this bill of rights ought to be carried farther, and some other principles established, as a part of this fundamental compact between the people of the United States and their federal rulers.

. . . There are other essential rights, which we have justly understood to be the rights of freemen. . . . The trials by jury in civil causes, it is said, varies [*sic*] so much in the several states, that no words could be found for the uniform establishment of it. If so the federal legislation will not be able to establish it by any general laws. I confess I am of opinion it may be established, but not in that beneficial manner in which we may enjoy it, for the reasons beforementioned. When I speak of the jury trial of the vicinage, or the trial of the fact in the neighbourhood, — I do not lay so much stress upon the circumstance of our being tried by our neighbors: in this enlightened country men may be probably impartially tried by those who do not live very near them: but the trial of facts in the neighborhood is of great importance in other respects. Nothing can be more essential than the cross examining witnesses, and generally before the triers of the facts in question. The common people can establish facts with much more ease with oral than written evidence; when trials of fact are removed to a distance from the homes of the parties and witnesses, oral evidence becomes intolerably expensive, and the parties must depend on written evidence, which to the common people is expensive and almost useless; it must be frequently taken ex-parte, and but very seldom leads to the proper discovery of truth.

The trial by jury is very important in another point of view. It is essential in every free country, that common people should have a part and share of influence, in the judicial as well as in the legislative department. To hold open to them the offices of senators, judges, and offices to fill which an expensive education is required, cannot answer any valuable purposes for them; they are not in a situation to be brought forward and to fill those offices; these, and most other offices of any considerable importance, will be occupied by the few. The few, the well born, &c. as Mr. Adams calls them, in judicial decisions as well as in legislation, are generally disposed, and very naturally too, to favour those of their own description.

The trial by jury in the judicial department, and the collection of the people by their representatives in the legislature, are those fortunate inventions which have procured for them, in this country, their true proportion of influence, and the wisest and most fit means of protecting themselves in the community. Their situation, as jurors and representatives, enables them to acquire information and knowledge in the affairs and government of the society; and to come forward, in turn, as the centinels and guardians of each other. I am very sorry that even a few of our countrymen should consider jurors and representatives in a different point of view, as ignorant, troublesome bodies, which ought not to have any share in the concerns of government.

Kaminski & Saladino, vol. 14, pp. 45–47.

13.2.4.9 A Democratic Federalist, October 17, 1787

The second and most important objection to the federal plan, which Mr. Wilson pretends to be made *in a disingenuous form*, is the entire *abolition of the trial by jury in civil cases.* It seems to me that Mr. Wilson's pretended answer, is much more *disingenuous* than the objection itself, which I maintain to be strictly founded in fact. He says "that the cases open to trial by jury differing in the different States, it was therefore impracticable to have made a general rule." This answer is extremely futile, because a reference might easily have been made to the *common law of England,* which obtains through every State, and cases in the maritime and civil law courts would of course have been excepted. I must also directly contradict Mr. Wilson when he asserts that there is no trial by jury in the courts of chancery — It cannot be unknown to a man of his high professional learning, that whenever a difference arises about a matter of fact in the courts of equity in America or England, the fact is sent down to the courts of common law to be tried by a jury, and it is what the lawyers call a *feigned issue.* This method will be impracticable under the proposed form of judicial jurisdiction for the United States.

But setting aside the equivocal answers of Mr. Wilson, I have it in my power to prove that under the proposed Federal Constitution, *the trial of facts in civil cases by a jury of the Vicinage* is entirely and effectually abolished, and will be absolutely impracticable. I wish the learned gentleman had explained to us what is meant by the *appellate* jurisdiction as to law and *fact* which is vested in the superior court of the United States? As he has not thought proper to do it, I shall endeavour to explain it to my fellow citizens, regretting at the same time that it has not been done by a man whose abilities are so much superior to mine. The word *appeal,* if I understand it right, in its proper legal signification includes the *fact* as well as the *law,* and precludes every idea of a trial by jury — It is a word of *foreign growth,* and is only known in England and America in those courts which are governed by the civil or ecclesiastical law of the *Romans*. Those courts have always been considered in England as a grievance, and have all been established by the usurpations of the *ecclesiastical* over the *civil* power. It is well known that the courts of chancery in England were formerly entirely in the hands of *ecclesiastics*, who took advantage of the strict forms of the common law, to introduce a foreign mode of jurisprudence under the specious name of *Equity*. Pennsylvania, the freest of the American States[,] has wisely rejected this establishment, and knows not even the name of a court of chancery — And in fact, there can not be any thing more absurd than a distinction between LAW and EQUITY. It might perhaps have suited those barbarous times when the law of England, like almost every other science, was perplexed with quibbles and *Aristotelian* distinctions, but it would be shameful to keep it up in these more enlightened days. At any rate, it seems to me that there is much more *equity* in a trial by jury, than in an appellate jurisdiction from the fact.

An *appeal* therefore is a thing unknown to the common law. Instead of an appeal from facts, it admits of a second, or even third trial by different juries, and mistakes in points of *law*, are rectified by superior courts in the form of a *writ of error* — and to a mere common lawyer, unskilled in the forms of the *civil law* courts, the words *appeal from law and fact*, are mere nonsense, and unintelligible absurdity.

But even supposing that the superior court of the United States had the authority to try facts by *juries of the vicinage*, it would be impossible for them to carry it into execution. It is well known that the supreme courts of the different states, at stated times in every year, go round the different counties of their respective states to try issues of fact, which is called *riding the circuits*. Now, how is it possible that the supreme continental court, which we will suppose to consist at most of five or six judges, can travel at least twice in every year, through the different counties of America, from New-Hampshire to Kentuckey [*sic*] and from Kentuckey to Georgia, to try facts by juries of the vicinage. Common sense will not admit of such a supposition. I am therefore right in my assertion, that *trial by jury in civil cases, is, by the proposed constitution entirely done away, and effectually abolished.*

Pennsylvania Herald, Storing, vol. 3, pp. 59–61.

13.2.4.10   One of the People, October 17, 1787

The . . . trials by jury are not infringed on. The Constitution is silent, and with propriety too, on these and every other subject relative to the internal government of the states. These are secured by the different state constitutions.

Pennsylvania Gazette, Jensen, vol. 2, p. 190.

13.2.4.11   A Citizen of Philadelphia, October 18, 1787

. . . Another objection is, that the new constitution *abolishes tryals by jury in civil causes*. I answer, I don't see one word in the constitution, which by any candid construction can support even the remotest suspicion that this ever entered the heart of one member of the convention. I therefore set down the suggestion for sheer malice, and so dismiss it.

Kaminski & Saladino, vol. 13, p. 303.

13.2.4.12 An Old Whig, No. 3, October 20, 1787

. . . As to the trial by jury, the question may be decided in a few words. Any future Congress sitting under the authority of the proposed new constitution, may, if they chuse, enact that there shall be no more trial by jury, in any of the United States; except in the trial of crimes; and this "SUPREME LAW" will at once annul the trial by jury, in all other cases. The author of the speech supposes that no danger "can possibly ensue, since the proceedings of the supreme court are to be regulated by the Congress, which is a faithful representation of the people; and the oppression of government is effectually barred; by declaring that in all criminal cases the trial by jury shall be preserved." Let us examine the last clause of this sentence first. — I know that an affected indifference to the trial by jury has been expressed, by some persons high in the confidence of the present ruling party in some of the states; — and yet for my own part I cannot change the opinion I had early formed of the excellence of this mode of trial even in civil causes. On the other hand I have no doubt that whenever a settled plan shall be formed for the extirpation of liberty, the banishment of jury trials will be one of the means adopted for the purpose. — But how is it that "the oppression of government is effectually barred by declaring that in all criminal cases the trial by jury shall be preserved?" —Are there not a thousand civil cases in which the government is a party? — In all actions for penalties, forfeitures and public debts, as well as many others, the government is a party and the whole weight of government is thrown into the scale of the prosecution[,] yet there are all of them civil causes. — These penalties, forfeitures and demands of public debts may be multiplied at the will and pleasure of government. — These modes of harassing the subject have perhaps been more effectual than direct criminal prosecutions. . . . The reason that is pretended in the speech why such a declaration; as a bill of rights requires, cannot be made for the protection of the trial by jury; — "that we cannot with any propriety say 'that the trial by jury shall be as heretofore'" in the case of a federal system of jurisprudence, is almost too contemptible to merit notice. — Is this the only form of words that language could afford on such an important occasion? Or if it were to what did these words refer when adopted in the constitutions of the states? — Plainly sir, to the trial by juries as established by the common law of England in the state of its purity; — That common law for which we contended so eagerly at the time of the revolution, and which now after the interval of a very few years, by the proposed new constitution we seem ready to abandon forever; at least in that article which is the most invaluable part of it; the trial by jury.

[Philadelphia] Independent Gazetteer, Kaminski & Saladino, vol. 13, pp. 427–28.

13.2.4.13 An American Citizen, No. 4, October 21, 1787

. . . Both the old and new foederal constitutions, and indeed *the constitution of Pennsylvania*, admit of courts in which no use is made of a jury. The board of property, the court of admiralty, and the high court of errors and appeals, in the state of Pennsylvania, as also the court of appeals under the old confederation, exclude juries. *Tryal by jury will therefore be in the express words of the Pennsyl-*

vania constitution, "as heretofore," — almost always used, though sometimes omitted. Trials for lands lying in any state between persons residing in such state, for bonds, notes, book debts, contracts, trespasses, assumptions, and all other matters between two or more citizens of any state, will be held in the state courts by juries, *as now.* In these cases, the foederal courts *cannot interfere.* But when a dispute arises between the citizens of any state about lands lying out of the bounds *thereof,* or when a trial is to be had between the citizens of any state and those of another, or the government of another, the private citizen will not be obliged to go into a court *constituted by the state,* with which, or with the citizens of which, *his dispute is. He can appeal to a disinterested foederal court.* This is surely a *great advantage,* and promises a *fair trial,* and an *impartial judgement.* The trial by jury is *not excluded* in these foederal courts. In all *criminal* cases, where the property or life of the citizen is at stake, he has the benefit of a jury. If convicted on impeachment, which is never done by a jury in any country, he cannot be fired, imprisoned or punished, but only may be *disqualified* from doing public mischief by losing his office, and his capacity to hold another. If the nature of his offence, besides its danger to his country, should be *criminal* in itself — should involve a charge of fraud, murder or treason — he may be tried for such crime, but cannot be convicted *without a jury.* In trials about property in the foederal courts, which can only be *as above stated,* there is nothing in the new constitution *to prevent a trial by jury.* No doubt it will be the mode in every case, wherein it is practicable. This will be adjusted by law, and it could not be done otherwise. In short, the sphere of jurisdiction for the foederal courts *is limited,* and that sphere only is subject to the regulations of our foederal government. The known principles of justice, the attachment to trial by jury whenever it can be used, the instructions of the state legislatures, the instructions of the people at large, the operation of the foederal regulations on the property of a president, a senator, a representative, a judge, as well as on that of a private citizen, will certainly render those regulations as favorable as possible to *property; for life and liberty are put more than ever into the hands of the juries.* Under the *present* constitution of all the states, a public officer may be condemned *to imprisonment or death* on impeachment, *without a jury;* but the new foederal constitution protects the accused, till he shall be convicted, from the hands of power, by rendering *a jury the indispensible judges of all crimes.*

Pennsylvania Gazette (October 24), Kaminski & Saladino,
vol. 13, pp. 434–35.

13.2.4.14 Centinel, No. 2, October 24, 1787

Mr. *Wilson* says, that it would have been impracticable to have made a general rule for jury trial in the civil cases assigned to the federal judiciary, because of the want of uniformity in the mode of jury trial, as practiced by the several states. This objection proves too much, and therefore amounts to nothing. If it precludes the mode of common law in civil cases, it certainly does in criminal. Yet in these we are told "the oppression of government is effectually barred by declaring that in all criminal cases *trial by jury* shall be preserved." Astonishing, that provision could not be made for a jury in civil controversies, of 12 men, whose verdict should be unanimous, *to be taken from the vicinage*; a precaution which is omitted as to trial of crimes, which may be any where in the state within which they have been committed. So that an inhabitant of *Kentucky* may be tried for treason at *Richmond*.

[Philadelphia] Freeman's Journal, Kaminski & Saladino, vol. 13, p. 466.

13.2.4.15   Proclamation, Wat Tyler, October 24, 1787

. . . Thus it may be argued . . . because the federal representation of the people will possess the power to declare in what civil cases the trial shall be by jury, *therefore* the trial by jury is abolished in all civil cases. . . .

Pennsylvania Herald, Jensen, vol. 2, p. 203.

13.2.4.16   Timothy Meanwell, October 29, 1787

. . . I was informed that the trial by jury, which was guaranteed to us by the constitution of Pennsylvania, was in many instances abolished; this I did not believe when I heard it — I could not entertain an opinion that men so enlightened as those of the convention, among whose names I saw friend — and friend — , could be inattentive to the preservation of the trial by jury. I immediately took the constitution in my hand, and began to search it from end to end, and was in hopes of finding some clause like that in the Bill of Rights in the constitution of Pennsylvania, that would secure the trial by juries in all cases whatsoever, but I was disappointed.

[Philadelphia] Independent Gazetteer, Kaminski & Saladino, vol. 14, p. 512.

13.2.4.17   Cincinnatus, No. 1, November 1, 1787

Let us suppose then, that what has happened, may happen again: That a patriotic printer, like Peter Zenger, should incur the resentment of our new rulers, by publishing to the world, transactions which they wish to conceal. If he should be prosecuted, if his judges should be as desirous of punishing him, *at all events,* as the judges were to punish Peter Zenger, what would his innocence or his virtue avail him? This constitution is so admirably framed for tyranny, that, by clear construction, the judges might put the verdict of a jury out of the question. Among the cases in which the court is to have appellate jurisdiction, are — controversies, to which the United States are a party: — In this appellate jurisdiction, the judges are to determine, *both law and fact.* That is, the court is both judge and jury. The attorney general then would have only to move a question of law in the court below, to ground an appeal to the supreme judicature, and the printer would be delivered up to the mercy of his judges. Peter Zenger's case will teach us, what mercy he might expect. Thus, if the president, vice-president, or any other officer, or favorite of state, should be censured in print, he might effectually deprive the printer, or author, of his trial by jury, and subject him to something, that will probably very much resemble the Star Chamber of former times. The freedom of the press, the sacred palladium of public liberty, would be pulled down; — all useful knowledge on the conduct of government would be withheld from the people — the press would become subservient to the purposes of bad and arbitrary rulers, and imposition, not information, would be its object.

. . . Yet it was the jury only, that saved Zenger, it was a jury only, that saved Woodfall, it can only be a jury that will save any future printer from the fangs of power.

New York Journal, Kaminski & Saladino, vol. 13, pp. 532–33.

13.2.4.18   **Timoleon, November 1, 1787**

". . . With as little ceremony, and similar constructive doctrine, the inestimable trial by jury can likewise be depraved and destroyed — because the Constitution in the 2d section of the 3d article, by expressly assuming the trial by jury in *criminal cases,* and being silent about it in *civil causes,* evidently declares it to be unnecessary in the latter. And more strongly so, by giving the supreme court jurisdiction in appeals, *'both as to law and fact.'* If this be added, that the trial by jury in criminal cases is only stipulated to be *'in the state,'* not in the county where the crime is supposed to have been committed; one excellent part of the jury trial, from the vicinage, or at least from the county, is even in criminal cases rendered precarious, and at the mercy of rulers under the new Consitution. — Yet the danger to liberty, peace, and property, from restraining and injuring this excellent mode of trial, will clearly appear from the following observations of the learned Dr. Blackstone, in his commentaries on the laws of England, Art. Jury Trial Book 3. chap. 33. — 'The establishment of jury trial was always so highly esteemed and valued by the people, that no conquest, *no change of government,* could ever prevail to abolish it. In the magna charta it is more than once insisted upon *as the principle bulwark of our liberties* — And this is a species of knowledge most absolutely necessary for every gentleman; as well, because he may be frequently called upon to determine in this capacity the rights of others, his fellow subjects; as, *because his own property, his liberty, and his life, depend upon maintaining in its legal force the trial by jury* . . . And in every country as the trial by jury has been *gradually disused,* so the great have increased in power, until the state has been torn to pieces by rival factions, and oligarchy in effect has been established, though under the shadow of regal government; unless where the miserable people have taken shelter under absolute monarchy, as the lighter evil of the two. . . . *It is therefore upon the whole, a duty which every man owes to his country, his friends, his posterity, and himself, to maintain, to the utmost of his power, this valuable trial by jury in all its rights'.*" Thus far the learned Dr. Blackstone, — "Could the Doctor, if he were here, at this moment," . . . "have condemned those parts of the new Constitution in stronger terms, which give the supreme court jurisdiction both as to law and *fact;* which have weakened the jury trial in criminal cases and which have discountenanced it in all civil causes? At first I wondered at the complaint that some people made of this new Constitution, because it led to the government of a few; but it is fairly to be concluded, from this injury to the trial by jury, that *some* who framed this new system, saw with Dr. Blackstone, how operative jury trial was in preventing the tyranny of the great ones, and therefore frowned upon it, as this new Constitution does. . . ."

New York Journal, Extraordinary, Kaminski & Saladino,
vol. 13, pp. 536–38.

13.2.4.19 Brutus, No. 2, November 1, 1787

It has been said, in answer to this objection, that such declaration of rights, however requisite they might be in the constitutions of the states, are not necessary in the general constitution, because, "in the former case, every thing which is not reserved is given, but in the latter the reverse of the proposition prevails, and every thing which is not given is reserved." It requires but little attention to discover, that this mode of reasoning is rather specious than solid. The powers, rights, and authority, granted to the general government by this constitution, are as complete, with respect to every object to which they extend, as that of any state government—It reaches to every thing which concerns human happiness—Life, liberty, and property, are under its controul. There is the same reason, therefore, that the exercise of power, in this case, should be restrained within proper limits, as in that of the state governments. To set this matter in a clear light, permit me to instance some of the articles of the bills of rights of the individual states, and apply them to the case in question.

* * *

For the purpose of securing the property of the citizens, it is declared by all the states, "that in all controversies at law, respecting property, the ancient mode of trial by jury is one of the best securities of the rights of the people, and ought to remain sacred and inviolable."

Does not the same necessity exist of reserving this right, under this national compact, as in that of this state? Yet nothing is said respecting it.

New York Journal, Kaminski & Saladino, vol. 13, pp. 526–27.

13.2.4.20 An Old Whig, No. 5, November 1, 1787

. . . It is needless to repeat the necessity of securing other personal rights in the forming a new government. The same argument which proves the necessity of securing one of them shews also the necessity of securing others. Without a bill of rights we are totally insecure in all of them; and no man can promise himself with any degree of certainty that his posterity will enjoy the inestimable blessings of liberty of conscience, of freedom of speech and of writing and publishing their thoughts on public matters, of trial by jury, of holding themselves, their houses and papers free from seizure and search upon general suspicion or general warrants; or in short that they will be secured in the enjoyment of life, liberty and property without depending on the will and pleasure of their rulers.

[Philadelphia] Independent Gazetteer, Kaminski & Saladino, vol. 13, p. 541.

13.2.4.21 An Officer of the Late Continental Army, November 6, 1787

. . . The objections that have been made to the new Constitution are these: . . .

8. TRIAL BY JURY, that sacred bulwark of liberty, is ABOLISHED IN CIVIL CASES, and Mr. [James] W[ilson], one of the Convention, has told you, that not being able to agree as to the FORM of establishing this point, they have left you deprived of the SUBSTANCE. Here are his own words: *"The subject was involved*

560

in difficulties. The Convention found the task too DIFFICULT *for them, and left
the business as it stands.*" [Philadelphia] Independent Gazetteer, Jensen, vol. 2, p. 211.

13.2.4.22 Cincinnatus, No. 2, November 8, 1787

. . . I come now to the consideration of the trial by jury in civil cases. . . . The
objection you impute to your opponents is — the trial by jury is abolished in civil
cases. This you call a disingenuous form — and truly it is very much so on your
part and of your own fabrication. The objection in its true form is, that — trial by
jury is not secured in civil cases. To this objection, you could not possibly give an
answer; you therefore ingeniously coined one to which you could make a plausible
reply. We expected, and we had a right to expect, that such an inestimable privilege as this would have been secured — that it would not have been less dependent
on the arbitrary exposition of future judges, who, when it may suit the arbitrary
views of the ruling powers will explain it away at pleasure. . . .

But, if taken even on your own ground it is not so clearly tenable. In point of
legal construction, the trial by jury does seem to be taken away in civil cases. It is a
law maxim, that the expression of one part is an exclusion of the other. In legal
construction therefore, the preservation of trial by jury in criminal, is an exclusion
of it in civil cases. Why else should it be mentioned at all? Either it followed of
course in both cases, or it depended on being stipulated. If the first, then the
stipulation was nugatory — if the latter, then it was in part given up. Therefore,
either we must suppose the Convention did a nugatory thing; or that by the
express mention of jury in criminal, they meant to exclude it in civil cases. And
that they did intend to exclude it, seems the more probable, as in the appeal they
have taken special care to render the trial by jury of no effect by expressly making
the court judges both of law and fact. And though this is subjected to the future
regulation of Congress, yet it would be absurd to suppose, that the regulation
meant its annihilation. We must therefore conclude, that in appeals the trial by
jury is expressly taken away, and in original process it is by legal implication taken
away in all civil cases.

Here then I must repeat — that you ought to have stated fairly to the people,
that the trial by jury was not secured; that they might know what, it was they were
to consent to; and if knowing it, they consented, the blame could not fall on
you. . . . The trial by [jury in] our country, is in my opinion, the great bulwark
of freedom, and for certain, the admiration of all foreign writers and nations. The
last writer of any distinguished note, upon the principles of government, the
celebrated Montesquieu, is in raptures with this peculiar perfection in the English
policy. . . .

Such are the opinions of Lord Camden and Vaughan, and multitudes of the first
names, both English and other foreigners might be cited, who bestow unbounded
approbation on this best of all human modes for protecting, life, liberty, and
property.

I own then, it alarms me, when I see these Doctors of our constitutions cutting in
twain this sacred shield of public liberty and justice. Surely my countrymen will
think a little before they resign this strong hold of freedom. Our state constitutions

have held it sacred in all its parts. They have anxiously secured it. But that these may not shield it from the intended destruction in the new constitution, it is therein as anxiously provided, that "this constitution, and the laws of the United States, which shall be made in pursuance thereof; or which shall be made under the authority of the United States, shall be the supreme laws of the land; and the judges of every state, shall be bound thereby; any thing in constitution and the laws of any state, to the contrary notwithstanding."

Thus this new system, with one sweeping clause, bears down every constitution in the union, and establishes its arbitrary doctrines, supreme and paramount to all the bills and declarations of rights, in which we vainly put our trust, and on which we rested the security of our often declared, unalienable liberties. But I trust the whole people of this country, will unite, in crying out, as did our sturdy ancestors of old — *Nolumus leges anglica mutari.* — We will not part with our birthright.

New York Journal, Kaminski & Saladino, vol. 14, pp. 12–14.

13.2.4.23 A Son of Liberty, November 8, 1787

MR. GREENLEAF, Having observed in your paper of the 25th ult. that a writer under the signature of *A Slave,* has pointed out a number of advantages or blessings, which, he says, will result from an adoption of the new government, proposed by the Convention: — I have taken the liberty to request, that you will give the following a place in your next paper, it being an enumeration of a *few* of the *curses* which will be entailed on the people of America, by this preposterous and newfangled system, if they are ever so infatuated as to receive it. . . . 3d. A suppression of trial by jury of your peers, in all civil cases, and even in criminal cases, the loss of the trial in the vicinage, where the fact and the credibility of your witnesses are known, and where you can command their attendance without insupportable expence, or inconveniences.

New York Journal, Kaminski & Saladino, vol. 13, p. 481.

13.2.4.24 Uncus, November 9, 1787

Mr. GODDARD, When you began publishing the *Centinel* in numbers, I expected we should have had one in each of your papers for some weeks, hoping, that after he had done finding fault with the doings of the late convention, the members of which were either too designing, — of too aristocratic principles, — too old, — or too ignorant, "inexperienced and fallible," for business of such magnitude; *he* would, by the *perfect rule* existing in his own mind, by which he has tried and condemned the proposed constitution, exhibit to the world a perfect model; which these States would have only to read, and invite "those who are competent to the task of developing the principles of government," to come forward, approve and adopt.

. . .

I believe, there is not a single article, wherein the *new plan* has proposed any amendment to the *old,* but what would be objected to by *Centinel.* To some he has objected, where they have made no amendment; as the power of Congress to try causes without a jury, which they have ever possessed.

[Baltimore] Maryland Journal, Kaminski & Saladino, vol.14, pp. 76, 79.

13.2.4.25 Gentleman in New-York, November 14, 1787

". . . I have not only no objection to, but am extremely desirous of, a strong and general government, provided the fundamental principles of liberty be well secured. These I take to be, trial by jury as has been and is practised. . . . In all these great points the proposed constitution requires amendment, before it can be adopted even with safety.

"In the constitution of the foederal court, where its jurisdiction is original, the securing jury trial in criminal, is, according to all legal reasoning, an exclusion of it in civil matters — and in its appellant function it is expressly said the court shall judge both of *law* and *fact*. This of course renders the finding of a jury below, totally nugatory.

Virginia Independent Chronicle, Kaminski & Saladino,
vol. 14, p. 103.

13.2.4.26 A Georgian, November 15, 1787

And now we come to the point which at once teems with numberless enormous innovations by introducing strange and new courts of almost any denomination into any of the states whereby our own courts will soon be annihilated, and abolishing the only pledge of liberty, the trial by jury, to tryants only formidable, in all civil cases, countenancing the greatest injustice to be lawfully, nay constitutionally, committed by the rich against their brave fellow citizens whose only misfortune is to be, perhaps, not so rich as they, by dragging their lawsuits of any denomination and of any sum, however small, if they choose, before the GRAND TRIBUNAL OF APPEAL to which the poor will be unable to follow with their evidences and witnesses, and on account of the great expenses. Therefore, fellow citizens, pray restrain this encroachment so destructive to the inestimable rights the more numerous part of middle-circumstanced citizens now enjoy. With horror beware of the precipice before you; and, if you will, please join me in amending the third Article in the Federal Consitution thus:

. . .

"The trial of all civil and criminal causes, except in cases of impeachment (as provided for in Article I, section 3) shall be by jury, drawn by lot out of a box from among the freeholders of that state where Congress shall reside, and within five miles thereof; and, when a crime against the United States has been committed within no state, the Supreme Court of Congress shall have the trial of the same where Congress then resides.

Gazette of the State of Georgia, Kaminski & Saladino, vol. 3, pp. 241–42.

13.2.4.27 Cincinnatus, No. 3, November 15, 1787

Sir, Your speech has varnished an iron trap, bated with some illustrious names, to catch the liberties of the people. And this you are pleased to call a constitution — "the best form of government that was ever offered to the world." May Heaven then have mercy on the world and on us. . . .

In my former papers, I have shewn, . . . that the sacred trial by jury, in civil cases, is at best doubtful; and in all cases of appeal expressly taken away. . . . Upon the omission of the trial by jury in civil cases, you observe — "when this subject was in discussion, we were involved in difficulties which pressed on all sides, and no precedent could be discovered to direct our course. The cases open to trial by jury differed in the different states, it was therefore impracticable on that ground to have made a general rule." — So, because the extent of the trial by jury varied in the different states, therefore it was proper to abolish it in all. For what else can your words — "it was impracticable to have made a general rule" mean? — If ever the rule is made, it must be general. And if this is impracticable — it surely follows, that in the foederal court we must go without it in civil cases. What sense is there in supposing, that what, for the reasons you alledge, was impracticable with the Convention, will be practicable with the Congress? What faculty can the one body have more than the other, of reconciling contradictions? . . . It is not possible to say, that the Convention could not have proposed, that there should be one similar general mode of trial by jury in the Foederal court in all cases whatever. If the states would not have acceded to the proposition, we should only be where we are. And that this trial by jury is best, even in courts where the civil law process now prevails, I think no unbigoted man can doubt. . . .

New York Journal, Kaminski & Saladino, vol. 14, pp. 124–26.

13.2.4.28 Letter, November 21, 1787

. . . The State of Rhode-Island refused to send delegates to the State Convention, and the event has manifested that their refusal was a happy one, as the New Constitution, which the Convention has proposed to us, is an elective monarchy, which is proverbially the worst government. . . . [T]he supreme continental court is to have, almost in every case, "appellate jurisdiction both as to law and fact," which signifies, if there is any meaning in words, the setting aside the trial by jury; . . . Our correspondent, therefore, thinks it the part of wisdom to abide, like the state of Rhode-Island, by the old articles of confederation, which, if re-examined with attention, we shall find worthy of great regard . . . .

[Philadelphia] Freeman's Journal, Kaminski & Saladino, vol. 14, p. 165.

13.2.4.29 Demosthenes Minor, November 22, 1787

Article 3, section 1. The comments made upon this Article are merely vain exclamations against the Constitution for abolishing the trial by jury. In civil cases, surely, all causes that should be determined by a court of equity do not require the intervention of that tribunal. . . .

Gazette of the State of Georgia, Jensen, vol. 3, pp. 246–47.

13.2.4.30 A Countryman, No. 2, November 22, 1787

Of a very different nature, tho' only one degree better than the other reasoning, is all that sublimity of *nonsense* and *alarm,* that has been thundered against it in every shape of *metaphoric terror,* on the subject of a *bill of rights,* the *liberty of the press, rights of conscience, rights of taxation and election, trials in the vicinity, freedom of speech, trial by jury,* and a *standing army.* These last are undoubtedly important points, much too important to depend on mere paper protection. For, guard such privileges by the strongest expressions, still if you leave the legislative and executive power in the hands of those who are or may be disposed to deprive you of them — you are but slaves. Make an absolute monarch — give him the supreme authority, and guard as much as you will by bills of right, your liberty of the press, and trial by jury; — he will find means either to take them from you, or to render them useless.

Your General Assembly under your present constitution are supreme. They may keep troops on foot in the most profound peace, if they think proper. They have heretofore abridged the trial by jury in some cases, and they can again in all. They can restrain the press, and may lay the most burdensome taxes if they please, and who can forbid? But still the people are perfectly safe that not one of these events shall take place so long as the members of the General Assembly are as much interested, and interested in the same manner, as the other subjects.

On examining the new proposed constitution, there can not be a question, but that there is authority enough lodged in the proposed federal Congress, if abused, to do the greatest injury. And it is perfectly idle to object to it, that there is no bill of rights, or to propose to add to it a provision that a trial by jury shall in no case be omitted, or to patch it up by adding a stipulation in favor of the press, or to guard it by removing the paltry objection to the right of Congress to regulate the time and manner of elections.

New Haven Gazette, Kominski & Saladino, vol. 14, pp. 172–74.

13.2.4.31 A Well-Informed Correspondent, November 28, 1787

. . . "The judicial powers of the Fœderal Courts have, also, been grossly misrepresented. It is said 'that the trial by jury is to be abolished, and the courts of the several states are to be annihilated.' But these, Sir, are mistaken notions, scandalous perversions of truth. The courts of judicature in each state will still continue in their present situation. The trial by jury in all disputes between man and man in each state will still remain inviolate, and in all cases of this description, there can be no appeal to the Fœderal Courts. It is only in particular specified cases, of which each state cannot properly take cognizance, that the judicial authority of the Fœderal Courts can be exercised. Even in the congressional courts of judicature, the trial of all crimes except in cases of impeachment, shall be by jury. How then can any man say that the trial by jury will be abolished, and that the courts of the several states will be annihilated by the adoption of the Fœderal Government? Must not the man who makes this assertion be either consummately impudent, or consummately ignorant? My God! what can he mean by such bareface representations? Can he be the friend to his country? Can he be a friend to the happiness of mankind? Is he not some insidious foe? Some emissary, hired by *British Gold* — plotting the ruin of both, by disseminating the seeds of suspicion and discontent among us?

Virginia Independent Chronicle, Kaminski & Saladino, vol. 14, pp. 244–45.

13.2.4.32 James McHenry, Speech to the Maryland House, November 29, 1787

. . . 1st. The judicial power of the United States underwent a full investigation — it is impossible for me to Detail the observations that were delivered on that subject — The right of tryal by Jury was left open and undefined from the difficulty attending any limitation to so valuable a priviledge, and from the persuasion that Congress might hereafter make provision more suitable to each respective State — To suppose that mode of Tryal intended to be abolished would be to suppose the Representatives in Convention to act contrary to the Will of their Constituents, and Contrary to their own Interest. —

Kaminski & Saladino, vol. 14, p. 284.

13.2.4.33 Luther Martin, Speech to the Maryland House, November 29, 1787

[T]hey would either trust your Juries for altho matters of fact are triable by juries in the Inferior Courts the Judges of the Supreme Court on *appeal* are to decide on *Law* and *fact* both. . . . [I]t is very doubtful if we are to have the priviledge of Tryal by Jury at all, where the cause originates in the supreme Court. . . .

Kaminski & Saladino, vol. 14, p. 290.

13.2.4.34 A Countryman, No. 3, November 29, 1787

. . . Last week I endeavoured to evince, that the only surety you could have for your liberties must be in the nature of your government; that you could derive no security from bills of rights, or stipulations, on the subject of . . . trial by jury, or on any other subject. Did you ever hear of an absolute monarchy, where those rights which are proposed by the pygmy politicians of this day, to be secured by stipulation, were ever preserved? Would it not be mere trifling to make any such stipulations, in any absolute monarchy?

On the other hand, if your interest and that of your rulers are the same, your liberties are abundantly secure. . . .

No people can be more secure against tyranny and oppression in their rulers than you are at present; and no rulers can have more supreme and unlimited authority than your general assembly have.

New Haven Gazette, Kaminski & Saladino, vol. 14, p. 296.

13.2.4.35 Cincinnatus, No. 5, November 29, 1787

Sir [James Wilson], In my former observations on your speech, to your fellow-citizens, explanatory and defensive of the new constitution; it has appeared, by arguments to my judgment unanswerable, that by ratifying the constitution, as the convention proposed it, the people will leave the liberty of the press, and the trial by jury, in civil cases, to the mercy of their rulers —

. . .

. . . Do not the several states harmonize in trial by jury of the vicinage. . . . Are not these the great principles on which every constitution is founded? In these the laws and habits of the several states are uniform.

New York Journal, Kaminski & Saladino, vol. 14, pp. 303–06.

13.2.4.36 Essay by One of the Common People, December 3, 1787

Never was the trial by jury in civil cases thought so lightly of in America as at this day: we have bled for it, and are now almost ready to trifle it away — because in cases of default (which implies a consent of parties) there is no trial by jury, we must give up that inestimable privilege in all civil cases whatever. — This is fine reasoning sure; because we will not have a jury when we do not want them, we shall not when we do — This gentleman cannot be serious when he asserts, that *"if it were to be expressed WHAT civil causes should be tried by jury, it might take a volume of laws, instead of an article of rights;"* If it did I would have the volume, rather than hazard the priviledge. [*sic*] — But I will ask whether it requires this volume of laws to express that privilege in our state constitution? and whether there would be any difficulty in having it declared, that the citizens of each state shall enjoy it conformably to the usage in the state where the tribunal shall be established? he [*sic*] says, *"doubtless congress will make some general regulations in this matter,"* but it will be well to recollect that they may *unmake* them, or *not* make them too, if they please, and *when* they please; but if it is a part of the constitution, the *people alone* will have the power to change or annul it. — It is too great a privilege to be left at loose. I sincerely believe if the federal constitution which shall be *given*, be *clearly defined,* and a *boundary line* be marked out, declaratory of the extent of their jurisdiction, of the rights which the state hold [*sic*] unalienable, and the privilege which the citizens thereof can never part with, the republick of America will last for ages, and be free.

Boston Gazette, Storing, vol. 4, p. 122.

13.2.4.37 Philadelphiensis, No. 3, December 5, 1787

. . . The only thing in which a government should be efficient, is to protect the *liberties, lives,* and *property* of the people governed, from foreign and domestic violence. This, and this only is what every government should do effectually. For any government to do more than this is impossible, and every one that falls short of it is defective. Let us now compare the new constitution with this legitimate definition of an efficient government, and we shall find that it has scarce a particle of an efficient government in its whole composition.

In the first place then it does not protect the people in those liberties and privileges that all freemen should hold sacred — The *liberty of conscience,* the *liberty of the press,* the *liberty of trial by jury,* &c. are all unprotected by this constitution.

[Philadelphia] Freeman's Journal, Kaminski & Saladino, vol. 14, p. 351.

13.2.4.38 Cumberland County Petition to the Pennsylvania Convention, December 5, 1787

Secondly: . . . This, as we conceive, unlimited powers given to Congress, in which they are to be the judges of what laws shall be necessary and proper, uncontrolled by a bill of rights, submits every right of the people of these states, both civil and sacred to the disposal of Congress, who may exercise their power to the expulsion of the jury — trial in civil causes — to the total suppression of the liberty of the press; and to setting up and establishing of a cruel tyranny, if they should be so disposed, over all the dearest and most sacred rights of the citizens.

Carlisle Gazette, Jensen, vol. 2, p. 310.

13.2.4.39 The People: Unconstitutionalism, December 10, 1787

We know of no reason why they should interfere with our common law courts (which have stood an hundred and fifty years equal in rectitude to any in the world) and impose upon us a court of appeals in the common law to judge in equity law and fact denying the benefit of a jury, on credit the only security of property to the common or poor people; and as it is the only thing that has saved the British people from tyranny, we think it is the only thing that will save us as to that high court.

Middlesex Gazette, Jensen, vol. 3, pp. 494–95.

13.2.4.40 Address and Reasons of Dissent of the Minority of the Pennsylvania Convention, December 12, 1787

The first consideration that this review suggests, is the omission of a BILL of RIGHTS, ascertaining and fundamentally establishing those unalienable and personal rights of men, without the full, free, and secure enjoyment of which there can be no liberty, and over which it is not necessary for a good government to have the controul. The principal of which are the rights of conscience, personal liberty by the clear and unequivocal establishment of the writ of *habeas corpus*, jury trial in civil and criminal cases; . . . the stipulations heretofore made in favor of them in the state constitutions, are entirely superseded by this constitution.

. . .

We have before noticed the judicial power as it would effect a consolidation of the states into one government; we will now examine it, as it would affect the liberties and welfare of the people, supposing such a government were practicable and proper.

The judicial power, under the proposed constitution, is founded on the well-known principles of the *civil law*, by which the judge determines both on law and fact, and appeals are allowed from the inferior tribunals to the superior, upon the whole question; so that *facts* as well as *law*, would be re-examined, and even new facts brought forward in the court of appeals; and to use the words of a very eminent Civilian. — "The cause is many times another thing before the court of appeals, than what it was at the time of the first sentence."

That this mode of proceeding is the one which must be adopted under this constitution, is evident from the following circumstances: — 1st. That the trial by jury, which is the grand characteristic of the common law, is secured by the constitution, only in criminal cases. — 2d. That the appeal from both *law* and *fact* is expressly established, which is utterly inconsistent with the principles of common law, and trials by jury. The only mode in which an appeal from law and fact can be established, is, by adopting the principles and practice of the civil law; unless the United States should be drawn into the absurdity of calling and swearing juries, merely for the purpose of contradicting their verdicts, which would render juries contemptible and worse than useless. — 3d. That the courts to be established would decide on all cases *of law and equity*, which is a well known characteristic of the civil law. . . .

Not to enlarge upon the loss of the invaluable right of trial by an unbiased jury, so dear to every friend of liberty, the monstrous expense and inconveniences of the mode of proceedings to be adopted, are such as will prove intolerable to the people of this country. . . . We abhor the idea of losing the transcendent privilege of trial by jury, with the loss of which, it is remarked by the same learned author, that in Sweden, the liberties of the commons were extinguished by an aristocratic senate: and that *trial by jury* and the liberty of the people went out together.

Kaminski & Saladino, vol. 15, pp. 25, 27–28.

13.2.4.41 A Countryman, No. 5, December 20, 1787

. . . The great power and influence of an hereditary monarch of Britain has spread many alarms, from an apprehension that the commons would sacrifice the liberties of the people to the money or influence of the crown: But the influence of a powerful *hereditary monarch,* with the national Treasury — Army — and fleet at his command — and the whole executive government — and one third of the legislative in his hands, — constantly operating on a house of commons, whose duration is never less than *seven years,* unless this same monarch should *end* it, (which he can do in an hour) has never yet been sufficient to obtain one vote of the house of commons which has taken from the people the liberty of the press, — trial by jury, — the rights of conscience, or of private property.

— Can you then apprehend danger of oppression and tyranny from too great duration of the power of *your* rulers.

New Haven Gazette, Kaminski & Saladino, vol. 15, p. 55.

13.2.4.42 Reply to George Mason's Objections to a Constitution, December 19 and 26, 1787

. . . Another important and weighty objection brought against the Constitution is that there is no security for the right of trial by jury in civil cases. The right of trial by jury most certainly is not taken away, neither is there anything in the Constitution that looks to that point; it is altogether left to the general government to dilate the subject as they please. It is in their power, by a law to be enacted for that purpose, to suit the temper and dispositions of the different states as they please. . . . The appellate jurisdiction of the Supreme Court, I acknowledge, is both of law and fact; but this by no means excludes the idea of trial by jury. . . . The people are terrified with the idea that by means of this constitutional plan, justice will be unattainable here, as it is in England. If we can hope to have civil justice administered here to as great perfection and with as much integrity as it is in England, I will be content. . . . There is no part of the world wherein the laws relating to property are more judiciously and ably administered than in the courts of Great Britain. Had their conduct in every other department been equally wise and conducted with equal integrity, the good people of America would not this day been [*sic*] forming a government for themselves.

New Jersey Journal, Jensen, vol. 3, p. 158.

13.2.4.43 America, December 31, 1787

. . . But you will say, that trial by jury, is an unalienable right, that ought not to be trusted with our rulers. Why not? If it is such a darling privilege, will not Congress be as fond of it, as their constituents? An elevation into that Council, does not render a man insensible to his privileges, nor place him beyond the necessity of securing them. A member of Congress is liable to all the operations of law, except during his attendance on public business; and should he consent to a law, annihilating any right whatever, he deprives himself, his family and estate, of the benefit resulting from that right, as well as his constituents. This circumstance alone, is a sufficient security.

But, why this outcry about juries? If the people esteem them so highly, why do they ever neglect them, and suffer the trial by them to go into disuse? In some States, *Courts of Admiralty* have no juries — nor Courts of Chancery at all. In the City-Courts of some States, juries are rarely or never called, altho' the parties may demand them; and one State, at least, has lately passed an act, empowering the parties to submit both *law* and *fact* to the Court. It is found, that the judgment of a Court, gives as much satisfaction, as the verdict of a jury, as the Court are as good judges of fact, as juries, and much better judges of law. I have no desire to abolish trials by jury, although the original design and excellence of them, is in many cases superseded. — While the people remain attached to this mode of deciding causes, I am confident, that no Congress can wrest the privilege from them.

[New York] Daily Advertiser, Kaminski & Saladino,
vol. 15, p. 197.

13.2.4.44 John Nicholson, Petition Against Confirmation of the Ratification of the Constitution, January 1788

That your petitioners are much alarmed at an instrument called a Constitution for the United States of America; framed by a Convention which had been appointed by several of the states, "solely to revise the Articles of the Confederation, and report such alterations and provisions therein as should when agreed to in Congress, And confirmed by the several states, render the Federal Constitution Adequate to the exigencies of government, and the preservation of the Union" inasmuch as the liberties, lives and property of your petitioners are not secured thereby.

That the powers therein proposed to be granted to the government of the United States are too great, and that the proposed distribution of those powers are dangerous and inimical to liberty and equality amongst the people. . . .

That the right of trial by jury should be secured both in civil and criminal cases.

Jensen, vol. 2, pp. 710–11.

13.2.4.45 A Citizen of New Haven, January 7, 1788

[N]or is their any thing in the constitution to deprive them of trial by jury in cases where that mode of trial has been heretofore used. All cases in the courts of common law between citizens of the same state, except those claiming lands under grants of different states, must be finally decided by the courts of the state to which they belong, so that it is not probable that more than one citizen to a thousand will ever have a cause that can come before a federal court.

Connecticut Courant, Jensen, vol. 3, p. 527;
Kaminski & Saladino, vol. 15, p. 283.

13.2.4.46   Curtiopolis, January 18, 1788

Fathers, Friends, Countrymen, Brethren, and Fellow Citizens, The happiness and existence of America being now suspended upon your wise deliberations; three or four sly Aristocrats having lashed the public passions, like wild horses, to the car of Legislation, and driving us all in the midst of political clouds of error, into that ditch of despotism lately dug by the Convention: Such dismal circumstances have induced a private citizen to lay before you, in as concise a manner as possible, the objections that have been made, by the Pennsylvania Secession, Brutus, Cato, Cincinnatus, Farmer, An Officer, &c. &c. our best men.

   . . .

26. It allows of other modes of trial besides that by jury, and of course this is *abolished:* such modes will be instituted under the direction of Congress, as will leave offenders, traitors, *malcontents,* or such of us as fall under the lash, *no chance at all.*

New York Daily Advertiser, Kaminski & Saladino,
vol. 15, pp. 399–400, 402.

13.2.4.47   The Federal Farmer, No. 15, January 18, 1788

As the trial by jury is provided for in criminal causes, I shall confine my observations to civil causes — and in these, I hold it is the established right of the jury by the common law, and the fundamental laws of this country, to give a general verdict in all cases when they chuse to do it, to decide both as to law and fact, whenever blended together in the issue put to them.

   . . .

But it is said, that no words could be found by which the states could agree to establish the jury-trial in civil causes. I can hardly believe men to be serious, who make observations to this effect. The states have all derived judicial proceedings principally from one source, the British system; from the same common source the American lawyers have almost universally drawn their legal information. All the states have agreed to establish the trial by jury, in civil as well as in criminal causes. The several states, in congress, found no difficulty in establishing it in the Western Territory, in the ordinance passed in July 1787. Storing, vol. 2, pp. 319–21.

13.2.4.48   The Federalist, No. 41, January 19, 1788

Had no other enumeration or definition of the powers of the Congress been found in the Constitution than the general expressions just cited, the authors of the objection might have had some color for it; though it would have been difficult to find a reason for so awkward a form of describing an authority to legislate in all possible cases. A power to destroy the freedom of the press, the trial by jury, or even to regulate the course of descents, or the forms of conveyances, must be very singularly expressed by the terms "to raise money for the general welfare."

Kaminski & Saladino, vol. 15, p. 424.

13.2.4.49   The Federal Farmer, No. 16, January 20, 1788

The trial by jury in criminal as well as in civil causes, has long been considered as one of our fundamental rights, and has been repeatedly recognized and confirmed by most of the state conventions. But the constitution expressly establishes this trial in criminal, and wholly omits it in civil causes. The jury trial in criminal causes, and the benefit of the writ of habeas corpus, are already as effectually established as any of the fundamental or essential rights of the people in the United States. . . . [I]nstead of establishing it in criminal causes only; we ought to establish it generally; — instead of the clause of forty or fifty words relative to this subject, why not use the language that has always been used in this country, and say, "the people of the United States shall always be entitled to the trial by jury." This would shew the people still hold the right sacred, and enjoin it upon congress substantially to preserve the jury trial in all cases, according to the usage and custom of the country. I have observed before, that it is *the jury trial* we want; the little different appendages and modifications tacked to it in the different states, are no more than a drop in the ocean: the jury trial is a solid uniform feature in a free government; it is the substance we would save, not the little articles of form.

Security against expost [*sic*] facto laws, the trial by jury, and the benefits of the writs of habeas corpus, are but a part of those inestimable rights the people of the United States are entitled to, even in judicial proceedings, by the course of the common law. These may be secured in general words, as in New-York, the Western Territory, &c. by declaring the people of the United States shall always be entitled to judicial proceedings according to the course of the common law, as used and established in the said states. Perhaps it would be better to enumerate the particular essential rights the people are entitled to in these proceedings, as has been done in many of the states, and as has been done in England. . . . We certainly, in federal processes, might as well claim the benefits of the writ of habeas corpus, as to claim trial by a jury — the right to have council — to have witnesses face to face — to be secure against unreasonable search warrrants, &c. was the constitution silent as to the whole of them: — but the establishment of the former, will evince that we could not claim them without it; and the omission of the latter, implies they are relinquished, or deemed of no importance. These are rights and benefits individuals acquire by compact; they must claim them under compacts, or immemorial usage — it is doubtful, at least, whether they can be claimed under immemorial usage in this country; and it is, therefore, we generally claim them under compacts, as charters and constitutions.

Storing, vol. 2, pp. 325–26.

13.2.4.50 Philadelphiensis, No. 18, January 23, 1788

. . . But the matter now in debate has no relation to that: the men opposed to the new constitution have the same cause to defend, that the people of America had during the period of a seven years war. Who is he so base, that will peaceably submit to a government that will eventually destroy his sacred *rights and privileges*? The liberty of conscience, the liberty of the press, the liberty of trial by jury, &c. must lie at the mercy of a few despots — an infernal junto, that are for changing our *free republican government* into a tyrannical and absolute monarchy. These are what roused the sons of America to oppose Britain, and from the nature of things, they must have a similar effect now.

[Philadelphia] Freeman's Journal, Kaminski & Saladino, vol. 15, p. 461.

13.2.4.51 Aristides, January 31, 1788

The institution of trial by jury has been sanctified by the experience of ages. It has been recognised by the constitution of every state in the union. It is deemed the birthright of Americans; and it is imagined, that liberty cannot subsist without it. The proposed plan expressly adopts it, for the decision of all criminal accusations, except impeachment; and is silent with respect to the determination of facts in civil causes.

The inference, hence drawn by many, is not warranted by the premises. By recognising the jury trial in criminal cases, the constitution effectually provides, that it shall prevail, so long as the constitution itself shall remain unimpaired and unchanged. But, from the great variety of civil cases, arising under this plan of government, it would be unwise and impolitic to say ought about it, in regard to these. Is there not a great variety of cases, in which this trial is taken away in each of the states? Are there not many more cases, where it is denied in England? For the convention to ascertain in what cases it shall prevail, and in what others it may be expedient to prefer other modes, was impracticable. On this subject, a future congress is to decide; and I see no foundation under Heaven for the opinion, that congress will despise the known prejudices and inclination of their countrymen. A very ingenious writer of Philadelphia has mentioned the objections without deigning to refute that, which he conceives to have originated "in sheer malice." —

Kaminski & Saladino, vol. 15, p. 536.

13.2.4.52 Luther Martin, Genuine Information, No. 10, February 1, 1788

. . . And in all those cases where the general government has jurisdiction in civil questions, the proposed constitution *not only* makes *no provision for the trial by jury* in the *first* instance, but by its appellate jurisdiction *absolutely takes away that inestimable privilege,* since it expressly declares the supreme court shall have appellate jurisdiction both as to law and fact. — Should, therefore, a jury be adopted in the *inferior* court, it would only be a *needless expence,* since on an appeal the *determination* of that jury *even on questions of fact,* however honest and upright, is to be of *no possible effect* — the supreme court is to take up *all questions of fact* — to *examine the evidence relative* thereto — to *decide upon* them in the *same manner* as if they had *never been tried by a jury* — . . .

Thus, Sir, *jury trials,* which have ever been the *boast* of the English constitution, which have been by our several *State constitutions* so *cautiously secured* to us, — *jury trials* which have so long been considered the *surest barrier* against *arbitrary power,* and the *palladium* of *liberty,* — with the *loss* of *which* the *loss* of our *freedom* may be dated, are *taken away* by the proposed form of government, not *only* in a *great variety* of questions between *individual* and *individual,* but in *every case* whether *civil* or *criminal* arising *under the laws of* the United States or the *execution* of those laws. — It is *taken away* in *those very cases* where *of all others* it is *most essential for our liberty,* to have it *sacredly guarded* and *preserved* — in *every case* whether *civil* or *criminal,* between *government* and *its officers* on the one part and the *subject or citizen* on the other. — Nor was this the effect of inattention, nor did it arise from any real difficulty in establishing and securing

jury trial by the proposed constitution, if the convention had wished so to do —
But the *same reason* influenced *here* as in the case of the establishment of inferior
courts; — as they could not trust *State judges,* so would they not confide in *State
juries.* — They alleged that the general government and the State governments
would always be at variance — that the citizens of the different States would enter
into the views and interests of their respective States, and therefore ought not to be
trusted in determining causes in which the general government was any way
interested, without giving the general government an opportunity, if it disapproved the verdict of the jury, to appeal, and to have the *facts examined* into *again*
and *decided upon* by *its own judges,* on whom it was thought a reliance might be
had by the general government, they being appointed under its authority.

[Baltimore] Maryland Gazette, Kaminski & Saladino, vol. 16, pp. 9–10.

13.2.4.53 Philadelphiensis, No. 9, February 6, 1788

To such lengths have these bold conspirators carried their scheme of despotism,
that your most sacred rights and privileges are surrendered at discretion. When
government thinks proper, under the pretence of writing a libel, &c. it may
imprison, inflict the most cruel and unusual punishment, seize property, carry on
prosecutions, &c. and the unfortunate citizen has no *magna charta,* no *bill of
rights,* to protect him; nay, the prosecution may be carried on in such a manner
that even a *jury* will not be allowed him.

[Philadelphia] Freeman's Journal, Kaminski & Saladino, vol. 16, p. 59.

13.2.4.54 An Old Whig, No. 8, February 6, 1788

First then, the general expectation seems to be that our future rulers will rectify
all that is amiss. If a bill of rights is wanting, they will frame a bill of rights. If too
much power is vested in them, they will not abuse it; nay, they will divest themselves of it. The very first thing they will do, will be to establish the liberties of the
people by good and wholesome ordinances, on so solid a foundation as to baffle
all future encroachments from themselves or their successors. Much good no
doubt might be done in this way; if Congress should possess the most virtuous
inclinations, yet there are some things which it will not be in their power to rectify.
For instance; *the appellate jurisdiction both as to law and fact,* which is given to
the supreme court of the continent, and which annihilates the trial by jury in all
civil causes, the Congress can only modify: — They cannot extinguish this power,
so destructive to the principles of real liberty. It would not by any means be
extravagant to say, that a new continental convention ought to be called, if it were
only for the sake of preserving that sacred palladium — THE INESTIMABLE RIGHT
OF TRIAL BY JURY.

. . .

. . . Again; how could the stripping people [*sic*] of the right of trial by jury
conduce to the strength of the state? Do we find the government in England at all
weakened by the people retaining the right of trial by jury? Far from it. Yet these
things which merely tend to oppress the people, without conducing at all to the
strength of the state, are the last which aristocratic rulers would consent to restore

to the people; because they encrease the personal power and importance of the rulers.

[Philadelphia] Independent Gazetteer, Kaminski & Saladino,
vol. 16, pp. 53, 55.

13.2.4.55 Letter, February 21, 1788

The same accounts say, that the *British merchants* are very much pleased with this scheme of government; they are laughing in their sleeves, at the prospect of now having it in their power to collect all their *old American debts with interest*: for foreigners are by the 2d article of the new constitution, allowed to sue in the courts of Congress, and to drag the citizens of America from the remotest parts of the continent, *on an appeal* to the *supreme court* at the national seat of government, where jury trial in civil cases is abolished: hitherto juries have been favorable to fellow citizens, they have considered their distresses; but a court of law will not attend to *such trifles*.

[Philadelphia] Independent Gazetteer, Kaminski & Saladino,
vol. 16, p. 519.

13.2.4.56 Hugh Williamson, Speech, February 25, 1788

It seems to be generally admitted, that the system of Government which has been proposed by the late Convention, is well calculated to relieve us from many of the grievances under which we have been laboring. If I might express my particular sentiments on this subject, I should describe it as more free and more perfect than any form of government that ever has been adopted by any nation; but I would not say it has no faults. Imperfection is inseparable from every human device. Several objections were made to this system by two or three very respectable characters in the Convention, which have been the subject of much conversation; and other objections, by citizens of this State, have lately reached our ears. It is proper that you should consider of these objections. They are of two kinds; they respect the things that are in the system, and the things that are not in it. We are told that there should have been a section for securing the Trial by Jury in Civil cases, . . . that there should also have been a Declaration of Rights. In the new system it is provided, that "*The trial of all crimes*, except in cases of Impeachment," *shall be by Jury*, but this provision could not possibly be extended to all *Civil* cases. For it is well known that the Trial by Jury is not general and uniform throughout the United States, . . . hence it became necessary to submit the question to the General Legislature, who might accommodate their laws on this occasion to the desires and habits of the nation. Surely there is no prohibition in a case that is untouched.

New York Daily Advertiser, Kaminski & Saladino, vol. 16, p. 202.

13.2.4.57 The Impartial Examiner, No. 1, February 27 and March 5, 1788

I believe, it is acknowledged that the establishment of excises has been one of the greatest grievances, under which the English nation has labored for almost a century and an half. . . . If this branch of revenue takes place, all the consequent rigour of excise laws will necessarily be introduced in order to enforce a due collection. On any charges or offence in this instance you will see yourselves deprived of your boasted trial by jury. The much admired common law process will give way to some quick and summary mode, by which the unhappy defendant will find himself reduced, perhaps to ruin, in less time than a charge could be exhibited against him in the usual course. . . .

And what is that "appellate jurisdiction both as to law and fact," but an establishment, which may in effect operate as original jurisdiction? — Or what is an appeal to enquire into facts after a solemn adjudication in any court below, but a trial *de novo? . . .* Add to all, that this high prerogative court establishes no fundamental rule of proceeding, except that the trial by jury is allowed in some criminal cases. All other cases are left open — and subject "to such regulations as the Congress shall make." — Under these circumstances I beseech you all, as citizens of Virginia, to consider seriously whether you will not endanger the solemn trial by jury, which you have long revered, as a sacred barrier against injustice — which has been established by your ancestors many centuries ago, and transmitted to you, as one of the greatest bulwarks of civil liberty — which you have to this day maintained inviolate: — I beseech you, I say, as members of this commonwealth, to consider whether you will not be in danger of losing this inestimable mode of trial in all those cases, wherein the constitution does not provide for its security. Nay, does not that very provision, which is made, by being confined to a few particular cases, almost imply a total exclusion of the rest? Let it, then, be a reflection deeply impressed on your minds — that if this noble privilege, which by long experience has been found the most exquisite method of determining controversies according to the scale of equal liberty, should once be taken away, it is unknown what new species of trial may be substituted in its room. Perhaps you may be surprised with some strange piece of judicial polity, — some arbitrary method, perhaps confining all trials to the entire decision of the magistracy, and totally excluding the great body of the people from any share in the administration of public justice.

. . . For instance, if Congress should pass a law that persons charged with capital crimes shall not have a *right to demand the cause or nature of the accusation,* shall not be *confronted with the accusers or witnesses, or call for evidence in their favor;* and a question should arise respecting their authority therein, — can it be said that they have exceeded the limits of their jurisdiction, when *that* has no limits; when no provision has been made for such a right?

Virginia Independent Chronicle, Storing, vol. 5, pp. 181–83, 185.

13.2.4.58 Brutus, No. 14, February 28 and March 6, 1788

The second paragraph of sect. 2d. art. 3. . . .

. . .

It has been the fate of this clause, as it has of most of those, against which unanswerable objections have been offered, to be explained different ways, by the advocates and opponents to the constitution. I confess I do not know what the advocates of the system, would make it mean, for I have not been fortunate enough to see in any publication this clause taken up and considered. It is certain however, they do not admit the explanation which those who oppose the constitution give it, or otherwise they would not so frequently charge them with want of candor, for alledging that it takes away the trial by jury, appeals from an inferior to a superior court, as practised in the civil law courts, are well understood. In these courts, the judges determine both on the law and the fact; and appeals are allowed from the inferior to the superior courts, on the whole merits: the superior tribunal will re-examine all the facts as well as the law, and frequently new facts will be introduced, so as many times to render the cause in the court of appeals very different from what it was in the court below.

. . .

It may still be insisted that this clause does not take away the trial by jury on appeals, but that this may be provided for by the legislature, under that paragraph which authorises them to form regulations and restrictions for the court in the exercise of this power.

. . . But supposing the Congress may under this clause establish the trial by jury on appeals. It does not seem to me that it will render this article much less exceptionable. An appeal from one court and jury, to another court and jury, is a thing altogether unknown in the laws of our state, and in most states in the union. A practice of this kind prevails in the eastern states; actions are there commenced in the inferior courts, and an appeal lies from them on the whole merits to the superior courts: the consequence is well known, very few actions are determined in the lower courts; it is rare that a case of any importance is not carried by appeal to the supreme court, and the jurisdiction of the inferior courts is merely nominal; this has proved so burthensome to the people in Massachusetts, that it was one of the principal causes which excited the insurrection in that state, in the year past; very few sensible and moderate men in that state but what will admit, that the inferior courts are almost entirely useless, and answer very little purpose, save only to accumulate costs against the poor debtors who are already unable to pay their just debts.

. . .

This method would preserve the good old way of administering justice, would bring justice to every man's door, and preserve the inestimable right of trial by jury. It would be following, as near as our circumstances will admit, the practice of the courts in England, which is almost the only thing I would wish to copy in their government.

But as this system now stands, their is to be as many inferior courts as Congress may see fit to appoint, who are to be authorised to originate and in the first instance to try all the cases falling under the description of this article; there is no security that a trial by jury shall be had in these courts, but the trial here will soon become, as it is in Massachusetts' inferior courts, mere matter of form; for an appeal may be had to the supreme court on the whole merits. This court is to have power to determine in law and in equity, on the law and the fact, and this court is exalted above all other power in the government, subject to no controul, and so fixed as not to be removeable, but upon impeachment, which I shall hereafter shew, is much the same thing as not to be removeable at all.

New York Journal, Storing, vol. 2, pp. 431–37.

13.2.4.59 A Columbian Patriot, February 1788

5. The abolition of trial by jury in civil causes. — This mode of trial the learned Judge Blackstone observes, "has been coeval with the first rudiments of civil government, that property, liberty and life, depend on maintaining in its legal force the constitutional trial by jury." He bids his readers pauze, and with Sir Matthew Hale observes, how admirably this mode is adapted to the investigation of truth beyond any other the world can produce. Even the party who have been disposed to swallow, without examination, the proposals of the *secret conclave*, have started on a discovery that this essential right was curtailed; and shall a privilege, the origin of which may be traced to our Saxon ancestors — that has been a part of the law of nations, even in the fewdatory systems of France, Germany, and Italy — and from the earliest records has been held so sacred, both in ancient and modern Britain, that it could never be shaken by the introduction of Norman customs, or any other conquests or change of government — shall this inestimable privilege be relinquished in America — either thro' the fear of inquisition for unaccounted thousands of public monies in the hands of some who have been officious in the fabrication of the *consolidated system*, or from the apprehension that some future delinquent possessed of more power than integrity, may be called to a trial by his peers in the hour of investigation?

Kaminski & Saladino, vol. 16, p. 279.

13.2.4.60 The Landholder, No. 10, February 29, 1788

To the Honourable LUTHER MARTIN, Esq;

. . .

Since the publication of the Constitution, every topic of vulgar declamation has been employed to persuade the people, that it will destroy the *trial by jury*, and is defective for being without a *bill of rights*. You, Sir, had more candour in the Convention than we can allow to those declaimers out of it; there you never signified by any motion or expression whatsoever, that it stood in need of a bill of rights, or in any wise endangered the trial by jury. In these respects the Constitution met your entire approbation: for had you believed it defective in these essentials, you ought to have mentioned it in Convention, or had you thought that it wanted further guards, it was your *indispensable duty to have proposed them.* I hope to hear that the same candour that influenced you on this occasion, has induced you to obviate any improper impressions such publications may have excited in your constituents, when you had the honour to appear before the General Assembly.

[Baltimore] Maryland Journal, Kaminski & Saladino, vol. 16, pp. 267–68.

13.2.4.61 Publicola, March 20, 1788

. . . The constitution of the respective states, and the rights of the people, are to remain as under the confederation, excepting such parts as interfere with the express powers given to Congress by the new constitution. All the clamour therefore, which has been raised about the trial by jury, and the liberty of the press, might have been spared, as altogether unfounded. To those who wish to trust themselves under separate state governments, which may, as they have hitherto done, disregard the recommendations and requisitions of the union, I would recommend an attentive perusal of history, and as they do not seem to place any dependance on the reasoning of their fellow citizens, learn to be wise from the experience of past ages. They will find that in all countries, a strict union among the people, has been the only means of preserving liberty. . . .

State Gazette of North Carolina, Kaminski & Saladino,
vol. 16, pp. 436–37.

13.2.4.62   A Farmer, No. 4, March 21, 1788

. . . But moreover does not *Aristedes,* and every lawyer, know that in the interpretation of all political as well as civil laws, this fundamental maxim must be observed, *That where there are two objects in contemplation of any legislature, the express adoption of one, is the total exclusion of the other;* and that the adoption of juries in civil *criminal* cases, in every legal interpretation, amounts to be an absolute rejection in *civil* cases: — If the right of establishing juries, by a *Congressional* law is admitted at all, it must be admitted, as an *inherent legislative right,* paramount to the constitution, as it is not derived from it, and then the power that can make, can by law unmake; so that referring this power to a source of authority *superior* to the act of government, would leave us without any juries at all (even in *criminal* cases) if Congress should so please; which position can never be the object of either friends or enemies to the system at present. — If it is defective, it is still bad policy to make it worse; but still in every view, we must reflect, that the establishment of trials by jury, belongs to *political,* not to *civil* legislation. It includes the right of organizing government, not of regulating the conduct of individuals, as the following enquiry will prove; we must never give an assembly the power of giving itself power.

As the worth and excellence of this mode of trial, preserved and handed down from generation to generation for near two thousand years, has drawn down the enthusiastic encomiums of the most enlightened lawyers and statesmen of every age; as it has taken deep root in the breast of every freeman, encompassed by the defences of affection and veneration, a repetition of its praises would be as tedious as useless: Some remarks however, still remain to be made, which will place this subject in a more important and conspicuous view.

The trial by jury, is the only remaining power which the Commons of England have retained in their own hands, of all that plentitude of authority and freedom, which rendered their northern progenitors irresistible in war, and flourishing in peace. — The usurpations of *the few,* gradually effected by artifice and force, have robbed *the many,* of that power which once formed the basis of those governments, so celebrated by mankind. — The government of Sparta, the form of which, it is said, has continued from the days of Lycurgus to our age, preserving its model amidst those overwheming tides of revolution and shipwrecks of governments, which Greece has sustained for near three thousand years; the same form of government among the Saxons and other Germans, consisting of King, Lords and Commons, applauded by Tacitus and Machiavelli, were thus distinguished from the present goverment of England — The power of the Commons resided with them, not in representatives but in the body of the people. — *De minoribus rebus, principes consultant; de majoribus omnes,* are either the words of Tacitus or Caesar. The administration of *ordinary* affairs was committed to the select men; but all important subjects were deliberated on by the whole body of the people. — Such was the consitution of Sparta, and of England, when Machiavelli gives them as a model, for there can be no doubt but that the *folk-motes* of the Saxons were not formed by representation — The venerable remembrance of which assemblies, hung long about the affections of Englishmen, and it was to restore them that they offered such frequent libations of their noblest blood; but the usurpations of *the few* have been unwearied and irresistible, and the trial by jury is all that now remains to *the many.*

The trial by jury is — the democratic branch of the judiciary power — more necessary than representatives in legislature; for those usurpations, which silently undermine the spirit of liberty, under the sanction of law, are more dangerous than direct and open legislative attacks; in the one case the treason is never discovered until liberty, and with it the power of defence is lost; the other is an open summons to arms, and then if the people will not defend their rights, they do not deserve to enjoy them.

The *judiciary* power, has generally been considered as a *branch* of the *executive,* because these two powers, have been so frequently united; — but where united, there is no liberty. — in every *free* State, the judiciary is kept separate, independent, and considered as an intermediate power; — and it certainly partakes more of a *legislative,* than an *executive* nature — The sound definition which Delolme applied to one branch may be justly extended to the whole judiciary, — *That it is a subordinate legislation in most instance, supplying by analogy, and precedent in each particular case, the defects of general legislative acts,* — [W]ithout then the check of the *democratic branch - the jury,* to ascertain those facts, to which the judge is to apply the law, and even in many cases to determine the cause by a *general* verdict — the latitude of judicial power, combined with the various and uncertain nature of evidence, will render it impossible to convict a judge of corruption, and ascertain his guilt. — Remove the fear of punishment, give hopes of impunity, and vice and tyranny come scowling from their dark abodes in the human heart. — Destroy juries and every thing is prostrated to judges, who may easily disguise law, by suppressing and varying fact: — Whenever therefore the trial by juries has been abolished, the liberties of the people were soon lost — The judiciary power is immediately absorbed, or placed under the direction of the executive, as example teaches in most of the States of Europe. — So formidable an engine of power, defended only by the gown and the robe, is soon seized and engrossed by the power that wields the sword. — Thus we find the judiciary and executive branches united, or the *former* totally dependent on the *latter* in most of the governments in the world. — It is true, where the judges will put on the sword and wield it with success, they will subject both princes and legislature to their despotism, as was the case in the memorable usurpation of the Justizia of Arragon, where the judiciary erected themselves into a frightful tyranny.

Why then shall we risque this important check to judiciary usurpation, provided by the wisdom of antiquity? Why shall we rob the Commons of the only remaining power they have been able to preserve, for their personal exercise? Have they ever abused it? — I know it has and will be said — they have — that they are too ignorant — that they cannot distinguish between right and wrong — that decisions on property are submitted to chance; and that the last word, commonly determines the cause: — There is some truth in these allegations — but whence comes it — The Commons are much degraded in the powers of the mind: — They were deprived of the use of understanding, when they were robbed of the power of employing it. — Men no longer cultivate, what is no longer useful, — should every opportunity be taken away, of exercising their reason, you will reduce them to that state of mental baseness, in which they appear in nine-tenths of this globe — distinguished from brutes, only by form and the articulation of sound — *Give them power and they will find understanding to us it* — But taking juries with all their real and attributed defects, it is not better to submit a cause to an impartial tribunal, who would at least, as soon do you right as wrong — than for every man to become subservient to government and those in power? — Would any man oppose government, where his property would be wholly at the mercy and decision of those that govern? — We know the influence that property has over the minds of men — they will risque their lives rather than their property; and a government, where there is no trial by jury, has an unlimited command over every man who has any thing to loose. — It is by the attacks on private property through the judiciary, that despotism becomes as irresistible as terrible. I could relate numerous examples of the greatest and best men in all countries, who have been driven to despair, by vexatious lawsuits, commenced at the instigation of the court, of favorites and of minions, and all *from the loss of juries*. — France was reduced to the brink of destruction in one instance. — The Queen mother Louise of Savoy, piqued at the constable of Bourbon, a young and amiable man, who refused to marry her, commenced a suit against him for all his estate — The judges were ready at the beck of the court, and without a shadow of justice deprived him by law of every shilling he was worth; and drove from this country an unfortunate hero, whose mad revenge carried desolation into her bosom. — In Denmark a despicable minion, who came in rags to the court, after the estblishment of their new government, which they solicited Frederick the IIId to make for them, acquired an immense fortune by plunder, sheltered by the favour of the Sovereign. At last he fixed his eyes on a most delightful estate, and offered to buy it — The owner did not want money, and could not think of selling the patrimony of an ancient family; this wretch then spirited up law-suits against him, and after the most cruel vexations obliged him to sell the estate for much less than he at first offered him. This unfortunate gentleman was driven from the country which gave him birth, and a once happy society of relations and friends. — Such would have been the fate of England, from those courts without juries, which took cognizance of causes arising in the revenues and imports in Charles the first's time, the court fortunately for the liberties of England, seized the bull by the horns, when they attacked that wonderful man John Hampden. He spent 20,000 *l.* rather than pay an illegal tax of twenty shillings, brought the case before the Parliament, roused the spirit of the nation, and finally overturned courts, King, and even the constitution for many years. These dreadful examples may teach us the importance of juries in *civil* cases — they may recal [*sic*] to my countrymen a maxim which their ancestors, as wise, and more virtuous than their posterity, held ever in view — *That if the people creep like tortoises, they will still find themselves too fast in giving away power.*   [Baltimore] Maryland Gazette, Storing, vol. 5, pp. 37–40.

13.2.4.63 Aristocrotis, April 1788

. . . Another privilege which the people possesses at present, and which the new congress will find it their interest to deprive them of, is trial by jury — for of all the powers which the people have wrested from government, this is the most absurd; it is even a gross violation of common sense, and most destructive to energy. In the first place it is absurd, that twelve ignorant plebians, should be constituted judges of a law, which passed through so many learned hands; — first a learned legislature after many learned animadversions and criticisms have enacted it — Second, learned writers have explained and commented on it. — Third, lawyers twisted, turned and new modeled it — and lastly, a learned judge opened up and explained it. Yet after all these learned discussions, an illiterate jury (who have scarce a right to think for themselves instead of judging for others) must determine whether it applies to the fact or not; and by their verdict the learned judge must be governed in passing sentence; and perhaps a learned gentleman be cast in an action with an insignificant cottager.

Secondly. Common sense recoils at the very idea of such a pernicious practice as this, because it makes no difference between the virtuous and the vicious, the precious and the vile; between those of noble birth, and illustrious descent, and those of base blood, and ignoble obscure pedigree — for an ignorant stupid jury, cannot discern the merit of persons — it is the merits of the cause they examine; which is just reversing the question, and beginning at the wrong end. Thirdly. This custom is fatal to energy, for tho' a law should be expressed in the most pointed terms, a jury may soften and mitigate, and in a great measure destroy the spirit of it. . . .   Storing, vol. 3, pp. 204–05.

13.2.4.64 Address of a Minority of the Maryland Convention, May 1, 1788

The great objects of these amendments were, 1st. To secure the trial by jury in all cases, the boasted birth-right of Englishmen, and their descendants, and the palladium of civil liberty; and to prevent the *appeal from fact,* which not only destroys that trial in civil cases, but by *construction,* may also elude it in criminal cases; a mode of proceeding both expensive and burthensome; and also by blending law with fact, will destroy all check on the judiciary authority, render it almost impossible to convict judges of corruption, and may lay the foundation of that gradual and silent attack on individuals, by which the approaches of tyranny become irresistable.   [Baltimore] Maryland Gazette, Kaminski & Saladino, vol. 17, p. 243.

13.2.4.65 The Federalist, No. 81, May 28, 1788

. . . To avoid all inconveniences, it will be safest to declare generally that the Supreme Court shall possess appellate jurisdiction both as to law and *fact,* and that this jurisdiction shall be subject to such *exceptions* and regulations as the national legislature may prescribe. This will enable the government to modify it in such a manner as will best answer the ends of public justice and security.

This view of the matter, at any rate puts it out of all doubt that the supposed abolition of the trial by jury by the operation of this provision is fallacious and untrue. The legislature of the United States would certainly have full power to provide that in appeals to the Supreme Court there should be no reexamination of facts where they had been tried in the original causes by juries. This would certainly be an authorised exception; but if for the reason already intimated it should be thought too extensive, it might be qualified with a limitation to such causes only as are determinable at common law in that mode of trial.

The amount of the observations hitherto made on the authority of the judicial department is this — . . . that this appellate jurisdiction does, in no case, *abolish* the trial by jury; and that an ordinary degree of prudence and integrity in the national councils will insure us solid advantages from the establishment of the proposed judiciary, without exposing us to any of the inconveniences which have been predicted from that source.

Kaminski & Saladino, vol. 18, p. 110.

13.2.4.66   The Federalist, No. 83, May 28, 1788

The objection to the plan of the convention, which has met with most success in this state, and perhaps in several of the other states, is *that* relative to *the want of a constitutional provision* for the trial by jury in civil cases. The disingenuous form in which this objection is usually stated, has been repeatedly adverted to and exposed; but continues to be pursued in all the conversations and writings of the opponents of the plan. The mere silence of the constitution in regard to *civil causes,* is represented as an abolition of the trial by jury; and the declamations to which it has afforded a pretext, are artfully calculated to induce a persuasion that this pretended abolition is complete and universal; extending not only to every species of civil, but even to *criminal causes.* To argue with respect to the latter, would, however, be as vain and fruitless, as to attempt the serious proof of the *existence* of *matter,* or to demonstrate any of those propositions which by their own internal evidence force conviction, when expressed in language adapted to convey their meaning.

With regard to civil causes, subtleties almost too contemptible for refutation, have been adopted to countenance the surmise that a thing, which is only *not provided for,* is entirely *abolished.* Every man of discernment must at once perceive the wide difference between *silence* and *abolition.* But as the inventors of this fallacy have attempted to support it by certain *legal maxims* of interpretation, which they have perverted from their true meaning, it may not be wholly useless to explore the ground they have taken.

The maxims on which they rely are of this nature, "a specification of particulars is an exclusion of generals"; or, "the expression of one thing is the exclusion of another." Hence, say they, as the constitution has established the trial by jury in criminal cases, and is silent in respect to civil, this silence is an implied prohibition of trial by jury in regard to the latter.

The rules of legal interpretation are rules of *common sense,* adopted by the courts in the construction of the laws. The true test therefore, of a just application of them, is its conformity to the source from which they are derived. This being the case, let me ask if it is consistent with reason or common sense to suppose, that a provision obliging the legislative power to commit the trial of criminal causes to juries, is a privation of its right to authorise or permit that mode of trial in other cases? Is it natural to suppose, that a command to do one thing, is a prohibition to the doing of another, which there was a previous power to do, and which is not incompatible with the thing commanded to be done? If such a supposition would be unnatural and unreasonable, it cannot be rational to maintain that an injunction of the trial by jury in certain cases is an interdiction of it in others.

A power to constitute courts, is a power to prescribe the mode of trial; and consequently, if nothing was said in the constitution on the subject of juries, the legislature would be at liberty either to adopt that institution, or to let it alone. This discretion in regard to criminal causes is abridged by the express injunction of trial by jury in all such cases; but it is of course left at large in relation to civil causes, there being a total silence on this head. The specification of an obligation to try all criminal causes in a particular mode, excludes indeed the obligation or necessity of employing the same mode in civil causes, but does not abridge *the power* of the legislature to exercise that mode if it should be thought proper. The pretence therefore, that the national legislature would not be at full liberty to submit all the civil causes of federal cognizance to the determination of juries, is a pretence destitute of all just foundation.

From these observations, this conclusion results, that the trial, by jury in civil cases would not be abolished, and that the use attempted to be made of the maxims which have been quoted, is contrary to reason and common sense, and therefore not admissible. Even if these maxims had a precise technical sense, corresponding with the ideas of those who employ them upon the present occasion, which, however, is not the case, they would still be inapplicable to a constitution of government. In relation to such a subject, the natural and obvious sense of its provisions, apart from any technical rules, is the true criterion of construction.

. . .

The friends and adversaries of the plan of the convention, if they agree in nothing else, concur at least in the value they set upon the trial by jury: Or if there is any difference between them, it consists in this; the former regard it as a valuable safeguard to liberty, the latter represent it as the very palladium of free government. For my own part, the more the operation of the institution has fallen under my observation, the more reason I have discovered for holding it in high estimation; and it would be altogether superfluous to examine to what extent it deserves to be esteemed useful or essential in a representative republic, or how much more merit it may be entitled to as a defence against the oppressions of an hereditary monarch, than as a barrier to the tyranny of popular magistrates in a popular government. Discussions of this kind would be more curious than beneficial, as all are satisfied of the utility of the institution, and of its friendly aspect to liberty. But I must acknowledge that I cannot readily discern the inseparable connnection between the existence of liberty and the trial by jury in civil cases. Arbitrary impeachments, arbitrary methods of prosecuting pretended offences, and arbitrary punishments upon arbitrary convictions have ever appeared to me to be the great engines of judicial despotism; and these have all relation to criminal proceedings. The trial by jury in criminal cases, aided by the *habeas corpus* act, seems therefore to be alone concerned in the question. And both of these are provided for in the most ample manner in the plan of the convention.

. . .

It is evident that it can have no influence upon the legislature, in regard to the *amount* of the taxes to be laid, to the *objects* upon which they are to be imposed, or to the *rule* by which they are to be apportioned. If it can have any influence therefore, it must be upon the mode of collection, and the conduct of the officers entrusted with the execution of the revenue laws.

As to the mode of collection in this state, under our own constitution, the trial by jury is in most cases out of use. . . .

And as to the conduct of the officers of the revenue, the provision in favor of trial by jury in criminal cases, will afford the security aimed at. Wilful abuses of a public authority, to the oppression of the subject, and every species of official extortion, are offences against the government; for which, the persons who commit them, may be indicted and punished according to the circumstances of the case.

The excellence of the trial by jury in civil cases, appears to depend on circumstances foreign to the preservation of liberty. The strongest argument in its favour is, that it is a security against corruption. As there is always more time and better opportunity to tamper with a standing body of magistrates than with a jury summoned for the occasion, there is room to suppose, that a corrupt influence would more easily find its way to the former than to the latter. The force of this consideration, is however, diminished by others. The sheriff who is the summoner of ordinary juries, and the clerks of courts who have the nomination of special juries, are themselves standing officers, and acting individually, may be supposed more accessible to the touch of corruption than the judges, who are a collective body. It is not difficult to see that it would be in the power of those officers to select jurors who would serve the purpose of the party as well as a corrupted bench. In the next place, it may fairly be supposed that there would be less difficulty in gaining some of the jurors promiscuously taken from the public mass, than in gaining men who had been chosen by the government for their probity and good character. But making every deduction for these considerations the trial by jury must still be a valuable check upon corruption. It greatly multiplies the impediments to its success. As matters now stand, it would be necessary to corrupt both court and jury; for where the jury have gone evidently wrong, the court will generally grant a new trial, and it would be in most cases of little use to practice upon the jury, unless the court could be likewise gained. Here then is a double security; and it will readily be perceived that this complicated agency tends to preserve the purity of both institutions. By increasing the obstacles to success it discourages attempts to seduce the integrity of either. The temptations to prostitution, which the judges might have to surmount, must certainly be much fewer while the co-operation of a jury is necessary, than they might be if they had themselves the exclusive determination of all causes.

Notwithstanding therefore the doubts I have expressed as to the essentiality of trial by jury, in civil cases, to liberty, I admit that it is in most cases, under proper regulations, an excellent method of determining questions of property; and that on this account alone it would be entitled to a constitutional provision in its favour, if it were possible to fix the limits within which it ought to be comprehended. There is however, in all cases, great difficulty in this; and men not blinded by enthusiasm, must be sensible that in a federal government which is a composition of societies whose ideas and institutions in relation to the matter materially vary from each other, that difficulty must be not a little augmented. For my own part, at every new view I take of the subject, I become more convinced of the reality of the obstacles, which we are authoritatively informed, prevented the insertion of a provision on this head in the plan of the convention.

. . .

From this sketch it appears, that there is a material diversity as well in the modification as in the extent of the institution of trial by jury in civil cases in the several states; and from this fact, these obvious reflections flow. First, that no general rule could have been fixed upon by the convention which would have corresponded with the circumstances of all the states; and secondly, that more, or at least as much might have been hazarded, by taking the system of any one state for a standard, as by omitting a provision altogether, and leaving the matter as it has been left, to legislative regulation.   Kaminski & Saladino, vol. 18, pp. 115–21.

13.2.4.67   The Federalist, No. 84, May 28, 1788

[T]he Constitution proposed by the convention contains, as well as the constitution of this state, a number of such provisions [in favor of rights and privileges].

Independent of those which relate to the structure of the government, we find the following: . . . Article 3, section 2, clause 3 "The trial of all crimes, except in cases of impeachment, shall be by jury; and such trial shall be held in the State where the said crimes shall have been committed; but when not committed within any State, the trial shall be at such place or places as the Congress may by law have directed."   Kaminski & Saladino, vol. 18, p. 128.

13.2.4.68   A [New Hampshire] Farmer, No. 3, June 6, 1788

I shall now make some observations on the unjust and illiberal sarcasms, passed by Mr. Alfredus, on our jurors: — And, as he has such a peculiar nack of leaping over important things, by saying "they are nothing to the purpose," or by stigmatizing them, "as impertinent observations, groundless assertions," etc. I shall copy his own words, and then follow, with the sentiments of the Hon. Justice Blackstone, who is one of the most celebrated Authors now extant.

Sir, in your publication of Friday, January 18th, ult. you say, "What are the advantages of this boasted trial by jury, and on which side do they lie? *Not certainly on the side of justice,* for one unprincipled juror, secured in the interest of the opposite party, will frequently divert her course, and in four cases out of five where injustice is done, it is by *the ignorance or knavery of the jury.*" This, I may venture to affirm, is an impudent and bold stroke; it attacks the whole community at once, and has a tendency to sap and undermine the best preservative of liberty, and therefore ought to be held in abhorrence by every freeman; it is totally repugnant to the sense of the best writers on the subject, and especially to the ideas of the renowned author above mentioned, whose sentiments I shall now quote, vol. 3, page 378. *"When the jury have delivered in their verdict, and it is recorded in court, that ends the trial by jury; a trial which besides the other vast advantages which we have occasionally observed in its progress, is also as expeditious and cheap as it is convenient, equitable and certain: upon these accounts — the trial by jury has been, as I trust ever will be looked upon as the glory of the English law; and if it has so great an advantage over individuals in regulating civil property, how much must that advantage be heightened, when it is applied* to criminal *cases; it is the most transcendant privilege which any subject can enjoy or wish for; he cannot be affected either in his property, his liberty or his person, but by the unanimous consent of twelve of his neighbors and equals; a Constitution that I may venture to affirm has, under Providence, secured the just liberties of the English nation for a long succession of ages; and therefore a celebrated French writer (Montesque) who concludes, that because Rome, Sparta, and Carthage have lost their liberties, therefore those of England in time must perish, should have recollected that Rome, Sparta and Carthage, at the time when their liberties were lost, were strangers to the trial by jury.*

Great as this eulogium may seem, it is no more than this admirable Constitution, when traced to its principles, will be found, in sober reason, to deserve. The impartial administration of justice, which secures both our persons and properties, is the great end of civil society; but if that be entirely entrusted to the magistracy of a select body of men, and those generally selected by the Prince, or those who enjoy the highest offices in the state, their decision, in spite of their own natural integrity, will have frequently an involuntary bias toward those of their own rank and dignity; here therefore, a competent number of sensible and upright jurymen, chosen by lot from among those of the middle rank, will be found the best investigators of truth, and the surest guardians of public justice; for the most powerful individual in the state, will be cautious of committing any flagrant invasion of another's right, when he knows that the fact of his oppression, must be examined, and decided by twelve indifferent men, not appointed till near the hour of trial: and that, when once the fact is ascertained, the law must of course redress it — This therefore preserves, in the hands of the people, that share which they ought to have, in the administration of public justice; and prevents the encroachments of the more powerful and wealthy citizens.

Every new tribunal erected for the decision of facts, without the intervention of a jury, whether composed of justices of the peace; commissioners of the revenue; judges of a court of conscience; or any other standing magistrate, is a step towards establishing aristocracy, the most oppressive of absolute government. It is, therefore, upon the whole, the duty which every man owes to his country, his friends, his posterity, and himself, to maintain to the utmost of his power, this valuable Constitution in all its rights, and above all to guard with the most jealous circumspection against the introduction of new, and arbitrary methods of trial, which, under a variety of plausible pretenses, may in time, imperceptibly undermine this best preservative of LIBERTY," — Added to this, there is a late law of this state, which puts the pay, and travel of our jurors upon a very respectable footing — And lest Mr. Alfredus should say, this is nothing to the purpose, because the trial, by jury, under the English Constitution, — may be very different from what it is in ours, I will just mention, wherein they differ, under the English Constitution, — The jurors are returned by the sheriff. — under ours they are draughted by lot, from each town, which, I think, is the most equitable method, and as to the modes of process through the trials, they are nearly the same, both endeavor to do justice to the parties.

[New Hampshire] Freeman's Oracle and New Hampshire Advertiser, Storing, vol. 4, pp. 213–14.

13.2.4.69 Sydney, Address, June 13 & 14, 1788

By the 13th paragraph "no member of this State shall be disfranchised, or deprived of any of the rights or privileges secured to the subjects of the State by this constitution, unless by the law of the land, or judgment of its peers."

. . .

The 41st provides "that the trial by jury remain inviolate forever; that no acts of attainder shall be passed by the legislature of this State for crimes other than those committed before the termination of the present war. . . ."

There can be no doubt that if the new government be adopted in all its latitude, every one of these paragraphs will become a dead letter. . . .

New York Journal, Storing, vol. 6, p. 116.

13.2.5 LETTERS AND DIARIES

13.2.5.1 David Redick to William Irvine, September 24, 1787

The new plan of government proposed by the convention has made a bustle in the city and its vicinity. All people, almost, are for swallowing it down at once without examining its tendencies.

. . . Why is the trial by jury destroyed in civil causes before Congress? . . . I hope Congress will be very deliberate and digest it thoroughly before they send it recommended to the states.

Jensen, vol. 2, p. 134.

13.2.5.2 William Pierce to St. George Tucker, September 28, 1787

. . . "A defect is found by some people in this new Constitution, because it has not provided, except in criminal cases, for Trial by Jury. I ask if the trial by jury in civil cases is really and substantially of any security to the liberties of a people. In my idea the opinion of its utility is founded more in prejudice than in reason. I cannot but think that an able Judge is better qualified to decide between man and man than any twelve men possibly can be. The trial by jury appears to me to have been introduced originally to soften some of the rigors of the feodal system. . . . An Englishman to be sure will talk of it in raptures; it is a virtue in him to do so, because it is insisted on in Magna Charta (that favorite instrument of English liberty) as the great bulwark of the nation's happiness. . . .["]

Kaminski & Saladino, vol. 16, pp. 444–45.

13.2.5.3   James Madison to George Washington, September 30, 1787

An attempt was made in the next place by R.H. Lee to amend the act of the convention before it should go forth from Congress. He proposed a bill of Rights, — provision for juries in civil cases and several other things corresponding with the ideas of Colonel Mason. . . . It was amendments, and it was their duty to make use of it in a case where the essential guards of liberty had been omitted.

Hobson & Rutland, vol. 10, pp. 179–181.

13.2.5.4   Arthur Lee to John Adams, October 3, 1787

. . . The omission of a Declaration of rights — . . . securing trial by Jury in criminal cases only — . . . are errors, if errors, gross as a mountain.

Kaminski & Saladino, vol. 13, pp. 307–08.

13.2.5.5   Louis Guillaume Otto to Comte de Montmorin, October 20, 1787

. . . The Constitution is not even accompanied by a *Declaration of rights*, so that no recourse remains for the Citizen against oppression. . . . In England the right of resistance is part of the Constitution, here it is not even mentioned. — All civil cases will be decided in the supreme Court without benefit of Juries; but Judges will be named by Congress; what an unjust way of applying unjust laws!

Kaminski & Saladino, vol. 13, p. 424.

13.2.5.6   Richard Henry Lee to Samuel Adams, October 27, 1787

Our mutual friend Mr. Gerry furnishes me with an opportunity of writing to you without danger of my letter being stopt on its passage, as I have some reason to apprehend has been the case with letters written by me and sent by the Post — . . . . In my letter to you . . . , I sent you the amendments that I proposed in Congress. . . . [Mr. Wilson's] principal Sophism is, that bills of rights were necessary in the State Constitutions because every thing not reserved was given to the State Legislatures, but in the Federal government, every thing was reserved that was not given to the federal Legislature. This is clearly a distinction without difference. Because Independent States are in the same relation to each other as Individuals are with respect to uncreated government. So that if reservations were necessary in one case, they are equally necessary in the other. But the futility of this distinction appears from the conduct of the Convention itself, for they have made several reservations — every one of which proves the Rule in Conventional ideas to be, that what was not reserved was given — . . . But they have no reservation in favor of the Press, Rights of Conscience, Trial by Jury in Civil Cases, or Common Law securities. Kaminski & Saladino, vol. 13, pp. 484–85.

13.2.5.7   William Grayson to William Short, November 10, 1787

I have received your favor, for which I am much obliged; the Convention at Philada. about which I wrote you, have at length produced (contrary to expectation) an entire new constitution; This has put us all in an uproar: — Our public papers are full of attacks and justifications of the new system: And if you go into private companies, you hear scarcely any thing else: — In the Eastern states the thing is well recieved; the enemies to the Constitution say that this is no wonder, as they have overreached the Southern people so much in it's [*sic*] formation: In this State, I believe there is a great majority against it: the reason assigned by it's favorers is that they derives [*sic*] great advantages by imposing duties on ye. imports of Jersey & Connecticut, — In Jersey, nothing is more popular

. . .

With respect to my own sentiments I own I have important objections: — In the first place I think liberty a thing of too much importance to be trusted on the ground of *implication*: it should rest on principles expressed in the clearest & most unequivocal manner. A bill of rights ought then to have preceded. tryals [*sic*] by jury should have been expressly reserved in Civil as well as Criminal cases.

Kaminski & Saladino, vol. 14, pp. 81–82.

13.2.5.8 David Ramsay to Benjamin Rush, November 10, 1787

As I suppose your convention is about convening & that you are a member I shall take the liberty of suggesting my wishes on the subject.

I am ready & willing to adopt the constitution without any alteration but still think objections might be obviated if the first state convention after accepting in its present form would nevertheless express their approbation of some alterations being made on the condition that Congress & the other States concurred with them. . . . I wish also that there might be added some declaration in favor of the Press and trial by Jury. I assent to Mr Wilsons reasoning that all is retained which is not ceded; but think that an explicit declaration on this subject might do good at least so far as to obviate objections. . . .

Kaminski & Saladino, vol. 14, pp. 83–84.

13.2.5.9 Town of Preston, Connecticut, to the Connecticut Convention, November 12, 1787

5th. We observe that the right of trial by jury in civil causes is not secured in the federal courts. This is repugnant to the custom handed down from our ancestors and always set easy on the people and esteemed as a privilege.

Jensen, vol. 3, p. 441.

13.2.5.10 James White to Richard Caswell, November 13, 1787

. . . I must in candor confess, that I have regretted that the proposed constitution was not more explicit with respect to several essentials: but the great clamor is, that no express provision is made for the TRYAL BY JURY, and LIBERTY OF THE PRESS; things so interwoven with our political, or legal ideas, that I conceive the sacred immutability of these rights to be such, as never to have occurred as questionable objects to the convention. . . . Whatever may be our wish in theory, we find in practice, by our own example, that states in confederacy, like individuals in society, must part with some of their privileges for the preservation of the rest. In proof of which, it cannot be denied that, for want of attention to, or knowledge of that maxim, these states are now tottering on the brink of anarchy.

Kaminski & Saladino, vol. 14, p. 96.

13.2.5.11   William Shippen, Jr., to Thomas Lee Shippen, November 22, 1787

. . . There certainly should be a bill of rights prefixed securing the liberty of the press, the liberty of conscience and trial by jury. . . . It would then be an excellent Constitution don't you think so my son?

Jensen, vol. 2, p. 288.

13.2.5.12   From Roger Sherman, December 8, 1787

I am informed that you wish to know my opinion with respect to the new Constitution lately formed by the federal convention, and the Objections made against it.

. . .

To form a just opinion of the new constitution it Should be considered, whether the powers to be thereby vested in the federal government are Sufficient, and only Such as are necessary to Secure the Common interests of the States; and whether the exercise of those powers is placed in Safe hands. — In every government there is a trust, which may be abused; but the greatest Security against abuse is, that the interest of those in whom the powers of government are vested is the Same as that of the people they govern, and that they are dependent on the Suffrage of the people for their appointment to, and continuance in Office. this [*sic*] is a much greater Security than a declaration of rights, or restraining clauses upon paper.

The rights of the people under the new constitution will be Secured by a representation in proportion to their numbers in one branch of the legislature, and the rights of the particular State governments by their equal representation in the other branch.

. . .

It was thought necessary in order to carry into efect [*sic*] the laws of the union, and to preserve justice and harmony among the States to extend the judicial powers of the confederacy, they cannot be extended beyond the enumerated cases, but may be limited by Congress, and doubtless will be restricted to Such cases of importance & magnitude as cannot Safely be trusted to the final decision of the courts of the particular States, the Supreme court may have a circuit through the States to make the trials as convenient, and as little expensive to the parties as may be; and the trial by jury will doubtless be allowed in Cases proper for that mode of trial, . . .

Kaminski & Saladino, vol. 14, pp. 386–88.

13.2.5.13   George Lee Turberville to James Madison, December 11, 1787

. . . The operation of the Judiciary is a matter so far beyond the reach of most of our fellow Citizens that we are bounden to receive — & not to originate our opinions upon this branch of ye Federal government — Lawyers alone conceive themselves masters of this subject & they hold it forth to us *danger & distress* as the inevitable result of the new system — & that this will proceed from the immense power of the general Judiciary — which will pervade the states from one extremity to the other & will finally absorb — & destroy the state Courts — But to me their power seem's very fairly defined by the clauses that constitute them — & the mention of Juries, in criminal cases — seeming therefor by implication in civil cases — not to be allowed, is the only objection *I* have to this Branch —

Kaminski & Saladino, vol. 14, pp. 406–07.

13.2.5.14 Thomas Jefferson to William Carmichael, December 15, 1787

Our new constitution is powerfully attacked in the American newspapers. the objections are that it's effect would be to form the 13. states into one: that proposing to melt all down into one general government they have fenced the people by no declaration of rights, they have . . . reserved a power of abolishing trials by jury in civil cases. . . . You will perceive that these objections are serious, and some of them not without foundation. The constitution however has been received with a very general enthusiasm, and as far as can be judged from external demonstrations the bulk of the people are eager to adopt it.

Boyd, vol. 12, p. 425.

13.2.5.15 Thomas Jefferson to James Madison, December 20, 1787

. . . I will now add what I do not like. First the omission of a bill of rights providing clearly and without the aid of sophisms for . . . trials by jury in all matters of fact triable by the laws of the land and not by the law of Nations. To say, as Mr. Wilson does that a bill of rights was not necessary because all is reserved in the case of the general government which is not given, while in the particular ones all is given which is not reserved might do for the Audience to whom it was addressed, but is surely gratis dictum, opposed by strong inferences from the body of the instrument, as well as from the omission of the clause of our present confederation which had declared that in express terms. It was a hard conclusion to say because there has been no uniformity among the states as to cases triable by jury, because some have been so incautious as to abandon this mode of trial, therefore the more prudent states shall be reduced to the same level of calamity. It would have been much more just and wise to have concluded the other way that as most of the states had judiciously preserved this palladium, those who had wandered should be brought back to it, and to have established general right instead of wrong. Let me add that a bill of rights is what the people are entitled to against every government on earth, general or particular, and what no just government should refuse, or rest on inference.

Boyd, vol. 12, p. 440.

13.2.5.16 Timothy Pickering to Charles Tillinghast, December 24, 1787

. . . The trial by jury in civil cases, I grant, is not explicitly secured by the constitution: but we have been told the reason of the omission; and to me it is satisfactory. In many of the civil causes subject to the jurisdiction of the federal courts, trial by jury would evidently be improper; in others, it was found impracticable in the convention to fix on the mode of constituting juries. But we may assure ourselves that the first Congress will make provision for introducing it in every case in which it shall be proper & practicable. . . . So if the Convention had positively fixed a trial by jury in all the civil cases in which it is contended that it ought to have been established, — it might have been found as highly inconvenient in practice as the case above stated; but being fixed by the *constitution*, the inconvenience must be endured (whatever mischief might arise from it) until the Constitution itself should be altered.   Kaminski & Saladino, vol. 14, pp. 204–05.

13.2.5.17 Thomas Paine to George Clymer, December 29, 1787

. . . There are many excellent things in the new System. I perceive the difficulties you must have found in debating on certain points, such as the trial by Juries, because in some cases, such for instance as that of the United States against any particular State, for if the trial is to be held in the delinquent State, a Jury composed from that State, would be a part of the delinquent, and consequently Judges in their own case.   Kaminski & Saladino, vol. 14, p. 487.

13.2.5.18 Thomas Jefferson to Uriah Forrest, December 31, 1787

. . . I will now tell you what I do not like. — First the Omission of a Bill of rights, providing clearly, and without the aid of sophisms, for . . . trials by jury in all matters of fact triable by the laws of the land, and not by the law of Nations. To say, as Mr. Wilson does, that a bill of rights was not necessary, because all is reserved in the case of the general government which is not given, while in the particular ones all is given which is not reserved, might do for the audience to which it was addressed: but is surely a gratis dictum, the reverse of which might as well be said; and it is opposed by strong inferences from the body of the instrument, as well as from the omission of the clause of our present confederation which had made the reservation in express terms. It was hard to conclude because there has been a want of uniformity among the states as to cases triable by jury, because some have been so incautious as to abandon this mode of trial in certain cases, therefore the more prudent states shall be reduced to the same level of calamity. It would have been much more just and wise to have concluded the other way, that as most of the states had preserved with jealousy this sacred palladium of liberty, those who had wandered should be brought back to it: and to have established general right instead of general wrong, for I consider all the ill as established, which may be established. I have a right to nothing which another has a right to take away; and Congress will have a right to take away trials by jury in all civil cases. Let me add that a bill of rights is what the people are entitled to against every government on earth, general or particular; and what no just government should refuse, or rest on inferences.   Boyd, vol. 12, pp. 476–477.

13.2.5.19 Thomas B. Wait to George Thatcher, January 8, 1788

. . . How can you, after *perusing* the arguments of Crazy Jonathan, approve of the abolition of juries in civil causes — If the Genl. Court of this state are insurgents for depriving the subject of that right in 110 actions out of 120 — what shall we say to the Constitution that evidently deprives the subject of that right altogether? — O, my good friend, that cursed Small pox has made a crazy Jonathan of you in good earnest. — But your life is spared — and I am happy —   Kaminski & Saladino, vol. 15, p. 286.

13.2.5.20 Samuel Holden Parsons to William Cushing, January 11, 1788

Trial by jury is said to be taken away. No such inference can be drawn from the Constitution. All civil [cases] were never tried by jury in this country or in Great Britain. . . . The mode of ascertaining the fact will be pointed out by law, and we cannot suppose Congress to divest themselves of all good sense as well as honesty so as to adopt measures totally repugnant to the habits and feelings of the people as the objection supposes.

Jensen, vol. 3, p. 572.

13.2.5.21 Charles Johnson to James Iredell, January 14, 1788

. . . For my part I will candidly, and in confidence, declare to you that it is a doubtful point with me, and which I cannot yet bring to a decision, whether it will be better to receive the new Constitution, with all its seeming imperfections on its head, or run the risk of obtaining another Convention, which may revise and amend, expunge those articles that seem repugnant to the liberties of the people — . . . and explicitly secure the trial by jury, according to former usage — . . . with all the other rights of the individual which are not necessary to be given up to government, and which ought not and cannot be required for any good purpose.

Kaminski & Saladino, vol. 15, p. 364.

13.2.5.22 Letter from Centinel, January 19, 1788

. . . Whilst I am issuing number after number of my Centinel, all written with a freedom and spirit sufficient, one would think, to rouse the people — I say, while I am doing this, the states, one after another, either unanimously or by large majorities, are ratifying the new constitution. . . . I have rung the changes upon — the liberty of the press — trial by jury — despotism and tyranny — and am reduced to the necessity of repeating in different words the same railings against the constitution. . . .

Pennsylvania Gazette, Kaminski & Saladino, vol. 15, p. 451.

13.2.5.23 Thomas Jefferson to William Stephen Smith, February 2, 1788

. . . But I own it astonishes me to find such a change wrought in the opinions of our countrymen since I left them, as that threefourths of them should be contented under a system which leaves to their governors the power of taking from them the trial by jury in civil cases. . . . This is degeneracy in the principles of liberty to which I had given four centuries instead of four years.

Boyd, vol. 12, p. 558.

13.2.5.24 Marquis de Lafayette to George Washington, February 4, 1788

. . . We are Anxiously Waiting for the Result of the State Conventions — the New Constitution Has Been Much Examined and Admired By European Philosophers — It Seems the Want of a declaration of Rights, of An Insurance for the trial By juries, . . . are, . . . the Principal Points objected to. . . .

Kaminski & Saladino, vol. 14, p. 501.

13.2.5.25   George Washington to Marquis de Lafayette, April 28, 1788

. . . For example: there was not a member in the convention, I believe, who had the least objection to what is contended for by the Advocates for a *Bill of Rights* and *Tryal by Jury*. The first, where the people evidently retained every thing which they did not in express terms give up, was considered nugatory as you will find to have been more fully explained by Mr. Wilson and others: — And as to the second, it was only the difficulty of establishing a mode which should not interfere with the fixed modes of any of the States, that induced the Convention to leave it, as a matter of future adjustment.   *Kaminski & Saladino, vol. 17, p. 235.*

13.2.5.26   William R. Davie to James Madison, June 10, 1789

. . .

I have collected with some attention the objections of the honest and serious — they are but few & perhaps necessary alterations. — . . . they also insist on the trial by jury being expressly secured to them in all cases. . . .   *Hobson & Rutland, vol. 12, p. 211.*

13.2.5.27   Fisher Ames to Thomas Dwight, June 11, 1789

Mr. Madison has introduced his long expected Amendments. It contains a Bill of Rights — the right . . . of juries . . . at least this is the substance. There is too much of it.   *Veit, p. 246.*

13.2.5.28   Diary of William Maclay, July 10–11, 1789

. . . Well and What now, is the fact to be tryed by Chancery powers. I am bold to say no Issue of fact ever was tryed or found for or against in Chancery. facts often were carried into Chancery, as evidence but if they were doubted of, issue was joined on them, and directed to be tryed by a Jury. But now the ~~fact~~ Business unfolds itself, now we see what Gentlemen would be at, it is to try Facts on civil law principles, without the aid of a Jury, and this I promise You never will be submitted to. The question was put and wee carried it. But the House seemed rather to break up in a Storm.

. . .

As we came down the Stairs Docr. Johnson was by my side. Doctor (said I) I wish you would leave off, using these side Winds, and boldly at once bring in a Clause for deciding all Causes on civil law principles without the aid of a Jury. No No said he the Civil law name I am not very found of. I reply'd, you need not care about the name, since you have got the thing.   *Bowling & Veit, pp. 105–06.*

13.2.5.29   Thomas Jefferson to the Abbé Arnoux, July 19, 1789

With respect to the value of this institution [trial by jury] I must make a general observation. We think in America that it is necessary to introduce people into every department of government as far as they are capable of exercising it; and that this is the only way to insure a long continued and honest administration of its powers. . . . They are not qualified to judge questions of law, but they are capable of judging questions of fact. In the form of juries they determine all matters of fact, leaving to the permanent judges to decide the law resulting from those facts. But we all know that permanent judges acquire an Esprit de corps, that being known they are liable to be tempted by bribery, that they are misled by favor, by relationship, by spirit of party, by a devotion to the Executive or Legislative, that it is better to leave a cause to the decision of cross and pile, than to that of a judge biased to one side, and that the opinion of 12 honest jurymen gives still a better hope of right, than cross and pile does. It is therefore left to the juries, if they think the permanent judges are under any bias whatever in any cause, to take upon themselves to judge the law as well as the fact. Were I called upon to decide whether the people had best be omitted in the Legislative or Judiciary department, I would say it is better to leave them out of the legislative. The execution of the laws is more important than the making of them.

Boyd, vol. 15, pp. 282–83.

13.3 DISCUSSION OF RIGHTS

13.3.1 TREATISES

13.3.1.1 Giles Duncombe, 1695

And first as to their number twelve: and this number is no less esteemed by our Law than by Holy Writ. If the twelve Apostles on their twelve Thrones, must try us in our Eternal State, good reason hath the Law to appoint the number of twelve to try our Temporal. The Tribes of Israel were twelve, the Patriarchs were twelve, and Solomon's Officers were twelve, I Kings, 4.7. . . . Therefore not only matters of Fact were tried by twelve, but of ancient times twelve Judges were to try matters in Law, in the Exchequer Chamber, and there were twelve Counsellors of State for matters of State; and he that wageth his Law must have eleven others with him, which think he says true. And the Law is so precise in this number of twelve, that if the tryal be by more or less, it is a mis-Tryal.

Tryals Per Pais, 3rd ed. (London:
Richard and Edward Atkins, 1795), pp. 69–70.

13.3.1.2 Montesquieu, 1748

Book XI: Of the Laws Which Establish Political Liberty, with Regard to the Constitution

. . .

It is true that in democracies the people seem to act as they please; but political liberty does not consist in an unrestrained freedom. In governments, that is, in societies directed by laws, liberty can consist only in the power of doing what we ought to will, and in not being constrained to do what we ought not to will.

We must have continually present in our minds the difference between independence and liberty. Liberty is a right of doing whatever the laws permit; and if a citizen could do what they forbid, he would be no longer possessed of liberty, because all his fellow citizens would have the same power.

Democratic and aristocratic states are not necessarily free. Political liberty is to be met with only in moderate governments; yet even in these it is not always met with. It is there only when there is no abuse of power: but constant experience shews us, that every man invested with power is apt to abuse it; he pushes on till he comes to the utmost limit. Is it not strange, tho' true, to say that virtue itself has need of limits?

To prevent this abuse, 'tis necessary that by the very disposition of things power should be a check to power. A government may be so constituted, as no man shall be compelled to do things to which the law does not oblige him, nor forced to abstain from things which the law permits.

. . .

In every government there are three sorts of power: the legislative; the executive in respect to things dependent on the law of nations; and the executive, in regard to matters that depend on civil laws.

. . .

The political liberty of the subject is a tranquillity of mind, arising from the opinion each person has of his safety. In order to have this liberty, it is requisite the government be so constituted as one man need not be afraid of another.

When the legislative and executive powers are united in the same person, or in the same body of magistracy, there can be then no liberty; because apprehensions may arise, lest the same monarch or senate should enact tyrannical laws, to execute them in a tyrannical manner.

Again, there is no liberty, if the power of judging be not separated from the legislative and executive powers. Were it joined with the legislative, the life and liberty of the subject would be exposed to arbitrary control; for the judge would be then the legislator. Were it joined to the executive power, the judge might behave with all the violence of an oppressor.

. . .

The judiciary power ought not to be given to a standing senate; it should be exercised by persons taken from the body of the people, at certain times of the year, and pursuant to a form and manner prescribed by law, in order to erect a tribunal that should last only as long as necessity requires.

By this method the power of judging, a power so terrible to mankind, not being annexed to any particular state or profession, becomes, as it were, invisible. People have not then the judges continually present to their view; they fear the office, but not the magistrate.

In accusations of a deep or criminal nature, it is proper the person accused should have the privilege of chusing in some measure his judges in concurrence with the law; or at least he should have the right to except against so great a number, that the remaining part may be deemed his own choice.

The other two powers may be given rather to magistrates or permanent bodies, because they are not exercised on any private subject; one being no more than the general will of the state, and the other the execution of the general will.

But tho' the tribunals ought not to be fixt, yet the judgments ought, and to such a degree as to be ever conformable to the exact letter of the law. Were they to be the private opinion of the judge, people would then live in society without knowing exactly the obligations it lays them under.

Spirit of Laws, bk. 11, chs. 3, 4, 6.

13.3.1.3 William Blackstone, 1768

THE subject of our next enquiries will be the nature and method of the trial *by jury;* called also the trial *per pais,* or *by the country.* A trial that hath been used time out of mind in this nation, and seems to have been co-eval with the first civil government thereof. Some authors have endeavoured to trace the original of juries up as high as the Britons themselves, the first inhabitants of our island; but certain it is, that they were in use among the earliest Saxon colonies, their institution being ascribed by bishop Nicolson to Woden himself, their great legislator and captain. Hence it is, that we may find traces of juries in the laws of all those nations which adopted the feodal system, as in Germany, France, and Italy; who had all of them a tribunal composed of twelve good men and true, *"boni homines,"* usually the vasals or tenants of the lord, being the equals or peers of the parties litigant: and, as the lord's vasals judged each other in the lord's courts, so the king's vasals, or the lords themselves, judged each other in the king's court. In England we find actual mention of them so early as the laws of king Ethelred, and that not as a new invention. Stiernhook ascribes the invention of the jury, which in the Teutonic languages is denominated *nembda,* to Regner, king of Sweden and Denmark, who was co-temporary with our king Egbert. Just as we are apt to impute the invention of this, and some other pieces of juridical polity, to the superior genius of Alfred the great; to whom, on account of his having done much, it is usual to attribute every thing: and as the tradition of antient Greece placed to the account of their one Hercules whatever atchievement [*sic*] was performed superior to the ordinary prowess of mankind. Whereas the truth seems to be, that this tribunal was universally established among all the northern nations, and so interwoven in their very constitution, that the earliest accounts of the one give us also some traces of the other. It's establishment however and use, in this island, of what date soever it be, though for a time greatly impaired and shaken by the introduction of the Norman trial by battel, was always so highly esteemed and valued by the people, that no conquest, no change of government, could ever prevail to abolish it. In *magna carta* it is more than once insisted on as the principal bulwark of our liberties; but especially by chap. 29. that no freeman shall be hurt in either his person or property, *"nisi per legale judicium parium suorum vel per legem terrae.* ["] A privilege which is couched in almost the same words with that of the emperor Conrad, two hundred years before: *"nemo beneficium suum perdat, nisi secundum consuetudinem antecessorum nostrorum et per judicium parium suorum."* And it was ever esteemed, in all countries, a privilege of the highest and most beneficial nature.

. . .

TRIALS by jury in civil causes are of two kinds; *extraordinary,* and *ordinary.* The extraordinary I shall only briefly hint at, and confine the main of my observations to that which is more usual and ordinary.

. . .

WITH regard to the *ordinary* trial by jury in civil cases, I shall pursue the same method in considering it, that I set out with in explaining the nature of prosecuting actions in general, *viz.* by following the order and course of the proceedings themselves, as the most clear and perspicuous way of treating it.

WHEN there an issue is joined, by these words, "and this the said A prays may be enquired of by the country," or, "and of this he puts himself upon the country, and the said B does the like," the court awards a writ of *venire facias* upon the roll or record, commanding the sheriff "that he cause to come *here* on such day, twelve free and lawful men, *liberos et legales homines,* of the body of his county, by whom the truth of the matter may be better known, and who are neither of kin to the aforesaid A, nor the aforesaid B, to recognize the truth of the issue between the said parties." And such writ is accordingly issued to the sheriff.

THUS the cause stands ready for the trial *at the bar* of the court itself: for all trials were there antiently had, in actions which were there first commenced; which never happened but in matters of weight and consequence, all trifling suits being ended in the court-baron, hundred, or county courts: and all causes of great importance or difficulty are still usually retained upon motion, to be tried at the bar in the superior courts. But when the usage began, to bring actions of any trifling value in the courts of Westminster-hall, it was found to be an intolerable burthen to compel the parties, witnesses, and jurors, to come from Westmorland perhaps or Cornwall, to try an action of assault at Westminster. Therefore the legislature took into consideration, that the king's justices came usually twice in the year into the several counties, *ad capiendas assisas,* to take or try writs of assise, of *mort d'ancestor, novel disseisin, nusance,* and the like. The form of which writs we may remember was stated to be, that they commanded the sheriff to summon an assise or jury, and go to view the land in question; and then to have the said jury ready at the next coming of the justices of assise (together with the parties) to recognize and determine the disseisin, or other injury complained of. As therefore these judges were ready in the country to administer justice in real actions of assise, the legislature thought proper to refer other matters in issue to be also determined before them, whether of a mixed or personal kind. And therefore it was enacted by statute Westm. 2. 13 Edw. I. c. 30. that a clause of *nisi prius* should be inserted in all the aforesaid writs of *venire facias;* that is, "that the sheriff should cause the jurors to come to Westminster (or wherever the king's courts should be held) on such a day in easter and michaelmas terms; *nisi prius,* unless before that day the justices assigned to take assises shall come into his said county." By virtue of which the sheriff returned his jurors to the court of the justices of assise, which was sure to be held in the vacation before easter and michaelmas terms; and there the trial was had.

. . .

LET us now pause awhile, and observe (with sir Matthew Hale) in these first preparatory stages of the trial, how admirably this constitution is adapted and framed for the investigation of truth, beyond any other method of trial in the world. For, first the *person returning* the jurors is a man of some fortune and consequence; that so he may be not only the less tempted to commit wilful errors, but likewise be responsible for the faults of either himself or his officers: and he is also bound by the obligation of an oath faithfully to execute his duty. Next, as to the *time of their return:* the panel is returned to the court upon the original *venire,* and the jurors are to be summoned and brought in many weeks afterwards to the trial, whereby the parties may have notice of the jurors, and of their sufficiency or insufficiency, characters, connections, and relations, that so they may be challenged upon just cause; while at the same time by means of the compulsory process (of *distringas* or *habeas corpora*) the cause is not like to be retarded through defect of jurors. Thirdly, as to the *place* of their appearance: which in causes of weight and consequence is at the bar of the court; but in ordinary cases at the assises, held in the county where the cause of action arises, and the witnesses and jurors live: a provision most excellently calculated for the saving of expense to the parties. For, though the preparation of the causes in point of pleading is transacted at Westminster, whereby the order and uniformity of proceeding is preserved throughout the kingdom, and multiplicity of forms is prevented; yet this is no great charge or trouble, one attorney being able to transact the business of forty clients. But the troublesome and most expensive attendance is that of jurors and witnesses at the trial; which therefore is brought home to them, in the country where most of them inhabit. Fourthly, the *persons before whom* they are to appear, and before whom the trial is to be held, are the judges of the superior court, if it be a trial at bar; or the judges of assise, delegated from the courts at Westminster by the king, if the trial be held in the country: persons, whose learning and dignity secure their jurisdiction from contempt, and the novelty and very parade of whose appearance have no small influence upon the multitude. The very point of their being strangers in the county is of infinite service, in preventing those factions and parties, which would intrude in every cause of moment, were it tried only before persons resident on the spot, as justices of the peace, and the like. And, the better to remove all suspicion of partiality, it was wisely provided by the statutes 4 Edw. III. c. 2. 8 Ric. II. c. 2. and 33 Hen. VIII. c. 24. that no judge of assise should hold pleas in any county wherein he was born or inhabits. And, as this constitution prevents party and faction from intermingling in the trial of right, so it keeps both the rule and the administration of the laws uniform. These justices, though thus varied and shifted at every assises, are all sworn to the same laws, have had the same education, have pursued the same studies, converse and consult together, communicate their decisions and resolutions, and preside in those courts which are mutually connected and their judgments blended together, as they are interchangeably courts of appeal or advice to each other. And hence their administration of justice, and conduct of trials, are consonant and uniform; whereby that confusion and contrariety are avoided, which would naturally arise from a variety of uncommunicating judges, or from any provincial establishment. . . .

. . .

A COMMON jury is one returned by the sheriff according to the directions of the statute 3 Geo. II. c. 25. which appoints, that the sheriff shall not return a separate panel for every separate cause, as formerly; but one and the same panel for every cause to be tried at the same assises, containing not less than forty eight, nor more than seventy two, jurors: and that their names, being written on tickets, shall be put into a box or glass; and when each cause is called, twelve of these persons, whose names shall be first drawn out of the box, shall be sworn upon the jury, unless absent, challenged, or excused; and unless a previous view of the lands, or tenements, or other matters in question, shall have been thought necessary by the court: in which case six or more of the jurors returned, to be agreed on by the parties, or named by a judge or other proper officer of the court, shall be appointed to take such view; and then such of the jury as have appeared upon the view (if any) shall be sworn on the inquest previous to any other jurors. These acts are well calculated to restrain any suspicion of partiality in the sheriff, or any tampering with the jurors when returned.

As the jurors appear, when called, they shall be sworn, unless *challenged* by either party. Challenges are of two sorts; challenges to the *array,* and challenges to the *polls.*

. . .

BUT challenges to the polls of the jury (who are judges of fact) are reduced to four heads by sir Edward Coke: *propter honoris respectum; propter defectum; propter affectum;* and *propter delictum.*

. . .

3. JURORS may be challenged *propter affectum,* for suspicion of biass or partiality. This may be either a *principal* challenge, or *to the favour.* A *principal* challenge is such, where the cause assigned carries with it *prima facie* evident marks of suspicion, either of malice or favour: as, that a juror is of kin to either party within the ninth degree; that he has been arbitrator on either side; that he has an interest in the cause; that there is an action depending between him and the party; that he has taken money for his verdict; that he has formerly been a juror in the same cause; that he is the party's master, servant, counsellor, steward or attorney, or of the same society or corporation with him: all these are principal causes of challenge; which, if true, cannot be overruled, for jurors must be *omni exceptione majores.* Challenges *to the favour,* are where the party hath no principal challenge; but objects only some probable circumstances of suspicion, as acquaintance, and the like; the validity of which must be left to the determination of *triors,* whose office it is to decide whether the juror be favourable or unfavourable. The triors, in case the first man called be challenged, are two indifferent persons named by the court; and, if they try one man and find him indifferent, he shall be sworn; and then he and the two triors shall try the next; and when another is found indifferent and sworn, and two triors shall be superseded, and the two first sworn on the jury shall try the rest.

4. CHALLENGES *propter delictum* are for some crime of misdemesnor, that affects the juror's credit and renders him infamous. As for a conviction of treason, felony, perjury, or conspiracy; or if he hath received judgment of the pillory, tumbrel, or the like; or to be branded, whipt, or stigmatized; or if he be outlawed or excommunicated, or hath been attainted of false verdict, *praemunire,* or forgery; or lastly, if he hath proved recreant when champion in the trial by battel, and thereby hath lost his *liberam legem.* A juror may himself be examined on oath of *voir dire, veritatem dicere,* with regard to the three former of these causes of challenge, which are not to his dishonour; but not with regard to his head of challenge, *propter delictum,* which would be to make him either forswear or accuse himself, if guilty.

. . .

WHEN the evidence is gone through on both sides, the judge in the presence of the parties, the counsel, and all others, sums up the whole to the jury; omitting all superfluous circumstances, observing wherein the main question and principal issue lies, stating what evidence has been given to support it, with such remarks as he thinks necessary for their direction, and giving them his opinion in matters of law arising upon that evidence.

THE jury, after the proofs are summed up, unless the case be very clear, withdraw from the bar to consider of their verdict: and, in order to avoid intemperance and causeless delay, are to be kept without meat, drink, fire, or candle, unless by permission of the judge, till they are all unanimously agreed. A method of accelerating unanimity not wholly unknown in other constitutions of Europe, and in matters of greater concern. For by the golden bulle of the empire, if, after the congress is opened, the electors delay the election of a king of the Romans for thirty days, they shall be fed only with bread and water, till the same is accomplished. But if our juries eat or drink at all, or have any eatables about them, without consent of the court, and before verdict, it is fineable; and if they do so at his charge for whom they afterwards find, it will set aside the verdict. Also if they speak with either of the parties or their agents, after they are gone from the bar; or if they receive any fresh evidence in private; or if to prevent disputes they cast lots for whom they shall find; any of these circumstances will entirely vitiate the verdict. And it has been held, that if the jurors do not agree in their verdict before the judges are about to leave the town, though they are not to be threatened or imprisoned, the judges are not bound to wait for them, but may carry them round the circuit from town to town in a cart. This necessity of a total unanimity seems to be peculiar to our own constitution; or, at least, in the *nembda* or jury of the antient Goths, there was required (even in criminal cases) only the consent of the major part; and in case of an equality, the defendant was held to be acquitted.

WHEN they are all unanimously agreed, the jury return back to the bar; and, before they deliver their verdict, the plaintiff is bound to appear in court, by himself, attorney, or counsel, in order to answer the amercement to which by the old law he is liable, as has been formerly mentioned, in case he fails in his suit, as a punishment for his false claim. To be *amerced*, or *a mercie*, is to be at the king's mercy with regard to the fine to be imposed; *in misericordia domini regis pro falso clamore suo.* The amercement is disused, but the form still continues; and if the plaintiff does not appear, no verdict can be given, but the plaintiff is said to be *nonsuit, non sequitur clamorem suum.* Therefore it is usual for a plaintiff, when he or his counsel perceives that he has not given evidence sufficient to maintain his issue, to be voluntarily nonsuited, or withdraw himself: whereupon the crier is ordered to *call the plaintiff;* and if neither he, nor any body for him, appears, he is nonsuited, the jurors are discharged, the action is at an end, and the defendant shall recover his costs. The reason of this practice is, that a nonsuit is more eligible for the plaintiff, than a verdict against him: for after a nonsuit, which is only a default, he may commence the same suit again for the same cause of action; but after a verdict had, and judgment consequent thereupon, he is for ever barred from attacking the defendant upon the same ground of complaint. But, in case the plaintiff appears, the jury by their foreman deliver in their verdict.

A VERDICT, *vere dictum,* is either *privy,* or *public.* A *privy* verdict is when the judge hath left or adjourned the court; and the jury, being agreed, in order to be delivered from their confinement, obtain leave to give their verdict privily to the judge out of court: which privy verdict is of no force, unless afterwards affirmed by a public verdict given openly in court; wherein the jury may, if they please, vary from their privy verdict. So that the privy verdict is indeed a mere nullity; and yet it is a dangerous practice, allowing time for the parties to tamper with the jury, and therefore very seldom indulged. But the only effectual and legal verdict is the *public* verdict; in which they openly declare to have found the issue for the plaintiff, or for the defendant; and if for the plaintiff, they assess the damages also sustained by the plaintiff, in consequence of the injury upon which the action is brought.   Commentaries, bk. 3, ch. 23; vol. 3, pp. 349–77 (footnotes omitted).

13.3.2 CASELAW

13.3.2.1 Den dem. Bayard v. Singleton, 1787

That by the constitution every citizen has undoubtedly a right to a decision of his property by a trial by jury. For that if the Legislature could take away this right, and require him to stand condemned in his property without a trial, it might with as much authority require his life to be taken way without a trial by jury, and that he should stand condemned to die, without the formality of any trial at all: that if the members of the General Assembly could do this, they might with equal authority, not only render themselves the Legislators of the State for life, without any further election of the people, from thence transmit the dignity and authority of legislation down to their heirs male forever.   1 N.C. (1 Mart.) 5, 7 (Super. Ct.)

Chapter 14

AMENDMENT VIII
BAIL/PUNISHMENT CLAUSES

14.1 TEXTS
14.1.1 DRAFTS IN FIRST CONGRESS

14.1.1.1 Proposal by Madison in House, June 8, 1789

14.1.1.1.a   Fourthly. That in article 1st, section 9, between clauses 3 and 4 [of the Constitution], be inserted these clauses, to wit, . . .

. . .

Excessive bail shall not be required, nor excessive fines imposed, nor cruel and unusual punishments inflicted.   Congressional Register, June 8, 1789, vol. 1, pp. 427–28.

14.1.1.1.b   *Fourthly.* That in article 1st, section 9, between clauses 3 and 4 [of the Constitution], be inserted these clauses, to wit:

. . .

Excessive bail shall not be required, nor excessive fines imposed, nor cruel and unusual punishments inflicted.

   Daily Advertiser, June 12, 1789, p. 2, col. 1.

14.1.1.1.c   *Fourth.* That in article 1st, section 9, between clauses 3 and 4 [of the Constitution], be inserted these clauses, to wit: . . .

. . .

Excessive bail shall not be required, nor excessive fines imposed, nor cruel and unusual punishments inflicted.   New-York Daily Gazette, June 13, 1789, p. 574, col. 3.

14.1.1.2 Proposal by Sherman to House Committee of Eleven, July 21–28, 1789

[Amendment] 7 Excessive bail shall not be required, nor excessive fines imposed, nor cruel & unusual punishments be inflicted in any case.

   Madison Papers, DLC.

14.1.1.3 House Committee of Eleven Report, July 28, 1789

ART. 1, SEC. 9 — Between PAR. 2 and 3 insert, . . .

. . .

"Excessive bail shall not be required, nor excessive fines imposed, nor cruel and unusual punishments inflicted."

   Broadside Collection, DLC.

14.1.1.4 House Consideration, August 17, 1789

14.1.1.4.a   [The Committee of the Whole House] then proceeded to the 6th clause of the 4th proposition in these words, "excessive bail shall not be required, nor excessive fines imposed, nor cruel and unusual punishments inflicted."

> Congressional Register, August 17, 1789, vol. 2, p. 225 ("The question was put on the clause, and it was agreed to by a considerable majority.").

14.1.1.4.b   Ninth Amendment — "Excessive bail shall not be required, nor excessive fines imposed, nor cruel and unusual punishments inflicted."

> Daily Advertiser, August 18, 1789, p. 2, col. 4 ("This amendment was adopted.").

14.1.1.4.c   Ninth amendment — "Excessive bail shall not be required, nor excessive fines imposed, nor cruel and unusual punishments inflicted."

> New-York Daily Gazette, August 19, 1789, p. 802, col. 4 ("This amendment was adopted.").

14.1.1.4.d   9th Amendment. "Excessive bail shall not be required, nor excessive fines imposed, nor cruel and unusual punishments inflicted."

> Gazette of the U.S., August 22, 1798, p. 249, col. 3 ("This amendment was adopted.").

14.1.1.5 House Consideration, August 18, 1789

Eighth. Excessive bail shall not be required; nor excessive fines imposed; nor cruel and unusual punishments inflicted.

> HJ, p. 107 ("read and debated . . . agreed to by the House, . . . two-thirds of the members present concurring").[1]

14.1.1.6 House Resolution, August 24, 1789

ARTICLE the THIRTEENTH.

Excessive bail shall not be required, nor excessive fines imposed, nor cruel and unusual punishments inflicted.

> House Pamphlet, RG 46, DNA.

14.1.1.7 Senate Consideration, August 25, 1789

14.1.1.7.a   The Resolve of the House of Representatives of the 24th of August, upon certain "Articles to be proposed to the Legislatures of the several States as Amendments to the Constitution of the United States" was read as followeth: . . .

Article the thirteenth

"Excessive bail shall not be required, nor excessive fines imposed, nor cruel and unusual punishments inflicted.

> Rough SJ, pp. 218–19.

14.1.1.7.b   The Resolve of the House of Representatives of the 24th of August, was read as followeth:

. . .

---

[1]On August 22, 1789, the following motion was agreed to:
ORDERED, That it be referred to a committee of three, to prepare and report a proper arrangement of, and introduction to the articles of amendment to the Constitution of the United States, as agreed to by the House; and that Mr. Benson, Mr. Sherman, and Mr. Sedgwick be of the said committee.

> HJ, p. 112.

"Article the Thirteenth.

"Excessive bail shall not be required, nor excessive fines imposed, nor cruel and unusual punishments inflicted.

Smooth SJ, p. 196.

14.1.1.7.c The Resolve of the House of Representatives of the 24th of August, was read as followeth:

. . .

"ARTICLE the THIRTEENTH.

"Excessive bail shall not be required, nor excessive fines imposed, nor cruel and unusual punishments inflicted.

Printed SJ, p. 105.

14.1.1.8 Further Senate Consideration, September 7, 1789

14.1.1.8.a On Motion to adopt the thirteenth article of amendments proposed by the House of Representatives.

Rough SJ, p. 256 ("It passed in the affirmative.").

14.1.1.8.b On motion, To adopt the thirteenth Article of Amendments proposed by the House of Representatives —

Smooth SJ, pp. 228–29 ("It passed in the Affirmative.").

14.1.1.8.c On motion, To adopt the thirteenth Article of Amendments proposed by the House of Representatives —

Printed SJ, p. 121 ("It passed in the Affirmative.").

14.1.1.8.d   that the Senate do

Resolved ~~to~~ /\ concur with the House of Representatives in

Article thirteenth,

Senate MS, 4, RG 46, DNA.

14.1.1.9 Further Senate Consideration, September 9, 1789

14.1.1.9.a On motion to number the remaining articles agreed to by the Senate tenth, eleventh and twelfth instead of the numbers affixed by the Resolve of the House of Representatives.

Rough SJ, p. 277 ("It passed in the affirmative.";
motion renumbered thirteenth article as tenth article).

14.1.1.9.b On motion, To number the remaining articles agreed to by the Senate, tenth, eleventh and twelfth, instead of the numbers affixed by the Resolve of the House of Representatives —

Smooth SJ, p. 246 (" It passed in the Affirmative.";
motion renumbered thirteenth article as tenth article).

14.1.1.9.c On motion, To number the remaining Articles agreed to by the Senate, tenth, eleventh and twelfth, instead of the numbers affixed by the Resolve of the House of Representatives —

Printed SJ, p. 131 ("It passed in the Affirmative.";
motion renumbered thirteenth article as tenth article).

14.1.1.9.d To erase the word "Thirteenth" & insert — Tenth.

Ellsworth MS, p. 4, RG 46, DNA.

14.1.1.10 Senate Resolution, September 9, 1789

ARTICLE THE TENTH.

Excessive bail shall not be required, nor excessive fines imposed, nor cruel and unusual punishments inflicted.

Senate Pamphlet, RG 46, DNA.

14.1.1.11 Further House Consideration, September 21, 1789

RESOLVED, That this House doth agree to the second, fourth, eighth, twelfth, thirteenth, sixteenth, eighteenth, nineteenth, twenty-fifth, and twenty-sixth amendments, and doth disagree to the first, third, fifth, sixth, seventh, ninth, tenth, eleventh, fourteenth, fifteenth, seventeenth, twentieth, twenty-first, twenty-second, twenty-third, and twenty-fourth amendments proposed by the Senate to the said articles, two thirds of the members present concurring on each vote.

RESOLVED, That a conference be desired with the Senate on the subject matter of the amendments disagreed to, and that Mr. Madison, Mr. Sherman, and Mr. Vining, be appointed managers at the same on the part of this House.

HJ, p. 146.

14.1.1.12 Further Senate Consideration, September 21, 1789

14.1.1.12.a   A message from the House of Representatives —

Mr. Beckley, their Clerk, brought up a Resolve of the House of this date, to agree to the 2nd, 4th, 8th, 12th, 13th, 16th, 18th, 19th, 25th, and 26th Amendments proposed by the Senate, "To articles of Amendment to be proposed to the Legislatures of the several States, as Amendments to the Constitution of the United States," and to disagree to the 1st, 3d, 5th, 6th, 7th, 9th, 10th, 11th, 14th, 15th, 17th, 20th, 21st, 22d, 23d, and 24th amendments: Two thirds of the members present concurring on each vote: And "That a conference be desired with the Senate on the subject matter of the amendments disagreed to," and that Mr. Madison, Mr. Sherman, and Mr. Vining, be appointed managers of the same, on the part of the House of Representatives —

And he withdrew.

Smooth SJ, pp. 265–66.

14.1.1.12.b   A message from the House of Representatives —

Mr. Beckley, their Clerk, brought up a Resolve of the House of this date, to agree to the 2d, 4th, 8th, 12th, 13th, 16th, 18th, 19th, 25th, and 26th Amendments proposed by the Senate, "To Articles of Amendment to be proposed to the Legislatures of the several States, as Amendments to the Constitution of the United States," and to disagree to the 1st, 3d, 5th, 6th, 7th, 9th, 10th, 11th, 14th, 15th, 17th, 20th, 21st, 22d, 23d, and 24th Amendments: Two thirds of the members present concurring on each vote: And "That a conference be desired with the Senate on the subject matter of the Amendments disagreed to," and that Mr. Madison, Mr. Sherman, and Mr. Vining, be appointed managers of the same, on the part of the House of Representatives —

And he withdrew.

Printed SJ, pp. 141–42.

14.1.1.13   Further Senate Consideration, September 21, 1789

14.1.1.13.a   The Senate proceeded to consider the Message of the House of Representatives disagreeing to the Amendments made by the Senate "To Articles to be proposed to the Legislatures of the several States, as Amendments to the Constitution of the United States" And

RESOLVED, That the Senate do recede from their third Amendment, and do insist on all the others.

RESOLVED, That the Senate do concur with the House of Representatives in a conference on the subject matter of disagreement on the said Articles of Amendment, and that Mr. Ellsworth Mr. Carroll and Mr. Paterson be managers of the conference on the part of the Senate.

Smooth SJ, p. 267.

14.1.1.13.b   The Senate proceeded to consider the message of the House of Representatives disagreeing to the Amendments made by the Senate "To Articles to be proposed to the Legislatures of the several States, as Amendments to the Constitution of the United States" — And

RESOLVED, That the Senate do recede from their third Amendment, and do insist on all the others.

RESOLVED, That the Senate do concur with the House of Representatives in a conference on the subject matter of disagreement on the said Articles of Amendment, and that Mr. Ellsworth, Mr. Carroll, and Mr. Paterson be managers of the conference on the part of the Senate.

Printed SJ, p. 142.

14.1.1.14   Conference Committee Report, September 24, 1789

[T]hat it will be proper for the House of Representatives to agree to the said Amendments proposed by the Senate, with an Amendment to their fifth Amendment, so that the third Article shall read as follows: "Congress shall make no Law respecting an establishment of Religion, or prohibiting the free exercise thereof; or abridging the freedom of Speech, or of the Press; or the right of the people peaceably to assemble and ~~to~~ petition the Government for a redress of grievances;" And with an Amendment to the fourteenth Amendment proposed by the Senate, so that the eighth Article, as numbered in the Amendments proposed by the Senate, shall read as follows "In all criminal prosecutions, the accused shall enjoy the right to a speedy & publick trial by an impartial jury of the district wherein the crime shall have been committed, as the district shall have been previously ascertained by law, and to be informed of the nature and cause of the accusation; to be confronted with the witnesses against him, and to have com

pulsory process for obtaining witnesses ~~against him~~ in his favour, & ⋀ have the assistance of counsel for his defence."

Conference MS, RG 46, DNA (Ellsworth's handwriting).

14.1.1.15   House Consideration of Conference Committee Report, September 24 [25], 1789

RESOLVED, That this House doth recede from their disagreement to the first, third, fifth, sixth, seventh, ninth, tenth, eleventh, fourteenth, fifteenth, seven-

teenth, twentieth, twenty-first, twenty-second, twenty-third, and twenty-fourth amendments, insisted on by the Senate: PROVIDED, That the two articles which by the amendments of the Senate are now proposed to be inserted as the third and eighth articles, shall be amended to read as followeth;

Article the third. "Congress shall make no law respecting an establishment of religion, or prohibiting the free exercise thereof; or abridging the freedom of speech, or of the press; or the right of the people peaceably to assemble, and to petition the government for a redress of grievances."

Article the eighth. "In all criminal prosecutions, the accused shall enjoy the right to a speedy and public trial by an impartial jury of the state and district wherein the crime shall have been committed, which district shall have been previously ascertained by law, and to be informed of the nature and cause of the accusation, to be confronted with the witnesses against him, to have compulsory process for obtaining witnesses in his favor, and to have the assistance of council for his defence."

> HJ, p. 152 ("On the question, that the House do agree to the alteration and amendment of the eighth article, in manner aforesaid, It was resolved in the affirmative. Ayes 37 Noes 14").

14.1.1.16 Senate Consideration of Conference Committee Report, September 24, 1789

14.1.1.16.a   Mr. Ellsworth, on behalf of the managers of the conference on "articles to be proposed to the several States as Amendments to the Constitution of the United States," reported as follows:

That it will be proper for the House of Representatives to agree to the said amendments proposed by the Senate, with an Amendment to their fifth Amendment, so that the third Article shall read as follows: "Congress shall make no law respecting an establishment of Religion, or prohibiting the free exercise thereof; or abridging the freedom of Speech, or of the Press; or the right of the people peaceably to assemble and petition the Government for a redress of Grievances;" And with an Amendment to the fourteenth Amendment proposed by the Senate, so that the eighth article, as numbered in the Amendments proposed by the Senate, shall read as follows; "In all criminal prosecutions, the accused shall enjoy the right to a speedy and public trial by an impartial Jury of the district wherein the Crime shall have been committed, as the district shall have been previously ascertained by law, and to be informed of the nature and cause of the accusation, to be confronted with the witnesses against him, and to have compulsory process for obtaining witnesses in his favor, and to have the assistance of Counsel for defence."

> Smooth SJ, pp. 272–73.

14.1.1.16.b   Mr. Ellsworth, on behalf of the managers of the conference on "Articles to be proposed to the several States as Amendments to the Constitution of the United States," reported as follows:

That it will be proper for the House of Representatives to agree to the said Amendments proposed by the Senate, with an Amendment to their fifth Amendment, so that the third Article shall read as follows: "Congress shall make no Law RESPECTING AN ESTABLISHMENT OF RELIGION, or prohibiting the free exercise thereof; or abridging the freedom of Speech, or of the Press; or the right of the People peaceably to assemble and petition the Government for a redress of Grievances;" And with an Amendment to the fourteenth Amendment proposed by the Senate, so that the eighth Article, as numbered in the Amendments proposed by the Senate, shall read as follows; "In all criminal prosecutions, the accused shall enjoy the right to a speedy and public trial BY AN IMPARTIAL JURY OF THE DISTRICT WHEREIN THE CRIME SHALL HAVE BEEN COMMITTED, AS THE DISTRICT SHALL HAVE BEEN PREVIOUSLY ASCERTAINED BY LAW, and to be informed of the nature and cause of the accusation, to be confronted with the witnesses against him, and to have compulsory process for obtaining witnesses in his favor, and to have the assistance of Counsel for defence."

Printed SJ, p. 145.

14.1.1.17 Further Senate Consideration of Conference Committee Report, September 24, 1789

14.1.1.17.a   A Message from the House of Representatives —

Mr. Beckley, their Clerk, brought up the Amendments to the "Articles to be proposed to the Legislatures of the several States, as Amendments to the Constitution of the United States;" and informed the Senate, that the House of Representatives had receded from their disagreement to the 1st, 3d, 5th, 6th, 7th, 9th, 10th, 11th, 14th, 15th, 17th, 20th, 21st, 22d, 23d, and 24th Amendments, insisted on by the Senate: Provided that the "Two Articles, which by the Amendments of the Senate are now proposed to be inserted as the third and eighth Articles," shall be amended to read as followeth:

Article the Third. "Congress shall make no Law respecting an establishment of Religion, or prohibiting the free exercise thereof; or abridging the freedom of Speech, or of the Press; or the right of the people peaceably to assemble, and petition the Government for a redress of Grievances."

Article the Eighth. "In all criminal prosecutions the accused shall enjoy the right to a speedy and public trial by an impartial Jury of the State and District, wherein the crime shall have been committed, which District shall have been previously ascertained by law, and to be informed of the nature and cause of the accusation, to be confronted with the witnesses against him, and to have compulsory process for obtaining witnesses in his favor, and to have the assistance of Counsel for his defence."

Smooth SJ, pp. 278–79.

14.1.1.17.b   A Message from the House of Representatives —

Mr. Beckley, their Clerk, brought up the Amendments to the "Articles to be proposed to the Legislatures of the several States, as Amendments to the Constitution of the United States;" and informed the Senate, that the House of Representatives had receded from their disagreement to the 1st, 3d, 5th, 6th, 7th, 9th, 10th, 11th, 14th, 15th, 17th, 20th, 21st, 22d, 23d, and 24th Amendments, insisted on by the Senate: Provided that the "Two Articles, which by the Amendments of the Senate are now proposed to be inserted as the third and eighth Articles," shall be amended to read as followeth:

Article the Third. "Congress shall make no Law respecting an establishment of Religion, or prohibiting the free exercise thereof; or abridging the freedom of

Speech, or of the Press; or the right of the People peaceably to assemble, and petition the Government for a redress of Grievances."

Article the Eighth. "In all criminal prosecutions the accused shall enjoy the right to a speedy and public trial by an impartial Jury of the State and District, wherein the crime shall have been committed, which District shall have been previously ascertained by law, and to be informed of the nature and cause of the accusation, to be confronted with the witnesses against him, and to have compulsory process for obtaining witnesses in his favor, and to have the assistance of Counsel for his defence."

Printed SJ, p.148.

14.1.1.18 Further Senate Consideration of Conference Committee Report, September 25, 1789

14.1.1.18.a   The Senate proceeded to consider the Message from the House of Representatives of the 24th, with Amendments to the Amendments of the Senate, to "Articles to be proposed to the Legislatures of the several States, as Amendments to the Constitution of the United States" — And

RESOLVED, That the Senate do concur in the Amendments proposed by the House of Representatives, to the Amendments of the Senate. Smooth SJ, p. 283.

14.1.1.18.b   The Senate proceeded to consider the Message from the House of Representatives of the 24th, with Amendments to the Amendments of the Senate, to "Articles to be proposed to the Legislatures of the several States, as Amendments to the Constitution of the United States" — And

RESOLVED, That the Senate do concur in the Amendments proposed by the House of Representatives, to the Amendments of the Senate.

Printed SJ, pp. 150–51.

14.1.1.19 Agreed Resolution, September 25, 1789

14. 1.1.19.a   Article the Tenth.

Excessive bail shall not be required, nor excessive fines imposed, nor cruel and unusual punishments inflicted. Smooth SJ, Appendix, p. 294.

14.1.1.19.b   ARTICLE THE TENTH.

Excessive bail shall not be required, nor excessive fines imposed, nor cruel and unusual punishments inflicted. Printed SJ, Appendix, p. 164.

14.1.1.20 Enrolled Resolution, September 28, 1789

Article the tenth . . . Excessive bail shall not be required, nor excessive fines imposed, nor cruel and unusual punishments inflicted.

Enrolled Resolutions, RG 11, National Archives.

14.1.1.21 Printed Versions

14.1.1.21.a   ART. VIII. Excessive bail shall not be required, nor excessive fines imposed, nor cruel and unusual punishments inflicted. Statutes at Large, vol. 1, p. 21.

14.1.1.21.b   ART. X. Excessive bail shall not be required, nor excessive fines imposed, nor cruel and unusual punishments inflicted.

Statutes at Large, vol. 1, p. 98.

14.1.2 PROPOSALS FROM THE STATE CONVENTIONS

14.1.2.1   New York, July 26, 1788

That excessive Bail ought not to be required; nor excessive Fines imposed; nor Cruel or unusual Punishments inflicted.

State Ratifications, RG 11, DNA.

14.1.2.2   North Carolina, August 1, 1788

13th. That excessive bail ought not to be required, nor excessive fines imposed, nor cruel and unusual punishments inflicted, [*sic*]

State Ratifications, RG 11, DNA.

14.1.2.3   Pennsylvania Minority, December 12, 1787

4. That excessive bail ought not to be required nor excessive fines imposed, nor cruel or unusual punishments inflicted.

Pennsylvania Packet, December 18, 1787.

14.1.2.4   Rhode Island, May 29, 1790

13th. That excessive bail ought not to be required, nor excessive fines imposed, nor cruel or unusual punishments inflicted.

State Ratifications, RG 11, DNA.

14.1.2.5   Virginia, June 27, 1788

Thirteenth, That excessive Bail ought not be required, nor excessive fines imposed, nor cruel and unusual punishments inflicted.

State Ratifications, RG 11, DNA.

14.1.3 STATE CONSTITUTIONS AND LAWS; COLONIAL CHARTERS AND LAWS

14.1.3.1   Connecticut: Declaration of Rights, 1776

[¶ 4] And that no Man's Person shall be restrained, or imprisoned, by any Authority whatsoever, before the Law hath sentenced him thereunto, if he can and will give sufficient Security, Bail, or Mainprize for his Appearance and good Behaviour in the mean Time, unless it be for Capital Crimes, Contempt in open Court, or in such Cases wherein some express Law doth ·allow of, or order the same.

Connecticut Acts, p. 2.

14.1.3.2   Delaware: Declaration of Rights, 1776

Sect. *16.* That excessive bail ought not be required, nor excessive fines imposed, nor cruel or unusual punishment inflicted.

Delaware Laws, vol. 1, p. 81.

14.1.3.3   Georgia: Constitution, 1777

LIX. Excessive fines shall not be levied, nor excessive bail demanded.

Georgia Laws, p. 15.

14.1.3.4 Maryland: Declaration of Rights, 1776

22. That excessive bail ought not to be required, nor excessive fines imposed, nor cruel or unusual punishments inflicted by the courts of law.

Maryland Laws, November 3, 1776.

14.1.3.5 Massachusetts

14.1.3.5.a Body of Liberties, 1641

[18] No mans person shall be restrained or imprisoned by any Authority whatsoever, before the law hath sentenced him thereto, If he can put in sufficient securitie, bayle or mainprise, for his appearance, and good behaviour in the meane time, unlesse it be in Crimes Capital, and Contempts in open Court, and in such cases where some expresse act of Court doth allow it.

. . .

[43] No man shall be beaten with above 40 stripes, nor shall any true gentleman, nor any man equall to a gentleman be punished with whipping, unles his crime be very shamefull, and his course of life vitious and profligate.

. . .

[45] No man shall be forced by Torture to confesse any Crime against himselfe nor any other unless it be some Capitall case where he is first fullie convicted by cleare and suffitient evidence to be guilty, After which if the cause be of that nature, That it is very apparent there be other conspiratours, or confederates with him, Then he may be tortured, yet not with such Tortures as be Barbarous and inhumane.

[46] For bodilie punishments we allow amongst us none that are inhumane Barbarous or cruel.

Massachusetts Colonial Laws, pp. 37, 43.

14.1.3.5.b Constitution, 1780

[Part I, Article] XXVI. No magistrate or court of law, shall demand excessive bail or sureties, impose excessive fines, or inflict cruel or unusual punishments.

Massachusetts Perpetual Laws, p. 7.

14.1.3.6 New Hampshire: Bill of Rights, 1783

[Part I, Article] XVIII. All penalties ought to be proportioned to the nature of the offence. No wise legislature will affix the same punishment to the crimes of theft, forgery and the like, which they do to those of murder and treason; where the same undistinguishing severity is exerted against all offences, the people are led to forget the real distinction in the crimes themselves, and to commit the most flagrant with as little compunction as they do those of the lightest dye: For the same reason a multitude of sanguinary laws is both impolitic and unjust. The true design of all punishments being to reform, not to exterminate mankind.

. . .

[Part I, Article] XXXIII. No magistrate or court of law shall demand excessive bail or sureties, impose excessive fines, or inflict cruel or unusual punishments.

New Hampshire Laws, pp. 25–26, 27.

14.1.3.7   New York

14.1.3.7.a   Act Declaring . . . Rights & Priviledges, 1691

That a Free-man shall not be amerced for a small Fault, but after the manner of his Fault, and for a great Fault after the greatness thereof, saving to him his Free-hold; and a Husband-man, saving to him his Wainage; and a Merchant, saving to him his Merchandize; and none of these Amercements shall be assessed, but by the Oath of Twelve Honest and Lawful men of the Vicinage. Provided, the Faults and Misdemeanours be not in Contempt of Courts of Judicature. All Tryals shall be by the Verdict of Twelve Men, and as near as may be Peers or Equals, and of the Neighbourhood of the place where the fact shall arise or grow, whether the same be by Indictments, Declaration, Information, or otherwayes, against the Person Offender or Defendant.

. . .

That in all Cases whatsoever, Bayl by sufficient Sureties shall be allowed and taken, unless for Treason and Fellony, plainly and specially expressed and mentioned in the Warrant of Commitment, and that the Fellony be such as is restrained from Bayl by the Laws of *England*.   New York Acts, pp. 17–18.

14.1.3.7.b   Bill of Rights, 1787

Seventh, That no Citizens of this State shall be fined or amerced without reasonable Cause, and such Fine or Amerciament shall always be according to the Quantity of his or her Trespass or Offence, and saving to him or her his or her Contentement; *That is to say,* Every Freeholder saving his Freehold, a Merchant saving his Merchandize, and a Mechanic saving the Implements of his Trade.

Eighth, That excessive Bail ought not to be required, nor excessive Fines imposed, nor cruel and unusual Punishments inflicted.   New York Laws, vol. 2, p. 2.

14.1.3.8   North Carolina: Declaration of Rights, 1776

Sect. X. That excessive Bail should not be required, nor excessive Fines imposed, nor cruel or unusual punishments inflicted.   North Carolina Laws, p. 275.

14.1.3.9   Pennsylvania

14.1.3.9.a   Laws Agreed Upon in England, 1682

XI. That all *Prisoners* shall be Baylable by sufficient Sureties, unless for *Capital Offences,* where the Proof is evident, or the Presumption great.

. . .

XVIII. That all **Fines** shall be moderate, and saving mens Contenements, Merchandize or Wainage.   Pennsylvania Frame, pp. 8, 9.

14.1.3.9.b   Constitution, 1776

CHAPTER II.

. . .

Sect. 29. Excessive bail shall not be exacted for bailable offences: And all fines shall be moderate.

. . .

SECT. 38. The penal laws as heretofore used shall be reformed by the legislature of this state, as soon as may be, and punishments made in some cases less sanguinary, and in general more proportionate to the crimes.

SECT. 39. To deter more effectually from the commission of crimes, by continued visible punishments of long duration, and to make sanguinary punishments less necessary; houses ought to be provided for punishing by hard labour, those who shall be convicted of crimes not capital; wherein the criminals shall be employed for the benefit of the public, or for the reparation of injuries done to private persons: And all persons at proper times shall be admitted to see the prisoners at their labour.

Pennsylvania Acts, McKean, pp. xviii, xix.

14.1.3.9.c Constitution, 1790

ARTICLE IX.

. . .

SECT. XIII. That excessive bail shall not be required, nor excessive fines imposed, nor cruel punishments inflicted.

SECT. XIV. That all prisoners shall be bailable by sufficient sureties, unless for capital offences, when the proof is evident or presumption great; and the privilege of the writ of habeas corpus shall not be suspended, unless when, in cases of rebellion or invasion, the public safety may require it.

Pennsylvania Acts, Dallas, p. xxxv.

14.1.3.10 South Carolina

14.1.3.10.a Constitution, 1778

XL. That the penal Laws, as heretofore used, shall be reformed, and Punishments made, in some Cases, less sanguinary, and, in general, more proportionate to the Crime.

South Carolina Constitution, p. 15.

14.1.3.10.b Constitution, 1790

ARTICLE IX.

. . .

Section 4. Excessive bail shall not to be required, nor excessive fines imposed, nor cruel punishments inflicted.

South Carolina Laws, App., p. 41.

14.1.3.11 Vermont: Constitution, 1777

CHAPTER II.

. . .

SECTION XXV.

THE Person of a Debtor, where there is not a strong Presumption of Fraud, shall not be continued in Prison, after delivering up, *bona fide,* all his Estate, real and personal, for the Use of his Creditors, in such manner as shall be hereafter regulated by Law. All Prisoners shall be bailable by sufficient Sureties, unless for capital Offences, when the Proof is evident, or Presumption great.

SECTION XXVI.

EXCESSIVE bail shall not be exacted for bailable Offences: And all Fines shall be moderate.

Vermont Acts, p. 9.

14.1.3.12   Virginia: Declaration of Rights, 1776

IX. THAT excessive bail ought not to be required, nor excessive fines imposed, nor cruel and unusual punishments inflicted.

Virginia Acts, p. 33.

14.1.4 OTHER TEXTS

14.1.4.1   English Bill of Rights, 1689

. . . That excessive baile ought not to be required nor excessive fines imposed nor cruell and unusuall punishments inflicted.

1 Will. & Mar., sess. 2, c. 2.

14.1.4.2   Northwest Territory Ordinance, 1787

Article of the Second. The inhabitants of the said territory shall always be entitled to the benefits of the writ of habeas corpus, and of the trial by jury: of a proportionate representation of the people in the legislature, and of judicial proceedings according to the course of common law; all persons shall be bailable unless for Capital Offences, where the proof shall be evident, or the presumption great; all fines shall be moderate, and no cruel or unusual punishments shall be inflicted; no man shall be deprived of his liberty or property but by the judgment of his peers, or the law of the land; and should the public exigencies make it Necessary for the common preservation to take any persons property, or to demand his particular services, full compensation shall be made for the same; and in the just preservation of rights and property it is understood and declared, that no law ought ever to be made, or have force in the said territory, that shall in any manner whatever interfere with, or affect private contracts or engagements bona fide and without fraud, previously formed.

Continental Congress Papers, DNA.

14.1.4.3   Richard Henry Lee to Edmund Randolph, Proposed Amendments, October 16, 1787

. . . That excessive Bail, excessive fines, or cruel and unusual punishments, should not be demanded or inflicted. . . .

Virginia Gazette, December 22, 1787.

14.2 DISCUSSION OF DRAFTS AND PROPOSALS

14.2.1 THE FIRST CONGRESS

14.2.1.1   June 8, 1789[2]

14.2.1.2   August 17, 1789

14.2.1.2.a   The house went into a committee of the whole, on the subject of amendments. . . .

[T]he committee . . . then proceeded to the 6th clause of the 4th proposition

---

[2]For the reports of Madison's speech in support of his proposals, *see* 1.2.1.1.a–c.

in these words, "excessive bail shall not be required, nor excessive fines imposed, nor cruel and unusual punishments inflicted."

MR. SMITH (of S.C.) objected to the words "nor cruel and unusual punishments," the import of them being too indefinite.

MR. LIVERMORE.

The clause seems to express a great deal of humanity, on which account I have no objection to it; but as it seems to have no meaning in it, I do not think it necessary. What is meant by the terms excessive bail? Who are to be the judges? What is understood by excessive fines? It lays with the court to determine. No cruel and unusual punishment is to be inflicted; it is sometimes necessary to hang a man, villains often deserve whipping, and perhaps having their ears cut off; but are we in future to be prevented from inflicting these punishments because they are cruel? If a more lenient mode of correcting vice and deterring others from the commission of it could be invented, it would be very prudent in the legislature to adopt it, but until we have some security that this will be done, we ought not to be restrained from making necessary laws by any declaration of this kind.

The question was put on the clause, and it was agreed to by a considerable majority.

Congressional Register, August 17, 1789, vol. 2, pp. 219, 225–26.

14.2.1.2.b   Ninth Amendment — "Excessive bail shall not be required, nor excessive fines imposed, nor cruel and unusual punishments inflicted."

Daily Advertiser, August 18, 1789, p. 2, col. 4
("This amendment was adopted.").

14.2.1.2.c   The house resolved itself into a committee of the whole on the subject of amendments to the constitution.

. . .

Ninth amendment — "Excessive bail shall not be required, nor excessive fines imposed, nor cruel and unusual punishments inflicted."

New-York Daily Gazette, August 19, 1789, p. 802, col. 4
("This amendment was adopted.").

14.2.1.2.d   In COMMITTEE of the whole HOUSE.

. . .

9th Amendment. "Excessive bail shall not be required, nor excessive fines imposed, nor cruel and unusual punishments inflicted."

Mr. LIVERMORE said, the clause appears to express much humanity, as such, he liked it; but as it appeared to have no meaning, he did not like it: As to bail, the term is indefinite, and must be so from the nature of things; and so with respect to fines; and as to punishments, taking away life is sometimes necessary, but because it may be thought cruel, will you therefore never hang any body — the truth is, matters of this kind must be left to the discretion of those who have the administration of the laws.

This amendment was adopted.

Gazette of the U.S., August 22, 1789, p. 249, col. 3.

14.2.2 STATE CONVENTIONS

14.2.2.1 Massachusetts, January 30, 1788

Mr. HOLMES. . . .

. . .

What gives an additional glare of horror to these gloomy circumstances is the consideration, that Congress have to ascertain, point out, and determine, what kind of punishments shall be inflicted on persons convicted of crimes. They are nowhere restrained from inventing the most cruel and unheard-of punishments, and annexing them to crimes; and there is no constitutional check on them, but that *racks* and *gibbets* may be amongst the most mild instruments of their discipline.

Elliot, vol. 2, p. 111.

14.2.2.2 Virginia

14.2.2.2.a June 14, 1788

Mr. HENRY. . .

. . . Congress, from their general powers, may fully go into business of human legislation. They may legislate, in criminal cases, from treason to the lowest offence — petty larceny. They may define crimes and prescribe punishments. In the definition of crimes, I trust they will be directed by what wise representatives ought to be governed by. But when we come to punishments, no latitude ought to be left, nor dependence put on the virtue of representatives. What says our bill of rights? — "that excessive bail ought not to be required, nor excessive fines imposed, nor cruel and unusual punishments inflicted." Are you not, therefore, now calling on those gentlemen who are to compose Congress, to prescribe trials and define punishments without this control? Will they find sentiments there similar to this bill of rights? You let them loose; you do more — you depart from the genius of your country. . . .

In this business of legislation, your members of Congress will lose the restriction of not imposing excessive fines, demanding excessive bail, and inflicting cruel and unusual punishments. These are prohibited by your declaration of rights. What has distinguished our ancestors? — That they would not admit of tortures, or cruel and barbarous punishment. But Congress may introduce the practice of the civil law, in preference to that of the common law. They may introduce the practice of France, Spain, and Germany — of torturing, to extort a confession of the crime. They will say that they might as well draw examples from those countries as from Great Britain, and they will tell you that there is such a necessity of strengthening the arm of government, that they must have a criminal equity, and extort confession by torture, in order to punish with still more relentless severity. We are then lost and undone. . . .

. . .

Mr. GEORGE NICHOLAS. . . .

. . . But the gentleman says that, by this Constitution, they have power to make laws to define crimes and prescribe punishments; and that, consequently, we are not free from torture. . . . If we had no security against torture but our declaration of rights, we might be tortured to-morrow; for it has been repeatedly infringed and disregarded. A bill of rights is only an acknowledgement of the preëxisting claim to rights in the people. . . .

Mr. GEORGE MASON replied that the worthy gentleman was mistaken in his assertion that the bill of rights did not prohibit torture; for that one clause expressly provided that no man can give evidence against himself; and that the worthy gentleman must know that, in those countries where torture is used, evidence was extorted from the criminal himself. Another clause of the bill of rights provided that no cruel or unusual punishments shall be inflicted; therefore, torture was included in the prohibition.

Mr. NICHOLAS acknowledged the bill of rights to contain that prohibition, and that the gentleman was right with respect to the practice of extorting confession from the criminal in those countries where torture is used; but still he saw no security arising from the bill of rights as separate from the Constitution, for that it had been frequently violated with impunity. Elliot, vol. 3, pp. 447–48, 451–52.

14.2.2.2.b June 15, 1788

Gov. RANDOLPH. . . .

As to the exclusion of excessive bail and fines, and cruel and unusual punishments, this would follow of itself, without a bill of rights. Observations have been made about watchfulness over those in power which deserve our attention. There must be a combination; we must presume corruption in the House of Representatives, Senate, and President, before we can suppose that excessive fines can be imposed or cruel punishments inflicted. Their number is the highest security. Numbers are the highest security in our own Constitution, which has attracted so many eulogiums from the gentlemen. Here we have launched into a sea of suspicions. How shall we check power? By their numbers. Before these cruel punishments can be inflicted, laws must be passed, and judges must judge contrary to justice. This would excite universal discontent and detestation of the members of the government. They might involve their friends in the calamities resulting from it, and could be removed from office. I never desire a greater security than this, which I believe to be absolutely sufficient. Elliot, vol. 3, pp. 467–68.

14.2.3 PHILADELPHIA CONVENTION

None.

14.2.4 NEWSPAPERS AND PAMPHLETS

14.2.4.1 George Mason, Objections to the Constitution, October 7, 1787

Under their own Construction of the general Clause at the End of the enumerated Powers, the Congress may grant Monopolies in Trade & Commerce, constitute new Crimes, inflict unusual & severe Punishments, and extend their Power as far as they shall think proper; so that the State Legislatures have no Security for the Powers now presumed to remain to them; or the People for their Rights. —
Kaminski & Saladino, vol. 13, p. 350.

14.2.4.2   Centinel, No. 2, October 24, 1787

The new plan, it is true, does propose to secure the people of the benefit of personal liberty by the *habeas corpus;* and trial by jury for all crimes, except in case of impeachment; but there is no declaration . . . that the requiring of excessive bail, imposing of excessive fines and cruel and unusual punishments be forbidden. . . .

[Philadelphia] Freeman's Journal, Kaminski & Saladino, vol. 13, p. 466.

14.2.4.3   Brutus, No. 2, November 1, 1787

For the security of liberty it has been declared, "that excessive bail should not be required, nor excessive fines imposed, nor cruel or unusual punishments inflicted — That all warrants, without oath or affirmation, to search suspected places, or seize any person, his papers or property, are grievous and oppressive."

These provisions are as necessary under the general government as under that of the individual states; for the power of the former is as complete to the purpose of requiring bail, imposing fines, inflicting punishments, granting search warrants, and seizing persons, papers, or property, in certain cases, as the other.

New York Journal, Kaminski & Saladino, vol. 13, p. 527.

14.2.4.4   Philadelphiensis, No. 9, November 7, 1787

To such lengths have these bold conspirators carried their scheme of despotism, that your most sacred rights and privileges are surrendered at discretion. When government thinks proper, under the pretense of writing a libel, &c. it may imprison, inflict the most cruel and unusual punishment, seize property, carry on prosecutions, &c. and the unfortunate citizen has no *magna charta,* no *bill of rights,* to protect him; nay, the prosecution may be carried on in such a manner that even a *jury* will not be allowed him. Where is that *base slave* who would not appeal to the *ultima ratio,* before he submits to this government?

[Philadelphia] Independent Gazetteer, Storing, vol. 3, p. 129.

14.2.4.5   The Impartial Examiner, No. 1, February 27, and March 5, 1788

. . . For instance, if Congress should pass a law that persons charged with capital crimes shall not have a *right to demand the cause or nature of the accusation,* shall not be *confronted with the accusers or witnesses, or call for evidence in their own favor;* and a question should arise respecting their authority therein, — can it be said that they have exceeded the limits of their jurisdiction, when *that* has no limits; when no provision has been made for such a right? — When no responsibility on the part of Congress has been required by the constitution? The same observation may be made on any arbitrary or capricious imprisonments *contrary to the law of the land.* The same may be made, if *excessive bail should be required; if excessive fines should be imposed; if cruel and unusual punishments should be inflicted; if the liberty of the press should be restrained;* in a word — if laws should be made totally derogatory to the whole catalogue of rights, which are now secured under your present form of government.

Virginia Independent Chronicle, Storing, vol. 5, p. 185.

14.2.4.6 Marcus, No. 4, March 12, 1788

As to the constituting of new crimes, and inflicting unusual and severe punishment, certainly the cases enumerated wherein the Congress are empowered either to define offences, or prescribe punishments, are such as are proper for the exercise of such authority in the general Legislature of the Union. They only relate to "counterfeiting the securities and current coin of the United States; to piracies and felonies committed on the high seas, and offences against the law of nations, and to treason against the United States." These are offences immediately affecting the security, the honor or the interest of the United States at large, and of course must come within the sphere of the Legislative authority which is entrusted with their protection. Beyond these authorities Congress can exercise no other power of this kind, except in the enacting of penalties, to enforce their acts of Legislation in the cases where express authority is delegated to them, and if they could not enforce such acts by the enacting of penalties those powers would be altogether useless, since a legislative regulation without some sanction would be an absurd thing indeed. The Congress having, for these reasons, a just right to authority in the above particulars, the question is, whether it is practicable and proper to prescribe the limits to its exercise, for fear that they should inflict punishments unusual and severe? It may be observed, in the first place, that a declaration against "cruel and unusual punishments," formed part of an article in the Bill of Rights at the Revolution in England, in 1688. The prerogative of the Crown having been grossly abused in some preceding reigns, it was thought proper to notice every grievance they had endured, and those declarations went to an abuse of power in the crown only, but were never intended to limit the authority of Parliament. Many of these articles of the Bill of Rights in England, without a due attention to the difference of the cases, were eagerly adopted when our Constitutions were formed, the minds of men then being so warmed with their exertions in the cause of liberty, as to lean too much perhaps towards a jealousy of power to repose a proper confidence in their own government. From these articles in the State Constitutions, many things were attempted to be transplanted into our new Constitution, which would either have been nugatory or improper: This is one of them. The expressions "unusual and severe," or "cruel and unusual," surely would have been too vague to have been of any consequence, since they admit of no clear and precise signification. If to guard against punishments being too severe, the Convention had enumerated a vast variety of cruel punishments, and prohibited the use of any of them, let the number have been ever so great, an inexhaustible fund must have been unmentioned, and if our government had been disposed to be cruel, to their invention would only have been put to a little more trouble. If to avoid this difficulty, they had determined, not negatively, what punishments should not be exercised, but positively what punishments should, this must have led them into a labyrinth of detail which in the original constitution of a government would have appeared perfectly ridiculous, and not left a room for such changes according to circumstances, as must be in the power of every Legislature that is rationally formed. Thus, when we enter into particulars, we must be convinced that the proposition of such a restriction would have led to nothing useful, or to something dangerous, and therefore that its omission is not chargeable as a fault in the new Constitution. Let us also remember, that as those who are to make those laws must themselves be subject to them, their own interest and feelings will dictate to them not to make them unnecessarily severe; and that in the case of treason, which usually in every country exposes men most to the avarice and rapacity of government, care is taken that the innocent family of the offender shall not suffer for the treason of their relation. This is the crime with respect to which a jealousy is of the most importance, and accordingly it is defined with great plainness and accuracy, and the temptations to abusive prosecutions guarded against as much as possible. . . .

Norfolk and Portsmouth Journal, Kaminski & Saladino,
vol. 16, pp. 381–82.

14.2.5 LETTERS AND DIARIES

None.

14.3 DISCUSSION OF RIGHTS

14.3.1 TREATISES

14.3.1.1 Montesquieu, 1748

Of the Powers of Punishment

Experience shows that in countries remarkable for the lenity of penal laws, the spirit of the inhabitants is as much thereby affected, as in other countries, with severer punishments.

If an inconveniency or abuse arises in the state, a violent government endeavors suddenly to redress it; and instead of putting the old laws in execution, it establishes some cruel punishment which instantly puts a stop to the evil. But the spring of government hereby loses its elasticity; the imagination grows accustomed to the severe as well as the milder punishment; and as the fear of the latter diminishes, they are soon obliged in every case to have recourse to the other.

. . .

Of the Just Proportion Betwixt Punishments and Crimes

It is an essential point that there should be a certain proportion in punishments, because it is essential that a great crime should be avoided rather than a lesser, and that which is more pernicious to society rather than that which is less.

. . .

It is a great abuse amongst us to subject to the same punishment a person that only robs on the high-way, and another that robs and murders. Obvious it is that for the public security some difference should be made in the punishment.

. . .

Where there is no difference in the punishment, there should be some in the expectation of pardon. . . .

Spirit of Laws, bk. 6, chs. 12, 16.

14.3.1.2 William Blackstone, 1769

AND, first, to refuse or delay to bail any person bailable, is an offence against the liberty of the subject, in any magistrate, by the common law; as well as by the statute Westm. 1. 3 Edw. I. c. 15 and the *habeas corpus* act, 31 Car. II c. 2. And lest the intention of the law should be frustrated by the justices requiring bail to a greater amount than the nature of the case demands, it is expressly declared by statute 1 W. & M. st. 2. c. 1. that excessive bail ought not be required: though what bail shall be called excessive, must be left to the courts, on considering the circumstances of the case, to determine. And on the other hand, if the magistrate takes insufficient bail, he is liable to be fined, if the criminal doth not appear. Bail may be taken either in court, or in some particular cases by the sheriff, coroner, or other magistrate; but most usually by the justices of the peace. Regularly, in all offences either against the common law or act of parliament, that are below felony, the offender ought to be admitted to bail, unless it be prohibited by some special act of parliament. . . .

. . . But, where the imprisonment is only for safe custody *before* the conviction, and not for punishment *afterwards,* in such cases bail is ousted or taken away, wherever the offence is of a very enormous nature: for then the public is entitled to demand nothing less than the highest security that can be given; *viz.* the body of the accused, in order to ensure that justice shall be done upon him, if guilty.

Commentaries, bk. 4, ch. 22; vol. 4, pp. 294–95.

14.3.2 CASELAW

14.3.2.1 Titus Oates' Case, 1685

[Upon Titus Oates' conviction upon two indictments for perjury, the Court pronounced sentence:]

"First, the Court does order for a fine, that you pay 1000 marks upon each Indictment.

"Secondly, That you be stripped of all your Canonical Habits.

"Thirdly, The Court does award, That you do stand upon the Pillory, and in the Pillory, here before Westminster-hall gate, upon Monday next, for an hour's time, between the hours of 10 and 12; with a paper over your head (which you must first walk with round about to all the Courts in Westminster-hall) declaring your crime." And that is upon the first indictment.

"Fourthly, (on the Second Indictment), upon Tuesday, you shall stand upon, and in the Pillory, at the Royal Exchange in London, for the space of an hour, between the hours of twelve and two; with the same inscription.

"You shall upon the next Wednesday, be whipped from Aldgate to Newgate.

"Upon Friday, you shall be whipped from Newgate to Tyburn, by the hands of the common hangman."

But, Mr. Oates, we cannot but remember, there were several particular times you swore false about; and therefore, as annual commemoration, that it may be known to all people as long as you live, we have taken special care of you for an annual punishment.

"Upon the 24th of April every year, as long as you live, you are to stand upon the Pillory, and in the Pillory, at Tyburn, just opposite to the gallows, for the space of an hour, between the hours of ten and twelve.

"You are to stand upon, and in the Pillory, here at Westminster-hall gate, every 9th of August, in every year, so long as you live. And that it may be known what we mean by it, 'tis to remember, what he swore about Mr. Ireland's being in town between the 8th and 12th of August.

"You are to stand upon, and in the Pillory, at Charing-cross, on the 10th of August, every year, during your life, for an hour, between ten and twelve.

"The like over-against the Temple gate, upon the 11th.

"And upon the 2d of September, . . . you are to stand upon, and in the Pillory, for the space of one hour, between twelve and two, at the Royal Exchange; and all this you are to do every year, during your life; and to be committed close prisoner, as long as you live.

[Following the Revolution, Oates sought reversal unsuccessfully in the House of Lords. Several lords entered this dissent:]

"1. For that the king's bench, being a temporal court, made it part of the judgment, that Titus Oates, being a clerk, should for his said perjuries, be divested of his canonical and priestly habit, and to continue divested all his life; which is a matter wholly out of their power, belonging to the ecclesiastical courts only.

"2. For that the said judgments are barbarous, inhuman, and unchristian; and there is [*sic*] no precedents to warrant the punishments of whipping and committing to prison for life, for the crime of perjury; which yet were but part of the punishments inflicted upon him.

"3. For that the particular matters upon which the indictments were found, were the points objected against Mr. Titus Oates' own testimony in several of the trials, in which he was allowed to be a good and credible witness, though testified against him by most of the same persons, who witnessed against him on those indictments.

"4. For that this will be an encouragement and allowance for giving the like cruel, barbarous, and illegal judgements [*sic*] hereafter, unless this judgment be reversed.

"5. Because sir John Holt, sir Henry Pollexfen, the two chief justices, and sir Robert Atkins chief baron, with six judges more, (being all that were then present), for these and many other reasons, did, before us, solemnly deliver their opinions, and unanimously declare, That the said judgements [*sic*] were contrary to law and ancient practice, and therefore erroneous, and ought to be reversed.

"6. Because it is contrary to the declaration on the twelfth of February last, which was ordered by the Lords Spiritual and Temporal and Commons assembled, and by their declarations engrossed in parchment, and enrolled among the records of parliament, and recorded in chancery; whereby it doth appear, that excessive bail ought not be required, nor excessive fines imposed, nor cruel nor unusual punishments inflicted. . . ."

10 How. St. Tr. 1079, 1316–17 (K.B. 1685), 1325 (H.L. 1689).

Chapter 15

AMENDMENT IX
UNENUMERATED RIGHTS CLAUSE

15.1 TEXTS

15.1.1 DRAFTS IN FIRST CONGRESS

15.1.1.1 **Proposal by Madison in House, June 8, 1789**

15.1.1.1.a Fourthly. That in article 1st, section 9, between clauses 3 and 4 [of the Constitution], be inserted these clauses, to wit, . . .

. . .

The exceptions here or elsewhere in the constitution, made in favor of particular rights, shall not be so construed as to diminish the just importance of other rights retained by the people; or as to enlarge the powers delegated by the constitution; but either as actual limitations of such powers, or as inserted merely for greater caution.

Congressional Register, June 8, 1789, vol. 1, pp. 427–28.

15.1.1.1.b *Fourthly.* That in article 1st, section 9, between clauses 3 and 4 [of the Constitution], be inserted these clauses, to wit: . . .

. . .

The exceptions here or elsewhere in the constitution, made in favor of particular rights, shall not be so construed as to diminish the just importance of other rights retained by the people; or as to enlarge the powers delegated by the constitution; but either as actual limitations of such powers, or as inserted merely for greater caution.

Daily Advertiser, June 12, 1789, p. 2, col. 2.

15.1.1.1.c *Fourth.* That in article 1st, section 9, between clauses 3 and 4 [of the Constitution], be inserted these clauses, to wit: . . .

. . .

The exceptions here or elsewhere in the constitution, made in favour of particular rights, shall not be so construed as to diminish the just importance of other rights retained by the people; or as to enlarge the powers delegated by the constitution; but either as actual limitations of such powers, or as inserted merely for greater caution.

New-York Daily Gazette, June 13, 1789, p. 574, col. 4.

15.1.1.2 House Committee of Eleven Report, July 28, 1789

ART. 1, SEC. 9 — Between PAR. 2 and 3 insert, . . .

. . .

"The enumeration in this Constitution of certain rights shall not be construed to deny or disparage others retained by the people."

Broadside Collection, DLC.

15.1.1.3 House Consideration, August 17, 1789

15.1.1.3.a   The 8th clause of the 4th proposition was taken up, which was "The enumeration in this constitution of certain rights shall not be construed to deny or disparage others retained by the people."

Congressional Register, August 17, 1789, vol. 2, p. 226 (After the failure of the following motion, "the question was taken on the clause, and it passed in the affirmative.").

15.1.1.3.b   Eleventh Amendment — The enumeration in this constitution of certain rights shall not be construed to deny or disparage others retained by the people."

Daily Advertiser, August 18, 1789, p. 2, col. 4 ("This was agreed to without amendment.").

15.1.1.3.c   Eleventh amendment — "The enumeration in this constitution of certain rights shall not be construed to deny or disparage others retained by the people."

New-York Daily Gazette, August 19, 1789, p. 802, col. 4 ("This was agreed to without amendment.").

15.1.1.3.d   11th Amendment. The enumeration in this constitution of certain rights shall not be construed to deny or disparage others retained by the people."

Gazette of the U.S., August 22, 1789, p. 249, col. 3 ("This was agreed to without amendment.").

15.1.1.4 Motion by Gerry in House, August 17, 1789

Mr. GERRY said it ought to be "deny or impair," for the word "disparage" was not of plain import. . . .

Congressional Register, August 17, 1789, p. 226 ("[H]e therefore moved to make that alteration, but not being seconded, . . .").

15.1.1.5 House Consideration, August 21, 1789

Tenth. The enumeration in this Constitution of certain rights, shall not be construed to deny or disparage others retained by the people.

HJ, p. 108 ("read and debated . . . agreed to by the House, . . . two-thirds of the members present concurring").[1]

[1]On August 22, 1789, the following motion was agreed to:
ORDERED, That it be referred to a committee of three, to prepare and report a proper arrangement of, and introduction to the articles of amendment to the Constitution of the United States, as agreed to by the House; and that Mr. Benson, Mr. Sherman, and Mr. Sedgwick be of the said committee.

HJ, p. 112.

15.1.1.6   House Resolution, August 24, 1789

ARTICLE THE FIFTEENTH.

The enumeration in the Constitution of certain rights, shall not be construed to deny or disparage others retained by the people.   House Pamphlet, RG 46, DNA.

15.1.1.7   Senate Consideration, August 25, 1789

15.1.1.7.a   The Resolve of the House of Representatives of the 24th of August, upon certain "Articles to be proposed to the Legislatures of the several States as Amendments to the Constitution of the United States" was read as followeth: . . .

Article the fifteenth

The enumeration in the Constitution of certain rights, shall not be construed to deny or disparage others retained by the people.   Rough SJ, p. 219.

15.1.1.7.b   The Resolve of the House of Representatives of the 24th of August, was read as followeth:

. . .

"Article the Fifteenth.

"The enumeration in the Constitution of certain rights, shall not be construed to deny or disparage others retained by the people.   Smooth SJ, p. 196.

15.1.1.7.c   The Resolve of the House of Representatives of the 24th of August, was read as followeth:

. . .

"ARTICLE THE FIFTEENTH.

"The enumeration in the Constitution of certain rights, shall not be construed to deny or disparage others retained by the people.   Printed SJ, p. 106.

15.1.1.8   Further Senate Consideration, September 7, 1789

15.1.1.8.a   On Motion to adopt the fifteenth Article of amendments to the Constitution of the United States, proposed by the House of Representatives.
Rough SJ, p. 259 ("It passed in the Affirmative.").

15.1.1.8.b   On motion, To adopt the fifteenth Article of Amendments to the Constitution of the United States, proposed by the House of Representatives —
Smooth SJ, p. 231 ("It passed in the Affirmative.").

15.1.1.8.c   On motion, To adopt the fifteenth Article of Amendments to the Constitution of the United States, proposed by the House of Representatives —
Printed SJ, p. 122 ("It passed in the Affirmative.").

15.1.1.8.d   that the Senate do
Resolved ~~to~~ ∧ concur with the House of Representatives in
Article fifteenth.   Senate MS, p. 4, RG 46, DNA.

15.1.1.9 Further Senate Consideration, September 9, 1789

15.1.1.9.a On motion to number the remaining articles agreed to by the Senate tenth, eleventh and twelfth instead of the numbers affixed by the Resolve of the House of Representatives.

Rough SJ, p. 277 ("It passed in the affirmative.";
motion renumbered fifteenth article as eleventh article).

15.1.1.9.b On motion, To number the remaining articles agreed to by the Senate, tenth, eleventh and twelfth, instead of the numbers affixed by the Resolve of the House of Representatives —

Smooth SJ, p. 246 ("It passed in the Affirmative.";
motion renumbered fifteenth article as eleventh article).

15.1.1.9.c On motion, To number the remaining Articles agreed to by the Senate, tenth, eleventh and twelfth, instead of the numbers affixed by the Resolve of the House of Representatives —

Printed SJ, p. 131 ("It passed in the Affirmative.";
motion renumbered fifteenth article as eleventh article).

15.1.1.9.d To erase the word — "Fifteenth" — & insert Eleventh.

Ellsworth MS, p. 4, RG 46, DNA.

15.1.1.10 Senate Resolution, September 9, 1789

[ARTICLE THE] ELEVENTH.

The en[umeration in the Constitution of certain] rights, shall not be construed to deny or disparage others retained by the people.

Senate Pamphlet, RG 46, DNA [material in brackets not legible].

15.1.1.11 Further House Consideration, September 21, 1789

RESOLVED, That this House doth agree to the second, fourth, eighth, twelfth, thirteenth, sixteenth, eighteenth, nineteenth, twenty-fifth, and twenty-sixth amendments, and doth disagree to the first, third, fifth, sixth, seventh, ninth, tenth, eleventh, fourteenth, fifteenth, seventeenth, twentieth, twenty-first, twenty-second, twenty-third, and twenty-fourth amendments proposed by the Senate to the said articles, two thirds of the members present concurring on each vote.

RESOLVED, That a conference be desired with the Senate on the subject matter of the amendments disagreed to, and that Mr. Madison, Mr. Sherman, and Mr. Vining, be appointed managers at the same on the part of this House.

HJ, p. 146.

15.1.1.12 Further Senate Consideration, September 21, 1789

15.1.1.12.a A message from the House of Representatives —

Mr. Beckley, their Clerk, brought up a Resolve of the House of this date, to agree to the 2nd, 4th, 8th, 12th, 13th, 16th, 18th, 19th, 25th, and 26th Amendments proposed by the Senate, "To articles of Amendment to be proposed to the Legislatures of the several States, as Amendments to the Constitution of the United States," and to disagree to the 1st, 3d, 5th, 6th, 7th, 9th, 10th, 11th, 14th, 15th, 17th, 20th, 21st, 22d, 23d, and 24th amendments: Two thirds of the members present concurring on each vote: And "That a conference be desired with the

Senate on the subject matter of the amendments disagreed to," and that Mr. Madison, Mr. Sherman, and Mr. Vining, be appointed managers of the same, on the part of the House of Representatives —

And he withdrew.

Smooth SJ, pp. 265–66.

15.1.1.12.b   A message from the House of Representatives —

Mr. Beckley, their Clerk, brought up a Resolve of the House of this date, to agree to the 2d, 4th, 8th, 12th, 13th, 16th, 18th, 19th, 25th, and 26th Amendments proposed by the Senate, "To Articles of Amendment to be proposed to the Legislatures of the several States, as Amendments to the Constitution of the United States," and to disagree to the 1st, 3d, 5th, 6th, 7th, 9th, 10th, 11th, 14th, 15th, 17th, 20th, 21st, 22d, 23d, and 24th Amendments: Two thirds of the members present concurring on each vote: And "That a conference be desired with the Senate on the subject matter of the Amendments disagreed to," and that Mr. Madison, Mr. Sherman, and Mr. Vining, be appointed managers of the same, on the part of the House of Representatives —

And he withdrew.

Printed SJ, pp. 141–42.

15.1.1.13   Further Senate Consideration, September 21, 1789

15.1.1.13.a   The Senate proceeded to consider the Message of the House of Representatives disagreeing to the Amendments made by the Senate "To Articles to be proposed to the Legislatures of the several States, as Amendments to the Constitution of the United States" And

Resolved, That the Senate do recede from their third Amendment, and do insist on all the others.

RESOLVED, That the Senate do concur with the House of Representatives in a conference on the subject matter of disagreement on the said Articles of Amendment, and that Mr. Ellsworth Mr. Carroll and Mr. Paterson be managers of the conference on the part of the Senate.

Smooth SJ, p. 267.

15.1.1.13.b   The Senate proceeded to consider the message of the House of Representatives disagreeing to the Amendments made by the Senate "To Articles to be proposed to the Legislatures of the several States, as Amendments to the Constitution of the United States" — And

RESOLVED, That the Senate do recede from their third Amendment, and do insist on all the others.

RESOLVED, That the Senate do concur with the House of Representatives in a conference on the subject matter of disagreement on the said Articles of Amendment, and that Mr. Ellsworth, Mr. Carroll, and Mr. Paterson be managers of the conference on the part of the Senate.

Printed SJ, p. 142.

15.1.1.14   Conference Committee Report, September 24, 1789

[T]hat it will be proper for the House of Representatives to agree to the said Amendments proposed by the Senate, with an Amendment to their fifth Amendment, so that the third Article shall read as follows: "Congress shall make no Law

respecting an establishment of <u>Religion</u>, or prohibiting the free exercise thereof; or abridging the freedom of Speech, or of the Press; or the right of the people peaceably to assemble and ~~to~~ petition the Government for a redress of grievances;" And with an Amendment to the fourteenth Amendment proposed by the Senate, so that the eighth Article, as numbered in the Amendments proposed by the Senate, shall read as follows "In all criminal prosecutions, the accused shall enjoy the right to a speedy & publick trial <u>by an impartial jury of the district wherein the crime shall have been committed, as the district shall have been previously ascertained by law</u>, and to be informed of the nature and cause of the accusation; to be confronted with the witnesses against him, and to have com
to
pulsory process for obtaining witnesses ~~against him~~ in his favour, & $\wedge$ have the assistance of council for his defence."

Conference MS, RG 46, DNA (Ellsworth's handwriting).

15.1.1.15 House Consideration of Conference Committee Report, September 24 [25], 1789

RESOLVED, That this House doth recede from their disagreement to the first, third, fifth, sixth, seventh, ninth, tenth, eleventh, fourteenth, fifteenth, seventeenth, twentieth, twenty-first, twenty-second, twenty-third, and twenty-fourth amendments, insisted on by the Senate: PROVIDED, That the two articles which by the amendments of the Senate are now proposed to be inserted as the third and eighth articles, shall be amended to read as followeth;

Article the third. "Congress shall make no law respecting an establishment of religion, or prohibiting the free exercise thereof; or abridging the freedom of speech, or of the press; or the right of the people peaceably to assemble, and to petition the government for a redress of grievances."

Article the eighth. "In all criminal prosecutions, the accused shall enjoy the right to a speedy and public trial by an impartial jury of the state and district wherein the crime shall have been committed, which district shall have been previously ascertained by law, and to be informed of the nature and cause of the accusation, to be confronted with the witnesses against him, to have compulsory process for obtaining witnesses in his favor, and to have the assistance of council for his defence."

HJ, p. 152 ("On the question, that the House do agree to the alteration
and amendment of the eighth article, in manner aforesaid, It was resolved
in the affirmative. Ayes 37 Noes 14").

15.1.1.16 Senate Consideration of Conference Committee Report, September 24, 1789

15.1.1.16.a   Mr. Ellsworth, on behalf of the managers of the conference on "articles to be proposed to the several States as Amendments to the Constitution of the United States," reported as follows:

That it will be proper for the House of Representatives to agree to the said amendments proposed by the Senate, with an Amendment to their fifth Amendment, so that the third Article shall read as follows: "Congress shall make no law respecting an establishment of <u>Religion</u>, or prohibiting the free exercise thereof; or abridging the freedom of Speech, or of the Press; or the right of the people peaceably to assemble and petition the Government for a redress of Grievances;" And with an Amendment to the fourteenth Amendment proposed by the Senate, so that the eighth article, as numbered in the Amendments proposed by the Senate, shall read as follows; "In all criminal prosecutions, the accused shall enjoy the right to a speedy and public trial by an impartial <u>Jury</u> of the district wherein the <u>Crime</u> shall have been committed, as the district shall have been previously ascertained by law, and to be informed of the nature and cause of the accusation, to be confronted with the witnesses against him, and to have compulsory process for obtaining witnesses in his favor, and to have the assistance of Counsel for defence."

Smooth SJ, pp. 272–73.

15.1.1.16.b   Mr. Ellsworth, on behalf of the managers of the conference on "Articles to be proposed to the several States as Amendments to the Constitution of the United States," reported as follows:

That it will be proper for the House of Representatives to agree to the said Amendments proposed by the Senate, with an Amendment to their fifth Amendment, so that the third Article shall read as follows: "Congress shall make no Law RESPECTING AN ESTABLISHMENT OF RELIGION, or prohibiting the free exercise thereof; or abridging the freedom of Speech, or of the Press; or the right of the People peaceably to assemble and petition the Government for a redress of Grievances;" And with an Amendment to the fourteenth Amendment proposed by the Senate, so that the eighth Article, as numbered in the Amendments proposed by the Senate, shall read as follows; "In all criminal prosecutions, the accused shall enjoy the right to a speedy and public trial BY AN IMPARTIAL JURY OF THE DISTRICT WHEREIN THE CRIME SHALL HAVE BEEN COMMITTED, AS THE DISTRICT SHALL HAVE BEEN PREVIOUSLY ASCERTAINED BY LAW, and to be informed of the nature and cause of the accusation, to be confronted with the witnesses against him, and to have compulsory process for obtaining witnesses in his favor, and to have the assistance of Counsel for defence."

Printed SJ, p. 145.

15.1.1.17   Further Senate Consideration of Conference Committee Report, September 24, 1789

15.1.1.17.a   A Message from the House of Representatives —

Mr. Beckley, their Clerk, brought up the Amendments to the "Articles to be proposed to the Legislatures of the several States, as Amendments to the Constitution of the United States;" and informed the Senate, that the House of Representatives had receded from their disagreement to the 1st, 3d, 5th, 6th, 7th, 9th, 10th, 11th, 14th, 15th, 17th, 20th, 21st, 22d, 23d, and 24th Amendments, insisted on by the Senate: Provided that the "Two Articles, which by the Amendments of the Senate are now proposed to be inserted as the third and eighth Articles," shall be amended to read as followeth:

Article the Third. "Congress shall make no Law respecting an establishment of Religion, or prohibiting the free exercise thereof; or abridging the freedom of Speech, or of the Press; or the right of the people peaceably to assemble, and petition the Government for a redress of Grievances."

Article the Eighth. "In all criminal prosecutions the accused shall enjoy the right to a speedy and public trial by an impartial Jury of the State and District, wherein the crime shall have been committed, which District shall have been previously ascertained by law, and to be informed of the nature and cause of the accusation, to be confronted with the witnesses against him, and to have compulsory process for obtaining witnesses in his favor, and to have the assistance of Counsel for his defence."

Smooth SJ, pp. 278–79.

15.1.1.17.b A Message from the House of Representatives —

Mr. Beckley, their Clerk, brought up the Amendments to the "Articles to be proposed to the Legislatures of the several States, as Amendments to the Constitution of the United States;" and informed the Senate, that the House of Representatives had receded from their disagreement to the 1st, 3d, 5th, 6th, 7th, 9th, 10th, 11th, 14th, 15th, 17th, 20th, 21st, 22d, 23d, and 24th Amendments, insisted on by the Senate: Provided that the "Two Articles, which by the Amendments of the Senate are now proposed to be inserted as the third and eighth Articles," shall be amended to read as followeth:

Article the Third. "Congress shall make no Law respecting an establishment of Religion, or prohibiting the free exercise thereof; or abridging the freedom of Speech, or of the Press; or the right of the People peaceably to assemble, and petition the Government for a redress of Grievances."

Article the Eighth. "In all criminal prosecutions the accused shall enjoy the right to a speedy and public trial by an impartial Jury of the State and District, wherein the crime shall have been committed, which District shall have been previously ascertained by law, and to be informed of the nature and cause of the accusation, to be confronted with the witnesses against him, and to have compulsory process for obtaining witnesses in his favor, and to have the assistance of Counsel for his defence."

Printed SJ, p. 148.

15.1.1.18 Further Senate Consideration of Conference Committee Report, September 25, 1789

15.1.1.18.a The Senate proceeded to consider the Message from the House of Representatives of the 24th, with Amendments to the Amendments of the Senate, to "Articles to be proposed to the Legislatures of the several States, as Amendments to the Constitution of the United States" — And

RESOLVED, That the Senate do concur in the Amendments proposed by the House of Representatives, to the Amendments of the Senate. Smooth SJ, p. 283.

15.1.1.18.b The Senate proceeded to consider the Message from the House of Representatives of the 24th, with Amendments to the Amendments of the Senate, to "Articles to be proposed to the Legislatures of the several States, as Amendments to the Constitution of the United States" — And

RESOLVED, That the Senate do concur in the Amendments proposed by the House of Representatives, to the Amendments of the Senate.

Printed SJ, pp. 150–51.

15.1.1.19   Agreed Resolution, September 25, 1789

15.1.1.19.a   Article the Eleventh.

The enumeration in the Constitution, of certain rights, shall not be construed to deny or disparage others retained by the people.   Smooth SJ, Appendix, p. 294.

15.1.1.19.b   ARTICLE the ELEVENTH.

The enumeration in the Constitution, of certain rights, shall not be construed to deny or disparage others retained by the people.   Printed SJ, Appendix, p. 164.

15.1.1.20   Enrolled Resolution, September 28, 1789

Article the eleventh . . . The enumeration in the Constitution, of certain rights, shall not be construed to deny or disparage others retained by the people.

Enrolled Resolutions, RG 11, DNA.

15.1.1.21   Printed Versions

15.1.1.21.a   ART. IX. The enumeration in the Constitution of certain rights, shall not be construed to deny or disparage others retained by the people.

Statutes at Large, vol. 1, p. 21.

15.1.1.21.b   ART. XI. The enumeration in the Constitution, of certain rights, shall not be construed to deny or disparage others retained by the people.

Statutes at Large, vol. 1, p. 98.

15.1.2 PROPOSALS FROM THE STATE CONVENTIONS

15.1.2.1   New York, July 26, 1788

That all Power is originally vested in and consequently derived from the People, and that Government is instituted by them for their common Interest Protection and Security.

That the enjoyment of Life, Liberty and the pursuit of Happiness are essential rights which every Government ought to respect and preserve.

That the Powers of Government may be reassumed by the People, whensoever it shall become necessary to their Happiness; that every Power, Jurisdiction and right, which is not by the said Constitution clearly delegated to the Congress of the United States, or the departments of the Government thereof, remains to the People of the several States, or to their respective State Governments to whom they may have granted the same; And that those Clauses in the said Constitution, which declare, that Congress shall not have or exercise certain Powers, do not imply that Congress is entitled to any Powers not given by the said Constitution; but such Clauses are to be construed either as exceptions to certain specified Powers, or as inserted merely for greater Caution.   State Ratifications, RG 11, DNA.

15.1.2.2   North Carolina, August 1, 1788

1st. That there are certain natural rights of which men, when they form a social compact, cannot deprive or divest their posterity, among which are the enjoyment of life, and liberty, with the means of acquiring, possessing and protecting property, and pursuing and obtaining happiness and safety.

2d. That all power is naturally vested in, and consequently derived from the people; that magistrates therefore are their trustees, and agents, and at all times amenable to them.

. . .

State Ratifications, RG 11, DNA.

15.1.2.3 Virginia, June 27, 1788

First, That there are certain natural rights of which men, when they form a social compact cannot deprive or divest their posterity, among which are the enjoyment of life and liberty, with the means of acquiring, possessing and protecting property, and pursuing and obtaining happiness and safety. Second, That all power is naturally vested in and consequently derived from the people; that Magestrates, therefore, are their trustees and agents at all times amenable to them. . . .

State Ratifications, RG 11, DNA.

15.1.3 STATE CONSTITUTIONS AND LAWS; COLONIAL CHARTERS AND LAWS

15.1.3.1 Delaware: Constitution, 1776

ART. 30. No article of the declaration of rights and fundamental rules of this state, agreed to by this convention, . . . ought ever be violated on any pretence whatever. No other part of this constitution shall be altered, changed or diminished without the consent of five parts in seven of the Assembly, and seven Members of the Legislative Council.

Delaware Laws, vol. 1, App., p. 91.

15.1.3.2 Georgia: Constitution, 1777

WHEREAS the conduct of the legislature of Great-Britain for many years past, has been so oppressive on the people of America, that of late years, they have plainly declared, and asserted a right to raise taxes upon the people of America, and to make laws to bind them in all cases whatsoever, without their consent; which conduct being repugnant to the common rights of mankind, hath obliged the Americans, as freemen, to oppose such oppressive measures, and to assert the rights and privileges they are entitled to, by the laws of nature and reason. . . .

. . .

We therefore the representatives of the people, from whom all power originates, and for whose benefit all government is intended, by virtue of the power delegated to us, Do ordain and declare, and it is hereby ordained and declared, that the following rules and regulations be adopted for the future government of this State.

Georgia Laws, p. 7.

15.1.3.3 Maryland: Declaration of Rights, 1776

3. That the inhabitants of Maryland are entitled to the common law of England, and the trial by jury, according to the course of that law, and to the benefit of such of the English statutes as existed at the time of their first emigration, and which by

experience have been found applicable to their local and other circumstances, and of such others as have been since made in England or Great-Britain, and have been introduced, used, and practised by the courts of law or equity; and also to all acts of assembly in force on the first of June seventeen hundred and seventy-four, except such as may have since expired, or have been, or may be altered by acts of convention, or this declaration of rights; subject nevertheless to the revision of, and amendment or repeal by, the legislature of this state; and the inhabitants of Maryland are also entitled to all property derived to them from or under the charter granted by his majesty Charles the first, to Caecilius Calvert, baron of Baltimore.

. . .

42. That this declaration of rights, or the form of government to be established by this convention, or any part of either of them, ought not to be altered, changed or abolished, by the legislature of this state, but in such manner as this convention shall prescribe and direct.

Maryland Laws, November 3, 1776.

15.1.3.4 Massachusetts: Constitution, 1780

PREAMBLE.

THE end of the institution, maintenance, and administration of government, is to secure the existence of the body politick; to protect it; and to furnish the individuals who compose it, with the power of enjoying, in safety and tranquillity, their natural rights, and the blessings of life: And whenever these great objects are not obtained, the people have a right to alter the government, and to take measures necessary for their safety, prosperity and happiness.

. . .

PART I.
A Declaration Of The Rights Of The Inhabitants
Of The Commonwealth Of Massachusetts.
ARTICLE

I. ALL men are born free and equal, and have certain natural, essential and unalienable rights; among which may be reckoned the right of enjoying and defending their lives and liberties; that of acquiring, possessing, and protecting property; in fine, that of seeking and obtaining their safety and happiness.

. . .

IV. The people of this Commonwealth, have the sole and exclusive right of governing themselves, as a free, sovereign, and independent state; and do, and forever hereafter shall, exercise and enjoy every power, jurisdiction and right, which is not, or may not hereafter, be by them expressly delegated to the United States of America, in Congress assembled.

Massachusetts Perpetual Laws, pp. 5–6.

15.1.3.5 New Hampshire: Constitution, 1783

[Part I, Article I.] ALL men are born equally free and independent; therefore, all government of right originates from the people, is founded in consent, and instituted for the general good.

II. All men have certain natural, essential, and inherent rights; among which are

637

— the enjoying and defending life and liberty — acquiring, possessing and protecting property — and in a word, of seeking and obtaining happiness.

III. When men enter into a state of society, they surrender up some of their natural rights to society, in order to secure the protection of others; and, without such an equivalent, the surrender is void.

IV. Among the natural rights, some are in their very nature unalienable, because no equivalent can be given or received for them. Of this kind are the RIGHTS OF CONSCIENCE.

. . .

VII. The people of this State, have the sole and exclusive right of governing themselves as a free, sovereign, and independent State, and do, and forever hereafter shall, exercise, and enjoy every power, jurisdiction and right pertaining, thereto, which is not, or may not hereafter be by them expressly delegated to the United States of America in Congress assembled.   New Hampshire Laws, pp. 22–24.

15.1.3.6   New Jersey: Constitution, 1776

WHEREAS all the constitutional Authority ever possessed by the Kings of *Great Britain* over these Colonies, . . . was by Compact, derived from the People, and held for them, for the common Interest of the whole Society. . . .
New Jersey Acts, p. iii.

15.1.3.7   New York: Constitution, 1777

"We hold these Truths to be self-evident, that all Men are created equal; that they are endowed by their Creator with certain unalienable Rights; that among these are, Life, Liberty and the Pursuit of Happiness. . . ."
New York Laws, vol. 1, p. 3.

15.1.3.8   North Carolina: Constitution, 1776

Sect. XLIV. That the Declaration of Rights is hereby declared to be Part of the Constitution of this State, and ought never to be violated on any Pretence whatever.   North Carolina Laws, p. 280.

15.1.3.9   Pennsylvania

15.1.3.9.a   Constitution, 1776

WHEREAS all government ought to be instituted and supported for the security and protection of the community as such, and to enable the individuals who compose it to enjoy their natural rights, and the other blessings which the author of existence has bestowed upon man; and whenever these great ends of government are not obtained, the people have a right, by common consent to change it, and take such measures as to them may appear necessary to promote their safety and happiness. And whereas the inhabitants of this commonwealth have, in consideration of protection only, heretofore acknowledged allegiance to the king of Great Britain; and the said king has not only withdrawn that protection, but commenced, and still continues to carry on, with unabated vengeance, a most cruel and unjust war against them employing therein, not only the troops of Great

Britain, but foreign mercenaries, savages and slaves, for the avowed purpose of reducing them to a total and abject submission to the despotic domination of the British parliament, with many other acts of tyranny, (more fully set forth in the declaration of congress) whereby all allegiance and fealty to the said king and his successors, are dissolved and at an end, and all power and authority derived from him ceased in these colonies. And whereas it is absolutely necessary for the welfare and safety of the inhabitants of said colonies, that they be henceforth free and independent states, and that just, permanent, and proper forms of government exist in every part of them derived from and founded on the authority of the people only, agreeable to the directions of the honourable American congress. We, the representatives of the freemen of Pennsylvania, in general convention met, for the express purpose of framing such a government, confessing the goodness of the great Governor of the universe (who alone knows to what degree of earthly happiness mankind may attain, by perfecting the arts of government) in permitting the people of this state, by common consent, and without violence, deliberately to form for themselves such just rules as they shall think best, for governing their future society; and being fully convinced, that it is our indispensible duty to establish such original principles of government, as will best promote the general happiness of the people of this state, and their posterity, and provide for future improvements, without partiality for, or prejudice against any particular class, sect, or denomination of men whatever, do, by virtue of the authority vested in us by our constituents, ordain, declare, and establish, the following *Declaration of Rights,* and *Frame of Government,* to be the CONSTITUTION of this commonwealth, and to remain in force therein for ever, unaltered, except in such articles as shall hereafter on experience be found to require improvement, and which shall by the same authority of the people, fairly delegated as this frame of government directs, be amended or improved for the more effectual obtaining and securing the great end and design of all government, herein before mentioned.

CHAPTER I.
A DECLARATION of the RIGHTS of the Inhabitants
of the State of Pennsylvania.

I. THAT all men are born equally free and independent, and have certain natural, inherent and unalienable rights, amongst which are, the enjoying and defending life and liberty, acquiring, possessing and protecting property, and pursuing and obtaining happiness and safety.

. . .

IV. That all power being originally inherent in, and consequently derived from, the people; therefore all officers of government, whether legislative or executive, are their trustees and servants, and at all times accountable to them.

V. That government is, or ought to be, instituted for the common benefit, protection and security of the people, nation or community; and not for the particular emolument or advantage of any single man, family, or set of men, who are a part only of that community: And that the community hath an indubitable, unalienable and indefeasible right to reform, alter or abolish government in such manner as shall be by that community judged most conducive to the public weal.

Pennsylvania Acts, McKean, pp. vii–ix.

15.1.3.9.b Constitution, 1790

ARTICLE IX.

THAT *the general, great, and essential Principles of Liberty and free Government may be recognized and unalterably established,* WE DECLARE,

SECTION I. THAT all men are born equally free and independent, and have certain inherent and indefeasible rights, among which are those of enjoying and defending life and liberty, of acquiring, possessing, and protecting property and reputation, and of pursuing their own happiness.

SECT. II. That all power is inherent in the people, and all free governments are founded on their authority, and instituted for their peace, safety and happiness: For the advancement of those ends they have, at all times, an unalienable and indefeasible right to alter, reform, or abolish their government, in such manner as they may think proper.

· · ·

SECT. XXVI. To guard against transgressions of the high powers which we have delegated, WE DECLARE, That every thing in this article is excepted out of the general powers of government, and shall for ever remain inviolate.

Pennsylvania Acts, Dallas, pp. xxxiii, xxxvi.

15.1.3.10 South Carolina: Constitution, 1790

ARTICLE IX.

Section 1. All power is originally vested in the people; and all free governments are founded on their authority, and are instituted for their peace, safety and happiness.

South Carolina Laws, App., p. 41.

15.1.3.11 Vermont: Constitution, 1777

WHEREAS all Government ought to be instituted and supported for the Security and Protection of the Community as such, and to enable the Individuals who compose it to enjoy their natural Rights, and the other Blessings which the Author of Existence has bestowed upon Man; and whenever those great Ends of Government are not obtained, the People have a Right by common Consent to change it, and take such Measures as to them may appear necessary to promote their Safety and Happiness.

A DECLARATION OF THE RIGHTS OF THE INHABITANTS OF THE STATE OF *VERMONT*

I. That all Men are born equally free and independent, and have certain natural, inherent and unalienable Rights, amongst which are the enjoying and defending Life and Liberty; acquiring, possessing and protecting Property, and pursuing and obtaining Happiness and Safety.

· · ·

5. THAT all Power being originally inherent in, and consequently derived from the People; therefore all Officers of Government, whether legislative or executive, are their Trustees and Servants, and at all Times accountable to them.

Vermont Acts, pp. 1, 3.

15.1.3.12 Virginia: Declaration of Rights, 1776

I. THAT all men are by nature equally free and independent, and have certain inherent rights, of which, when they enter into a state of society, they cannot, by any compact, deprive or devest their posterity; namely, the enjoyment of life and liberty, with the means of acquiring and possessing property, and pursuing and obtaining happiness and safety.

Virginia Acts, p. 33.

15.1.4 OTHER TEXTS

15.1.4.1 Declaration of Independence, July 4, 1776

. . . We hold these truths to be self-evident, that all men are created equal, that they are endowed by their Creator with certain unalienable Rights, that among these are Life, Liberty and the pursuit of Happiness. — That to secure these rights, Governments are instituted among Men, deriving their just powers from the consent of the governed, — That whenever any Form of Government becomes destructive of these ends, it is the Right of the People to alter or to abolish it; and to institute new Government, laying its foundation on such principles and organizing its powers in such form, as to them shall seem most likely to effect their Safety and Happiness.

Engrossed Manuscripts, DNA.

15.1.4.2 Articles of Confederation, November 15, 1777

Article II. Each state retains its sovereignty, freedom and independence, and every Power, Jurisdiction and right, which is not by this confederation expressly delegated to the United States, in Congress assembled.

Continental Congress Papers, DNA.

15.1.4.3 Richard Henry Lee to Edmund Randolph, Proposed Amendments, October 16, 1787

It having been found from universal experience that the most express declarations and reservations are necessary to protect the just rights and liberty of mankind from the silent, powerful and ever active conspiracy of those who govern; and it appearing to be the sense of the good people of America, by the various bills or declarations of rights whereon the governments of the greater number of the states are founded. That such precautions are necessary to restrain and regulate the exercise of the great powers given to rulers, In conformity with these principles, and from respect for the public sentiment on this subject, it is submitted, — That the new Constitution proposed for the government of the United States be bottomed upon a declaration, or bill of rights, clearly and precisely stating the principles upon which this social compact is founded. . . .

Virginia Gazette, December 22, 1787.

15.2 DISCUSSION OF DRAFTS AND PROPOSALS
15.2.1 THE FIRST CONGRESS

15.2.1.1 **June 8, 1789**[2]

15.2.1.1.a

Mr. JACKSON.

The more I consider the subject of amendments, the more, mr. speaker, I am convinced it is improper. I revere the rights of my constituents as much as any gentleman in congress, yet, I am against inserting a declaration of rights in the constitution, and that upon some of the reasons referred to by the gentleman last up. If such an addition is not dangerous or improper, it is at least unnecessary: that is a sufficient reason for not entering into the subject at a time when there are urgent calls for our attention to important business. Let me ask, gentlemen, what reason there is for the suspicions which are to be removed by this measure? Who are congress that such apprehensions should be entertained of them? Do we not belong to the mass of the people? Is there a single right but, if infringed, will affect us and our connections as much as any other person? Do we not return at the expiration of two years into private life, and is not this a security against encroachment? Are we not sent here to guard those rights which might be endangered, if the government was an aristocracy or a despotism? View for a moment the situation of Rhode-Island and, say whether the people's rights are more safe under state legislatures than under a government of limited powers? Their liberty is changed to licentiousness. But do gentlemen suppose bills of rights necessary to secure liberty? If they do, let them look at New York, New Jersey, Virginia, South Carolina, and Georgia. Those states have no bills of rights, and are the liberty of the citizens less safe in those states, than in the other of the United States? I believe they are not.

There is a maxim in law, and it will apply to bills of rights, that when you enumerate exceptions, the exceptions operate to the exclusion of all circumstances that are omitted; consequently, unless you except every right from the grant of power, those omitted are inferred to be resigned to the discretion of the government.

Congressional Register, June 8, 1789, vol. 1, p. 437.

15.2.1.1.b MR. JACKSON observed, That the Hon. Gentleman's ingenious detail, so far from convincing him of the expediency of bringing forward the subject of amendments at this time, had confirmed him in the contrary opinion: The prospect which such a discussion opened, was wide and extensive, and would preclude other benefits, of much greater moment, at the present juncture — He differed widely from the Gentleman, with regard to bills of rights — several of the States had no such bills — Rhode-Island had none — there, liberty was carried to excess, and licentiousness triumphed — In some States, which had such a nominal security, the encroachments upon the rights of the people had been most complained of. . . .

Gazette of the U.S., June 10, 1787, p. 67, col. 2.

[2]For Madison's speech in support of his proposals, *see* 1.2.1.1.a–c.

15.2.1.2 **August 17, 1789**

15.2.1.2.a   The 8th clause of the 4th proposition was taken up, which was "The enumeration in this constitution of certain rights shall not be construed to deny or disparage others retained by the people."

Mr. GERRY said it ought to be "deny or impair," for the word "disparage" was not of plain import; he therefore moved to make that alteration, but not being seconded, the question was taken on the clause, and it passed in the affirmative.

Congressional Register, August 17, 1789, vol. 2, p. 226.

15.2.1.2.b   11th Amendment. ["]The enumeration in this constitution of certain rights shall not be construed to deny or disparage others retained by the people."

This was agreed to without amendment.

Gazette of the U.S., August 22, 1787, p. 249, col. 3.

15.2.2 STATE CONVENTIONS

15.2.2.1 **Massachusetts**

15.2.2.1.a **February 4, 1788**

Rev. Mr. THACHER. . . . There are other restraints, which, though not directly named in this Constitution, yet are evidently discerned by every man of common observation. These are, the government of the several states, and the spirit of liberty in the people.

Elliot, vol. 2, p. 145.

15.2.2.1.b **February 5, 1788**

Mr. PARSONS demonstrated the impracticability of forming a bill, in a national constitution, for securing individual rights, and showed the inutility of the measure, from the ideas, that no power was given to Congress to infringe on any one of the natural rights of the people by this Constitution; and, should they attempt it without constitutional authority, the act would be a nullity, and could not be enforced.

Elliot, vol. 2, pp. 161–62.

15.2.2.2 **New York, July 1, 1788**

Mr. TREDWELL. Sir, little accustomed to speak in public, and always inclined, in such an assembly as this, to be a hearer rather than a speaker, on a less important occasion than the present I should have contented myself with a silent vote; but when I consider the nature of this dispute, that it is a contest, not between little states and great states, (as we have been told,) between little folks and great folks, between patriotism and ambition, between the navigating and non-navigating individuals, (for not one of the amendments we contend for has the least reference to the clashing interests of the states;) when I consider, likewise, that a people jealous of their liberties, and strongly attached to freedom, have reposed so entire a confidence in this assembly, that upon our determination depends their future enjoyment of those invaluable rights and privileges, which they have so lately and so gallantly defended at every risk and expense, both of life and property, — it appears to me so interesting and important, that I cannot be totally silent on the occasion, lest lisping babes should be taught to curse my name, as a betrayer of their freedom and happiness.

The gentleman who first opened this debate did (with an emphasis which I believe convinced every one present of the propriety of the advice) urge the necessity of proceeding, in our deliberations on this important subject, coolly and dispassionately. With how much candor this advice was given, appears from the subsequent parts of a long speech, and from several subsequent speeches almost totally addressed to our fears. The people of New Jersey and Connecticut are so exceedingly exasperated against us, that, totally regardless of their own preservation, they will take the two rivers of Connecticut and Delaware by their extremities, and, by dragging them over our country, will, by a sweeping deluge, wash us all into the Hudson, leaving neither house nor inhabitant behind them. But if this event should not happen, doubtless the Vermontese, with the British and tories our natural enemies, would, by bringing down upon us the great Lake Ontario, sweep hills and mountains, houses and inhabitants, in one deluge, into the Atlantic. These, indeed, would be terrible calamities; but terrible as they are, they are not to be compared with the horrors and desolation of tyranny. The arbitrary courts of Philip in the Netherlands, in which life and property were daily confiscated without a jury, occasioned as much misery and a more rapid depopulation of the province, before the people took up arms in their own defence, than all the armies of that haughty monarch were able to effect afterwards; and it is doubtful, in my mind, whether governments, by abusing their powers, have not occasioned as much misery and distress, and nearly as great devastations of the human species, as all the wars which have happened since Milton's battle of the angels to the present day. The end or design of government is, or ought to be, the safety, peace, and welfare of the governed. Unwise, therefore, and absurd in the highest degree, would be the conduct of that people, who, in forming a government, should give to their rulers power to destroy them and their property, and thereby defeat the very purpose of their institutions; or, in other words, should give unlimited power to their rulers, and not retain in their own hands the means of their own preservation. The first governments in the world were parental, the powers of which were restrained by the laws of nature; and doubtless the early succeeding governments were formed on the same plan, which, we may suppose, answered tolerably well in the first ages of the world, while the moral sense was strong, and the laws of nature well understood, there being then no lawyers to explain them away. But in after times, when kings became great, and courts crowded, it was discovered that governments should have a right to tyrannize, and a power to oppress; and at the present day, when the *juris periti* are become so skilful in their profession, and quibbling is reduced to a science, it is become extremely difficult to form a constitution which will secure liberty and happiness to the people, or laws under which property is safe. Hence, in modern times, the design of the people, in forming an original constitution of government, is not so much to give powers to their rulers, as to guard against the abuse of them; but, in a federal one, it is different.

Sir, I introduce these observations to combat certain principles which have been daily and confidently advanced by the favorers of the present Constitution, and which appear to me totally indefensible. The first and grand leading, or rather misleading, principle in this debate, and on which the advocates for this system of unrestricted powers must chiefly depend for its support, is that, in forming a constitution, whatever powers are not expressly granted or given the government, are reserved to the people, or that rulers cannot exercise any powers but those expressly given to them by the Constitution. Let me ask the gentleman who advanced this principle, whether the commission of a Roman dictator, which was in these few words — to take care that the state received no harm — does not come up fully to their ideas of an energetic government; or whether an invitation from the people to one or more to come and rule over them, would not clothe the rulers with sufficient powers. If so, the principle they advance is a false one. Besides, the absurdity of this principle will evidently appear, when we consider the great variety of objects to which the powers of the government must necessarily extend, and that an express enumeration of them all would probably fill as many volumes as Pool's Synopsis of the Critics. But we may reason with sufficient certainty on the subject, from the sense of all the public bodies in the United States, who had occasion to form new constitutions. They have uniformly acted upon a direct and contrary principle, not only in forming the state constitutions and the old Confederation, but also in forming this very Constitution, for we do not find in every state constitution express resolutions made in favor of the people; and it is clear that the late Convention at Philadelphia, whatever might have been the sentiments of some of its members, did not adopt the principle, for they have made certain reservations and restrictions, which, upon that principle, would have been totally useless and unnecessary; and can it be supposed that wise body, whose only apology for the great ambiguity of many parts of that performance, and the total omission of some things which many esteem essential to the security of liberty, was a great desire for brevity, should so far sacrifice that great and important object, as to insert a number of provisions which they esteemed totally useless? Why is it said that the privilege of the writ of *habeas corpus* shall not be suspended, unless, in cases of rebellion or invasion, the public safety may require it? What clause in the Constitution, except this very clause itself, gives the general government a power to deprive us of that great privilege, so sacredly secured to us by our state constitutions? Why is it provided that no bill of attainder shall be passed, or that no title of nobility shall be granted? Are there any clauses in the Constitution extending the powers of the general government to these objects? Some gentlemen say that these, though not necessary, were inserted for greater caution. I could have wished, sir, that a greater caution had been used to secure to us the freedom of election, a sufficient and responsible representation, the freedom of the press, and the trial by jury both in civil and criminal cases.

These, sir, are the rocks on which the Constitution should have rested; no other foundation can any man lay, which will secure the sacred temple of freedom against the power of the great, the undermining arts of ambition, and the blasts of profane scoffers — for such there will be in every age — who will tell us that all religion is in vain; that is, that our political creeds, which have been handed down to us by our forefathers as sacredly as our Bibles, and for which more of them have suffered martyrdom than for the creed of the apostles, are all nonsense; who will tell us that paper constitutions are mere paper, and that parchment is but parchment, that jealousy of our rulers is a sin, &c. I could have wished also that sufficient caution had been used to secure to us our religious liberties, and to have prevented the general government from tyrannizing over our consciences by a religious establishment — a tyranny of all others most dreadful, and which will assuredly be exercised whenever it shall be thought necessary for the promotion and support of their political measures. It is ardently to be wished, sir, that these and other invaluable rights of freemen had been as cautiously secured as some of the paltry local interests of some of the individual states. But it appears to me, that, in forming this Constitution, we have run into the same error which the lawyers and Pharisees of old were charged with; that is, while we have secured the tithes of mint, anise, and cumin, we have neglected to weightier matters of the law, judgment, mercy, and faith. . . .

. . .

In this Constitution, sir, we have departed widely from the principles and political faith of '76, when the spirit of liberty ran high, and danger put a curb on ambition. Here we find no security for the rights of individuals, no security for the existence of our state governments; here is no bill of rights, no proper restriction of power; our lives, our property, and our consciences, are left wholly at the mercy of the legislature, and the powers of the judiciary may be extended to any degree short of almighty. Sir, in this Constitution we have not only neglected, — we have done worse, — we have openly violated, our faith, — that is our public faith.

Elliot, vol. 2, pp. 396–401.

15.2.2.3 North Carolina, July 29, 1788

Mr. MACLAINE. Mr. Chairman, I beg leave to make a few observations. One of the gentleman's objections to the Constitution now under consideration is, that it is not the act of the states, but of the people; but that it ought to be the act of the states; and he instances the delegation of power by the states to the Confederation, at the commencement of the war, as a proof of this position. I hope, sir, that all power is in the people, and not in the state governments. If he will not deny the authority of the people to delegate power to agents, and to devise such a government as a majority of them thinks will promote their happiness, he will withdraw his objection. The people, sir, are the only proper authority to form a government. They, sir, have formed their state governments, and can alter them at pleasure. Their transcendent power is competent to form this or any other government which they think promotive of their happiness. But the gentleman contends that there ought to be a bill of rights, or something of that kind — something declaring expressly, that all power not expressly given to the Constitution ought to be retained by the states; and he produces the Confederation as authority for its necessity. When the Confederation was made, we were by no means so well acquainted with the principles of government as we are now. We were then jealous of the power of our rulers, and had an idea of the British government when we entertained that jealousy. There is no people on earth so well acquainted with the nature of government as the people of America generally are. We know now that it is agreed upon by most writers, and men of judgment and reflection, that all power is in the people, and immediately derived from them. The gentleman surely must know that, if there be certain rights which never can, nor ought to, be given up, these rights cannot be said to be given away, merely because we have omitted to say that we have not given them up. Can any security arise from declaring that we have a right to what belongs to us? Where is the necessity of such a declaration? If we have this inherent, this unalienable, this indefeasible title to those rights, if they are not given up, are they not retained? If Congress should make a law beyond the powers and the spirit of the Constitution, should we not say to Congress, "You have no authority to make this law. There are limits beyond which you cannot go. You cannot exceed the power prescribed by the Constitution. You are amenable to us for your conduct. This act is unconstitutional. We will disregard it, and punish you for the attempt."

But the gentleman seems to be most tenacious of the judicial power of the states. The honorable gentleman must know, that the doctrine of reservation of power not relinquished, clearly demonstrates that the judicial power of the states is not impaired. . . .

     . . .

MR. SPENCER answered, that the gentleman last up had misunderstood him. He did not object to the caption of the Constitution, but he instanced it to show that the United States were not, merely as states, the objects of the Constitution; but that the laws of Congress were to operate upon individuals, and not upon states. He then continued: I do not mean to contend that the laws of the general government should not operate upon individuals. I before observed that this was necessary, as laws could not be put in execution against states without the agency of the sword, which, instead of answering the ends of government, would destroy it. I endeavored to show that, as the government was not to operate against states, but against individuals, the rights of individuals ought to be properly secured. In order to constitute this security, it appears to me there ought to be such a clause in the Constitution as there was in the Confederation, expressly declaring, that every power, jurisdiction, and right, which are not given up by it, remain in the states. Such a clause would render a bill of rights unnecessary. But as there is no such clause, I contend that there should be a bill of rights, ascertaining and securing the great rights of the states and people. Besides my objection to the revision of facts by the federal court, and the insecurity of jury trial, I consider the concurrent jurisdiction of those courts with the state courts as extremely dangerous. . . .

Elliot, vol. 4, pp. 160–64.

15.2.2.4   Pennsylvania

15.2.2.4.a   October 28, 1787

MR. WILSON. . . . In a government possessed of enumerated powers, such a measure [adopting a bill of rights] would be not only unnecessary, but preposterous and dangerous. Whence comes this notion, that in the United States there is no security without a bill of rights? Have the citizens of South Carolina no security for their liberties? They have no bill of rights. Are the citizens on the eastern side of the Delaware less free, or less secured in their liberties, than those on the western side? The state of New Jersey has no bill of rights. The state of New York has no bill of rights. The states of Connecticut and Rhode Island have no bill of rights. I know not whether I have exactly enumerated the states who have not thought it necessary to add *a bill of rights* to their constitutions; but this enumeration, sir, will serve to show by experience, as well as principle, that, even in single governments, a bill of rights is not an essential or necessary measure. But in a government consisting of enumerated powers, such as is proposed for the United States, a bill of rights would not only be unnecessary, but, in my humble judgement, highly imprudent. In all societies, there are many powers and rights which cannot be particularly enumerated. A bill of rights annexed to a constitution is *an enumeration of the powers* reserved. If we attempt an enumeration, every thing that is not enumerated is presumed to be given. The consequence is, that an imperfect enumeration would throw all implied power into the scale of the government, and the rights of the people would be rendered incomplete. On the other hand, an imperfect enumeration of the powers of government reserves all implied power to the people; and by that means the constitution becomes incomplete. But of the two, it is much safer to run the risk on the side of the constitution; for an omission in the enumeration of the powers of government is neither so dangerous nor important as an omission in the enumeration of the rights of the peop e [*sic*].

Elliot, vol. 2, pp. 436–37.

15.2.2.4.b **December 4, 1787**

MR. WILSON. . . . I consider that there are very few who understand the whole of these rights. All the political writers, from *Grotius* and *Puffendorf* down to *Vattel*, have treated on this subject; but in no one of those books, nor in the aggregate of them all, can you find a complete enumeration of rights appertaining to the people as men and as citizens.

. . . Enumerate all the rights of men! I am sure, sir, that no gentleman in the late Convention would have attempted such a thing. . . .

Elliot, vol. 2, p. 454.

15.2.2.4.c **September 3, 1788**

PROCEEDINGS OF THE MEETING [of citizens]
AT HARRISBURG, IN PENNSYLVANIA

We, the conferees, . . . agree in opinion, — . . .

I. That Congress shall not exercise any powers whatever, but such as are expressly given to that body by the Constitution of the United States: nor shall any authority, power, or jurisdiction, be assumed or exercised by the executive or judiciary departments of the Union, under color or pretence of construction or fiction; but all the rights of sovereignty, which are not by the said Constitution expressly and plainly vested in the Congress, shall be deemed to remain with, and shall be exercised by, the several states in the Union, according to their respective constitutions; and that every reserve of the rights of individuals, made by the several constitutions of the states in the Union, shall remain inviolate, except so far as they are expressly and manifestly yielded or narrowed by the national Constitution.

Elliot, vol. 2, pp. 543, 545.

15.2.2.5 North Carolina, July 29, 1788

Mr. IREDELL. . . . The gentleman says that unalienable rights ought not to be given up. Those rights which are unalienable are not alienated. They still remain with the great body of the people. If any right be given up that ought not to be, let it be shown. Say it is a thing which affects your country, and that it ought not be surrendered: this would be reasonable. But when it is evident that the exercise of any power not given up would be a usurpation, it would be not only useless, but dangerous, to enumerate a number of rights which are not intended to be given up; because it would be implying, in the strongest manner, that every right not included in the exception might be impaired by the government without usurpation; and it would be impossible to enumerate every one. Let anyone make what collection or enumeration of rights he pleases, I will immediately mention twenty or thirty more rights not contained in it.

Mr. BLOODWORTH. . . . By its not being provide for, it is expressly provided against. I still see the necessity of a bill of rights. Gentlemen use contradictory arguments on this subject, if I recollect right. Without the most express restrictions, Congress may trample on your rights. Every possible precaution should be taken when we grant powers. Rulers are always disposed to abuse them.

Elliot, vol. 4, pp. 166–67.

15.2.2.6 South Carolina, May 20, 1788

Mr. PATRICK DOLLARD. . . . They are nearly all, to a man, opposed to this new Constitution, because, they say, they have omitted to insert a bill of rights therein, ascertaining and fundamentally establishing, the unalienable rights of men, without a full, free, and secure enjoyment of which there can be no liberty, and over which it is not necessary that a good government should have the control. They say that they are by no means against vesting Congress with ample and sufficient powers; but to make over to them, or any set of men, their birthright, comprised in Magna Carta, which this new Constitution absolutely does, they can never agree to.

Elliot, vol. 4, p. 337.

15.2.2.7 Virginia

15.2.2.7.a June 12, 1788

Mr. HENRY. . . . When we see men of such talents and learning compelled to use their utmost abilities to convince themselves that there is no danger, is it not sufficient to make us tremble? Is it not sufficient to fill the minds of the ignorant part of men with fear? If gentlemen believe that the apprehensions of men will be quieted, they are mistaken, since our best-informed men are in doubt with respect to the security of our rights. Those who are not so well informed will spurn at the government. When our common citizens, who are not possessed with such extensive knowledge and abilities are called upon to change their bill of rights (which, in plain, unequivocal terms, secures their most valuable rights and privileges) for construction and implication, will they implicitly acquiesce? Our declaration of rights tells us that "all men are by nature free and independent," &c. . . . Will they exchange these rights for logical reasons?

Elliot, vol. 3, pp. 317–18.

June 14, 1788

MR. GEORGE MASON. Mr. Chairman, gentlemen say there is no new power given by this clause. Is there any thing in this Constitution which secures to the states the powers which are said to be retained? Will powers remain to the states which are not expressly guarded and reserved? I will suppose a case. Gentlemen may call it an impossible case, and suppose that Congress will act with wisdom and integrity. Among the enumerated powers, Congress are to lay and collect taxes, duties, imposts, and excises, and to pay the debts, and to provide for the general welfare and common defence; and by that clause (so often called the *sweeping clause*) they are to make all laws necessary to execute those laws. Now, suppose oppressions should arise under this government, and any writer should dare to stand forth, and expose to the community at large the abuses of those powers; could not Congress, under the idea of providing for the general welfare, and under their own construction, say that this was destroying the general peace, encouraging sedition, and poisoning the minds of the people? And could they not, in order to provide against this, lay a dangerous restriction on the press? Might they not even bring the trial of this restriction within the ten miles square, when there is no prohibition against it? Might they not thus destroy the trial by jury? Would they not extend their implication? It appears to me that they may and will. And shall the support of our rights depend on the bounty of men whose interest it may be to oppress us? That Congress should have the power to provide for the general welfare of the Union, I grant. But I wish a clause in the Constitution, with respect to all powers which are not granted, that they are retained by the states. Otherwise, the power of providing for the general welfare may be perverted to its destruction.

Many gentlemen, whom I respect, take different sides of this question. We wish this amendment to be introduced, to remove our apprehensions. There was a clause in the Confederation reserving to the states respectively every power, jurisdiction, and right, not expressly delegated to the United States. This clause has never been complained of, but approved by all. Why not, then, have a similar clause in this Constitution, in which it is the more indispensably necessary than in the Confederation, because of the great augmentation of power vested in the former? In my humble apprehension, unless there be some such clear and finite expression, this clause now under consideration will go to any thing our rulers may think proper. Unless there be some express declaration that every thing not given is retained, it will be carried to any power Congress may please.

MR. HENRY moved to read from the 8th to the 13th article of the declaration of rights; which was done.

MR. GEORGE NICHOLAS, in reply to the gentlemen opposed to the clause under debate, went over the same grounds, and developed the same principles, which Mr. Pendleton and Mr. Madison had done. The opposers of the clause, which gave the power of providing for the general welfare, supposed its dangers to result from its connection with, and extension of, the powers granted in the other clauses. He endeavored to show the committee that it only empowered Congress to make such laws as would be necessary to enable them to pay the public debts and provided for the common defence; that this general welfare was united, not to the general power of legislation, but to the particular power of laying and collecting taxes, imposts, and excises, for the purpose of paying the debts and providing for the common defence, — that is, that they could raise as much money as would pay the debts and provide for the common defence, in consequence of this power. The clause which was affectedly called the *sweeping clause* contained no new grant of power. To illustrate this position, he observed that, if it had been added at the end of every one of the enumerated powers, instead of being inserted at the end of all, it would be obvious to any one that it was not augmentation of power. If, for instance, at the end of the clause granting power to lay and collect taxes, who could suspect it to be an addition of power? As it would grant no new power if inserted at the end of each clause, it could not when subjoined to the whole.

He then proceeded thus: But, says he, who is to determine the extent of such powers? I say, the same power which, in all well-regulated communities, determines the extent of legislative powers. If they exceed these powers, the judiciary will declare it void or else the people will have a right to declare it void. Is this depending on any man? But, says the gentleman, it may go to any thing. It may destroy the trial by jury; and they may say it is necessary for providing for the general defence. The power of providing for the general defence only extends to raise any sum of money they may think necessary, by taxes, imposts, &c. But, says he, our only defence against oppressive laws consists in the virtue of our representatives. This was misrepresented. If I understand it right, no new power can be exercised. As to those which are actually granted, we trust to the fellow-feelings of our representatives; and if we are deceived, we then trust to altering our government. It appears to me, however, that we can confide in their discharging their powers rightly, from the peculiarity of their situation, and connection with us. If, sir, the powers of the former Congress were very inconsiderable, that body did not deserve to have great powers.

It was so constructed that it would be dangerous to invest it with such. But why were the articles of the bill of rights read? Let him show us that those rights are given up by the Constitution. Let him prove them to be violated. He tells us that the most worthy characters of the country differ as to the necessity of a bill of rights. It is a simple and plain proposition. It is agreed upon by all that the people have all power. If they part with any of it, is it necessary to declare that they retain the rest? Liken it to any similar case. If I have one thousand acres of land, and I grant five hundred of it, must I declare that I retain the other five hundred? Do I grant the whole thousand acres, when I grant five hundred, unless I declare that the five hundred I do not give belong to me still? It is so in this case. After granting some powers, the rest must remain with the people.

Gov. RANDOLPH observed that he had some objections to the clause. He was persuaded that the construction put upon it by the gentlemen, on both sides, was erroneous; but he thought any construction better than going into anarchy.

Mr. GEORGE MASON still thought that there ought to be some express declaration in the Constitution, asserting that rights not given to the general government were retained by the states. He apprehended that, unless this was done, many valuable and important rights would be concluded to be given up by implication. All governments were drawn from the people, though many were perverted to their oppression. The government of Virginia, he remarked, was drawn from the people; yet there were certain great and important rights, which the people, by their bill of rights, declared to be paramount to the power of the legislature. He asked, Why should it not be so in this Constitution? Was it because we were more substantially represented in it than in the state government? If, in the state government, where the people were substantially and fully represented, it was necessary that the great rights of human nature should be secure from the encroachments of the legislature, he asked if it was not more necessary in this government, where they were but inadequately represented? He declared that artful sophistry and evasions could not satisfy him. He could see no clear distinction between rights relinquished by a positive grant, and lost by implication. Unless there were a bill of rights, implication might swallow up all our rights.

Mr. HENRY. Mr. Chairman, the necessity of a bill of rights appears to me to be greater in this government than ever it was in any government before. I have observed already, that the sense of the European nations, and particularly Great Britain, is against the construction of rights being retained which are not expressly relinquished. I repeat, that all nations have adopted this construction — that all rights not expressly and unequivocally reserved to the people are impliedly and incidentally relinquished to rulers, as necessarily inseparable from the delegated powers. It is so in Great Britain; for every possible right, which is not reserved to the people by some express provision or compact, is within the king's prerogative. It is so in that country which is said to be in such full possession of freedom. It is so in Spain, Germany, and other parts of the world. Let us consider the sentiments which have been entertained by the people of America on this subject. At the revolution, it must be admitted that it was their sense to set down those great rights which ought, in all countries, to be held inviolable and sacred. Virginia did so, we all remember. She made a compact to reserve, expressly, certain rights.

When fortified with full, adequate, and abundant representation, was she satisfied with that representation? No. She most cautiously and guardedly reserved and secured those invaluable, inestimable rights and privileges, which no people, inspired with the least glow of patriotic liberty, ever did, or ever can, abandon. She is called upon now to abandon them, and dissolve that compact which secured them to her. She is called upon to accede to another compact, which most infallibly supersedes and annihilates her present one. Will she do it? This is the question. If you intend to reserve your unalienable rights, you must have the most express stipulation; for, if implication be allowed, you are ousted of those rights. If the people do not think it necessary to reserve them, they will be supposed to be given up. How were the congressional rights defined when the people of America united by a confederacy to defend their liberties and rights against the tyrannical attempts of Great Britain? The states were not then contented with implied reservation. No, Mr. Chairman. It was expressly declared in our Confederation that every right was retained by the states, respectively, which was not given up to the government of the United States. But there is no such thing here. You, therefore, by a natural and unavoidable implication, give up your rights to the general government.

Your own example furnishes an argument against it. If you give up these powers, without a bill of rights, you will exhibit the most absurd thing to mankind that ever the world saw — a government that has abandoned all its powers — the powers of direct taxation, the sword, and the purse. You have disposed them to Congress, without a bill of rights — without check, limitation, or control. And still you have checks and guards; still you keep barriers — pointed where? Pointed against your weakened, prostrated, enervated state government! You have a bill of rights to defend you against the state government, which is bereaved of all power, and yet you have none against Congress, though in full and exclusive possession of all power! You arm yourselves against the weak and defenceless, and expose yourselves naked to the armed and powerful. Is not this a conduct of unexampled absurdity? What barriers have you to oppose to this most strong, energetic government? To that government you have nothing to oppose. All your defence is given up. This is a real, actual defect. It must strike the mind of every gentleman. When our government was first instituted in Virginia, we declared the common law of England to be in force.

That system of law which has been admired, and has protected us and our ancestors, is excluded by that system. Added to this, we adopted a bill of rights. By this Constitution, some of the best barriers of human rights are thrown away. Is there not an additional reason to have a bill of rights? By the ancient common law, the trial of all facts is decided by a jury of impartial men from the immediate vicinage. This paper speaks of different juries from the common law in criminal cases; and in civil controversies excludes trial by jury altogether. There is, therefore, more occasion for the supplementary check of a bill of rights now than then. Congress, from their general powers, may fully go into business of human legislation. They may legislate, in criminal cases, from treason to the lowest offence — petty larceny. They may define crimes and prescribe punishments. In the definition of crimes, I trust they will be directed by what wise representatives ought to be governed by. But when we come to punishments, no latitude ought to be left, nor dependence put on the virtue of representatives. What says our bill of rights? — "that excessive bail ought not to be required, nor excessive fines imposed, nor cruel and unusual punishments inflicted." Are you not, therefore, now calling on those gentlemen who are to compose Congress, to prescribe trials and define punishments without this control? Will they find sentiments there similar to this bill of rights? You let them loose; you do more — you depart from the genius of your country. That paper tells you that the trial of crimes shall be by jury, and held in the state where the crime shall have been committed. Under this extensive provision, they may proceed in a manner extremely dangerous to liberty: a person accused may be carried from one extremity of the state to another, and be tried, not by an impartial jury of the vicinage, acquainted with his character and the circumstances of the fact, but by a jury unacquainted with both, and who may be biased against him. Is not this sufficient to alarm men? How different is this from the immemorial practice of your British ancestors, and your own! I need not tell you that, by the common law, a number of hundredors were required on a jury, and that afterwards it was sufficient if the jurors came from the same county. With less than this the people of England have never been satisfied. That paper ought to have declared the common law in force.

In this business of legislation, your members of Congress will loose the restriction of not imposing excessive fines, demanding excessive bail, and inflicting cruel and unusual punishments. These are prohibited by your declaration of rights. What has distinguished our ancestors? — That they would not admit of tortures, or cruel and barbarous punishment. But Congress may introduce the practice of the civil law, in preference to that of the common law. They may introduce the practice of France, Spain, and Germany — of torturing, to extort a confession of the crime. They will say that they might as well draw examples from those countries as from Great Britain, and they will tell you that there is such a necessity of strengthening the arm of government, that they must have a criminal equity, and extort confession by torture, in order to punish with still more relentless severity. We are then lost and undone. And can any man think it troublesome, when we can, by a small interference, prevent our rights from being lost? If you will, like the Virginian government, give them knowledge of the extent of the rights retained by the people, and the powers of themselves, they will, if they be honest men, thank you for it. Will they not wish to go on sure grounds? But if you leave them otherwise, they will not know how to proceed; and, being in a state of uncertainty, they will assume rather than give up powers by implication.

A bill of rights may be summed up in a few words. What do they tell us? — That our rights are reserved. Why not say so? Is it because it will consume too much paper? Gentlemen's reasoning against a bill of rights does not satisfy me. Without saying which has the right side, it remains doubtful. A bill of rights is a favorite thing with the Virginians and the people of the other states likewise. It may be their prejudice, but the government ought to suit their geniuses; otherwise, its operation will be unhappy. A bill of rights, even if its necessity be doubtful, will exclude the possibility of dispute; and, with great submission, I think the best way is to have no dispute. In the present Constitution, they are restrained from issuing general warrants to search suspected places, or seize persons not named, without evidence of the commission of a fact, &c. There was certainly some celestial influence governing those who deliberated on that Constitution; for they have, with the most cautious and enlightened circumspection, guarded those indefeasible rights which ought ever to be held sacred! The officers of Congress may come upon you now, fortified with all the terrors of paramount federal authority. Excisemen may come in multitudes; for the limitation of their numbers no man knows. They may, unless the general government be restrained by a bill of rights, or some similar restriction, go into your cellars and rooms, and search, ransack, and measure, every thing you eat, drink, and wear. They ought to be restrained within proper bounds. With respect to the freedom of the press, I need say nothing; for it is hoped that the gentlemen who shall compose Congress will take care to infringe as little as possible the rights of human nature. This will result from their integrity. They should, from prudence, abstain from violating the rights of their constituents. They are not, however, expressly restrained. But whether they will intermeddle with that palladium of our liberties or not, I leave you to determine.

MR. GRAYSON thought it questionable whether rights not given up were reserved. A majority of the states, he observed, had expressly reserved certain important rights by bills of rights, and that in the Confederation there was a clause declaring expressly that every power and right not given up was retained by the states. It was the general sense of America that such a clause which was necessary; otherwise, why did they introduce a clause which was totally unnecessary? It had been insisted, he said, in many parts of America, that a bill of rights was only necessary between a prince and people, and not in such a government as this, which was a compact between the people themselves. This did not satisfy his mind; for so extensive was the power of legislation, in his estimation, that he doubted whether, when it was once given up, *any thing* was retained. He further remarked, that there were some negative clauses in the Constitution, which refuted the doctrine contended for by the other side. For instance; the 2d clause of the 9th section of the 1st article provided that "the privilege of the writ of *habeas corpus* shall not be suspended, unless when, in cases of rebellion or invasion, the public safety may require it." And, by the last clause of the same section, "no title of nobility shall be granted by the United States." Now, if these restrictions had not been here inserted, he asked whether Congress would not most clearly have had a right to suspend that great and valuable right, and to grant titles of nobility. When, in addition to these considerations, he saw they had an indefinite power to provide for the general welfare, he thought there were great reasons to apprehend great dangers. He thought, therefore, that there ought to be a bill of rights.

Elliot, vol. 3, pp. 441–49.

15.2.2.7.c **June 24, 1788**

Mr. HENRY. . . . What is the inference when you enumerate the rights which you are to enjoy? That those not enumerated are relinquished.

. . .

Mr. HENRY. . . . Other essential rights — what are they? The world will say that you intend to give them up. When you go into an enumeration of your rights, and stop that enumeration, the inevitable conclusion is, that what is omitted is intended to be surrendered.

. . .

Mr. MADISON. With respect to the proposition of the honorable gentleman to my left, (Mr. Wythe) gentlemen apprehend that, by enumerating three rights, it implied there were no more. The observations made by a gentleman lately up, on that subject, correspond precisely with my opinion. That resolution declares that the powers granted by the proposed Constitution are the gift of the people, and may be resumed by them when perverted to their oppresion, and every power not granted thereby remains with the people, and at their will. It adds, likewise, that not right, of any denomination, can be cancelled, abridged, restrained, or modified, by the general government, or any of its officers, except in those instances in which power is given by the Constitution for these purposes. There cannot be a more positive and unequivocal declaration of the principle of the adoption — that everything not granted is reserved. This is obviously and self-evidently the case, without the declaration. Can the general government exercise any power not delegated? If an enumeration be made of our rights, will it not be implied that everything omitted is given to the general government? Has not the honorable gentleman himself admitted that an imperfect enumeration is dangerous? Does the Constitution say that they shall not alter the law of descents, or do those things which would subvert the whole system of the state laws? If it did, what was not excepted would be granted. Does it follow, from the omission of such restrictions, that they can exercise powers not delegated? The reverse of the proposition holds. The delegation alone warrants the exercise of any power.

Elliot, vol. 3, pp. 587–88, 594, 620.

15.2.3 PHILADELPHIA CONVENTION

None.

15.2.4 NEWSPAPERS AND PAMPHLETS

15.2.4.1 John DeWitt, October 1787

The Compact itself is a recital upon paper of that proportion of the subject's natural rights, intended to be parted with, for the benefit of adverting to it in case of dispute. Miserable indeed would be the situation of those individual States who have not prefixed to their Constitutions a Bill of Rights, if, as a very respectable, learned Gentleman at the Southward observes, "the People, when they established the powers of legislation under their separate Governments, invested their Representatives with every right and authority which they did not, in explicit terms, reserve; and therefore upon every question, respecting the jurisdiction of the House of Assembly, if the Frame of Government is silent, the jurisdiction is efficient and complete." In other words, those powers which the people by their Constitutions expressly give them, they enjoy by positive grant, and those remaining ones, which they never meant to give them, and which the Constitutions say nothing about, they enjoy by tacit implication, so that by one means and by the other, they became possessed of the whole. — This doctrine is but poorly calculated for the meridian of America, where the nature of compact, the mode of construing them, and the principles upon which society is founded, are so accurately known and universally diffused. That insatiable thirst for unconditional controul over our fellow-creatures, and the facility of sounds to convey essentially different ideas, produced the first Bill of Rights ever prefixed to a Frame of Government. The people, altho' fully sensible that they reserved every title of power they did not expressly grant away, yet afraid that the words made use of, to express those rights so granted might convey more than they originally intended, they chose at the same moment to express in different language those rights which the agreement did not include, and which they never designed to part with, endeavoring thereby to prevent any cause for future altercation and the intrusion into society of that doctrine of tacit implication which has been the favorite theme of every tyrant from the origin of all governments to the present day.

[Boston] American Herald, Storing, vol. 4, p. 22.

15.2.4.2   James Wilson, October 6, 1787

It will be proper however, before I enter into the refutation of the charges that are alledged, to mark the leading descrimination [*sic*] between the state constitutions, and the constitution of the United States. When the people established the powers of legislation under their separate governments, they invested their representatives with every right and authority which they did not in explicit terms reserve; and therefore upon every question, respecting the jurisdiction of the house of assembly, if the frame of government is silent, the jurisdiction is efficient and complete. But in delegating fœderal powers, another criterion was necessarily introduced, and the congressional authority is to be collected, not from tacit implication, but from the positive grant expressed in the instrument of union. Hence it is evident, that in the former case every thing which is not reserved is given, but in the latter the reverse of the proposition prevails, and every thing which is not given, is reserved. This distinction being recognized, will furnish an answer to those who think the omission of a bill of rights, a defect in the proposed constitution: for it would have been superfluous and absurd to have stipulated with a fœderal body of our own creation, that we should enjoy those privileges, of which we are not divested either by the intention or the act, that has brought that body into existence.   Pennsylvania Herald (October 9, 1787), Kaminski & Saladino, vol. 13, pp. 339–40.

15.2.4.3   The Federal Farmer, No. 4, October 12, 1787

DEAR SIR, . . . It is said, that when the people make a constitution, and delegate powers, that all powers not delegated by them to those who govern, is reserved to the people; and that the people, in the present case, have reserved in themselves, and in there [*sic*] state governments, every right and power not expressly given by the federal constitution to those who shall administer the national government. It is said on the other hand, that the people, when they make a constitution, yield all power not expressly reserved to themselves. The truth is, in either case, it is mere matter of opinion, and men usually take either side of the argument, as will best answer their purposes: But the general assumption being, that men who govern, will, in doubtful cases, construe laws and constitutions most favourably for encreasing their own powers; all wise and prudent people, in forming constitutions, have drawn the line, and carefully described the powers parted with and the powers reserved.   Kaminski & Saladino, vol. 14, pp. 44–45.

15.2.4.4   An Old Whig, No. 2, October 17, 1787

MR. PRINTER, . . . The principle is this: that "in *delegating federal powers*, the congressional authority is to be collected, *not from tacit implication*, but from *the positive grant* expressed in the instrument of union," "*that everything which is not given is reserved.*" *If this* be a just representation of the matter, the authority of the several states will be sufficient to protect our liberties from the encroachments of

Congress, without any continental bill of rights; *unless* the powers which are *expressly given* to Congress are *too large*.

[Philadelphia] Independent Gazetteer, Kaminski & Saladino,
vol. 13, p. 400.

15.2.4.5 The Federal Farmer, No. 16, January 20, 1788

. . . We must consider this constitution, when adopted, as the supreme act of the people, and in construing it hereafter, we and our posterity must strictly adhere to the letter and spirit of it, and in no instance depart from them: . . . by the people's now establishing certain fundamental rights, it is strongly implied, that they are of opinion, that they would not otherwise be secured as a part of the federal system, or be regarded in the federal administration as fundamental. . . . — Further, the people, thus establishing some few rights, and remaining totally silent about others similarly circumstanced, the implication indubitably is, that they mean to relinquish the latter, or at least feel indifferent about them. Rights, therefore, inferred from general principles of reason, being precarious and hardly ascertainable in the common affairs of society, and the people, in forming a federal constitution, explicitly shewing they conceive these rights to be thus circumstanced, and accordingly proceed to enumerate and establish some of them, the conclusion will be, that they have established all which they esteem valuable and sacred. On every principle, then, the people especially having began, ought to go through enumerating, and establish particularly all the rights of individuals, which can by any possibility come in question in making and executing federal laws.

Storing, vol. 2, pp. 326–27.

15.2.4.6 The Federalist, No. 84, May 28, 1788

I go further, and affirm that the bills of rights, in the sense and to the extent in which they are contended for, are not only unnecessary in the proposed Constitution, but would even be dangerous. They would contain various exceptions to powers not granted; and, on this very account, would afford a colorable pretext to claim more than were granted. For why declare that things shall not be done which there is no power to do? Why, for instance, should it be said that liberty of the press shall not be restrained, when no power is given by which restrictions may be imposed? I will not contend that such a provision would confer a regulating power; but it is evidence that it would furnish, to men disposed to usurp, a plausible pretense for claiming that power.

Kaminski & Saladino, vol. 18, p. 130.

15.2.5 LETTERS AND DIARIES

15.2.5.1 George Washington to President of Congress, September 17, 1787

. . . Individuals entering into society, must give up a share of liberty to preserve the rest. The magnitude of the sacrifice must depend, as well on situation and circumstance, as on the object to be obtained. It is at all times difficult to draw with precision the line between those rights which must be surrendered, and those which may be reserved; and on the present occasion this difficulty was encreased [*sic*] by a difference among the several States as to their situation, extent, habits, and particular interests.

Kaminiski and Saladino, vol. 13, p. 211.

15.2.5.2   James Madison to Thomas Jefferson, October 24, 1787

. . . A reform therefore which does not make provision for private rights, must be materially defective. The restraints agst. paper emissions, and violations of contracts are not sufficient. Supposing them to be effectual as far as they go, they are short of the mark. Injustice may be effected by such an infinitude of legislative expedients, that where the disposition exists it can only be controuled by some provision which reaches all cases whatsoever. The partial provision made, supposes the disposition which will evade it. . . . The great desideratum in Government is, so to modify the sovereignty as that it may be sufficiently neutral between different parts of the Society to controul one part from invading the rights of another, and at the same time sufficiently controuled itself, from setting up an interest adverse to that of the entire Society. . . .

Kaminski & Saladino, vol. 13, pp. 447, 449.

15.2.5.3   Thomas Jefferson to James Madison, December 20, 1787

To say, as mr Wilson does that a bill of rights was not necessary because all is reserved in the case of the general government which is not given, while in the particular ones all is given which is not reserved, might do for the Audience to whom it was addressed, but is surely gratis dictum, opposed by strong inferences from the body of the instrument, as well as from the omission of the clause of our present confederation which had declared that in express terms. It was a hard conclusion to say because there has been no uniformity among the states as to cases triable by jury, because some have been so incautious as to abandon this mode of trial, therefore the more prudent states shall be reduced to the same level of calamity. It would have been much more just and wise to have concluded the other way that as most of the states had judiciously preserved this palladium, those who had wandered should be brought back to it, and to have established general right instead of wrong. Let me add that a bill of rights is what the people are entitled to against every government on earth, general or particular, and what no just government should refuse, or rest on inference.

Boyd, vol. 12, p. 440.

15.2.5.4   George Washington to Marquis de Lafayette, April 28, 1788

. . . For example: there was not a member of the convention, I believe, who had the least objection to what is contended for by the Advocates for a *Bill of Rights* and *Tryal by Jury*. The first, where the people evidently retained every thing which they did not in express terms give up, was considered nugatory as you will find to have been more fully explained by Mr. Wilson and others: — And as to the second, it was only the difficulty of establishing a mode which should not interfere with the fixed modes of any of the States, that induced the Convention to leave it, as a matter of future adjustment.

Kaminski and Saladino, vol. 17, p. 235.

15.2.5.5 James Madison to Thomas Jefferson, October 17, 1788

. . . It is true nevertheless that not a few, particularly in Virginia have contended for the proposed alterations from the most honorable & patriotic motives; and that among the advocates for the Constitution, there are some who wish for further guards to public liberty & individual rights. As far as these may consist of a constitutional declaration of the most essential rights, it is probable they will be added; though there are many who think such addition unnecessary, and not a few who think it misplaced in such a Constitution. There is scarce any point on which the party in opposition is so much divided as to its importance and its propriety. My own opinion has always been in favor of a bill of rights; provided it be so framed as not to imply powers not meant to be included in the enumeration. At the same time I have never thought the omission a material defect, nor been anxious to supply it even by *subsequent* amendment, for any other reason than that it is anxiously desired by others. I have favored it because I supposed it might be of use, and if properly executed could not be of disservice. I have not viewed it in an important light 1. because I conceive that in a certain degree, though not in the extent argued by Mr. Wilson, the rights in question are reserved by the manner in which the federal powers are granted. 2. because there is great reason to fear that a positive declaration of some of the most essential rights could not be obtained in the requisite latitude. I am sure that the rights of Conscience in particular, if submitted to public definition would be narrowed much more than they are likely ever to be by an assumed power. One of the objections in New England was that the Constitution by prohibiting religious tests opened a door for Jews Turks & infidels. 3. because the limited powers of the federal Government and the jealousy of the subordinate Governments, afford a security which has not existed in the case of the State Governments, and exists in no other. 4 because experience proves the inefficacy of a bill of rights on those occasions when its controul is most needed. Repeated violations of these parchment barriers have been committed by overbearing majorities in every State.

Rutland & Hobson, vol. 11, p. 297.

15.2.5.6 Thomas Jefferson to James Madison, March 15, 1789

. . . In the arguments in favor of a declaration of rights, you omit one which has great weight to me, the legal check which it puts into the hands of the judiciary. This is a body, which if rendered independent, and kept strictly to their own department merits great confidence for their learning and integrity. . . . The Declaration of rights is like all other human blessings alloyed with some inconveniences, and not accomplishing fully it's [*sic*] object. But the good in this instance vastly overweighs the evil. I cannot refrain from making short answers to the objections which your letter states to have been raised. I. That the rights in question are reserved by the manner in which the federal powers are granted. Answer. a constitutive act may certainly be so formed as to need no declaration of rights. The act itself has the force of a declaration as far as it goes: and if it goes to all material points nothing more is wanting.

Boyd, vol. 14, pp. 659–60.

15.2.5.7   Tench Coxe to James Madison, June 18, 1789

I observe you have brought forward the amendments you proposed to the federal Constitution. I have given them a very careful perusal, and have attended particularly to their reception by the public. The most decided friends of the constitution admit (generally) that they will meliorate the government by removing some points of litigation and jealousy, and by heightening and strengthening the barriers between necessary power and indispensable liberty. . . . Those who are honest are well pleased at the footing on which the press, liberty of conscience, original right & power, trial by jury &ca. are rested.

Veit, p. 253.

15.2.5.8   Richard Parker to Richard Henry Lee, July 6, 1789

I observe the slip of the newspaper sent me and know the design, but I still think a Bill of rights not necessary here. . . . However I have no objection to such a bill of Rights as has been proposed by Mr. Maddison [*sic*] because we declare that we do not abridge our Rights by the reservation that we retain all that we have not specifically given. . . .

Veit, p. 260.

15.2.5.9   Henry Gibbs to Roger Sherman, July 16, 1789

. . . All Ambiguity of Expression certainly ought to be remov'd; Liberty of Conscience in religious matters, right of trial by Jury, Liberty of the Press &c. may perhaps be more explicitly secur'd to the Subject & a general reservation made to the States respectively of all the powers not expressly delegated to the general Government. . . .

Veit, p. 263.

15.2.5.10   William L. Smith to Edward Rutledge, August 10, 1789

. . . I shall support the Amendmts [*sic*] proposed to the Constitution that any exception to the powers of Congress shall not be so construed as to give it any powers not *expressly* given, & the enumeration of certain rights shall not be so construed as to deny others retained by the people — & the powers not delegated by this Constn. nor prohibited by it to the States, are reserved to the States respectively. . . .

Veit, p. 273.

15.2.5.11   James Madison to George Washington, December 5, 1789

[Randolph's] principle objection was pointed agst. the word '*retained*,' in the eleventh proposed amendment [Ninth Amendment], and his argument if I understood it applied in this manner — that as the rights declared in the first ten of the proposed amendments were not all that a free people would require the exercise of, and that as there was no criterion by which it could be determined whether any other particular right was retained or not, it would be more safe and more consistent with the spirit of the 1st & 17th amendts. proposed by Virginia that this reservation agst. constructive power, should operate rather as a provision agst. extending the powers of Congs. by their own authority, than a protection to rights reducible to no definitive certainty. But others, among whom I am one, see not the force of this distinction. . . .

If a line can be drawn between the powers granted and the rights retained, it would seem to be the same thing whether the latter be secured by declaring that they shall not be abridged, or that the former shall not be extended. If no such line can be drawn, a declaration in either form would amount to nothing.

Hobson & Rutland, vol. 12, pp. 458–59.

15.3 DISCUSSION OF RIGHTS

15.3.1 TREATISES

15.3.1.1 William Blackstone, 1765

For the principal aim of society is to protect individuals in the enjoyment of those absolute rights, which were vested in them by the immutable laws of nature; but which could not be preserved in peace without that mutual assistance and intercourse, which is gained by the institution of friendly and social communities. Hence it follows, that the first and primary end of human laws is to maintain and regulate these *absolute* rights of individuals. Such rights as are social and *relative* result from, and are posterior to, the formation of states and societies: so that to maintain and regulate these, is clearly a subsequent consideration. And therefore the principle view of human laws is, or ought to be, to explain, protect, and enforce such rights as are absolute. . . .

The absolute rights of man, considered as a free agent, endowed with discernment to know good from evil, and with power of choosing those measures which appear to him to be most desirable, are usually summed up in one general appellation, and denominated the natural liberty of mankind.

Commentaries, bk. 1, ch. 1; vol. 1, p. 120.

15.3.2 CASELAW

None.

Chapter 16

AMENDMENT X

RESERVATION OF POWERS CLAUSE

16.1 TEXTS

16.1.1 DRAFTS IN FIRST CONGRESS

16.1.1.1 Proposal by Madison in House, June 8, 1789

16.1.1.1.a   Eighthly. That immediately after article 6th [of the Constitution], be inserted, as article 7th, the clauses following, to wit:

The powers delegated by this constitution, are appropriated to the departments to which they are respectively distributed: so that the legislative department shall never exercise the powers vested in the executive or judicial; nor the executive exercise the powers vested in the legislative or judcial; [sic] nor the judicial exercise the powers vested in the legislative or executive departments.

The powers not delegated by this constitution, nor prohibited by it to the states, are reserved to the States respectively.

Congressional Register, June 8, 1789, vol. 1, p. 429.

16.1.1.1.b   *Eighthly.* That immediately after article 6th [of the Constitution], be inserted, as article 7th, the clauses following, to wit:

The powers delegated by this constitution, and [sic; are] appropriated to the departments to which they are respective [sic] distributed: so that the legislatively [sic] department shall never exercise the powers vested in the executive or judicial; nor the executive exercise the powers vested in the legislative or judicial; nor the judicial exercise the powers vested in the legislative or executive departments.

The powers not delegated by this constitution, nor prohibited by it to the states, are reserved to the states respectively.

Daily Advertiser, June 12, 1789, p. 2, col. 2.

16.1.1.1.c   *Eighth.* That immediately after article 6th [of the Constitution], be inserted, as article 7th, the clause following, to wit:

The powers delegated by this constitution, and [sic; are] appropriated to the departments to which they are respectively distributed: so that the legislatively [sic] department shall never exercise the powers vested in the executive or judicial; [nor the executive exercise the powers vested in the legislative or judicial;] nor the judicial exercise the powers vested in the legislative or executive departments.

New-York Daily Gazette, June 13, 1789, p. 574, col. 4.

16.1.1.2 Proposal by Sherman to House Committee of Eleven, July 21–28, 1789

[Amendment] 11 The legislative, executive and judiciary powers vested by the Constitution in the respective branches of the government of the united States, shall be exercised according to the distribution therein made, so that neither of said branches shall assume or exercise any of the powers peculiar to either of the other branches.

And the powers not delegated to the government of the united States by the Constitution, nor prohibited by it to the particular States, are retained by the States respectively. nor Shall any the exercise power by the government of the united States the particular instances here in enumerated by way of caution be construed to imply the contrary.

Madison Papers, DLC.

16.1.1.3 House Committee of Eleven Report, July 28, 1789

"Immediately after ART. 6, the following to be inserted as ART. 7."

"The powers delegated by this Constitution to the government of the United States, shall be exercised as therein appropriated, so that the Legislative shall never exercise the powers vested in the Executive or the Judicial; nor the Executive the powers vested in the Legislative or Judicial; nor the Judicial the powers vested in the Legislative or Executive."

"The powers not delegated by this Constitution, nor prohibited by it to the States, are reserved to the States respectively."

Broadside Collection, DLC.

16.1.1.4 House Consideration, August 18, 1789

The 8th proposition in the words following, was considered, "Immediately after art. 6, the following to be inserted as art. 7."

16.1.1.4.a "The powers delegated by this constitution to the government of the United States, shall be exercised as therein appropriated, so that the legislative shall not exercise the powers vested in the executive or the judicial; nor the executive the power vested in the legislative or judicial; nor the judicial the powers vested in the legislative or executive."

Congressional Register, August 18, 1789, vol. 2, pp. 233–34
("On the motion being put, the proposition was carried.").

16.1.1.4.b Seventeenth amendment — Immediately after Art. 6, the following to be inserted as Art. 7. "The powers delegated by this Constitution, to the government of the United States shall be exercised as therein appropriated, so that the Legislative shall never exercise the powers vested in the Executive or the Judicial; nor the Executive the powers vested in the Legislative or Judicial; nor the Judicial the powers vested in the Legislative or Executive."

Daily Advertiser, August 19, 1789, p. 2, col. 3
("This was agreed to.").

16.1.1.4.c 17th amendment: Immediately after art. 6, the following to be inserted as art. 7. "The powers delegated by this Constitution, to the government of the United States shall be exercised as therein appropriated, so that the Legislative shall never exercise the powers vested in the Executive or the Judicial; nor the Executive the powers vested in the Legislative or Judicial; nor the Judicial the powers vested in the Legislative or Executive."

> Gazette of the U.S., August 22, 1789, p. 250, col. 1
> ("[This amendment] was finally carried.").

16.1.1.5 House Consideration, August 18, 1789

16.1.1.5.a The 9th proposition in the words following was considered, "The powers not delegated by the constitution, nor prohibited by it to the states, are reserved to the states respectively."

> Congressional Register, August 18, 1789, vol. 2, p. 234.

16.1.1.5.b Eighteenth amendment — "The powers not delegated by this Constitution, nor prohibited by it to the States, are reserved to the States respectively."

> Daily Advertiser, August 19, 1789, p. 2, col. 3.

16.1.1.5.c 18th Amendment: "The powers not delegated by this Constitution, nor prohibited by it to the States, are reserved to the States respectively."

> Gazette of the U.S., August 22, 1789, p. 250, col. 1.

16.1.1.6 Motion by Tucker in House, August 18, 1789

16.1.1.6.a   Mr. TUCKER

Proposed to amend the proposition by prefixing to it, "all powers being derived from the people." . . . He extended his motion also, to add the word "expressly" so as to read "The powers not expressly delegated by this constitution."

> Congressional Register, August 18, 1789, vol. 2, p. 234
> ("Mr. TUCKER's motion being negatived. . . .").

16.1.1.6.b Mr. TUCKER proposed an introductory clause to this amendment, viz. *all power being derived from the people.*

> Gazette of the U.S., August 22, 1789, p. 250
> ("This motion was negatived.").

16.1.1.7 Motion by Carroll or Gerry in House, August 18, 1789

16.1.1.7.a Mr. CARROLL proposed to add to the end of the proposition, "or to the people," this was agreed to.

> Congressional Register, August 18, 1789, vol. 2, p. 235.

16.1.1.7.b Mr. GERRY then proposed to add, after the word "States," *and people thereof.*

> Gazette of the U.S., August 22, 1789, p. 250, col. 1
> ("The motion was negatived, and the amendment agreed to.").

16.1.1.8 Motion by Gerry in House, August 21, 1789

The 9th proposition, mr. Gerry proposed to amend by inserting the word "expressly" so as to read the powers not expressly delegated by the constitution, nor prohibited to the states, are reserved to the states respectively or to the people. . . .

> Congressional Register, August 21, 1789, vol. 2, pp. 243–44
> ("He was supported in this by one fifth of the members present,
> whereupon they were taken.").

16.1.1.9 Motion by Sherman in House, August 21, 1789

Mr. SHERMAN

Moved to alter the last clause so as to make it read, the powers not delegated to the United States, by the constitution, nor prohibited by it to the states, are reserved to the states respectively, or to the people.

Congressional Register, August 21, 1789, vol. 2, p. 244
("This motion was adopted without debate.").[1]

16.1.1.10 House Resolution, August 24, 1789

ARTICLE THE SIXTEENTH.

The powers delegated by the Constitution to the government of the United States, shall be exercised as therein appropriated, so that the Legislative shall never exercise the powers vested in the Executive or Judicial; nor the Executive the powers vested in the Legislative or Judicial; nor the Judicial the powers vested in the Legislative or Executive.

ARTICLE THE SEVENTEENTH.

The powers not delegated by the Constitution, nor prohibited by it, to the States, are reserved to the States respectively. House Pamphlet, RG 46, DNA.

16.1.1.11 Senate Consideration, August 25, 1789

16.1.1.11.a   The Resolve of the House of Representatives of the 24th of August, upon certain "Articles to be proposed to the Legislatures of the several States as Amendments to the Constitution of the United States" was read as followeth: . . .

Article the sixteenth

"The powers delegated by the Constitution to [the Government of the United States, shall be exercised as therein appropriated, so that the Legislative shall never exercise the powers vested in the Executive or Judicial; nor the Executive the powers vested in the Legislative or Judicial;] nor the Judicial the powers vested in the Legislative or Executive.

Article the seventeenh [sic]

"The powers not delegated by the Constitution, nor prohibited by it to the States, are reserved to the States respectively;"

Rough SJ, pp. 219–20 [material in brackets not legible].

16.1.1.11.b   The Resolve of the House of Representatives of the 24th of August, was read as followeth:

. . .

Article the Sixteenth.

"The powers delegated by the Constitution to the Government of the United States, shall be exercised as therein appropriated, so that the Legislative shall never exercise the powers vested in the Executive or Judicial; nor the Executive the

---

[1]On August 22, 1789, the following motion was agreed to:
ORDERED, That it be referred to a committee of three, to prepare and report a proper arrangement of, and introduction to the articles of amendment to the Constitution of the United States, as agreed to by the House; and that Mr. Benson, Mr. Sherman, and Mr. Sedgwick be of the said committee.
HJ, p. 112.

powers vested in the Legislative or Judicial; nor the Judicial the powers vested in the Legislative or Executive.

Article the Seventeenh. [*sic*]

"The powers not delegated by the Constitution, nor prohibited by it to the States, are reserved to the States respectively;"

Smooth SJ, pp. 196–97.

16.1.1.11.c   The Resolve of the House of Representatives of the 24th of August, was read as followeth:

. . .

ARTICLE THE SIXTEENTH.

"The powers delegated by the Constitution to the Government of the United States, shall be exercised as therein appropriated, so that the Legislative shall never exercise the powers vested in the Executive or Judicial; nor the Executive the powers vested in the Legislative or Judicial; nor the Judicial the powers vested in the Legislative or Executive.

ARTICLE THE SEVENTEENH. [*sic*]

"The powers not delegated by the Constitution, nor prohibited by it to the States, are reserved to the States respectively;"

Printed SJ, p. 106.

16.1.1.12 Further Senate Consideration, September 7, 1789

16.1.1.12.a   On Motion to adopt the sixteenth Article of Amendments to the Constitution of the United States, proposed by the House of Representatives.

Rough SJ, p. 259 ("It passed in the negative.").

16.1.1.12.b   On motion, To adopt the sixteenth Article of Amendments to the Constitution of the United States, proposed by the House of Representatives —

Smooth SJ, p. 231 ("It passed in the Negative.").

16.1.1.12.c   On motion, To adopt the sixteenth Article of Amendments to the Constitution of the United States, proposed by the House of Representatives —

Printed SJ, p. 122 ("It passed in the Negative.").

16.1.1.13 Further Senate Consideration, September 7, 1789

16.1.1.13.a   On Motion to amend the seventeenth Article, by inserting the word, "<u>ex-pressly</u>", before the word "delegated" —

Rough SJ, p. 259 ("It passed in the negative.").

16.1.1.13.b   On motion, To amend the seventeenth Article, by inserting the word "Ex-pressly", before the word "delegated" —

Smooth SJ, p. 231 ("It passed in the Negative.").

16.1.1.13.c   On motion, To amend the seventeenth Article, by inserting the word "EX-PRESSLY", before the word "delegated" —

Printed SJ, p. 233 ("It passed in the Negative.").

16.1.1.14 Further Senate Consideration, September 7, 1789

16.1.1.14.a   On motion, To adopt the seventeenth Article of amendments to the Constitution of the United States, proposed by the House of Representatives, to read as follows,

"The powers not delegated <u>to the United States</u> by the Constitution, nor prohibited by it, to the States, are reserved to the States respectively, <u>or to the People</u>."

Rough SJ, pp. 259–60 ("It passed in the affirmative.").

16.1.1.14.b   On motion, To adopt the seventeenth article of Amendments to the Constitution of the United States, proposed by the House of Representatives, to read as follows,

"The powers not delegated to the United States by the Constitution, nor prohibited by it to the States, are reserved to the States respectively, or to the people,"

Smooth SJ, p. 231 ("It passed in the Affirmative.").

16.1.1.14.c   On motion, To adopt the seventeenth article of Amendments to the Constitution of the United States, proposed by the House of Representatives, to read as follows,

"The powers not delegated to the United States by the Constitution, nor prohibited by it to the States, are reserved to the States respectively, or to the people,"

Printed SJ, p. 123 ("It passed in the Affirmative.").

16.1.1.14.d   that the Senate do

Resolved ∧ <u>not</u> t̶o̶ concur with the House of Representatives in
Article sixteenth.

that the Senate do

Resolved t̶o̶ ∧ concur with the House of Representatives in
Article seventeenth.

to read as follows:

"The powers not delegated to <u>the United States</u> by the Constitution, nor prohibited by it, to the States, are reserved to the States respectively, <u>or to the people</u>."

Senate MS, pp. 4–5, RG 46, DNA.

16.1.1.15 Further Senate Consideration, September 9, 1789

16.1.1.15.a   On motion to number the remaining articles agreed to by the Senate tenth, eleventh and twelfth instead of the numbers affixed by the Resolve of the House of Representatives.

Rough SJ, p. 277 ("It passed in the affirmative.";
motion renumbered seventeenth article as twelfth article).

16.1.1.15.b   On motion, To number the remaining articles agreed to by the Senate, tenth, eleventh and twelfth, instead of the numbers affixed by the Resolve of the House of Representatives —

Smooth SJ, p. 246 ("It passed in the Affirmative.";
motion renumbered seventeenth article as twelfth article).

16.1.1.15.c   On motion, To number the remaining Articles agreed to by the Senate, tenth, eleventh and twelfth, instead of the numbers affixed by the Resolve of the House of Representatives —

Printed SJ, p. 131 ("It passed in the Affirmative.";
motion renumbered seventeenth article as twelfth article).

16.1.1.15.d   To erase the word — "Seventeenth" — & insert Twelfth.

To insert in the Seventeenth Article after the word "delegated" — to the United States. — &

To insert at the end of the same article — or to the people; —

Ellsworth MS, p. 4, RG 46, DNA.

16.1.1.16   Senate Resolution, September 9, 1789

ARTICLE THE TWELFTH.

The powers not delegated to the United States by the Constitution, nor prohibited by it to the States, are reserved to the States respectively, or to the people.

Senate Pamphlet, RG 46, DNA.

16.1.1.17   Further House Consideration, September 21, 1789

RESOLVED, That this House doth agree to the second, fourth, eighth, twelfth, thirteenth, sixteenth, eighteenth, nineteenth, twenty-fifth, and twenty-sixth amendments, and doth disagree to the first, third, fifth, sixth, seventh, ninth, tenth, eleventh, fourteenth, fifteenth, seventeenth, twentieth, twenty-first, twenty-second, twenty-third, and twenty-fourth amendments proposed by the Senate to the said articles, two thirds of the members present concurring on each vote.

RESOLVED, That a conference be desired with the Senate on the subject matter of the amendments disagreed to, and that Mr. Madison, Mr. Sherman, and Mr. Vining, be appointed managers at the same on the part of this House.

HJ, p. 146.

16.1.1.18   Further Senate Consideration, September 21, 1789

16.1.1.18.a   A message from the House of Representatives —

Mr. Beckley, their Clerk, brought up a Resolve of the House of this date, to agree to the 2nd, 4th, 8th, 12th, 13th, 16th, 18th, 19th, 25th, and 26th Amendments proposed by the Senate, "To articles of Amendment to be proposed to the Legislatures of the several States, as Amendments to the Constitution of the United States," and to disagree to the 1st, 3d, 5th, 6th, 7th, 9th, 10th, 11th, 14th, 15th, 17th, 20th, 21st, 22d, 23d, and 24th amendments: Two thirds of the members present concurring on each vote: And "That a conference be desired with the Senate on the subject matter of the amendments disagreed to," and that Mr. Madison, Mr. Sherman, and Mr. Vining, be appointed managers of the same, on the part of the House of Representatives —

And he withdrew.

Smooth SJ, pp. 265–66.

16.1.1.18.b   A message from the House of Representatives —

Mr. Beckley, their Clerk, brought up a Resolve of the House of this date, to agree to the 2d, 4th, 8th, 12th, 13th, 16th, 18th, 19th, 25th, and 26th Amendments proposed by the Senate, "To Articles of Amendment to be proposed to the Legislatures of the several States, as Amendments to the Constitution of the United States," and to disagree to the 1st, 3d, 5th, 6th, 7th, 9th, 10th, 11th, 14th, 15th, 17th, 20th, 21st, 22d, 23d, and 24th Amendments: Two thirds of the members present concurring on each vote: And "That a conference be desired with the Senate on the subject matter of the Amendments disagreed to," and that Mr. Madison, Mr. Sherman, and Mr. Vining, be appointed managers of the same, on the part of the House of Representatives —

And he withdrew.

Printed SJ, pp. 141–42.

16.1.1.19 Further Senate Consideration, September 21, 1789

16.1.1.19.a The Senate proceeded to consider the Message of the House of Representatives disagreeing to the Amendments made by the Senate "To Articles to be proposed to the Legislatures of the several States, as Amendments to the Constitution of the United States" And

RESOLVED, That the Senate do recede from their third Amendment, and do insist on all the others.

RESOLVED, That the Senate do concur with the House of Representatives in a conference on the subject matter of disagreement on the said Articles of Amendment, and that Mr. Ellsworth Mr. Carroll and Mr. Paterson be managers of the conference on the part of the Senate.

Smooth SJ, p. 267.

16.1.1.19.b The Senate proceeded to consider the message of the House of Representatives disagreeing to the Amendments made by the Senate "To Articles to be proposed to the Legislatures of the several States, as Amendments to the Constitution of the United States" — And

RESOLVED, That the Senate do recede from their third Amendment, and do insist on all the others.

RESOLVED, That the Senate do concur with the House of Representatives in a conference on the subject matter of disagreement on the said Articles of Amendment, and that Mr. Ellsworth, Mr. Carroll, and Mr. Paterson be managers of the conference on the part of the Senate.

Printed SJ, p. 142.

16.1.1.20 Conference Committee Report, September 24, 1789

[T]hat it will be proper for the House of Representatives to agree to the said Amendments proposed by the Senate, with an Amendment to their fifth Amendment, so that the third Article shall read as follows: "Congress shall make no Law respecting an establishment of Religion, or prohibiting the free exercise thereof; or abridging the freedom of Speech, or of the Press; or the right of the people peaceably to assemble and to petition the Government for a redress of grievances;" And with an Amendment to the fourteenth Amendment proposed by the Senate, so that the eighth Article, as numbered in the Amendments proposed by the Senate, shall read as follows "In all criminal prosecutions, the accused shall enjoy the right to a speedy & publick trial by an impartial jury of the district wherein the crime shall have been committed, as the district shall have been previously ascertained by law, and to be informed of the nature and cause of the accusation; to be confronted with the witnesses against him, and to have com

to pulsory process for obtaining witnesses against him in his favour, & ∧ have the assistance of counsel for his defence."

Conference MS, RG 46, DNA (Ellsworth's handwriting).

16.1.1.21 House Consideration of Conference Committee Report, September 24 [25], 1789

RESOLVED, That this House doth recede from their disagreement to the first, third, fifth, sixth, seventh, ninth, tenth, eleventh, fourteenth, fifteenth, seventeenth, twentieth, twenty-first, twenty-second, twenty-third, and twenty-fourth amendments, insisted on by the Senate: PROVIDED, That the two articles which by the amendments of the Senate are now proposed to be inserted as the third and eighth articles, shall be amended to read as followeth;

Article the third. "Congress shall make no law respecting an establishment of religion, or prohibiting the free exercise thereof; or abridging the freedom of speech, or of the press; or the right of the people peaceably to assemble, and to petition the government for a redress of grievances."

Article the eighth. "In all criminal prosecutions, the accused shall enjoy the right to a speedy and public trial by an impartial jury of the state and district wherein the crime shall have been committed, which district shall have been previously ascertained by law, and to be informed of the nature and cause of the accusation, to be confronted with the witnesses against him, to have compulsory process for obtaining witnesses in his favor, and to have the assistance of council for his defence."

> HJ, p. 152 ("On the question, that the House do agree to the alteration and amendment of the eighth article, in manner aforesaid, It was resolved in the affirmative. Ayes 37 Noes 14").

16.1.1.22 Senate Consideration of Conference Committee Report, September 24, 1789

16.1.1.22.a   Mr. Ellsworth, on behalf of the managers of the conference on "articles to be proposed to the several States as Amendments to the Constitution of the United States," reported as follows:

That it will be proper for the House of Representatives to agree to the said amendments proposed by the Senate, with an Amendment to their fifth Amendment, so that the third Article shall read as follows: "Congress shall make no law respecting an establishment of Religion, or prohibiting the free exercise thereof; or abridging the freedom of Speech, or of the Press; or the right of the people peaceably to assemble and petition the Government for a redress of Grievances;" And with an Amendment to the fourteenth Amendment proposed by the Senate, so that the eighth article, as numbered in the Amendments proposed by the Senate, shall read as follows; "In all criminal prosecutions, the accused shall enjoy the right to a speedy and public trial by an impartial Jury of the district wherein the Crime shall have been committed, as the district shall have been previously ascertained by law, and to be informed of the nature and cause of the accusation, to be confronted with the witnesses against him, and to have compulsory process for obtaining witnesses in his favor, and to have the assistance of Counsel for defence."

> Smooth SJ, pp. 272–73.

16.1.1.22.b   Mr. Ellsworth, on behalf of the managers of the conference on "Articles to be proposed to the several States as Amendments to the Constitution of the United States," reported as follows:

That it will be proper for the House of Representatives to agree to the said

Amendments proposed by the Senate, with an Amendment to their fifth Amendment, so that the third Article shall read as follows: "Congress shall make no Law RESPECTING AN ESTABLISHMENT OF RELIGION, or prohibiting the free exercise thereof; or abridging the freedom of Speech, or of the Press; or the right of the People peaceably to assemble and petition the Government for a redress of Grievances;" And with an Amendment to the fourteenth Amendment proposed by the Senate, so that the eighth Article, as numbered in the Amendments proposed by the Senate, shall read as follows; "In all criminal prosecutions, the accused shall enjoy the right to a speedy and public trial BY AN IMPARTIAL JURY OF THE DISTRICT WHEREIN THE CRIME SHALL HAVE BEEN COMMITTED, AS THE DISTRICT SHALL HAVE BEEN PREVIOUSLY ASCERTAINED BY LAW, and to be informed of the nature and cause of the accusation, to be confronted with the witnesses against him, and to have compulsory process for obtaining witnesses in his favor, and to have the assistance of Counsel for defence."

Printed SJ, p. 145.

16.1.1.23   Further Senate Consideration of Conference Committee Report, September 24, 1789

16.1.1.23.a   A Message from the House of Representatives —

Mr. Beckley, their Clerk, brought up the Amendments to the "Articles to be proposed to the Legislatures of the several States, as Amendments to the Constitution of the United States;" and informed the Senate, that the House of Representatives had receded from their disagreement to the 1st, 3d, 5th, 6th, 7th, 9th, 10th, 11th, 14th, 15th, 17th, 20th, 21st, 22d, 23d, and 24th Amendments, insisted on by the Senate: Provided that the "Two Articles, which by the Amendments of the Senate are now proposed to be inserted as the third and eighth Articles," shall be amended to read as followeth:

Article the Third. "Congress shall make no Law respecting an establishment of Religion, or prohibiting the free exercise thereof; or abridging the freedom of Speech, or of the Press; or the right of the people peaceably to assemble, and petition the Government for a redress of Grievances."

Article the Eighth. "In all criminal prosecutions the accused shall enjoy the right to a speedy and public trial by an impartial Jury of the State and District, wherein the crime shall have been committed, which District shall have been previously ascertained by law, and to be informed of the nature and cause of the accusation, to be confronted with the witnesses against him, and to have compulsory process for obtaining witnesses in his favor, and to have the assistance of Counsel for his defence."

Smooth SJ, pp. 278–79.

16.1.1.23.b   A Message from the House of Representatives —

Mr. Beckley, their Clerk, brought up the Amendments to the "Articles to be proposed to the Legislatures of the several States, as Amendments to the Constitution of the United States;" and informed the Senate, that the House of Representatives had receded from their disagreement to the 1st, 3d, 5th, 6th, 7th, 9th, 10th, 11th, 14th, 15th, 17th, 20th, 21st, 22d, 23d, and 24th Amendments, insisted on by the Senate: Provided that the "Two Articles, which by the Amendments of the

Senate are now proposed to be inserted as the third and eighth Articles," shall be amended to read as followeth:

Article the Third. "Congress shall make no Law respecting an establishment of Religion, or prohibiting the free exercise thereof; or abridging the freedom of Speech, or of the Press; or the right of the People peaceably to assemble, and petition the Government for a redress of Grievances."

Article the Eighth. "In all criminal prosecutions the accused shall enjoy the right to a speedy and public trial by an impartial Jury of the State and District, wherein the crime shall have been committed, which District shall have been previously ascertained by law, and to be informed of the nature and cause of the accusation, to be confronted with the witnesses against him, and to have compulsory process for obtaining witnesses in his favor, and to have the assistance of Counsel for his defence."

Printed SJ, p.148.

16.1.1.24 Further Senate Consideration of Conference Committee Report, September 25, 1789

16.1.1.24.a   The Senate proceeded to consider the Message from the House of Representatives of the 24th, with Amendments to the Amendments of the Senate, to "Articles to be proposed to the Legislatures of the several States, as Amendments to the Constitution of the United States" — And

RESOLVED, That the Senate do concur in the Amendments proposed by the House of Representatives, to the Amendments of the Senate. Smooth SJ, p. 283.

16.1.1.24.b   The Senate proceeded to consider the Message from the House of Representatives of the 24th, with Amendments to the Amendments of the Senate, to "Articles to be proposed to the Legislatures of the several States, as Amendments to the Constitution of the United States" — And

RESOLVED, That the Senate do concur in the Amendments proposed by the House of Representatives, to the Amendments of the Senate.

Printed SJ, pp. 150–51.

16.1.1.25 Agreed Resolution, September 25, 1789

16.1.1.25.a   Article the Twelfth.

The powers not delegated to the United States by the Constitution, nor prohibited by it to the States, are reserved to the States respectively, or to the people.

Smooth SJ, Appendix, p. 294.

16.1.1.25.b   ARTICLE THE TWELFTH.

The powers not delegated to the United States by the Constitution, nor prohibited by it to the States, are reserved to the States respectively, or to the people.

Printed SJ, Appendix, p. 164.

16.1.1.26 Enrolled Resolution, September 28, 1789

Article the Twelfth. . . . The powers not delegated to the United States by the Constitution, nor prohibited by it to the States, are reserved to the States respectively, or to the people.

Enrolled Resolutions, RG 11, DNA.

16.1.1.27 **Printed Versions**

16.1.1.27.a   ART. X. The powers not delegated to the United States by the Constitution, nor prohibited by it to the States, are reserved to the States respectively or to the people.

Statues at Large, vol. 1, p. 21–22.

16.1.1.27.b   ART. XII. The powers not delegated to the United States by the Constitution, nor prohibited by it to the States, are reserved to the States respectively, or to the people.

Statutes at Large, vol. 1, p. 98.

16.1.2 PROPOSALS FROM THE STATE CONVENTIONS

16.1.2.1 **Maryland Minority, April 26, 1788**

1. That congress shall exercise no power but what is expressly delegated by this constitution.

Maryland Gazette, May 1, 1788 (committee majority).

16.1.2.2 **Massachusetts, February 6, 1788**

First, That it be explicitly declared that all Powers not expressly delegated by the aforesaid Constitution are reserved to the several States to be by them exercised.

State Ratifications, RG 11, DNA.

16.1.2.3 **New Hampshire, June 21, 1788**

First that it be Explicitly declared that all Powers not expressly & particularly Delegated by the aforesaid Constitution are reserved to the several States to be, by them Exercised. —

State Ratifications, RG 11, DNA.

16.1.2.4 **New York, July 26, 1788**

That all Power is originally vested in and consequently derived from the People, and that Government is instituted by them for their common Interest Protection and Security.

That the enjoyment of Life, Liberty and the pursuit of Happiness are essential rights which every Government ought to respect and preserve.

That the Powers of Government may be reassumed by the People, whensoever it shall become necessary to their Happiness; that every Power, Jurisdiction and right, which is not by the said Constitution clearly delegated to the Congress of the United States, or the departments of the Government thereof, remains to the People of the several States, or to their respective State Governments to whom they may have granted the same; And that those Clauses in the said Constitution, which declare, that Congress shall not have or exercise certain Powers, do not imply that Congress is entitled to any Powers not given by the said Constitution; but such Clauses are to be construed either as exceptions to certain specified Powers, or as inserted merely for greater Caution. *State Ratifications, RG 11, DNA.*

16.1.2.5 **North Carolina, August 1, 1788**

1st. That there are certain natural rights of which men, when they form a social compact, cannot deprive or divest their posterity, among which are the enjoyment of life, and liberty, with the means of acquiring, possessing and protecting property, and pursuing and obtaining happiness and safety.

2d. That all power is naturally vested in, and consequently derived from the people; . . .

I. THAT each state in the union shall, respectively, retain every power, jurisdiction and right, which is not by this constitution delegated to the Congress of the United States, or to the departments of the Federal Government.

. . .

XVIII. That those clauses which declare that Congress shall not exercise certain powers, be not interpreted in any manner whatsoever to extend the powers of Congress; but that they be construed either as making exceptions to the specified powers where this shall be the case, or otherwise, as inserted merely for greater caution.

State Ratifications, RG 11, DNA.

16.1.2.6 Pennsylvania Minority, December 12, 1787

15. That the sovereignty, freedom, and independency of the several states shall be retained, and every power, jurisdiction and right which is not by this Constitution expressly delegated to the United States in Congress assembled.

Pennsylvania Packet, December 18, 1787.

16.1.2.7 South Carolina, May 23, 1788

This Convention doth also declare that no Section or paragraph of the said Constitution warrants a Construction that the states do not retain every power not expressly relinquished by them and vested in the General Government of the Union.

State Ratifications, RG 11, DNA.

16.1.2.8 Virginia, June 27, 1788

First, That there are certain natural rights of which men, when they form a social compact cannot deprive or divest their posterity, among which are the enjoyment of life and liberty, with the means of acquiring, possessing and protecting property, and pursuing and obtaining happiness and safety. Second, That all power is naturally vested in and consequently derived from the people; that Magestrates, therefore, are their trustees and agents at all times amenable to them. . . .

Amendments to the Body of the Constitution.

First, That each State in the Union shall respectively retain every power, jurisdiction and right which is not by this Constitution delegated to the Congress of the United States or to the departments of the Foederal Government. . . . Seventeeth, That those clauses which declare that Congress shall not exercise certain powers be not interpreted in any manner whatsoever to extend the powers of Congress. But that they may be construed either as making exceptions to the specified powers where this shall be the case, or otherwise as inserted merely for greater caution.

State Ratifications, RG 11, DNA.

16.1.3 STATE CONSTITUTIONS AND LAWS;
COLONIAL CHARTERS AND LAWS

16.1.3.1 Delaware, 1776

ART. 30. No article of the declaration of rights and fundamental rules of this state, agreed to by this convention, . . . ought ever be violated on any pretence whatever. No other part of this constitution shall be altered, changed or diminished without the consent of five parts in seven of the Assembly, and seven Members of the Legislative Council.

16.1.3.2 Georgia, 1777

WHEREAS the conduct of the legislature of Great-Britain for many years past, has been so oppressive on the people of America, that of late years, they have plainly declared, and asserted a right to raise taxes upon the people of America, and to make laws to bind them in all cases whatsoever, without their consent; which conduct being repugnant to the common rights of mankind, hath obliged the Americans, as freemen, to oppose such oppressive measures, and to assert the rights and privileges they are entitled to, by the laws of nature and reason. . . .

. . .

We therefore the representatives of the people, from whom all power originates, and for whose benefit all government is intended, by virtue of the power delegated to us, Do ordain and declare, and it is hereby ordained and declared, that the following rules and regulations be adopted for the future government of this State.

Georgia Laws, p. 7.

16.1.3.3 Maryland: Declaration of Rights, 1776

1. That all government of right originates from the people, is founded in compact only, and instituted solely for the good of the whole.

Maryland Laws, November 3, 1776.

16.1.3.4 Massachusetts: Constitution, 1780

Preamble.

THE end of the institution, maintenance, and administration of government, is to secure the existence of the body politick; to protect it; and to furnish the individuals who compose it, with the power of enjoying, in safety and tranquility, their natural rights, and the blessings of life: And whenever these great objects are not obtained, the people have a right to alter the government, and to take measures necessary for their safety, prosperity, and happiness.

. . .

PART I.
A Declaration Of The Rights Of The Inhabitants
Of The Commonwealth Of Massachusetts.
ARTICLE

I. ALL men are born free and equal, and have certain natural, essential and unalienable rights: among which may be reckoned the right of enjoying and defending their lives and liberties: that of acquiring, possessing, and protecting property: in fine, that of seeking and obtaining their safety and happiness.

. . .

IV. The people of this Commonwealth, have the sole and exclusive right of governing themselves, as a free, sovereign, and independent state: and do, and forever herafter shall, exercise and enjoy every power, jurisdiction and right, which is not, or may not hereafter, be by them expressly delegated to the United States of America, in Congress assembled.

V. All power residing originally in the people, and being derived from them, the several magistrates and officers of government, vested with authority, whether legislative, executive, or judicial, are their substitutes and agents, and are at all times accountable to them.

. . .

VII. Government is instituted for the common good; for the protection, safety, prosperity and happiness of the people; and not for the profit, honour, or private interest of any one man, family, or class of men: Therefore the people alone have an incontestible, unalienable, and indefeasible right to institute government; and to reform, alter, or totally change the same, when their protection, safety, prosperity and happiness require it.

. . .

XXX. In the government of this Commonwealth, the legislative deparment shall never exercise the executive and judicial powers, or either of them: The executive shall never exercise the legislative and judicial powers, or either of them: The judicial shall never exercise the legislative and executive powers, or either of them: To the end it may be a government of laws and not of men.

Massachusetts Perpetual Laws, pp. 5–6, 8.

16.1.3.5 New Hampshire: Constitution, 1783

[Part I, Article I.] ALL men are born equally free and independent; therefore, all government of right originates from the people, is founded in consent, and instituted for the general good.

II. All men have certain natural, essential, and inherent rights; among which are — the enjoying and defending life and liberty — acquiring, possessing and protecting property — and in a word, of seeking and obtaining happiness.

III. When men enter into a state of society, they surrender up some of their natural rights to society, in order to secure the protection of others; and, without such an equivalent, the surrender is void.

IV. Among the natural rights, some are in their very nature unalienable, because no equivalent can be given or received for them. Of this kind are the RIGHTS OF CONSCIENCE.

. . .

VII. The people of this State, have the sole and exclusive right of governing themselves as a free, sovereign, and independent State, and do, and forever hereafter shall, exercise, and enjoy every power, jurisdiction and right pertaining thereto, which is not, or may not hereafter be by them expressly delegated to the United States of America in Congress assembled.

New Hampshire Laws, pp. 22–24.

16.1.3.6 New Jersey: Constitution, 1776

WHEREAS all the constitutional Authority ever possessed by the Kings of *Great Britain* over these Colonies, . . . was by Compact, derived from the People, and held for them, for the common Interest of the whole Society. . . .

New Jersey Acts, p. iii.

16.1.3.7 New York: Constitution, 1777

I. THIS Convention, therefore, in the name and by the Authority of the good People of this State, doth ORDAIN, DETERMINE AND DECLARE, That no Authority shall, on any Pretence whatever, be excercised [*sic*] over the People or Members of this State, but such as shall be derived from and granted by them.

New York Laws, vol. 1, p. 5.

16.1.3.8 North Carolina: Declaration of Rights, 1776

Sect. I. That all political Power is vested in and derived from the People only.

North Carolina Laws, p. 275.

16.1.3.9 Pennsylvania

16.1.3.9.a Constitution, 1776

WHEREAS all government ought to be instituted and supported for the security and protection of the community as such, and to enable the individuals who compose it to enjoy their natural rights, and the other blessings which the author of existence has bestowed upon man; and whenever these great ends of government are not obtained, the people have a right, by common consent to change it, and take such measures as to them may appear necessary to promote their safety and happiness. And whereas the inhabitants of this commonwealth have, in consideration of protection only, heretofore acknowledged allegiance to the king of Great Britain: and the said king has not only withdrawn that protection, but commenced, and still continues to carry on, with unabated vengeance, a most cruel and unjust war against them employing therein, not only the troops of Great Britain, but foreign mercenaries, savages and slaves, for the avowed purpose of reducing them to a total and abject submission to the despotic domination of the British parliament, with many other acts of tyranny, (more fully set forth in the declaration of congress) whereby all allegiance and fealty to the said king and his successors, are dissolved and at an end, and all power and authority derived from him ceased in these colonies. And whereas it is absolutely necessary for the welfare and safety of the inhabitants of said colonies, that they be henceforth free and independent states, and that just, permanent, and proper forms of government exist in every part of them derived from and founded on the authority of the people only, agreeable to the directions of the honourable American congress. We, the representatives of the freemen of Pennsylvania, in general convention met, for the express purpose of framing such a government, confessing the goodness of the great Governor of the universe (who alone knows to what degree of earthly happiness mankind may attain, by perfecting the arts of government) in permitting the people of this state, by common consent, and without violence, deliberately to form for themselves such just rules as they shall think best, for governing their future society; and being fully convinced, that it is our indispensible duty to establish such original principles of government, as will best promote the general happiness of the people of this state, and their posterity, and provide for future improvements, without partiality for, or prejudice against any particular class, sect, or denomination of men whatever, do, by virtue of the authority vested in us by our constituents, ordain, declare, and establish, the following *Declaration of Rights,* and *Frame of Government,* to be the CONSTITUTION of this common-wealth, and to remain in force therein for ever, unaltered, except in such articles as shall hereafter on experience be found to require improvement, and which shall by the same authority of the people, fairly delegated as this frame of government directs, be amended or improved for the more effectual obtaining and securing the great end and design of all government, herein before mentioned.

CHAPTER I.

A DECLARATION of the RIGHTS of the Inhabitants
of the State of Pennsylvania.

I. THAT all men are born equally free and independent, and have certain natural, inherent and unalienable rights, amongst which are, the enjoying and defending life and liberty, acquiring, possessing and protecting property, and pursuing and obtaining happiness and safety.

. . .

IV. That all power being originally inherent in, and consequently derived from, the people; therefore all officers of government, whether legislative or executive, are their trustees and servants, and at all times accountable to them.

V. That government is, or ought to be, instituted for the common benefit, protection and security of the people, nation or community; and not for the particular emolument or advantage of any single man, family, or set of men, who are a part only of that community: And that the community hath an indubitable, unalienable and indefeasible right to reform, alter or abolish government in such manner as shall be by that community judged most conducive to the public weal.

Pennsylvania Acts, McKean, pp. vii–ix.

16.1.3.9.b Constitution, 1790

ARTICLE IX.

THAT *the general, great, and essential Principles of Liberty and free Government may be recognized and unalterably established,* WE DECLARE,

SECTION I. THAT all men are born equally free and independent, and have certain inherent and indefeasible rights, among which are those of enjoying and defending life and liberty, of acquiring, possessing, and protecting property and reputation, and of pursuing their own happiness.

SECT. II. That all power is inherent in the people, and all free governments are founded on their authority, and instituted for their peace, safety and happiness: For the advancement of those ends they have, at all times, an unalienable and indefeasible right to alter, reform, or abolish their government, in such manner as they may think proper.

. . .

SECT. XXVI. To guard against transgressions of the high powers which we have delegated, WE DECLARE, That every thing in this article is excepted out of the general powers of government, and shall for ever remain inviolate.

Pennsylvania Acts, Dallas, pp. xxxiii, xxxvi.

16.1.3.10 South Carolina: Constitution, 1790

ARTICLE IX.

Section 1. All power is originally vested in the people; and all free governments are founded on their authority, and are instituted for their peace, safety and happiness.

South Carolina Laws, App., p. 41.

16.1.3.11 Vermont: Constitution, 1777

WHEREAS all government ought to be instituted and supported for the Security and Protection of the Community as such, and to enable the Individuals who compose it to enjoy their natural Rights, and the other Blessings which the Author of Existence has bestowed upon Man; and whenever those great Ends of Government are not obtained, the People have a Right by common Consent to change it, and take such Measures as to them may appear necessary to promote their Safety and Happiness.

A DECLARATION of the RIGHTS of the INHABITANTS of the state of *VERMONT*

I. That all Men are born equally free and independent, and have certain natural, inherent and unalienable Rights, amongst which are the enjoying and defending Life and Liberty; acquiring, possessing and protecting Property, and pursuing and obtaining Happiness and Safety.

. . .

V. THAT all Power being originally inherent in, and consequently derived from the People; therefore all Officers of Government, whether legislative or executive, are their Trustees and Servants, and at all Times accountable to them.

Vermont Acts, pp. 1, 3.

16.1.3.12 Virginia: Declaration of Rights, 1776

I. THAT all men are by nature equally free and independent, and have certain inherent rights, of which, when they enter into a state of society, they cannot, by any compact, deprive or devest their posterity; namely, the enjoyment of life and liberty, with the means of acquiring and possessing property, and pursuing and obtaining happiness and safety.

SEC. 2. That all power is vested in, and consequently derived from the people; that Magistrates are their trustees and servants, and at all times amenable to them.

Virginia Acts, p. 33.

16.1.4 OTHER TEXTS

16.1.4.1 Declaration of Independence, July 4, 1776

. . . We hold these truths to be self-evident, that all men are created equal, that they are endowed by their Creator with certain unalienable Rights, that among these are Life, Liberty and the pursuit of Happiness. — That to secure these rights, Governments are instituted among Men, deriving their just powers from the consent of the governed, — That whenever any Form of Government becomes destructive of these ends, it is the Right of the People to alter or to abolish it; and to institute new Government, laying its foundation on such principles and organizing its powers in such form, as to them shall seem most likely to effect their Safety and Happiness.

Engrossed Manuscripts, DNA.

16.1.4.2 Articles of Confederation, November 15, 1777

Article II. Each state retains its sovereignty, freedom and independence, and every Power, Jurisdiction and right, which is not by this confederation expressly delegated to the United States, in Congress assembled.

Continental Congress Papers, DNA.

16.1.4.3 Richard Henry Lee to Edmund Randolph, Proposed Amendments, October 16, 1787

It having been found from universal experience that the most express delarations and reservations are necessary to protect the just rights and liberty of mankind from the silent, powerful and ever active conspiracy of those who govern; and it appearing to be the sense of the good people of America, by the various bills or declarations of rights whereon the governments of the greater number of the states are founded. That such precautions are necessary to restrain and regulate the exercise of the great powers given to rulers. In conformity with these principles, and from respect for the public sentiment on this subject, it is submitted, — That the new Constitution proposed for the government of the United States be bottomed upon a declaration or bill of rights, clearly and precisely stating the principles upon which this social compact is founded. . . .

Virginia Gazette, December 22, 1787.

16.2 DISCUSSION OF DRAFTS AND PROPOSALS

16.2.1 THE FIRST CONGRESS

16.2.1.1 June 8, 1789[2]

16.2.1.1.a

Mr. JACKSON.

The more I consider the subject of amendments, the more, mr. speaker, I am convinced it is improper. I revere the rights of my constituents as much as any gentleman in congress, yet, I am against inserting a declaration of rights in the constitution, and that upon some of the reasons referred to by the gentleman last up. If such an addition is not dangerous or improper, it is at least unnecessary: that is a sufficient reason for not entering into the subject at a time when there are urgent calls for our attention to important business. Let me ask gentlemen, what reason there is for the suspicions which are to be removed by this measure? Who are congress that such apprehensions should be entertained of them? Do we not belong to the mass of the people? Is there a single right but, if infringed, will affect

[2]For Madison's speech in support of his proposals, *see* 1.2.1.1.a–c.

us and our connections as much as any other person? Do we not return at the expiration of two years into private life, and is not this a security against encroachment? Are we not sent here to guard those rights which might be endangered, if the government was an aristocracy or a despotism? View for a moment the situation of Rhode-Island and, say whether the people's rights are more safe under state legislatures than under a government of limited powers? Their liberty is changed to licentiousness. But do gentlemen suppose bills of rights necessary to secure liberty? If they do, let them look at New York, New Jersey, Virginia, South Carolina, and Georgia. Those states have no bills of rights, and are the liberty of the citizens less safe in those states, than in the other of the United States? I believe they are not.

There is a maxim in law, and it will apply to bills of rights, that when you enumerate exceptions, the exceptions operate to the exclusion of all circumstances that are omitted; consequently, unless you except every right from the grant of power, those omitted are inferred to be resigned to the discretion of the government.

Congressional Register, June 8, 1789, vol. 1, p. 437.

16.2.1.1.b Mr. Jackson observed, That the Hon. Gentleman's ingenious detail, so far from convincing him of the expediency of bringing forward the subject of amendments at this time, had confirmed him in the contrary opinion: The prospect which such a discussion opened, was wide and extensive, and would preclude other benefits, of much greater moment, at the present juncture — He differed widely from the Gentleman, with regard to bills of rights — several of the States had no such bills — Rhode-Island had none — there, liberty was carried to excess, and licentiousness triumphed — In some States, which had such a nominal security, the encroachments upon the rights of the people had been most complained of. . . .

Gazette of U.S., June 10, 1787, p. 67, col. 2.

16.2.1.2 August 15, 1789

Mr. Hartley

Observed that it had been asserted in the convention of Pennsylvania, by the friends of the Constitution, that all the rights and powers that were not given to the government, were retained by the states and the people thereof; this was also his own opinion, but as four or five states had required to be secured in those rights by an express declaration in the constitution, he was disposed to gratify them; he thought every thing that was not incompatible with the general good ought to be granted, if it would tend to obtain the confidence of the people in the government, and, upon the whole, he thought these words were as necessary to be inserted in the declaration of rights as most in the clause.

Congressional Register, August 15, 1789, vol. 2, pp. 198–99.

16.2.1.3 August 18, 1789

16.2.1.3.a The 9th proposition, in the words following was considered, "The powers not delegated by the constitution, nor prohibited by it to the states, are reserved to the states respectively."

MR. TUCKER

Proposed to amend the proposition, by prefixing to it, "all powers being derived from the people," thought this a better place to make this assertion than the introductory clause of the constitution, where a similar sentiment was proposed by the committee. He extended his motion also, to add the word "expressly," so as to read "The powers not expressly delegated by this constitution."

MR. MADISON

Objected to this amendment, because it was impossible to confine a government to the exercise of express powers, there must necessarily be admitted powers by implication, unless the constitution descended to recount every minutiae. He remembered the word "expressly" had been moved in the convention of Virginia, by the opponents to the ratification, and after full and fair discussion was given up by them, and the system allowed to retain its present form.

MR. SHERMAN

Coincided with mr. Madison in opinion, observing that corporate bodies are supposed to possess all powers incident to a corporate capacity, without being absolutely expressed.

MR. TUCKER

Did not view the word "expressly" in the same light with the gentleman who opposed him; he thought every power to be expressly given that could be clearly comprehended within any accurate definition of the general power.

Mr. TUCKER's motion being negatived,

Mr. CARROLL proposed to add to the end of the proposition, "or to the people," this was agreed to.

Congressional Record, August 18, 1789, vol. 2, pp. 234–35.

16.2.1.3.b   18th Amendment: "The powers not delegated by this Constitution, nor prohibited by it to the States, are reserved to the States respectively."

MR. TUCKER proposed an introductory clause to this amendment, viz. *all power being derived from the people.*

MR. MADISON objected to this, as confining the government within such limits as to admit of no implied powers, and I believe, he said, that no government ever existed which was not necessarily obliged to exercise powers by implication. This question was agitated in the Convention of Virginia; it was brought forward by those who were opposed to the Constitution, and was finally given up by them.

MR. SHERMAN observed, that all corporations are supposed to possess all the powers incidental to their corporate capacity: It is not in human wisdom to provide for every possible contingency.

This motion was negatived.

MR. GERRY then proposed to add, after the word "States," *and people thereof.*

MR. CARROLL objected to the addition, as it tended to create a distinction between the people and their legislatures.

The motion was negatived, and the amendment agreed to.

Gazette of the U.S., August 22, 1789, p. 250, col. 1.

16.2.1.4   August 21, 1789

The house proceeded in the consideration of the amendments to the constitution reported by the committee of the whole. . . .

. . .

The 9th proposition, mr. Gerry proposed to amend by inserting the word "expressly" so as to read the powers not expressly delegated by the constitution, nor prohibited to the states, are reserved to the states respectively or to the people; as he thought this an amendment of great importance, he requested the ayes and noes might be taken. He was supported in this by one fifth of the members present, whereupon they were taken. . . .

Mr. Sherman

Moved to alter the last clause so as to make it read, the powers not delegated to the United States, by the constitution, nor prohibited by it to the states, are reserved to the states respectively, or to the people.

The motion was adopted without debate.

Congressional Register, August 21, 1789, vol. 2, p. 243.

16.2.2 STATE CONVENTIONS

16.2.2.1   Massachusetts

16.2.2.1.a   February 4, 1788

Rev. Mr. THACHER. . . . There are other restraints, which, though not directly named in this Constitution, yet are evidently discerned by every man of common observation. These are, the government of the several states, and the spirit of liberty in the people.

Elliot, vol. 2, p. 145.

16.2.2.1.b   February 5, 1788

Mr. PARSONS demonstrated the impracticability of forming a bill, in a national constitution, for securing individual rights, and showed the inutility of the measure, from the ideas, that no power was given to Congress to infringe on any one of the natural rights of the people by this Constitution; and, should they attempt it without constitutional authority, the act would be a nullity, and could not be enforced.

Elliot, vol. 2, pp. 161–62.

16.2.2.2   New York, July 1, 1788

Mr. TREDWELL. Sir, little accustomed to speak in public, and always inclined, in such an assembly as this, to be a hearer rather than a speaker, on a less important occasion than the present I should have contented myself with a silent vote; but when I consider the nature of this dispute, that it is a contest, not between little states and great states, (as we have been told,) between little folks and great folks, between patriotism and ambition, between freedom and power; not so much between the navigating and the non-navigating individuals, (for not one of the amendments we contend for has the least reference to the clashing interests of the states;) when I consider, likewise, that a people jealous of their liberties, and strongly attached to freedom, have reposed so entire a confidence in this assembly, that upon our determination depends their future enjoyment of those invaluable rights and privileges, which they have so lately and so gallantly defended at every risk and expense, both of life and property, — it appears to me so interesting and important, that I cannot be totally silent on the occasion, lest lisping babes should be taught to curse my name, as a betrayer of their freedom and happiness.

The gentleman who first opened this debate did (with an emphasis which I believe convinced every one present of the propriety of the advice) urge the necessity of proceeding, in our deliberations on this important subject, coolly and dispassionately. With how much candor this advice was given, appears from the subsequent parts of a long speech, and from several subsequent speeches almost totally addressed to our fears. The people of New Jersey and Connecticut are so exceedingly exasperated against us, that, totally regardless of their own preservation, they will take the two rivers of Connecticut and Delaware by their extremities, and, by dragging them over our country, will, by a sweeping deluge, wash us all into the Hudson, leaving neither house nor inhabitant behind them. But if this event should not happen, doubtless the Vermontese, with the British and tories our natural enemies, would, by bringing down upon us the great Lake Ontario, sweep hills and mountains, houses and inhabitants, in one deluge, into the Atlantic. These, indeed, would be terrible calamities; but terrible as they are, they are not to be compared with the horrors and desolation of tyranny. The arbitrary courts of Philip in the Netherlands, in which life and property were daily confiscated without a jury, occasioned as much misery and a more rapid depopulation of the province, before the people took up arms in their own defence, than all the armies of that haughty monarch were able to effect afterwards; and it is doubtful, in my mind, whether governments, by abusing their powers, have not occasioned as much misery and distress, and nearly as great devastations of the human species, as all the wars which have happened since Milton's battle of the angels to the present day. The end or design of government is, or ought to be, the safety, peace, and welfare of the governed. Unwise, therefore, and absurd in the highest degree, would be the conduct of that people, who, in forming a government, should give to their rulers power to destroy them and their property, and thereby defeat the very purpose of their institutions; or, in other words, should give unlimited power to their rulers, and not retain in their own hands the means of their own preservation. The first governments in the world were parental, the powers of which were restrained by the laws of nature; and doubtless the early succeeding governments were formed on the same plan, which, we may suppose, answered tolerably well in the first ages of the world, while the moral sense was strong, and the laws of nature well understood, there being then no lawyers to explain them away. But in after times, when kings became great, and courts crowded, it was discovered that governments should have a right to tyrannize, and a power to oppress; and at the present day, when the *juris periti* are become so skilful in their profession, and quibbling is reduced to a science, it is become extremely difficult to form a constitution which will secure liberty and happiness to the people, or laws under which property is safe. Hence, in modern times, the design of the people, in forming an original constitution of government, is not so much to give powers to their rulers, as to guard against the abuse of them; but, in a federal one, it is different.

Sir, I introduce these observations to combat certain principles which have been daily and confidently advanced by the favorers of the present Constitution, and which appear to me totally indefensible. The first and grand leading, or rather misleading, principle in this debate, and on which the advocates for this system of unrestricted powers must chiefly depend for its support, is that, in forming a constitution, whatever powers are not expressly granted or given the government, are reserved to the people, or that rulers cannot exercise any powers but those expressly given to them by the Constitution. Let me ask the gentleman who advanced this principle, whether the commission of a Roman dictator, which was in these few words — to take care that the state received no harm — does not come up fully to their ideas of an energetic government; or whether an invitation from the people to one or more to come and rule over them, would not clothe the rulers with sufficient powers. If so, the principle they advance is a false one. Besides, the absurdity of this principle will evidently appear, when we consider the great variety of objects to which the powers of the government must necessarily extend, and that an express enumeration of them all would probably fill as many volumes as Pool's Synopsis of the Critics. But we may reason with sufficient certainty on the subject, from the sense of all the public bodies in the United States, who had occasion to form new constitutions. They have uniformly acted upon a direct and contrary principle, not only in forming the state constitutions and the old Confederation, but also in forming this very Constitution, for we do not find in every state constitution express resolutions made in favor of the people; and it is clear that the late Convention at Philadelphia, whatever might have been the sentiments of some of its members, did not adopt the principle, for they have made certain reservations and restrictions, which, upon that principle, would have been totally useless and unnecessary; and can it be supposed that wise body, whose only apology for the great ambiguity of many parts of that performance, and the total omission of some things which many esteem essential to the security of liberty, was a great desire of brevity, should so far sacrifice that great and important object, as to insert a number of provisions which they esteemed totally useless? Why is it said that the privilege of the writ of *habeas corpus* shall not be suspended, unless, in cases of rebellion or invasion, the public safety may require it? What clause in the Constitution, except this very clause itself, gives the general government a power to deprive us of that great privilege, so sacredly secured to us by our state constitutions? Why is it provided that no bill of attainder shall be passed, or that no title of nobility shall be granted? Are there any clauses in the Constitution extending the powers of the general government to these objects? Some gentlemen say that these, though not necessary, were inserted for greater caution. I could have wished, sir, that a greater caution had been used to secure to us the freedom of election, a sufficient and responsible representation, the freedom of the press, and the trial by jury both in civil and criminal cases.

These, sir, are the rocks on which the Constitution should have rested; no other foundation can any man lay, which will secure the sacred temple of freedom against the power of the great, the undermining arts of ambition, and the blasts of profane scoffers — for such there will be in every age — who will tell us that all religion is in vain; that is, that our political creeds, which have been handed down to us by our forefathers as sacredly as our Bibles, and for which more of them have suffered martyrdom than for the creed of the apostles, are all nonsense; who will tell us that paper constitutions are mere paper, and that parchment is but parchment, that jealousy of our rulers is a sin, &c. I could have wished also that sufficient caution had been used to secure to us our religious liberties, and to have prevented the general government from tyrannizing over our consciences by a religious establishment — a tyranny of all others most dreadful, and which will assuredly be exercised whenever it shall be thought necessary for the promotion and support of their political measures. It is ardently to be wished, sir, that these and other invaluable rights of freemen had been as cautiously secured as some of the paltry local interests of some of the individual states. But it appears to me, that, in forming this Constitution, we have run into the same error which the lawyers and Pharisees of old were charged with; that is, while we have secured the tithes of mint, anise, and cumin, we have neglected the weightier matters of the law, judgment, mercy, and faith. . . .

In this Constitution, sir, we have departed widely from the principles and political faith of '76, when the spirit of liberty ran high, and danger put a curb on ambition. Here we find no security for the rights of individuals, no security for the existence of our state governments; here is no bill of rights, no proper restriction of power; our lives, our property, and our consciences, are left wholly at the mercy of the legislature, and the powers of the judiciary may be extended to any degree short of almighty. Sir, in this Constitution we have not only neglected, — we have done worse, — we have openly violated, our faith, — that is our public faith.
. . .

Respecting the power to make all *laws necessary* for the carrying the Constitution into execution, —

"*Provided,* That no power shall be exercised by Congress, but such as is expressly given by this Constitution; and all others, not expressly given, shall be reserved to the respective states, to be by them exercised."

Moved by Mr. LANSING.

Elliot, vol. 2, pp. 396–401, 406.

16.2.2.3   North Carolina

16.2.2.3.a   July 29, 1788

Mr. MACLAINE. Mr. Chairman, I beg leave to make a few observations. One of the gentleman's objections to the Constitution now under consideration is, that it is not the act of the states, but of the people; but that it ought to be the act of the states; and he instances the delegation of power by the states to the Confederation, at the commencement of the war, as a proof of this position. I hope, sir, that all power is in the people, and not in the state governments. If he will not deny the authority of the people to delegate power to agents, and to devise such a government as a majority of them thinks will promote their happiness, he will withdraw his objection. The people, sir, are the only proper authority to form a government. They, sir, have formed their state governments, and can alter them at pleasure.

Their transcendent power is competent to form this or any other government which they think promotive of their happiness. But the gentleman contends that there ought to be a bill of rights, or something of that kind — something declaring expressly, that all power not expressly given to the Constitution ought to be retained by the states; and he produces the Confederation as an authority for its necessity. When the Confederation was made, we were by no means so well acquainted with the principles of government as we are now. We were then jealous of the power of our rulers, and had an idea of the British government when we entertained that jealousy. There is no people on earth so well acquainted with the nature of government as the people of America generally are. We know now that it is agreed upon by most writers, and men of judgment and reflection, that all power is in the people, and immediately derived from them. The gentleman surely must know that, if there be certain rights which never can, nor ought to, be given up, these rights cannot be said to be given away, merely because we have omitted to say that we have not given them up. Can any security arise from declaring that we have a right to what belongs to us? Where is the necessity of such a declaration? If we have this inherent, this unalienable, this indefeasible title to those rights, if they are not given up, are they not retained? If Congress should make a law beyond the powers and the spirit of the Constitution, should we not say to Congress, "You have no authority to make this law. There are limits beyond which you cannot go. You cannot exceed the power prescribed by the Constitution. You are amenable to us for your conduct. This act is unconstitutional. We will disregard it, and punish you for the attempt."

But the gentleman seems to be most tenacious of the judicial power of the states. The honorable gentleman must know, that the doctrine of reservation of power not relinquished, clearly demonstrates that the judicial power of the states is not impaired. . . .

. . .

Mr. SPENCER answered, that the gentleman last up had misunderstood him. He did not object to the caption of the Constitution, but he instanced it to show that the United States were not, merely as states, the objects of the Constitution; but that the laws of Congress were to operate upon individuals, and not upon states. He then continued: I do not mean to contend that the laws of the general government should not operate upon individuals. I before observed that this was necessary, as laws could not be put in execution against states without the agency of the sword, which, instead of answering the ends of government, would destroy it. I endeavored to show that, as the government was not to operate against states, but against individuals, the rights of individuals ought to be properly secured. In order to constitute this security, it appears to me there ought to be such a clause in the Constitution as there was in the Confederation, expressly declaring, that every power, jurisdiction, and right, which are not given up by it, remain in the states. Such a clause would render a bill of rights unnecessary. But as there is no such clause, I contend that there should be a bill of rights, ascertaining and securing the great rights of the states and people. Besides my objection to the revision of facts by the federal court, and the insecurity of jury trial, I consider the concurrent jurisdiction of those courts with the state courts as extremely dangerous. . . .

Elliot, vol. 4, pp. 160–64.

16.2.2.3.b **August 1, 1788**

Mr. IREDELL. . . .

"1. Each state in the Union shall respectively retain every power, jurisdiction, and right, which is not by this Constitution delegated to the Congress of the United States, or to the departments of the general government; nor shall the said Congress, nor any department of the said government, exercise any act of authority over any individual in any of the said states, but such as can be justified under some power particularly given in this Constitution; but the said Constitution shall be considered at all times a solemn instrument, defining the extent of their authority, and the limits of which they cannot rightfully in any instance exceed.["]

Elliot, vol. 4, p. 249.

16.2.2.4 **Pennsylvania**

16.2.2.4.a **October 28, 1787**

Mr. WILSON. . . . In a government possessed of enumerated powers, such a measure [adopting a bill of rights] would be not only unnecessary, but preposterous and dangerous. Whence comes this notion, that in the United States there is no security without a bill of rights? Have the citizens of South Carolina no security for their liberties? They have no bill of rights. Are the citizens on the eastern side of the Delaware less free, or less secured in their liberties, than those on the western side? The state of New Jersey has no bill of rights. The state of New York has no bill of rights. The states of Connecticut and Rhode Island have no bill of rights. I know not whether I have exactly enumerated the states who have not thought it necessary to add a *bill of rights* to their constitutions; but this enumeration, sir, will serve to show by experience, as well as principle, that, even in single governments, a bill of rights is not an essential or necessary measure. But in a government consisting of enumerated powers, such as is proposed for the United States, a bill of rights would not only be unnecessary, but, in my humble judgement, highly imprudent. In all societies, there are many powers and rights which cannot be particularly enumerated. A bill of rights annexed to a constitution is *an enumeration of the powers* reserved. If we attempt an enumeration, every thing that is not enumerated is presumed to be given. The consequence is, that an imperfect enumeration would throw all implied power into the scale of the government, and the rights of the people would be rendered incomplete. On the other hand, an imperfect enumeration of the powers of government reserves all implied power to the people; and by that means the constitution becomes incomplete. But of the two, it is much safer to run the risk on the side of the constitution; for an omission in the enumeration of the powers of government is neither so dangerous nor important as an omission in the enumeration of the rights of the peop e. [*sic*]

Elliot, vol. 2, pp. 436–37.

16.2.2.4.b **December 4, 1787**

Mr. WILSON. . . . I consider that there are very few who understand the whole of these rights. All the political writers, from *Grotius* and *Puffendorf* down to *Vattel*, have treated on this subject; but in no one of those books, nor in the aggregate of them all, can you find a complete enumeration of rights appertaining to the people as men and as citizens.

. . . Enumerate all the rights of men! I am sure, sir, that no gentleman in the late Convention would have attempted such a thing. . . .

Sir, I think there is another subject with regard to which this Constitution deserves approbation. I mean the accuracy with which the *line is drawn* between the powers of the *general government* and those of the *particular state governments*. We have heard some general observations, on this subject, from the gentlemen who conduct the opposition. They have asserted that these powers are unlimited and undefined. These words are as easily pronounced as *limited* and *defined*. They have already been answered by my honorable colleague, (Mr. M'Kean;) therefore I shall not enter into an explanation. But it is not pretended that the line is drawn with mathematical precision; the inaccuracy of language must, to a certain degree, prevent the accomplishment of such a desire. Whoever views the matter in a true light, will see that the powers are as minutely enumerated and defined as was possible, and will also discover that the general clause, against which so much exception is taken, is nothing more than what was necessary to render effectual the particular powers that are granted.

But let us suppose — and the supposition is very easy in the minds of the gentlemen on the other side — that there is some difficulty in ascertaining where the true line lies. Are we therefore thrown into despair? Are *disputes* between the *general* government and the *state* governments to be necessarily the consequence of inaccuracy? I hope, sir, they will not be the enemies of each other, or resemble comets in conflicting orbits, mutually operating destruction; but that their motion will be better represented by that of the planetary system, where each part moves harmoniously within its proper sphere, and no injury arises by interference or opposition. Every part, I trust, will be considered as a part of the United States. Can any cause of distrust arise here? Is there any increase of risk? Or, rather, are not the enumerated powers as well defined here, as in the present Articles of Confederation?

Elliot, vol. 2, pp. 454, 481–82.

16.2.2.4.c **September 3, 1788**

PROCEEDINGS OF THE MEETING [of citizens]
AT HARRISBURG, IN PENNSYLVANIA

We, the conferees, . . . agree in opinion, — . . .

I. That Congress shall not exercise any powers whatever, but such as are expressly given to that body by the Constitution of the United States: nor shall any authority, power, or jurisdiction, be assumed or exercised by the executive or judiciary departments of the Union, under color or pretense of construction or fiction; but all the rights of sovereignty, which are not by the said Constitution expressly and plainly vested in the Congress, shall be deemed to remain with, and shall be exercised by, the several states in the Union, according to their respective constitutions; and that every reserve of the rights of individuals, made by the several constitutions of the states in the Union, to the citizens and inhabitants of each state respectively, shall remain inviolate, except so far as they are expressly and manifestly yielded or narrowed by the national Constitution.

Elliot, vol. 2, pp. 543–45.

16.2.2.5 North Carolina, July 29, 1788

Mr. IREDELL. . . . The gentleman says that unalienable rights ought not to be given up. Those rights which are unalienable are not alienated. They still remain with the great body of the people. If any right be given up that ought not to be, let it be shown. Say it is a thing which affects your country, and that it ought not to be surrendered: this would be reasonable. But when it is evident that the exercise of any power not given up would be a usurpation, it would be not only useless, but dangerous, to enumerate a number of rights which are not intended to be given up; because it would be implying, in the strongest manner, that every right not included in the exception might be impaired by the government without usurpation; and it would be impossible to enumerate every one. Let anyone make what collection or enumeration of rights he pleases, I will immediately mention twenty or thirty more rights not contained in it.

Mr. BLOODWORTH. . . . By its not being provided for, it is expressly provided against. I still see the necessity of a bill of rights. Gentlemen use contradictory arguments on this subject, if I recollect right. Without the most express restrictions, Congress may trample on your rights. Every possible precaution should be taken when we grant powers. Rulers are always disposed to abuse them.

Elliot, vol. 4, pp. 166–67.

16.2.2.6 South Carolina, May 20, 1788

Mr. PATRICK DOLLARD. . . . They are nearly all, to a man, opposed to this new Constitution, because, they say, they have omitted to insert a bill of rights therein, ascertaining and fundamentally establishing, the unalienable rights of men, without a full, free, and secure enjoyment of which there can be no liberty, and over which it is not necessary that a good government should have the control.

Elliot, vol. 4, p. 337.

16.2.2.7 Virginia

16.2.2.7.a June 12, 1788

Mr. HENRY. . . . When we see men of such talents and learning compelled to use their utmost abilities to convince themselves that there is no danger, is it not sufficient to make us tremble? Is it not sufficient to fill the minds of the ignorant part of men with fear? If gentlemen believe that the apprehensions of men will be quieted, they are mistaken, since our best-informed men are in doubt with respect to the security of our rights. Those who are not so well informed will spurn at the government. When our common citizens, who are not possessed with such extensive knowledge and abilities, are called upon to change their bill of rights (which, in plain, and unequivocal terms, secure their most valuable rights and privileges) for construction and implication, will they implicitly acquiesce? Our declaration of rights tells us that "all men are by nature free and independent," &c. . . . Will they exchange these rights for logical reasons?   Elliot, vol. 3, pp. 317–18.

16.2.2.7.b **June 14, 1788**

Mr. GEORGE MASON. Mr. Chairman, gentlemen say there is no new power given by this clause. Is there any thing in this Constitution which secures to the states the powers which are said to be retained? Will powers remain to the states which are not expressly guarded and reserved? I will suppose a case. Gentlemen may call it an impossible case, and suppose that Congress will act with wisdom and integrity. Among the enumerated powers, Congress are to lay and collect taxes, duties, imposts, and excises, and to pay the debts, and to provide for the general welfare and common defence; and by that clause (so often called the *sweeping clause*) they are to make all laws necessary to execute those laws. Now, suppose oppression should arise under this government, and any writer should dare to stand forth, and expose to the community at large the abuses of those powers; could not Congress, under the idea of providing for the general welfare, and under their own construction, say that this was destroying the general peace, encouraging sedition, and poisoning the minds of the people? And could they not, in order to provide against this, lay a dangerous restriction on the press? Might they not even bring the trial of this restriction within the ten miles square, when there is no prohibition against it? Might they not thus destroy the trial by jury? Would they not extend their implication? It appears to me that they may and will. And shall the support of our rights depend on the bounty of men whose interest it may be to oppress us? That Congress should have power to provide for the general welfare of the Union, I grant. But I wish a clause in the Constitution, with respect to all powers which are not granted, that they are retained by the states. Otherwise, the power of providing for the general welfare may be perverted to its destruction.

Many gentlemen, whom I respect, take different sides of this question. We wish this amendment to be introduced, to remove our apprehensions. There was a clause in the Confederation reserving to the states respectively every power, jurisdiction, and right, not expressly delegated to the United States. This clause has never been complained of, but approved by all. Why not, then, have a similar clause in this Constitution, in which it is the more indispensably necessary than in the Confederation, because of the great augmentation of power vested in the former? In my humble apprehension, unless there be some such clear and finite expression, this clause now under consideration will go to any thing our rulers may think proper. Unless there be some express declaration that every thing not given is retained, it will be carried to any power Congress may please.

Mr. HENRY moved to read from the 8th to the 13th article of the declaration of rights; which was done.

Mr. GEORGE NICHOLAS, in reply to the gentlemen opposed to the clause under debate, went over the same grounds, and developed the same principles, which Mr. Pendleton and Mr. Madison had done. The opposers of the clause, which gave the power of providing for the general welfare, supposed its dangers to result from its connection with, and extension of, the powers granted in the other clauses. He endeavored to show the committee that it only empowered Congress to make such laws as would be necessary to enable them to pay the public debts and provide for the common defence; that this general welfare was united, not to the general power of legislation, but to the particular power of laying and collecting taxes, imposts, and excises, for the purpose of paying the debts and providing for the common defence, — that is, that they could raise as much money as would pay the debts and provide for the common defence, in consequence of this power. The clause which was affectedly called the *sweeping clause* contained no new grant of power. To illustrate this position, he observed that, if it had been added at the end of every one of the enumerated powers, instead of being inserted at the end of all, it would be obvious to any one that it was no augmentation of power. If, for instance, at the end of the clause granting power to lay and collect taxes, it had been added that they should have power to make necessary and proper laws to lay and collect taxes, who could suspect it to be an addition of power? As it would grant no new power if inserted at the end of each clause, it could not when subjoined to the whole.

He then proceeded thus: But, says he, who is to determine the extent of such powers? I say, the same power which, in all well-regulated communities, determines the extent of legislative powers. If they exceed these powers, the judiciary will declare it void, or else the people will have a right to declare it void. Is this depending on any man? But, says the gentleman, it may go to any thing. It may destroy the trial by jury; and they may say it is necessary for providing for the general defence. The power of providing for the general defence only extends to raise any sum of money they may think necessary, by taxes, imposts, &c. But, says he, our only defence against oppressive laws consists in the virtue of our representatives. This was misrepresented. If I understand it right, no new power can be exercised. As to those which are actually granted, we trust to the fellow-feelings of our representatives; and if we are deceived, we then trust to altering our government. It appears to me, however, that we can confide in their discharging their powers rightly, from the peculiarity of their situation, and connection with us. If, sir, the powers of the former Congress were very inconsiderable, that body did not deserve to have great powers.

It was so constructed that it would be dangerous to invest it with such. But why were the articles of the bill of rights read? Let him show us that those rights are given up by the Constitution. Let him prove them to be violated. He tells us that the most worthy characters of the country differ as to the necessity of a bill of rights. It is a simple and plain proposition. It is agreed upon by all that the people have all power. If they part with any of it, is it necessary to declare that they retain the rest? Liken it to any similar case. If I have one thousand acres of land, and I grant five hundred acres of it, must I declare that I retain the other five hundred? Do I grant the whole thousand acres, when I grant five hundred, unless I declare that the five hundred I do not give belong to me still? It is so in this case. After granting some powers, the rest must remain with the people.

Gov. RANDOLPH observed that he had some objections to the clause. He was persuaded that the construction put upon it by the gentlemen, on both sides, was erroneous; but he thought any construction better than going into anarchy.

Mr. GEORGE MASON still thought that there ought to be some express declaration in the Constitution, asserting that rights not given to the general government were retained by the states. He apprehended that, unless this was done, many valuable and important rights would be concluded to be given up by implication. All governments were drawn from the people, though many were perverted to their oppression. The government of Virginia, he remarked, was drawn from the people; yet there were certain great and important rights, which the people, by their bill of rights, declared to be paramount to the power of the legislature. He asked, Why should it not be so in this Constitution? Was it because we were more substantially represented in it than in the state government? If, in the state government, where the people were substantially and fully represented, it was necessary that the great rights of human nature should be secure from the encroachments of the legislature, he asked if it was not more necessary in this government, where they were but inadequately represented? He declared that artful sophistry and evasions could not satisfy him. He could see no clear distinction between rights relinquished by a positive grant, and lost by implication. Unless there were a bill of rights, implication might swallow up all our rights.

Mr. HENRY. Mr. Chairman, the necessity of a bill of rights appears to me to be greater in this government than ever it was in any government before. I have observed already, that the sense of the European nations, and particularly Great Britain, is against the construction of rights being retained which are not expressly relinquished. I repeat, that all nations have adopted this construction — that all rights not expressly and unequivocally reserved to the people are impliedly and incidentally relinquished to rulers, as necessarily inseparable from the delegated powers. It is so in Great Britain; for every possible right, which is not reserved to the people by some express provision or compact, is within the king's prerogative. It is so in that country which is said to be in such full possession of freedom. It is so in Spain, Germany, and other parts of the world. Let us consider the sentiments which have been entertained by the people of America on this subject. At the revolution, it must be admitted that it was their sense to set down those great rights which ought, in all countries, to be held inviolable and sacred. Virginia did so, we all remember. She made a compact to reserve, expressly, certain rights.

When fortified with full, adequate, and abundant representation, was she satisfied with that representation? No. She most cautiously and guardedly reserved and secured those invaluable, inestimable rights and privileges, which no people, inspired with the least glow of patriotic liberty, ever did, or ever can, abandon. She is called upon now to abandon them, and dissolve that compact which secured them to her. She is called upon to accede to another compact, which most infallibly supersedes and annihilates her present one. Will she do it? This is the question. If you intend to reserve your unalienable rights, you must have the most express stipulation; for, if implication be allowed, you are ousted of those rights. If the people did not think it necessary to reserve them, they will be supposed to be given up. How were the congressional rights defined when the people of America united by a confederacy to defend their liberties and rights against the tyrannical attempts of Great Britain? The states were not then contented with implied reservation. No, Mr. Chairman. It was expressly declared in our Confederation that every right was retained by the states, respectively, which was not given up to the government of the United States. But there is no such thing here. You, therefore, by a natural and unavoidable implication, give up your rights to the general government.

Your own example furnishes an argument against it. If you give up these powers, without a bill of rights, you will exhibit the most absurd thing to mankind that ever the world saw — a government that has abandoned all its powers — the powers of direct taxation, the sword, and the purse. You have disposed them to Congress, without a bill of rights — without check, limitation, or control. And still you have checks and guards; still you keep barriers — pointed where? Pointed against your weakened, prostrated, enervated state government! You have a bill of rights to defend you against the state government, which is bereaved of all power, and yet you have none against Congress, though in full and exclusive possession of all power! You arm yourselves against the weak and defenseless, and expose yourselves naked to the armed and powerful. Is not this a conduct of unexampled absurdity? What barriers have you to oppose to this most strong, energetic government? To that government you have nothing to oppose. All your defence is given up. This is a real, actual defect. It must strike the mind of every gentleman. When our government was first instituted in Virginia, we declared the common law of England to be in force.

That system of law which has been admired, and has protected us and our ancestors, is excluded by that system. Added to this, we adopted a bill of rights. By this Constitution, some of the best barriers of human rights are thrown away. Is there not an additional reason to have a bill of rights? By the ancient common law, the trial of all facts is decided by a jury of impartial men from the immediate vicinage. This paper speaks of different juries from the common law in criminal cases; and in civil controversies excludes trial by jury altogether. There is, therefore, more occasion for the supplementary check of a bill of rights now than then. Congress, from their general powers, may fully go into business of human legislation. They may legislate, in criminal cases, from treason to the lowest offence — petty larceny. They may define crimes and prescribe punishments. In the definition of crimes, I trust they will be directed by what wise representatives ought to be governed by. But when we come to punishments, no latitude ought to be left, nor dependence put on the virtue of representatives. What says our bill of rights? — "that excessive bail ought not to be required, nor excessive fines imposed, nor cruel and unusual punishments inflicted." Are you not, therefore, now calling on those gentlemen who are to compose Congress, to prescribe trials and define punishments without this control? Will they find sentiments there similar to this bill of rights? You let them loose; you do more — you depart from the genius of your country. That paper tells you that the trial of crimes shall be by jury, and held in the state where the crime shall have been committed. Under this extensive provision, they may proceed in a manner extremely dangerous to liberty: a person accused may be carried from one extremity of the state to another, and be tried, not by an impartial jury of the vicinage, acquainted with his character and the circumstances of the fact, but by a jury unacquainted with both, and who may be biased against him. Is this not sufficient to alarm men? How different is this from the immemorial practice of your British ancestors, and your own! I need not tell you that, by the common law, a number of hundredors were required on a jury, and that afterwards it was sufficient if the jurors came from the same county. With less than this the people of England have never been satisfied. That paper ought to have declared the common law in force.

In this business of legislation, your members of Congress will loose the restriction of not imposing excessive fines, demanding excessive bail, and inflicting cruel and unusual punishments. These are prohibited by your declaration of rights. What has distinguished our ancestors? — That they would not admit of tortures, or cruel and barbarous punishment. But Congress may introduce the practice of the civil law, in preference to that of the common law. They may introduce the practice of France, Spain, and Germany — of torturing, to extort a confession of the crime. They will say that they might as well draw examples from those countries as from Great Britain, and they will tell you that there is such a necessity of strengthening the arm of government, that they must have a criminal equity, and extort confession by torture, in order to punish with still more relentless severity. We are then lost and undone. And can any man think it troublesome, when we can, by a small interference, prevent our rights from being lost? If you will, like the Virginian government, give them knowledge of the extent of the rights retained by the people, and the powers of themselves, they will, if they be honest men, thank you for it. Will they not wish to go on sure grounds? But if you leave them otherwise, they will not know how to proceed; and, being in a state of uncertainty, they will assume rather than give up powers by implication.

A bill of rights may be summed up in a few words. What do they tell us? — That our rights are reserved. Why not say so? Is it because it will consume too much paper? Gentlemen's reasoning against a bill of rights does not satisfy me. Without saying which has the right side, it remains doubtful. A bill of rights is a favorite thing with the Virginians and the people of the other states likewise. It may be their prejudice, but the government ought to suit their geniuses; otherwise, its operation will be unhappy. A bill of rights, even if its necessity be doubtful, will exclude the possibility of dispute; and, with great submission, I think the best way is to have no dispute. In the present Constitution, they are restrained from issuing general warrants to search suspected places, or seize persons not named, without evidence of the commission of a fact, &c. There was certainly some celestial influence governing those who deliberated on that Constitution; for they have, with the most cautious and enlightened circumspection, guarded those indefeasible rights which ought ever to be held sacred! The officers of Congress may come upon you now, fortified with all the terrors of paramount federal authority. Excisemen may come in multitudes; for the limitation of their numbers no man knows. They may, unless the general government be restrained by a bill of rights, or some similar restriction, go into your cellars and rooms, and search, ransack, and measure, every thing you eat, drink, and wear. They ought to be restrained within proper bounds. With respect to the freedom of the press, I need say nothing; for it is hoped that the gentlemen who shall compose Congress will take care to infringe as little as possible the rights of human nature. This will result from their integrity. They should, from prudence, abstain from violating the rights of their constituents. They are not, however, expressly restrained. But whether they will intermeddle with that palladium of our liberties or not, I leave you to determine.

Mr. GRAYSON thought it questionable whether rights not given up were reserved. A majority of the states, he observed, had expressly reserved certain important rights by bills of rights, and that in the Confederation there was a clause declaring expressly that every power and right not given up was retained by the states. It was the general sense of America that such a clause was necessary; otherwise, why did they introduce a clause which was totally unnecessary? It had been insisted, he said, in many parts of America, that a bill of rights was only necessary between a prince and people, and not in such a government as this, which was a compact between the people themselves. This did not satisfy his mind; for so extensive was the power of legislation, in his estimation, that he doubted whether, when it was once given up, *any thing* was retained. He further remarked, that there were some negative clauses in the Constitution, which refuted the doctrine contended for by the other side. For instance; the 2d clause of the 9th section of the 1st article provided that "the privilege of the writ of *habeas corpus* shall not be suspended, unless when, in cases of rebellion or invasion, the public safety may require it." And, by the last clause of the same section, "no title of nobility shall be granted by the United States." Now, if these restrictions had not been here inserted, he asked whether Congress would not most clearly have had a right to suspend that great and valuable right, and to grant titles of nobility. When, in addition to these considerations, he saw they had an indefinite power to provide for the general welfare, he thought there were great reasons to apprehend great dangers. He thought, therefore, that there ought to be a bill of rights.

Elliot, vol. 3, pp. 441–49.

16.2.2.7.c **June 24, 1788**

Mr. HENRY. . . . What is the inference when you enumerate the rights which you are to enjoy? That those not enumerated are relinquished.

. . .

Mr. HENRY. . . . Other essential rights — what are they? The world will say that you intended to give them up. When you go into an enumeration of your rights, and stop that enumeration, the inevitable conclusion is, that what is omitted is intended to be surrendered.

Mr. MADISON. . . . With respect to the proposition of the honorable gentleman to my left, (Mr. Wythe,) gentlemen apprehend that, by enumerating three rights, it implied there were no more. The observations made by a gentleman lately up, on that subject, correspond precisely with my opinion. That resolution declares that the powers granted by the proposed Constitution are the gift of the people, and may be resumed by them when perverted to their oppression, and every power not granted thereby remains with the people, and at their will. It adds, likewise, that no right, of any denomination, can be cancelled, abridged, restrained, or modified, by the general government, or any of its officers, except in those instances in which power is given by the Constitution for these purposes. There cannot be a more positive and unequivocal declaration of the principle of the adoption — that everything not granted is reserved. This is obviously and self-evidently the case, without the declaration. Can the general government exercise any power not delegated? If an enumeration be made of our rights, will it not be implied that every thing omitted is given to the general government? Has not the honorable gentleman himself admitted that an imperfect enumeration is dangerous? Does the Constitution say that they shall not alter the law of descents, or do those things which would subvert the whole system of the state laws? If it did, what was not excepted would be granted. Does it follow, from the omission of such restrictions, that they can exercise powers not delegated? The reverse of the proposition holds. The delegation alone warrants the exercise of any power.

Elliot, vol. 3, pp. 587–88, 594, 620.

16.2.3 PHILADELPHIA CONVENTION

16.2.3.1 Charles Pinckney's Plan, May 29, 1787

10. Each State retains its Rights not expressly delegated — . . . .

Jensen, vol. 1, p. 246.

16.2.4 NEWSPAPERS AND PAMPHLETS

16.2.4.1 John DeWitt, No. 2, October 1787

The Compact itself is a recital upon paper of that proportion of the subject's natural rights, intended to be parted with, for the benefit of adverting to it in case of dispute. Miserable indeed would be the situation of those individual States who have not prefixed to their Constitutions a Bill of Rights, if, as a very respectable, learned Gentleman at the Southward observes, "the People, when they established the powers of legislation under their separate Governments, invested their Representatives with every right and authority which they did not, in explicit terms, reserve; and therefore upon every question, respecting the jurisdiction of the House of Assembly, if the Frame of Government is silent, the jurisdiction is efficient and complete." In other words, those powers which the People by their Constitutions expressly give them, they enjoy by positive grant, and those remaining ones, which they never meant to give them, and which the Constitutions say nothing about, they enjoy by tacit implication, so that by one means and by the other, they become possessed of the whole. — This doctrine is but poorly calculated for the meridian of America, where the nature of compact, the mode of construing them, and the principles upon which society is founded, are so accurately known and universally diffused. That insatiable thirst for unconditional controul over our fellow-creatures, and the facility of sounds to convey essentially different ideas, produced the first Bill of Rights ever prefixed to a Frame of Government. The people, altho' fully sensible that they reserved very title of power that they did not expressly grant away, yet afraid that the words made use of, to express those rights so granted might convey more than they originally intended, they choose at the same moment to express in different language those rights which the agreement did not include, and which they never designed to part with, endeavoring thereby to prevent any cause for future altercation and the intrusion into society of that doctrine of tacit implication which has been the favorite theme of every tyrant from the origin of all governments to the present day.

[Boston] American Herald, Storing, vol. 4, p. 22.

16.2.4.2   James Wilson, October 6, 1787

It will be proper however, before I enter into the refutation of the charges that are alledged, to mark the leading descrimination [*sic*] between the state constitutions, and the constitution of the United States. When the people established the powers of legislation under their separate governments, they invested their representatives with every right and authority which they did not in explicit terms reserve; and therefore upon every question, respecting the jurisdiction of the house of assembly, if the frame of government is silent, the jurisdiction is efficient and complete. But in delegating fœderal powers, another criterion was necessarily introduced, and the congressional authority is to be collected, not from tacit implication, but from the positive grant expressed in the instrument of union. Hence it is evident, that in the former case every thing which is not reserved is given, but in the latter the reverse of the proposition prevails, and every thing which is not given, is reserved. This distinction being recognized, will furnish an answer to those who think the omission of a bill of rights, a defect in the proposed constitution: for it would have been superfluous and absurd to have stipulated with a fœderal body of our own creation, that we should enjoy those privileges, of which we are not divested either by the intention or the act, that has brought that body into existence.

Pennsylvania Herald (October 9, 1787), Kaminski & Saladino, vol. 13, pp. 339–40.

16.2.4.3   The Federal Farmer, No. 4, October 12, 1787

DEAR SIR, . . . It is said, that when the people make a constitution, and delegate powers, that all powers not delegated by them to those who govern, is reserved to the people; and that the people, in the present case, have reserved in themselves, and in there [*sic*] state governments, every right and power not expressly given by the federal constitution to those who shall administer the national government. It is said on the other hand, that the people, when they make a constitution, yield all power not expressly reserved to themselves. The truth is, in either case, it is mere matter of opinion, and men usually take either side of the argument, as will best answer their purposes: But the general assumption being, that men who govern, will, in doubtful cases, construe laws and constitutions most favourably for encreasing their own powers; all wise and prudent people, in forming constitutions, have drawn the line, and carefully described the powers parted with and the powers reserved.

Kaminski & Saladino, vol. 14, pp. 44–45.

16.2.4.4   An Old Whig, No. 2, October 17, 1787

MR. PRINTER, . . . The principle is this: that "in *delegating federal powers,* the congressional authority is to be collected, *not from tacit implication,* but from *the positive grant* expressed in the instrument of union," *"that everything which is not given is reserved." If this* be a just representation of the matter, the authority of the several states will be sufficient to protect our liberties from the encroachments of Congress, without an continental bill of rights; *unless* the powers which are *expressly given* to Congress are *too large.*

[Philadelphia] Independent Gazetteer, Kaminski & Saladino, vol. 13, p. 400.

16.2.4.5 Centinel, No. 2, October 24, 1787

In the plan of Confederation of 1778, it was thought proper by Article the 2d, to declare that "each State retains its sovereignty, freedom and independence, and every power, jurisdiction and right, which is not by this Confederation expressly delegated to the United States in Congress assembled." Positive grant was not then thought sufficiently descriptive and restraining upon Congress, and the omission of such a declaration now, when such great devolutions of power are proposed, manifests the design of reducing the several States to shadows. But Mr. Wilson will tell you that every right and power not specially granted to Congress is considered as withheld. . . . The lust for power is so universal, that a speculative unascertained rule of construction would be a poor security for the liberties of the people.

[Philadelphia] Freeman's Journal, Kaminski & Saladino, vol. 13, p. 460.

16.2.4.6 Cincinnatus, No. 1, November 1, 1787

. . . The confederation, in its very outset, declares — that what is not expressly given, is reserved. This constitution makes no such reservation. The presumption therefore is, that the framers of the proposed constitution, did not mean to subject it to the same exception.

New York Journal, Kaminski & Saladino, vol. 13, p. 531.

16.2.4.7 A Landholder, No. 6, December 10, 1787

There is no declaration of rights. Bills of rights were introduced in England when its kings claimed all power and jurisdiction, and were considered by them as grants *to the people.* They are insignificant since government is considered as originating from the people, and all the power government now has is a grant *from the people.* The constitution they establish with powers limited and defined becomes now, to the legislator and magistrate, what originally a bill of rights was to the people. To have inserted in this Constitution a bill of rights for the states would suppose them to derive and hold their rights from the federal government, when the reverse is the case.

Connecticut Courant, Jensen, vol. 3, pp. 487, 489.

16.2.4.8 Address and Reasons of Dissent of the Minority of the Pennsylvania Convention, December 18, 1787

The new constitution, consistently with the plan of consolidation, contains no reservation of the rights and privileges of the state governments, which was made in the confederation of the year 1778, by Article the 2d. . . .

. . .

Kaminski & Saladino, vol. 15, p. 25.

16.2.4.9   A Citizen of New Haven, January 7, 1788

The powers vested in the federal government are particularly defined, so that each state still retains its sovereignty in what concerns its own internal government and a right to exercise every power of a sovereign state not particularly delegated to the government of the United States.

Connecticut Courant, Jensen, vol. 3, p. 525.

16.2.4.10   The Federal Farmer, No. 16, January 20, 1788

We must consider this constitution, when adopted, as the supreme act of the people, and in construing it hereafter, we and our posterity must strictly adhere to the letter and spirit of it, and in no instance depart from them. . . . By the people's now establishing certain fundamental rights, it is strongly implied, that they are of opinion, that they would not otherwise be secured as a part of the federal system, or be regarded in the federal administration as fundamental. . . . Further, the people, thus establishing some few rights, and remaining totally silent about others similarly circumstanced, the implication indubitably is, that they mean to relinquish the latter, or at least feel indifferent about them. Rights, therefore, inferred from general principles of reason, being precarious and hardly ascertainable in the common affairs of society, and the people, in forming the constitution, explicitly shewing they conceive these rights to be thus circumstanced, and accordingly proceed to enumerate and establish all which they esteem valuable and sacred. On every principle, then, the people especially having began, ought to go through enumerating, and establish particularly all the rights of individuals, which can by any possibility come in question in making and executing federal laws.

Storing, vol. 2, pp. 326–27.

16.2.4.11   The Federalist, No. 84, May 28, 1788

I go further, and affirm that the bills of rights, in the sense and to the extent in which they are contended for, are not only unnecessary in the proposed Constitution, but would even be dangerous. They would contain various exceptions to powers not granted; and, on this very account, would afford a colorable pretext to claim more than were granted. For why declare that things shall not be done which there is no power to do? Why, for instance, should it be said that liberty of the press shall not be restrained, when no power is given by which restrictions may be imposed? I will not contend that such a provision would confer a regulating power; but it is evidence that it would furnish, to men disposed to usurp, a plausible pretense for claiming that power.

Kaminski & Saladino, vol. 18, p. 130.

16.2.5   LETTERS AND DIARIES

16.2.5.1   George Washington to President of Congress, September 17, 1787

. . . Individuals entering into society, must give up a share of liberty to preserve the rest. The magnitude of the sacrifice must depend as well on situation and circumstance, as on the object to be obtained. It is at all times difficult to draw with precision the line between those rights which must be surrendered, and those which may be reserved; and on the present occasion this difficulty was encreased

701

[*sic*] by a difference among the several States as to their situation, extent, habits, and particular interests.

Kaminski and Saladino, vol. 13, p. 211.

16.2.5.2 Roger Sherman and Oliver Ellsworth to Governor Huntington, September 26, 1787

. . . Some additional powers are vested in Congress, which was a principle object the states had in view in appointing the Convention; those powers extend only to matters respecting the common interests of the Union and are specially defined, so that the particular states retain their *Sovereignty* in all other matters.

Jensen, vol. 3, p. 351.

16.2.5.3 James Madison to Thomas Jefferson, October 24, 1787

. . . A reform therefore which does not make provision for private rights, must be materially defective. The restraints agst. paper emissions, and violations of contracts are not sufficient. Supposing them to be effectual as far as they go, they are short of the mark. Injustice may be effected by such an infinitude of legislative expedients, that where the disposition exists it can only be controuled by some provision which reaches all cases whatsoever. The partial provision made, supposes the disposition which will evade it. . . . The great desideratum in Government is, so to modify the sovereignty as that it may be sufficiently neutral between different parts of the Society to controul one part from invading the rights of another, and at the same time sufficiently controuled itself, from setting up an interest adverse to that of the entire Society.

Kaminski & Saladino, vol. 13, pp. 447, 449.

16.2.5.4 Thomas Jefferson to James Madison, December 20, 1787

To say, as mr Wilson does that a bill of rights was not necessary because all is reserved in the case of the general government which is not given, while in the particular ones all is given which is not reserved, might do for the Audience to whom it was addressed, but is surely gratis dictum, opposed by strong inferences from the body of the instrument, as well as from the omission of the clause of our present confederation which had declared that in express terms. It was a hard conclusion to say because there has been no uniformity among the states as to cases triable by jury, because some have been so incautious as to abandon this mode of trial, therefore the more prudent states shall be reduced to the same level of calamity. It would have been much more just and wise to have concluded the other way that as most of the states had judiciously preserved this palladium, those who had wandered should be brought back to it, and to have established general right instead of wrong. Let me add that a bill of rights is what the people are entitled to against every government on earth, general or particular, and what no just government should refuse, or rest on inference. . . .

Boyd, vol. 12, p. 440.

16.2.5.5 George Washington to Marquis de Lafayette, April 28, 1788

. . . For example: there was not a member of the convention, I believe, who had the least objection to what is contended for by the Advocates for a *Bill of Rights* and *Tryal by Jury*. The first, where the people evidently retained everything which they did not in express terms give up, was considered nugatory as you will find to have been more fully explained by Mr. Wilson and others: — And as to the second, it was only the difficulty of establishing a mode which should not interfere with the fixed modes of any of the States, that induced the Convention to leave it, as a matter of future adjustment.

Kaminski & Saladino, vol. 17, p. 235.

16.2.5.6 Thomas Jefferson to James Madison, March 15, 1789

. . . In the arguments in favor of a declaration of rights, you omit one which has great weight to me, the legal check which it puts into the hands of the judiciary. This is a body, which if rendered independent, and kept strictly to their own department merits great confidence for their learning and integrity. . . . The Declaration of rights is like all other human blessings alloyed with some inconveniences, and not accomplishing fully it's [*sic*] object. But the good in this instance vastly overweighs the evil. I cannot refrain from making short answers to the objections which your letter states to have been raised. I. That the rights in question are reserved by the manner in which the federal powers are granted. Answer. a constitutive act may certainly be so formed as to need no declaration of rights. The act itself has the force of a declaration as far as it goes: and if it goes to all material points nothing more is wanting.

Boyd, vol. 14, pp. 659–60.

16.2.5.7 Abraham Baldwin to Joel Barlow, June 14, 1789

A few days since, Madison brought before us propositions of amendment agreeably to his promise to his constituents. Such as he supposed would tranquillize the minds of honest opposers without injuring the system. viz. That what is not given is reserved, that liberty of the press & trial by jury shall remain *inviolable*. We are too busy at present in cutting away at the whole cloth, to stop to do any body's patching. There is no such thing as antifederalism heard of.

Veit, p. 250.

16.2.5.8 Tench Coxe to James Madison, June 18, 1789

I observe you have brought forward the amendments you proposed to the federal Constitution. I have given them a very careful perusal, and have attended particularly to their reception by the public. The most decided friends of the constitution admit (generally) that they will meliorate the government by removing some points of litigation and jealousy, and by heightening and strengthening the barriers between necessary power and indispensable liberty. . . . Those who are honest are well pleased at the footing on which the press, liberty of conscience, original right & power, trial by jury &ca. are rested.

Veit, p. 253.

16.2.5.9 Richard Parker to Richard Henry Lee, July 6, 1789

I observe the slip of the newspaper sent me and know the design, but I still think a Bill if rights not necessary here. . . . However I have no objection to such a bill of Rights as has been proposed by Mr. Maddison [*sic*] because we declare that we do not abridge our Rights by the reservation that we retain all that we have not specifically given. . . .

Veit, p. 260.

16.2.5.10 Henry Gibbs to Roger Sherman, July 16, 1789

. . . All Ambiguity of Expression certainly ought to be remov'd; Liberty of Conscience in religious matters, right of trial by Jury, Liberty of the Press &c. may perhaps be more explicitly secur'd to the Subject & a general reservation made to the States respectively of all the powers not expressly delegated to the general Government. . . .

Veit, p. 263.

16.2.5.11 William L. Smith to Edward Rutledge, August 10, 1789

. . . I shall support the Amendmts. [*sic*] proposed to the Constitution that any exception to the powers of Congress shall not be so construed as to give it any powers not *expressly* given, & the enumeration of certain rights shall not be so construed as to deny others retained by the people — & the powers not delegated by this Constn. nor prohibited by it to the States, are reserved to the States respectively. . . .

Veit, p. 273.

16.2.5.12 James Madison to George Washington, December 5, 1789

[Randolph's] principle objection was pointed agst. the word *'retained,'* in the eleventh proposed amendment [Ninth Amendment], and his argument if I understood it applied in this manner — that as the rights declared in the first ten of the proposed amendments were not all that a free people would require the exercise of, and that as there was no criterion by which it could be determined whether any other particular right was retained or not, it would be more safe and more consistent with the spirit of the 1st & 17th amendts. proposed by Virginia that this reservation agst. constructive power, should operate rather as a provision agst. extending the powers of Congs. by their own authority, than a protection to rights reducible to no definitive certainty. But others, among whom I am one, see not the force of this distinction. . . .

If a line can be drawn between the powers granted and the rights retained, it would seem to be the same thing whether the latter be secured by declaring that they shall not be abridged, or that the former shall not be extended. If no such line can be drawn, a declaration in either form would amount to nothing.

Hobson & Rutland, vol. 12, pp. 458–59.

16.3 DISCUSSION OF RIGHTS

16.3.1 TREATISES

16.3.1.1 William Blackstone, 1765

For the principal aim of society is to protect individuals in the enjoyment of those absolute rights, which were vested in them by the immutable laws of nature; but which could not be preserved in peace without that mutual assistance and intercourse, which is gained by the institution of friendly and social communities.

Hence it follows, that the first and primary end of human laws is to maintain and regulate these *absolute* rights of individuals. Such rights as are social and *relative* result from, and are posterior to, the formation of states and societies: so that to maintain and regulate these, is clearly a subsequent consideration. And therefore the principle view of human laws is, or ought to be, to explain, protect, and enforce such rights as are absolute. . . .

THE absolute rights of man, considered as a free agent, endowed with discernment to know good from evil, and with power of choosing those measures which appear to him to be most desirable, are usually summed up in one general appellation, and denominated the natural liberty of mankind.

Commentaries, bk. 1, ch. 1; vol. 1, p. 120.

16.3.2 CASELAW

None.

APPENDIX

Bill of Rights[1]

Article the third . . . Congress shall make no law respecting an establishment of religion, or prohibiting the free exercise thereof; or abridging the freedom of speech, or of the press, or the right of the people peaceably to assemble, and to petition the Government for a redress of grievances.

Article the fourth . . . A well regulated militia, being necessary to the security of a free State, the right of the people to keep and bear arms, shall not be infringed.[2]

Article the fifth . . . No soldier shall, in time of peace be quartered in any house, without the consent of the owner, nor in time of war, but in a manner prescribed by law.[3]

Article the sixth . . . The right of the people to be secure in their persons, houses, papers, and effects, against unreasonable searches and seizures, shall not be violated, and no warrants shall issue, but upon probable cause, supported by oath or affirmation, and particularly describing the place to be searched, and the persons or things to be seized.[4]

Article the seventh . . . No person shall be held to answer for a capital, or otherwise infamous crime, unless on a presentment or indictment of a Grand Jury, except in cases arising in the land or naval forces, or in the militia, when in actual service in time of war or public danger; nor shall any person be subject for the same offence to be twice put in jeopardy of life or limb, nor shall be compelled in any criminal case to be a witness against himself, nor be deprived of life, liberty, or property, without due process of law; nor shall private property be taken for public use without just compensation.[5]

Article the eighth . . . In all criminal prosecutions, the accused shall enjoy the right to a speedy and public trial, by an impartial jury of the State and district wherein the crime shall have been committed, which district shall have been previously ascertained by law, and to be informed of the nature and cause of the

---

[1]These ten articles were ratified by 1791. Article the First was never ratified. Article the Second was ratified in 1992 and became the Twenty-Seventh Amendment.

[2]In some transcriptions, the first letters of *militia* and *arms* are capitalized. However, while the first letters of each word are slightly elevated above the remaining letters, they are not nearly as elevated as letters that are plainly capitalized.

[3]In some transcriptions, the first letter of *owner* is capitalized. But see footnote 2.

[4]In some transcriptions, the first letters of *warrant* and *oath* are capitalized. But see footnote 2.

[5]In some transcriptions, the first letters of *militia* and *war* are capitalized. But see footnote 2.

accusation; to be confronted with the witnesses against him; to have compulsory process for obtaining witnesses in his favor, and to have the assistance of counsel for his defence.

Article the Ninth . . . In suits at common law, where the value in controversy shall exceed twenty dollars, the right of trial by jury shall be preserved, and no fact tried by a jury shall be otherwise re-examined in any Court of the United States, than according to the rules of the common law.

Article the tenth . . . Excessive bail shall not be required, nor excessive fines imposed, nor cruel and unusual punishments inflicted.

Article the eleventh . . . The enumeration in the Constitution, of certain rights, shall not be construed to deny or disparage others retained by the people.

Article the Twelfth . . . The powers not delegated to the United States by the Constitution, nor prohibited by it to the States, are reserved to the States respectively, or to the people.